# Essentials of Abnormal Psychology

## FIRST CANADIAN EDITION

# Essentials of Abnormal Psychology

FIRST CANADIAN EDITION

V. Mark Durand
*University of South Florida, St. Petersburg*

David H. Barlow
*Boston University*

Sherry H. Stewart
*Dalhousie University*

THOMSON

NELSON

Australia    Canada    Mexico    Singapore    Spain    United Kingdom    United States

**Essentials of Abnormal Psychology, First Canadian Edition**

by V. Mark Durand, David H. Barlow, and Sherry H. Stewart

**Associate Vice President, Editorial Director:**
Evelyn Veitch

**Editor-in-Chief, Higher Education:**
Anne Williams

**Executive Marketing Manager:**
Lenore Taylor

**Managing Developmental Editor:**
Alwynn Pinard

**Photo Researcher/Permissions Coordinator:**
Terri Rothman

**Content Production Manager:**
Imoinda Romain

**Production Service:**
GEX Publishing Services

**Copy Editor:**
GEX Publishing Services

**Proofreader:**
GEX Publishing Services

**Indexer:**
GEX Publishing Services

**Production Coordinator:**
Ferial Suleman

**Design Director:**
Ken Phipps

**Cover Design:**
Jack Steiner

**Cover Image:**
Connie Coleman/Photographer's Choice/Getty Images

**Compositor:**
GEX Publishing Services

**Printer:**
Quebecor World

**Library and Archives Canada Cataloguing in Publication**

Durand, Vincent Mark
Essentials of abnormal psychology / V. Mark Durand, David H. Barlow, Sherry H. Stewart. — 1st Canadian ed.

Includes index.
ISBN-13: 978-0-17-610388-0
ISBN-10: 0-17-610388-0

1. Psychology, Pathological—Textbooks.  I. Barlow, David H. II. Stewart, Sherry H. (Sherry Heather), 1965-  III. Title.

RC454.D87 2007          616.89
C2006-907051-2

■ *To Wendy, for three decades of love.*

*V. M. D.*

■ *I dedicate this book to my mother, Doris Elinor Barlow-Lanigan,*
  *for her multidimensional influence across my life span.*

*D. H. B.*

■ *To my adored daughter, Laila Xiu Tao, who has provided me the balance*
  *I needed to complete this ambitious project.*

*S. H. S.*

# About the Authors

**V. Mark Durand** is known worldwide as an authority in the area of autism and related disabilities and is currently Regional Vice Chancellor for Academic Affairs at the University of South Florida St. Petersburg. Dr. Durand was previously the founding Dean of Arts & Sciences. Dr. Durand is a fellow of the American Psychological Association. He has administered more than $4 million in federal research and training grants and currently has a 5-year federally funded project focused on the prevention of severe behavior problems in children with disabilities.

He taught from 1984 to 2003 at SUNY's University at Albany. He served in a variety of leadership positions at the University at Albany, including associate director for clinical training for the doctoral psychology program from 1987 to 1990, chair of the psychology department from 1995 to 1998, and interim dean of Arts and Sciences from 2001 to 2002. He established the Center for Autism and Related Disabilities at the University at Albany, SUNY. He received his B.A., M.A., and Ph.D.—all in psychology—from the State University of New York–Stony Brook.

Dr. Durand was awarded the University Award for Excellence in Teaching at SUNY–Albany in 1991 and in 1989 was named Distinguished Reviewer of the Year for the *Journal of the Association for Persons with Severe Handicaps*. He has served on various editorial boards, reviewed for numerous journals, and written more than 100 scholarly articles and book chapters on the assessment and treatment of problem behaviour. His five books include *Severe Behavior Problems: A Functional Communication Training Approach* and, most recently, *Sleep Better! A Guide to Improving Sleep for Children with Special Needs.*

Dr. Durand developed a unique treatment for severe behaviour problems that is currently mandated by several U.S. states and is used worldwide. He also developed an assessment tool that is used internationally and has been translated into more than 15 languages. In 1993 he was the keynote speaker for the Australian National Conference on Behaviour Modification; he has also lectured throughout Norway. He has been consulted by the departments of education in numerous U.S. states and by the U.S. Departments of Justice and Education. His current research program includes the study of prevention models and treatments for such serious problems as self-injurious behaviour.

In his leisure time he enjoys long-distance running and is in training for his first marathon race.

**David H. Barlow** is an internationally recognized pioneer and leader in clinical psychology. A professor at Boston University, Dr. Barlow also directs the Center for Anxiety and Related Disorders, one of the largest research clinics of its kind in the world. From 1979 to 1996, he was distinguished professor at the University at Albany–State University of New York. From 1975 to 1979, he was professor of psychiatry and psychology at Brown University, where he also founded the clinical psychology internship program. From 1969 to 1975, he was professor of psychiatry at the University of Mississippi, where he founded the Medical School psychology residency program. Dr. Barlow received his B.A. from the University of Notre Dame, his M.A. from Boston College, and his Ph.D. from the University of Vermont.

A fellow of every major psychological association, Dr. Barlow has received many awards in honour of his excellence in scholarship, including the National Institute of Mental Health Merit Award for long-term contributions to the clinical research effort; the 2000 Distinguished Scientist Award for applications of psychology from the American Psychological Association; the Distinguished Scientist Award from the Society of Clinical Psychology of the American Psychological Association; and a certificate of appreciation from the APA section on the clinical psychology of women, for "outstanding commitment to the advancement of women in psychology." In 2004, he received the C. Charles Burlingame Award from the Institute of Living and was awarded an Honorary Doctorate of Humane Letters degree from the Massachusetts School of Professional Psychology. He also received career contribution awards from the Massachusetts, California, and Connecticut Psychological Associations and, in 2000, was named Honorary Visiting Professor at the Chinese People's Liberation Army General Hospital and Postgraduate Medical School. In addition, the annual Grand Rounds in Clinical Psychology at Brown University was named in his honour, and he was awarded the first graduate alumni scholar award at the University of Vermont. During the 1997–1998 academic year he was Fritz Redlich Fellow at the Center for Advanced Study in the Behavioral Sciences in Menlo Park, California.

Dr. Barlow has served on the editorial boards of 19 different journals, published more than 500 scholarly articles, and written 25 books, including *Anxiety and Its Disorders,* 2nd edition, Guilford Press; *Clinical Handbook of Psychological Disorders: A Step-by-Step Treatment Manual,* 3rd edition, Guilford Press; *Single-Case Experimental Designs: Strategies for Studying Behavior Change,* 2nd edition, Allyn & Bacon (with Michael Herson); *The Scientist-Practitioner: Research and Accountability in the Age of Managed Care,* 2nd edition, Allyn & Bacon (with Steve Hayes and Rosemery Nelson); and *Mastery of Your Anxiety and Panic,* Oxford University Press (with Michelle Craske).

From 1990 to 1994, Dr. Barlow was one of three psychologists on the task force that was responsible for reviewing the work of more than 1000 mental-health professionals who participated in the creation of the new DSM-IV. He also chaired the APA Task Force on Psychological Intervention Guidelines, which created a template for clinical practice guidelines. His current research program focuses on the nature and treatment of anxiety and related emotional disorders.

At leisure he plays golf, skis, and retreats to his home in Nantucket, where he loves to write, walk on the beach, and visit with his island friends.

**Sherry H. Stewart** has an international reputation for her work in the areas of addictions, anxiety disorders, and the comorbidity of mental health and substance use disorders. She is a professor of psychiatry and psychology at Dalhousie University. She served as the coordinator of the Dalhousie doctoral training program in clinical psychology from 2004 to 2006. Dr. Stewart has a cross-appointment as a professor in community health and epidemiology at Dalhousie; she also holds research appointments at local teaching hospitals in the Halifax metropolitan area. She is currently visiting faculty at the University of British Columbia in Vancouver where she is taking her second sabbatical. She received her B.Sc. (honours) in psychology from Dalhousie University in 1987 and her Ph.D. in clinical psychology from McGill University in 1993. She completed her clinical internship at the Toronto Hospital in 1992–1993. Dr. Stewart has been registered as a clinical psychologist in Nova Scotia since 1995. She ran a part-time private practice in the metropolitan Halifax area until 2003, when she left her practice to become a mother.

Dr. Stewart is currently the associate editor of the international journal *Cognitive Behaviour Therapy* and serves on the editorial board of the *Canadian Journal of Behavioural Science.* She has provided reviews for numerous scientific journals and granting agencies. Dr. Stewart has published close to 140 scientific articles, 3 books, and 16 book chapters. She has also served as the guest editor for several special issues of scholarly journals covering such topics as the comorbidity of alcohol abuse and pathological gambling, side effects of benzodiazepine medications, state-of-the-art cognitive-behavioural treatments for substance use disorders, the comorbidity of mental health and substance use disorders, the role of anxiety sensitivity in pain experiences and conditions, the relationship of anxiety sensitivity to substance misuse, and the psychological impact of the events of September 11, 2001.

Her research has been funded by a variety of local, national, and international granting agencies. Currently, Dr. Stewart heads or is involved with projects funded by agencies such as the Social Sciences and Humanities Research Council of Canada, the Canadian Tobacco Control Research Initiative, the Nova Scotia Health Research Foundation, the Nova Scotia Gaming Foundation, the Ontario Problem Gambling Research Centre, and the National Institute on Alcohol Abuse and Alcoholism. She has received the prestigious Investigator Award from the Canadian Institutes of Health Research for her important health-related research on a novel approach to the prevention of alcohol abuse in adolescents, and she currently holds a Killam Research Professorship from the Dalhousie Faculty of Science for her innovations in addictions research. The quality of her research has also been recognized through numerous other awards including the Young Investigator Award from the Anxiety Disorders Association of America in 1998, the New Investigator Award from the Association for Advancement of Behavior Therapy Women's Special Interest Group in 1998, the President's New Researcher Award from the Canadian Psychological Association in 1998, and the Killam Prize in Science in 1997.

In her leisure time, Dr. Stewart enjoys international cuisine and travel. In the summer, she loves to spend time at her family cottage with her daughter, Laila, where they partake in walks on the beach and icy dips in the Atlantic.

# Brief Contents

**1** Abnormal Behaviour in Historical Context  1

**2** An Integrative Approach to Psychopathology  34

**3** Clinical Assessment, Diagnosis, and Research Methods  75

**4** Anxiety Disorders  126

**5** Somatoform and Dissociative Disorders  177

**6** Mood Disorders and Suicide  215

**7** Physical Disorders and Health Psychology  270

**8** Eating and Sleep Disorders  308

**9** Sexual and Gender Identity Disorders  355

**10** Substance-Related Disorders  400

**11** Personality Disorders  445

**12** Schizophrenia and Other Psychotic Disorders  485

**13** Developmental and Cognitive Disorders  522

**14** Mental Health Services: Legal and Ethical Issues  577

# Contents

Preface   *xvii*
Culture Index   *xxiii*
Gender Index   *xxiv*

## 1

# Abnormal Behaviour in Historical Context   1

**Understanding Psychopathology**   2

   **Jody:** The Boy Who Fainted at the Sight of Blood   2

   *What Is a Psychological Disorder?*   2

   *The Science of Psychopathology*   5

   *Historical Conceptions of Abnormal Behaviour*   8

**The Supernatural Tradition**   9

   *Demons and Witches*   9

   *Stress and Melancholy*   9

   **Charles VI:** The Mad King   10

   *Treatments for Possession*   11

   *The Moon and the Stars*   11

   *Comments*   11

**The Biological Tradition**   12

   *Hippocrates and Galen*   12

   *The 19th Century*   13

   *The Development of Biological Treatments*   14

   *Consequences of the Biological Tradition*   15

**The Psychological Tradition**   15

   *Moral Therapy*   16

   *Asylum Reform and the Decline of Moral Therapy*   16

   *Psychoanalytic Theory*   18

   *Humanistic Theory*   24

   *The Behavioural Model*   25

**The Present: The Scientific Method and an Integrative Approach**   29

*Summary*   30

*Key Terms*   31

*Answers to Concept Checks*   31

*Chapter Quiz*   33

## 2

# An Integrative Approach to Psychopathology   34

**One-Dimensional or Multidimensional Models**   35

   *What Caused Jody's Phobia?*   35

   *Outcome and Comments*   37

**Biological Contributions to Psychopathology**   38

   *The Nature of Genes*   39

   *New Developments in the Study of Genes and Behaviour*   40

   *The Interaction of Genetic and Environmental Effects*   40

   *Nongenomic "Inheritance" of Behaviour*   43

   *The Central Nervous System*   44

   *The Structure of the Brain*   46

   *The Peripheral Nervous System*   48

   *Neurotransmitters*   50

   *Implications for Psychopathology*   54

   *Psychosocial Influences on Brain Structure and Function*   55

   *Interactions of Psychosocial Factors with Brain Structure and Function*   56

   *Comments*   57

**Behavioural Contributions to Psychopathology  57**

*Conditioning and Cognitive Processes  57*

*Learned Helplessness and Learned Optimism  58*

*Social Learning  59*

*Prepared Learning  60*

*Cognitive Science and the Unconscious  60*

*Cognitive-Behavioural Therapy  62*

**Emotional Contributions to Psychopathology  62**

*The Physiology and Purpose of Fear  62*

*Emotional Phenomena  63*

*The Components of Emotion  63*

*Anger and Your Heart  65*

**Social Contributions to Psychopathology  65**

*Voodoo, the Evil Eye, and Other Fears  65*

*Gender  66*

*Social Effects on Health and Behaviour  67*

*Social and Interpersonal Influences on the Elderly  68*

*Global Incidence of Psychological Disorders  68*

**Developmental Contributions to Psychopathology  69**

*The Principle of Equifinality  70*

**Conclusions  70**

*Summary  71*

*Key Terms  72*

*Answers to Concept Checks  72*

*Chapter Quiz  74*

*The Clinical Interview  79*

*Physical Examination  81*

*Behavioural Assessment  82*

*Psychological Testing  84*

*Neuropsychological Testing  88*

*Neuroimaging: Pictures of the Brain  89*

*Psychophysiological Assessment  90*

**Diagnosing Psychological Disorders  92**

*Classification Issues  93*

*DSM-IV  96*

**Conducting Research in Psychopathology  99**

*Basic Components of a Research Study  100*

*Statistical versus Clinical Significance  102*

*The "Average" Client  103*

**Types of Research Methods  104**

*Studying Individual Cases  104*

*Research by Correlation  104*

*Research by Experiment  107*

*Single-Case Experimental Designs  109*

**Genetics and Research across Time and Cultures  112**

*Studying Genetics  112*

*Studying Behaviour over Time  115*

*Studying Behaviour across Cultures  117*

*The Power of a Program of Research  119*

*Replication  120*

*Research Ethics  120*

*Summary  121*

*Key Terms  122*

*Answers to Concept Checks  123*

*Chapter Quiz  125*

# 3
# Clinical Assessment, Diagnosis, and Research Methods  75

**Assessing Psychological Disorders  76**

**Frank:** Young, Serious, and Anxious  76

**Brian:** Unwanted Thoughts of Harm  77

*Key Concepts in Assessment  78*

# 4
# Anxiety Disorders  126

**The Complexity of Anxiety Disorders  127**

*Anxiety, Fear, and Panic: Some Definitions  127*

**Gretchen:** Attacked by Panic  128

*Causes of Anxiety Disorders  129*

*Comorbidity of Anxiety Disorders  132*

**Generalized Anxiety Disorder  132**

*Clinical Description  133*

**Irene:** Ruled by Worry  133

*Statistics  134*

*Causes  135*

*Treatment  136*

**Panic Disorder With and Without Agoraphobia  138**

**Mrs. M.:** Self-Imprisoned  139

*Clinical Description  139*

*Statistics  141*

*Causes  143*

*Treatment  145*

**Specific Phobia  149**

**Bob:** Too Scared to Fly  149

*Clinical Description  149*

*Statistics  152*

*Causes  153*

*Treatment  155*

**Social Phobia  155**

**Billy:** Too Shy  156

*Clinical Description  156*

*Statistics  156*

*Causes  157*

*Treatment  159*

**Posttraumatic Stress Disorder  160**

*Clinical Description  160*

**The Joneses:** One Victim, Many Traumas  160

*Statistics  162*

*Causes  162*

*Treatment  164*

**Obsessive-Compulsive Disorder  166**

*Clinical Description  167*

**Richard:** Enslaved by Ritual  167

*Statistics  169*

*Causes  169*

*Treatment  170*

*Summary  172*

*Key Terms  173*

*Answers to Concept Checks  173*

*Chapter Quiz  174*

# 5

# Somatoform and Dissociative Disorders  177

**Somatoform Disorders  178**

*Hypochondriasis  179*

**Kirsten:** Invisibly Ill  179

*Somatization Disorder  183*

**Linda:** Full-Time Patient  183

*Conversion Disorder  186*

**Ms. A.:** Loss of Voice  187

**Celia:** Seeing Through Blindness  189

*Pain Disorder  191*

**The Medical Student:** Temporary Pain  192

**The Woman with Cancer:** Managing Pain  192

*Body Dysmorphic Disorder  192*

**Jim:** Ashamed to Be Seen  192

**Dissociative Disorders  197**

*Depersonalization Disorder  198*

**Bonnie:** Dancing Away from Herself  198

*Dissociative Amnesia  199*

**The Woman Who Lost Her Memory**  199

*Dissociative Fugue  200*

**The Misbehaving Sheriff**  201

*Dissociative Trance Disorder  201*

*Dissociative Identity Disorder  202*

**Jonah:** Bewildering Blackouts  202

**The Hillside Strangler**  203

**Sybil:** A Childhood Drama  205

*Summary  210*

*Key Terms  210*

*Answers to Concept Checks  211*

*Chapter Quiz  212*

# 6

# Mood Disorders and Suicide 215

**Understanding and Defining Mood Disorders 216**

Katie: Weathering Depression 216

An Overview of Depression and Mania 217

The Structure of Mood Disorders 218

Depressive Disorders 219

Jack: A Life Kept Down 220

Bipolar Disorders 223

Jane: Funny, Smart, and Desperate 223

Billy: The World's Best at Everything 224

**Prevalence of Mood Disorders 229**

In Children and Adolescents 230

In the Elderly 231

Across Cultures 232

Among the Creative 233

The Overlap of Anxiety and Depression 233

**Causes of Mood Disorders 235**

Biological Dimensions 235

Brain Wave Activity 238

Psychological Dimensions 239

Katie: No Easy Transitions 240

Social and Cultural Dimensions 243

An Integrative Theory 246

**Treatment of Mood Disorders 247**

Medications 248

Electroconvulsive Therapy and Transcranial Magnetic Stimulation 251

Phototherapy for Seasonal Affective Disorder 251

Psychological Treatments 252

Beck and Irene: A Dialogue 252

Combined Treatments 254

Preventing Relapse 255

Psychological Treatments for Bipolar Disorder 256

Katie: The Triumph of the Self 257

**Suicide 258**

Statistics 258

Causes 260

Risk Factors 260

Is Suicide Contagious? 262

Treatment 262

Summary 264

Key Terms 265

Answers to Concept Checks 265

Chapter Quiz 267

# 7

# Physical Disorders and Health Psychology 270

**Psychological and Social Factors that Influence Health 271**

Health and Health-Related Behaviour 272

The Nature of Stress 273

The Physiology of Stress 274

Contributions to the Stress Response 274

Stress, Anxiety, Depression, and Excitement 275

Stress and the Immune Response 276

**Psychosocial Effects on Physical Disorders 279**

AIDS 279

Cancer 281

Cardiovascular Problems 283

John: The Human Volcano 283

Hypertension 284

Coronary Heart Disease 286

Chronic Pain 288

Preepi: Resigned to Pain 289

Chronic Fatigue Syndrome 292

**Psychological Treatment of Physical Disorders 294**

Biofeedback 295

Relaxation and Meditation 296

A Comprehensive Stress- and Pain-Reduction Program 296

Sally: Improving Her Perception 297

Drugs and Stress-Reduction Programs 298

Denial as a Means of Coping 298

Modifying Behaviours to Promote Health 299

Summary 302

Key Terms 303

Answers to Concept Checks 303

Chapter Quiz 305

# 8

# Eating and Sleep Disorders 308

## Major Types of Eating Disorders 309

Bulimia Nervosa 310

Phoebe: Apparently Perfect 310

Anorexia Nervosa 313

Julie: The Thinner the Better 314

Binge-Eating Disorder 316

Statistics 317

## Causes of Eating Disorders 320

Social Dimensions 320

Phoebe: Dancing to Destruction 324

Biological Dimensions 325

Psychological Dimensions 326

An Integrative Model 327

## Treatment of Eating Disorders 328

Drug Treatments 328

Psychological Treatments 328

Phoebe: Taking Control 330

Preventing Eating Disorders 333

## Sleep Disorders: The Major Dyssomnias and Parasomnias 334

An Overview of Sleep Disorders 335

Primary Insomnia 337

Sonja: School on Her Mind 338

Primary Hypersomnia 340

Ann: Sleeping in Public 341

Narcolepsy 342

Breathing-Related Sleep Disorders 342

Circadian Rhythm Sleep Disorders 343

## Treatment of Sleep Disorders 344

Medical Treatments 344

Environmental Treatments 345

Psychological Treatments 346

Preventing Sleep Disorders 347

Parasomnias and Their Treatment 347

Summary 349

Key Terms 350

Answers to Concept Checks 350

Chapter Quiz 352

# 9

# Sexual and Gender Identity Disorders 355

## What Is Normal Sexuality? 356

Gender Differences 357

Cultural Differences 358

The Development of Sexual Orientation 358

## Gender Identity Disorder 359

Joe: Trapped in the Wrong Body 360

Defining Gender Identity Disorder 360

Causes 361

David/Brenda: Nature over Nurture 362

Treatment 362

## Overview of Sexual Dysfunctions 365

Sexual Desire Disorders 366

Mr. and Mrs. C.: Getting Started 367

Lisa: The Terror of Sex 367

Sexual Arousal Disorders 368

Bill: Long Marriage, New Problem 368

Orgasm Disorders 369

Greta and Will: Loving Disunion 370

Gary: Running Scared 371

Sexual Pain Disorders 371

Jill: Sex and Spasms 372

Assessing Sexual Behaviour 373

## Causes and Treatment of Sexual Dysfunction 374

Causes of Sexual Dysfunction 374

Treatment of Sexual Dysfunction 378

Carl: Never Too Late 379

## Paraphilia: Clinical Descriptions 383

Fetishism 384

Voyeurism and Exhibitionism 384

Robert: Outside the Curtains 384

Transvestic Fetishism 385

Mr. M.: Strong Man in a Dress 385

Sexual Sadism and Sexual Masochism 385

Pedophilia and Incest 387

Tony: More and Less a Father 387

Paraphilia in Women   389
Causes of Paraphilia   389

**Robert:** Revenge on Repression   389

**Tony:** Trained Too Young   389

## Assessing and Treating Paraphilia   391
Psychological Treatment   391

**Tony:** Imagining the Worst   391
Drug Treatments   393
Summary   393
Summary   394
Key Terms   395
Answers to Concept Checks   395
Chapter Quiz   397

## 10 Substance-Related Disorders   400

## Perspectives on Substance-Related Disorders   401
**Danny:** Multiple Dependencies   401
Levels of Involvement   402
Diagnostic Issues   406

## Depressants   408
Alcohol Use Disorders   408
Sedative, Hypnotic, or Anxiolytic Substance Use Disorders   413

## Stimulants   415
Amphetamine Use Disorders   416
Cocaine Use Disorders   417
Nicotine Use Disorders   419
Caffeine Use Disorders   420

## Opioids   421

## Hallucinogens   422
Marijuana   422
LSD and Other Hallucinogens   423

## Other Drugs of Abuse   425

## Causes of Substance-Related Disorders   427
Biological Dimensions   427
Psychological Dimensions   428
Cognitive and Learning Factors   429

Social Dimensions   430
Cultural Dimensions   431
An Integrative Model   431

## Treatment of Substance-Related Disorders   433
Biological Treatments   434
Psychosocial Treatments   435
Prevention   439
Summary   440
Key Terms   441
Answers to Concept Checks   441
Chapter Quiz   443

## 11 Personality Disorders   445

## An Overview of Personality Disorders   446
Aspects of Personality Disorders   446
Categorical and Dimensional Models   447
Personality Disorder Clusters   448
Statistics and Development   448
Gender Differences   450
Comorbidity   451

## Cluster A Personality Disorders   452
Paranoid Personality Disorder   452

**Jake:** Victim of Conspiracy?   452
Schizoid Personality Disorder   454

**Mr. Z.:** All on His Own   454
Schizotypal Personality Disorder   456

**Mr. S.:** Man with a Mission   456

## Cluster B Personality Disorders   458
Antisocial Personality Disorder   459

**Ryan:** The Thrill Seeker   459
Borderline Personality Disorder   467

**Claire:** A Stranger Among Us   467
Histrionic Personality Disorder   470

**Pat:** Always Onstage   470
Narcissistic Personality Disorder   472

**Willie:** It's All About Me   472

**Cluster C Personality Disorders   474**
Avoidant Personality Disorder   474

**Jane:** Not Worth Noticing   474
Dependent Personality Disorder   476

**Karen:** Whatever You Say   476
Obsessive-Compulsive Personality Disorder   477

**Daniel:** Getting It Exactly Right   477

**Personality Disorders Under Study   479**
Summary   479
Key Terms   480
Answers to Concept Checks   480
Chapter Quiz   482

**12**

# Schizophrenia and Other Psychotic Disorders   485

**Perspectives on Schizophrenia   486**
Early Figures in Diagnosing Schizophrenia   486
Identifying Symptoms   487

**Arthur:** Saving the Children   487

**Clinical Description, Symptoms, and Subtypes   488**
Positive Symptoms   489

**David:** Missing Uncle Bill   490
Negative Symptoms   491
Disorganized Symptoms   493
Schizophrenia Subtypes   494
Other Psychotic Disorders   495

**Prevalence and Causes of Schizophrenia   498**
Statistics   498
Development   499
Cultural Factors   500
Genetic Influences   500
Neurobiological Influences   503
Psychological and Social Influences   508

**Treatment of Schizophrenia   510**
Biological Interventions   511
Psychosocial Interventions   513
Treatment across Cultures   516
Prevention   516

Summary   516
Key Terms   517
Answers to Concept Checks   517
Chapter Quiz   519

**13**

# Developmental and Cognitive Disorders   522

**Common Developmental Disorders   523**
Attention Deficit/Hyperactivity Disorder   524

**Danny:** The Boy Who Couldn't Sit Still   524
Learning Disorders   528

**Alice:** Taking a Reading Disorder to College   528

**Pervasive Developmental Disorders   533**
Autistic Disorder   533

**Amy:** In Her Own World   534
Treatment of Pervasive Developmental Disorders   538

**Mental Retardation   540**
**James:** Up to the Challenge   541
Clinical Description   542
Statistics   544
Causes   544
Treatment of Mental Retardation   547
Prevention of Developmental Disorders   549

**Cognitive Disorders   550**
Delirium   551

**Mr. J.:** Sudden Distress   551
Dementia   553

**Diana:** Humiliation and Fear   554
Amnestic Disorder   567

**S.T.:** Remembering Fragments   567
Summary   569
Key Terms   570
Answers to Concept Checks   570
Chapter Quiz   572

# 14

# Mental Health Services: Legal and Ethical Issues   577

**Arthur:** A Family's Dilemma   578

## Civil Commitment   578
*Criteria for Civil Commitment*   579
*Defining Mental Illness*   581
*Dangerousness*   581
*Deinstitutionalization and Homelessness*   582
*An Overview of Civil Commitment*   583

## Criminal Commitment   584
*The Insanity Defence*   585
**Wayne Sullivan:** Not Criminally Responsible or "Getting Off Easy"?   586
*Reactions to the Insanity Defence*   587
*Fitness to Stand Trial*   588
*Duty to Warn*   589
*Mental Health Professionals as Expert Witnesses*   589

## Patients' Rights and Clinical Practice Guidelines   590
*The Right to Treatment*   591
*The Right to Refuse Treatment*   591
**George Reid:** Asserting the Right to Refuse Treatment   591
*Ethics of Research Involving Human Participants*   592
**Greg Aller:** Concerned about Rights   592
*Clinical Practice Guidelines*   594

## Conclusions   596
*Summary*   596
*Key Terms*   597
*Answers to Concept Checks*   597
*Chapter Quiz*   599

## Answers to Chapter Quizzes   601
## Glossary   602
## References   610
## Name Index   684
## Subject Index   708

# Preface

Until several years ago, the science of psychopathology had been compartmentalized, with psychopathologists examining the separate effects of psychological, biological, and social influences. This approach is still reflected in popular media accounts that describe, for example, a newly discovered gene, a biological dysfunction (chemical imbalance), or early childhood experiences as a "cause" of a psychological disorder. This way of thinking still dominates discussions of causality and treatment in some psychology textbooks: "The psychoanalytic views of this disorder are ... ," "the biological views are ... ," and, often in a separate chapter, "psychoanalytic treatment approaches for this disorder are ... ," "cognitive behavioural treatment approaches are ... ," or "biological treatment approaches are...."

In the first U.S. edition of this text we tried to do something very different. We thought the field had advanced to the point that it was ready for an integrative approach in which the intricate interactions of biological, psychological, and social factors are explicated in as clear and convincing a manner as possible. Recent explosive advances in knowledge confirm this approach as the only viable way of understanding psychopathology. To take just one example, Chapter 2 now contains a description of a study demonstrating that stressful life events can lead to depression, but not everyone shows this response. Rather, stress is more likely to cause depression in individuals who already carry a particular gene that influences serotonin at the brain synapses. These results confirm the integrative approach in this book: Psychological disorders cannot be explained by genetic or environmental factors alone, but rather by their interaction. We now understand that psychological and social factors directly affect neurotransmitter function and even genetic expression. Similarly, we cannot study behavioural, cognitive, or emotional processes without appreciating the contribution of biological and social factors to psychological and psychopathological expression. Instead of compartmentalizing psychopathology, we use a more accessible approach that accurately reflects the current state of our clinical science.

## Integrative Approach

As noted above, the first U.S. edition of our text pioneered a new generation of abnormal psychology textbooks that offer an integrative and multidimensional perspective. (We acknowledge such one-dimensional approaches as biological, psychosocial, and supernatural as historic trends.) We include substantial current evidence of the reciprocal influences of biology and behaviour and of psychological and social influences on biology. Our examples hold students' attention; for example, we discuss genetic contributions to trauma exposure, the effects of early social and behavioural experience on later brain function and structure, new information on the relation of social networks to the common cold, and new data on psychosocial treatments for cancer. We emphasize the fact that in the phenomenon of implicit memory and blind sight, which may have parallels in dissociative experiences, psychological science verifies the existence of the unconscious (although it does not much resemble the seething cauldron of conflicts envisioned by Freud). We present new evidence confirming the effects of psychological treatments on neurotransmitter flow and brain function. We acknowledge the often neglected area of emotion theory for its rich contributions to psychopathology, for example, the effects of anger on cardiovascular disease. We weave scientific findings from the study of emotions together with behavioural, biological, cognitive, and social discoveries to create an integrated tapestry of psychopathology.

## Life-Span Developmental Influences

No modern view of abnormal psychology can ignore the importance of life-span developmental factors to the manifestation and treatment of psychopathology. Accordingly, we consider the importance of development throughout the text; we discuss childhood and geriatric anxiety, for example, in the context of the anxiety disorders chapter. This organization, which is for the most part consistent with DSM-IV, helps students appreciate the need to study each disorder from childhood through adulthood. We note findings on developmental considerations in separate sections of each disorder chapter and, as appropriate, discuss how specific developmental factors affect causation and treatment.

## Scientist-Practitioner Approach

We go to some lengths to explain why the scientist-practitioner approach to psychopathology is both practical and ideal. Like most of our colleagues, we view this as something more than simple awareness of how scientific findings apply to psychopathology. We show how every clinician contributes to general scientific knowledge through astute and systematic clinical observations, functional analyses of individual case studies, and systematic observations of series of cases in clinical settings. We also describe the formal methods used by scientist-practitioners, showing how abstract research designs are actually implemented in research programs.

## Clinical Cases of Real People

We have enriched the book with authentic clinical histories to illustrate scientific findings on the causes and treatment of psychopathology. We have all run active clinics for years, so most of the cases are from our own files, with supplements from case reports published by several noted Canadian practitioners. These clinical cases provide a fascinating frame of reference for the findings we describe. Most chapters begin with a case description, and most discussions of the latest theory and research are related to these very human cases.

## Disorders in Detail

We cover the major psychological disorders in 10 chapters, focusing on 3 broad categories: clinical description, causal factors, and treatment and outcomes. We pay considerable attention to case studies and DSM-IV-TR criteria, and we include statistical data, such as prevalence and incidence rates, sex ratio, age of onset, and the general course or pattern for the disorder as a whole. Throughout, we explore how biological, psychological, and social dimensions may interact to cause a particular disorder. Finally, by covering treatment and outcomes within the context of specific disorders, we provide a realistic sense of clinical practice.

## Treatment

One of the best-received innovations in the first four U.S. editions of this text is that we discuss treatment in the same chapter as the disorders themselves instead of in a separate chapter, an approach that is supported by the development of specific psychosocial and pharmacological treatment procedures for specific disorders. We have retained this integrative format and have improved on it in the present edition, and we include treatment procedures in the key terms and glossary.

## Legal and Ethical Issues

In our closing chapter we integrate many of the approaches and themes that have been discussed throughout the text. We include case studies of people who have been involved directly with many legal and ethical issues and with the delivery of mental health services in Canada. We also provide a historical context for current perspectives so students will understand the effects of social and cultural influences on legal and ethical issues.

## Diversity

Issues of culture and gender are integral to the study of psychopathology. Throughout the text we describe current thinking about which aspects of the disorders are culturally specific and which are universal, and about the strong and sometimes puzzling effects of gender roles. For instance, we discuss the current information on topics such as the gender imbalance in depression, how social phobia may be expressed differently in Japanese culture, the ethnic differences in eating disorders, and the diagnosis of ADHD outside North America. Clearly, our field will grow in depth and detail as these subjects and others become standard research topics. For example, why do some disorders overwhelmingly affect females and others appear predominantly in males? And why does this apportionment sometimes change from one culture to another? In answering questions like these, we adhere closely to science, emphasizing that gender and culture are each one dimension among several that may influence psychopathology.

The Culture Index and Gender Index on pages xxiii and xxiv will help you locate specific areas of the text where issues of culture and gender are discussed.

---

# New to the Canadian Edition

## A Thorough Update

This exciting field moves at a rapid pace, and we take particular pride in how our book reflects the most recent developments. This first Canadian edition of *Essentials of Abnormal Psychology* has been carefully revised to reflect the very latest research studies on psychological disorders and their treatment. Hundreds of recent references from 2001 to

2006 (and some still in the press) appear in this edition, and some of the information they contain stuns the imagination. Nonessential material has been eliminated, some new headings have been added, and DSM-IV-TR disorder criteria summary tables are once again included in the chapters on specific types of disorders.

## Canadian Content

Our goal in writing this edition was to retain all the best features of the earlier U.S. versions, while producing a textbook that is more relevant for the Canadian college student. The original text was written by two American authors for American college students and instructors. Thus, it tended to focus on statistics, legal issues, cultural issues, and clinical issues that were specific to the American context. Although widely employed in Canadian colleges, earlier versions of this text did not specifically include information relevant to the Canadian context. In this edition, we have remedied this situation.

In particular, we provide Canadian statistics on prevalence rates in the chapters on specific disorders, including reference to Canadian epidemiological studies. We also provide information on the Canadian health-care system and the types of mental health practitioners employed within the Canadian system. Throughout the text, we provide examples of important Canadian contributions in various areas of abnormal psychology. This actually proved to be a fairly easy task, given the abundance and very high quality of research being conducted in Canadian institutions and by Canadian researchers on various aspects of abnormal behaviour, from studies on etiology to investigations of novel treatment approaches. We have also attempted to highlight cultural influences most relevant to the Canadian context. In particular, we have included research that focuses on the mental health of Canadian Aboriginal peoples and other cultural groups strongly represented in Canadian culture (e.g., Canadians of Asian descent). Finally, we have provided coverage of the Canadian legal context with respect to mental health law, since these laws vary somewhat from those in other countries, including the United States.

## DSM-IV, DSM-IV-TR, and DSM-V

Much has been said about the mix of political and scientific considerations that resulted in DSM-IV, and naturally we have our own opinions. (David H. Barlow had the interesting experience of sitting on the task force.) Psychologists are often concerned about turf issues in what has become, for better or worse, the nosological standard in our field, and with

good reason: In previous DSM editions, scientific findings sometimes gave way to personal opinions. However, this time most professional biases were left at the door while the task force almost endlessly debated the data. This process produced enough new information to fill every psychopathology journal for a year with integrative reviews, reanalysis of existing databases, and new data from field trials. From a scholarly point of view, the process was both stimulating and exhausting.

In this book are highlights of various debates that created the nomenclature and recent updates. For example, we summarize and update the data and discussion of sadistic personality disorder and self-defeating personality disorder, two previously proposed personality disorders that did not make it into the final diagnostic criteria, and two other proposed personality disorders that are currently under study for possible inclusion in DSM-V (i.e., depressive and negativistic personality disorders, respectively). Students can thus see the process of making diagnoses, as well as the mix of data and inference that are part of it.

In 2000, the American Psychiatric Association published a revision of the text accompanying the DSM-IV diagnostic criteria that updates the scientific literature with few changes to the criteria themselves. Several senior clinical investigators from one of our research centres (DHB) participated in the text revision, and much of this information has found its way into the first Canadian edition of this textbook. For example, the text revision (DSM-IV-TR) discusses the intense continuing debate on categorical and dimensional approaches to classification. We discuss this ongoing debate in Chapter 11 as it applies to the optimal classification of personality disorders.

Now the planning process has begun for DSM-V. The first phase of this massive project involved a joint effort by the U.S. National Institute of Mental Health and the American Psychiatric Association focused on delineating needed research efforts to provide crucial information for the DSM-V process. Research planning workgroups were formed in areas such as neuroscience, problems/gaps in the current system, cross-cultural issues, and developmental issues, with the charge of producing "white papers" outlining the required research agenda. The white papers, along with an article summarizing important recommendations, were published in 2002. The Planning Committee has now organized a series of conferences to further these efforts. Eleven conferences are planned through 2007, chaired by members of the North American and international research communities on topics such as externalizing disorders of childhood, personality disorders, and stress-induced and fear circuitry disorders. In 2007, the DSM-V task force will convene with the goal of producing DSM-V by 2011–2012. It is already clear that DSM-V will incorporate a more dimensional approach to classification, as described in Chapter 3 of this textbook.

## Prevention

Looking ahead into the future of abnormal psychology as a field, the prospect of helping the most people who display psychological disorders may lie in our ability to prevent these difficulties. Although this has long been a goal of many, we are now at the beginning of what appears to be a new age in prevention research. Numerous scientists from all over the globe are developing the methodologies and techniques that may finally provide us with the means to interrupt the debilitating toll of emotional distress caused by the disorders chronicled in this book. We therefore highlight these cutting-edge prevention efforts—such as preventing eating disorders, suicide, substance abuse, and health problems like HIV and injuries—in appropriate chapters as a means of celebrating these important events as well as to spur on the field to continue this important work.

## Retained Features
### Visual Summaries

At the end of each chapter on disorders is a colourful two-page visual chart that succinctly summarizes the causes, development, symptoms, and treatment of each disorder covered in the chapter. Our integrative approach is instantly evident in these diagrams, which show the interaction of biological, psychological, and social factors in the etiology and treatment of disorders. The visual summaries will help instructors wrap up discussions, and students will appreciate them as study aids.

## Outstanding Pedagogy

- *Chapter Quizzes* are included at the end of every chapter, providing students with a valuable opportunity to measure their mastery of key chapter material. Answers to these quizzes appear at the end of the text.
- *Concept Checks* appear regularly at the end of nearly every major section in each chapter, offering a mini-test of the material just covered.
- Study aids built into each chapter and retained from the previous edition include *Learning Objectives*, a bulleted list placed at the beginning of every major section; *boldfacing of Key Terms* and a *Running Glossary* that appears at the bottom of the pages; and *Disorder Criteria Summary tables* that provide a digested version of many of the disorders listed in the DSM-IV-TR.

- Also retained from the previous U.S. edition are end-of-chapter study aids: a detailed, bulleted *Chapter Summary*, organized by major section; a list of *Key Terms*, with page references included; *answers to the Concept Check questions; InfoTrac® College Edition search terms* for researching articles related to key topics in the chapter; a list of *relevant video clips* pertaining to the chapter's topics on the Abnormal Psychology Live CD-ROM that is included with every new edition of the text; and a prompt to the student to find additional study help on the *book companion website*.
- As in the previous U.S. edition, the end-of-chapter material includes a prompt to special *Video Concept Reviews* on the *Abnormal PsychologyNow* product, where one or two particularly difficult concepts in the chapter are explained by author V. Mark Durand.

## Learning Aids for the Student

 ### Abnormal Psychology Live Student CD-ROM

Every new copy of the Canadian edition is packaged with a free CD-ROM, *Abnormal Psychology Live*, which includes video clips of actual clients discussing their disorders. Each video clip has specific questions written about it, and students can write their responses on screen as well as print them out. New clips have been added, and questions are posed to students to help them better understand the nature of disorders. Sample videos included in the Canadian edition CD-ROM are as follows:

- Virtual Reality Therapy (Chapter 4)
- Snake Phobia Treatment (Chapter 4)
- Studying the Effects of Emotions on Physical Health (Chapter 7)
- Breast Cancer Support and Education (Chapter 7)
- Research on Exercise and Weight Control (Chapter 7)
- Nicotine Dependence (Chapter 10)
- Edward: ADHD in a Gifted Student (Chapter 13)
- Rebecca: A First-Grader with Autistic Disorder (Chapter 13)
- Lauren: A Kindergartener with Down Syndrome (Chapter 13)
- Computer Simulations and Senile Dementia (Chapter 13)

**Thomson NOW! (0-17-644218-9)**

ThomsonNOW is an **online learning and homework assessment program** created in concert with the text to present a seamless, integrated learning tool.

- With ThomsonNOW, instructors can dramatically affect student success. Assigning text-specific tutorials requires no instructor set-up. In addition, faculty can use the same system to **create tailored homework assignments, quizzes, and tests** that **auto-grade** and **flow directly into the instructor's gradebook!** This means instructors can actually assign marks to homework assignments, motivating students to study the material and come to class prepared.
- Students can improve their grades and save study time with ThomsonNOW. It isn't just reading—it provides a **customized study plan** that lets students **master what they need to know without spending time on what they already know!** The study plan provides a road map to interactive exercises, videos, ebook and other resources that help students master the subject. Pretests and posttests allow students to monitor their progress. Focused studying via ThomsonNow will minimize student efforts and yet maximize results.

Within *ThomsonNOW*, V. Mark Durand provides a brief **Video Concept Review** for each chapter. In these onscreen videos, he briefly reviews difficult concepts that may need additional explanation so students can "hear them again" before the test.

##  InfoTrac® College Edition

Instructors in Canada and the United States can order InfoTrac College Edition, an online library offering instant access (through a password) to the latest research and new articles on subjects related to abnormal psychology. At the end of every chapter of this text, InfoTrac College Edition search terms are suggested.

## Companion Website

The book's website (at **www.essentialsabnormal psych.nelson.com**) offers students practice quizzes and links to related sites for each chapter of the text, as well as flash cards, glossaries, research activities, and more.

## Teaching Aids for the Instructor
### Videos

- *Abnormal Psychology: Inside Out*, Volume I 0-534-20359-0
- *Abnormal Psychology: Inside/Out*, Volume II 0-534-36480-2
- *Abnormal Psychology: Inside/Out*, Volume III 0-534-50759-X

- *Abnormal Psychology: Inside/Out*, Volume IV 0-534-63369-2
- *Deficits of the Mind and the Brain for Abnormal Psychology* 0-534-20356-6

## Classroom Presentation Materials

*Multimedia Manager Instructor's Resource CD*, a Microsoft® PowerPoint® Link Tool: This CD-ROM, adapted by Joseph Mior, includes lecture outlines that are built around this first Canadian edition. It also includes most of the figures from the text, relevant video clips, and a direct link to the Durand/Barlow/Stewart website. Also on the CD-ROM are Microsoft Word files for the print *Instructor's Manual* and the ExamView® *Computerized Test Bank*. ISBN: 0-17-644194-8

## Additional Resources

- *Test Bank* adapted by Anastasia Bake contains 100–125 items per chapter in multiple-choice, true/false, and essay formats that are sorted into factual, conceptual, and applied questions. The items are all page-referenced to the main text, and each chapter contains at least 10 items that are located on the student portion of the book's website. ISBN: 0-17-644202-2
- *Instructor's Manual* adapted by Katrina Gantly contains learning objectives, chapter outlines, chapter summaries, key terms, classroom activities, demonstrations, lecture topics, supplemental reading material, book reviews, video resources, and Internet resources. ISBN: 0-17-644186-7
- *InfoTrac College Edition:* Instructors can order this fully searchable online university library for students that offers complete articles from more than 600 scholarly and popular publications. InfoTrac College Edition access is available on a password-protected website that is updated daily.

## Titles of Interest

- *Looking into Abnormal Psychology: Contemporary Readings* by Scott O. Lilienfeld is a fascinating 234-page reader comprised of 40 articles from popular magazines and journals. Each article explores ongoing controversies regarding mental illness and its treatment.
- *Casebook in Abnormal Psychology* by Timothy A. Brown and David H. Barlow is a comprehensive casebook that reflects the integrative approach, which considers the multiple influences of genetics, biology, familial, and environmental factors within a unified model of causality, as well as maintenance and treatment of the disorder. The casebook describes treatment methods that are

the most effective interventions developed for a particular disorder. It also presents two undiagnosed cases in order to give students an appreciation for the complexity of disorders. The cases are strictly teaching/learning exercises similar to what many instructors use on their examinations.

## Acknowledgments

It is always amazing that so many people, some of whom we never have the privilege to meet, contribute so much of themselves to the success of this book. This first Canadian edition would not have begun and certainly would not have been finished without the inspiration and coordination of Joanna Cotton, my former publisher at Thomson Nelson. Joanna was involved in the early ideas stage of the book, and it was she who convinced me that writing a Canadian edition of this popular college text was an achievable goal and that it would result in a product that would be truly appreciated by abnormal psychology students and course instructors at colleges across Canada. Joanna's replacements, Ann Millar and now Anne Williams, my current publisher at Thomson Nelson, were both invaluable in terms of their considerable efforts and encouragement at later stages of the process of putting this textbook together. Many thanks to my senior developmental editor Alwynn Pinard for her tireless commitment to the project. Alwynn especially has "looked over my shoulder" to guide me throughout the development of this book and to keep me on track (or get me back on track!) with various project deadlines. Her considerable patience has been very much appreciated, and her assistance has resulted in an even better book. I am truly in her debt.

In the production process, many individuals worked as hard as I did to complete this project in a timely manner. I am indebted to Jaime Smith and Imoinda Romain, my content production managers at Thomson Nelson, and Kelly Morrison, my project manager, for coordinating the production process so that things always ran efficiently. I also want to thank Lisa Berland, my copy editor, for her attention to detail, her uncanny ability to spot inconsistencies, and her extraordinary gift in smoothing awkward prose. I also extend my thanks to Terri Rothman for her commitment to finding the best photos possible, and for her assistance in seeking permissions. Kathy MacDonald, Allison Eisner, and Pamela Collins, my research assistants in Halifax, deserve enormous credit for their organizational assistance and for their

help in researching the Canadian content, compiling the reference list, and locating missing references. It is an understatement to say that I couldn't have done it without them. In addition, I extend my thanks to Lenore Taylor, executive marketing manager at Thomson Nelson, for her important contributions in heading the marketing team for this text. And finally, I must acknowledge the fine work of the originating authors of the U.S. edition, Dr. V. Mark Durand and Dr. David H. Barlow, and their skilled editorial team at Wadsworth for providing me with such a wonderful text to work with!

*Sherry H. Stewart*
Vancouver, British Columbia, November 2006

## Reviewers

Creating this Canadian edition has been both stimulating and exhausting, and we could not have done without the valuable assistance of the reviewers who provided superb feedback. To them we express our deepest gratitude. The reviewers read the previous U.S. edition and provided extraordinarily perceptive critical comments, pointed to relevant information (Canadian content and otherwise), and offered new insights, all of which helped us immensely in revising the previous U. S. edition to make it suitable for a Canadian college market. Although not all comments were favourable, all were important. Readers who take the time to communicate their thoughts offer the greatest reward to writers and scholars.

For the first Canadian edition of *Essentials of Abnormal Psychology*, we thank the following reviewers:

Anastasia Bake, *St. Clair College*
Jean Brown, *Cambrian College*
Larry Costello, *Fanshawe College*
Pat Dockrill, *Loyalist College*
Jill Esmonde-Moore, *Georgian College*
Marilyn Hadad, *Ryerson University*
Ian McBain, *Langara College*

We also thank the reviewers of the first Canadian edition of *Abnormal Psychology: An Integrative Approach* (Barlow, Durand, & Stewart, 2006), who were enormously helpful with Canadian content suggestions—content that has also been incorporated into the current text.

# Culture Index

Aboriginal peoples: 97, 142, 201, 233, 259, 318, 361, 419
Alcohol use disorders: 411–412
Asians: 142–143, 195, 259, 301–302, 318–319, 559, 564
Blacks: 194, 201, 318, 500, 564
Body dysmorphic disorder: 194–195
Conversion disorder: 189–190
Coronary heart disease: 287
Dementia: 564
Depression: 221, 232–233, 259
Developmental disorders: 532
Diagnostic guidelines: 97
Dissociative trance disorder: 189, 201–202
Eating disorders: 310, 318–319

Fear: 65–66
Gender identity disorders: 360–361
Obsessive-compulsive disorder: 169–170
Panic disorder: 142–143
Personality disorders: 453–454, 465
Phobias: 153
Psychological disorders, differences in: 3–4
Research: 117–118
Schizophrenia: 500, 509–510, 516
Sexual dysfunctions: 376–378
Sexuality: 358
Smoking: 301–302
Somatization disorder: 166–167
Substance-related disorders: 417–418, 431
Suicide: 258–259

# Gender Index

Agoraphobia: 141–142
Body dysmorphic disorder: 194
Conversion disorder: 189
Dementia: 556, 559
Developmental disorders: 525, 531, 535
Eating disorders: 310, 313–334
Gender identity disorders: 359–364
Generalized anxiety disorder: 135
Hypochondriasis: 180
Insomnia: 338
Mood disorders: 229, 230–231, 236, 244–245

Obsessive-compulsive disorder: 169
Pain: 292
Paraphilias: 389–390
Personality disorders: 449–451, 471–472
Phobias: 152
Sexual dysfunctions: 365–373, 379–382
Sexuality: 357–358
Social phobia: 156
Somatization disorder: 184–185
Substance-related disorders: 411
Suicide: 259

# 1

# Abnormal Behaviour in Historical Context

Bert Hardy/Hulton Archive/Getty Images

## Understanding Psychopathology
*What Is a Psychological Disorder?*
*The Science of Psychopathology*
*Historical Conceptions of Abnormal Behaviour*

## The Supernatural Tradition
*Demons and Witches*
*Stress and Melancholy*
*Treatments for Possession*
*The Moon and the Stars*
*Comments*

## The Biological Tradition
*Hippocrates and Galen*
*The 19th Century*
*The Development of Biological Treatments*
*Consequences of the Biological Tradition*

## The Psychological Tradition
*Moral Therapy*
*Asylum Reform and the Decline of Moral Therapy*
*Psychoanalytic Theory*
*Humanistic Theory*
*The Behavioural Model*

## The Present: The Scientific Method and an Integrative Approach

 **Abnormal Psychology Live CD-ROM**
*Roots of Behaviour Therapy*

# Understanding Psychopathology

■ *Define abnormal behaviour (psychological disorder) and describe psychological dysfunction, distress, and atypical or culturally unexpected responses.*

■ *Describe the scientist-practitioner model.*

Today you may have gotten out of bed, had breakfast, gone to class, studied, and, at the end of the day, enjoyed the company of your friends before falling asleep. It probably did not occur to you that many physically healthy people are unable to do some or any of these things. What they have in common is a **psychological disorder,** a psychological dysfunction within an individual associated with distress or impairment in functioning and a response that is not typical or culturally expected. Before examining exactly what this means, let's look at one individual's situation.

## Jody
### The Boy Who Fainted at the Sight of Blood

Jody, a 16-year-old, was referred to our anxiety disorders clinic after increasing episodes of fainting. About two years earlier, in his first biology class, the teacher showed a movie of a frog dissection to illustrate various points about anatomy. The film was particularly graphic, with vivid images of blood, tissue, and muscle. About halfway through, Jody felt a bit lightheaded and left the room. But the images did not leave him. He continued to be bothered by them and occasionally felt slightly queasy. He began to avoid situations where he might see blood or injury. He stopped looking at magazines that might have gory pictures. He found it difficult to look at raw meat, or even Band-Aids, because they brought the feared images to mind. Eventually, anything his friends or parents said that evoked an image of blood or injury caused Jody to feel lightheaded. It got so bad that if one of his friends exclaimed, "Cut it out!" he felt faint. Beginning about six months before his visit to the clinic, Jody actually fainted when he unavoidably encountered something bloody. His family physician could find nothing wrong with him, nor could several other physicians. By the time he was referred to

our clinic he was fainting 5 to 10 times a week, often in class. Clearly, this was problematic for him and disruptive in school; each time he fainted, the other students flocked around him, trying to help, and class was interrupted. Because no one could find anything wrong with him, the principal finally concluded that he was being manipulative and suspended him from school, even though he was an honour student.

Jody was suffering from what we now call *blood-injury-injection phobia.* His reaction was quite severe, thereby meeting the criteria for **phobia,** a psychological disorder characterized by marked and persistent fear of an object or situation. But many people have similar reactions that are not as severe when they receive an injection or see someone who is injured, whether blood is visible or not. For people who react as severely as Jody, this phobia can be very disabling. They may avoid certain careers, such as medicine or nursing, and, if they are so afraid of needles and injections that they avoid them even when necessary, they put their health at risk.

## What Is a Psychological Disorder?

Keeping in mind the real-life problems faced by Jody, let's look more closely at the definition of *psychological disorder,* or abnormal behaviour: It is a *psychological dysfunction* within an individual associated with *distress or impairment* in functioning and a *response that is not typical or culturally expected* (see Figure 1.1). On the surface, these three criteria may seem obvious, but they were not easily arrived at, and it is worth a moment to explore what they mean. You will see, importantly, that no one criterion has yet been developed that fully defines abnormality.

---

**psychological disorder** Psychological dysfunction associated with distress or impairment in functioning that is not a typical or culturally expected response.

**phobia** Psychological disorder characterized by marked and persistent fear of an object or situation.

**Figure 1.1** ■ The three criteria defining a psychological disorder.

## Psychological Dysfunction

*Psychological dysfunction* refers to a breakdown in cognitive, emotional, or behavioural functioning. For example, if you are out on a date, it should be fun. But if you experience severe fear all evening and just want to go home, even though there is nothing to be afraid of, and the severe fear happens on every date, your emotions are not functioning properly. However, if all your friends agree that the person who asked you out is dangerous, then it would not be "dysfunctional" for you to be fearful and avoid the date.

A dysfunction was present for Jody: He fainted at the sight of blood. But many people experience a mild version of this reaction (feeling queasy at the sight of blood) without meeting the criteria for the disorder, so knowing where to draw the line between normal and abnormal dysfunction is often difficult. For this reason, these problems are often considered to be on a *continuum* or as a *dimension*, rather than as categories that are either present or absent. This, too, is a reason why just having a dysfunction is not enough to meet the criteria for a psychological disorder.

## Personal Distress

That the disorder or behaviour must be associated with *distress* adds an important component and seems clear: The criterion is satisfied if the individual is extremely upset. We can certainly say that Jody was very distressed and even suffered with his phobia. But remember, by itself this criterion does not define abnormal behaviour. It is often normal to be distressed—for example, if someone close to you dies. The human condition is such that suffering and distress are part of life. This is not likely to change. Furthermore, for some disorders, by definition, suffering and distress are absent. Consider the person who feels extremely elated and acts impulsively as part of a manic episode. As we see in Chapter 6, one of the major difficulties with this

problem is that people enjoy the manic state so much they are reluctant to begin treatment or stay in treatment long. Thus, defining psychological disorder by distress alone doesn't work, although the concept of distress contributes to a good definition.

The concept of *impairment* is useful, though not entirely satisfactory. For example, many people consider themselves shy or lazy. This doesn't mean that they're abnormal. But if you are so shy that you find it impossible to date or even interact with people, and you make every attempt to avoid interactions even though you would like to have friends, then your social functioning is impaired. Jody was clearly impaired by his phobia, but many people with similar, less severe reactions are not impaired. This difference again illustrates the important point that most psychological disorders are simply extreme expressions of otherwise normal emotions, behaviours, and cognitive processes.

## Atypical or Not Culturally Expected

Finally, the criterion that the response be *atypical or not culturally expected* is important but also insufficient to determine abnormality. At times, something is considered abnormal because it occurs infrequently; it deviates from the average. The greater the deviation, the more abnormal it is. You might say that someone is abnormally short or abnormally tall, meaning that the person's height deviates substantially from average, but this obviously isn't a definition of disorder. Many people are far from the average in their behaviour, but few would be considered disordered. We might call them talented or eccentric. Many artists, movie stars, and athletes fall in this category. For example, Ashley MacIsaac is a rebellious and outspoken fiddler and bandleader who pushes the limits in terms of his behaviour on stage and with the media. Although his behaviour is atypical, he is usually considered simply eccentric. Celebrities like MacIsaac are well paid and seem to enjoy their careers. In most cases, the more productive you are in the eyes of society, the more eccentricities society will tolerate. Therefore, "deviating from the average" doesn't work well as a definition.

Another view is that your behaviour is abnormal if you are violating social norms, even if a number of people are sympathetic to your point of view. This definition is useful in considering important cultural differences in psychological disorders. For example, to enter a trance state and believe you are possessed reflects a psychological disorder in most Western cultures. But in many other societies this behaviour is accepted and expected (see Chapter 5). Social norm violation, as a definition of abnormal behaviour, is particularly problematic in a multicultural society such as Canada.

We accept extreme behaviours by entertainers, such as eccentric fiddler and bandleader Ashley MacIsaac, that would not be tolerated in other members of our society.

A social standard of *normal* has also been misused. Consider, for example, the practice of committing political dissidents to mental institutions because they protest the policies of their government, which was common in the former Soviet Union before the fall of communism. Although such dissident behaviour clearly violates social norms, it should not alone be cause for commitment.

In a thoughtful analysis of the matter, Wakefield (1992, 1999) uses the shorthand definition "harmful dysfunction." A related concept that is also useful is to determine whether or not the behaviour is out of the individual's control (something he or she doesn't want to do; Widiger & Sankis, 2000). Variants of these approaches are most often used in current diagnostic practice, as outlined in the fourth edition, text revision, of the *Diagnostic and Statistical Manual* (DSM-IV-TR, American Psychiatric Association, 2000a), which contains the current listing of criteria for psychological disorders. These approaches guide our thinking in this book.

Some religious behaviours may seem unusual to us but are culturally or individually appropriate.

## An Accepted Definition

In conclusion, it is difficult to define "normal" and "abnormal" (Lilienfeld & Marino, 1995, 1999)—and the debate continues (Clark, 1999; Houts, 2001; Klein, 1999; Spitzer, 1999; Wakefield, 2003). The most widely accepted definition used in DSM-IV-TR describes *behavioural, emotional, or cognitive dysfunctions that are unexpected in their cultural context and associated with personal distress or substantial impairment in functioning* as abnormal. This definition can be useful across cultures and subcultures if we pay careful attention to what is "functional" or "dysfunctional" (or out of control) in a given society. But it is never easy to decide what represents dysfunction or dyscontrol, and some scholars have argued persuasively that the health professions will never be able to satisfactorily define "disease" or "disorder" (e.g., Lilienfeld & Marino, 1995, 1999). The best we may be able to do is to consider how the apparent disease or disorder matches a "typical" profile of a disorder—for example, major depression or schizophrenia—when most or all of the symptoms that experts would agree are part of the disorder are present. We call this typical profile a *prototype* and, as described in Chapter 3, the diagnostic criteria from DSM-IV-TR found throughout this book are all prototypes. This means that the patient may have only some of the features or symptoms of the disorder (a minimum number), but not all of them, and still meet criteria for the disorder because his or her set of symptoms is close to the "prototype." Once again this concept is described more fully in Chapter 3, where the diagnosis of psychological disorders is discussed.

The planning process for the fifth edition of the *Diagnostic and Statistical Manual* (DSM-V) has begun (Kupfer, First, & Regier, 2002), and the planning committees have already begun to wrestle with improvements they can make to definitions of "disorder." To assist this process, the planning committees have conceptualized three research questions that will form the basis for further investigation. First, they propose to do a careful analysis of the concepts that currently underlie disorders that are accepted in DSM-IV-TR, evaluating the degree to which they might conform (or not) to the numerous ways we have of understanding disorders. Second, they propose to conduct surveys of mental health professionals around the world to attempt to get a better idea of the concepts of mental disorders used worldwide and to see if some striking commonalities emerge. Finally, using the same survey process, they would look at what, in the eyes of mental health professionals, separates those people who would truly meet criteria for a disorder from other individuals who might have a mild form of the same problem such that it would not interfere with their functioning (Rounsaville et al., 2002). It is hoped that these surveys will shed light on the difficult problem of defining a psychological disorder.

To leave you with a final challenge, take the problem of defining abnormal behaviour a step further and consider this: What if Jody passed out so often that after a while neither his classmates nor his teachers even noticed because he regained consciousness quickly? Furthermore, what if Jody continued to get good grades? Would fainting all the time at the mere thought of blood be a disorder? Would it be impairing? dysfunctional? distressing? What do you think?

## The Science of Psychopathology

**Psychopathology** is the scientific study of psychological disorders. Within this field are specially trained professionals, including clinical and counselling psychologists, psychiatrists, psychiatric social workers, and psychiatric nurses, as well as marriage and family therapists and mental health counsellors. *Clinical psychologists* typically receive a Ph.D. degree following a course of graduate-level study that lasts approximately five years. This education prepares them to conduct research into the causes and treatment of psychological disorders and to diagnose, assess, and treat these disorders. Instead of a Ph.D. degree, clinical psychologists sometimes receive a Psy.D. (Doctor of Psychology) degree for which the training is similar to the Ph.D. but with more emphasis on clinical practice and less on research training. Psy.D. programs are rare in Canada; they currently exist or are in development only in Quebec (Dobson, 2003; Hunsley & Johnston, 2000). In Canada, regulation of the psychology profession is under the jurisdiction of the provinces and territories. Depending on the jurisdiction, a psychologist may have either a doctoral or a master's degree (Hunsley & Johnston, 2000). Largely to protect the public, but also in the interest of the profession (Goodman, 2000), only those who are licensed or registered with their provincial board or college are permitted to call themselves "psychologists" (e.g., such as in advertising). Note that the labels "psychotherapist" and "therapist" are not regulated by the provincial and territorial psychology boards or colleges.

Psychologists with other specialty training, such as experimental and social psychologists, concentrate on investigating the basic determinants of behaviour but do not assess or treat psychological disorders. In addition, although there is a great deal of overlap, *counselling psychologists* (who can receive a Ph.D., Psy.D., or Ed.D—Doctor of Education) tend to study and treat adjustment and vocational issues encountered by relatively healthy individuals, whereas clinical psychologists usually concentrate on more severe psychological disorders.

Psychiatrists first earn an M.D. degree in medical school and then specialize in psychiatry during a three- to four-year residency training. Psychiatrists also investigate the nature and causes of psychological disorders, often from a biological point of view, make diagnoses, and offer treatments. Many psychiatrists emphasize drugs or other biological treatments, although most use psychosocial treatments as well.

*Psychiatric social workers* typically earn a master's degree in social work as they develop expertise in collecting information relevant to the social and family situation of the individual with a psychological disorder. Social workers also treat disorders, often concentrating on family problems associated with them. *Psychiatric nurses* have advanced degrees, such as a master's or a Ph.D., and specialize in the care and treatment of patients with psychological disorders, usually in hospitals as part of a treatment team. Finally, *marriage and family therapists* and *mental health counsellors* typically spend one to two years earning a master's degree and provide clinical services in hospitals or clinics, usually under the supervision of a doctoral-level clinician. According to the research of Paula Goering and her colleagues at the Centre for Addictions and Mental Health in Toronto, there are currently 3600 psychiatrists, 13 000 psychologists and psychological associates, 11 000 psychiatric nurses, and thousands of psychiatric social workers currently practising in Canada today (Goering, Wasylenki, & Durbin, 2000).

### The Scientist-Practitioner

The most important development in the recent history of psychopathology is the adoption of scientific methods to learn more about the nature of psychological disorders, their causes, and their treatment. Many mental health professionals take a scientific approach to their clinical work and therefore earn the title **scientist-practitioner** (Barlow, Hayes, & Nelson, 1984; Hayes, Barlow, & Nelson-Gray, 1999).

Mental health practitioners may function as scientist-practitioners in one or more of three ways (see Figure 1.2). First, they may keep up with the

---

**psychopathology** Scientific study of psychological disorders.

**scientist-practitioner model** Expectation that mental health professionals will apply scientific methods to their work. They must keep current in the latest research on diagnosis and treatment, they must evaluate their own methods for effectiveness, and they may generate their own research to discover new knowledge of disorders and their treatment.

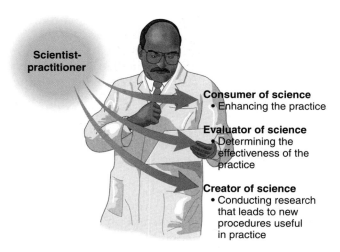

**Figure 1.2** ■ How a mental health professional can function as a scientist-practitioner.

latest scientific developments in their field and therefore use the most current diagnostic and treatment procedures. In this sense, they are consumers of the science of psychopathology to the advantage of their patients. Second, scientist-practitioners evaluate their own assessments or treatment procedures to see if they work. They are accountable not only to their patients but also to the government agencies and insurance companies that pay for the treatments, so they must demonstrate clearly that their treatments work. Third, scientist-practitioners might conduct research, often in clinics or hospitals, that produces new information about disorders or their treatment, thus becoming immune to the fads that plague our field, often at the expense of patients and their families. For example, new "miracle cures" for psychological disorders that are reported several times a year in popular media would not be used by a scientist-practitioner if there were no sound scientific data showing that they work. Such data flow from research that attempts three basic things: to describe psychological disorders, to determine their causes, and to treat them (see Figure 1.3). These three categories compose an organizational structure that recurs throughout this book and that is formally evident in the discussions of specific disorders beginning in Chapter 4. A general overview of them now will give you a clearer perspective on our efforts to understand abnormality.

## Clinical Description

In hospitals and clinics we often say that a patient "presents" with a specific problem or set of problems, or we discuss the **presenting problem.** *Presents* is a traditional shorthand way of indicating why the person came to the clinic. Describing Jody's presenting problem is the first step in determining

his **clinical description,** which represents the unique combination of behaviours, thoughts, and feelings that make up a specific disorder. The word *clinical* refers both to the types of problems or disorders that you would find in a clinic or hospital and to the activities connected with assessment and treatment. Throughout this text are excerpts from many more individual cases, most of them from our personal files.

Clearly, one important function of the clinical description is to specify what makes the disorder different from normal behaviour or from other disorders. Statistical data may also be relevant. For example, how many people in the population as a whole have the disorder? This figure is called the **prevalence** of the disorder. Statistics on how many new cases occur during a given period, such as a year, represent the **incidence** of the disorder. Other statistics include the *sex ratio*—that is, what percentage of males and females have the disorder—and the typical *age of onset*, which often differs from one disorder to another.

In addition to having different symptoms, age of onset, and possibly a different sex ratio and prevalence, most disorders follow a somewhat individual pattern, or **course.** For example, some disorders, such as schizophrenia (see Chapter 12), follow a *chronic course,* meaning that they tend to last a long time, sometimes a lifetime. Other disorders, such as mood disorders (see Chapter 6), follow an *episodic course,* in that the individual is likely to recover within a few months, only to suffer a recurrence of the disorder later. This pattern may repeat throughout a person's

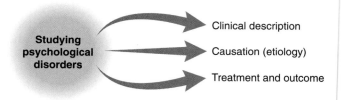

**Figure 1.3** ■ Three major categories make up the study and discussion of psychological disorders.

---

**presenting problem**   Original complaint reported by the client to the therapist. The actual treated problem may sometimes be a modification derived from the presenting problem.

**clinical description**   Details of the combination of behaviours, thoughts, and feelings of an individual that make up a particular disorder.

**prevalence**   Number of people displaying a disorder in the total population at any given time.

**incidence**   Number of new cases of a disorder appearing during a specific time period.

**course**   Pattern of development and change of a disorder over time.

life. Still other disorders may have a *time-limited course,* meaning the disorder will improve without treatment in a relatively short period.

Closely related to differences in the course of disorders are differences in the onset. Some disorders have an *acute onset,* meaning that they begin suddenly; others develop gradually over an extended period, which is sometimes called an *insidious onset.* It is important to know the typical course of a disorder so that we can know what to expect in the future and how best to deal with the problem. This is an important part of the clinical description. For example, if someone has a mild disorder with acute onset that we know is time limited, we might advise the individual not to bother with expensive treatment, because the problem will be over soon enough, like a common cold. However, if the disorder is likely to last a long time (become chronic), the individual might want to seek treatment and take other appropriate steps. The anticipated course of a disorder is called the **prognosis.** So we might say, "the prognosis is good," meaning the individual will probably recover, or "the prognosis is guarded," meaning the probable outcome doesn't look good.

The patient's age may be an important part of the clinical description. A specific psychological disorder occurring in childhood may present differently from the same disorder in adulthood or old age. Children experiencing severe anxiety and panic often assume that they are physically ill because they have difficulty understanding that there is nothing physically wrong. Because their thoughts and feelings are different from those experienced by adults with anxiety and panic, children are often misdiagnosed and treated for a medical disorder.

## Causation, Treatment, and Outcomes

**Etiology,** or the study of origins, has to do with why a disorder begins (what causes it) and includes biological, psychological, and social dimensions. Because the etiology of psychological disorders is so important to this field, we devote an entire chapter (Chapter 2) to it. Treatment is often important to the study of psychological disorders. If a new drug or psychosocial treatment is successful in treating a disorder, it may give us some hints about the nature of the disorder and its causes. For example, if a drug with a specific known effect within the nervous system alleviates a certain psychological disorder, we know that something in that part of the nervous system might be either causing the disorder or helping maintain it. Similarly, if a psychosocial treatment designed to help clients regain a sense of control over their lives is effective with a certain disorder, a diminished sense of control may be an important psychological component of the disorder itself.

© Royalty-Free/CORBIS

Children experience panic and anxiety differently from adults, so their reactions may be mistaken for symptoms of physical illness.

As we see in the next chapter, psychology is never that simple. This is because the *effect* does not necessarily imply the *cause.* To use a common example, you might take an aspirin to relieve a tension headache you developed during a gruelling day of taking exams. If you then feel better, that does not mean that the headache was caused by a lack of aspirin. Nevertheless, many people seek treatment for psychological disorders, and treatment can provide interesting hints about the nature of the disorder.

In the past, textbooks emphasized treatment approaches in a general sense, with little attention to the disorder being treated. For example, a mental health professional might be thoroughly trained in a single theoretical approach, such as psychoanalysis or behaviour therapy (both described later in the chapter), and then use that approach on every disorder. More recently, as our science has

**prognosis** Predicted future development of a disorder over time.

**etiology** Cause or source of a disorder.

advanced, we have developed specific effective treatments that do not always adhere neatly to one theoretical approach or another but have grown out of a deeper understanding of the disorder in question. For this reason, there are no separate chapters in this book on such types of treatment approaches as psychodynamic, cognitive behavioural, or humanistic. Rather, the latest and most effective drug and psychosocial treatments are described in the context of specific disorders in keeping with our integrative multidimensional perspective.

We now survey many early attempts to *describe* and *treat* abnormal behaviour, and more still to comprehend its *causes*, which will give you a better perspective on current approaches. In Chapter 2, we examine exciting contemporary views of causation and treatment. In Chapter 3, we discuss efforts to describe, or classify, abnormal behaviour, then we review research methods—our systematic efforts to discover the truths underlying description, cause, and treatment that allow us to function as scientist-practitioners. In Chapters 4 through 13, we examine specific disorders; our discussion is organized in each case in the now familiar triad of description, cause, and treatment. Finally, in Chapter 14 we examine legal, professional, and ethical issues that are relevant to psychological disorders and their treatment in Canada today. With that overview in mind, let us turn to the past.

## Historical Conceptions of Abnormal Behaviour

For thousands of years, humans have tried to explain and control problematic behaviour. But our efforts always derive from the theories or models of behaviour that are popular at the time. The purpose of these models is to explain why someone is "acting like that." Three major models that have guided us date back to the beginnings of civilization.

Humans have always supposed that agents outside our bodies and environment influence our behaviour, thinking, and emotions. These agents, which might be divinities, demons, spirits, or other phenomena such as magnetic fields, the moon, or the stars, are the driving forces behind the *supernatural model*. In addition, since ancient Greece, the mind has often been called the *soul* or the *psyche* and considered separate from the body. Although many have thought that the mind can influence the body and, in turn, the body can influence the mind, most philosophers looked for causes of abnormal behaviour in one or the other. This split gave rise to two traditions of thought about abnormal behaviour, summarized as the *biological model* and the *psychological model*.

These three models—the supernatural, the biological, and the psychological—are very old but continue to be used today.

## Concept Check 1.1

**Part A** Write the letter for any or all of the following definitions of abnormality in the blanks: (a) societal norm violation, (b) impairment in functioning, (c) dysfunction, and (d) distress.

1. Miguel recently began feeling sad and lonely. Although still able to function at work and fulfill other responsibilities, he finds himself feeling down much of the time and he worries about what is happening to him. Which of the definitions of abnormality apply to Miguel's situation? _____

2. Three weeks ago, Jane, a 35-year-old business executive, stopped showering, refused to leave her apartment, and started watching television talk shows. Threats of being fired have failed to bring Jane back to reality, and she continues to spend her days staring blankly at the television screen. Which of the definitions seems to describe Jane's behaviour? _____

**Part B** Match the following words that are used in clinical descriptions with their corresponding examples: (a) presenting problem, (b) prevalence, (c) incidence, (d) prognosis, (e) course, or (f) etiology.

3. Maria should recover quickly with no intervention necessary. Without treatment, John will deteriorate rapidly. _____

4. Three new cases of bulimia have been reported in this county, and only one in the next county, during the past month. _____

5. Elizabeth visited the campus mental health centre because of her increasing feelings of guilt and anxiety. _____

6. Biological, psychological, and social influences all contribute to a variety of disorders. _____

7. The pattern a disorder follows can be chronic, time limited, or episodic. _____

8. How many people in the population as a whole suffer from obsessive-compulsive disorder? _____

# The Supernatural Tradition

■ *Place psychopathology in its historical context by identifying historical conceptions of abnormal behaviour in terms of supernatural influences.*

For much of our recorded history, deviant behaviour has been considered a reflection of the battle between good and evil. When confronted with unexplainable, irrational behaviour and by suffering and upheaval, people perceived evil. A noted historian, Barbara Tuchman, chronicled the second half of the 14th century, a particularly difficult time for humanity, in *A Distant Mirror* (Tuchman, 1978). She ably captures the conflicting tides of opinion on the origins and treatment of insanity during that bleak and tumultuous period.

## Demons and Witches

One strong current of opinion put the causes and treatment of psychological disorders squarely in the realm of the supernatural. During the last quarter of the 14th century, religious and lay authorities supported these popular superstitions, and society began to believe in the reality and power of demons and witches. The Catholic Church had split, and a second centre, complete with a pope, emerged in the south of France to compete with Rome. In reaction to this schism, the Roman church fought back against the evil in the world that must have been behind this heresy.

People turned increasingly to magic and sorcery to solve their problems. During these turbulent times, the bizarre behaviour of people afflicted with psychological disorders was seen as the work of the devil and witches. It followed that individuals possessed by evil spirits were probably responsible for any misfortune experienced by the townspeople, which inspired drastic action against the possessed. Treatments included *exorcism*, in which various religious rituals were performed to rid the victim of evil spirits. Other approaches included shaving the pattern of a cross in the hair of the victim's head and securing sufferers to a wall near the front of a church so that they might benefit from hearing Mass.

The conviction that sorcery and witches are causes of madness and other evils continued into the 15th century, and evil continued to be blamed for unexplainable behaviour, even after the European founding of the New World, as evidenced by the Salem witch trials.

Mary Evans Picture Library

During the Middle Ages, individuals with psychological disorders were sometimes thought to be possessed by evil spirits that had to be exorcised through rituals.

## Stress and Melancholy

An equally strong opinion, even during this period, reflected the enlightened view that insanity was a natural phenomenon, caused by mental or emotional stress, and that it was curable (Alexander & Selesnick, 1966; Maher & Maher, 1985). Mental depression and anxiety were recognized as illnesses (Kemp, 1990; Schoeneman, 1977), although symptoms such as despair and lethargy were often identified by the church with the sin of *acedia*, or sloth (Tuchman, 1978). Common treatments were rest, sleep, and a healthy and happy environment. Other treatments included baths, ointments, and various potions. Indeed, during the 14th and 15th centuries, people with mental illnesses, along with people who had physical deformities or disabilities, were often moved from house to house in medieval villages as neighbours took turns caring for them. We now know that this medieval practice of keeping people who have psychological disturbances in their own community is beneficial (see Chapter 12).

One of the chief advisers to the king of France, a bishop and philosopher named Nicholas Oresme, suggested that the disease of melancholy (depression) was the source of some bizarre behaviour, rather than demons. Oresme pointed out that much of the evidence for the existence of sorcery and witchcraft, particularly among people with psychological disorders, was obtained from people who were tortured and who, quite understandably, confessed to anything.

These conflicting crosscurrents of natural and supernatural explanations for mental disorders are represented more or less strongly in various historical works, depending on the sources consulted by historians. Some assumed that demonic influences were the predominant explanations of abnormal behaviour during the Middle Ages (e.g., Zilboorg & Henry, 1941); others believed that the supernatural had little or no influence. As we see in the handling of the severe psychological disorder experienced by the late-14th-century King Charles VI of France, both influences were strong, sometimes alternating in the treatment of the same case.

## Charles VI
### The Mad King

In the summer of 1392, King Charles VI of France was under a great deal of stress, due in part to the division of the Catholic Church. As he rode with his army to the province of Brittany, a nearby aide dropped his lance with a loud clatter and the king, thinking he was under attack, turned on his own army, killing several prominent knights before being subdued from behind. The army immediately marched back to Paris. The king's lieutenants and advisers concluded that he was mad.

During the following years, at his worst the king hid in a corner of his castle believing he was made of glass or roamed the corridors howling like a wolf. At other times he couldn't remember who or what he was. He became fearful and enraged whenever he saw his own royal coat of arms and would try to destroy it if it were brought near him.

The people of Paris were devastated by their leader's apparent madness. Some thought it reflected God's anger, because the king failed to take up arms to end the schism in the Catholic Church; others thought it was God's warning against taking up arms; and still others thought it was divine punishment for heavy taxes (a conclusion some people might make today). But most thought the king's madness was caused by sorcery, a belief strengthened by a great drought that dried up the ponds and rivers, causing cattle to die of thirst. Merchants claimed their worst losses in 20 years.

Naturally, the king was given the best care available. The most famous healer in the land was a 92-year-old physician whose treatment program included moving the king to one of his residences in the country where the air was thought to be the cleanest in the land. The physician prescribed rest, relaxation, and recreation. After some time, the king seemed to recover. The physician recommended that the king not be burdened with the responsibilities of running the kingdom, claiming that if he had few worries or irritations, his mind would gradually strengthen and further improve.

Unfortunately, the physician died and the insanity of King Charles VI returned more seriously than before. This time, however, he came under the influence of the conflicting crosscurrent of supernatural causation. "An unkempt evil-eyed charlatan and pseudo-mystic named Arnaut Guilhem was allowed to treat Charles on his claim of possessing a book given by God to Adam by means of which man could overcome all affliction resulting from original sin" (Tuchman, 1978, p. 514). Guilhem insisted that the king's malady was caused by sorcery, but his treatments failed to produce a cure.

A variety of remedies and rituals of all kinds were tried, but none worked. High-ranking officials and doctors of the university called for the "sorcerers" to be discovered and punished. "On one occasion, two Augustinian friars, after getting no results from magic incantations and a liquid made from powdered pearls, proposed to cut incisions in the king's head. When this was not allowed by the king's council, the friars accused those who opposed their recommendation of sorcery" (Tuchman, 1978, p. 514). Even the king, during his lucid moments, came to believe that the source of madness was evil and sorcery. "In the name of Jesus Christ," he cried, weeping in his agony, "if there is any one of you who is an accomplice to this evil I suffer, I beg him to torture me no longer but let me die!" (Tuchman, 1978, p. 515).

*Mary Evans Picture Library*

If Jody had lived during the late 14th century, it is possible that he would have been seen as possessed and subjected to exorcism. You may remember the movie *The Exorcist*, in which a young girl, behaving very strangely, was screened for every possible mental and physical disorder before authorities reluctantly resorted to an exorcism.

## Treatments for Possession

With a perceived connection between evil deeds and sin on the one hand and psychological disorders on the other, it is logical to conclude that the person is largely responsible for the disorder, which might well be a punishment for evil deeds. Does this sound familiar? The acquired immune deficiency syndrome (AIDS) epidemic is associated with a similar belief among some people. Because the human immuno-deficiency virus (HIV) is, in Western societies, most prevalent among practising homosexuals, many people believe it is a divine punishment for what they consider abhorrent behaviour. This view has dissipated as the AIDS virus spreads to other "less sinful" segments of the population, but it still persists.

Possession, however, is not always connected with sin but may be seen as involuntary, and the possessed individual may be seen as blameless. Furthermore, exorcisms at least have the virtue of being relatively painless. Interestingly, they sometimes work, as do other forms of faith healing, for reasons we will explore in subsequent chapters. But what if they did not? In the Middle Ages, if exorcism failed, some authorities thought that steps were necessary to make the body uninhabitable by evil spirits, and many people were subjected to confinement, beatings, and other forms of torture (Kemp, 1990).

Somewhere along the way, a creative "therapist" decided that hanging people over a pit full of poisonous snakes might scare the evil spirits right out of their bodies (to say nothing of terrifying the people themselves). Strangely, this approach sometimes worked; that is, the most disturbed, oddly behaving individuals would suddenly come to their senses and experience relief from their symptoms, if only temporarily. Naturally, this was reinforcing to the therapist, so snake pits were built in many institutions. Many other treatments based on the hypothesized therapeutic element of shock were developed, including dunkings in ice-cold water.

## The Moon and the Stars

The Swiss physician Paracelsus (1493–1541) rejected notions of possession by the devil, suggesting instead that the movements of the moon

In hydrotherapy, patients were shocked back to their senses by being submerged in ice-cold water.

and stars had profound effects on people's psychological functioning. This influential theory inspired the word *lunatic*, which is derived from the Latin word for "moon," *luna*. You might hear some of your friends explain something crazy they did last night by saying, "It must have been the full moon." The belief that heavenly bodies affect human behaviour still exists, although there is no scientific evidence to support it. This belief is most noticeable today in followers of astrology, who hold that their behaviour and the major events in their lives can be predicted by their day-to-day relationship to the position of the planets. However, no serious evidence has ever confirmed such a connection.

## Comments

The supernatural tradition in psychopathology is alive and well, although it is relegated, for the most part, to some cultures outside North America and to small religious sects within North America. Members of organized religions in most parts of the world look to psychology and medical science for help with major psychological disorders; in fact, the Roman Catholic Church requires that all health-care resources be exhausted before spiritual solutions such as exorcism can be considered. Nonetheless, miraculous cures are sometimes achieved by exorcism, magic potions, rituals, and other methods that seem to have little connection with modern science. It is fascinating to explore them when they do occur, and we will return to this topic in subsequent chapters. But such cases are relatively rare, and almost no one would advocate supernatural treatment for severe psychological disorders except, perhaps, as a last resort.

# The Biological Tradition

■ *Trace the major historical developments and underlying assumptions of the biological approach to understanding abnormal behaviour.*

Physical causes of mental disorders have been sought since early in history. Important to the biological tradition are a man, Hippocrates; a disease, syphilis; and the early consequences of believing that psychological disorders are biologically caused.

## Hippocrates and Galen

The Greek physician Hippocrates (460–377 B.C.E.) is considered to be the father of modern medicine. He and his associates left a body of work called the *Hippocratic Corpus* written between 450 and 350 B.C.E. (Maher & Maher, 1985), in which they suggested that psychological disorders could be treated like any other disease. They did not limit their search for the causes of psychopathology to the general area of "disease," because they believed that psychological disorders might also be caused by brain pathology or head trauma and could be influenced by heredity (genetics). These were remarkably astute deductions for the time, and they have been supported in recent years. Hippocrates considered the brain to be the seat of wisdom, consciousness, intelligence, and emotion. Therefore, disorders involving these functions would logically be located in the brain. Hippocrates also recognized the importance of psychological and interpersonal contributions to psychopathology, such as the sometimes negative effects of family stress; on some occasions, he removed patients from their families.

The Roman physician Galen (ca. 129–198 C.E.) later adopted the ideas of Hippocrates and his associates and developed them further, creating a powerful and influential school of thought within the biological tradition that extended well into the 19th century. One of the more interesting and influential legacies of the Hippocratic-Galenic approach is the *humoral theory* of disorders. Hippocrates assumed that normal brain functioning was related to four bodily fluids or *humours:* blood, black bile, yellow bile, and phlegm. Blood came from the heart, black bile from the spleen, phlegm from the brain, and choler or yellow bile from the liver. Physicians believed that disease resulted from too much or too little of one of the humours; for example, too much black bile was thought to cause melancholia (depression). In fact, the term *melancholer,* which means black bile, is still used today in its derivative form *melancholy* to refer to aspects of depression. The humoral theory was, perhaps, the first example of associating psychological disorders with chemical imbalance, an approach that is widespread today.

The four humours were related to the Greeks' conception of the four basic qualities: heat, dryness, moisture, and cold. Each humour was associated with one of these qualities. Terms derived from the four humours are still sometimes applied to personality traits. For example, *sanguine* (red, like blood) describes someone who is ruddy in complexion (presumably from copious blood flowing through the body), and cheerful and optimistic. Nonetheless, insomnia and delirium were also thought to be caused by excessive blood in the brain. *Melancholic,* of course, means depressive (depression was thought to be caused by black bile flooding the brain). A *phlegmatic* personality (from the humour phlegm) indicates apathy and sluggishness but can also mean being calm under stress. A *choleric* person (from yellow bile or choler) is hot tempered (Maher & Maher, 1985).

Excesses of one or more humours were treated by regulating the environment to increase or decrease heat, dryness, moisture, or cold, depending on which humour was out of balance. One reason King Charles VI's physician moved him to the less stressful countryside was to restore the balance in his humours (Kemp, 1990). In addition to rest, good nutrition, and exercise, two treatments were developed. In one, *bleeding* or *bloodletting,* a carefully measured amount of blood was removed from the body, often with leeches. The other was to induce vomiting; indeed, in a well-known treatise on depression published in 1621, *Anatomy of Melancholy,* Burton recommended eating tobacco and a half-boiled cabbage to induce vomiting (Burton, 1621/1977). Three hundred years ago, Jody might have been diagnosed with an illness, a brain disorder, or some other physical problem and given the proper medical treatments of the day, including bed rest, a healthful diet, exercise, and other ministrations as indicated.

Hippocrates also coined the word *hysteria* to describe a concept he learned about from the Egyptians, who had identified what we now call the *somatoform disorders* (see Chapter 5). In these disorders, the physical symptoms appear to be the result of an organic pathology for which no organic cause can be found, such as paralysis and some kinds of blindness. Because these disorders occurred primarily in women, the Egyptians (and

National Library of Medicine

*Breathing a vein*

Bloodletting, the extraction of blood from patients, was intended to restore the balance of humours in the body.

Hippocrates) mistakenly assumed that they were restricted to women. They also presumed a cause: The empty uterus wandered to various parts of the body in search of conception (the Greek for "uterus" is *hysteron*). Numerous physical symptoms reflected the location of the wandering uterus. The prescribed cure might be marriage or, occasionally, fumigation of the vagina to lure the uterus back to its natural location (Alexander & Selesnick, 1966). Knowledge of physiology eventually disproved the wandering uterus theory; however, the tendency to stigmatize dramatic women as "hysterical" continued unabated well into the 1970s, when mental health professionals became sensitive to the prejudicial stereotype the term implied.

## The 19th Century

The biological tradition waxed and waned during the centuries after Hippocrates and Galen but was reinvigorated in the 19th century by two factors: the discovery of the nature and cause of syphilis, and strong support from the well-respected North American psychiatrist John P. Grey.

### Syphilis

Behavioural and cognitive symptoms of what we now know as advanced syphilis, a sexually transmitted disease caused by a bacterial microorganism entering the brain, include believing that everyone is plotting against you (delusion of persecution) or

that you are God (delusion of grandeur), as well as other bizarre behaviours. Although these symptoms are similar to those of psychosis—psychological disorders characterized in part by beliefs that are not based in reality (delusions) and/or perceptions that are not based in reality (hallucinations)—researchers recognized that a subgroup of apparently psychotic patients deteriorated steadily, becoming paralyzed and dying within five years of onset. This course of events contrasted with that of most psychotic patients, who remained fairly stable. In 1825, the condition was designated a disease, *general paresis,* because it had consistent symptoms (presentation) and a consistent course that resulted in death. The relationship between general paresis and syphilis was only gradually established. Louis Pasteur's germ theory of disease, around 1870, facilitated the identification of the specific bacterial microorganism that caused syphilis. Pasteur stated that all the symptoms of a disease were caused by a germ (bacterium) that had invaded the body.

Of equal importance was the discovery of a cure for general paresis. Physicians observed a surprising recovery in patients who had contracted malaria, and deliberately injected others with blood from a soldier who was ill with malaria. Many recovered, because the high fever "burned out" the syphilis bacteria. Obviously, this type of experiment would not be ethically possible today. Ultimately, clinical investigators discovered that penicillin cures syphilis, but with the malaria cure, "madness" and associated behavioural and cognitive symptoms for the first time were traced directly to a curable infection. Many mental health professionals then assumed that comparable causes and cures might be discovered for all psychological disorders.

### John P. Grey

The champion of the biological tradition in North America was a very influential psychiatrist named John P. Grey who was appointed superintendent of a large hospital in New York in 1854 (Bockoven, 1963). Grey also became editor of the *American Journal of Insanity,* the precursor of the current *American Journal of Psychiatry,* the flagship publication of the American Psychiatric Association. Grey's position was that insanity was *always* due to physical causes. Therefore, the mentally ill patient should be treated as physically ill. The emphasis was again on rest, diet, and proper room temperature and ventilation, approaches used for centuries by previous therapists in the biological tradition. Grey even invented the rotary fan to ventilate his large hospital.

Under Grey's leadership, the conditions in hospitals greatly improved, and they became more humane, livable institutions. But in subsequent years they also became so large and impersonal that individual attention was not possible.

In fact, leaders in psychiatry at the end of the 19th century were alarmed at the increasing size and impersonality of mental hospitals and recommended that they be downsized. It was almost 100 years before the community mental health movement was successful in reducing the population of mental hospitals with the controversial policy of "deinstitutionalization," in which patients were released into their communities. Unfortunately, this practice has as many negative consequences as positive ones, including a large increase in the number of chronically disabled patients homeless on the streets of our cities.

## The Development of Biological Treatments

On the positive side, renewed interest in the biological origin of psychological disorders led, ultimately, to greatly increased understanding of biological contributions to psychopathology and to the development of new treatments. In the 1930s, the physical interventions of electric shock and brain surgery were often used. Their effects, and the effects of new drugs, were discovered by accident. For example, insulin was occasionally given to stimulate appetite in psychotic patients who were not eating, but it also seemed to calm them down. In 1927, a Viennese physician, Manfred Sakel, began using higher and higher dosages until patients convulsed and became temporarily comatose (Sakel, 1958). Some recovered their mental health, much to the surprise of everybody, and their recovery was attributed to the

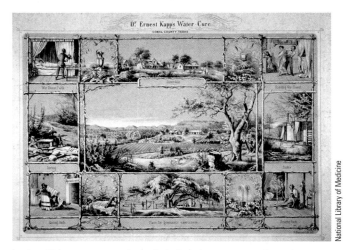

In the 19th century, psychological disorders were attributed to mental or emotional stress, so patients were often treated sympathetically in a restful and hygienic environment.

*National Library of Medicine*

convulsions. The procedure became known as *insulin shock therapy*, but it was abandoned because it was too dangerous, often resulting in prolonged coma or even death. Other methods of producing convulsions had to be found.

In the 1920s, Joseph von Meduna observed that schizophrenia was rarely found in epileptics (which ultimately did not prove to be true). Some of his followers concluded that induced brain seizures might cure schizophrenia. Following suggestions on the possible benefits of applying electric shock directly to the brain—notably, by two Italian physicians, Cerletti and Bini, in 1938—a surgeon in London treated a depressed patient by sending six small shocks directly through his brain, producing convulsions (Hunt, 1980). The patient recovered. Though greatly modified, shock treatment is still with us today. The controversial modern uses of *electroconvulsive therapy* (ECT) are described in Chapter 6. It is interesting that even now we have little knowledge of how it works.

During the 1950s, the first effective drugs for severe psychotic disorders were developed in a systematic way. These drugs were introduced to Canada by psychiatrist Hans Lehman. Before that time, a number of medicinal substances, including opium (derived from poppies), had been used as sedatives, along with countless herbs and folk remedies (Alexander & Selesnick, 1966). With the discovery of *Rauwolfia serpentine* (later renamed reserpine) and another class of drugs called *neuroleptics* (major tranquillizers), for the first time hallucinatory and delusional thought processes could be diminished; these drugs also controlled agitation and aggressiveness. Other discoveries included *benzodiazepines* (minor tranquillizers), which seemed to reduce anxiety. By the 1970s, the benzodiazepines (known by brand names such as Valium and Librium) were among the most widely prescribed drugs in the world. As drawbacks and side effects of tranquillizers became apparent, along with their limited effectiveness, prescriptions decreased somewhat (we discuss the benzodiazepines in more detail in Chapters 4 and 10).

Throughout the centuries, as Alexander and Selesnick (1966) point out, "The general pattern of drug therapy for mental illness has been one of initial enthusiasm followed by disappointment" (p. 287). For example, bromides, a class of sedating drugs, were used at the end of the 19th and the beginning of the 20th century to treat anxiety and other psychological disorders. By the 1920s, they were reported as being effective for many serious psychological and emotional symptoms. By 1928, one of every five prescriptions in the United States was for bromides. When their side effects, including various undesirable physical symptoms, became widely known, and experience began to show that their overall effectiveness was relatively modest, bromides largely disappeared from the scene.

Neuroleptics have also been used less as attention has focused on their many side effects, such as tremors and shaking. However, the positive side effects of these drugs on some patients' psychotic symptoms of hallucinations, delusions, and agitation revitalized both the search for biological contributions to psychological disorders and the search for new and more powerful drugs, a search that has paid many dividends, as documented in later chapters.

### Consequences of the Biological Tradition

In the late 19th century, John P. Grey and his colleagues ironically reduced or eliminated interest in treating mental patients because they thought that mental disorders were due to some as yet undiscovered brain pathology and were therefore incurable. The only available course of action was to hospitalize these patients. In fact, around the turn of the century some nurses documented clinical success in treating mental patients with psychological methods but were prevented from treating others for fear of raising hopes of a cure among family members. In place of treatment, interest centred on diagnosis, legal questions concerning the responsibility of patients for their actions during periods of insanity, and the study of brain pathology itself.

Emil Kraepelin (1856–1926) was the dominant figure during this period and one of the founding fathers of modern psychiatry. He was extremely influential in advocating the major ideas of the biological tradition, but he was not very involved in treatment. His lasting contribution was in the area of diagnosis and classification, which we'll discuss in detail in Chapter 3. Kraepelin (1913) was one of the first to distinguish among various psychological

disorders, seeing that each may have a different age of onset and course, with somewhat different clusters of presenting symptoms and probably a different cause. Many of his descriptions of schizophrenic disorders are still useful today.

By the end of the 1800s, a scientific approach to psychological disorders and their classification had begun with the search for biological causes. Furthermore, treatment was based on humane principles. However, there were many drawbacks, the most unfortunate being that active intervention and treatment were all but eliminated in some settings even though some effective approaches were available. It is to these that we now turn.

---

**Concept Check 1.2**

For thousands of years, humans have tried to understand and control abnormal behaviour. Check your understanding of these historical theories and match them to the treatments used to "cure" abnormal behaviour: (a) marriage, fumigation of the vagina; (b) hypnosis; (c) bloodletting, induced vomiting; (d) patient placed in socially facilitative environments; and (e) exorcism, burning at the stake.

1. Supernatural causes; evil demons took over the victims' bodies and controlled their behaviours. _____
2. The humoral theory reflected the belief that normal functioning of the brain required a balance of four bodily fluids or humours. _____
3. Maladaptive behaviour was caused by poor social and cultural influences within the environment. _____

---

# The Psychological Tradition

■ *Describe the different approaches of the psychological tradition (i.e., psychoanalysis, humanism, and behavioural) with regard to their explanations of abnormal behaviour.*

It is a long leap from evil spirits to brain pathology as causes of psychological disorders. In the intervening centuries, where was the body of thought that put psychological development, both normal and abnormal, in an interpersonal and social context? In fact, this approach has a long and distinguished tradition.

Plato, for example, thought that the two causes of maladaptive behaviour were the social and cultural influences in one's life and the learning that took place in that environment. If something was wrong in the environment, such as abusive parents, one's impulses and emotions would overcome reason. The best treatment was to reeducate the individual through rational discussion so that the power of reason would predominate (Maher & Maher, 1985). This was a precursor to modern **psychosocial** approaches, which focus not only on psychological factors but also on social and cultural ones. Other well-known early philosophers, including Aristotle, also emphasized the influence of social environment and early learning on later psychopathology. These philosophers wrote about the importance of fantasies, dreams, and cognitions and thus anticipated, to some extent, later developments in psychoanalytic thought and cognitive science. They also advocated humane and responsible care for people with psychological disturbance.

## Moral Therapy

During the first half of the 18th century, a strong psychosocial approach to mental disorders called **moral therapy** became influential. The term *moral* really meant "emotional" or "psychological." Its basic tenets included treating institutionalized patients as normally as possible in a setting that provided them with many opportunities for appropriate social and interpersonal contact (Bockoven, 1963). Relationships were carefully nurtured. Individual attention clearly emphasized positive consequences for appropriate interactions and behaviour; the staff made a point of modelling this behaviour. Restraint and seclusion were eliminated.

Moral therapy as a system originated with the well-known French psychiatrist Philippe Pinel (1745–1826; Zilboorg & Henry, 1941). A former patient, Pussin, long since recovered, was working in a Parisian hospital when Pinel took over. Pussin had already instituted remarkable reforms, remembering, perhaps, being shackled as a patient himself. Pussin persuaded Pinel to go along with the changes. Much to Pinel's credit, he did, providing a humane, socially facilitative atmosphere that produced "miraculous" results.

After William Tuke (1732–1822) followed Pinel's lead in England, Benjamin Rush (1745–1813), often considered the founder of North American psychiatry, introduced moral therapy to the New World. It then became the treatment of choice in the leading hospitals. *Asylums* had appeared in the 16th century in Europe, but they were more like prisons than hospitals. It was the rise of moral therapy in Europe and North America that made asylums habitable and even therapeutic.

Institutionalizing people with mental illness in Canada began with humane intentions, to relieve the neglect and suffering of these individuals who had previously been placed in jails or poorhouses, or left to care for themselves in the community (Sussman,

Patients with psychological disorders were freed from chains and shackles as a result of the influence of Philippe Pinel (1745–1826), a pioneer in making mental institutions more humane.

1998). In the 19th century, Canadian provinces proceeded relatively independently to develop separate and more adequate provisions for people with mental illness in the form of mental hospitals or "asylums" (see Table 1.1 for a summary). Asylum development in most provinces was influenced to a great extent by systems and movements in Great Britain and to a lesser extent by those in the United States. The involvement of religious orders in the care of people with mental illnesses in Quebec was influenced by practices occurring in France. The development of asylums through the moral therapy movement did bring some relief to many people with mental illnesses (Sussman, 1998).

## Asylum Reform and the Decline of Moral Therapy

Unfortunately, after the mid-19th century, humane treatment declined because of a convergence of factors. First, it was widely recognized that moral therapy worked best when the number of patients in an institution was 200 or fewer, allowing for a great deal of individual attention. However, patient loads in existing hospitals increased to 1000, 2000, and more with the enormous waves of immigrants arriving in North America at the time.

**psychosocial treatment** Treatment practices that focus on social and cultural factors (such as family experience) and on psychological influences. These approaches include cognitive, behavioural, and interpersonal methods.

**moral therapy** Nineteenth-century psychosocial approach to treatment that involved treating patients as normally as possible in normal environments.

**TABLE 1.1** Development of the First Asylums in Canada

| Province | Date | Notes |
|---|---|---|
| Quebec | 1845 | Beauport, or the Quebec Lunatic Asylum, was opened. |
| New Brunswick | 1847 | The Provincial Lunatic Asylum was erected. |
| Ontario | 1850 | The Provincial Lunatic Asylum in Toronto admitted patients. |
| Newfoundland | 1854 | An asylum for mentally ill patients was erected and admitted its first patients. |
| Nova Scotia | 1857 | The first patients were admitted to the Provincial Hospital for the Insane. |
| British Columbia | 1872 | A remodelled provincial general hospital (the Old Royal Hospital) was opened as the Asylum for the Insane in British Columbia. |
| Prince Edward Island | 1877 | The Prince Edward Island Hospital for the Insane was built. |
| Manitoba | 1886 | The Selkirk Lunatic Asylum admitted patients. |
| Saskatchewan | 1911 | The Saskatchewan Provincial Hospital admitted its first patients. |
| Alberta | 1914 | The Insane Asylum in Ponoka was opened. |

*Asylum Hospital, Hamilton, Ont.*

*Vintage Postcards of Hamilton, Ontario, by Janet Forjan-Freedman www.hamiltonpostcards.com*

*Source:* Adapted from Table 1 of: Sussman, S. The First Asylums in Canada: A Response to Neglectful Community Care and Current Trends. *Can J Psychiatry* 1998; 43(3): 260–264.

A second reason for the decline of moral therapy has an unlikely source. The great crusader Dorothea Dix (1802–1887) campaigned endlessly for reform in the treatment of the insane throughout Canada and the United States. A schoolteacher who had worked in various institutions, she had firsthand knowledge of the deplorable conditions imposed on people with mental disorders, and she made it her life's work to inform the public and their leaders of these abuses. Her work became known as the **mental hygiene movement.** Dix visited Canada in 1843 and 1844 and discovered appalling conditions involving the incarceration of lunatics at Beauport in Quebec and in the Toronto jail. She was involved in the construction of the asylum in St. John's, Newfoundland, in 1854. The most notable of her contributions to the mental hygiene movement in Canada was her appeal to the Nova Scotia Legislature in 1850. In this appeal, she described the deplorable conditions for people with mental illnesses at the time and argued for the development of an asylum in Nova Scotia (Hurd, 1916).

In addition to improving the standards of care, Dix worked hard to make sure that everyone who needed care received it, including the homeless. Through her efforts, humane treatment became more widely available in North American institutions.

Unfortunately, an unforeseen consequence of Dix's heroic efforts was a substantial increase in the number of mental patients. This influx led to a rapid transition from moral therapy to custodial care because hospitals were inadequately staffed. Dix reformed our asylums and single-handedly inspired the construction of numerous new institutions. But

*Stock Montage*

Dorothea Dix (1802–1887) began the mental hygiene movement and spent much of her life campaigning for reform in the treatment of the mentally ill.

even her tireless efforts and advocacy could not ensure sufficient staffing to allow the individual attention necessary to moral therapy. Unfortunately, institutionalization in Canada eventually "became a synonym for an inhumane response to mentally ill people" (Sussman, 1998, p. 262).

An important mental health reformer and crusader who followed Dix's example was Clarence Hincks, a University of Toronto medical school graduate who cofounded the Canadian Committee for Mental Hygiene in 1918. Early in his career, he toured mental institutions in Manitoba and documented continued appalling conditions for patients (Griffin, 1989; Roland, 1990). Having suffered and recovered from depression himself, Hincks advocated for the position that mental illness was treatable. His position stood in contrast to the prevailing

**mental hygiene movement** Mid-19th-century effort to improve care of the mentally disordered by informing the public of their mistreatment.

view, in the middle of the 19th century, that mental illness was caused by brain pathology and, therefore, was incurable. This latter view is illustrated by the fact that one mental institution of that time in Portage La Prairie, Manitoba, was named the "Home for Incurables" (Roland, 1990).

The psychological tradition lay dormant for a time only to reemerge in several different schools of thought in the 20th century. The first major approach was **psychoanalysis,** based on Sigmund Freud's (1856–1939) elaborate theory of the structure of the mind and the role of unconscious processes in determining behaviour. The second was **behaviourism,** associated with John B. Watson, Ivan Pavlov, and B. F. Skinner, which focuses on how learning and adaptation affect the development of psychopathology.

## Psychoanalytic Theory

Have you ever felt as if someone cast a spell on you? Have you ever been mesmerized by a look across the classroom from a beautiful man or woman or by a stare from a rock musician as you sat in front at a concert? If so, you have something in common with the patients of Austrian physician Anton Mesmer (1734–1815) and with millions of people since his time who have been hypnotized. Mesmer suggested to his patients that their problem was due to an undetectable bodily fluid called *animal magnetism,* which could become blocked. Mesmer had his

patients sit in a dark room around a large vat of chemicals with rods extending from the vat and touching the patients. Dressed in flowing robes, he might then identify and tap various areas of their bodies where their animal magnetism was blocked and suggest strongly that they were being cured. Because of his rather unusual techniques, Mesmer was considered a charlatan, strongly opposed by the medical establishment (Winter, 1998). Benjamin Franklin put animal magnetism to the test by conducting a brilliant experiment in which patients received either magnetized water or non-magnetized water with strong suggestions that they would get better. Neither the patient nor the therapist knew which water was which, making it a "double-blind" experiment (see Chapter 3). When both groups got better, Franklin concluded that animal magnetism, or mesmerism, was nothing more than strong suggestion (Gould, 1991; McNally, 1999). Nevertheless, Mesmer is widely regarded as the father of hypnosis, a state in which suggestible subjects sometimes appear to be in a trance.

Many distinguished scientists and physicians were interested in Mesmer's powerful methods of suggestion. One of the best known, Jean Charcot (1825–1893), was head of the hospital in Paris where Pinel had introduced psychological treatments several generations earlier. A distinguished

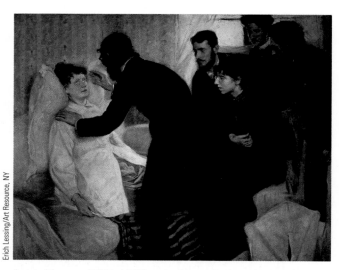

Anton Mesmer (1734–1815) and other early therapists used strong suggestions to cure their patients, who were often hypnotized.

*From In Search of Sanity: A Chronicle of the Canadian Mental Health Association 1918–1988, by John D. Griffin MD, MA, DPM(E), FRCP(C). Courtesy of the Canadian Mental Health Association.*

Clarence Hincks (1885–1964) was an early crusader for the mental hygiene movement in Canada. In 1918, he cofounded the Canadian Committee for Mental Hygiene—a precursor to today's Canadian Mental Health Association.

*Erich Lessing/Art Resource, NY*

**psychoanalysis** Psychoanalytic assessment and therapy, which emphasizes exploration of, and insight into, unconscious processes and conflicts, pioneered by Sigmund Freud.

**behaviourism** Explanation of human behaviour, including dysfunction, based on principles of learning and adaptation derived from experimental psychology.

neurologist, Charcot demonstrated that some of the techniques of mesmerism were effective with a number of psychological disorders. He did much to legitimize the fledgling practice of hypnosis. In 1885, a young man named Sigmund Freud came from Vienna to study with Charcot.

After returning from France, Freud teamed up with Josef Breuer (1842–1925), who had experimented with a somewhat different hypnotic procedure. While his patients were in the highly suggestible state of hypnosis, Breuer asked them to describe their problems, conflicts, and fears in as much detail as they could. Breuer observed two important phenomena during this process. First, patients often became extremely emotional as they talked and felt quite relieved and improved after emerging from the hypnotic state. Second, seldom would they have gained an understanding of the relationship between their emotional problems and their psychological disorder. In fact, it was difficult or impossible for them to recall some of the details they had described under hypnosis. In other words, the material seemed to be beyond the awareness of the patient. With this observation, Breuer and Freud had "discovered" the **unconscious** mind and its apparent influence on the production of psychological disorders. Together, Breuer and Freud also discovered that it is therapeutic to recall and relive emotional trauma that has been made unconscious and to release the accompanying tension. This process became known as **catharsis.** A fuller understanding of the relationship between current emotions and earlier events is referred to as *insight.* As we shall see throughout this book, particularly in Chapters 4 and 5 on anxiety and somatoform disorders, the existence of "unconscious" memories and feelings and the importance of "processing" emotion-laden information have been verified and reaffirmed.

Freud and Breuer's theories were based on case observations, some of which were made in a surprisingly systematic way for those times. An excellent example is Breuer's classic description of his treatment of "hysterical" symptoms in Anna O. in 1895 (Breuer & Freud, 1957). Anna O. was a young woman who was perfectly healthy until she turned 21. Shortly before her problems began, her father developed a serious chronic illness that led to his death. Throughout his illness, Anna O. had cared for him, spending endless hours at his bedside. Five months after her father became ill, Anna noticed that during the day her vision blurred and that from time to time she had difficulty moving her right arm and both legs. Soon, additional symptoms such as speech difficulties appeared.

In a series of treatment sessions, Breuer dealt with one symptom at a time through hypnosis and subsequent "talking through," tracing each symptom to its hypothetical causation in circumstances surrounding the death of Anna's father. One at a time her "hysterical" ailments disappeared, but only after treatment was administered to each respective behaviour. This process of treating one behaviour at a time fulfills a basic requirement for drawing scientific conclusions about the effects of treatment in an individual case study.

Bertha Pappenheim (1859–1936), famous as "Anna O.," was described as "hysterical" by Josef Breuer.

*Mary Evans Picture Library*

Freud took these basic observations and expanded them into the **psychoanalytic model,** the most comprehensive theory yet constructed on the development and structure of our personalities. He also speculated on where this development could go wrong and produce psychological disorders.

Jean Charcot (1825–1893) studied hypnosis and influenced Sigmund Freud to consider psychosocial approaches to psychological disorders.

*Erich Lessing/Art Resource, NY*

**unconscious**  Part of the psychic makeup that is outside the awareness of the person.

**catharsis**  Rapid or sudden release of emotional tension thought to be an important factor in psychoanalytic therapy.

**psychoanalytic model**  Complex and comprehensive theory originally advanced by Sigmund Freud that seeks to account for the development and structure of personality, as well as the origin of abnormal behaviour, based primarily on inferred inner entities and forces.

Although most of it remains unproved, psychoanalytic theory has had a strong influence, and being familiar with its basic ideas is still important; what follows is a brief outline of the theory. We focus on its three major facets: (1) the *structure of the mind* and the distinct functions of personality that sometimes clash with one another, (2) the *defense mechanisms* with which the mind defends itself from these clashes or conflicts, and (3) the *stages of early psychosexual development* that provide grist for the mill of our inner conflicts.

Sigmund Freud (1856–1939) is considered the founder of psychoanalysis.

*© Bettmann/CORBIS*

## The Structure of the Mind

The mind, according to Freud, has three major parts or functions: the *id, ego,* and *superego* (see Figure 1.4). These terms, like many from psychoanalysis, have found their way into our common vocabulary, but you may not be aware of their meaning.

The **id** is the source of our strong sexual and aggressive feelings or energies. It is, basically, the animal within us. The positive energy or drive within the id is the *libido.* Even today, some people explain low sex drive as an absence of libido. Another source of energy is the death instinct, or *thanatos.* Much like matter and antimatter, these two basic drives are continually in opposition.

The id operates according to the *pleasure principle,* with an overriding goal of maximizing pleasure and eliminating any associated tension or conflicts. The goal of pleasure, which is particularly prominent in childhood, often conflicts with social rules and regulations, as we shall see later. The id has its own characteristic way of processing information; referred to as *primary process,* this type of thinking is emotional, irrational, illogical, filled with fantasies, and preoccupied with sex, aggression, selfishness, and envy.

Fortunately for all of us, in Freud's view, the id's selfish and sometimes dangerous drives do not go unchecked. In fact, only a few months into life, we know we must adapt our basic demands to the real world. In other words, we must find ways to meet our basic needs without offending everyone around us. The part of our mind that ensures that we act

realistically is called the **ego.** It operates according to the *reality principle.* The thinking styles of the ego are characterized by logic and reason and are referred to as *secondary process.*

The third important structure within the mind, the **superego,** or what we might call conscience, represents the *moral principles* instilled in us by our parents and our culture. It is the voice within us that nags at us when we know we're doing something wrong. Because the purpose of the superego is to counteract the potentially dangerous aggressive and sexual drives of the id, the basis for conflict is readily apparent.

The role of the ego is to mediate conflict between the id and the superego, juggling their demands with the realities of the world. The ego is often referred to as the executive or manager of our minds. If it mediates successfully, we can go on to the higher intellectual and creative pursuits of life. If it is unsuccessful, and the id or superego becomes too strong, conflict will overtake us and psychological disorders will develop. Because these conflicts are all within the mind, they are referred to as **intrapsychic conflicts.** Finally, Freud believed that the id and the superego are almost entirely unconscious.

## Defence Mechanisms

The ego fights a continual battle to stay on top of the warring id and superego. Occasionally, their conflicts produce anxiety that threatens to overwhelm the ego. The anxiety is a signal that alerts the ego to marshal **defence mechanisms,** unconscious protective processes that keep primitive emotions associated with conflicts in check so that the ego can continue its coordinating function.

We all use defence mechanisms—they are sometimes adaptive and at other times maladaptive. For example, have you ever done poorly on a test because the professor was unfair in her grading? And then when you got home you yelled at your

**id** In psychoanalysis, the unconscious psychic entity present at birth representing basic drives.

**ego** In psychoanalysis, the psychic entity responsible for finding realistic and practical ways to satisfy id drives.

**superego** In psychoanalysis, the psychic entity representing the internalized moral standards of parents and society.

**intrapsychic conflicts** In psychoanalysis, the struggles among the id, ego, and superego.

**defence mechanisms** Common patterns of behaviour, often adaptive coping styles when they occur in moderation, observed in response to particular situations. In psychoanalysis, these are thought to be unconscious processes originating in the ego. Although Freud first conceptualized defence mechanisms, it was his daughter, Anna Freud, who developed the ideas more fully.

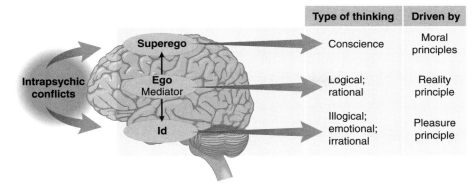

| Type of thinking | Driven by |
|---|---|
| Conscience | Moral principles |
| Logical; rational | Reality principle |
| Illogical; emotional; irrational | Pleasure principle |

**Figure 1.4** ■ Freud's structure of the mind.

brother or perhaps even your dog? This is an example of the defence mechanism of *displacement.* The ego adaptively "decides" that expressing primitive anger at your professor might not be in your best interest. Because your brother and your dog don't have the authority to affect you in a negative way, your anger is "displaced" onto one of them.

Defence mechanisms have been subjected to scientific study. There is some evidence that they may be potentially important in both psychopathology and health (MacGregor, Davidson, Rowan, Barksdale, & MacLean, 2003; McGregor, Zanna, Holmes, & Spencer, 2001; Vaillant, Bond, & Vaillant, 1986). For example, different psychological disorders seem to be associated with different defence mechanisms (Pollack & Andrews, 1989), which might be important in planning treatment. Indeed, the DSM-IV-TR includes an axis of defence mechanisms in the appendix. The concept of defence mechanisms—"coping styles," in contemporary terminology—continues to be important to the study of psychopathology.

Examples of defence mechanisms are as follows (based on DSM-IV-TR, APA, 2000a):

- *Denial:* Refuses to acknowledge some aspect of objective reality or subjective experience that is apparent to others
- *Displacement:* Transfers a feeling about, or a response to, an object that causes discomfort onto another, usually less threatening, object or person
- *Projection:* Falsely attributes own unacceptable feelings, impulses, or thoughts to another individual or object
- *Rationalization:* Conceals the true motivations for actions, thoughts, or feelings through elaborate reassuring or self-serving but incorrect explanations
- *Reaction formation:* Substitutes behaviour, thoughts, or feelings that are the direct opposite of unacceptable ones

- *Repression:* Blocks disturbing wishes, thoughts, or experiences from conscious awareness
- *Sublimation:* Directs potentially maladaptive feelings or impulses into socially acceptable behaviour

Psychosexual Stages of Development

Freud also theorized that during infancy and early childhood we pass through a number of **psychosexual stages of development** that have a profound and lasting impact. This makes Freud one of the first to take a developmental perspective of the study of abnormal behaviour, which we will look at in more detail throughout this book. The stages—oral, anal, phallic, latency, and genital—represent distinctive patterns of gratifying our basic needs and satisfying our drive for physical pleasure. For example, the oral stage, typically extending for approximately two years from birth, is characterized by a central focus on the need for food. In the act of sucking, necessary for feeding, the lips, tongue, and mouth become the focus of libidinal drives and, therefore, the principal source of pleasure. Freud hypothesized that if we did not receive appropriate gratification during a specific stage or if a specific stage left a particularly strong impression (which he termed *fixation*), an individual's personality would reflect the stage throughout adult life. For example, fixation at the oral stage might result in excessive thumb sucking and emphasis on oral stimulation through overeating, chewing pencils, or biting fingernails. Adult personality characteristics theoretically associated with oral fixation include dependency and passivity or, in reaction to these tendencies, rebelliousness and cynicism.

---

**psychosexual stages of development** In psychoanalysis, the sequence of phases a person passes through during development. Each stage is named for the location on the body where id gratification is maximal at that time.

One of the more controversial and frequently mentioned psychosexual conflicts occurs during the phallic stage (from age 3 to age 5 or 6), which is characterized by early genital self-stimulation. This conflict is the subject of the Greek tragedy *Oedipus Rex*, in which Oedipus is fated to kill his father and, unknowingly, to marry his mother. Freud asserted that all young boys fantasize about sexual interactions with their mothers. These fantasies, in turn, are accompanied by strong feelings of envy and anger toward their fathers, whose place they wish to take. Furthermore, strong fears develop that the father may punish that lust by removing the son's penis—thus the phenomenon of *castration anxiety*. This fear helps the boy keep his lustful impulses toward his mother in check. The battle of the lustful impulses on the one hand and castration anxiety on the other creates an intrapsychic conflict called the *Oedipus complex*. The phallic stage passes uneventfully only if the child resolves his ambivalent relationship with his parents. If this happens, he will go on to channel his libidinal impulses into heterosexual relationships and retain harmless affection for his mother.

The counterpart conflict in girls, called the *Electra complex*, is even more controversial. Freud viewed the young girl as wanting to replace her mother and possess her father. Central to this possession is the girl's desire for a penis, so as to be more like her father—hence the term *penis envy*. According to Freud, the conflict is successfully resolved when females develop healthy heterosexual relationships and look forward to having a baby, which he viewed as a healthy substitute for having a penis. Needless to say, this particular theory has provoked marked criticism over the years as being sexist and demeaning. Remember that it is theory, not fact; no systematic research exists to support it.

In Freud's view, all non-psychotic psychological disorders resulted from underlying unconscious conflicts, the anxiety that resulted from those conflicts, and the implementation of ego defence mechanisms. Freud called such disorders **neuroses,** or *neurotic disorders,* from an old term referring to disorders of the nervous system.

## Later Developments in Psychoanalytic Thought

Freud's original psychoanalytic theories have been greatly modified and developed by his students and followers.

Anna Freud (1895–1982), Freud's daughter, concentrated on the way in which the defensive reactions of the ego determine our behaviour. She was the first proponent of the modern field of **ego psychology** or self-psychology. Her book *Ego and the Mechanisms of Defense* (1946) is still influential. According to Anna

© Hulton-Deutsch Collection/CORBIS

Anna Freud (1895–1982), here with her father, contributed the concept of defence mechanisms to the field of psychoanalysis.

Freud, the individual slowly accumulates adaptational capacities, skill in reality testing, and defences. Abnormal behaviour develops when the ego is deficient in regulating functions such as delaying and controlling impulses or in marshalling appropriate normal defences to strong internal conflicts.

A related area popular today is referred to as **object relations.** In this school of thought are theorists Melanie Klein and Otto Kernberg. Kernberg's work on borderline personality disorder, in which some behaviour "borders" on being out of touch with reality and thus psychotic, has been widely applied (see Chapter 11). Object relations is the study of how children incorporate the images, memories, and sometimes the values of a person who was important to them and to whom they were (or are) emotionally attached (e.g., a parent). *Object* in this sense refers to these important people. Incorporated objects can become an integrated part of the ego or may assume conflicting roles in determining the identity, or self.

**neurosis** Obsolete psychodynamic term for psychological disorder thought to result from unconscious conflicts and the anxiety they cause. Plural is *neuroses.*

**ego psychology** Derived from psychoanalysis, this theory emphasizes the role of the ego in development and attributes psychological disorders to failure of the ego to manage impulses and internal conflicts.

**object relations** Modern development in psychodynamic theory involving the study of how children incorporate the memories and values of people who are close and important to them.

According to object relations theory, you tend to see the world through the eyes of the person incorporated into your self. Object relations theorists focus on how these disparate images come together to make up a person's identity and on the conflicts that may emerge.

Carl Jung (1875–1961) and Alfred Adler (1870–1937) were students of Freud who came to reject his ideas and form their own schools of thought. Unlike Freud, both Jung and Adler believed that the basic quality of human nature is positive and that there is a strong drive toward self-actualization. Jung and Adler believed that by removing barriers to both internal and external growth, the individual would improve and flourish.

Others took psychoanalytical theorizing in different directions, emphasizing development over the life span and the influence of culture and society on personality. Karen Horney (1885–1952) and Erich Fromm (1900–1980) are associated with these ideas, but the best-known theorist is Erik Erikson (1902–1994). Erikson's greatest contribution was his theory of development across the life span, in which he described in some detail the crises and conflicts that accompany eight specific stages. For example, in the last of these stages, the *mature age*, beginning at about 65, individuals review their lives and attempt to make sense of them, experiencing both the satisfaction of having completed some lifelong goals and the despair of having failed at others. Scientific developments have borne out the wisdom of considering psychopathology from a developmental point of view.

## Psychoanalytic Psychotherapy

Many techniques of psychoanalytic psychotherapy, or psychoanalysis, are designed to reveal the nature of unconscious mental processes and conflicts through catharsis and insight. Freud developed techniques of **free association** in which patients are instructed to say whatever comes to mind without the usual socially required censoring. This is intended to reveal emotionally charged material that may be repressed because it is too painful to bring into consciousness. Freud's patients lay on a couch, and he sat behind them so that they would not be distracted. This is how the couch became the symbol of psychotherapy. Other techniques include **dream analysis** (still popular today), in which the content of dreams, supposedly reflecting the primary process thinking of the id, is systematically related to symbolic aspects of unconscious conflicts. The therapist interprets the patient's thoughts and feelings from free association and the content of dreams and relates them to various unconscious conflicts. This procedure is often difficult because the patient may resist the efforts of the therapist to uncover repressed and sensitive conflicts and may *deny* the interpretations. The goal of this stage of therapy is to help the patient gain insight into the nature of the conflicts.

The relationship between the therapist, or **psychoanalyst,** and the patient is important. In a phenomenon called **transference,** patients come to relate to the therapist very much as they did toward important figures in their childhood, particularly their parents. Patients who resent the therapist but can verbalize no good reason for it may be reenacting childhood resentment toward a parent. More often, the patient will fall deeply in love with the therapist, which reflects strong positive feelings that existed earlier for a parent. In *countertransference,* therapists project some of their own personal issues and feelings onto the patient. Therapists are trained to deal with their own feelings and their patients', whatever the mode of therapy. It is strictly against all ethical canons of the mental health professions to accept overtures from patients that might lead to relationships outside therapy.

Classical psychoanalysis requires therapy four to five times a week for several years to analyze unconscious conflicts, resolve them, and restructure the personality to put the ego back in charge. A study conducted at the Canadian Institute of Psychoanalysis in Toronto showed that the mean length of treatment for patients undergoing psychoanalysis was 4.8 years in Canada, 5.7 years in the United States, and 6.6 years in Australia (Doidge et al., 2002). Reduction of "symptoms" (psychological disorders) is relatively inconsequential, because they are only expressions of underlying intrapsychic conflicts that arise from psychosexual developmental stages. Thus, eliminating a phobia or depressive episode would be of little use unless the underlying conflict was dealt with adequately, because another set of "symptoms" would almost certainly emerge (*symptom substitution*). Because of the extraordinary expense of psychoanalysis, and the lack of evidence that it is effective in alleviating psychological disorders, this approach is seldom used today.

**free association** Psychoanalytic therapy technique intended to explore threatening material repressed into the unconscious. The patient is instructed to say whatever comes to mind without censoring.

**dream analysis** Psychoanalytic therapy method in which dream contents are examined as symbolic of id impulses and intrapsychic conflicts.

**psychoanalyst** Therapist who practises psychoanalysis after earning either an M.D. or a Ph.D. degree and receiving additional specialized postdoctoral training.

**transference** Psychoanalytic concept suggesting that clients may seek to relate to the therapist as they do to important authority figures, particularly their parents.

Classical psychoanalysis is still practised, particularly in some large cities, but many psychotherapists employ a loosely related set of approaches referred to as **psychodynamic psychotherapy.** Although conflicts and unconscious processes are still emphasized, and efforts are made to identify trauma and active defence mechanisms, therapists use an eclectic mixture of tactics with a social and interpersonal focus (Blagys & Hilsenroth, 2000). Two main features distinguish psychodynamic psychotherapy from classic psychoanalysis. First, psychodynamic psychotherapy is significantly briefer. Second, psychodynamic therapists de-emphasize the goal of personality reconstruction, focusing instead on relieving the suffering associated with psychological disorders.

### Comments

Pure psychoanalysis is of historical more than current interest, and classical psychoanalysis as a treatment has been diminishing in popularity for years. In 1980, the term *neurosis,* which specifically implied a psychoanalytic view of the causes of psychological disorders, was dropped from the DSM, the official diagnostic system of the American Psychiatric Association.

A major criticism of psychoanalysis is that it is basically unscientific, relying on reports by the patient of events that happened years ago. These events have been filtered through the experience of the observer and then interpreted by the psychoanalyst in ways that might differ from one analyst to the next. Finally, there has been no careful measurement of any of these psychological phenomena and no obvious way to prove or disprove the basic hypotheses of psychoanalysis. This is important, because measurement and the ability to prove or disprove a theory are the foundations of the scientific approach.

Nevertheless, psychoanalytic concepts and observations have been valuable, not only to the study of psychopathology and psychodynamic psychotherapy but also to the history of ideas in Western civilization. Careful scientific studies of psychopathology have supported the observation of unconscious mental processes and the understanding that memories of life events can be repressed and otherwise avoided in a variety of ingenious ways. The relationship of the therapist and the patient, called the *therapeutic alliance,* is an important area of study across most therapeutic strategies. These concepts, along with the importance of various coping styles or defence mechanisms, appear repeatedly throughout this book.

Freud's revolutionary ideas that pathological anxiety emerges in connection with some of our deepest and darkest instincts brought us a long way from witch trials and incurable brain pathology. Before Freud, the source of good and evil and of urges and prohibitions was conceived as external and spiritual, usually in the guise of demons confronting the forces of good. Since Freud, the mind has become the battleground for these forces, and we are inexorably caught up in the battle, sometimes for better and sometimes for worse.

## Humanistic Theory

We have already seen that Jung and Adler broke sharply with Freud. Their fundamental disagreement concerned the very nature of humanity. Freud portrayed life as a battleground where we are continually in danger of being overwhelmed by our darkest forces. Jung and Adler, by contrast, emphasized the positive, optimistic side of human nature. Jung talked about setting goals, looking toward the future, and realizing one's fullest potential. Adler believed that human nature reaches its fullest potential when we contribute to other individuals and to society. He believed that we all strive to reach superior levels of intellectual and moral development. Nevertheless, both Jung and Adler retained many of the principles of psychodynamic thought. Their general philosophies were adopted in the middle of the 20th century by personality theorists and became known as *humanistic psychology.*

**Self-actualizing** was the watchword for this movement. The underlying assumption is that all of us could reach our highest potential, in all areas of functioning, if only we had the freedom to grow. Inevitably, a variety of conditions may block our actualization. Because every person is basically good and whole, most blocks originate outside the individual. Difficult living conditions or stressful life or interpersonal experiences may move you from your true self.

Abraham Maslow (1908–1970) was most systematic in describing the structure of personality. He postulated a *hierarchy of needs,* beginning with our most basic physical needs for food and sex and ranging upward to our needs for self-actualization, love, and self-esteem. Social needs such as friendship fall somewhere between. Maslow hypothesized that we cannot progress up the hierarchy until we have satisfied the needs at lower levels.

---

**psychodynamic psychotherapy**    Contemporary version of psychoanalysis that still emphasizes unconscious processes and conflicts but is briefer and more focused on specific problems.

**self-actualizing**    Process emphasized in humanistic psychology in which people strive to achieve their highest potential against difficult life experiences.

Carl Rogers (1902–1987) is, from the point of view of therapy, the most influential humanist. Rogers originated client-centred therapy, later known as **person-centred therapy** (Rogers, 1961). In this approach, the therapist takes a passive role, making as few interpretations as possible. The point is to give the individual a chance to develop during the course of therapy, unfettered by threats to the self. Humanist theorists have great faith in the ability of human relations to foster this growth. **Unconditional positive regard,** the complete and almost unqualified acceptance of most of the client's feelings and actions, is critical to the humanistic approach. *Empathy* is the sympathetic understanding of the individual's particular view of the world. The hoped-for result of person-centred therapy is that clients will be more straightforward and honest with themselves and will access their innate tendencies toward growth.

Like psychoanalysis, the humanistic approach has had a substantial effect on theories of interpersonal relationships. For example, the human potential movements so popular in the 1960s and 1970s were a direct result of humanistic theorizing. This approach also emphasized the importance of the therapeutic relationship in a way quite different from Freud's. Rather than seeing the relationship as a means to an end (transference), humanistic therapists believed that relationships, including the therapeutic relationship, were the single most positive influence in facilitating human growth. In fact, Rogers made substantial contributions to the scientific study of therapist–client relationships. And research by W. H. Coons and colleagues in Hamilton, Ontario (Coons, 1957, 1967; Coons & Peacock, 1970) provided evidence for the importance of the humanistic concept of empathy or "the opportunity for interpersonal interaction in a consistently warm and accepting social environment" (Coons, 1957, p. 1) in explaining the success of psychotherapy.

Proponents of the humanistic model stress the unique, non-quantifiable experiences of the individual, emphasizing that people are more different than alike. Thus, it does not come as a surprise that many humanistic model proponents have not been much interested in doing research that would discover or create new knowledge. A major exception is Carl Rogers himself, who conducted important work on understanding how psychotherapy works.

As Maslow noted, the humanistic model found its greatest application among individuals without psychological disorders. The application of person-centred therapy to more severe psychological disorders has decreased substantially over the decades, although certain variations have periodically arisen in some areas of psychopathology. For example, Les

Greenberg and his colleagues at York University in Toronto have developed experiential and emotion-focused therapies that have their roots in the person-centred approach (Greenberg & Paivio, 1997; Greenberg, Watson, & Lietaer, 1998). These variations of traditional humanistic therapy have demonstrated effectiveness in treating certain psychological disorders, including mood and anxiety disorders (see Chapters 4 and 6).

## *The Behavioural Model*

As psychoanalysis swept the world at the beginning of the 20th century, events in Russia and North America would eventually provide an alternative psychological model that was every bit as powerful. The **behavioural model,** which is also known as the *cognitive-behavioural* (e.g., Meichenbaum, 1995) or *social learning model* (e.g., Bandura, 1973, 1986), brought the systematic development of a more scientific approach to psychological aspects of psychopathology.

### Ivan Pavlov and Classical Conditioning

In his classic study examining why dogs salivate before the presentation of food, Russian physiologist Ivan Petrovich Pavlov (1849–1936) initiated the study of **classical conditioning,** a type of learning in which a neutral stimulus is paired with a response until it elicits that response. Conditioning is one way we acquire new information, particularly information that is somewhat emotional in nature. Let's look at a powerful contemporary example.

Psychologists working in oncology units have studied a phenomenon well known to many cancer patients, their nurses and physicians, and their families. Chemotherapy, a common treatment for some forms of cancer, has some side effects, including severe nausea and vomiting. But as documented in the research of Patricia Dobkin at the University of Montreal and others, these patients often experience

---

**person-centred therapy**  Therapy method in which the client, rather than the counsellor, primarily directs the course of discussion, seeking self-discovery and self-responsibility.

**unconditional positive regard**  Acceptance by the counsellor of the client's feelings and actions without judgment or condemnation.

**behavioural model**  Explanation of human behaviour, including dysfunction, based on principles of learning and adaptation derived from experimental psychology.

**classical conditioning**  Fundamental learning process first described by Ivan Pavlov. An event that automatically elicits a response is paired with another stimulus event that does not (a neutral stimulus). After repeated pairings, the neutral stimulus becomes a conditioned stimulus that by itself can elicit the desired response.

severe nausea and, occasionally, vomiting when they merely see the medical personnel who administered the chemotherapy or any equipment associated with the treatment, even on days when their treatment is not delivered (Morrow & Dobkin, 1988). For some patients, this reaction becomes associated with a variety of stimuli that evoke people or things present during chemotherapy—anybody in a nurse's uniform or even the sight of the hospital. This phenomenon is called *stimulus generalization* because the response "generalizes" to similar stimuli. This particular reaction is obviously distressing and uncomfortable, particularly if it is associated with a variety of objects or situations. Psychologists have had to develop specific treatments to overcome this response (Redd & Andrykowski, 1982); they are described more fully in Chapter 7.

Ivan Pavlov (1849–1936) identified the process of classical conditioning, which is important to many emotional disorders.

Whether the stimulus is food, as in Pavlov's laboratory, or chemotherapy, the classical conditioning process begins with a stimulus that would elicit a response in almost anyone and requires no learning; no conditions must be present for the response to occur. For these reasons, the food or chemotherapy is called the *unconditioned stimulus (UCS)*. The natural or unlearned response to this stimulus—in these cases, salivation or nausea—is called the *unconditioned response (UCR)*. Now the learning comes in. As we have already seen, any person or object *associated* with the unconditioned stimulus (food or chemotherapy) acquires the power to elicit the same response, but the response, because it was elicited by the *conditioned stimulus (CS)*, is termed a *conditioned response (CR)*. Thus, the nurse who is associated with the chemotherapy becomes a CS. The nauseous sensation, which is almost the same as that experienced during chemotherapy, becomes the CR.

With a UCS as powerful as chemotherapy, a CR can be learned in one trial. However, most learning of this type requires repeated pairing of the UCS (for example, chemotherapy) and the CS (for instance, nurses' uniforms or hospital equipment). When Pavlov began to investigate this phenomenon, he substituted a metronome for the footsteps of his laboratory assistants so that he could quantify the stimulus more accurately and, therefore, study the approach more precisely. What he also learned is

that presentation of the CS (for example, the metronome) *without* the food for a long enough period would eventually eliminate the CR to the food. In other words, the dog learned that the metronome no longer meant that a meal might be on the way. This process was called **extinction.**

Because Pavlov was a physiologist, it was natural for him to study these processes in a laboratory and to be scientific about it. This required precision in measuring and observing relationships and in ruling out alternative explanations. This approach was not common in psychology at that time. For example, it was impossible for psychoanalysts to measure unconscious conflicts precisely or even observe them. Even early experimental psychologists such as Edward Titchener (1867–1927) emphasized the study of **introspection.** Subjects simply reported on their inner thoughts and feelings after experiencing certain stimuli, but the results of this "armchair" psychology were inconsistent and discouraging to many experimental psychologists.

### Watson and the Rise of Behaviourism

An early North American psychologist, John B. Watson (1878–1958), is considered the founder of behaviourism. Strongly influenced by the work of Pavlov, Watson decided that psychology could be made as scientific as physiology, and that psychology no more needs introspection or other non-quantifiable methods than do chemistry and physics (Watson, 1913). This, then, was the beginning of behaviourism and, like most revolutionaries, Watson took his cause to extremes. For example, he wrote that "thinking," for purposes of science, could be equated with subvocal talking and that we need only measure movements around the larynx to study this process objectively.

Most of Watson's time was spent developing behavioural psychology as a radical empirical science, but he did dabble briefly in the study of psychopathology. In 1920, he and a student, Rosalie Rayner, presented to an 11-month-old boy named Albert a harmless fluffy white rat to play with. Albert was not afraid of the small animal and enjoyed playing with it. However, every time Albert reached for the rat, the experimenters made a loud noise behind him. After only five trials, Albert showed the

**extinction** Learning process in which a response maintained by reinforcement in operant conditioning or pairing in classical conditioning decreases when that reinforcement or pairing is removed; also the procedure of removing that reinforcement or pairing.

**introspection** Early, non-scientific approach to the study of psychology involving systematic attempts to report thoughts and feelings that specific stimuli evoked.

first signs of fear if the white rat came near. The experimenters then determined that Albert displayed mild fear of any white furry object, even a Santa Claus mask with a white fuzzy beard. You may not think that this is surprising, but keep in mind that this was one of the first examples ever recorded in a laboratory of actually producing fear of an object not previously feared. Of course, this experiment would be considered unethical by today's standards.

Another student of Watson's, Mary Cover Jones thought that if fear could be learned or classically conditioned in this way, perhaps it could also be unlearned or "extinguished." She worked with a boy named Peter, who at 2 years, 10 months old was already afraid of furry objects. Jones decided to bring a white rabbit into the room where Peter was playing for a short time each day. She also arranged for other children, whom she knew did not fear rabbits, to be in the same room. She noted that Peter's fear gradually diminished. Each time it diminished, she brought the rabbit closer. Eventually Peter was touching and even playing with the rabbit (Jones, 1924a, 1924b), and years later the fear had not returned.

### The Beginnings of Behaviour Therapy

The implications of Jones's research were largely ignored for two decades, given the fervour associated with more psychoanalytic conceptions of the development of fear. But in the late 1940s and early 1950s, Joseph Wolpe (1915–1997), a pioneering psychiatrist from South Africa, became dissatisfied with prevailing psychoanalytic interpretations of psychopathology and began looking for something else. He turned to the work of Pavlov and became familiar with the wider field of behaviourism. He developed a variety of behavioural procedures for treating his patients, many of whom had phobias.

Mary Cover Jones (1896–1987) was one of the first psychologists to use behavioural techniques to free a patient from phobia.

Archives of the History of American Psychology

Wolpe's best-known technique was termed **systematic desensitization.** Individuals were gradually introduced to the objects or situations they feared so that their fear could extinguish; that is, they could learn that nothing bad happened in the presence of the phobic object or scene. Wolpe added another element by having his patients do something that was *incompatible with fear* while they were in the presence of the dreaded object or situation. Because he could not always reproduce the phobic object in his office, Wolpe had his patients carefully and systematically *imagine* the phobic scene, and the response he chose was relaxation, because it was convenient. For example, Wolpe treated a young man with a phobia of dogs by training him first to relax deeply and then imagine he was looking at a dog across the park. Gradually, the young man could imagine the dog across the park and remain relaxed, experiencing little or no fear; Wolpe then had him imagine that he was closer to the dog. Eventually the young man imagined that he was touching the dog while maintaining a relaxed state.

Wolpe reported success with systematic desensitization, one of the first wide-scale applications of the new science of behaviourism to psychopathology. Wolpe, working with fellow pioneers Hans Eysenck and Stanley J. Rachman in London, called this approach **behaviour therapy.** Wolpe eventually moved to the United States and Rachman to Canada, while Eysenck remained in the United Kingdom, which contributed to the dissemination of behaviour therapy throughout North America and Europe.

### B. F. Skinner and Operant Conditioning

Freud's influence extended far beyond psychopathology into many aspects of our cultural and intellectual history. Only one other behavioural scientist has made a similar impact, Burrhus Frederic Skinner (1904–1990). In 1938, he published *The Behaviour of Organisms* in which he laid out, in a comprehensive manner, the principles of operant conditioning, a type of learning in which behaviour changes as a function of what follows the behaviour. Skinner observed early on that a large part of our

---

**systematic desensitization**  Behavioural therapy technique to diminish excessive fears, involving gradual exposure to the feared stimulus paired with a positive coping experience, usually relaxation.

**behaviour therapy**  Array of therapy methods based on the principles of behavioural and cognitive science, as well as principles of learning as applied to clinical problems. It considers specific behaviours rather than inferred conflict as legitimate targets for change.

behaviour is not automatically elicited by a UCS and that we must account for this. Skinner ranged far and wide in his writings, describing, for example, the potential applications of a science of behaviour to our culture. Some of the best-known examples of his ideas are in the novel *Walden Two* (1948), in which he depicts a fictional society run on the principles of operant conditioning. In another well-known work, *Beyond Freedom and Dignity* (1971), Skinner lays out a broader statement of problems facing our culture and suggests solutions based on his own view of a science of behaviour.

B. F. Skinner (1904–1990) studied operant conditioning, a form of learning that is central to psychopathology.

Skinner was strongly influenced by Watson's conviction that a science of human behaviour must be based on observable events and relationships among those events. The work of psychologist Edward L. Thorndike (1874–1949) also influenced Skinner. Thorndike is best known for the *law of effect,* which states that behaviour is either strengthened (likely to be repeated more frequently) or weakened (likely to occur less frequently) depending on the consequences of that behaviour. Skinner took the simple notions that Thorndike had tested in the animal laboratories, using food as a reinforcer, and developed them in a variety of complex ways to apply to much of our behaviour. For example, if a 5-year-old boy starts shouting at the top of his lungs in McDonald's, much to the annoyance of the people around him, it is unlikely that his behaviour was automatically elicited by a UCS. Also, he will be less likely to do it in the future if his parents scold him, take him out to the car to sit for a bit, or consistently reinforce more appropriate behaviour. Then again, if the parents think his behaviour is cute and laugh, chances are he will do it again.

Skinner coined the term *operant conditioning* because behaviour "operates" on the environment and changes it in some way. For example, the boy's behaviour affects his parents' behaviour and probably the behaviour of other customers. Therefore, he changes his environment. Skinner preferred the term **reinforcement** to "reward" because it connotes the effect on the behaviour. But he pointed out that all of our behaviour is governed to some degree by reinforcement, which can be arranged in an endless variety of ways in *schedules of reinforcement* (Ferster & Skinner, 1957). Skinner also believed that using punishment as a consequence is relatively ineffective in the long run and that the primary way to develop new behaviour is to positively reinforce desired behaviour. Much like Watson, Skinner did not see the need to go beyond the observable and quantifiable to establish a satisfactory science of behaviour. He did not deny the influence of biology or the existence of subjective states of emotion or cognition; he simply explained these phenomena as relatively inconsequential side effects of a particular history of reinforcement.

The subjects of Skinner's research were usually animals, mostly pigeons and rats. Using his new principles, Skinner and his disciples actually taught the animals a variety of tricks, including dancing, playing Ping-Pong, and playing a toy piano. To do this, he used a procedure called **shaping,** a process of reinforcing successive approximations to a final behaviour or set of behaviours. If you want a pigeon to play Ping-Pong, first you provide it with a pellet of food every time it moves its head slightly toward a Ping-Pong ball tossed in its direction. Gradually you require the pigeon to move its head ever closer to the Ping-Pong ball until it touches it. Finally, receiving the food pellet is contingent on the pigeon actually hitting the ball back with its head.

Pavlov, Watson, and Skinner contributed significantly to behaviour therapy (e.g., Wolpe, 1958), in which scientific principles of psychology are applied to clinical problems. Many psychologists and other mental health professionals quickly picked up on behaviour therapy techniques and began applying them with their patients in the 1950s and 1960s. For example, an early study conducted at the Saskatchewan Hospital in Weyburn showed that the use of reinforcements by nursing staff could produce substantial reductions in psychiatric patients' undesirable behaviour and increases in patients' desirable behaviour (Ayllon & Michael, 1959). The ideas of Pavlov, Watson, and Skinner have substantially contributed to current psychosocial treatments, so they will be referred to repeatedly in this book.

**reinforcement** In operant conditioning, consequences for behaviour that strengthen it or increase its frequency. Positive reinforcement involves the contingent delivery of a desired consequence; negative reinforcement is the contingent escape from an aversive consequence. Unwanted behaviours may result from their reinforcement or the failure to reinforce desired behaviours.

**shaping** In operant conditioning, the development of a new response by reinforcing successively more similar versions of that response. Both desirable and undesirable behaviours may be learned in this manner.

## Comments

The behavioural model has contributed greatly to the understanding and treatment of psychopathology, as will be apparent in the chapters that follow. Nevertheless, this model is incomplete in itself and inadequate to account for what we now know about psychopathology. In the past there was little or no room for biology in behaviourism, because disorders were considered to be, for the most part, environmentally determined reactions. The model also fails to account for development of psychopathology across the life span. Recent advances in our knowledge of how information is processed, both consciously and subconsciously, have added a layer of complexity. We also now know that learning can occur indirectly or vicariously through observing others in social interactions (Bandura, Jeffrey, & Bachicha, 1974; Bandura & MacDonald, 1963; Bandura, Ross, & Ross, 1963). Integrating all these dimensions requires a new model of psychopathology.

# The Present: The Scientific Method and an Integrative Approach

■ *Explain the importance of science and the scientific method as applied to abnormal behaviour.*

■ *Describe the multidimensional-integrative approach to diagnosing and evaluating abnormal behaviour and explain why it is important.*

As William Shakespeare wrote, "What's past is prologue." We have just reviewed three different traditions or ways of thinking about causes of psychopathology: the supernatural, the biological, and the psychological (further subdivided into two major historical components: psychoanalytic and behavioural).

Supernatural explanations of psychopathology are still with us. Superstitions prevail, including beliefs in the effects of the moon and the stars on our behaviour. However, this tradition has little influence on scientists and other professionals. Biological, psychoanalytic, and behavioural models, by contrast, continue to further our knowledge of psychopathology, as we will see in the next chapter.

Each tradition has failed in at least one important way. First, scientific methods were not often applied to the theories and treatments within a tradition, mostly because methods that would have produced the evidence necessary to confirm or disconfirm the theories and treatments had not been developed. Lacking such evidence, various fads and superstitions were widely accepted that ultimately proved to be untrue or useless. New fads often superseded truly useful theories and treatment procedures. This trend was at work in the "discovery" of the drug reserpine, which, in fact, had been around for thousands of years. King Charles VI was subjected to a variety of procedures, some of which have since been proved useful and others that were mere fads or even harmful. How we use scientific methods to confirm or disconfirm findings in psychopathology will be described in Chapter 3.

Second, health professionals tend to look at psychological disorders narrowly, from their own point of view alone. John P. Grey assumed that psychological disorders were the result of brain disease and that other factors had no influence. John Watson assumed that all behaviours, including disordered behaviour, were the result of psychological and social influences and that the contribution of biological factors was inconsequential.

In the 1990s, two developments came together as never before to shed light on the nature of psychopathology: (1) the increasing sophistication of scientific tools and methodology (e.g., neuroimaging—see Chapter 3) and (2) the realization that no one influence—biological, behavioural, cognitive, emotional, or social—ever occurs in isolation. Literally, every time we think, feel, or do something, the brain and the rest of the body are hard at work. Perhaps not as obvious, however, is that our thoughts, feelings, and actions inevitably influence the function and even the structure of the brain, sometimes permanently. In other words, our behaviour, both normal and abnormal, is the product of a continual interaction of psychological, biological, and social influences.

The view that psychopathology is multiply determined had its early adherents. Perhaps the most notable was psychiatrist Adolf Meyer (1866–1950). Whereas most professionals during the first half of the century held narrow views of the cause of psychopathology, Meyer steadfastly emphasized the equal contributions of biological, psychological, and sociocultural determinism. Although Meyer had some proponents, it was 100 years before the wisdom of his advice was fully recognized in the field.

By 2000, a veritable explosion of knowledge about psychopathology had occurred. The young fields of cognitive science and neuroscience began to grow exponentially as we learned more about the brain and about how we process, remember, and use information. At the same time, startling new findings from behavioural science revealed the importance of early experience in determining later development. It was clear that a new model was needed that would consider biological, psychological, and social influences on behaviour. This approach to psychopathology would combine findings from all areas with our rapidly growing understanding of how we experience life during different developmental periods, from infancy to old age. In the remainder of this book we explore some of these reciprocal influences and demonstrate that the only currently valid model of psychopathology is multidimensional and integrative.

**Concept Check 1.3**

Match the treatment with the corresponding psychological theory of behaviour: (a) behavioural model, (b) moral therapy, (c) psychoanalytic theory, (d) humanistic theory.

1. Treating institutionalized patients as normally as possible and encouraging social interaction and relationship development. _____

2. Hypnosis; psychoanalysis such as free association and dream analysis; and balance of the id, ego, and superego. _____
3. Person-centred therapy with unconditional positive regard. _____
4. Classical conditioning, systematic desensitization, and operant conditioning. _____

# Summary

## Understanding Psychopathology

- A psychological disorder is (1) a psychological dysfunction within an individual that is (2) associated with distress or impairment in functioning and (3) a response that is not typical or culturally expected. All three basic criteria must be met; no one criterion has yet been identified that defines the essence of abnormality.
- The field of psychopathology is concerned with the scientific study of psychological disorders. Trained mental health professionals range from clinical and counselling psychologists to psychiatrists and psychiatric social workers and nurses. Each profession requires a specific type of training.
- Using scientific methods, mental health professionals can function as scientist-practitioners. They not only keep up with the latest findings but also use scientific data to evaluate their own work, and they often conduct research within their clinics or hospitals.
- Research about psychological disorders falls into three basic categories: description, causation, and treatment and outcomes.

## The Supernatural, Biological, and Psychological Traditions

- Historically, there have been three prominent approaches to abnormal behaviour. In the supernatural tradition, abnormal behaviour is

attributed to agents outside our bodies or social environment, such as demons, spirits, or the influence of the moon and stars; though still alive, this tradition has been largely replaced by biological and psychological perspectives. In the biological tradition, disorders are attributed to disease or biochemical imbalances; in the psychological tradition, abnormal behaviour is attributed to faulty psychological development and to social context.

- Each tradition has its own way of treating individuals who have psychological disorders. Supernatural treatments include exorcism to rid the body of the supernatural spirits. Biological treatments typically emphasize physical care and the search for medical cures, especially drugs. Psychological approaches use psychosocial treatments, beginning with moral therapy and including modern psychotherapy.
- Sigmund Freud, the founder of psychoanalytic therapy, offered an elaborate conception of the unconscious mind, much of which is still conjecture. In therapy, Freud focused on tapping into the mysteries of the unconscious through techniques such as catharsis, free association, and dream analysis. Though Freud's followers veered from his path in many ways, Freud's influence can still be felt today.
- One outgrowth of Freudian therapy is humanistic psychology, which focuses more on human potential and self-actualizing than on psychological

disorders. Therapy that has evolved from this approach is known as person-centred therapy; the therapist shows almost unconditional positive regard for the client's feelings and thoughts.

- The behavioural model moved psychology into the realm of science. Both research and therapy focus on things that are measurable, including such techniques as systematic desensitization, reinforcement, and shaping.

## The Present: The Scientific Method and an Integrative Approach

- With the increasing sophistication of our scientific tools, and new knowledge from cognitive science, behavioural science, and neuroscience, we now realize that no contribution to psychological disorders ever occurs in isolation. Our behaviour, both normal and abnormal, is a product of a continual interaction of psychological, biological, and social influences.

## Key Terms

| | | | |
|---|---|---|---|
| psychological disorder, 2 | moral therapy, 16 | psychosexual stages of development, 21 | unconditional positive regard, 25 |
| phobia, 2 | mental hygiene movement, 17 | neurosis, 22 | behavioural model, 25 |
| psychopathology, 5 | psychoanalysis, 18 | ego psychology, 22 | classical conditioning, 25 |
| scientist-practitioner model, 5 | behaviourism, 18 | object relations, 22 | extinction, 26 |
| presenting problem, 6 | unconscious, 19 | free association, 23 | introspection, 26 |
| clinical description, 6 | catharsis, 19 | dream analysis, 23 | systematic desensitization, 27 |
| prevalence, 6 | psychoanalytic model, 19 | psychoanalyst, 23 | behaviour therapy, 27 |
| incidence, 6 | id, 20 | transference, 23 | reinforcement, 28 |
| course, 6 | ego, 20 | psychodynamic psychotherapy, 24 | shaping, 28 |
| prognosis, 7 | superego, 20 | self-actualizing, 24 | |
| etiology, 7 | intrapsychic conflicts, 20 | person-centred therapy, 25 | |
| psychosocial treatment, 16 | defence mechanisms, 20 | | |

## Answers to Concept Checks

**1.1**  **Part A**  1. d  2. b, c

  **Part B**  3. d  4. c  5. a  6. f  7. e  8. b

**1.2**  1. e  2. c  3. d

**1.3**  1. b  2. c  3. d  4. a

 **InfoTrac College Edition**

If your instructor ordered your book with InfoTrac College Edition, please explore this online library for additional readings, review, and a handy resource for short assignments. Go to:

**http://infotrac.thomsonlearning.com**

Enter these search terms: psychopathology, defense mechanisms, operant conditioning, mental health

 **The Abnormal Psychology Book Companion Website**

Go to **www.essentialsabnormalpsych.nelson.com** for practice quiz questions, Internet links, critical thinking exercises, and more.

 **Abnormal Psychology Live CD-ROM**

- **Roots of Behaviour Therapy:** This combined clip shows the historical progression of classical conditioning and the behavioural model from Pavlov through Watson and Skinner.

**Thomson NOW!** **http://hed.nelson.com** Go to this site for the link to ThomsonNow™, your one-stop study shop. Take a Pretest for this chapter and ThomsonNow™ will generate a personalized Study Plan based on your test results! The Study Plan will identify the topics you need to review and direct you to online resources to help you master those topics. You can then take a Posttest to help you determine the concepts you have mastered and what you still need work on.

## Video Concept Review

For challenging concepts that typically need more than one explanation, Mark Durand provides a video review via ThomsonNow™ of the following topics:

- Defining abnormality.
- Explaining the integrative approach.

# Chapter Quiz

1. Dr. Roberts, a psychiatrist, often prescribes medication to his patients for their psychological problems. Dr. Roberts has what type of degree?

   a. Ph.D.
   b. M.D.
   c. Psy.D.
   d. Ed.D.

2. All of the following are part of a clinical description EXCEPT:

   a. thoughts.
   b. feelings.
   c. causes.
   d. behaviours.

3. The _____ describes the number of people in a population who have a disorder, whereas the _____ describes how many new cases of a disorder occur within a given period.

   a. ratio; prevalence
   b. incidence; ratio
   c. incidence; prevalence
   d. prevalence; incidence

4. Which of the following is NOT a historical model of abnormal behaviour?

   a. the psyche model
   b. the supernatural model
   c. the biological model
   d. the psychological model

5. During the 19th century, the biological tradition of psychological disorders was supported by the discovery that a bacterial microorganism, _____, could result in psychotic symptoms and bizarre behaviours in advanced stages.

   a. malaria
   b. yellow fever
   c. dengue
   d. syphilis

6. Which of the following describes the order in which biological treatments for mental disorders were introduced?

   a. neuroleptic drug therapy, insulin therapy, electroconvulsive therapy
   b. insulin therapy, electroconvulsive therapy, neuroleptic drug therapy
   c. electroconvulsive therapy, neuroleptic drug therapy, insulin therapy
   d. electroconvulsive therapy, insulin therapy, neuroleptic drug therapy

7. _____ is the release of tension following the disclosure of emotional trauma, whereas _____ is the increased understanding of current feelings and past events.

   a. Insight; catharsis
   b. Catharsis; insight
   c. Catharsis; mediation
   d. Mediation; catharsis

8. Which of the following is an example of the Freudian defence mechanism known as displacement?

   a. Terry despises the fact that his brother is a star athlete. Instead of letting his brother know how he feels, Terry cheers him on at every game.
   b. Erika is attracted to her friend's husband and flirts with him. When her friend confronts her, Erika disagrees and refuses to believe what her friend is saying.
   c. Adam is criticized by his teacher in front of other students. When he goes home, his dog runs to him, and Adam kicks the dog.
   d. Judith feels uncomfortable around people with ethnic backgrounds different from her own. During a group discussion at work, she tells a co-worker that his ideas are racist.

9. Before feeding her dog, Anna always gets his food out of the pantry. When she opens the pantry door, her dog begins to salivate. The dog's salivation is a(n):

   a. unconditioned stimulus.
   b. unconditioned response.
   c. conditioned stimulus.
   d. conditioned response.

10. B. F. Skinner is known for introducing the concept of _____, the belief that behaviour can influence and change the environment.

   a. classical conditioning
   b. systematic desensitization
   c. operant conditioning
   d. extinction

*(See the Appendix on page 601 for answers.)*

# 2 An Integrative Approach to Psychopathology

© Photorake Inc./Alamy

**One-Dimensional or Multidimensional Models**
*What Caused Jody's Phobia?*
*Outcome and Comments*

**Biological Contributions to Psychopathology**
*The Nature of Genes*
*New Developments in the Study of Genes and Behaviour*
*The Interaction of Genetic and Environmental Effects*
*Nongenomic "Inheritance" of Behaviour*
*The Central Nervous System*
*The Structure of the Brain*
*The Peripheral Nervous System*
*Neurotransmitters*
*Implications for Psychopathology*
*Psychosocial Influences on Brain Structure and Function*
*Interactions of Psychosocial Factors with Brain
    Structure and Function*
*Comments*

**Behavioural Contributions to Psychopathology**
*Conditioning and Cognitive Processes*
*Learned Helplessness and Learned Optimism*
*Social Learning*
*Prepared Learning*
*Cognitive Science and the Unconscious*
*Cognitive-Behavioural Therapy*

**Emotional Contributions to Psychopathology**
*The Physiology and Purpose of Fear*
*Emotional Phenomena*
*The Components of Emotion*
*Anger and Your Heart*

**Social Contributions to Psychopathology**
*Voodoo, the Evil Eye, and Other Fears*
*Gender*
*Social Effects on Health and Behaviour*
*Social and Interpersonal Influences on the Elderly*
*Global Incidence of Psychological Disorders*

**Developmental Contributions to
Psychopathology**
*The Principle of Equifinality*

**Conclusions**

 **Abnormal Psychology Live CD-ROM**
*Integrative Approach*

Remember Jody from Chapter 1? We knew he had a blood-injury-injection phobia, but we did not know why. Here we address the issue of causation. In this chapter we examine the specific components of a **multidimensional integrative approach** to psychopathology. *Biological* dimensions include causal factors from the fields of genetics and neuroscience. *Psychological* dimensions include causal factors from behavioural and cognitive processes, including learned helplessness, social learning, prepared learning, and even unconscious processes (in a different guise than in the days of Freud). *Emotional* influences contribute in a variety of ways to psychopathology, as do *social* and *interpersonal* influences. Finally, *developmental* influences figure in any discussion of causes of psychological disorders. You will become familiar with these areas as they relate to psychopathology and learn about some of the latest developments that are relevant to psychological disorders. But keep in mind what we confirmed in the last chapter: No influence operates in isolation. Each dimension, biological or psychological, is strongly influenced by the others and by development, and they weave together in various complex and intricate ways to create a psychological disorder.

We explain briefly why we have adopted a multidimensional integrative model of psychopathology. Then we preview various causal influences and interactions, using Jody's case as background. After that we look more deeply at specific causal influences in psychopathology, examining both the latest research and the integrative ways of viewing what we know.

# One-Dimensional or Multidimensional Models

- ■ *Distinguish between multidimensional and unidimensional models of causality.*
- ■ *Identify the main influences comprising the multidimensional model.*

To say that psychopathology is caused by a physical abnormality or by conditioning is to accept a linear or one-dimensional model, which attempts to trace the origins of behaviour to a single cause. A linear causal model might hold that schizophrenia or a phobia is caused by a chemical imbalance or by growing up surrounded by overwhelming conflicts among family members. In psychology and psychopathology, we still encounter this type of thinking occasionally, but most scientists and clinicians believe abnormal behaviour results from multiple influences. A system, or feedback loop, may have independent inputs at many different points, but as each input becomes part of the whole it can no longer be considered independent. This perspective on causality is *systemic*, which derives from the word *system;* it implies that any particular influence contributing to psychopathology cannot be considered out of context. Context, in this case, is the biology and behaviour of the individual, as well as the cognitive, emotional, social, and cultural environment, because any one component of the system inevitably affects the other components. This is a multidimensional model.

## *What Caused Jody's Phobia?*

From a multidimensional perspective, let's look at what might have caused Jody's phobia (see Figure 2.1).

### Behavioural Influences

The cause of Jody's phobia might at first seem obvious. He saw a movie with graphic scenes of blood and injury and had a bad reaction to it. His reaction, an unconditioned response, became associated with situations similar to the scenes in the movie, depending on how similar they were. But Jody's reaction reached such an extreme that even hearing someone say, "Cut it out!" evoked queasiness. Is Jody's phobia a straightforward case of classical conditioning? It might seem so, but one puzzling question arises: Why didn't the other kids in Jody's class develop the same phobia? As far as Jody knew, nobody else even felt queasy!

### Biological Influences

We now know that much more is involved in blood-injury-injection phobia than a simple conditioning experience, although, clearly, conditioning and stimulus generalization contribute. We have learned a lot about this phobia (Marks, 1988; Page, 1994, 1996). Physiologically, Jody experienced a *vasovagal syncope*, which is a common cause of fainting. When he saw

---

**multidimensional integrative approach** Approach to the study of psychopathology that holds that psychological disorders are always the products of multiple interacting causal factors.

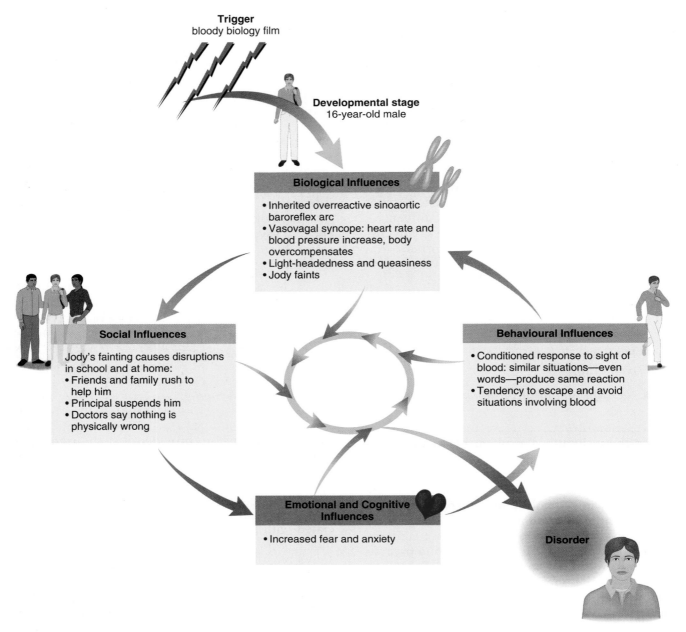

**Trigger**
bloody biology film

**Developmental stage**
16-year-old male

**Biological Influences**

- Inherited overreactive sinoaortic baroreflex arc
- Vasovagal syncope: heart rate and blood pressure increase, body overcompensates
- Light-headedness and queasiness
- Jody faints

**Social Influences**

Jody's fainting causes disruptions in school and at home:
- Friends and family rush to help him
- Principal suspends him
- Doctors say nothing is physically wrong

**Behavioural Influences**

- Conditioned response to sight of blood: similar situations—even words—produce same reaction
- Tendency to escape and avoid situations involving blood

**Emotional and Cognitive Influences**

- Increased fear and anxiety

**Disorder**

**Figure 2.1** ■ Jody's case, as seen from a multidimensional perspective.

the film he became mildly distressed, as many people would, and his heart rate and blood pressure increased accordingly, which he probably did not notice. Then his body took over, immediately compensating by decreasing his vascular resistance, lowering his heart rate and, eventually, lowering his blood pressure. The amount of blood reaching his brain diminished until he lost consciousness. *Syncope* means "sinking feeling" or "swoon" because of low blood pressure in the head. If Jody had bent down and put his head between his knees, he might have avoided fainting, but it happened so quickly he had no time to use this strategy.

A possible cause of the vasovagal syncope is an overreaction of a mechanism that compensates for

sudden increases in blood pressure by lowering it. Interestingly, the tendency to overcompensate seems to be inherited, a trait that may account for the high rate of blood-injury-injection phobia in families (Öst, 1992). Do you ever feel queasy at the sight of blood? If so, chances are your mother, your father, or someone else in your immediate family has the same reaction. But many people with rather severe syncope reaction tendencies do *not* develop phobias. They cope with their reaction in various ways, including tensing their muscles whenever they are confronted with blood. Tensing the muscles quickly raises blood pressure and prevents the fainting response. Furthermore, some people with little or no syncope reaction develop the phobia anyway

(Öst, 1992). Therefore, the cause of blood-injury-injection phobia is complicated. If we said that the phobia is caused by a biological dysfunction (an overactive vasovagal reaction) or a traumatic experience (seeing a gruesome film) and subsequent conditioning, we would be partly right on both counts, but in adopting a one-dimensional causal model we would miss the most important point: To cause blood-injury-injection phobia, a complex *interaction* must occur between behavioural and biological factors. Inheriting a strong syncope reaction definitely puts a person at risk for developing this phobia, but other influences are at work.

### Emotional Influences

Jody's case is a good example of biology influencing behaviour. But behaviour, thoughts, and feelings can also influence biology, sometimes dramatically. What role did Jody's fear and anxiety play in the development of his phobia, and where did they come from? Emotions can affect physiological responses such as blood pressure, heart rate, and respiration, particularly if we know rationally there is nothing to fear, as Jody did. In his case, rapid increases in heart rate, caused by his emotions, may have triggered a stronger and more intense vasovagal reaction. Emotions also changed the way he thought about situations involving blood and injury and motivated him to behave in ways he didn't want to, avoiding all situations connected with blood and injury even if it was important not to avoid them. As we see throughout this book, emotions play a substantial role in the development of many disorders.

### Social Influences

We are all social animals; by our very nature we tend to live in groups such as families. Social and cultural factors make direct contributions to biology and behaviour. Jody's friends and family rushed to his aid when he fainted. Did their support help or hurt? His principal rejected him and dismissed his problem. What effect did this behaviour have on his phobia? Rejection, particularly by authority figures, can make psychological disorders worse than they otherwise would be. Then again, being supportive only when somebody is experiencing symptoms is not always helpful because the strong effects of social attention may increase the frequency and intensity of the reaction.

### Developmental Influences

One more influence affects us all—the passage of time. As time passes, many things about ourselves and our environments change in important ways, causing us to react differently at different ages. Thus, at certain times we may enter a *developmental*

People who experience the same traumatic event will have different long-term reactions.

Mark Wallheiser/Reuters/Landov

*critical period* when we are more or less reactive to a given situation or influence than at other times. To go back to Jody, it is possible he was previously exposed to other situations involving blood. Important questions to ask are these: Why did this problem develop when he was 16 years old and not before? Is it possible that his susceptibility to having a vasovagal reaction was highest in his teenage years? It may be that the timing of his physiological reaction, along with viewing the disturbing biology film, provided just the right (but unfortunate) combination to initiate his severe phobic response.

## *Outcome and Comments*

Fortunately for Jody, he responded well to brief but intensive treatment at one of our clinics, and he was back in school within 7 days. Jody was gradually exposed, with his full cooperation, to words, images, and situations describing or depicting blood and injury while a sudden drop in blood pressure was prevented using applied muscle tension. Applied muscle tension is a simple behavioural technique that reduces vasovagal reactions by maintaining blood pressure. It has been used successfully in the treatment of people with blood and injury phobias, like Jody (Ditto, Wilkins, France, Lavoie, & Adler, 2003). For Jody's exposure treatment, we began with something mild, such as the phrase "cut it out!" By the end of the week Jody was witnessing surgical procedures at the local hospital while practising applied muscle tension. Jody required close therapeutic supervision during this program. At one point, while driving home with his parents from an evening session, he had the bad luck to pass a car crash, and he saw a bleeding accident victim. That night, he dreamed about bloody accident victims coming through the walls of his bedroom. This experience made him call the clinic and request emergency intervention to reduce his distress, but it did not slow his progress. (Programs for treating phobias and related anxiety disorders are described more fully in Chapter 4. It is the issue of etiology or causation that concerns us here.)

As you can see, finding the causes of abnormal behaviour is a complex and fascinating process. Focusing on biological or behavioural factors would not have given us a full picture of the causes of Jody's disorder; we had to consider a variety of other influences and how they might interact. A discussion in more depth follows, examining the research underlying the many biological, psychological, and social influences that must be considered as causes of any psychological disorder.

## Concept Check 2.1

Theorists have abandoned the notion that any one factor can explain abnormal behaviour in favour of an integrative model. Match each of the following scenarios to its most likely influence(s): (a) behavioural, (b) biological, (c) emotional, (d) social, and (e) developmental.

1. The fact that some phobias are more common than others (e.g., fear of heights and snakes) and may have contributed to the survival of the species in the past suggests that phobias may be genetically prewired. This is evidence for which influence? _____
2. Jan's husband, Jinx, was an unemployed jerk who spent his life chasing women other than his wife. Jan, happily divorced for years, cannot understand why the smell of Jinx's brand of aftershave causes her to become nauseated. Which influence best explains her response? _____
3. Sixteen-year-old Nathan finds it more difficult than his 7-year-old sister to adjust to his parents' recent separation. This may be explained by what influences? _____
4. A traumatic ride on a Ferris wheel at a young age was most likely the initial cause of Jennifer's fear of heights. Her strong emotional reaction to heights is likely to maintain or even increase her fear. The initial development of the phobia is likely a result of _____ influences; however, _____ influences are likely perpetuating the behaviour.

# Biological Contributions to Psychopathology

- *Define and describe how genes interact with environmental factors to affect behaviour.*

- *Identify the different models proposed to describe how genes interact with environmental factors to affect behaviour.*

- *Explain the role of neurotransmitters and their involvement in abnormal behaviour.*

- *Identify the functions of different brain regions and their role in psychopathology.*

What causes you to look like one or both of your parents or, perhaps, your grandparents? Obviously, it is the genes you inherit from your parents and from your ancestors before them. **Genes** are long molecules of deoxyribonucleic acid (DNA) at various locations on chromosomes within the cell nucleus. In this section on biological contributions to psychopathology, we consider the role of genetic factors. Ever since Gregor Mendel's

pioneering work in the 19th century, we have known that physical characteristics such as hair and eye colour and, to a certain extent, height and weight are determined—or at least strongly

**genes**  Long deoxyribonucleic acid (DNA) molecules, the basic physical units of heredity that appear as locations on chromosomes.

influenced—by our genetic endowment. However, other factors in the environment influence our physical appearance as well. To some extent, our weight and even our height are affected by nutritional, social, and cultural factors. Consequently, our genes seldom determine our physical development in any absolute way. They do provide some boundaries to our development. Exactly where we go within these boundaries depends on environmental influences.

Except for identical twins, every person has a unique set of genes unlike those of anyone else in the world. Because there is plenty of room for the environment to influence our development within the constraints set by our genes, there are many reasons for the development of individual differences.

What about our behaviour and traits, our likes and dislikes? Do genes influence personality and, by extension, abnormal behaviour? This question of nature (genes) versus nurture (upbringing and other environmental influences) is age-old in psychology, and the answers beginning to emerge are fascinating. Before discussing them, let's review briefly what we know.

## The Nature of Genes

We have known for a long time that each normal human cell has 46 chromosomes arranged in 23 pairs. One chromosome in each pair comes from your father, and one from your mother. We can actually see these chromosomes through a microscope, and we can sometimes tell when one is faulty and predict what problems it will cause.

The first 22 pairs of chromosomes provide programs for the development of the body and brain, and the last pair, called the *sex chromosomes*, determines an individual's sex. In females, both chromosomes in the 23rd pair are called *X chromosomes*. In males, the mother contributes an X chromosome but the father contributes a *Y chromosome*. This one difference is responsible for the variance in biological sex. Abnormalities in the sex chromosomal pair can cause ambiguous sexual characteristics (see Chapter 9).

The DNA molecules that contain genes have a certain structure, a double helix that was discovered only a few decades ago. The shape of a helix is like a spiral staircase. A double helix is two spirals intertwined, turning in opposite directions. Located on this double spiral are simple pairs of molecules bound together and arranged in different orders. On the X chromosome are approximately 160 million pairs. The ordering of these base pairs determines how the body develops and works.

If something is wrong in the ordering of these molecules on the double helix, we have a *defective*

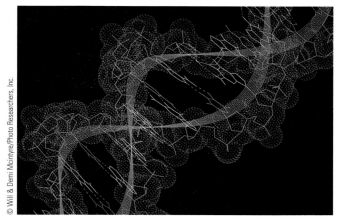

A DNA molecule, which contains genes, resembles a double spiral, or helix.

*gene*, which may or may not lead to problems. If it is a single dominant gene, such as the type that controls hair or eye colour, the effect can be quite noticeable. A *dominant gene* is one of a pair of genes that determines a particular trait. A *recessive gene*, by contrast, must be paired with another recessive gene to determine a trait. When we have a dominant gene, using Mendelian laws of genetics we can predict fairly accurately how many offspring will develop a certain trait, characteristic, or disorder, depending on whether one or both of the parents carry that dominant gene.

Most of the time, predictions are not so simple. Much of our development and, interestingly, most of our behaviour, personality, and even intelligence quotient (IQ) is probably *polygenic*—that is, influenced by many genes, each contributing only a tiny effect. For this reason, most scientists have decided that we must look for patterns of influence across these genes, using procedures called *quantitative genetics* (Plomin, 1990; Plomin, DeFries, McClearn,

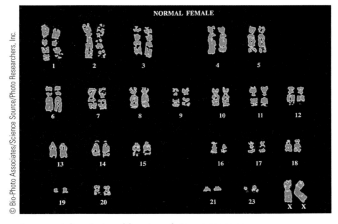

A normal female has 23 pairs of chromosomes.

& Rutter, 1997). Quantitative genetics basically sums up all the tiny effects across many genes without necessarily telling us which genes are responsible for which effects, although researchers are now using molecular genetic techniques (the study of the actual structure of genes) in an attempt to identify some of the specific genes that contribute to individual differences (e.g., Gershon, Kelsoe, Kendler, & Watson, 2001; Gottesman, 1997; Hariri et al., 2002; Plomin et al., 1995). In Chapter 3, we look at the actual methods scientists use to study the influence of genes. Here, our interest is on what they are finding.

## New Developments in the Study of Genes and Behaviour

Scientists have now identified, in a preliminary way, the genetic contribution to psychological disorders and related behavioural patterns. The best estimates attribute about half of our enduring personality traits and cognitive abilities to genes. For example, it now seems quite clear that the heritability of general cognitive ability (IQ) is approximately 62%, and this figure is relatively stable throughout adult life (Gottesman, 1997). This estimate is based on a landmark study by McClearn et al. (1997), who compared 110 Swedish identical twin pairs, at least 80 years old, with 130 same-sex fraternal twin pairs of a similar age. This work built on earlier important twin studies with different age groups showing similar results (e.g., Bouchard, Lykken, McGue, Segal, & Tellegen, 1990). In the McClearn et al. (1997) study, heritability estimates for specific cognitive abilities, such as memory, or ability to perceive spatial relations ranged from 32% to 62%. In other studies, the same calculation

Genetic contributions to behaviour are evident in twins who were raised apart. When these brothers were finally reunited, they were both firefighters, and they discovered many other shared characteristics and interests.

for personality traits such as shyness or activity levels ranges between 30% and 50% (Bouchard et al., 1990; Kendler, 2001; Loehlin, 1992; Saudino & Plomin, 1996; Saudino, Plomin, & DeFries, 1996). For psychological disorders, the evidence indicates that genetic factors make some contribution to all disorders but account for less than half of the explanation. If one of a pair of identical twins has schizophrenia, there is a less than 50% likelihood that the other twin will also (Gottesman, 1991). Similar or lower rates exist for other psychological disorders (Plomin et al., 1997), with the possible exception of alcoholism (Kendler et al., 1995).

Behavioural geneticists have reached general conclusions in the past several years on the role of genes and psychological disorders that are relevant to our purposes. First, it is likely that specific genes or small groups of genes may ultimately be found to be associated with certain psychological disorders, as suggested in several important studies described in this chapter. But much of the current evidence suggests that contributions to psychological disorders come from many genes, each having a relatively small effect. It is extremely important that we recognize this probability and continue to make every attempt to track the group of genes implicated in various disorders. Advances in gene mapping and molecular genetics help with this difficult research (e.g., Gershon et al., 2001; Plomin et al., 1997).

Second, it has become increasingly clear that genetic contributions cannot be studied in the absence of interactions with events in the environment that trigger genetic vulnerability or "turn on" specific genes. It is to this fascinating topic that we now turn.

## The Interaction of Genetic and Environmental Effects

In 1983, the distinguished neuroscientist and Nobel Prize winner Eric Kandel speculated that the process of learning affects more than behaviour. He suggested that the very genetic structure of cells may change as a result of learning, if genes that were inactive or dormant interact with the environment in such a way that they become active. In other words, the environment may occasionally turn on certain genes. This type of mechanism may lead to changes in the number of receptors at the end of a neuron, which, in turn, would affect biochemical functioning in the brain.

Although Kandel was not the first to propose this idea, it had enormous impact. Most of us assume that the brain, like other parts of the body, may be influenced by environmental changes during development. But we also assume that once maturity is reached, the structure and function of our internal organs and most of our physiology are pretty much set or, in the case of the brain, hard-wired. The competing idea is that the brain and its functions are plastic, subject to continual change in response to the environment, even at the level of genetic structure. Now there is evidence supporting that view (Kolb, Gibb, & Robinson, 2003; Owens, Mulchahey, Stout, & Plotsky, 1997).

With these new findings in mind, we can now explore gene–environment interactions as they relate to psychopathology. Two models have received the most attention, the diathesis–stress model and reciprocal gene–environment model.

## The Diathesis–Stress Model

For years, scientists have assumed a specific method of interaction between genes and environment. According to this **diathesis–stress model,** individuals inherit tendencies to express certain traits or behaviours, which may then be activated under conditions of stress (see Figure 2.2). Each inherited tendency is a *diathesis,* which means, literally, a condition that makes a person susceptible to developing a disorder. When the right kind of life event, such as a certain type of stressor, comes along, the disorder develops. For example, according to the diathesis–stress model, Jody inherited a *tendency* to faint at the sight of blood. This tendency is the diathesis, or **vulnerability.** It would not become prominent until certain environmental events occurred. For Jody, this event was the sight of an animal being dissected when he was in a situation in which escape, or at least closing his eyes, was not acceptable. The stress of seeing the dissection under these conditions activated his genetic tendency to faint. Together, these factors led to him developing a disorder. If he had not taken biology, he might have gone through life without ever knowing he had the tendency, at least to such an extreme, although he might have felt queasy about minor cuts and bruises. You can see that the "diathesis" is genetically based and the "stress" is environmental, but they must interact to produce a disorder.

This relationship has been demonstrated in an elegant way in a landmark study by Caspi et al. (2003). These investigators are studying a group of 847 New Zealand individuals who have undergone a variety of assessments for more than 2 decades, starting at the age of 3. They noted whether the subjects, at age 26, had been depressed during the past year. Overall, 17% of the study participants reported that they had experienced a major depressive episode during the prior year. The investigators also identified the genetic makeup of the individuals and, in particular, a gene that produces a substance called a *chemical transporter* that affects the transmission of serotonin in the brain. Serotonin, one of the four neurotransmitters we will talk about later in the chapter, is particularly implicated in depression. But the gene that Caspi et al. were studying comes in two common versions or alleles, the long allele (L) and the short allele (S). There was reason to believe, from prior work with animals, that individuals with at least two copies of the L allele were able to cope better with stress than individuals with two copies of the S allele. Because the investigators have been recording stressful life events in these individuals all of their lives, they were able to test this relationship. In fact, in people with two S alleles, the risk for having a major depressive episode doubled if they had at least four stressful life events, compared with people experiencing four stressful events who had two L alleles. But the really interesting finding occurs when we look at the childhood experience of these individuals. In people with the two S alleles, severe and stressful maltreatment during childhood more than doubled their risks of depression in adulthood compared with

**diathesis–stress model**   Hypothesis that both an inherited tendency (a vulnerability) and specific stressful conditions are required to produce a disorder.

**vulnerability**   Susceptibility or tendency to develop a disorder.

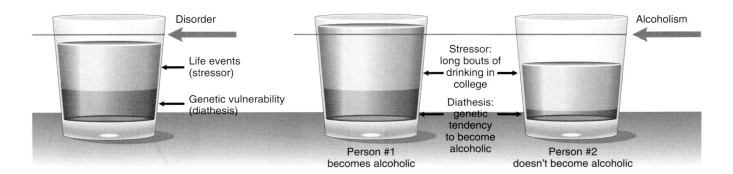

**Figure 2.2**  ■  In the diathesis–stress model, the greater the underlying vulnerability, the less stress is needed to trigger a disorder.

those individuals carrying the two S alleles who were not maltreated or abused (63% versus 30%). For individuals carrying the two L alleles, on the other hand, stressful childhood experiences did not affect the incidence of depression in adulthood, because 30% of this group became depressed whether or not they had experienced stressful childhood maltreatment. This relationship is shown in Figure 2.3. Therefore, unlike the group with two S alleles, depression in the two L alleles group seems related to stress in their recent past rather than childhood experiences. This study is by far the most important yet in demonstrating clearly that neither genes nor life experiences (environmental events) can explain the onset of a disorder such as depression. It takes a complex interaction of the two factors as suggested in the diathesis–stress model.

## The Reciprocal Gene–Environment Model

Some evidence now indicates that genetic endowment may *increase the probability* that an individual will experience stressful life events (e.g., Kendler, 2001; Saudino, Pedersen, Lichtenstein, McClearn, & Plomin, 1997). For example, people with a genetic vulnerability to develop a certain disorder, such as blood-injury-injection phobia, may also have a personality trait—let's say impulsiveness—that makes them more likely to be involved in minor accidents that would result in their seeing blood. In other

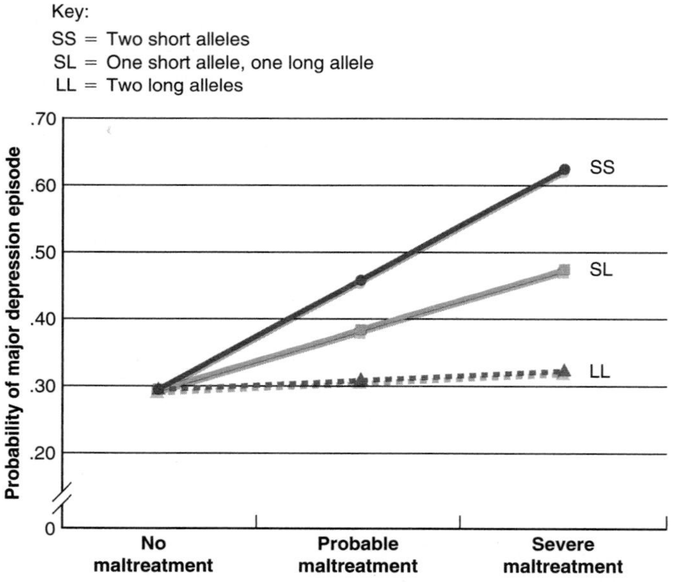

words, they may be accident prone because they are continually rushing to complete things or to get to places without regard for their physical safety. These people, then, might have a genetically determined tendency to create the very environmental risk factors that trigger a genetic vulnerability to blood-injury-injection phobia.

This **reciprocal gene–environment model,** or gene–environment correlation model (Kendler, 2001), has been proposed fairly recently (Rende & Plomin, 1992). Nonetheless, the work of Toronto psychologist Randy Katz and his colleagues (McGuffin, Katz, & Bebbington, 1988) and other research teams has provided some evidence that it applies to the development of depression. Specifically, some people may tend to seek out difficult relationships or other circumstances that lead to depression (Bebbington et al., 1988; Kendler et al., 1995; McGuffin et al., 1988). However, this did not seem to be the case in the New Zealand study described previously (Caspi et al., 2003), since stressful episodes during adulthood occurred at about the same frequency in the two S alleles and the two L alleles groups.

An interesting study by Kerry Jang and his colleagues at the University of British Columbia examined the influences of genes on exposure to various types of trauma or extremely stressful, life-threatening events (Stein, Jang, Taylor, Vernon, & Livesley, 2002). Using a large twin study, they found that whether or not genetic factors were involved depended on the type of trauma being considered. Both genetic and environmental factors affected whether or not people were exposed to traumas involving assault, such as robbery and rape. In contrast, only environmental factors seemed to influence whether or not people were exposed to traumas that did not involve assault, such as motor vehicle accidents and natural disasters. Again, obviously no one gene leads people to be victims of crimes involving assault. It is more likely that genes influence inherited personality traits such as impulsiveness that cause people to enter dangerous situations in which such types of traumas are most likely to occur.

It is important to issue a word of caution that the reciprocal gene–environment model might be misinterpreted as a model involving victim blaming. The model does not claim, for example, that depressed people bring on depression themselves by purposely seeking out situations that lead to depression. Nor does it claim that survivors of

Key:
SS = Two short alleles
SL = One short allele, one long allele
LL = Two long alleles

**Figure 2.3** ■ Interaction of genes and early environment in producing adult major depression. (Reprinted with permission from Caspi, A., Sugden, K., Moffitt, T. E., Taylor, A., Craig, I. W., Harrington, H., et al. (2003). Influence of life stress on depression: Moderation by polymorphism in the 5-HTT gene. *Science, 301,* 386–389. Copyright © 2003 AAAS.)

**reciprocal gene–environment model** Hypothesis that people with a genetic predisposition for a disorder may also have a genetic tendency to create environmental risk factors that promote the disorder.

traumas involving assault are to blame for their problems because they sought out dangerous situations to begin with. In fact, a fine line exists between simply blaming the victim and understanding that genetic influences on personality can contribute to the types of life experiences a person has, which in turn contribute to the development of psychopathology.

## Nongenomic "Inheritance" of Behaviour

To make things a bit more interesting but also more complicated, a number of recent reports suggest that studies to date have overemphasized the extent of genetic influence on our personalities, our temperaments, and their contribution to the development of psychological disorders. This overemphasis may be due, in part, to the manner in which these studies have been conducted (Moore, 2001; Turkheimer & Waldron, 2000). Several intriguing lines of evidence have come together in the past several years to buttress this conclusion.

For example, in a fascinating study with rats, Michael Meaney of McGill University and his colleagues used a powerful experimental procedure called "cross fostering" to study stress reactivity and how it is passed on through generations (Francis, Diorio, Liu, & Meaney, 1999). They first demonstrated, as had many other investigators, that maternal behaviour affected how the young rats tolerated stress. If the mothers were calm and supportive, their rat pups were less fearful and better able to tolerate stress. Of course, we don't know if this effect is caused by genetic influences or the effects of being raised by calm mothers. This is where cross fostering comes in. Meaney and his colleagues took some newly born rat pups of fearful and easily stressed mothers and placed them for rearing with calm mothers. Other young rats remained with their easily stressed mothers (Francis et al., 1999). With this interesting scientific twist, they demonstrated that calm and supportive behaviour by the mothers could be passed down through generations of rats *independent of genetic influences*, because rats born to easily stressed mothers but reared by calm mothers grew up more calm and supportive. The authors conclude "these findings suggest that individual differences in the expression of genes in brain regions that regulate stress reactivity can be transmitted from one generation to the next through behaviour.... The results ... suggest that the mechanism for this pattern of inheritance involves differences in maternal care" (p. 1158). Meaney and his colleagues have reported similar results in other studies as well (e.g., Anisman, Zaharia,

Meaney, & Merali, 1998; see also review by Meaney, 2001).

Suomi (1999) has reported similar results in his work with rhesus monkeys, using the cross fostering strategies just described. Suomi (1999) showed that if genetically reactive and emotional young monkeys are reared by calm mothers for the first 6 months of their lives, the animals behaved, in later life, as if they were non-emotional and not reactive to stress at birth. In other words, the environmental effects of early parenting seem to override any genetic contribution to be anxious, emotional, or reactive to stress. Suomi (1999) also demonstrated that these emotionally reactive monkeys raised by "calm, supportive" parents were also calm and supportive when raising their own children, thereby influencing and even reversing the genetic contribution to the expression of personality traits or temperaments.

Strong effects of the environment have also been observed in humans. For example, Tienari et al. (1994) found that children of parents with schizophrenia who were adopted away as babies demonstrated a tendency to develop psychiatric disorders (including schizophrenia) themselves only if they were adopted into dysfunctional families. Those children adopted into functional families with high-quality parenting did not develop the disorders. Collins and colleagues (Collins, Maccoby, Steinberg, Hetherington, & Bornstein, 2000), in reviewing the contributions of nature (genes) versus nurture (environment), conclude, with respect to the influence of parenting, that "this new generation of evidence on the role of parenting should add to the conviction, long held by many scholars, that broad general main effects for either heredity or environment are unlikely in research on behaviour and personality" (p. 228). That is, a specific genetic predisposition, no matter how strong, may never express itself in behaviour unless the individual is exposed to a certain kind of environment. On the other hand, a certain kind of (maladaptive) environment may have little effect on a child's development unless that child carries a particular genetic endowment. Thus, it is too simplistic to say the genetic contribution to a personality trait or to a psychological disorder is approximately 50%. We can talk of a heritable (genetic) contribution only in the context of the individual's past and present environment.

These new conceptualizations of the role of genetic contributions as constraining environmental influences have implications for preventing unwanted personality traits or temperaments and even psychological disorders, a theme of this edition. That is, it seems that environmental manipulations, particularly early in life, may do much to override the genetically influenced tendency to develop undesirable behavioural emotional reactions. Although current research suggests the influence of everything in our environment in its totality, such as peer groups, schools, and so on, affects this genetic expression, the strongest evidence exists for the effects of early parenting influences and other early experiences (Collins et al., 2000).

In summary, a complex interaction between genes and environment plays an important role in every psychological disorder (Kendler, 2001; Rutter, 2002; Turkheimer, 1998). Our genetic endowment does contribute to our behaviour, our emotions, and our cognitive processes and constrains the influence of environmental factors, such as upbringing, on our later behaviour, as is evident in the New Zealand study (Caspi et al., 2003). Environmental events, in turn, seem to affect our very genetic structure by determining whether certain genes are activated or not (Gottlieb, 1998). Furthermore, strong environmental influences alone may be sufficient to override genetic diatheses. Thus, neither nature (genes) nor nurture (environmental events) alone, but a complex interaction of the two, influences the development of our behaviour and personalities.

In the following, we continue to consider the role of biological factors, but we switch our focus to consideration of neuroscience and its contributions to psychopathology.

## Concept Check 2.2

Determine whether these statements relating to the genetic contributions of psychopathology are True (T) or False (F).

1. _____ The first 20 pairs of chromosomes program the development of the body and brain.
2. _____ No individual genes have been identified that cause any major psychological disorders.
3. _____ According to the diathesis–stress model, people inherit a vulnerability to express certain traits or behaviours that may be activated under certain stress conditions.
4. _____ The idea that individuals may have a genetic endowment to increase the probability that they will experience stressful life events and therefore trigger a vulnerability is in accordance with the diathesis–stress model.
5. _____ Environmental events alone influence the development of our behaviour and personalities.

Knowing how the nervous system and, especially, how the brain works is central to any understanding of our behaviour, emotions, and cognitive processes. This is the focus of **neuroscience.** To comprehend the newest research in this field, we first need an overview of how the brain and the nervous system function. The human nervous system includes the *central nervous system*, consisting of the brain and the spinal cord, and the *peripheral nervous system*, consisting of the somatic nervous system and the autonomic nervous system (see Figure 2.4).

## The Central Nervous System

The central nervous system (CNS) processes all information received from our sense organs and reacts as necessary. It sorts out what is relevant, such as a certain taste or a new sound, from what isn't, such as a familiar view or ticking clock; checks the memory banks to determine why the information is relevant; and implements the right reaction, whether it is to answer a question or to play a Chopin étude. This is a lot of exceedingly complex work. The spinal cord is part of the CNS, but its primary function is to facilitate the sending of messages to and from the brain, which is the other major component of the CNS and the most complex organ in the body. The brain uses an average of 140 billion nerve cells, called **neurons,** to control our every thought and action. Neurons transmit information throughout the nervous system. Understanding how they work is important for our purposes because current research has confirmed that neurons contribute to psychopathology.

The typical neuron contains a central cell body with two kinds of branches. One kind of branch is called a *dendrite*. Dendrites have numerous *receptors* that receive messages in the form of chemical impulses from other nerve cells, which are converted into electrical impulses. The other kind of branch, called an *axon*, transmits these impulses to other neurons. Any one nerve cell may have multiple connections to other neurons. The brain has billions of nerve cells, so you can see how complicated the system becomes, far more complicated than the most powerful computer that has ever been built (or will be for some time).

Nerve cells are not actually connected. There is a small space through which the impulse must pass to get to the next neuron. The space between the axon of

**neuroscience** Study of the nervous system and its role in behaviour, thoughts, and emotions.

**neuron** Individual nerve cell responsible for transmitting information.

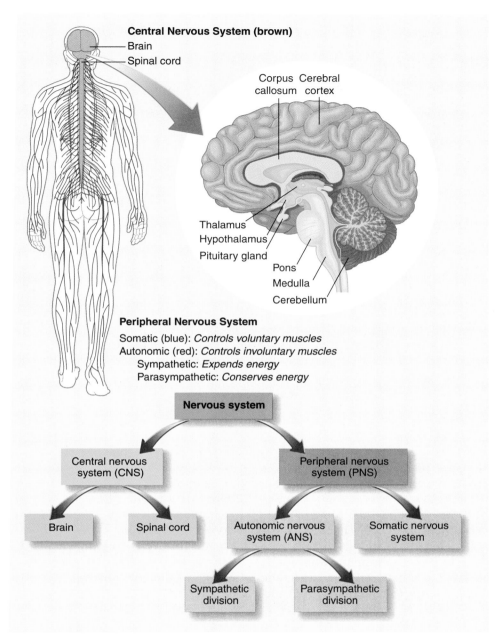

**Figure 2.4  ■**  Divisions of the nervous system. (From *Psychology* by E. Bruce Goldstein. © 1994 Brooks/Cole Publishing Company.)

one neuron and the dendrite of another is called the **synaptic cleft** (see Figure 2.5). What happens in this space is of great interest to psychopathologists. The chemicals that are released from the axon of one nerve cell and transmit the impulse to the receptors of another nerve cell are called **neurotransmitters.** These were mentioned briefly when we described the genetic contribution to depression in the New Zealand study. Only in the past several decades have we begun to understand their complexity. Now, using increasingly sensitive equipment and techniques, scientists have identified many different types of neurotransmitters.

Major neurotransmitters relevant to psychopathology include *norepinephrine* (also known as noradrenaline), *serotonin, dopamine,* and *gamma aminobutyric acid (GABA).* You will see these terms

**synaptic cleft**  Space between nerve cells where chemical transmitters act to move impulses from one neuron to the next.

**neurotransmitters**  Chemicals that cross the synaptic cleft between nerve cells to transmit impulses from one neuron to the next. Their relative excess or deficiency is involved in several psychological disorders.

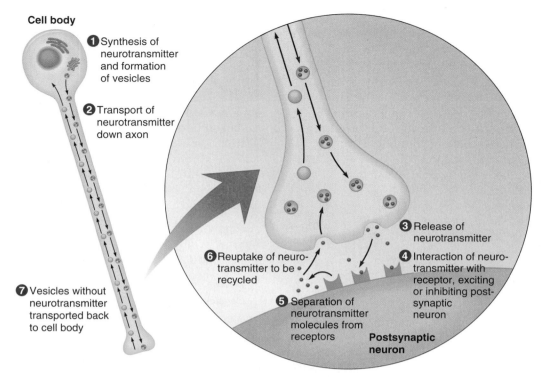

**Cell body**

**1** Synthesis of neurotransmitter and formation of vesicles

**2** Transport of neurotransmitter down axon

**7** Vesicles without neurotransmitter transported back to cell body

**3** Release of neurotransmitter

**4** Interaction of neurotransmitter with receptor, exciting or inhibiting post-synaptic neuron

**5** Separation of neurotransmitter molecules from receptors

**6** Reuptake of neurotransmitter to be recycled

**Postsynaptic neuron**

**Figure 2.5** ■ The transmission of information from one neuron to another. (From *Psychology* by E. Bruce Goldstein. © 1994 Brooks/Cole Publishing Company.)

many times in this book. Excesses or insufficiencies in some neurotransmitters are associated with different groups of psychological disorders. For example, reduced levels of GABA were initially thought to be associated with excessive anxiety (Costa, 1985). Early research (Snyder, 1976, 1981) linked increases in dopamine activity to schizophrenia. Other early research found correlations between depression and high levels of norepinephrine (Schildkraut, 1965) and,

possibly, low levels of serotonin (Siever, Davis, & Gorman, 1991). However, more recent research, described later in this chapter, indicates that these early interpretations were much too simplistic. Many types and subtypes of neurotransmitters are just being discovered, and they interact in complex ways. In view of their importance, we will return to the subject of neurotransmitters shortly.

The central nervous system screens out information that is irrelevant to the current situation. From moment to moment we notice what moves or changes more than what remains the same.

© David Young-Wolff/PhotoEdit

## The Structure of the Brain

Having an overview of the brain is useful because many of the structures described here are mentioned later in the context of specific disorders. One way to view the brain (see Figure 2.6) is to see it in two parts—the *brain stem* and the *forebrain*. The brain stem is the lower and more ancient part of the brain. Found in most animals, this structure handles most of the essential automatic functions such as breathing, sleeping, and moving around in a coordinated way. The forebrain is more advanced and has evolved more recently.

The lowest part of the brain stem, the *hindbrain*, regulates many automatic activities, such as breathing, the pumping action of the heart (heartbeat), and digestion. It also contains a structure that controls motor coordination.

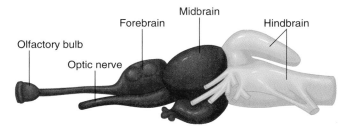

**Figure 2.6a** ■ Divisions of the brain. (From *Biological Psychology* (with CD-ROM and InfoTrac), 7th edition by J.W. Kalat © 2001. Reprinted with permission of Wadsworth, a division of Thomson Learning. www.thomsonrights.com. Fax 800-730-2215.)

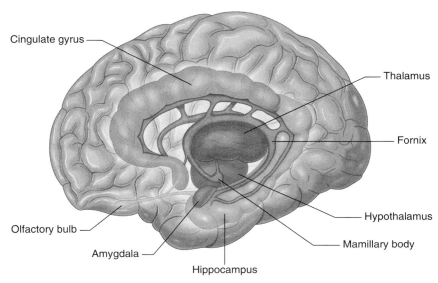

**Figure 2.6b** ■ The limbic system. (From *Biological Psychology* (with CD-ROM and InfoTrac), 7th edition by J.W. Kalat © 2001. Reprinted with permission of Wadsworth, a division of Thomson Learning. www.thomsonrights.com. Fax 800-730-2215.)

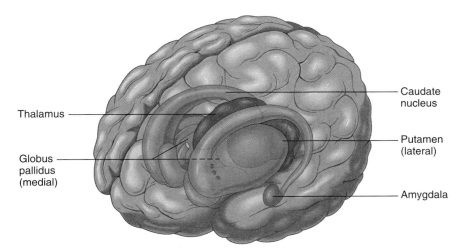

**Figure 2.6c** ■ The basal ganglia. (From *Biological Psychology* (with CD-ROM and InfoTrac), 7th edition by J.W. Kalat © 2001. Reprinted with permission of Wadsworth, a division of Thomson Learning. www.thomsonrights.com. Fax 800-730-2215.)

The *midbrain* coordinates movement with sensory input and contains parts of the *reticular activating system,* which contributes to processes of arousal and tension such as whether we are awake or asleep.

At the top of the brain stem are the *thalamus* and *hypothalamus,* which are involved broadly with regulating behaviour and emotion. These structures function primarily as a relay between the forebrain and the remaining lower areas of the brain stem. Some anatomists even consider the thalamus and hypothalamus to be parts of the forebrain.

At the base of the forebrain, just above the thalamus and hypothalamus, is the *limbic system. Limbic* means "border," so named because it is located around the edge of the centre of the brain. The limbic system, which figures prominently in much of psychopathology, includes structures such as the *hippocampus* (sea horse) and *amygdala* (almond), both of which are named for their approximate shapes. This system helps regulate our emotional experiences and expressions and, to some extent, our ability to learn and to control our impulses. It is also involved with the basic drives of sex, aggression, hunger, and thirst.

Damage to the *basal ganglia,* also at the base of the forebrain, may make us change our posture or twitch or shake. Thus, the basal ganglia are believed to control motor activity. Later in this chapter we review some interesting findings on the relationship of this area to obsessive-compulsive disorder.

The largest part of the forebrain is the *cerebral cortex,* which contains more than 80% of all the neurons in the CNS. This part of the brain provides us with our distinctly human qualities, allowing us to look to the future and plan, to reason, and to create. The cerebral cortex is divided into two hemispheres. Although the hemispheres look alike structurally and operate relatively independently (both are capable of perceiving, thinking, and remembering), recent research indicates that each has different specialties. The left hemisphere seems to be chiefly responsible for verbal processes. The right hemisphere seems to be better at creating images.

The hemispheres may play differential roles in specific psychological disorders. For example, current theories about dyslexia (a learning disability involving reading) suggest that it may be a result of the two hemispheres not specializing adequately or not communicating properly with each other (Shaywitz, 2003). Each hemisphere consists of four separate areas or lobes: *temporal, parietal, occipital,* and *frontal* (see Figure 2.7). Each is associated with different processes: the temporal lobe with recognizing various sights and sounds and with long-term memory storage; the parietal lobe with recognizing various sensations of touch; the occipital lobe with integrating and making sense of various visual inputs. These three

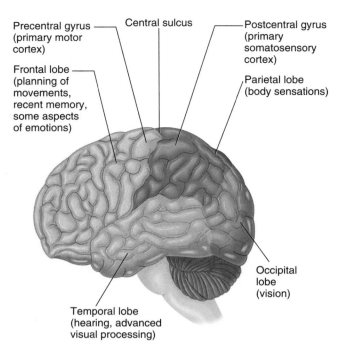

**Figure 2.7** ■ Some major subdivisions of the human cerebral cortex and a few of their primary functions. (From *Biological Psychology* (with CD-ROM and InfoTrac), 7th edition by J.W. Kalat © 2001. Reprinted with permission of Wadsworth, a division of Thomson Learning. www.thomsonrights.com. Fax 800-730-2215.)

lobes, located toward the back (posterior) of the brain, work together to process sight, touch, hearing, and other signals from our senses.

The frontal lobe is the most interesting from the point of view of psychopathology. It carries most of the weight of our thinking and reasoning abilities and of our memory. It also enables us to relate to the world around us and the people in it, to behave as social animals. When studying areas of the brain for clues to psychopathology, most researchers focus on the frontal lobe of the cerebral cortex, as well as on the limbic system and the basal ganglia.

## The Peripheral Nervous System

The peripheral nervous system coordinates with the brain stem to make sure the body is working properly. Its two major components are the *somatic nervous system* and the *autonomic nervous system (ANS).* The somatic nervous system controls the muscles, so damage in this area might make it difficult for us to engage in any voluntary movement, including talking. The autonomic nervous system includes the *sympathetic nervous system (SNS)* and *parasympathetic nervous system (PNS).* The primary duties of the ANS are to regulate the cardiovascular system (e.g., the heart and blood vessels) and the endocrine system (e.g., the pituitary, adrenal, thyroid, and gonadal glands) and to perform various other functions, including aiding digestion and regulating body temperature (see Figure 2.8).

The *endocrine system* works a bit differently from other systems in the body. Each endocrine gland produces its own chemical messenger, called a **hormone,** and releases it directly into the bloodstream. The adrenal glands produce epinephrine (also called *adrenaline*) in response to stress, as well as salt-regulating hormones; the thyroid gland produces thyroxine, which facilitates energy metabolism and growth; the pituitary is a master gland that produces a variety of regulatory hormones; and the gonadal glands produce sex hormones such as

estrogen and testosterone. The endocrine system is closely related to the immune system; it is also implicated in a variety of disorders, particularly the stress-related physical disorders discussed in Chapter 7.

The sympathetic and parasympathetic divisions of the ANS often operate in a complementary fashion. The SNS is primarily responsible for mobilizing the body during times of stress or danger, by rapidly activating the organs and glands under its control. When the sympathetic division goes on

**hormone**  Chemical messenger produced by the endocrine glands.

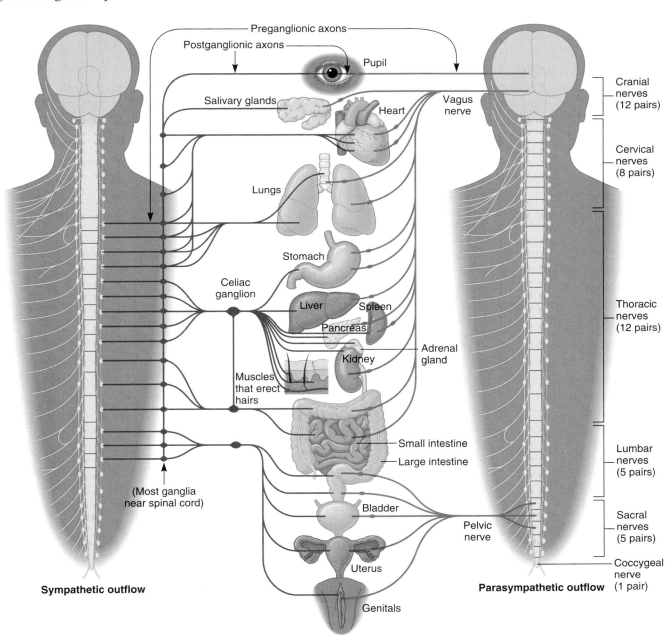

**Figure 2.8**  ■  The sympathetic nervous system (red lines) and parasympathetic nervous system (blue lines). (From *Biological Psychology* (with CD-ROM and InfoTrac), 7th edition by J.W. Kalat © 2001. Reprinted with permission of Wadsworth, a division of Thomson Learning. www.thomsonrights.com. Fax 800-730-2215.)

alert, the heart beats faster, thereby increasing the flow of blood to the muscles; respiration increases, allowing more oxygen to get into the blood and brain; and the adrenal glands are stimulated. All these changes help mobilize us for action. If we are threatened by some immediate danger, such as a mugger coming at us on the street, we are able to run faster or defend ourselves with greater strength than if the SNS had not innervated our internal organs. When you read in the newspaper that a woman lifted a heavy object to free a trapped child, you can be sure her sympathetic nervous system was working overtime. This system mediates a substantial part of our "emergency" or "alarm" reaction, discussed later in this chapter and in Chapter 4.

One of the functions of the PNS is to balance the SNS. In other words, because we could not operate in a state of hyperarousal and preparedness forever, the PNS takes over after the SNS has been active for a while, normalizing our arousal and facilitating the storage of energy by helping the digestive process.

One brain connection that is implicated in some psychological disorders involves the hypothalamus and the endocrine system. The hypothalamus connects to the adjacent pituitary gland, which is the master or coordinator of the endocrine system. The pituitary gland, in turn, may stimulate the cortical part of the adrenal glands on top of the kidneys. As we noted previously, surges of epinephrine tend to energize us, arouse us, and get our bodies ready for threat or challenge. When athletes say their adrenaline was really flowing, they mean they were highly aroused and up for the game. The cortical part of the adrenal glands also produces the stress hormone *cortisol.* This system is called the *hypothalamic-pituitary-adrenalcortical axis,* or *HPA axis* (see Figure 2.9); it has been implicated in several psychological disorders.

This brief overview should give you a general sense of the structure and function of the brain and nervous system. New procedures for studying brain structure and function that involve photographing the working brain are discussed in Chapter 3. Here, we focus on what these studies reveal about the nature of psychopathology.

## Neurotransmitters

The biochemical neurotransmitters in the brain and nervous system that carry messages from one neuron to another are receiving intense attention by psychopathologists (Bloom & Kupfer, 1995; Bloom, Nelson, & Lazerson, 2001; LeDoux, 2001). The first of these chemicals to be discovered was acetylcholine, in 1921, by a German biologist named Otto Loewi, who would later win the Nobel Prize for his work. Many more neurotransmitters have since been identified, but only in the past few years have we developed the extraordinarily sophisticated procedures necessary to

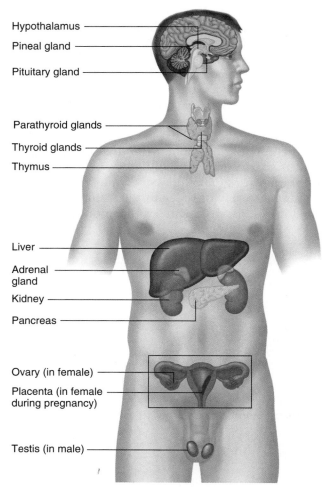

**Figure 2.9** ■ Location of some of the major endocrine glands. (From *Biological Psychology* (with CD-ROM and InfoTrac), 7th edition by J.W. Kalat © 2001. Reprinted with permission of Wadsworth, a division of Thomson Learning. www.thomsonrights.com. Fax 800-730-2215.)

study them. One way to think of neurotransmitters is as narrow currents flowing through the ocean of the brain. Neurons that are sensitive to one type of neurotransmitter cluster together and form paths from one part of the brain to the other.

Often these paths overlap with the paths of other neurotransmitters but, as often as not, they end up going their separate ways (Bloom et al., 2001; Dean, Kelsey, Heller, & Ciaranello, 1993). There are thousands, perhaps tens of thousands, of these **brain circuits,** and we are just beginning to discover and map them. Recently, neuroscientists have identified several that seem to play roles in various psychological disorders (LeDoux, 2001).

Almost all drug therapies work by either increasing or decreasing the flow of specific neurotransmitters. Some drugs directly inhibit, or block,

---

**brain circuits** Neurotransmitter currents or neural pathways in the brain.

the production of a neurotransmitter. Other drugs increase the production of competing biochemical substances that may deactivate the neurotransmitter. Yet other drugs do not affect neurotransmitters directly but prevent the chemical from reaching the next neuron by closing down, or occupying, the receptors in that neuron. After a neurotransmitter is released, it is quickly drawn back from the synaptic cleft into the same neuron. This process is called **reuptake.** Some drugs work by blocking the reuptake process, thereby causing continued stimulation along the brain circuit.

New neurotransmitters are frequently discovered, and existing neurotransmitter systems must be subdivided into separate classifications. Because this dynamic field of research is in a state of considerable flux, the neuroscience of psychopathology is an exciting area of study. However, research findings that seem to apply to psychopathology today may no longer be relevant tomorrow. Many years of study will be required before it is all sorted out.

You may still read reports that certain psychological disorders are "caused" by biochemical imbalances, excesses, or deficiencies in certain neurotransmitter systems. For example, abnormal activity of the neurotransmitter serotonin is often described as causing depression, and abnormalities in the neurotransmitter dopamine have been implicated in schizophrenia. However, increasing evidence indicates that this is an enormous oversimplification. We are now learning that the effects of neurotransmitter activity are more general and less specific. They often seem to be related to the way we process information (Bloom et al., 2001; Depue, Luciana, Arbisi, Collins, & Leon, 1994; Kandel, Schwartz, & Jessell, 2000; LeDoux, 2001). Changes in neurotransmitter activity may make people more or less likely to exhibit certain kinds of behaviour in certain situations without causing the behaviour directly. In addition, broad-based disturbances in our functioning are almost always associated with interactions of the various neurotransmitters rather than with alterations in the activity of any one system (Depue & Spoont, 1986; Depue & Zald, 1993; LeDoux, 2001; Owens et al., 1997).

Research on neurotransmitter function focuses primarily on what happens when activity levels change. We can study this in several ways. We can introduce substances called **agonists** that effectively *increase* the activity of a neurotransmitter by mimicking its effects; substances called **antagonists** that *decrease,* or block, a neurotransmitter; or substances called **inverse agonists** that produce effects *opposite* to those produced by the neurotransmitter. By systematically manipulating the production of a neurotransmitter in different parts of the brain, scientists are able to learn more about its effects. In fact, most drugs could be classified as either agonistic or antagonistic, although they may achieve these results in a variety of ways. We now describe the four neurotransmitter systems most often mentioned in connection with psychological disorders.

### Serotonin

The technical name for **serotonin** is 5-hydroxytryptamine (5-HT). Approximately six major circuits of serotonin spread from the midbrain, looping around its various parts (Azmitia, 1978; see Figure 2.10). Because of the widespread nature of these circuits, many of them ending up in the cortex, serotonin is believed to influence a great deal of our behaviour, particularly the way we process information (Depue & Spoont, 1986; Spoont, 1992). It was genetically influenced dysregulation in this system that contributed to depression in the New Zealand study described previously (Caspi et al., 2003).

The serotonin system regulates our behaviour, moods, and thought processes. Extremely low

**reuptake**   Action by which a neurotransmitter is quickly drawn back into the discharging neuron after being released into a synaptic cleft.

**agonist**   Chemical substance that effectively increases the activity of a neurotransmitter by imitating its effects.

**antagonist**   Chemical substance that decreases or blocks the effects of a neurotransmitter.

**inverse agonist**   Chemical substance that produces effects opposite those of a particular neurotransmitter.

**serotonin**   Neurotransmitter involved in information processing, coordination of movement, inhibition, and restraint; it also assists in the regulation of eating, sexual, and aggressive behaviours, all of which may be involved in different psychological disorders. Its interaction with dopamine is implicated in schizophrenia.

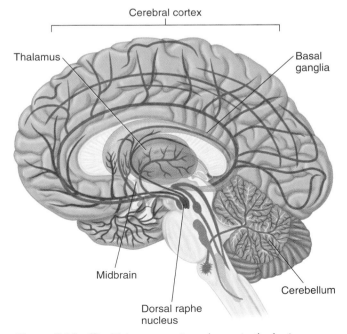

**Figure 2.10** ■ Major serotonin pathways in the brain.

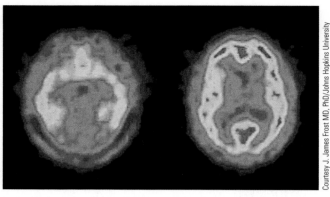

A PET scan shows the distribution of serotonergic neurons. This brain scanning method was recently used by researchers at the Toronto PET Centre to document increased serotonin receptor density in patients with schizophrenia (Tauscher et al., 2002).

activity levels of serotonin are associated with less inhibition and with impulsivity and the tendency to overreact to situations. Low serotonin activity has been associated with aggression, suicide, impulsive overeating, and excessive sexual behaviour. However,

these behaviours do not *necessarily* happen if serotonin activity is low. Other currents in the brain, or other psychological or social influences, may compensate for low serotonin activity. Therefore, low serotonin activity may make us more vulnerable to certain problematic behaviour without directly causing it. Several different classes of drugs primarily affect the serotonin system, including the tricyclic antidepressants such as imipramine (known by its brand name Tofranil). The class of drugs called selective serotonin reuptake inhibitors (SSRIs), including fluoxetine (Prozac; see Figure 2.11), affect serotonin more directly than other drugs. These drugs are used to treat a number of psychological disorders, particularly anxiety, mood, and eating disorders.

## Gamma Aminobutyric Acid

The neurotransmitter **gamma aminobutyric acid, GABA** for short, reduces postsynaptic activity, which, in turn, inhibits a variety of behaviours and emotions; its best-known effect, however, is to reduce anxiety (Charney & Drevets, 2002; Davis, 2002).

**How Neurotransmitters Work**
Neurotransmitters are stored in tiny sacs at the end of the neuron Ⓐ. An electric jolt makes the sacs merge with the outer membrane, and the neurotransmitter is released into the synapse Ⓑ. The molecules diffuse across the gap and bind to receptors, specialized proteins, on the adjacent neuron Ⓒ. When sufficient neurotransmitter has been absorbed, the receptors release the molecules, which are then broken down or reabsorbed by the first neuron and stored for later use Ⓓ.

**How Serotonin Drugs Work**
Prozac enhances serotonin's effects by preventing it from being absorbed Ⓔ. Redux and fenfluramine (antiobesity drugs) cause the release of extra serotonin into the synapse Ⓕ.

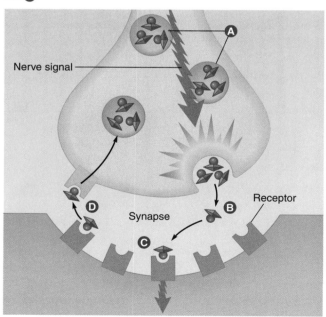

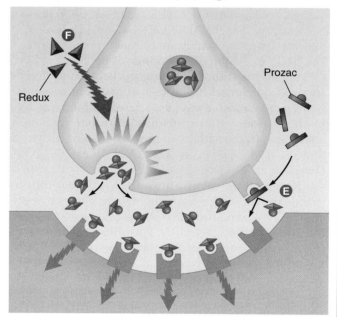

**Receptor Variation**
There are at least 15 different serotonin receptors, each associated with a different function.

**Figure 2.11** ■ Manipulating serotonin in the brain.

Scientists have discovered that a particular class of drugs, the *benzodiazepines,* or mild tranquillizers, makes it easier for GABA molecules to attach themselves to the receptors of specialized neurons. Thus, the higher the level of benzodiazepine, the more GABA becomes attached to neuron receptors and the calmer we become (to a point). Neuroscientists thus assume that we must have within us substances very much like the benzodiazepine class of drugs—in other words, natural benzodiazepines. However, we have yet to discover them (Bloom & Kupfer, 1995).

As with other neurotransmitter systems, we now know that GABA's effect is not specific to anxiety but has a much broader influence. Like serotonin, the GABA system rides on many circuits distributed widely throughout the brain. GABA seems to reduce overall arousal somewhat and to temper our emotional responses. For example, in addition to reducing anxiety, minor tranquillizers also have an anticonvulsant effect, relaxing muscle groups that may be subject to spasms. Furthermore, this system seems to reduce levels of anger, hostility, aggression, and, perhaps, even positive emotional states such as eager anticipation and pleasure (Bond & Lader, 1979; Lader, 1975).

### Norepinephrine

A third neurotransmitter system important to psychopathology is **norepinephrine** (also known as *noradrenaline*; see Figure 2.12). We have already seen that norepinephrine, like epinephrine (referred to as a *catecholamine*), is part of the endocrine system.

Norepinephrine seems to stimulate at least two groups (and probably several more) of receptors called *alpha-adrenergic* and *beta-adrenergic* receptors. Someone in your family may be taking a widely used class of drugs called *beta-blockers,* particularly if he or she has hypertension or difficulties with regulating heart rate. As the name indicates, these drugs block the beta-receptors so that their response to a surge of norepinephrine is reduced, which keeps blood pressure and heart rate down. In the CNS, a number of norepinephrine circuits have been identified. One major circuit begins in the hindbrain, in an area that controls basic bodily functions such as respiration. Another circuit appears to influence the body's emergency reactions or alarm responses (Charney & Drevets, 2002; Gray, 1987; Gray & McNaughton, 1996) that occur when we suddenly find ourselves in a dangerous situation. This suggests that norepinephrine may bear some relationship to states of panic (Charney et al., 1990; Gray & McNaughton, 1996). More likely, however, this system, with all its varying circuits coursing through the brain, acts in a general way to regulate or modulate certain

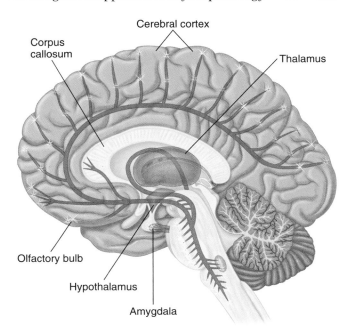

**Figure 2.12** ■ Major norepinephrine pathways in the human brain. (Adapted from *Biological Psychology* (with CD-ROM and InfoTrac), 7th edition by J.W. Kalat © 2001. Reprinted with permission of Wadsworth, a division of Thomson Learning. www.thomsonrights.com. Fax 800-730-2215.)

behavioural tendencies and is not directly involved in specific patterns of behaviour or in psychological disorders.

### Dopamine

Finally, **dopamine** is a major neurotransmitter also classified as a catecholamine, due to the similarity of its chemical structure to epinephrine and norepinephrine. Dopamine has been implicated in psychological disorders such as schizophrenia (see Figure 2.13). Remember the wonder drug reserpine mentioned in Chapter 1 that reduced psychotic behaviours associated with schizophrenia? This drug and more modern antipsychotic treatments affect a number of neurotransmitter systems, but their greatest impact

**gamma aminobutyric acid (GABA)** Neurotransmitter that reduces activity across the synapse and thus inhibits a range of behaviours and emotions, especially generalized anxiety.

**norepinephrine** Neurotransmitter that is active in the central and peripheral nervous systems, controlling heart rate, blood pressure, and respiration, among other functions. Because of its role in the body's alarm reaction, it may also contribute in general and indirectly to panic attacks and anxiety and mood disorders.

**dopamine** Neurotransmitter whose generalized function is to activate other neurotransmitters and to aid in exploratory and pleasure-seeking behaviours (thus balancing serotonin). A relative excess of dopamine is implicated in schizophrenia (though contradictory evidence suggests the connection is not simple), and its deficit is involved in Parkinson's disease.

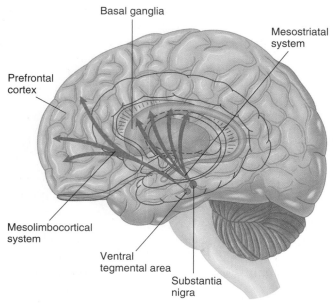

Basal ganglia

Mesostriatal system

Prefrontal cortex

Mesolimbocortical system

Ventral tegmental area

Substantia nigra

**Figure 2.13** ■ Two major dopamine pathways. The mesolimbic system is apparently implicated in schizophrenia; the path to the basal ganglia contributes to problems in the locomotor system, such as tardive dyskinesia, which sometimes results from use of neuroleptic drugs. (Adapted from *Biological Psychology* (with CD-ROM and InfoTrac), 7th edition by J.W. Kalat © 2001. Reprinted with permission of Wadsworth, a division of Thomson Learning. www.thomsonrights.com. Fax 800-730-2215.)

may be that they block specific dopamine receptors, lowering dopamine activity (e.g., Snyder, Burt, & Creese, 1976). Thus, it was long thought possible that in schizophrenia, dopamine circuits may be too active. The recent development of new antipsychotic drugs such as clozapine, which has only weak effects on certain dopamine receptors, suggests this idea may need revising. We explore the dopamine hypothesis in some detail in Chapter 12.

In its various circuits throughout specific regions of the brain, dopamine also seems to have a more general effect, best described as a *switch* that turns on various brain circuits possibly associated with certain types of behaviour. Once the switch is turned on, other neurotransmitters may then inhibit or facilitate emotions or behaviour (Oades, 1985; Spoont, 1992). Dopamine circuits merge and cross with serotonin circuits at many points and therefore influence many of the same behaviours. For example, dopamine activity is associated with exploratory, outgoing, pleasure-seeking behaviours, and serotonin is associated with inhibition and constraint; thus, in a sense they balance each other (Depue et al., 1994).

One of a class of drugs that affects the dopamine circuits specifically is L-dopa, which is a dopamine agonist (increases levels of dopamine). One of the systems that dopamine switches on is

the locomotor system, which regulates our ability to move in a coordinated way and, once turned on, is influenced by serotonin activity. Because of these connections, deficiencies in dopamine have been associated with disorders such as Parkinson's disease, in which a marked deterioration in motor behaviour includes tremors and rigidity of muscles. L-dopa has been successful in reducing some of these motor disabilities in individuals with Parkinson's disease.

## Implications for Psychopathology

Psychological disorders typically mix emotional, behavioural, and cognitive symptoms, so identifiable lesions (or damage) localized in *specific* structures of the brain do not, for the most part, cause them. Even widespread damage most often results in motor or sensory deficits, which are usually the province of the medical specialty of neurology; neurologists often work with neuropsychologists to identify specific lesions. But psychopathologists are also beginning to theorize about the more *general* role of brain function in the development of personality, considering how different types of biologically driven personalities might be more vulnerable to developing certain types of psychological disorders. For example, genetic contributions might lead to patterns of neurotransmitter activity that influence personality. Thus, some impulsive risk takers may have low serotonergic activity and high dopaminergic activity.

Procedures for studying images of the functioning brain have recently been applied to *obsessive-compulsive disorder (OCD)*. Individuals with this severe anxiety disorder suffer from intrusive, frightening thoughts—for example, that they might have become contaminated with poison and will poison their loved ones if they touch them. To prevent this drastic consequence, they engage in compulsive

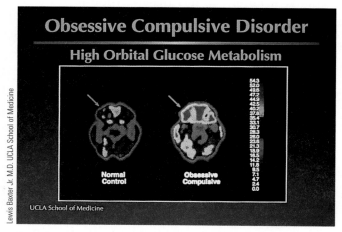

Brain function is altered in people with obsessive-compulsive disorder, but it normalizes after effective psychosocial treatment.

rituals such as frequent washing to try to scrub off the imagined poison. A number of investigators have found intriguing differences between the brains of patients with OCD and those of other people. Though the size and structure of the brain are the same, patients with OCD have increased activity in the part of the frontal lobe of the cerebral cortex called the *orbital surface*. Increased activity is also present in the cingulate gyrus and, to a lesser extent, in the caudate nucleus, a circuit that extends from the orbital section of the frontal area of the cortex to parts of the thalamus. Activity in these areas seems to be correlated; that is, if one area is active, the other areas are also. These areas contain several pathways of neurotransmitters, and one of the most concentrated is serotonin.

Remember that one of the roles of serotonin seems to be to moderate our reactions. Eating behaviour, sexual behaviour, and aggression are under better control with adequate levels of serotonin. Research, mostly on animals, demonstrates that lesions (damage) that interrupt serotonin circuits seem to impair the ability to ignore irrelevant external cues, making the organism overreactive. Thus, if we were to experience damage or interruption in this brain circuit, we might find ourselves acting on every thought or impulse that enters our heads.

## Psychosocial Influences on Brain Structure and Function

At the same time that psychopathologists are exploring the causes of psychopathology, whether in the brain or in the environment, people are suffering and require the best treatments we have. Sometimes the effects of treatment tell us something about the nature of psychopathology. For example, if a clinician thinks OCD is caused by a specific brain (dys)function or by learned anxiety to scary or repulsive thoughts, this view would determine choice of treatment, as we noted in Chapter 1. Directing a treatment at one or the other of these theoretical causes of the disorder and then observing whether the patient gets better will prove or disprove the accuracy of the theory. This common strategy has one overriding weakness. Successfully treating a patient's particular feverish state or toothache with aspirin does not mean the fever or toothache was caused by an aspirin deficiency, because an effect does not imply a cause. Nevertheless, this line of evidence gives us some hints about causes of psychopathology, particularly when it is combined with other, more direct experimental evidence.

If you knew that someone with OCD might have a somewhat faulty brain circuit, what treatment would you choose? Maybe you would recommend brain surgery. Psychosurgery to correct severe psychopathology is an option still chosen today on occasion, particularly in the case of OCD when the suffering is severe (Jenike et al., 1991). Precise surgical lesions might dampen the runaway activity in the faulty brain circuit in question. This result would probably be welcome if all other treatments have failed, although psychosurgery is used seldom and has not been studied systematically.

Nobody wants to do surgery if less intrusive treatments are available. To use the analogy of a television set that has developed the "disorder" of going fuzzy, if you had to rearrange and reconnect wires on the circuit board every time the disorder occurred, the correction would be a major undertaking. Alternatively, if you could simply push some buttons on the remote and eliminate the fuzziness, the correction would be simpler and less risky. The development of drugs affecting neurotransmitter activity has given us one of those buttons. We now have drugs that, although not a cure or even an effective treatment in all cases, seem to be beneficial in treating OCD. As you might suspect, most of them act by increasing serotonin activity.

But is it possible to get at this brain circuit without either surgery or drugs? Could psychological treatment be powerful enough to affect the circuit directly? The answer now seems to be yes. For example, Baxter and colleagues used brain imaging on patients who had not been treated and then took an additional, important scientific step (Baxter et al., 1992). They treated the patients with a cognitive-behavioural therapy known to be effective in OCD called *exposure and response prevention* (described more fully in Chapter 4) and then repeated the brain imaging. In a bellwether finding, widely noted in the world of psychopathology, Baxter and his colleagues discovered that the brain circuit had been changed (normalized) by a psychological intervention.

In another example, research by Helen Mayberg and her colleagues at the Rotman Institute in Toronto used brain imaging before and after cognitive-behavioural therapy in a group of depressed patients. They found changes suggesting that cognitive-behavioural therapy affects recovery from depression by modulating the functioning of limbic and cortical brain regions (Goldapple et al., 2004). Yet another team observed normalization of brain circuits after successful treatment for specific phobia, which they termed "re-wiring the brain" (Paquette et al., 2003). In yet another intriguing study, Leuchter, Cook, Witte, Morgan, and Abrams (2002) treated patients with major depressive disorder with either antidepressant medications or placebo medications. (Remember that it is common for inactive placebo medications, which are just sugar pills, to result in behavioural and emotional changes in patients, presumably as a result of psychological factors such as increasing hope and expectations.) Measures of brain function showed that *both* antidepressant medications and placebos changed brain function, but in somewhat different parts of the brain, suggesting different mechanisms of action for these two interventions. Placebos alone are not usually as effective as active medication, but every time clinicians prescribe pills, they are also treating the patient psychologically by inducing positive expectation for change, and this intervention changes brain function.

## Interactions of Psychosocial Factors with Brain Structure and Function

Several experiments illustrate the interaction of psychosocial factors and brain function on neurotransmitter activity, with implications for the development of psychological disorders. Some even indicate that psychosocial factors directly affect levels of neurotransmitters. For example, Insel, Scanlan, Champoux, and Suomi (1988) raised two groups of rhesus monkeys identically except for their ability to control things in their cages. One group had free access to toys and food treats, but the second group got these toys and treats only when the first group did. In other words, the second group had the same number of toys and treats but they could not choose when they got them. Therefore, they had less control over their environment. In psychological experiments we say the second group was "yoked" with the first group because their treatment depended entirely on what happened to the first group. In any case, the monkeys in the first group grew up with a sense of control over things in their lives and those in the second group didn't.

Later in their lives, all these monkeys were administered a benzodiazepine inverse agonist, a neurochemical that has the *opposite* effect of the neurotransmitter GABA; the effect is an extreme burst of anxiety. (The few times this neurochemical has been administered to people, usually scientists administering it to each other, the recipients have reported the experience—which lasts only a short time—to be one of the most horrible sensations they had ever endured.) When this substance was injected into the monkeys, the results were interesting. The monkeys that had been raised with little control over their environment ran to a corner of their cage where they crouched and displayed signs of severe anxiety and panic. But the monkeys that had a sense of control behaved quite differently. They did not seem anxious at all. Rather, they seemed angry and aggressive, even attacking other monkeys near them. Thus, the same level of a neurochemical substance, acting as a neurotransmitter, had very different effects, depending on the psychological histories of the monkeys.

Thomas Insel/1986 Study/National Institute of Mental Health

Rhesus monkeys injected with a specific neurotransmitter react with anger or fear, depending on their early psychological experiences.

The experiment by Insel and colleagues (1988) is an example of a significant interaction between neurotransmitters and psychosocial factors. Other experiments suggest that psychosocial influences directly affect the functioning and perhaps even the structure of the CNS. Scientists have observed that psychosocial factors routinely change the activity levels of many of our neurotransmitter systems, including norepinephrine and serotonin (Coplan et al., 1996, 1998; Heim & Nemeroff, 1999; Ladd et al., 2000; Sullivan, Kent, & Coplan, 2000). It also seems that the structure of neurons themselves, including the number of receptors on a cell, can be changed by learning and experience (Gottlieb, 1998; Kandel, 1983; Kandel, Jessell, & Schacter, 1991; Ladd et al., 2000; Owens et al., 1997) and that these effects on the CNS continue throughout our lives.

We are now beginning to learn how psychosocial factors affect brain function and structure (Kolb, Gibb, & Robinson, 2003; Kolb & Whishaw, 1998). For example, Greenough, Withers, and Wallace (1990) studied the cerebellum, which coordinates and controls motor behaviour. They discovered that the nervous systems of rats raised in a rich environment requiring a lot of learning and motor behaviour develop differently from those in rats that were couch potatoes. The active rats had many more connections between nerve cells in the cerebellum and grew many more dendrites. The researchers also observed that certain kinds of learning decreased the connections between neurons in other areas. In a follow-up study, Wallace, Kilman, Withers, and Greenough (1992) reported that these structural changes in the brain began in as little as 4 days in rats, suggesting enormous plasticity in brain structure as a result of experience. Similarly, stress during early development can lead to substantial changes in the functioning of the HPA axis described here that, in turn, make primates more or less susceptible to stress later in life (Barlow, 2002; Coplan et al., 1998; Suomi, 1999). It may be something similar to this mechanism that was responsible for the effects of early stress on the later development of depression in genetically susceptible individuals in the New Zealand study described previously (Caspi et al., 2003).

So, we can conclude that early psychological experience affects the development of the nervous system and thus determines vulnerability to psychological disorders later in life. As shown by the research of Bryan Kolb at the University of Lethbridge, and others, it seems that the very structure of our nervous system is constantly changing as a result of learning and experience, even into old age (e.g., Kolb, Gibb, & Gorny, 2003). Of course, this plasticity of the CNS helps us adapt more readily to our environment. These findings will be important when we discuss the causes of anxiety disorders and mood disorders in Chapters 4 and 6.

## Comments

The specific brain circuits involved in psychological disorders are complex systems identified by pathways of neurotransmitters traversing the brain. The existence of these circuits suggests that the structure and the function of the nervous system play major roles in psychopathology. But other research suggests the circuits are strongly influenced, perhaps even created, by psychological and social factors. Furthermore, both biological interventions, such as drugs, and psychological interventions or experience seem capable of altering the circuits. Therefore, we cannot consider the nature and cause of psychological disorders without examining both biological and psychological factors. We now turn to an examination of psychological factors.

## Concept Check 2.3

Check your understanding of the brain structures and neurotransmitters. Match each with its description below: (a) frontal lobe, (b) brain stem, (c) GABA, (d) midbrain, (e) serotonin, (f) dopamine, (g) norepinephrine, and (h) cerebral cortex.

1. Movement, breathing, and sleeping depend on the ancient part of the brain, which is present in most animals. _____
2. Which neurotransmitter binds to neuron receptor sites, inhibiting postsynaptic activity and reducing overall arousal? _____
3. Which neurotransmitter is a switch that turns on various brain circuits? _____
4. Which neurotransmitter seems to be involved in your emergency reactions or alarm responses? _____
5. This area contains part of the reticular activating system and coordinates movement with sensory output. _____
6. Which neurotransmitter is believed to influence the way we process information, as well as to moderate or inhibit our behaviour? _____
7. More than 80% of the neurons in the human central nervous system are contained in this part of the brain, which gives us distinct qualities. _____
8. This area is responsible for most of our memory, thinking, and reasoning capabilities and makes us social animals. _____

# Behavioural Contributions to Psychopathology

■ *Compare and contrast the behavioural and cognitive theories and how they are used to explain the origins of mental illness.*

Enormous progress has been made in understanding behavioural and cognitive influences in psychopathology. Some new information has come from the rapidly growing field of **cognitive science,** which is concerned with how we acquire and process information and how we store and ultimately retrieve it (one of the processes involved in memory). Scientists have also discovered that a great deal goes on inside our heads of which we are not necessarily aware. Because, technically, these cognitive processes are unconscious, some findings recall the unconscious mental processes that are so much a part of Freud's theory of psychoanalysis (although they do not look much like the ones he envisioned). A brief account of current thinking on what is happening during the process of classical conditioning will start us on our way.

## Conditioning and Cognitive Processes

During the 1960s and 1970s, behavioural scientists in animal laboratories began to uncover the complexity of the basic processes of classical conditioning

---

**cognitive science**  Field of study that examines how humans and other animals acquire, process, store, and retrieve information.

(Bouton, Mineka, & Barlow, 2001; Mineka & Zinbarg, 1996, 1998). Rescorla (1988) concluded that simply pairing two events closely in time (such as the food and the metronome in Pavlov's laboratories) is not what's important in this type of learning; at the very least, it is a simple summary. Rather, a variety of different judgments and cognitive processes combine to determine the final outcome of this learning, even in lower animals such as rats.

To take just one simple example, Pavlov would have predicted that if the food and the sound of the metronome were paired, say, 50 times, then a certain amount of learning would take place. But Rescorla and others discovered that if one animal never saw the food except for the 50 trials following the metronome sound, whereas the food was brought to the other animal many times *between* the 50 times it was paired with the metronome, the two animals would learn different things; that is, even though the metronome and the food were paired 50 times for each animal, the metronome was *much less meaningful* to the second animal (see Figure 2.14). Put another way, the first animal learned that the sound of the metronome meant food came next; the second animal learned that the food sometimes came after the sound and sometimes without the sound. That two different conditions produce two different learning outcomes demonstrates that basic classical (and operant) conditioning paradigms facilitate the learning of the *relationship* among events in the environment. This type of learning enables us to develop working ideas about the world that allow us to make appropriate judgments. We can then respond in a way that will benefit or at least not hurt us. In other words, complex cognitive and emotional processing of information is involved when conditioning occurs, even in animals.

## Learned Helplessness and Learned Optimism

Along similar lines, Seligman, also working with animals, described the phenomenon of **learned helplessness,** which occurs when rats or other

---

**learned helplessness** Seligman's theory that people become depressed when they make an *attribution* that they have no control over the stress in their lives (whether in reality they do or not).

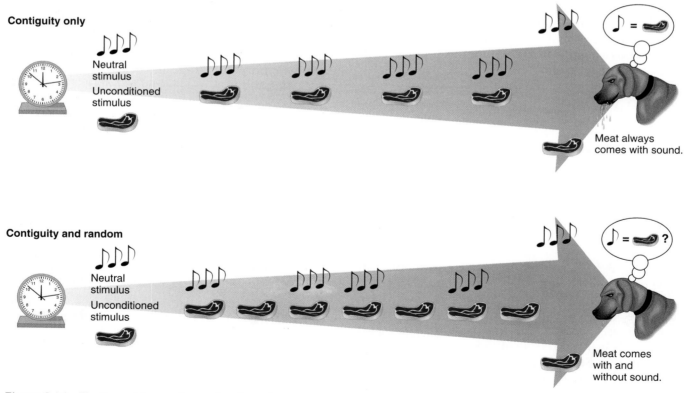

**Figure 2.14** ■ Rescorla's experiment that showed contiguity—pairing a neutral stimulus and an unconditioned stimulus—does not result in the same kind of conditioning. The dog in the contiguity-only group (top panel) experiences the usual conditioning procedure: Pairing a sound and food causes the sound to take on properties of the food. For the dog in the contiguity-and-random group, the fact that the food appeared away from the sound and with it makes the sound much less meaningful.

animals encounter conditions over which they have no control. If rats are confronted with a situation in which they receive occasional foot shocks, they can function well if they learn they can cope with these shocks by doing something to avoid them (say, pressing a lever). But if the animals learn their behaviour has no effect on their environment—sometimes they get shocked and sometimes they don't, no matter what they do—they become "helpless"; in other words, they give up attempting to cope and seem to develop the animal equivalent of depression.

Seligman theorized that the same phenomenon may happen with people who are faced with uncontrollable stress in their lives. Subsequent work revealed this to be true under one important condition: People become depressed if they "decide" or "think" they can do little about the stress in their lives, even if it seems to others that there is something they could do. People make an *attribution* that they have no control, and they become depressed (Abramson, Seligman, & Teasdale, 1978; Miller & Norman, 1979). We revisit this important psychological theory of depression in Chapter 6. It illustrates, once again, the necessity of recognizing that different people process information about events in the environment in different ways. These cognitive differences are an important component of psychopathology.

Lately, Seligman has turned his attention to a different set of attributions, which he terms *learned optimism* (Seligman, 1998, 2002). If people faced with considerable stress and difficulty in their lives nevertheless display an optimistic, upbeat attitude, they are likely to function better psychologically and physically. We will return to this theme repeatedly throughout this book but particularly in Chapter 7, when we talk about the effects of psychological factors on health. But consider one example: In a recent study, individuals between age 50 and age 94 who had positive views about themselves and positive attitudes toward aging lived seven and a half years longer than those without such positive, optimistic attitudes (Levy, Slade, Kunkel, & Kasl, 2002). This connection was still true after the investigators controlled for age, sex, income, loneliness, and physical capability to engage in household and social activities. This effect is extremely powerful and exceeds the 1–4 years of added life associated with other factors such as low blood pressure, low cholesterol levels, and no history of obesity or cigarette smoking. Studies such as this have created interest in a new field of study called *positive psychology* in which investigators explore factors that account for positive attitudes and happiness (Diener, 2000; Lyubomirsky, 2001). We will return to these themes in the chapters describing specific disorders.

## Social Learning

Another influential psychologist was Canadian Albert Bandura. Bandura (1973, 1986) observed that organisms, including lower animals, do not have to actually experience certain events in their environment to learn effectively. Rather, they can learn just as much by observing what happens to someone else in a given situation. This fairly obvious discovery came to be known as **modelling** or **observational learning.** What is important is that, even in animals, this type of learning requires a symbolic integration of the experiences of others with judgments of what might happen to oneself. In other words, even an animal that is not very intelligent by human standards, such as a rat, must make a decision about the conditions under which its own experiences would be similar to those of the animal it is observing. Bandura expanded his observations into a network of ideas in which behaviour, cognitive factors, and environmental influences converged to produce the complexity of behaviour that confronts us. He also specified in some detail the importance of the social context of our learning; that is, much of what we learn depends on our interactions with other people around us. Thus, his approach became known as *social learning theory*.

In the 1960s, Bandura made notable contributions to the understanding of children's aggressive behaviours. He and his students conducted a series of experiments using models interacting with a plastic Bobo doll (e.g., Bandura, Ross, & Ross, 1961, 1963). For example, Bandura and his colleagues (1963) conducted a study that was designed to examine the influence of consequences to the model on children's imitative learning of aggression. Nursery school children were randomly assigned to one of four groups. The first group observed a model who interacted aggressively with the Bobo doll and whose aggressive behaviour was rewarded. A second group of children observed a model who interacted aggressively with the Bobo doll but was punished. A third (control) group was exposed to highly expressive but non-aggressive models. An additional control group had no exposure to models. Children who had witnessed the aggressive model who was rewarded showed more imitative aggression. In contrast, children who had witnessed the aggressive model who was punished failed to reproduce the model's behaviour (Bandura et al., 1963). The results of these studies helped Bandura develop and refine his social learning theory.

---

**modelling** Learning through observation and imitation of the behaviour of other individuals and the consequences of that behaviour.

The basic idea in all Bandura's work is that a careful analysis of cognitive processes may produce the most accurate scientific predictions of behaviour. Concepts of probability learning, information processing, and attention have become increasingly important in psychopathology (Barlow, 2002; Craighead, Ilardi, Greenberg, & Craighead, 1997; Mathews & MacLeod, 1994).

## Prepared Learning

It is clear that biology and, probably, our genetic endowment influence what we learn. This conclusion is based on the fact that we learn to fear some objects much more easily than others, as is demonstrated in the important experiments of Swedish psychologist Arne Öhman. In other words, we learn fears and phobias selectively (Morris, Öhman, & Dolan, 1998; Öhman, Flykt, & Lundqvist, 2000; Öhman & Mineka, 2001). Why might this be? According to the concept of **prepared learning,** we have become *highly prepared* for learning about certain types of objects or situations over the course of evolution because this knowledge contributes to the survival of the species (Mineka, 1985b; Seligman, 1971). Even without any contact, we are more likely to learn to fear snakes or spiders than rocks or flowers, even if we know rationally that the snake or spider is harmless (e.g., Fredrikson, Annas, & Wik, 1997; Pury & Mineka, 1997). In the absence of experience, however, we are less likely to fear guns or electrical outlets, even though they are potentially much more deadly.

Why do we so readily learn to fear snakes or spiders? One possibility is that when our ancestors lived in caves, those who avoided snakes and spiders eluded deadly varieties and therefore survived in greater numbers to pass down their genes to us, thus contributing to the survival of the species. This is just a theory, of course, but it seems a likely explanation. Something within us recognizes the connection between a certain signal and a threatening event. In other words, certain UCSs and CSs "belong" to one another. If you've ever gotten sick on cheap wine or bad food, chances are you won't make the same mistake again. This quick or "one-trial" learning also occurs in animals that eat something that tastes bad, causes nausea, or may contain poison. It is easy to see that survival is associated with quickly learning to avoid poisonous food. Perhaps these selective associations are also facilitated by our genes (Barlow, 2002; Cook, Hodes, & Lang, 1986; Garcia, McGowan, & Green, 1972).

## Cognitive Science and the Unconscious

Advances in cognitive science have revolutionized our conceptions of the unconscious. We are not aware of much of what goes on inside our heads, but our unconscious is not necessarily the seething cauldron of primitive emotional conflicts envisioned by Freud. Rather, we simply seem able to process and store information, and act on it, without having the slightest awareness of what the information is or why we are acting on it (Bargh & Chartrand, 1999). Is this surprising? Consider briefly these two examples.

Weiskrantz (1992) describes a phenomenon called *blind sight* or *unconscious vision.* He relates the case of a young man who, for medical reasons, had a small section of his visual cortex (the centre for the control of vision in the brain) surgically removed. Though the operation was considered a success, the young man became blind in both eyes. Later, during routine tests, a physician raised his hand to the left of the patient who, much to the shock of his doctors, reached out and touched it. Subsequently, scientists determined that he not only could reach accurately for objects but also could distinguish among objects and perform most of the functions usually associated with sight. Yet, when asked about his abilities, he would say, "I couldn't see anything, not a darn thing," and that all he was doing was guessing.

The phenomenon in this case is associated with real brain damage. Much more interesting, from the point of view of psychopathology, is that the same thing seems to occur in healthy individuals who have been hypnotized (Hilgard, 1992; Kihlstrom, 1992); that is, normal individuals, provided with hypnotic suggestions that they are blind, are able to function visually but have no awareness or memory of their visual abilities. This condition, which illustrates a process of *dissociation* between behaviour and consciousness, is the basis of the dissociative disorders discussed in Chapter 5.

A second example, more relevant to psychopathology, is called **implicit memory** (Craighead et al., 1997; Graf, Squire, & Mandler, 1984; Kihlstrom, Barnhardt, & Tataryn, 1992; McNally, 1999; Schacter,

---

**prepared learning**   Certain associations can be learned more readily than others because this ability has been adaptive for evolution.

**implicit memory**   Condition of memory in which a person cannot recall past events even though he or she acts in response to them.

Chiu, & Ochsner, 1993). As has been described by cognitive psychologist Peter Graf and his colleagues at the University of British Columbia, implicit memory is apparent when someone clearly acts on the basis of things that have happened in the past but can't remember the events (Graf et al., 1984). In contrast, a good memory for events is called *explicit memory*. Much research attests to the distinctiveness of implicit and explicit memory processes, including evidence that they differ in their developmental patterns (e.g., Billingsley, Smith, & McAndrews, 2002), underlying brain structures (e.g., Billingsley, McAndrews, & Smith, 2002), and degree to which they are affected by certain drugs (e.g., Buffett-Jerrott, Stewart, Bird, & Teehan, 1998). Implicit memory can be selective for only certain events or circumstances. Clinically, we have already seen in Chapter 1 an example of implicit memory at work in the story of Anna O., the classic case first described by Breuer and Freud (1895/1957) to demonstrate the existence of the unconscious. It was only after therapy that Anna O. remembered events surrounding her father's death and the connection of these events to her paralysis. Thus, Anna O.'s behaviour (occasional paralysis) was evidently connected to implicit memories of her father's death. Many scientists have concluded that Freud's speculations on the nature and structure of the unconscious went beyond the evidence, but the existence of unconscious processes has since been demonstrated, and we must take them into account as we study psychopathology.

What methods do we have for studying the unconscious? In the Stroop colour-naming paradigm, subjects are shown a variety of words, each printed in a different colour. They are shown these words quickly and asked to name the colours in which they are printed while ignoring their meaning (see Figure 2.15). Colour naming is delayed when the meaning of the word attracts the subject's attention, despite his or her efforts to concentrate on the colour; that is, the meaning of the word interferes with the subject's ability to process colour information (see Kolb & Whishaw, 2003). For example, experimenters have determined that people with certain psychological disorders, such as Jody, are much slower at naming the colours of words associated with their problem (e.g., *blood, injury,* and *dissect*) than the colours of words that have no relation to the disorder. For instance, one of the authors of this book and her students (Francis, Stewart, & Hounsell, 1997) used the Stroop task in a study with women who were chronic dieters. On the Stroop, these researchers compared participants' colour-naming speeds for

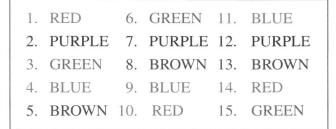

| 1. RED | 6. GREEN | 11. BLUE |
| 2. PURPLE | 7. PURPLE | 12. PURPLE |
| 3. GREEN | 8. BROWN | 13. BROWN |
| 4. BLUE | 9. BLUE | 14. RED |
| 5. BROWN | 10. RED | 15. GREEN |

**Figure 2.15** ■ The Stroop paradigm. Have someone keep time as you name the colour of ink in which each of the words is printed and not the words themselves, and again as you read the printed words.

words pertaining to food (e.g., *icing, chips,* and *cookie*) versus words unrelated to food (e.g., animal words like *snakes, insect, elephants*). Women who were chronic dieters, but not women who were normal eaters, showed substantially slowed colour naming for food words (i.e., for words pertaining to their eating problem; see Figure 2.16). Thus, psychologists can now uncover particular patterns of emotional significance, even if the subject cannot verbalize them or is not aware of them.

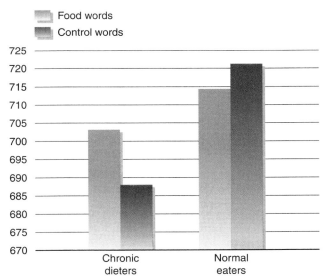

**Figure 2.16** ■ Average colour-naming speeds (in milliseconds) for food and control words in chronic dieters and normal eaters. Only the chronic dieters show substantially slowed colour naming for food words as compared with their colour-naming speeds for words not pertaining to food. (Adapted from Francis et al., 1997.)

## Cognitive-Behavioural Therapy

As scientists began to discover the important contributions of cognitive processes to behavioural development, psychologists began to integrate cognitive procedures and techniques directly into therapy. Among the originators of **cognitive-behavioural therapy (CBT)** was Aaron T. Beck (1976), who developed methods for dealing with faulty attributions and attitudes associated with learned helplessness and depression (see Chapter 6). CBT is a strong and growing therapy approach in Canada today, spearheaded by a number of internationally renowned scientist-practitioners including Zindel Segal in Toronto, David A. Clark in Fredericton, David Zuroff in Montreal, and Martin Antony in Hamilton (see Chapters 4 and 6). Another therapy approach that emphasizes cognitive procedures and techniques, called *rational-emotive therapy*, was developed by Albert Ellis (1962). This approach also focuses directly on the irrational beliefs Ellis thought were at the root of maladaptive feelings and behaviour. And clinical psychologist Donald Meichenbaum, recently retired from the University of Waterloo, developed a novel cognitive-behavioural approach he called *self-instructional training*. In this approach, he worked on modifying what clients say to themselves about the consequences of their behaviour (Meichenbaum, 1977; Meichenbaum & Cameron, 1974). Meichenbaum and his colleagues applied this technique with success to a variety of problems, including schizophrenics with attentional control problems (Meichenbaum & Cameron, 1973) and impulsive, hyperactive children (Meichenbaum, 1971; Meichenbaum & Goodman, 1971). How specific cognitive-behavioural methods are used is described in more detail in this book in the chapters on specific disorders.

**cognitive-behavioural therapy (CBT)** Group of treatment procedures aimed at identifying and modifying faulty thought processes, attitudes and attributions, and problem behaviours; often used synonymously with cognitive therapy.

# Emotional Contributions to Psychopathology

■ *Explain the nature and role of emotions in psychopathology.*

Emotions play an enormous role in our day-to-day lives and can contribute in major ways to the development of psychopathology (Gross, 1999). Consider the emotion of fear. Have you ever found yourself in a really dangerous situation? Have you ever almost crashed your car and known for several seconds beforehand what was going to happen? Have you ever been swimming in the ocean and realized you were out too far or caught in a current? Have you ever almost fallen from a height, such as a cliff or a roof? In any of these instances you would have felt an incredible surge of arousal. As the first great emotion theorist, Charles Darwin (1872), pointed out more than 100 years ago, this kind of reaction seems to be programmed in all animals, including humans, which suggests that it serves a useful function.

The alarm reaction that activates during potentially life-threatening emergencies is called the **fight or flight response.** If you are caught in ocean currents, your almost instinctual tendency is to struggle toward shore. You might realize rationally that you're best off just floating until the current runs its course and then, more calmly, swimming in. Yet somewhere, deep within, ancient instincts for survival won't let you relax, even though struggling against the ocean will only wear you out and increase your chance of drowning. Still, this same kind of reaction might momentarily give you the strength to lift a car off your trapped brother or fight off an attacker. The whole purpose of the physical rush of adrenaline that we feel in extreme danger is to mobilize us to escape the danger (flight) or to withstand it (fight).

## The Physiology and Purpose of Fear

How do physical reactions prepare us to respond this way? The great physiologist Walter Cannon (1929) speculated on the reasons. Fear activates your cardiovascular system. Your blood vessels constrict, thereby raising arterial pressure and decreasing the blood flow to your fingers and toes. Excess blood is redirected to the skeletal muscles, where it is available to the vital organs that may be needed in an emergency. Often people seem "white with fear"; that is, they turn pale as a result of decreased blood flow to the skin. "Trembling with fear," with your hair standing on end, may be the result of shivering and piloerection (in which body

**fight or flight response** Biological reaction to alarming stressors that musters the body's resources (e.g., blood flow, respiration) to resist or flee the threat.

Charles Darwin, *Evolution of the Species*, 1896

Charles Darwin (1809–1882) drew this cat frightened by a dog to show the fight or flight reaction.

hairs stand erect), reactions that conserve heat when your blood vessels are constricted.

These defensive adjustments can also produce the hot and cold spells that often occur during extreme fear. Breathing becomes faster and, usually, deeper to provide necessary oxygen to rapidly circulating blood. Increased blood circulation carries oxygen to the brain, stimulating cognitive processes and sensory functions, which makes you more alert and able to think more quickly during emergencies. An increased amount of glucose (sugar) is released from the liver into the bloodstream, further energizing various crucial muscles and organs, including the brain. Pupils dilate, presumably to allow a better view of the situation. Hearing becomes more acute, and digestive activity is suspended, resulting in a reduced flow of saliva (the "dry mouth" of fear). In the short term, voiding the body of all waste material and eliminating digestive processes further prepare the organism for concentrated action and activity, so there is often pressure to urinate and defecate.

It is easy to see why the fight or flight reaction is fundamentally important. Millennia ago, when our ancestors lived in tenuous circumstances, those with strong emergency reactions were more likely to live through attacks and other dangers than those with weak emergency responses, and the survivors passed their genes down to us.

## Emotional Phenomena

The **emotion** of fear is a subjective feeling of terror, a strong motivation for behaviour (escaping or fighting), and a complex physiological or arousal

response. To define *emotion* is difficult, but most theorists agree that it is an "action tendency" (Lang, 1985, 1995; Lang, Bradley, & Cuthbert, 1998); that is, a tendency to behave in a certain way (e.g., escape), elicited by an external event (a threat) and a feeling state (terror), accompanied by a (possibly) characteristic physiological response (Gross, 1999; Gross & Muñoz, 1995; Izard, 1992; Lazarus, 1991, 1995). One purpose of a feeling state is to *motivate* us to carry out a behaviour: If we escape, our terror, which is unpleasant, will be decreased, so decreasing unpleasant feelings motivates us to escape (Gross, 1999; Öhman, 1996).

Emotions are usually short-lived, temporary states lasting from several minutes to several hours, occurring in response to an external event. **Mood** is a more persistent period of affect or emotionality. Thus, in Chapter 6 we describe enduring or recurring states of depression or excitement (mania) as mood disorders. But anxiety disorders, described in Chapter 4, are characterized by enduring or chronic anxiety and, therefore, could be called *mood disorders*. Alternatively, both anxiety disorders and mood disorders could be called *emotional disorders*, a term not formally used in psychopathology. This is only one example of the occasional inconsistencies in the terminology of abnormal psychology.

A related term you will see occasionally is **affect,** which usually refers to the momentary emotional tone that accompanies what we say or do. For example, if you just got an A+ on your test but you look sad, your friends might think your reaction strange because your affect is not appropriate to the event. The term *affect* can also be used more generally to summarize commonalities among emotional states that are characteristic of an individual. Thus, someone who tends to be fearful, anxious, and depressed is experiencing negative affect. Positive affect would subsume tendencies to be pleasant, joyful, excited, and so on.

## The Components of Emotion

Emotion theorists now agree that emotion comprises three related components—*behaviour, physiology,* and *cognition*—but most emotion theorists tend to concentrate on one component or another (see Figure 2.17). Emotion theorists who concentrate on behaviour think that basic patterns of emotion differ from one another in fundamental ways; for

**emotion** Pattern of action elicited by an external event and a feeling state, accompanied by a characteristic physiological response.

**mood** Enduring period of emotionality.

**affect** Conscious, subjective aspect of an emotion that accompanies an action at a given time.

**Emotion and Behaviour**
- Basic patterns of emotional behaviour (freeze, escape, approach, attack) that differ in fundamental ways.
- Emotional behaviour is a means of communication.

**Cognitive Aspects of Emotion**
- Appraisals, attributions, and other ways of processing the world around you that are fundamental to emotional experience.

**Physiology of Emotion**
- Emotion is a brain function involving (generally) the more primitive brain areas.
- Direct connection between these areas and the eyes may allow emotional processing to bypass the influence of higher cognitive processes.

**Figure 2.17**    ■    Emotion has three important and overlapping components: behaviour, cognition, and physiology.

example, anger may differ from sadness not only in how it feels but also behaviourally and physiologically. These theorists also emphasize that emotion is a way of communicating between one member of the species and another. One function of fear is to motivate immediate and decisive action such as running away. But if you look scared, your facial expression will quickly communicate the possibility of danger to your friends, who may not have been aware that a threat is imminent. Your facial communication increases their chance for survival because they can now respond more quickly to the threat when it occurs.

Other scientists, most notably Cannon (1929), have concentrated on the physiology of emotions in some pioneering work, viewing emotion as primarily a brain function. Research in this tradition suggests that areas of the brain associated with emotional expression are generally more ancient and primitive than areas associated with higher cognitive processes such as reasoning.

Other research demonstrates direct neurobiological connections between the emotional centres of the brain and the parts of the eye (the retina) or ear that allow emotional activation without the influence of higher cognitive processes (LeDoux, 1996, 2001; Öhman, Flykt, & Lundqvist, 2000; Zajonc, 1984, 1998); in other words, you may experience various emotions quickly and directly without necessarily thinking about them or being aware of why you feel the way you do.

Finally, a number of prominent theorists concentrate on studying the cognitive aspects of emotion. Notable among these theorists was the late Richard S. Lazarus (e.g., 1968, 1991, 1995), who proposed that changes in a person's environment are appraised in terms of their potential impact on that person. The type of appraisal you make determines the emotion you experience. For example, if you see somebody holding a gun in a dark alley, you will probably appraise the situation as dangerous and experience fear. You would make a different appraisal if you saw a tour guide displaying an antique gun in a museum. Lazarus would suggest that thinking and feeling cannot be separated, but other cognitive scientists are concluding otherwise by suggesting that, although cognitive and emotional systems interact and overlap, they are fundamentally separate (Teasdale, 1993). In fact, all of these components of emotion—behaviour, physiology, and cognition—are important, and theorists

AP/Wide World Photos

© Danny Lehman/CORBIS

Our emotional reaction depends on context. Fire, for example, can be threatening or comforting.

are adopting more integrative approaches by studying their interaction (Gross, 1999; Gross & John, 2003).

### Anger and Your Heart

When we discussed Jody's blood phobia, we observed that behaviour and emotion may strongly influence biology. Scientists have made important discoveries about the familiar emotion of anger. We have known for years that negative emotions such as hostility and anger increase a person's risk of developing heart disease (Chesney, 1986; MacDougall, Dembroski, Dimsdale, & Hackett, 1985). In fact, sustained hostility with angry outbursts contributes more strongly to death from heart disease than other well-known risk factors, including smoking, high blood pressure, and high cholesterol levels (Finney, Stoney, & Engebretson, 2002; Suarez, Lewis, & Kuhn, 2002; Williams, Haney, Lee, Kong, & Blumenthal, 1980).

Why is this, exactly? Ironson and her colleagues (1992) asked a number of people with heart disease to recall something that made them very angry in the past. Sometimes these events had occurred many years earlier. In one case, an individual who had spent time in a Japanese prisoner-of-war camp during World War II became angry every time he thought about it. Ironson and her associates compared the experience of anger with stressful events that increased heart rate but were not associated with anger. For example, some participants imagined making a speech to defend themselves against a charge of shoplifting. Others tried to figure out difficult problems in arithmetic within a time limit. Heart rates during these angry situations and stressful ones were then compared with heart rates that increased as a result of exercise (riding a stationary bicycle).

The investigators found that the ability of the heart to pump blood efficiently through the body dropped significantly during anger but not during stress or exercise. In fact, remembering being angry was sufficient to cause the anger effect. If subjects were *really* angry, their heart-pumping efficiency dropped even more, putting them at risk for dangerous disturbances in heart rhythm (arrhythmias). This study was the first to prove that anger affects the heart through decreased pumping efficiency, at least in people who already have heart disease. Now, Suarez et al. (2002) have demonstrated how anger may cause this effect. Inflammation produced by an overactive immune system in particularly hostile individuals may contribute to clogged arteries (and decreased heart pumping efficiency).

## Concept Check 2.4

Check your understanding of behavioural and cognitive influences by identifying the descriptions. Choose your answers from (a) learned helplessness, (b) modelling, (c) prepared learning, and (d) implicit memory.

1. Karen noticed that every time Don behaved well at lunch, the teacher praised him. Karen decided to behave better to receive praise herself. _____

2. Josh stopped trying to please his father because he never knows whether his father will be proud or outraged. _____

3. Greg fell into a lake as a baby and almost drowned. Even though Greg has no recollection of the event, he hates to be around large bodies of water. _____

4. Christal was scared to death of the tarantula, even though she knew it wasn't likely to hurt her. _____

# Social Contributions to Psychopathology

■ *Describe social and cultural influences on abnormal behaviour.*

Given the welter of neurobiological and psychological variables impinging on our lives, is there any room for the influence of social, interpersonal, and cultural factors? Studies are beginning to demonstrate the substantial power and depth of such influences. In fact, researchers have now established that cultural and social influences can kill you. Consider the following example.

### Voodoo, the Evil Eye, and Other Fears

In many cultures around the world, individuals may experience *fright disorders*, exaggerated startle responses, and other observable fear reactions. One example is the Latin American *susto*, characterized by various anxiety-based symptoms, including

A "possessed" person receives treatment in a voodoo ritual.

insomnia, irritability, phobias, and the marked somatic symptoms of sweating and increased heart rate (tachycardia). But susto has only one cause: The individual becomes the object of black magic, or witchcraft, and is suddenly badly frightened. In some cultures, the sinister influence is called the *evil eye* (Good & Kleinman, 1985; Tan, 1980), and the resulting fright disorder can be fatal. Cannon (1942), examining the Haitian phenomenon of voodoo death, suggested that the sentence of death by a medicine man may create an intolerable autonomic arousal in the subject, who has little ability to cope because there is no social support. Ultimately, the condition leads to damage to internal organs and death. Thus, from all accounts, an individual who is from a physical and psychological point of view functioning in a perfectly healthy and adaptive way suddenly dies because of marked changes in the social environment.

Fears and phobias are universal, occurring across all cultures. But what we fear is strongly influenced by our social environment and cultural context. As noted by cross-cultural psychologist John Berry of Queen's University, although all human societies exhibit commonalities and share basic psychological processes, such underlying commonalities are expressed by various groups in vastly different ways from one time and place to another (Berry, 2003).

## Gender

Gender roles have a strong and sometimes puzzling effect on psychopathology. Everyone experiences anxiety and fear, and phobias are found all over the world. But phobias have a peculiar characteristic: The likelihood of your having a particular phobia is powerfully influenced by your gender! Someone who complains of an insect or small animal phobia severe enough to prohibit field trips or visits to friends in the country is almost certain to be female, as are 90% of the people with this phobia. But a social phobia strong enough to keep someone from attending parties or meetings affects men and women equally.

We think these substantial differences have to do with cultural expectations of men and women, or our *gender roles*. For example, an equal number of men and women may have an experience that could lead to an insect or small animal phobia, such as being bitten by one, but in our society it isn't always acceptable for a man to show or even admit fear. So a man is more likely to hide or endure the fear until he gets over it. It is more acceptable for women to acknowledge fearfulness, so a phobia develops. It is also more acceptable for a man to be shy than to show fear, so he is more likely to admit social discomfort.

To avoid or survive a panic attack, an extreme experience of fear, some males drink alcohol instead of admitting they're afraid (see Chapter 4). In many cases this attempt to cope may lead to alcoholism (Stewart, Samoluk, & MacDonald, 1999), a disorder that affects many more males than females (see Chapter 10). One reason for this gender imbalance is that males are more likely than females to self-medicate their fear and panic with alcohol and in so doing to start down the slippery slope to addiction.

Bulimia nervosa, the severe eating disorder, occurs almost entirely in young females. Why? As we see in Chapter 8, a cultural emphasis on female thinness plagues our society and, increasingly, societies around the world. The pressures for males to be thin are less apparent, and of the few males who develop bulimia a substantial percentage belong to the gay subculture where cultural imperatives to be thin are present.

Finally, in an exciting new finding, Taylor (2002; Taylor et al., 2000) describes a unique way that females in many different species respond to stress in their lives. This unique response to stress is called *tend and befriend* and refers to protecting themselves and their young through nurturing behaviour (tend) and forming alliances with larger social groups, particularly other females (befriend). Taylor et al. (2000) supposed that this response fits better with the way females respond to stress because it builds on the brain's attachment-caregiving system and leads to nurturing and affiliative behaviour. Furthermore, the response is characterized by identifiable neurobiological processes in the brain.

Our gender doesn't cause psychopathology. But because gender role is a social and cultural factor that influences the form and content of a disorder, we attend closely to it in the chapters that follow.

## Social Effects on Health and Behaviour

A large number of studies have demonstrated that the greater the number and frequency of social relationships and contacts, the longer you are likely to live. Conversely, the lower you score on a social index that measures the richness of your social life, the shorter your life expectancy. Studies documenting this finding have been reported in North America (Berkman & Syme, 1979; House, Robbins, & Metzner, 1982; Schoenbach, Kaplan, Fredman, & Kleinbaum, 1986), and in Sweden and Finland. The studies take into account existing physical health and other risk factors for dying young, such as high blood pressure, high cholesterol levels, and smoking habits, and still produce the same result. Studies also show that social relationships seem to protect individuals against many physical and psychological disorders, such as high blood pressure, depression, alcoholism, arthritis, the progression to AIDS, and low birth weight in newborns (Cobb, 1976; House, Landis, & Umberson, 1988; Leserman et al., 2000).

Even whether or not we come down with a cold is strongly influenced by the quality and extent of our social network. Cohen and colleagues (Cohen, Doyle, Skoner, Rabin, & Gwaltney, 1997) used nasal drops to expose 276 healthy volunteers to one of two different rhinoviruses (cold viruses), and then they quarantined the subjects for a week. The authors measured the extent of participation in 12 different types of social relationships (e.g., spouse, parent, friend, and colleague), as well as other factors, such as smoking and poor sleep quality, that are likely to increase susceptibility to colds. The surprising results were that the greater the extent of social ties, the smaller the chance of catching a cold, even after all other factors were taken into consideration (controlled for). In fact, those with the fewest social ties were more than four times more likely to catch a cold than those with the greatest number of ties. This effect also extends to pets! Compared with people without pets, those with pets evidenced lower resting heart rate and blood pressure and responded with smaller increases in these variables during laboratory stressors (Allen, Bloscovitch, & Mendes, 2002). What could account for this? Once again, social and interpersonal factors seem to influence psychological and neurobiological variables—for example, the immune system—sometimes to a substantial degree. Thus, we cannot really study psychological and biological aspects of psychological disorders (or physical disorders, for that matter) without taking into account the social and cultural context of the disorder.

How do social relationships have such a profound impact on our physical and psychological characteristics? We don't know for sure, but there are some intriguing hints. Some people think interpersonal relationships give meaning to life and that people who have something to live for can overcome physical deficiencies and even delay death. You may have known an elderly person who far outlived his or her expected time to witness a significant family event such as a grandchild's graduation from college. Once the event has passed, the person dies. Another common observation is that if one spouse in a long-standing marital relationship dies, particularly an elderly wife, the other often dies soon after, regardless of health status. It is also possible that social relationships facilitate health-promoting behaviours, such as restraint in the use of alcohol and drugs, getting proper sleep, and seeking appropriate health care (House, Landis, & Umberson, 1988; Leserman et al., 2000).

Sometimes social upheaval is an opportunity for studying the impact of social networks on individual functioning. For example, whether you live in a city or the country may be associated with your chances of developing schizophrenia, a severe disorder. Lewis, David, Andreasson, and Allsbeck (1992) found that the incidence of schizophrenia was 38% greater in men raised in cities than in those raised in rural areas. We have known for a long time that more schizophrenia exists in the city than in the country, but researchers thought people with schizophrenia who drifted to cities *after* developing schizophrenia or other endemic urban factors such as drug use or unstable family relationships might be the real culprit. But Lewis and associates carefully controlled for such factors, and it now seems that something about cities over and above those influences may contribute to the development of schizophrenia. We do not yet know what it is. This finding, if it is replicated and shown to be true, may be important in view of the mass migration of individuals to overcrowded urban areas, particularly in less developed countries.

In summary, we cannot study psychopathology independently of social and cultural influences, and we still have much to learn. Cheung (1998), Draguns (1990, 1995), and Kirmayer and Groleau (2001) have nicely summarized our knowledge in concluding that many major psychological disorders, such as schizophrenia and major depressive disorder, seem to occur in all cultures, but they may look different from one culture to another because individual symptoms are strongly influenced by social and interpersonal context. For example, as we see in Chapter 6, depression in Western culture is reflected in feelings of guilt and inadequacy, and in developing countries it appears with physical

A long and productive life usually includes strong social relationships and interpersonal relations.

distress such as fatigue or illness. In Canada, Asian immigrants represent 63% of all Canadian immigrants (Bowman, 2000; Statistics Canada, 1996a). Laurence Kirmayer, a cross-cultural psychiatrist at McGill University, has described how affective expressions of depression are often perceived as self-centred and threatening to the social structure in many Asian cultures, such as in Chinese society. This cultural context results in affective and cognitive dimensions of depression being less readily endorsed by depressed Chinese patients (Kirmayer & Groleau, 2001). These types of cultural differences likely contribute to the consistent underutilization of mainstream mental health services by Asian Canadians (Li & Browne, 2000).

As another clear example of social influences on mental health, consider the high rates of various psychological disorders and problems among Aboriginal Canadians relative to other groups of Canadians. As we will discuss in more detail in the chapters to come, rates of suicide (see Chapter 6), substance abuse (see Chapter 10), and familial violence are all elevated among Aboriginal peoples (Gotowiec & Beiser, 1993–1994). Poverty, an established risk factor for many psychological disorders (Richters, 1993), is higher among Aboriginal people (Lee, 2000), which very likely contributes substantially to their elevated rates of certain psychological disorders. However, the fact that more Aboriginal people live in poverty is not the only reason for the elevated rates of these psychological and social problems. Their unique experiences of a history of oppression by the majority culture also need to be considered as a contributing factor. These oppressive experiences include the maltreatment of Aboriginal children in the residential school system from the late 19th century to as recently as the 1980s (Grant, 1996; Haig-Brown, 1988) and the continued discrimination against, and reduced opportunities for, Aboriginal people.

## Social and Interpersonal Influences on the Elderly

Finally, the effect of social and interpersonal factors on the expression of physical and psychological disorders may differ with age. Grant, Patterson, and Yager (1988) studied 118 men and women 65 years or older who lived independently. Those with fewer meaningful contacts and less social support from relatives had consistently higher levels of depression and more reports of unsatisfactory quality of life. However, if these individuals became physically ill, they had more substantial support from their families than those who were not physically ill. This finding raises the unfortunate possibility that it may be advantageous for elderly people to become physically ill, because illness allows them to reestablish the social support that makes life worth living. If further research indicates this is true, involving their families before they get ill might help maintain their physical health (and significantly reduce health-care costs).

The study of older adults is growing at a rapid pace, in line with increases in the proportion of our population that is elderly. Frank Denton and his colleagues at McMaster University made projections of the age distribution of the Canadian population for the 45-year period from 1996–2041. They conclude that substantial aging of the Canadian population appears virtually certain (Denton, Feaver, & Spencer, 1998). Some have suggested that with this growth will come a corresponding increase in the number of older adults with mental health problems, many of whom will not receive appropriate care (e.g., Gatz & Smyer, 1992). As you can see, it is necessary and important to understand and treat the disorders experienced by older adults.

## Global Incidence of Psychological Disorders

Behavioural and mental health problems in developing countries are exacerbated by political strife, technological change, and massive movements from rural to urban areas. An important study from the World Health Organization (WHO) reveals that 10% to 20% of all primary medical services in poor countries are sought by patients with psychological disorders, principally anxiety and mood disorders (including suicide attempts), and those with alcoholism, drug abuse, and childhood developmental disorders (WHO, 2001). Record numbers of young men are committing suicide in Micronesia. Alcoholism levels among adults in Latin America have risen to 20%. Treatments for disorders such as depression and addictive behaviours that are successful in North

America can't be administered in countries where mental health care is limited. In China, more than 1 billion people are served by approximately 3000 mental health professionals. In contrast, Canada alone has more than 10 000 licensed psychologists (Adair, Paivio, & Ritchie, 1996) to serve just over 30 million people (Statistics Canada, 2001a). And yet, psychological services in Canada are very much underutilized, particularly by those Canadians with the greatest mental health needs (Hunsley, Lee, & Aubry, 1999). Using data collected during the 1994–1995 Population Health Survey, John Hunsley and his colleagues showed that only about 2% of those Canadians surveyed indicated that they had consulted a psychologist in the year before the survey (Hunsley et al., 1999). These shocking statistics suggest that in addition to their role in causation, social and cultural factors substantially maintain disorders, because most societies have not yet developed the social context for alleviating and ultimately preventing them. Changing society's attitude is just one of the challenges facing us.

# Developmental Contributions to Psychopathology

■ *Describe developmental influences on abnormal behaviour across the life span.*

Life-span developmental psychopathologists (e.g., Galambos & Leadbeater, 2002) point out that we tend to look at psychological disorders from a snapshot perspective: We focus on a particular point in a person's life and assume it represents the whole person. The inadequacy of this way of looking at people should be clear. Think back on your own life over the past few years. The person you were, say, 3 years ago, is very different from the person you are now, and the person you will be 3 years from now will have changed in important ways. To understand psychopathology, we must appreciate how experiences during different periods of development may influence our vulnerability to other types of stress or to differing psychological disorders (Rutter, 2002).

Important developmental changes occur at all points in life. For example, adulthood, far from being a relatively stable period, is highly dynamic, with important changes occurring into old age. Erik Erikson suggested that we go through eight major crises during our lives (Erikson, 1982), each determined by our biological maturation and the social demands made at particular times. Unlike Freud, who envisioned no developmental stages beyond adolescence, Erikson believed that we grow and change beyond the age of 65. During older adulthood, for example, we look back and view our lives either as rewarding or as disappointing. Although aspects of Erikson's theory of psychosocial development have been criticized as being too vague and not supported by research (Shaffer, 1993), it demonstrates the comprehensive approach to human development advocated by life-span developmentalists.

Basic research is beginning to confirm the importance of this approach. In one experiment by Bryan Kolb and his colleagues (Kolb, Gibb, & Gorny, 2003), animals were placed in complex environments, either as juveniles, as adults, or in old age when cognitive abilities were beginning to decline (senescence). What they found was that the environment had different effects on the brains of these animals depending on their developmental stage. Basically, the complex and challenging environments increased the size and complexity of neurons in the motor and sensory cortical regions in the adult and aged animals, but unlike the older groups, *decreased* the spine density of neurons in young animals. Nevertheless, this decrease was associated with enhanced motor and cognitive skills when the animals became adults. Even prenatal experience seems to affect brain structure, because the offspring of an animal housed in a rich and complex environment throughout pregnancy have the advantage of more complex cortical brain circuits after birth (Kolb, Gibb, & Robinson, 2003). Thus, we can infer that the influence of developmental stage and prior experience has a substantial impact on the development and presentation of psychological disorders, an inference that is receiving confirmation from sophisticated life-span developmental psychology research (e.g., Cartensen, Charles, Isaacowitz, & Kennedy, 2003; Isaacowitz, Smith, & Carstensen, 2003). For example, in depressive (mood) disorders, children and adolescents do not receive the same benefit from antidepressant drugs as do adults (Hazell, O'Connell, Heathcote, Robertson, & Henry, 1995). Also, the gender distribution in depression is approximately equal until puberty, when it becomes much more common in girls (Hankin et al., 1998).

## *The Principle of Equifinality*

Like a fever, a particular behaviour or disorder may have a number of causes. The principle of **equifinality** is used in developmental psychopathology to indicate that we must consider a number of paths to a given outcome (Cicchetti, 1991). There are many examples of this principle; for example, a delusional syndrome may be an aspect of schizophrenia, but it can also arise from amphetamine abuse. Delirium, which involves difficulty focusing attention, often occurs in older adults after surgery, but it can also result from thiamine deficiency or renal (kidney) disease. Autism can sometimes occur in children whose mothers are exposed to rubella during pregnancy, but it can also occur in children whose mothers experience difficulties during labour.

Different paths can also result from the interaction of psychological and biological factors during various stages of development. How someone copes with impairment due to organic causes may have a profound effect on that person's overall functioning. For example, people with documented brain damage may have different levels of disorder. Those with healthy systems of social support, consisting of family and friends, and highly adaptive personality characteristics, such as marked confidence in their abilities to overcome challenges, may experience only mild behavioural and cognitive disturbance despite an organic pathology. Those without comparable support and personality may be incapacitated. This may be clearer if you think of people you know with physical disabilities. Some, paralyzed from the waist down by accident or disease (paraplegics), have nevertheless become superb athletes or accomplished in business or the arts. Others with the same condition are depressed and hopeless; they have withdrawn from life or, even worse, ended their lives. Even the content of delusions and hallucinations that may accompany a disorder, and the degree to which they are frightening or difficult to cope with, is determined in part by psychological and social factors.

Researchers are exploring not only what makes people experience particular disorders but also what protects others from having the same difficulties. If you were interested in why someone would be depressed, for example, you would first look at people who display depression. But you could also study people in similar situations and from similar backgrounds who are not depressed. An excellent example of this approach is research on "resilient" children, which suggests that social factors may protect some children from being hurt by stressful experiences, such as one or both parents suffering a psychiatric disturbance (Garmezy & Rutter, 1983; Hetherington & Blechman, 1996; Weiner, 2000). The presence of a caring adult friend or relative can offset the negative stresses of this environment, as can the child's own ability to understand and cope with unpleasant situations. Those of us brought up in violent or otherwise dysfunctional families who have successfully gone on to university might want to look back for the factors that protected us. Perhaps if we better understand why some people do not encounter the same problems as others in similar circumstances, we can better understand particular disorders, assist those who suffer from them, and even prevent some cases from occurring.

---

**equifinality** Developmental psychopathology principle that a behaviour or disorder may have several different causes.

# Conclusions

We have examined modern approaches to psychopathology and we have found the field to be complex indeed. In this overview, we have seen that biological, behavioural, emotional, social, and developmental factors all must be considered when we think about psychopathology. Even though our knowledge is incomplete, you can see why we could never resume the one-dimensional thinking typical of the various historical traditions described in Chapter 1.

And yet, books about psychological disorders and news reports in the popular press often describe the causes of these disorders in one-dimensional terms without considering other influences. For example, how many times have you heard that a psychological disorder such as depression, or perhaps schizophrenia, is caused by a "chemical imbalance" without considering other possible causes? When you read that a disorder is *caused* by a chemical imbalance, it sounds like nothing else matters and all you have to do is correct the imbalance in neurotransmitter activity to "cure" the problem.

Based on research we will review when we talk about specific psychological disorders, there is no question that psychological disorders are associated with altered neurotransmitter activity and other aspects of brain function (a chemical imbalance). But we have learned in this chapter that a "chemical imbalance" could, in turn, be caused by psychological or social factors such as stress, strong emotional reactions, difficult family interactions, changes caused by aging, or, most likely, some interaction of all these factors. Therefore, it is inaccurate and misleading to say that a psychological disorder is "caused" by a chemical imbalance, even though chemical imbalances almost certainly exist.

Similarly, how many times have you heard that alcoholism or other addictive behaviours were caused by "lack of willpower," implying that if these individuals simply developed the right attitude they could overcome their addiction? There is no question that people with severe addictions may have faulty cognitive processes as indicated by rationalizing their behaviour, or other faulty appraisals, or by attributing their problems to stress in their lives, or some other "bogus" excuse. They may also misperceive the effects that alcohol has on them, and all of these cognitions and attitudes contribute to developing addictions. But considering only cognitive processes without considering other factors as causes of addictions would be as incorrect as saying that depression is caused by a chemical imbalance. Our genes play a role in the development of addictive behaviours, as we learn in Chapter 10. There is also evidence that brain function in people suffering from addictions may be different from brain function in those individuals who may ingest similar amounts of alcohol but do not develop addictive behaviour. Interpersonal, social, and cultural factors also contribute strongly to the development of addictive behaviours. To say, then, that addictive behaviours such as alcoholism are caused by lack of willpower or to certain faulty ways of thinking is highly simplistic and just plain wrong.

If you learn one thing from this book, it should be that psychological disorders do not have just one cause. They have many causes—these causes all interact—and we must understand this interaction to appreciate fully the origins of psychological disorders. To do this requires a multidimensional integrative approach. In chapters covering specific psychological disorders, we return to cases very much like Jody's and consider them from this multidimensional integrative perspective. But first we must explore the processes of assessment and diagnosis used to measure and classify psychopathology.

## Concept Check 2.5

Fill in the blanks to complete these statements relating to the cultural, social, and developmental factors influencing psychopathology.

1. What we _____ is strongly influenced by our social environments.
2. The likelihood of your having a particular phobia is powerfully influenced by your _____!
3. A large number of studies have demonstrated that the greater the number and frequency of relationships and _____, the longer you are likely to live.
4. The effect of social and interpersonal factors on the expression of physical and psychological disorders may differ with _____.
5. The principle of _____ is used in developmental psychopathology to indicate that we must consider a number of paths to a given outcome.

# Summary

## One-Dimensional or Multidimensional Models

- The causes of abnormal behaviour are complex and fascinating. You can say that psychological disorders are caused by nature (biology) and by nurture (psychosocial factors), and you would be right on both counts—but also wrong on both counts.
- To identify the causes of various psychological disorders, we must consider the interaction of all relevant dimensions: genetic contributions, the role of the nervous system, behavioural and cognitive processes, emotional influences, social and interpersonal influences, and developmental

factors. Thus, we have arrived at a multidimensional integrative approach to the causes of psychological disorders.

## Biological Contributions to Psychopathology

- The genetic influence on much of our development and most of our behaviour, personality, and even IQ is polygenic—that is, influenced by many genes. This is assumed to be the case in abnormal behaviour as well, although research is beginning to identify specific small groups of genes that relate to some major psychological disorders.

- In studying causal relationships in psychopathology, researchers look at the interactions of genetic and environmental effects. In the diathesis–stress model, individuals are assumed to inherit certain vulnerabilities that make them susceptible to a disorder when the right kind of stressor comes along. In the reciprocal gene-environment model, the individual's genetic vulnerability toward a certain disorder may make it more likely that he or she will experience the stressor that, in turn, triggers the genetic vulnerability and thus the disorder.

- The field of neuroscience promises much as we try to unravel the mysteries of psychopathology. Within the nervous system, levels of neurotransmitter and neuroendocrine activity interact in complex ways to modulate and regulate emotions and behaviour and contribute to psychological disorders.

- Critical to our understanding of psychopathology are the neurotransmitter currents called brain circuits. Of the neurotransmitters that may play a key role, we investigated four: serotonin, gamma aminobutyric acid (GABA), norepinephrine, and dopamine.

## Behavioural Contributions to Psychopathology

- The relatively new field of cognitive science provides a valuable perspective on how behavioural and cognitive influences affect the learning and adaptation each of us experience throughout life. Clearly, such influences not only contribute to psychological disorders but also may directly modify brain functioning, brain structure, and even genetic expression. We examined some of the research in this field by looking at learned helplessness, modelling, prepared learning, implicit memory, and cognitive-behavioural therapy.

## Emotional Contributions to Psychopathology

- Emotions have a direct and dramatic impact on our functioning and play a central role in many disorders. Mood, a persistent period of emotionality, is often evident in psychological disorders.

## Social Contributions to Psychopathology

- Social and cultural influences profoundly affect both psychological disorders and biology.

## Developmental Contributions to Psychopathology

- In considering a multidimensional integrative approach to psychopathology, it is important to remember the principle of equifinality, which reminds us that we must consider the various paths to a particular outcome, not just the result.

## Key Terms

| | | | |
|---|---|---|---|
| multidimensional integrative approach, 35 | neuron, 44 | serotonin, 51 | implicit memory, 60 |
| genes, 38 | synaptic cleft, 45 | gamma aminobutyric acid (GABA), 53 | cognitive-behavioural therapy (CBT), 62 |
| diathesis–stress model, 41 | neurotransmitters, 45 | norepinephrine, 53 | fight or flight response, 62 |
| vulnerability, 41 | hormone, 49 | dopamine, 53 | emotion, 63 |
| reciprocal gene–environment model, 42 | brain circuits, 50 | cognitive science, 57 | mood, 63 |
| | reuptake, 51 | learned helplessness, 58 | affect, 63 |
| | agonist, 51 | modelling, 59 | equifinality, 70 |
| neuroscience, 44 | antagonist, 51 | prepared learning, 60 | |
| | inverse agonist, 51 | | |

## Answers to Concept Checks

**2.1**  1. b  2. a (best answer) or c  3. e  4. a (initial), c (maintenance)

**2.2**  1. F (first 22 pairs) 2. T  3. T  4. F (reciprocal gene–environment model)  5. F (complex interaction of both nature and nurture)

**2.3**  1. b  2. c  3. f  4. g  5. d  6. e  7. h  8. a

**2.4**  1. b  2. a  3. d  4. c

**2.5**  1. fear  2. gender  3. social contacts  4. age  5. equifinality

**InfoTrac College Edition**

If your instructor ordered your book with InfoTrac College Edition, please explore this online library for additional readings, review, and a handy resource for short assignments. Go to:

**http://infotrac.thomsonlearning.com**

Enter these search terms: neuroscience, behaviour genetics, cognitive science, psychosocial development, developmental psychopathology, observational learning

 **The Abnormal Psychology Book Companion Website**

Go to **www.essentialsabnormalpsych.nelson.com** for practice quiz questions, Internet links, critical thinking exercises, and more.

 **Abnormal Psychology Live CD-ROM**

- **Integrative Approach:** This clip summarizes the integrative approach, showing how psychological factors affect our biology and how our brain influences our behaviour.

**Thomson NOW!** **http://hed.nelson.com** Go to this site for the link to ThomsonNow™, your one-stop study shop. Take a Pretest for this chapter and ThomsonNow™ will generate a personalized Study Plan based on your test results! The Study Plan will identify the topics you need to review and direct you to online resources to help you master those topics. You can then take a Posttest to help you determine the concepts you have mastered and what you still need work on.

## Video Concept Review

For challenging concepts that typically need more than one explanation, Mark Durand provides a video review via ThomsonNow of the following topic:

- Comparing the diathesis–stress model with the reciprocal gene–environment model.

# Chapter Quiz

1. Which approach to psychopathology considers biological, social, behavioural, emotional, cognitive, and developmental influences?

    a. genetic
    b. multidimensional
    c. interpersonal
    d. psychodynamic

2. Much of our development and most of our behaviour, personality, and IQ are influenced by many genes, each contributing only a portion of the overall effect. This type of influence is known as:

    a. reciprocal.
    b. polygenic.
    c. integrative.
    d. recessive.

3. Behavioural genetics research has concluded that:

    a. genetic factors do not contribute to most psychological disorders.
    b. genetic factors that contribute to psychological disorders account for most of the explanation.
    c. for any one psychological disorder there is probably one gene that explains most of its development.
    d. genetic factors that contribute to psychological disorders account for less than half of the explanation.

4. Which portion of the brain is responsible for complex cognitive activities such as reasoning, planning, and creating?

    a. limbic system
    b. basal ganglia
    c. hindbrain
    d. cerebral cortex

5. John is startled by a loud crash in his apartment. His heart immediately starts beating rapidly and the pace of his breathing increases. What part of the nervous system is responsible for this physiological response?

    a. central nervous system
    b. sympathetic nervous system
    c. limbic system
    d. parasympathetic nervous system

6. Which neurotransmitter appears to reduce overall arousal and dampen emotional responses?

    a. serotonin
    b. gamma aminobutyric acid
    c. norepinephrine
    d. dopamine

7. Seligman noted that when rats or other animals encounter conditions over which they have no control, they give up attempting to cope and seem to develop the animal equivalent of depression. This is referred to as:

    a. learned depression.
    b. learned fear.
    c. learned helplessness.
    d. learned defencelessness.

8. Which concept explains why fears of snakes and heights are more common (or more easily learned) than fears of cats and flowers?

    a. equifinality
    b. vulnerability
    c. prepared learning
    d. observational learning

9. Recent research on implicit memory suggests that:

    a. people can recall colours more quickly than words.
    b. memories can change based on the implicit structures of the brain.
    c. implicit memory is more relevant to psychopathology than explicit memory.
    d. memories outside our awareness may influence psychopathology, just as Freud speculated.

10. Emotion comprises all of the following components EXCEPT:

    a. behaviour.
    b. cognition.
    c. genetics.
    d. physiology.

*(See the Appendix on page 601 for answers.)*

# 3 Clinical Assessment, Diagnosis, and Research Methods

© Gary Conner/Phototake

**Assessing Psychological Disorders**
*Key Concepts in Assessment*
*The Clinical Interview*
*Physical Examination*
*Behavioural Assessment*
*Psychological Testing*
*Neuropsychological Testing*
*Neuroimaging: Pictures of the Brain*
*Psychophysiological Assessment*

**Diagnosing Psychological Disorders**
*Classification Issues*
*DSM-IV*

**Conducting Research in Psychopathology**
*Basic Components of a Research Study*
*Statistical versus Clinical Significance*
*The "Average" Client*

**Types of Research Methods**
*Studying Individual Cases*
*Research by Correlation*
*Research by Experiment*
*Single-Case Experimental Designs*

**Genetics and Research across Time and Cultures**
*Studying Genetics*
*Studying Behaviour over Time*
*Studying Behaviour across Cultures*
*The Power of a Program of Research*
*Replication*
*Research Ethics*

 **Abnormal Psychology Live CD-ROM**
*Arriving at a Diagnosis*
*Psychological Assessment*
*Research Methods*

# Assessing Psychological Disorders

- *Describe the nature and function of clinical assessment and the concepts that determine the value of assessment.*

- *Describe the nature and purpose of each of the principal methods of clinical assessment.*

The processes of clinical assessment and diagnosis are central to the study of psychopathology and, ultimately, to the treatment of psychological disorders. **Clinical assessment** is the systematic evaluation and measurement of psychological, biological, and social factors in an individual presenting with a possible psychological disorder. **Diagnosis** is the process of determining whether the particular problem afflicting the individual meets all the criteria for a psychological disorder, as set forth in the *Diagnostic and Statistical Manual of Mental Disorders,* Fourth Edition (Text Revision), or DSM-IV-TR (American Psychiatric Association, 2000a). In this chapter, after demonstrating assessment and diagnosis within the context of an actual case, we examine the development of the DSM into a widely used classification system for abnormal behaviour. Then we review the many assessment techniques available to the clinician. Next we turn to diagnostic issues and the related challenges of classification. Finally, we explore the research methods used to study the processes of assessment, diagnosis, and treatment.

## Frank
### Young, Serious, and Anxious

Frank was referred to one of our clinics for evaluation and possible treatment of severe distress and anxiety centring on his marriage. He arrived neatly dressed in his work clothes (he was a mechanic). He reported that he was 24 years old and that this was the first time he had seen a mental health professional. He wasn't sure that he really needed (or wanted) to be there, but he felt he was beginning to "come apart" because of his marital difficulties. What follows is a transcript of parts of this first interview.

**THERAPIST:** What sorts of problems have been troubling you during the past month?

**FRANK:** I'm beginning to have a lot of marital problems. I was married about 9 months ago, but I've been really tense around the house and we've having been a lot of arguments.

**THERAPIST:** Is this something recent?

**FRANK:** Well, it wasn't too bad at first, but it's been worse lately. I've also been really uptight in my job, and I haven't been getting my work done.

Note that we always begin by asking the patient to describe for us, in a relatively open-ended way, the major difficulties that brought him or her to the office. When dealing with adults, or children old enough (or verbal enough) to tell us their story, this strategy tends to break the ice. It also reveals the central problems as seen through the patient's eyes.

After Frank described this major problem in some detail, the therapist asked him about his marriage, his job, and other current life circumstances. Frank seemed to be quite tense and anxious and would often look down at the floor while he talked, glancing up only occasionally to make eye contact. Sometimes his right leg would twitch. Although it was not easy to see at first because he was looking down, Frank was also closing his eyes tightly for a period of 2 to 3 seconds. It was during these periods when his eyes were closed that his right leg would twitch.

The interview proceeded for the next half hour, exploring marital and job issues. It became increasingly clear that Frank was feeling inadequate and anxious about handling situations in his life. By this time he was talking freely and looking up a little more at the therapist, but he was continuing to close his eyes and twitch his right leg slightly.

---

**clinical assessment** Systematic evaluation and measurement of psychological, biological, and social factors in a person presenting with a possible psychological disorder.

**diagnosis** Process of determining whether a presenting problem meets the established criteria for a specific psychological disorder.

**THERAPIST:** Are you aware that once in a while you're closing your eyes while you're telling me this?

**FRANK:** I'm not aware all the time, but I know I do it.

**THERAPIST:** Do you know how long you've been doing that?

**FRANK:** Oh, I don't know, maybe a year or two.

**THERAPIST:** Are you thinking about anything when you close your eyes?

**FRANK:** Well, actually I'm trying not to think about something.

**THERAPIST:** What do you mean?

**FRANK:** Well, I have these really frightening and stupid thoughts, and … it's hard to even talk about it.

**THERAPIST:** The thoughts are frightening?

**FRANK:** Yes, I keep thinking I'm going to take a fit, and I'm just trying to get that out of my mind.

**THERAPIST:** Could you tell me more about this fit?

**FRANK:** Well, you know, it's those terrible things where people fall down and they froth at the mouth, and their tongues come out, and they shake all over. You know, seizures. I think they call it epilepsy.

**THERAPIST:** And you're trying to get these thoughts out of your mind?

**FRANK:** Oh, I do everything possible to get those thoughts out of my mind as quickly as I can.

**THERAPIST:** I've noticed you moving your leg when you close your eyes. Is that part of it?

**FRANK:** Yes, I've noticed if I really jerk my leg and pray real hard for a little while the thought will go away. (Excerpt from "Behavioural Assessment: Basic Strategies and Initial Procedures," by R. O. Nelson and D. H. Barlow. In D. H. Barlow (Ed.), *Behavioural Assessment of Adult Disorders,* 1981. Copyright © 1981 by Guilford Press. Reprinted by permission.)

---

What's wrong with Frank? The interview reveals an insecure young man experiencing substantial stress as he questions whether he is capable of handling marriage and a job. He reports that he loves his wife very much and wants the marriage to work and that he is attempting to be as conscientious as possible on his job, a job from which he derives a lot of satisfaction and enjoyment. Also, for some reason, he is having troubling thoughts about seizures. Now let's consider one more case for purposes of illustration. This case (we'll call him Brian) was described by Stanley J. Rachman, a clinical psychologist recently retired from the University of British Columbia (Rachman, 2003).

## Brian
### Unwanted Thoughts of Harm

A 30-year-old self-employed bookkeeper referred himself for treatment … having failed to benefit from a variety of previous treatments, both psychiatric and psychological. He complained of … thoughts and images of harming himself, thoughts of hurting other people, and unwanted sexual thoughts and images. The [thought] of causing harm to children was the most distressing [to Brian] and generally focused on his 5-year-old nephew. He described a recent example when he took his nephew out for a drive and had thoughts of "beating him up and dumping him on the side of the road." He also had thoughts of harming children who were unfamiliar to him, saying that these can be triggered by driving past a school or seeing children in a playground. He also had occasional thoughts of harming members of his family. His images of self-harm took two main forms. The first involved slashing his wrists, arms, and hands with a knife. The image usually lasted for 15–30 seconds and was triggered by the sight of sharp objects. The second image/thought involved placing his hand on a hot element when cooking on the stove. He also reported unwanted sexual thoughts but said that the associated images were not as intense as those involving aggressive themes.

He reported having the harm images about 3 times a week and the thoughts of self-harm about 4–5 times a day. The thoughts and images disturbed his concentration and ability to perform at work. He was depressed and slower than he used to be when performing tasks, partly because he had to repeat things too many times when he lost track of what he was doing. He tried to deal with the [thoughts] by deliberately thinking of more pleasant things but had little success with this method. He vigorously resisted the images of harming … children, but despite this, they persisted.

… He concealed his thoughts from everyone else because he expected that others would find them unacceptable and conclude that there was something wrong with him…. [H]e was extremely worried that he might be going crazy and losing his mental stability. He was particularly worried that the intense anxiety might one day cause him to "lose control and snap." (Rachman, 2003, pp. 149–150).

So where do we go from here? How do we determine whether Frank has a psychological disorder or he is simply one of many young men experiencing the normal stresses and strains of a new marriage who, perhaps, could benefit from some marital counseling? And what about Brian? Why is he having these troubling and persistent thoughts and mental images? The purpose of this chapter is to illustrate how mental health clinicians address these types of questions in a systematic way, assessing patients in order to study the basic nature of psychopathology as well as to make diagnoses and plan treatment.

## Key Concepts in Assessment

The process of clinical assessment in psychopathology has been likened to a funnel (Hawkins, 1979; Peterson, 1968). The clinician begins by collecting a lot of information across a broad range of the individual's functioning to determine where the source of the problem may lie. After getting a preliminary sense of the overall functioning of the person, the clinician narrows the focus by ruling out problems in some areas and concentrating on areas that seem most relevant.

To understand the different ways clinicians assess psychological problems, we need to understand three basic concepts that help determine the value of our assessments: *reliability, validity,* and *standardization* (see Figure 3.1). Assessment techniques are subject to a number of strict requirements, in particular, some evidence (research) that they do what they are designed to do. One of the more important requirements of these assessments is that they are reliable. **Reliability** is the degree to which a measurement is consistent (Asmundson,

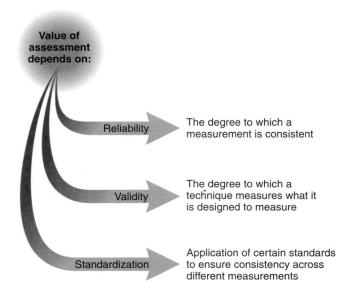

Value of assessment depends on:

Reliability → The degree to which a measurement is consistent

Validity → The degree to which a technique measures what it is designed to measure

Standardization → Application of certain standards to ensure consistency across different measurements

**Figure 3.1** ■ Concepts that determine the value of a clinical assessment.

Norton, & Stein, 2002). Imagine how irritated you would be if you had stomach pain and you went to four competent physicians and got four different diagnoses and four different treatments. The diagnoses would be said to be unreliable because two or more "raters" (the physicians) did not agree on the conclusion. We expect, in general, that presenting the same symptoms to different physicians will result in similar diagnoses. One way psychologists improve their reliability is by carefully designing their assessment devices and then conducting research on them to ensure that two or more raters will get the same answers (called *interrater reliability*). They also determine whether these techniques are stable across time. In other words, if you go to a clinician on Tuesday and are told you have an IQ of 110, you should expect a similar result if you take the same test again on Thursday. This is known as *test-retest reliability*. We return to the concept of reliability when we talk about diagnoses and classification.

**Validity** is whether something measures what it is designed to measure; in this case, whether a technique assesses what it is supposed to (Asmundson et al., 2002). Comparing the results of one assessment measure with the results of others that are better known allows you to begin to determine the validity of the first measure. This comparison is called *concurrent* or *descriptive validity*. For example, if the results from a standard, but long,

During their first meeting, the mental health professional focuses on the problem that brought the person to treatment.

© Mary Kate Denny/PhotoEdit

**reliability** Degree to which a measurement is consistent— for example, over time or among different raters.

**validity** Degree to which a technique actually measures what it purports to measure.

IQ test were essentially the same as the results from a new brief version, you could conclude that the brief version had concurrent validity. *Predictive validity* is how well your assessment tells you what will happen in the future. For example, does it predict who will succeed in school and who will not, which is one of the goals of an IQ test?

**Standardization** is the process by which a certain set of standards or norms is determined for a technique to make its use consistent across different measurements. The standards might apply to the procedures of testing, scoring, and evaluating data. To illustrate, the assessment might be given to large numbers of people who differ on important factors such as age, race, gender, socioeconomic status, and diagnosis; their scores would then be used as a standard, or norm, for comparison purposes. For example, if you are a First Nations male, 19 years old, and from a working-class background, your score on a psychological test should be compared with the scores of others like you and not with the scores of very different people, such as a group of women of Asian descent, in their 60s, from middle-class backgrounds. Reliability, validity, and standardization are important to all forms of psychological assessment.

Clinical assessment consists of a number of strategies and procedures that help clinicians acquire the information they need to understand their patients and assist them. These procedures include a *clinical interview* and, within the context of the interview, a *mental status exam* that can be administered either formally or informally; often a thorough *physical examination; behavioural observation and assessment;* and *psychological tests* (if needed).

## The Clinical Interview

The clinical interview, the core of most clinical work, is used by psychologists, psychiatrists, and other mental health professionals. The interviewer gathers information on current and past behaviour, attitudes, and emotions, as well as a detailed history of the individual's life in general and of the presenting problem. Clinicians determine when the specific problem started and identify other events (e.g., life stress, trauma, and physical illness) that might have occurred at about the same time. In addition, most clinicians gather at least some information about the patient's current and past interpersonal and social history, including family makeup (e.g., marital status, number of children, or college student currently living with parents), and about the individual's upbringing. Information on sexual development, religious attitudes (current and past), relevant cultural concerns (such as stress induced by discrimination), and educational

history are also routinely collected. To organize information obtained during an interview, many clinicians use a **mental status exam.**

### The Mental Status Exam

In essence, the mental status exam involves the systematic observation of somebody's behaviour. In the mental status exam, clinicians organize their observations of other people in a way that gives them sufficient information to determine whether a psychological disorder might be present (Nelson & Barlow, 1981). For the most part, these exams are performed relatively quickly by experienced clinicians in the course of interviewing or observing a patient. The exam covers five categories: appearance and behaviour, thought processes, mood and affect, intellectual functioning, and sensorium.

1. *Appearance and behaviour.* The clinician notes any overt physical behaviours such as Frank's leg twitch, as well as the individual's dress, general appearance, posture, and facial expression. For example, slow and effortful motor behaviour, like Brian's slowed performance on tasks, is sometimes referred to as psychomotor retardation and may indicate severe depression.

2. *Thought processes.* When clinicians listen to a patient talk, they're getting a good idea of that person's thought processes. They might look for several things here. For example, does the person talk really fast or really slowly? Does the patient make sense when he or she talks, or are ideas presented with no apparent connection? In some patients with schizophrenia, a disorganized speech pattern, referred to as "looseness of association," is quite noticeable. In addition to rate or flow and continuity of speech, what about the content? For example, a clinician would note Brian's intense and distressing thoughts of harming children in this part of the mental status exam. Is there any evidence of *delusions* (distorted views of reality)? A typical delusion involves *delusions of persecution,* where someone thinks people are after him or her and out to get him or her all the time. The individual might also have *ideas of reference,* where everything everyone else does somehow relates back

---

**standardization**  Process of establishing specific norms and requirements for a measurement technique to ensure it is used consistently across measurement occasions. This includes instructions for administering the measure, evaluating its findings, and comparing these with data for large numbers of people.

**mental status exam**  Relatively coarse preliminary test of a client's judgment, orientation to time and place, and emotional and mental state; typically conducted during an initial interview.

to him or her. *Hallucinations* are things that a person sees or hears but really aren't there. For example, the clinician might ask, "Do you ever see things or maybe hear things when you know there is nothing there?"

3. *Mood and affect.* *Mood* is the predominant feeling state of the individual, as we noted in Chapter 2. Does the person appear to be down in the dumps or continually elated? Does she or he talk in a depressed or hopeless fashion? Are there times when the depression seems to go away? For example, Brian's feelings of depression and his intense anxiety and worry about his thought patterns would be the clinician's focus in this part of the mental status exam. *Affect,* by contrast, refers to the feeling state that accompanies what we say at a given point in time. If a friend just told you his or her mother died and is laughing about it, or if your friend has just won the lottery and is crying, you would think it strange, to say the least. A mental health clinician would note that your friend's affect is "inappropriate."

4. *Intellectual functioning.* Clinicians make a rough estimate of others' intellectual functioning just by talking to them. Do they seem to have a reasonable vocabulary? Can they talk in abstractions and metaphors (as most of us do much of the time)? How is the person's memory? We usually make some gross or rough estimate of intelligence that is noticeable only if it deviates from normal, such as concluding the person is above or below average intelligence. In Brian's mental status exam, for example, the clinician might look at Brian's answers to questions about his occupational achievement (i.e., he is successfully self-employed as a bookkeeper) and infer from Brian's use of language that this client is of average to above-average intelligence.

5. *Sensorium.* *Sensorium* is our general awareness of our surroundings. Do the individuals know what the date is, what time it is, where they are, who they are, and who you are? People with permanent brain damage or dysfunction—or temporary brain damage or dysfunction, often due to drugs or other toxic states—may not know the answers to these questions. If the patient knows who he or she is and who the clinician is, and has a good idea of the time and place, the clinician would say that the patient's sensorium is "clear" and is "oriented times three" (to person, place, and time). In Brian's case, although his recurrent thoughts and images about harming himself and others were extremely distracting to him, he had no difficulties in terms of his awareness of his surroundings.

What can we conclude from these informal behavioural observations? Basically, they allow the clinician to make a preliminary determination about which areas of the patient's behaviour and condition should be assessed in more detail and perhaps more formally. If psychological disorders remain a possibility, the clinician may begin to hypothesize which disorders might be present. This process, in turn, provides more focus for the assessment and diagnostic activities to come.

We have already given examples of the type of information revealed by the mental status exam in the case of Brian. Let's now return to Frank's case. What have we learned from his mental status exam (see Figure 3.2)? Observing Frank's persistent motor behaviour in the form of a twitch led to the discovery of a connection (functional relationship) with some troublesome thoughts regarding seizures. Beyond this, his appearance was appropriate, and the flow and content of his speech was reasonable; his intelligence was well within normal limits, and he was oriented times three. He did display an anxious mood; however, his affect was appropriate to what he was saying. Observations during the mental status exam in both Frank's and Brian's cases suggested that we direct the remainder of the clinical interview and additional assessment and diagnostic activities to identify the possible existence of a disorder characterized by intrusive, unwanted thoughts and the attempt to resist them—in other words, *obsessive-compulsive disorder.* Later we describe some of the specific assessment strategies, from among many choices, that we would use with Frank or Brian.

Patients usually have a good idea of their major concerns in a general sense ("I'm depressed"; "I'm phobic"); occasionally, the problem reported by the patient may not, after assessment, be the major issue in the eyes of the mental health clinician. The case of Frank illustrates this point well: He complained of distress relating to marital problems, but the clinician decided, on the basis of the initial interview, that the principal difficulties lay elsewhere. Frank wasn't attempting to hide anything from the clinician. Frank just didn't think his intrusive thoughts were the major problem; in addition, talking about them was difficult for him because they were quite frightening, just as Brian's recurrent, unwanted thoughts were very distressing and anxiety-provoking for him.

These examples illustrate the importance of conducting the clinical interview in a way that elicits the patient's trust and empathy. Psychologists and other mental health professionals are trained extensively in methods that put patients at ease and facilitate communication, including non-threatening ways of seeking information and appropriate listening skills. Information provided by patients to psychologists and psychiatrists is protected by laws of "privileged communication" or confidentiality;

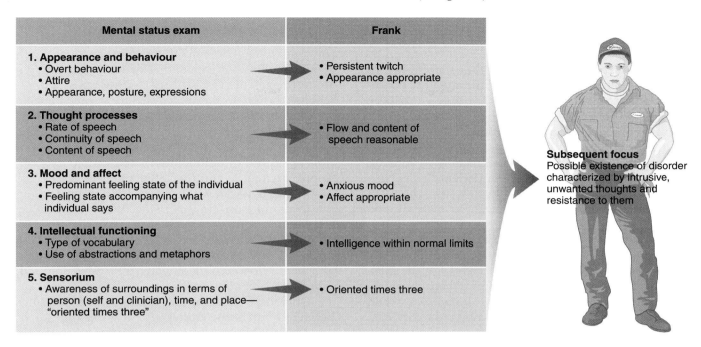

| Mental status exam | Frank |
|---|---|
| **1. Appearance and behaviour**<br>• Overt behaviour<br>• Attire<br>• Appearance, posture, expressions | • Persistent twitch<br>• Appearance appropriate |
| **2. Thought processes**<br>• Rate of speech<br>• Continuity of speech<br>• Content of speech | • Flow and content of<br>  speech reasonable |
| **3. Mood and affect**<br>• Predominant feeling state of the individual<br>• Feeling state accompanying what<br>  individual says | • Anxious mood<br>• Affect appropriate |
| **4. Intellectual functioning**<br>• Type of vocabulary<br>• Use of abstractions and metaphors | • Intelligence within normal limits |
| **5. Sensorium**<br>• Awareness of surroundings in terms of<br>  person (self and clinician), time, and place—<br>  "oriented times three" | • Oriented times three |

**Subsequent focus**
Possible existence of disorder characterized by intrusive, unwanted thoughts and resistance to them

**Figure 3.2** ■ Components of the mental status exam.

that is, even if authorities want the information the therapist has received from the patient, they cannot have access to it without the expressed consent of the patient. The only exception to this rule occurs when the clinician judges that, because of the patient's condition, some harm or danger to the patient or someone else is imminent. At the outset of the initial interview, the therapist should inform the patient of the confidential nature of their conversation and the (quite rare) conditions under which that confidence would not hold.

### Semistructured Clinical Interviews

Until relatively recently, most clinicians, after training, developed their own methods of collecting necessary information from patients. Different patients seeing different psychologists or other mental health professionals might encounter markedly different types and styles of interviews. *Unstructured interviews* follow no systematic format. *Semistructured interviews* are made up of questions that have been carefully phrased and tested to elicit useful information in a consistent manner, so clinicians can be sure they have inquired about the most important aspects of particular disorders. Clinicians may also depart from set questions to follow up on specific issues—thus the label "semistructured." Because the wording and sequencing of questions has been carefully worked out over a number of years, the clinician can feel confident that a semistructured interview will accomplish its purpose. The disadvantage is that it robs the interview of some of the spontaneous quality of two people talking

about a problem. Also, if applied too rigidly, this type of interview may inhibit the patient from volunteering useful information that is not directly relevant to the questions being asked. For these reasons, fully structured interviews administered wholly by a computer have not caught on, although they are used in some settings. An increasing number of mental health professionals routinely use semistructured interviews.

### *Physical Examination*

If the patient presenting with psychological problems has not had a physical exam in the past year, a clinician might recommend one, with particular attention to the medical conditions sometimes associated with the specific psychological problem. Many problems presenting as disorders of behaviour, cognition, or mood may, on careful physical examination, have a clear relationship to a temporary toxic state. This toxic state could be caused by bad food, the wrong amount or type of medicine, or the onset of a medical condition. For example, thyroid difficulties, particularly hyperthyroidism (overactive thyroid gland), may produce symptoms that mimic certain anxiety disorders, such as generalized anxiety disorder. Hypothyroidism (underactive thyroid gland) might produce symptoms consistent with depression. Certain psychotic symptoms, including delusions or hallucinations, might be associated with the development of a brain tumour. Withdrawal from cocaine often produces panic attacks, but many patients presenting with panic attacks are reluctant to volunteer information about their addiction, which may lead to an inappropriate diagnosis and improper treatment.

Usually, psychologists and other mental health professionals are well aware of the medical conditions and drug use and abuse that may contribute to the kinds of problems described by the patient. If a current medical condition or substance abuse situation exists, the clinician must ascertain whether it is merely coexisting or causal, usually by looking at the onset of the problem. If a patient has experienced severe bouts of depression for the past 5 years, but within the past year also developed hypothyroid problems or began taking a sedative drug, then we would not conclude the depression was caused by the medical or drug condition. If the depression developed simultaneously with the initiation of sedative drugs, and diminished considerably when the drugs were discontinued, we would be likely to conclude the depression was part of a substance-induced mood disorder.

## Behavioural Assessment

The mental status exam is one way to begin to sample how people think, feel, and behave, and how these actions might contribute to or explain their problems. **Behavioural assessment** takes this process one step further by using direct observation to assess formally an individual's thoughts, feelings, and behaviour in specific situations or *contexts*. Indeed, behavioural assessment may be much more appropriate than any interview in terms of assessing individuals who are not old enough or skilled enough to report their problems and experiences. Clinical interviews sometimes provide limited assessment information. Young children or individuals who are not verbal because of the nature of their disorder, or because of cognitive deficits or impairments, are not good candidates for clinical interviews. As we already mentioned, sometimes people deliberately withhold information because it is embarrassing or because they aren't aware it is important. In addition to talking with a client in an office about a problem, some clinicians go to the person's home or workplace or even into the local community to observe the person and the reported problems directly. Others set up role-play simulations in a clinical setting to see how people might behave in similar situations in their daily lives. These techniques are all types of behavioural assessment.

In behavioural assessment, *target behaviours* are identified and observed with the goal of determining the factors that seem to influence them. It may seem easy to identify what is bothering a particular person (i.e., the target behaviour), but even this aspect of assessment can be challenging. For example, when the mother of a 7-year-old child with a severe conduct disorder came to one of our clinics for assistance, she told the clinician, after much prodding, that her son "didn't listen to her" and he sometimes had an "attitude." The boy's schoolteacher, however, painted a different picture. She spoke candidly of his verbal violence—of his threats toward other children and to herself, threats she took seriously. To get a clearer picture of the situation at home, the clinician visited one afternoon. Approximately 15 minutes after the visit began, the boy got up from the kitchen table without removing the drinking glass he was using. When his mother meekly asked him to put the glass in the sink, he picked it up and threw it across the room, sending broken glass throughout the kitchen. He giggled and went into his room to watch TV. "See," she said. "He doesn't listen to me!"

Obviously, this mother's description of her son's behaviour at home didn't give a good picture of what he was really like. It also didn't accurately portray her response to his violent outbursts. Without the home visit, the clinician's assessment of the problem and recommendations for treatment would have been very different. Clearly this was more than simple disobedience. We developed strategies to teach the mother how to make requests of her son and how to follow up if he was violent.

But going into a person's home, workplace, or school isn't always possible or practical, so clinicians sometimes set up analogue settings (Roberts, 2001). For example, one of us studies children with autism (a disorder characterized by social withdrawal and communication problems; see Chapter 13). The reasons for self-hitting (called *self-injurious*) behaviour are discovered by placing the children in simulated classroom situations, such as sitting alone at a desk, working in a group, or being asked to complete a difficult task (Durand, 2003). Observing how they behave in these different situations helps us determine why they hit themselves so that we can design a successful treatment to eliminate the behaviour. Clinical child psychologist David Wolfe, a research chair at the Centre for Addictions and Mental Health in Toronto, uses contrived situations to assess the emotional reactions of parents with a history of abuse toward their children (e.g., Wolfe, 1991). By asking parents to have their children put away their favourite toys, which usually results in

---

**behavioural assessment**   Measuring, observing, and systematically evaluating (rather than inferring) the client's thoughts, feelings, and behaviour in the actual problem situation or context.

problem behaviour by the child, the therapist can see how the parents respond. These observations are later used to develop treatments.

### The ABCs of Observation

Observational assessment is usually focused on the here and now (Greene & Ollendick, 2000). Therefore, the clinician's attention is usually directed to the immediate behaviour, its antecedents (or what happened just before the behaviour), and its consequences (what happened afterward; Baer, Wolf, & Risley, 1968). To use the example of the young boy, an observer would note that the sequence of events was (1) his mother asking him to put his glass in the sink (antecedent), (2) the boy throwing the glass (behaviour), and (3) his mother's lack of response (consequence). This antecedent-behaviour-consequence sequence (the ABCs) might suggest that the boy was being reinforced for his violent outburst by not having to clean up his mess. And because there was no negative consequence for his behaviour (his mother didn't scold or reprimand him), he will probably act violently the next time he doesn't want to do something (see Figure 3.3).

This is an example of a relatively *informal observation*. During the home visit, the clinician took rough notes about what occurred. Later, in his office, he elaborated on the notes. A problem with this type of observation is that it relies on the observer's recollection and on his or her interpretation of the events. *Formal observation* involves identifying specific behaviours that are *observable* and *measurable* (called an *operational definition*). For example, it would be difficult for two people to agree on what "having an attitude" looks like. An operational definition, however, clarifies this behaviour by specifying that this is "any time the boy does not comply with his mother's reasonable requests." Once the target behaviour is selected and defined, an observer writes down each time it occurs, along with what happened just before (antecedent) and

just after (consequence). The goal of collecting this information is to see whether there are any obvious patterns of behaviour and then to design a treatment based on these patterns.

People can also observe their own behaviour to find patterns, a technique known as *self-monitoring* or *self-observation* (Haynes, 2000). People trying to quit smoking may write down the number of cigarettes they smoke and the times and places they smoke. This observation can tell them exactly how big their problem is (e.g., they smoke two packs a day) and what situations lead them to smoke more (e.g., talking on the phone). When behaviours occur only in private (such as purging by people with bulimia), self-monitoring is essential. Because the people with the problem are in the best position to observe their own behaviour throughout the day, clinicians often ask clients to self-monitor their behaviour to get more detailed information about the problem.

A more formal and structured way to observe behaviour is through checklists and *behaviour rating scales*, which are used as assessment tools before treatment and then periodically during treatment to assess changes in the patient's behaviour. Of the many such instruments for assessing a variety of behaviours, the Brief Psychiatric Rating Scale (Lachar et al., 2001), which can be completed by staff, assesses 18 general areas of concern. Each symptom is rated on a 7-point scale from 0 (not present) to 6 (extremely severe). The rating scale includes such items as *somatic concern* (preoccupation with physical health, fear of physical illness, hypochondriasis), *guilt feelings* (self-blame, shame, remorse for past behaviour), and *grandiosity* (exaggerated self-opinion, arrogance, conviction of unusual power or abilities).

A phenomenon known as *reactivity* can distort any observational data. Any time you observe how people behave, your mere presence may cause them to change their behaviour (Kazdin, 1979). To test reactivity, you can tell a friend you are going to record every time she or he says the word *like*. Just before you reveal your intent, however, count the times your friend uses this word in a 5-minute period. You will probably find that he or she uses the word much less when you are recording it. Your friend will *react* to the observation by changing the behaviour. The same phenomenon occurs if you observe your own behaviour, or self-monitor. Behaviours people want to increase, such as talking more in class, tend to increase, and behaviours people want to decrease, such as smoking, tend to decrease when they are self-monitored (e.g., Hufford, Shields, Shiffman, Paty, & Balabanis, 2002). Clinicians sometimes depend on the reactivity of self-monitoring to increase the effectiveness of their treatments.

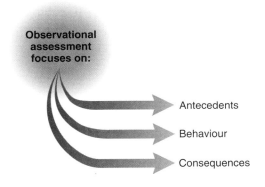

**Observational assessment focuses on:**

Antecedents

Behaviour

Consequences

**Figure 3.3** ■ The ABCs of observation.

## *Psychological Testing*

We are confronted with so-called psychological tests in the popular press almost every week: "12 Questions to Test Your Relationship," "New Test to Help You Assess Your Lover's Passion," "Are You a Type 'Z' Personality?" Although we may not want to admit it, many of us have probably purchased a magazine at some point to take one of these tests. Many are no more than entertainment, designed to make you think about the topic (and to make you buy the magazine). They are typically made up for the purposes of the article and include questions that, on the surface, seem to make sense. We are interested in these tests because we want to understand better why we and our friends behave the way we do. In reality, they usually tell us little.

In contrast, the tests used to assess psychological disorders must meet the strict standards we have noted. They must be *reliable*—so that two or more people administering the same test to the same person will come to the same conclusion about the problem—and they must be *valid*—so that they measure what they say they are measuring.

Psychological tests include specific tests to determine cognitive, emotional, or behavioural responses that might be associated with a specific disorder and more general tests that assess long-standing personality features. Specialized areas include *intelligence testing* to determine the structure and patterns of cognition. *Neuropsychological testing* determines the possible contribution of brain damage or dysfunction to the patient's condition. *Neurobiological procedures* use imaging to assess brain structure and function.

### Projective Testing

We saw in Chapter 1 how Freud brought to our attention the presence and influence of unconscious processes in psychological disorders. At this point we should ask, "If people aren't aware of these thoughts and feelings, how do we assess them?" To address this intriguing problem, psychoanalytic workers developed several assessment measures known as **projective tests.** They include a variety of methods in which ambiguous stimuli, such as pictures of people or things, are presented to a person who is asked to describe what he or she sees. The theory is that people project their own personality and unconscious fears onto other people and things—in this case, the ambiguous stimuli—and, without realizing it, reveal their unconscious thoughts to the therapist.

Because these tests are based in psychoanalytic theory, they have been, and remain, controversial. Even so, the use of projective tests is quite common, with a majority of clinicians administering them at least occasionally and most doctoral

programs providing training in their use (Durand, Blanchard, & Mindell, 1988). Two of the more widely used are the Rorschach inkblot test and the Thematic Apperception Test.

More than 80 years ago, a Swiss psychiatrist named Hermann Rorschach developed a series of inkblots, initially to study perceptual processes, then to diagnose psychological disorders. The *Rorschach inkblot test* is one of the early projective tests. In its current form, the test includes 10 inkblot pictures that serve as the ambiguous stimuli (see Figure 3.4). The examiner presents the inkblots one by one to the person being assessed, who responds by telling what he or she sees (Rorschach, 1951).

Unfortunately, much of the early use of the Rorschach is extremely controversial because of the lack of data on reliability or validity, among other things. Until relatively recently, therapists administered the test any way they saw fit, although one of the most important tenets of assessment is that the same test be given in the same way each time—that is, according to standardized procedures. If you encourage someone to give more detailed answers

**projective tests** Psychoanalytically based measures that present ambiguous stimuli to clients on the assumption that their responses will reveal their unconscious conflicts. Such tests are inferential and lack high reliability and validity.

**Figure 3.4** ■ This inkblot resembles the ambiguous figures presented in the Rorschach test.

during one testing session but not during a second session, you may get different responses as the result of your administering the test differently on the two occasions—not because of problems with the test or administration by another person (inter-rater reliability).

To respond to the concerns about reliability and validity, John Exner developed a standardized version of the Rorschach inkblot test, called the *Comprehensive System* (Exner, 1974, 1978, 1986; Exner & Weiner, 1982). Exner's system of administering and scoring the Rorschach specifies how the cards should be presented, what the examiner should say, and how the responses should be recorded (Erdberg, 2000). Varying these steps can lead to varying responses by the client. Unfortunately, despite the attempts to bring standardization to the use of the Rorschach test, its use remains controversial. Critics of the Rorschach question whether research on the Comprehensive System supports its use as a valid assessment technique for people with psychological disorders (Hunsley & Bailey, 1999; Wood, Nezworski, & Stejskal, 1996).

The *Thematic Apperception Test* (TAT) is perhaps the best known projective test after the Rorschach. It was developed in 1935 by Morgan and Murray (Bellak, 1975). The TAT consists of a series of 31 cards (see Figure 3.5): 30 with pictures on them and one blank card, although only 20 cards are typically used during each administration. Unlike the Rorschach, which involves asking for a fairly straightforward description of what the test taker sees, the instructions for the TAT ask the person to tell a dramatic story about the picture. Like the Rorschach, the TAT is based on the notion that people will reveal their unconscious mental processes in their stories about the pictures (Dana, 1996).

Unfortunately, unlike recent trends in the use of the Rorschach, the TAT continues to be used inconsistently. How the stories people tell about these pictures are interpreted depends on the examiner's frame of reference and on what the patient may say. It is not surprising, therefore, that there is little reliability across raters using this system and that questions remain about its use in psychopathology (Garb, Wood, Nezworski, Grove, & Stejskal, 2001; Gieser & Stein, 1999; Karon, 2000).

When used as icebreakers, for getting people to open up and talk about how they feel about things going on in their lives, the ambiguous stimuli in these tests can be valuable tools. However, their relative lack of reliability and validity makes them less useful as diagnostic tests (Anastasi, 1988). Concern over the inappropriate use of projective tests should remind you of the importance of the scientist-practitioner approach. Clinicians not only are responsible for knowing how to administer tests

**Figure 3.5** ■ Example of a picture resembling those in the Thematic Apperception Test.

but also need to be aware of research that suggests they have limited usefulness as a means of diagnosing psychopathology.

### Personality Inventories

Although many **personality inventories** are available, we look at the most widely used personality inventory in North America, the *Minnesota Multiphasic Personality Inventory* (MMPI; Hathaway & McKinley, 1943). In stark contrast to projective tests, which rely heavily on theory for an interpretation, the MMPI and similar inventories are based on an *empirical* approach, that is, the collection and evaluation of data. The administration of the MMPI is straightforward. The individual being assessed reads statements (e.g., "I cry easily," "I believe I am being followed") and answers either "true" or "false."

Individual responses on the MMPI are not examined; instead, the pattern of responses is reviewed to see whether it resembles patterns from groups of people who have specific disorders (e.g., a pattern similar to a group with schizophrenia).

**personality inventories** Self-report questionnaires that assess personal traits by asking respondents to identify descriptions that apply to them.

Each group is represented on separate standard scales (Butcher, Graham, Williams, & Ben-Porath, 1990). (See Table 3.1.)

The MMPI is one of the most extensively researched assessment instruments in psychology (Anastasi, 1988; Butcher, 2000). The original standardization sample—the people who first responded to the statements and set the standard for answers—included many people from Minnesota who had no psychological disorders, and several groups of people who had particular disorders. The more recent versions of this test, the MMPI-2 and the MMPI-A (Archer & Krishnamurthy, 1996), eliminate problems with the original version, problems caused partly by the original selective sample of people and partly by the wording of questions (Helmes & Reddon, 1993; Newmark & McCord, 1996). For example, some questions were sexist (Worell & Remer, 1992). Other items were criticized as insensitive to cultural diversity. Items dealing with religion, for example, referred almost exclusively to Christianity (Butcher et al., 1990). The MMPI-2 has also been standardized with a sample that reflects the composition of the general population, including Black people and Aboriginal people for the first time. In addition, new items have been added that deal with contemporary issues such as type A personality, low self-esteem, and family problems.

Reliability of the MMPI is excellent when it is interpreted according to standardized procedures, and thousands of studies on the original MMPI attest to its validity with a range of psychological problems (Butcher, 2000). But a word of caution is necessary here. Some clinicians look at an MMPI profile and interpret the scales on the basis of their own clinical experience and judgment only. By not relying on the standard means of interpretation, this practice compromises the instrument's reliability and validity.

In addition to the MMPI, another example of an instrument used to assess an important aspect of personality functioning is the Revised Psychopathy Checklist (PCL-R). A constellation of antisocial behaviours involving aggressiveness, unreliability, irresponsibility, and a failure to learn from experience are sometimes referred to as psychopathy (see Chapter 11). The PCL-R was developed by forensic psychologist Robert Hare and his colleagues at the University of British Columbia (Hare, 1991) to measure psychopathy directly. Since psychopaths are cunning and manipulative pathological liars (Hare, 1991), it is difficult to use self-report measures to assess psychopathy. This is because a psychopath would likely lie and deny the existence of characteristics that would place him or her in a bad light! Hare developed the PCL-R as an instrument to assess the characteristics of psychopathy using interviews with the client along with material from institutional files (e.g., records from correctional institutions) or significant others. The PCL-R consists of a checklist of 20 characteristics like pathological lying and superficial charm; this instrument is discussed in more detail in Chapter 11 on the personality disorders.

## Intelligence Testing

"She must be very smart. I hear her IQ is 180!" What is "IQ"? What is "intelligence"? And how are they important in psychopathology? As many of you know from your introductory psychology course, intelligence tests were developed for one specific purpose: to predict who would do well in school. In 1904, Alfred Binet and Théodore Simon were commissioned by the French government to develop a test that would identify "slow learners" who would benefit from remedial help. The two psychologists identified a series of tasks that presumably measured the skills children need to succeed in school, including tasks of attention, perception, memory, reasoning, and verbal comprehension. Binet and Simon gave their original series

## TABLE 3.1 Sample MMPI-2 Content Scales

| Scale | Description of Content and Correlates |
|---|---|
| ANX (Anxiety) | General symptoms of anxiety and tension, sleep and concentration problems, somatic correlates of anxiety, excessive worrying, difficulty making decisions, and willingness to admit to these problems. |
| FRS (Fears) | Many specific fears and phobias: animals, high places, insects, blood, fire, storms, water, the dark, being indoors, dirt, and so on. |
| OBS (Obsessiveness) | Excessive rumination, difficulty making decisions, compulsive behaviours, rigidity, feelings of being overwhelmed. |
| DEP (Depression) | Depressive thoughts, anhedonia, feelings of hopelessness and uncertainty, possible suicidal thoughts. |
| HEA (Health Concerns) | Many physical symptoms across several body systems: gastrointestinal, neurological, sensory, cardiovascular, dermatological, and respiratory. Reports of pain and general worries about health. |
| BIZ (Bizarre Mentation) | Psychotic thought processes; auditory, visual, or olfactory hallucinations; paranoid ideation; delusions. |
| ANG (Anger) | Anger-control problems, irritability, impatience, loss of control, past or potential abusiveness. |
| CYN (Cynicism) | Misanthropic beliefs, negative expectations about the motives of others, generalized distrust. |
| ASP (Antisocial Practices) | Cynical attitudes, problem behaviours, trouble with the law, stealing, belief in getting around rules and laws for personal gain. |

of tasks to a large number of children; they then eliminated those that did not separate the slow learners from the children who did well in school. After several revisions and sample administrations, they had a test that was relatively easy to administer and that did what it was designed to do—predict academic success. In 1916, Lewis Terman translated a revised version of this test for use in North America; it became known as the *Stanford-Binet*.

The test provided a score known as an **intelligence quotient,** or IQ. Initially, IQ scores were calculated by using the child's *mental age*. For example, a child who passed all the questions on the 7-year-old level and none of the questions on the 8-year-old level received a mental age of 7. This mental age was then divided by the child's *chronological age* and multiplied by 100 to get the IQ score. However, there were some problems with using this type of formula for calculating an IQ score (Bjorklund, 1989). Current tests use what is called a *deviation IQ*. A person's score is compared only with the scores of others of the same age. The IQ score, then, is really an estimate of how much a child's performance in school will deviate from the average performance of others of the same age.

In addition to the revised version of the Stanford-Binet (Caruso, 2001), there is another widely used set of intelligence tests, developed by psychologist David Wechsler. The Wechsler tests contain *verbal scales* (which measure vocabulary, knowledge of facts, short-term memory, and verbal reasoning skills) and *performance scales* (which assess psychomotor abilities, nonverbal reasoning, and ability to learn new relationships; Tulsky, Zhu, & Prifitera, 2000). Some researchers have raised concerns about the "portability" of these intelligence tests to people from other countries and cultures, since these tests were developed and standardized largely with people from the majority culture in the United States. For example, several studies have documented lower than average scores on the verbal scales of the first two versions of the Wechsler Intelligence Scale for Children (WISC) in Canadian First Nations children (e.g., King, 1967; St. John, Krichev, & Bauman, 1976; Seyfort, Spreen, & Lahmer, 1980). Moreover, the large majority of a sample of Canadian Inuit children scored in the mentally retarded range when their scores on the second version of the WISC were compared with the usual norms (Wilgosh, Mulcahy, & Watters, 1986). These data suggest that children from these groups may have some difficulty understanding many of the test items (Wilgosh et al.,

---

**intelligence quotient (IQ)**   Score on an intelligence test estimating a person's deviation from average test performance.

This child is concentrating on a standard psychological assessment test.

1986). The findings caution against the indiscriminate use of these tests with cultural groups outside those on whom the test was originally normed.

One of the biggest mistakes non-psychologists (and a distressing number of psychologists) make is to confuse IQ with intelligence. An IQ is a score on one of the intelligence tests we just described. An IQ score significantly higher than average means the person has a significantly greater than average chance of doing well in our educational system. By contrast, a score significantly lower than average suggests the person will probably not do well in school. Does a lower-than-average IQ score mean a person is not intelligent? Not necessarily. First, there are numerous reasons for a low score. If the IQ test is administered in English and that is not the person's native language, the results will be affected.

Perhaps more important, however, is the lack of general agreement about what constitutes intelligence (Weinberg, 1989). Remember that the IQ tests measure abilities such as attention, perception, memory, reasoning, and verbal comprehension. But do these skills represent the totality of what we consider intelligence? Some recent theorists believe that what we think of as intelligence involves much more, including the ability to adapt to the environment, the ability to generate new ideas, and the ability to process information efficiently (Sternberg, 1988). We will discuss disorders that involve cognitive impairment, such as delirium and mental retardation, and IQ tests are typically used in assessing these disorders. Keep in mind, however, that we will be discussing IQ and not necessarily intelligence. In general, however, IQ tests tend to be reliable, and to the extent that they predict academic success, they are valid assessment tools.

## Neuropsychological Testing

Sophisticated tests have been developed that can pinpoint the location of brain dysfunction (Goldstein, 2000). Fortunately, these techniques are generally available and relatively inexpensive. **Neuropsychological testing** measures abilities in areas such as receptive and expressive language, attention and concentration, memory, motor skills, perceptual abilities, and learning and abstraction in such a way that the clinician can make educated guesses about the person's performance and the possible existence of brain impairment. In other words, this method of testing assesses brain dysfunction by observing its effects on the person's ability to perform certain tasks. Although you do not see damage, you can see its effects.

A fairly simple neuropsychological test often used with children is the *Bender Visual-Motor Gestalt Test* (Canter, 1996). A child is given a series of cards on which are drawn various lines and shapes. The task is for the child to copy what is drawn on the card. The errors on the test are compared with test results of other children of the same age; if the number of errors exceeds a certain amount, then brain dysfunction is suspected. This test is less sophisticated than other neuropsychological tests because the nature or location of the problem cannot be determined with this test. It still can be useful for psychologists, however, because it provides a simple screening instrument that is easy to administer and can detect possible problems. Two of the most popular advanced tests of organic damage that allow more precise determinations of the location of the problem are the *Luria-Nebraska Neuropsychological Battery* (Golden, Hammeke, & Purisch, 1980) and the *Halstead-Reitan Neuropsychological Battery* (Reitan & Davison, 1974). These offer an elaborate battery of tests to assess a variety of skills. For example, the Halstead-Reitan Neuropsychological Battery includes the *Rhythm Test* (which asks the person to compare rhythmic beats testing sound recognition, attention, and concentration), the *Strength of Grip Test* (which compares the grip of the right and left hands), and the *Tactile Performance Test* (which requires the test taker to place wooden blocks in a form board while blindfolded, testing learning and memory skills; Macciocchi & Barth, 1996).

Research on the validity of neuropsychological tests suggests they may be useful for detecting organic damage and cognitive disorders (see Chapter 13). For example, one study by researchers at the University of Toronto found that a brief neuropsychological test battery was 94% correct in differentiating people with dementia from normal controls and about 74% correct in differentiating people with dementia of the Alzheimer's type from people with other types of dementia (Tierney, Snow, Szalai, Fisher, & Zorzitto, 1996). However, these types of studies raise the issue of **false positives** and **false negatives** (Boll, 1985). For any assessment strategy, there will be times when the test shows a problem when none exists (false positives) and times when no problem is found when some difficulty is present (false negatives). The possibility of false results is particularly troublesome for tests of brain dysfunction; a clinician who fails to find damage that exists might miss an important medical problem that

---

**neuropsychological testing**  Assessment of brain and nervous system functioning by testing an individual's performance on behavioural tasks.

**false positive**  Assessment error in which pathology is reported (i.e., test results are positive) when none is actually present.

**false negative**  Assessment error in which no pathology is noted (i.e., test results are negative) when it is actually present.

needs to be treated. Fortunately, neuropsychological tests are used primarily as screening devices and are routinely paired with other assessments to improve the likelihood that real problems will be found. They do well with regard to measures of reliability and validity, and they are often informed by recent developments in cognitive neuroscience (Stuss & Levine, 2002). On the downside, they can require hours to administer and are therefore not used routinely unless brain damage is suspected.

## Neuroimaging: Pictures of the Brain

For more than a century we have known that many of the things that we do, think, and remember are partially controlled by specific areas of the brain. In recent years we have developed the ability to look inside the brain and take increasingly accurate pictures of its structure and function, using a technique called **neuroimaging** (Adams, Kutcher, Antoniw, & Bird, 1996; Andreasen & Swayze, 1993; Baxter, Guze, & Reynolds, 1993). Neuroimaging can be divided into two categories. One category includes procedures that examine the *structure* of the brain, such as the size of various parts and whether there is any damage. In the second category are procedures that examine the actual *functioning* of the brain by mapping blood flow and other metabolic activity.

### Images of Brain Structure

The first technique, developed in the early 1970s, uses multiple X-ray exposures of the brain from different angles; that is, X-rays are passed directly through the head. As with any X-rays, these are partially blocked or attenuated more by bone and less by brain tissue. The degree of attenuation is picked up by detectors in

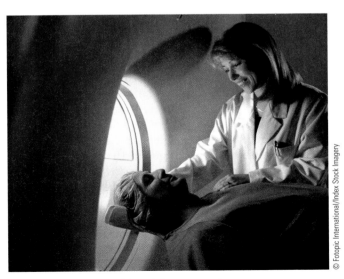

The patient is being positioned for a magnetic resonance imaging scan.

© Fotopic International/Index Stock Imagery

the opposite side of the head. A computer then reconstructs pictures of various slices of the brain. This procedure, which takes about 15 minutes, is called *computerized axial tomography* (*CAT*), *CAT scan,* or *CT scan*. It is relatively noninvasive and has proved useful in identifying and locating abnormalities in the structure or shape of the brain. It is particularly useful in locating brain tumours, injuries, and other structural and anatomical abnormalities. One difficulty, however, is that these scans, like all X-rays, involve repeated radiation, which poses some risk of cell damage (Baxter et al., 1993).

More recently, a procedure has been developed that gives greater resolution (specificity and accuracy) than a CT scan without the inherent risks of X-rays. This scanning technique is called nuclear *magnetic resonance imaging* (*MRI*). The patient's head is placed in a high-strength magnetic field through which radio frequency signals are transmitted. These signals "excite" the brain tissue, altering the protons in the hydrogen atoms. The alteration is measured, along with the time it takes the protons to "relax" or return to normal. Where there are lesions (or damage), the signal is lighter or darker (Andreasen & Swayze, 1993). Technology now exists that allows the computer to view the brain in layers, which enables precise examination of the structure. Although MRI is more expensive than a CT scan and originally took as long as 45 minutes, this is changing as technology improves. Newer versions of MRI procedures take as little as 10 minutes; the time and cost are decreasing yearly. Another disadvantage of MRI at present is that someone undergoing the procedure is totally enclosed inside a narrow tube with a magnetic coil surrounding the head. People who are somewhat claustrophobic often cannot tolerate an MRI, as demonstrated in a recent study by a team at the University of British Columbia (McIsaac, Thordarson, Shafran, Rachman, & Poole, 1998).

Although neuroimaging procedures are useful for identifying damage to the brain, only recently have they been used to determine structural or anatomical abnormalities that might be associated with various psychological disorders. We review some tantalizing preliminary studies in subsequent chapters on specific disorders.

### Images of Brain Functioning

Several widely used procedures are capable of measuring the actual functioning of the brain, as opposed to its structure. The first is called *positron emission tomography* (*PET*). Subjects undergoing a

**neuroimaging** Sophisticated computer-aided procedures that allow relatively non-invasive examination of nervous system structure and function.

PET scan are injected with a tracer substance attached to radioactive isotopes, groups of atoms that react distinctively. This substance interacts with blood, oxygen, or glucose. When parts of the brain become active, blood, oxygen, or glucose rushes to these areas of the brain, creating "hot spots" picked up by detectors that identify the location of the isotopes. Thus, we can learn what parts of the brain are working and what parts are not. To obtain clear images, the individual undergoing the procedure must remain motionless for 40 seconds or more. These images can be superimposed on MRI images to show the precise location of the active areas. The PET scans are also useful in supplementing MRI and CT scans in localizing the sites of trauma caused by head injury or stroke and in localizing brain tumours.

More important, PET scans are used increasingly to look at varying patterns of metabolism that might be associated with different disorders. Recent PET scans have demonstrated that many patients with early Alzheimer's-type dementia (see Chapter 13) show reduced glucose metabolism in the parietal lobes. Other intriguing findings have been reported for obsessive-compulsive disorder and bipolar disorder (see Chapters 4 and 6). For example, excess activity in the dopamine neurotransmitter system has been implicated in manic states among patients with bipolar mood disorder (see Chapter 6). Researchers at the University of British Columbia Mood Disorders Clinical Research Unit recently used PET to try to identify the brain regions involved in dopamine overactivity among a group of patients with bipolar disorder who were tested during the manic state (Yatham et al., 2002). In this same study, the researchers also used PET to examine the effects of drug therapy on dopamine activity in bipolar disorder by testing patients before and after drug treatment. Despite the exciting uses of PET for increasing understanding of many forms of abnormal behaviour,

PET scanning is very expensive: The cost is about $6 million to set up a PET facility and $500 000 a year to run it. Therefore, these facilities are available only in large medical centres.

A second procedure used to assess brain functioning is called *single photon emission computed tomography* (*SPECT*). It works much like PET, although a different tracer substance is used and it is somewhat less accurate. It is also less expensive, however, and requires far less sophisticated equipment to pick up the signals. Therefore, it is used more frequently. The most exciting advances involve MRI procedures that have been developed to work much more quickly than the regular MRI (Barinaga, 1997; Cohen, Rosen, & Brady, 1992). Using sophisticated computer technology, these procedures take only milliseconds and, therefore, can take pictures of the brain at work, recording its changes from one second to the next (e.g., Stern et al., 2000). Because these procedures measure the functioning of the brain, they are called functional MRI, or fMRI. For example, findings from a recent fMRI study by Robert Hare and his colleagues (Kiehl et al., 2001) suggest that the emotional deficits observed in psychopaths (see Chapter 11) may be linked to a weakened input from limbic structures—the part of the brain responsible for regulating our emotional experiences (see Chapter 2). Today, fMRI has largely replaced PET scans in the leading brain-imaging centres because it allows researchers to see the immediate response of the brain to a brief event, such as seeing a new face.

Brain imagery procedures hold enormous potential for illuminating the contribution of neurobiological factors to psychological disorders. For example, in Chapter 4 on anxiety disorders, you will learn what fMRI procedures reveal about brain functioning in individuals such as Frank and Brian, who have obsessive-compulsive disorder.

## *Psychophysiological Assessment*

Yet another method for assessing brain structure and function specifically, and nervous system activity more generally, is called **psychophysiological assessment.** As the term implies, *psychophysiology* refers to measurable changes in the nervous system that reflect emotional or psychological events. The measurements may be taken either directly from the brain or peripherally, from other parts of the body.

Frank feared that he might have seizures. If we had any reason to suspect he might really have periods of memory loss or exhibit bizarre, trance-like

UCI BRAIN IMAGING CENTER
PCP　SCHIZOPHRENIC　CONTROL

0.0　16.3　32.6　0.0　16.7　33.4　0.0　16.4　32.8
pmol/100gm/min　pmol/100gm/min　pmol/100gm/min

Dr. Monty Buchsbaum/Peter Arnold, Inc.

These PET scans compare activity in the brain of a drug abuser (left), in a person with schizophrenia (centre), and in a normal brain (right).

**psychophysiological assessment** Measurement of changes in the nervous system reflecting psychological or emotional events such as anxiety, stress, and sexual arousal.

(a)

(b)

(c)

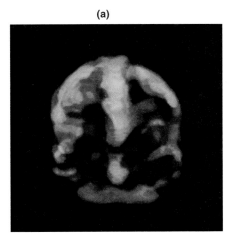
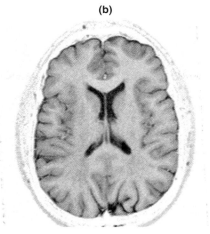
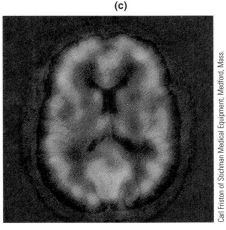

Carl Friston of Stichman Medical Equipment, Medford, Mass.

A horizontal brain section (a) in a SPECT image clearly reveals parietal lobe damage in a person with schizophrenia. Images (b) and (c) are MRI photographs. SPECT images show metabolic activity and thus indicate the relationship between brain and behaviour. The higher resolution MRI images show tissue variations.

behaviour, if only for a short period, it would be important for him to have an **electroencephalogram (EEG).** Measuring electrical activity in the head related to the firing of a specific group of neurons reveals brain wave activity, the low-voltage electrical current ongoing in the brain, usually from the cortex. A person's brain waves can be assessed in both waking and sleeping states. In an EEG, electrodes are placed directly on various places on the scalp to record the different low-voltage currents.

We have learned much about EEG patterns in the past decades (Fein & Callaway, 1993). Usually we measure ongoing electrical activity in the brain. When brief periods of EEG patterns are recorded in response to specific events, such as hearing a psychologically meaningful stimulus, the response is called an *event-related potential* or *evoked potential.* We have learned that EEG patterns are often affected by psychological or emotional factors and can be an index of these reactions, or a psychophysiological measure. In a normal, healthy, relaxed adult, waking activities are characterized by a very regular pattern of changes in voltage termed *alpha waves.*

Many types of stress-reduction treatments attempt to *increase* the frequency of the alpha waves, often by relaxing the patients in some way. The alpha wave pattern is associated with relaxation and calmness. During sleep, we pass through several different stages of brain activity, at least partially identified by EEG patterns. During the deepest, most relaxed stage, typically occurring 1 to 2 hours after a person falls asleep, EEG recordings show a pattern of *delta waves.* These brain waves are slower and more irregular than the alpha waves, which is normal for this stage of sleep. We see in Chapter 4 that panic attacks occurring while a person is sound asleep come almost exclusively during the delta wave stage. If

frequent delta wave activity occurred during the waking state, it might indicate dysfunction of localized areas of the brain.

Extremely rapid and irregular spikes on the EEG recordings of someone who is awake may reflect significant seizure disorders, depending on the pattern. The EEG recording is one of the primary diagnostic tools for identifying seizure disorders. Psychophysiological assessment of other bodily responses may also play a role in assessment. These responses include heart rate, respiration, and *electrodermal* activity, formerly referred to as *galvanic skin response,* which is a measure of sweat gland activity controlled by the peripheral nervous system. Remember from Chapter 2 that the peripheral nervous system and, in particular, the sympathetic division of the autonomic nervous system are responsive to stress and emotional arousal.

Assessing psychophysiological *responding* to emotional stimuli is important in many disorders, one being posttraumatic stress disorder. Stimuli such as sights and sounds associated with the trauma evoke strong psychophysiological responding, even if the patient is not fully aware that this is happening.

Psychophysiological assessment is also used with many sexual dysfunctions and disorders. For example, sexual arousal can be assessed through direct measurement of penile circumference in males or vaginal blood flow in females in response to erotic stimuli, usually movies or slides (see Chapter 9). Sometimes the individual might be unaware of specific patterns of sexual arousal.

**electroencephalogram (EEG)** Measure of electrical activity patterns in the brain, taken through electrodes placed on the scalp.

Physiological measures are also important in the assessment and treatment of conditions such as headaches and hypertension (Andrasik, 2000; E. B. Blanchard, 1992); they form the basis for the treatment we call *biofeedback*. In biofeedback, as we see in Chapter 7, levels of physiological responding, such as blood pressure readings, are fed back to the patient (provided on a continuous basis) by meters or gauges so that the patient can try to regulate these responses.

Nevertheless, physiological assessment is not without its limitations, because it requires a great deal of skill and some technical expertise. Even when administered properly, the measures sometimes produce inconsistent results because of procedural or technical difficulties or the nature of the response. For this reason, only clinicians specializing in certain disorders where these measures are particularly important are likely to make extensive use of psychophysiological recording equipment, although more straightforward applications such as monitoring heart rate during relaxation exercises are more common. More sophisticated psychophysiological assessment is most often used in theoretical investigations of the nature of certain psychological disorders, particularly emotional disorders (Barlow, 2002; Heller, Nitschke, & Miller, 1998).

## Concept Check 3.1

**Part A** The mental status exam includes five categories: appearance and behaviour, thought processes, mood and affect, intellectual functioning, and sensorium. Identify which part of the mental status exam is being performed in the following situations.

1. Dr. Swan listened carefully to Joyce's speech pattern, noting its speed, content, and continuity. She noticed no looseness of association but did hear indications of delusional thoughts and visual hallucinations. _____

2. Andrew arrived at the clinic accompanied by police, who had found him dressed only in shorts although the temperature was –5°C. He was reported to the police by someone who saw him walking slowly down the street, making strange faces, and talking to himself. _____

3. When Lisa was brought to Dr. Miller's office, he asked if she knew the date and time, her identity, and where she was. _____

4. Dr. Jones viewed Tim's laughter after discussing his near-fatal incident as inappropriate and noted that Tim appeared to be elated. _____

5. Mark's vocabulary and memory seemed adequate, leading Dr. Adams to estimate that Mark was of average intelligence. _____

**Part B** Check your understanding of reliability and validity by marking both R (reliable) or NR (not reliable) and V (valid) or NV (not valid) for each test.

6. EEG to show electrical activity in the brain of people who have seizures _____
7. Rorschach inkblots _____
8. Structured interviews with definite answers _____

# Diagnosing Psychological Disorders

■ *Explain the nature and purposes of psychiatric diagnosis and how the DSM is used to help therapists and counsellors make an accurate psychiatric diagnosis.*

Thus far, we have looked at Frank's and Brian's functioning on an individual basis; that is, we have closely observed their behaviour, cognitive processes, and mood, and we have conducted semistructured interviewing, behavioural assessment, and psychological tests. These operations tell us what is unique about Frank and about Brian, not what they may have in common with other individuals or even with each other.

Learning how Frank or Brian may resemble other people in terms of the problems each presents is important for several reasons. If, in the past, people came in with similar problems or psychological profiles, we can go back and find a lot of information from their cases that might be applicable to Frank's case or to Brian's. We can see how the problems began for those other individuals, what factors seemed influential, and how long the problem or disorder lasted. Did the problem in the other cases just go away on its own? If not, what kept it going? Did it need treatment? Most important, what treatments seemed to relieve the problem for those other individuals? These general questions are useful because they evoke a wealth of clinical and research information that enables the investigator to make certain inferences about what will happen next and what treatments may work. In other words, the clinician can establish a *prognosis,* a term we discussed in Chapter 1 that refers to the likely future course of a disorder under certain conditions.

Because classification is such an integral part of science and, indeed, of our human experience, we describe its various aspects individually (Millon, 1991). The term **classification** is broad, referring simply to any effort to construct groups or categories and to assign objects or people to these categories on the basis of their shared attributes or relations—a nomothetic strategy. If the classification is in a scientific context, it is most often called **taxonomy,** which is the classification of entities for scientific purposes, such as insects, rocks, or if the subject is psychology, behaviours. If you apply a taxonomic system to psychological or medical phenomena or other clinical areas, you use the word **nosology.** The term **nomenclature** describes the names or labels of the disorders that make up the nosology (e.g., anxiety or mood disorders). Most mental health professionals use the classification system contained in the *Diagnostic and Statistical Manual of Mental Disorders,* Fourth Edition, text revision (DSM-IV-TR). This is the official system in North America and is used widely throughout the world. However, it is not the only recognized system. Another system used widely in Europe is the *International Classification of Diseases and Health Related Problems*, Tenth Edition (ICD-10) published by the World Health Organization (WHO, 1992). A clinician refers to the DSM-IV-TR or the ICD-10 to identify a specific psychological disorder in the process of making a diagnosis.

During the past several years we have seen enormous changes in how we think about classifying psychopathology. Because these developments affect so much of what we do, we examine carefully the processes of classification and diagnosis as they are used in psychopathology. We look first at different approaches, examine the concepts of reliability and validity as they pertain to diagnosis, and then discuss our current system of classification in North America, the DSM-IV-TR.

## Classification Issues

Classification is at the heart of any science, and much of what we have said about it is common sense. If we could not order and label objects or experiences, scientists could not communicate with each other and our knowledge would not advance. Everyone would have to develop a personal system, which, of course, would mean nothing to anyone else. In your biology or geology courses, when you study insects or rocks, classification is fundamental. Knowing how one species of insects differs from another allows us to study its functioning and origins.

When we are dealing with human behaviour or human behavioural disorders, however, the subject of classification becomes controversial. Some people have questioned whether it is proper or ethical to classify human behaviour. Even among those who recognize the necessity of classification, major controversies have arisen in several areas. Within psychopathology, for example, definitions of "normal" and "abnormal" are questioned, and so is the assumption that a behaviour or cognition is part of one disorder and not another. Some would prefer to talk about behaviour and feelings on a continuum from happy to sad or fearful to non-fearful rather than to create such categories as mania, depression, and phobia. For better or worse, classifying behaviour and people is something we all do. Few of us talk about our own emotions or those of our friends by using a number on a scale (where 0 is totally unhappy and 100 is totally happy), although this approach might be more accurate. ("How do you feel about that?" "About 65.") Rather, we talk about being happy, sad, angry, depressed, fearful, and so on.

### Categorical and Dimensional Approaches

The **classical** (or pure) **categorical approach** to classification originates in the work of Emil Kraepelin (1856–1926) and the biological tradition in the study of psychopathology. Here we assume that every diagnosis has a clear underlying

**classification** Assignment of objects or people to categories on the basis of shared characteristics.

**taxonomy** System of naming and classification (e.g., of specimens) in science.

**nosology** Classification and naming system for medical and psychological phenomena.

**nomenclature** In a naming system or nosology, the actual labels or names that are applied. In psychopathology, these include mood disorders or eating disorders.

**classical categorical approach** Classification method founded on the assumption of clear-cut differences among disorders, each with a different known cause.

pathophysiological cause, such as a bacterial infection or a malfunctioning endocrine system, and that each disorder is unique. When diagnoses are thought of in this way, the causes could be psychological or cultural, instead of pathophysiological, but there is still only one set of causative factors per disorder, which does not overlap with other disorders. Because each disorder is fundamentally different from every other, we need only one set of defining criteria, which everybody in the category has to meet. If the criteria for a major depressive episode are the presence of depressed mood, significant weight loss when not dieting, diminished ability to think or concentrate, and 7 additional specific symptoms, then, to be diagnosed with depression, an individual would have to meet all 10 criteria. In that case, according to the classical categorical approach, the clinician would know the cause of the disorder.

Classical categorical approaches are quite useful in medicine. It is extremely important for a physician to make accurate diagnoses. If a patient has a fever accompanied by stomach pain, the doctor must determine quickly if the cause is stomach flu or an infected appendix. This is not always easy, but physicians are trained to examine the signs and symptoms closely, and they usually reach the correct conclusion. To understand the cause of symptoms (infected appendix) is to know what treatment will be effective (surgery). But if someone is depressed or anxious, is there a similar type of underlying cause? As we saw in Chapter 2, probably not. Most psychopathologists believe psychological and social factors interact with biological factors to produce a disorder. Therefore, despite the beliefs of Kraepelin and other early biological investigators, the mental health field has not adopted a classical categorical model of psychopathology.

A second strategy is a **dimensional approach,** in which we note the variety of cognitions, moods, and behaviours with which the patient presents and quantify them on a scale. For example, on a scale of 1 to 10, a patient might be rated as severely anxious (10), moderately depressed (5), and mildly manic (2) to create a profile of emotional functioning (10, 5, 2). Although dimensional approaches have been applied to psychopathology, they have been relatively unsatisfactory until now (First et al., 2002; Rounsaville et al., 2002). Most theorists have not been able to agree on how many dimensions are required: Some say 1 dimension is enough; others have identified as many as 33 (Millon, 1991).

A third strategy for organizing and classifying behavioural disorders has found increasing support in recent years as an alternative to classical categorical or dimensional approaches. It is a categorical approach but with the twist that it basically combines some of the features of each of the former approaches. Called a **prototypical approach,** this alternative identifies certain essential characteristics of an entity so you (and others) can classify it, but it also allows certain nonessential variations that do not necessarily change the classification. For example, if someone were to ask you to describe a dog, you could easily give a general description (the essential, categorical characteristics), but you might not exactly describe a specific dog. Dogs come in different colours, sizes, and even species (the nonessential, dimensional variations), but they all share certain doggish characteristics that allow you to classify them separately from cats. Thus, requiring a certain number of prototypical criteria and only some of an additional number of criteria is adequate. Of course, this system is not perfect because there is a greater blurring at the boundaries of categories, and some symptoms apply to more than one disorder. However, it has the advantage of fitting best with the current state of our knowledge of psychopathology, and it is relatively user friendly.

When this approach is used in classifying a psychological disorder, many of the different possible features or properties of the disorder are listed, and any candidate must meet enough (but not all) of them to fall into that category. Consider the DSM-IV-TR criteria defining a major depressive episode.

---

**dimensional approach**  Method of categorizing characteristics on a continuum rather than on a binary, either-or, or all-or-none basis.

**prototypical approach**  System for categorizing disorders using essential, defining characteristics and a range of variation on other characteristics.

Despite their wide physical variation, all dogs belong to the same class of animals.

Criteria for Major Depressive Episode   Five (or more) of the following symptoms have been present during the same 2-week period and represent a change from previous functioning; at least one of the symptoms is either (1) depressed mood or (2) loss of interest or pleasure.

*Note:* Symptoms that are clearly due to a general medical condition or mood-incongruent delusions or hallucinations should not be included.

1. Depressed mood most of the day
2. Markedly diminished interest or pleasure in all, or almost all, activities
3. Significant weight loss (when not dieting) or weight gain
4. Insomnia or hypersomnia nearly every day
5. Psychomotor agitation or retardation
6. Fatigue or loss of energy nearly every day
7. Feelings of worthlessness or excessive or inappropriate guilt
8. Diminished ability to think or concentrate, or indecisiveness
9. Recurrent thoughts of death

As you can see, the criteria include many non-essential symptoms, but if you have either depressed mood or marked loss of interest or pleasure in most activities and at least four of the remaining eight symptoms, you come close enough to the prototype to meet the criteria for a major depressive episode. One person might have depressed mood, significant weight loss, insomnia, psychomotor agitation, and loss of energy, whereas another person who also meets the criteria for major depressive episode might have markedly diminished interest or pleasure in activities, fatigue, feelings of worthlessness, difficulty thinking or concentrating, and suicidal ideation. Although both have the requisite five symptoms that bring them close to the prototype, they look different because they share only one symptom. This is a good example of a prototypical category. The DSM-IV-TR is based on this approach.

Diagnosing forms of mental disorders is one very important activity engaged in by clinical psychologists and some other mental health professionals. Errors in diagnosis can lead to serious consequences such as inappropriate treatments being used with a given client. In part, accurate diagnoses are dependent on the diagnostic system being used (e.g., DSM-IV-TR, ICD-10). But diagnostic accuracy is also dependent on the skills of the individual making the diagnosis. Therefore, only trained individuals are permitted to diagnose mental disorders, and the activity of diagnosis is often regulated to protect the public. For example, in Ontario, diagnosis is one activity that falls under the Regulated Health Professions Act (October 1999) that is relevant to all psychologists.

## Reliability

Any system of classification should describe specific subgroups of symptoms that are clearly evident and can be readily identified by experienced clinicians. If two clinicians interview the patient at separate times on the same day (and assuming the patient's condition does not change during the day), the two clinicians should see, and perhaps measure, the same set of behaviours and emotions. The psychological disorder can thus be identified reliably. Obviously, if the disorder is not readily apparent to both clinicians, the resulting diagnoses might represent bias. For example, someone's clothes might provoke some comment. One of your friends might later say, "She looked kind of sloppy tonight." Another might comment, "No, that's just a real funky look; she's right in style." Perhaps a third friend would say, "Actually, I thought she was dressed kind of neatly." You might wonder if they had all seen the same person. In any case, there would be no *reliability* to their observations. Getting your friends to agree about someone's appearance would require a careful set of definitions that you all accept.

One of the most unreliable categories in current classification is the area of personality disorders—chronic, trait-like sets of inappropriate behaviours and emotional reactions that characterize a person's way of interacting with the world. Although great progress has been made, particularly with certain personality disorders, determining the presence or absence of this type of disorder during one interview is still difficult. Morey and Ochoa (1989) asked 291 mental health professionals to describe an individual with a personality disorder they had recently seen, along with their diagnoses. Morey and Ochoa also collected from these clinicians detailed information on the actual signs and symptoms present in these patients. In this way, they were able to determine whether the actual diagnosis made by the clinicians matched the objective criteria for the diagnosis as determined by the symptoms. In other words, was the clinician's diagnosis accurate, based on the presence of symptoms that actually define the diagnosis?

Morey and Ochoa found substantial bias in making diagnoses. For example, patients who were white, female, or poor were diagnosed with borderline personality disorder more often than the criteria indicated. Although bias among clinicians is always a potential problem, the more reliable the nosology, or system of classification, the less likely it is to creep in during diagnosis.

## Validity

In addition to being reliable, a system of nosology must be valid. Earlier we described *validity* as whether something measures what it is designed to measure.

There are several different types of diagnostic validity. For one, the system should have *construct validity*. This means that the signs and symptoms chosen as criteria for the presence of the diagnostic category are consistently associated or hang together, and what they identify differs from other categories. Someone meeting the criteria for depression should be discriminable from someone meeting the criteria for social phobia. This discriminability might be evident not only in the presenting symptoms but also in the course of the disorder and possibly in the choice of treatment. It may also predict familial aggregation, the extent to which the disorder would be found among the patient's relatives (Blashfield & Livesley, 1991; Cloninger, 1989; Kupfer, First, & Regier, 2002).

In addition, a valid diagnosis tells the clinician what is likely to happen with the prototypical patient; it may predict the course of the disorder and the likely effect of one treatment or another. This type of validity is often referred to as *predictive validity* and sometimes *criterion validity*, when the outcome is the criterion by which we judge the usefulness of the category. Finally, there is *content validity*, which simply means that if you create criteria for a diagnosis of, say, social phobia, it should reflect the way most experts in the field think of social phobia as opposed to, say, depression. In other words, you need to get the label right.

## DSM-IV

In the late 1980s, clinicians and researchers realized the need for a consistent, worldwide system of nosology. The ICD-10 was published in 1993, and the United States was required by treaty obligations to use the ICD-10 codes in all matters related to health. To make the ICD-10 and DSM as compatible as possible, work proceeded on both the ICD-10 and the DSM-IV simultaneously. Concerted efforts were made to share research data and other information to create an empirically based worldwide system of nosology for psychological disorders. The DSM-IV task force decided to rely as little as possible on a consensus of experts. Any changes in the diagnostic system were to be based on sound scientific data. Work groups consisting of expert advisers in particular areas like eating disorders, anxiety disorders, and mood disorders, were created. These work groups attempted to review the voluminous literature in all areas pertaining to the diagnostic system (cf. Widiger et al., 1996; Widiger et al., 1998) and to identify large sets of data that might have been collected for other reasons but that, with reanalysis, would be useful to DSM-IV. Many Canadian researchers were part of these work groups, including Keith Dobson and Richard Swinson (anxiety disorders), Sid Kennedy and Janet Polivy (eating disorders), and Robert Hare and Paul Links (personality disorders), to name but a few. Finally, 12 different independent studies or field trials examined the reliability and validity of alternative sets of definitions or criteria and, in some cases, the possibility of creating a new diagnosis (see Widiger et al., 1998).

Perhaps the most substantial change in DSM-IV was that the distinction between organically based disorders and psychologically based disorders that was present in previous editions was eliminated. As we saw in Chapter 2, we now know that even disorders associated with known brain pathology are substantially affected by psychological and social influences. Similarly, disorders previously described as psychological in origin have biological components and, most likely, identifiable brain circuits.

A multiaxial system—reflecting the dimensional approach—had been introduced with DSM-III in 1980. A specific disorder, such as schizophrenia or a mood disorder, was represented only on the first axis. More enduring (chronic) disorders of personality were listed on Axis II. Axis III comprised physical disorders and conditions. On Axis IV the clinician rated, in a dimensional fashion, the amount of psychosocial stress the person reported, and the current level of adaptive functioning was given on Axis V.

The multiaxial system remains in DSM-IV, with some changes in the five axes. Specifically, only personality disorders and mental retardation are now coded on Axis II. Pervasive developmental disorders, learning disorders, motor skills disorders, and communication disorders, previously coded on Axis II, are now all coded on Axis I. Axis IV, which rated the patient's amount of psychosocial stress, was not useful and has been replaced. The new Axis IV is used for reporting psychosocial and environmental problems that might have an impact on the disorder. Axis V is essentially unchanged. In addition, optional axes have been included for rating dimensions of behaviour or functioning that may be important in some cases. There are axes for defence mechanisms or coping styles, social and occupational functioning, and relational functioning; a clinician might use them to describe the quality of relationships that provide the interpersonal context for the disorder. Finally, a number of new disorders were introduced in DSM-IV, and some disorders in DSM-III-R have been either deleted or subsumed into other DSM-IV categories.

### DSM-IV and Frank

In Frank's case, initial observations indicate an anxiety disorder on Axis I, specifically obsessive-compulsive disorder. However, he might also have long-standing personality traits that lead him systematically to avoid social contact. If so, there might be a diagnosis of schizoid personality disorder on Axis II. Unless Frank has an identifiable medical condition, there is nothing on Axis III. Job and marital difficulties would be coded on Axis IV, where we note psychosocial or environmental problems that are not part of the disorder but might make it worse. Frank's difficulties with work would be noted by checking "occupational problems" and specifying "threat of job loss"; for problems with the primary support group, marital difficulties would be noted. On Axis V, the clinician would rate the highest overall level of Frank's current functioning on a 0 to 100 scale (100 indicates superior functioning in a variety of situations). At present, Frank's score is 55, which indicates moderate interference with functioning at home and at work.

The multiaxial system organizes a range of important information that might be relevant to the likely course of the disorder and, perhaps, treatment. For example, two people, like the cases of Frank and Brian examined earlier, might both present with obsessive-compulsive disorder, which would be coded on Axis I. But Frank and Brian might look different on Axes II through V; such differences would greatly affect the clinician's recommendations for the two cases.

## Social and Cultural Considerations in DSM-IV

By emphasizing levels of stress in the environment, DSM-IV facilitates a more complete picture of the individual. Furthermore, DSM-IV corrects a previous omission by including a plan for integrating important social and cultural influences on diagnosis. The plan allows the disorder to be described from the perspective of the patient's personal experience and in terms of the primary social and cultural group, such as Chinese or First Nations. The following are suggestions for accomplishing these goals (Mezzich et al., 1993; Mezzich et al., 1999).

What is the primary cultural reference group of the patient? For recent immigrants to the country and other ethnic minorities, how involved are they with their "new" culture versus their old culture? Have they mastered the language of their "new" country (e.g., English or French in Canada) or is language a continuing problem?

Does the patient use terms and descriptions from his or her "old" country to describe the disorder? For example, as we will see in Chapter 4, *kayak-angst* in the Inuit culture is a type of anxiety disorder close to panic disorder with agoraphobia. Does the patient accept Western models of disease or disorder for which treatment is available in health-care systems, or does the patient also have an alternative health-care system in another culture (e.g., traditional herbal doctors in Chinese subcultures)?

What does it mean to have a disability? Which kinds of disabilities are acceptable in a given culture and which are not? For example, is it acceptable to be physically ill but not anxious or depressed? What are the typical family, social, and religious supports in the culture? Are they available to the patient? Does the clinician understand the first language of the patient and the cultural significance of the disorder?

These cultural considerations must not be overlooked in making diagnoses and planning treatment, and they are assumed throughout this book. We have a lot more work to do in this area to make our nosology truly culturally sensitive.

## Criticisms of DSM-IV

Because the collaboration among groups creating the ICD-10 and DSM-IV was largely successful, it is clear that DSM-IV (and the closely related ICD-10 mental disorder section) is the most advanced, scientifically based system of nosology ever developed. Nevertheless, we still cannot assume that the system

The DSM-IV diagnostic guidelines take cultural considerations into account.

is final, or even completely correct. Any nosological system should be considered a work in progress.

We still have "fuzzy" categories that blur at the edges, making diagnostic decisions difficult at times. As a consequence, individuals are often assigned more than one psychological disorder at the same time, sometimes as many as three or four. (Several disorders exist in a state of **comorbidity.**) How can we conclude anything definite about the course of a disorder, the response to treatment, or the likelihood of associated problems if we are dealing with combinations of disorders (Follette & Houts, 1996; Kupfer et al., 2002)? The answers to these difficult questions are hard to establish when only one disorder is present. In the future, people who require an assignment of three or four disorders may have an entirely new class in our nosological system. Resolution of these tough problems simply awaits the long, slow process of science.

Criticisms centre on two other aspects of DSM-IV and ICD-10. First, they strongly emphasize reliability, sometimes at the expense of validity. This is understandable, because reliability is so difficult to achieve unless you are willing to sacrifice validity. If the sole criterion for establishing depression were to hear the patient say at some point during an interview, "I feel depressed," one could theoretically achieve perfect reliability (unless the clinician didn't hear the client, which sometimes happens). But this achievement would be at the expense of validity because many people with differing psychological disorders, or none, occasionally say they are depressed. Thus, clinicians could agree that the statement occurred, but it would be of little use (Carson, 1991; Meehl, 1989). Second, as Carson (1996) points out, methods of constructing our nosology have a way of perpetuating definitions handed down to us from past decades, even if they might be fundamentally flawed. Carson (1991) makes a strong argument that it might be better to start fresh every once in a while and create a whole new system of disorders based on emerging scientific knowledge rather than simply fine-tune old definitions, but this is unlikely to happen.

In addition to the frightful complexity of categorizing psychopathology in particular and human behaviour in general, systems are subject to misuse, some of which can be dangerous and harmful. Diagnostic categories are just a convenient format for organizing observations that help professionals communicate, study, and plan. But if we reify a category, we literally make it a "thing," assuming it has a meaning that, in reality, does not exist. Categories may change with the advent of new knowledge, so none can be written in stone. If a case falls on the fuzzy borders between diagnostic categories, we should not expend all our energy attempting to force it into one category or another. It is a mistaken assumption that everything has to fit neatly somewhere.

## A Caution about Labelling

A related problem that occurs any time we categorize people is **labelling.** You may remember Kermit the Frog from *Sesame Street* sharing with us that "It's not easy being green." Something in human nature causes us to use a label, even one as superficial as skin colour, to characterize the totality of an individual ("He's green … he's different from me"). We see the same phenomenon among psychological disorders ("He's a schizo"). Furthermore, if the disorder

**comorbidity**   The presence of two or more disorders in an individual at the same time.

**labelling**   Applying a name to a phenomenon or a pattern of behaviour. The label may acquire negative connotations or be applied erroneously to the person rather than to his or her behaviours.

The kinds of disabilities accepted in a given culture are socially determined.

is associated with an impairment in cognitive or behavioural functioning, the label itself has negative connotations and becomes pejorative.

Once labelled, individuals with a disorder may identify with the negative connotations associated with the label. This affects their self-esteem. Attempts to document the detrimental effects of labelling have produced mixed results (Segal, 1978), but if you think of your own reactions to people with mental illness, you will probably recognize the tendency to generalize inappropriately from the label. We have to remember that terms in psychopathology do not describe people, but identify patterns of behaviour that may or may not occur in certain circumstances. Thus, whether the disorder is medical or psychological, we must resist the temptation to identify the person with the disorder: Note the different implications of "John is a diabetic" and "John is a person who has diabetes."

The current plan is that the work groups for DSM-V will be assembled around 2007, with the new criteria for DSM-V not appearing until approximately 2011 or later. This delay would give researchers the time to begin to answer some of the questions put forth in a research agenda for DSM-V (Kupfer et al., 2002).With this in mind, we can turn our attention to the current state of our knowledge about a variety of major psychological disorders. Beginning with Chapter 4, we attempt to predict the next major scientific breakthroughs affecting diagnostic criteria and definitions of disorders. But first we review the all-important area of research methods and strategies used to establish new knowledge of psychopathology.

# Conducting Research in Psychopathology

- *Describe the basic components of research in psychopathology.*
- *Explain the importance of ethical principles in the research process.*

Behavioural scientists explore human behaviour the same way other scientists study the path of a comet or the AIDS virus: They use the scientific method. As we've already seen, abnormal behaviour is a challenging subject because of the interaction of biological and psychological dimensions. Rarely are there any simple answers to such questions as "Why do some people have hallucinations?" or "How do you treat someone who is suicidal?"

In addition to the obvious complexity of human nature, another factor that makes an objective study of abnormal behaviour difficult is the inaccessibility of many important aspects of this phenomenon. We can't get inside the minds of people except indirectly. Fortunately, as University of Regina psychologist Gordon Asmundson and his colleagues describe in their clinical research textbook, some creative individuals have accepted this challenge and have developed many ingenious methods for studying scientifically what behaviours constitute problems, why people suffer from behavioural disorders, and how to treat these problems (Asmundson et al., 2002). Some of you will ultimately contribute to this important field by applying the methods described in this chapter. Understanding research methods is extremely important for all of you. You or someone close to you may need the services of a psychologist, psychiatrist, or other mental health provider. You may have questions such as these:

- Should childhood aggression be cause for concern, or is it a phase my child will grow out of?
- The *Canada AM* show just reported that increased exposure to sunlight alleviates depression. Instead of seeing a therapist, should I buy a ticket to Cuba?
- I read a story about the horrors of shock therapy. Should I advise my neighbour not to let her daughter have this treatment?
- My mother is still in her 50s but seems to be forgetting things. Friends tell me this is natural as you grow older. Should I be concerned?

To answer such questions you need to be a good consumer of research. When you understand the correct ways of obtaining information—that is, research methodology—you will know when you are dealing with fact and not fiction. Knowing the difference between a fad and an established approach to a problem can be the difference between months of suffering and a quick resolution to a disturbing problem.

## Basic Components of a Research Study

The basic research process is simple. You start with an educated guess, called a **hypothesis,** about what you expect to find. When you decide how you want to test this hypothesis, you have a **research design** that includes the aspects you want to measure in the people you are studying (the **dependent variable**) and the influences on their behaviours (the **independent variable**). Finally, two forms of validity are specific to research studies: **internal** and **external validity.** Internal validity is the extent to which we can be confident that the independent variable is causing the dependent variable to change. External validity refers to how well the results relate to things outside your study, in other words, how well your findings describe similar individuals who were not among the study participants.

Although we discuss a variety of research strategies, they all have these basic elements (see Asmundson et al., 2002). Table 3.2 shows the essential components of a research study.

### Hypothesis

Human beings look for order and purpose. We want to know why the world works as it does and why people behave the way they do.

Abnormal behaviour defies the regularity and predictability we desire. It is this departure from the norm that makes the study of abnormal behaviour so intriguing. In an attempt to make sense of these phenomena, behavioural scientists construct hypotheses and then test them. Hypotheses are nothing more than educated guesses about the world. You may believe that watching violent television programs will cause children to be more aggressive. You may think that bulimia is influenced by media depictions of supposedly ideal female body types. You may suspect that someone abused as a child is likely to become a spouse abuser and child abuser later on. These concerns are all testable hypotheses.

Once a scientist decides what to study, the next step is to put it in words that are unambiguous and in a form that is testable. Consider a study of the effects

**hypothesis**   Educated guess or statement to be tested by research.

**research design**   Plan of experimentation used to test a hypothesis.

**dependent variable**   In an experimental research study, the phenomenon that is measured and expected to be influenced.

**independent variable**   Phenomenon that is manipulated by the experimenter in a research study and expected to influence the dependent variable.

**internal validity**   Extent to which the results of a research study can be attributed to the independent variable after confounding alternative explanations have been ruled out.

**external validity**   Extent to which research study findings generalize, or apply, to people and settings not involved in the study.

---

| **TABLE 3.2** | The Basic Components of a Research Study |
|---|---|
| Component | Description |
| Hypothesis | An educated guess or statement to be supported by data. |
| Research design | The plan for testing the hypothesis. Affected by the question addressed, by the hypothesis, and by practical considerations. |
| Dependent variable | Some aspect of the phenomenon that is measured and is expected to be changed or influenced by the independent variable. |
| Independent variable | The aspect manipulated or thought to influence the change in the dependent variable. |
| Internal validity | The extent to which the results of the study can be attributed to the independent variable. |
| External validity | The extent to which the results of the study can be generalized or applied outside the immediate study. |

of drinking alcohol on gambling behaviour as an example. Michael Ellery and his colleagues at Dalhousie University observed a sample of 44 regular gamblers while they were playing a video poker game on a video lottery terminal (VLT) machine to examine the effects of alcohol on various aspects of gambling behaviour (Ellery, Stewart, & Loba, 2005). The researchers posed the hypothesis that administration of a mildly intoxicating dose of alcohol, relative to administration of a nonalcoholic control beverage, would lead to increases in several parameters of gambling behaviour (e.g., overall money spent, overall play time) among these regular gamblers. The way this hypothesis is stated suggests the researchers already know the answer to their question. Obviously, they won't know what they will find until the study is completed, but phrasing the hypothesis in this way makes it testable. For example, it is possible that this low dose of alcohol might have no impact on any aspect of gambling behaviour on the VLTs. This concept of **testability** (the ability to support the hypothesis) is important for science because it allows us to say that in this case, either (1) gambling behaviour is adversely affected by drinking alcohol, so let's study this more and consider the policy implications (e.g., should casinos be allowed to serve free drinks to gambling patrons?), or (2) gambling behaviour is not affected by a relatively low dose of alcohol, so let's look elsewhere for factors that might increase risk-taking during gambling.

When they develop an experimental hypothesis, researchers specify dependent and independent variables. A dependent variable is what is expected to change or be influenced by the study. Psychologists studying abnormal behaviour typically measure an aspect of the disorder, such as overt behaviours, thoughts, and feelings, or biological symptoms. In Ellery and colleagues' (2005) study on alcohol effects on gambling, the main dependent variables included overall average bet magnitude, overall money spent on VLT play, overall time spent playing, and rate of powerbets (i.e., the number of times per minute an initial bet was doubled after viewing only the first two cards of the five-card poker hand). Independent variables are those factors thought to affect the dependent variables. The independent variable in the study by Ellery et al. (2005) was alcohol consumption (mildly intoxicating dose of alcohol versus control beverage).

### Internal and External Validity

Suppose Ellery and colleagues (2005) found that, unknown to them, many of the gamblers assigned to the alcohol condition had consumed a lot of coffee just before they came into the lab. This would have affected the data in a way not related to alcohol effects, which would completely change the meaning of their results. This situation, which relates to internal validity, is called a **confound,** defined as any

factor occurring in a study that makes the results uninterpretable. For the Ellery et al. (2005) study, we wouldn't know how the caffeine use had affected the results. The degree to which confounds are present in a study is a measure of internal validity, the extent to which the results can be explained by the independent variable. Such a hypothetical confound in the Ellery et al. (2005) study would have made this research internally invalid because it would have reduced the ability to explain the results in terms of the independent variable—alcohol consumption.

Scientists use many strategies to ensure internal validity in their studies, three of which we discuss here: control groups, randomization, and analogue models. In a **control group,** people are similar to the experimental group in every way except that members of the experimental group are exposed to the independent variable and those in the control group are not. Because researchers can't prevent people from being exposed to many things around them that could affect the outcomes of the study, they try to compare people who receive the treatment with people who go through similar experiences except for the treatment (control group). Control groups help rule out alternative explanations for results, thereby strengthening internal validity. For example, in the Ellery et al. (2005) study, half the gamblers were assigned to the treatment group and given a mildly intoxicating dose of alcohol and the other half were assigned to the control group and given a nonalcoholic beverage.

**Randomization** is the process of assigning people to different research groups in such a way that each person has an equal chance of being placed in any group. Placing people in groups by flipping a coin or using a random number table helps improve internal validity by eliminating any systematic bias in assignment (Asmundson et al., 2002).

**Analogue models** create in the controlled conditions of the laboratory aspects that are comparable (analogous) to the phenomenon under study. A

**testability** Ability of a hypothesis, for example, to be subjected to scientific scrutiny and to be accepted or rejected, a necessary condition for the hypothesis to be useful.

**confound** Any factor occurring in a research study that makes the results uninterpretable because its effects cannot be separated from those of the variables being studied.

**control group** Group of individuals in a research study who are similar to the experimental participants in every way but are not exposed to the treatment received by the experimental group; their presence allows a comparison of the differential effects of the treatment.

**randomization** Method for placing individuals into research groups that assures each one of an equal chance of being assigned to any group, to eliminate any systematic differences across groups.

**analogue model** Approach to research employing participants who are similar to clinical clients, allowing replication of a clinical problem under controlled conditions.

bulimia researcher could ask volunteers to binge eat in the laboratory, questioning them before they ate, while they were eating, and after they finished to learn whether eating in this way made them feel more or less anxious, guilty, and so on. If she used volunteers of any age, gender, race, or background, she could rule out influences on the participants' attitudes about eating that she might not be able to dismiss if the group contained only people with bulimia. In this way, such "artificial" studies help improve internal validity.

One useful type of analogue model is the animal model. Animal models have been developed on the basis of laboratory research with animal participants to explain various types of psychological disorders, as we will learn in many of the coming chapters in this book. For example, University of Alberta researchers W. David Pierce and W. Frank Epling have developed an animal model of anorexia nervosa, a serious eating disorder. In research with rats, these researchers observed that when the animals were fed only one meal a day and allowed to run on an activity wheel, they exercised excessively, stopped eating, and died of starvation (Pierce & Epling, 1994). Pierce and Epling labelled this phenomenon "activity anorexia" and noted that it bears close resemblance to the symptoms of anorexia nervosa in humans. Pierce and Epling's animal model permits basic research on anorexia that for practical and ethical reasons cannot be conducted with humans.

In a research study, internal and external validity often seem to be in opposition. On the one hand, we want to be able to control as many different things as possible to conclude that the independent variable (the aspect of the study we manipulated) was responsible for the changes in the dependent variables (the aspects of the study we expected to change). On the other hand, we want the results to apply to people other than the subjects of the study and in other settings; this is **generalizability,** the extent to which results apply to *everyone* with a particular disorder. If we control the total environment of the people who participate in the study so that only the independent variable changes, the result is not relevant to the real world. Ellery and colleagues (2005) had their gamblers drink a specific amount of alcohol and waited a specific time to allow the alcohol to absorb into the gamblers' systems before they had them play the VLTs. This procedure ensured that all gamblers in the treatment group would be experiencing similar mild levels of intoxication at the time they were gambling. This procedure eliminates confounds related to variations in the level of alcohol in the blood across participants, thereby increasing internal validity. But it also prohibits conclusions about the effects of higher doses of alcohol or about the effects of drinking alcohol while playing the VLTs (both of which might be more common in the real world), thereby decreasing external validity. Internal and external validity are in this way often inversely related. Researchers constantly try to balance these two concerns and, as we see later in this chapter, the best solution for achieving both internal and external validity may be to conduct several related studies.

## Statistical versus Clinical Significance

The introduction of statistics is part of psychology's evolution from a prescientific to a scientific discipline. Statisticians gather, analyze, and interpret data from research. In psychological research, statistical significance typically means the probability of obtaining the observed effect by chance is small. As an example, consider a group of adults with mental retardation who also have self-injurious behaviour—hitting, slapping, or scratching themselves until they cause physical damage. Suppose they participate in an experimental treatment program and are observed to hurt themselves less often than a similar group of adults who do not receive treatment. If a statistical test of these results indicates the difference in behaviour is expected to occur by chance less than five times in every 100 experiments, then we can say the difference is statistically significant. But is it an *important* difference? The difficulty is in the distinction between **statistical** and **clinical significance.**

---

**generalizability**   Extent to which research results apply to a range of individuals not included in the study.

**statistical significance**   Probability that obtaining the observed research findings merely by chance is small.

**clinical significance**   Degree to which research findings have useful and meaningful applications to real problems.

Studying people as part of a group sometimes masks individual differences.

In the previous example, suppose we used a rating scale to note how frequently each person hit himself or herself. At the beginning of the study, all the participants hit themselves an average of 10 times per day. At the end of the study, we added all the scores on the rating scales and found that the treated group received lower scores than the untreated group and the results were statistically significant. Is this new treatment something we should recommend for all people who hit themselves?

Closer examination of the results leads to concern about *the size of the effect*. Let's say that when you look at the people who were rated as improved you find they still hit themselves about six times per day. Even though the frequency is lower, they are still hurting themselves. Some hit themselves just a few times but produce serious cuts, bruises, and contusions. This suggests that your statistically significant results may not be clinically significant, that is, important to the people who hurt themselves. The distinction would be particularly important if there were another treatment that did not reduce the incidence of self-hitting so much, but reduced the severity of the blows, causing less harm.

Fortunately, concern for the clinical significance of results has led researchers to develop statistical methods that address not just that groups are different, but how large these differences are, or *effect size*. Calculating the actual statistical measures involves fairly sophisticated procedures that take into account how much each treated and untreated person in a research study improves or worsens (Grissom & Kim, 2001). In other words, instead of just looking at the results of the group as a whole, individual differences are considered as well. Some researchers have used more subjective ways of determining whether truly important change has resulted from treatment. For example, Wolf (1978) has advocated the assessment of *social validity*. This technique involves obtaining input from the person being treated and from significant others about the importance of the changes that have occurred. In our example, we might ask employers and family members if they thought the treatment led to truly important reductions in self-injurious behaviour. If the effect of the treatment is large enough to impress those directly involved, the treatment effect is clinically significant. Statistical techniques of measuring effect size and assessing subjective judgments of change will let us better evaluate the results of our treatments.

## The "Average" Client

Too often we look at results from studies and make generalizations about the group, ignoring individual differences. Kiesler (1966) labelled the tendency to see all participants as one homogeneous group the *patient uniformity myth*. Comparing groups according to their mean scores ("Group A improved by 50% over Group B") hides important differences in individual reactions to our interventions.

The patient uniformity myth leads researchers to make inaccurate generalizations about disorders and their treatments. To continue with our previous example, it would not be surprising if a researcher studying the treatment of self-injurious behaviour concluded that the experimental treatment was a good approach. Yet suppose we found that, although some participants improved with treatment, others got worse. Such differences would be averaged out in the analysis of the group as a whole, but for the person whose head banging increased with the experimental treatment, it would make little difference that, "on the average," people improved. Because people differ in such ways as age, cognitive abilities, gender, and history of treatment, a simple group comparison may be misleading. Practitioners who deal with all types of disorders understand the heterogeneity of their clients and therefore do not know whether treatments that are statistically significant will be effective for a given individual. In our discussions of various disorders, we return to this issue.

## Concept Check 3.3

In each of the statements provided, fill in the blanks with one of the following: hypothesis, dependent variable, independent variable, internal validity, external validity, or confound.

1. In a treatment study, the introduction of the treatment to the participants is referred to as the _____ variable.
2. After the treatment study was completed, you found that many of the people in the control group received treatment outside of the study. This is called a _____.
3. A researcher's guess about what her study might find is labelled the _____.
4. Scores on a depression scale improved for a treatment group after therapy. The change in these scores would be referred to as a change in the _____ variable.
5. A relative lack of confounds in a study would indicate good _____ validity, whereas good generalizability of the results would be called good _____ validity.

# Types of Research Methods

■ *Compare and contrast different research designs, including the types of questions that are appropriate and inappropriate for each.*

Behavioural scientists use several different forms of research when studying the causes of behaviour. We now examine individual case studies, correlational research, experimental research, and single-case experimental studies.

## Studying Individual Cases

What is the best way to begin exploring a relatively unknown disorder? One method is to use the **case study method,** investigating intensively one or more individuals who display the behavioural and physical patterns of interest (Lowman, 2001).

One way to describe the case study method is by noting what it is not. It does not use the scientific method. Few efforts are made to ensure internal validity and, typically, many confounding variables are present that can interfere with conclusions. Instead, the case study method relies on a clinician's observations of differences among one person or group with a disorder, people with other disorders, and people with no psychological disorders. The clinician usually collects as much information as possible to obtain a detailed description of the person. Historically, interviewing the person under study yields a great deal of information about personal and family background, education, health, and work history, as well as the person's opinions about the nature and causes of the problems being studied.

Case studies are important in the history of psychology. Freud developed psychoanalytic theory and the methods of psychoanalysis on the basis of his observations of dozens of cases. Freud and Breuer's description of Anna O. (see Chapter 1) led to development of the clinical technique known as free association. Sex researchers Virginia Johnson and William Masters based their work on many case studies and helped shed light on numerous myths regarding sexual behaviour (Masters & Johnson, 1966). Joseph Wolpe, author of the landmark book *Psychotherapy by Reciprocal Inhibition* (1958), based his work with systematic desensitization on more than 200 cases. As our knowledge of psychological disorders has grown, we have relied less on the case study method.

We are constantly exposed to cases of abnormal behaviour through the media. For example, the case of child serial killer Clifford Olson, who raped and murdered at least 10 children and adolescents in British Columbia in the early 1980s, is known throughout the world. Olson himself has blamed his earlier experiences in the Canadian prison system (including a prison partnership with a convicted child rapist-murderer) for sparking his transition from a petty thief to a prolific killer. What conclusions should we draw? Did Olson have valuable insight into the causes of his own behaviour, or was he attempting to evade responsibility? We must be careful about concluding anything from such sensational portrayals. Remembering people's tendencies to be more highly influenced by dramatic accounts than by scientific evidence (Nisbett & Ross, 1980), we highlight research findings in this book.

## Research by Correlation

One of the fundamental questions posed by scientists is whether two variables relate to each other. A statistical relationship between two variables is called a **correlation.** For example, is schizophrenia related to the size of ventricles in the brain? Are people with depression more likely to have negative attributions? Is the frequency of hallucinations higher among older people? The answers depend on determining how one variable (number of hallucinations) is related to another (age). Unlike experimental designs, which involve manipulating or changing conditions, correlational designs are used to study phenomena just as they occur. The result of a correlational study—whether variables occur together—is important to the ongoing search for knowledge about abnormal behaviour.

One of the clichés of science is that a correlation does not imply a causation. Two things occurring together do not imply that one caused the other. For example, the occurrence of marital problems in families is correlated with behaviour problems in children (Emery, 1982; Harrist & Ainslie, 1998; Reid & Crisafulli, 1990). If you conduct a correlational study in this area you will find that in families with marital problems you tend to see children with behaviour problems; in families with

---

**case study method**   Research procedure in which a single person or small group is studied in detail. The method does not allow conclusions about cause-and-effect relationships, and findings can be generalized only with great caution.

**correlation**   Degree to which two variables are associated.

fewer marital problems, you are likely to find children with fewer behaviour problems. The most obvious conclusion is that having marital problems will cause children to misbehave. If only it were as simple as that! The nature of the relationship between marital discord and childhood behaviour problems can be explained in a number of ways. It may be that problems in a marriage cause disruptive behaviour in the children (Pagani, Tremblay, Vitaro, Kerr, & McDuff, 1998). However, some evidence suggests the opposite may be true as well: The disruptive behaviour of children may cause marital problems (Rutter & Giller, 1984). In addition, evidence suggests genetic influences may play a role in conduct disorders (Rutter et al., 1990) and in marital discord (McGue & Lykken, 1992).

This example points out the problems in interpreting the results of a correlational study. We know that variable A (marital problems) is correlated with variable B (child behaviour problems). We do not know from these studies whether A causes B (marital problems cause child problems), whether B causes A (child problems cause marital problems), or whether some third variable C causes both (genes influence both marital problems and child problems).

The association between marital discord and child problems represents a **positive correlation.** This means that great strength or quantity in one variable (a great deal of marital distress) is associated with great strength or quantity in the other variable (more child disruptive behaviour). At the same time, lower strength or quantity in one variable (marital distress) is associated with lower strength or quantity in the other (disruptive behaviour). If you have trouble conceptualizing statistical concepts, you can think about this mathematical relationship in the same way you would a social relationship. Two people who are getting along well tend to go places together: "Where I go, you will go!" The correlation (or **correlation coefficient**) is represented as +1.00. The plus sign means there is a

positive relationship, and the 1.00 means that it is a "perfect" relationship, in which the people are inseparable. Obviously, two people who like each other do not go everywhere together. The strength of their relationship ranges between 0.00 and 1.00 (0.00 means no relationship exists). The higher the number, the stronger the relationship, whether the number is positive or negative (e.g., a correlation of −.80 is "stronger" than a correlation of +.75). You would expect two strangers, for example, to have a relationship of 0.00 because their behaviour is not related; they sometimes end up in the same place together, but this occurs rarely and randomly. Two people who know each other but do not like each other would be represented by a negative sign, with the range of −1.00 to 0.00, and a strong negative relationship would be −1.00, which means "Anywhere you go, I won't be there!"

Using this analogy, marital problems in families and behaviour problems in children have a relatively strong positive correlation represented by a number such as +.50. They tend to go together. On the other hand, other variables are strangers to each other. Schizophrenia and height are not related, so they don't go together and probably would be represented by a number close to 0.00. If A and B have no correlation, their correlation coefficient would approximate 0.00. Other factors have negative relationships: As one increases, the other decreases. (See Figure 3.6 for an illustration of positive and negative correlations.) We used an example of **negative correlation** in Chapter 2,

**positive correlation** Association between two variables in which one increases as the other increases.

**correlation coefficient** Computed statistic reflecting the strength and direction of any association between two variables. It can range from +1.00 through 0 (indicating no association) to −1.00, with the absolute value indicating the strength and the sign reflecting the direction.

**negative correlation** Association between two variables in which one increases as the other decreases.

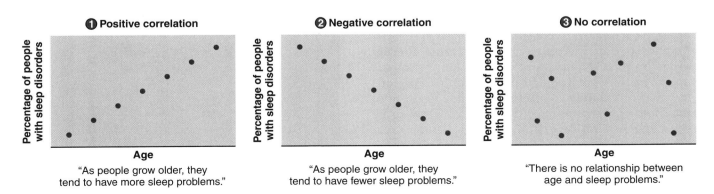

❶ Positive correlation  ❷ Negative correlation  ❸ No correlation

"As people grow older, they tend to have more sleep problems."

"As people grow older, they tend to have fewer sleep problems."

"There is no relationship between age and sleep problems."

**Figure 3.6** ■ These three graphs represent hypothetical correlations between age and sleep problems.

when we discussed social supports and illness. The more social supports that are present, the less likely it is that a person will become ill. The negative relationship between social supports and illness could be represented by a number such as –.40. The next time someone wants to break up with you, ask if the goal is to weaken the strength of your positive relationship to something like +.25 (friends), to become complete strangers at 0.00, or to have an intense negative relationship approximating –1.00 (enemies).

A correlation allows us to see whether a relationship exists between two variables, but not to draw conclusions about whether either variable causes the effects. This is a problem of **directionality.** In this case, it means that we do not know whether A causes B, B causes A, or a third variable, C, causes A and B. Therefore, even an extremely strong relationship between two variables (+.90) means nothing about the direction of causality.

## Epidemiological Research

Scientists often think of themselves as detectives, searching for the truth by studying clues. One type of correlational research that is like the efforts of detectives is called **epidemiology,** the study of the incidence, distribution, and consequences of a particular problem or set of problems in one or more populations. Epidemiologists expect that by tracking a disorder among many people, they will find important clues to why the disorder exists. One strategy involves determining *prevalence,* the number of people with a disorder at any one time. For example, the prevalence of alcohol dependence among Canadian adults is about 3% (Statistics Canada, 2002a). A related strategy is to determine the *incidence* of a disorder, the estimated number of new cases during a specific period of time. For example, as we see in Chapter 10, the incidence of new cases of cocaine use has been decreasing over the past decade among most age groups in Canada (Statistics Canada, 2002a). Although the primary goal of epidemiology is to determine the extent of medical problems, it is also useful in the study of psychological disorders. In the early 1900s, many people displayed symptoms of a strange mental disorder. Its symptoms were similar to those of organic psychosis, which is often caused by mind-altering drugs or great quantities of alcohol. Many patients appeared to be catatonic (immobile for long periods of time) or exhibited symptoms similar to those of paranoid schizophrenia. Victims were likely to be poor and African American, which led to speculation about class inferiority. However, using the methods of epidemiological research, Goldberger found correlations between the disorder and diet, and he identified the cause of the disorder as a deficiency of the B vitamin niacin among people with

poor diets. The symptoms were successfully eliminated by niacin therapy and improved diets. A long-term, widespread benefit of Goldberger's findings was the introduction of vitamin-enriched bread in the 1940s (Gottesman, 1991).

Researchers have used epidemiological techniques to study the effects of stress on psychological disorders. For example, researchers have examined the psychological effects of the September 11, 2001, terrorist attacks on the World Trade Center and the American Pentagon. Following those events, Blanchard et al. (2004) examined rates of two anxiety disorders—acute stress disorder and posttraumatic stress disorder (see Chapter 4)—in samples of students from three American universities, one of which was geographically closer to the attacks. They found higher rates of both acute stress disorder (28% vs. 10% and 19%) and posttraumatic stress disorder (11% vs. 3% and 7%) in the students attending the university that was closer to the site of the attacks. A similar study conducted in Saskatchewan showed that about 4% of the Canadian sample met criteria for posttraumatic stress disorder following the events of September 11 (Asmundson, Carleton, Wright, & Taylor, 2004). Taken together, these findings suggest a relationship between geographical proximity and impact of the trauma, with those living closer to the site of the terrorist attacks showing the greatest levels of distress. These are both correlational studies because the investigators

**directionality**   Possibility that, when two variables, A and B, are correlated, variable A causes variable B or B causes A.

**epidemiology**   Psychopathology research method examining the prevalence, distribution, and consequences of disorders in populations.

The more social supports people have, the less likely it is that they will become ill.

did not manipulate the independent variable. (They weren't involved in committing the terrorist acts!) Despite their correlational nature, these studies do show a relationship between stress and psychological problems.

Like other types of correlational research, epidemiological research can't tell us conclusively what causes a particular phenomenon. However, knowledge about the prevalence and course of psychological disorders is extremely valuable to our understanding because it points researchers in the right direction.

## Research by Experiment

An **experiment** involves the manipulation of an independent variable and the observation of its effects. We manipulate the independent variable to answer the question of causality. If we observe a correlation between social supports and psychological disorders, we can't conclude which of these factors influenced the other. We can, however, change the extent of social supports and see whether there is an accompanying change in the prevalence of psychological disorders—in other words, do an experiment.

What will this experiment tell us about the relationship between these two variables? If we increase social supports and find no change in the frequency of psychological disorders, it *may* mean that lack of such supports does not cause psychological problems. On the other hand, if we find that psychological disorders diminish with increased social support, we can be more confident that nonsupport does contribute to them. However, because we are never 100% confident that our experiments are internally valid—that no other explanations are possible—we are cautious about interpreting our results. In this section, we describe different ways researchers conduct experiments and consider how each one brings us closer to understanding abnormal behaviour.

### Group Experimental Designs

With correlational designs, researchers observe groups to see how different variables are associated. In group experimental designs, researchers are more active. They actually change an independent variable to see how the behaviour of the people in the group is affected. Suppose researchers design an intervention to help reduce insomnia in older adults, who are particularly affected by the condition (Ancoli-Israel, 2000; Morin, Savard, Ouellet, & Daley, 2003). They treat 20 individuals and follow them for 10 years to learn whether their sleep patterns improve. The treatment is the independent variable; that is, it would not have occurred naturally. They then assess the members to learn whether their behaviour changed as a function of what the researchers did.

Introducing or withdrawing a variable in a way that would not have occurred naturally is also called *manipulating a variable*.

Unfortunately, a decade later the researchers find that the adults treated for sleep problems still, as a group, sleep less than 8 hours per night. Is the treatment a failure? Maybe not. The question that can't be answered in this study is what would have happened to group members if they hadn't been treated. Perhaps their sleep patterns would have been worse. Fortunately, researchers have devised ingenious methods to help sort out these complicated questions.

### Control Groups

One answer to the what-if dilemma is to use a control group—people who are similar to the experimental group in every way except they are not exposed to the independent variable. The researchers also follow this group of people, assess them 10 years later, and look at their sleep patterns over this time. They probably observe that, without intervention, people tend to sleep fewer hours as they get older (Bootzin, Engle-Friedman, & Hazelwood, 1983; Foley, Monjan, Simonsick, Wallace, & Blazer, 1999; Morin & Edinger, 2003). Members of the control group, then, might sleep significantly less than people in the treated group, who might themselves sleep somewhat less than they did 10 years earlier. The control group allows the researchers to see that their treatment did help the treated subjects keep their sleep time from decreasing further.

Ideally, a control group is nearly identical to the treatment group in such areas as age, gender, socioeconomic backgrounds, and the problems they are reporting. Furthermore, a researcher would do the same assessments before and after the independent variable manipulation (e.g., a treatment) to people in both groups. Any later differences between the groups after the change would, therefore, be attributable only to what was changed.

People in a treatment group often expect to get better. When behaviour changes as a result of a person's expectation of change rather than as a result of any manipulation by an experimenter, the phenomenon is known as a **placebo effect.** Conversely, people in the control group may be disappointed that they are not receiving treatment. Depending on the type of disorder they experience

---

**experiment**   Research method that can establish causation by manipulating the variables in question and controlling for alternative explanations of any observed effects.

**placebo effect**   Behaviour change resulting from the person's expectation of change rather than from the experimental manipulation.

(e.g., depression), disappointment may make them worse. This phenomenon would also make the treatment group look better by comparison.

One way researchers address the expectation concern is through **placebo control groups.** The word *placebo* (which means "I shall please") typically refers to inactive medications such as sugar pills. The placebo is given to members of the control group to make them believe they are getting treatment (Hyman & Shore, 2000; MacDonald, Stewart, Hutson, Rhyno, & Loughlin, 2001; Parloff, 1986). A placebo control in a medication study can be carried out with relative ease because people in the untreated group receive something that *looks like* the medication administered to the treatment group. In psychological treatments, however, it is not always easy to devise something that people believe may help them but does not include the component the researcher believes is effective. Clients in these types of control groups are often given part of the actual therapy—for example, the same homework as the treated group—but not the portions the researchers believe are responsible for improvements.

Note that you can look at the placebo effect as one portion of any treatment (Lambert, Shapiro, & Bergin, 1986). If someone you provide with a treatment improves, you would have to attribute the improvement to a combination of your treatment and the client's expectation of improving (placebo effect). Therapists want their clients to expect improvement; this helps strengthen the treatment. However, when researchers conduct an experiment to determine the portion of a particular treatment responsible for the observed changes, the placebo effect is a confound that can dilute the validity of the research. Thus, researchers use a placebo control group to help distinguish the results of positive expectations from the results of actual treatment.

The **double-blind control** is a variant of the placebo control group procedure. As the name suggests, not only are the participants in the study "blind," or unaware of what group they are in or what treatment they are given (single blind), but so are the researchers or therapists providing treatment (double blind). This type of control is meant to eliminate the possibility that an investigator might bias the outcome (Basoglu, Marks, Livanou, & Swinson, 1997). For example, a researcher comparing two treatments who expected one to be more effective than the other might "try harder" if the "preferred" treatment wasn't working as well as expected. On the other hand, if the treatment that wasn't expected to work seemed to be failing, the researcher might not push as hard to see it succeed. This reaction might not be deliberate, but it does happen. This phenomenon is referred to as an *allegiance effect* (Quitkin, Rabkin, Gerald, Davis, &

Klein, 2000). If, however, both the participants and the researchers or therapists are "blind," there is less chance that bias will affect the results.

A double-blind placebo control does not work perfectly in all cases (Basoglu et al., 1997). If medication is part of the treatment, participants and researchers may be able to tell whether or not they have received it by the presence or absence of physical reactions (side effects). Even with purely psychological interventions, participants often know whether or not they are receiving a powerful treatment, and they may alter their expectations for improvement accordingly.

## Comparative Treatment Research

As an alternative to using no-treatment or placebo control groups to help evaluate results, some researchers compare different treatments. In this design, the researcher gives different treatments to two or more comparable groups of people with a particular disorder and then assesses how or whether each treatment helped the people who received it. This is called **comparative treatment research.** In the sleep study we discussed, two groups of older adults could be selected, with one group given medication for insomnia and the other given a cognitive–behavioural intervention, and the results could be compared.

The *process* and *outcome* of treatment are two important issues to be considered when different approaches are studied. Process research focuses on the mechanisms responsible for behaviour change or "why does it work?" In an old joke, someone goes to a physician for a new miracle cold cure. The physician prescribes the new drug and tells the patient the cold will be gone in 7 to 10 days. As most of us know, colds typically improve in 7 to 10 days without so-called miracle drugs. The new drug probably does nothing to further the improvement of the patient's cold. The process aspect of testing medical interventions involves evaluating biological mechanisms responsible for change. Does the medication cause lower serotonin levels, for example, and does this account for the changes we observe? Similarly, in looking at psychological interventions, we determine

---

**placebo control group** In an outcome experiment, a control group that does not receive the experimental manipulation but is given a similar procedure with an identical expectation of change, allowing the researcher to assess any placebo effect.

**double-blind control** Procedure in outcome studies that prevents bias by ensuring that neither the participants nor the providers of the experimental treatment know who is receiving treatment and who is receiving placebo.

**comparative treatment research** Outcome research that contrasts two or more treatment methods to determine which is most effective.

what is "causing" the observed changes. This is important for several reasons. First, if we understand what the "active ingredients" of our treatment are, we can often eliminate aspects that are not important, thereby saving clients time and money. In addition, knowing what is important about our interventions can help us create more powerful versions that may be more effective.

Outcome research focuses on the positive and/or negative results of the treatment. In other words, does it work? Remember, the treatment process involves finding out why or how your treatment works. In contrast, the treatment outcome involves finding out what changes occur *after* treatment. You probably have guessed by now that even this seemingly simple task becomes more complicated the closer we look at it. Depending on what dependent variables you select to measure, and when and where you assess them, your view of success may vary considerably. For example, Francis and Hart (1992), who described their work with depressed adolescents in an inpatient (hospital)

Scott T. Baxter/Photodisc

CP Photo/Tom Hanson

In comparative treatment research, different treatments are administered to comparable groups of people.

setting, used a treatment that includes "activity increase" strategies. The goal is to help adolescents become more involved in activities that give them access to positive experiences. Francis and Hart note that, although they observe improvements in depression when the adolescents are in the structured hospital environment, this improvement often disappears outside the hospital.

Do activity-increase strategies result in positive treatment outcomes for depressed adolescents? That depends on where you assess their depression. If you look at their outcomes in the hospital, you may see improvement. If you follow them home after discharge, you might conclude the treatment wasn't effective. Again, in evaluating whether a treatment is effective, researchers must carefully define success.

## Single-Case Experimental Designs

B. F. Skinner's innovations in scientific methodology were among his most important contributions to psychopathology. Skinner formalized the concept of **single-case experimental designs.** This method involves the systematic study of individuals under a variety of experimental conditions. Skinner thought it was much better to know a lot about the behaviour of one individual than to make only a few observations of a large group to present the "average" response. Psychopathology is concerned with the problems experienced by specific people, and this methodology has greatly helped us understand the factors involved in individual psychopathology (Hayes, Barlow, & Nelson-Gray, 1999). Many applications throughout this book reflect Skinnerian methods.

Single-case experimental designs differ from case studies in their use of various strategies to improve internal validity, thereby reducing the number of confounding variables. As we will see, these strategies have strengths and weaknesses in comparison with traditional group designs. Although we use examples from treatment research to illustrate the single-case experimental designs, they, like other research strategies, can help explain why people engage in abnormal behaviour and how to treat them.

### Repeated Measurements

One of the more important strategies used in single-case experimental design is *repeated measurement*, in which a behaviour is measured several times instead of only once before you change the independent variable and once afterward. The researcher takes the

**single-case experimental design**    Research tactic in which an independent variable is manipulated for a single individual, allowing cause-and-effect conclusions but with limited generalizability.

same measurements over and over to learn how variable the behaviour is (how much does it change day to day?) and whether it shows any obvious trends (is it getting better or worse?). Suppose a young woman, Wendy, comes into the office complaining about feelings of anxiety. When the clinician asks her to rate the level of her anxiety, she gives it a 9 (10 is the worst). After several weeks of treatment Wendy rates her anxiety at 6. Can we say that the treatment reduced her anxiety? Not necessarily.

Suppose the clinician had measured Wendy's anxiety each day during the weeks before her visit to the office (repeated measurement) and observed that it differed greatly. On particularly good days, she rated her anxiety from 5 to 7. On bad days, it was up between 8 and 10. Suppose further that, even after treatment, her daily ratings continued to range from 5 to 10. The rating of 9 before treatment and 6 after treatment may only have been part of the daily variations she experienced normally. Wendy could just as easily have had a good day and reported a 6 before treatment and then had a bad day and reported a 9 after treatment, which would imply that the treatment made her worse!

Repeated measurement is part of each single-subject experimental design. It helps identify how a person is doing before and after intervention, and whether the treatment accounted for any changes. Figure 3.7 summarizes Wendy's anxiety and the added information obtained by repeated measurement. The top graph shows Wendy's original before-and-after ratings of her anxiety. The middle graph shows that, with daily ratings, her reports are variable and that just by chance the previous measurement was probably misleading. She had good and bad days both before and after treatment and doesn't seem to have changed much.

The bottom graph shows a different possibility: Wendy's anxiety was on its way down before the treatment, which would also have been obscured with just before-and-after measurements. Maybe she was getting better on her own, and the treatment didn't have

much effect. Although the middle graph shows how the **variability** from day to day could be important in an interpretation of the effect of treatment, the bottom graph shows how the **trend** can also be important in determining the cause of any change. The three graphs illustrate important parts of repeated measurements: (1) the **level** or degree of behaviour change with different interventions (top), (2) the *variability* or degree of change over time (middle), and (3) the *trend* or direction of change (bottom). Again, before-and-after scores alone do not necessarily show what is responsible for behavioural changes.

---

**variability**  Degree of change in a phenomenon over time.

**trend**  The direction of change of a behaviour or behaviours (e.g., increasing or decreasing).

**level**  Degree of behaviour change with different interventions (e.g., high or low).

---

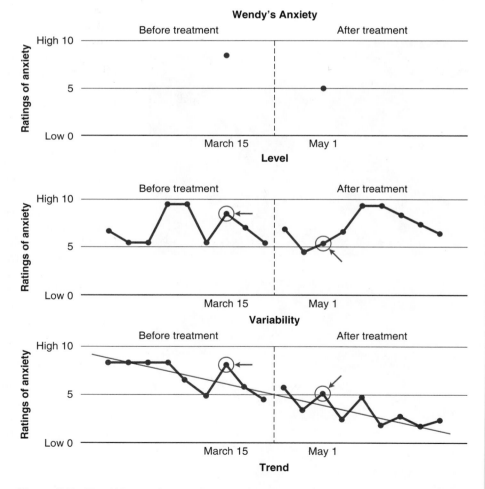

**Figure 3.7**  ■  Although the top graph gives the impression that Wendy's anxiety level changed significantly, the middle and bottom graphs demonstrate how examining variability and trend can provide much more information about the true nature of the change.

## Withdrawal Designs

One of the more common strategies used in single-case research is a **withdrawal design,** in which a researcher tries to determine whether the independent variable is responsible for changes in behaviour. The effect of Wendy's treatment could be tested by stopping it for a period of time to see whether her anxiety increased. A simple withdrawal design has three parts. First, a person's condition is evaluated before treatment, to establish a **baseline.** Then comes the change in the independent variable—in Wendy's case, the beginning of treatment. Last, treatment is withdrawn ("return to baseline") and the researcher assesses whether Wendy's anxiety level changes again as a function of this last step. If her anxiety lessens with the treatment in comparison with baseline, and then worsens again after treatment is withdrawn, the researcher can conclude the treatment has reduced Wendy's anxiety.

How is this design different from a case study? An important difference is that the change in treatment is designed specifically to show whether treatment caused the changes in behaviour. Although case studies often involve treatment, they don't include any effort to learn whether the person would have improved without the treatment. A withdrawal design gives researchers a better sense of whether or not the treatment caused behaviour change.

In spite of their advantages, withdrawal designs are not always appropriate. The researcher is required to remove what might be an effective treatment, a decision that is sometimes difficult to justify for ethical reasons. In Wendy's case, a researcher would have to decide there was a sufficient reason to deliberately make her anxious again. A withdrawal design is also unsuitable when the treatment can't be removed. Suppose Wendy's treatment involved visualizing herself on a beach on a tropical island. It would be difficult—if not impossible—to stop her from imagining something. Similarly, some treatments involve teaching people skills, which might be impossible to unlearn. If Wendy learned how to be less anxious in social situations, how could she revert to being socially apprehensive?

Several counterarguments support the use of withdrawal designs (Hayes et al., 1999). Treatment is routinely withdrawn when medications are involved. *Drug holidays* are periods when the medication is withdrawn so that clinicians can determine whether it is responsible for the treatment effects. Any medication can have negative side effects, and unnecessary medication should be avoided. Sometimes treatment withdrawal happens naturally. Withdrawal does not have to be prolonged; a brief withdrawal may still clarify the role of the treatment.

## Multiple Baselines

Another single-case experimental design strategy used frequently that doesn't have some of the drawbacks of a withdrawal design is the **multiple baseline.** Rather than stopping the intervention to see whether it is effective, the researcher starts treatment at different times across settings (home versus school), behaviours (yelling at spouse or boss), or people. After waiting a period of time and taking repeated measures of Wendy's anxiety both at home and at her office (the baseline), the clinician could treat her first at home. When the treatment begins to be effective, intervention could begin at work. If she improves only at home after beginning treatment, but improves at work after treatment is used there also, we could conclude the treatment was effective. This is an example of using a multiple baseline across settings.

Does internal validity improve with a multiple baseline? Yes. Any time other explanations for results can be ruled out, internal validity is improved. Wendy's anxiety improved only in the settings where it was treated, which rules out competing explanations. For example, if she had won the lottery at the same time treatment started and her anxiety decreased in all situations, we couldn't conclude her condition was affected by treatment.

Suppose a researcher wanted to assess the effectiveness of a treatment for a child's problem behaviours. Treatment could focus first on the child's crying then on a second problem, such as fighting with siblings. If the treatment was first effective only in reducing crying and effective for fighting only after the second intervention, the researcher could conclude that the treatment, not something else, accounted for the improvements. This is a multiple baseline conducted across behaviours.

An example of a multiple baseline across individuals design is a study by Jaye Wald (2002) at the University of British Columbia, who reported results

---

**withdrawal design** Removing a treatment to note whether it has been effective. In single-case experimental designs, a behaviour is measured (baseline), an independent variable is introduced *(intervention),* and then the intervention is withdrawn. Because the behaviour continues to be measured throughout *(repeated measurement),* any effects of the intervention can be noted. Also called reversal design.

**baseline** Measured rate of a behaviour before introduction of an intervention that allows comparison and assessment of the effects of the intervention.

**multiple baseline** Single-case experimental research design in which measures are taken on two or more behaviours or on a single behaviour in two or more situations. A particular intervention is introduced for each at different times. If behaviour change is coincident with each introduction, this is strong evidence that the intervention caused the change.

obtained with a set of people whose fear and avoidance of driving was treated with gradual exposure to driving via virtual reality technology. This design typically involves demonstrating the effects of a treatment on two or more participants. Before the treatment is administered, participants complete a baseline phase, where they provide information on the problem behaviour for a specified period. The experimenter concludes that a causal effect of the independent variable (treatment) on the dependent variable (levels of the problem behaviour) exists when the problem improves only after the treatment is administered. When this effect is replicated across individuals, the conclusion about a causal relationship becomes stronger. In Wald's (2002) study on driving phobia, each patient completed a baseline phase, 8 weekly virtual reality therapy sessions (the treatment), and posttreatment and follow-up assessments to examine levels of driving anxiety and avoidance. Only when treatment began did each patient's driving phobia show improvement. This design allowed Wald to rule out coincidence or some other change in the patients' lives as explanations for their improvements.

Single-case experimental designs are sometimes criticized because they tend to involve only a small number of cases, leaving their external validity in doubt. In other words, we can't say the results we saw with a few people would be the same for everyone. However, although they are called *single-case* designs, researchers can and often do use them with several people at once, just as Wald (2002) did in her multiple baseline study, in part to address the issue of external validity.

Among the advantages of the multiple baseline design in evaluating treatments is that it does not require withdrawal of treatment and, as we've seen, withdrawing treatment is sometimes difficult or impossible. Furthermore, the multiple baseline typically resembles the way treatment would naturally be implemented. A clinician can't help a client with numerous problems simultaneously, but can take repeated measures of the relevant behaviours and observe when they change. A clinician who sees predictable and orderly changes related to where and when the treatment is used can conclude the treatment is causing the change.

## Concept Check 3.4

Check your understanding of research methods by indicating which would be most appropriate in each of the following situations. Choose from (a) case study, (b) correlation, (c) epidemiology, (d) experiment, and (e) single-case experimental design.

1. A researcher is interested in how noise levels affect a person's concentration. _____
2. A researcher wants to investigate the hypothesis that as children go through adolescence, they listen to louder music. _____
3. A researcher is interested in studying a woman who had no contact with civilization and created her own language. _____
4. A researcher wants to know how different kinds of music will affect a 5-year-old who has never spoken. _____

# Genetics and Research across Time and Cultures

■ *Explain the advantages and disadvantages of family, adoption, twin, genetic linkage, and association studies.*

■ *Explain how studying behaviour over time and across cultures fits within the research design and the research process more generally.*

Examining the origin and strategies for treating an individual's behaviour problem or disorder requires that several factors be considered so that multiple possible influences are taken into account. The factors include determining any inherited influences, how behaviour will change or remain the same over time, and the effects of culture. We discuss these issues, as well as research replication and ethics, as key elements in the research process.

## Studying Genetics

We tend to think of genetics in terms of what we inherit from our parents: "He's got his mother's eyes!" "She's thin just like her dad." "She's stubborn like her mother." This simple view of how we become the people we are suggests that how we look, think, feel, and behave is predetermined. Yet, as we saw in Chapter 2, we now know that the interaction between our genetic makeup and our experiences is what determines how we will develop. The goal of behavioural geneticists (people who study the genetics of behaviour) is to tease out the role of genetics in these interactions.

Genetic researchers examine both **phenotypes,** the observable characteristics or behaviour of the individual, and **genotypes,** the unique genetic makeup of individual people. For example, a person with Down syndrome typically has some level of mental retardation and a variety of other physical characteristics such as slanted eyes and a thick tongue. These characteristics are the phenotype. The genotype is the extra 21st chromosome that causes Down syndrome.

Our knowledge of the phenotypes of different psychological disorders exceeds our knowledge of the genotypes, but that may soon change. Since the discovery of the double helix, scientists have known we have to map the structure and location of every gene on all 46 chromosomes if we are to fully understand our genetic endowment. Beginning in 1990, scientists around the world, in a coordinated effort, began the **human genome project** (*genome* means all the genes of an organism). Using the latest advances in molecular biology, scientists working on this project have completed a rough draft of the mapping of all human genes. For example, geneticists Steve Scherer, Lap-Chee Tsui, and Johanna Rommens at the Hospital for Sick Children in Toronto have been making substantial success in mapping chromosome 7. You can view their website at www.chr7.org. Such work from laboratories worldwide has identified hundreds of genes that contribute to inherited diseases. These exciting findings represent truly astounding progress in deciphering the nature of genetic endowment and its role in psychological disorders.

What follows is a brief review of common research strategies scientists use as they study the interaction between environment and genetics in psychological disorders: family, adoption, twin, genetic linkage, and association studies.

### Family Studies

In **family studies,** scientists simply examine a behavioural pattern or emotional trait in the context of the family. The member with the trait singled out for study is called the **proband.** If there is a genetic influence, presumably the trait should occur more often in first-degree relatives (parents, siblings, or offspring) than in second-degree or more distant relatives. The presence of the trait in distant relatives, in turn, should be somewhat greater than in the population as a whole. In Chapter 1, we met Jody, the adolescent with blood-injury-injection phobia who fainted at the sight of blood. The tendency of a trait to run in families, or

*familial aggregation,* is as high as 60% for this disorder; that is, 60% of the first-degree relatives of someone with blood-injury-injection phobia have the same reaction at least to some degree. This is one of the highest rates of familial aggregation for any psychological disorder we have studied.

The problem with family studies is that family members tend to live together, and there might be something in their shared environment that causes the high familial aggregation. For example, Mom might have developed a bad reaction to blood as a young girl after witnessing a serious accident. Every time she sees blood she has a strong emotional response. Because emotions are contagious, the young children watching Mom probably react similarly. In adulthood, they pass it on, in turn, to their own children.

### Adoption Studies

How do we separate environmental from genetic influences in families? One way is through **adoption studies.** Scientists identify adoptees who have a particular behavioural pattern or psychological disorder

**phenotype** Observable characteristics or behaviours of an individual.

**genotype** Specific genetic makeup of an individual.

**human genome project** Ongoing scientific attempt to develop a comprehensive map of all human genes.

**family studies** Genetic studies that examine patterns of traits and behaviours among relatives.

**proband** In genetics research, the individual displaying the trait or characteristic being studied. Also known as *index case.*

**adoption studies** In genetics research, studies of first-degree relatives reared in different families and environments. If they share common characteristics, such as a disorder, this finding suggests that those characteristics have a genetic component.

Although family members often resemble each other, genetics has to do with far more than what we inherit from our parents.

and attempt to locate first-degree relatives who were raised in different family settings. Suppose a young man has a disorder and scientists discover his brother was adopted as a baby and brought up in a different home. The researchers would then examine the brother to see whether he also displays signs of the disorder. If they can identify enough sibling pairs (and they usually do, after a lot of hard work), they can assess whether siblings brought up in different families display the disorder to the same extent as the original participant. If the siblings raised with different families have the disorder more frequently than would be expected by chance, the researchers can infer that genetic endowment is a contributor.

## Twin Studies

Nature presents an elegant experiment that gives behavioural geneticists their closest possible look at the role of genes in development: identical (monozygotic) twins. These twins not only look alike but also have identical genes. Fraternal (dizygotic) twins, on the other hand, come from different eggs and have only about 50% of their genes in common, as do all first-degree relatives. In **twin studies,** the obvious scientific question is whether identical twins share the same trait—say, fainting at the sight of blood—more often than fraternal twins. Determining whether a trait is shared is easy with some physical traits, such as height. As Robert Plomin from the Institute of Psychiatry in London, England, points out, correlations in height for both first-degree relatives and fraternal twins are .45, and they are .90 for identical twins (Plomin, 1990). These findings show that heritability of height is about 90%, so approximately 10% of the variance is due to environmental factors. But the 90% estimate is the *average* contribution. An identical twin who was severely physically abused or selectively deprived of proper foods might be substantially different in height from the other twin.

Behaviour genetics researchers Kerry Jang, John Livesley, and Philip Vernon (1998) conducted a study on the heritability of conduct problems. The individuals in the study were 681 twin pairs in the University of British Columbia's twin database. The investigators found that monozygotic (identical) male twins had a greater degree of resemblance for conduct problems than did dizygotic (fraternal) male twins, suggesting a significant heritable component for conduct problems in males. In contrast, conduct problems were not found to be heritable in females. The researchers concluded that genetic factors exert a stronger influence on conduct problems in males than in females. This way of studying genetics isn't perfect. You can assume monozygotic twins have the same genetic makeup and dizygotic twins do not. However, a complicating concern is whether monozygotic twins have the same experiences or environment as dizygotic twins. Some identical twins are dressed alike and are even given similar names. Yet the twins influence each other's behaviour, and in some cases, monozygotic twins may affect each other more than dizygotic twins (Carey, 1992).

One way to address this problem is by combining the adoption study and twin study methods. If you can find identical twins, one of whom was adopted as an infant, you can estimate the relative roles of genes and the environment (nature versus nurture) in the development of behavioural patterns.

## Genetic Linkage and Association Studies

The results of a series of family, twin, and adoption studies may suggest that a particular disorder has a genetic component, but they can't provide the location of the implicated gene or genes. To locate a defective gene, there are two general strategies: **genetic linkage** and **association studies** (Merikangas & Risch, 2003).

The basic principle of genetic linkage studies is simple. When a family disorder is studied, other inherited characteristics are assessed at the same time. These other characteristics—called **genetic markers**—are selected because we know their exact location. If a match or *link* is discovered between the inheritance of the disorder and the inheritance of a genetic marker, the genes for the disorder and the genetic marker are probably close together on the same chromosome. For example, bipolar disorder (manic depression) was studied in a large Amish family (Egeland et al., 1987). Researchers found that two markers on chromosome 11, genes for insulin and a known cancer gene, were linked to the presence of mood disorder in this family, suggesting that a gene for bipolar disorder might be on chromosome 11. Unfortunately, although this is a genetic linkage study, it also illustrates the danger of drawing premature conclusions from research. This

**twin studies**   In genetics research, comparisons of twins with unrelated or less closely related individuals. If twins, particularly monozygotic twins who share identical genotypes, share common characteristics such as a disorder, even if they were reared in different environments, this is strong evidence of genetic involvement in those characteristics.

**genetic linkage studies**   Studies that seek to match the inheritance pattern of a disorder to that of a genetic marker; this helps researchers establish the location of the gene responsible for the disorder.

**association studies**   Research strategies for comparing genetic markers in groups of people with and without a particular disorder.

**genetic marker**   Inherited characteristic for which the chromosomal location of the responsible gene is known.

linkage study and a second study that purported to find a linkage between the bipolar disorder and the X chromosome (Biron et al., 1987) have yet to be replicated; that is, different researchers have not been able to show similar linkages in other families (Craddock & Jones, 2001).

The inability to replicate findings in these studies is common (Altmuller, Palmer, Fischer, Scherb, & Wjst, 2001). This type of failure casts doubt on conclusions that only one gene is responsible for such complex disorders. Be mindful of such limitations the next time you read in a newspaper or hear on TV that a gene has been identified as causing some disorder.

The second strategy for locating specific genes, association studies, also uses genetic markers. Whereas linkage studies compare markers in a large group of people with a particular disorder, association studies compare such people and people without the disorder. If certain markers occur significantly more often in the people with the disorder, it is assumed the markers are close to the genes involved with the disorder. Association studies are thus better able to identify genes that may only weakly be associated with a disorder. Both strategies for locating specific genes shed new light on the origins of specific disorders and may inspire new approaches to treatment (Merikangas & Risch, 2003).

## *Studying Behaviour over Time*

Sometimes we want to ask, "How will a disorder or behaviour pattern change (or remain the same) over time?" This question is important for several reasons. First, the answer helps us decide whether to treat a particular person. For example, should we begin an expensive and time-consuming program for a young adult who is depressed over the loss of a grandparent? You might not if you knew that, with normal social supports, the depression is likely to diminish over the next few months without treatment. On the other hand, if you have reason to believe a problem isn't likely to go away on its own, you might decide to begin treatment. For example, as we see later, aggression among very young children does not usually go away naturally and should be dealt with as early as possible.

It is also important to understand the developmental changes in abnormal behaviour, because sometimes these can provide insight into how problems are created and become more serious. For example, we will see that some researchers identify people who are at risk for schizophrenia by their family histories and follow them through the entire risk period (18–45 years of age; see Tsuang, Stone, & Faraone, 2002). The goal is to discover the factors (e.g., social status and family psychopathology) that

predict who will manifest the disorder. (This complex and fascinating research is described in Chapter 12.)

### Prevention Research

An additional reason for studying behaviour over time and therefore improving our understanding of the very nature of certain clinical problems is that we may be able to design interventions and services to prevent these problems (Conrod & Stewart, 2005). Clearly, preventing mental health difficulties would save countless families significant emotional distress, and the financial savings could be substantial. Prevention research includes the study of biological, psychological, and environmental risk factors for developing later problems (called *preintervention* research); treatment interventions to help prevent later problems (called *prevention intervention* research); and more widespread structural issues such as governmental policies that could assist with prevention efforts (called *preventive service systems* research; NAMHC Workgroup on Mental Disorders Prevention Research, 1998). The research strategies used in prevention research for examining psychopathology across time combine individual and group research methods, including both correlational and experimental designs. We look next at two of the most frequently used: cross-sectional and longitudinal designs.

### Cross-Sectional Designs

A variation of correlation research is to compare different people at different ages. For a **cross-sectional design,** researchers take a cross section of a population across the different age groups and compare them on some characteristic. For example, if they were trying to understand the development of alcohol abuse and dependence, they could take groups of adolescents at 12, 15, and 17 years of age and assess their beliefs about alcohol use. In such a comparison, Brown and Finn (1982) made some interesting discoveries. They found that 36% of the 12-year-olds thought the primary purpose of drinking was to get drunk. This percentage increased to 64% with 15-year-olds but dropped again to 42% for the 17-year-old students. The researchers also found that 28% of the 12-year-olds reported drinking with their friends at least sometimes, a rate that increased to 80% for the 15-year-olds and to 88% for the 17-year-olds. Brown and Finn used this information to develop the hypothesis that the reason for excessive drinking among teens is a deliberate attempt to get drunk rather than a

---

**cross-sectional design** Methodology to examine a characteristic by comparing different individuals of different ages.

mistake in judgment once they are under the influence of alcohol. In other words, teenagers do not, as a group, appear to drink too much because once they've had a drink or two they show poor judgment and drink excessively. Instead, their attitudes before drinking seem to influence how much they drink later.

In cross-sectional designs, the participants in each age group are called **cohorts;** Brown and Finn (1982) studied three cohorts: 12-year-olds, 15-year-olds, and 17-year-olds. The members of each cohort are the same age at the same time and thus have all been exposed to similar experiences. Meanwhile, members of one cohort differ from members of other cohorts in age and in their exposure to cultural and historical experiences. You would expect a group of 12-year-olds in the early 1990s to have received a great deal of education about drug and alcohol use, whereas the 17-year-olds may not have. Differences among cohorts in their opinions about alcohol use may be related to their respective cognitive and emotional development at these different ages and to their dissimilar experiences. This **cohort effect,** the confounding of age and experience, is a limitation of the cross-sectional design.

Researchers prefer cross-sectional designs to study changes over time partly because they are easier to use than longitudinal designs (discussed next). In addition, some phenomena are less likely to be influenced by different cultural and historical experiences and therefore are less susceptible to cohort effects. For example, the prevalence of Alzheimer's disease among people at ages 60 and 70—assumed to be strongly influenced by biology—is not likely to be greatly affected by different experiences among the study participants.

One question not answered by cross-sectional designs is how problems develop in individuals. For example, do children who refuse to go to school grow up to have anxiety disorders? A researcher cannot answer this question simply by comparing adults with anxiety problems and children who refuse to go to school. He could ask the adults whether they were anxious about school when they were children, but this **retrospective information** (looking back) may be less than accurate (Watt, Stewart, & Cox, 1998). To get a better picture of how individuals develop over the years, researchers use longitudinal designs.

## Longitudinal Designs

Rather than looking at different groups of people of differing ages, researchers may follow one group over time and assess change in its members directly. The advantages of **longitudinal designs** are that they do not suffer from cohort effect problems and they allow the researchers to assess individual

change. (Figure 3.8 illustrates both longitudinal and cross-sectional designs.) Daniel Nagin and Richard Tremblay at the University of Montreal conducted a longitudinal study on physical aggression in boys. They followed more than 1000 boys from low socioeconomic neighbourhoods in Montreal from age 6 to age 15, examining their levels of physical aggression over this period. Using this method, Nagin and Tremblay were able to identify four distinct groups of boys based on their levels and stability of aggression over this period. The first group was a *chronic physical aggression* group comprising boys who displayed persistently high levels of aggression over the 9 years of the study. The second

**cohort**   Participants in each age group of a cross-sectional research study.

**cohort effect**   Observation that people of different age groups also differ in their values and experiences.

**retrospective information**   Literally "the view back," data collected by examining records or recollections of the past. It is limited by the accuracy, validity, and thoroughness of the sources.

**longitudinal design**   Systematic study of changes in the same individual or group examined over time.

**Longitudinal design**

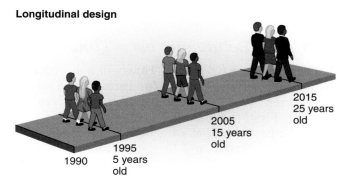

Same people followed across time

**Cross-sectional design**

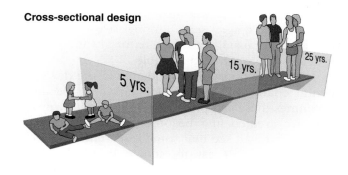

People of different ages viewed at the same time

**Figure 3.8** ■ Two research designs.

group was a *high but declining* group comprising boys who displayed a high levels of aggression in kindergarten but showed a decrease thereafter. A third group was a *moderate but declining* group whose members showed moderate levels of aggression in kindergarten but a decrease thereafter. The final group was a *low* group whose members rarely displayed aggression during the study (Nagin & Tremblay, 1999).

In addition to measuring levels of physical aggression, the researchers also measured parental and early childhood variables that might help explain which boys would show persistently high aggression from childhood to adolescence. The researchers found that the only characteristic that distinguished boys in the chronic physical aggression group from boys in the high but declining group was having a teenage mother or a mother with less education than other mothers (Nagin & Tremblay, 2001). The longitudinal research of Tremblay and his colleagues is discussed in Chapter 11.

Imagine conducting a major longitudinal study. Not only must the researcher persevere over months and years, but so must the people who participate in the study. They must remain willing to continue in the project, and the researcher must hope they will not move away or die! Longitudinal research is costly and time consuming; it is also subject to the possibility that the research question will have become irrelevant by the time the study is complete. Finally, longitudinal designs can suffer from a phenomenon similar to the cohort effect on cross-sectional designs. The **cross-generational effect** involves trying to generalize the findings to groups whose experiences are very different from those of the study participants. For example, the drug-use histories of people who were young adults in the 1960s and early 1970s are vastly different from those of people born in the 1990s.

Sometimes psychopathologists combine longitudinal and cross-sectional designs in a strategy called the **sequential design,** which involves repeated study of different cohorts over time. One example is some recent research conducted on children's beliefs about cigarette smoking (Chassin, Presson, Rose, & Sherman, 2001). These researchers used the sequential design to follow 10 cohorts of junior high- and senior high-school-age children (cross-sectional design) since the early 1980s (longitudinal design). Through questionnaires they have tracked how these children (and later, adults) viewed the health risks associated with smoking from their youth into their mid-30s. For example, the researchers would ask if they believed in the following statement: "A person who eats right and exercises regularly can smoke without harming his/her health." The results suggest that, in junior high (ages 11–14), the children viewed smoking as less risky to them personally and believed that there were positive psychological benefits (e.g., making them appear more mature). These beliefs changed as the children went into senior high school and entered adulthood, but point to the importance of targeting smoking prevention programs during the junior high school years (Chassin et al., 2001).

## Studying Behaviour across Cultures

Just as we can become narrowly focused when we study people only at a certain age, we can also miss important aspects by studying people from only one culture. Studying the differences in behaviour of people from different cultures can tell us a great deal about the origins and possible treatments of abnormal behaviours. Unfortunately, most research literature originates in Western cultures (Lambert et al., 1992), producing an ethnocentric view of psychopathology that can limit our understanding of disorders in general and can restrict the way we approach treatment (Draguns & Tanaka-Matsumi, 2003). Researchers in Malaysia—where psychological disorders are commonly believed to have supernatural origins—have

Longitudinal studies can be complicated by the cross-generational effect; for example, young people in the 1960s shared experiences that were very different from those of young people today.

Don Dutton/Toronto Star

**cross-generational effect**   Limit to the generalizability of longitudinal research because the group under study may differ from others in culture and experience.

**sequential design**   Combination of the cross-sectional and longitudinal research methods involving repeated study of different cohorts over time.

The same behaviours—for example, those of individuals in public—may be viewed very differently in different cultures.

In cross-cultural research, we can't randomly assign infants to different cultures and observe how they develop. People from varying cultures can differ in any number of important ways—their genetic backgrounds, for one—that could explain variations in their behaviour for reasons other than culture.

The characteristics of different cultures can also complicate research efforts. Symptoms or descriptions of them can be very dissimilar in different societies. Nigerians who are depressed complain of heaviness or heat in the head, crawling sensations in the head or legs, burning sensations in the body, and a feeling the belly is bloated with water (Ebigno, 1982). In contrast, people in North America report feeling worthless, being unable to start or finish anything, losing interest in usual activities, and thinking of suicide. Natives of China, on the other hand, do not report the loss of pleasure, helplessness or hopelessness, guilt, or suicidal thoughts seen in depressed North Americans (Kleinman, 1982). These few examples illustrate that applying a standard definition of depression across different cultures will result in vastly different outcomes.

An additional complicating factor is varying tolerances, or *thresholds*, for abnormal behaviour. If people in different cultures see the same behaviours differently, researchers will have trouble comparing incidence and prevalence rates. Lambert and colleagues (1992) found that Jamaican parents and teachers report fewer incidents of abnormal child behaviour than do their North American counterparts. Does this represent a biological or environmental difference in the children, the effects of different thresholds of tolerance in the societies, or a combination of all three? Understanding cultural attitudes and customs is essential to such research.

Finally, treatment research is also complicated by cross-cultural differences. Cultures develop treatment models that reflect their own values. In Japan, psychiatric hospitalization is organized in terms of a family model, with caregivers assuming parental roles. A family model was also common in psychiatric institutions in 19th-century North America until it was replaced with the medical model common today (Blue & Gaines, 1992; Dwyer, 1992). In Saudi Arabia, women are veiled when outside the home, which prevents them from uncovering their faces in the presence of therapists; custom thus complicates efforts to establish a trusting and intimate therapeutic client–therapist relationship (Dubovsky, 1983). Because medicine and religion are inseparable in the Islamic view, medical and religious treatments are combined (Baasher, 2001). As you can see, something as basic as comparing treatment outcomes is highly complex in a cross-cultural context.

described a disorder they call *gila*, which has some of the features of schizophrenia but differs in important ways (Razali, Hasanah, Khan, & Subramaniam, 2000; Razali, Khan, & Hasanah, 1996; Resner & Hartog, 1970). Could we learn more about schizophrenia (and *gila*) by comparing the disorders *and* the cultures in which they are found? Increasing awareness of the limited cultural scope of our research is creating a corresponding increase in cross-cultural research on psychopathology.

The designs we have described are adapted for studying abnormal behaviour across cultures. Some researchers view the effects of different cultures as though they were different treatments (Malpass & Poortinga, 1986). In other words, the independent variable is the effect of different cultures on behaviour rather than, say, the effect of cognitive therapy versus simple exposure for the treatment of fears. The difference between looking at culture as a "treatment" and our typical design, however, is important.

# Concept Check 3.5

1. List the four traditional research strategies scientists use to study the interaction between environment and genetics in psychological disorders.
2. The following are some of the advantages and limitations of methods used in research across time. Sort them out by marking CS for cross-sectional designs and L for longitudinal designs.

Benefits:
   a. _____ shows individual development
   b. _____ easier
   c. _____ no cohort effects

Limitations:
   d. _____ cohort effects
   e. _____ cross-generational effect
   f. _____ no individual development data

3. Describe some problems associated with cross-cultural research.

## The Power of a Program of Research

When we examine different research strategies independently, as we have done here, we often have the impression that some approaches are better than others. It is important to understand that this is not true. Depending on the type of question you are asking and the practical limitations inherent in the inquiry, any of the research techniques would be appropriate. Significant issues often are resolved not by one perfectly designed study but by a *series* of studies that examine different aspects of the problem—in a *program* of research. In an outstanding example of this approach, Patterson and his colleagues have studied the aggressive behaviour of children.

Their earliest research focused on basic concerns, such as why children are aggressive. The researchers first did a series of correlational studies to determine what variables were associated with aggression in children. One study was conducted in a state institution for girls with various problem behaviours (Buehler, Patterson, & Furniss, 1966). Researchers found that the delinquent behaviours—including rule breaking, criticizing adults, and aggressiveness—were likely to be reinforced by the girls' peers, who encouraged them.

Using strategies from epidemiology, Patterson also looked at the prevalence of aggression in children. He found that the likelihood of inappropriate

behaviour among children who are identified as *not* having a disorder ranged from 41% to 11%, with a mean of approximately 25% (Patterson, Cobb, & Ray, 1972). In other words, some level of aggression appears to be normal. Children are seen as "deviant" not for displaying a behaviour but when that behaviour exceeds an acceptable level of frequency or intensity.

As you remember, interpreting the results from correlation studies can be difficult, especially if the intent is to determine causation. To forestall this criticism, Patterson also conducted experimental studies. One strategy he used was a single-case experimental design (withdrawal design), in which he observed how a 5-year-old boy reacted to his mother's attempts to change his problem behaviour (Patterson, 1982). Patterson asked the boy's mother to restrain the child if he was aggressive but not to talk to him during this time. Patterson observed that the boy whined and complained when he was restrained. In the experimental condition, Patterson asked the mother to talk with her son in a positive way when he complained. Later, Patterson had her again ignore her son's complaints (a withdrawal design). He found the boy was more likely to complain about being restrained when his mother talked with him. One conclusion was that reinforcement (verbal communication) from the mother encouraged the boy to try to escape her restraint by complaining. By observing both the boy's behaviour (the dependent variable) and the mother's behaviour (the independent variable), Patterson could make stronger conclusions about the role of the mother in influencing her son's behaviour.

How does aggressiveness change over time? Patterson used cross-sectional research to observe children at different ages. In one study he found that the rate of aggression decreases as children get older (Patterson, 1982). It seems that children are less often aggressive as they get older, but for some, their aggression persists, as shown in the longitudinal research of Richard Tremblay and his colleagues.

Using treatment outcome research, Patterson's research team has also examined the effects of a treatment package on the aggressive behaviour of children. Patterson and Fleischman (1979) introduced a behavioural treatment involving parent training (see Chapter 11) and described the results of the treatment on the behaviour of both parents and their children. The researchers found they could reduce inappropriate child behaviour and improve the parenting skills of the parents, and these changes persisted a year after treatment.

As this example indicates, research is conducted in stages, and a complete picture of any behaviour can be seen only after looking at it from many different perspectives. An integrated program of research can help researchers explore various aspects of abnormal behaviour.

## Replication

Scientists in general, and behavioural scientists in particular, are never really convinced something is "true." People are skeptical when it comes to claims about causes or treatment outcomes. Replicating findings is what makes researchers confident that what they are observing isn't a coincidence. We noted when we described the case study method that if we look at a disorder in only one person, no matter how carefully we describe and document what we observe, we cannot draw strong conclusions.

The strength of a research program is in its ability to replicate findings in different ways to build confidence in the results. If you look back at the research strategies we have described, you will find that replication is one of the most important aspects of each. The more times a researcher repeats a process (and the behaviour he or she is studying changes as expected) the more sure he or she is about what caused the changes.

## Research Ethics

A final issue, though not the least important, involves the ethics of doing research in abnormal psychology. For example, the appropriateness of a clinician's delaying treatment to people who need it, just to satisfy the requirements of an experimental design, is frequently questioned. One single-case experimental design, the withdrawal design, can involve removing treatment for a period. Treatment is also withheld when placebo control groups are used in group experimental designs. Researchers across the world—in an evolving code of ethics referred to as the Declaration of Helsinki—are developing guidelines to determine just when it would be appropriate to use placebo-controlled trials (Carpenter, Appelbaum, & Levine, 2003). The fundamental question is this: When does a scientist's interest in preserving the internal validity of a study outweigh a client's right to treatment?

One answer to this question involves **informed consent**—a research participant's formal agreement to cooperate in a study following full disclosure of the nature of the research and the participant's role in it (Simon, 1999). The ethical requirement of informed consent helps to prevent tragedies such as those resulting from the "psychic driving" experiments conducted by Dr. Ewan Cameron on vulnerable psychiatric patients (without their consent) at the Allan Memorial Institute in Montreal from 1957

to 1964 (see Chapter 14 for more information). Informed consent procedures used today would also have prevented the unfortunate psychological consequences experienced by a Western Canadian boy who was, without his knowledge or consent about the situation, raised as a girl following a botched circumcision operation in 1966. This famous real-life experiment, conducted by sexologist Dr. John Money, is described in detail in Chapter 9. Today, because of ethical requirements of informed consent, in studies using some form of treatment delay or withdrawal, the participant is told why it will occur and the risks and benefits, and permission to proceed is then obtained. In placebo control studies, participants are told they may not receive an active treatment (all participants are blind to or unaware of which group they are placed in), but they are usually given the option of receiving treatment after the study ends.

True informed consent is at times elusive. The basic components are competence, voluntarism, full information, and comprehension on the part of the subject (Imber et al., 1986). In other words, research participants must be capable of consenting to participation in the research, they must volunteer or not be coerced into participating, they must have all the information they need to make the decision, and they must understand what their participation will involve. In some circumstances, all these conditions are difficult to attain. Children, for example, often do not fully appreciate what will occur during research. Similarly, individuals with cognitive impairments such as mental retardation or schizophrenia may not understand their role or their rights as participants. In institutional settings participants should not feel coerced into taking part in research.

Certain general protections help ensure that these concerns are properly addressed. First, according to the Tri-Council Policy Statement for the *Ethical Conduct for Research Involving Humans*, prepared by the former Medical Research Council of Canada (now replaced by the Canadian Institutes of Health Research), the Natural Sciences and Engineering Research Council of Canada, and the Social Sciences and Humanities Research Council of Canada, research in Canadian university and medical settings must be approved by a research ethics board (REB; CIHR, NSERC, SSHRC, 2003). These are committees made up of university faculty

---

**informed consent** Ethical requirement whereby research participants agree to participate in a research study only after they receive full disclosure about the nature of the study and their role in it.

and non-academic people from the community, and their purpose is to see that the rights of research participants are protected. The committee structure allows people other than the researcher to look at the research procedures to determine whether sufficient care is being taken to protect the welfare and dignity of the participants.

To safeguard those who participate in psychological research and to clarify the responsibilities of researchers, the Canadian Psychological Association (CPA) published the *Canadian Code of Ethics for Psychologists*, third edition, which includes general guidelines that apply to the various activities engaged in by psychologists, including conducting research (CPA, 2000; see also O'Neill, 1998b). People in research experiments must be protected from both physical and psychological harm. In addition to the issue of informed consent, the CPA Code stresses that the welfare of the research participants is given priority over any other consideration, including experimental design. The CPA Code of Ethics is discussed in detail in Chapter 14.

Psychological harm is difficult to define, but its definition remains the responsibility of the investigator. Researchers must hold in confidence all information obtained from participants, who have the right to concealment of their identity on all data, either written or informal. Whenever deception is considered essential to research, the investigator must satisfy a committee of peers that this judgment is correct. If deception is used, participants must be debriefed—that is, told in language they can understand the true purpose of the study and why it was necessary to deceive them.

The Society for Research in Child Development (1990) has endorsed ethical guidelines for research that address some of the issues unique to research with children. For example, not only do these guidelines call for confidentiality, protection from harm, and debriefing, but they also require informed consent from children's caregivers and from the children themselves if they are age 7 and older. These guidelines specify that the research must be explained to children in language they can understand so that they can decide whether they wish to participate. Many other ethical issues extend beyond protection of the participants, including how researchers deal with errors in their research, fraud in science, and the proper way to give credit to others. Doing a study involves much more than selecting the appropriate design. Researchers must be aware of numerous concerns that involve the rights of the people in the experiment and their own conduct.

## Concept Check 3.6

True or False?

1. _____ After the nature of the experiment and their role in it are disclosed to the participants, they must be allowed to refuse or agree to sign an informed consent form.
2. _____ If the participant is in the control group or taking a placebo, an informed consent is not needed.
3. _____ Research in universities or medical settings must be approved by the institution's research ethics board whether or not the participants lack the cognitive skills to protect themselves from harm.
4. _____ Participants have a right to concealment of their identity on all data collected and reported.
5. _____ When deception is essential to the research, participants do not have to be debriefed regarding the true purpose of the study.

# Summary

## Assessing Psychological Disorders

- Clinical assessment is the systematic evaluation and measurement of psychological, biological, and social factors in an individual with a possible psychological disorder; diagnosis is the process of determining that those factors meet all the criteria for a specific psychological disorder.

- Reliability, validity, and standardization are important components in determining the value of a psychological assessment.
- To assess various aspects of psychological disorders, clinicians may first interview and take an informal mental status exam of the patient. More systematic observations of behaviour are called behavioural assessment.

- A variety of psychological tests can be used during assessment, including projective tests, in which the patient responds to ambiguous stimuli by projecting unconscious thoughts; personality inventories, in which the patient takes a self-report questionnaire designed to assess personal traits; and intelligence testing that provides a score known as an intelligence quotient.
- Biological aspects of psychological disorders may be assessed through neuropsychological testing that is designed to identify possible areas of brain dysfunction. Neuroimaging can be used more directly to identify brain structure and function. Finally, psychophysiological assessment refers to measurable changes in the nervous system reflecting emotional or psychological events that might be relevant to a psychological disorder.

## Diagnosing Psychological Disorders

- The term *classification* refers to any effort to construct groups or categories and to assign objects or people to the categories on the basis of their shared attributes or relations. Methods of classification include classical categorical, dimensional, and prototypical approaches. Our current system of classification, the *Diagnostic and Statistical Manual of Mental Disorders,* Fourth Edition, Text Revision (DSM-IV-TR), is based on a prototypical approach, in which certain essential characteristics are identified, but certain "nonessential" variations do not necessarily change the classification. The DSM-IV-TR categories are based on empirical findings to identify the criteria for each diagnosis. Although this system is the best to date in terms of scientific underpinnings, it is far from perfect, and research continues on the most useful way to classify psychological disorders as we begin to plan for DSM-V.

## Conducting Research in Psychopathology

- Research involves establishing a hypothesis that is then tested. In abnormal psychology, research focuses on hypotheses meant to explain the nature, the causes, or the treatment of a disorder.

## Types of Research Methods

- The individual case study is used to study one or more individuals in depth. Though case studies have an important role in the theoretical development of psychology, they are not subject to experimental control and must necessarily be suspect in terms of both internal and external validity.
- Research by correlation can tell us whether a relationship exists between two variables, but it does not tell us if that relationship is a causal one. Epidemiological research is a type of correlational research that reveals the incidence, distribution, and consequences of a particular problem in one or more populations.
- Research by experiment can follow one of two designs: group or single case. In both designs, a variable (or variables) is manipulated and the effects are observed to determine the nature of a causal relationship.

## Genetics and Research across Time and Cultures

- Genetic research focuses on the role of genetics in behaviour. These research strategies include family studies, adoption studies, twin studies, genetic linkage analyses, and association studies.
- Research strategies that examine psychopathology across time include cross-sectional and longitudinal designs. Both focus on differences in behaviour or attitudes at different ages, but the former does so by looking at different individuals at different ages, while the latter looks at the same individuals at different ages.
- The clinical picture, causal factors, and treatment process and outcome can all be influenced by cultural factors.
- The more the findings of a research program are replicated, the more they gain credibility.
- Ethics are important to the research process, and ethical guidelines are spelled out by many professional organizations and research funding bodies in an effort to ensure the well-being of research participants.

## Key Terms

| | | | |
|---|---|---|---|
| clinical assessment, 76 | mental status exam, 79 | personality inventories, 85 | neuropsychological testing, 88 |
| diagnosis, 76 | behavioural assessment, 82 | intelligence quotient (IQ), 87 | false positives, 88 |
| reliability, 78 | projective tests, 84 | | false negatives, 88 |
| validity, 78 | | | |
| standardization, 79 | | | |

neuroimaging, 89
psychophysiological
    assessment, 90
electroencephalogram
    (EEG), 91
classification, 93
taxonomy, 93
nosology, 93
nomenclature, 93
classical categorical
    approach, 93
dimensional
    approach, 94
prototypical
    approach, 94
comorbidity, 98
labelling, 98
hypothesis, 100
research design, 100

dependent variable, 100
independent variable, 100
internal validity, 100
external validity, 100
testability, 101
confound, 101
control group, 101
randomization, 101
analogue model, 101
generalizability, 102
statistical
    significance, 102
clinical significance, 102
case study method, 104
correlation, 104
positive correlation, 105
correlation
    coefficient, 105
negative correlation, 105
directionality, 106

epidemiology, 106
experiment, 107
placebo effect, 107
placebo control
    group, 108
double-blind control, 108
comparative treatment
    research, 108
single-case experimental
    design, 109
variability, 110
trend, 110
level, 110
withdrawal design, 111
baseline, 111
multiple baseline, 111
phenotype, 113
genotype, 113
human genome
    project, 113

family studies, 113
proband, 113
adoption studies, 113
twin studies, 114
genetic linkage
    studies, 114
association studies, 114
genetic marker, 114
cross-sectional
    design, 115
cohort, 116
cohort effect, 116
retrospective
    information, 116
longitudinal design, 116
cross-generational
    effect, 117
sequential design, 117
informed consent, 120

---

## Answers to Concept Checks

**3.1**   **Part A**   1. thought processes  2. appearance and behaviour  3. sensorium  4. mood and affect  5. intellectual functioning

  **Part B**   6. R, V  7. NR, NV  8. R, V

**3.2**   1. T  2. F  3. F (still a problem) 4. F (reliability)  5. T

**3.3**   1. independent  2. confound  3. hypothesis 4. dependent  5. internal, external

**3.4**   1. d  2. b  3. a  4. e

**3.5**   1. family studies, adoption studies, twin studies, and genetic linkage and association studies
  2. a. L  b. CS  c. L  d. CS  e. L  f. CS
  3. no random assignment, symptoms and treatments vary from one place to another, and tolerances vary

**3.6**   1. T  2. F  3. T  4. T  5. F

 **InfoTrac College Edition**

If your instructor ordered your book with InfoTrac College Edition, please explore this online library for additional readings, review, and a handy resource for short assignments. Go to:

**http://infotrac.thomsonlearning.com**

Enter these search terms: psychological assessment, Diagnostic and Statistical Manual, neuropsychological testing, research methods, experimental design, epidemiology, placebo effect, twin studies, cross-sectional design

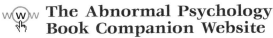 **The Abnormal Psychology Book Companion Website**

Go to **www.essentialsabnormalpsych.nelson.com** for practice quiz questions, Internet links, critical thinking exercises, and more.

 **Abnormal Psychology Live CD-ROM**

• **Arriving at a Diagnosis:** A team discusses how they arrive at the conclusion that a client has panic disorder.
• **Psychological Assessment:** The psychological team discusses factors in dysfunctional beliefs, family relationships and behaviour patterns that might be contributing to a woman's major depressive disorder.
• **Research Methods:** David Barlow discusses the protocols and procedures in doing ethical research on clients with psychological problems. He explains the safeguards and the changes in the practices over time.

**Thomson NOW!** **http://hed.nelson.com** Go to this site for the link to ThomsonNow™, your one-stop study shop. Take a Pretest for this chapter and ThomsonNow™ will generate a personalized Study Plan based on your test results! The Study Plan will identify the topics you need to review and direct you to online resources to help you master those topics. You can then take a Posttest to help you determine the concepts you have mastered and what you still need work on.

## Video Concept Review

For challenging concepts that typically need more than one explanation, Mark Durand provides a video review via ThomsonNow™ of the following topics:

- The importance of a data-based psychosocial approach.
- Categorical versus dimensional approaches to diagnosis.

# Chapter Quiz

1. During a clinical interview a psychologist notes that a client is not aware of what the date is or even where she is. The psychologist has gained information about what aspect of the client's mental status?

   a. reliability
   b. affect
   c. sensorium
   d. intellectual functioning

2. One criticism of the Rorschach inkblot test and other projective assessment techniques is that different therapists administer and interpret them in different ways. Because of that variability, the tests lack what key attribute?

   a. random sampling
   b. standardization
   c. validity
   d. testability

3. What type of test would you use to explore whether an individual might have some sort of brain damage or injury?

   a. neuropsychological test
   b. projective test
   c. electrodermal test
   d. personality test

4. Measuring electrical activity in the brain with an electroencephalogram (EEG) would be most appropriate to answer which of the following questions?

   a. Will this client perform at the same level with his peers in school?
   b. Does this client have excessive fears and worries?
   c. Is this client well-suited to pursue a career in the creative arts?
   d. Is this client benefiting from relaxation training?

5. Which approach to diagnostic classification identifies both essential characteristics of a disorder that everyone with the disorder shares and nonessential characteristics that might vary from person to person?

   a. prototypical
   b. standardized
   c. dimensional
   d. categorical

6. Despite improvements in the DSM-IV-TR, which of the following criticisms can still be levelled at that classification system?

   a. It provides no opportunity to describe biological or social factors that might influence psychological health.
   b. It relies on a purely dimensional approach, and the number of relevant dimensions on which to describe clients is infinite.
   c. The system emphasizes validity at the expense of reliability.
   d. It categorizes and labels people, which can be pejorative or even self-fulfilling.

7. In most experiments, researchers explore the expected influence of the _____ on the _____.

   a. incidence; prevalence
   b. independent variable; dependent variable
   c. external validity; internal validity
   d. testability; generalizability

8. When behaviour change occurs because of a person's expectation of change rather than (or in addition to) the result of any manipulation by the experimenter, it is known as the:

   a. clinical significance.
   b. cohort effect.
   c. placebo effect.
   d. prevalence.

9. What type of research design is used if an experiment examines life satisfaction in different groups of 20-, 40-, and 60-year-olds to draw conclusions about age differences?

   a. cross-sectional
   b. longitudinal
   c. multiple baseline
   d. case study

10. One way that participants in research projects are protected from harm is by making sure they are not coerced into participating and that they have full knowledge of what their participation will involve. What is that ethical protection called?

    a. internal validity
    b. positive correlation
    c. informed consent
    d. clinical significance

*(See the Appendix on page 601 for answers.)*

# 4 Anxiety Disorders

## The Complexity of Anxiety Disorders
Anxiety, Fear, and Panic: Some Definitions
Causes of Anxiety Disorders
Comorbidity of Anxiety Disorders

## Generalized Anxiety Disorder
Clinical Description
Statistics
Causes
Treatment

## Panic Disorder With and Without Agoraphobia
Clinical Description
Statistics
Causes
Treatment

## Specific Phobia
Clinical Description
Statistics
Causes
Treatment

## Social Phobia
Clinical Description
Statistics
Causes
Treatment

## Posttraumatic Stress Disorder
Clinical Description
Statistics
Causes
Treatment

## Obsessive-Compulsive Disorder
Clinical Description
Statistics
Causes
Treatment

## Visual Summary: Exploring Anxiety Disorders

## Abnormal Psychology Live CD-ROM
Panic Disorder: Steve
Virtual Reality Therapy
Snake Phobia Treatment
Obsessive-Compulsive Disorder: Chuck

© Erich Lessing/Art Resource, NY

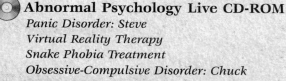

# The Complexity of Anxiety Disorders

- *Describe psychological and biological similarities and differences among anxiety, fear, and a panic attack.*

- *Identify the genetic and biological vulnerability factors that are known to influence the development of anxiety disorders.*

Anxiety is complex and mysterious, as Freud realized many years ago. "Anxiety" is a specific type of disorder, but it is much more than that. It is an emotion implicated so heavily across the full range of psychopathology that we begin by exploring its general nature, both biological and psychological. Next, we consider fear, a somewhat different but clearly related emotion. We suggest that panic is fear that occurs when there is nothing to be afraid of and, therefore, at an inappropriate time. With these important ideas clearly in mind, we focus on specific anxiety disorders.

## *Anxiety, Fear, and Panic: Some Definitions*

Have you ever experienced anxiety? A silly question, you might say, because most of us feel some anxiety almost every day of our lives. But have you ever stopped to think about the nature of anxiety? What is it? What causes it?

**Anxiety** is a negative mood state characterized by bodily symptoms of physical tension and by apprehension about the future (American Psychiatric Association, 1994; Barlow, 2002). Anxiety is very hard to study. In humans it can be a subjective sense of unease, a set of behaviours (looking worried and anxious, fidgeting), or a physiological response originating in the brain and reflected in elevated heart rate and muscle tension. Because anxiety is difficult to study in humans, much of the research has been done with animals. For example, we might teach laboratory rats that a light signals an impending shock. The animals look and act anxious when the light comes on. They may fidget, tremble, and perhaps cower in a corner. We might give them an anxiety-reducing drug and notice a reduction of anxiety in their reaction to the light. But is the rats' experience of anxiety the same as humans'? It seems to be similar, but we don't know for sure; research with animals provides only general information about the nature of anxiety in humans. Thus, anxiety remains a mystery, and we are only beginning our journey of discovery. Anxiety is also closely related to depression (Barlow, 2000, 2002; Barlow, Chorpita, & Turovsky, 1996; Cox, Enns, Walker, Kjernisted, & Pidlubny, 2001; Mineka,

**Panic Disorder: Steve**
*"First time it happened to me, I was driving down the highway, and I had a kind of a knot in my chest. I felt like I had swallowed something and it got stuck, and it lasted pretty much overnight.... I felt like I was having a heart attack.... I assumed that's what was happening. I felt very panicky. A flushed feeling came over my whole body. I felt as though I was going to pass out."*

Thomson Learning

Watson, & Clark, 1998), so much of what we say here is relevant to Chapter 6.

Anxiety is not very pleasant, so why do we seem programmed to experience it almost every time we do something important? Surprisingly, anxiety is good for us, at least in moderate amounts. Psychologists have known for nearly a century that we perform better when we are a little anxious (Yerkes & Dodson, 1908). You would not have done so well on that test the other day if you had had no anxiety. You were a little more charming and lively on that date last weekend because you were anxious. And you will be better prepared for that job interview coming up if you are anxious. In short, physical and intellectual performances are driven and enhanced by anxiety. Without it, very few of us would get much done.

But what happens when you have too much anxiety? You might actually fail the exam because you can't concentrate on the questions. All you can think about when you're too anxious is how terrible it will be if you fail. You might blow the interview for the same reason. On that date with a new person, you might spend the evening with perspiration running off your face, a sick feeling in your

**anxiety**   Mood state characterized by marked negative affect and bodily symptoms of tension in which a person apprehensively anticipates future danger or misfortune. Anxiety may involve feelings, behaviours, and physiological responses.

CP Photo/AP/Ed Bailey

Even successful performers like Alanis Morissette can experience excessive anxiety.

stomach, and unable to think of even one reasonably interesting thing to say. Too much of a good thing can be harmful, and few sensations are more harmful than severe anxiety that is out of control.

What makes the situation worse is that severe anxiety usually doesn't go away—that is, even if we "know" there is really nothing to be afraid of, we remain anxious. We constantly see examples of this kind of irrationality. Well-known singer and song-writer Alanis Morissette reportedly experiences severe anxiety. In one interview, she recounted an episode of anxiety that occurred shortly after she had moved to Los Angeles. Morissette was returning home to Canada for the holidays, and while writing cards on the plane, she suddenly began crying and shaking uncontrollably, and she felt as if she was going to faint. This experience scared her and she sought treatment ("The People's Courtney," 1995).

Morissette and countless other individuals who have anxiety-based disorders are well aware that they have little to fear in the situations they find so stressful. She should know, for example, that flying is the safest way to travel and that no objective danger existed in the situation when she experienced this anxiety attack. And yet Morissette, like others dealing with anxiety disorders, cannot seem to shake her excessive fear. All the disorders discussed in this chapter are characterized by excessive anxiety, which takes many different forms.

In Chapter 2 we saw that **fear** is an immediate alarm reaction to danger. Like anxiety, fear can be good for us. It protects us by activating a massive response from the autonomic nervous system (increased heart rate and blood pressure, for

example), which, along with our subjective sense of terror, motivates us to escape (flee) or, possibly, to attack (fight). As such, this emergency reaction is often called the flight or fight response.

Although not all emotion theorists agree, there is much evidence that fear and anxiety reactions differ psychologically and physiologically (Barlow, 2002). As noted earlier, anxiety is a future-oriented mood state, characterized by apprehension because we cannot predict or control upcoming events. Fear, on the other hand, is an immediate emotional reaction to current danger characterized by strong escapist action tendencies and, often, a surge in the sympathetic branch of the autonomic nervous system (Barlow, Brown, & Craske, 1994). Someone experiencing fear might say, "I've got to get out of here right now or I may not make it."

What happens if you experience the alarm response of fear when there is nothing to be afraid of? Alanis Morissette's episode of unexpected crying, shaking, and feeling faint on the airplane is a good example of this kind of false alarm. Consider also the case of Gretchen, who appeared at one of our clinics.

## Gretchen
### Attacked by Panic

I was 25 when I had my first attack. It was a few weeks after I'd come home from the hospital. I had had my appendix out. The surgery had gone well, and I wasn't in any danger, which is why I don't understand what happened. But one night I went to sleep and I woke up a few hours later—I'm not sure how long—but I woke up with this vague feeling of apprehension. Mostly I remember how my heart started pounding. And my chest hurt; it felt like I was dying—that I was having a heart attack. And I felt kind of queer, as if I were detached from the experience. It seemed like my bedroom was covered with a haze. I ran to my sister's room, but I felt like I was a puppet or a robot who was under the control of somebody else while I was running. I think I scared her almost as much as I was frightened myself. She called an ambulance (Barlow, 2002).

---

**fear**   Emotional response consisting of an immediate alarm reaction to present danger or life-threatening emergencies.

The roots of the panic experience are deeply embedded in our cultural myths. Pan, the Greek god of nature, lived in the country, presiding over rivers, woods, streams, and grazing animals. But Pan did not look like the typical god. He was very ugly and short, with legs resembling a goat's. Unfortunately for travellers, Pan habitually napped in a small cave or thicket near the road. When travelling Greeks disturbed him, he let out a blood-curdling scream so intense that many terrified travellers died of fright. This sudden, overwhelming reaction came to be known as **panic,** after the irate god. In psychopathology, a **panic attack** is defined as an abrupt experience of intense fear or acute discomfort, accompanied by physical symptoms that usually include heart palpitations, chest pain, shortness of breath, and, possibly, dizziness.

Three basic types of panic attacks are described in DSM-IV: situationally bound, unexpected, and situationally predisposed. If you know you are afraid of high places, like the top of the CN Tower in Toronto, or of driving over long bridges, like the Confederation Bridge to Prince Edward Island, you might have a panic attack in these situations but not anywhere else; this is a *situationally bound* (cued) panic attack. By contrast, you might have an *unexpected* (uncued) panic attack like the one Alanis Morissette experienced on the plane. The third type of panic attack, the *situationally predisposed*, is between these types. You are more likely to, but will not inevitably, have an attack where you have had one before, for example, in a large mall. If you don't know whether it will happen today, and it does, the attack is situationally predisposed. We mention these types of attacks because they play a role in several anxiety disorders. Unexpected and situationally predisposed attacks are important in *panic disorder*. Situationally bound attacks are more common in *specific phobias* or *social phobia* (see Figure 4.1).

Remember that fear is an intense emotional alarm accompanied by a surge of energy in the autonomic nervous system that motivates us to flee from danger. Does Gretchen's panic attack sound like it could be the emotion of fear? A variety of evidence suggests it is (Barlow, 2002; Barlow et al., 1996), including similarities in reports of the experience of fear and panic, similar behavioural tendencies to escape, and similar underlying neurobiological processes.

## Causes of Anxiety Disorders

You learned in Chapters 1 and 2 that excessive emotional reactions have no simple one-dimensional cause but come from multiple sources.

---

**panic**   Sudden overwhelming fright or terror.

**panic attack**   Abrupt experience of intense fear or discomfort in the absence of danger accompanied by a number of physical symptoms, such as dizziness or heart palpitations.

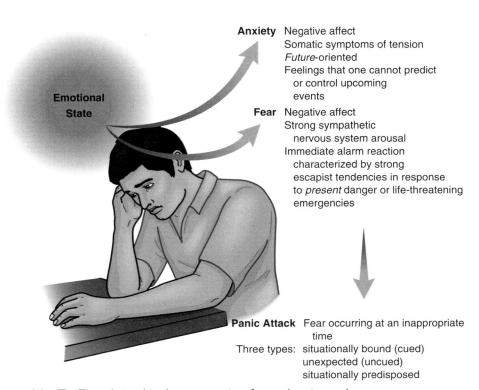

**Anxiety**   Negative affect
Somatic symptoms of tension
*Future*-oriented
Feelings that one cannot predict or control upcoming events

**Fear**   Negative affect
Strong sympathetic nervous system arousal
Immediate alarm reaction characterized by strong escapist tendencies in response to *present* danger or life-threatening emergencies

**Panic Attack**   Fear occurring at an inappropriate time
Three types:   situationally bound (cued)
unexpected (uncued)
situationally predisposed

**Emotional State**

**Figure 4.1** ■ The relationships between anxiety, fear, and panic attack.

## Biological Contributions

Increasing evidence shows that we inherit a tendency to be tense or uptight (Eysenck, 1967; Gray & McNaughton, 1996; Lader & Wing, 1964; McGuffin & Reich, 1984). As with almost all psychological disorders, and unlike hair or eye colour, no single gene seems to cause anxiety. Instead, contributions from many genes in several different areas on chromosomes collectively make us vulnerable to anxiety (Kendler et al., 1995; Lesch et al., 1996; Plomin et al., 1997) when the right psychological and social factors are in place. The tendency to panic also seems to run in families and may have a genetic component (Barlow, 2002).

Anxiety is also associated with specific brain circuits and neurotransmitter systems. For example, depleted levels of GABA are associated with increased anxiety, although the relationship is not quite so direct. Increasing attention in the last several years has focused on the role of the corticotropin-releasing factor (CRF) system as central to the expression of anxiety (and depression; Heim & Nemeroff, 1999; Ladd et al., 2000; Sullivan et al., 2000). This is because CRF activates the HPA axis, described in Chapter 2. This CRF system has wide-ranging effects on areas of the brain implicated in anxiety including the emotional brain (the limbic system). The CRF system is also directly related to the GABA-benzodiazepine system and the serotonergic and noradrenergic neurotransmitter systems.

The area of the brain most often associated with anxiety is the limbic system (Charney & Drevets, 2002; Gray & McNaughton, 1996; LeDoux, 1995,

1996), which acts as a mediator between the brain stem and the cortex. The more primitive brain stem monitors and senses changes in bodily functions and relays these potential danger signals to higher cortical processes through the limbic system.

The late Jeffrey Gray, a prominent British neuropsychologist, identified a brain circuit in the limbic system of animals that seems heavily involved in anxiety (Gray, 1982, 1985; McNaughton & Gray, 2000) and may be relevant to humans. This circuit leads from the septal and hippocampal area in the limbic system to the frontal cortex. The system that Gray called the **behavioural inhibition system (BIS)** is activated by signals from the brain stem of unexpected events, such as major changes in body functioning that might signal danger. Danger signals in response to something we see that might be threatening descend from the cortex to the septal-hippocampal system. The BIS also receives a big boost from the amygdala (Davis, 1992; LeDoux, 1996). When the BIS is activated by signals that arise from the brain stem or descend from the cortex, our tendency is to freeze, experience anxiety, and apprehensively evaluate the situation to confirm that danger is present.

The BIS circuit is distinct from the circuit involved in panic. Gray (1982; Gray & McNaughton, 1996) and Graeff (1987, 1993; Deakin & Graeff, 1991) identified what Gray calls the **fight/flight system (FFS).** This circuit originates in the brain stem and travels through several midbrain structures, including the amygdala. When stimulated in animals, this circuit produces an immediate alarm-and-escape response that looks very much like panic in humans (Gray & McNaughton, 1996). Gray and McNaughton (1996) and Graeff (1993) think the FFS is activated in part by deficiencies in serotonin.

It is likely that factors in your environment can change the sensitivity of these brain circuits, making you more or less susceptible to developing anxiety and its disorders (Francis, Diorio, Plotsky, & Meaney, 2002). An important study has appeared suggesting that cigarette smoking as a teenager is associated with greatly increased risk for developing anxiety disorders as adults, particularly panic disorder and generalized anxiety disorder (Johnson et al., 2000; see also review by Zvolensky, Schmidt, & Stewart, 2003). Nearly 700 adolescents were followed into adulthood. Teens who smoked 20 or more cigarettes daily were 15 times more likely to develop panic disorder and

---

### Disorder Criteria Summary
#### Panic Attack

A panic attack involves experiencing four or more of the following symptoms during a specific period of time:

- Palpitations or pounding heart
- Sweating
- Trembling or shaking
- Shortness of breath
- Feeling of choking
- Chest pain
- Nausea
- Dizziness
- Feeling of unreality
- Fear of losing control
- Fear of dying
- Numbness or tingling sensations
- Chills or hot flashes

*Source:* Reprinted with permission from the *Diagnostic and Statistical Manual of Mental Disorders,* Fourth Edition, Text Revision. (Copyright © 2000) American Psychiatric Association.

---

**behavioural inhibition system (BIS)**   Brain circuit in the limbic system that responds to threat signals by inhibiting activity and causing anxiety.

**fight/flight system (FFS)**   Brain circuit in animals that when stimulated causes an immediate alarm and escape response resembling human panic.

5 times more likely to develop generalized anxiety disorder than teens who smoked less or not at all. One possible explanation is that chronic exposure to nicotine, a drug that increases anxiety, as well as respiratory problems, somehow sensitizes the brain circuits associated with anxiety and increases one's biological vulnerability to develop severe anxiety disorders. Research into the neurobiology of anxiety and panic is very new, but we have made exciting progress.

## Psychological Contributions

In Chapter 2 we reviewed some theories on the nature of psychological causes of anxiety. Remember that Freud thought anxiety was a psychic reaction to danger surrounding the reactivation of an infantile fearful situation. Behavioural theorists view anxiety as a product of early classical conditioning, modelling, or other forms of learning (Bandura, 1986). Evidence is accumulating (e.g., Barlow, 2002) that supports an integrated model of anxiety involving a variety of factors. In childhood we may acquire an awareness that events are not always in our control (Chorpita & Barlow, 1998). The continuum of this perception may range from total confidence in our control of all aspects of our lives to deep uncertainty about ourselves and our ability to deal with upcoming events. The perception that events may be out of our control is most evident as a set of danger-laden beliefs. If you are anxious about schoolwork, you may think you will do poorly on the next exam and that there is no way you can pass the course, even though all your grades have been As and Bs. A general "sense of uncontrollability" may develop early as a function of upbringing and other environmental factors.

Interestingly, the actions of parents in early childhood seem to do a lot to foster this sense of control or, conversely, a sense of uncontrollability (Chorpita & Barlow, 1998; MacPherson, Stewart, & McWilliams, 2001; Watt & Stewart, 2003; Watt et al., 1998). Generally, it seems that parents who interact in a positive and predictable way with their children by responding to their needs, particularly when the child communicates his or her needs for attention, food, relief from pain, and so on, perform an important function. These parents teach their children that they have control over their environment and their responses have an effect on their parents and their environment. In addition, parents who allow their children to explore their world and develop the necessary skills to cope with unexpected occurrences enable their children to develop a healthy sense of control. What seems to be important is providing a "secure home base" for your children so that you are there for them if they need you while they explore their world (Chorpita & Barlow, 1998). In contrast, parents who are overprotective and overintrusive and who "clear the way" for their children, never letting them experience any adversity,

also create a situation where children never learn how to cope with adversity when it comes along. Therefore, these children don't learn that they can control their environment. A variety of evidence has accumulated supporting these ideas (Barlow, 2002; Chorpita & Barlow, 1998; Chorpita, Brown, & Barlow, 1998; Lieb et al., 2000; Nolen-Hoeksema, Wolfson, Mumme, & Guskin, 1995).

Most psychological accounts of panic invoke *conditioning* and *cognitive* explanations that are difficult to separate (Bouton, Mineka, & Barlow, 2001). Thus, a strong fear response initially occurs during extreme stress or perhaps as a result of a dangerous situation in the environment (a true alarm). This emotional response then becomes associated with a variety of external and internal cues. In other words, the cues provoke the fear response and an assumption of danger, whether or not danger is actually present (Bouton et al., 2001; Martin, 1983; Razran, 1961). External cues are places or situations similar to the one where the initial panic attack occurred. Internal cues are increases in heart rate or respiration that were associated with the initial panic attack, even if they are now due to perfectly normal circumstances, such as exercise. Thus, when your heart is beating fast you are more likely to think of and, perhaps, experience a panic attack than when it is beating normally.

## Social Contributions

Stressful life events trigger our biological and psychological vulnerabilities to anxiety. Most are interpersonal in nature—marriage, divorce, difficulties at work, death of a loved one, and so on. Some might be physical, such as an injury or illness. Social pressures, perhaps to excel in school, might also provide sufficient stress to trigger anxiety.

The same stressors can trigger physical reactions such as headaches or hypertension and emotional reactions such as panic attacks (Barlow, 2002). The particular way we react to stress seems to run in families. If you get headaches when under stress, chances are other people in your family also get headaches. If you have panic attacks, other members of your family probably do also. This finding suggests a possible genetic contribution, at least to initial panic attacks.

## An Integrated Model

Putting the factors together in an integrated way, we can see that a tendency to be uptight or high-strung might be inherited. But a *generalized biological vulnerability* to develop anxiety is not anxiety itself. You might also grow up believing the world is dangerous and out of control, and you might not be able to cope when things go wrong based on your early experiences. If this perception is strong, you have a *generalized psychological vulnerability* to anxiety.

Finally, you might be under a lot of pressure, particularly from interpersonal stressors. A given stressor could activate your biological tendencies to anxiety and your psychological tendencies to feel you might not be able to deal with the situation and control the stress. Once this cycle starts, it tends to feed on itself, so it might not stop even when the particular life stressor has long since passed. Anxiety can be very general, evoked by many aspects of your life. But it is usually focused on one area, such as grades (Barlow, 2002).

Panic is also a characteristic response to stress that runs in families and may have a genetic component. Because an individual associates the panic attack with internal or external cues (conditioning is one form of learning), the attacks are called *learned alarms*. Even if you have a legitimate fear response to a dangerous situation (true alarm), your reaction can become associated with a variety of cues that may then trigger an attack *in the absence* of any danger, making it a learned alarm. Furthermore, anxiety and panic are closely related (Barlow, 2002) in that anxiety increases the likelihood of panic. This relationship makes sense from an ethological point of view, because sensing possible future threat or danger (anxiety) should prepare us to react instantaneously with an alarm response if the danger becomes imminent. Anxiety and panic need not occur together, but it makes sense that they often do.

### Comorbidity of Anxiety Disorders

Before describing the specific anxiety disorders, it is important to note that they often co-occur. As we described in Chapter 3, the co-occurrence of two or more disorders in a single individual is referred to as *comorbidity*. The fact that rates of comorbidity among anxiety disorders (and depression) are high emphasizes that all of these disorders share the common features of anxiety and panic described here. They also share the same vulnerabilities, biological and psychological, to develop anxiety and panic. They differ only in the focus of anxiety (what are they anxious about?) and, perhaps, the patterning of panic attacks. Of course, if each patient with an anxiety disorder also had every other anxiety

disorder, there would be little sense in distinguishing among the specific disorders. It would be enough to say, simply, that the patient had an anxiety disorder. But this is not the case, and, although rates of comorbidity are high, they vary somewhat from disorder to disorder. By far, the most common additional diagnosis for all anxiety disorders is major depression, which occurrs in 50% of anxiety disordered cases over the course of the patient's life (Brown & Barlow, 2002; Brown, Campbell, Lehman, Grisham, & Mancill, 2001). This becomes important when we discuss the relationship between anxiety and depression later in this chapter.

We now turn to a description of the individual anxiety disorders. But keep in mind that approximately 50% of individuals with these disorders will present with one or more additional anxiety or depressive disorders and, perhaps, some other disorders, particularly substance use disorders, as described later.

---

## Concept Check 4.1

Complete the following statements about anxiety and its causes with the following terms: (a) comorbidity, (b) panic attack, (c) situationally bound, (d) neurotransmitter, (e) brain circuits, (f) stressful.

1. A _____ is an abrupt experience of intense fear or acute discomfort accompanied by physical symptoms, such as chest pain and shortness of breath.
2. A _____ panic attack often occurs in certain situations but not anywhere else.
3. Anxiety is associated with specific _____ (e.g., behavioural inhibition system or fight/flight system) and _____ systems (e.g., noradrenergic).
4. The rates of _____ among anxiety disorders are high because they share the common features of anxiety and panic.
5. _____ life events can trigger our biological and psychological vulnerabilities to anxiety.

---

# Generalized Anxiety Disorder

■ *Describe the essential features of generalized anxiety disorder, its proposed causal factors, and available treatment approaches.*

Specific anxiety disorders are complicated by panic attacks or other features that are the focus of the anxiety. In generalized anxiety disorder, the

focus is generalized to the events of everyday life. For that reason, we consider generalized anxiety disorder first.

## Clinical Description

Is somebody in your family a worrywart? Is somebody in your family perfectionistic? Perhaps it is you! Most of us worry to some extent. As we have said, worry can be useful. It helps us plan for the future, make sure that we're prepared for that test, or double-check that we've thought of everything before we head home for the holidays. The worry process itself is not pleasant, but without it nothing would go smoothly. But what if you worry indiscriminately about everything? Furthermore, what if worrying is unproductive: No matter how much you worry, you can't seem to decide what to do about an upcoming problem or situation. And what if you *can't stop* worrying, even if you know it is doing you no good and probably making everyone else around you miserable? These features characterize **generalized anxiety disorder (GAD).** Consider the case of Irene.

### Irene
#### Ruled by Worry

Irene was a 20-year-old university student with an engaging personality but not many friends. She came to the clinic complaining of excessive anxiety and general difficulties in controlling her life. Everything was a catastrophe for Irene. Although she carried a 3.7 grade point average, she was convinced she would flunk every test she took. As a result, she repeatedly threatened to drop courses after only several weeks of classes because she feared that she would not understand the material.

Irene worried until she dropped out of the first university she attended after 1 month. She felt depressed for a while, then she decided to take a couple of courses at a local college, believing she could handle the work there better. After achieving straight As at the college for 2 years, she enrolled once again in university as a third-year student. After a short time she began calling the clinic in a state of extreme agitation, saying she had to drop this or that course because she couldn't handle it. With great difficulty, her therapist and parents persuaded her to stay in the courses and to seek further help. In any course Irene completed, her grade was between an A and a B-minus, but she still worried about every test and every paper, afraid she would fall apart and be unable to understand and complete the work.

Irene did not worry only about school. She was also concerned about relationships with her friends, and whenever she was with her new boyfriend she feared making a fool of herself and losing his interest. In fact, she reported that each date went extremely well, but she knew the next one would probably be a disaster. As the relationship progressed and some sexual contact seemed natural, Irene was worried sick that her inexperience would make her boyfriend consider her naive and stupid. Nevertheless, she reported enjoying the early sexual contact and admitted that he seemed to enjoy it also, but she was convinced that the next time a catastrophe would happen.

Irene was also concerned about her health. She had minor hypertension, probably because she was somewhat overweight. She then approached every meal as if death itself might result if she ate the wrong types or amounts of food. She became reluctant to have her blood pressure checked for fear it would be very high or to weigh herself for fear she was not losing weight. She severely restricted her eating and as a result had an occasional episode of binge eating, although not often enough to warrant concern.

In addition, Irene worried about her religious faith and about her relationships with her family, particularly her mother and sister. Although Irene had an occasional panic attack, this was not a major issue to her. As soon as the panic subsided she focused on the next possible catastrophe. In addition to high blood pressure, Irene had tension headaches and a "nervous stomach," with a lot of gas, occasional diarrhea, and some abdominal pain. Irene's life was a series of impending catastrophes. Her mother reported that she dreaded a phone call from Irene, let alone a visit, because she knew she would have to see her daughter through a crisis. For the same reason, Irene had few friends. Even so, when she temporarily gave up her anxiety she was really fun to be with.

---

Irene had GAD, which is, in many ways, the basic syndrome that characterizes every anxiety disorder considered in this chapter (Brown, Barlow, & Liebowitz, 1994). The DSM-IV-TR criteria specify

---

**generalized anxiety disorder (GAD)**   Anxiety disorder characterized by intense, uncontrollable, unfocused, chronic, and continuous worry that is distressing and unproductive accompanied by physical symptoms of tenseness, irritability, and restlessness.

that at least 6 months of excessive anxiety and worry (apprehensive expectation) must be ongoing more days than not. Furthermore, it must be very difficult to turn off or control the worry process. This is what distinguishes pathological worrying from the normal kind we all experience from time to time as we get ready for an upcoming event or challenge. Most of us worry for a time but can set the problem aside and go on to another task. Even if the upcoming challenge is a big one, as soon as it is over, the worrying stops. For Irene, it never stopped. She turned to the next crisis as soon as the current one was over.

The physical symptoms associated with generalized anxiety and GAD differ somewhat from those associated with panic attacks and panic disorder (covered next). Whereas panic is associated with autonomic arousal, presumably as a result of a sympathetic nervous system surge (for instance, heart rate increases and palpitations, perspiration, and trembling), GAD is characterized by muscle tension, mental agitation (Brown, Marten, & Barlow, 1995), susceptibility to fatigue (probably the result of chronic excessive muscle tension), some irritability, and difficulty sleeping. Focusing attention is difficult as the mind quickly switches from crisis to crisis. For children, only one physical symptom is required for diagnosis.

People with GAD worry about minor, everyday life events for the most part, a characteristic that distinguishes GAD from other anxiety disorders. When asked, "Do you worry excessively about minor things?" 100% of individuals with GAD respond "yes" compared with approximately 50% of individuals with other anxiety disorder categories, as displayed in Figure 4.2. Such a difference is statistically significant. Of course, major events quickly become the focus of anxiety and worry, too. Adults typically focus on possible misfortune to their children, family health, job responsibilities, and more minor things such as household chores or being on time for appointments. Children with GAD most often worry about academic, athletic, or social performance and physical injury (Silverman, La Greca, & Wasserstein, 1995; Weems, Silverman, & La Greca, 2000). The elderly tend to focus, understandably, on health (Person & Borkovec, 1995); they also have difficulty sleeping, which seems to make the anxiety worse (Beck & Stanley, 1997).

## Statistics

Although worry and physical tension are common, the severe generalized anxiety experienced by Irene is quite rare. According to a community survey conducted in Edmonton, approximately 8% of the population meets criteria for GAD during a given 1-year

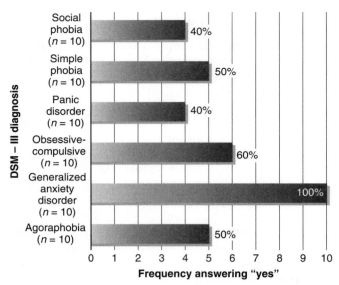

**Figure 4.2** ■ Clients' answers to interviewer's question "Do you worry excessively about minor things?" (From "Description of Patients Diagnosed with DSM-III-R Generalized Anxiety Disorder," by W. C. Sanderson and D. H. Barlow, 1990, *Journal of Nervous and Mental Disease*, 178: 590.)

**Disorder Criteria Summary**
Generalized Anxiety Disorder (GAD)

Features of generalized anxiety disorder include:
- Excessive anxiety and worry for 6 months or more about a number of events or activities
- Difficulty in controlling the worry
- At least three of these symptoms: (1) restlessness or feeling all keyed up; (2) becoming fatigued easily; (3) difficulty concentrating; (4) irritability; (5) muscle tension; (6) sleep disturbance
- Significant distress or impairment
- Anxiety is not limited to one specific issue

*Source:* Reprinted with permission from the *Diagnostic and Statistical Manual of Mental Disorders,* Fourth Edition, Text Revision. (Copyright © 2000) American Psychiatric Association.

period (Newman & Bland, 1994). This is still quite a large number, making GAD one of the most common anxiety disorders. Similar rates are reported from around the world, for example, rural South Africa (Bhagwanjee, Parekh, Paruk, Petersen, & Subedar, 1998) and the United States (Blazer, Hughes, George, Swartz, & Boyer, 1991; Carter, Wittchen, Pfister & Kessler, 2001; Kessler et al., 1994). However, relatively few people with GAD come for treatment compared with patients with panic disorder. Anxiety clinics like ours report that only approximately 10% of their patients meet criteria for GAD compared with 30% to 50% for panic disorder. This may be because most patients with GAD seek help from their primary care doctors, where they are found in large numbers (Roy-Byrne & Katon, 2000).

About two-thirds of individuals with GAD are female in both clinical samples (Woodman, Noyes, Black, Schlosser, & Yagla, 1999; Yonkers, Warshaw, Massion, & Keller, 1996) and epidemiological studies, which include people who do not necessarily seek out treatment (Blazer, George, & Hughes, 1991; Carter et al., 2001; Wittchen, Zhao, Kessler, & Eaton, 1994). But this sex ratio may be specific to developed countries. In a South African study mentioned later, GAD was more common in males (see p. 142).

Some people with GAD report onset in early adulthood. Stressful life events may play some role in the development of GAD. For example, Newman and Bland (1994) showed that a person with GAD is likely to have experienced an excess of life stressors compared with someone without this disorder. Nevertheless, most studies find that GAD is associated with an earlier and more gradual onset than most other anxiety disorders (Anderson, Noyes, & Crowe, 1984; Barlow, 2002; Brown, Barlow, & Liebowitz, 1994; Sanderson & Barlow, 1990; Woodman et al., 1999). Like Irene, many people have felt anxious and tense all their lives. Once it develops, GAD is chronic. One study found only an 8% probability of becoming symptom free after 2 years of follow-up (Yonkers et al., 1996). Another found that patients with GAD retained their symptoms more consistently over 5 years than patients with panic disorder (Woodman et al., 1999).

GAD is prevalent among the elderly (Flint, 1994; Wittchen et al., 1994). We also know that the use of minor tranquillizers in the elderly is very high, ranging from 17% to 50% in one study (Salzman, 1991). It is not entirely clear why drugs are prescribed with such frequency for the elderly. One possibility is that the drugs may not be entirely intended for anxiety. Prescribed drugs may be primarily for sleeping problems or other secondary effects of medical illnesses. In any case, benzodiazepines interfere with cognitive function (Buffett-Jerrott & Stewart, 2002) and put the elderly at greater risks for falling down and breaking bones, particularly their hips (Barlow, 2002).

The elderly may be particularly susceptible to anxiety about failing health or other life situations that begin to diminish whatever control they retain over events in their lives. This increasing lack of control, failing health, and the gradual loss of meaningful functions may be a particularly unfortunate by-product of the way the elderly are treated in Western culture. If it were possible to change our attitudes and behaviour, we might well reduce the frequency of anxiety, depression, and early death among our elderly citizens.

## Causes

What causes GAD? We have learned a great deal in the past several years. As with most anxiety disorders, there may be a genetic contribution. This conclusion is based on studies showing that GAD tends to run in families (Noyes, Clarkson, Crowe, Yates, & McChesney, 1987; Noyes et al., 1992). Twin studies strengthen this suggestion. Kendler, Neale, Kessler, Heath, and Eaves (1992a) found that the risk of GAD was somewhat greater for both members of monozygotic (identical) female twin pairs than for dizygotic female twins when one twin already had GAD. But in a later, more broadly focused study, Kendler et al. (1995) confirmed that what seems to be inherited is the tendency to become anxious rather than GAD itself. As noted at the beginning of this chapter, investigations of anxiety as a human trait show a clear heritable factor, and there is every reason to think that, when all the appropriate studies are done, GAD will be proved at least as strongly heritable as is the trait of anxiety (Barlow, 2001).

For a long time, GAD has posed a real puzzle to investigators. Although the definition of the disorder is relatively new, originating in 1980 with DSM-III, clinicians and psychopathologists were working with people with generalized anxiety long before diagnostic systems were developed. For years, clinicians thought that people who were generally anxious had simply not focused their anxiety on anything specific. Thus, such anxiety was described as "free floating." But now scientists have looked more closely and have discovered some interesting distinctions.

The first hints of difference were found in the physiological responsivity of individuals with GAD. It is interesting that individuals with GAD do not respond as strongly as individuals with anxiety disorders in which panic is more prominent. In fact, several studies have found that individuals with GAD show *less responsiveness* on most physiological measures, such as heart rate, blood pressure, skin conductance, and respiration rate (Borkovec & Hu, 1990; Hoehn-Saric, McLeod, & Zimmerli, 1989; Roemer, Orsillo, & Barlow, 2002) than do individuals with other anxiety disorders.

Several distinct cognitive characteristics of people with GAD are outlined in a model developed by Quebec researchers Michel Dugas and Robert Ladouceur and their colleagues (see Dugas, Gagnon, Ladouceur, & Freeston, 1998) including intolerance of uncertainty and erroneous beliefs about worry. Although unpredictable events are known to produce anxiety (Seligman & Binik, 1977), people with GAD are less tolerant of situations involving uncertainty than people with other anxiety disorders or non-clinical controls (Ladouceur et al., 1999). People with GAD also hold stronger erroneous beliefs that worrying is effective in avoiding negative outcomes and promoting positive outcomes. These beliefs might maintain their tendencies to worry. For example, they might believe that worrying about a family member's health is useful because if something should happen to the family member, then at least the worrier would not be taken by surprise (Ladouceur et al., 1999). This model has been helpful in developing cognitive methods for treating people with GAD, as we will describe later.

With new methods from cognitive science, we are beginning to uncover the sometimes unconscious mental processes ongoing in GAD (McNally, 1996). Evidence from this type of research, being conducted largely in Britain, indicates that individuals with GAD are highly sensitive to threat in general, particularly to a threat that has personal relevance. That is, they allocate their attention much more readily to sources of threat than people who are not anxious (Bradley, Mogg, White, Groom, & de Bono, 1999; Butler & Mathews, 1983; MacLeod, Mathews, & Tata, 1986; Mathews, 1997; Mogg, Mathews, & Weinman, 1989). Furthermore, this acute awareness of potential threat, particularly if it is personal, seems to be entirely automatic or unconscious.

In summary, some people inherit a tendency to be tense (generalized biological vulnerability), and they develop a sense early on that important events in their lives may be uncontrollable and potentially dangerous (generalized psychological vulnerability). Significant stress makes them apprehensive and vigilant. This sets off intense worry with resulting physiological changes, leading to generalized anxiety disorder (Roemer et al., 2002; Turovsky & Barlow, 1996). Cognitive factors such as intolerance of uncertainty and erroneous beliefs about worry also seem to play contributing roles in causing and maintaining GAD (Ladouceur, Gosselin, & Dugas, 2000). This model is very current, as it combines findings from cognitive science with biological data from both the central and the peripheral nervous systems. Time will tell if the model is correct, although supporting data continue to come in (Craske, 1999; DiBartolo, Brown, & Barlow, 1997). In any case, it is consistent with our view of anxiety as a future-oriented mood state focused on potential danger or threat, as opposed to an emergency or alarm reaction to actual present danger. A model of the development of generalized anxiety disorder is presented in Figure 4.3.

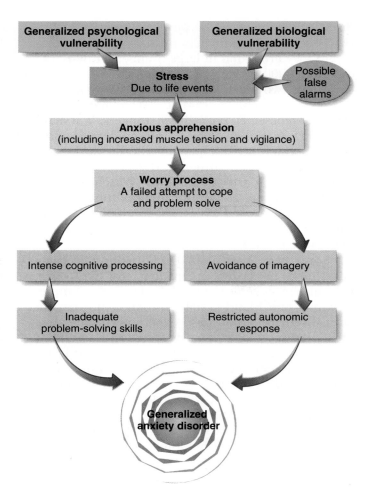

**Figure 4.3** ■ An integrative model of generalized anxiety disorder.

## Treatment

GAD is quite common, and available treatments, both drug and psychological, are reasonably effective. Benzodiazepines (minor tranquillizers) are most frequently prescribed for generalized anxiety, and the evidence indicates that they give some relief, at least in the short term. Few studies have looked at the effects of these drugs for a period longer than 8 weeks. Those that have suggest benefits seem to continue for approximately 6 months (Schweizer & Rickels, 1996). But the therapeutic effect is relatively modest. Furthermore, benzodiazepines carry some risks. First, they seem to impair both cognitive and motor functioning (e.g., Hindmarch, 1986, 1990; O'Hanlon, Haak, Blaauw, & Riemersma, 1982; Van Laar, Volkerts, & Verbaten, 2001). For example, people don't seem to be as alert on the job or at school when they are taking benzodiazepines. Research has shown that these drugs are associated with memory impairments, slowing of psychomotor functions, and attentional impairments (e.g., Buffett-Jerrott, Stewart, Bird, & Teehan, 1998;

Buffett-Jerrott, Stewart, & Teehan, 1998; Stewart, Rioux, Connolly, Dunphy, & Teehan, 1996; see also review by Buffett-Jerrott & Stewart, 2002). Thus, these drugs may impair driving, and in the elderly they seem to be associated with falls resulting in hip fractures (Ray, Gurwitz, Decker, & Kennedy, 1992; Wang, Bohn, Glynn, Mogun & Avorn, 2001). More important, benzodiazepines seem to produce both psychological and physical dependence, making it difficult for people to stop taking them (Noyes, Garvey, Cook, & Suelzer, 1991; Rickels, Schweizer, Case, & Greenblatt, 1990; Schweizer, Rickels, Case, & Greenblatt, 1990; Westra & Stewart, 1998, 2002).

There is reasonably wide agreement that the optimal use of benzodiazepines is for the short-term relief of anxiety associated with a temporary crisis or stressful event, such as a family problem. Under these circumstances, a physician may prescribe a benzodiazepine until the crisis is resolved but for no more than several days or a week or two at most. There is increasing evidence for the usefulness of antidepressants in the treatment of GAD (e.g., Rickels, Downing, Schweizer, & Hassman, 1993; Rickels et al., 2003; Schatzberg, 2000). These drugs may, ultimately, prove to be a better choice (Brawman-Mintzer, 2001).

In the short term, psychological treatments seem to confer about the same benefit as drugs in the treatment of GAD but are probably better in the long term (Barlow & Lehman, 1996; Borkovec & Whisman, 1996; Borkovec, Newman, Pincus, & Lytle, 2002; Gould, Otto, Pollack, & Yap, 1997; Roemer et al., 2002; Westra & Stewart, 1998).

For example, in the early 1990s, we developed a cognitive-behavioural treatment (CBT) for GAD in which patients evoke the worry process during therapy sessions and confront anxiety-provoking images and thoughts head-on. The patient learns to use cognitive therapy and other coping techniques to counteract and control the worry process (Craske, Barlow, & O'Leary, 1992; Wetherell, Gatz, & Craske, 2003). Borkovec and his colleagues found such a treatment to be significantly better than a placebo psychological treatment, not only at post-treatment but also at a 1-year follow-up (Borkovec & Costello, 1993).

Ladouceur and his colleagues have developed and tested a GAD psychological treatment that targets the factors identified in their cognitive model of GAD described earlier (Ladouceur et al., 2000). For example, to combat erroneous believes about worry, the therapist used cognitive-behavioural strategies to help patients reevaluate the actual usefulness of worry. Twenty-six GAD patients were randomly assigned to either a treatment condition or a waiting list control condition. Relative to those on the waiting list, those receiving the active treatment showed significant change in self-report, clinician, and significant-other ratings of GAD symptoms after treatment (see Figure 4.4). Gains were maintained at 6 and 12 months after treatment. Moreover, 77% of the patients no longer met GAD diagnostic criteria following treatment. A more recent study showed that this intervention is also effective when delivered in a group format, thereby increasing its cost-effectiveness (Dugas et al., 2003).

Borkovec and Ruscio (2001) reviewed 13 controlled studies evaluating CBTs for GAD and found substantial gains compared with no treatment or alternative treatment such as psychodynamic

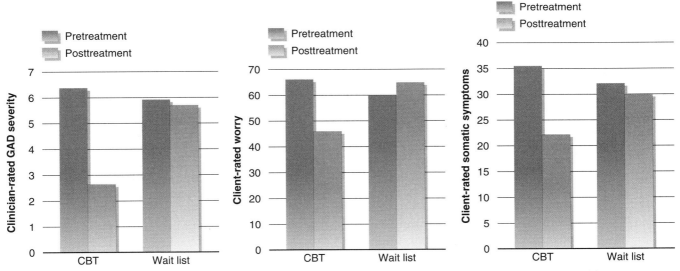

**Figure 4.4** ■ Pretreatment to posttreatment changes in clinician-rated GAD severity, client-rated worry, and client-rated somatic symptoms in patients receiving cognitive behavioural therapy (CBT) versus wait-list controls. (From Ladouceur, R., Gosselin, P., & Dugas, M.J. (2000). Experimental manipulation of intolerance of uncertainty: A study of a theoretical model of worry. *Behavior Research and Therapy*, 38, 933–941. Used with permission.)

therapy. Studies indicate that brief psychological treatments such as these alter the sometimes unconscious cognitive biases associated with GAD (Mathews, Mogg, Kentish, & Eysenck, 1995; Mogg, Bradley, Millar, & White, 1995). Recent studies also suggest that psychological interventions with GAD are effective to the extent that they focus on increasing the patient's ability to tolerate uncertainty (e.g., Ladouceur et al., 2000). Despite this success, it is clear we need more powerful treatments, both drug and psychological, for this chronic, treatment-resistant condition. Recently we have been developing a new psychological treatment for GAD that incorporates procedures focusing on acceptance rather than avoidance of distressing thoughts and feelings. Meditational approaches help teach the patient to be more tolerant of these feelings (Orsillo, Roemer & Barlow, 2003; Roemer & Orsillo, 2002; Roemer et al., 2002). Preliminary results are encouraging.

There is particularly encouraging evidence that psychological treatments are effective with children who have generalized anxiety. In Australia, Barrett, Dadds, and Rapee (1996) found significant benefit in children with severe GAD when cognitive-behavioural procedures were combined with family therapy. After treatment, 95% of the children receiving this combination of therapies no longer met criteria for the diagnosis. Even more encouraging was a 6-year follow-up showing that the gains were largely maintained with 85.7% still not meeting criteria for diagnosis (Barrett, Duffy, Dadds, & Rapee, 2001). Similarly, we are making progress in adapting our treatments for the elderly,

as important new studies show (Beck & Stanley, 1997; Stanley, Beck, & Glassco, 1997).

After trying a number of different drugs, Irene was treated with the CBT approach developed at our clinic and found herself much more able to cope with life. She completed college and graduate school, married, and is successful in her career as a counsellor in a nursing home. But even now, Irene finds it difficult to relax and stop worrying. She continues to experience mild to moderate anxiety, particularly when under stress; she takes minor tranquillizers on occasion to support her psychological coping skills.

## Concept Check 4.2

True or False?
1. _____ GAD is characterized by muscle tension, mental agitation, irritability, sleeping difficulties, and susceptibility to fatigue.
2. _____ Most studies show that in the majority of cases of GAD onset is early in adulthood as an immediate response to a life stressor.
3. _____ GAD is very prevalent in the elderly and in females in our society.
4. _____ GAD has no genetic basis.
5. _____ Cognitive-behavioural treatment and other psychological treatments for GAD are probably better than drug therapies in the long run.

# Panic Disorder With and Without Agoraphobia

■ *Describe the essential features of panic disorder.*

Do you have a relative, an eccentric aunt, for example, who never seems to leave the house? Family reunions or visits always have to be at her house. She never goes anywhere else. Like most people, you may attribute your old aunt's behaviour to her being a little odd or perhaps just not fond of travel. She is warm and friendly when people come to visit, so she retains contact with the family.

In fact, your aunt may not be just odd or eccentric. She may have a debilitating anxiety disorder called **panic disorder with agoraphobia (PDA),** in which individuals experience severe unexpected panic attacks; they may think they're dying or otherwise losing control. Because they never know when an attack might occur, they

develop **agoraphobia,** fear and avoidance of situations in which they would feel unsafe in the event of a panic attack or symptoms. These situations include those from which it would be hard or embarrassing to escape, to get home, or to get to a hospital. In severe cases, people with PDA are unable to leave the house, sometimes for years, as in the example of Mrs. M.

**panic disorder with agoraphobia (PDA)** Fear and avoidance of situations the person believes might induce a dreaded panic attack.

**agoraphobia** Anxiety about being in places or situations from which escape might be difficult.

## Mrs. M.
### Self-Imprisoned

Mrs. M. was 67 years old and lived in a second-floor walk-up apartment in a lower-middle-class section of the city. Her adult daughter, one of her few remaining contacts with the world, had requested an evaluation with Mrs. M.'s consent. I rang the bell and entered a narrow hallway; Mrs. M. was nowhere in sight. Knowing that she lived on the second floor, I walked up the stairs and knocked on the door at the top. When I heard Mrs. M. ask me to come in, I opened the door. She was sitting in her living room, and I could quickly see the layout of the rest of the apartment. The living room was in the front; the kitchen was in the back, adjoining a porch. To the right of the stairs was the one bedroom, with a bathroom opening from it.

Mrs. M. was glad to see me and very friendly, offering me coffee and homemade cookies. I was the first person she had seen in 3 weeks. In fact, Mrs. M. had not left that apartment in 20 years, and she had suffered from panic disorder with agoraphobia for over 30 years.

As she told her story, Mrs. M. conveyed vivid images of a wasted life. And yet she continued to struggle in the face of adversity and to make the best she could of her limited existence. Even areas in her apartment signalled the potential for terrifying panic attacks. She had not answered the door herself for the past 15 years because she was afraid to look into the hallway. She could enter her kitchen and go into the areas containing the stove and refrigerator, but for the past 10 years she had not been to the part of the room that overlooked the backyard or out onto the back porch. Thus, her life for the past decade had been confined to her bedroom, her living room, and the front half of her kitchen. She relied on her adult daughter to bring groceries and visit once a week. Her only other visitor was the parish priest, who came to deliver communion every 2 to 3 weeks when he could. Her only other contact with the outside world was through the television and the radio. Her husband, who had abused both alcohol and Mrs. M., had died 10 years earlier of alcohol-related causes. Early in her very stressful marriage she had her first terrifying panic attack and had gradually withdrawn from the world. As long as she stayed in her apartment, she was relatively free of panic. For this reason, and because in her mind there were few reasons left near the end of her life to venture out, she declined treatment.

## Clinical Description

At the beginning of the chapter we talked about the related phenomena of anxiety and panic. In PDA, anxiety and panic are combined with *phobic avoidance* in an intricate relationship that can become as devastating as it was for Mrs. M. Many people who have panic attacks do not necessarily develop panic disorder. Similarly, many people experience anxiety and panic without developing agoraphobia. In those cases, the disorder is called **panic disorder without agoraphobia (PD).**

To meet criteria for panic disorder (with or without agoraphobia), a person must experience an unexpected panic attack and develop substantial anxiety over the possibility of having another attack or about the implications of the attack or its consequences. In other words, he or she must think that each attack is a sign of impending death or incapacitation. A few individuals do not report concern about another attack but still change their behaviour in a way that indicates the distress the attacks cause them. They may avoid going to certain places or neglect their duties around the house for fear an attack might occur if they are too active.

### The Development of Agoraphobia

Many people with panic disorder develop agoraphobia. The term *agoraphobia* was coined in 1871 by Westphal and, in the original Greek, refers to fear of the marketplace. This is a very appropriate term because the *agora,* the Greek marketplace, was a busy, bustling area. One of the most stressful places for individuals with agoraphobia today is the shopping mall, the modern-day agora.

As noted by Stanley J. Rachman, "the consequences of panic can constitute a more serious problem than the panic itself" (Rachman, 1988, p. 259). All the evidence now points to the conclusion that agoraphobic avoidance behaviour is simply one complication of severe, unexpected panic attacks (Barlow, 2002; Craske & Barlow, 1988, 2001). Simply put, if you have had unexpected panic attacks and are afraid you may have another one, you want to be in a safe place or at

---

**panic disorder without agoraphobia (PD)** Panic attacks experienced without development of agoraphobia.

least with a safe person who knows what you are experiencing if another attack occurs so that you can quickly get to a hospital or at least go into your bedroom and lie down (the home is usually a safe place). We know that anxiety is diminished for individuals with agoraphobia if they think a location or person is "safe" (Rachman, 1984), even if there is nothing effective the person could do if something bad did happen. If you are in a shopping mall or a crowded movie theatre or church, not only is it difficult to leave but you also are probably going to embarrass yourself if you try. You may think you will have to climb over everyone in church to get out, get up in the middle of the movie and run out, or worse, faint in the movie theatre (in fact, individuals with agoraphobia seldom do any of these things). For these reasons, when they do go to church or to the movies, people with agoraphobia always plan for rapid escape (e.g., by sitting near the door). A list of typical situations commonly avoided by someone with agoraphobia is found in Table 4.1.

Though agoraphobic behaviour initially is closely tied to the occasions of panic, it can become relatively independent of panic attacks (Craske & Barlow, 1988; Craske, Rapee, & Barlow, 1988). In other words, an individual who has not had a panic attack for years may still have strong agoraphobic avoidance, like Mrs. M. Agoraphobic avoidance seems to be determined by the extent to which you think or expect you might have another attack rather than by how many attacks you actually have or how severe they are. Thus, agoraphobic avoidance is simply one way of coping with unexpected panic attacks.

Other methods of coping with panic attacks include using (and eventually abusing) alcohol or drugs. Winnipeg psychologist Brian Cox and his colleagues demonstrated that a high comorbidity exists

### Disorder Criteria Summary
#### Panic Disorder with Agoraphobia (PDA)

Features of panic disorder with agoraphobia include:
- Recurring unexpected panic attacks
- One or more of the following during the month after a panic attack: (1) persistent worry about having an additional attack; (2) worry about the implications of an attack; (3) a significant change in behaviour related to the attack
- Anxiety about being in places or social situations from which escape might be difficult or embarrassing, such as being in a crowd, travelling on a bus, or waiting in line

*Source:* Reprinted with permission from the *Diagnostic and Statistical Manual of Mental Disorders*, Fourth Edition, Text Revision. (Copyright © 2000) American Psychiatric Association.

between panic disorder and alcohol abuse or dependence (Cox, Norton, Swinson, & Endler, 1990; see also review by Norton et al., in press). An experimental study by MacDonald, Baker, Stewart, and Skinner (2000) at Dalhousie University showed that panic-prone individuals may be more susceptible than others to the anxiety-reducing effects of alcohol when they are experiencing panic-like bodily sensations. This may explain why these individuals are more likely to develop alcohol abuse and dependence.

Some individuals do not avoid agoraphobic situations but endure them with "intense dread." For example, people who simply must go to work each day or, perhaps, travel as part of the job will endure untold agonies of anxiety and panic simply to achieve their goals. Thus, DSM-IV-TR notes that agoraphobia may be characterized either by avoiding the situations or by enduring them with marked distress.

Canadian hockey player Shayne Corson, a forward who has played 20 NHL seasons, won a Stanley Cup, and served as a member of Canada's 1998 Olympic hockey team, experiences crippling panic attacks. His panic attacks would come on suddenly and unexpectedly. He experienced uncomfortable sensations in his chest which he worried might be signs of a heart attack. Corson would try to distract himself, but he found these attacks to be extremely distressing. When out at a restaurant or nightclub, he reportedly wouldn't last more than 4 to 5 minutes before he would flee, fearful that he might experience a panic attack in public. Corson's panic attacks often occurred right on the Maple Leafs bench in front of unsuspecting teammates and fans. Corson was prescribed antianxiety medication and saw a psychiatrist for treatment of his panic attacks (Hornby, 2001; Kennedy, 2001). Unfortunately, his

| **TABLE 4.1** | Typical Situations Avoided by People with Agoraphobia | |
|---|---|---|
| Shopping malls | Being far from home |
| Cars (as driver or passenger) | Staying at home alone |
| Buses | Waiting in line |
| Trains | Supermarkets |
| Subways | Stores |
| Wide streets | Crowds |
| Tunnels | Planes |
| Restaurants | Elevators |
| Theaters | Escalators |

*Source:* From *Mastery of Your Anxiety and Panic III* (p. 5), by D. H. Barlow and M. G. Craske, 2000, Boulder, CO: Graywind Publications. Copyright © 2000 by Graywind Publications. Adapted with permission.

Photo by Graig Abel/Toronto Maple Leafs

NHL player Shayne Corson has revealed publicly that he has endured repeated panic attacks.

agoraphobic avoidance. A list of situations or activities typically avoided within the interoceptive cluster is found in Table 4.2.

## Statistics

Panic disorder with or without agoraphobia is fairly common. Approximately 3.5% of the population meet the criteria for panic disorder at some point during their lives, two-thirds of them women (Eaton, Kessler, Wittchen, & Magee, 1994), and another 5.3% meet the criteria for agoraphobia (Kessler et al., 1994). The rates of agoraphobia may be somewhat overestimated as a result of methodological difficulties, but most people with panic disorder do have agoraphobic avoidance.

Onset of panic disorder usually occurs in early adult life—from mid-teens through about 40 years of age. The mean age of onset is between 25 and 29 (Craske & Barlow, 2001; Öst, 1987).

Most initial unexpected panic attacks begin at or after puberty. In fact, puberty seems a better predictor of unexpected panic attacks than age, because higher rates of panic attacks are found in girls after puberty compared with before puberty (Hayward et al., 1992). Furthermore, many prepubertal children who are

symptoms reemerged and interfered so much with the effectiveness of his game that Corson decided to quit the Maple Leafs team during the 2003 playoffs (Hockey Hall of Fame and Museum, 2001). Corson eventually recovered sufficiently to return to his hockey career in 2004 (Foster, 2004).

Most patients with severe agoraphobic avoidance (and some with little) also display another cluster of avoidant behaviours that we call *interoceptive avoidance* or avoidance of internal physical sensations (Barlow & Craske, 2000; Brown, White, & Barlow, 2005; Craske & Barlow, 2001; Shear et al., 1997; Watt, Stewart, Lefaivre, & Uman, 2006). These behaviours involve removing yourself from situations or activities that might produce the physiological arousal that somehow resembles the beginnings of a panic attack. Some patients might avoid exercise because it produces increased cardiovascular activity or faster respiration that reminds them of panic attacks and makes them think one might be beginning. In fact, Lachlan McWilliams at Acadia University in Nova Scotia showed that panic-prone university males reported engaging in exercise less frequently than other university males, consistent with the possibility that they might be avoiding exercise because of their fear of arousal sensations (McWilliams & Asmundson, 2001). Other patients might avoid sauna baths or any rooms in which they might perspire. Psychopathologists are beginning to recognize that this cluster of avoidance behaviours is every bit as important as more classical

| **TABLE 4.2** Interoceptive Daily Activities Typically Avoided by People with Agoraphobia |
| --- |
| Running up flights of stairs |
| Walking outside in intense heat |
| Hot, stuffy rooms |
| Hot, stuffy cars |
| Hot, stuffy stores or shopping malls |
| Walking outside in very cold weather |
| Aerobics |
| Lifting heavy objects |
| Dancing |
| Sexual relations |
| Watching horror movies |
| Eating heavy meals |
| Watching exciting movies or sports events |
| Getting involved in "heated" debates |
| Having showers with the doors and windows closed |
| Having a sauna |
| Hiking |
| Sports |
| Drinking coffee or any caffeinated beverages |
| Eating chocolate |
| Standing quickly from a sitting position |
| Getting angry |

*Source:* From *Mastery of Your Anxiety and Panic III* (p. 11), by D. H. Barlow and M. G. Craske, 2000, Boulder, CO: Graywind Publications. Copyright © 2000 by Graywind Publications. Adapted with permission.

seen by general medical practitioners have symptoms of hyperventilation that may well be panic attacks. However, these children do not report fear of dying or losing control—perhaps because they are not at a stage of their cognitive development where they can make these attributions (Nelles & Barlow, 1988).

As we have said, 75% or more of those who have agoraphobia are women (Barlow, 2002; Myers et al., 1984; Thorpe & Burns, 1983). For a long time we didn't know why, but now it seems the most logical explanation is cultural (Arrindell et al., 2003a). It is more accepted for women to report fear and to avoid numerous situations. Men, however, are expected to be stronger and braver, to "tough it out." Another possible reason pertains to gender differences in fear of anxiety. Research conducted at Dalhousie University has shown that women are more fearful of anxiety symptoms than are men (Stewart, Taylor, & Baker, 1997). Schmidt and Koselka (2000) showed that panic-disordered women have greater agoraphobia because they believe panic attacks are more likely and because they are more afraid of the consequences of a panic attack (e.g., fearing that they will have a heart attack).

What happens to men who have severe unexpected panic attacks? Is cultural disapproval of fear in men so strong that most of them simply endure panic? The answer seems to be "no." A large proportion of males with unexpected panic attacks cope in a culturally acceptable way: They consume large amounts of alcohol (see reviews by Cox et al., 1990; Norton et al., in press). A study by Cox, Swinson, Shulman, Kuch, and Reichman (1993), conducted at the Centre for Addiction and Mental Health in Toronto, compared 74 men and 162 women with panic disorder. Although the women reported higher levels of agoraphobic avoidance, the men reported higher levels of weekly alcohol intake, and greater beliefs in alcohol as an effective way to cope with anxiety. The problem is that these men with panic disorder can become dependent on alcohol, and many begin the long downward spiral into serious addiction. Thus, males may end up with an even more severe problem than PDA. Because these men are so impaired by alcohol abuse, clinicians may not realize they also have PDA. And even if they are successfully treated for their addiction, the anxiety disorder still requires treatment (Chambless, Cherney, Caputo, & Rheinstein, 1987; Cox, Swinson, Schulman, Kuch, & Reichman, 1993; Kushner, Abrams, & Borchardt, 2000; Kushner, Sher, & Beitman, 1990; Stewart & Conrod, in press).

## Cultural Influences

Panic disorder exists worldwide, although its expression may vary from place to place. In Lesotho, Africa, the prevalence of panic disorder (and generalized anxiety disorder) was found to be equal to or greater than in North America (Hollifield, Katon, Spain, & Pule, 1990). In a more comprehensive study, prevalence rates for panic disorder were remarkably similar in Canada, the United States, Puerto Rico, New Zealand, Italy, Korea, and Taiwan, with only Taiwan showing somewhat lower rates (Horwath & Weissman, 1997) perhaps because of a stigma about admitting to psychological problems in Taiwanese culture (Weissman et al., 1997). In this cross-national study, the 1-year prevalence rates in the Canadian sample were 0.9% for men and 1.9% for women (Weissman et al., 1997).

In another large-scale study, the Cross-National Collaborative Panic Study (1992), panic disorder patients from clinics in 14 countries were examined, including those from Europe, Latin America, and North America. Although panic disorder occurred in all the countries studied, some interesting differences in the prominent features of the disorder were observed cross-nationally. For example, phobic avoidance was more common in panic disorder patients in Canada and the United States relative to panic patients in Latin American clinics. In addition, fear of dying and choking or smothering sensations were more common in panic patients from southern countries relative to those in other countries.

Somatic symptoms of anxiety may be emphasized in people from developing countries. Subjective feelings of dread or angst may not be part of the cultural idiom; that is, individuals do not attend to these feelings and do not report them, focusing only on bodily sensations. In Chapter 2 we described a fright disorder called *susto* in Latin America characterized by sweating, increased heart rate, and insomnia but not by reports of anxiety or fear, even though a severe fright is the cause. Another culture-bound syndrome that bears some relation to panic disorder occurs among the Inuit of northern Canada and Western Greenland. This syndrome is called *kayak-angst* and involves episodes of intense fear, worries about drowning, physical arousal sensations (rapid heartbeat and trembling), and intense disorientation that occur when a seal hunter or fisherman is alone at sea (Amering & Katschnig, 1990; Boag, 1970). Like the relation of panic disorder to agoraphobic avoidance, kayak-angst can cause the hunter or fisherman to avoid travel in the kayak, which can obviously lead to significant impairments in his or her livelihood (Katschnig & Amering, 1990).

## Nocturnal Panic

Think back to the case of Gretchen, whose panic attack was described earlier. Is there anything unusual about her report? She was sound asleep when it happened! Approximately 60% of the people with panic disorder have experienced such nocturnal attacks (Craske & Rowe, 1997; Uhde, 1994). In fact, panic attacks occur more frequently between 1:30 a.m. and 3:30 a.m. than at any other time (C. B. Taylor et al., 1986). In some cases, people are afraid to go to sleep at night! Are they having nightmares? Research indicates they are not. Nocturnal attacks are studied in a sleep laboratory. Patients spend a few nights sleeping while attached to an electroencephalograph (EEG) machine that monitors their brain waves (see Chapter 3). We all go through various stages of sleep that are reflected by different patterns on the EEG. (Stages of sleep are discussed fully in Chapter 8.) We have learned that nocturnal panics occur during delta wave or slow wave sleep, which typically occurs several hours after we fall asleep and is the deepest stage of sleep. People with panic disorder often begin to panic when they start sinking into delta sleep, and then they awaken in the midst of an attack. Because there is no obvious reason for them to be anxious or panicky when they are sound asleep, most of these individuals think they are dying (Craske & Barlow, 1988; Craske & Rowe, 1997).

What causes nocturnal panic? Our best information at the current time is that the change in stages of sleep to the beginning of slow wave sleep produces physical sensations of "letting go" that are frightening to an individual with panic disorder (Craske et al., 2002). This process is described more fully later when we discuss causes of panic disorder. Several other events also occur during sleep that resemble nocturnal panic and are mistakenly thought to be the cause of nocturnal panic by some. Initially, we thought it might be nightmares, but nightmares and other dreamlike activity occur only during a stage of sleep characterized by rapid eye movement (REM) sleep, which typically occurs much later in the sleep cycle. Therefore, people are not dreaming when they have nocturnal panics, a conclusion consistent with patient reports. Some therapists are not aware of the stage of sleep associated with nocturnal panic attacks and assume that patients are "repressing" their dream material, perhaps because it might relate to an early trauma too painful to be admitted to consciousness. As we've seen, this is virtually impossible because nocturnal panic attacks do not occur during REM sleep, so there is no well-developed dream or nightmare activity going on when they happen. Thus, it is not possible for these patients to be dreaming anything.

A fascinating condition that at first glance appears similar to nocturnal panic is called isolated sleep paralysis. Have you ever found yourself awake at night, unable to move, your heart pounding as you stare at aspects of the room—maybe the clock, maybe the window—feeling that a presence is in the room with you? If you were from Newfoundland and Labrador, you would refer to this experience as being visited by the "Old Hag" (Hufford, 1982) and if you were from an African or Caribbean culture, this experience would be captured by the expression "the witch is riding you" (Bell, Dixie-Bell, & Thompson, 1986). Isolated sleep paralysis occurs during the transitional state between sleep and waking, when a person is either falling asleep or waking up, but mostly when waking up. During this period the individual is unable to move and experiences a surge of terror that resembles a panic attack; occasionally, the person also has vivid hallucinations. One possible explanation is that REM sleep is spilling over into the waking cycle. This seems likely because one feature of REM sleep is lack of bodily movement. Another is vivid dreams, which could account for the experience of hallucination. The "Old Hag" is mentioned twice in E. Annie Proulx's novel *The Shipping News*, set in Newfoundland and Labrador.

## Causes

It is not possible to understand panic disorder (with or without agoraphobia) without referring to the triad of contributing factors mentioned throughout this book: biological, psychological, and social. Strong evidence indicates that agoraphobia develops

Miramax/Columbia/The Kobal Collection/Doane Gregory

The character Quoyle (played by actor Kevin Spacey) is visited by the "Old Hag" in *The Shipping News*, providing an illustration of myths surrounding isolated sleep paralysis symptoms in Newfoundland culture.

after a person has unexpected panic attacks (or panic-like sensations); but whether agoraphobia develops and how severe it becomes seem to be socially and culturally determined, as we noted earlier. Panic attacks and panic disorder, however, seem to be related most strongly to biological and psychological factors and their interaction.

At the beginning of the chapter we discussed how biological, psychological, and social factors may contribute to the development and maintenance of anxiety and to an initial unexpected panic attack (Bouton et al., 2001; White & Barlow, 2002; see Figure 4.5).

As noted earlier, we all inherit—some more than others—a vulnerability to stress, which is a tendency to be generally neurobiologically overreactive to the events of daily life (generalized biological vulnerability). But some people are also more likely than others to have an emergency alarm reaction (unexpected panic attack) when confronted with stress-producing events. These may include stress on the job or at school, death of a loved one, divorce, and positive events that are nevertheless stressful, such as graduating from school and starting a new career, getting married, or changing jobs. (Other people

might be more likely to have headaches or high blood pressure in response to the same kinds of stress.) Particular situations quickly become associated in an individual's mind with external and internal cues that were present during the panic attack (Bouton et al., 2001). The next time the person's heart rate increases during exercise, that person might assume he or she is having a panic attack (conditioning). Harmless exercise is an example of an internal cue or a conditioned stimulus (CS) for a panic attack. Being in a movie theatre when panic first occurred would be an external cue that might become a CS for future panics. Because these cues become associated with a number of different internal and external stimuli through a learning process, we call them learned alarms.

But none of this would make much difference without the next step. The individuals must be susceptible to developing anxiety over the possibility of having another panic attack (a generalized psychological vulnerability). That is, they think the physical sensations associated with the panic attack mean something terrible is about to happen, perhaps death. This is what creates panic disorder. In

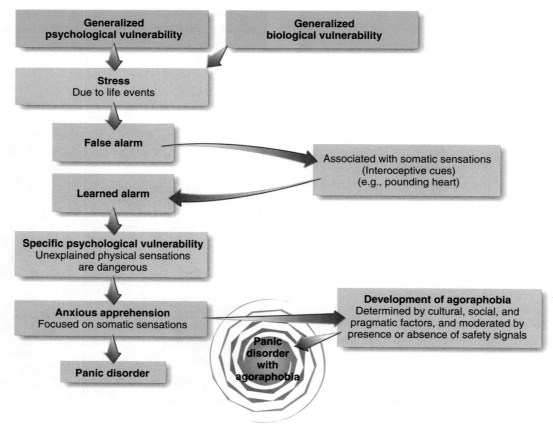

**Figure 4.5** ■ A model of the causes of panic disorder with or without agoraphobia. (From "Panic Disorder and Agoraphobia," by K. S. White and D. H. Barlow [2002], in *Anxiety and Its Disorders: The Nature and Treatment of Anxiety and Panic,* by D. H. Barlow, 2nd ed. New York: Guilford Press. Copyright © 2002 by Guilford Press. Reprinted by permission.)

other words, when people have a tendency to expect the worst when they experience strong physical sensations, some of them focus their anxiety on the possibility of *future* panic attacks—perhaps because they've been taught in childhood that unexpected bodily sensations may be dangerous, whereas other people experiencing these attacks do not. This tendency to believe that unexpected bodily sensations are dangerous reflects a specific psychological vulnerability to develop panic and related disorders.

Research using a self-report measure called the Panic Attack Questionnaire, developed by researchers in Winnipeg, has established that about one-third of individuals in the general population have experienced a panic attack (Norton, Dorward, & Cox, 1986; Norton, Harrison, Hauch, & Rhodes, 1985). An even smaller number (approximately 8% to 12% of the population) has an occasional unexpected panic attack, often during a period of intense stress (Mattis & Ollendick, 2002; Norton et al., 1985; Salge, Beck, & Logan, 1988; Telch, Lucas, & Nelson, 1989; Wilson, Sandler, Asmundson, Larsen, & Ediger, 1991). Most of these people do not develop anxiety (Telch et al., 1989). Only approximately 3% go on to develop anxiety over future panic attacks and thereby meet the criteria for panic disorder.

What happens to those individuals who don't develop anxiety? They seem to attribute the attack to events of the moment, such as an argument with a friend, something they ate, or a bad day, and go on with their lives, perhaps experiencing an occasional panic attack when they are under stress again. These "non-clinical panickers" are similar to patients with panic disorder in terms of the kinds of symptoms that occur during a panic attack (e.g., heart palpitations, difficulty concentrating, dizziness, feeling helpless). But panic disorder patients experience these symptoms to a greater extent. Phobic avoidance and lifestyle restriction are also much greater in panic disorder patients relative to non-clinical panickers (Cox, Endler, & Norton, 1994; Cox, Endler, & Swinson, 1991).

We can now measure one aspect of the psychological vulnerability for panic disorder, using an instrument known as the *Anxiety Sensitivity Index* (Reiss, Peterson, Gursky, & McNally, 1986). Anxiety sensitivity refers to the tendency to catastrophize the meaning of anxiety-related bodily sensations (S. Taylor, 1999). Anxiety sensitivity levels are higher in panic disorder than in any other anxiety disorder save posttraumatic stress disorder (Taylor, Koch, & McNally, 1992). One of the best tests of anxiety sensitivity as a vulnerability to experience panic attacks was demonstrated in an experiment conducted by Schmidt, Lerew, and Jackson (1997; see also Schmidt et al., 1999). Schmidt et al. (1997) administered the Anxiety Sensitivity Index to a large number of military recruits undergoing a stressful basic training regimen. High scores on the Anxiety Sensitivity Index prior to basic training predicted the onset of unexpected panic attacks in the 5 weeks following basic training.

The influential cognitive theories of British psychologist David M. Clark (1986, 1996) explicate in more detail some of the cognitive processes that may be ongoing in panic disorder. Clark emphasizes the specific psychological vulnerability of people with this disorder to interpret normal physical sensations in a catastrophic way. In other words, although we all typically experience rapid heartbeat after exercise, if you have a psychological or cognitive vulnerability, you might interpret the response as dangerous and feel a surge of anxiety. This anxiety, in turn, produces more physical sensations because of the action of the sympathetic nervous system; you perceive these additional sensations as even more dangerous; and a vicious cycle begins that results in a panic attack. Thus, Clark emphasizes the cognitive process as most important in panic disorder.

## Treatment

As we noted in Chapter 1, research on the effectiveness of new treatments is important to psychopathology. Responses to certain specific treatments, whether drug or psychological, may indicate the causes of the disorder. We now discuss the benefits and some drawbacks of medication, psychological interventions, and a combination of these two treatments.

### Medication

While studies strongly suggest that anxiety and panic may well be separate processes, it seems that some high-potency benzodiazepines are just as effective for panic disorder as are tricyclic antidepressants such as imipramine, as well as the newer selective serotonin reuptake inhibitors (SSRIs) such as Prozac and Paxil. In fact, a large number of drugs affecting either the noradrenergic, serotonergic, or GABA-benzodiazepine neurotransmitter systems or some combination seem effective in treating panic disorder (Barlow, 2002; Spiegel, Wiegel, Baker, & Greene, 2000).

There are advantages and disadvantages to each class of drugs. Imipramine, one of the tricyclic antidepressants, produces strong side effects that include dizziness, dry mouth, and, on occasion, sexual dysfunction, so many patients refuse to stay on it for long. But a person who can become accustomed to the side effects or wait until they wear off may find the drug can reduce panic attacks and associated anxiety. SSRIs are just as effective but produce fewer immediate side effects, so individuals usually continue taking their pills (e.g., Lecrubier, Bakker, et al., 1997; Lecrubier, Judge, et al., 1997). SSRIs are currently the preferred drug for panic disorder, although sexual dysfunction seems to occur in 75% or more of people taking these medications. On the other hand, high-potency benzodiazepines such as *alprazolam* (Xanax), commonly used for panic disorder, work very fast but are hard to stop taking due to psychological and physical dependence and addiction. Also, all benzodiazepines adversely affect cognitive and motor functions to some degree. Therefore, people taking them in high doses often find their ability to drive a car or study somewhat reduced.

Approximately 60% of patients with panic disorder are free of panic as long as they stay on an effective drug (Ballenger et al., 1988; Klosko, Barlow, Tassinari, & Cerny, 1990; Lecrubier, Bakker, et al., 1997), but relapse rates are high once the medication is stopped. Approximately 20% to 50% of patients relapse after stopping tricyclic antidepressants (Spiegel et al., 2000; Telch, 1988; Telch, Tearnan, & Taylor, 1983). The relapse rate is closer to 90% for those who stop taking benzodiazepines (e.g., Fyer et al., 1987).

***Virtual Reality: A New Technique in the Treatment of Anxiety Disorders***
*"I just feel really closed in, I feel like my heart is going to start beating really fast.... I won't be able to get enough air, I won't be able to breathe, and I'll pass out."*

## Psychological Intervention

Psychological treatments have proven quite effective for panic disorder. Originally, such treatments concentrated on reducing agoraphobic avoidance, using strategies based on exposure to feared situations. The strategy of exposure-based treatments is to arrange conditions in which the patient can gradually face the feared situations and learn there is really nothing to fear. Of course, most patients with phobias are well aware of this rationally, but they must be convinced on an emotional level by "reality testing" the situation. Sometimes the therapist accompanies the patients on their exposure exercises. At other times, the therapist simply helps patients structure their own exercises and provides them with a variety of psychological coping mechanisms to help them complete the exercises, which are typically arranged from least to most difficult.

The therapist identifies situations relevant to the patient and then arranges them in order of difficulty.

Gradual exposure exercises, sometimes combined with anxiety-reducing coping mechanisms such as relaxation or breathing retraining, have proved effective in helping patients overcome agoraphobic behaviour. As many as 70% of patients undergoing these treatments substantially improve as their anxiety and panic are reduced and their agoraphobic avoidance is greatly diminished. Few, however, are cured, because many still experience some anxiety and panic attacks, though at a less severe level.

Effective psychological treatments have recently been developed that treat panic attacks directly (Barlow & Craske, 1989, 2000; Clark et al., 1994; Klosko et al., 1990). **Panic control treatment (PCT)** developed at one of our clinics (DHB) concentrates on exposing patients with panic disorder to the cluster of interoceptive sensations that remind them of their panic attacks. The therapist attempts to create "mini" panic attacks in the office by having the patients exercise to elevate their heart rates or perhaps by spinning them in a chair to make them dizzy. A variety of exercises have been developed for this purpose (see Table 4.3). Patients also receive cognitive therapy. Basic attitudes and perceptions concerning the dangerousness of the feared but objectively harmless situations are identified and modified. As we learned earlier, many of these attitudes and perceptions are beyond the patient's awareness. Uncovering these unconscious cognitive processes requires a great deal of therapeutic skill. Sometimes, in addition to exposure to interoceptive sensations and cognitive therapy, patients are taught relaxation or breathing retraining to help them cope with increases in anxiety and to reduce excess arousal.

These psychological procedures are highly effective for panic disorder. Follow-up studies of patients who receive PCT indicate that most of them remain better after at least 2 years (Barlow & Lehman, 1996; Craske, Brown, & Barlow, 1991). Researchers have begun attempting to understand which aspects of PCT (i.e., exposure to interoceptive sensations, cognitive therapy, or relaxation and breathing retraining) are the most or least important components of the treatment. For example, as described by Hamilton researchers Randi McCabe and Martin Antony (2002), concerns have been raised about the breathing retraining component in that it does not seem to add to the effectiveness of

**panic control treatment (PCT)**  Cognitive-behavioural treatment for panic attacks, involving gradual exposure to feared somatic sensations and modification of perceptions and attitudes about them.

**TABLE 4.3**  Exercises to Create the Sensation of Panic

1. Shake your head loosely from side to side for 30 seconds (to produce dizziness or disorientation).

2. Place your head between your legs for 30 seconds and then lift it quickly (to produce lightheadedness or blood rushing).

3. Take one step up—using stairs, a box, or a footstool—and immediately step down. Do this repeatedly at a fast enough rate to notice your heart pumping quickly for 1 minute (to produce racing heart and shortness of breath).

4. Hold your breath for as long as you can or about 30 to 45 seconds (to produce chest tightness and smothering feelings).

5. Tense every part of your body for 1 minute without causing pain. Tense your arms, legs, stomach, back, shoulders, face—everything. Alternatively, try holding a push-up position for 1 minute or for as long as you can (to produce muscle tension, weakness, and trembling).

6. Spin in a chair for 1 minute. If you have a chair that spins, such as a desk chair, this is ideal. It's even better if someone is there to spin you around. Otherwise, stand up and turn around quickly to make yourself dizzy. Be near a soft chair or couch that you can sit in after 1 minute is up. This will produce dizziness and perhaps nausea.

7. Hyperventilate for 1 minute. Breathe deep and fast, using a lot of force. Sit down as you do this. This exercise might produce unreality, shortness of breath, tingling, cold or hot feelings, dizziness, or headache.

8. Breathe through a thin straw for 1 minute. Don't allow any air through your nose; hold your nostrils together (to produce feelings of restricted air flow or smothering).

9. Stare at a small spot on the wall or stare at yourself in the mirror for 2 minutes. Stare as hard as you can to produce feelings of unreality.

*Source:* From *Mastery of Your Anxiety and Panic III*, by D. H. Barlow and M. G. Craske, 2000. Boulder, CO: Graywind Publications. Reprinted by permission.

PCT. In fact, some patients may misuse it as a means of escaping from or avoiding their feared bodily sensations (Taylor, 2001).

Although psychological treatments like PCT are quite effective, they are not yet available to many individuals who have panic disorder (Barlow, Levitt, & Bufka, 1999). In part, this is because specialized anxiety disorder clinics are located in large urban areas like Toronto, Hamilton, Winnipeg, and Vancouver, meaning that a person with PDA living in a rural area may have particular difficulty accessing effective services for anxiety disorders. For this reason, Swinson, Fergus, Cox, and Wickwire (1995) conducted an important study on

telephone-administered CBT for patients with PDA that was designed to reduce these barriers to effective treatment. Forty-two patients with PDA who were living in rural Ontario were randomly assigned to either the active CBT group (consisting of 8 telephone-administered sessions) or to a wait list control. The CBT group, but not the wait list control group, showed significant declines from before to after treatment on agoraphobic avoidance, fear of agoraphobic situations, and anxiety sensitivity (see Figure 4.6). All treatment gains were maintained 3 and 6 months after the treatment had been completed. Thus, delivering CBT by telephone appears to be a promising method for

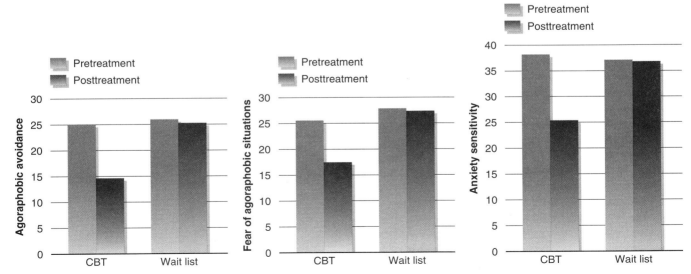

**Figure 4.6**  ■  Levels of agoraphobic avoidance, fear of agoraphobic situations, and anxiety sensitivity at pretreatment and posttreatment in patients with PDA who received telephone-administered CBT versus those in a wait list control group. (Adapted from "Efficacy of Telephone Administered Behavioral Therapy for Panic Disorder and Agoraphobia" by R.P. Swinson, K.D. Fergus, B.J. Cox, & K. Wickwire, 1995, *Behavior Research and Therapy, 33*, 465–469.)

making effective treatment available to patients with PDA who live in remote regions of Canada where specialized anxiety disorder services are not readily available (Swinson et al., 1995).

## New Evidence on Combined Treatment

Results have now been published from a major study sponsored by the U.S. National Institute of Mental Health that looked at the separate and combined effects of psychological and drug treatments (Barlow, Gorman, Shear, & Woods, 2000). In this double-blind study, 312 carefully screened patients with panic disorder were treated at four different sites, two known for their expertise with medication treatments and two known for their expertise with psychological treatments. The purpose of this arrangement was to control for any bias that might affect the results because of the allegiance of investigators committed to one type of treatment or the other. Patients were randomized into five different treatment conditions: psychological treatment alone (CBT); drug treatment alone (imipramine—IMI—a tricyclic antidepressant, was used); a combined treatment condition (CBT + IMI); and two "control" conditions, one using placebo alone (PBO), and one using CBT + PBO (to determine the extent to which any advantage for combined treatment was due to placebo contribution).

Figure 4.7 shows the results in terms of the patients who had responded to treatment by the end of 3 months of active treatment, during which patients were seen weekly (acute response). Data were based on the judgment of an independent evaluator using a standardized panic disorder severity scale and include patients who dropped out along the way and were counted as failures. The data indicate that all treatment groups were significantly better than placebo, with some evidence that, among those who responded to treatment, people taking the drug alone did a little bit better than those receiving the CBT alone, but approximately the same number of patients responded to both treatments. Combined treatment was no better than individual treatments.

Figure 4.7 also presents the results after 6 additional months of maintenance treatment (9 months after treatment was initiated) during which patients were seen once per month. At this point the results looked very much as they did after initial treatment, except there was a slight advantage for combined treatment at this point, and the number of people responding to placebo had diminished. Six months after treatment was discontinued, patients on medication, whether

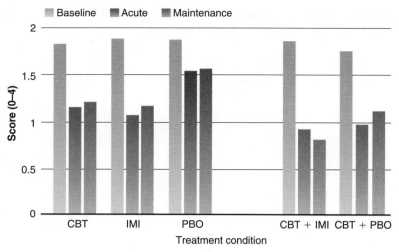

**Figure 4.7** ▪ Responders based on the Panic Disorder Severity Scale average item score after acute and after maintenance conditions. (From Barlow et al., 2000.)

combined with CBT or not, had deteriorated somewhat, and those receiving CBT without the drug had retained most of their gains.

Conclusions from this large and important study suggest no advantage to combining drug and CBT treatments because any incremental effect of combined treatment seems to be a placebo effect, not a true drug effect. Furthermore, the psychological treatments seemed to perform better in the long run (6 months after treatment had stopped). The public health recommendation emanating from this study, based on the principle of utilizing the least intrusive treatment first, suggests the psychological treatment should be offered initially, followed by drug treatment for those patients who do not respond adequately or for whom psychological treatment is not available. Because this was such a large study involving so many different research centres, it has had a substantial impact on health care policy.

## Concept Check 4.3

True or False?

1. _____ Panic disorder without agoraphobia (PD) is a disorder in which an individual experiences anxiety and panic with phobic avoidance of what he or she considers an "unsafe" situation.

2. _____ About 40% of the population meets the criteria for panic disorder at some point in their lives.

3. _____ Psychological treatments like panic control treatment or CBT are highly effective for treating this disorder.

# Specific Phobia

■ *Identify the principal causes of specific phobias and the most typical strategies used to treat them.*

Remember Jody in Chapter 1? When he saw a film of the frog being dissected, Jody began feeling queasy. Eventually he reached the point of fainting if someone simply said, "Cut it out." Consider next the case of Bob who has difficulties with flying. Bob's case and his treatment were described by Robert Ladouceur (1982). Jody and Bob have in common what we call a **specific phobia.**

## Bob
### Too Scared to Fly

Bob was a 29-year-old Caucasian man who worked as a translator. His main complaint was a fear of flying. Although his work as a translator did not necessitate air travel, the places he could travel for vacations were severely limited by his flying phobia. Bob had always been very interested in art and history and he had long dreamed of travelling in Europe. However, his intense fear of flying had prevented him from making the trip.

Bob had tried psychoanalytically oriented psychotherapy mainly to help with his phobia. However, despite being in therapy for 6 years, he reported that it had not been particularly helpful. Although his overall level of general anxiety was somewhat reduced, his flying phobia remained. He had ended this therapy a year earlier. He was not taking any medications for his anxiety.

Three years earlier, in an attempt to overcome his avoidance behaviour, he had purchased an airline ticket for a trip from Quebec to Paris. He purchased the ticket well in advance of his planned travel dates. However, Bob became increasingly anxious as the day of the trip approached. Eventually, he became so overwhelmed by his anxiety about the flight that he cancelled his trip and returned the ticket to the travel agent. He was even willing to pay a hefty financial penalty for his late cancellation—anything to avoid having to fly! The therapist learned that Bob had never flown in his lifetime. This provided evidence that his fear of flying was not due to a direct traumatic experience during some previous flight (i.e., his phobia was not acquired through classical conditioning). Instead, it appeared that he had developed his flying phobia from various vicarious sources (e.g., seeing dangerous flights depicted in films or airplane crashes described in the news).

From Ladouceur, R. (1982). In vivo cognitive desensitization of flight phobia: A case study. *Psychological Reports,* 50, 459–462. Adapted with permission.

## Clinical Description

A specific phobia is an irrational fear of a specific object or situation that markedly interferes with an individual's ability to function. Prior to DSM-IV this category was called "simple" phobia to distinguish it from the more complex agoraphobia condition, but we now recognize there is nothing simple about it. Many of you might be afraid of something that is not dangerous, such as going to the dentist, or have a greatly exaggerated fear of something that is only slightly dangerous, such as driving a car or flying. For this reason, most people can identify to some extent with a phobia. Recent surveys indicate that specific fears of a variety of objects or situations occur in a majority of the population (Myers et al., 1984). But the very commonness of fears, even severe fears, often causes people to trivialize the psychological disorder known as a specific phobia. These phobias, in their severe form, can be extremely disabling, as we saw with Jody.

In contrast to the devastating effects of phobias for some people, for others like Bob, phobias are simply a nuisance—sometimes an extremely inconvenient nuisance—but they can adapt to life with a phobia by simply working around it somehow. In the Atlantic provinces and New England where two of us live and work, some people are afraid to drive in the snow. We have had people come to our clinics who have been so severely phobic that during the winter they were ready to uproot, change their jobs and their lives, and move to a warmer climate. That is one way of dealing with a phobia. We discuss some other ways at the end of this chapter.

---

**specific phobia** Unreasonable fear of a specific object or situation that markedly interferes with daily life functioning.

## Disorder Criteria Summary
Specific Phobia

Features of specific phobia include:
- Marked and persistent fear that is excessive or unreasonable of a specific object or situation (e.g., heights, animals, seeing blood), with a duration of at least 6 months
- Immediate anxious or fearful response to exposure of phobic object or situation
- Recognition that the fear is excessive and unreasonable or marked distress about having the phobia
- The phobic situation or object is avoided or is endured with intense anxiety or distress

*Source:* Reprinted with permission from the *Diagnostic and Statistical Manual of Mental Disorders*, Fourth Edition, Text Revision. (Copyright © 2000) American Psychiatric Association.

The major characteristic held in common by Jody and Bob, of course, is the DSM-IV-TR criterion of marked and persistent fear that is set off by a specific object or situation. Both have also recognized that their fear and anxiety are excessive or unreasonable. Finally, both went to considerable lengths to avoid situations where their phobic response might occur.

The similarities end there. In fact, there are as many phobias as there are objects and situations. The variety of Greek and Latin names contrived to describe phobias stuns the imagination. Table 4.4 gives only the phobias beginning with the letter *a* from a long list compiled from medical dictionaries and other diverse sources (Maser, 1985). Of course, this sort of list has little or no value for people studying psychopathology, but it does show the extent of the named phobias.

Before the publication of DSM-IV in 1994, no meaningful classification of specific phobias existed. However, we have now learned that the cases of Jody and Bob represent types of specific phobia that differ in major ways. Four major subtypes of specific phobia have been identified: (1) animal type, (2) natural environment type (e.g., heights, storms, and water), (3) blood-injury-injection type, and (4) situational type (such as planes, elevators, or enclosed places). A fifth category, "other," includes phobias that do not fit any of the four major subtypes (e.g., situations that may lead to choking, vomiting, or contracting an illness, or, in children, avoidance of loud sounds or costumed characters). Although this subtyping strategy is useful, we also know that most people who have a phobia tend to have multiple phobias of several types (Hofmann, Lehman, & Barlow, 1997). This fact weakens the utility of subtyping a bit.

## Blood-Injury-Injection Phobia

How do phobia subtypes differ from each other? We have already seen one major difference in the case of Jody. Rather than the usual surge of activity in the sympathetic nervous system and increased heart rate and blood pressure, Jody experienced a marked drop in heart rate and blood pressure and fainted as a consequence. Many people who suffer from phobias and experience panic attacks in their feared situations report that they feel like they are going to faint but they never do, because their heart rate and blood pressure are actually increasing. Therefore, those with **blood-injury-injection phobias** almost always differ in their physiological reaction from

| TABLE 4.4 | Phobias Beginning with "A" |
|---|---|
| **Term** | **Fear of:** |
| Acarophobia | Insects, mites |
| Achluophobia | Darkness, night |
| Acousticophobia | Sounds |
| Acrophobia | Heights |
| Aerophobia | Air currents, drafts, wind |
| Agoraphobia | Open spaces |
| Agyiophobia | Crossing the street |
| Aichmophobia | Sharp, pointed objects; knives; being touched by a finger |
| Ailurophobia | Cats |
| Algophobia | Pain |
| Amathophobia | Dust |
| Amychophobia | Laceration; being clawed, scratched |
| Androphobia | Men (and sex with men) |
| Anemophobia | Air currents, wind, drafts |
| Anginophobia | Angina pectoris |
| Anthropophobia | Human society |
| Antlophobia | Floods |
| Apeirophobia | Infinity |
| Aphephobia | Physical contact, being touched |
| Apiphobia | Bees, bee stings |
| Astraphobia | Thunderstorms, lightning |
| Ataxiophobia | Disorder |
| Atephobia | Ruin |
| Auroraphobia | Northern lights |
| Autophobia | Being alone; solitude; oneself; being egotistical |

*Source:* From "List of Phobias" by J. D. Maser, in *Anxiety and the Anxiety Disorders* (p. 805), edited by A. H. Tuma and J. D. Maser, 1985, Mahwah, NJ: Lawrence Erlbaum Associates. Copyright © 1985 by Lawrence Erlbaum Associates. Reprinted with permission.

**blood-injury-injection phobia** Unreasonable fear and avoidance of exposure to blood, injury, or the possibility of an injection. Victims often experience fainting and a drop in blood pressure.

people with other types of phobia (Barlow & Liebowitz, 1995; Öst, 1992). We also noted in Chapter 2 that blood-injury-injection phobia runs in families more strongly than any phobic disorder we know. This is probably because people with this phobia inherit a strong vasovagal response to blood, injury, or the possibility of an injection, all of which cause a drop in blood pressure and a tendency to faint. The phobia develops over the possibility of having this response. The average age of onset for this phobia is approximately 9 years (Antony, Brown, & Barlow, 1997a; Öst, 1989).

### Situational Phobia

Phobias characterized by fear of public transportation or enclosed places are called **situational phobias.** Claustrophobia, a fear of small enclosed places (see Radomsky, Rachman, Thordarson, McIsaac, & Teachman, 2001), is situational, as is a phobia of planes (Ladouceur, 1982). Situational phobia tends to emerge in an individual's early to mid-20s and has been shown to run in families (Curtis, Hill, & Lewis, 1990). The main difference between situational phobia and panic disorder with agoraphobia is that people with situational phobia never experience panic attacks outside the context of their phobic object or situation (Antony et al., 1997a; Antony, Brown, & Barlow, 1997b). Therefore, they can relax when they don't have to confront their phobic situation. People with panic disorder, in contrast, might experience unexpected, uncued panic attacks at any time.

### Natural Environment Phobia

Sometimes very young people develop fears of situations or events occurring in nature. These fears are called **natural environment phobias.** The major examples are heights, storms, and water. These fears also seem to cluster together (Antony & Barlow, 2002; Hofmann et al., 1997): If you fear one situation or event, such as deep water, you are likely to fear another, such as storms. Many of these situations have some danger associated with them and, therefore, mild to moderate fear can be adaptive. For example, we should be careful in a high place or in deep water. It is entirely possible that we are somewhat prepared to be afraid of these situations; as we discussed in Chapter 2, something in our genes makes us sensitive to these situations if any sign of danger is present. In any case, these phobias have a peak age of onset of about 7 years. They are not phobias if they are only passing fears. They have to be persistent and to interfere substantially with the person's functioning,

Corel

People who develop a natural environment phobia intensely fear such places as heights and events such as lightning.

leading to avoidance of boat trips or summer vacations in the mountains where there might be a storm.

### Animal Phobia

Fears of animals and insects are called **animal phobias.** Once again, these fears are common but become phobic only if severe interference with functioning occurs. For example, we have seen cases in our clinic where people with snake or mice phobias are unable to read magazines for fear of unexpectedly coming across a picture of one of these animals. There are many places that these people are unable to go, even if they want to very much, such as to the country to visit someone. The fear experienced by people with animal phobias is very different from an ordinary mild revulsion. The age of onset for these phobias, like that of natural environment phobias, peaks around 7 years (Antony et al., 1997a; Öst, 1987).

---

**situational phobia**   Fear of enclosed places (e.g., claustrophobia) or public transportation (e.g., fear of flying).

**natural environment phobia**   Fear of situations or events in nature, especially heights, storms, and water.

**animal phobia**   Unreasonable, enduring fear of animals or insects that usually develops early in life.

### Separation Anxiety Disorder

All the anxiety disorders described in this chapter may occur during childhood, and there is one additional anxiety disorder unique to children. **Separation anxiety disorder** is characterized by children's unrealistic and persistent worry that something will happen to their parents or other important people in their life or that something will happen to the children themselves that will separate them from their parents (e.g., they will be lost, kidnapped, killed, or hurt in an accident). Children often refuse to go to school or even to leave home, not because they are afraid of school but because they are afraid of separating from loved ones. These fears can result in nightmares involving possible separation and by physical symptoms, distress, and anxiety (Barlow, Pincus, Heinrichs, & Choate, 2003).

Of course, all young children experience separation anxiety to some extent; this fear usually decreases as the child grows older. Therefore, a clinician must judge whether the separation anxiety is greater than would be expected at that particular age (Barlow et al., 2003; Ollendick & Huntzinger, 1990). A study by late researcher Norman Endler at York University showed that adolescents high in

A child with separation anxiety disorder persistently worries that parting with an important person drastically endangers either the loved one or the child.

separation anxiety are those most prone to feeling homesick in their first year of university (Endler & Flett, 2002).

### *Statistics*

Specific fears occur in a majority of people. Not surprisingly, fears of snakes and heights are the most common (Agras, Sylvester, & Oliveau, 1969). The sex ratio among common fears is overwhelmingly female with a couple of exceptions. Among these exceptions is fear of heights, for which the sex ratio is approximately equal. Few people who report specific fears qualify as having a phobia, but for approximately 7% of the Canadian population, their fears are at some point severe enough to be classified as disorders and earn the label "phobia" (Bland, Orn, & Newman, 1988). These numbers seem to be increasing in younger generations (Magee, Eaton, Wittchen, McGonagle, & Kessler, 1996). This is a very high percentage, making specific phobia one of the most common psychological disorders around the world (Arrindell et al., 2003b).

As with common fears, the sex ratio for specific phobias is overwhelmingly female. In the Bland et al. (1988) survey of more than 3000 adults in Edmonton, the lifetime prevalence rate was twice as high in women as in men (i.e., 9.8% versus 4.6%). As noted by leading anxiety investigator Martin Antony, specific phobias represent an interesting paradox (Antony & Barlow, 2002). Despite the fact that specific phobia is a common, treatable, and well-understood condition, people with this disorder rarely present for treatment. For example, of a sample of 522 patients with anxiety disorders referred to a Canadian anxiety disorders clinic, only 6% received a principal diagnosis of specific phobia (Antony & Barlow, 2002).

Thus, even though phobias may interfere with an individual's functioning, only the most severe cases actually come for treatment, because affected people tend to work around their phobias. For example, someone with a fear of heights arranges her life so she never has to be in a tall building or other high place, just as Bob arranged his life so that he never had to fly. People with situational phobias of such things as driving, flying, or small enclosed places most frequently come for treatment. However, there is reason to believe that people with blood-injury-injection phobias are quite prevalent in the population (Agras et al., 1969; Myers et al., 1984); people with this phobia

**separation anxiety disorder** Excessive, enduring fear in some children that harm will come to them or their parents while they are apart.

might seek help if they knew good treatments are available.

As noted by Antony, Brown, and Barlow (1997a), once a phobia develops, it tends to last a lifetime (run a chronic course). Thus, the issue of treatment, described shortly, becomes important.

Although most anxiety disorders look much the same in adults and children, clinicians must be aware of the types of normal fears and anxieties experienced throughout childhood so that they can distinguish them from specific phobias (Albano, Chorpita, & Barlow, 1996; King, 1993; Silverman & Rabian, 1993). Infants, for example, show marked fear of loud noises and strangers. At 1 to 2 years of age, children quite normally are anxious about separating from parents, and fears of animals and the dark develop and may persist into the fourth or fifth year of life. Fear of various monsters and other imaginary creatures may begin about age 3 and last for several years. At age 10, children may fear evaluation by others and feel anxiety over their physical appearance. Generally, reports of fear decline with age, although performance-related fears of such activities as taking a test or talking in front of a large group may increase with age. Specific phobias seem to decline with old age (Blazer, George, & Hughes, 1991; Sheikh, 1992).

The prevalence of specific phobias varies from one culture to another. A variant of phobia in Chinese cultures is called *Pa-leng*, sometimes *frigo phobia* or "fear of the cold." Pa-leng can be understood only in the context of traditional ideas—in this case the Chinese concept of *yin* and *yang* (Tan, 1980). Chinese medicine holds that there must be a balance of yin and yang forces in the body for health to be maintained. Yin represents the cold, dark, windy, energy-sapping aspects of life; yang refers to the warm, bright, energy-producing aspects of life. Individuals with Pa-leng have a morbid fear of the cold. They ruminate over loss of body heat and may wear several layers of clothing even on a hot day. They may complain of belching and flatulence (passing gas), which indicate the presence of wind and therefore of too much yin in the body.

## Causes

For a long time we thought that most specific phobias began with an unusual traumatic event. For example, if you were bitten by a dog you would develop a phobia of dogs. We now know this is not always the case (Barlow, 2002; Öst, 1985; Rachman, 2002). This is not to say that traumatic conditioning experiences do not result in subsequent phobic behaviour. Almost every person with a choking phobia has had some kind of a choking experience.

An individual with claustrophobia who recently came to our clinic reported being trapped in an elevator for an extraordinarily long period of time. These are examples of phobias acquired by *direct experience*, where real danger or pain results in an alarm response (a true alarm). As noted by Stanley J. Rachman, such direct conditioning is merely one way of developing a phobia. There are at least two others: *observing* someone else experience severe fear (vicarious experience), or, under the right conditions, *being told* about danger. In fact, vicarious and informational transmission of fears can take place in he absence of any direct contact with the phobic object or situation (Rachman, 1977).

People develop phobias in at least one other way: by experiencing a false alarm (panic attack) in a specific situation. Remember our earlier discussion of unexpected panic attacks? Studies show that many people with phobias do not necessarily experience a true alarm resulting from real danger at the onset of their phobia. Many initially have an unexpected panic attack in a specific situation, related, perhaps, to current life stress. A phobia of that situation may then develop. Munjack (1984) studied people with specific phobias of driving. He noted that about 50% of the people who could remember when their phobia started had experienced a true alarm due to a traumatic experience such as a car accident. The others had had nothing terrible happen to them while they were driving, but they had experienced an unexpected panic attack during which they felt they were going to lose control of the car and wipe out half the people on the highway. In fact, their driving was not impaired and their catastrophic thoughts were simply part of the panic attack.

We also learn fears vicariously (Rachman, 1977). Seeing someone else have a traumatic experience or endure intense fear may be enough to instill a phobia in the watcher. Öst (1985) describes how a severe dental fear developed in this way. An adolescent boy sat in the waiting room at the school dentist's office partly observing, but fully hearing, his friend who was being treated. Evidently, the boy's reaction to pain caused him to move suddenly, and the drill punctured his cheek. The boy in the waiting room who overheard the accident bolted from the room and developed a severe and long-lasting fear of dental situations. Nothing actually happened to the second person, but you can certainly understand why he developed his phobia.

Sometimes just being warned repeatedly about a potential danger is sufficient for someone to develop a phobia. Öst (1985) describes the case of a woman with an extremely severe snake phobia who had never encountered a snake. Rather, she had been told repeatedly while growing up about the dangers of snakes in the high grass. She was encouraged to

wear high rubber boots to guard against this imminent threat—and she did so even when walking
down the street. Rachman (1977) calls this mode of
developing a phobia *information transmission*.

Terrifying experiences alone do not create phobias. As we have said, a true phobia also requires
anxiety over the possibility of another extremely
traumatic event or false alarm. Remember, when we
are anxious, we persistently anticipate something
terrible, and we are likely to avoid situations where
that terrible thing might occur. If we don't develop
anxiety, our reaction would presumably be in the
category of normal fears experienced by more than
half the population. Normal fear can cause mild
distress, but it is usually ignored and forgotten. A
diagram of the etiology of specific phobia is presented in Figure 4.8.

In summary, several things have to occur for a
person to develop a phobia. First, a traumatic conditioning experience often plays a role (even
hearing about a frightening event is sufficient for
some individuals). Second, fear is more likely to
develop if we are "prepared"; that is, we seem to
carry an inherited tendency to fear situations that
have always been dangerous to the human race,
such as being threatened by wild animals or
trapped in small places (see Chapter 2).

We also have to be susceptible to developing
anxiety focused on the possibility that the event
will happen again. We have discussed the biological and psychological reasons for anxiety and
have seen that at least one phobia, blood-injury-
injection phobia, is highly heritable (Öst, 1989;
Page & Martin, 1998). Patients with blood phobia
probably also inherit a strong vasovagal response
that makes them susceptible to fainting. This alone
would not be sufficient to ensure their becoming
phobic but combines with anxiety to produce
strong vulnerability.

Several years ago, Fyer et al. (1990) demonstrated that approximately 31% of the first-degree
relatives of people with specific phobias also had a
phobia, compared with 11% of the first-degree relatives of normal controls. Interestingly, it seems that
each subtype of phobia "bred true," in that relatives
were likely to have identical types of phobia.
Kendler, Karkowski, and Prescott (1999a) and Page
and Martin (1998) found relatively high estimates
for heritability of individual specific phobias. As
Antony and Barlow (2002) have pointed out, we do
not know for sure whether the tendency for phobias
to run in families is due to genes or to modelling,
but the findings are at least suggestive of a unique
genetic contribution to specific phobia.

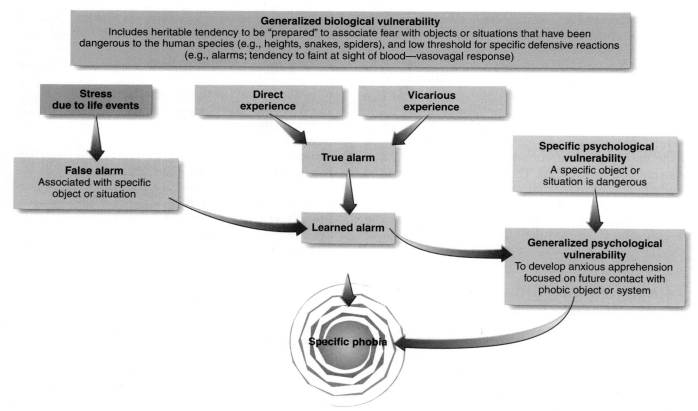

**Figure 4.8** ■ A model of the various ways a specific phobia may develop. (From "Specific Phobias" by M. M. Antony & D. H. Barlow
[2002], in *Anxiety and Its Disorders: The Nature and Treatment of Anxiety and Panic*, by D. H. Barlow, 2nd ed. New York:
Guilford Press. Copyright © 2002 by Guilford Press. Reprinted by permission.)

Finally, social and cultural factors are strong determinants of who develops and reports a specific phobia. In most societies, it is almost unacceptable for males to express fears and phobias. Thus, the overwhelming majority of reported specific phobias occur in women (Arrindell, et al. 2003b). What happens to the males? Possibly, they work hard to overcome their fears by repeatedly exposing themselves to their feared situations. A more likely possibility is that they simply endure their fears without telling anyone about them and without seeking any treatment (Antony & Barlow, 2002).

### Treatment

Although the development of phobias is relatively complex, the treatment is fairly straightforward. Almost everyone agrees that specific phobias require structured and consistent exposure-based exercises. This approach was used successfully by Ladouceur (1982) in the treatment of Bob's flying phobia (described earlier). At a follow-up 14 months after this treatment had ended, Bob had made two overseas trips without any incapacitating anxiety. Nevertheless, most patients who expose themselves gradually to what they fear must be under therapeutic supervision. As was illustrated in Bob's case, individuals who attempt to carry out the exercises alone often attempt to do too much too soon and end up escaping the situation, which may strengthen the phobia. In addition, if they fear having another unexpected panic attack in this situation, it is helpful to direct therapy at panic attacks in the manner described for panic disorder (Antony, Craske, & Barlow, 1995; Craske, Antony, & Barlow, 1997). Finally, in cases of blood-injury-injection phobia, where fainting is a real possibility, graduated exposure-based exercises must be done in specific ways. Individuals must tense various muscle groups during exposure exercises to keep

*Rapid Behavioural Treatment of a Specific Phobia (Snakes)*
"Since I remember, I remember being afraid of snakes.... I have dreams of snakes, it's horrible."

Thomson Learning

their blood pressure sufficiently high to complete the practice (Öst & Sterner, 1987).

New developments make it possible to treat many specific phobias in a single, day long session (e.g., Antony & Barlow, 2002; Antony et al., 1995; Craske et al., 1997; Öst, Ferebee, & Furmark, 1997; Öst, Svensson, Hellström, & Lindwall, 2001). Basically, the therapist spends most of the day with the individual, working through exposure exercises with the phobic object or situation. The patient then practises approaching the phobic situation at home, checking in occasionally with the therapist. For example, in a recent study by Antony, McCabe, Leuw, Sano, and Swinson (2001), 60 individuals with a specific phobia of spiders underwent a single, 2-hour session of exposure treatment. Based on measures of heart rate, subjective reports of fear, and the ability to approach a spider, participants improved after 1 hour of treatment, and further improved after the second hour. It appears that blood-injury-injection phobia can also be treated in a single day-long session (Hellstrom, Fellenius, & Öst, 1996). In these cases not only does the phobia disappear but the tendency to experience the vasovagal response at the sight of blood also lessens considerably. It is also now clear, based on brain imaging work, that these treatments change brain functioning by modifying neural circuitry. That is, these treatments "rewire" the brain (Paquette et al., 2003).

# Social Phobia

■ *Identify the principal causes of social phobias and the most typical strategies used to treat them.*

Are you shy? If so, you have something in common with 20% to 50% of university students, depending on which survey you read. In fact, the vast majority of university students experience symptoms of anxiety in social situations from time to time (Purdon, Antony, Monteiro, & Swinson, 2001). A much smaller number of

people, who suffer severely around others, have **social phobia.** Consider the case of Billy, a 13-year-old boy.

---

**social phobia**  Extreme, enduring, irrational fear and avoidance of social or performance situations.

## Billy
### Too Shy

Billy was the model boy at home. He did his homework, stayed out of trouble, obeyed his parents, and was generally so quiet and reserved he didn't attract much attention. However, when he got to junior high school, something his parents had noticed earlier became painfully evident. Billy had no friends. He was unwilling to attend social or sporting activities connected with school, even though most of the other kids in his class went to these events. When his parents decided to check with the guidance counsellor, they found that she had been about to call them. She reported that Billy did not socialize or speak up in class and was sick to his stomach all day if he knew he was going to be called on. His teachers had difficulty getting anything more than a yes-or-no answer from him. More troublesome was that he had been found hiding in a stall in the boy's restroom during lunch, which he said he had been doing for several months instead of eating. After Billy was referred to our clinic, we diagnosed a severe case of social phobia, an irrational and extreme fear of social situations. Billy's phobia took the form of extreme shyness. He was afraid of being embarrassed or humiliated in the presence of almost everyone except his parents.

## Clinical Description

Social phobia is more than exaggerated shyness (McCabe & Antony, 2002; Schneier et al., 1996). Billy's case holds some characteristics in common with many cases that appear periodically in the press. Some well-known athletes and performers have debilitating performance anxiety. The inability of a skilled athlete to throw a baseball to first base or a seasoned performer to appear on stage certainly does not match the concept of "shyness" with which we are all familiar. In fact, many of these performers may well be among our more gregarious citizens. What holds these two seemingly different conditions of debilitating and pervasive shyness and performance anxiety together? Billy experienced marked and persistent fear of various social situations. In fact, he was extremely fearful of any situation in which he might have to interact with people. For other people, their social fears are quite specific to performing in public. Individuals with performance anxiety usually have no difficulty with social interaction, but when they must do something in front of people, anxiety takes over and they focus on the possibility that they will embarrass themselves.

The most common type of performance anxiety, to which most people can relate, is public speaking. In a community survey conducted in Winnipeg by Stein, Walker, and Forde (1996), about one-third of respondents indicated that they experienced excessive anxiety about public speaking. Other common situations are eating in a restaurant; signing a paper in front of a clerk; or, for males, urinating in a public rest room ("bashful bladder"). Males with this last problem must wait until a stall is available, a difficult task at times. What these examples have in common is that the individual is required to *do* something while others are watching and, to some extent, evaluating their behaviour. This is truly a social phobia because the people have no difficulty eating, writing, or urinating in private. Only when others are watching does the behaviour deteriorate.

Individuals who are extremely and painfully shy in almost all social situations meet DSM-IV-TR criteria for the subtype *social phobia generalized type*, occasionally called *social anxiety disorder*. It is particularly prominent in children. In the child program in one of our clinics, 100% of children and adolescents with social phobia met criteria for generalized type (Albano, DiBartolo, Heimberg, & Barlow, 1995). Billy also fits this subtype (Schneier et al., 1996).

## Statistics

According to the National Comorbidity Survey in the United States, as many as 13.3% of the general population experience social phobia at some point in their lives (Kessler et al., 1994). This makes social phobia the most prevalent psychological disorder in the United States. Similarly high rates of social phobia were revealed in a recent community survey by Stein, Torgrud, and Walker (2002). They interviewed about 2000 people in Winnipeg, Calgary, Edmonton, and rural Alberta and found a 1-year prevalence of 7.2% for social phobia. Of course, many more people are shy but not severely enough to meet criteria for social phobia. The sex ratio favours females only somewhat (1.4:1.0), unlike other anxiety disorders where females predominate (Magee et al., 1996). This distribution differs a bit from the sex ratio of social phobics appearing at clinics, which is nearly 50:50 (Hofmann & Barlow, 2002; Marks, 1985), suggesting that males may seek help more frequently, perhaps because of career-related issues.

Social phobia usually begins during adolescence, with a peak age of onset about 15 years.

Social phobia also tends to be more prevalent in people who are young (18–29 years), undereducated, single, and of low socioeconomic status. Prevalence declines slightly among the elderly (Magee et al., 1996; Sheikh, 1992). Considering their difficulty in meeting people, it is not surprising that a greater percentage of individuals with social phobia are single than in the population at large (Stein & Kean, 2000).

## Disorder Criteria Summary
### Social Phobia

Features of social phobia include:
- Marked and persistent fear of one or more social or performance situations that involve exposure to unfamiliar people or possible scrutiny by others, with the fear that one will be embarrassed or humiliated
- Exposure to the feared social situation almost always provokes anxiety, sometimes as a panic attack
- Recognition (in adults) that the fear is excessive and unreasonable
- The feared social or performance situation is avoided or endured with intense anxiety or distress
- The avoidance, anxious anticipation, or distress interferes significantly with the person's life and healthy functioning

*Source:* Reprinted with permission from the *Diagnostic and Statistical Manual of Mental Disorders*, Fourth Edition, Text Revision. (Copyright © 2000) American Psychiatric Association.

Social phobias distribute relatively equally among different ethnic groups (Magee et al., 1996). In a cross-national study of the rates of social phobia in Canada, the United States, Puerto Rico, and Korea, the lifetime prevalence of the disorder was found to be quite similar across the four countries surveyed. They did find, however, some different expressions of social phobia cross-culturally (Weissman et al., 1996a). In Japan, the clinical presentation of anxiety disorders is best summarized under the label *shinkeishitsu*. One of the most common subcategories is referred to as *taijin kyofusho* (Kirmayer, 1991; Kleinknecht, Dinnel, Kleinknecht, Hiruma, & Harada, 1997). Japanese people with this form of social phobia strongly fear looking people in the eye and are afraid that some aspect of their personal presentation (blushing, stuttering, body odour, and so on) will appear reprehensible. Thus, the focus of anxiety in this disorder is on offending or embarrassing others rather than embarrassing oneself as in social phobia. Japanese males with this disorder outnumber females by a 3:2 ratio (Takahasi, 1989).

## Causes

We have noted that we seem to be prepared by evolution to fear certain wild animals and dangerous situations in the natural environment. Similarly, it seems we are prepared to fear angry, critical, or rejecting people (Mineka & Zinbarg, 1995, 1996; Öhman, 1986). In a series of studies, Öhman and colleagues (e.g., Dimberg & Öhman, 1983; Öhman & Dimberg, 1978) noted that we learn more quickly to fear angry expressions than other facial expressions, and this fear diminishes much more slowly than other types of learning. More recently, Lundh and Öst (1996) demonstrated that people with social phobia who saw a number of pictures of faces were likely to remember critical expressions, whereas those without social phobia remembered the accepting expressions.

In a new study that uses functional neuroimaging, Canadian psychiatrist Murray Stein and colleagues showed that individuals with generalized social phobia react to angry faces with greater activation of the amygdala than normals (Stein, Golden, Sareen, Zorrilla, & Brown, 2002). This finding is intriguing given the established role of the limbic system in anxiety (as described earlier in this chapter) and suggests that the amygdala may be crucially involved in people with social phobia's exaggerated tendency to fear angry faces. Why should we inherit a tendency to fear angry faces? Our ancestors probably avoided hostile, angry, domineering people who might attack or kill them. In fact, in all species, dominant aggressive individuals, high in the social hierarchy, tend to be avoided. Possibly, individuals who avoided people with angry faces were more likely to survive and pass their genes down to us. Of course, this is just a theory.

Research has demonstrated that some infants are born with a temperamental profile or trait of inhibition or shyness that is evident as early as 4 months of age (e.g., Kagan, 1994, 1997; Kagan, Reznick, & Snidman, 1988; Kagan & Snidman, 1991, 1999). Four-month-old infants with this trait become more agitated and cry more frequently when presented with toys or other normal stimuli than infants without the trait. There is now evidence that individuals with excessive behavioural inhibition are at increased risk for developing phobic behaviour (Biederman et al., 1990; Hirschfeld et al., 1992). In any case, inhibition relates more to generalized social phobia than to discrete performance anxiety such as public speaking. A model of the etiology of social phobia would look somewhat like models of panic disorder and specific phobia.

Three pathways to social phobia are possible, as depicted in Figure 4.9. First, one could inherit a generalized biological vulnerability to develop anxiety

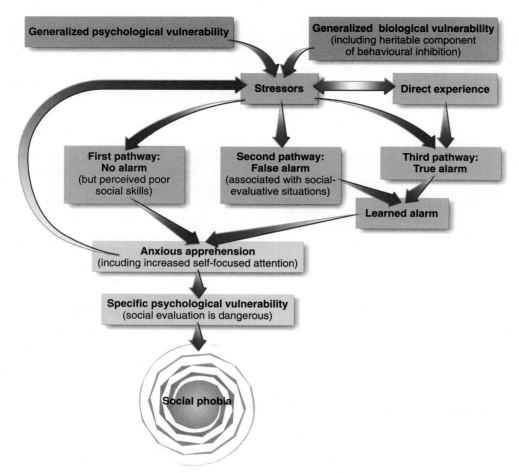

**Figure 4.9** ■ A model of the various ways a social phobia may develop. (From "Social Phobia [Social Anxiety Disorder]" by S. G. Hofmann & D. H. Barlow [2002], in *Anxiety and Its Disorders: The Nature and Treatment of Anxiety and Panic*, by D. H. Barlow, 2nd ed. New York: Guilford Press. Copyright © 2002 by Guilford Press. Reprinted by permission.)

and/or a biological tendency to be socially inhibited. The existence of a generalized psychological vulnerability as reflected in a sense that events, particularly stressful events, are potentially uncontrollable would increase an individual's vulnerability. When under stress, anxiety and self-focused attention could increase to the point of disrupting performance, even in the absence of an alarm (panic attack). Second, when under stress, one might have an unexpected panic attack (false alarm) in a social situation that would become associated (conditioned) to social cues. The individual would then become anxious about having additional (learned) alarms (panic attacks) in the same or similar social situations. Third, someone might experience a real social trauma resulting in a true alarm. Anxiety would then develop (be conditioned) in the same or similar social situations. Traumatic social experiences may also extend back to difficult periods in childhood. Early adolescence—usually ages 12 through 15—is when children may be brutally taunted by peers who are attempting to assert their own dominance. In

fact, some recent evidence suggests that those with social phobia may indeed have experienced more bullying and teasing in childhood than individuals with other anxiety disorders (McCabe, Antony, Summerfeldt, Liss, & Swinson, 2003). Such experiences may produce anxiety and panic that are reproduced in future social situations and might also lead them to develop biased perceptions about the likelihood that others will treat them similarly in future (Alden, 2001).

But one more factor must fall into place to make it a social anxiety disorder. The individual with the vulnerabilities and experiences just described must also have learned growing up that social evaluation in particular can be dangerous. In fact, evidence indicates that some people with social phobia are predisposed to focus their anxiety on events involving social evaluation. Some investigators (Bruch & Heimberg, 1994; Rapee & Melville, 1997) suggest that the parents of patients with social phobia are significantly more socially fearful and concerned with the opinions of others than are the parents of patients with panic disorder and that they pass this concern on to their children (Lieb et al., 2000). Fyer, Mannuzza, Chapman, Liebowitz, and Klein (1993) reported that the relatives of people with social phobia had a significantly greater risk of developing it than the relatives of individuals without social phobia (16% versus 5%)—thus, the specific psychological vulnerability depicted in Figure 4.9. Interestingly, this psychological vulnerability factor may itself have a biological basis. A recent twin study by Stein, Jang, and Livesley (2002) showed that the tendency to fear being negatively evaluated by others is moderately heritable. Thus, as you can see, a combination of biological and psychological events seem to lead to the development of social phobia.

## Treatment

Effective treatments have been developed for social phobia only in the past several years (Barlow & Lehman, 1996; Cox, Walker, Enns, & Karpinski, 2002; Hofmann, 2004; Radomsky & Otto, 2001; Taylor, 1996; Turk, Heimberg, & Hope, 2001). For example, in cognitive-behavioural group therapy (CBGT), groups of patients rehearse or role-play their socially phobic situations in front of one another (Heimberg et al., 1990; Turk et al., 2001). The group members participate in the role-playing, for example, acting as audience for someone who has extreme difficulty giving a speech. At the same time the therapist conducts rather intensive cognitive therapy aimed at uncovering and changing the automatic or unconscious perceptions of danger that the socially phobic client assumes to exist. These treatments have been much more effective than education about anxiety and social phobia and social support for stressful life events. More important, a follow-up after 5 years indicates that the therapeutic gains are maintained (Heimberg, Salzman, Holt, & Blendell, 1993).

Some studies have suggested that the exposure-based behavioural rehearsal of anxiety-provoking situations is a more important part of treatment than the cognitive therapy component (Feske & Chambless, 1995; Gould, Buckminster, Pollack, Otto, & Yap, 1997; Hofmann & Barlow, 2002). We have adapted these protocols for use with adolescents, directly involving parents in the group treatment process. Preliminary results suggest that adolescents with severe social phobia can attain relatively normal functioning in school and other social settings (Albano & Barlow, 1996).

Effective drug treatments have been discovered as well. Tricyclic antidepressants and, particularly, monoamine oxidase (MAO) inhibitors have been found to be more effective than placebo in the treatment of severe social anxiety (Liebowitz et al., 1992). Since 1999, the SSRIs, Paxil, Zoloft, and Effexer have received approval for treatment of social anxiety disorder based on studies showing effectiveness compared with placebo (e.g., Stein et al., 1998).

One large and important study compared MAO inhibitors, among the most powerful drugs for social anxiety disorder, with the psychological treatments described earlier. In this study (Heimberg et al., 1998; Liebowitz et al., 1999) 133 patients were randomly assigned to phenelzine, CBGT, drug placebo, or an educational-supportive group therapy that served as a placebo for the psychological treatment because it did not contain the cognitive-behavioural component. Results show that both treatments are highly and equally effective compared with the two placebo conditions but that relapse tends to be more common after treatment stops among those taking medication.

A meta-analysis on the relative effectiveness of psychological and pharmacological treatments for social phobia concluded that pharmacotherapies were in fact the most consistently effective treatments for social phobia. However, these authors were unable to compare the durability of treatment gains for the psychological versus pharmacological treatments, because too few drug studies included follow-up after the medications had been discontinued (Fedoroff & Taylor, 2001).

## Concept Check 4.4

Identify the following specific phobias: (a) blood-injury-injection, (b) acrophobia, (c) animal, (d) social, (e) natural environment.

1. _____ Mark had no friends at school and hid in the boys' bathroom during both lunch and recess.
2. _____ Dennis fears and strenuously avoids storms. Not surprisingly, on his first oceangoing cruise, he found that deep water terrified him, too.
3. _____ Rita was comfortable at the zoo until the old terror gripped her at the insect display.
4. _____ John had to give up his dream of becoming a surgeon because he faints at the sight of blood.
5. _____ Rachel turned down several lucrative job offers that involved public speaking for a low-paying desk job.
6. _____ Farrah can't visit her rural friends because of her fear of snakes.

# Posttraumatic Stress Disorder

■ *Describe the essential features of posttraumatic stress disorder, its proposed causal factors, and available treatment approaches.*

In recent years we have heard a great deal about the severe and long-lasting emotional disorders that can occur after a variety of traumatic events. Perhaps the most impressive traumatic event is war, but emotional disorders also occur after physical assault (particularly rape), car accidents, natural catastrophes, or the sudden death of a loved one. One emotional disorder that follows a trauma is known as **posttraumatic stress disorder (PTSD).**

## Clinical Description

DSM-IV-TR describes the setting event for PTSD as exposure to a traumatic event during which one feels fear, helplessness, or horror. Afterward, victims re-experience the event through memories and nightmares. When memories occur suddenly and the victims find themselves reliving the event, they are having a *flashback*. Victims avoid anything that reminds them of the trauma. They display a characteristic restriction or numbing of emotional responsiveness, which may be disruptive to interpersonal relationships. They are sometimes unable to remember certain aspects of the event. It is possible that victims unconsciously attempt to avoid the experience of emotion, like people with panic disorder, because intense emotions could bring back memories of the trauma. Finally, victims typically are chronically overaroused, easily startled, and quick to anger.

We conducted a study on the psychological impact of an airline disaster on community volunteers in a rural community (Mitchell, Stewart, Griffin, & Loba, 2004). Swissair Flight 111 crashed off the coast of Peggy's Cove in Nova Scotia on September 2, 1998. When local residents heard the crash, many went out in their boats and attempted to rescue survivors. Unfortunately, none of the 229 passengers and crew survived the crash, and these community volunteers unexpectedly were confronted with airplane debris, passengers' personal effects, and gruesome human remains. In some cases, they were faced with dismembered body parts, and the crash victims' skin had often separated from the rest of the body, a phenomenon called degloving.

Many volunteers continued assisting with the recovery work (e.g., volunteering for ground search and rescue) over the ensuing weeks and were continually exposed to these sights and smells. Well

© T. Caldwell/Ottawa Sun/Corbis Sygma

Exposure to a traumatic event may create profound fear, helplessness, and an emotional re-experiencing of the event—all symptoms of PTSD.

after their exposure to the disaster had ended, many volunteers reported psychological symptoms attributable to their trauma exposure. Many reported having intrusive memories of the horrors they had encountered in their volunteer work, avoiding reminders of the disaster, experiencing emotional numbing, and having difficulties sleeping. These are all common symptoms in PTSD. The percentage of volunteers reporting each of the 17 DSM-IV-TR PTSD symptoms is illustrated in Table 4.5.

Consider next the case of the Joneses from one of our clinics.

## The Joneses
### One Victim, Many Traumas

Mrs. Betty Jones and her four children arrived at a farm to visit a friend. (Mr. Jones was at work.) Jeff, the oldest child, was 8 years old. Marcie, Cathy, and Susan were 6, 4, and 2 years of age,

---

**posttraumatic stress disorder (PTSD)** Enduring, distressing emotional disorder that follows exposure to a severe helplessness or fear-inducing threat. The victim re-experiences the trauma, avoids stimuli associated with it, and develops a numbing of responsiveness and an increased vigilance and arousal.

respectively. Mrs. Jones parked the car in the driveway, and they all started across the yard to the front door. Suddenly Jeff heard growling somewhere near the house. Before he could warn the others, a large German shepherd charged and leapt at Marcie, the 6-year-old, knocking her to the ground and tearing viciously at her face. The family, too stunned to move, watched the attack helplessly. After what seemed like an eternity, Jeff lunged at the dog and it moved away. The owner, in a state of panic, ran to a nearby house to get help. Mrs. Jones immediately put pressure on Marcie's facial wounds in an attempt to stop the bleeding. The owner had neglected to retrieve the dog, and it stood a short distance away, growling and barking at the frightened family. Eventually the dog was restrained and Marcie was rushed to the hospital. Marcie, who was hysterical, had to be restrained on a padded board so emergency room physicians could stitch her wounds.

**TABLE 4.5** Percentage of Swissair Disaster Volunteers Reporting Each DSM-IV-TR PTSD Symptom on a Self-Report Scale

| Symptom Domain | Item | % Reporting |
|---|---|---|
| **Cognitive** | | |
| Re-experiencing | Intrusive thoughts | 69% |
| | Nightmares | 39% |
| | Flashbacks | 46% |
| | Emotional reactivity | 77% |
| | Physiological reactivity | 31% |
| Avoidance | Avoid thoughts of trauma | 46% |
| | Avoid trauma reminders | 39% |
| | Inability to recall trauma | 31% |
| Emotional Numbing | Loss of interest | 39% |
| | Detachment | 53% |
| | Restricted affect | 15% |
| | Foreshortened future | 23% |
| **Somatic** | | |
| Hyper-Arousal | Sleep disturbance | 31% |
| | Increased irritability | 23% |
| | Difficulty concentrating | 46% |
| | Hypervigilance | 46% |
| | Excessive startle | 31% |

*Source:* From "We Will Never Forget..:The Swissair Flight 111 Disaster and Its Impact on Volunteers and Communities," by T.L. Mitchell, S.H. Stewart, K. Griffin, and P. Loba (2004). *Journal of Health Psychology, 9,* 245–262. Reprinted with permission.

This case is unusual because not only did Marcie develop PTSD but so did her 8-year-old brother. In addition, Cathy, 4, and Susan, 2, although quite young, also showed symptoms of the disorder, as did their mother (Albano, Miller, Zarate, Côté, & Barlow, 1997). Jeff evidenced classic survivor guilt symptoms, reporting that he should have saved Marcie or at least put himself between Marcie and the dog. Both Jeff and Marcie regressed developmentally, wetting the bed and experiencing nightmares and separation fears. In addition, Marcie, having been strapped down and given local anesthetic and stitches, became frightened of any medical procedures and even of such routine daily events as having her nails trimmed or taking a bath. Furthermore, she refused to be tucked into bed, something she had enjoyed all her life, probably because it reminded her of the hospital board. Jeff started sucking his fingers, which he had not done for years. These behaviours, along with intense separation anxiety, are common, particularly in younger children (Eth, 1990; Silverman & La Greca, 2002). Cathy, the 4-year-old, evidenced considerable fear and avoidance when tested but denied having any problem when she was interviewed by a child psychologist. Susan, the 2-year-old, also had some symptoms, but was too young to talk about them. However, for several months following the trauma she repeatedly said, without provocation, "Doggy bit sister."

Children's memories of traumatic events can become embellished over the years. For example, some children incorporate a superhero coming to the rescue. These intense memories are malleable and subject to distortion (e.g., Porter, Yuille, & Lehman, 1999).

PTSD is subdivided into *acute* and *chronic. Acute PTSD* can be diagnosed 1 month after the event occurs. When PTSD continues longer than 3 months, it is considered chronic. *Chronic PTSD* is usually associated with more prominent avoidance behaviours (Davidson, Hughes, Blazer, & George, 1991), as well as with the more frequent co-occurrence of additional diagnoses such as social phobia. In *PTSD with delayed onset,* individuals show few if any symptoms immediately after a trauma, but later, perhaps years afterward, they develop full-blown PTSD. Why onset is delayed in some individuals is not yet clear.

As we noted, PTSD cannot be diagnosed until a month after the trauma. New to DSM-IV-TR is a disorder called **acute stress disorder.** This is really

**acute stress disorder** Severe reaction immediately following a terrifying event, often including amnesia about the event, emotional numbing, and derealization. Many victims later develop posttraumatic stress disorder.

PTSD occurring within the first month after the trauma, but the different name emphasizes the very severe reaction that some people have immediately. PTSD-like symptoms are accompanied by severe dissociative symptoms, such as amnesia for all or part of the trauma, emotional numbing, and derealization, or feelings of unreality. According to one Australian study, 63% to 70% of individuals with acute stress disorder from motor vehicle accidents went on to develop PTSD up to 2 years after the trauma. In addition, 13% who did not meet criteria for acute stress disorder went on to develop PTSD. If the victim experienced very strong arousal and emotional numbing as part of his or her acute stress disorder, the likelihood of later developing PTSD was greater (Harvey & Bryant, 1998). Acute stress disorder was included in DSM-IV because many people with very severe early reactions to trauma could not otherwise be diagnosed and, therefore, could not receive insurance coverage for immediate treatment.

## Statistics

Determining the prevalence rates for PTSD seems relatively straightforward: Simply observe victims of a trauma and see how many develop PTSD. But a number of studies have demonstrated the remarkably low prevalence of PTSD in populations of trauma victims. Stanley J. Rachman (1978) studied the British citizenry who endured numerous life-threatening air raids during Word War II. He concluded that "a great majority of people endured the air raids extraordinarily well, contrary to the universal expectation of mass panic. Exposure to repeated bombings did not produce a significant increase in psychiatric disorders. Although short-lived fear reactions were common, surprisingly few persistent phobic reactions emerged" (Rachman, 1991, p. 162). Similar results have been observed after disastrous fires, earthquakes, and floods (Green, Grace, Lindy, Titchener, & Lindy, 1983).

On the other hand, some studies have found a very high incidence of PTSD after trauma. Kilpatrick et al. (1985) sampled more than 2000 adult women who had personally experienced such trauma as rape, sexual molestation, robbery, and aggravated assault. Participants were asked whether they had thought about suicide after the trauma, attempted suicide, or had a *nervous breakdown* (a lay term that has no meaning in psychopathology but is commonly used to refer to a severe psychological upset). The authors also analyzed the results based on whether the attack was completed or attempted. Rape had the most significant emotional impact. Compared with 2.2% of non-victims, 19.2% of rape victims had attempted suicide, and 44% reported suicidal ideation at some time following the rape. Similarly, Resnick, Kilpatrick, Dansky, Saunders, and Best (1993) found that 32% of rape victims met criteria for PTSD at some point in their lives. Looking at all types of trauma (e.g., physical assault and accidents) in a large sample of U.S. adult women, Resnick et al. (1993) found that 17.9% experienced PTSD. Taylor and Koch (1995) found that 15% to 20% of Canadian adults experiencing severe auto accidents developed PTSD. Other surveys indicate that among the population as a whole, 7.8% have experienced PTSD (Kessler, Sonnega, Bromet, Hughes, & Nelson, 1995), and combat and sexual assault are the most common traumas.

What accounts for the discrepancies between the low rate of PTSD in citizens who endured bombing and shelling in London, England, and the relatively high rate in victims of crime? Investigators have now concluded that during air raids many people *may not have directly experienced the horrors of dying, death, and direct attack.* Close exposure to the trauma seems to be necessary to developing this disorder (Keane & Barlow, 2002; King, King, Foy, & Gudanowski, 1996).

But is this the whole story? It seems not. Some people experience the most horrifying traumas imaginable and emerge psychologically healthy. For others, even relatively mild stressful events are sufficient to produce a full-blown disorder. To understand how this can happen we must consider the etiology of PTSD.

## Causes

PTSD is the one disorder for which we are sure of the etiology: Someone personally experiences a trauma and develops a disorder. However, whether a person develops PTSD or not is a surprisingly complex issue involving biological, psychological, and social factors. Foy, Sipprelle, Rueger, and Carroll (1984) concluded that the intensity of combat exposure contributed to the etiology of PTSD in a group of war veterans but did not account for all of it. For example, approximately 67% of prisoners of war developed PTSD (Foy, Resnick, Sipprelle, & Carroll, 1987). This means that 33% of the prisoners who endured long-term deprivation and torture *did not* develop the disorder. Similarly, Resnick, Kilpatrick, Dansky, Saunders, and Best (1993) demonstrated that the percentage of female crime victims who developed PTSD increased as a function of the severity of the trauma (see Figure 4.10). At lower levels of trauma, some people develop PTSD but most do not. In our sample of Swissair recovery volunteers, the longer the individual was involved in recovery work (presumably

## Disorder Criteria Summary
### Posttraumatic Stress Disorder (PTSD)

Features of PTSD include:
- Exposure to a traumatic event in which the person experienced, witnessed, or was confronted by a situation involving death, threatened death, or serious injury, in response to which the person reacted with intense fear, helplessness, or horror
- The traumatic event is persistently re-experienced in one or more of the following ways: (1) recurrent and intrusive distressing recollections of the event, including images, thoughts, or perceptions; (2) recurrent distressing dreams of the event; (3) a sense that the traumatic event is recurring, including illusions, hallucinations, and dissociative flashbacks; (4) intense psychological distress at exposure to cues that call to mind the event; (5) physiological reaction to cues that call to mind the event
- Persistent avoidance of stimuli associated with the trauma, and numbing of general responsiveness
- Persistent symptoms of increased arousal, such as difficulty sleeping, irritability, and hypervigilance
- Clinically significant distress or impairment in social, occupational, or other important areas of functioning
- Duration of the disturbance for more than 1 month

*Source:* Reprinted with permission from the *Diagnostic and Statistical Manual of Mental Disorders*, Fourth Edition, Text Revision. (Copyright © 2000) American Psychiatric Association.

reflecting more severe exposure), the more severe and frequent were the PTSD symptoms; yet not all volunteers developed PTSD, despite exposure to such an awful event (Mitchell et al., 2004). What accounts for these differences?

As with other disorders, we bring our own generalized biological and psychological vulnerabilities with us. The greater the vulnerability, the more likely we are to develop PTSD. If certain characteristics run in your family, you have a much greater chance of developing the disorder (Davidson, Swartz, Storck, Krishnan, & Hammett, 1985; Foy et al., 1987). A family history of anxiety suggests a generalized biological vulnerability for PTSD. True et al. (1993) reported that, given the same amount of combat exposure and one twin with PTSD, a monozygotic (identical) twin was more likely than a dizygotic twin to develop PTSD. This suggests some genetic influence in the development of PTSD. A recent twin study by Stein, Jang, Taylor, Vernon, and Livesley (2002) showed that PTSD symptoms after non-combat trauma are also moderately heritable. Interestingly, they further found that exposure to

certain types of traumas (i.e., assaultive trauma like robbery, but not non-assaultive trauma like car accidents) was also contributed by genetics. In other words, genetic factors seem to influence the risk of being exposed to certain kinds of trauma, perhaps through inherited personality characteristics that affect what kinds of environments (e.g., risky versus safe) a person will choose. Recall the reciprocal gene–environment model we described in Chapter 2, in which existing vulnerabilities, some of them heritable, may help determine the kind of environment in which someone lives and, therefore, the type of psychological disorder that person may develop.

Also, there seems to be a *generalized psychological vulnerability* described in the context of other disorders based on early experiences with unpredictable or uncontrollable events. Foy et al. (1987) discovered that at very high levels of trauma, these vulnerabilities did not matter as much, because most prisoners (67%) developed PTSD. However, at low levels of stress or trauma, vulnerabilities matter a great deal in determining whether the disorder will develop. Family instability is one factor that may instill a sense that the world is an uncontrollable, potentially dangerous place (Chorpita & Barlow, 1998), so it is not surprising that individuals

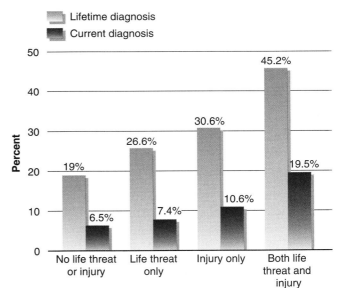

**Figure 4.10** ■ Prevalence of lifetime and current posttraumatic stress disorder associated with assault characteristics. (From "Prevalence of Civilian Trauma and Posttraumatic Stress Disorder in a Representative National Sample of Women" by H. S. Resnick, D. G. Kilpatrick, B. S. Dansky, B. E. Sanders, and C. L. Best, 1993, *Journal of Consulting and Clinical Psychology*, 61, 984–991. Figure 2, p. 989. Copyright © 1993 by the American Psychological Association. Reprinted with permission.)

from unstable families are at risk for developing PTSD if they experience trauma. This factor was relevant in a study of more than 1600 male and female war veterans (King et al., 1996).

Finally, social and cultural factors play a major role in the development of PTSD (e.g., Carroll, Rueger, Foy, & Donahoe, 1985). The results from a number of studies are consistent in showing that, if you have a strong and supportive group of people around you, it is much less likely you will develop PTSD after a trauma. In a particularly interesting study, Vernberg, La Greca, Silverman, and Prinstein (1996) studied 568 elementary school children 3 months after Hurricane Andrew hit the coast of south Florida. More than 55% of these children reported moderate to very severe levels of PTSD symptoms, a typical result for this type of disaster (La Greca & Prinstein, 2002). When the authors examined factors contributing to who developed PTSD symptoms and who didn't, social support from parents, close friends, classmates, and teachers was an important protective factor. Similarly, positive coping strategies involving active problem solving seemed to be protective, whereas becoming angry and placing blame on others were associated with higher levels of PTSD. The broader and deeper the network of social support, the less chance of developing PTSD.

Why is this? We are all social animals and something about having a loving, caring group of people around us directly affects our biological and psychological responses to stress. In fact, a number of studies show that support from loved ones reduces cortisol secretion and HPA axis activity in children during stress (e.g., Nachmias, Gunnar, Mangelsdorf, Parritz, & Buss, 1996). It is likely that one reason for the very high prevalence of PTSD in Vietnam veterans is the tragic absence of social support when they returned from the war.

It seems clear that PTSD involves a number of neurobiological systems (Charney, Deutch, Krystal, Southwick, & Davis, 1993; Heim & Nemeroff, 1999; Ladd et al., 2000; Southwick, Krystal, Johnson, & Charney, 1992; Sullivan et al., 2000). Charney and colleagues conducted research on animals, mostly rats who were exposed to strong uncontrollable stress such as repeated shock. Their findings revealed that stressful and threatening cues may activate input from several regions of the brain. These inputs then activate the CRF system, as noted earlier in the chapter.

Evidence of damage to the hippocampus has appeared in groups of patients with war-related PTSD (Gurvits et al., 1996) and adult survivors of childhood sexual abuse (Bremner et al., 1995). The hippocampus is a part of the brain that plays an important role in learning and memory. Thus, if there is damage to the hippocampus, we might expect some disruptions in learning and memory. In fact, disruptions in memory functions, including short-term memory and recalling events, have been demonstrated in patients with PTSD (Sass et al., 1992). These memory deficits are also evident in veterans of the Gulf War (Vasterling, Brailey, Constans, & Sotker, 1998).

Earlier we described a panic attack as an adaptive fear response occurring at an inappropriate time. It is not surprising that Southwick et al. (1992) trace a brain circuit for PTSD that is similar to the brain circuit for panic attacks, originating in the locus coeruleus in the brain stem. We have speculated that the alarm reaction is much the same in both panic disorder and PTSD, but in panic disorder the alarm is false. In PTSD, the initial alarm is true in that real danger is present (Keane & Barlow, 2002; Jones & Barlow, 1990). If the alarm is severe enough, we may develop a conditioned or learned alarm reaction to stimuli that remind us of the trauma (e.g., being tucked into bed reminded Marcie of the emergency room board). We may also develop anxiety about the possibility of additional uncontrollable emotional experiences (such as flashbacks, which are common in PTSD). Whether or not we develop anxiety depends in part on our vulnerabilities. This model of the etiology of PTSD is presented in Figure 4.11.

## Treatment

From the psychological point of view, most clinicians agree that victims of PTSD should face the original trauma to develop effective coping procedures and thus overcome the debilitating effects of the disorder (Barlow & Lehman, 1996; Foa & Meadows, 1997; Keane & Barlow, 2002). In psychoanalytic therapy, reliving emotional trauma to relieve emotional suffering is called *catharsis*. The trick, of course, is in arranging the re-exposure so it will be therapeutic rather than traumatic again. Unlike the object of a specific phobia, a traumatic event is difficult to recreate, and few therapists want to try. Therefore, *imaginal exposure*, in which the content of the trauma and the emotions associated with it are worked through systematically, has been used for decades under a variety of names.

A complication is that trauma victims often repress the emotional side of their memories of the event and sometimes, it seems, the memory itself. This happens automatically and unconsciously. On occasion, with treatment, the memories flood back and the patient dramatically relives the episode. Although this may be frightening to both patient and therapist, it can be therapeutic if handled appropriately.

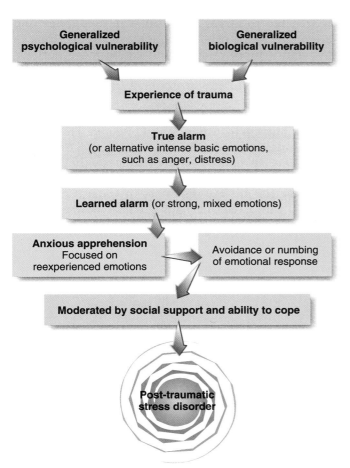

**Figure 4.11** ■ A model of the causes of posttraumatic stress disorder. (From "Posttraumatic Stress Disorder" by T. M. Keane & D. H. Barlow [2002], in *Anxiety and Its Disorders: The Nature and Treatment of Anxiety and Panic*, by D. H. Barlow, 2nd ed. New York: Guilford Press. Copyright © 2002 by Guilford Press. Reprinted by permission.)

Both Marcie, the young girl bitten by the dog, and her brother were treated simultaneously. The primary difficulty was Marcie's reluctance to be seen by a doctor or to undergo any physical examinations, so a series of experiences was arranged from least to most intense (see Table 4.6). Mildly anxiety-provoking procedures for Marcie included having her pulse taken, lying on an examination table, and taking a bath after accidentally cutting herself. The most intense challenge was being strapped on a restraining board. First Marcie watched her brother go through these exercises. He was not afraid of these particular procedures, although he was anxious about being strapped to a board because of Marcie's terror at the thought. After she watched her brother experience these situations with little or no fear, Marcie tried each one in turn. The therapist took instant photographs of her that she kept after completing

the procedures. Marcie was also asked to draw pictures of the situations. The therapist and her family warmly congratulated her as she completed each exercise. Because of Marcie's age, she was not adept at imaginatively re-creating memories of the traumatic medical procedures. Therefore, her treatment offered experiences designed to alter her current perceptions of the situations. Marcie's PTSD was successfully treated, and her brother's guilt was greatly reduced as a function of helping in her treatment.

A recent modification to traditional imaginal exposure therapy is Donald Meichenbaum's CBT treatment for PTSD. Meichenbaum (1994) uses a constructivist-narrative approach for treating individuals who have been traumatized (e.g., through rape). In this approach, the therapist assists the client in reconstructing his or her "story" about the traumatic event—changing the meaning the client has attached to the traumatic event and helping the client develop adaptive coping strategies and a sense of survivorship (Meichenbaum, 1994).

Another newer psychological treatment for PTSD is known as eye-movement desensitization and reprocessing (EMDR; Shapiro, 1995, 1999).

| **TABLE 4.6** Fear and Avoidance Hierarchy for Marcie | | |
|---|---|---|
| | Pretreatment Fear Rating | Posttreatment Fear Rating |
| Being strapped on a board | 4 | 0 |
| Having an electrocardiogram | 4 | 0 |
| Having a chest X-ray | 4 | 0 |
| Having a doctor listen to heart with stethoscope | 3 | 0 |
| Lying on examination table | 3 | 0 |
| Taking a bath after sustaining an accidentally inflicted cut | 3 | 0 |
| Allowing therapist to put Band-Aid on a cut | 2 | 0 |
| Letting therapist listen to heart with stethoscope | 1 | 0 |
| Having pulse taken | 1 | 0 |
| Allowing therapist to examine throat with tongue depressor | 1 | 0 |

*Source:* From "Behavioral Assessment and Treatment of PTSD in Prepubertal Children: Attention to Developmental Factors and Innovative Strategies in the Case Study of a Family," by A. M. Albano, P. P. Miller, G. Côté, and D. H. Barlow, 1997, *Cognitive and Behavioral Practice*, 4: 254. Copyright © 1997 by Association for Advancement of Behavior Therapy.

Lieutenant-General (Retired) Romeo Dallaire, who is an activist promoting recognition of stress reactions in Canadian military personnel, has PTSD related to his experiences on a peacekeeping mission in Rwanda.

that it led to larger reductions in avoidance and cognitive re-experiencing, achieved reductions in avoidance more quickly, and led to more patients who were PTSD-free after treatment. EMDR did not differ on any outcomes from relaxation training.

Some drug treatments have also been tried with PTSD, but the investigation of effective ones is just beginning (Lydiard, Brawman-Mintzer, & Ballenger, 1996). Preliminary experience suggests that some of the same drugs, such as SSRIs (Prozac and Paxil), effective for anxiety disorders in general might be helpful with PTSD, perhaps because they relieve the severe anxiety and panic attacks so prominent in this disorder.

## Concept Check 4.5

Match the correct preliminary diagnosis with the following cases: (a) acute posttraumatic stress disorder, (b) acute stress disorder, (c) delayed onset posttraumatic stress disorder.
1. Judy witnessed a horrific tornado level her farm 3 weeks ago. Since then, she's had many flashbacks of the incident, trouble sleeping, and a fear of going outside in storms. _____
2. Jack was involved in a car accident 6 weeks ago in which the driver of the other car was killed. Since then, Jack has been unable to get in a car because it brings back the horrible scene he witnessed. Nightmares of the incident haunt him and interfere with his sleep. He is irritable and has lost interest in his work and hobbies. _____
3. Patricia was raped at the age of 17, 30 years ago. Just recently, she has been having flashbacks of the event, difficulty sleeping, and fear of sexual contact with her husband. _____

While thinking about the traumatic experience in therapy, the client is asked to follow the therapist's moving fingers with his or her eyes, all the while keeping the image of the trauma in mind. This unusual technique is said by proponents to facilitate rapid reprocessing of the traumatic event (Shapiro, 1999). Recently, a group of researchers at the University of British Columbia compared the efficacy of this newer approach to imaginal exposure and to relaxation training (Taylor et al., 2003). Sixty patients with PTSD were randomly assigned to one of three treatment modalities. Exposure therapy was superior to the other two treatments in

# Obsessive-Compulsive Disorder

■ *Describe the symptoms, defining characteristics, and integrative model of obsessive-compulsive disorder.*

**Obsessive-compulsive disorder (OCD)** is the devastating culmination of the anxiety disorders. It is not uncommon for someone with OCD to experience severe generalized anxiety, recurrent panic attacks, debilitating avoidance, and major depression, all

**obsessive-compulsive disorder (OCD)**  Anxiety disorder involving unwanted, persistent, intrusive thoughts and impulses as well as repetitive actions intended to suppress them.

occurring simultaneously with obsessive-compulsive symptoms. With OCD, establishing even a foothold of control and predictability over the dangerous events in life seems so utterly hopeless that victims resort to magic and rituals.

## *Clinical Description*

In other anxiety disorders the danger is usually in an external object or situation, or at least in the memory of one. In OCD the dangerous event is a thought, image, or impulse that the client attempts to avoid as completely as someone with a snake phobia avoids snakes. For example, has anyone ever told you not to think of pink elephants? If you really concentrate on not thinking of pink elephants, using every mental means possible, you will realize how difficult it is to suppress a suggested thought or image. Individuals with OCD fight this battle all day, every day, sometimes for most of their lives, and they usually fail miserably. In Chapter 3 we discussed the case of Frank, who experienced involuntary thoughts of epilepsy or seizures and prayed or shook his leg to try to distract himself. **Obsessions** are intrusive and mostly nonsensical thoughts, images, or urges that the individual tries to resist or eliminate. **Compulsions** are the thoughts or actions used to suppress the obsessions and provide relief. Frank had both obsessions and compulsions, but his disorder was mild compared with the case of Richard.

## Richard
### Enslaved by Ritual

Richard, a 19-year-old first-year university student majoring in philosophy, withdrew from school because of incapacitating ritualistic behaviour. He abandoned personal hygiene because the compulsive rituals that he had to carry out during washing or cleaning were so time consuming that he could do nothing else. Almost continual showering gave way to no showering. He stopped cutting and washing his hair and beard, brushing his teeth, and changing his clothes. He left his room infrequently and, to avoid rituals associated with the toilet, defecated on paper towels, urinated in paper cups, and stored the waste in the closet. He ate only late at night when his family was asleep. To be able to eat he had to exhale completely, making a lot of hissing noises, coughs, and hacks, and then fill his mouth with as much food as he could while no air was in his lungs. He would eat only a mixture of peanut butter, sugar, cocoa, milk, and mayonnaise. All other foods he considered contaminants. When he walked he took very small steps on his toes while continually looking back, checking and rechecking. On occasion he ran quickly in place. He withdrew his left arm completely from his shirt sleeve as if he were crippled and his shirt was a sling.

**Obsessive-Compulsive Disorder: Chuck**
*"I'm a little bit obsessive-compulsive.... It's a little difficult to deal with. The obsessive part—I'll get a thought in my head, and I can't put it out. It's just there all the time. I think about it when I go to bed, I think about it when I get up.... I'm a 'checker'— I have to check things.... I don't cook, but I have to check the stove every morning ... not always really rational."*

Thomson Learning

Like everyone with OCD, Richard experienced intrusive and persistent thoughts and impulses; in his case they were about sex, aggression, and religion. His various behaviours were efforts to suppress sexual and aggressive thoughts or to ward off the disastrous consequences he thought would ensue if he did not perform his rituals. Richard performed most of the repetitive behaviours and mental acts mentioned in the DSM-IV-TR criteria. Compulsions can be either behavioural (handwashing or checking) or mental (thinking about certain words in a specific order, counting, praying, and so on; Foa et al., 1996; Steketee & Barlow, 2002). The important thing is that they are believed to reduce stress or prevent a dreaded event. Compulsions are often "magical" in that they frequently bear no logical relation to the obsession.

---

**obsessions**   Recurrent intrusive thoughts or impulses a person seeks to suppress or neutralize while recognizing they are not imposed by outside forces

**compulsions**   Repetitive, ritualistic, time-consuming behaviours or mental acts a person feels driven to perform

## Disorder Criteria Summary
Obsessive-Compulsive Disorder (OCD)

Features of OCD include:

- Obsessions: Recurrent and persistent thoughts, impulses, or images that are experienced as intrusive and inappropriate and that cause marked anxiety or distress; more than just excessive worries about real-life problems; the person attempts to ignore or suppress or neutralize them; the person recognizes that the thoughts, impulses, or images are a product of her or his own mind
- Compulsions: Repetitive behaviours (e.g., frequent handwashing or checking) or mental acts (e.g., praying or counting) that the person feels driven to perform in response to an obsession or according to rules that must be applied rigidly
- Recognition that the obsessions or compulsions are excessive or unreasonable
- The thoughts, impulses, or behaviours cause marked distress, consume more than an hour a day, or significantly interfere with a person's normal functioning or relationships

*Source:* Reprinted with permission from the *Diagnostic and Statistical Manual of Mental Disorders,* Fourth Edition, Text Revision. (Copyright © 2000) American Psychiatric Association.

## Obsessions

Jenike, Baer, and Minichiello (1986) noted that the most common obsessions in a sample of 100 patients were contamination (55%), aggressive impulses (50%), sexual content (32%), somatic concerns (35%), and the need for symmetry (37%). Sixty percent of those sampled displayed multiple obsessions. "Need for symmetry" refers to keeping things in perfect order or doing something in a very specific way. As a child were you careful not to step on cracks in the sidewalk? You and your friends might have kept this up for a few minutes before tiring of it. But what if you had to spend your whole life avoiding cracks, on foot or in a car? You wouldn't have much fun. People with obsessive impulses may feel they are about to yell out a swear word in church.

## Compulsions

Leckman et al. (1997a) analyzed types of compulsions in several large groups of patients and found that checking, ordering, and arranging, along with washing and cleaning, were the major categories of rituals. Most patients with OCD present with cleaning and washing or checking rituals. For people who fear contact with objects or situations that may be contaminating, washing or cleaning restores a sense of safety and control. Checking rituals prevent

an imagined disaster or catastrophe. Most are logical, such as repeatedly checking the stove to see whether you turned it off, but severe cases can be illogical. For example, Richard thought that if he did not eat in a certain way he might become possessed. If he didn't take small steps and look back, some disaster might happen to his family. A mental act, such as counting, can also be a compulsion. Like Richard, many patients have both kinds of rituals.

Certain kinds of obsessions are strongly associated with certain kinds of rituals (Leckman et al., 1997a). A recent study of OCD symptom subgroups by Summerfeldt, Richter, Antony, and Swinson (1999) supported four factors: (1) obsessions/checking, (2) symmetry/ordering, (3) contamination/cleaning, and (4) hoarding. More specifically, aggression and sexual obsessions seem to lead to checking rituals. Obsessions with symmetry lead to ordering and arranging or repeating rituals; obsessions with contamination lead, of course, to washing rituals. In addition, a small group of patients compulsively hoard things, fearing that if they throw something away, even a 10-year-old newspaper, they then might urgently need it (Black et al., 1998; Frost, Steketee, & Williams, 2002; Samuels et al., 2002). One patient's house and yard were condemned by the city because junk was piled so high it was both unsightly and a fire hazard. Among her hoard was a 20-year collection of used sanitary napkins!

On rare occasions, patients, particularly children, will present with few if any identifiable obsessions. We saw an 8-year-old child who felt compelled to undress, put on his pyjamas, and turn down the covers in a time-consuming fashion each night; he always repeated the ritual three times! He could give no particular reason for his behaviour; he simply had to do it.

Toronto-born comedian Howie Mandel reportedly has OCD characterized by obsessions of becoming contaminated by germs.

## Statistics

A large epidemiological study put the lifetime prevalence of OCD at approximately 2.6% (Karno & Golding, 1991), although recent studies like that by Murray Stein and colleagues suggest that this may be a bit of an overestimate (Stein, Forde, Anderson, & Walker, 1997). A cross-national study of rates of OCD in Canada and six other countries found that rates were remarkably similar across cultures (Weissman et al., 1994). Of course, not all cases meeting criteria for OCD are as severe as Richard's. Obsessions and compulsions can be arranged along a continuum, like most clinical features of anxiety disorders. Between 10% and 15% of "normal" university students engaged in checking behaviour substantial enough to score within the range of patients with OCD (Frost, Sher, & Geen, 1986).

It would also be unusual *not* to have an occasional intrusive or strange thought. Many people have bizarre, sexual, or aggressive thoughts, particularly if they are bored—for example, when sitting in class. Some examples of such thoughts from ordinary people who do not have OCD are listed in Table 4.7.

Have you had any of these thoughts? Most people do, but they let these thoughts go in one ear and out the other, so to speak. Certain individuals, however, are horrified by such thoughts, considering them signs of an alien, intrusive, evil force. The majority of individuals with OCD are female, but the ratio is not as large as for some other anxiety disorders. Rasmussen and Tsuang (1984, 1986) reported that 55% of 1630 patients were female. The ECA epidemiology study noted 60% females in their sample of OCD (Karno & Golding, 1991). Interestingly, in children the sex ratio is reversed, with more males than females (Hanna, 1995). This seems to be because boys tend to develop OCD earlier. By mid-adolescence the sex ratio is approximately equal before becoming predominantly female in adulthood (Albano et al., 1996). Average age of onset ranges from early adolescence to mid-20s but typically peaks earlier in males (13 to 15) than in females (20 to 24; Rasmussen & Eisen, 1990). Once OCD develops, it tends to become chronic (Eisen & Steketee, 1998; Steketee & Barlow, 2002).

In Arabic countries, OCD is easily recognizable, although as always cultural beliefs and concerns influence the content of the obsessions and the nature of the compulsions. In Saudi Arabia and Egypt, obsessions are primarily related to religious practices, specifically the Muslim emphasis on cleanliness. Contamination themes are also highly prevalent in India. Nevertheless, OCD looks remarkably similar across cultures. Insel (1984)

| **TABLE 4.7** | Obsessions and Intrusive Thoughts Reported by Non-clinical Samples* |
|---|---|

**Harming**

Impulse to jump out of a high window
Idea of jumping in front of a car
Impulse to push someone in front of a train
Wishing a person would die
While holding a baby, having a sudden urge to kick it
Thoughts of dropping a baby
Thought that if I forget to say goodbye to someone, they might die
Thought that thinking about horrible things happening to a child will cause it

**Contamination or Disease**

Thought of catching a disease from public pools or other public places
Thoughts I may have caught a disease from touching a toilet seat
Idea that dirt is always on my hand

**Inappropriate or Unacceptable Behaviour**

Idea of swearing or yelling at my boss
Thought of doing something embarrassing in public, like forgetting to wear a top
Hoping someone doesn't succeed
Thought of blurting out something in church
Thought of "unnatural" sexual acts

**Doubts about Safety, Memory, Etc.**

Thought that I haven't locked the house up properly
Idea of leaving my curling iron on the carpet and forgetting to pull out the plug
Thought that I've left the heater and stove on
Idea that I've left the car unlocked when I know I've locked it
Idea that objects are not arranged perfectly

*Examples were obtained from Rachman and deSilva (1978) and from unpublished research by Dana Thordarson, Ph.D., and Michael Kyrios, Ph.D. (personal communications, 2000), at the University of British Columbia.

*Source:* From "Obsessive-Compulsive Disorder," by G. Steketee and D. H. Barlow, in *Anxiety and Its Disorders: The Nature and Treatment of Anxiety and Panic* (2nd ed., p. 529). Copyright © 2002 by Guilford Press. Reprinted by permission.

reviewed studies from England, Hong Kong, India, Egypt, Japan, and Norway and found essentially similar types and proportions of obsessions and compulsions, as did Weissman et al. (1994) reviewing studies from Canada, Finland, Taiwan, Africa, Puerto Rico, Korea, and New Zealand.

## Causes

Many of us sometimes have intrusive, even horrific thoughts (Rachman & deSilva, 1978) and occasionally engage in ritualistic behaviour, especially when we are under stress (Parkinson & Rachman, 1981a,

1981b). But few of us develop OCD. Once again, as with panic disorder and PTSD, one must develop anxiety focused on the possibility of having additional intrusive thoughts.

The repetitive, intrusive, unacceptable thoughts of OCD may be regulated by the hypothetical brain circuit described in Chapter 2. However, the tendency to develop anxiety over having additional compulsive thoughts may have the same generalized biological and psychological precursors as anxiety in general.

Why would people with OCD focus their anxiety on the occasional intrusive thought rather than on the possibility of a panic attack or some other external situation? One hypothesis is that early experiences taught them that some thoughts are dangerous and unacceptable because the terrible things they are thinking might actually happen and they would be responsible. The experiences would result in a specific psychological vulnerability to develop OCD. They learn this through the same process of misinformation that convinced the person with snake phobia that snakes were dangerous and could be everywhere.

Clients with OCD equate thoughts with the specific actions or activity represented by the thoughts. Rachman and his colleagues call this *thought-action fusion* (e.g., Rachman & Shafran, 1998; Shafran, Thordarson, & Rachman, 1996). Thought-action fusion may, in turn, be caused by attitudes of excessive responsibility and resulting guilt developed during childhood, where even a bad thought is associated with evil intent (Salkovskis, Shafran, Rachman, & Freeston, 1999; Steketee & Barlow, 2002). One patient believed thinking about abortion was the moral equivalent of having an abortion.

Richard finally admitted to having strong homosexual impulses that were unacceptable to him and to his minister father, and he believed the impulses were as sinful as actual acts. Many people with OCD who believe in the tenets of fundamental religions, whether Christian, Jewish, or Islamic, present with similar attitudes of inflated responsibility and thought-action fusion. Several studies showed that the strength of religious belief, but not the type of belief, was associated with thought-action fusion and severity of OCD (Rassin & Koster, 2003; Steketee, Quay, & White, 1991). Of course, the vast majority of people with fundamental beliefs do not develop OCD.

But what if the most frightening thing in your life was not a snake, or speaking in public, but a terrible thought that happened to pop into your head? You can't avoid it as you would a snake, so you resist this thought by attempting to suppress it or "neutralize" it using mental or behavioural

strategies such as distraction, praying, or checking. These strategies become compulsions, but they are doomed to fail in the long term, because these strategies backfire and actually increase the frequency of the thought (Purdon, 1999; Wegner, 1989). In fact, Christine Purdon at the University of Waterloo and David A. Clark at the University of New Brunswick have conducted a large body of research in this area. On the basis of their work and a review of the literature, they conclude that there is indeed an association between attempted thought suppression and obsessional thinking (Clark & Purdon, 1995; Purdon, 1999; Purdon & Clark, 2000). Once again, generalized biological and psychological vulnerabilities must be present for this disorder to develop. Believing some thoughts are unacceptable and therefore must be suppressed (a *specific psychological vulnerability*) may put people at greater risk of OCD (Amir, Cashman, & Foa, 1997; Parkinson & Rachman, 1981b; Salkovskis & Campbell, 1994). A model of the etiology of OCD that is somewhat similar to other models of anxiety disorders is presented in Figure 4.12.

## Treatment

Studies evaluating the effects of drugs on OCD are showing some promise (Steketee & Barlow, 2002; Zohar et al., 1996). The most effective seem to be those that specifically inhibit the reuptake of serotonin, such as clomipramine or the SSRIs, which benefit up to 60% of patients with OCD with no particular advantage to one drug over another. However, the average treatment gain is moderate at best (Greist, 1990), and relapse frequently occurs when the drug is discontinued (Lydiard et al., 1996).

Highly structured psychological treatments work somewhat better than drugs, but they are not readily available. The most effective approach is called exposure and ritual prevention (ERP), a process whereby the rituals are actively prevented and the patient is systematically and gradually exposed to the feared thoughts or situations (Barlow & Lehman, 1996; Foa & Franklin, 2001; Steketee & Barlow, 2002). Richard would be systematically exposed to harmless objects or situations that he thought were contaminated, including certain foods and household chemicals, and his washing and checking rituals would be prevented. Usually this can be done by simply working closely with patients to see that they do not wash or check. In severe cases, patients may be hospitalized and the faucets removed from the bathroom sink for a time to discourage repeated

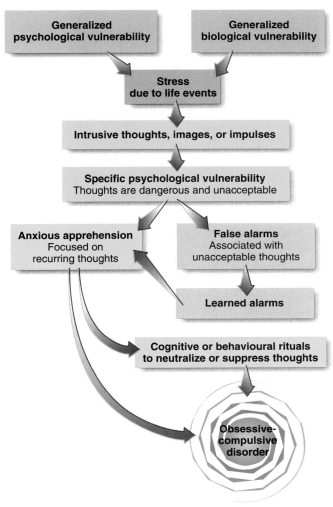

**Figure 4.12** ■ A model of the causes of obsessive-compulsive disorder. (From "Obsessive-Compulsive Disorder," by G. Steketee and D. H. Barlow, in *Anxiety and Its Disorders: The Nature and Treatment of Anxiety and Panic* (2nd ed.), by D. H. Barlow (p. 536). Copyright © 2002 by Guilford Press. Reprinted by permission.)

washing. However the rituals are prevented, the procedures seem to facilitate "reality testing," because the patient soon learns, at an emotional level, that no harm will result whether he carries out the rituals or not.

A recent study led by Peter McLean at the University of British Columbia compared ERP to a CBT that targeted the dysfunctional cognitions characteristic of OCD such as inflated responsibility (McLean et al., 2001). Patients were randomized to either the ERP or CBT conditions and half in each group received their treatment immediately, while the other half served as a waiting list control (and received their treatment later). Both types of treatment were better than the wait list control in terms of reducing symptoms of OCD.

The ERP treatment was slightly more effective than CBT both immediately after the treatment and at a 3-month follow up. Unexpectedly, inflated responsibility beliefs decreased in both the CBT and the ERP conditions. Thus, preventing rituals does seem to allow for cognitive change in people with OCD.

Studies are now available examining the combined effects of medication and psychological treatments. In the largest study to date (Kozak, Liebowitz, & Foa, 2000), ERP was compared with the drug clomipramine and to a combined condition. ERP, with or without the drug, produced superior results to the drug alone, with 85% responding to ERP alone versus 50% to the drug alone. Combining the treatments did not produce any additional advantage. Also, relapse rates were high from the medication-only group when the drug was withdrawn.

Psychosurgery is the most radical treatment for OCD. "Psychosurgery" is a misnomer that refers to neurosurgery for a psychological disorder. Jenike et al. (1991) reviewed the records of 33 patients with OCD, most of them extremely severe cases who had failed to respond to either drug or psychological treatment. After a specific surgical lesion to the cingulate bundle (cingulotomy), approximately 30% benefited substantially. Considering that these patients seemed to have no hope from other treatments, surgery deserves consideration as a last resort. Each year we understand more about the causes of OCD, and our treatments are improving. Before long, such radical treatments as psychosurgery will no longer be employed.

## Concept Check 4.6

Fill in the blanks to form facts about obsessive-compulsive disorder.

1. _____ are intrusive and nonsensical thoughts, images, or urges an individual tries to eliminate or suppress.
2. The practices of washing, counting, and hoarding to suppress obsessions and provide relief are called _____.
3. The lifetime prevalence of OCD is approximately _____%, or even lower.
4. _____ is a radical treatment for OCD involving a surgical lesion to the cingulate bundle.

# Summary

## The Complexity of Anxiety Disorders

- Anxiety is a future-oriented state characterized by negative affect in which a person focuses on the possibility of uncontrollable danger or misfortune; in contrast, fear is a present-oriented state characterized by strong escapist tendencies and a surge in the sympathetic branch of the autonomic nervous system in response to current danger.
- A panic attack represents the alarm response of real fear, but there is no actual danger.
- Panic attacks may be (1) unexpected (without warning), (2) situationally bound (always occurring in a specific situation), or (3) situationally predisposed (likely but unpredictable in a specific situation).
- Panic and anxiety combine to create different anxiety disorders.

## Generalized Anxiety Disorder

- In generalized anxiety disorder (GAD), anxiety focuses on minor everyday events, not one major worry or concern.
- Both genetic and psychological vulnerabilities seem to contribute to the development of GAD.
- Though drug and psychological treatments may be effective in the short term, drug treatments are no more effective in the long term than placebo treatments. Successful treatment may help individuals with GAD focus on what is really threatening to them in their lives.

## Panic Disorder with and without Agoraphobia

- In panic disorder with or without agoraphobia (a fear and avoidance of situations considered to be "unsafe"), anxiety is focused on the next panic attack.
- We all have some genetic vulnerability to stress, and many of us have had a neurobiological over-reaction to some stressful event—that is, a panic attack. Individuals who develop panic disorder then develop *anxiety* over the possibility of having another panic attack.
- Both drug and psychological treatments have proved successful in the treatment of panic disorder. One psychological method, *panic control treatment*, concentrates on exposing patients to clusters of sensations that remind them of their panic attacks.

## Specific Phobia

- In phobic disorders, the individual avoids situations that produce severe anxiety and/or panic. In specific phobia, the fear is focused on a particular object or situation.
- Phobias can be acquired by experiencing some traumatic event; they can also be learned vicariously or even be taught.
- Treatment of phobias is rather straightforward, with a focus on structured and consistent exposure-based exercises.

## Social Phobia

- Social phobia is a fear of being around others, particularly in situations that call for some kind of "performance" in front of other people.
- Though the causes of social phobia are similar to those of specific phobias, treatment has a different focus that includes rehearsing or role-playing socially phobic situations. In addition, drug treatments have been effective.

## Posttraumatic Stress Disorder

- Posttraumatic stress disorder (PTSD) focuses on avoiding thoughts or images of past traumatic experiences.
- The underlying cause of PTSD is obvious—a traumatic experience. But mere exposure is not enough. The intensity of the experience seems to be a factor in whether an individual develops PTSD; biological vulnerabilities, as well as social and cultural factors, appear to play a role.
- Treatment involves re-exposing the victim to the trauma to overcome the debilitating effects of PTSD.

## Obsessive-Compulsive Disorder

- Obsessive-compulsive disorder (OCD) focuses on avoiding frightening or repulsive intrusive thoughts (obsessions) or neutralizing these thoughts through the use of ritualistic behaviour (compulsions).
- As with all anxiety disorders, biological and psychological vulnerabilities seem to be involved in the development of OCD.
- Drug treatment seems to be only modestly successful in treating OCD. The most effective treatment approach is exposure and response prevention.

## Key Terms

anxiety, 127
fear, 128
panic, 129
panic attack, 129
behavioural inhibition
   system (BIS), 130
fight/flight system
   (FFS), 130
generalized anxiety
   disorder (GAD), 133

panic disorder with
   agoraphobia
   (PDA), 138
agoraphobia, 138
panic disorder without
   agoraphobia
   (PD), 139
panic control treatment
   (PCT), 146
specific phobia, 149

blood-injury-injection
   phobia, 150
situational phobia, 151
natural environment
   phobia, 151
animal phobia, 151
separation anxiety
   disorder, 152
social phobia, 155

posttraumatic stress
   disorder (PTSD), 160
acute stress disorder, 161
obsessive-compulsive
   disorder (OCD), 166
obsessions, 167
compulsions, 167

## Answers to Concept Checks

**4.1**  1. b  2. c  3. e, d  4. a  5. f

**4.2**  1. T  2. F (more gradual)  3. T  4. F  5. T

**4.3**  1. F (with agoraphobia)  2. F (3.5%)  3. T

**4.4**  1. d  2. e  3. c  4. a  5. d  6. c

**4.5**  1. b  2. a  3. c

**4.6**  1. obsessions  2. compulsions  3. 2.6
4. psychosurgery

 ## InfoTrac College Edition

If your instructor ordered your book with InfoTrac College Edition, please explore this online library for additional readings, review, and a handy resource for short assignments. Go to:

**http://infotrac.thomsonlearning.com**

Enter these search terms: anxiety, panic disorder, phobia, generalized anxiety disorder, agoraphobia, separation anxiety disorder, posttraumatic stress disorder, obsessive-compulsive disorder

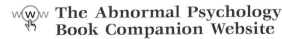 ## The Abnormal Psychology Book Companion Website

Go to **www.essentialsabnormalpsych.nelson.com** for practice quiz questions, Internet links, critical thinking exercises, and more.

 ## Abnormal Psychology Live CD-ROM

- **Steve, a Patient with Panic Disorder:** Steve discusses how panic attacks have disrupted his life.
- **Virtual Reality Therapy:** A virtual reality program helps one woman overcome her fear of riding the subway.
- **Snake Phobia Treatment:** A demonstration of exposure therapy that helps a snake phobic overcome her severe fear of snakes in just 3 hours.
- **Chuck, a Client with Obsessive-Compulsive Disorder:** Chuck discusses how his obsessions affect his everyday life, going to work, planning a vacation, and so on.

**Thomson NOW! http://hed.nelson.com** Go to this site for the link to ThomsonNow™, your one-stop study shop. Take a Pretest for this chapter and ThomsonNow™ will generate a personalized Study Plan based on your test results! The Study Plan will identify the topics you need to review and direct you to online resources to help you master those topics. You can then take a Posttest to help you determine the concepts you have mastered and what you still need work on.

## Video Concept Review

For challenging concepts that typically need more than one explanation, Mark Durand provides a video review via ThomsonNow™ of the following topic:

- Describing the value of medical versus psychological treatments of anxiety disorders.

# Chapter Quiz

1. _____ is a psychological experience characterized by concern about future events, and _____ is characterized by concern about current circumstances.
   a. Panic; anxiety
   b. Fear; anxiety
   c. Anxiety; fear
   d. Depression; anxiety

2. In an integrated model of anxiety, which childhood experience appears to make an individual more vulnerable to anxiety in adulthood?
   a. negative and inconsistent attention from parents
   b. exposure to situations that reinforce a rigid sense of personal control
   c. interactions with peers that are violent
   d. academic failures in preschool

3. Which of the following is true about generalized anxiety disorder?
   a. It is most common in individuals aged 15–24 years.
   b. Its course tends to be chronic.
   c. It is the least common of the anxiety disorders.
   d. It is more common in men.

4. Why are the majority of people who suffer from agoraphobia women?
   a. Chromosomal features related to sensitivity of the hypothalamus–pituitary axis are more common in women.
   b. Women are more likely to employ cognitive distortions in which they appraise events as threatening.
   c. The hormonal system in women sensitizes the female nervous system to stress.
   d. Cultural factors make it more acceptable for women to avoid situations and to report their fears.

5. Marty has a fear of dogs. Which of the following suggests that his fear qualifies as a specific phobia rather than just an everyday fear?
   a. Marty's fear of dogs comes and goes following an episodic pattern.
   b. Marty owns a cat but no dog.
   c. Marty believes that his fear of dogs is reasonable and appropriate.
   d. Marty will only work night shifts, a time when he thinks all dogs will be safely inside.

6. Which technique appears to be the most effective treatment for phobias?
   a. exposure to the feared stimulus under therapeutic supervision
   b. rapid and repeated exposure to the feared stimulus followed by immediate escape
   c. hypnosis during which fear-related conflicts are banished from the unconscious
   d. challenging the client to see that the fears are irrational, unrealistic, and excessive

7. Which of the following is the most essential characteristic of social phobia?
   a. fear of being in public places
   b. fear of being left alone
   c. fear of evaluation by other people
   d. fear of having a panic attack

8. Which feature differentiates posttraumatic stress disorder from acute stress disorder?
   a. the time since the traumatic event occurred
   b. the severity of the symptoms
   c. the nature of the symptoms
   d. the presence of emotional numbing

9. Every morning when he leaves for work Anthony has recurring doubts about whether he locked his front door. He continues thinking about this throughout the day, to the distraction of his work. Anthony is experiencing:
   a. obsessions.
   b. derealization.
   c. panic.
   d. compulsions.

10. When a person believes that thinking about hurting someone is just as bad as actually hurting someone, that person is experiencing:
    a. an obsession.
    b. a false alarm.
    c. a panic attack.
    d. thought-action fusion.

*(See the Appendix on page 601 for answers.)*

# Exploring Anxiety Disorders

People with anxiety disorders:

- Feel overwhelming tension, apprehension, or fear when there is no actual danger
- May take extreme action to avoid the source of their anxiety

Photodisc/Getty Images

### Biological Influences

- Inherited vulnerability to experience anxiety and/or panic attacks
- Activation of specific brain circuits, neurotransmitters, and neurohormonal systems

**TRIGGER**

Photodisc/Getty Images

### Social Influences

- Social support reduces intensity of physical and emotional reactions to triggers or stress
- Lack of social support intensifies symptoms

**CAUSES**

### Behavioural Influences

- Marked avoidance of situations and/or people associated with fear, anxiety, or panic attack

Eyewire/Getty Images

### Emotional and Cognitive Influences

- Heightened sensitivity to situations or people perceived as threats
- Unconscious feeling that physical symptoms of panic are catastrophic (intensifies physical reaction)

## TREATMENT FOR ANXIETY DISORDERS

Photodisc/Getty Images

### Cognitive–Behavioural Therapy

- Systematic exposure to anxiety-provoking situations or thoughts
- Learning to substitute positive behaviours and thoughts for negative ones
- Learning new coping skills: relaxation exercises, controlled breathing, etc.

### Drug Treatment

- Reduces the symptoms of anxiety disorders by influencing brain chemistry
    - —antidepressants (Tofranil, Paxil, Effexor)
    - —benzodiazepines (Xanax, Klonapin)

### Other Treatments

- Managing stress through a healthy lifestyle: rest, exercise, nutrition, social support, moderate alcohol or other drug intake

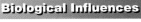

# TYPES OF ANXIETY DISORDERS

## Panic Disorders

People with panic disorders have had one or more panic attacks and are very anxious and fearful about having future attacks.

**What is a panic attack?**
A person having a panic attack feels:
- Apprehension leading to intense fear
- Sensation of "going crazy," or of losing control
- Physical signs of distress: racing heartbeat, rapid breathing, dizziness, nausea, sensation of heart attack or imminent death

**When/why do panic attacks occur?**
Panic attacks can be:
- *Situationally bound:* always occurring in the same situation, which may lead to extreme avoidance of triggering persons, places, or events (see specific and social phobias)
- *Unexpected:* can lead to extreme avoidance of any situation or place felt to be unsafe (agoraphobia)
- *Situationally predisposed:* attacks may or may not occur in specific situations (between situationally bound and unexpected)

## Phobias

People with phobias avoid situations that produce severe anxiety and/or panic. There are three main types:

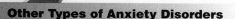

### Agoraphobia
- Fear and avoidance of situations, people, or places where it would be unsafe to have a panic attack: malls, grocery stores, buses, planes, tunnels, etc.
- In the extreme, inability to leave the house or even a specific room
- Begins after a panic attack, but can continue for years even if no other attacks occur

### Specific Phobia
- Fear of specific object or situation that triggers attack: heights, closed spaces, insects, snakes, flying
- Develops from personal or vicarious experience of traumatic event with the triggering object or situation, or from misinformation

### Social Phobia
Fear of being called for some kind of "performance" that may be judged: speaking in public, using a public restroom (for males), or generally interacting with people

## Other Types of Anxiety Disorders

**Generalized Anxiety Disorder**
- Uncontrollable unproductive worrying about everyday events
- Feeling impending catastrophe even after successes
- Inability to stop the worry/anxiety cycle: e.g., Irene's fear of failure about school relationships and health even though everything seemed fine
- Physical symptoms of muscle tension

**Posttraumatic Stress Disorder**
- Fear of reexperiencing a traumatic event: rape, war, life-threatening situation, etc.
- Nightmares or flashbacks (of the traumatic event)
- Avoidance of the intense feelings of the event and emotional numbing

**Obsessive–Compulsive Disorder**
- Fear of unwanted and intrusive thoughts (obsessions)
- Repeated ritualistic actions or thoughts (compulsions) designed to neutralize the unwanted thoughts: e.g., Richard's attempts to suppress "dangerous" thoughts about sex, aggression, and religion with compulsive washing and cleaning rituals

# 5 Somatoform and Dissociative Disorders

© Yoav Levy/Phototake

**Somatoform Disorders**
*Hypochondriasis*
*Somatization Disorder*
*Conversion Disorder*
*Pain Disorder*
*Body Dysmorphic Disorder*

**Dissociative Disorders**
*Depersonalization Disorder*
*Dissociative Amnesia*
*Dissociative Fugue*
*Dissociative Trance Disorder*
*Dissociative Identity Disorder*

**Visual Summary: Exploring Somatoform and Dissociative Disorders**

 **Abnormal Psychology Live CD-ROM**
*Body Dysmorphic Disorder: Doug*
*Dissociative Identity Disorder: Rachel*

Many people continually run to the doctor even though there is nothing really wrong with them. This is usually a harmless tendency that may even be worth some good-natured jokes. But for a few individuals, the preoccupation with their health or appearance becomes so great that it dominates their lives. Their problems fall under the general heading of **somatoform disorders.** *Soma* means body, and the problems preoccupying these people seem, initially, to be physical disorders. What the disorders have in common, however, is that there is usually no identifiable medical condition causing the physical complaints.

Have you ever felt "detached" from yourself or your surroundings? ("This isn't really me," or "That doesn't really look like my hand," or "There's something unreal about this place.") During these experiences some people feel as if they are dreaming. These mild sensations that most people experience occasionally are slight alterations, or detachments, in consciousness or identity, and they are known as *dissociative experiences* or *dissociation*. For a few people, these experiences are so intense and extreme that they lose their identity entirely and assume a new one or they lose their memory or sense of reality and are unable to function. We discuss several types of **dissociative disorders** in the second half of this chapter.

Somatoform and dissociative disorders are strongly linked historically, and increasing evidence indicates they share common features (Kihlstrom, 1994; Prelior, Yutzy, Dean, & Wetzel, 1993). They used to be categorized under one general heading, *hysterical neurosis*. You may remember (from Chapter 1) that the term *hysteria*, which dates back to the Greek Hippocrates, and the Egyptians before him, suggests that the cause of these disorders, which were thought to occur primarily in women,

can be traced to a "wandering uterus." But the term *hysterical* came to refer more generally to physical symptoms without known organic cause or to dramatic or "histrionic" behaviour thought to be characteristic of women. Freud (1894/1962) suggested that in a condition called *conversion hysteria* unexplained physical symptoms indicated the conversion of unconscious emotional conflicts into a more acceptable form. The historical term *conversion* remains with us (without the theoretical implications); however, the prejudicial and stigmatizing term *hysterical* is no longer used.

The term *neurosis*, as defined in psychoanalytic theory, suggested a specific cause for certain disorders. Specifically, neurotic disorders resulted from underlying unconscious conflicts, anxiety that resulted from those conflicts, and the implementation of ego defence mechanisms. *Neurosis* was eliminated from the diagnostic system in 1980 because it was too vague, applying to almost all non-psychotic disorders, and because it implied a specific but unproved cause for these disorders.

Somatoform and dissociative disorders are not well understood, but they have intrigued psychopathologists and the public for centuries. A fuller understanding provides a rich perspective on the extent to which normal, everyday traits found in all of us can evolve into distorted, strange, and incapacitating disorders.

---

**somatoform disorders**   Pathological concerns of individuals with the appearance or functioning of their bodies, usually in the absence of any identifiable medical condition.

**dissociative disorders**   Disorders in which individuals feel detached from themselves or their surroundings, and reality, experience, and identity may disintegrate.

# Somatoform Disorders

- *Identify the defining features of somatoform disorders and distinguish the major features of hypochondriasis from illness phobia and somatization disorder.*

- *Describe sensory, motor, and visceral symptoms that characterize conversion disorder.*

DSM-IV-TR lists five basic somatoform disorders: hypochondriasis, somatization disorder, conversion disorder, pain disorder, and body dysmorphic

disorder. In each, individuals are pathologically concerned with the appearance or functioning of their bodies.

## *Hypochondriasis*

Like many terms in psychopathology, **hypochondriasis** has ancient roots. To the Greeks, the "hypochondria" was the region below the ribs, and the organs in this region affected mental state. For example, ulcers and abdominal disorders were once considered part of the hypochondriac syndrome. As the actual causes of such disorders were discovered, physical complaints without a clear cause continued to be labelled *hypochondriasis* (Barsky, Wyshak, & Klerman, 1986). In hypochondriasis, severe anxiety is focused on the possibility of having a serious disease. The threat seems so real that reassurance from physicians does not seem to help. Consider the case of Kirsten—a woman seen at one of the authors' clinics whose case is described in more detail by Stewart and Watt (2001).

### Kirsten
Invisibly Ill

Kirsten was a 42-year-old married mother of three daughters who worked part time as a bank teller. She presented with a persistent fear of breast cancer and a preoccupation with the belief that she may have developed malignant tumours in her breasts.

Before the onset of Kirsten's illness, a female relative had developed breast cancer and had undergone a radical mastectomy. Kirsten herself had discovered small lumps in her breasts and had consulted her physician, fearing that she had developed breast cancer. Medical tests revealed that her physical symptoms were indicative of non-malignant fibroid masses and did not require intervention.

For several months before her psychological assessment, Kirsten had been visiting her family physician two times per month for breast examinations. These tests would temporarily allay her fears, but worries that she had developed breast cancer would return within days or even hours of her visits to the physician.

These concerns were exerting significant effects on her interpersonal and work life. Intrusive thoughts about breast cancer would interfere with her ability to concentrate at her bank job. She was so highly distressed by touching or looking at her own breasts that she had her husband assist her in putting on her brassiere and in applying creams or sunscreen in any area around her chest. Kirsten reported that she avoided the news and women's magazines

for fear that she would come across an article or news item on breast cancer, which she found extremely distressing. She also avoided visiting her relative who had had the mastectomy because she found such contact to be upsetting.

Kirsten reported a strong fear of death, involving concerns that she would die from breast cancer and leave her three children motherless. Her husband was becoming exasperated with the demands she was placing on him. Her family physician was also becoming frustrated about Kirsten's constant need for reassurance and referred her for psychological assessment and possible cognitive-behavioural therapy.

### Disorder Criteria Summary
Hypochondriasis

Features of hypochondriasis include:
- Preoccupation with fears of having a serious disease
- Preoccupation persists despite appropriate medical evaluation and reassurance
- Preoccupation is not of delusional intensity and is not restricted to concern over physical appearance
- Clinically significant distress or impairment because of preoccupation
- Duration of at least 6 months

*Source:* Reprinted with permission from the *Diagnostic and Statistical Manual of Mental Disorders*, Fourth Edition, Text Revision. (Copyright © 2000) American Psychiatric Association.

### Clinical Description

Gail's problems are fairly typical of hypochondriasis. Research indicates that hypochondriasis shares many features with the anxiety and mood disorders, particularly panic disorder (Asmundson, Taylor, & Cox, 2001; Craske et al., 1996), including similar age of onset, personality characteristics, and patterns of familial aggregation (running in families). Indeed, research by Quebec psychologist Guylaine Côté and her colleagues (1996) revealed that anxiety and mood disorders are frequently comorbid with hypochondriasis; that is, if individuals with a hypochondriacal disorder have additional diagnoses, these are most likely to be anxiety

---

**hypochondriasis** Somatoform disorder involving severe anxiety over the belief that one has a disease process without any evident physical cause.

or mood disorders (see also Rief, Hiller, & Margraf, 1998; Simon, Gureje, & Fullerton, 2001).

Hypochondriasis is characterized by anxiety or fear that one has a serious disease. Therefore, the essential problem is anxiety, but its expression is different from that of the other anxiety disorders. In hypochondriasis, the individual is preoccupied with bodily symptoms, misinterpreting them as indicative of illness or disease. Almost any physical sensation may become the basis for concern for individuals with hypochondriasis. Some may focus on normal bodily functions such as heart rate or perspiration, others on minor physical abnormalities such as a cough. Some individuals complain of vague symptoms, such as aches or fatigue. Because a key feature of this disorder is preoccupation with physical symptoms, individuals with hypochondriasis almost always go initially to family physicians. They come to the attention of mental health professionals only after family physicians have ruled out realistic medical conditions as a cause.

Another important feature of hypochondriasis is that reassurances from numerous doctors that the individual is healthy have, at best, only a short-term effect. It isn't long before patients like Kirsten are back in the office of another doctor on the assumption that the previous doctors have missed something. In studying this feature for purposes of modifying the diagnostic criteria in DSM-IV, Côté et al. (1996) confirmed a subtle but interesting distinction (see also Craske et al., 1996; Kellner, Hernandez, & Pathak, 1992). Individuals who fear *developing* a disease, and therefore avoid situations they associate with contagion, are different from those who are anxious that they *have* the disease like Kirsten. Individuals who have marked fear of *developing* a disease are classified as having an *illness phobia*. Individuals who mistakenly believe they *have* a disease are diagnosed with hypochondriasis.

The work of Côté and her colleagues (1996) shows that these two groups differ further. Individuals with high disease conviction are more likely to misinterpret physical symptoms and display higher rates of checking behaviours and trait anxiety than individuals with illness phobia (see also Haenen, de Jong, Schmidt, Stevens, & Visser, 2000). Individuals with illness phobia have an earlier age of onset than those with *disease conviction*. Disease conviction has become the core feature of hypochondriasis. Of course, some people may have both a disease conviction and a fear of developing additional diseases (Kellner, 1986). In one study, 60% of a group of patients with illness phobia went on to develop hypochondriasis and panic disorder (Benedetti et al., 1997).

If you have just read Chapter 4, you may think that patients with panic disorder resemble patients with hypochondriasis. In fact, the two conditions co-occur quite commonly. For example, a study by a group of researchers in Winnipeg (Furer, Walker, Chartier, & Stein, 1997) found that nearly half of a group of patients with panic disorder also met diagnostic criteria for hypochondriasis and that hypochondriasis was more common in patients with panic disorder (48%) than in either a group of patients with social phobia (17%) or controls (14%).

Like those with hypochondriasis, patients with panic disorder also misinterpret physical symptoms as the beginning of the next panic attack, which they believe may kill them. However, panic disorder and hypochondriasis do have some important differences. Steven Taylor, a clinical psychologist at the University of British Columbia, suggested that, although both disorders include characteristic concern with physical symptoms, patients with panic disorder typically fear immediate symptom-related catastrophes that may occur during the few minutes they are having a panic attack. Individuals with hypochondriacal concerns, on the other hand, focus on a long-term process of illness and disease (e.g., cancer or AIDS). In addition, the anxieties of individuals with panic disorder tend to focus on the specific set of 10 or 15 sympathetic nervous system symptoms associated with a panic attack. Hypochondriacal concerns range much wider (Taylor, 1994, 1995).

### Statistics

We know little about the prevalence of hypochondriasis in the general population. Early estimates indicate that anywhere between 1% and 14% of medical patients are diagnosed with hypochondriasis (Barsky, Wyshak, Klerman, & Latham, 1990). A more recent large study in which almost 1400 patients in primary-care settings were carefully interviewed suggests that about 3% met criteria for hypochondriasis (Escobar, Waitzkin, Silver, Gara, & Holman, 1998). Although historically considered one of the "hysterical" disorders unique to women, the sex ratio is actually 50:50 (Asmundson, Taylor, Sevgur, & Cox, 2001; Kirmayer & Robbins, 1991; Kirmayer, Looper, & Taillefer, 2003). It was thought for a long time that hypochondriasis was more prevalent in elderly populations, but this does not seem to be true (Barsky, Frank, Cleary, Wyshak, & Klerman, 1991). In fact, hypochondriasis is spread fairly evenly across various phases of adulthood. Naturally, more elderly people go to see physicians, making the *absolute number* of patients with hypochondriasis in this age group somewhat higher than in the younger population, but among those people seeing a doctor, a similar proportion of elderly versus younger people have hypochondriasis. Hypochondriasis may emerge at any time of life, with the peak age periods found in adolescence, middle age (40s and 50s), and after age 60 (Kellner, 1986). As with most anxiety and mood disorders, hypochondriasis is chronic.

Culture-specific syndromes seem to fit comfortably with hypochondriasis. Among these is the disorder of *koro*, in which there is the belief, accompanied by severe anxiety and sometimes panic, that the genitals are retracting into the abdomen. Most victims of this disorder are Chinese males, although it is also reported in females; there are few reports of the problem in Western cultures. Rubin (1982) points to the central importance of sexual functioning among Chinese males. Typical sufferers are guilty about excessive masturbation, unsatisfactory intercourse, or promiscuity. These kinds of events may predispose men to focus their attention on their sexual organs, which could exacerbate anxiety and emotional arousal, much as it does in the anxiety disorders, thereby setting off an "epidemic."

Another culture-specific disorder, prevalent in India, is an anxious concern about losing semen, something that obviously occurs during sexual activity. The disorder, called *dhat*, is associated with a vague mix of physical symptoms including dizziness, weakness, and fatigue that are not so specific as in koro. These low-grade depressive or anxious symptoms are simply attributed to a physical factor, semen loss. Other specific culture-bound somatic symptoms associated with emotional factors would include hot sensations in the head or a sensation of something crawling in the head, specific to African patients (Ebigno, 1986), and a sensation of burning in the hands and feet in Pakistani or Indian patients (Kirmayer & Weiss, 1993).

Somatic symptoms may be among the more challenging manifestations of psychopathology.

First, a physician must rule out a physical cause for the somatic complaints before referring the patient to a mental health professional. Second, the mental health professional must determine the nature of the somatic complaints to know whether they are associated with a specific somatoform disorder or are part of some other psychopathological syndrome, such as a panic attack. Third, the clinician must be acutely aware of the specific culture or subculture of the patient, which often requires consultation with experts in cross-cultural presentations of psychopathology.

### Causes

Investigators with generally differing points of view agree on psychopathological processes ongoing in hypochondriasis. Faulty interpretation of physical signs and sensations as evidence of physical illness is central, so almost everyone agrees that hypochondriasis is basically a *disorder of cognition or perception* with strong emotional contributions (Adler, Côté, Barlow, & Hillhouse, 1994; Barsky & Wyshak, 1990; Salkovskis & Clark, 1993).

Individuals with hypochondriasis experience physical sensations common to all of us, but they quickly focus their attention on these sensations. Remember that the very act of focusing on yourself increases arousal and makes the physical sensations seem more intense than they are (see Chapter 4). If you also tend to misinterpret these as symptoms of illness, your anxiety will increase further. Increased anxiety produces additional physical symptoms in a vicious cycle (see Figure 5.1; Salkovskis & Warwick, 2001; Warwick & Salkovskis, 1990).

Using procedures from cognitive science such as the Stroop test (see Chapter 2), a number of investigators (Hitchcock & Mathews, 1992; Pauli & Alpers,

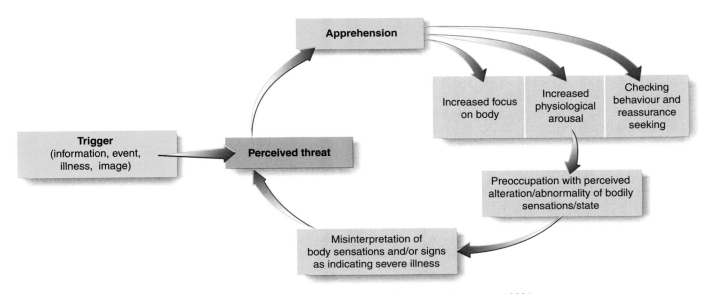

**Figure 5.1** ■ Integrative model of causes in hypochondriasis. (Based on Warwick & Salkovskis, 1990.)

2002) have confirmed that subjects with hypochondriasis show enhanced perceptual sensitivity to illness cues. They also tend to interpret ambiguous stimuli as threatening (Haenen et al., 2000; Stewart & Watt, 2000). Thus, they quickly become aware (and frightened) of any sign of possible illness or disease. A minor headache, for example, might be interpreted as a sure sign of a brain tumour. Individuals with hypochondriasis, compared with normals, take a "better safe than sorry" approach to dealing with even minor physical symptoms by getting them checked out as soon as possible (Smeets, de Jong, & Mayer, 2000). More fundamentally, they have a restrictive concept of health as being totally symptom free (Rief et al., 1998).

What causes individuals to develop this pattern of somatic sensitivity and distorted beliefs? There is every reason to believe the fundamental causes of hypochondriasis are similar to those implicated in the anxiety disorders. For example, evidence shows that hypochondriasis runs in families (Kellner, 1985), suggesting (but not proving) a possible genetic contribution. But this contribution may be non-specific, such as a tendency to overrespond to stress, and thus may be indistinguishable from the nonspecific genetic contribution to anxiety disorders. Hyperresponsivity might combine with a tendency to view negative life events as unpredictable and uncontrollable and, therefore, to be guarded against at all times.

Why does this anxiety focus on physical sensations and illness? We know that children with hypochondriacal concerns often report the same kinds of symptoms that other family members may have reported at one time (Kellner, 1985; Pilowsky, 1970). It is therefore possible, as in panic disorder, that individuals who develop hypochondriasis have *learned* from family members to focus their anxiety on specific physical conditions and illness. A recent study by Margo Watt found that adults with elevated hypochondriacal concerns reported more learning experiences in childhood around negative reactions to bodily symptoms than did adults with lower levels of hypochondriacal concerns (Watt & Stewart, 2000). These learning experiences involved being rewarded by parents (i.e., instrumental learning) when the child expressed bodily complaints (e.g., being allowed to miss school or receiving increased attention). These experiences also involved observing a parent or other family member verbally instructing the child that all bodily sensations are dangerous and signs of serious illness.

Three other factors may contribute to this etiological process (Côté et al., 1996; Kellner, 1985). First, hypochondriasis seems to develop in the context of a stressful life event, as do many disorders, including anxiety disorders. Such events often involve death or illness. Recall that the beginning of Kirsten's disorder seemed to coincide with the serious illness (breast cancer) of a female relative. Second, people who develop hypochondriasis tend to have had a disproportionate incidence of disease in their family when they were children. Thus, even if they did not develop hypochondriasis until adulthood, they carry strong memories of illness that could easily become the focus of anxiety. Third, an important social and interpersonal influence may be operating (Noyes et al., 2003). Some people who come from families in which illness is a major issue seem to have learned that an ill person is often paid increased attention (Watt & Stewart, 2000). The "benefits" of being sick might contribute to the development of the disorder. A "sick person" who thus receives more attention and less responsibility is described as adopting a "sick role." These issues may be even more significant in somatization disorder.

## Treatment

Unfortunately, we know little about treating hypochondriasis. For people with hypochondriasis who are willing to be referred to a mental health professional, emerging work suggests that cognitive-behavioural therapy can be very effective. Preliminary results from the work of psychologists Patricia Furer, John Walker, and Mark Freeston (2001) show that 83% of patients no longer meet diagnostic criteria for hypochondriasis after cognitive-behavioural therapy. Scientifically controlled studies have appeared only recently. Warwick, Clark, Cobb, and Salkovskis (1996) randomly assigned 32 patients to either cognitive-behavioural therapy or a no-treatment wait-list control group. Treatment focused on identifying and challenging illness-related misinterpretations of physical sensations and on showing patients how to create "symptoms" by focusing attention on certain body areas. Bringing on their own symptoms persuaded many patients that such events were under their control.

Patients were also coached to seek less reassurance regarding their concerns. Patients in the treatment group improved an average of 76%, and those in the wait-list group improved only 5%; benefits were maintained for 3 months. David M. Clark et al. (1998) replicated this result in a larger study and found that a general stress-management treatment (see Chapter 7) was substantially more effective than assignment to the wait-list group. Both the cognitive-behavioural and stress-management treatments retained their gain at 1-year follow-up. Although it is common clinical practice to uncover unconscious conflicts through psychodynamic psychotherapy, results on the effectiveness of this kind of treatment have seldom been reported. In one study, only 4 of

23 patients seemed to derive any benefit (Ladee, 1966). Finally, in a review of the scant available literature on the pharmacological treatment of hypochondriasis, Murray Enns and his colleagues concluded that some preliminary evidence exists of the effectiveness of antidepressant medications, especially the selective serotonin reuptake inhibitors (SSRIs; Enns, Kjernisted, & Lander, 2001).

Steven Taylor and his colleagues recently completed a review of psychological and pharmacological treatments, in order to identify the most promising interventions for treating patients with hypochondriasis. They found that cognitive behavioural therapy is the most effective treatment. They also found that fluoxetine (an SSRI) appears promising. Psychoeducation was sufficient only for mild cases of hypchondriasis. It is likely we will see more research on the treatment of hypochondriasis in the future (Taylor, Asmundson, & Coons, 2003).

## Somatization Disorder

In 1859, Pierre Briquet, a French physician, described patients who came to see him with seemingly endless lists of somatic complaints for which he could find no medical basis (American Psychiatric Association, 1980). Despite his negative findings, patients returned shortly with either the same complaints or new lists containing slight variations. For more than 100 years this disorder was called *Briquet's syndrome,* before being changed in 1980 to **somatization disorder.** Consider the case of Linda.

### Linda
Full-Time Patient

Linda, an intelligent woman in her 30s, came to our clinic looking distressed and pained. As she sat down she noted that coming into the office was difficult for her because she had trouble breathing and considerable swelling in the joints of her legs and arms. She was also in some pain from chronic urinary tract infections and might have to leave at any moment to go to the restroom, but she was extremely happy she had kept the appointment. At least she was seeing someone who could help alleviate her considerable suffering. She said she knew we would have to go through a detailed initial interview, but she had something that might save time. At this point she pulled out several sheets of paper and handed them over. One section, some five pages long, described her contacts with the health-care system for *major difficulties only.* Times, dates, potential diagnoses, and days hospitalized were noted. The second section, one and a half single-spaced pages, consisted of a list of all the medications she had taken for various complaints.

Linda felt she had any one of a number of chronic infections that nobody could properly diagnose. She had begun to have these problems in her teenage years. She often discussed her symptoms and fears with doctors and clergy. Drawn to hospitals and medical clinics, she had entered nursing school after high school. However, during hospital training, she noticed her physical condition deteriorating rapidly: She seemed to pick up the diseases she was learning about. A series of stressful emotional events resulted in her leaving nursing school.

After developing unexplained paralysis in her legs, Linda was admitted to a psychiatric hospital, and after a year she regained her ability to walk. On discharge she obtained disability status, which freed her from having to work full time, and she volunteered at the local hospital. With her chronic but fluctuating incapacitation, on some days she could go in and on some days she could not. She was seeing a family practitioner and six specialists, who monitored various aspects of her physical condition. She was also seeing two ministers for pastoral counselling.

## Clinical Description

Linda easily met and exceeded all the DSM-IV-TR diagnostic criteria for somatization disorder. Do you notice any differences between Linda, who presented with somatization disorder, and Kirsten, who presented with hypochondriacal disorder? Linda was more severely impaired and had suffered in the past from symptoms of paralysis (which we now call *conversion symptoms;* see p. 186). But the more telling difference is that Linda was *not so afraid* as Kirsten that she had a disease. Linda was concerned with the symptoms themselves, not with what they might mean. Individuals with hypochondriasis most often take immediate action on noticing a symptom by calling the doctor or taking medication. People with somatization disorder, on the other hand, do not feel the urgency to take

---

**somatization disorder** Somatoform disorder involving extreme and long-lasting focus on multiple physical symptoms for which no medical cause is evident.

action but continually feel weak and ill, and they avoid exercising, thinking it will make them worse (Rief et al., 1998). Furthermore, Linda's entire life revolved around her symptoms; she once said her symptoms were her identity: Without them she would not know who she was. By this she meant that she would not know how to relate to people except in the context of discussing her symptoms, much as other people might talk about their day at the office or their kids' accomplishments at school. Her few friends who were not health-care professionals had the patience to relate to her sympathetically, through the veil of her symptoms, and she thought of them as friends because they "understood" her suffering.

## Statistics

Somatization disorder is rare. DSM-III-R criteria required 13 or more symptoms from a list of 35, making diagnosis difficult. The criteria were greatly simplified for DSM-IV with only 8 symptoms required (Cloninger, 1996). These criteria have been validated as easier to use and more accurate than alternative or past criteria (Yutzy et al., 1995). Katon et al. (1991) demonstrated that somatization disorder occurs on a continuum: People with only a few somatic symptoms of unexplained origin may experience sufficient distress and impairment of functioning to be considered to have a "disorder." Although it has its own name, undifferentiated somatoform disorder, it is really just somatization disorder with fewer than eight symptoms. Using between four and six symptoms as criteria, Escobar and Canino (1989) found a prevalence of somatization disorder of 4.4% in one large city and approximately 20% of a large number of patients in a primary-care setting meeting these criteria (Escobar et al., 1998).

Linda's disorder developed during adolescence, apparently the typical age of onset. A number of

studies have demonstrated that individuals with somatization disorder tend to be women, unmarried, and from lower socioeconomic groups (e.g., Lieb et al., 2002; Swartz, Blazer, George, & Landerman, 1986a; Swartz, Blazer, Woodbury, George, & Landerman, 1986b). For instance, 68% of the patients in a large sample studied by Kirmayer and Robbins (1991) were female. In addition to a variety of somatic complaints, individuals may have psychological complaints, usually anxiety or mood disorders (Kirmayer & Robbins, 1991; Lieb et al., 2002). The rates are relatively uniform around the world for somatic complaints, as is the sex ratio (Gureje, Simon, Ustun, & Goldberg, 1997).

### Disorder Criteria Summary
#### Somatization Disorder

Features of somatization disorder include:
- History of many physical complaints beginning before the age of 30 that occur over years and result in treatment being sought or significant impairment in important areas of functioning
- Each of the following: (a) four pain symptoms; (b) two gastrointestinal symptoms other than pain (e.g., nausea, diarrhea, bloating); (c) one sexual symptom (e.g., excessive menstrual bleeding, erectile dysfunction); (d) one pseudoneurologic symptom (e.g., double vision, impaired coordination or balance, difficulty swallowing)
- Physical complaints cannot be fully explained by a known general medical condition or the effects of a substance (e.g., a medication or drug of abuse) *or* where there is a general medical condition, the physical complaints or impairment are in excess of what would be expected
- Complaints or impairment are not intentionally produced or feigned

*Source:* Reprinted with permission from the *Diagnostic and Statistical Manual of Mental Disorders,* Fourth Edition, Text Revision. (Copyright © 2000) American Psychiatric Association.

## Causes

Somatization disorder shares some features with hypochondriasis, including a history of family illness or injury during childhood. But this is a minor factor at best because countless families experience chronic illness or injuries without passing on the sick role to children. Similar to etiological models of hypochondriasis, Laurence Kirmayer and his colleagues have theorized that patients with somatization disorder are more sensitive to physical sensations or overattend to them (Kirmayer, Robbins, & Paris, 1994).

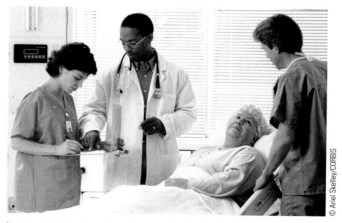

In somatization disorder, primary relationships are often with medical caregivers; one's symptoms are one's identity.

© Ariel Skelley/CORBIS

Given the past difficulty in making a diagnosis, few etiological studies of somatization disorder have been done. Early studies of possible genetic contributions had mixed results. For example, in a sophisticated twin study, Torgersen (1986) found no increased prevalence of somatization disorder in monozygotic pairs, but most studies find substantial evidence that the disorder runs in families and may have a heritable basis (Bell, 1994; Guze, Cloninger, Martin, & Clayton, 1986). A more startling finding emerged from these studies, however. Somatization disorder is strongly linked in family and genetic studies to antisocial personality disorder (ASPD; see Chapter 11), which is characterized by vandalism, persistent lying, theft, irresponsibility with finances and at work, and outright physical aggression. Individuals with ASPD seem insensitive to signals of punishment and to the negative consequences of their often impulsive behaviour, and they apparently experience little anxiety or guilt.

ASPD occurs primarily in males and somatization disorder in females, but they share a number of features. Both begin early in life, typically run a chronic course, predominate among lower socioeconomic classes, are difficult to treat, and are associated with marital discord, drug and alcohol abuse, and suicide attempts, among other complications (Cloninger, 1978; Goodwin & Guze, 1984). Both family and adoption studies suggest that ASPD and somatization disorder tend to run in families and may have a heritable component (e.g., Bohman, Cloninger, von Knorring, & Sigvardsson, 1984; Cadoret, 1978), although it is also possible that the behavioural patterns could be learned in a maladaptive family setting.

Yet, the aggressiveness, impulsiveness, and lack of emotion characteristic of ASPD seem to be at the other end of the spectrum from somatization disorder. What could these two disorders possibly have in common? Although we don't yet have the answers, Lilienfeld (1992; Lilienfeld & Hess, 2001) reviews a number of hypotheses; we look at some of them here because they are a fascinating example of integrative biopsychosocial thinking about psychopathology.

One model with some support suggests that somatization disorder and ASPD share a neurobiologically based disinhibition syndrome characterized by impulsive behaviour (e.g., Cloninger, 1987; Gorenstein & Newman, 1980). Evidence indicates that impulsiveness is common in ASPD (e.g., Newman, Widom, & Nathan, 1985). Many of the behaviours and traits associated with somatization disorder also seem to reflect the impulsive characteristic of short-term gain at the expense of long-term problems. The continual development of new somatic symptoms gains immediate sympathy and attention (for a while) but eventually social isolation (Goodwin & Guze, 1984).

If individuals with ASPD and somatization disorder share the same underlying neurophysiological vulnerability, why do they behave so differently? The explanation is that social and cultural factors exert a strong effect. The major difference between the disorders is their degree of *dependence* (Cloninger, 1987; Widom, 1984). Aggression is strongly associated with males in most mammalian species, including rodents (Gray & Buffery, 1971). Dependence and lack of aggression are strongly associated with females. Gender roles are among the strongest components of identity. It is possible that gender socialization accounts almost entirely for the profound differences in the expression of the same biological vulnerability among men and women.

These theoretical models are still preliminary and require a great deal more data before we can have confidence in their validity. But such ideas are at the forefront of our knowledge and reflect the kinds of integrative approaches to psychopathology that will inevitably emerge as our knowledge increases.

Might these assumptions apply to Linda or her family? Linda's sister had been married briefly and had two children. She had been in therapy for most of her adult life. Occasionally, Linda's sister visited doctors with various somatic complaints, but her primary difficulty was unexplained periods of recurring amnesia that might last several days; these spells alternated with blackout periods during which she was rushed to the hospital.

Were there signs of impulsivity or ASPD in this family? The sister's older daughter, after a stormy adolescence characterized by truancy and delinquency, was sentenced to jail for violations involving drugs and assault. In the midst of one session with us, Linda noted that she had kept a list of people with whom she had had sexual intercourse. The list numbered well over 20, suggesting substantial sexual impulsivity. Most of the sexual episodes occurred in the offices of mental health professionals or clergy!

This development in Linda's relationship with caregivers was important because she saw it as the ultimate sign that the caregivers were concerned about her as a person and she was important to them. But the relationships almost always ended tragically. And Linda herself was never satisfied or fulfilled by the relationships but was greatly hurt when they inevitably ended. The Canadian Psychological Association has decreed that it is *always* unethical to have *any* sexual contact with a patient at any time during treatment. Violations of this ethical canon have nearly always resulted in tragic consequences.

## Treatment

Somatization disorder is exceedingly difficult to treat, and there are no treatments with proven effectiveness that seem to "cure" the syndrome. In our clinics we concentrate on providing reassurance, reducing stress, and, in particular, reducing the frequency of help-seeking behaviours. One of the most common patterns is the person's tendency to visit numerous medical specialists according to the symptom of the week. There is an extensive medical and physical workup with every visit to a new physician (or to one who has not been seen for a while). In treatment, to limit these visits, a gatekeeper physician is assigned to each patient to screen all physical complaints. Subsequent visits to specialists must be specifically authorized by this gatekeeper. In the context of a positive therapeutic relationship, most patients are amenable to this arrangement.

Additional therapeutic attention is directed at reducing the supportive consequences of relating to significant others on the basis of physical symptoms alone. More appropriate methods of interacting with others are encouraged. Because Linda, like many patients with this disorder, had become eligible for disability payments, additional goals involved encouraging at least part-time employment with the goal of discontinuing disability. In a recent review of behavioural medicine approaches to treatment, Karl Looper and Laurence Kirmayer (2002) of McGill University discuss the current state of research knowledge on the treatment of somatization disorder. Some interventions have been aimed at physicians working with these patients and others have been aimed at the patients themselves. Randomized controlled studies demonstrate that written consultation letters sent to referring physicians to educate them about somatization disorder are effective in reducing the excessive and costly help seeking associated with this type of somatoform disorder. Unfortunately, this kind of intervention does not improve the psychological distress of somatization patients (e.g., Rost, Kashner, & Smith, 1994). In terms of interventions aimed at the patients themselves, group cognitive-behavioural therapy has been shown to provide additional benefit not only in reducing health care costs, but also in improving somatization disorder patients' psychological well-being (e.g., Lidbeck, 1997).

## *Conversion Disorder*

The term *conversion* has been used off and on since the Middle Ages (Mace, 1992) but was popularized by Freud, who believed the anxiety resulting from unconscious conflicts somehow was "converted" into physical symptoms to find expression. This allowed the individual to discharge some anxiety without actually experiencing it. As in phobic disorders, the anxiety resulting from unconscious conflicts might be "displaced" onto another object.

### Clinical Description

**Conversion disorders** generally have to do with physical malfunctioning, such as paralysis, blindness, or difficulty speaking (aphonia), without any physical or organic pathology to account for the malfunction. Most conversion symptoms suggest that some kind of neurological disease is affecting sensory-motor systems, although conversion symptoms can mimic the full range of physical malfunctioning.

Conversion disorders provide us with some of the most intriguing, sometimes astounding, examples of psychopathology. What could possibly account for somebody going blind when all visual processes are perfectly normal or experiencing paralysis of the arms or legs when there is no neurological damage?

**Disorder Criteria Summary**
Conversion Disorder

Features of conversion disorder include:
- One or more conditions affecting voluntary motor or sensory function that suggest a neurological or general medical condition
- Psychological factors are judged to be associated with the condition because of preceding conflicts or other stressors
- Condition cannot otherwise be explained by a general medical condition, effects of a substance, or as a culturally sanctioned behaviour or experience
- Clinically significant distress or impairment caused by condition

*Source:* Reprinted with permission from the *Diagnostic and Statistical Manual of Mental Disorders*, Fourth Edition, Text Revision. (Copyright © 2000) American Psychiatric Association.

In addition to blindness (see Fraser, 1994), and paralysis or weakness in the limbs, conversion symptoms may include the loss of the sense of touch. Some people have seizures, which may be psychological in origin, because no significant EEG changes can be documented. Another relatively common symptom is *globus hystericus*, the sensation of a lump in the throat that makes it difficult to swallow, eat, or sometimes talk. Conversion symptoms can

---

**conversion disorder** Physical malfunctioning, such as blindness or paralysis, suggesting neurological impairment but with no organic pathology to account for it.

also include aphonia or even total mutism. Consider the symptoms of Ms. A. described in the following case study (Wald, Taylor, & Scamvougeras, 2004).

## Ms. A.
### Loss of Voice

Ms. A. was a retired emergency services worker whose work had exposed her to severe accidents and homicides. She presented with intermittent episodes of speech disruption that had been present for about a year. These periods of disruption in her speech usually lasted a few minutes and they were occurring several times per week. Between these episodes, her speech was completely normal. Although an extensive medical and neurological evaluation was performed, a physical basis for the speech problems could not be found.

During the episodes, Ms. A. was either unable to speak at all or she experienced difficulty speaking properly. Sometimes her speaking was markedly slowed down. At other times she was only able to say "mmmm-mmmm-mmmm." These episodes began with a sensation of a "lump in the throat" (globus hystericus).

The condition was causing Ms. A. distress and it was interfering with her social life. She was very embarrassed about these episodes and consequently began to avoid social situations in case she might experience an episode of speech disruption in public.

Ms. A. was more likely to experience speech disruption when she was tired or stressed but the episodes could occur very unexpectedly as well. Remembering the traumatic events she had witnessed in her prior job in which she had been exposed to severely mutilated victims could also trigger speech disruption episodes, even though she reported that she had not been greatly upset at the time of witnessing the actual events.

### Closely Related Disorders

Distinguishing among conversion reactions, real physical disorders, and outright **malingering** (faking) is sometimes difficult. Several factors can help.

First, conversion reactions often have the same quality of indifference to the symptoms that is present in somatization disorder. This attitude, referred to as *la belle indifférence*, is considered a hallmark of conversion reactions, but, unfortunately, it is not a foolproof sign. A blasé attitude toward illness is sometimes displayed by people with actual physical disorders, and some people with conversion symptoms become quite distressed.

Second, conversion symptoms are often precipitated by marked stress. C. V. Ford (1985) noted that the incidence of marked stress preceding a conversion symptom occurred in 52% to 93% of the cases. Thus, if a clinician cannot identify a stressful event preceding the onset of the conversion symptom, he or she might more carefully consider the presence of a true physical condition. Finally, although people with conversion symptoms can usually function normally, they seem truly unaware either of this ability or of sensory input. For example, individuals with the conversion symptom of blindness can usually avoid objects in their visual field, but they will tell you they can't see the objects. Similarly, individuals with conversion symptoms of paralysis of the legs might suddenly get up and run in an emergency, and then be astounded they were able to do this. It is possible that at least some people who experience miraculous cures during religious ceremonies may have been experiencing conversion reactions. These factors may help in distinguishing between conversion and organically based physical disorders, but clinicians sometimes make mistakes. For example, Stone, Zeidler, and Sharpe (2003), summarizing a number of studies, estimate the rate of misdiagnosis of conversion disorders that are really physical problems is between 5% and 10%.

It can also be difficult to distinguish between individuals who are experiencing conversion symptoms in a seemingly involuntary way and malingerers who are good at faking symptoms. Once malingerers are exposed, their motivation is clear: They are either trying to get out of something, such as work or legal difficulties, or they are attempting to gain something, such as a financial settlement. Malingerers are fully aware of what they are doing and are clearly attempting to manipulate others to gain a desired end.

More puzzling is a set of conditions called **factitious disorders,** which fall somewhere between malingering and conversion disorders. The symptoms are under voluntary control, as with malingering, but there is *no obvious reason* for voluntarily producing the symptoms except, possibly, to assume the sick role and receive increased attention.

**malingering**  Deliberate faking of a physical or psychological disorder motivated by gain.

**factitious disorder**  Nonexistent physical or psychological disorder deliberately faked for no apparent gain except possibly sympathy and attention.

Tragically, this disorder may extend to producing symptoms in other members of the family. An adult, almost always a mother, may purposely make her child sick, evidently for the attention and pity then given to the mother who is causing the symptoms. When an individual deliberately makes someone else sick, the condition is called *factitious disorder by proxy* or *Munchausen syndrome by proxy*, but it is really an atypical form of child abuse (Check, 1998). Table 5.1 presents differences between typical child abuse and Munchausen syndrome by proxy.

**Disorder Criteria Summary**
Factitious Disorders

Features of factitious disorders include:
- Intentional production or feigning of physical or psychological problems
- Behaviour motivated by desire to assume the sick role
- Absence of external incentives (such as economic gain, avoiding physical responsibility)

*Source:* Reprinted with permission from the *Diagnostic and Statistical Manual of Mental Disorders*, Fourth Edition, Text Revision. (Copyright © 2000) American Psychiatric Association.

The offending parent may resort to extreme tactics to create the appearance of illness in the child. For example, one mother stirred a vaginal tampon obtained during menstruation in her child's urine specimen. Another mother mixed feces into her child's vomit (Check, 1998). Because the parent typically establishes a positive relationship with a medical staff, the true nature of the illness is most often unsuspected and the staff perceive the parent as remarkably caring and totally involved in providing for her child's well-being. Therefore, the parent is often successful at eluding suspicion. Helpful procedures to assess the possibility of Munchausen syndrome by proxy include a trial separation of the parent and the child or video surveillance of the child while in the hospital. An important study has appeared validating the utility of surveillance in hospital rooms of children with suspected Munchausen syndrome by proxy. In this study, video surveillance was the method used to establish the diagnosis in many cases. In one case a child was suffering from recurring *E. coli* infections, and cameras caught the mother injecting her own urine into the child's intravenous line (Hall, Eubanks, Meyyazhagan, Kenney, & Johnson, 2000).

Not only can cases of Munchausen's syndrome by proxy be missed by medical professionals and child welfare services, but errors in the opposite direction can also be made. A recent example is the case of a mother who was investigated by the Children's Aid Society of Ottawa for more than a year over allegations that she may have subjected her daughter to too many medical procedures. The agency had suspicions that the woman had Munchausen's syndrome by proxy. The case was closed without any finding of wrongdoing on this woman's part (Priest, 2003).

## Unconscious Mental Processes

Unconscious cognitive processes seem to play a role in much of psychopathology (although not necessarily as Freud envisioned it), but nowhere is this phenomenon more readily and dramatically apparent than when we attempt to distinguish between conversion disorders and related conditions.

New information (reviewed in Chapter 2) on unconscious cognitive processes becomes important. We are all capable of receiving and processing information in a number of sensory channels (such as vision and hearing) without being aware of it. Remember the phenomenon of blind sight or unconscious vision (see chapter 2)? Weiskrantz (1980) and others discovered that people with small, localized damage to certain parts of their brains could identify

| TABLE **5.1** | Munchausen Syndrome by Proxy versus Typical Child Abuse | |
|---|---|---|
| | Typical Child Abuse | Munchausen Syndrome by Proxy |
| Physical presentation of the child | Results from direct physical contact with the child; signs often detected on physical examination. | Misrepresentation of an acute or accidental medical or surgical illness not usually obvious on physical examination. |
| Obtaining the diagnosis | Perpetrator does not invite the discovery of the manifestation of the abuse. | Perpetrator usually presents the manifestations of the abuse to the health-care system. |
| The victims | Children are either the objects of frustration and anger or are receiving undue or inappropriate punishment. | Children serve as the vector in gaining the attention the parent desires. Anger is not the primary causal factor. |
| Awareness of abuse | Usually present. | Not usually present. |

*Source:* From "Munchausen Syndrome by Proxy: An Atypical Form of Child Abuse," by J. R. Cheek 1998, *Journal of Practical Psychiatry and Behavioral Health*, 341, Table 6.2. Copyright © 1998. Reprinted by permission of Lippincott Williams & Wilkins.

objects in their field of vision, but they had no awareness that they could see. Could this happen to people without brain damage? Consider the case of Celia.

## Celia
### Seeing Through Blindness

A 15-year-old girl named Celia suddenly was unable to see. Shortly thereafter she regained some of her sight, but her vision was so severely blurred that she could not read. When she was brought to a clinic for testing, psychologists arranged a series of sophisticated vision tests that did not require her to report when she could or could not see. One of the tasks required her to examine three triangles displayed on three separate screens and to press a button under the screen containing an upright triangle. Celia performed perfectly on this test without being aware that she could see anything (Grosz & Zimmerman, 1970). Was Celia faking? Evidently not, or she would have purposely made a mistake.

Sackeim, Nordlie, and Gur (1979) evaluated the potential difference between real unconscious process and faking by hypnotizing two participants and giving each a suggestion of total blindness. One participant was also told it was extremely important that she appear to everyone to be blind. The second participant was not given further instructions. The first participant, evidently following instructions to appear blind at all costs, performed far below chance on a visual discrimination task similar to the upright triangle task. On almost every trial she chose the wrong answer. The second participant, with the hypnotic suggestion of blindness but no instructions to appear blind at all costs, performed perfectly on the visual discrimination tasks—although she reported she could not see anything.

How is this relevant to identifying malingering? In an earlier case, Grosz and Zimmerman (1965) evaluated a male who seemed to have conversion symptoms of blindness. They discovered that he performed much more poorly than chance on a visual discrimination task. Subsequent information from other sources confirmed that he was almost certainly malingering. To review these distinctions, someone who is truly blind would perform at a chance level on visual discrimination tasks. People with conversion symptoms, on the other hand, can see objects in their visual field and therefore would perform well on

these tasks, but this experience is dissociated from their awareness of sight. Malingerers and, perhaps, individuals with factitious disorders simply do everything possible to pretend they can't see.

### Statistics

We have already seen that conversion disorder may occur with other disorders, particularly somatization disorder, as in the case of Linda. Linda's paralysis passed after several months and did not return, although on occasion she would report "feeling as if" it were returning. Conversion disorders are relatively rare in mental health settings, but remember that people who seek help for this condition are more likely to consult neurologists or other specialists. The prevalence estimates in neurological settings vary dramatically from 1% to 30% (Marsden, 1986; Trimbell, 1981), with a recent study estimating that 10% to 20% of all patients referred to epilepsy centres have psychogenic, non-epileptic seizures (Benbadis & Allen-Hauser, 2000).

Like somatization disorder, conversion disorders are found primarily in women (Folks, Ford, & Regan, 1984; Rosenbaum, 2000) and typically develop during adolescence or slightly thereafter. However, they occur relatively frequently in males at times of extreme stress (Chodoff, 1974). Conversion reactions are not uncommon in soldiers exposed to combat (Mucha & Reinhardt, 1970). The symptoms often disappear after a time, only to return later in the same or similar form when a new stressor occurs. A recent longitudinal study by University of Toronto researchers suggests that, in the case of conversion disorders involving movement disturbances, long-term prognosis is quite poor (Feinstein, Stergiopoulos, Fine, & Lang, 2001).

In other cultures, some conversion symptoms are common aspects of religious or healing rituals. Seizures, paralysis, and trances are common in some rural fundamentalist religious groups in North

The seizures and trances that may be symptomatic of conversion disorder are also common in some fundamentalist religious groups in North America.

America (Griffith, English, & Mayfield, 1980), and they are often seen as evidence of contact with God. Individuals who exhibit such symptoms are thus held in high esteem by their peers. These symptoms do not meet criteria for a "disorder" unless they persist and interfere with an individual's functioning.

## Causes

Freud described four basic processes in the development of conversion disorder. First, the individual experiences a traumatic event—in Freud's view, an unacceptable, unconscious conflict. Second, because the conflict and the resulting anxiety are unacceptable, the person represses the conflict, making it unconscious. Third, the anxiety continues to increase and threatens to emerge into consciousness, and the person "converts" it into physical symptoms, thereby relieving the pressure of having to deal directly with the conflict. This reduction of anxiety is considered the *primary gain* or reinforcing event that maintains the conversion symptom. Fourth, the individual receives greatly increased attention and sympathy from loved ones and may be allowed to avoid a difficult situation or task. Freud considered such attention or avoidance to be the *secondary gain*, the secondarily reinforcing set of events.

We believe Freud was basically correct on at least three counts and possibly a fourth, although firm evidence supporting any of these ideas is sparse and Freud's views were far more complex than represented here. What seems to happen is that individuals with conversion disorder have experienced a traumatic event that must be escaped. This might be combat, where death is imminent, or being exposed to an accident or homicide (as in the case of Ms. A.; Wald et al., 2004). Because simply running away is unacceptable in most cases, the socially acceptable alternative of getting sick is substituted; but getting sick on purpose is also unacceptable, so this motivation is detached from the person's consciousness. Finally, because the escape behaviour (the conversion symptoms) is successful to an extent in obliterating the traumatic situation, the behaviour continues until the underlying problem is resolved.

One recent study confirms these hypotheses, at least partially (Wyllie, Glazer, Benbadis, Kotagal, & Wolgamuth, 1999). In this study, 34 child and adolescent patients, 25 of them girls, were evaluated after receiving a diagnosis of psychologically based pseudoseizures (psychogenic non-epileptic seizures). Many of these children and adolescents presented with additional psychological disorders, including 32% with mood disorders and 24% with separation anxiety and school refusal. Other anxiety disorders were present in some additional patients.

When the extent of psychological stress in the lives of these children was examined, it was found that most of the patients had substantial stress, including a history of sexual abuse, recent parental divorce or death of a close family member, and physical abuse. The authors conclude that major mood disorders and severe environmental stress, especially sexual abuse, are common among children and adolescents with the conversion disorder of pseudoseizures, as have other studies (Roelofs, Keijsers, Hoogduin, Naring, & Moene, 2002).

The one step in Freud's progression of events about which some questions remain is the issue of primary gain. The notion of primary gain accounts for the feature of *la belle indifférence* (cited previously), where individuals seem not the least bit distressed about their symptoms. In other words, Freud thought that because symptoms reflected an unconscious attempt to resolve a conflict, the patient would not be upset by them. But as illustrated in the case of Ms. A. (Wald et al., 2004), patients with conversion disorder are in fact often quite distressed by their symptoms. (Recall that Ms. A. was so embarrassed by her episodes of speech disruption that she began to avoid social gatherings.) Formal tests of this feature of indifference also provide little support for Freud's claim. For example, Lader and Sartorius (1968) compared patients with conversion disorder with control groups of anxious patients without conversion symptoms. The patients with conversion disorder showed equal or greater anxiety and physiological arousal than the control group. The impression of indifference may be more in the mind of the therapist than true of the patient.

Social and cultural influences also contribute to conversion disorder, which, like somatization disorder, tends to occur in less educated, lower socioeconomic groups where knowledge about disease and medical illness is not well developed (Kirmayer et al., 2003; Swartz, Blazer, Woodbury, George, & Landerman, 1986). For example, Binzer, Andersen, and Kullgren (1997) noted that 13% of their series of 30 patients with motor disabilities because of conversion disorder had attended high school compared with 67% in a control group of motor symptoms resulting from a physical cause. Prior experience with real physical problems, usually among other family members, tends to influence the later choice of specific conversion symptoms; that is, patients tend to adopt symptoms with which they are familiar (e.g., Brady & Lind, 1961). Furthermore, the incidence of these disorders has decreased over the decades (Kirmayer et al., 2003). The most likely explanation is that increased knowledge of the real causes of physical problems by both patients and loved ones eliminates much of the possibility of secondary gain so important in these disorders.

Finally, many conversion symptoms seem to be part of a larger constellation of psychopathology. In some cases, individuals may have a marked biological vulnerability to develop the disorder when under stress, with biological processes like those discussed in the context of somatization disorder. In other cases, exposure to traumatic events may play a large contributing role as in the case of Ms. A. (Wald et al., 2004). For countless other cases, however, biological contributory factors seem to be less important than the overriding influence of interpersonal factors, including the actions of family members and loved ones, as we will see. We talk about Ms. A.'s treatment in the next section. There you will see that the extent of her suffering and its successful resolution point primarily to a psychological and social etiology.

## Treatment

Although few systematic controlled studies have evaluated the effectiveness of treatment for conversion disorders, we often treat these conditions in our clinics, as do others (e.g., Campo & Negrini, 2000; Moene, Spinhoven, Hoogduin, & van Dyck, 2002), and our methods closely follow our thinking on etiology. Because conversion disorder has much in common with somatization disorder, many of the treatment principles are similar.

A principal strategy is to identify and attend to the traumatic or stressful life event, if it is still present (either in real life or in memory), and remove, if possible, sources of "secondary gain." As in the case of Anna O. described in Chapter 1, therapeutic assistance in reexperiencing or "reliving" the event (catharsis) is a reasonable first step. In the case of Ms. A., Wald and colleagues (2004) employed cognitive-behavioural therapy involving imaginal exposure to trauma memories. The frequency of speech disturbance episodes decreased during the treatment until Ms. A. was virtually symptom free. Her distress also declined during therapy.

The therapist must also work hard to reduce any reinforcing or supportive consequences of the conversion symptoms (secondary gain). For example, conversion symptoms are often strongly reinforced by attention and concern from loved ones. The therapist must collaborate with both the patient and the family to eliminate such self-defeating patterns.

Cognitive-behavioural programs appear to hold promise in the treatment of conversion disorder. In a recent study, 65% of a group of 45 patients with mostly motor behaviour conversions (e.g., difficulty walking) responded well to such treatment. Interestingly, hypnosis, which was administered to approximately half the patients, did not confer any additional benefit to the cognitive-behavioural treatment (Moene et al., 2002).

## *Pain Disorder*

A related somatoform disorder about which little is known is **pain disorder.** In pain disorder there may have been clear physical reasons for pain, at least initially, but psychological factors play a major role in maintaining it. In the placement of this disorder in DSM-IV-TR, serious consideration was given to removing it entirely from the somatoform disorders and putting it in a separate section, because a person rarely presents with localized pain without some physical basis, such as an accident or illness. Therefore, it was difficult to separate the cases where the causes were judged to be primarily psychological from the ones where the causes are primarily physical. Because pain disorder fits most closely within the somatoform cluster (an individual presents with physical symptoms judged to have strong psychological contributions), the decision was made to leave pain disorder in the somatoform section. However, the subtypes of pain disorder run the gamut from pain judged to be due *primarily to psychological factors* to pain judged to be due *primarily to a general medical condition.*

### Disorder Criteria Summary
Pain Disorder

Features of pain disorder include:
- Presence of serious pain in one or more anatomical sites
- Pain causes clinically significant distress or impairment in functioning
- Psychological factors judged to play primary role in onset, severity, exacerbation, or maintenance of the pain
- Pain is not feigned or intentionally produced

*Source:* Reprinted with permission from the *Diagnostic and Statistical Manual of Mental Disorders,* Fourth Edition, Text Revision. (Copyright © 2000) American Psychiatric Association.

The prevalence of pain disorder is unclear. One study from Germany suggests that this is a fairly common condition, with from 5% to 12% of the population meeting criteria for pain disorder (Grabe et al., 2003). An important feature of pain disorder is

---

**pain disorder** Somatoform disorder featuring true pain but for which psychological factors play an important role in onset, severity, or maintenance.

that the pain is real and it hurts, regardless of the causes (Aigner & Bach, 1999; King & Strain, 1991). Consider the two cases described here.

## The Medical Student
### Temporary Pain

During her first clinical rotation, a 25-year-old third-year medical student in excellent health was seen at her student health service for intermittent abdominal pain of several weeks' duration. The student claimed no past history of similar pain. Physical examination revealed no physical problems, but she told the physician that she had recently separated from her husband. The student was referred to the health service psychiatrist. No other psychiatric problems were found. She was taught relaxation techniques and given supportive therapy to help her cope with her stressful situation. The student's pain subsequently disappeared, and she successfully completed medical school.

## The Woman with Cancer
### Managing Pain

A 56-year-old woman with metastatic breast cancer who appeared to be coping appropriately with her disease had severe pain in her right thigh for a month. She initially obtained relief from a combination of drugs and subsequently received hypnotherapy and group therapy. These treatment modalities provided additional pain relief and enabled the patient to decrease her narcotic intake with no increase in pain.

The medical student's pain was seen as largely psychological. In the case of the second woman, the pain was probably related to cancer. But we now know that whatever its cause, pain has a strong psychological component (Gagliese & Katz, 2000; Melzack, 1993). If medical treatments for existing physical conditions are in place and pain remains, or if the pain seems clearly related to psychological factors, psychological interventions are appropriate. Because of the complexity of pain and the variety of narcotics and other medications prescribed for it,

multidisciplinary pain clinics are part of most large hospitals (see Sullivan, 2003). (In Chapter 7, we discuss health psychology and the contribution of psychological factors to physical disorders, and we delve more deeply into types of pain disorders, their causes, and treatment.)

## Body Dysmorphic Disorder

Did you ever wish you could change part of your appearance? Maybe your weight or the size of your nose or the way your ears stick out? Most people fantasize about improving something, but some relatively normal-looking people imagine they are so ugly they are unable to interact with others or otherwise function normally for fear that people will laugh at their ugliness. This curious affliction is called **body dysmorphic disorder (BDD),** and at its centre is a preoccupation with some imagined defect in appearance by someone who looks reasonably normal, or even in someone whose appearance is judged by others as very attractive. In fact, actress Uma Thurman, who is well known for her striking Scandinavian features, recently admitted that she has BDD (Kahn, 2001). Thus, the disorder has also been referred to as "imagined ugliness" (Phillips, 1991). Consider the case of Jim.

## Jim
### Ashamed to Be Seen

In his mid-20s, Jim was diagnosed with suspected social phobia; he was referred to one of our clinics by another professional. Jim had just finished rabbinical school and had been offered a position at a synagogue in a nearby city. However, he found himself unable to accept because of marked social difficulties. Lately he had given up leaving his small apartment for fear of running into people he knew and being forced to stop and interact with them.

Jim was a good-looking young man of about average height, with dark hair and eyes. Although he was somewhat depressed, a mental status exam and a brief interview focusing on current functioning and past history did not reveal any remarkable problems. There was no sign of a psychotic process (he was not out of

---

**body dysmorphic disorder (BDD)**   Somatoform disorder featuring a disruptive preoccupation with some imagined defect in appearance ("imagined ugliness").

touch with reality). We then focused on Jim's social difficulties. We expected the usual kinds of anxiety about interacting with people or "doing something" (performing) in front of them. But this was not Jim's concern. Rather, he was convinced that everyone, even his good friends, were staring at a part of his body that he himself found absolutely grotesque. He reported that strangers would never mention his deformity and his friends felt too sorry for him to mention it. Jim thought his head was square! Like the Beast in *Beauty and the Beast* who could not imaging people reacting to him with anything less than abhorrence, Jim could not imagine people getting past the fact that his head was square. To hide his condition as well as he could, Jim wore soft floppy hats and was most comfortable in winter, when he could all but completely cover his head with a large stocking cap. To us, Jim looked perfectly normal.

## Clinical Description

To give you a better idea of the types of concerns people with BDD present to health professionals, the locations of imagined defects in 30 patients are shown in Table 5.2. In another series of 23 adolescents with BDD, 61% focused on their skin and 55% on their hair (Albertini & Phillips, 1999). Many people with this disorder become fixated on mirrors (Veale &Riley, 2001). They frequently check their presumed ugly feature to see whether any change has taken place. Others avoid mirrors to an almost phobic extent. Understandably, suicidal ideation, suicide attempts, and suicide itself are frequent consequences of this disorder (Phillips, 1991; Zimmerman & Mattia, 1998). People with BDD also have "ideas of reference," which means they think everything that goes on in their world somehow is related to them—in this case, to their imagined defect. This disorder can cause considerable disruption in the patient's life. Many patients with severe BBD become housebound for fear of showing themselves to other people.

If this disorder seems strange to you, you are not alone. For decades, this condition, previously known as *dysmorphophobia* (literally, fear of ugliness), was thought to represent a psychotic delusional state because the affected individuals were unable to realize, even for a fleeting moment, that their ideas were irrational. Whether this is true is still debated.

In the context of obsessive-compulsive disorder (OCD; see Chapter 4), a similar issue arose as to whether patients really believe in their obsessions

| TABLE **5.2** Location of Imagined Defects in 30 Patients with Body Dysmorphic Disorder* | | |
|---|---|---|
| Location | N | % |
| Hair† | 19 | 63 |
| Nose | 15 | 50 |
| Skin‡ | 15 | 50 |
| Eyes | 8 | 27 |
| Head/face§ | 6 | 20 |
| Overall body build/bone structure | 6 | 20 |
| Lips | 5 | 17 |
| Chin | 5 | 17 |
| Stomach/waist | 5 | 17 |
| Teeth | 4 | 13 |
| Legs/knees | 4 | 13 |
| Breasts/pectoral muscles | 3 | 10 |
| Ugly face (general) | 3 | 10 |
| Ears | 2 | 7 |
| Cheeks | 2 | 7 |
| Buttocks | 2 | 7 |
| Penis | 2 | 7 |
| Arms/wrists | 2 | 7 |
| Neck | 1 | 3 |
| Forehead | 1 | 3 |
| Facial muscles | 1 | 3 |
| Shoulders | 1 | 3 |
| Hips | 1 | 3 |

*Total is greater than 100% because most patients had "defects" in more than one location.
†Involved head hair in 15 cases, beard growth in 2 cases, and other body hair in 3 cases.
‡Involved acne in 7 cases, facial lines in 3 cases, and other skin concerns in 7 cases.
§Involved concerns with shape in 5 cases and size in 1 case.

*Source:* From K.A. Phillips, S.L. McElroy, P.E. Keck, Jr., H.G. Pope, Jr. and J.I. Hudson, Body Dysmorphic Disorder: 30 Cases of Imagined Ugliness, *Am J Psychiatry,* 1993, 150: 302–308. Reprinted with permission from the American Journal of Psychiatry, © 1993 American Psychiatric Association.

or realize they are irrational. A minority (10% or less) of people with OCD believe their fears about contaminating others or their need to prevent catastrophes with their rituals are realistic and reasonable. This brings up the major issue of what is "delusional" and what isn't, which is even more important in BDD.

For example, in the 30 cases examined by Phillips, McElroy, Keck, Pope, and Hudson (1993) and in 50 cases reported by Veale and colleagues

(1996), about half the subjects were convinced their imagined bodily defect was real and a reasonable source of concern. Is this delusional? Psychopathologists, including those on the DSM-IV task force, have wrestled long and hard with this issue only to conclude there are no clear answers and more research is needed. For now, individuals with BDD whose beliefs are so firmly held that they could be called delusional receive a second diagnosis of delusional disorder: somatic type (see Chapter 12).

## Statistics

The prevalence of BDD is hard to estimate because by its very nature it tends to be kept secret. However, the best estimates are that it is far more common than we had previously thought. Without some sort of treatment, it tends to run a lifelong course (Phillips, 1991; Veale et al., 1996). One of the patients with BDD reported in Phillips et al. (1993) had suffered from her condition for 71 years, since the age of 9. If you think a university friend seems to have at least a mild version of BDD, you're probably correct. One study suggested that as many as 70% of university students report at least some dissatisfaction with their bodies; 28% of these appear to meet all the criteria for the disorder (Fitts, Gibson, Redding, & Deiter, 1989). However, this study was done by questionnaire and may have reflected the large percentage of students who are concerned simply with weight.

Another, more recent study investigated the prevalence of BDD specifically in an ethnically diverse sample of 566 adolescents between age 14 and age 19. The overall prevalence of BDD in this group was 2.2%, with adolescent girls more dissatisfied with their bodies than boys and Blacks of both genders less dissatisfied with their bodies than Caucasians, Asians, and Hispanics (Mayville, Katz, Gipson, & Cabral, 1999).

**Body Dysmorphic Disorder: Doug**
*"I didn't want to talk to anybody.... I was afraid because what I saw on my face ... they saw.... If I could see it, they could see it. And I thought there was like an arrow pointing at it. And I was very self-conscious. And I felt like the only time I felt comfortable was at night, because it was dark time."*

BDD is not strongly associated with one sex or the other. According to published reports, slightly more females than males are affected in North America, but 62% of a large number of individuals with BDD in Japan were males. As you might suspect, few people with this disorder get married. Age of onset ranges from early adolescence through the 20s, peaking at the age of 18 or 19 (Phillips et al., 1993; Zimmerman & Mattia, 1998). Individuals are somewhat reluctant to seek treatment. In many cases a relative will force the issue, demanding the individual get help; this insistence may reflect the disruptiveness of the disorder for family members. Severity is also reflected in the high percentage (24%) of past suicide attempts among the 50 cases described by Veale et al. (1996); 29% of the 30 cases described by Phillips et al. (1993); and 21% of a group of 33 adolescents (Albertini & Phillips, 1999).

## Disorder Criteria Summary
### Body Dysmorphic Disorder (BDD)

Features of body dysmorphic disorder include:
- Preoccupation with an imagined defect in appearance, or gross exaggeration of a slight physical anomaly
- Preoccupation causes significant distress or impairment in functioning
- Preoccupation is not better accounted for by another disorder (e.g., anorexia nervosa)

*Source:* Reprinted with permission from the *Diagnostic and Statistical Manual of Mental Disorders*, Fourth Edition, Text Revision. (Copyright © 2000) American Psychiatric Association.

One study of 62 consecutive outpatients with BDD found that the degree of psychological stress and impairment was generally worse than comparable indices in patients with depression, diabetes, or a recent myocardial infarction (heart attack) on several questionnaire measures (Phillips, 2000). Thus, BDD is among the more serious of psychological disorders. Further reflecting the intense suffering that accompanies this disorder, Veale (2000) collected information on 25 patients with BDD who had sought cosmetic surgery in the past. Nine patients who could not afford surgery, or were turned down for other reasons, had attempted by their own hand to alter their appearance dramatically, often with tragic results. One example was a man preoccupied by his skin, who believed it was too "loose." He used a staple gun on both sides of his face to try to keep his skin taut. The staples fell out after 10 minutes and he narrowly missed damaging his facial nerve. In a second example, a woman was preoccupied by her skin and the shape of her face. She filed down her teeth to alter the appearance of her jaw line.

Individuals with BDD react to what they think is a horrible or grotesque feature. Thus, the psychopathology lies in their reacting to a deformity that others cannot perceive. Of course, social and cultural determinants of beauty and body image largely define what is "deformed." Nowhere is this more evident than in the greatly varying cultural standards for body weight and shape, factors that play a major role in eating disorders, as we see in Chapter 8.

For example, in most cultures it is desirable for a woman's skin to be lighter and more perfectly smooth than a man's skin (Fallon, 1990; Liggett, 1974). Over the centuries freckles have not been popular, and in many cultures chemical solutions were used to remove them. Unfortunately, whole layers of skin disappeared and the underlying flesh was severely damaged (Liggett, 1974). Concerns with the width of the face, so common in BDD, can also be culturally determined. Until recently, in some areas of France, Africa, Greenland, and Peru, the head of a newborn infant was reshaped, either by hand or by tight caps secured by strings. Sometimes the face was elongated; other times it was widened. Similarly, attempts were made to flatten the noses of newborn infants, usually by hand (Fallon, 1990; Liggett, 1974). In Burma, women wear brass neck rings from an early age to lengthen the neck. One woman's neck was nearly 40 centimetres long (Morris, 1985).

In various cultures a child's head or face is manipulated to produce desirable features, as in the addition of rings to lengthen the neck of this Burmese girl.

Finally, many are aware of the old practice in China of binding girls' feet, often preventing the foot from growing to more than one-third of its normal size. Women's bound feet forced them to walk in a way that was thought seductive. As Brownmiller (1984) points out, the myth that an unnaturally small foot signifies extraordinary beauty and grace is still with us. Can you think of the fairy tale in which a small foot becomes the identifying feature of the beautiful heroine? What can we learn about BDD from such practices of mutilation around the world? The behaviour of individuals with BDD seems remarkably strange, because they go *against* current cultural practices that put less emphasis on altering facial features. In other words, people who simply conform to the expectations of their culture do not have a disorder (as noted in Chapter 1). Nevertheless, aesthetic plastic surgery, particularly for the nose and lips, is still widely accepted and, because it is most often undertaken by the wealthy, carries an aura of elevated status. In this light, BDD may not be so strange. As with most psychopathology, its characteristic attitudes and behaviour may simply be an exaggeration of normal culturally sanctioned behaviour.

### Causes and Treatment

We know little about either the etiology or the treatment of BDD. We have almost no information on whether it runs in families, so we can't investigate a specific genetic contribution. Similarly, we do not have any meaningful information on biological or psychological predisposing factors or vulnerabilities. Psychoanalytic speculations are numerous, but most centre on the defensive mechanism of displacement—that is, an underlying unconscious conflict would be too anxiety provoking to admit into consciousness, so the person displaces it onto a body part.

What little evidence we do have on etiology comes from a weak source: the pattern of comorbidity of BDD with other disorders. BDD is a somatoform disorder because its central feature is a psychological preoccupation with somatic issues. For example, in hypochondriasis the focus is on physical sensations, and in BDD the focus is on physical appearance. We have already seen that many of the somatoform disorders tend to co-occur. Linda presented with somatization disorder but also had a history of conversion disorder. However, BDD does not tend to co-occur with the other somatoform disorders, nor does it occur in family members of patients with other somatoform disorders.

A disorder that does frequently co-occur with BDD and is found among other family members is OCD (Tynes, White, & Steketee, 1990; Zimmerman & Mattia, 1998). Is BDD a variant of OCD? There

Michael Jackson as a child and as an adult. Many people alter their features through surgery. However, people with body dysmorphic disorder are seldom satisfied with the results.

are a lot of similarities (Yeh, Taylor, Thordarson, & Corcoran, 2003). People with BDD complain of persistent, intrusive, and horrible thoughts about their appearance, and they engage in such compulsive behaviours as repeatedly looking in mirrors to check their physical features. BDD and OCD also have approximately the same age of onset and run the same course. One recent brain-imaging study demonstrated similar abnormal brain functioning between patients with BDD and patients with OCD (Rauch et al., 2003). Perhaps most significantly, there are two, and only two, treatments for BDD with any evidence of effectiveness.

First, drugs that block the reuptake of serotonin, such as clomipramine (Anafranil) and fluvoxamine (Luvox), provide relief to at least some people (Hollender, Cohen, Simeon, & Rosen, 1994; Phillips, Dwight, & McElroy, 1998). One controlled study of the effects of drugs on BDD demonstrated that clomipramine was significantly more effective than desipramine, a drug that does not specifically block reuptake of serotonin, for the treatment of BDD (Hollander et al., 1999). These are the same drugs that have the strongest effect in OCD. Second, exposure and response prevention, the type of cognitive-behavioural therapy effective with OCD, has been successful with BDD (McKay et al., 1997; Wilhelm, Otto, Lohr, & Deckersbach, 1999). In the Rosen, Reiter, and Orosan (1995) study, 82% of patients treated with this approach responded, although these patients may have been somewhat less severe than other series (Wilhelm et al., 1999). Furthermore, patients with BDD and OCD have similar rates of response to these treatments (Saxena et al., 2001). If BDD does turn out to be a variant of OCD, we will know a lot more about some of the biological and psychological factors that may lead to its development (Veale et al., 1996).

Another interesting lead on causes of BDD comes from cross-cultural explorations of similar disorders. You may remember the Japanese variant of social phobia, *taijin kyofusho* (see Chapter 4), in which individuals may believe they have horrendous bad breath or body odor and thus avoid social interaction. But people with *taijin kyofusho* also have all the other characteristics of social phobia. Patients who would be diagnosed with BDD in our culture might simply be considered to have severe social phobia in Japan and Korea. Possibly, then, social anxiety is fundamentally related to BDD, a connection that would give us further hints on the nature of the disorder.

## Plastic Surgery

Because the concerns of people with BDD involve mostly the face or head, it is not surprising that the disorder is big business for the plastic surgery profession—but it's bad business. These patients do not benefit from surgery and may return for additional surgery or, on occasion, file malpractice lawsuits. Even worse, a study found that the preoccupation with imagined ugliness increased in people who had plastic surgery, dental work, or special skin treatments for their perceived problems (Phillips et al., 1993).

Some investigators estimate that as many as 2% of all patients who request plastic surgery may have BDD (Andreasen & Bardach, 1977), and recent direct surveys suggest a much higher percentage, perhaps up to 25% (Barnard, 2000). The most common procedures are rhinoplasties (nose jobs), face-lifts, eyebrow elevations, liposuction, breast augmentation, and surgery to alter the jaw line. Surgery of this type is increasing rapidly. Between 1992 and 1999, according to the American Society of Plastic Surgeons, eyelid surgery increased 139% to 142 033 surgeries annually and breast enlargement increased 413% to 167 318 surgeries annually. The problem is that surgery on the proportion of these people with BDD seldom produces the desired results. These individuals return for additional surgery on the same defect or concentrate on some new defect. Hollander, Liebowitz, Winchel, Klumker, and Klein (1989) describe one patient who had four separate rhinoplasties and then became concerned about his thinning hair and sloped shoulders. Phillips et al. (1993) report that of 25 surgical or dental procedures, only 2 gave relief. In more than 20 cases, the severity of the disorder and accompanying distress *increased* after surgery. Clinical psychologists Randi McCabe and Martin

Antony in Hamilton have recommended that assessments of BDD symptoms routinely be made and that surgery outcomes, including quality of life, should be monitored in a standardized manner in the plastic surgery context (Ching, Thoma, McCabe, & Antony, 2003).

## Concept Check 5.1

Diagnose the somatoform disorders described here by choosing one of the following: (a) pain disorder, (b) hypochondriasis, (c) somatization disorder, (d) conversion disorder, (e) body dysmorphic disorder.

1. Emily constantly worries about her health. She has been to numerous doctors for her concerns about cancer and other serious diseases only to be reassured of her well-being. Emily's anxiousness is exacerbated by each small ailment (headaches, stomach pains, etc.) that she considers indications of a major illness. _____

2. D. J. arrived at Dr. Blake's office with a folder crammed full of medical records, symptom documentation, and lists of prescribed treatments and drugs. Several doctors are monitoring him for his complaints, ranging from chest pain to difficulty swallowing. D. J. recently lost his job for using too many sick days. _____

3. Sixteen-year-old Chad suddenly lost the use of his arms with no medical cause. The complete paralysis slowly improved to the point that he could slightly raise them. However, Chad cannot drive, pick up objects, or perform most tasks necessary for day-to-day life. _____

4. Loretta is 32 and has been preoccupied with the size and shape of her nose for 2 years. She has been saving money for plastic surgery, after which, she is sure, her career will improve. Trouble is, three honest plastic surgeons have told her that her nose is fine as it is. _____

5. Betty had considerable pain when she broke her arm. A year after it healed and all medical tests indicate her arm is fine, she still complains of the pain. It seems to intensify when she fights with her husband. _____

# Dissociative Disorders

■ *Describe and distinguish among the five types of dissociative disorders.*

■ *Describe important etiological and treatment factors, including important known cultural influences on each disorder.*

■ *Discuss false memory syndrome in the context of trauma associated with dissociative disorders.*

At the beginning of the chapter we said that when individuals feel detached from themselves or their surroundings, almost as if they are dreaming or living in slow motion, they are having dissociative experiences. Morton Prince, the founder of the *Journal of Abnormal Psychology*, noted more than 90 years ago that many people experience something like dissociation occasionally (Prince, 1906–1907). It is most likely to happen after an extremely stressful event, such as an accident. It might also happen when you're very tired or under physical or mental pressure from, say, staying up all night cramming for an exam. Perhaps because you knew the cause, the dissociation may not have bothered you much (Dixon, 1963; Noyes, Hoenk, Kuperman, & Slymen,

1977). On the other hand, it may have been extremely frightening.

These kinds of dissociative experiences can be divided into two types. During an episode of *depersonalization,* your perception alters so that you temporarily lose the sense of your own reality. During an episode of **derealization,** your sense of the reality of the external world is lost. Things may seem to change shape or size; people may seem dead or mechanical. These sensations of unreality are characteristic of the dissociative disorders

---

**derealization** Situation in which the individual loses his or her sense of the reality of the external world.

because, in a sense, they are psychological mechanisms whereby the person "dissociates" from reality. Depersonalization is often part of a serious set of conditions with which reality, experience, and even the person's identity seem to disintegrate. As we go about our day-to-day lives, we ordinarily have an excellent sense of who we are and a general knowledge of the identity of other people. We are also aware of events around us, of where we are, and of why we are there. Finally, except for occasional small lapses, our memories remain intact so that events leading up to the current moment are clear in our minds.

But what happens if we can't remember why we are in a certain place or even who we are? What happens if we lose our sense that our surroundings are real? Finally, what happens if we not only forget who we are but also begin thinking we are somebody else—somebody who has a different personality, different memories, and even different physical reactions, such as allergies we never had? These are examples of disintegrated experience (Cardeña & Gleaves, 2003; Putnam, 1991). In each case there are alterations in our relationship to the self, to the world, or to memory processes.

Although we have much to learn about these disorders, we briefly describe four of them—depersonalization disorder, dissociative amnesia, dissociative fugue, and dissociative trance disorder—before examining the fascinating condition of dissociative identity disorder. As you will see, the influence of social and cultural factors is strong in dissociative disorders. Even in severe cases, the expression of the pathology does not stray far from socially and culturally sanctioned forms.

## Depersonalization Disorder

When feelings of unreality are so severe and frightening that they dominate an individual's life and prevent normal functioning, clinicians may diagnose the rare **depersonalization disorder.** Trying to describe the uncomfortable feeling of depersonalization can be very difficult to convey in words. A 40-year old female patient of Ottawa psychiatrist George Fraser described the experience as follows:

> Very often, I feel that I can't make contact with people, as if we are existing in different dimensions. I think they hear me speaking, but are puzzled about what I'm saying and, as I talk, I feel a gap between my intentions and my voice, as if my thoughts were a high slow-moving gear and way out the top of my consciousness is a little tiny gear going at top speed, which is my voice and I can't feel the connection. Sometimes I feel like I don't overlap with people. (Fraser, 1994, p. 142).

Consider next the case of Bonnie.

### Bonnie
#### Dancing Away from Herself

Bonnie, a dance teacher in her late 20s, was accompanied by her husband when she first visited the clinic and complained of "flipping out." When asked what she meant, she said, "It's the most scary thing in the world. It often happens when I'm teaching my modern dance class. I'll be up in front and I will feel focused on. Then, as I'm demonstrating the steps, I just feel like it's not really me and that I don't really have control of my legs. Sometimes I feel like I'm standing in back of myself just watching. Also I get tunnel vision. It seems like I can only see in a narrow space right in front of me and I just get totally separated from what's going on around me. Then I begin to panic and perspire and shake." It turns out that Bonnie's problems began after she smoked marijuana for the first time about 10 years before. She had the same feeling then and found it very scary, but with the help of friends she got through it. Lately the feeling recurred more frequently and more severely, particularly when she was teaching dance class.

You may remember from Chapter 4 that during an intense panic attack many people (approximately 50%) experience feelings of unreality. People undergoing intense stress or experiencing a traumatic event may also experience these symptoms, which characterize the newly defined *acute stress disorder.* Feelings of depersonalization and derealization are part of several different disorders (Boon & Draijer, 1991). But when severe depersonalization and derealization are the primary problem, the individual meets criteria for depersonalization disorder (Steinberg, 1991).

Montreal researchers Jean Charbonneau and Kieron O'Connor (1999) interviewed 20 individuals who were self-referred from the general population as experiencing depersonalization. They found that in the majority of cases, onset occurred following a traumatic life event, after sexual abuse, or after giving birth. Simeon et al. (1997) described 30 consecutive cases, 19 women and 11 men. Mean age of onset was 16.1 years and the course tended to be

**depersonalization disorder**   Dissociative disorder in which feelings of depersonalization are so severe they dominate the client's life and prevent normal functioning.

chronic, lasting an average of 15.7 years so far in those cases. All the patients were substantially impaired. Although none had any additional dissociative disorders, more than 50% suffered from additional mood and anxiety disorders.

---

### Disorder Criteria Summary
#### Depersonalization Disorder

Features of depersonalization disorder include:
- Persistent or recurrent feelings of being detached from one's body or mental processes (e.g., feeling like one is in a dream)
- Reality testing remains intact during the depersonalization experience
- Depersonalization causes clinically significant distress or impairment in functioning
- Condition does not occur exclusively as part of another mental disorder such as schizophrenia, panic disorder, or acute stress disorder.

*Source:* Reprinted with permission from the *Diagnostic and Statistical Manual of Mental Disorders,* Fourth Edition, Text Revision. (Copyright © 2000) American Psychiatric Association.

---

Guralnick, Schmeidler, and Simeon (2000) compared 15 patients with depersonalization disorder with 15 matched normal comparison subjects on a comprehensive neuropsychological test battery that assessed cognitive function. Although both groups were of equal intelligence, the subjects with depersonalization disorder showed a distinct cognitive profile, reflecting some specific cognitive deficits on measures of attention, short-term memory, and spatial reasoning. Basically, these patients were easily distracted and had some trouble perceiving three-dimensional objects because they tended to "flatten" these objects into two dimensions.

It is not clear how these cognitive and perceptual deficits develop, but they seem to correspond with reports of "tunnel vision" (perceptual distortions) and "mind emptiness" (difficulty absorbing new information) that characterize these patients. Although the search has begun for specific aspects of brain functioning that might correlate with depersonalization (e.g., Sierra & Berrios, 1998), most of this work is currently speculative.

### Dissociative Amnesia

Perhaps the easiest to understand of the severe dissociative disorders is one called **dissociative amnesia,** which includes several different patterns. People who are unable to remember anything, including who they are, are said to have **generalized amnesia.** Generalized amnesia may be lifelong or may extend from a period in the more recent past, such as 6 months or a year previously.

## The Woman Who Lost Her Memory

Several years ago a woman in her early 50s brought her daughter to one of our clinics because of the girl's refusal to attend school and other severely disruptive behaviour. The father, who refused to come to the session, was quarrelsome, a heavy drinker, and, on occasion, abusive. The girl's brother, now in his mid-20s, lived at home and was a burden on the family. Several times a week a major battle erupted, complete with shouting, pushing, and shoving, as each member of the family blamed the others for all their problems. The mother, a strong woman, was clearly the peacemaker responsible for holding the family together. Approximately every 6 months, usually after a family battle, the mother totally lost her memory and the family had her admitted to the hospital. After a few days away from the turmoil, the mother regained her memory and went home, only to repeat the cycle in the coming months. Although we did not treat this family (they lived too far away), the situation resolved itself when the children moved away and the stress decreased.

---

Far more common than general amnesia is **localized,** or *selective* **amnesia,** a failure to recall specific events, usually traumatic, that occur during a specific period (Fraser, 1994). Dissociative amnesia is common during war (Cardeña & Gleaves, 2003; Loewenstein, 1991). Sackeim and Devanand (1991) describe the interesting case of a woman whose father had deserted her when she was young. She had also been forced to have an abortion at the age

---

**dissociative amnesia**   Dissociative disorder featuring the inability to recall personal information, usually of a stressful or traumatic nature.

**generalized amnesia**   Condition in which the person loses memory of all personal information, including his or her own identity.

**localized amnesia**   Memory loss limited to specific times and events, particularly traumatic events. Also known as *selective amnesia.*

of 14. Years later, she came for treatment for frequent headaches. In therapy she reported early events (e.g., the abortion) rather matter of factly; but under hypnosis she would relive, with intense emotion, the early abortion and remember that subsequently she was raped by the abortionist. She also had images of her father attending a funeral for her aunt, one of the few times she ever saw him. Upon awakening from the hypnotic state she had no memory of emotionally reexperiencing these events, and she wondered why she had been crying. In this case the woman did not have amnesia for the *events themselves* but rather for her intense *emotional reactions to the events*. In most cases of dissociative amnesia, the forgetting is selective for traumatic events or memories rather than generalized.

A possible case of dissociative amnesia that arose fairly recently in the Canadian legal system is the first degree murder trial of Kenneth Mackay in Saskatoon (CBC Saskatchewan, 2003). Mackay was charged with killing Crystal Paskemin in 2000. Although Mackay admitted to having run over the victim with his truck, which he claims was an accident, he cannot explain why the victim's body was found burned. His defence lawyer claimed that Mackay had forgotten about burning the victim's body because of the trauma of the accident. In fact, a memory expert testified in court that Mackay may have had dissociative amnesia (CBC Saskatchewan, 2003). Despite the expert witness testimony, the jury rejected his defence, and Mackay was sentence to life in prison with no possibility of parole for 25 years (O'Hara, 2004).

## Disorder Criteria Summary
### Dissociative Amnesia

Features of dissociative amnesia include:

- One or more episodes of inability to recall important personal information, usually of a traumatic or stressful nature, that is too extensive to be explained as ordinary forgetfulness
- Episodes are not related to a medical condition, psychological effects of a substance (e.g., a drug of abuse), or a separate psychological disorder
- Inability to recall causes clinically significant distress or impairment in functioning

*Source:* Reprinted with permission from the *Diagnostic and Statistical Manual of Mental Disorders*, Fourth Edition, Text Revision. (Copyright © 2000) American Psychiatric Association.

## Dissociative Fugue

A related disorder is referred to as **dissociative fugue,** with *fugue* literally meaning "flight" (*fugitive* is from the same root). In these curious cases,

memory loss revolves around a specific incident—an unexpected trip (or trips). Mostly, individuals just take off and later find themselves in a new place, unable to remember why or how they got there. Usually they have left behind an intolerable situation. During these trips a person sometimes assumes a new identity or at least becomes confused about the old identity. One famous case of likely dissociative fugue is that of British writer Agatha Christie who disappeared from her home with associated memory loss after the death of her mother and learning of her husband's extramarital affair (Phillip, 2003). In a similar case, Alderwoman Darlene (Dar) Heatherington from Lethbridge, Alberta, vanished while on business in Great Falls, Montana, in May 2003. She went missing after renting a bicycle for a ride in the park, and Great Falls launched a large-scale search for her. Three days later she was found disoriented in a Las Vegas

© Bettmann/CORBIS

Famous British mystery writer Agatha Christie once disappeared from her home for 11 days. Her memory loss and flight from home were reportedly triggered by the stresses of the recent death of her mother and knowledge of her husband's extramarital affair.

**dissociative fugue** Dissociative disorder featuring sudden, unexpected travel from home, along with an inability to recall one's past, sometimes with assumption of a new identity.

hotel parking lot (CTV.ca, 2003). Although the circumstances surrounding Dar Heatherington's trip to Las Vegas remain unclear, at first glance her story bears some striking similarities to the disappearance of Agatha Christie (Phillip, 2003). For example, before her disappearance, Ms. Heatherington was stressed because of overwork and reportedly being stalked (c-News, 2003; Harrington, 2003). However, later evidence emerged that suggest that Dar Heatherington likely did not experience a dissociative fugue, although Agatha Christie may have.

Consider next the case of the misbehaving sheriff.

## The Misbehaving Sheriff

Aktar and Brenner (1979) describe a 46-year-old sheriff who reported at least three episodes of dissociative fugue. On each occasion he found himself as far as 300 kilometres from his home. When he came to he immediately called his wife, but he was never able to completely recall what he did while he was away, sometimes for several days. During treatment the sheriff remembered who he was during these trips. Despite his occupation, he became the outlaw type he had always secretly admired. He adopted an alias, drank heavily, mingled with a rough crowd, and went to brothels and wild parties.

---

Dissociative amnesia and fugue states seldom appear before adolescence and usually occur in adulthood. It is rare for these states to appear for the first time after an individual reaches the age of 50 (Sackeim & Devanand, 1991). However, once they do appear, they may continue well into old age.

Fugue states usually end rather abruptly, like those of the misbehaving sheriff, and the individual returns home recalling most, if not all, of what happened. In this disorder, the disintegrated experience is more than memory loss, involving at least some disintegration of identity if not the complete adoption of a new one.

An apparently distinct dissociative disorder not found in Western cultures is called *amok* (as in "running amok"). Most people with this disorder are males. Amok has attracted attention because individuals in this trancelike state often brutally assault and sometimes kill people or animals. If the person is not killed himself, he probably will not remember the episode. Running amok is only one of a number of "running" syndromes in which an individual enters a trancelike state and suddenly, imbued with a mysterious source of energy, runs or

flees for a long time. Except for amok, the prevalence of running disorders is somewhat greater in women, as with most dissociative disorders. Among the Inuit, for example, running disorder is termed *pivloktoq*. Despite their different culturally determined expression, running disorders seem to meet criteria for dissociative fugue, with the possible exception of amok.

**Disorder Criteria Summary**
Dissociative Fugue

Features of dissociative fugue include:
• Sudden, unexpected travel from home or customary place of work, with inability to recall one's past
• Confusion about personal identity or assumption of new identity (partial or complete)
• Disturbance doesn't occur exclusively during the course of dissociative identity disorder and is not caused by a substance or a general medical condition
• Disturbance causes clinically significant distress or impairment of functioning

*Source:* Reprinted with permission from the *Diagnostic and Statistical Manual of Mental Disorders*, Fourth Edition, Text Revision. (Copyright © 2000) American Psychiatric Association.

## *Dissociative Trance Disorder*

Dissociative disorders differ in important ways across cultures. In many areas of the world, dissociative phenomena may occur as a trance or possession. The usual sorts of dissociative symptoms, such as sudden changes in personality, are attributed to possession by a spirit important in the particular culture. Often this spirit demands and receives presents or favours from the family and friends of the victim. Like other dissociative states, trance disorder seems to be most common in women and is often associated with stress or trauma, which, as in dissociative amnesia and fugue states, is current rather than in the past.

Trance and possession are a common part of some traditional religious and cultural practices and are not considered abnormal in that context. Dissociative trances commonly occur in India, Nigeria (where they are called *vinvusa*), Thailand *(phii pob)*, and other Asian and African countries (Mezzich et al., 1992; Saxena & Prasad, 1989). In North America, culturally accepted dissociation commonly occurs during African American prayer meetings (Griffith et al., 1980), First Nations sweat lodge ceremonies (Jilek, 1982), and Puerto Rican spiritist sessions (Comas-Diaz, 1981). Among Bahamians and Blacks from the southern United States, trance syndromes are often referred to colloquially as "falling out."

Only when the state is *undesirable* and considered pathological by members of the culture is it defined as a **dissociative trance disorder.** Although trance and possession are almost never seen in Western cultures, they are among the most common forms of dissociative disorders elsewhere. A category to include these states has been proposed for a future edition of DSM.

## Disorder Criteria Summary
### Trance and Possession Disorder

Features of trance and possession disorder include:
- (1) Trance—a temporary, marked alteration in the state of consciousness or loss of customary sense of personal identity associated with a narrowing or awareness of immediate surroundings or stereotyped behaviours or movements that are experienced as being beyond the person's control
- (2) Possession trance—a single or episodic alteration in the state of consciousness characterized by the replacement of customary sense of personal identity by a new identity, often a spirit, power, deity, or other person
- The condition is not accepted as a normal part of a collective cultural or religious practice
- The trance or possession state causes clinically significant distress or impairment in functioning

*Source:* Reprinted with permission from the *Diagnostic and Statistical Manual of Mental Disorders,* Fourth Edition, Text Revision. (Copyright © 2000) American Psychiatric Association.

## Dissociative Identity Disorder

People with **dissociative identity disorder (DID)** may adopt as many as 100 new identities, all simultaneously coexisting. In some cases, the identities are complete, each with its own behaviour, tone of voice, and physical gestures. But in many cases, only a few characteristics are distinct, because the identities are only partially independent. Consider the case of Jonah, originally reported by Ludwig, Brandsma, Wilbur, Bendfeldt, and Jameson (1972).

## Jonah
### Bewildering Blackouts

Jonah, a 27 year old Black man, experienced severe headaches that were unbearably painful and lasted for increasingly longer periods. Furthermore, he couldn't remember things that happened while he had a headache, except that sometimes a great deal of time passed. Finally, after a particularly bad night, when he could stand it no longer, he arranged for admission to the local hospital. What really prompted Jonah to come to the hospital, however, was that other people told him what he did during his severe headaches. For example, he was told that the night before he had a violent fight with another man and attempted to stab him. He fled the scene and was shot at during a high-speed chase by the police. His wife told him that during a previous headache he chased her and his 3-year-old daughter out of the house, threatening them with a butcher knife. During his headaches, and while he was violent, he called himself "Usoffa Abdulla, son of Omega." Once he attempted to drown a man in a river. The man survived and Jonah escaped by swimming half a kilometre upstream. He woke up the next morning in his own bed, soaking wet, with no memory of the incident.

### Clinical Description

During Jonah's hospitalization, the staff was able to observe his behaviour directly, both when he had headaches and during other periods that he did not remember. He claimed other names at these times, acted differently, and generally seemed to be another person entirely. The staff distinguished three separate identities, or **alters,** in addition to Jonah. (*Alters* is the shorthand term for the different identities or personalities in DID.) The first alter was named Sammy. Sammy seemed rational, calm, and in control. The second alter, King Young, seemed to be in charge of all sexual activity and was particularly interested in having as many heterosexual interactions as possible. The third alter was the violent and dangerous Usoffa Abdulla. Characteristically, Jonah knew nothing of the three alters. Sammy was most aware of the other personalities. King Young and Usoffa Abdulla knew a little bit about the others but only indirectly.

---

**dissociative trance disorder (DTD)** Altered state of consciousness in which the person believes firmly that he or she is possessed by spirits; considered a disorder only where there is distress and dysfunction.

**dissociative identity disorder (DID)** Formerly known as multiple personality disorder; a disorder in which as many as 100 personalities or fragments of personalities coexist within one body and mind.

**alters** Shorthand term for alter egos, the different personalities or identities in dissociative identity disorder.

In the hospital, psychologists determined that Sammy first appeared when Jonah was about 6, immediately after Jonah saw his mother stab his father. Jonah's mother sometimes dressed him as a girl in private. On one of these occasions, shortly after Sammy emerged, King Young appeared. When Jonah was 9 or 10 he was brutally attacked by a group of White youths. At this point Usoffa Abdulla emerged, announcing that his sole reason for existence was to protect Jonah.

DSM-IV-TR criteria for DID include amnesia, as in dissociative amnesia and dissociative fugue. Here, however, identity has also fragmented. How many personalities live inside one body is relatively unimportant, whether there are 3, 4, or even 100 of them. Rather, the defining feature of this disorder is that certain aspects of the person's identity are dissociated. For this reason, the name was changed in DSM-IV from multiple personality disorder to DID. This change also corrects the notion that multiple people somehow live inside one body.

## Characteristics

The person who becomes the patient and asks for treatment is usually a "host" identity. Host personalities usually attempt to hold various fragments of identity together but end up being overwhelmed. The first personality to seek treatment is seldom the original personality of the person. Usually the host personality develops later (Putnam, 1992). Many patients have at least one impulsive alter who handles sexuality and generates income, sometimes by acting as a prostitute. In other cases all alters may abstain from sex. Cross-gendered alters are not uncommon. For example, a small agile woman might have a strong powerful male alter who serves as a protector.

The transition from one personality to another is called a *switch*. Usually the switch is instantaneous (although in movies and television it is often drawn out for dramatic effect). Physical transformations may occur during switches. Posture, facial expressions, patterns of facial wrinkling, and even physical disabilities may emerge. In one study, changes in handedness occurred in 37% of the cases (Putnam, Guroff, Silberman, Barban, & Post, 1986).

## Can DID Be Faked?

Are the fragmented identities "real," or is the person faking them to avoid responsibility or stress? As with conversion disorders, it is difficult to answer this question, for several reasons (Kluft, 1999). First, evidence indicates that individuals with DID are suggestible (Bliss, 1984). It is possible that alters are created in response to leading questions from therapists, either during psychotherapy or while the person is in a hypnotic state.

### Disorder Criteria Summary
#### Dissociative Identity Disorder (DID)

Features of DID include:
- The presence of two or more distinct identities or personality states, each with its own relatively enduring pattern
- At least two of these identities or personality states recurrently take control of the person's behaviour
- Inability to recall important information that is too extensive to be explained by ordinary forgetfulness
- Disturbance not caused by direct physiological effects of a substance (e.g., alcohol intoxication) or general medical condition

*Source:* Reprinted with permission from the *Diagnostic and Statistical Manual of Mental Disorders*, Fourth Edition, Text Revision. (Copyright © 2000) American Psychiatric Association.

## The Hillside Strangler

During the late 1970s, Kenneth Bianchi brutally raped and murdered 10 young women in the Los Angeles area and left their bodies naked and in full view on the sides of various hills. Despite overwhelming evidence that Bianchi was the "Hillside Strangler," he continued to assert his innocence, prompting some professionals to think he might have DID. His lawyer brought in a clinical psychologist, who hypnotized him and asked whether there were another part of Ken with whom he could speak. Guess what? Somebody called "Steve" answered and said he had done all the killing. Steve also said that Ken knew nothing about the murders. With this evidence, the lawyer entered a plea of not guilty by reason of insanity.

The defence called on the late Martin Orne, a distinguished clinical psychologist and psychiatrist who was one of the world's leading experts on hypnosis and dissociative disorders (Orne, Dinges, & Orne, 1984). Orne used procedures similar to those we described in the context of conversion blindness to determine whether Bianchi was simulating DID or had a true psychological disorder. For example, Orne suggested during an in-depth interview with Bianchi that a true multiple personality disorder included at least three personalities. Bianchi soon produced a third personality. By interviewing Bianchi's friends and relatives, Orne established that there was no independent corroboration of different personalities before

Bianchi's arrest. Psychological tests also failed to show significant differences among the personalities; true fragmented identities often score differently on personality tests. Several textbooks on psychopathology were found in Bianchi's room; therefore, he presumably had studied the subject. Orne concluded that Bianchi responded like someone simulating hypnosis, not someone deeply hypnotized. On the basis of Orne's testimony, Bianchi was found guilty and sentenced to life in prison.

Some investigators have studied the ability of individuals to fake dissociative experiences. Carleton University psychologist Nicholas Spanos (now deceased) conducted important work on this issue. Spanos, Weeks, and Bertrand (1985) demonstrated in an experiment that a university student could simulate an alter if it was suggested that faking was plausible, as in the interview with Bianchi. All the students in the group were told to play the role of an accused murderer claiming his innocence. The subjects received exactly the same interview as Bianchi, word for word. More than 80% simulated an alternate personality to avoid conviction. Groups that were given vaguer instructions, and no direct suggestion an alternate personality might exist, were much less likely to use one in their defence.

These findings on faking and the effect of hypnosis led Spanos (1996) to suggest that the symptoms of DID could be accounted for by therapists who inadvertently suggested the existence of alters to suggestible individuals, a model known as the *sociocognitive model* because the possibility of identity fragments and early trauma is socially reinforced by a therapist (Lilienfeld et al., 1999). A recent survey of American psychiatrists showed little consensus on the scientific validity of DID, with only one-third in the sample believing that the diagnosis should have been included without reservation in DSM-IV-TR (Pope, Oliva, Hudson, Bodkin, & Gruber, 1999). A similar study of Canadian psychiatrists showed that fewer than one-third had no reservations about including DID in the DSM-IV-TR (Lalonde, Hudson, Gigante, & Pope, 2001). Canadian psychiatrists were significantly more skeptical about the legitimacy of the DID diagnosis than were the American psychiatrists. (We return to this point of view when we discuss false memories.)

On the other hand, some objective tests suggest that many people with fragmented identities are not consciously and voluntarily simulating (Kluft, 1991, 1999). For example, a study by University of British Columbia psychologist Eric Eich and his colleagues (Eich, Macaulay, Loewenstein, & Dihle, 1997a) compared the performance of real DID patients and simulators on objective memory tests. They found that "interpersonality amnesia" (i.e., in which events experienced by a particular personality state of identity are retrievable by the same identity but not by a different one; Eich et al., 1997b) could not be explained by deliberate simulating. In another study, Condon, Ogston, and Pacoe (1969) examined a film about Chris Sizemore, the real-life subject of the book and movie *The Three Faces of Eve*. They determined that one of the personalities (Eve Black) showed a *transient microstrabismus* (divergence in conjugant lateral eye movements) that was not observed in the other personalities.

### Statistics

Jonah had 4 identities, but the average number of alter personalities is reported by clinicians as closer to 15 (Ross, 1997; Sackeim & Devanand, 1991). Of people with DID, the ratio of females to males is as high as 9:1, although these data are based on accumulated case studies rather than survey research (Maldonado, Butler, & Spiegel, 1998). The onset is almost always in childhood, often as young as 4 years of age, although it is usually approximately 7 years after the appearance of symptoms before the disorder is identified (Maldonado et al., 1998; Putnam et al., 1986). Once established, the disorder tends to last a lifetime in the absence of treatment. The form it takes does not seem to vary substantially over the person's life span, although some evidence indicates the frequency of switching decreases with age (Sackeim & Devanand, 1991). Different personalities may emerge in response to new life situations, as was the case with Jonah.

Chris Sizemore's history of dissociative identity disorder was dramatized in *The Three Faces of Eve*.

AP/Wide World Photos

We don't have good epidemiological studies on the prevalence of the disorder in the population at large, although investigators think it is more common than previously estimated (Kluft, 1991; Ross, 1997). Semistructured interviews of large numbers of inpatients with severe disturbances found prevalence rates of DID of between 3% and 6% in Canada and the United States (Horen, Leichner, & Lawson, 1995; Ross, Anderson, Fleisher, & Norton, 1991) and approximately 2% in Holland (Friedl & Draijer, 2000). Additional studies in non-clinical samples, conducted in Winnipeg (Ross, 1991, 1997), suggest that between 0.5% and 1% of these large samples (more than 400 in each) suffer from DID.

A very large percentage of DID patients have simultaneous psychological disorders that may include substance abuse, depression, somatization disorder, borderline personality disorder, panic attacks, and eating disorders (Kluft, 1999; Ross et al., 1990). In one sample of over 100 patients, more than seven additional diagnoses were noted on the average (Ellason & Ross, 1997). Another study of 42 patients documented a pattern of severe comorbid personality disorders, including severe borderline pathology (Dell, 1998). It seems likely that different personalities will present with differing patterns of comorbidity, but the research has not yet been done. In some cases this high rate of comorbidity may reflect that certain disorders, such as borderline personality disorder, share many features with DID—for example, self-destructive, sometimes suicidal behaviour and emotional instability. For the most part, however, the high frequency of additional disorders accompanying DID simply reflects an intensely severe reaction to what seems to be in almost all cases horrible child abuse.

Because auditory hallucinations are common, DID is often misdiagnosed as a psychotic disorder. But the voices in DID are reported by patients as coming from inside their heads, not outside as in psychotic disorders. Because patients with DID are usually aware the voices are hallucinations, they don't report them and try to suppress them. These voices often encourage doing something against the person's will, so some individuals, particularly in other cultures, appear to be possessed by demons (Putnam, 1997). Although systematic studies are lacking, DID seems to occur in a variety of cultures throughout the world (Boon & Draijer, 1993; Ross, 1997). For example, Coons, Bowman, Kluft, and Milstein (1991) found reports of DID in 21 countries.

## Causes

It is informative to examine current evidence on causes for all dissociative disorders, as we do later, but our emphasis here is on the etiology of DID. Life circumstances that encourage the development of DID seem clear in at least one respect. Almost every patient presenting with this disorder reports that he or she was horribly, often unspeakably, abused as a child.

## Sybil
### A Childhood Drama

You may have seen the movie that was based on Sybil's biography (Schreiber, 1973). Sybil's mother had schizophrenia and her father refused or was unable to intervene in the mother's brutality. Day after day throughout her childhood, Sybil was sexually tortured and occasionally nearly murdered. Before she was 1 year old, her mother began tying her up in various ways and, on occasion, suspending her from the ceiling. Many mornings her mother placed Sybil on the kitchen table and forcefully inserted various objects into her vagina. Sybil's mother reasoned, psychotically, that she was preparing her daughter for adult sex. In fact, she so brutally tore the child's vaginal canal that scars were evident during adult gynecological exams. Sybil was also given strong laxatives but prohibited from using the bathroom. Because of her father's detachment and the normal appearance of the family, the abuse continued without interruption throughout Sybil's childhood.

Imagine you are a child in a situation like this. What can you do? You're too young to run away. You're too young to call the authorities. Although the pain may be unbearable, you have no way of knowing it is unusual or wrong. But you can do one thing! You can escape into a fantasy world; you can be somebody else. If the escape blunts the physical and emotional pain just for a minute or makes the next hour bearable, chances are you'll escape again. Your mind learns there is no limit to the identities that can be created as needed. Fifteen? A hundred? Such numbers have been recorded in some cases. You do whatever it takes to get through life. Most surveys report a very high rate of childhood trauma in cases of DID (Gleaves, 1996; Ross, 1997). Putnam et al. (1986) examined 100 cases and found that 97% of the patients had experienced significant trauma, usually sexual or physical abuse. Sixty-eight percent reported incest. A four-site study by Colin Ross and colleagues (1990) was conducted on identified cases of DID from Winnipeg, Utah, California, and Ottawa. They found that, of 102 cases, 95% reported physical or sexual abuse. Unfortunately, the abuse seems often as bizarre and sadistic as what Sybil suffered. Some children were buried alive. Some were tortured with matches, steam irons, razor blades, or glass. Investigators have corroborated the existence of at least some early sexual abuse in 12 patients with DID, whose backgrounds were extensively investigated by examining early records, interviewing relatives and acquaintances, and so on (Lewis, Yeager, Swica, Pincus, & Lewis, 1997). Nonetheless, Kluft (1996, 1999) notes that some reports by patients are not true but have been confabulated (made up).

Not all the trauma is caused by abuse. Putnam (1992) describes a young girl in a war zone who saw both her parents blown to bits in a minefield. In a heart-wrenching response, she tried to piece the bodies back together, bit by bit.

Such observations have led to wide-ranging agreement that DID is rooted in a natural tendency to escape or "dissociate" from the unremitting negative affect associated with severe abuse (Kluft, 1984, 1991). A lack of social support during or after the abuse also seems implicated. A study of 428 adolescent twins by Waller and Ross (1997) demonstrated that a surprisingly high 33% to 50% of the variance in dissociative experience could be attributed to a chaotic, non-supportive family environment. The remainder of the variance was associated with individual experience and personality factors.

The behaviour and emotions that make up disorders seem related to otherwise normal tendencies present in all of us to some extent. It is common for otherwise normal individuals to escape in some way from emotional or physical pain (Butler, Duran, Jasiukaitis, Koopman, & Spiegel, 1996; Spiegel & Cardeña, 1991). Noyes and Kletti (1977) surveyed more than 100 survivors of various life-threatening situations and found that most had experienced some type of dissociation, such as feelings of unreality, a blunting of emotional and physical pain, and even separation from their bodies. Dissociative amnesia and fugue states are clearly reactions to severe life stress. But the life stress or trauma is in the present rather than in the past, as in the case of the overwrought mother who suffered from dissociative amnesia. Many patients are escaping legal difficulties or severe stress at home or on the job (Sackeim & Devanand, 1991). But sophisticated statistical analyses indicate that "normal" dissociative reactions differ substantially from the pathological experiences we've described (Waller, Putnam, & Carlson, 1996; Waller & Ross, 1997) and that at least some people do not develop severe pathological dissociative experiences no matter how extreme the stress. These findings are consistent with our diathesis–stress model in that only with the appropriate vulnerabilities (the diathesis) will a person react to stress with pathological dissociation.

You may have noticed that DID seems similar in its etiology to posttraumatic stress disorder (PTSD). Both conditions feature strong emotional reactions to experiencing a severe trauma (Butler et al., 1996). But remember that not everyone goes on to experience PTSD after severe trauma. Only people who are biologically and psychologically vulnerable to anxiety are at risk for developing PTSD in response to moderate levels of trauma.

There is a growing body of opinion that DID is an extreme subtype of PTSD, with a much greater emphasis on the process of dissociation than on symptoms of anxiety, although both are present in each disorder (Butler et al., 1996). Some evidence also shows that the "developmental window" of vulnerability to the abuse that leads to DID closes around 9 years of age (Putnam, 1997). After that, DID is unlikely to develop, although severe PTSD might. If true, this is a particularly good example of the role of development in the etiology of psychopathology.

We also must remember that we know relatively little about DID. Our conclusions are based on retrospective case studies or correlations rather than on the prospective examination of people who may have undergone the severe trauma that seems to lead to DID (Kihlstrom, Glisky, & Anguilo, 1994). Therefore, it is hard to say what psychological or biological factors might contribute, but there are hints concerning individual differences that might play a role.

**Suggestibility**   Suggestibility is a personality trait distributed normally across the population, much like weight and height. Some people are much more suggestible than others, some are relatively immune to suggestibility, and the majority fall in the midrange.

Did you ever have an imaginary childhood playmate? Many people did, and it is one sign of the ability to lead a rich fantasy life, which can be helpful and adaptive. But it also seems to correlate with being suggestible or easily hypnotized (some people equate the terms *suggestibility* and *hypnotizability*). A hypnotic trance is also similar to dissociation (Bliss, 1986; Butler et al., 1996). People in a trance tend to be focused on one aspect of their world, and they become vulnerable to suggestions by the hypnotist. There is also the phenomenon of self-hypnosis, in which individuals can dissociate from most of the world around them and "suggest" to themselves that, for example, they won't feel pain in one of their hands.

According to the *autohypnotic model*, people who are suggestible may be able to use dissociation as a defence against extreme trauma (Putnam, 1991). According to the work of Colin Ross and his colleagues, as many as 50% of DID patients clearly remember imaginary playmates in childhood (Ross et al., 1990); whether they were created before or

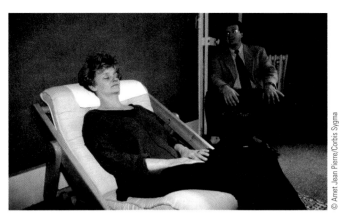

A person in a hypnotic trance is suggestible and may become absorbed in a particular experience.

after the trauma is not entirely clear. When the trauma becomes unbearable, the person's very identity splits into multiple dissociated identities. Children's ability to distinguish clearly between reality and fantasy as they grow older may be what closes the developmental window for developing DID around age 9. People who are less suggestible may develop a severe posttraumatic stress reaction but not a dissociative reaction. Once again, these explanations are speculative because there are no controlled studies of this phenomenon (Kihlstrom et al., 1994).

**Biological Contributions**   As in PTSD, where the evidence is more solid, there is almost certainly a biological vulnerability to DID, but it is difficult to pinpoint. For example, in the large twin study mentioned earlier (Waller & Ross, 1997), none of the variance or identifiable causal factors were attributable to heredity: All of them were environmental. In contrast, another twin study by Kerry Jang, John Livesley, and their colleagues found evidence for a strong genetic contribution to dissociative disorder symptoms. About half the variance in dissociative symptoms was attributable to genetic factors (Jang, Paris, Zweig-Frank, & Livesley, 1998). Given these inconsistent findings, more research is clearly needed on the role of genetic factors.

Interesting observations may provide some hints about brain activity during dissociation. Individuals with certain neurological disorders, particularly seizure disorders, experience many dissociative symptoms (Bowman & Coons, 2000; Cardeña, Lewis-Fernandez, Bear, Pakianathan, & Spiegel, 1996). Devinsky, Feldman, Burrowes, and Bromfield (1989) reported that approximately 6% of patients with temporal lobe epilepsy reported "out of body" experiences. About 50% of another series of patients with temporal lobe epilepsy displayed some kinds of dissociative symptoms (Schenk & Bear, 1981), including alternate identities or identity fragments.

Patients with dissociative experiences who have seizure disorders are clearly different from those who do not (Ross, 1997). The patients with seizures develop dissociative symptoms in adulthood that are not associated with trauma, in clear contrast to DID patients without seizure disorders. This is certainly an area for future study (Putnam, 1991).

Head injury and resulting brain damage may induce amnesia or other types of dissociative experience. But these conditions are usually easily diagnosed because they are generalized and irreversible and associated with an identifiable head trauma (Butler et al., 1996).

### Real Memories and False

One of the most controversial issues in the field of abnormal psychology today concerns the extent to which memories of early trauma, particularly sexual abuse, are accurate. Some suggest that many such memories are simply the result of strong suggestions by careless therapists. The stakes in this controversy are enormous, with considerable opportunity for harm to innocent people on each side of the controversy, as has been noted by Clare MacMartin and A. Daniel Yarmey (1999) at the University of Guelph.

On the one hand, if early sexual abuse occurred but is not remembered because of dissociative amnesia, it is crucially important to re-experience aspects of the trauma under the direction of a skilled therapist to relieve current suffering. Without therapy, the patient is likely to suffer from PTSD or a dissociative disorder indefinitely. It is also important that perpetrators are held accountable for their actions, perhaps through the legal system, because abuse of this type is a crime, and prevention is an important goal. Connie Kristiansen and her colleagues at Carleton University have expressed concern that because of the validity of recovered memories has been questioned, this may discourage those who have been abused from speaking out about their abuse, decreasing the chance that perpetrators of abuse will be punished for their crimes (e.g., Kristiansen, Gareau, Mittlehold, DeCourville, & Hovdestad, 1999).

On the other hand, if memories of early trauma are inadvertently created in response to a careless therapist, but seem real to the patient, false accusations against loved ones could lead to irreversible family breakup and, perhaps, unjust prison sentences for those falsely accused as perpetrators. In recent years, allegedly inaccurate accusations as a result of false memories have led to substantial lawsuits against therapists and awards of millions of dollars in damages. As with most issues that reach this level of contention and disagreement, it is clear that the final answer will not involve an all-or-none resolution. There is incontrovertible evidence that false memories *can* be created by reasonably well-understood psychological processes (Ceci, 2003; Loftus, 2003). But there is also good evidence that early traumatic experiences can cause selective dissociative amnesia, with substantial implications for psychological functioning (Gleaves, Smith, Butler, & Spiegel, 2004; Kluft, 1999).

Victims of accusations deriving from allegedly false memories have formed a society called the False Memory Syndrome Foundation. One goal is to educate the legal profession and the public about false memories after psychotherapy so that, in the absence of other objective evidence, such "memories" cannot be used to convict innocent people.

Evidence supporting the existence of distorted or illusory memories comes from lab-based experiments conducted by cognitive psychologists. For example, a study by Stephen Porter at Dalhousie University and John Yuille and Darrin Lehman (1999) at the University of British Columbia tested whether it is possible to "remember" a highly emotional event that never actually occurred. These researchers first contracted participants' parents to learn about which of a variety of stressful events (e.g., being seriously attacked by an animal) each participant had actually been exposed to as a child. Then, participants were brought into the laboratory and were encouraged by interviewers to "recover" a memory for a false event using guided imagery and repeated attempts to retrieve the memory. The false events were presented to the participants as actually having happened to them, according to their parents' reports. A shockingly large number of participants "recovered" a full (26%) or partial (another 30%) memory for the false experience.

But there is also plenty of evidence that therapists need to be sensitive to signs of trauma that may not be fully remembered in patients presenting with symptoms of dissociative or posttraumatic stress disorders. Even if patients are unable to report or remember early trauma, it can sometimes be confirmed through corroborating evidence (Coons, 1994). In one study, Williams (1994) interviewed 129 women with previously documented histories, such as hospital records, of having been sexually abused as children. Thirty-eight percent did not recall the incidents that had been reported to authorities at least 17 years earlier, even with extensive probing of their abuse histories. Although "forgetting" or other reasons for not disclosing are present, it is possible that some subjects "repressed" their memories.

In another study, Elliot (1997) surveyed 364 individuals out of a larger group who had experienced substantial trauma such as a natural disaster, car accident, or physical abuse. Fully 32% reported delayed recall of the event, which suggested at least temporary dissociative amnesia. The severity of the trauma predicted the extent of the amnesia, and the most common trigger for recalling the trauma was a media presentation, such as a movie. As Brewin, Andrews, and Gotlib (1993) also point out, the available data from cognitive science do not necessarily support an extreme reconstructive model of (false) memory induced by careless therapists, because most individuals can recall important details of their childhood, particularly if they are unique and unexpected.

How will this controversy be resolved? Because false memories can be created through strong repeated suggestions by an authority figure, therapists must be fully aware of the conditions under which this is likely to occur, particularly when dealing with young children. This requires extensive knowledge of the workings of memory and other aspects of psychological functioning and illustrates, once again, the dangers of dealing with inexperienced or inadequately trained psychotherapists. Elaborate tales of satanic abuse of children under the care of elderly women in daycare centres are most likely cases of memories implanted by aggressive and careless therapists or law enforcement officials (Lilienfeld et al., 1999). In some cases, elderly caregivers have been sentenced to life in prison.

On the other hand, many people with dissociative and posttraumatic stress disorders have suffered documented extreme abuse and trauma, which could then become dissociated from awareness. It may be that future research will find that the severity of dissociative amnesia is directly related to the severity of the trauma in vulnerable individuals, and it is likely to be proved as qualitatively different from "normal" dissociative experiences (e.g., Kluft, 1999; Waller et al., 1996). In other words, are there two kinds of memories: traumatic memories that can be dissociated and "normal" memories that cannot? At present, this is the scientific crux of the issue.

Advocates on both sides of this issue agree that clinical science must proceed as quickly as possible to specify the processes under which the implantation of false memories is likely and to define the presenting features that indicate a real but dissociated traumatic experience (Lilienfeld et al., 1999; Pope, 1997). Until then, mental health professionals must be extremely careful not to prolong unnecessary suffering among both victims of actual abuse and victims falsely accused as abusers (Prout & Dobson, 1998).

## Treatment

Individuals who experience dissociative amnesia or a fugue state usually get better on their own and remember what they have forgotten. The episodes are so clearly related to current life stress that prevention of future episodes usually involves therapeutic resolution of the distressing situations and increasing the strength of personal coping mechanisms. When necessary, therapy focuses on recalling what happened during the amnesic or fugue states, often with the help of friends or family who know what happened, so that patients can confront the information and integrate it into their conscious experience. For more difficult cases, hypnosis or benzodiazepines (minor tranquillizers) have been used, with suggestions from the therapist that it is OK to remember the events (Maldonado et al., 1998).

For DID, however, the process is not so easy. With the person's very identity shattered into many different elements, reintegrating the personality might seem hopeless. Fortunately, this is not always the case. Although no controlled research has been reported on the effects of treatment, there are many documented successes of attempts to reintegrate identities through long-term psychotherapy (Ellason & Ross, 1997; Putnam, 1989). Nevertheless, the prognosis for most people remains guarded. Coon (1986) found that only 5 of 20 patients achieved a full integration of their identities. More recently, Ellason and Ross (1997) reported that 12 of 54 (22.2%) patients in Canada and the United States had achieved integration 2 years after presenting for treatment, which in most cases had been continuous. Russell Powell and his colleague have pointed out that these results could, of course, be attributed to other factors than therapy because no experimental comparison was present (Powell & Howell, 1998).

The strategies that therapists use today in treating DID are based on accumulated clinical wisdom and on procedures that have been successful with PTSD (Maldonado et al., 1998; see Chapter 4). The fundamental goal is to identify cues or triggers that provoke memories of trauma and/or dissociation and to neutralize them. More importantly, the patient must confront and relive the early trauma and gain control over the horrible events, at least as they recur in the patient's mind (Kluft, 1999; Ross, 1997). To instill this sense of control, the therapist must skillfully, and slowly, help the patient visualize and relive aspects of the trauma until it is simply a terrible memory instead of a current event. Because the memory is unconscious, aspects of the experience are often not known to either the patient or the therapist until they emerge during treatment. Hypnosis is often used to access unconscious memories and bring various alters into awareness. Because the process of dissociation may be similar to the process of hypnosis, the latter may be a particularly efficient way to access traumatic memories (Maldonado et al., 1998). (There is as yet no evidence that hypnosis is a *necessary* part of treatment.) We know that DID seems to run a chronic course and seldom improves spontaneously, which confirms that current treatments, primitive as they are, have some effectiveness.

It is possible that reemerging memories of trauma may trigger further dissociation. The therapist must guard against this happening. Trust is important to any therapeutic relationship, but it is essential in the treatment of DID. Occasionally, medication is combined with therapy, but there is little indication that it helps much. What little clinical evidence there is indicates that antidepressant drugs might be appropriate in some cases (Coon, 1986; Putnam & Loewenstein, 1993).

## Concept Check 5.2

Diagnose the dissociative disorders described here by choosing one of the following: (a) dissociative fugue, (b) depersonalization disorder, (c) generalized amnesia, (d) dissociative identity disorder, (e) localized amnesia.

1. Henry is 64 and recently arrived in town. He does not know where he is from or how he got here. His driver's licence proves his name, but he is unconvinced it is his. He is in good health and not taking any medication. _____

2. Karl was brought to a clinic by his mother. She was concerned because at times his behaviour was strange. His speech and his way of relating to people and situations would change dramatically, almost as if he were a different person. What bothered her and Karl most was that he could not recall anything he did during these periods. _____

3. Terry complained about feeling out of control. She said she felt sometimes as if she were floating under the ceiling and just watching things happen to her. She also experienced tunnel vision and felt uninvolved in the things that went on in the room around her. This always caused her to panic and perspire. _____

4. Ann was found wandering the streets, unable to recall any important personal information. After searching her purse and finding an address, doctors were able to contact her mother. They learned that Ann had just been in a terrible accident and was the only survivor. Ann could not remember her mother or any details of the accident. She was very distressed. _____

5. Carol cannot remember what happened last weekend. On Monday she was admitted to a hospital, suffering from cuts, bruises, and contusions. It also appeared that she had been sexually assaulted. _____

# Summary

## Somatoform Disorders

- Individuals with somatoform disorders are pathologically concerned with the appearance or functioning of their bodies and bring these concerns to the attention of health professionals, who usually find no identifiable medical basis for the physical complaints.
- There are several types of somatoform disorders. Hypochondriasis is a condition in which individuals believe they are seriously ill and become anxious over this possibility. Somatization disorder is characterized by a seemingly unceasing and wide-ranging pattern of physical complaints that dominate the individual's life and interpersonal relationships. In conversion disorder, there is physical malfunctioning, such as paralysis, without apparent physical problems. In pain disorder, psychological factors are judged to play a major role in maintaining physical suffering. In body dysmorphic disorder (BDD), a person who looks normal is obsessively preoccupied with some imagined defect in appearance (imagined ugliness).
- Distinguishing among conversion reactions, real physical disorders, and outright malingering, or faking, is sometimes difficult. Even more puzzling can be factitious disorder, in which the person's symptoms are feigned and under voluntary control, as with malingering, but for no apparent reason.
- The causes of somatoform disorders are not well understood, but some, including hypochondriasis and BDD, seem closely related to anxiety disorders.
- Treatment of somatoform disorders ranges from basic techniques of reassurance and social support to those meant to reduce stress and remove any secondary gain for the behaviour. Recently, specifically tailored cognitive-behavioural therapy has proved successful with hypochondriasis. Patients with BDD often turn to plastic surgery, which more often than not increase their preoccupation and distress.

## Dissociative Disorders

- Dissociative disorders are characterized by alterations in perceptions: a sense of detachment from the self, the world, or memories.
- Dissociative disorders include depersonalization disorder, in which the individual's sense of personal reality is temporarily lost (depersonalization), as is the reality of the external world (derealization). In dissociative amnesia, the individual may be unable to remember important personal information. In generalized amnesia, the individual is unable to remember anything; more commonly, the individual is unable to recall specific events that occur during a specific period (localized or selective amnesia). In dissociative fugue, memory loss is combined with an unexpected trip (or trips). In the extreme, new identities, or alters, may be formed, as in dissociative identity disorder (DID). Finally, the newly defined dissociative trance disorder is considered to cover dissociations that may be culturally determined.
- The causes of dissociative disorders are not well understood but often seem related to the tendency to escape psychologically from memories of traumatic events.
- Treatment of dissociative disorders involves helping the patient reexperience the traumatic events in a controlled therapeutic manner to develop better coping skills. In the case of DID, therapy is often long term and may include antidepressant drugs. Particularly essential with this disorder is a sense of trust between therapist and patient.

## Key Terms

| | | | |
|---|---|---|---|
| somatoform disorders, 178 | conversion disorder, 186 | derealization, 197 | dissociative fugue, 200 |
| dissociative disorders, 178 | malingering, 187 | depersonalization disorder, 198 | dissociative trance disorder (DTD), 202 |
| hypochondriasis, 179 | factitious disorder, 187 | dissociative amnesia, 199 | dissociative identity disorder (DID), 202 |
| somatization disorder, 183 | pain disorder, 191 | generalized amnesia, 199 | alters, 202 |
| | body dysmorphic disorder (BDD), 192 | localized amnesia, 199 | |

## Answers to Concept Checks

**5.1**  1. b  2. c  3. d  4. e  5. a

**5.2**  1. a  2. d  3. b  4. c  5. e

 ## InfoTrac College Edition

If your instructor ordered your book with InfoTrac College Edition, please explore this online library for additional readings, review, and a handy resource for short assignments. Go to:

**http://infotrac.thomsonlearning.com**

Enter these search terms: somatoform disorders, dissociation (psychology), body dysmorphic disorder, dissociative identity disorder, factitious disorder, somatization

 ## The Abnormal Psychology Book Companion Website

Go to **www.essentialsabnormalpsych.nelson.com** for practice quiz questions, Internet links, critical thinking exercises, and more.

 ## Abnormal Psychology Live CD-ROM

- **Doug, an Example of Body Dysmorphic Disorder:** This interview by Dr. Katharine Phillips, an authority on this disorder, shows how it cripples this man's life until he seeks treatment for it.

- **Rachel, an Example of Dissociative Identity Disorder:** These three clips explore her multiple personalities, how she copes with them, and how they emerge in response to threats within the environment.

**Thomson NOW!** **http://hed.nelson.com** Go to this site for the link to ThomsonNow™, your one-stop study shop. Take a Pretest for this chapter and ThomsonNow™ will generate a personalized Study Plan based on your test results! The Study Plan will identify the topics you need to review and direct you to online resources to help you master those topics. You can then take a Posttest to help you determine the concepts you have mastered and what you still need work on.

## Video Concept Review

For challenging concepts that typically need more than one explanation, Mark Durand provides a video review via ThomsonNow™ of the following topic:

- The differences among hypochondriasis, illness phobia, and the fear associated with panic disorder.

# Chapter Quiz

1. The primary symptom of hypochondriasis is:
   a. fear of developing a disease.
   b. fear of spreading a disease.
   c. fear of contact with diseased individuals.
   d. fear of currently having a disease.

2. Someone who presents with the following symptoms might have hypochondriasis.
   a. interpreting momentary flutters in the stomach as a sign of illness
   b. reluctance to visit the doctor for fear of having a panic attack
   c. enjoyment of the immediate attention received when visiting a doctor
   d. realization that the presence of an illness could qualify the individual for full-time disability benefits

3. Choose the scenario that best demonstrates a somatization disorder.
   a. Lisa reports that she has continuous nausea and is unable to work, but a medical exam finds no sign of illness. Lisa claims she only feels better when her husband stays home to nurse her.
   b. Eddie visits 11 different physicians in 6 months but is frustrated that no doctor seems able to make an adequate diagnosis.
   c. Sherry has physical complaints that have lasted at least 10 years. Her symptoms include pain in her feet, hands, and neck; alternating diarrhea and constipation; and difficulty walking. Sherry's physician cannot find any illness to account for these complaints.
   d. Pedro stops working because he thinks that his ears are twice the size they should be and that he looks like a freak. His therapist observes, however, that Pedro's ears are a normal size.

4. Hypochondriasis is related to _____, whereas somatization disorder is linked to _____.
   a. obsessive-compulsive disorder; schizotypal personality disorder
   b. dissociative disorder; obsessive-compulsive disorder
   c. psychotic disorders; anxiety disorders
   d. anxiety disorder; antisocial personality disorder

5. In factitious disorder:
   a. the individual is faking symptoms for personal gain.
   b. the individual is voluntarily producing the symptoms without any obvious financial or other external incentives.
   c. the individual is not in control of the symptoms but there is no physical explanation.
   d. the symptoms are caused by a yet-to-be-identified virus.

6. Jorge, a 19-year-old male, was hospitalized after his legs collapsed under him while walking to class. He could not regain his stance and has been unable to walk since, although he desperately wants to walk again. A neurological exam revealed no medical problem. Jorge's behaviour is consistent with:
   a. somatization disorder.
   b. conversion disorder.
   c. malingering.
   d. body dysmorphic disorder.

7. Mrs. Thompson brought her 4-year-old daughter, Carmen, to the emergency room, stating that the child had been vomiting nonstop throughout the morning. Carmen's condition improved over the course of several days. On the day of her discharge from the hospital, a nurse walked in as Mrs. Thompson was giving Carmen a drink of floor cleaner. Mrs. Thompson's behaviour is consistent with:
   a. parental hypochondriasis.
   b. Munchausen syndrome by proxy.
   c. conversion syndrome by proxy.
   d. parental somatization.

8. _____ describes the experience of losing a sense of your own reality, whereas _____ describes losing your sense of reality of the external world.
   a. Depersonalization; derealization
   b. Derealization; somatization
   c. Derealization; depersonalization
   d. Somatization; derealization

9. Michael's wife, Jennifer, reported him missing to the police in 1998. Two years later she saw Michael in an airport. He lived two states away from Jennifer, was married to another woman, and had two children with her. Michael told Jennifer that his name was Danny, not Michael, and that he had never met her before. Michael's presentation is consistent with:
   a. multiple personality disorder.
   b. dissociative trance disorder.
   c. dissociative identity disorder.
   d. dissociative fugue.

10. The different identities or personalities in dissociative identity disorder are called _____, whereas the change from one personality to another is called a _____.
    a. masks; transition
    b. faces; switch
    c. façades; transition
    d. alters; switch

*(See the Appendix on page 601 for answers.)*

# Exploring Somatoform and Dissociative Disorders

These two sets of disorders share some common features and are strongly linked historically as "hysterical neuroses." Both are relatively rare and not yet well understood.

## SOMATOFORM DISORDERS
Characterized by a pathological concern with physical functioning or appearance

### HYPOCHONDRIASIS

**Characteristics**

- Severe anxiety over physical problems that are medically undetectable
- Affects women and men equally
- May emerge at any age
- Evident in diverse cultures

Faulty interpretation of physical sensations

Additional physical symptoms

**CAUSES**

Intensified focus on symptoms

Increased anxiety

**Treatment**

- Psychotherapy to challenge illness perceptions
- Counseling and/or support groups to provide reassurance

### SOMATIZATION DISORDER

**Characteristics**

- Reports of multiple physical symptoms without a medical basis
- Runs in families; probably heritable basis
- Very rare—most prevalent among unmarried women in low socioeconomic groups
- Onset usually in adolescence; often persists into old age

Continual development of new symptoms

Eventual social isolation

**CAUSES**

Immediate sympathy and attention

**Treatment**

- Very hard to treat
- Cognitive-behavioural therapy (CBT) to provide reassurance, reduce stress, and minimize help-seeking behaviours
- Therapy to broaden basis for relating to others

### CONVERSION DISORDER

**Characteristics**

- Severe physical dysfunctioning (e.g., paralysis, blindness) without corresponding physical pathology
- Affected people are genuinely unaware that they can function normally
- May coincide with other problems, especially somatization disorder
- Most prevalent in low socio-economic groups, women, and men under extreme stress (e.g., soldiers)

Life stresses or psychological conflict

Social influences (symptoms learned from observing real illness or injury)

**CAUSES**

Reduced by incapacitating symptoms

**Treatment**

- Same as for somatization disorder, with emphasis on resolving life stress or conflict and reducing help-seeking behaviors

### BODY DYSMORPHIC DISORDER (BDD)

**Characteristics**

- Socially disabling preoccupation with a normal physical feature that is believed to be hideous ("imagined ugliness")
- Prevalence is not known; affects men and women equally
- Associated with obsessive-compulsive disorder

Intrusive, anxiety-provoking idea that individual has a physical defect apparent to everyone

Pathological attempts to "fix" the problem that prevents a more reality-based appraisal of the "defect"

**CAUSES**

Intensified focus on imagined defects accompanied by extreme self-consciousness

Increased anxiety

**Treatment**

- CBT treatments seem most effective
- Drug treatments can provide relief for some sufferers
- Without treatment, BDD lasts a lifetime

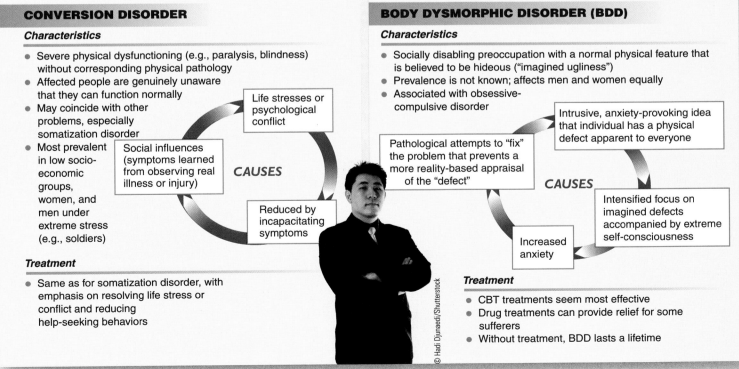

© Hadi Djunaedi/Shutterstock

# DISSOCIATIVE DISORDERS
Characterized by detachment from the self (depersonalization) and objective reality (derealization)

## DISSOCIATIVE IDENTITY DISORDER (DID)

### Characteristics

- Affected person adopts new identities, or alters, that coexist simultaneously. The alters may be complete and distinct personalities, or only partly independent.
- Average number of alters is 15
- Childhood onset; affects more women than men
- Patients often suffer from other psychological disorders simultaneously
- Rare outside of Western cultures

### Treatment

- Long-term psychotherapy may reintegrate separate personalities in 25% of patients
- Treatment of associated trauma similar to PTSD. Lifelong condition without treatment.

**CAUSES**

Similar etiology to posttraumatic stress disorder

Severe abuse during childhood
- Fantasy life is the only "escape"
- Practice becomes automatic, and then involuntary

High suggestibility a possible trait

Biological vulnerability likely

_Photodisc/Getty Images_

**CONTROVERSY**

The scientific community is divided over the question of whether multiple identities are a genuine experience or faked. Studies have shown that "false memories" can be created ("implanted") by therapists. Other tests confirm that various alters are physiologically distinct.

## DEPERSONALIZATION DISORDER

_© Brand X Pictures/Alamy_

### Characteristics

- Severe and frightening feelings of detachment dominate the person's life
- Affected person feels like an outside observer of his/her own mental or body processes
- Causes significant distress or impairment in functioning, especially emotional expression and deficits in perception
- Some symptoms are similar to those of panic disorder
- Very rare; onset usually in adolescence

### Treatment

- Psychological treatments similar to those for panic disorder may be helpful
- Stresses associated with onset of disorder should be addressed
- Tends to be lifelong

## DISSOCIATIVE FUGUE

### Characteristics

- Memory loss accompanies an unplanned journey
- Person sometimes assumes a new identity, or becomes confused about old identity
- Usually associated with an intolerable situation
- Fugue states usually end abruptly
- Typically adult onset

### Treatment

- Usually self-correcting when current life stress is resolved
- If needed, therapy focuses on retrieving lost information

## DISSOCIATIVE AMNESIA

### Characteristics

- Generalized: Inability to remember anything, including identity; comparatively rare
- Localized: Inability to remember specific events (usually traumatic); frequently occurs in war; more common than general amnesia
- Usually adult onset for both types

### Treatment

- Usually self-correcting when current life stress is resolved
- If needed, therapy focuses on retrieving lost information

_Photodisc/Getty Images_

## DISSOCIATIVE TRANCE DISORDER

### Characteristics

- Sudden changes in personality accompany a trance or "possession"
- Causes significant distress and/or impairment in functioning
- Often associated with stress or trauma
- Prevalent worldwide, usually in a religious context; rarely seen in Western cultures
- More common in women than men

### Treatment

- Little is known

# 6

# Mood Disorders and Suicide

Lawrence M Sawyer/Photodisc

**Understanding and Defining Mood Disorders**
*An Overview of Depression and Mania*
*The Structure of Mood Disorders*
*Depressive Disorders*
*Bipolar Disorders*

**Prevalence of Mood Disorders**
*In Children and Adolescents*
*In the Elderly*
*Across Cultures*
*Among the Creative*
*The Overlap of Anxiety and Depression*

**Causes of Mood Disorders**
*Biological Dimensions*
*Brain Wave Activity*
*Psychological Dimensions*
*Social and Cultural Dimensions*
*An Integrative Theory*

**Treatment of Mood Disorders**
*Medications*
*Electroconvulsive Therapy and Transcranial Magnetic Stimulation*
*Phototherapy for Seasonal Affective Disorder*
*Psychological Treatments*
*Combined Treatments*
*Preventing Relapse*
*Psychological Treatments for Bipolar Disorder*

**Suicide**
*Statistics*
*Causes*
*Risk Factors*
*Is Suicide Contagious?*
*Treatment*

**Visual Summary: Exploring Mood Disorders**

 **Abnormal Psychology Live CD-ROM**
*Bipolar Disorder: Mary*
*Major Depressive Disorder: Barbara*
*Major Depressive Disorder: Evelyn*

# Understanding and Defining Mood Disorders

- ▪ *Differentiate a depressive episode from a manic and hypomanic episode.*
- ▪ *Describe the clinical symptoms of major depression and bipolar disorder.*
- ▪ *Differentiate major depression from dysthymic disorder and distinguish bipolar disorder from cyclothymic disorder.*

Think back over the last month of your life. It may seem normal in most respects; you studied during the week, socialized on the weekend, and thought about the future once in a while. Perhaps you were anticipating with some pleasure the next school break or seeing an old friend or a lover. But maybe sometime during the past month you also felt kind of down, because you broke up with your boyfriend or girlfriend or, worse yet, somebody close to you died. Think about your feelings during this period. Were you sad? Perhaps you remember crying. Maybe you felt listless, and you couldn't seem to get up the energy to go out with your friends. It may be that you feel this way once in a while for no good reason you can think of, and your friends think you're moody.

If you are like most people, you know your mood will pass. You will be back to your old self in a day or two. If you never felt down and always saw only what was good in a situation, it might be more remarkable than if you were depressed once in a while. Feelings of depression (and joy) are universal, which makes it all the more difficult to understand disorders of mood, disorders that can be so incapacitating that suicide may seem by far a better option than living. Consider the case of Katie.

## Katie
### Weathering Depression

Katie was an attractive but shy 16-year-old who came to one of our clinics with her parents. For several years, Katie had seldom interacted with anybody outside her family because of her considerable social anxiety. Going to school was difficult, and as her social contacts decreased her days became empty and dull. By the time she was 16, a deep, all-encompassing depression blocked the sun from her life. Here is how she described it later.

*The experience of depression is like falling into a deep, dark hole that you cannot climb out of. You scream as you fall, but it seems like no one hears you. Some days you float upward without even trying; on other days, you wish that you would hit bottom so that you would never fall again.*

*Depression affects the way you interpret events. It influences the way you see yourself and the way you see other people. I remember looking in the mirror and thinking that I was the ugliest creature in the world. Later in life, when some of these ideas would come back, I learned to remind myself that I did not have those thoughts yesterday and chances were that I would not have them tomorrow or the next day. It is a little like waiting for a change in the weather.*

But at 16, in the depths of her despair, Katie had no such perspective. She often cried for hours at the end of the day. She had begun drinking alcohol the year before, with the blessing of her parents, strangely enough, because the pills prescribed by her family doctor did no good. A glass of wine at dinner had a temporary soothing effect on Katie, and both she and her parents, in their desperation, were willing to try anything that might make her a more functional person. But one glass was not enough. She drank more often. She began drinking herself to sleep. It was a means of escaping what she felt: "I had very little hope of positive change. I do not think that anyone close to me was hopeful, either. I was angry, cynical, and in a great deal of emotional pain." Katie's life continued to spiral downward.

For several years, Katie had thought about suicide as a solution to her unhappiness. At 13, in the presence of her parents, she reported these thoughts to a psychologist. Her parents wept, and the sight of their tears deeply affected Katie. From that point on she never expressed her suicidal thoughts again, but they remained with her. By the time she was 16, her preoccupation with her own death had increased.

*I think this was just exhaustion. I was tired of dealing with the anxiety and depression day in and day out. Soon I found myself trying to sever the few interpersonal connections that I did have, with my closest friends, with my mother, and my oldest brother. I was almost impossible to talk to. I was angry and frustrated all the time. One day I went over the edge. My mother and I had a disagreement about some unimportant little thing. I went to my bedroom where I kept a bottle of whiskey or vodka or whatever I was drinking at the time. I drank as much as I could until I could pinch myself as hard as I could and feel nothing. Then I got out a very sharp knife that I had been saving and slashed my wrist deeply. I did not feel anything but the warmth of the blood running from my wrist.*

*The blood poured out onto the floor next to the bed that I was lying on. The sudden thought hit me that I had failed, that this was not enough to cause my death. I got up from the bed and began to laugh. I tried to stop the bleeding with some tissues. I stayed calm and frighteningly pleasant. I walked to the kitchen and called my mother. I cannot imagine how she felt when she saw my shirt and pants covered in blood. She was amazingly calm. She asked to see the cut and said that it was not going to stop bleeding on its own and that I needed to go to the doctor immediately. I remember as the doctor shot Novocaine into the cut he remarked that I must have used an anesthetic before cutting myself. I never felt the shot or the stitches.*

*After that, thoughts of suicide became more frequent and much more real. My father asked me to promise that I would never do it again and I said I would not, but that promise meant nothing to me. I knew it was to ease his pains and fears and not mine, and my preoccupation with death continued.*

Think for a moment about your own experience of depression. What are the major differentiating factors between your feelings and Katie's? Clearly, Katie's depression was outside the boundaries of normal experience because of its intensity and duration. In addition, her severe or "clinical" depression interfered substantially with her ability to function. Finally, a number of associated psychological and physical symptoms accompany clinical depression.

Because of their sometimes tragic consequences, we need to develop as full an understanding as possible of mood disorders. In the following sections, we describe how various emotional experiences and symptoms interrelate to produce specific mood disorders. We offer detailed descriptions of different mood disorders and examine the many criteria that define them. We discuss the relationship of anxiety and depression and the causes and treatment of mood disorders. We conclude with a discussion of suicide.

## An Overview of Depression and Mania

The disorders described in this chapter used to be categorized under several different general labels, such as "depressive disorders," "affective disorders,"

or even "depressive neuroses." Beginning with DSM-III, these problems have been grouped under the heading **mood disorders** because they are characterized by gross deviations in mood.

The fundamental experiences of depression and mania contribute, either singly or together, to all the mood disorders. We describe each state and discuss its contributions to the various mood disorders. Then we briefly describe the additional criteria, features, or symptoms that define the specific disorders.

The most commonly diagnosed and most severe depression is called a **major depressive episode.** The DSM-IV-TR criteria indicate an extremely depressed mood state that lasts at least 2 weeks and includes cognitive symptoms (such as feelings of worthlessness and indecisiveness) and disturbed physical functions (such as altered sleeping patterns, significant changes in appetite and weight, or a notable loss of energy) to the point that even the slightest activity or movement requires an overwhelming effort. The episode is typically accompanied by a general loss of interest and an inability to experience any pleasure from life, including interactions with family or friends or accomplishments at work or at school. (The inability to experience pleasure or have any "fun" is termed *anhedonia.*) Although all symptoms are important, evidence suggests that the most central indicators of a full major depressive episode (Keller et al., 1995; Sayer, Kirmayer, & Taillefer, 2003) are the physical changes (sometimes called somatic or *vegetative* symptoms) and the behavioural and emotional "shutdown," or anhedonia (Kasch, Rottenberg, Arnow, & Gotlib, 2002), rather than reports of sadness or distress or the tendency to cry. This anhedonia reflects that these episodes represent a state of low positive affect and not just high negative affect (Kasch et al., 2002). The average duration of a major depressive episode, if untreated, is approximately 9 months (Eaton et al., 1997; Tollefson, 1993).

The second fundamental state in mood disorders is abnormally exaggerated elation, joy, or euphoria. In **mania,** individuals find extreme pleasure in every activity; some patients compare their daily experience of mania to a continuous sexual orgasm. They become extraordinarily active (hyperactive), require little sleep, and may develop grandiose plans, believing they can accomplish anything they desire.

**mood disorders** Group of disorders involving severe and enduring disturbances in emotionality ranging from elation to severe depression.

**major depressive episode** Most common and severe experience of depression, including feelings of worthlessness, disturbances in bodily activities such as sleep, loss of interest, and the inability to experience pleasure, persisting at least 2 weeks.

**mania** Period of abnormally excessive elation or euphoria, associated with some mood disorders.

Speech is typically rapid and may become incoherent because the individual is attempting to express so many exciting ideas at once; this feature is typically referred to as *flight of ideas*.

DSM-IV-TR criteria for a manic episode require a duration of only 1 week, less if the episode is severe enough to require hospitalization. Hospitalization could occur, for example, if the individual was engaging in self-destructive buying sprees, charging thousands of dollars in the expectation of making a million dollars the next day. Irritability is often part of a manic episode, usually near the end. Paradoxically, being anxious or depressed is also commonly part of mania, as described later. The average duration of an untreated manic episode is 3 to 6 months (Angst & Sellaro, 2000).

DSM-IV-TR also defines a **hypomanic episode,** a less severe version of a manic episode that does not cause marked impairment in social or occupational functioning. (*Hypo* means "below"; thus, the episode is below the level of a manic episode.) A hypomanic episode is not necessarily problematic, but it contributes to the definition of several mood disorders.

---

**Disorder Criteria Summary**
Major Depressive Episode

Features of a major depressive episode include:
- Depressed mood most of the day (or irritable mood in children or adolescents)
- Markedly diminished interest or pleasure in most daily activities
- Significant weight loss when not dieting or weight gain, or significant decrease or increase in appetite
- Ongoing insomnia or hypersomnia
- Psychomotor agitation or retardation
- Fatigue or loss of energy
- Feelings of worthlessness or excessive guilt
- Diminished ability to think or concentrate
- Recurrent thoughts of death, suicide ideation, or suicide attempt
- Clinically significant distress or impairment
- Not associated with bereavement
- Persistence for longer than 2 months

*Source:* Reprinted with permission from the *Diagnostic and Statistical Manual of Mental Disorders,* Fourth Edition, Text Revision. (Copyright © 2000) American Psychiatric Association.

---

## The Structure of Mood Disorders

Individuals who experience either depression or mania are said to suffer from a *unipolar mood disorder,* because their mood remains at one "pole" of the usual depression–mania continuum. Mania by itself (unipolar mania) does occur (Solomon et al., 2003) but is rare. Almost everyone with a

unipolar mood disorder suffers from unipolar depression. Someone who alternates between depression and mania is said to have a *bipolar mood disorder* travelling from one "pole" of the depression–elation continuum to the other and back again. However, this label is somewhat misleading, because depression and elation may not be at opposite ends of the same mood state; though related, they are often relatively independent. An individual can experience manic symptoms but feel somewhat depressed or anxious at the same time. This combination is called a **mixed manic** (or *dysphoric manic*) **episode** (Angst & Sellaro, 2000; Freeman & McElroy, 1999). The patient usually experiences the symptoms of mania as being out of control or dangerous and becomes anxious or depressed about his or her uncontrollability. Recent research suggests that manic episodes are characterized by dysphoric (anxious or depressive) features more commonly than was thought, and dysphoria can be severe (Cassidy, Forest, Murry, & Carroll, 1998). The rare individual who suffers from manic episodes alone also meets criteria for bipolar mood disorder in the DSM-IV-TR because experience shows that most of these individuals can be expected to become depressed later (Goodwin & Jamison, 1990).

---

**Disorder Criteria Summary**
Manic Episode

Features of a manic episode include:
- Distinct period of abnormally and persistently elevated, expansive, or irritable mood, lasting at least 1 week
- Significant degree of at least three of the following: inflated self-esteem, decreased need for sleep, excessive talkativeness, flight of ideas or sense that thoughts are racing, easy distractibility, increase in goal-directed activity or psychomotor agitation, excessive involvement in pleasurable but risky behaviours
- Mood disturbance is severe enough to cause impairment in normal functioning or requires hospitalization, or there are psychotic features
- Symptoms are not caused by the direct physiological effects of a substance or a general medical condition

*Source:* Reprinted with permission from the *Diagnostic and Statistical Manual of Mental Disorders,* Fourth Edition, Text Revision. (Copyright © 2000) American Psychiatric Association.

---

**hypomanic episode**   Less severe and less disruptive version of a manic episode that is one of the criteria for several mood disorders.

**mixed manic episode**   Condition in which the individual experiences both elation and depression or anxiety at the same time. Also known as *dysphoric manic episode.*

Depression and mania may differ from one person to another in terms of their severity, their course (or the frequency with which they tend to recur), and, occasionally, the accompanying symptoms. For example, in a manic episode, one individual may present with clear and extreme euphoria and elation accompanied by inflated self-esteem or grandiosity, and another may appear irritable and exhibit flight of ideas. In reality, it is more common to see patients with a mix of such symptoms. As noted previously, an important feature of major depressive episodes is that they are *time limited,* lasting from as little as 2 weeks to more than 9 months if untreated (Tollefson, 1993). Almost all major depressive episodes eventually remit on their own without treatment, although approximately 10% last 2 years or longer. Manic episodes remit on their own without treatment after approximately 6 months (Goodwin & Jamison, 1990). Therefore, it is important to determine the course or temporal patterning of the episodes. For example, do they tend to recur? If they do, does the patient recover fully between episodes? Do the depressive episodes alternate with manic or hypomanic episodes? All these different patterns come under the DSM-IV-TR general heading of course modifiers for mood disorders.

## *Depressive Disorders*

DSM-IV-TR describes several types of depressive disorders. These disorders differ from each other in the frequency with which depressive symptoms occur and the severity of the symptoms.

### Clinical Descriptions

The most easily recognized mood disorder is **major depressive disorder, single episode,** defined by the absence of manic or hypomanic episodes before or during the disorder. We now know that an occurrence of just one isolated depressive episode in a lifetime is rare (Judd, 2000; Solomon et al., 2000).

If two or more major depressive episodes occurred and were separated by at least 2 months during which the individual was not depressed, **major depressive disorder, recurrent,** is diagnosed. Otherwise, the criteria are the same as for major depressive disorder, single episode. Recurrence is important in predicting the future course of the disorder and in choosing appropriate treatments. Individuals with recurrent major depression usually have a family history of depression, unlike people who experience single episodes. As many as 85% of single-episode cases later experience a second episode and thus meet criteria for major depressive disorder, recurrent (Judd, 1997; Keller et al., 1992), based on follow-ups as long as 15 years (Mueller et al., 1999). Because of this finding and others

reviewed later, clinical scientists in just the last several years have concluded that unipolar depression is almost always a chronic condition that waxes and wanes over time but seldom disappears. The median lifetime number of major depressive episodes is four; in one large sample, 25% experienced six or more episodes (Angst, 1988; Angst & Preizig, 1996). The median duration of recurrent major depressive episodes is 4 to 5 months (Kessler et al., 2003; Solomon et al., 1997), somewhat shorter than the average length of the first episode (Eaton et al., 1997).

On the basis of these criteria, how would you diagnose Katie? Katie experienced severely depressed mood, feelings of worthlessness, difficulty concentrating, recurrent thoughts of death, sleep difficulties, and loss of energy. She clearly met the criteria for major depressive disorder, recurrent. Katie's depressive episodes were severe when they occurred, but she tended to cycle in and out of them.

**Dysthymic disorder** shares many of the symptoms of major depressive disorder but differs in its course. The symptoms are somewhat milder but

Canadian singer and songwriter Sarah McLachlan has reportedly had bouts of depression. Her music provides her fans a window into her emotional pain. She has said of her early work that "it was almost as if I needed to be depressed to be creative" (Waliszewski & Smithouser, 1997).

**major depressive disorder, single or recurrent episode** Mood disorder involving one (single episode) or more (separated by at least 2 months without depression–recurrent) major depressive episodes.

**dysthymic disorder** Mood disorder involving persistently depressed mood, with low self-esteem, withdrawal, pessimism, or despair, and present for at least 2 years with no absence of symptoms for more than 2 months.

remain relatively unchanged over long periods, sometimes 20 or 30 years or more (Akiskal & Cassano, 1997; Klein, Schwartz, Rose, & Leader, 2000).

Dysthymic disorder is defined as a persistently depressed mood that continues for at least 2 years, during which the patient cannot be symptom free for more than 2 months at a time. Dysthymic disorder differs from a major depressive episode only in the severity, chronicity, and number of its symptoms, which are milder and fewer but last longer. It seems that most people suffering from dysthymia eventually experience a major depressive episode (Klein, Lewinsohn, & Seeley, 2001).

### Double Depression

Recently, individuals have been studied who experience both major depressive episodes and dysthymic disorder, and who are therefore said to have **double depression.** Typically, dysthymic disorder develops first, perhaps at an early age, and one or more major depressive episodes occur later (Eaton et al., 1997; Klein et al., 2000). Identifying this particular pattern is important because it is associated with severe psychopathology and a problematic future course (Akiskal & Cassano, 1997; Keller, Hirschfeld, & Hanks, 1997; Klein et al., 2000). For example, Keller, Lavori, Endicott, Coryell, and Klerman (1983) found that 61% of patients with double depression had not recovered from the underlying dysthymic disorder 2 years after follow-up. The investigators also found that patients who had recovered from the superimposed major depressive episode experienced high rates of relapse and recurrence. Consider the case of Jack.

## Jack
### A Life Kept Down

Jack was a 49-year-old divorced white man who lived at his mother's home with his 10-year-old son. He complained of chronic depression, saying he finally realized he needed help. Jack reported that he had been a pessimist and a worrier for much of his adult life. He consistently felt kind of down and depressed and did not have much fun. He had difficulty making decisions, was generally pessimistic about the future, and thought little of himself. During the past 20 years, the longest period he could remember in which his mood was "normal" or less depressed lasted only 4 or 5 days.

Despite his difficulties, Jack had managed to finish university and obtain a master's degree in public administration. People told him his future was bright and he would be highly valued in government. Jack did not think so. He took a job as a low-level clerk in a provincial government agency, thinking he could always work his way up. He never did, remaining at the same desk for 20 years.

Jack's wife, fed up with his continued pessimism, lack of self-confidence, and relative inability to enjoy day-to-day events, became discouraged and divorced him. Jack moved in with his mother so that she could help care for his son and share expenses.

About 5 years before coming to the clinic, Jack had experienced a bout of depression worse than anything he had previously known. His self-esteem went from low to nonexistent. From indecisiveness, he became unable to decide anything. He was exhausted all the time and felt as if lead had filled his arms and legs, making it difficult even to move. He became unable to complete projects or to meet deadlines. Seeing no hope, he began to consider suicide. After tolerating a listless performance for years from someone they had expected to rise through the ranks, Jack's employers finally fired him.

After about 6 months, the major depressive episode resolved and Jack returned to his chronic but milder state of depression. He could get out of bed and accomplish some things, although he still doubted his own abilities. However, he was unable to obtain another job. After several years of waiting for something to turn up, he realized he was unable to solve his own problems and that without help his depression would certainly continue. After a thorough assessment, we determined that Jack suffered from a classic case of double depression.

### Onset and Duration

The mean age of onset for major depressive disorder is 25 years in community samples of participants who are not in treatment (Burke, Burke,

**double depression**  Severe mood disorder typified by major depressive episodes superimposed over a background of dysthymic disorder.

Regier, & Rae, 1990) and 29 years for patients who are in treatment (Judd et al., 1998a), but the average age of onset seems to be decreasing (Kessler et al., 2003; Weissman, Bruce, Leaf, Florio, & Holzer, 1991). In fact, the prevalence of major depression increases dramatically during the adolescent years (e.g., Offord et al., 1987), particularly in adolescent girls (see review in Santor & Kusumakar, 2001). A frightening finding is that the incidence of depression and consequent suicide seem to be steadily increasing (Kessler et al., 2003; Lewinsohn, Rohde, Seeley, & Fischer, 1993). In 1989, a survey of people in five American cities (Klerman & Weissman, 1989; Wickramaratne, Weissman, Leaf, & Holford, 1989) revealed a greatly increased risk of developing depression in younger people. Among those born before 1905, only 1% had developed depression by age 75; of those born since 1955, 6% had become depressed by age 24. Another study based on similar surveys conducted in Canada, Puerto Rico, Italy, Germany, France, Taiwan, Lebanon, and New Zealand (see Figure 6.1) suggests that this trend toward developing depression at increasingly earlier ages is occurring worldwide (Cross-National Collaborative Group, 1992). This trend can be observed by comparing the similar patterns in the four panels of Figure 6.1 that compare data collected from the American, Puerto Rican, Taiwanese, and Lebanese samples, respectively.

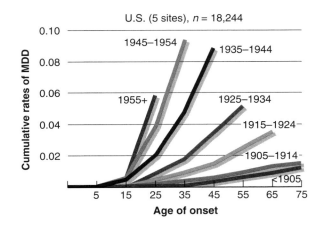

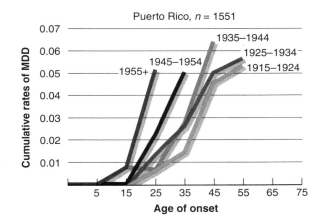

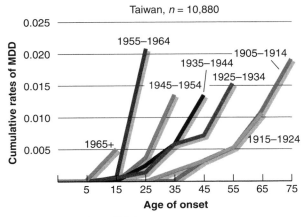

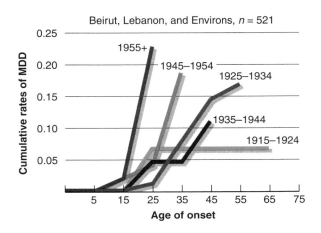

*Years indicate date of birth.

**Figure 6.1** ■ Cross-cultural data on the onset of major depressive disorder (MDD). (From "The Changing Rate of Major Depression: Cross-National Comparisons," by the Cross-National Collaborative Group, 1992, *Journal of the American Medical Association*, 268, 3098–3105. Copyright © 1992 by the American Medical Association. Reprinted by permission.)

## Disorder Criteria Summary
### Dysthymic Disorder

Features of dysthymic disorder include:

- Depressed mood for most of the day, on most days, for at least 2 years (or at least 1 year in children and adolescents)
- The presence, while depressed, of at least two of the following: poor appetite or overeating, insomnia or hypersomnia, low energy or fatigue, low self-esteem, poor concentration or difficulty making decisions, feelings of hopelessness
- During the 2 years or more of disturbance, the person has not been without the symptoms for more than 2 months at a time
- No major depressive episode has been present during this period
- No manic episode has occurred, and criteria have not been met for cyclothymic disorder
- The symptoms are not caused by the direct physiological effects of a substance or a medical condition
- Clinically significant distress or impairment of functioning

*Source:* Reprinted with permission from the *Diagnostic and Statistical Manual of Mental Disorders,* Fourth Edition, Text Revision. (Copyright © 2000) American Psychiatric Association.

As we noted previously, the length of depressive episodes is variable, with some lasting as little as 2 weeks; in more severe cases, an episode might last for several years, with the average duration of the first episode being 4 to 9 months if untreated (Eaton et al., 1997; Kessler et al., 2003). Although 9 months is a long time to endure a severe depressive episode, evidence indicates that even in the most severe cases, the probability of remission of the episode approaches 90% (Thase, 1990) within a 5-year period (Keller, Lavori, et al., 1992). Even in those severe cases where the episode lasts 5 years or longer, 38% can be expected to recover (Mueller et al., 1996). On occasion, however, episodes may not entirely clear up, leaving some residual symptoms. In this case, the likelihood of a subsequent episode is much higher (Judd et al., 1998b). It is also likely that subsequent episodes will be associated with incomplete interepisode recovery. Knowing this is important to treatment planning, because treatment should be continued much longer in these cases.

Recent evidence also identifies important subtypes of dysthymic disorder. Although the typical age of onset has been estimated to be in the early 20s, onset before 21 years of age, and often much earlier, is associated with three characteristics: (1) greater chronicity (it lasts longer), (2) relatively poor prognosis (response to treatment), and (3) a stronger likelihood of the disorder running in the family of the affected individual (Klein, Taylor, Dickstein, &

Harding, 1988; Santor & Kusumakar, 2001). A greater prevalence of current personality disorders has been found in patients with early onset dysthymia than in patients with major depressive disorder (Pepper et al., 1995). Adolescents who have recovered from dysthymic disorder still have a lower level of social support and higher levels of stress than adolescents with major depressive disorders or other non-mood disorders (Klein, Lewisohn, & Seely, 1997). These findings may further reflect the insidiousness of the psychopathology in early-onset dysthymia. Investigators have found a rather high prevalence of dysthymic disorder in children (Kovacs, Gatsonis, Paulauskas, & Richards, 1989), and Kovacs, Akiskal, Gatsonis, and Parrone (1994) found that 76% of a sample of dysthymic children later developed major depressive disorder.

Dysthymic disorder may last 20 to 30 years or more, although a preliminary study reported a median duration of approximately 5 years in adults (Rounsaville, Sholomskas, & Prusoff, 1988) and 4 years in children (Kovacs et al., 1994). Klein et al. (2000) conducted a 5-year naturalistic follow-up of 86 adults with dysthymic disorder and found that 53% had recovered at some point, but 45% of those had relapsed. The whole sample of 86 patients spent approximately 70% of the 5-year follow-up period meeting full criteria for a mood disorder. These findings demonstrate the chronicity of dysthymia. Even worse, patients with dysthymia were more likely to attempt suicide than a comparison group with episodes of major depressive disorder during the 5-year period. Kovacs et al. (1994), on the other

Queen Victoria remained in such deep mourning for her husband, Prince Albert, that she was unable to perform as monarch for several years after his death.

hand, found that almost all children with dysthymia in their sample eventually recovered from it. It is relatively common for major depressive episodes and dysthymic disorder to co-occur (double depression; McCullough et al., 2000). Among those who have had dysthymia, as many as 79% have also had a major depressive episode at some point in their lives.

## From Grief to Depression

At the beginning of the chapter, we asked if you had ever felt down or depressed. Almost everyone has. But if someone you love has died—particularly if the death was unexpected and the person was a member of your immediate family—you may, after your initial reaction to the trauma, have experienced most of the symptoms of a major depressive episode: anxiety, emotional numbness, and denial. The frequency of severe depression following the death of a loved one is so high (approximately 62%) that mental health professionals do not consider it a disorder unless severe symptoms appear, such as psychotic features or suicidal ideation, or the less alarming symptoms last longer than 2 months (Jacobs, 1993). Some grieving individuals require immediate treatment because they are so incapacitated by their symptoms (e.g., severe weight loss or no energy) that they cannot function.

We must confront death and process it emotionally. All religions and cultures have rituals, such as funerals and burial ceremonies, to help us work through our losses with the support and love of our relatives and friends (Bonanno & Kaltman, 1999). Usually the natural grieving process resolves within the first several months, although some people grieve for a year or longer (Clayton & Darvish, 1979; Jacobs, Hansen, Berkman, Kasl, & Ostfeld, 1989). Grief often recurs at significant anniversaries, such as the birthday of the loved one, holidays, and other meaningful occasions, including the anniversary of the death. Mental health professionals are concerned when someone does *not* grieve after a death, because grieving is our natural way of confronting and handling loss.

When grief lasts beyond the normal time, mental health professionals become concerned (Blanchard, Blanchard, & Becker, 1976). After a year or so, the chance of recovering from severe grief without treatment is considerably reduced and, for approximately 10% to 20% of bereaved individuals (Jacobs, 1993; Middleton, Burnett, Raphael, & Martinek, 1996), a normal process becomes a disorder. Many of the psychological and social factors related to mood disorders in general, including a history of past depressive episodes (Horowitz et al., 1997; Jacobs et al., 1989), also predict the development of a normal grief response into a **pathological grief reaction** or **impacted grief reaction.** Particularly prominent

symptoms include intrusive memories and distressingly strong yearnings for the loved one and avoiding people or places that are reminders of the loved one (Horowitz et al., 1997). Recent brain-imaging studies indicate that areas of the brain associated with close relationships and attachment are active in grieving people, in addition to areas of the brain associated with more general emotional responding (Gündel, O'Connor, Littrell, Fort, & Lane, 2003). In cases of long-lasting grief, the rituals intended to help us face and accept death were ineffective. As with victims suffering from posttraumatic stress, one therapeutic approach is to help grieving individuals re-experience the trauma under close supervision. Usually the grieving person is encouraged to talk about the loved one, the death, and the meaning of the loss, while experiencing all the associated emotions, until he or she can come to terms with reality. This would include finding some meaning in the traumatic loss, incorporating positive emotions associated with memories of the relationship into the intense negative emotions connected with the loss, and arriving at the position that he or she can cope with the pain and life will go on (Bonanno & Kaltman, 1999).

## *Bipolar Disorders*

The key identifying feature of *bipolar disorders* is the tendency of manic episodes to alternate with major depressive episodes in an unending roller-coaster ride from the peaks of elation to the depths of despair. Beyond that, bipolar disorders are parallel in many ways to depressive disorders. For example, a manic episode might occur only once or repeatedly. Consider the case of Jane.

### Jane
#### Funny, Smart, and Desperate

Jane was the wife of a well-known surgeon and the loving mother of three children. They lived in an old country house on the edge of town with plenty of room for the family and pets. Jane was nearly 50; the older children had moved out; the youngest son, 16-year-old Mike, was having substantial academic difficulties in school and seemed anxious. Jane brought Mike to the clinic to find out why he was having problems.

---

**pathological or impacted grief reaction** Extreme reaction to the death of a loved one that involves psychotic features, suicidal ideation, or severe loss of weight or energy, or that persists more than 2 months.

As they entered the office, I observed that Jane was well dressed, neat, vivacious, and personable; she had a bounce to her step. She began talking about her wonderful and successful family before she and Mike even reached their seats. Mike, by contrast, was quiet and reserved. He seemed resigned and perhaps relieved that he would have to say little during the session. By the time Jane sat down, she had mentioned the personal virtues and material achievement of her husband, and the brilliance and beauty of one of her older children, and she was proceeding to describe the second child. But before she finished she noticed a book on anxiety disorders and, having read voraciously on the subject, began a litany of various anxiety-related problems that might be troubling Mike.

In the meantime, Mike sat in the corner with a small smile on his lips that seemed to be masking considerable distress and uncertainty over what his mother might do next. It became clear as the interview progressed that Mike suffered from obsessive-compulsive disorder, which disturbed his concentration both in and out of school. He was failing all his courses.

It also became clear that Jane was in the midst of a *hypomanic* episode, evident in her unbridled enthusiasm, grandiose perceptions, "uninterruptable" speech, and report that she needed little sleep these days. She was also easily distracted, such as when she quickly switched from describing her children to the book on the table. When asked about her own psychological state, Jane readily admitted that she was a "manic depressive" (the old name for *bipolar disorder*) and that she alternated rather rapidly between feeling on top of the world and feeling very depressed; she was taking medication for her condition. I immediately wondered if Mike's obsessions had anything to do with his mother's condition.

Mike was treated intensively for his obsessions and compulsions but made little progress. He said that life at home was difficult when his mother was depressed. She sometimes went to bed and stayed there for 3 weeks. During this time, she seemed be in a depressive stupor, essentially unable to move for days. It was up to the children to care for themselves and their mother, whom they fed by hand. Because the older children had now left home, much of the burden had fallen on Mike. Jane's profound depressive episodes would remit after about 3 weeks, and she would immediately enter a hypomanic episode that might last several months or more. During hypomania, Jane was, for the most part, funny and entertaining and a

delight to be with—if you could get a word in edgewise. Consultation with her therapist, an expert in the area, revealed that he had prescribed a number of medications but was so far unable to bring her mood swings under control.

Jane had **bipolar II disorder,** in which major depressive episodes alternate with hypomanic episodes rather than full manic episodes. As we noted earlier, hypomanic episodes are less severe. Although she was noticeably "up," Jane functioned pretty well while in this mood state. The criteria for **bipolar I disorder** are the same, except the individual experiences a full manic episode. As in the criteria set for depressive disorder, for the manic episodes to be considered separate, there must be a symptom-free period of at least 2 months between episodes. Otherwise, one episode is seen as a continuation of the last.

The case of Billy illustrates a full manic episode. This individual was first encountered when he was admitted to a hospital.

## Billy
### The World's Best at Everything

Before Billy reached the ward you could hear him laughing and carrying on in a deep voice; it sounded like he was having a wonderful time. As the nurse brought Billy down the hall to introduce him to the staff, he spied the Ping-Pong table. Loudly, he exclaimed, "Ping-Pong! I love Ping-Pong! I have only played twice but that is what I am going to do while I am here; I am going to become the world's greatest Ping-Pong player! And that table is gorgeous! I am going to start work on that table immediately and make it the finest Ping-Pong table in the world. I am going to sand it down, take it apart, and rebuild it until it gleams and every angle is perfect!" Billy soon went on to something else that absorbed his attention.

The previous week, Billy had emptied his bank account, taken his credit cards and those of his elderly parents with whom he was living, and bought every piece of fancy stereo equipment he could find. He thought that he would

**bipolar II disorder** The alternation of major depressive episodes with hypomanic (not full manic) episodes.

**bipolar I disorder** The alternation of major depressive episodes with full manic episodes.

set up the best sound studio in the city and make millions of dollars by renting it to people who would come from far and wide. This episode had precipitated his admission to the hospital.

---

During manic or hypomanic phases, patients often deny they have a problem, which was characteristic of Billy. Even after spending inordinate amounts of money or making foolish business decisions, these individuals, particularly if they are in the midst of a full manic episode, are so wrapped up in their enthusiasm and expansiveness that their behaviour seems reasonable to them. The high during a manic state is so pleasurable, people may stop taking their medication during periods of distress or discouragement in an attempt to bring on a manic state once again; this is a serious challenge to professionals.

Returning to the case of Jane, we continued to treat Jane's son Mike for several months. We made little progress before the school year ended. Because Mike was doing so poorly, the school administrators informed his parents that he would not be accepted back the next year. Mike and his parents wisely decided it might be a good idea if he got away from the house and did something different for a while, and he began working and living at a ski and tennis resort. Several months later, his father called to tell us that Mike's obsessions and compulsions had completely lifted since he'd been away from home. The father thought Mike should continue living at the resort, where he had entered school and was doing better academically. He now agreed with our previous assessment that Mike's condition might be related to his relationship with his mother. Several years later, we heard that Jane, in a depressive stupor, had killed herself, an all-too-tragic outcome in bipolar disorder.

## Disorder Criteria Summary
### Bipolar II Disorder

Features of bipolar II disorder include:
- Presence (or history) of one or more major depressive episodes
- Presence (or history) of at least one hypomanic episode
- No history of a full manic episode or a mixed episode
- Mood symptoms are not better accounted for by schizoaffective disorder or superimposed on another disorder such as schizophrenia
- Clinically significant distress or impairment of functioning

*Source:* Reprinted with permission from the *Diagnostic and Statistical Manual of Mental Disorders*, Fourth Edition, Text Revision. (Copyright © 2000) American Psychiatric Association.

A milder but more chronic version of bipolar disorder called *cyclothymic disorder* is similar in many ways to dysthymic disorder. Like dysthymic disorder, **cyclothymic disorder** is a chronic alternation of mood elevation and depression that does not reach the severity of manic or major depressive episodes. Individuals with cyclothymic disorder tend to be in one mood state or the other for years with relatively few periods of neutral (or euthymic) mood. This pattern must last for at least 2 years (1 year for children and adolescents) to meet criteria for the disorder. Individuals with cyclothymic disorder alternate between the kinds of mild depressive symptoms Jack experienced during his dysthymic states and the sorts of hypomanic episodes Jane experienced. In neither case was the behaviour severe enough to require hospitalization or immediate intervention. Much of the time, such individuals are just considered moody. However, the chronically fluctuating mood states are, by definition, substantial enough to interfere with functioning. Furthermore, people with cyclothymia should be treated because of their increased risk to develop the more severe bipolar I or bipolar II disorder (Akiskal & Pinto, 1999; Goodwin & Jamison, 1990).

***Bipolar Disorder: Mary***
*"Whoo, whoo, whoo—on top of the world!... It's going to be one great day!... I'm incognito for the Lord God Almighty. I'm working for him. I have been for years. I'm a spy. My mission is to fight for our way of life.... for liberty.... I can bring up the wind, I can bring the rain, I can bring the sunshine, I can do lots of things.... I love the outdoors...."*

### Onset and Duration

The average age of onset for bipolar I disorder is 18, and for bipolar II disorder it is 22, although cases of both can begin in childhood (Weissman et al., 1991). This is somewhat younger than the average age of onset for major depressive disorder, and bipolar disorders begin more acutely (Angst & Sellaro, 2000; Weissman et al., 1991; Winokur, Coryell, Endicott, & Akiskal, 1993). About one-third of the cases of bipolar disorder begin in adolescence (Taylor & Abrams, 1981), and the onset is often preceded by minor oscillations in mood or mild cyclothymic mood swings (Goodwin & Ghaemi, 1998; Goodwin & Jamison, 1990). Only 10% to 13% of bipolar II disorder cases progress to full bipolar I syndrome (Coryell et al., 1995; Depression Guideline Panel, 1993). The distinction

---

**cyclothymic disorder** Chronic (at least 2 years) mood disorder characterized by alternating mood elevation and depression levels that are not as severe as manic or major depressive episodes.

between unipolar and bipolar mood disorder also seems well defined because only 5.2% of a large group of 381 patients with unipolar depression experienced a manic episode during a 10-year follow-up period (Coryell et al., 1995), although Angst and Sellaro (2000), in reviewing some older studies, estimated the rate of depressed individuals later experiencing mania as closer to 25%. In any case, if unipolar and bipolar disorders were more closely related, we would expect to see more individuals moving from one to the other.

**Disorder Criteria Summary**
Cyclothymic Disorder

Features of cyclothymic disorder include:
- For at least 2 years, numerous periods with hypomanic symptoms and numerous periods with depressive symptoms that do not meet the criteria for a major depressive episode
- Since onset, the person has not been without the symptoms for more than 2 months at a time
- No major depression episode, manic episode, or mixed episode has been present during the first 2 years of the disturbance
- Mood symptoms are not better accounted for by schizoaffective disorder, or superimposed on another disorder such as schizophrenia
- The symptoms are not caused by the physiological effects of a substance or a general medical condition
- Clinically significant distress or impairment of functioning

*Source:* Reprinted with permission from the *Diagnostic and Statistical Manual of Mental Disorders,* Fourth Edition, Text Revision. (Copyright © 2000) American Psychiatric Association.

It is relatively rare for someone to develop bipolar disorder after the age of 40. Once it does appear, the course is chronic; that is, mania and depression alternate indefinitely. Therapy usually involves managing the disorder with ongoing drug regimens that prevent recurrence of episodes. Suicide is an all-too-common consequence of bipolar disorder, almost always occurring during depressive episodes, as it did in the case of Jane. Estimates of suicide attempts in bipolar disorder range from an average of 17% for bipolar I to 24% for bipolar II, as compared to 12% in unipolar depression (Rihmer & Pestality, 1999). Even with treatment, patients with bipolar disorder tend to do poorly, with one study showing 60% of a large group experiencing poor adjustment during the first 5 years after treatment (Goldberg, Harrow, & Grossman, 1995; Goodwin et al., 2003). A more comprehensive and longer follow-up of 219 patients reported that only 16% recovered; 52% endured recurrent episodes, 16% had become chronically disabled, 8% had an incomplete recovery, and another 8% had committed suicide (Angst & Sellaro, 2000).

In typical cases, cyclothymia is chronic and life-long. In about one-third of patients, cyclothymic mood swings develop into full-blown bipolar disorder (Waters, 1979). In one sample of cyclothymic patients, 60% were female, and the age of onset was quite young, often during the teenage years or before, with some data suggesting the most common age of onset to be 12 to 14 years (Depue et al., 1981). The disorder is often not recognized, and those experiencing it are thought to be high strung, explosive, moody, or hyperactive (Biederman et al., 2000; Goodwin & Jamison, 1990). One subtype of cyclothymia is based on the predominance of mild depressive symptoms, one on the predominance of hypomanic symptoms, and another on an equal distribution of both.

### Postpartum Depression

Diagnosing a mood disorder is not a straightforward task; great diversity of symptoms is possible within any of the diagnostic categories. Other symptoms, or *specifiers*, may or may not accompany a mood disorder. When they do, they are often helpful in determining the most effective treatment. For example, the *postpartum onset specifier* can apply to both major depressive and manic episodes. It is characterized by severe manic or depressive episodes that first occur during the postpartum period (the 4 weeks immediately following childbirth), typically 2 to 3 days after delivery. The postpartum incidence, however, is quite low, approximately one per one thousand deliveries (Dean & Kendell, 1981). If a new mother experiences one of these severe postpartum episodes, the chances are approximately 50% that she will experience another episode with subsequent births (Davidson & Robertson, 1985; Depression Guideline Panel, 1993).

Celebrities like singer and songwriter Sarah McLaughlin and politician Maureen McTeer (wife of former prime minister Joe Clark) have spoken publicly about their battles with postpartum depression. For example, in her recent autobiography, *In My Own Name*, McTeer describes her struggle in trying to juggle the multiple roles of new mother, prime minister's wife, feminist role model, and lawyer, all within the public spotlight of politics. In her book, she describes her postpartum depression symptoms: "After the initial euphoria following Catherine's birth, I felt alone and depressed. I cried a great deal and seemed unable to pull out of my funk" (McTeer, 2003, p. 84).

Postpartum depression expert Valerie Whiffen at the University of Ottawa concluded that the risks for developing mood disorders during the postpartum period might be overestimated (Whiffen, 1992). One study found no differences in the rates of minor and major depression in a group of childbearing women, either during pregnancy or after delivery, and in a well-matched control group (O'Hara, Zekoski,

Phillipps, & Wright, 1990). A close examination of women with postpartum depression by Whiffen and her colleagues revealed no essential differences between the characteristics of this mood disorder and others (Gotlib, Whiffen, Wallace, & Mount, 1991; Whiffen, 1992; Whiffen & Gotlib, 1993). In other words, postpartum depression does not seem to require a separate category in the DSM-IV-TR (Purdy & Frank, 1993).

Some research is emerging on the risk factors for postpartum depression that may ultimately assist in early identification. For example, Whiffen's work suggests that having an infant with a difficult temperament is an important type of stressor that can contribute to postpartum depression (Whiffen & Gotlib, 1989a). Moreover, recent work by McGill University researchers Phyllis Zelkowitz and Tamara Milet (2001) indicates that low socioeconomic status and high levels of life stress are also related to the persistence of postpartum depression following birth of the child. Early recognition is very important (Steiner, 2002) because in a few tragic cases, a mother in the midst of an episode has killed her newborn child (Purdy & Frank, 1993). One well-known such case is the Killinger-Johnson murder-suicide that took place in Toronto in August of 2000. Suzanne Killinger-Johnson, a psychiatrist, jumped in front of a train with her 6-month-old son. The baby died instantly and the mother died the next day. Killinger-Johnson was believed to have been suffering from postpartum depression.

## Differences in the Course of Mood Disorders

Three other specifiers may accompany recurrent mania or depression: longitudinal course, rapid cycling, and seasonal pattern. Differences in course or temporal pattern may require different treatment strategies.

1. *Longitudinal course specifiers.* Whether the individual has had major episodes of depression or mania in the past is important, as is whether the individual fully recovered between past episodes. Other important determinations are whether the patient with a major depressive episode had dysthymia before the episode (double depression) and whether the patient with bipolar disorder experienced a previous cyclothymic disorder. Antecedent dysthymia or cyclothymia predicts a *decreasing* chance of full interepisode recovery (Judd et al., 1998b). Most likely, the patient will require a long and intense course of treatment to maintain a normal mood state for as long as possible after recovering from the current episode (Mueller et al., 1999; Solomon et al., 2000).

***Major Depressive Disorder: Barbara***
*" ... I've been sad, depressed most of my life.... I had a headache in high school for a year and a half.... There have been different periods in my life when I wanted to end it all.... I hate me, I really hate me. I hate the way I look, I hate the way I feel. I hate the way I talk to people.... I do everything wrong.... I feel really hopeless."*

Thomson Learning

2. *Rapid-cycling specifier.* This temporal specifier applies only to bipolar I and bipolar II disorders. Some people move quickly in and out of depressive or manic episodes. An individual with bipolar disorder who experiences at least four manic or depressive episodes within a year is considered to have a *rapid-cycling pattern,* which is apparently a severe variety of bipolar disorder that does not respond well to standard treatments (Bauer et al., 1994; Kilzieh & Akiskal, 1999) and which is associated with a higher probability of suicide attempts (Coryell et al., 2003). Some evidence indicates that alternative drug treatment such as anticonvulsants and mood stabilizers rather than antidepressants may be more effective with this group of patients (Kilzieh & Akiskal, 1999; Post et al., 1989).

Approximately 20% to 25% of bipolar patients experience rapid cycling. As many as 90% are female, a higher rate than in other variations of bipolar disorder (e.g., Coryell et al., 2003; Wehr, Sack, Rosenthal, & Cowdry, 1988), and this finding is consistent across 10 studies (Kilzieh & Akiskal, 1999). Unlike bipolar patients in general, most people with rapid cycling begin with a depressive episode rather than a manic episode (McElroy & Keck, 1993). In most cases, rapid cycling tends to increase in frequency over time and can reach severe states in which patients cycle between mania and depression without any break. When this direct transition from one mood state to another happens, it is referred to as "rapid switching" or "rapid mood switching" and is a particularly severe and treatment-resistant form of the disorder (MacKinnon, Zandi, Gershon, Nurnberger, & DePaulo, 2003; Maj, Pirozzi, Magliano, & Bartoli, 2002). Fortunately, rapid cycling does not seem to be permanent, because fewer than 3% of patients continue with rapid cycling across a 5-year period (Coryell, Endicott, & Keller, 1992), with 80% returning to a non-rapid-cycling pattern within 2 years (Coryell et al., 2003).

3. *Seasonal pattern specifier.* This temporal specifier applies both to bipolar disorders and to recurrent major depressive disorder. It accompanies episodes that occur during certain seasons (e.g., winter depression). Some mood disorders seem tied to seasons of the year. The most usual pattern is a depressive episode that begins in the late fall and ends with the beginning of spring. In bipolar disorder, individuals may become depressed during the winter and manic during the summer. This condition is called **seasonal affective disorder (SAD).**

Although some studies have reported seasonal cycling of manic episodes, the overwhelming majority of seasonal mood disorders involve winter depression (Lewy, 1993). A community-based telephone survey conducted in Toronto found that the prevalence of the seasonal subtype of major depression (i.e., winter depression SAD) was about 3% (Levitt, Boyle, Joffe, & Baumal, 2000). Unlike more severe melancholic types of depression, people with winter depressions tend toward excessive sleep (rather than decreased sleep) and increased appetite (rather than decreased appetite), and weight gain (rather than weight loss), symptoms shared with atypical depressive episodes. Although SAD seems a bit different from other major depressive episodes, family studies conducted by Raymond Lam and his colleagues at the University of British Columbia have not yet revealed any differential aggregation that would suggest winter depressions are a separate type (Allen, Lam, Remick, & Sadovnick, 1993).

Emerging evidence suggests that SAD may be related to daily and seasonal changes in the production of melatonin, a hormone secreted by the pineal gland. Because exposure to light suppresses melatonin production, it is produced only at night.

Melatonin production also tends to increase in winter, when there is less sunlight. One theory is that increased production of melatonin might trigger depression in vulnerable people (Goodwin & Jamison, 1990; Lee et al., 1998). Wehr et al. (2001) have shown that melatonin secretion *does* increase in winter, but only in patients with SAD and not in healthy controls. (We return to this topic when we discuss biological contributions to depression.) Another possibility is that circadian rhythms, which are thought to have some relationship to mood, are delayed in winter (Lewy & Sack, 1987; Wirtz-Justice, 1998).

As you might expect, the prevalence of SAD is higher in extreme northern and southern latitudes because there is less winter sunlight. For example, a study conducted in Toronto showed that SAD occurred in 11% of those in the sample who were diagnosed with depression (Levitt et al., 2000). In contrast, a study conducted in the northern city of Thompson, Manitoba, showed that SAD occurred in about 20% of those with depression (Williams & Schmidt, 1993). SAD is quite prevalent in Fairbanks, Alaska, where 9% of the population appear to meet criteria for the disorder and another 19% have some seasonal symptoms of depression (Schwartz, Brown, Wehr, & Rosenthal, 1996). However, the causes of SAD are more complex than simply living in a northern climate, as is illustrated in a study by Magnusson and Axelsson (1993). These researchers studied rates of SAD in 252 descendants of Icelanders who had immigrated to northern Manitoba. They found very low rates of SAD in this group (i.e., 1.2% prevalence rate, which is lower than rates observed on the east coast of the United States!). It is possible that this group has somehow genetically adapted to the reduced number of daylight hours in their environment, which provides some protection from the development of SAD (Magnusson & Axelsson, 1993).

SAD also seems quite stable. In one group of 59 patients, 86% experienced a depressive episode each winter during a 9-year period of observation, with only 14% recovering during that time. For 26 (44%) of these patients, whose symptoms were more severe to begin with, depressive episodes began to occur during other seasons as well (Schwartz, Brown, Wehr, & Rosenthal, 1996). Rates in children and adolescents are between 1.7% and 5.5%, according to one study, with higher rates in postpubertal girls (Swedo et al., 1995), but the study needs replication.

Most seasonal affective disorders involve depression in winter, when the light is low and the days are short.

CP Photo/Kevin Frayer

**seasonal affective disorder (SAD)** Mood disorder involving a cycling of episodes corresponding to the seasons of the year, typically with depression occurring during the winter.

## Concept Check 6.1

Match each description or case by choosing its corresponding disorder: (a) mania, (b) double depression, (c) dysthymic disorder, (d) major depressive episode, (e) bipolar I disorder.

1. Last week, as he does about every 3 months, Ryan went out with his friends, buying rounds of drinks, socializing until early morning, and feeling on top of the world. Today Ryan will not get out of bed to go to work, see his friends, or even turn on the lights. _____

2. Feeling certain he would win the lottery, Charles went on an all-night shopping spree, maxing out all his credit cards without a worry. We know he's done this several times, feeling abnormally extreme elation, joy, and euphoria. _____

3. Heather has had some mood disorder problems in the past, although some days she's better than others. All of a sudden, though, she seems to have fallen into a rut. She can't make any decisions because she doesn't trust herself. _____

4. For the past few weeks, Jennifer has been sleeping a lot. She feels worthless, can't get up the energy to leave the house, and has lost a lot of weight. Her problem is the most common and extreme mood disorder. _____

5. Sanchez is always down and a bit blue, but occasionally he seems so depressed that nothing pleases him. _____

# Prevalence of Mood Disorders

■ *Describe the differences in prevalence of mood disorders across the life span.*

Several large epidemiological studies estimating the prevalence of mood disorder have been carried out in recent years (Kessler et al., 1994; Weissman et al., 1991). Prevalence rates in Canadian studies have been quite variable, ranging from 4.1% in the Ontario Health Survey, to 10.3% and 11% in surveys in Toronto and Calgary, respectively (De Marco, 2000; Offord et al., 1996; Patten, 2000). As Roger Bland, a leading psychiatric epidemiologist from the University of Alberta, has pointed out, different research methods may account for the differing rates of prevalence (Bland, 1997). Scott Patten at the University of Calgary provides another explanation. He argues that prevalence rates for depression in Canada appear to be decreasing, suggesting progress in public health efforts toward combating depression in our country (Patten, 2002).

Wittchen, Knauper, and Kessler (1994) compiled a summary of major prevalence studies from around the world. The figures for major depressive disorder of 16% lifetime and 6.5% in the last 10 months have recently been confirmed in the most sophisticated study to date (Kessler et al., 2003). The studies agree that women are twice as likely to have mood disorders as men.

Table 6.1 breaks down lifetime prevalence by four principal mood disorders. Notice here that the imbalance in prevalence between males and females is accounted for solely by major depressive disorder and dysthymia, because bipolar disorders are distributed approximately equally across gender.

| **TABLE 6.1** | Lifetime Prevalence Of Mood Disorder Subtypes By Age and Sex | | | |
|---|---|---|---|---|
| | Lifetime Prevalence in % | | | |
| | Bipolar I | Bipolar II | Major Depression | Dysthymia |
| Total | 0.8 | 0.5 | 4.9 | 3.2 |
| **Age** | | | | |
| 18–29 | 1.1 | 0.7 | 5.0 | 3.0 |
| 30–44 | 1.4 | 0.6 | 7.5 | 3.8 |
| 45–64 | 0.3 | 0.2 | 4.0 | 3.6 |
| 65+ | 0.1 | 0.1 | 1.4 | 1.7 |
| **Sex** | | | | |
| Men | 0.7 | 0.4 | 2.6 | 2.2 |
| Women | 0.9 | 0.5 | 7.0 | 4.1 |

Note: Significant variation within groups, adjusted for age, sex, or ethnicity.

*Source:* Adapted with permission of The Free Press, a Division of Simon & Schuster Adult Publishing Group, from *Psychiatric Disorders in America: The Epidemiologic Catchment Area Study,* by Lee N. Robbins, Ph.D., and Darrel A. Regier, M.D. Copyright © 1991 by Lee N. Robbins and Darrel A. Regier. All rights reserved.

## In Children and Adolescents

You might assume that depression requires some experience with life, that an accumulation of negative events or disappointments might create pessimism, which then leads to depression. Like many reasonable assumptions in psychopathology, this one is not uniformly correct. We now have evidence that 3-month-old babies can become depressed! Infants of depressed mothers display marked depressive behaviours (sad faces, slow movement, lack of responsiveness) even when interacting with a non-depressed adult (Field et al., 1988). Whether this behaviour or temperament is caused by a genetic tendency inherited from the mother, the result of early interaction patterns with a depressed mother, or a combination is not yet clear.

Most investigators agree that mood disorders are fundamentally similar in children and in adults (Lewinsohn, Hops, Roberts, Seeley, & Andrews, 1993; Pataki & Carlson, 1990). Therefore, no "childhood" mood disorders in DSM-IV-TR are specific to a developmental stage, unlike anxiety disorders. However, it seems clear that the "look" of depression changes with age (see Table 6.2). For example, children under 3 years of age might manifest depression by their facial expressions and by their eating, sleeping, and play behaviour, quite differently from children between age 9 and age 12. The work of psychologist Ian Gotlib, formerly at the University of Western Ontario, and his colleagues has shown that adolescents who are forced to limit their activities because of illness or injury are at high risk for depression (Lewinsohn, Gotlib, & Seeley, 1997).

Estimates on the prevalence of mood disorders in children and adolescents vary widely, although more sophisticated studies are beginning to appear. The general conclusion is that depressive disorders occur *less frequently* in children than in adults but rise dramatically in adolescence, when, if anything, depression is *more frequent* than in adults (Kashani, Hoeper, Beck, & Corcoran, 1987; Lewinsohn et al., 1993). Furthermore, some evidence indicates that, in young children, dysthymia is more prevalent than major depressive disorder, but this ratio reverses in adolescence. Like adults, adolescents experience major depressive disorder more frequently than dysthymia (Kashani et al., 1983, 1987). Major depressive disorder in adolescents is also a largely female disorder (Santor & Kusumakar, 2001), as it is in adults, although interestingly, this is not true for more mild depression. Only among the adolescents referred to treatment

**TABLE 6.2** Speculative Manifestations of Depressive Symptoms through Childhood

| Adult Symptom | Childhood Symptom | | | | |
| | 0–36 Months | 3–5 Years | 6–8 Years | 9–12 Years | 13–18 Years |
|---|---|---|---|---|---|
| Dysphoric mood | Sad or expressionless face, gaze aversion, staring, irritability | Sad expression, somberness or labile mood, irritability | Prolonged unhappiness, somberness, irritability | Sad expression, apathy, irritability | Sad expression, apathy, irritability, increasing complaints of depression |
| Loss of interest or pleasure | No social play | Decreased socialization | Decreased socialization | Adult presentation | Adult presentation |
| Appetite or weight change | Feeding problems | Feeding problems | Adult presentation | Adult presentation | Adult presentation |
| Insomnia or hypersomnia | Sleep problems | Sleep problems | Sleep problems | Adult presentation | Adult presentation |
| Psychomotor agitation | Tantrums, irritability | Irritability, tantrums | Irritability, tantrums | Aggressive behaviour | Aggressive behaviour |
| Psychomotor retardation | Lethargy | Lethargy | Lethargy | Lethargy | Adult presentation |
| Loss of energy | Lethargy | Lethargy | Lethargy | Lethargy | Adult presentation |
| Feelings of worthlessness | | Low self-esteem | Low self-esteem | Guilt, low self-esteem | Guilt |
| Diminished concentration | | | Poor school performance | Poor school performance | Poor school performance |
| Recurrent thoughts of death or suicide | | Accident proneness | Accident proneness, morbid outlook | Adult presentation | Adult presentation |
| Anxiety | Separation/attachment problems | School phobia | Phobias, separation anxiety | Phobias, separation anxiety | Adult presentation |
| Somatic complaints | | Present | Present | Present | Present |

*Source:* From "Phenomenology of Major Depression from Childhood through Adulthood: Analysis of Three Studies," by G. A. Carlson and J. H. Kashani, *American Journal of Psychiatry,* 145 (10), 1222–1225. Copyright © 1988 by the American Psychiatric Association. Reprinted with permission.

Among adolescents, severe major depressive disorder occurs mostly in girls.

does the gender imbalance exist (Compas et al., 1997), though why more girls reach a more severe state requiring referral to treatment is not clear.

Looking at mania, children below the age of 9 seem to present with more irritability and emotional swings rather than classic manic states, and they are often mistaken as being hyperactive. In addition, their symptoms are more chronic in that they are always present rather than episodic as in adults (Biederman et al., 2000). This presentation seems to continue through adolescence (Faraone et al, 1997), although adolescents may appear more typically manic. Bipolar disorder seems to be rare in childhood, although case studies of children as young as 4 years of age displaying bipolar symptoms have been reported (Poznanski, Israel, & Grossman, 1984), and the diagnosis may be mistaken for conduct disorder or attention deficit/hyperactivity disorder (ADHD). However, the prevalence of bipolar disorder rises substantially in adolescence, which is not surprising in that many adults with bipolar disorder report a first onset during the teen years (Keller & Wunder, 1990).

One developmental difference between children and adolescents on the one hand and adults on the other is that children, especially boys, tend to become aggressive and even destructive during depressive episodes. For this reason, childhood depression (and mania) is sometimes misdiagnosed as hyperactivity or, more often, conduct disorder in which aggression and even destructive behaviour are common. Often conduct disorder and depression co-occur (Lewinsohn et al., 1993; Petersen et al., 1993). Puig-Antich (1982) found that one-third of prepubertal depressed boys met full criteria for a conduct disorder, which developed at approximately the same time as the depressive disorder and remitted with the resolution of the depression. Biederman and colleagues (1987) found that 32% of children with ADHD also met criteria for major

depression, and between 60% and 90% of children and adolescents with mania also have ADHD (Biederman et al., 2000). In any case, successful treatment of the underlying depression (or spontaneous recovery) resolves the associated problems in these specific cases. Adolescents with bipolar disorder may also become aggressive, impulsive, sexually provocative, and accident prone (Carlson, 1990; Keller & Wunder, 1990).

Whatever the presentation, mood disorders in children and adolescents are serious because of their likely consequences. In an important prospective study, conducted as part of the Ontario Child Health Study, Fleming, Boyle, and Offord (1993) followed 652 adolescents with either a major depressive disorder or a conduct disorder for 4 years. These adolescents largely continued to experience serious psychopathology and markedly impaired functioning. Lewinsohn, Rohde, Seeley, Klein, and Gotlib (2000) also followed 274 adolescents with major depressive disorder into adulthood and identified several risk factors for additional depressive episodes as adults. Prominent among these were conflicts with parents, being female, and a higher proportion of family members experiencing depressive episodes. Finally, Weissman et al. (1999) identified a group of 83 children with an onset of major depressive disorder before puberty and followed them for 10 to 15 years. Generally there was also a poor adult outcome in this group, with high rates of suicide attempts and social impairment compared with children without major depressive disorder. Interestingly, these prepubertal children were more likely to develop substance abuse or other disorders as adults rather than continue with their depression, unlike adolescents with major depressive disorder.

## In the Elderly

Only recently have we seriously considered the problem of depression in the elderly. A Canadian study by Dalhousie University researcher Kenneth Rockwood and colleagues estimated that 18% to 20% of nursing home residents may experience major depressive episodes (Rockwood, Stolee, & Brahim, 1991; see also Katz, Leshen, Kleban, & Jethanandani, 1989), which are likely to be chronic if they appear first after the age of 60 (Rapp, Parisi, & Wallace, 1991). Late-onset depressions are associated with marked sleep difficulties, hypochondriasis, and agitation. It can be difficult to diagnose depression in the elderly because the presentation of mood disorders is often complicated by the presence of medical illnesses or symptoms of dementia (e.g., Blazer, 1989; Small, 1991). That is, elderly people who become physically ill or begin to show signs of dementia might become depressed about it, but the signs of depression would be attributed to the illness or dementia and thus missed. Nevertheless, the overall prevalence of major depressive disorder in the elderly is the same as or slightly lower than in the general population (Kessler et al., 1994; Weissman et al., 1991), perhaps because stressful life events that trigger major depressive episodes decrease with age. But, as noted by Ian Gotlib, milder symptoms that do not meet criteria for major depressive disorder seem to be more common among the elderly (Gotlib & Nolan, 2001), perhaps because of illness and infirmity (Roberts, Kaplan, Shema, & Strawbridge, 1997).

Anxiety disorders accompany depression in the elderly (in about a third of cases), particularly generalized anxiety disorder and panic disorder (Lenze et al., 2000), and when they do, patients are more severely depressed. Depression can also contribute to physical disease in the elderly (Grant, Patterson, & Yager, 1988; House, Landis, & Umberson, 1988). In fact, being depressed doubles the risk of death in elderly patients who have suffered a heart attack or stroke (Schultz, Drayer, & Rollman, 2002). An even more tragic finding is that symptoms of depression are increasing substantially in our growing population of elderly people. Wallace and O'Hara (1992) in a longitudinal study found that elderly citizens became increasingly depressed over a 3-year period. They suggest, with some evidence, that this trend is related to increasing illness and reduced social support; in other words, as we become frailer and more alone, the psychological result is depression, which increases the probability that we will become even frailer and have even less social support. This vicious cycle is deadly.

The earlier gender imbalance in depression disappears after the age of 65. In early childhood, boys are no more likely to be depressed than girls, but an overwhelming surge of depression in adolescent girls produces an imbalance in the sex ratio (Santor & Kusumakar, 2001) that is maintained until old age, when just as many women are depressed but increasing numbers of men are affected (Wallace & O'Hara, 1992). From the perspective of the life span, this is the first time since early childhood that the sex ratio for depression is balanced.

## Across Cultures

We noted the strong tendency of anxiety to take physical or somatic forms in some cultures; instead of talking about fear, panic, or general anxiety, many people describe stomachaches, chest pains or heart distress, and headaches. According to the research of Laurence Kirmayer (2001), much the same tendency exists across cultures for mood disorders, which is not surprising given the close relationship of anxiety and depression. Feelings of weakness or tiredness particularly characterize depression that is accompanied by mental or physical slowing or retardation.

Although somatic symptoms that characterize mood disorders seem roughly equivalent across cultures, it is difficult to compare subjective feelings. The way people think of depression may be influenced by the cultural view of the individual and the role of the individual in society (Jenkins, Kleinman, & Good, 1990). For example, in societies that focus on the *individual* instead of the *group*, it is common to hear statements such as "I feel blue" or "I am depressed." However, in cultures where the individual is tightly integrated into the larger group, someone might say, "Our life has lost its meaning," referring to the group in which the individual resides (Manson & Good, 1993). Despite these influences, it is generally agreed that the best way to study the nature and prevalence of mood disorders (or any other psychological disorder) in other cultures is first to determine their prevalence using standardized criteria (Neighbors, Jackson, Campbell, & Williams, 1989). The DSM criteria are increasingly used, along with semistructured interviews in which the same questions are asked, with some allowances for different words that might be specific to a culture or subculture.

One such study is the Cross-National Collaborative Study, which used the same structured interview and diagnostic criteria in 10 countries including Canada (Weissman et al., 1994). The Canadian data were collected in Edmonton by a team led by Roger Bland. As can be seen in Figure 6.1, the highest rates of major depression were observed in Beirut, Lebanon (19% prevalence), and the lowest in Taiwan (1.5% prevalence). Compared with the prevalence rates in the other countries, the rates in the Canadian sample were

Depression among the elderly is a serious problem that can be difficult to diagnose because the symptoms are often similar to those of physical illness or dementia.

Photodisc

moderate (4.6% prevalence). Since depression is often related to stress levels, the high rates of major depression in Lebanon may be related to the stresses of living under the unrest and violence that is characteristic of Beirut's current political climate.

Kinzie, Leung, Boehnlein, and Matsunaga (1992) used a structured interview to determine the percentage of adult members of a First Nations reserve who met criteria for mood disorders. The lifetime prevalence for any mood disorder was 19.4% in men, 36.7% in women, and 28% overall, approximately four times higher than in the general population. Examined by disorder, almost all the increase is accounted for by greatly elevated rates of major depression. Findings in the same reserve for substance abuse are similar to the results for major depressive disorder (see Chapter 10). A study of mental health services use among the Cree of James Bay, Quebec, indicated that depression was the most common psychiatric illness, occurring in 16.5% of the 242 Cree who were receiving treatment by nursing or other medical professionals in the region (Lavallee, Robinson, & Laverdure, 1991). Depression was the most common problem for women and alcohol abuse the most common for men (Lavallee et al., 1991). As noted by Laurence Kirmayer (1994; Kirmayer, Boothroyd, Tanner, Adelson, & Robinson, 2000), the appalling social and economic conditions faced by many groups of Native peoples in North America fulfill all the requirements for chronic major life stress, which is so strongly related to the onset of mood disorders, particularly major depressive disorder.

## Among the Creative

Is there truth in the enduring belief that genius is allied to madness? Several researchers have attempted to find out. The results are surprising. Table 6.3 lists a group of famous North American poets, many of whom won the coveted Pulitzer Prize. As you can see, all almost certainly had bipolar disorder. Many committed suicide. These 8 poets are among the 36 born in the 20th century who are represented in *The New Oxford Book of American Verse*, a collection reserved for only the most distinguished poets. It is certainly striking that about 20% of these 36 poets exhibited bipolar disorders, given the population prevalence of slightly less than 1%.

Many artists and writers, whether suspected of mood disorders or not, speak of periods of inspiration when thought processes quicken, moods lift, and new associations are generated (Jamison, 1989, 1993). Perhaps something inherent in manic states fosters creativity. But, as noted by the late Norman Endler, "it is one thing to have the high degree of energy that exists in a manic state; it is another thing to channel it in a direction that creates new works and accomplishes effective tasks" (Endler, 1990, p. 19). Endler was an internationally respected authority on emotional disorders who endured bipolar disorder himself and wrote about his experiences with this disorder in a book entitled *Holiday of Darkness* (Endler, 1990). It is also possible that the genetic vulnerability to mood disorders is independently accompanied by a predisposition to creativity (Richards, Kinney, Lunde, Benet, & Merzel, 1988). In other words, the genetic patterns associated with bipolar disorder may also carry the spark of creativity. These ideas are little more than speculations at present, but the study of creativity and leadership, so highly valued in all cultures, may be enhanced by a deeper understanding of "madness" (Endler, 1990; Ludwig, 1995).

## The Overlap of Anxiety and Depression

One of the mysteries faced by psychopathologists is the apparent overlap of anxiety and depression. Some of the latest theories on the causes of depression are

**TABLE 6.3** Partial Listing of Major 20th-Century North American Poets, Born between 1895 and 1935, with Documented Histories of Manic-Depressive Illness

| Poet | Pulitzer Prize in Poetry | Treated for Major Depressive Illness | Treated for Mania | Committed Suicide |
|------|--------------------------|--------------------------------------|-------------------|-------------------|
| Hart Crane (1899–1932) | | X | X | X |
| Theodore Roethke (1908–1963) | X | X | X | |
| Delmore Schwartz (1913–1966) | | X | X | |
| John Berryman (1914–1972) | X | X | X | X |
| Randall Jarrell (1914–1965) | | X | X | X |
| Robert Lowell (1917–1977) | X | X | X | |
| Anne Sexton (1928–1974) | X | X | X | X |
| Sylvia Plath* (1932–1963) | X | X | | X |

*Plath, although not treated for mania, was probably bipolar II.

*Source:* Goodwin & Jamison, 1990.

based, in part, on this research. Several theorists have concluded that the two moods are more alike than different. This may seem strange, because you probably do not feel the same when you are anxious as when you are depressed. However, we now know that almost everyone who is depressed, particularly to the extent of having a disorder, is also anxious (Barlow, 2002; Brown, Campbell, Lehman, Grisham, & Mancill, 2001), but not everyone who is anxious is depressed.

Let's examine this fact for a moment: *Almost all depressed patients are anxious, but not all anxious patients are depressed.* This means that certain core symptoms of depression are *not* found in anxiety and, therefore, reflect what is "pure" about depression. These core symptoms are the inability to experience pleasure *(anhedonia)* and a depressive "slowing" of both motor and cognitive functions until they are extremely laboured and effortful (Moras et al., 1996; Rottenberg et al., 2002). Cognitive content (what one is thinking about) is usually more negative in depressed individuals than in anxious ones (Greenberg & Beck, 1989).

Recently, our own ongoing research has identified symptoms that seem central to panic and anxiety. In panic, the symptoms reflect primarily autonomic activation (excessive physiological symptoms such as heart palpitations and dizziness); muscle tension and apprehension (excessive worrying about the future) seem to reflect the essence of anxiety (Brown, Chorpita, & Barlow, 1998; Zinbarg & Barlow, 1996). Many people with depression and even bipolar disorder also have symptoms of anxiety or panic (Frank et al., 2002; MacKinnon et al., 2003). More important, a large number of symptoms help define both anxiety and depressive disorders. Because these symptoms are *not specific* to either kind of disorder, they are called symptoms of *negative affect* (Brown et al., 1998; Tellegen, 1985).

Symptoms specific to anxiety, specific to depression, and common to both states are presented in Table 6.4. Ultimately, research in this area may cause us to rethink our diagnostic criteria and combine anxiety and mood disorders into one larger category. Symptoms of negative affect alone are often less severe than full-blown anxiety or mood disorders, but their presence increases the risk of more severe disorders, suggesting that these symptoms are on a continuum with major depression and anxiety disorders (Nolen-Hoeksema, 2000b; Solomon & Haaga, 2003).

Now think back for a minute to the case of Katie. You remember she was severely depressed and clearly had experienced a major depressive episode and serious suicidal ideation. A review of the list of depressive symptoms shows that Katie

had all of them, thus meeting the criteria for major depressive disorder outlined in DSM-IV-TR. However, remember that Katie's difficulty began with her dread of interacting with her classmates or teachers for fear of making a fool of herself. Finally, she became so anxious that she stopped going to school. After seeing a doctor who recommended she be "persuaded" to attend school, her parents became firmer. As Katie explained, however,

> I felt nauseated and sick each time that I went into the school building and so each day I was sent home. Uncomfortable physical experiences like sweaty palms, trembling, dizziness, and nausea accompanied my anxiety and fear. For me, being in a classroom, being in the school building, even the anticipation of being in school, triggered anxiety and illness. All of the sensations of anxiety draw your attention away from your surroundings and toward your own physical feelings. All of this would be bearable if it wasn't so extremely intense. I found myself battling the desire to escape and

**TABLE 6.4** Symptoms Specific to Anxiety and to Depression as Well as Symptoms Shared by Both States

**Pure Anxiety Symptoms**

Apprehension
Tension
Edginess
Trembling
Excessive worry
Nightmares

**Pure Depression Symptoms**

Helplessness
Depressed mood
Loss of interest
Lack of pleasure
Suicidal ideation
Diminished libido

**Mixed Anxiety and Depression Symptoms (Negative Affect)**

Anticipating the worst
Worry
Poor concentration
Irritability
Hypervigilance
Unsatisfying sleep
Crying
Guilt
Fatigue
Poor memory
Middle/late insomnia
Sense of worthlessness
Hopelessness
Early insomnia

*Source:* Adapted from "The DSM-IV Field Trial for Mixed Anxiety Depression" by R.E. Zinbarg, D. H. Barlow, M. Liebowitz, L. Street, E. Broadhead, W. Katon, P. Roy-Byrne, J.P. Lepine, M. Teherani, J. Richards, P.J. Brantley, and H. Kraemer, 1994, *American Journal of Psychiatry* 151(8), 1153–62.

seek comfort. And, each escape brings with it a sense of failure and guilt. I understood that my physical sensations were inappropriate for the situation but I couldn't control them. I blamed myself for my lack of control.

Katie's case is rather typical in that severe anxiety eventually turned into depression. She never really lost the anxiety; she just became depressed, too. Epidemiological studies have confirmed that major depression almost always follows anxiety and may be a consequence of it (Breslau, Schultz, & Peterson, 1995; Kessler et al., 1996). Merikangas et al. (2003) followed almost 500 individuals for 15 years and found relatively few people experienced depression (or anxiety) alone. When they did, they usually ended up later with both anxiety and depression. The finding that depression often follows anxiety leads us to the causes of depression and other mood disorders.

# Causes of Mood Disorders

■ *Describe the biological, psychological, and sociocultural contributions to the development of unipolar and bipolar mood disorders.*

In Chapter 2 we described *equifinality* as the same end product resulting from possibly different causes. Just as there may be many reasons for a fever, there may be a number of reasons for depression. For example, a depressive disorder that arises in winter has a different precipitant than a severe depression following a death, even though the episodes might look similar. Nevertheless, psychopathologists are identifying biological, psychological, and social factors that seem strongly implicated in the etiology of mood disorders, whatever the precipitating factor. An integrative theory of the etiology of mood disorders considers the interaction of biological, psychological, and social dimensions and notes the strong relationship of anxiety and depression. Before describing this, we review evidence pertaining to each contributing factor.

## Biological Dimensions

Studies that would allow us to determine the genetic contribution to a particular disorder or class of disorders are complex and difficult to do. But several strategies—such as family studies and twin studies—can help us estimate this contribution.

### Familial and Genetic Influences

In *family studies*, we look at the prevalence of a given disorder in the first-degree relatives of an individual known to have the disorder (the *proband*). As noted in a review by Randy Katz, family studies have shown that both unipolar depression and bipolar disorder run in families (Katz & McGuffin, 1993). Despite wide variability, the rate in relatives of probands with mood disorders is consistently about two to three times greater than in relatives of controls who don't have mood disorders (Gershon, 1990; Klein, Lewinsohn, Rohde, Seeley, & Durbin, 2002). Klein et al. (2002) also demonstrated that increasing severity and recurrence of major depression in the proband was associated with higher rates of depression in relatives.

The best evidence that genes have something to do with mood disorders comes from *twin studies*, in which we examine the frequency with which identical twins (with identical genes) have the disorder compared with fraternal twins who share only 50% of their genes (as do all first-degree relatives). If a genetic contribution exists, the disorder should be present in identical twins to a much greater extent than in fraternal twins. A number of recent twin studies, including those by Randy Katz and colleagues, suggest that mood disorders are heritable (e.g., McGuffin & Katz, 1989; McGuffin et al., 2003). The strongest of the new studies is presented in Figure 6.2 (McGuffin et al., 2003). As you can see, an identical twin is two to three times more likely to present with a mood disorder than a fraternal twin if the first twin has a mood disorder (66.7% of identical

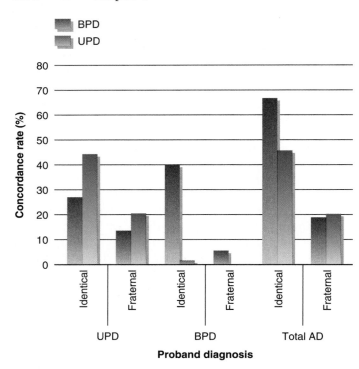

**Figure 6.2** ▪ Co-occurrence of types of mood disorders in twins for unipolar (UPD) and bipolar (BPD) affective disorder (AD). (From "The Heritability of Bipolar Affective Disorder and the Genetic Relationship to Unipolar Depression" by P. McGuffin, F. Rijsdijk, M. Andrew, P. Sham, R. Katz, and A. Cardno, *Archives of General Psychiatry, 60,* 497–502. Copyright © 2003 by the American Medical Association. Adapted with permission.)

twins compared with 18.9% of fraternal twins if the first twin has bipolar disorder; 45.6% versus 20.2% if the first twin has unipolar disorder). But notice that if one twin has unipolar disorder the chances of a co-twin having bipolar disorder are slim to none. Severity may also be related to amount of concordance (the degree to which something is shared). For example, one study showed that if one twin had severe depression (defined as three or more major depressive episodes), then 59% of the identical twins and 30% of the fraternal twins also presented with a mood disorder. If the individual presented with fewer than three episodes, the concordance rate dropped to 33% in identical twins and 14% in fraternal twins (Bertelsen, Harvald, & Jauge, 1977). This means severe mood disorders may have a stronger genetic contribution than less severe disorders, a finding that holds true for most psychological disorders.

Kendler, Neale, Kessler, Heath, and Eaves (1993) also estimated heritability of major depressive disorders in a large number of female twins to be from 41% to 46%, well within the range reported in Figure 6.2. Even in older adults, estimates of heritability remain in the moderate range of approximately 35% (McGue & Christensen, 1997).

Two recent reports have appeared suggesting sex differences in genetic vulnerability to depression. Bierut et al. (1999) studied 2662 twin pairs in the Australian twin registry and found the characteristically higher rate of depressive disorders in women. Estimates of heritability in women ranged from 36% to 44%, consistent with other studies. But estimates for men were lower and ranged from 18% to 24%. These results mostly agree with an important study of men in North America by Lyons et al. (1998). The authors conclude that environmental events play a larger role in causing depression in men than in women.

Although these findings raise continuing questions about the relative contributions of psychosocial and genetic factors to mood disorders, overwhelming evidence suggests that such disorders are familial and almost certainly reflect an underlying genetic vulnerability, particularly for women. As described in some detail in Chapter 2 (see pp. 41–42), studies are now beginning to identify a small group of genes that confer this vulnerability, at least for some types of depression (Caspi et al., 2003). In this complex field it is likely that many additional patterns of gene combinations will be found to contribute to varieties of depression.

In conclusion, the best estimates of genetic contributions to depression fall in the range of approximately 40% for women but seem to be significantly less for men. Genetic contributions to bipolar disorder seem to be somewhat higher. This means that from 60% to 80% of the causes of depression can be attributed to environmental factors. Behavioural geneticists break down environmental factors into events shared by twins (experiencing the same upbringing in the same house and, perhaps, experiencing the same stressful events) and events not shared. What part of our experience causes depression? There is wide agreement that it is the unique non-shared events rather than what is shared that interacts with biological vulnerability to cause depression (Bierut et al., 1999; Plomin et al., 1997).

### Depression and Anxiety: Same Genes?

Although most studies have looked at specific disorders in isolation, a growing trend is to examine the heritability of related groups of disorders. Evidence supports the supposition of a close relationship among depression, anxiety, and panic. For example, data from family studies indicate that the more signs and symptoms of anxiety and depression there are in a given patient, the greater the rate of anxiety, depression, or both in first-degree relatives and children (Hammen, Burge, Burney, & Adrian, 1990; Hudson et al., 2003). In several important reports from a major set of data on more than 2000 female twins, Kendler and his colleagues (Kendler, Heath, Martin, & Eaves, 1987; Kendler et al., 1995) found that the same genetic factors contribute to both anxiety and depression. Social and psychological explanations rather than genes seemed to account for the factors that differentiate anxiety from depression. These findings suggest, once again, that with the possible exception of mania, the biological vulnerability for mood disorders may not be specific to that disorder but may reflect a more general predisposition to anxiety or mood disorders. The specific form of the disorder would be determined by unique psychological, social, or additional biological factors (Akiskal, 1997; Lyons et al., 1998).

## Neurotransmitter Systems

Mood disorders have been the subject of more intense neurobiological study than almost any other area of psychopathology, with the possible exception of schizophrenia. New findings describing the relationship of specific neurotransmitters to mood disorders appear almost monthly and are punctuated by occasional reports of so-called breakthroughs. In this difficult area, most breakthroughs prove to be illusory, but false starts provide us with an ever-deeper understanding of the enormous complexity of the neurobiological underpinnings of mood disorders (Garlow & Nemeroff, 2004; National Institute of Mental Health, 2003).

In Chapter 2, we observed that we now know that neurotransmitter systems have many subtypes and interact in many complex ways, with each other and with neuromodulators (products of the endocrine system). Research implicates low levels of serotonin in the etiology of mood disorders (Benkelfat, Ellenbogen, Dean, Palmour, & Young, 1994; Sokolov & Kutcher, 2001), but only in relation to other neurotransmitters, including norepinephrine and dopamine (e.g., Goodwin & Jamison, 1990; Spoont, 1992). Remember that the apparent primary function of serotonin is to regulate our emotional reactions. For example, we are more impulsive, and our moods swing more widely, when our levels of serotonin are low. This may be because one of the functions of serotonin is to regulate systems involving norepinephrine and dopamine (Mandell & Knapp, 1979). According to the "permissive" hypothesis, when serotonin levels are low, other neurotransmitters are "permitted" to range more widely, become dysregulated, and contribute to mood irregularities, including depression. A drop in norepinephrine would be one of the consequences. Mann et al. (1996) used sophisticated brain-imaging procedures (PET scans) to confirm impaired serotonergic transmission in patients with depression. This theory is undoubtedly overly simplistic, but it does represent current strategies in the study of neurotransmitters and psychopathology. Current thinking is that the balance of the various neurotransmitters and their subtypes is more important than the absolute level of any one neurotransmitter.

In the context of this delicate balance, there is continued interest in the role of dopamine, particularly in relationship to manic episodes (Depue & Iacono, 1989) or psychotic features (Garlow & Nemeroff, 2004). For example, the dopamine agonist L-dopa seems to produce hypomania in bipolar patients (e.g., Van Praag & Korf, 1975), along with other dopamine agonists (Silverstone, 1985). But, as with other research in this area, it is difficult to pin down any relationships with certainty.

### The Endocrine System

Investigators became interested in the endocrine system when they noticed that patients with diseases affecting this system sometimes became depressed. For example, hypothyroidism, or Cushing's disease, affects the adrenal cortex. This disease leads to excessive secretion of cortisol and, often, to depression (and anxiety).

In Chapter 2, and again in Chapter 4 on anxiety disorders, we discussed the brain circuit called the HPA axis. This axis begins in the hypothalamus and runs through the pituitary gland, which coordinates the endocrine system (see Figure 2.9; p. 50). One of the glands influenced by the pituitary is the cortical section of the adrenal gland, which produces the stress hormone cortisol that completes the HPA axis. Cortisol is called a *stress hormone* because it is elevated during stressful life events. (We discuss this system in more detail in Chapter 7.) For now, it is enough to know that cortisol levels are elevated in depressed patients, a finding that makes sense considering the relationship between depression and severe life stress (Gold, Goodwin, & Chrousos, 1988; Ladd, Owens, & Nemeroff, 1996).

This connection led to the development of what was thought to be a biological test for depression, the *dexamethasone suppression test*. Dexamethasone suppresses cortisol secretion in normal subjects. However, when this substance was given to patients who were depressed, much *less* suppression was noticed, and what did occur didn't last long (Carroll, Martin, & Davies, 1968; Carroll et al., 1980). Approximately 50% of patients show this reduced suppression, particularly if their depression is severe (Rush et al., 1997). The thinking was that in depressed patients, the adrenal cortex secreted enough cortisol to overwhelm the suppressive effects of dexamethasone. This theory was heralded as important because it promised the first biological laboratory test for a psychological disorder. However, later research demonstrated that individuals with other disorders, particularly anxiety disorders, also demonstrate non-suppression (Feinberg & Carroll, 1984; Goodwin & Jamison, 1990), which eliminated its usefulness as a test to diagnose depression.

Recent research has taken some exciting new turns. Recognizing that stressful hormones are elevated in patients with depression (and anxiety), researchers have begun to focus on the harmful consequences of these elevations. We saw in Chapter 4 on anxiety disorders that individuals experiencing long-term heightened levels of stress hormones undergo some shrinkage of a brain structure called the *hippocampus*. The hippocampus, among other things, is responsible for down-regulating stress hormones and serves important functions in facilitating cognitive processes such as short-term memory. But the new finding, at least in animals, is that long-term overproduction of stress hormones makes the organism unable to develop new neurons (neurogenesis). This suppression of neurogenesis in the hippocampus might contribute to depression (McEwen, 1999). In fact, successful treatments for depression, including electroconvulsive therapy, seem to produce neurogenesis in the hippocampus, thereby reversing this process (Santarelli et al., 2003). This is just a theory that must now undergo the slow process of scientific confirmation.

## Sleep and Circadian Rhythms

Earlier we discussed the interesting new findings on SAD, noting that a characteristic symptom is an *increase* in sleeping. We have known for several years that sleep disturbances are a hallmark of most mood disorders. Most important, in people who are depressed there is a significantly shorter period after falling asleep before rapid eye movement (REM) sleep begins. Depressed individuals have diminished slow wave sleep, which is the deepest, most restful part of sleep (Jindal et al., 2002; Kupfer, 1995). (We discuss the process of sleep in more detail in Chapter 8.) In addition to entering REM sleep *much more quickly*, depressed patients experience REM activity that is much more intense, and the stages of deepest sleep don't occur until later and sometimes not at all. It is not yet clear whether sleep disturbances also characterize bipolar patients (Goodwin & Jamison, 1990), although preliminary evidence suggests patterns of *increased* rather than *decreased* sleep (Kupfer, 1995) and a longer rather than shorter REM latency (Rao et al., 2002).

Another interesting finding is that *depriving* depressed patients of sleep, particularly during the second half of the night, causes temporary improvement in their condition (Giedke & Schwarzler, 2002; Wehr & Sack, 1988), although the depression returns when the patients start sleeping normally again. In any case, because sleep patterns reflect a biological rhythm, there may be a relationship among SAD, sleep disturbances in depressed patients, and a more *general* disturbance in biological rhythms. This would not be surprising if it were true, because most mammals are exquisitely sensitive to day length at the latitudes at which they live, and this "biological clock" controls eating, sleeping, and weight changes. Thus, substantial disruption in circadian rhythm might be particularly problematic for some vulnerable individuals (Moore, 1999).

An additional interesting finding is that patients with bipolar disorder and their children (who are at risk for the disorder) show increased sensitivity to *light* (e.g., Nurnberger et al., 1988); that is, they show greater suppression of melatonin when they are exposed to light at night. Evidence also indicates that extended bouts of insomnia trigger manic episodes (Wehr, Goodwin, Wirz-Justice, Breitmeier, & Craig, 1982). These findings and others suggest that mood disorders may be related to disruptions in our circadian (daily) rhythms. For example, sleep deprivation may temporarily readjust the biological rhythms of depressed patients. Light therapy for SAD may have a similar effect (we'll discuss this later in this chapter). Goodwin and Jamison (1990) suggest that the specific genetic vulnerability to mood disorders may be related to low levels of serotonin, which somehow affect the regulation of our daily biological rhythms (Kupfer, 1995). Many of the results cited here are preliminary, and this theory, although fascinating, is still only speculative.

## *Brain Wave Activity*

A new and promising area of investigation focuses on characteristics of brain waves in depressed and anxious individuals. Measuring electrical activity in the brain with EEG was described in Chapter 3, where we also described a type of brain wave activity, alpha waves, that indicate calm, positive feelings. Davidson (1993) and Heller and Nitschke (1997) noted differential alpha activity in the two hemispheres of the brain in depressed individuals. These investigations demonstrated that depressed individuals exhibit greater right-side anterior activation of their cerebral hemispheres (and less left-side activation) than non-depressed individuals. Furthermore, the research of Ian Gotlib and his colleagues indicates that right-sided anterior activation is also found in patients who are no longer depressed (Gotlib, Ranganath, & Rosenfeld, 1998), suggesting this brain function might exist *before* the individual becomes depressed and represent a vulnerability to depression. If these findings are confirmed (Gotlib & Abramson, 1999), this type of brain functioning could become an indicator of a biological vulnerability to depression.

## Psychological Dimensions

In reviewing genetic contribution to the causes of depression, we noted that fully 60% to 80% of the causes of depression could be attributed to psychological experiences. Furthermore, most of those experiences are unique to the individual.

### Stressful Life Events

Stress and trauma are among the most striking unique contributions to the etiology of all psychological disorders. This is reflected throughout psychopathology and is evident in the wide adoption of the diathesis–stress model of psychopathology presented in Chapter 2 (and referred to throughout this book), which describes possible genetic and psychological vulnerabilities. But in seeking what activates this vulnerability (diathesis), we usually look for a stressful or traumatic life event.

You would think it would be sufficient to ask people whether anything major had happened in their lives before they developed depression or some other psychological disorder. Most people who develop depression report losing a job, getting divorced, having a child, or graduating from school and starting a career. But, as with most issues in the study of psychopathology, the significance of a major event is not easily discovered (Kessler, 1997), so most investigators have stopped simply asking patients whether something bad (or good) happened, and they have begun to look at the *context* of the event and the *meaning* it has for the individual.

For example, losing a job is stressful for most people, but it is far more difficult for some than others. A few people might even see it as a blessing. If you were laid off as a manager in a large corporation because of a restructuring, but your wife is the president of another corporation and makes more than enough money to support the family, it might not be so bad. Furthermore, if you are an aspiring writer or artist who has not had time to pursue your art, becoming jobless might be the opportunity you have been waiting for, particularly if your wife has been telling you for years to devote yourself to your creative pursuits.

Now consider losing your job if you are a single mother of two young children living from day to day and, on account of a recent credit card bill, you have to choose between paying the electric bill or buying food. The stressful life event is the same, but the context is very different and transforms the significance of the event substantially. To complicate the scenario further, think for a minute about how such a woman might react to losing her job. One woman might decide she is a total failure and thus becomes unable to carry on and provide for her children. Another woman might realize the job loss was not her fault and take advantage of a job training program while scraping by somehow. Thus, both the *context* of the life event and its *meaning* are important. This approach to studying life events, developed by George W. Brown (1989) and associates in England, is represented in Figure 6.3.

Brown's considerable advance in studying life events is difficult to carry out, and the methodology is still evolving. Many psychologists are actively developing new methods (e.g., Monroe & Roberts, 1990; Monroe, Rohde, Seeley, & Lewinsohn, 1999). One crucial issue is the bias inherent in remembering events. If you ask people who are currently depressed what happened when they first became depressed more than 5 years ago, you will probably get different answers from those they would give if they were *not* currently depressed. Because current moods distort memories, many investigators have concluded that the only useful way to study stressful life events is to follow people *prospectively*, to determine more accurately the precise nature of events and their relation to subsequent psychopathology.

In any case, in summarizing a large amount of research it is clear that stressful life events are strongly related to the onset of mood disorders (Kessler, 1997; Kendler, Karkowski, & Prescott, 1999b; Mazure, 1998). Measuring the *context* of events and their impact in a random sample of the population, a number of studies have found a marked relationship between severe and, in some cases, traumatic life events and the onset of depression (Brown, Harris, & Hepworth, 1994; Mazure, 1998). Severe events precede nearly *all* types of depression (Brown et al., 1994). The work of Ian Gotlib and colleagues indicates that major life stress is a somewhat stronger predictor for initial episodes of depression compared with recurrent episodes (Lewinsohn, Allen, Seeley, & Gotlib, 1999). In addition, for people with recurrent depression, the clear occurrence of a severe life stress before or early in the latest episode predicts a much

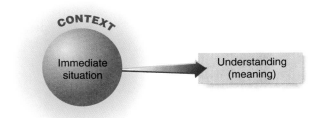

**Figure 6.3**  ■  Context and meaning in life stress situations. (From "Life Events and Measurement," by G. W. Brown. In G. W. Brown and T. O. Harris, Eds., *Life events and illness*, 1989. Copyright © 1989 by Guilford Press. Reprinted by permission.)

poorer response to treatment and a longer time before remission (Monroe, Kupfer, & Frank, 1992), as well as a greater likelihood of recurrence (Monroe, Roberts, Kupfer, & Frank, 1996).

Although the context and meaning are often more important than the exact nature of the event, there are some events that are particularly likely to lead to depression. One of them is the breakup of a relationship, which is difficult for both adolescents (Monroe et al., 1999) and adults (Kendler, Hettema, Butera, Gardner, & Prescott, 2003). The work of Zindel Segal and colleagues in Toronto indicates that romantic relationships play a key role in vulnerability to depression in adolescent girls (Williams, Connolly, & Segal, 2001). Despite this strong relationship between stress and depression, scientists are discovering that not all stressful events are independent of the depression. Remember in Chapter 2 where we noted that our genetic endowment might actually increase the probability that we will experience stressful life events? We referred to this as the reciprocal gene–environment model (Saudino et al., 1997). One example would be people who tend to seek out difficult relationships because of genetically based personality characteristics that then lead to depression. Now, Kendler et al. (1999b) report that about one-third of the association between stressful life events and depression is not the usual arrangement in which stress triggers depression; rather, individuals vulnerable to depression are placing themselves in high-risk stressful environments such as difficult relationships or other risky situations where bad outcomes are common.

The relationship of stressful events to the onset of episodes in bipolar disorder is also strong (Ellicott, 1988; Goodwin & Jamison, 1990; Johnson & Roberts, 1995; Reilly-Harrington, Alloy, Fresco, & Whitehouse, 1999). However, several issues may be particularly relevant to the etiology of bipolar disorders (Goodwin & Ghaemi, 1998). First, stressful life events seem to trigger early mania and depression, but as the disorder progresses these episodes seem to develop a life of their own. In other words, once the cycle begins, a psychological or pathophysiological process takes over and ensures the disorder will continue (e.g., Post, 1992; Post et al., 1989). Second, some of the precipitants of manic episodes seem related to loss of sleep, as in the postpartum period (Goodwin & Jamison, 1990), or as a result of jet lag, that is, disturbed circadian rhythms. In most cases of bipolar disorder, nevertheless, stressful life events are substantially indicated not only in provoking relapse but also in preventing recovery (Johnson & Miller, 1997).

Finally, although almost everyone who becomes depressed has experienced a significant stressful event, most people who experience such events do not become depressed. Although the data are not yet as precise as we would like, somewhere between 20% and 50% of individuals who experience severe events become depressed. Thus, between 50% and 80% of individuals do *not* develop depression or, presumably, any other psychological disorder. Again, data strongly support the *interaction* of stressful life events with some kind of vulnerability: genetic, psychological, or, more likely, a combination of the two influences (Barlow, 2002; Hankin & Abramson, 2001).

Given a genetic vulnerability (diathesis) and a severe life event (stress), what happens then? Research has isolated a number of psychological and biological processes. To illustrate one, let's return to Katie. Her life event was attending a new school.

## Katie
### No Easy Transitions

*I was a serious and sensitive 11-year-old at the edge of puberty and at the edge of an adventure that many teens and preteens embark on—the transition from elementary to junior high school. A new school, new people, new responsibilities, new pressures. Academically, I was a good student up to this point but I didn't feel good about myself and generally lacked self-confidence.*

Katie began to experience severe anxiety reactions. Then she became quite ill with the flu. After recovering and attempting to return to school, Katie discovered that her anxieties were worse than ever. More important, she began to feel she was losing control.

*As I look back I can identify events that precipitated my anxieties and fears, but then everything seemed to happen suddenly and without cause. I was reacting emotionally and physically in a way that I didn't understand. I felt out of control of my emotions and body. Day after day I wished, as a child does, that whatever was happening to me would magically end. I wished that I would awake one day to find that I was the person I was several months before.*

Katie's feeling of loss of control leads to another important psychological factor in depression: learned helplessness.

## Learned Helplessness

To review our discussion in Chapter 2, Seligman discovered that dogs and rats have an emotional reaction to events over which they have no control. If rats receive occasional shocks, they can function reasonably well if they can cope with the shocks by doing something to avoid them, such as pressing a lever. But if they learn that nothing they do helps them avoid the shocks, they eventually become helpless, give up, and manifest an animal equivalent of depression (Seligman, 1975).

Do humans react the same way? Seligman suggests we seem to, but only under one important condition: People become anxious and depressed when they decide, or make an *attribution*, that they have no control over the stress in their lives (Abramson, Seligman, & Teasdale, 1978; Miller & Norman, 1979). These findings evolved into an important model called the **learned helplessness theory of depression.** Often overlooked is Seligman's point that anxiety is the first response to a stressful situation. Depression may follow marked hopelessness about coping with the difficult life events (Barlow, 1988, 2002). The depressive attributional style is (1) *internal,* in that the individual attributes negative events to personal failings ("it is all my fault"); (2) *stable,* in that, even after a particular negative event passes, the attribution that "additional bad things will always be my fault" remains; and (3) *global,* in that the attributions extend across a variety of issues. Research continues on this interesting concept, but you can see how it applies to Katie. Early in her difficulties with attending school, she began to believe that events were out of her control and that she was unable even to begin to cope. More important, in her eyes the bad situation was all her fault: "I blamed myself for my lack of control." A downward spiral into a major depressive episode followed.

But a major question remains: Is learned helplessness a cause of depression or a correlated side effect of becoming depressed? If it were a *cause,* learned helplessness would have to exist *before* the depressive episode. Results from a 5-year longitudinal study in children may shed some light on this issue. Nolen-Hoeksema, Girgus, and Seligman (1992) reported that negative attributional style did not predict later symptoms of depression in *young* children; rather, stressful life events seemed to be the major precipitant of symptoms. However, as they *grew older,* they tended to develop more negative cognitive styles, which did tend to predict symptoms of depression in reaction to additional negative events. Nolen-Hoeksema and colleagues speculate that meaningful negative events early in childhood may give rise to negative attributional styles in a developmental fashion, making these children more vulnerable to future depressive episodes when stressful events occur.

This thinking recalls the types of psychological vulnerabilities theorized to contribute to the development of anxiety disorders (Barlow, 1988, 2002). That is, in a person who has a non-specific genetic vulnerability to either anxiety or depression, stressful life events activate a psychological sense that life events are uncontrollable (Barlow, 2002; Chorpita & Barlow, 1998). Evidence suggests that negative attributional styles are not specific to depression but characterize anxiety patients as well (Hankin & Abramson, 2001; Heimberg, Klosko, Dodge, & Shadick, 1989; Barlow, 2002). This may indicate that a psychological (cognitive) vulnerability is no more specific for mood disorders than a genetic vulnerability. Both types of vulnerabilities may underlie numerous disorders.

Abramson, Metalsky, and Alloy (1989) revised the learned helplessness theory to de-emphasize specific attributions and highlight the development of *a sense of hopelessness* as a crucial cause of many forms of

According to the learned helplessness theory of depression, people become depressed when they believe they have no control over the stress in their lives.

**learned helplessness theory of depression** Seligman's theory that people become anxious and depressed when they make an *attribution* that they have no control over the stress in their lives (whether in reality they do or not).

depression. Attributions are important only to the extent that they contribute to a sense of hopelessness. This fits well with recent thinking on crucial differences between anxiety and depression. Both anxious and depressed individuals feel helpless and believe they lack control, but only in depression do they give up and become hopeless about ever regaining control (Alloy, Kelly, Mineka, & Clements, 1990; Barlow, 1991, 2002; Chorpita & Barlow, 1998).

Evidence from the work of Ian Gotlib and his colleagues indicates that a pessimistic style of attributing negative events to one's own character flaws results in hopelessness (Gotlib & Abramson, 1999). This style may predate and therefore, in a sense, contribute to depressive episodes that follow negative or stressful events (Gotlib & Abramson, 1999). In fact, a recent longitudinal study by McGill University psychologists John Abela and Sabina Sarin (2002) followed children in grade 7 for 10 weeks, obtaining information on their initial attributional styles, negative life events, and later symptoms of depression. This study obtained results supporting the hopelessness theory of depression.

## Negative Cognitive Styles

Forty years ago, Aaron T. Beck (1967, 1976) suggested that depression may result from a tendency to interpret everyday events in a negative way, wearing grey instead of rose-coloured glasses. According to Beck, people with depression make the worst of everything; for them, the smallest setbacks are major catastrophes. In his extensive clinical work, Beck observed that all of his depressed patients thought this way, and he began classifying the types of "cognitive errors" that characterized this style. From the long list he compiled, two representative examples are *arbitrary inference* and *overgeneralization*. Arbitrary inference is evident when a depressed individual emphasizes the negative rather than the positive aspects of a situation. A high-school teacher may assume he is a terrible instructor because two students in his class fell asleep. He fails to consider other reasons they might be sleeping (up all night partying) and "infers" that his teaching style is at fault. As an example of overgeneralization, when your professor makes one critical remark on your paper you then assume you will fail the class despite a long string of positive comments and good grades on other papers. You are overgeneralizing from one small remark. According to Beck, people who are depressed think like this all the time. They make cognitive errors in thinking negatively about *themselves*, their *immediate world*, and their *future*, three areas that together are called the **depressive cognitive triad** (see Figure 6.4).

In addition, Beck theorized, after a series of negative events in childhood, individuals may

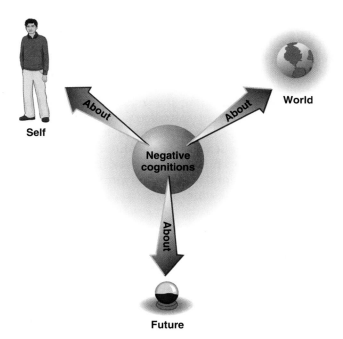

**Figure 6.4** ■ Beck's cognitive triad for depression.

develop a deep-seated *negative schema*, an enduring negative cognitive belief system about some aspect of life (Gotlib & Krasnoperova, 1998; Gotlib, Kurtzman, & Blehar, 1997; Gotlib & MacLeod, 1997). In a "self-blame" schema, individuals feel personally responsible for every bad thing that happens. With a negative self-evaluation schema, they believe they can never do anything correctly. In Beck's view, these cognitive errors and schemas are automatic, that is, not necessarily conscious. Indeed, an individual might not even be aware of thinking negatively and illogically. Thus, minor negative events can lead to a major depressive episode.

A variety of evidence supports a cognitive theory of emotional disorders in general and depression in particular (Goodman & Gotlib, 1999; Mazure, Bruce, Maciejewski, & Jacobs, 2000; Reilly-Harrington et al., 1999), and Canadian researchers have been at the forefront of developments in testing Beck's cognitive theory of depression (Rector, Segal, & Gemar, 1998). The thinking of depressed individuals is consistently more negative than that of non-depressed individuals (Dobson & Shaw, 1987; Gotlib & Abramson, 1999; Zuroff, Blatt, Sanislow, Bondi, & Pilkonis, 1999) in each dimension of the cognitive triad—the self, the world, and the future (e.g., Bradley & Mathews, 1988; Segal, Hood, Shaw, & Higgins, 1988).

---

**depressive cognitive triad** Thinking errors in depressed people negatively focused in three areas: themselves, their immediate world, and their future.

Research by Nicholas Kuiper and his colleagues at the University of Western Ontario has focused on the self component of Beck's cognitive triad. For example, Derry and Kuiper (1981) asked depressed and non-depressed individuals to complete a "self-referent encoding task" in which they rated a series of adjectives as to whether or not each described him or her. The depressed group viewed adjectives with depressive content (e.g., stupid, boring) as being significantly more applicable to themselves than did non-depressed participants. Conversely, the depressed group viewed adjectives with non-depressive content (e.g., nice, attractive) as being significantly less applicable to themselves.

Findings from a variety of prominent Canadian research teams suggest that depressive cognitions seem to emerge from distorted and probably automatic methods of processing information. People are more likely to recall negative events when they are depressed than when they are not depressed or than non-depressed individuals (Gotlib, Roberts, & Gilboa, 1996; Lewinsohn & Rosenbaum, 1987). A study by Marlene Moretti at Simon Fraser University and her colleagues (1996) used a cognitive task involving faces displaying different emotions to examine the processing of socially relevant information in depression. Participants were instructed to select the target expression that was most informative about how the person in the picture felt about the participant. The non-depressed participants showed a bias toward selecting faces with positive expressions as most informative, whereas the depressed participants selected both negative and positive faces. These results suggest that depressed people have less access to positive social information about themselves (Moretti et al., 1996).

The implications of Beck's theory are important. By recognizing cognitive errors and the underlying schemas, we can correct them and alleviate depression and related emotional disorders. In developing ways to do this, Beck became the father of cognitive therapy, one of the most important developments in psychotherapy in the last 50 years.

## Cognitive Vulnerability for Depression: An Integration

Seligman and Abramson, on the one hand, and Beck, on the other, developed their theories independently, and good evidence indicates their models are independent, in that some people may have a negative outlook (dysfunctional attitudes), whereas others may explain things negatively (hopeless attributions; Joiner & Rudd, 1996; Spangler, Simons, Monroe, & Thase, 1997). Nevertheless, the basic premises overlap a great deal, and considerable evidence suggests depression is always associated with a pessimistic explanatory style and negative cognitions.

Evidence also exists that cognitive vulnerabilities predispose some people to view events in a negative way, putting them at risk for depression (e.g., Mazure et al., 2000; Reilly-Harrington et al., 1999).

## Social and Cultural Dimensions

A number of social and cultural factors contribute to the onset or maintenance of depression. Among these, marital relationships, gender, and social support are most prominent.

### Marital Relations

Marital dissatisfaction and depression are strongly related. Findings from a number of studies also indicate that marital disruption often precedes depression. Bruce and Kim (1992) collected data on 695 women and 530 men and then reinterviewed them up to 1 year later. During this period a number of participants separated from or divorced their spouses, though the majority reported stable marriages. Approximately 21% of the women who reported a marital split during the study experienced severe depression, a rate three times higher than that for women who remained married. Nearly 17% of the men who reported a marital split developed severe depression, a rate *nine* times higher than that for men who remained married. However, when the researchers considered only those participants with no history of severe depression, 14% of the men who separated or divorced during the period experienced severe depression, as did approximately 5% of the women. In other words, *only the men* faced a heightened risk of developing a mood disorder for the first time immediately following a marital split. Is remaining married more important to men than to women? It would seem so.

Monroe, Bromet, Connell, and Steiner (1986), as well as O'Hara (1986), also implicated factors in the marital relationship as predicting the later onset of depression. Important findings from the Monroe group's (1986) study emphasize the necessity of separating *marital conflict* from *marital support*. In other words, it is possible that high marital conflict and strong marital social support may both be present at the same time or may both be absent. The work of Ian Gotlib and his colleagues indicates that high conflict, low support, or both are particularly important in generating depression (Barnett & Gotlib, 1988; Gotlib & Beach, 1995).

Another finding with considerable support is that depression, particularly if it continues, may lead to substantial deterioration in marital relationships (Gotlib & Beach, 1995; Whiffen & Gotlib, 1989b). It is not hard to figure out why. Being around someone who is continually negative, ill tempered, and pessimistic becomes tiring after a while. Because emotions are contagious, the spouse probably begins to feel bad also. These kinds of interactions precipitate arguments or, worse, make the non-depressed spouse want to leave (Biglan et al., 1985).

But conflict within a marriage seems to have different effects on men and women. Depression seems to cause men to withdraw or otherwise disrupt the relationship. For women, on the other hand, problems in the relationship most often cause depression. Thus, for both men and women, depression and problems in marital relations are associated, but the causal direction is different (Fincham, Beach, Harold, & Osborne, 1997), a result also found by Spangler, Simons, Monroe, and Thase (1996). Given these factors, Beach, Sandeen, and O'Leary (1990) suggest that therapists treat disturbed marital relationships at the same time as the mood disorder to ensure the highest level of success for the patient and the best chance of preventing future relapses.

## Mood Disorders in Women

As noted by psychiatric epidemiologist Roger Bland and others, data on the prevalence of mood disorders indicate dramatic gender imbalances (Bland, 1997). Although bipolar disorder is evenly divided between men and women, almost 70% of the individuals with major depressive disorder and dysthymia are women (Bland, 1997; Hankin & Abramson, 2001). What is particularly striking is that this gender imbalance is constant around the world, even though overall rates of disorder may vary from country to country (Weissman & Olfson,

1995; see Figure 6.5). For example, data from the Canadian site of the Cross-National Collaborative Study indicated that the lifetime prevalence of major depression was 12% for women as compared with only 7% for men (Weissman et al., 1994; see Figure 6.5). Often overlooked is the similar ratio for most anxiety disorders, particularly panic disorder and generalized anxiety disorder. Women represent an even greater proportion of specific phobias, as we noted in Chapter 2. What could account for this?

It may be that gender differences in the development of emotional disorders are strongly influenced by perceptions of uncontrollability (Barlow, 1988, 2002). If you feel a sense of mastery over your life and the difficult events we all encounter, you might experience occasional stress but you will not feel the helplessness central to anxiety and mood disorders. The source of these differences is cultural, in the sex roles assigned to men and women in our society. Males are strongly encouraged to be independent, masterful, and assertive; females, by contrast, are expected to be more passive, to be sensitive to other people, and, perhaps, to rely on others more than males do (Cyranowski, Frank, Young, & Shear, 2000; Hankin & Abramson, 2001). Although these stereotypes are slowly changing, they still describe current sex roles to a large extent. But this culturally induced dependence and passivity may put women at severe risk for emotional disorders by increasing their feelings of uncontrollability and helplessness. Evidence has accumulated that parenting styles encouraging stereotypic gender roles are implicated in the development of early psychological vulnerability to later depression

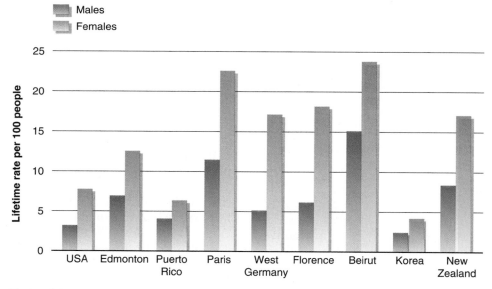

**Figure 6.5** ■ Lifetime international rate per 100 people for major depression. (Adapted with permission from "Depression in Women: Implications for Health Care Research," by M.M. Weissman and M. Olfson, 1995, *Science*, 269: 799–801. © 1995 AAAS.)

or anxiety (Chorpita & Barlow, 1998), specifically, a smothering overprotective style that prevents the child from developing initiative.

The value women place on intimate relationships may also put them at risk (Hammen, Marks, Maulo, & DeMayo, 1985). Disruptions in such relationships, combined with an inability to cope with the disruptions, may be far more damaging to women than to men. Data from Fincham et al. (1997) and Spangler et al. (1996), described earlier, seem to support this view. Cyranowski et al. (2000) note that the tendency for adolescent girls to express aggression by rejecting other girls, combined with a greater sensitivity to rejection, may precipitate more depressive episodes in these adolescent girls compared with boys. However, data from Bruce and Kim (1992), reviewed earlier, suggest that if the disruption in a marital relationship reaches the stage of divorce, men who had previously been functioning well are at greater risk for depression.

Another potentially important gender difference is that women tend to ruminate more than men about their situation and blame themselves for being depressed (Nolen-Hoeksema, 1987, 1990, 2000b; Nolen-Hoeksema, Larson, & Grayson, 1999). Men tend to ignore their feelings, perhaps engaging in activity to take their minds off them. This male behaviour may be therapeutic because "activating" people (getting them busy doing something) is a common element of successful therapy for depression (Lau & Segal, 2003; Lewinsohn & Gotlib, 1995).

As Janet Stoppard at the University of New Brunswick points out, women *are* at a disadvantage in our society (Stoppard, 1989, 1999, 2000; Stoppard & McMullen, 2003): They experience more discrimination, poverty, sexual harassment, and abuse than do men. They also earn less respect and accumulate less power. The majority of the people living in poverty in North America are women and children. Women, particularly single mothers, have a difficult time entering the workplace. Therefore, the meaning of conflict in a relationship is greater for women than for men, who are likely to respond more to problems at work. Data from the Canadian National Population Health Survey indicate that rates of depression are 2.5 times higher in single women with a child under 5 years old than among married mothers (Cairney, Thorpe, Rietschlin, & Avison, 1999). In fact, married women employed full time outside the home report levels of depression no greater than those of employed married men. Single, divorced, and widowed women experience significantly more depression than men in the same categories (Weissman & Klerman, 1977). This does not necessarily mean that anyone should get a job to avoid becoming depressed. Indeed, for a man or woman, feeling mastery, control, and value in the

Of the impoverished people in North America, the majority are women and children.

strongly socially supported role of homemaker and parent should be associated with low rates of depression. Moreover, recent findings from the Canadian National Population Health Survey show that work stress can be associated with depression in both men and women. It is just that gender might alter the type of work stress that is most strongly associated with depression (i.e., psychological demands predict depression in men whereas physical demands do so in women; Wang & Patten, 2001).

Finally, other disorders may reflect gender role stereotypes, but in the opposite direction. Disorders associated with aggressiveness, overactivity, and substance abuse occur far more frequently in men than in women (Barlow, 1988, 2002). Identifying the reasons for gender imbalances across the full range of psychopathological disorders may prove important in discovering causes of disorders.

### Social Support

In Chapter 2, we examined the powerful effect of social influences on our psychological and biological functioning. We cited several examples of how social influences seem to contribute to early death, such as the evil eye or lack of social support in old age. In general, the greater the number and frequency of your social relationships and contacts, the longer you are likely to live (e.g., House et al., 1988). It is not surprising, then, that social factors influence whether we become depressed.

In an early landmark study, Brown and Harris (1978) first suggested the important role of social support in the onset of depression. In a study of a large number of women who had experienced a serious life stress, they discovered that only 10% of the women who had a friend in whom they could confide became depressed compared with 37% of the women who did not have a close supportive relationship. Later prospective studies have also confirmed the importance of social support (or lack of it) in predicting the onset of depressive symptoms later (e.g., Joiner, 1997; Monroe, Imhoff, Wise, & Harris, 1983). Other studies have established the importance of social support in speeding recovery from depressive episodes (Keitner et al., 1995; Sherbourne, Hays, & Wells, 1995).

A recent Canadian randomized control study by Misri, Kostaras, Fox, and Kostaras (2000) examined the effects of partner support on the treatment of women with postpartum depression. Relative to control group patients, women who received the treatment involving partner support showed a significant decrease in their symptoms of depression, attesting to the importance of social support in recovery from postpartum depression. Johnson, Winett, Meyer, Greenhouse, and Miller (1999) examined the effects of social support in speeding recovery from both manic and depressive episodes in patients with bipolar disorder, and they came up with a surprising finding. A socially supportive network of friends and family helped speed recovery from depressive episodes but not from manic episodes. This finding highlights the uniquely different quality of manic episodes (McGuffin et al., 2003). In any case, these and related findings on the importance of social support have led to an exciting new psychological therapeutic approach for emotional disorders called *interpersonal psychotherapy*, which we discuss later in this chapter.

## An Integrative Theory

How do we put all this together? Basically, depression and anxiety may often share a common, genetically determined biological vulnerability (Barlow, 2002; Barlow et al., 1996) that can be described as an overactive neurobiological response to stressful life events. Again, this vulnerability is simply a general tendency to develop depression (or anxiety) rather than a specific vulnerability for depression or anxiety itself. Interestingly, this biological vulnerability to develop depression seems stronger for women than for men (Bierut et al., 1999). But only between 20% and 40% of the causes of depression can be attributed to genes. For the remainder, we look at life experience.

People who develop mood disorders also possess a psychological vulnerability experienced as feelings of inadequacy for coping with the difficulties confronting them. As with anxiety, we may develop this sense of control in childhood (Barlow, 2002; Chorpita & Barlow, 1998). It may range on a continuum from total confidence to complete inability to cope. When vulnerabilities are triggered, the "giving up" process seems crucial to the development of depression (Alloy et al., 1990, 2000).

A variety of evidence indicates that these attitudes and attributions correlate rather strongly with such biochemical markers of stress and depression as by-products of norepinephrine (e.g., Samson, Mirin, Hauser, Fenton, & Schildkraut, 1992) and with hemispheric lateral asymmetry (R. J. Davidson 1993; Heller & Nitschke, 1997).

The causes of this psychological vulnerability can be traced to early adverse experience in the form of childhood adversity and/or exposure to caregivers with psychopathology perhaps years before the onset of mood disorders. For example, Taylor and Ingram (1999) demonstrated that children of depressed mothers possess a less positive self-concept and more negative information processing, and Hammen and Brennan (2001) showed greater interpersonal deficits in this group of children. Jaffee et al. (2002) demonstrated that more severe childhood anxiety was associated with an earlier onset of depression. This enduring psychological vulnerability intensifies the biochemical and cognitive response to stress later in life (Goodman & Gotlib, 1999; Nolen-Hoeksema, 2000a).

There is also good evidence that stressful life events trigger the onset of depression in most cases, particularly initial episodes. How do these factors interact? The best current thinking is that stressful life events activate stress hormones, which, in turn, have wide-ranging effects on neurotransmitter systems, particularly those involving serotonin, norepinephrine, and the CRF system. Evidence also indicates that activation of stress hormones over the long term may actually turn on certain genes, producing long-term structural and chemical changes in the brain. For example, processes triggered by long-term stress seem to lead to atrophy of neurons in the hippocampus that help regulate emotions, or, more importantly, an inability to generate new neurons (neurogenesis). Such structural change might permanently affect the regulation of neurotransmitter activity. The extended effects of stress may also disrupt the circadian rhythms in certain individuals, who then become susceptible to the recurrent episodic cycling that seems so uniquely characteristic of the mood disorders (Moore, 1999; Post, 1992).

As noted earlier, triggering stressful life events also activate a dormant psychological vulnerability characterized by negative thinking and a sense of helplessness and hopelessness. What we have so far is a possible mechanism for the diathesis–stress model. Finally, it seems clear that factors such as interpersonal relationships or our gender may protect us from the effects of stress and therefore from developing mood disorders. Alternatively, these factors may at least determine whether we quickly recover from these disorders or not.

In summary, biological, psychological, and social factors all influence the development of mood disorders, as depicted in Figure 6.6. This

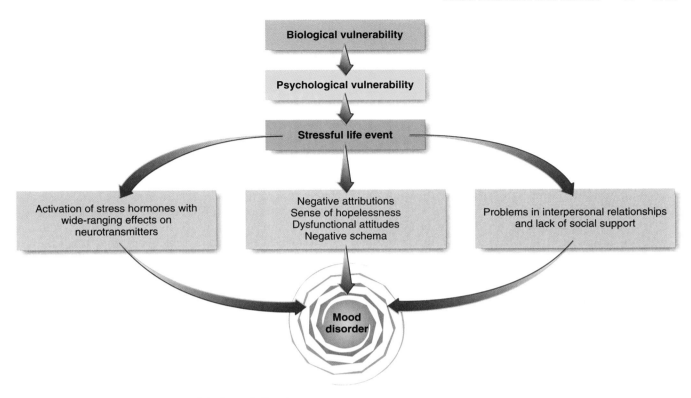

**Figure 6.6** ■ An integrative model of mood disorders.

model does not account for the varied presentation of mood disorders—unipolar, bipolar, and so on—although mania in bipolar disorder may be associated with unique genetic contributions. But why would someone with an underlying genetic vulnerability who experiences a stressful life event develop a bipolar disorder rather than a unipolar disorder or, for that matter, an anxiety disorder? As with the anxiety disorders and other stress disorders, specific psychosocial circumstances, such as early learning experiences, may interact with specific genetic vulnerabilities and personality characteristics to produce the rich variety of emotional disorders. Only time will tell.

**Concept Check 6.3**

Answer these questions about the various causes of mood disorders:
1. What are some of the biological causes of mood disorders? _____
2. What psychological factors can have an impact on these disorders? _____
3. Do social and cultural dimensions exist as causes? If so, which ones? _____

# Treatment of Mood Disorders

■ *Describe medical and psychological treatments that have been successful in treating mood disorders.*

We have learned a great deal about the neurobiology of mood disorders during the past several years. Findings on the complex interplay of neurochemicals are beginning to shed light on the nature of mood disorders. As we have noted, the principal effect of medications is to alter levels of these neurotransmitters and other related neurochemicals. Other biological treatments, such as electroconvulsive therapy (ECT),

dramatically affect brain chemistry. A more interesting development, however, alluded to throughout this book, is that powerful psychological treatments also alter brain chemistry. Despite these advances, most cases of depression go untreated because neither health-care professionals nor patients recognize and correctly identify or diagnose depression. Similarly, many professionals and patients are unaware of the existence of successful treatments (Hirschfeld et al., 1997). For this reason, it is important to learn about treatments for depression.

## Medications

### Antidepressants

Three basic types of antidepressant medications are used to treat depressive disorders: *tricyclic antidepressants, monoamine oxidase (MAO) inhibitors,* and the newer *selective serotonin reuptake inhibitors (SSRIs).*

*Tricyclic antidepressants* are widely used treatments for depression. The best-known variants are probably *imipramine* (Tofranil) and *amitriptyline* (Elavil). It is not yet clear how these drugs work, but initially, at least, they block the reuptake of certain neurotransmitters, allowing them to pool in the synapse and, as the theory goes, desensitize or *down-regulate* the transmission of that particular neurotransmitter (so less of the neurochemical is transmitted). Tricyclic antidepressants seem to have their greatest effect by down-regulating norepinephrine, although other neurotransmitter systems, particularly serotonin, are also affected. This process then has a complex effect on both presynaptic and postsynaptic regulation of neurotransmitter activity, eventually restoring appropriate balance. Ultimately, as noted previously, these drugs and other antidepressants may promote new nerve growth (neurogenesis) in the hippocampus (Santarelli et al., 2003). This process takes a while to work, often between 2 and 8 weeks. During this time, many patients feel a bit worse and develop a number of side effects such as blurred vision, dry mouth, constipation, difficulty urinating, drowsiness, weight gain (at least 6 kilograms

[13 pounds] on average), and, perhaps, sexual dysfunction. For this reason, as many as 40% of these patients may stop taking the drug, thinking the cure is worse than the disease. Nevertheless, with careful management, many side effects disappear. Tricyclics alleviate depression in approximately 50% of patients compared with approximately 25% to 30% of patients taking placebo pills, based on a summary analysis of more than 100 studies (American Psychiatric Association, 2000a; Depression Guideline Panel, 1993; see Table 6.5). If dropouts are excluded and only those who complete treatment are counted, success rates increase to between 65% and 70%. Another issue clinicians must consider is that tricyclics are *lethal* if taken in excessive doses; therefore, they must be prescribed with great caution to patients with suicidal tendencies.

*MAO inhibitors* work very differently; as their name suggests, they block the MAO enzyme that breaks down such neurotransmitters as norepinephrine and serotonin. The result is roughly equivalent to the effect of the tricyclics. Because they are not broken down, the neurotransmitters pool in the synapse, ultimately leading to a down-regulation or desensitization. The MAO inhibitors seem to be as effective as or slightly more effective than the tricyclics (American Psychiatric Association, 2000b; Depression Guideline Panel, 1993) with somewhat fewer side effects. But MAO inhibitors are used far less often because of two potentially serious consequences: Consuming foods and beverages containing tyramine, such as cheese, red wine, or beer, can lead to severe hypertensive episodes and, occasionally, death. In addition, many other drugs that people take daily, such as cold medications, are dangerous and even fatal in interaction with an MAO inhibitor. For this reason, MAO inhibitors are

| **TABLE 6.5** | Efficacy of Various Antidepressant Drugs for Major Depressive Disorder | | | |
|---|---|---|---|---|
| | **Drug Efficacy** | | **Drug Placebo** | |
| Drug | Inpatient | Outpatient | Inpatient | Outpatient |
| Tricyclics | 50.0% | 51.5% | 25.1% | 21.3% |
| SD | (6.5) | (5.2) | (11.5) | (3.9) |
| N | [33] | [102] | [8] | [46] |
| Monoamine oxidase inhibitors | 52.7% | 57.4% | 18.4% | 30.9% |
| SD | (9.7) | (5.5) | (22.6) | (17.1) |
| N | [14] | [21] | [9] | [13] |
| Selective serotonin reuptake inhibitors | 54.0% | 47.4% | 25.5% | 20.1% |
| SD | (10.1) | (12.5) | (21.7) | (7.8) |
| N | [8] | [39] | [2] | [23] |

Note: The percentage shown in the *Drug Efficacy* column is the anticipated percentage of patients provided the treatment shown who will respond. The *Drug Placebo* column shows the expected percentage difference in patients given a drug versus a placebo based on direct drug–placebo comparisons in trials that included at least these two cells. The numbers in parentheses are the standard deviations of the estimated percentage of responders. The bracketed numbers give the number of studies for which these estimates are calculated.

*Source:* Adapted from Depression Guideline Panel, 1993.

usually prescribed only when tricyclics are not effective (see Endler, 1990).

Pharmaceutical companies have developed a new generation of more selective MAO inhibitors that are short acting and do not interact negatively with tyramine (Baldessarini, 1989). Testing is still continuing on these new drugs.

Another class of drugs seems to have a specific effect on the serotonin neurotransmitter system (although they affect other systems to some extent). These SSRIs specifically block the presynaptic reuptake of serotonin. This temporarily increases levels of serotonin at the receptor site, but again the precise long-term mechanism of action is unknown, although levels of serotonin are eventually increased. Perhaps the best-known drug in this class is fluoxetine (Prozac). Like many other medications, Prozac was initially hailed as a breakthrough drug. Then reports began to appear that it might lead to suicidal preoccupation, paranoid reactions, and, occasionally, violence (e.g., Mandalos & Szarek, 1990; Teicher, Glod, & Cole, 1990). Prozac went from being a wonder drug in the eyes of the press to a potential menace to modern society. Neither conclusion was true. Findings indicate that the risks of suicide with this drug are no greater than with any other antidepressant, and the effectiveness is about the same (Fava & Rosenbaum, 1991). However, Prozac has its own set of side effects, the most prominent of which are physical agitation, sexual dysfunction, low sexual desire (which is very prevalent, occurring in 50% to 75% of cases), insomnia, and gastrointestinal upset. But these side effects, on the whole, seem to bother most patients less than the side effects associated with tricyclic antidepressants, with the possible exception of the sexual dysfunction. Studies suggest similar effectiveness of SSRIs and tricyclics with dysthymia (Lapierre, 1994).

Two new antidepressants seem to have somewhat different mechanisms of neurobiological action. Venlafaxine is related to tricyclic antidepressants but acts in a slightly different manner, reducing some of the associated side effects and the risk of damage to the cardiovascular system. Other typical side effects remain, including nausea and sexual dysfunction. Nefazodone is closely related to the SSRIs but seems to improve sleep efficiency instead of disrupting sleep. Both drugs are roughly comparable in effectiveness to older antidepressants (American Psychiatric Association, 2000b; Preskorn, 1995).

Finally, there has been a great deal of interest lately in the antidepressant properties of the natural herb St. John's wort *(hypericum)*. St. John's wort is popular in Europe and it began catching on in Canada and the United States around 1995 (Canterbury Farms, 1997). Unfortunately, a large North American study showed no specific effectiveness for the herb compared with placebo treatments or other medications (Hypercium Depression Trial Study Group, 2002). This study has been criticized, however, because it included only severely depressed patients, and St. John's wort might work better with people who are only mildly depressed. In any case, St. John's wort is available only in health food stores and similar outlets, and there is no guarantee that any given brand of St. John's wort contains the appropriate ingredients, since this herb is not regulated by any government agency. Moreover, Health Canada issued a letter to Canadian physicians, pharmacists, and alternative medicine practitioners warning them about the possibility of negative drug interactions with St. John's wort (e.g., with drug treatments for HIV, immunosuppressant drugs taken by transplant patients, antidepressants, and oral contraceptives; Health Canada, 2000a).

Current studies indicate that drug treatments effective with adults are *not* necessarily effective with children (Geller et al., 1992; Ryan, 1992). Sudden deaths of children under 14 who were taking tricyclic antidepressants have been reported, particularly during exercise, as in routine school athletic competition (Tingelstad, 1991). The causes imply cardiac side effects. Traditional antidepressant drug treatments are usually effective with the elderly, but administering them takes considerable skill because older people may experience a variety of side effects not experienced by younger adults, including memory impairment and physical agitation (e.g., Deptula & Pomara, 1990; Marcopulos & Graves, 1990).

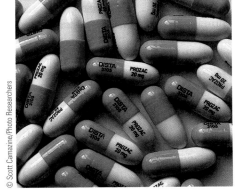

Of the synthetic drugs for depression, fluoxetine (Prozac, *left*), is the most widely used; the common groundcover hypericum (St. John's wort, *right*) is popular as a natural treatment in Europe and in North America.

Clinicians and researchers have concluded that recovery from depression, although important, may not be the most important therapeutic outcome (Frank et al., 1990; Prien & Kupfer, 1986). The large majority of people eventually recover from a major depressive episode, some rather quickly. A more important goal is often to delay the next depressive episode or even prevent it entirely (National Institute of Mental Health, 2003; Thase & Kupfer, 1996). This is particularly important for patients who retain some symptoms of depression or have a past history of chronic depression or multiple depressive episodes. Because all these factors put people at risk for relapse, it is recommended that drug treatment go well beyond the termination of a depressive episode, continuing perhaps 6 to 12 months after the episode is over or even longer (American Psychiatric Association, 2000b). The drug is then gradually withdrawn over weeks or months. (We return later to strategies for *maintaining* therapeutic benefits.)

Antidepressant medications have relieved severe depression and undoubtedly prevented suicide in tens of thousands of patients around the world. Although these medications are readily available, many people refuse or are not eligible to take them. Some are wary of long-term side effects. Women of childbearing age must protect themselves against the possibility of conceiving while taking antidepressants, because they can damage the fetus. In addition, 40% to 50% of patients do not respond adequately to these drugs, and a substantial number of the remainder are left with residual symptoms. A recent review of the literature by Michael Bagby in Toronto indicates that response to antidepressant medications appears to be better in those with high social support and worse in those with co-occurring anxiety disorders (Bagby, Ryder, & Cristi, 2002).

## Lithium

A fourth type of equally effective antidepressant drug, *lithium*, is a common salt widely available in the natural environment. It is found in our drinking water in amounts too small to have any effect. However, the side effects of therapeutic doses of lithium are potentially more serious than those of other antidepressants. Dosage has to be carefully regulated to prevent toxicity (poisoning) and lowered thyroid functioning, which might intensify the lack of energy associated with depression. Substantial weight gain is also common. Lithium, however, has one major advantage that distinguishes it from other antidepressants: It is often effective in preventing and treating manic episodes. For this reason it is most often referred to as a mood-stabilizing drug. Because tricyclic antidepressants can induce manic episodes, even in individuals without preexisting bipolar disorder (Goodwin &

Ghaemi, 1998; Goodwin & Jamison, 1990), lithium is the treatment of choice for bipolar disorder.

We are not sure how lithium works (Endler, 1990). It may limit the availability of dopamine and norepinephrine, but it may have more important effects on some of the **neurohormones** in the endocrine system, particularly those that influence the production and availability of sodium and potassium, electrolytes found in body fluids (Goodwin & Jamison, 1990). Results indicate that 30% to 60% of bipolar patients respond well to lithium initially, 30% to 50% show evidence of a partial response, and 10% to 20% have a poor response (Prien & Potter, 1993; Show, 1985). Thus, although effective, lithium provides many people with inadequate therapeutic benefit. Patients who don't respond can take other drugs with antimanic properties, including anticonvulsants such as carbamazepine and valproate (Divalproex), and calcium channel blockers such as verapamil (Keck & McElroy, 2002; Sachs & Rush, 2003). Valproate has recently overtaken lithium as the most frequently prescribed mood stabilizer (Goodwin et al., 2003; Keck & McElroy, 2002). But newer studies show that these drugs have one distinct disadvantage: They are less effective than lithium in preventing suicide (Tondo, Jamison, & Baldessarini, 1997; Goodwin et al., 2003).

For those patients who *do* respond to lithium, some studies suggest that maintaining adequate doses can prevent recurrence of manic episodes in approximately 66% of individuals (with 34% relapsing), based on 10 major double-blind studies comparing lithium with placebo. Relapse rates in the placebo group averaged a high 81% over periods ranging from several months to several years (Goodwin & Jamison, 1990; Suppes, Baldessarini, Faedda, & Tohen, 1991). But newer studies following patients for up to 5 years report that approximately 70% ultimately relapse, even if they continue to take the lithium (Frank et al., 1999; Gitlin, Swendsen, Heller, & Hammen, 1995; Peselow, Fieve, Difiglia, & Sanfilipo, 1994). Nevertheless, for almost anyone with recurrent manic episodes, maintenance on lithium or a related drug is recommended to prevent relapse. Another problem with drug treatment of bipolar disorder is that people usually like the euphoric or high feeling that mania produces, and they often stop taking lithium to maintain or regain the state; that is, they do not comply with the medication regimen. Because the evidence now clearly indicates that individuals who stop their

---

**neurohormones**   Hormones that affect the brain and are increasingly the focus of study in psychopathology.

medication are at considerable risk for relapse, other methods, usually psychological in nature, are used to increase compliance.

## Electroconvulsive Therapy and Transcranial Magnetic Stimulation

When someone does not respond to medication (or in an extremely severe case), clinicians may consider a more dramatic treatment, **electroconvulsive therapy (ECT),** the most controversial treatment for psychological disorders, after psychosurgery. In Chapter 1, we described how ECT was used in the early 20th century. Despite many unfortunate abuses along the way, ECT is considerably changed today. It is now a safe and reasonably effective treatment for severe depression that has not improved with other treatments (American Psychiatric Association, 2000a; Black, Winokur, & Nasrallah, 1987; NIMH, 2003; Crowe, 1984; Klerman, 1988).

In current administrations, patients are anesthetized to reduce discomfort and given muscle-relaxing drugs to prevent bone breakage from convulsions during seizures. Electric shock is administered directly through the brain for less than a second, producing a seizure and a series of brief convulsions that usually lasts for several minutes. In current practice, treatments are administered once every other day for a total of 6 to 10 treatments (fewer if the patient's mood returns to normal). Side effects are surprisingly few and generally limited to short-term memory loss and confusion that disappear after a week or two, although some patients may have long-term memory problems. For severely depressed inpatients with psychotic features, controlled studies (including some in which the control group undergoes a "sham" ECT procedure and doesn't actually receive shocks) indicate that approximately 50% of those not responding to medication will benefit. Continued treatment with medication or psychotherapy is then necessary because the relapse rate approaches 60% (American Psychiatric Association, 2000a; Brandon et al., 1984; Depression Guideline Panel, 1993; Fernandez, Levy, Lachar, & Small, 1995; Prudic, Sackheim, & Devanand, 1990). It may not be in the best interest of acutely suicidal inpatients to wait 3 to 6 weeks to determine whether a drug or psychological treatment is working; in these cases, immediate ECT may be appropriate.

We do not really know why ECT works (Endler, 1990). Obviously, repeated seizures induce massive functional and perhaps structural changes in the brain, which seems to be therapeutic. There is some evidence that ECT increases levels of serotonin, blocks stress hormones, and promotes neurogenesis in the hippocampus. Because of the controversial nature of this treatment, its use declined considerably during the 1970s and 1980s (American Psychiatric Association, 1990).

Recently, another method for altering electrical activity in the brain by setting up a strong magnetic field has been introduced. This procedure is called *transcranial magnetic stimulation (TMS)*, and it works by placing a magnetic coil over the individual's head to generate a precisely localized electromagnetic pulse. Anesthesia is not required, and side effects are usually limited to headaches. Initial reports, as with most new procedures, showed promise in treating depression (George, Lisanby, & Sackheim, 1999). Double-blind trials, in which some patients received a "sham" procedure leading both clinician and patient to think they are getting TMS, demonstrated the effectiveness of TMS compared with this sham procedure (Fitzgerald et al., 2003). Now results from several important clinical trials suggest that TMS is equally effective to ECT in patients with severe or psychotic depression that is treatment resistant (has not responded to drugs or psychological treatments; Grunhaus, Schreiber, Dolberg, Polak, & Dannon, 2003; Janicak et al., 2002). If these results are confirmed, we would have a good alternative to ECT.

## Phototherapy for Seasonal Affective Disorder

A specific therapy has been developed for the treatment of the seasonal subtype of depression (i.e., SAD). Recall from our earlier discussion of SAD the role of increased production of melatonin in this disorder. Some clinicians reasoned that exposure to bright light might slow melatonin production in individuals with SAD (Blehar & Rosenthal, 1989; Lewy, Kern, Rosenthal, & Wehr, 1982). In phototherapy, the specific treatment developed for SAD, most patients are exposed to 2 hours of very bright light immediately on awakening (Lam & Levitt, 1999). The work of Raymond Lam and colleagues indicates that not only is phototherapy effective in treating depression in SAD patients, it is also effective in reducing suicidality (Lam, 1994; Lam, Tam, Shiah, Yatham, & Zis, 2000). But this treatment is not without side effects, as illustrated by the work of Anthony Levitt and colleagues at the Sunnybrook Health Sciences Centre in Toronto. Approximately 19% of patients experience headaches, 17% eyestrain, and 14% just feel "wired" (Levitt et al., 1993). The mechanism of action of phototherapy in

---

**electroconvulsive therapy (ECT)**   Biological treatment for severe, chronic depression involving the application of electrical impulses through the brain to produce seizures. The reasons for its effectiveness are unknown.

treating SAD is not yet fully established. One recent study suggested that advances in circadian rhythms are an important factor in the effectiveness of this relatively new form of treatment for SAD (Terman, Terman, Lo, & Cooper, 2001).

## Psychological Treatments

Of the effective psychological treatments now available for depressive disorders, two major approaches have the most evidence supporting their efficacy. The first is cognitive-behavioural; Aaron T. Beck, the founder of *cognitive therapy*, is most closely associated with this approach. The second approach, *interpersonal psychotherapy*, was developed by Myrna Weissman and Gerald Klerman.

### Cognitive-Behavioural Therapy

Beck's **cognitive therapy** grew directly out of his observations of the role of deep-seated negative thinking in generating depression (Beck, 1967, 1976; D. A. Clark, Beck, & Alford, 1999; Young, Weinberger, & Beck, 2001). David A. Clark describes the approach as follows. First, clients are taught to examine carefully their thought processes while they are depressed and to recognize "depressive" errors in thinking. This task is not always easy, because many thoughts are automatic and beyond clients' awareness. Negative thinking seems natural to them. Clients are taught that errors in thinking can directly cause depression. Treatment involves correcting cognitive errors and substituting less depressing and (perhaps) more realistic thoughts and appraisals. Later in therapy, underlying *negative cognitive schemas* (characteristic ways of viewing the world) that trigger specific cognitive errors are targeted, not only in the office but also as part of the client's day-to-day life. The therapist purposefully takes a Socratic approach, making it clear that therapist and client are working as a team to uncover faulty thinking patterns and the underlying schemas from which they are generated. Therapists must be skillful and highly trained (see D. A. Clark et al., 1999). Following is an example of an actual interaction between Beck and a client named Irene.

## Beck and Irene
### A Dialogue

Because an intake interview had already been completed by another therapist, Beck did not spend time reviewing Irene's symptoms in detail

or taking a history. Irene began by describing her "sad states." Beck almost immediately started to elicit her automatic thoughts during these periods.

**THERAPIST:** What kind of thoughts were you having during these 4 days when you said your thoughts kept coming over and over again?

**PATIENT:** Well, they were just—mostly, "Why is this happening again"—because, you know, this isn't the first time he's been out of work. You know, "What am I going to do"—like I have all different thoughts. They are all in different things like being mad at him, being mad at myself for being in this position all the time. Like I want to leave him or if I could do anything to make him straighten out and not depend so much on him. There's a lot of thoughts in there.

**T:** Now can we go back a little bit to the sad states that you have? Do you still have that sad state?

**P:** Yeah.

**T:** You have it right now?

**P:** Yeah, sort of. They were sad thoughts about— I don't know—I get bad thoughts, like a lot of what I'm thinking is bad things. Like not—there is like, ah, it isn't going to get any better, it will stay that way. I don't know. Lots of things go wrong, you know, that's how I think.

**T:** So one of the thoughts is that it's not going to get any better?

**P:** Yeah.

**T:** And sometimes you believe that completely?

**P:** Yeah, I believe it, sometimes.

**T:** Right now do you believe it?

**P:** I believe—yeah, yeah.

**T:** Right now you believe that things are not going to get better?

**P:** Well, there is a glimmer of hope but it's mostly....

**T:** What do you kind of look forward to in terms of your own life from here on?

---

**cognitive therapy**   Treatment approach that involves identifying and altering negative thinking styles related to psychological disorders such as depression and anxiety and replacing them with more positive beliefs and attitudes— and, ultimately, more adaptive behaviour and coping styles.

**P:** Well, what I look forward to—I can tell you but I don't want to tell you. *(Giggles)*. Um, I don't see too much.

**T:** You don't want to tell me?

**P:** No, I'll tell you but it's not sweet and great what I think. I just see me continuing on the way I am, the way I don't want to be, like not doing anything, just being there, like sort of with no use, that like my husband will still be there and he will, you know, he'll go in and out of drugs or whatever he is going to do, and I'll just still be there, just in the same place.

By inquiring about Irene's automatic thoughts, the therapist began to understand her perspective—that she would go on forever, trapped, with her husband in and out of drug centres. This hopelessness about the future is characteristic of most depressed patients. A second advantage to this line of inquiry is that the therapist introduced Irene to the idea of looking at her own thoughts, which is central to cognitive therapy. (Young et al., 2001, pp. 287–288)

---

Between sessions, clients are instructed to *monitor and log* their thought processes carefully, particularly in situations where they might feel depressed. They also attempt to change their behaviour by carrying out specific activities assigned as homework, such as tasks in which clients can test their faulty thinking. For example, a client who has to participate in an upcoming meeting might think, "If I go to that meeting, I'll just make a fool of myself and all my colleagues will think I'm stupid." The therapist might instruct the client to go to the meeting, predict ahead of time the reaction of her colleagues, and then see what really happens. This part of treatment is called *hypothesis testing* because the client makes a hypothesis about what's going to happen (usually a depressing outcome) and then, most often, discovers it is incorrect ("My colleagues congratulated me on my presentation"). The therapist typically schedules other activities to *reactivate* depressed patients who have given up most activities, helping them put some fun back into their lives. Cognitive therapy typically takes from 10 to 20 sessions, scheduled weekly.

## Interpersonal Psychotherapy

We have seen that major disruptions in our interpersonal relationships are an important category of stresses that can trigger mood disorders (Barnett & Gotlib, 1988; Kendler, Hettema, et al., 2003). In addition, people with few, if any, important social relationships seem at risk for developing and sustaining mood disorders (Sherbourne, Hays, & Wells, 1995). **Interpersonal psychotherapy (IPT**; Gillies, 2001; Weissman, 1995) focuses on resolving problems in existing relationships and learning to form important new interpersonal relationships.

Therapist Laurie Gillies of the Ontario Institute for Studies in Education and the University of Toronto has described the approach as follows (Gillies, 2001). Like cognitive-behavioural approaches, IPT is highly structured and seldom takes longer than 15 to 20 sessions, usually scheduled once a week. After identifying life stressors that seem to precipitate the depression, the therapist and patient work collaboratively on the patient's current interpersonal problems. Typically, these include one or more of four interpersonal issues: *dealing with interpersonal role disputes,* such as marital conflict; *adjusting to the loss of a relationship,* such as grief over the death of a loved one; *acquiring new relationships,* such as getting married or establishing professional relationships; and *identifying and correcting deficits in social skills* that prevent the person from initiating or maintaining important relationships (Gillies, 2001).

To take a common example, the therapist's first job is to identify and define an interpersonal dispute (Gillies, 2001; Weissman, 1995), perhaps with a wife who expects her spouse to support her but has had to take an outside job to help pay bills. The husband might expect the wife to share equally in generating income. If this dispute seems to be associated with the onset of depressive symptoms and to result in a continuing series of arguments and disagreements without resolution, it would become the focus for IPT.

After helping identify the dispute, the next step is to bring it to a resolution. First, the therapist helps the patient determine the stage of the dispute.

1. *Negotiation Stage:* Both partners are aware it is a dispute, and they are trying to renegotiate it.
2. *Impasse Stage:* The dispute smoulders beneath the surface and results in low-level resentment, but no attempts are made to resolve it.
3. *Resolution Stage:* The partners are taking some action, such as divorce or separation.

The therapist works with the patient to define the dispute clearly for both parties and develop specific strategies for resolving it.

---

**interpersonal psychotherapy (IPT)** Newer brief treatment approach that emphasizes resolution of interpersonal problems and stressors such as role disputes in marital conflict or forming relationships in marriage or a new job. It has demonstrated effectiveness for such problems as depression.

Recent studies comparing the results of cognitive therapy and IPT with those of tricyclic antidepressants and other control conditions have found that psychological approaches and medication are equally effective, and all treatments are more effective than placebo conditions, brief psychodynamic treatments, or other appropriate control conditions for both major depressive disorder and dysthymia (Beck, Hollon, Young, Bedrosian, & Budenz, 1985; Blackburn & Moore, 1997; Hollon et al., 1992; Miller, Norman, & Keitner, 1989; Schulberg et al., 1996; Shapiro et al., 1995). Depending on how "success" is defined, approximately 50% to 70% or more of people benefit from treatment to a significant extent, compared with approximately 30% in placebo or control conditions (Craighead, Hart, Craighead, & Ilardi, 2002).

Studies, including one conducted by Peter McLean at the University of British Columbia, have not found a difference in treatment effectiveness based on severity of depression (Hollon et al., 1992; McLean & Taylor, 1992). DeRubeis, Gelfand, Tang, and Simons (1999) carefully evaluated the effects of cognitive therapy versus medication in severely depressed patients only, across four studies, and found no advantage for one treatment or the other. Recently, O'Hara, Stuart, Gorman, and Wenzel (2000) demonstrated more positive effects for IPT in a group of women with postpartum depression, demonstrating that this approach is a worthwhile strategy in patients with postpartum depression who are reluctant to go on medication because, for example, they are breastfeeding. In one important related study, Spinelli and Endicott (2003) compared IPT with an alternative psychological approach in 50 depressed pregnant women unable to take drugs because of potential harm to the fetus. Fully 60% of these women recovered, leading the authors to recommend that IPT should be the first choice for pregnant depressed women.

Recent work by Darcy Santor and Vivek Kusumakar (2001) at Dalhousie University evaluated the effectiveness of 12 weeks of IPT in 25 depressed adolescents. The majority of teens improved substantially on both self-ratings and clinician-ratings of depression symptoms with 80% to 84% no longer showing meaningful levels of depression by therapy completion. The study suggests that IPT may be effective for treating depression in adolescents, and should be followed up with a randomized controlled trial (Santor & Kusumakar, 2001).

### Prevention

In view of the seriousness of mood disorders in children and adolescents, work has begun on preventing these disorders in these age groups (Muñoz, 1993). Most researchers focus on instilling social and problem-solving skills in children that are adequate to prevent the kinds of social stress so often associated with depression. Sanders, Dadds, Johnston, and Cash (1992) and Dadds, Sanders, Morrison, and Rebgetz (1992) determined that disordered communication and problem-solving skills, particularly within the family, are characteristic of depressed children and a natural target for preventive intervention.

Beardslee et al. (1997) have observed sustained effects from a preventive program directed at families with children between age 8 and age 15 in which one parent had experienced a recent episode of depression. Eighteen months after participating in 6 to 10 family sessions, these families were doing substantially better on most measures than the control families. In an even more intriguing preventive effort, Gilham, Reivich, Jaycox, and Seligman (1995) taught cognitive and social problem-solving techniques to 69 children in grades 5 and 6 who were at risk for depression. Compared with children in a matched no-treatment control group, the prevention group reported fewer depressive symptoms during the 2 years they were followed. More importantly, moderate to severe symptoms were reduced by half and the positive effects of this program increased during the period of follow-up. In an interesting replication, Seligman, Schulman, DeRubeis, and Hollon (1999) conducted a similar course for university students who were at risk for depression based on a pessimistic cognitive style. After 3 years, students taking the eight-session program experienced less anxiety and depression than a control group receiving the assessments only. This suggests that it might be possible to "psychologically immunize" at-risk children and adolescents against depression by teaching appropriate cognitive and social skills.

### Combined Treatments

A few studies have tested the important question of whether combining psychosocial treatments with medication is effective in treating depression (e.g., Blackburn & Moore, 1997; Hollon et al., 1992). With one exception, the results thus far do not strongly suggest any immediate advantage of combined treatment over separate drug or psychological treatment. The exception to this finding is a large study recently reported by Keller et al. (2000) on the treatment of chronic major depression that was conducted at 12 different clinics in North America. In this, the largest study ever conducted on the treatment of depression, 681 patients were assigned to receive antidepressant medication (nefazodone), cognitive-behavioural therapy constructed specifically for chronically depressed patients, or the combination of two treatments.

Forty-eight percent of patients receiving each of the individual treatments were either remitted or responded in a clinically satisfactory way compared with 73% of the patients receiving combined treatment. Because this study was conducted with only a subset of depressed patients, those with chronic depression, the findings would need to be replicated before we could say combined treatment was useful for depression generally. In addition, because the study did not include a fifth condition in which the cognitive-behavioural treatment was combined with placebo, we cannot determine whether the enhanced effectiveness of the combined treatment was due to placebo factors. A recent review by Zindel Segal and his colleagues at the Centre for Addiction and Mental Health in Toronto suggests that combined treatment is generally just as effective as separate drug or psychological therapies in the treatment of depression. However, when the depression is severe, combined drug and psychological treatments appear to have some additional benefits over either treatment administered separately (Segal, Vincent, & Levitt, 2002).

In any case, drugs and cognitive-behavioural treatments clearly operate in different ways. Medication, when it works, does so more quickly than psychological treatments, which in turn have the advantage of increasing the patient's long-range social functioning (particularly in the case of IPT) and protecting against relapse or recurrence (particularly cognitive therapy). Combining treatments, therefore, might take advantage of the drugs' rapid action and the psychosocial protection against recurrence or relapse, thereby allowing eventual discontinuation of the medications. For example, Fava, Grandi, Zielezny, Rafanelli, and Canestrari (1996) assigned patients who had been successfully treated with antidepressant drugs to either cognitive-behavioural treatment of residual symptoms or standard clinical management. Four years later, patients treated with cognitive-behavioural procedures had a substantially lower relapse rate (35%) than patients given the clinical management treatment (70%). In a second study, with patients with recurrent depressive episodes, the authors essentially replicated the results (Fava, Rafanelli, Grandi, Conti, & Belluardo, 1998).

## *Preventing Relapse*

Given the high rate of recurrence in depression, it is not surprising that well over 50% of patients on antidepressant medication relapse if their medication is stopped within 4 months after their last depressive episode (Hollon, Shelton, & Loosen, 1991; Thase, 1990). Therefore, one important question has to do with **maintenance treatment** to *prevent* relapse or recurrence over the long term.

In a number of studies, cognitive therapy reduced rates of subsequent relapse in depressed patients by more than 50% over groups treated with antidepressant medication (e.g., Evans et al., 1992; Simons, Murphy, Levine, & Wetzel, 1986). Evans et al. (1992) found that cognitive therapy prevented subsequent relapse to the same extent as did continuing medication over a 2-year period. Data on relapse presented in Figure 6.7 show that 50% of a group whose medication was stopped relapsed during the same period, compared with 32% of a group whose medication was continued at least 1 year. Relapse rates were only 21% for the group receiving cognitive therapy alone and 15% for those receiving cognitive therapy combined with medication. It is interesting that the cognitive therapy was *not* continued beyond the initial 12-week period.

Zindel Segal and his colleagues have been collaborating with researchers in the United Kingdom on a variant of traditional cognitive therapy that is specifically designed to prevent depressive relapse. This new therapy is called *mindfulness-based cognitive therapy* (Segal, Williams, & Teasdale, 2002). It is a group therapy designed to teach recovered depressed patients to disengage from the kinds of negative thinking that can precipitate a relapse to depression. More specifically, they are trained in mindfulness meditation to help them become more aware of their thoughts and

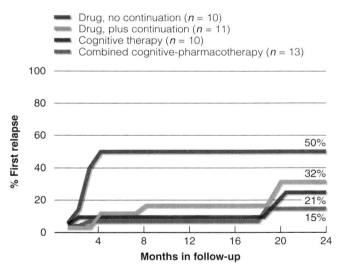

**Figure 6.7** ■ Data on relapse after treatment for depression. (From "Differential Relapse Following Cognitive Therapy and Pharmacotherapy for Depression," by M. D. Evans, S. D. Hollon, R. J. DeRubeis, J. M. Piasecki, W. M. Grove, M. J. Garvey, and V. B. Tuason, 1992, *Archives of General Psychiatry*, 49, 802–808. Copyright © 1992 by the American Medical Association. Reprinted by permission.)

**maintenance treatment** Combination of continued psychosocial treatment and/or medication designed to prevent relapse following therapy.

feelings and to view their thoughts as mental events rather than as accurate reflections of reality. In a recent randomized controlled study, Teasdale et al. (2000) treated a group of 145 patients with particularly severe recurrent depression, most of whom had already experienced three or more depressive episodes but were in remission from their depression after successful drug treatment. These patients were then treated with either cognitive therapy combined with a mindfulness meditation approach or treatment as usual, which included medication for about half of the patients over the course of 14 months. Among those with three or more past episodes, the group receiving the cognitive therapy experienced substantially and significantly fewer relapses than the group receiving treatment as usual. The proportion of patients not relapsing in both groups is presented in Figure 6.8.

Because psychosocial treatments affect biological aspects of disorders and drug treatments affect psychological components, the integrative model of mood disorders is helpful in studying the effects of treatment. Evidence suggests that psychological treatments alter neurochemical correlates of depression. McKnight, Nelson-Gray, and Barnhill (1992) used either cognitive therapy or tricyclic medication to treat groups of patients with major depressive disorder. They found that an abnormal pretreatment response to the dexamethasone suppression test (DST) of cortisol secretion did *not* predict which treatment would be more effective, and both produced a normalization of posttreatment DST responses. Similarly, the work of Zindel Segal and his colleagues has shown that successful cognitive therapy and tricyclic medication both decrease thyroid hormone levels (Joffe, Segal, & Singer, 1996).

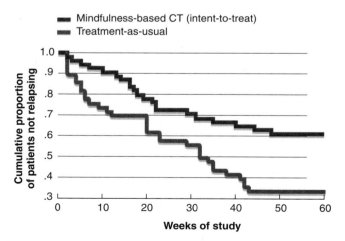

**Figure 6.8**    ■    Survival (nonrelapse/nonrecurrence) curves comparing relapse/recurrence with major depression for treatment as usual and mindfulness-based cognitive therapy in patients with three or more previous episodes of major depression. CT = cognitive therapy. (From Teasdale et al., 2000.)

## Psychological Treatments for Bipolar Disorder

Although medication, particularly lithium, seems a necessary treatment for bipolar disorder, most clinicians emphasize the need for psychological interventions to manage interpersonal and practical problems (e.g., marital and job difficulties that result from the disorder; Clarkin, Haas, & Glick, 1988). Until recently, the principal objective of psychological intervention was to increase compliance with medication regimens such as lithium (Cochran, 1984). We noted before that the "pleasures" of a manic state make refusal to take lithium a major therapeutic obstacle. Giving up drugs between episodes or skipping dosages during an episode significantly undermines treatment. Therefore, increasing compliance with drug treatments is important (Goodwin & Jamison, 1990; Scott, 1995). For example, Clarkin, Carpenter, Hull, Wilner, and Glick (1998) evaluated the advantages of adding a psychological treatment to medication in inpatients and found it improved adherence to medication for all patients and resulted in better overall outcomes for the most severe patients compared with medication alone.

More recently, psychological treatments have also been directed at psychosocial aspects of bipolar disorder. In a new approach, Frank and colleagues are testing a psychological treatment that regulates circadian rhythms by helping patients regulate their sleep cycles and other daily schedules (Craighead, Miklowitz, Frank & Vajk, 2002; Frank et al., 1997, 1999). Miller and colleagues, in a small pilot study, added family therapy to a drug regimen and reported a significant increase in the percentage of patients with bipolar disorder who fully recovered (56%) over those who had drug treatment alone (20%). During a 2-year follow-up, patients who received psychological treatment and medication had less than half the relapse rate of those who had drug treatment alone (Miller, Keitner, Epstein, Bishop, & Ryan, 1991).

David Miklowitz and his colleagues found that family tension is associated with relapse in bipolar disorder. Preliminary studies indicate that treatments, directed at helping families understand symptoms and develop new coping skills and communication styles, change communication styles (Simoneau, Miklowitz, Richards, Saleem, & George, 1999) and prevent relapse (Miklowitz, 2001; Miklowitz & Goldstein, 1997). More recently, Miklowitz, George, Richards, Simoneau, and Suddath (2003) demonstrated that their family-focused treatment combined with medication results in significantly less relapse 1 year following initiation of treatment than patients receiving crisis management and medication over the same period of time (see Figure 6.9). In another important study, Lam et al. (2003) showed that

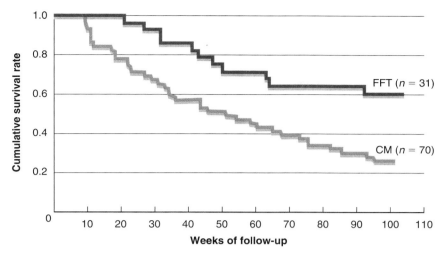

Cumulative survival rate

FFT (*n* = 31)

CM (*n* = 70)

Weeks of follow-up

**Figure 6.9** ■ Survival curves for bipolar patients assigned to family-focused treatment (FFT) and medication or crisis management (CM) and medication (intent-to-treat analysis, N = 101). Comparison of the curves revealed that patients undergoing FFT had longer survival intervals without experiencing disease relapse than patients undergoing CM (Wilcoxon $X^2_1$ = 8.71, P = 0.003). (From "A Randomized Study of Family-Focused Psychoeducation and Pharmacotherapy in the Outpatient Management of Bipolar Disorder," by D. J. Miklowitz, E. L. George, J. A. Richards, T. L. Simoneau, and R. L. Suddath, *Archives of General Psychiatry*, 60, 604–912. Copyright © 2003 American Medical Association. Adapted with permission.)

patients with bipolar disorders treated with cognitive therapy plus medication relapsed significantly less over 1 year than a control group receiving just medication, replicating, in part, earlier results from Perry, Tarrier, Morriss, McCarthy, and Limb (1999).

Let us now return to Katie, who, you will remember, had made a serious suicide attempt in the midst of a major depressive episode.

## Katie
### The Triumph of the Self

Like the overwhelming majority of people with serious psychological disorders, Katie had never received an adequate course of treatment, although she was evaluated from time to time by various mental health professionals. She lived in a rural area where competent professional help was not readily available. Her life ebbed and flowed with her struggle to subdue anxiety and depression. When she could manage her emotions sufficiently, she took an occasional course in the high school independent study program. Katie discovered that she was fascinated by learning. She enrolled in a local community college at the age of 19 and did extremely well, despite the fact that she had not progressed beyond her first year in high school. At the college she earned a high school equivalency degree. She went to work in a local factory. But she continued to drink heavily and to take Valium; on occasion, anxiety and depression would return and disrupt her life.

Finally, Katie left home, attended college full time, and fell in love. But the romance was one-sided, and she was rejected.

*One night after a phone conversation with him, I nearly drank myself to death. I lived in a single room alone in the dorm. I drank as much vodka as quickly as I could. I fell asleep. When I awoke, I was covered in vomit and couldn't recall falling asleep or being sick. I was drunk for much of the next day. When I awoke the following morning, I realized I could have killed myself by choking on my own vomit. More importantly, I wasn't sure if I fully wanted to die. That was the last of my drinking.*

Katie decided to make some changes. Taking advantage of what she had learned in the little treatment she had received, she began looking at life and herself differently. Instead of dwelling on how inadequate and evil she was, she began to pay attention to her strengths. "But I now realized that I needed to accept myself as is, and work with any stumbling blocks that I faced. I needed to get myself through the world as happily and as comfortably as I could. I had a right to that."

Other lessons learned in treatment now became valuable, and Katie became more aware of her mood swings:

*I learned to objectify periods of depression as [simply] periods of "feeling." They are a part of who I am, but not the whole. I recognize when I feel that way, and I check my perceptions with someone that I trust when I feel uncertain of them. I try to hold on to the belief that these periods are only temporary.*

Katie developed other strategies for coping successfully with life:

*I try to stay focused on my goals and what is important to me. I have learned that if one strategy to achieve some goal doesn't work there are other strategies that probably will. My endurance is one of my blessings. Patience, dedication, and discipline are also important. None of the changes that I have been through occurred instantly or automatically. Most of what I have achieved has required time, effort, and persistence.*

Katie dreamed that if she worked hard enough she could help other people who had problems similar to her own. Katie pursued that dream and earned her Ph.D. in psychology.

## Concept Check 6.4

Indicate which type of treatment for mood disorders is being described in each statement.
1. The controversial but somewhat successful treatment involving the production of seizures through electrical shock to the brain. _____
2. This teaches clients to carefully examine their thought process and recognize "depressive" errors in thinking. _____
3. These come in three main types (tricyclics, MAO inhibitors, and SSRIs), are often prescribed, but have numerous side effects. _____
4. This antidepressant must be carefully regulated to avoid illness but has the advantage of affecting manic episodes. _____
5. It is crucial to focus on resolving problems in existing relationships and learn to form new interpersonal relationships. _____
6. This is an effort to prevent relapse or recurrence over the long run. _____

# Suicide

■ *Describe the relationship between suicide and mood disorders, including known risk factors and approaches to suicide prevention and treatment.*

Most days we are confronted with news about the war on cancer or the frantic race to find a cure for AIDS. We also hear never-ending admonitions to improve our diet and to exercise more to prevent heart disease. But another cause of death ranks right up there with the most frightening and dangerous medical conditions. This is the inexplicable decision to kill themselves made by more than one million people per year worldwide (World Health Organization, 2000). Around the world, suicide causes more deaths per year than homicide or war (World Health Organization, 2002).

## Statistics

Most epidemiologists agree that the actual number of suicides may be even higher than official statistics suggest. Many of these unreported suicides occur when people purposefully drive into a bridge or off a cliff (Blumenthal, 1990). According to the work of Isaac Sakinofsky, head of the high-risk consultation clinic at the Centre for Addiction and Mental Health in Toronto, suicide rates in Canada are highest in Alberta, Quebec, and the Northwest Territories and lowest in Newfoundland and Labrador (Sakinofsky, 1998). A comparison of suicides in Canada and the United States pertains to rates of suicides by gunshot, given that the two countries have very different national policies on gun control. Suicides by gunshot continue to account for the majority of suicides in the United States. In Canada, we implemented restrictive gun control legislation in the 1970s, which was associated with long-lasting reductions in suicide rates. There have not been corresponding increases in suicide by other means in Canada since we implemented this legislation (Carrington, 1999; Leenaars & Lester, 1996).

As you might expect from the incidence of depression in Aboriginal people, their suicide rate is extremely high, although great variability exists across specific groups of Indigenous peoples. Some groups have rates up to 800 times the national average (Chandler & Lalonde, 1998). Elevated suicide rates appear to be specific to Natives living on reserves

(Cooper, Corrado, Karlberg, & Adams, 1992), which is likely the result of stressful conditions associated with life on the reserve (e.g, low income, overcrowding). Other studies suggest that alcohol abuse is also a likely contributing factor (Malchy, Enns, Young, & Cox, 1997; Wilkie, Macdonald, & Hildahl, 1998).

The suicide rate among Canadian Inuit has been alarmingly high in recent years. Boothroyd, Kirmayer, Spreng, Malus, and Hodgins (2001) studied cases of completed suicides in Nunavik to identify risk factors. Most cases were young males aged 15 to 24 who usually completed suicide by hanging or gunshot. Psychiatric problems such as depression, personality disorder, and drug abuse were very common in these cases.

Even more frightening is the dramatic *increase* in death by suicide in recent years, most evident among adolescents. Between 1960 and 1988 the suicide rate in adolescents rose from 3.6 to 11.3 per 100 000 population, an increase of 200% compared with a general population increase of 17%, before levelling off a bit. For teenagers, suicide is the *third* leading cause of death behind motor vehicle accidents and homicide (Minino, Arias, Kochanek, Murphy, & Smith, 2002; Ventura, Peters, Martin, & Maurer, 1997). Suicide rates among the elderly have also increased dramatically. This rise has been connected to the growing incidence of medical illness in our oldest citizens and to their increasing loss of social support (Conwell, Duberstein, & Caine, 2002). As we have noted, a strong relationship exists between illness or infirmity and hopelessness or depression (Brown, Beck, Steer, & Grisham, 2000; Centers for Disease Control, 2003). Suicide is not attempted only by adolescents and adults: Rosenthal and Rosenthal (1984) described 16 children 2 to 5 years of age who had attempted suicide at least once, many injuring themselves severely.

Regardless of age, males are four to five times more likely to *commit* suicide than females (American Psychiatric Association, 2003). This startling fact seems to be related in part to gender differences in the types of suicide *attempts*. Males generally choose far more violent methods, such as guns and hanging; females tend to rely on less violent options, such as drug overdose (Buda & Tsuang, 1990; Gallagher-Thompson & Osgood, 1997). More men commit suicide during old age and more women during middle age, in part because most attempts by older women are unsuccessful (Kuo, Gallo, & Tien, 2001). The suicide rate for young men in the United States is now the highest in the world, even surpassing rates in Japan and Sweden, countries long known for high rates of suicide (Blumenthal, 1990). But, as we noted, older men (over 65) in all countries are most at risk for completing suicide worldwide (McIntosh, Santos, Hubbard, & Overholser, 1994).

Men often choose violent methods of completing suicide. Nirvana's Kurt Cobain shot himself.

In China, and uniquely in China, more women commit suicide than men, particularly in rural settings (Murray, 1996; Phillips, Li, & Zhang, 2002). What accounts for this culturally determined reversal? Chinese scientists agree that China's suicide rates, probably the highest in the world, are the result of an absence of stigma. Suicide, particularly among women, is often portrayed in classical Chinese literature as a reasonable solution to problems. A rural Chinese woman's family is her entire world, and suicide is an honourable solution if the family collapses. Furthermore, highly toxic farm pesticides are readily available and it is possible that many women who did not necessarily intend to kill themselves die after accidentally swallowing poison.

In addition to completed suicides, two other important indices of suicidal behaviour are **suicidal attempts** (the person survives) and **suicidal ideation** (the person thinks seriously about suicide). Although males *commit* suicide more often than females in most of the world, females *attempt* suicide at least three times as often (Berman & Jobes, 1991; Kuo et al., 2001). This high incidence may reflect that more women than men are depressed and that depression is strongly related to suicide attempts (Frances, Franklin, & Flavin, 1986). Some estimates place the ratio of attempted to completed suicides from 50:1 to 200:1 or higher (Garland & Zigler, 1993; Moscicki, 1997). In addition, results from another study (Kovacs, Goldston, & Gatsonis, 1993) suggested that among adolescents the ratio of *thoughts* about suicide

---

**suicidal attempts** Efforts made to kill oneself.
**suicidal ideation** Serious thoughts about committing suicide.

to *attempts* is between 3:1 and 6:1. In other words, between 16% and 30% of adolescents in this study who had thought about killing themselves attempted it. "Thoughts" in this context does not refer to a fleeting philosophical type of consideration but rather to a serious contemplation of the act. The first step down the dangerous road to suicide is thinking about it.

In a study of university students (among whom suicide is the second leading cause of death), approximately 10% to 25% had thoughts about suicide during the past 12 months (Brener, Hassan, & Barrios, 1999; Meehan, Lamb, Saltzman, & O'Carroll, 1992). Only a minority of these university students with thoughts of suicide (perhaps around 15%) attempt to kill themselves, and only a few succeed (Kovacs et al., 1993). Nevertheless, given the enormity of the problem, suicidal thoughts are taken seriously by mental health professionals.

## Causes

In the spring of 2003, Bernard Loiseau, one of the all-time great French chefs, learned that an important French restaurant guide, GaultMillau, was reducing the rating on one of his restaurants. This was the first time in his career that any of his restaurants had a rating reduced. Later that week he killed himself. Although police quickly ruled his death a suicide, most people in France did not consider it a suicide and thought that his killer was still at large. His fellow chefs accused the guidebook of murder! They claimed that he had been deeply affected by the ratings demotion, as well as speculation in the press that he might lose one of his three Michelin stars (Michelin publishes the most famous French restaurant guide). This series of events caused a sensation throughout France and, indeed, throughout the culinary world. But did GaultMillau kill Loiseau? Let's examine the causes of suicide.

Individuals, usually volunteers, are highly trained to help desperate people thinking of harming themselves on suicide hotlines.

### Past Conceptions

The great sociologist Emile Durkheim (1951) defined a number of suicide types based on the social or cultural conditions in which they occurred. One type is "formalized" suicides that were approved of, such as the ancient custom of *hara-kiri* in Japan, in which an individual who brought dishonour to himself or his family was expected to impale himself on a sword. Durkheim referred to this as *altruistic suicide*. Durkheim also recognized the loss of social supports as an important provocation for suicide; he called this *egoistic suicide*. (Elderly citizens who kill themselves after losing touch with their friends or family fit into this category.) Magne-Ingvar, Ojehagen, and Traskman-Bendz (1992) found that only 13% of 75 individuals who had seriously attempted suicide had an adequate social network of friends and relationships. *Anomic suicides* are the result of marked disruptions, such as the sudden loss of a high-prestige job. ("Anomie" is feeling lost and confused.) Finally, *fatalistic suicides* result from a loss of control over one's own destiny. The mass suicide of 39 Heaven's Gate cult members is an example of this type because the lives of those people were largely in the hands of Marshall Applewhite, a supreme and charismatic leader. Durkheim's work was important in alerting us to the social contribution to suicide. Freud (1917/1957) believed that suicide (and depression, to some extent) indicated unconscious hostility directed inward to the self rather than *outward* to the person or situation causing the anger. Indeed, suicide victims often seem to be psychologically "punishing" others who may have rejected them or caused some other personal hurt. Current thinking considers social and psychological factors but also highlights the potential importance of biological contributions.

### Risk Factors

Edward Shneidman pioneered the study of risk factors for suicide (Shneidman, 1989; Shneidman, Farberow, & Litman, 1970). Among the methods he and others have used to study those conditions and events that make a person vulnerable is **psychological autopsy.** The psychological profile of the person who committed suicide is reconstructed through extensive interviews with friends and family members who are likely to know what the individual was thinking and doing in the

**psychological autopsy**  Postmortem psychological profile of a suicide victim constructed from interviews with people who knew the person before death.

period before death. This and other methods have allowed researchers to identify a number of risk factors for suicide.

## Family History

If a family member committed suicide, there is an increased risk that someone else in the family will also (Kety, 1990; Mann, Waternaux, Haas, & Malone, 1999). This may not be surprising, because so many people who kill themselves are depressed, and depression runs in families. Nevertheless, the question remains: Are people who kill themselves simply adopting a familiar solution, or does an inherited trait, such as impulsivity, account for increased suicidal behaviour in families? The possibility that something is inherited is supported by several adoption studies. One found an increased rate of suicide in the biological relatives of adopted individuals who had committed suicide compared with a control group of adoptees who had not committed suicide (Schulsinger, Kety, & Rosenthal, 1979; Wender et al., 1986). In a small study of people whose twins had committed suicide, 10 of 26 surviving monozygotic (identical) co-twins, and *none* of 9 surviving dizygotic (fraternal) co-twins had attempted suicide (Roy, Segal, & Sarchiapone, 1995). This suggests some biological (genetic) contribution to suicide, even if it is relatively small.

## Neurobiology

A variety of evidence suggests that low levels of serotonin may be associated with suicide and with violent suicide attempts (Asberg, Nordstrom, & Traskman-Bendz, 1986; Cremniter et al., 1999; Winchel, Stanley, & Stanley, 1990). As we have noted, extremely low levels of serotonin are associated with impulsivity, instability, and the tendency to overreact to situations (Spoont, 1992). It is possible then, that low levels of serotonin may contribute to creating a vulnerability to act impulsively. This impulsiveness may include suicide, which is sometimes an impulsive act.

## Existing Psychological Disorders

More than 90% of people who kill themselves have a psychological disorder (Conwell et al., 1996; Orbach, 1997). Suicide is often associated with mood disorders, and for good reason. As many as 60% of suicides (75% of adolescent suicides) are associated with an existing mood disorder (Brent & Kolko, 1990; Frances et al., 1986). Lewinsohn, Rohde, and Seeley (1993) concluded that in adolescents suicidal behaviour is largely an expression of severe depression. But many people with mood disorders do not attempt suicide, and, conversely, many people who attempt suicide do not have mood disorders. Therefore, depression and suicide, although strongly related, are

still independent. Looking more closely at the relationship between mood disorder and suicide, some investigators have isolated hopelessness, a specific component of depression, as strongly predicting suicide (Beck, 1986; Beck, Steer, Kovacs, & Garrison, 1985; Kazdin, 1983), at least among Caucasians (Enns, Inayatulla, Cox, & Cheyne, 1997).

Alcohol use and abuse are associated with approximately 25% to 50% of suicides (e.g., Frances et al., 1986) and are particularly evident in adolescent suicides (Brener et al., 1999; Hawton, Houston, Haw, Townsend, & Harriss, 2003). Brent and colleagues (1988) found that about one-third of adolescents who commit suicide were intoxicated when they died and that many more might have been under the influence of drugs. Combinations of disorders, such as substance abuse and mood disorders in adults or mood disorders and conduct disorder in children and adolescents, seem to create a stronger vulnerability than any one disorder alone (Conwell et al., 1996; Woods et al., 1997). For example, Hawton et al. (2003) noticed that the prevalence of previous attempts and repeated attempts doubled if a combination of disorders were present. For adolescents, Woods et al. (1997) found that substance abuse combined with other risk-taking behaviours such as getting into fights, carrying a gun, or smoking were predictive of teenage suicide, possibly reflecting impulsivity in these troubled adolescents. Esposito and Clum (2003) also noted that the presence of anxiety and mood (internalizing) disorders predicted suicide attempts in adolescents. Past suicide attempts are another strong risk factor and must be taken seriously.

A disorder characterized more by impulsivity than depression is borderline personality disorder (see Chapter 11). Frances and Blumenthal (1989) suggest that these individuals, known for making manipulative and impulsive suicidal gestures without necessarily wanting to destroy themselves, kill themselves by mistake in as many as 10% of the cases. The combination of borderline personality disorder and depression is particularly deadly (Soloff, Lynch, Kelly, Malone, & Mann, 2000).

The association of suicide with severe psychological disorders, especially depression, belies the myth that it is a response to disappointment in people who are otherwise healthy.

## Stressful Life Events

Perhaps the most important risk factor for suicide is a severe, stressful event experienced as shameful or humiliating, such as a failure (real or imagined) in school or at work, an unexpected arrest, or a rejection by a loved one (Blumenthal, 1990; Brent et al., 1988; Conwell et al., 2002; Joiner & Rudd, 2000; Shaffer, Garland, Gould, Fisher, & Trautmen,

1988). Physical and sexual abuse are also important sources of stress (Kirmayer, Malus, & Boothroyd, 1996; Wagner, 1997). Recent evidence confirms that the stress and disruption of natural disasters increase the likelihood of suicide (Krug et al., 1998). Based on data from 337 countries experiencing natural disasters in the 1980s, the authors concluded that the rates of suicide increased 13.8% in the 4 years after severe floods, 31% in the 2 years after hurricanes, and 62.9% in the first year after an earthquake. Given preexisting vulnerabilities—including psychological disorders, traits of impulsiveness, and lack of social support—a stressful event can often put a person over the edge. An integrated model of the causes of suicidal behaviour is presented in Figure 6.10.

## Is Suicide Contagious?

We hear all too often of the suicide of a teenager or celebrity. Most people react with sadness and curiosity. Some people react by attempting suicide themselves, often by the same method they have just heard about. Gould (1990) reported an increase in suicides during a 9-day period after widespread publicity about a suicide. Clusters of suicides (several people copying one person) seem to predominate among teenagers, with as many as 5% of all teenage suicides reflecting an imitation (Gould, 1990).

Why would anyone want to copy a suicide? First, suicides are often romanticized in the media: An attractive young person under unbearable pressure commits suicide and becomes a martyr to friends and peers by getting even with the (adult) world for creating such a difficult situation. Also, media accounts often describe in detail the methods used in the suicide, thereby providing a guide to potential victims. Little is reported about the paralysis, brain damage, and other tragic consequences of the incomplete or failed suicide, or that suicide is almost always associated with a severe psychological disorder. More important, even less is said about the futility of this method of solving problems (Gould, 1990; O'Carroll, 1990). To prevent these tragedies, the media should not inadvertently glorify suicides in any way, and mental health professionals must intervene immediately in schools and other locations with people who might be depressed or otherwise vulnerable to the contagion of suicide. But it isn't clear that suicide is "contagious" in the infectious disease sense. Rather, the stress of a friend's suicide or some other major stress may affect several individuals who are vulnerable because of existing psychological disorders (Joiner, 1999). Nevertheless, effective intervention is essential.

## Treatment

Despite the identification of important risk factors, predicting suicide is still an uncertain art. Individuals with few precipitating factors unexpectedly kill themselves, and many who live with seemingly insurmountable stress and illness and have little social support or guidance somehow survive and overcome their difficulties.

Mental health professionals are thoroughly trained in assessing for possible suicidal ideation. Others might be reluctant to ask leading questions for fear of putting the idea in someone's head. However, we know it is far more important to check

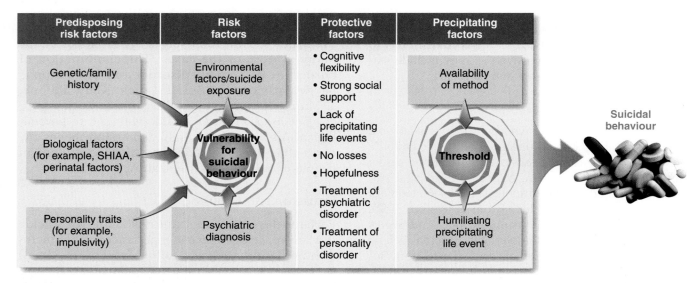

**Figure 6.10**　■　Threshold model for suicidal behaviour. (From "Clinical Assessment and Treatment of Youth Suicide," by S. J. Blumenthal and D. J. Kupfer, 1988, *Journal of Youth and Adolescence, 17,* 1–24. Copyright © 1988 by Plenum Publishing Corporation. Reprinted with kind permission of Springer Science and Business Media.)

for these "secrets" than to do nothing, because the risk of inspiring suicidal thoughts is small and the risk of leaving them undiscovered is enormous. Therefore, if there is any indication that someone is suicidal, the mental health professional will inquire, "Has there been any time recently when you've had some thoughts about hurting yourself or possibly killing yourself?"

The mental health professional will also check for possible recent humiliations and determine whether any of the factors are present that might indicate a high probability of suicide. For example, does a person who is thinking of suicide have a detailed plan or just a vague fantasy? If a plan is discovered that includes a specific time, place, and method, the risk is high. Does the detailed plan include putting all personal affairs in order, giving away possessions, and other final acts? If so, the risk is higher still. What specific method is the person considering? Generally, the more lethal and violent the method (guns, hanging, poison, and so on), the greater the risk it will be used. Does the person understand what might actually happen? Many people do not understand the effects of the pills on which they might overdose. Finally, has the person taken any precautions against being discovered? If so, the risk is extreme (American Psychiatric Association, 2003).

If a risk is present, clinicians attempt to get the individual to agree to or even sign a "no-suicide contract." Usually this includes a promise not to do anything remotely connected with suicide without contacting the mental health professional first. If the person at risk refuses a contract (or the clinician has serious doubts about the patient's sincerity) and the suicidal risk is judged to be high, immediate hospitalization is indicated, even against the will of the patient. Whether the person is hospitalized or not, treatment aimed at resolving underlying life stressors and treating existing psychological disorders should be initiated immediately.

In view of the public health consequences of suicide, a number of programs have been implemented to reduce the rates of suicide both in Canada and in other parts of the world. They include curriculum-based programs in which teams of professionals go into schools or other organizations to educate people about suicide and provide information on handling life stress. The United Kingdom targeted reducing suicide rates by 15%, and policymakers and mental health professionals are determining the best methods for achieving this goal (Lewis, Hawton, & Jones, 1997). More than 2000 suicide prevention and crisis centres across Canada provide 24-hour phone service to people in crisis, including those considering suicide (Dyck & White, 1998). Some findings are encouraging, such as a study showing that suicide rates declined in the years following the establishment of suicide prevention centres in several cities (Lester, 1991). Unfortunately, most research indicates that such educational and crisis phone line programs are not effective (Garfield & Zigler, 1993; Shaffer, Garland, Vieland, Underwood, & Busner, 1991). As Garfield and Zigler (1993) point out, hotline volunteers must be backed up by competent mental health professionals who can identify potentially serious risks.

More helpful are programs targeted to at-risk individuals, including adolescents in schools where a student has committed suicide. The Institute of Medicine (2002) recommends making services available immediately to friends and relatives of victims. In an important study following a suicide in a high school, Brent and colleagues (1989) identified 16 students as strongly at risk and referred them for treatment. Another important step is limiting access to lethal weapons for anyone at risk for suicide.

Specific treatments for people at risk have also been developed. For example, British psychologist Paul Salkovskis and his colleagues (Salkovskis, Atha, & Storer, 1990) treated 20 patients at high risk for *repeated* suicide attempts with a cognitive-behavioural problem-solving approach. Results indicated that they were significantly less likely to attempt suicide in the 6 months following treatment. Marsha Linehan and her colleagues (e.g., Linehan & Kehrer, 1993) developed a noteworthy treatment for the type of impulsive suicidal behaviour associated with borderline personality disorder (see Chapter 11). In an important study, M. David Rudd and colleagues developed a brief psychological treatment targeting young adults who were at risk for suicide because of the presence of suicidal ideation accompanied by previous suicidal attempts and/or mood or substance use disorders (Rudd et al., 1996). They randomly assigned 264 young people to either a new treatment or treatment as usual in the community. Patients spent approximately 9 hours each day for 2 weeks at a hospital treatment facility. Treatment consisted of problem solving, developing social competence, coping more adaptively with life's problems, and recognizing emotional and life experiences that may have precipitated the suicide attempt or ideation. Patients were assessed up to 2 years following treatment, and results indicated reductions in suicidal ideation and behaviour and marked improvement in problem-solving ability. Furthermore, the brief experimental treatment was significantly more effective at retaining the highest risk young adults in the program. This program has now been expanded into the first psychological treatment for suicidal behaviour with empirical support for its efficacy (Rudd, Joiner, & Rajab, 2001). With the increased rate of suicide, particularly in adolescents, the tragic and paradoxical act is receiving increased scrutiny from public health authorities. The quest will go on to determine more effective and efficient ways of preventing the most serious consequences of any psychological disorder, the taking of one's own life.

## Concept Check 6.5

Match each of the following summaries with the correct suicide type, choosing from (a) altruistic, (b) egoistic, (c) anomic, (d) fatalistic.

1. Ralph's wife left him and took the children. He is a well-known TV personality, but, because of a conflict with the new station owners, he was recently fired. If Ralph kills himself, what would his suicide be considered? _____

2. Sam killed himself while a prisoner of war in Vietnam. _____
3. Sheiba lives in a remote village in Africa. She was recently caught in an adulterous affair with a man in a nearby village. Her husband wants to kill her but won't have to because of a tribal custom that requires her to kill herself. She leaps from the nearby "sinful woman's cliff." _____
4. Mabel lived in a nursing home for many years. At first, her family and friends visited her often; now they come only at Christmas. Her two closest friends in the nursing home died recently. She has no hobbies or other interests. Mabel's suicide would be identified as what type? _____

# Summary

## Understanding and Defining Mood Disorders

- Mood disorders are among the most common psychological disorders, and the risk of developing them is increasing worldwide, particularly in younger people.
- Two fundamental experiences can contribute either singly or in combination to all the specific mood disorders: a major depressive episode and mania. A less severe episode of mania that does not cause impairment in social or occupational functioning is known as a *hypomanic episode*. An episode of mania coupled with anxiety or depression is known as a dysphoric manic or mixed manic episode.
- An individual who suffers from episodes of depression only is said to have a unipolar disorder. An individual who alternates between depression and mania has a bipolar disorder.
- Major depressive disorder may be a single episode or recurrent, but it is always time limited; in another form of depression, dysthymic disorder, the symptoms are somewhat milder but remain relatively unchanged over long periods. In cases of double depression, an individual experiences both depressive episodes and dysthymic disorder.
- Approximately 20% of bereaved individuals may experience pathological grief reaction, in which the normal grief response develops into a full-blown mood disorder.
- The key identifying feature of bipolar disorders is an alternation of manic episodes and major depressive episodes. Cyclothymic disorder is a milder but more chronic version of bipolar disorder.

- Patterns of additional features that sometimes accompany mood disorders, called *specifiers*, may predict the course or patient response to treatment, as does the temporal patterning or course of mood disorders. One pattern, seasonal affective disorder, often occurs in winter.

## Prevalence of Mood Disorders

- Mood disorders in children are fundamentally similar to mood disorders in adults.
- Symptoms of depression are increasing dramatically in our elderly population.
- The experience of anxiety across cultures varies, and it can be difficult to make comparisons, especially, for example, when we attempt to compare subjective feelings of depression.
- Some of the latest theories on the causes of depression are based, in part, on research into the relationship between anxiety and depression. Anxiety almost always precedes depression, and almost everyone with depression is also anxious.

## Causes of Mood Disorders

- The causes of mood disorders lie in a complex interaction of biological, psychological, and social factors. From a biological perspective, researchers are particularly interested in the stress hypothesis and the role of neurohormones. Psychological theories of depression focus on learned helplessness, depressive cognitive schemas, and interpersonal disruptions.

## Treatment of Mood Disorders

- A variety of treatments, both biological and psychological, have proven effectiveness for the mood disorders, at least in the short term. For those individuals who do not respond to antidepressant drugs or psychosocial treatments, a more dramatic physical treatment, electroconvulsive therapy (ECT) is sometimes used. Two psychosocial treatments—cognitive therapy and interpersonal therapy (IPT)—seem effective in treating depressive disorders.

- Relapse and recurrence of mood disorders are common in the long term, and treatment efforts must focus on maintenance treatment, that is, on preventing relapse or recurrence.

## Suicide

- Suicide is often associated with mood disorders but can occur in their absence. In any case, the incidence of suicide has been increasing in recent years, particularly among adolescents.

- In understanding suicidal behaviour, two indices are important: suicidal attempts (that are not successful) and suicidal ideation (serious thoughts about committing suicide). Important, too, in learning about risk factors for suicides is the psychological autopsy, in which the psychological profile of an individual who has committed suicide is reconstructed and examined for clues.

## Key Terms

| | | | |
|---|---|---|---|
| mood disorders, 217 | dysthymic disorder, 219 | learned helplessness theory of depression, 241 | interpersonal psychotherapy (IPT), 253 |
| major depressive episode, 217 | double depression, 220 | | maintenance |
| mania, 217 | pathological or impacted grief reaction, 223 | depressive cognitive triad, 242 | treatment, 255 |
| hypomanic episode, 218 | bipolar II disorder, 224 | neurohormones, 250 | suicidal attempts, 259 |
| mixed manic episode, 218 | bipolar I disorder, 224 | electroconvulsive therapy (ECT), 251 | suicidal ideation, 259 |
| major depressive disorder, single or recurrent episode, 219 | cyclothymic disorder, 225 seasonal affective disorder (SAD), 228 | cognitive therapy, 252 | psychological autopsy, 260 |

## Answers to Concept Checks

**6.1**  1. e  2. a  3. c  4. d  5. b

**6.2**  1. T  2. F (it does not require life experience)
        3. T  4. T

**6.3**  1. genetics, neurotransmitter system, endocrine system, circadian/sleep rhythms, neurohormones, etc.

   2. stressful life events, learned helplessness, depressive cognitive triad, negative schema, cognitive vulnerability

   3. marital dissatisfaction, gender, few social supports

**6.4**  1. electroconvulsive therapy (ECT)

   2. cognitive therapy

   3. antidepressants

   4. lithium

   5. interpersonal psychotherapy (IPT)

   6. maintenance treatment

**6.5**  1. c  2. d  3. a  4. b

 **InfoTrac College Edition**

If your instructor ordered your book with InfoTrac College Edition, please explore this online library for additional readings, review, and a handy resource for short assignments. Go to:

**http://infotrac.thomsonlearning.com**

Enter these search terms: major depression, bipoplar disorder, seasonal affective disorder, mood disorder, mania, dysphoria, electro convulsive therapy, cognitive therapy, suicide

 **The Abnormal Psychology Book Companion Website**

Go to **www.essentialsabnormalpsych.nelson.com** for practice quiz questions, Internet links, critical thinking exercises, and more.

## Abnormal Psychology
## Live CD-ROM

- **Mary, Bipolar Disorder:** We see the client in both a manic and a depressive phase of her illness. You may notice the similarity of the delusions in both phases of her illness.
- **Barbara, Major Depressive Disorder:** Barbara suffers from a major depressive disorder that's rather severe and long-lasting.
- **Evelyn, Major Depressive Disorder:** Evelyn has a major depressive disorder that gives a more positive view of long-term prospects for change.

**Thomson NOW!** **http://hed.nelson.com** Go to this site for the link to ThomsonNow™, your one-stop study shop. Take a Pretest for this chapter and ThomsonNow™ will generate a personalized Study Plan based on your test results! The Study Plan will identify the topics you need to review and direct you to online resources to help you master those topics. You can then take a Posttest to help you determine the concepts you have mastered and what you still need work on.

## Video Concept Review

For challenging concepts that typically need more than one explanation, Mark Durand provides a video review via ThomsonNow™ of the following topic:

- The differences between dysthmyia and depression.

# Chapter Quiz

1. An individual who is experiencing an elevated mood, a decreased need for sleep, and distractibility is most likely experiencing:
   a. panic disorder.
   b. mania.
   c. depersonalization.
   d. hallucinations.

2. What is the general agreement among mental health professionals about the relationship between bereavement and depression?
   a. Bereavement is less severe than depression in all cases.
   b. Depression can lead to bereavement in many cases.
   c. Bereavement can lead to depression in many cases.
   d. Symptoms of bereavement and depression rarely overlap.

3. Bipolar I disorder is characterized by _____, whereas bipolar II is characterized by _____.
   a. full manic episodes; hypomanic episodes
   b. hypomanic episodes; full manic episodes
   c. both depressive and manic episodes; full manic episodes
   d. full manic episodes; both depressive and manic episodes

4. Treatment for bereavement often includes:
   a. finding meaning in the loss.
   b. replacing the lost person with someone else.
   c. finding humour in the tragedy.
   d. replacing sad thoughts about the lost person with more happy thoughts.

5. Which statement best characterizes the relationship between anxiety and depression?
   a. Anxiety usually precedes the development of depression.
   b. Depression usually precedes the development of anxiety.
   c. Almost all depressed patients are anxious, but not all anxious patients are depressed.
   d. Almost all anxious patients are depressed, but not all depressed patients are anxious.

6. Which theory suggests that depression occurs when individuals believe that they have no control over the circumstances in their lives?
   a. attribution theory
   b. learned helplessness
   c. social learning theory
   d. theory of equifinality

7. In treating depressed clients, a psychologist helps them think more positively about themselves, about their place in the world, and about the prospects for the future. This psychologist is basing her techniques on whose model of depression?
   a. Sigmund Freud
   b. Carl Rogers
   c. Rollo May
   d. Aaron Beck

8. Maintenance treatment for depression can be important because it can prevent:
   a. transmission.
   b. bereavement.
   c. incidence.
   d. relapse.

9. Which of the following explains why some people refuse to take medications to treat their depression or take those medications and then stop?
   a. The medications are in short supply and are unavailable.
   b. The medications don't work for most people.
   c. For some people the medications cause serious side effects.
   d. The medications work in the short term but not the long term.

10. Which of the following is a risk factor for suicide?
    a. having a relative who committed suicide
    b. playing aggressive, full-contact sports
    c. a history of multiple marriages
    d. an abstract, philosophical cognitive style

*(See the Appendix on page 601 for answers.)*

# Exploring Mood Disorders

People with mood disorders experience one or both of the following:

• Mania: a frantic "high" with extreme overconfidence and energy, often leading to reckless behaviour
• Depression: a devastating "low" with extreme lack of energy, interest, confidence, and enjoyment of life

## TRIGGER

• Negative or positive life changes (death of a loved one, promotion, etc.)
• Physical illness

## Biological Influences

• Inherited vulnerability
• Altered neurotransmitters, and neurohormonal systems
• Sleep deprivation
• Circadian rhythm disturbances

## Social Influences

• Women and minorities: social inequality and oppression and a diminished sense of control
• Social support can reduce symptoms
• Lack of social support can aggravate symptoms

## CAUSES

## Behavioural Influences

**Depression**
• General slowing down
• Neglect of responsibilities and appearance
• Irritability; complaints about matters that used to be taken in stride

**Mania**
• Hyperactivity
• Reckless or otherwise unusual behaviour

## Emotional and Cognitive Influences

**Depression**
• Emotional flatness or emptiness
• Inability to feel pleasure
• Poor memory
• Inability to concentrate
• Hopelessness and/or learned helplessness
• Loss of sexual desire
• Loss of warm feelings for family and friends
• Exaggerated self-blame or guilt
• Overgeneralization
• Loss of self-esteem
• Suicidal thoughts or actions

**Mania**
• Exaggerated feelings of euphoria and excitement

# TYPES OF MOOD DISORDERS

## DEPRESSIVE DISORDERS

### Major Depressive Disorder
Symptoms of major depressive disorder:

- begin suddenly, often triggered by a crisis, change, or loss
- are extremely severe, interfering with normal functioning
- can be long term, lasting months or years if untreated

Some people have only one episode, but the pattern usually involves repeated episodes or lasting symptoms.

Brand X Pictures/Getty Images

### Dysthymia
Long-term unchanging symptoms of mild depression, sometimes lasting 20 to 30 years if untreated. Daily functioning not as severely affected, but over time impairment is cumulative.

### Double Depression
Alternating periods of major depression and dysthymia

## BIPOLAR DISORDERS

**People who have a bipolar disorder live on an unending emotional roller coaster.**

During the **Depressive Phase** the person may:

- lose all interest in pleasurable activities and friends
- feel worthless, helpless, and hopeless
- have trouble concentrating
- lose or gain weight without trying
- have trouble sleeping, or sleep more than usual
- feel tired all the time
- feel physical aches and pains that have no medical cause
- think about death or attempt suicide

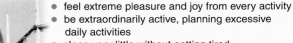

Photodisc/Getty Images

During the **Manic Phase** the person may:

- feel extreme pleasure and joy from every activity
- be extraordinarily active, planning excessive daily activities
- sleep very little without getting tired
- develop grandiose plans leading to reckless behaviour: unrestrained buying sprees, sexual indiscretions, foolish business investments, etc.
- have "racing thoughts" and talk on and on
- be easily irritated and distracted

Brand X Pictures/Getty Images

### Types of Bipolar Disorders

- **Bipolar I**: major depression and full mania
- **Bipolar II**: major depression and hypomania
- **Cyclothymia**: mild depression with hypomania, chronic and long term

## TREATMENT OF MOOD DISORDERS

Treatment for mood disorders is most effective and easiest when it's started early. Most people are treated with a combination of these methods.

Photodisc/Getty Images

*MEDICATION* Antidepressants can help to control symptoms and restore neurotransmitter functioning.
Common types of antidepressants:

- Tricyclics (Tofranil, Elavil)
- Monamine oxidase inhibitors (MAOIs): (Nardil, Parnate). MAOIs can have severe side effects, especially when combined with certain foods or over-the-counter medications.
- Selective serotonergic reuptake inhibitors or SSRIs (Prozac, Zoloft) are newer and cause fewer side effects than tricyclics or MAOIs.
- Lithium is the preferred drug for bipolar disorder. Side effects can be serious and dosage must be carefully regulated.

*COGNITIVE–BEHAVIOURAL THERAPY* Helps depressed people:

- learn to replace negative depressive thoughts and attributions with more positive ones
- develop more effective coping behaviours and skills

*INTERPERSONAL PSYCHOTHERAPY* Helps depressed people:

- focus on the social and interpersonal triggers for their depression (such as the loss of a loved one)
- develop skills to resolve interpersonal conflicts and build new relationships

*ECT (ELECTROCONVULSIVE THERAPY)*

- For severe depression, used when other treatments have been ineffective. Usually has temporary side effects such as memory loss and lethargy. In some patients, certain intellectual and/or memory functions may be permanently lost.

*LIGHT THERAPY*

- For seasonal affective disorder

Photodisc/Getty Images

# 7 Physical Disorders and Health Psychology

## Psychological and Social Factors that Influence Health

*Health and Health-Related Behaviour*
*The Nature of Stress*
*The Physiology of Stress*
*Contributions to the Stress Response*
*Stress, Anxiety, Depression, and Excitement*
*Stress and the Immune Response*

## Psychosocial Effects on Physical Disorders

*AIDS*
*Cancer*
*Cardiovascular Problems*
*Hypertension*
*Coronary Heart Disease*
*Chronic Pain*
*Chronic Fatigue Syndrome*

## Psychological Treatment of Physical Disorders

*Biofeedback*
*Relaxation and Meditation*
*A Comprehensive Stress- and Pain-Reduction Program*
*Drugs and Stress-Reduction Programs*
*Denial as a Means of Coping*
*Modifying Behaviours to Promote Health*

## Visual Summary: Exploring Physical Disorders and Health Psychology

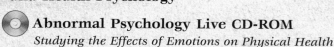 ## Abnormal Psychology Live CD-ROM

*Studying the Effects of Emotions on Physical Health*
*Breast Cancer Support and Education*
*Social Support/HIV: Orel*
*Research on Exercise and Weight Control*

© Simon Marcus/Corbis

# Psychological and Social Factors that Influence Health

■ *Distinguish between behavioural medicine and health psychology.*

■ *Identify the relationships among immune system function, stress, and physical disorders.*

At the beginning of the 20th century, the leading causes of death were influenza, pneumonia, diphtheria, tuberculosis, and gastrointestinal infections. Since then, the yearly death rate from these diseases has been reduced greatly (see Table 7.1). This reduction represents a revolution in public health that eliminated many infectious diseases and mastered many more. But the enormous success of our health-care system in reducing mortality from disease has revealed a more complex and challenging problem: Some major contributing factors to illness and death in this country are *psychological and behavioural.*

In Chapter 2, we described the profound effects of psychological and social factors on brain structure and function. These factors seem to influence neurotransmitter activity, the secretion of neurohormones in the endocrine system, and, at a more fundamental level, gene expression. We have repeatedly looked at the complex interplay of biological, psychological, and social factors in the production and maintenance of psychological disorders. It will come as no surprise that psychological and social factors are important to a number of additional disorders, including endocrinological disorders such as diabetes and disorders of the immune system such as AIDS. The difference between these and the other disorders discussed in this chapter is that they are

clearly *physical disorders.* They have known (or strongly inferred) physical causes and, for the most part, observable physical pathology (e.g., genital herpes, damaged heart muscle, malignant tumours, measurable hypertension). Contrast this with the somatoform disorders discussed in Chapter 5: In conversion disorders, for example, clients complain of physical damage or disease but show no physical pathology. In DSM-IV-TR, physical disorders such as hypertension and diabetes are coded separately on Axis III. However, there is a provision for recognizing *psychological factors affecting medical condition.*

The study of how psychological and social factors affect physical disorders used to be distinct and somewhat separate from the remainder of psychopathology. Early on, the field was called *psychosomatic medicine* (Alexander, 1950), which meant that *psychological* factors affected *somatic* (physical) function. *Psychophysiological disorders* was a label used to communicate a similar idea. Such terms are less often used today because they are misleading. Describing as psychosomatic a disorder with an obvious physical component gave the impression that psychological ("mental") disorders of mood and anxiety did not have a strong biological component. As we now know, this assumption is not viable. Dividing the *causes* of mental disorders and physical disorders is not

| **TABLE 7.1** The Leading Causes of Death in Canada, 1921–1925 and 1997 (Rates per 100 000 Population) | | | |
|---|---|---|---|
| 1921–1925 | Rate | 1997 | Rate |
| 1. Cardiovascular and renal diseases | 222 | 1. Diseases of the circulatory system | 265 |
| 2. Influenza, bronchitis and pneumonia | 141 | 2. Cancer | 196 |
| 3. Diseases of early infancy | 111 | 3. Respiratory diseases | 67 |
| 4. Tuberculosis | 85 | 4. Unintentional injuries | 28 |
| 5. Cancer | 76 | 5. Diseases of the digestive system | 25 |
| 6. Gastritis, duodenitis, entritis, colitis | 72 | 6. Endocrine diseases, etc. | 24 |
| 7. Accidents | 52 | 7. Diseases of the nervous system | 22 |
| 8. Communicable diseases: Diptheria, whooping cough, measles, scarlet fever, and typhoid fever | 47 | 8. Mental disorders | 20 |
| | | 9. Suicide | 12 |
| | | 10. Genito-urinary diseases | 12 |

*Source:* Figures for 1921–1925 from *Historical Statistics of Canada,* Section B. Vital Statistics and Health (B35-50) by Statistics Canada, 2002b, Ottawa. Figures for 1997 from *Leading Causes of Death and Hospitalization in Canada,* by Health Canada, Population and Public Health Branch, 2000b, Ottawa.

supported by current evidence. Biological, psychological, and social factors are implicated in the cause and maintenance of every disorder.

The contribution of psychosocial factors to the etiology and treatment of physical disorders is widely studied. Some of the discoveries are among the more exciting findings in all of psychology and biology. For example, in Chapter 2, we described briefly the specific harmful influences of anger on heart function. The tentative conclusion from that research was that the pumping efficiency of an angry person's heart is reduced, risking dangerous disturbances of heart rhythms (Ironson et al., 1992; Robins & Novaco, 2000). Remember, too, the tragic physical and mental deterioration among elderly people who are removed from social networks of family and friends (Broadhead, Kaplan, & James, 1983; Grant, Patterson, & Yager, 1988). Also, long-term unemployment among men who previously held steady jobs is associated with a doubling of the risk of death over the following 5 years compared with men who continued working (Morris, Cook, & Shaper, 1994). Researchers isolated stress caused by economic uncertainty as the principal cause of plummeting ages of life expectancy in eastern Europe after the fall of communism (Stone, 2000).

## Health and Health-Related Behaviour

The shift in focus from infectious disease to psychological factors has been called the second revolution in public health. Two closely related new fields of study have developed. In the first, **behavioural medicine** (Meyers, 1991; Rachman & Philips, 1980), knowledge derived from behavioural science is applied to the prevention, diagnosis, and treatment of medical problems. This is an interdisciplinary field in which psychologists, physicians, and other health professionals work closely together to develop new treatments and preventive strategies (Schwartz & Weiss, 1978). A second field, **health psychology,** is not interdisciplinary, and it is usually considered a subfield of behavioural medicine. Practitioners study psychological factors that are important to the promotion and maintenance of health; they also analyze and recommend improvements in health-care systems and health policy formation within the discipline of psychology (Kazarian & Evans, 2001; Stone, 1987).

Psychological and social factors influence health and physical problems in *two* distinct ways (see Figure 7.1). First, they can affect the basic biological processes that lead to illness and disease. Second, long-standing behaviour patterns may put people at risk to develop certain physical disorders. Sometimes both of these avenues contribute to the

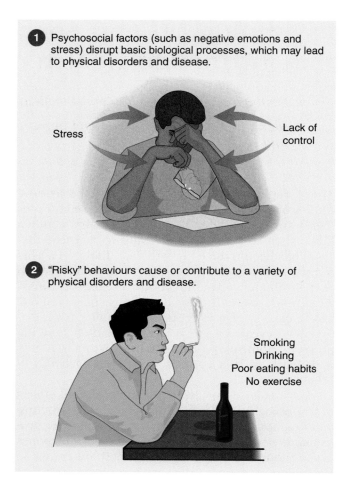

**① Psychosocial factors** (such as negative emotions and stress) disrupt basic biological processes, which may lead to physical disorders and disease.

Stress

Lack of control

**② "Risky" behaviours** cause or contribute to a variety of physical disorders and disease.

Smoking
Drinking
Poor eating habits
No exercise

**Figure 7.1** ▪ Psychosocial factors directly affect physical health in two ways.

etiology or maintenance of disease (Kiecolt-Glaser & Newton, 2001; Williams, Barefoot, & Schneiderman, 2003). Consider the tragic example of AIDS. AIDS is a disease of the immune system that is directly affected by stress (Cohen & Herbert, 1996; Kennedy, 2000), so stress may promote the deadly progression of AIDS (a conclusion pending confirmation from additional studies). This is an example of how psychological factors may directly influence biological processes. We also know that a variety of things we may choose to do put us at risk for AIDS—for example, having unprotected sex or sharing dirty needles. Because there is no medical cure for AIDS yet, our best weapon is large-scale behaviour modification to *prevent acquisition* of the disease.

**behavioural medicine** Interdisciplinary approach applying behavioural science to the prevention, diagnosis, and treatment of medical problems.

**health psychology** Subfield of behavioural medicine that studies psychological factors important in health promotion and maintenance.

Other behavioural patterns contribute to disease. Fully 50% of deaths from the 10 leading causes of death today can be traced to behaviours common to certain lifestyles (Centers for Disease Control, 2003). Cigarette smoking is a major behavioural contributor to mortality (Brannon & Feist, 1997; McGinnis & Foege, 1993). Smoking is estimated to have caused more than 45 000 deaths in Canada in 1999 alone (Canadian Council on Smoking & Health and Physicians for a Smoke-Free Canada, 2003). Behavioural patterns subsumed under unhealthy lifestyles also include poor eating habits, lack of exercise, and insufficient injury control (e.g., not wearing seat belts). These behaviours are grouped under the label *lifestyle* because they are, for the most part, enduring habits that are an integral part of a person's daily living pattern (Faden, 1987; Oyama & Andrasik, 1992). We return to lifestyles in the closing pages of this chapter when we look at efforts to modify them and promote health.

We have much to learn about how psychological factors affect physical disorders and disease. Available evidence suggests that the same kinds of causal factors active in psychological disorders—social, psychological, and biological—play a role in some physical disorders (Mostofsky & Barlow, 2000; Taylor, Repetti, & Seeman, 1997). But the factor attracting the most attention is *stress*, particularly the neurobiological components of the stress response.

## The Nature of Stress

In 1936, a young scientist in Montreal named Hans Selye noticed that one group of rats he injected with a certain chemical extract developed ulcers and other physiological problems, including atrophy of immune system tissues. But a control group of rats who received a daily saline (salty water) injection that should not have had any effect developed the *same* physical problems. Selye pursued this unexpected finding and discovered that the daily injections themselves seemed to be the culprit rather than the injected substance. Furthermore, many different types of environmental changes produced the same results. Borrowing a term from engineering, he decided the cause of this non-specific reaction was *stress*. As so often happens in science, an accidental or serendipitous observation led to a new area of study, in this case, *stress physiology* (Selye, 1936).

Selye theorized that the body goes through several stages in response to *sustained* stress. The first phase is a type of *alarm* response to immediate danger or threat. With continuing stress, we seem to pass into a stage of *resistance*, in which we mobilize various coping mechanisms to respond to the

Hans Selye, a scientist at McGill University, suggested in 1936 that stress contributes to certain physical problems.

stress. Finally, if the stress is too intense or lasts too long, we may enter a stage of *exhaustion*, in which our bodies suffer permanent damage or death (Selye, 1936, 1950). Selye called this sequence the **general adaptation syndrome (GAS).** Although Selye was not correct in all of the details of his theory, the idea that chronic stress may inflict permanent bodily damage or contribute to disease has been confirmed and elaborated on in recent years (Kemeny, 2003; Sapolsky, 2000a). The word *stress* means many things in modern life. In engineering, stress is the strain on a bridge when a heavy truck drives across it; stress is the *response* of the bridge to the truck's weight. But stress is also a *stimulus*. The truck is a "stressor" for the bridge, just as being fired from a job or facing a difficult final exam is a stimulus or stressor for a person. These varied meanings can create some confusion, but we concentrate on **stress** as the physiological response of the individual to a stressor.

---

**general adaptation syndrome (GAS)** Sequence of reactions to sustained stress described by Hans Selye. These stages are alarm, resistance, and exhaustion, which may lead to death.

**stress** Body's physiological response to a stressor, which is any event or change that requires adaptation.

## The Physiology of Stress

In Chapter 2, we described the physiological effects of the early stages of stress, noting in particular its activating effect on the sympathetic nervous system, which mobilizes our resources during times of threat or danger by activating internal organs to prepare the body for immediate action, either fight or flight. These changes increase our strength and mental activity. We also noted in Chapter 2 that the activity of the endocrine system increases when we are stressed, primarily through activation of the HPA axis. Although a variety of neurotransmitters begin flowing in the nervous system, much attention has focused on the endocrine system's neuro-modulators or neuropeptides, hormones affecting the nervous system that are secreted by the glands directly into the bloodstream (Brown, 1994; Krishnan, Doraiswamy, Venkataraman, Reed, & Richie, 1991). These neuromodulating hormones act much like neurotransmitters in carrying the brain's messages to various parts of the body. One of the neurohormones, *corticotropin-releasing factor (CRF)*, is secreted by the hypothalamus and stimulates the pituitary gland. Farther down the chain of the HPA axis, the pituitary gland (along with the autonomic nervous system) activates the adrenal gland, which secretes, among other things, the hormone *cortisol.* Because of their close relationship to the stress response, cortisol and other related hormones are known as the *stress hormones.*

Remember that the HPA axis is closely related to the limbic system. The hypothalamus, at the top of the brain stem, is right next to the limbic system, which contains the hippocampus and seems to control our emotional memories. The hippocampus is very responsive to cortisol. When stimulated by this hormone during HPA axis activity, the hippocampus helps to *turn off* the stress response, completing a feedback loop between the limbic system and the various parts of the HPA axis.

This loop may be important for a number of reasons. Working with primates, Robert Sapolsky and his colleague Michael Meany at McGill University (e.g., Sapolsky & Meaney, 1986) showed that increased levels of cortisol in response to chronic stress may kill nerve cells in the hippocampus. If hippocampal activity is thus compromised, excessive cortisol is secreted and, over time, the ability to turn off the stress response decreases, which leads to further aging of the hippocampus. These findings indicate that chronic stress leading to chronic secretion of cortisol may have long-lasting effects on physical function, including brain damage. Cell death may, in turn, lead to deficient problem-solving abilities among the aged and, ultimately, dementia. This physiological process may also affect our susceptibility to infectious disease

and our recovery from it in other pathophysiological systems. This work is important because we now know that hippocampal cell death associated with chronic stress and anxiety occurs in humans with, for example, posttraumatic stress disorder (see Chapter 4) and depression (see Chapter 6). The long-term effects of this cell death are not yet known.

## Contributions to the Stress Response

Stress physiology is profoundly influenced by psychological and social factors (Kemeny, 2003; Taylor et al., 1997). This link has been demonstrated in work with baboons living freely in a national reserve in Kenya (Sapolsky, 1990, 2000b). Baboons are investigated because their primary sources of stress, like humans', are psychological rather than physical. As with many species, baboons arrange themselves in a social hierarchy with dominant members at the top and submissive members at the bottom. And life is tough at the bottom! The lives of subordinate animals are made difficult (or "stressful") by continual bullying from the dominant animals, and they have less access to food, preferred resting places, and sexual partners.

Particularly interesting are findings on levels of cortisol in the baboons as a function of their social rank in a dominance hierarchy. Remember from our description of the HPA axis that the secretion of cortisol from the adrenal glands is the final step in a cascade of hormone secretion that originates in the limbic system in the brain during periods of stress. The secretion of cortisol contributes to our arousal and mobilization in the short run but, if produced chronically, it can damage the hippocampus. In addition, muscles atrophy, fertility is affected by declining testosterone, hypertension develops in the cardiovascular system, and the immune response is impaired. It has been discovered that dominant males in the baboon hierarchy ordinarily have *lower* resting levels of cortisol than subordinate males. When an emergency occurs, however, cortisol levels rise more quickly in the dominant males than in the subordinate males (Sapolsky, 1990, 2000b).

Researchers have sought the causes of these differences by working backward up the HPA axis. They found an excess secretion of CRF by the hypothalamus in subordinate animals combined with a diminished sensitivity of the pituitary gland (which is stimulated by CRF). Therefore, subordinate animals, unlike dominant animals, continually secrete cortisol, probably because their lives are so stressful. In addition, their HPA system is less sensitive to the effects of cortisol and therefore less efficient in turning off the stress response. This line of research also shows that subordinate males are at

Baboons at the top of the social hierarchy have a sense of predictability and control that allows them to cope with problems and maintain physical health; baboons at the bottom of the hierarchy experience the symptoms of stress because they have little control over access to food, resting places, and mates.

higher risk for atherosclerosis and coronary heart disease, a subject we discuss later in this chapter.

What is it about being on top that produces positive effects? It appears to be primarily the psychological benefits of having *predictability* and *controllability* concerning events in one's life. Parts of the data supporting this conclusion were gathered during years in which a number of male baboons were at the top of the hierarchy, with no clear "winner." Although these males dominated the rest of the animals in the group, they constantly attacked each other. Under these conditions they displayed hormonal profiles more like those of subordinate males. Thus, dominance combined with stability produced optimal stress hormone profiles. But the most important factor in regulating stress physiology seems to be a sense of control (Kemeny,

2003; Sapolsky & Ray, 1989). Control of social situations and the ability to cope with any tension that arises go a long way toward blunting the long-term effects of stress.

## Stress, Anxiety, Depression, and Excitement

If you have read the chapters on anxiety, mood, and related psychological disorders, you might conclude, correctly, that stressful life events combined with psychological vulnerabilities such as an inadequate sense of control are a factor in psychological and physical disorders. Is there any relationship between emotional and physical disorders? A very strong one seems to exist. Vaillant (1979) studied more than 200 male university undergraduates between 1942 and 1944 who were mentally and physically healthy. He followed these men closely for more than 30 years. Those who developed psychological disorders or who were highly stressed became chronically ill or died at a significantly higher rate than men who remained well adjusted and free from psychological disorders, a finding that has been repeatedly confirmed (e.g., Katon, 2003). This suggests that the same types of stress-related psychological factors that contribute to psychological disorders may contribute to the later development of physical disorders and that stress, anxiety, and depression are closely related. Can you tell the difference among feelings of stress, anxiety, depression, and excitement? You might say, "No problem," but these four states have a lot in common. Which one you experience may depend on your *sense of control* at the moment or how well you think you can cope with the threat or challenge you are facing (Barlow, 2002; Barlow, Rapee, & Reisner, 2001). This continuum of feelings from excitement to stress to anxiety to depression is shown in Figure 7.2.

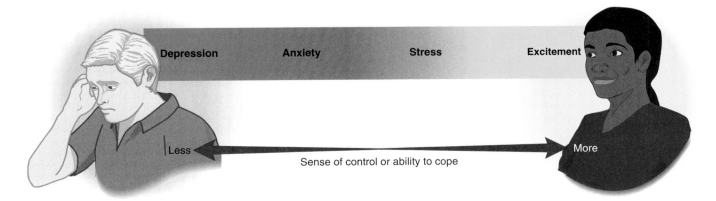

**Figure 7.2** ■ Responses to threats and challenges. Our feelings range along a continuum from depression to anxiety to stress to excitement, depending in part on our sense of control and ability to cope. (From *Mastering Stress 2001: A Lifestyle Approach*, by D. H. Barlow, R. M. Rapee, and L. C. Reisner, 2001. Copyright © 2001 by the American Health Publishing Co. Adapted with permission.)

Consider how you feel when you are excited. You might experience a rapid heartbeat, a sudden burst of energy, or a jumpy stomach. But if you're well prepared for the challenge—for example, if you're an athlete, really up for the game and confident in your abilities, or a musician, sure you are going to give an outstanding performance—these feelings of *excitement* can be pleasurable.

Sometimes when you face a challenging task, you feel you could handle it if you only had the time or help you need, but because you don't have these resources, you feel pressured. In response, you may work harder to do better and be perfect, even though you think you will be all right in the end. If you are under too much pressure, you may become tense and irritable or develop a headache or an upset stomach. This is what *stress* feels like. If something is threatening and you believe there is little you can do about it, you may feel *anxiety*. The threatening situation could be anything from a physical attack to making a fool of yourself in front of someone. As your body prepares for the challenge, you worry about it incessantly. Your sense of control is considerably less than if you were stressed. In some cases, there may not be any difficult situation. Sometimes we are anxious for no reason except that we feel certain aspects of our lives are out of control. Finally, individuals who always perceive life as threatening may lose hope about ever having control and slip into a state of *depression*, no longer trying to cope.

To sum up, the underlying physiology of these particular emotional states seems relatively similar. This is why we refer to a similar pattern of sympathetic arousal and activation of specific neurotransmitters and neurohormones in discussing anxiety, depression, and stress-related physical disorders. Nevertheless, it is psychological factors—specifically, a sense of control and confidence that we can cope with stress or challenges, called **self-efficacy** by Albert Bandura (1986)—that differ most markedly among these emotions, leading to different feelings (Taylor et al., 1997).

## Stress and the Immune Response

Have you had a cold during the past several months? How did you pick it up? Did someone sneeze nearby while you were sitting in class? Exposure to cold viruses is a necessary factor in developing a cold, but the level of stress you are experiencing at the time seems to play a major role in whether the exposure results in a cold. Researchers exposed volunteer participants to a specific dosage of a cold virus and followed them closely (Cohen, 1996; Cohen, Doyle, & Skoner, 1999). They found that the chance a participant would get sick was directly related to how

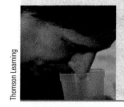

### Studying the Effects of Emotions on Physical Health

*"People with the lowest level of sociability are most likely to get a cold, while people with the highest level of sociability are least likely to develop a cold."*

Thomson Learning

much stress the person had experienced during the past year. A later study linked the intensity of stress and negative affect at the time of exposure to the later *severity* of the cold, as measured by mucus production (Cohen et al., 1995). Cohen, Doyle, Turner, Alper, and Skoner (2003) have also demonstrated that how sociable you are—that is, the quantity and quality of your social relationships—affects whether you come down with a cold when exposed to the virus, perhaps because socializing with friends relieves stress. These are among the first well-controlled studies to demonstrate that stress and related factors increase the risk of infection.

Think back to your last exam. Did you (or your roommate) have a cold? Exam periods are stressors that have been shown to produce increased infections, particularly of the upper respiratory tract (Glaser et al., 1987, 1990). Therefore, if you are susceptible to colds, maybe one way out is to skip final exams! A better solution is to learn how to control your stress before and during exams. Almost certainly, the effect of stress on susceptibility to infections is mediated through the **immune system,** which protects the body from any foreign materials that may enter it.

Research dating back to the original reports of Hans Selye (1936) demonstrates the detrimental effects of stress on immune system functioning. Humans under stress show clearly increased rates of infectious diseases, including colds, herpes, and mononucleosis (e.g., Cohen & Herbert, 1996; Vander Plate, Aral, & Magder, 1988). Direct evidence links a number of stressful situations to lowered immune system functioning, including marital discord or relationship difficulties (Kiecolt-Glaser & Newton, 2001; Uchino, Uno, & Holt-Lunstad, 1999), job loss, and the death of a loved one (Morris et al., 1994; Pavalko, Elder, & Clipp, 1993).

---

**self-efficacy** Perception that one has the ability to cope with stress or challenges.

**immune system** The body's means of identifying and eliminating any foreign materials (e.g., bacteria, parasites, even transplanted organs) that enter.

We have already noted that emotional disorders seem to make us more susceptible to developing physical disorders (Katon, 2003; Vaillant, 1979). Now direct evidence indicates that depression lowers immune system functioning (Herbert & Cohen, 1993; Stone, 2000), particularly in the aged (Herbert & Cohen, 1993; Schleifer, Keller, Bond, Cohen, & Stein, 1989). Weisse (1992) suggests that the level of depression (and perhaps the underlying sense of uncontrollability that accompanies depression) is a more potent factor in lowering immune system functioning than are specific stressful life events, such as job loss. Depression can also lead to poor self-care and a tendency to engage in more risky behaviours. For humans, like baboons, the ability to retain a sense of control over events in our lives may be one of the most important psychological contributions to good health.

*Chronic stress* may be more problematic than acute or sudden stress for the immune system because the effects are, by definition, longer lasting. In the 1970s, the nuclear power plant at Three Mile Island in Pennsylvania leaked. Many residents feared that any exposure to radiation they might have sustained would lead to cancer or other illnesses, and they lived with this fear for years. More than 6 years after the event, some individuals who had been in the area during the crisis still had lowered immune system functioning (McKinnon, Weisse, Reynolds, Bowles, & Baum, 1989). A similar finding of lower immune system functioning has been reported for people who care for chronically ill family members, such as Alzheimer's disease patients (Kiecolt-Glaser & Glaser, 1987).

To understand how the immune system protects us, we must first understand how it works. We take a brief tour of the immune system next, using Figure 7.3 as a visual guide, and then we examine psychological contributions to the biology of two diseases strongly related to immune system functioning: AIDS and cancer.

## How the Immune System Works

The immune system identifies and eliminates foreign materials, called **antigens,** in the body. Antigens can be any of a number of substances, usually bacteria, viruses, or parasites. But the immune system also targets the body's own cells that have become aberrant or damaged in some way, perhaps as part of a malignant tumour. Donated organs are foreign, so the immune system attacks them after surgical transplant; consequently, it is necessary to suppress the immune system temporarily after surgery.

The immune system has two main parts: the *humoral* and the *cellular*. Specific types of cells function as agents of both. White blood cells (macrophages), called *leukocytes*, do most of the work. They surround identifiable antigens and destroy them. They also signal *lymphocytes*, which consist of B cells and T cells.

---

**antigens**   Foreign materials that enter the body, including bacteria and parasites.

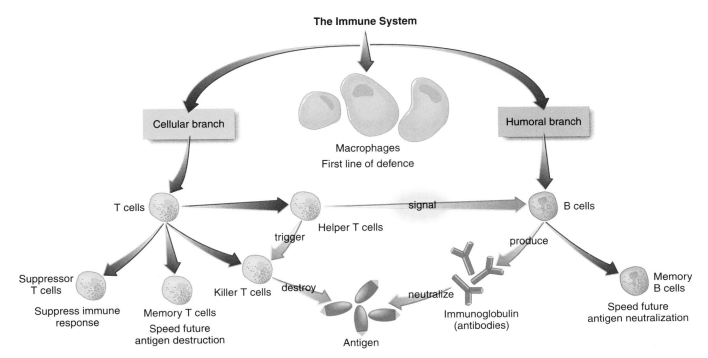

**Figure 7.3** ■ An overview of the immune system.

*B cells* operate within the humoral part of the immune system, releasing molecules that seek out antigens with the purpose of neutralizing them. B cells produce *antibodies,* which combine with the antigens to neutralize them. After the antigens are neutralized, *memory B cells* are created so that the next time that antigen is encountered, the immune system response will be even faster. This action accounts for the success of inoculations you may have received for mumps or measles as a child. An inoculation contains small amounts of the targeted organism but not enough to make you sick. Your immune system then "remembers" this antigen and prevents you from coming down with the full disease when you are exposed to it.

*T cells* operate in the cellular branch of the immune system. These cells don't produce antibodies. One subgroup, called *killer T cells,* was discovered in 1973 in Winnipeg by cancer researcher Arnold H. Greenberg (Bleackley, Green, Lockshin, Melino, & Zakeri, 2001; Greenberg, 1994). Killer T cells directly destroy viruses and cancerous processes (O'Leary, 1990; Roitt, 1988). Then *memory T cells* are created to speed future responses to the same antigen. Other subgroups of T cells help regulate the immune system. For example, *helper T cells* enhance the immune system response by signalling B cells to produce antibodies and telling killer T cells to destroy the antigen. *Suppressor T cells* suppress the production of antibodies by B cells when they are no longer needed.

We should have twice as many helper T cells as suppressor T cells. With too many helper T cells, the immune system may attack the body's normal cells rather than antigens. When this happens, we have what is called an **autoimmune disease,** such as **rheumatoid arthritis.** With too many suppressor T cells, the body is subject to invasion by a number of antigens. The human immunodeficiency virus (HIV) directly attacks the helper T cells, thereby severely weakening the immune system and causing AIDS.

Until the mid-1970s, most scientists believed the brain and the immune system operate independently. However, in 1974, Ader and Cohen (1975, 1993) made a startling discovery. Working with a classical conditioning paradigm, they gave sugar-flavoured water to rats, together with a drug that suppresses the immune system. Ader and Cohen then demonstrated that giving the same rats only the sweet-tasting water produced similar changes in the immune system. In other words, the rats had "learned" (through classical conditioning) to respond to the water by suppressing their immune systems. We now know there are many connections between the nervous system and the immune system. These findings have generated a

new field known as **psychoneuroimmunology (PNI)** (Ader & Cohen, 1993; Brown, 1994), which simply means the object of study is *psycho*logical influences on the *neuro*logical responses implicated in our *immune* response.

Cohen and Herbert (1996) illustrate pathways through which psychological and social factors may influence immune system functioning. Direct connections between the brain (the central nervous system) and HPA axis (hormonal) and the immune system have already been described. Behavioural changes in response to stressful events, such as increased smoking or poor eating habits, may also suppress the immune system (Figure 7.4).

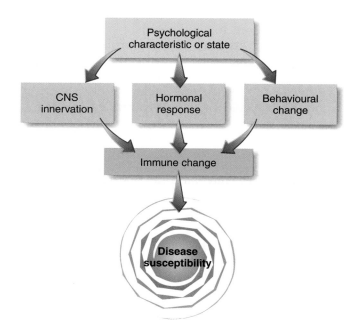

**Figure 7.4** ◼ Pathways through which psychological factors might influence onset and progression of immune system-mediated disease. For simplicity, arrows are drawn in only one direction, from psychological characteristics to disease. No lack of alternative paths is implied. (From Cohen & Herbert, 1996.) (CNS = central nervous system.)

**autoimmune disease** Condition in which the body's immune system attacks healthy tissue rather than antigens.

**rheumatoid arthritis** Painful, degenerative disease in which the immune system essentially attacks itself, resulting in stiffness, swelling, and even destruction of the joints. Cognitive-behavioural treatments can help relieve pain and stiffness.

**psychoneuroimmunology (PNI)** Study of psychological influences on the neurological responses involved in the body's immune response.

Assess your knowledge of the immune system by matching components of the immune system with their function in the body: (a) B cells, (b) antibodies, (c) killer T cells, (d) suppressor T cells, (e) memory cells.

1. This subgroup targets viral infections within the cells by directly destroying the antigens. _____

2. Highly specific molecules that combine with antigens to neutralize them. _____
3. Lymphocytes that operate within the humoral part of the immune system. _____
4. These are created so that when a specific antigen is encountered in the future, the immune response will be faster. _____
5. These T cells stop the production of antibodies by B cells when they are no longer needed. _____

# Psychosocial Effects on Physical Disorders

■ *Describe the relationships between stress and cardiovascular disease, AIDS, and cancer.*

■ *Define acute and chronic pain and their potential causes.*

With an enhanced understanding of the effects of emotional and behavioural factors on the immune system, we can now examine how these factors influence specific physical disorders. We begin with AIDS.

## AIDS

The ravages of the AIDS epidemic have made this disease a very high priority within the health-care system. In 2000, the total number of people around the world living with HIV was estimated at 34.3 million. By the end of 2003, the figure was 40 million, with 5 million new cases and 3 million deaths in 2003 alone (Stephenson, 2003). In the hardest-hit regions in southern Africa, between 20% and 40% of the adult population are believed to be HIV-positive. Furthermore, it is spreading rapidly to the densely populated regions of India and China, where the prevalence is expected to rise from "a few thousand" in 2000 to 10 million in 2010 (China UN Theme Group, 2001; Schwartlander, Garnett, Walker, & Anderson, 2000).

Once a person is infected with HIV, the course of the disease is variable. After several months to several years with no symptoms, patients may develop minor health problems such as weight loss, fever, and night sweats, symptoms that make up the condition known as **AIDS-related complex (ARC).** A diagnosis of AIDS itself is not made until one of several serious diseases appears, such as pneumocystis pneumonia, cancer, dementia, or a wasting syndrome in which the body literally withers away. The median time from initial infection to the development of full-blown AIDS has been estimated to range from 7.3 to 10 years or more (Moss & Bacchetti, 1989; Pantaleo, Graziosi, & Fauci, 1993). Although most people with AIDS die within 1 year of diagnosis, as many as 15% survive 5 years or longer (Kertzner & Gorman, 1992). Recently, clinical scientists have developed powerful new combinations of drugs referred to as *highly active antiretroviral therapy* (HAART) that seem to suppress the virus in those infected with HIV, even in advanced cases (Brechtl, Breitbart, Galietta, Krivo, & Rosenfeld, 2001). Although this is a hopeful development, it does not seem to be a cure, because the most recent evidence suggests the virus is seldom if ever eliminated but rather lies dormant in reduced numbers; thus, infected patients face a lifetime of taking multiple medications (Cohen, 2002). Also, the percentage who drop out of HAART because of severe side effects is very high, 61% in one study (O'Brien, Clark, Besch, Myers, & Kissinger, 2003). Even more discouraging is that drug-resistant strains of HIV are now being transmitted.

Because AIDS is a relatively new disease, with a long latency to development, we are still learning

**AIDS-related complex (ARC)**  Group of minor health problems such as weight loss, fever, and night sweats that appear after HIV infection but before development of full-blown AIDS.

about the factors, including possible psychological factors, that extend survival and well-being (Kennedy, 2000). Investigators identified a group of people who have been exposed repeatedly to HIV but have not contracted AIDS. A major distinction of these people is that their immune systems, particularly the cellular branch, are robust and strong (Ezzel, 1993). Therefore, efforts to boost the immune system may contribute to the prevention of AIDS.

Learning we have an incurable terminal illness is extremely stressful for anyone. This happens every day to individuals stricken with HIV. The stress of learning you are carrying HIV can be devastating as can be dealing with the emergence of AIDS-related symptoms in those who are infected with the virus. In a study by Montreal researchers José Côté and Carolyn Pepler, 90 hospitalized HIV-positive men were randomly assigned to one of two psychological interventions intended to help regulate emotional responses to an exacerbation of AIDS symptoms, or to a control group. One intervention was skills-based in which the men learned cognitive coping skills for dealing with their illness and the other an emotion-focused intervention in which the men were encouraged to express their feelings about their illness. Before and after the intervention, all men were assessed for mood, distress, and anxiety levels.

Both active interventions produced beneficial effects on overall negative mood (see Figure 7.5) compared with the control group. The cognitive coping skills group showed some additional benefits, including an overall decrease in distress and intrusive thoughts about their illness, as well as decreases in anxiety after each session. These findings point to the importance of psychological factors like cognitive coping in regulating emotional reactions to the emergence of symptoms among those infected with HIV (Côté & Pepler, 2002).

But can such psychological interventions actually affect not only distress levels in HIV-positive patients but also the course of the illness? Antoni et al. (1991) studied the effects of administering a psychological stress-reduction treatment to a group of individuals who believed they might have HIV during the weeks before they were tested for HIV. Half of the group received the stress-reduction program; the other half received the usual medical and psychological care. Unfortunately, many individuals in this group turned out to be HIV-positive. However, similar to the findings in the Côté and Pepler (2002) study, of those in the Antoni et al. (1991) study, only those who had undergone the psychological stress-reduction procedures did *not* show substantial increases in anxiety and depression. Furthermore—and more importantly—they demonstrated *increases* in their immune system functioning as measured by such indices as helper T and killer T cells. In addition, participants in the stress-reduction program showed significant increases in antibodies to two herpes viruses, suggesting improved functioning of the immune system (Esterling et al., 1992). This is important because herpes viruses are closely related to HIV and seem to promote further activation of HIV-infected cells, resulting in a faster and deadlier spread of HIV. What was most encouraging about this study, however, was that a follow-up showed less disease progression in the stress-reduction group 2 years later (Ironson et al., 1994). A more recent study has confirmed that high levels of stress and low social support are associated with a faster progression to disease in a group of HIV-infected men without AIDS who were followed for 7.5 years (Leserman et al., 2000).

Remember, though, that the participants in the Antoni et al. (1991) study were in an early asymptomatic stage of the disease, which stands in contrast to the participants in the Côté and Pepler (2002) study, who were at an advanced stage of the illness and required hospitalization. Important new studies suggest the same cognitive-behavioural stress-management program may have positive effects on the immune systems of individuals who are already symptomatic (Antoni et al., 2000; Lutgendorf et al., 1997). Specifically, the intervention program used in the Lutgendorf et al. (1997) study significantly decreased depression and anxiety compared with a control group that did not receive the treatment. Goodkin et al. (2001) reported that a 10-week psychological treatment significantly buffered against an increase in HIV viral load, which is a powerful and reliable predictor of progression to full-blown AIDS, when compared with a control group. Thus, even in progressed symptomatic HIV, psychological interventions may not only enhance psychological

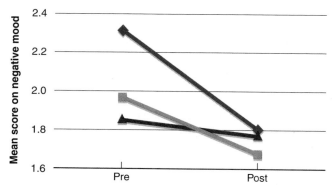

**Figure 7.5** ■ Means for negative mood for the coping skills training intervention (diamond), the emotional expression intervention (square), and the control condition (triangle) at preintervention (Pre) and postintervention (Post). (From Côté and Pepler, 2002.)

adjustment but also influence immune system functioning, and this effect may be long lasting.

It is too early to tell whether these results will be strong or persistent enough to translate into increased survival time for AIDS patients, although results from Ironson et al. (1994) and Antoni et al. (2000) suggest they might. But note that some earlier studies of stress-reduction procedures on AIDS patients found no effect on other aspects of the immune system (e.g., Coates, McKusick, Kuno, & Stites, 1989). If stress and related variables *are* clinically significant to immune response in HIV-infected patients, as suggested by Ironson et al. (1994) and Antoni et al. (2000), then psychological interventions to bolster the immune system might increase survival rates and, in the most optimistic scenario, prevent the slow deterioration of the immune system (Kennedy, 2000; Kiecolt-Glaser & Glaser, 1992).

If stress-reduction procedures do affect the disease process directly, perhaps through the immune system, it is not clear why they are effective. Among the possibilities are that stress-reduction procedures may give patients a greater sense of control, decrease their hopelessness, build active coping responses, change negative cognitions, help them use social support networks more effectively, or some combination of these factors (Uchino, Cacioppo, & Kiecolt-Glaser, 1996; Uchino et al., 1999). We don't know the answer, but few areas of study in behavioural medicine and health psychology are more urgent.

## Cancer

Among the more mind-boggling developments in the study of illness and disease is the discovery that the development and course of different varieties of **cancer** are subject to psychological influences (Williams & Schneiderman, 2002). This has resulted in a new field of study called **psycho-oncology** (Anderson & Baum, 2001; Greer, 1999). *Oncology* means the study of cancer. Spiegel and colleagues (1989) studied 86 women with advanced breast cancer that had metastasized to other areas of their bodies and was expected to kill them within 2 years. Clearly, the prognosis was poor. Although the researchers had little hope of affecting the disease, they thought that by treating these people in group psychotherapy at least they could relieve some of their anxiety, depression, and pain.

All patients had routine medical care for their cancer. In addition, 50 (of the 86) patients met with their therapist for psychotherapy once a week in small groups. Much to everyone's surprise, the therapy group's survival time was significantly longer than that of the control group that did not

***Breast Cancer Support and Education:*** *"Women who had low self-esteem, low body image, feelings of low control, low optimism, and a lack of support at home were even more likely to benefit from an education intervention."*

receive psychotherapy but otherwise benefited from the best care available. In fact, the group receiving therapy lived twice as long on average (approximately 3 years) as the controls (approximately 18 months). Four years after the study began, one-third of the therapy patients were still alive, and all the patients receiving the best medical care available *without* psychotherapy had died (see Figure 7.6). These findings do not mean that psychological interventions cured advanced cancer. At 10 years, only three patients in the therapy group still survived.

Spiegel and colleagues (1996) later demonstrated that this brief psychological treatment can be implemented relatively easily in oncology clinics everywhere. Clinical trials involving large numbers of patients with cancer are in progress to evaluate more thoroughly the life-prolonging and life-enhancing effects of psychological treatments for cancer. One such study confirmed that psychological treatments reduced depression and pain and increased well-being but failed to replicate the

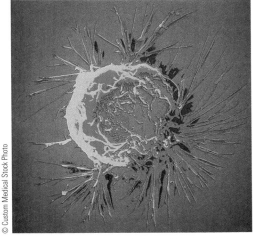

Breast cancer cell

**cancer**   Category of often-fatal medical conditions involving abnormal cell growth and malignancy.

**psycho-oncology**   Study of psychological factors involved in the course and treatment of cancer.

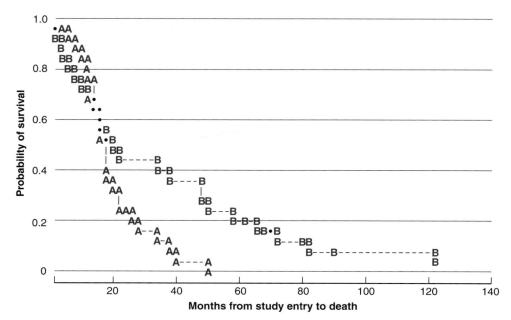

**Figure 7.6** ■ Survival time for women with advanced breast cancer. In a study of women being treated for advanced breast cancer, researchers found that women in a treatment group (N = 50) who received psychological intervention survived significantly longer than did women in a control group (N = 36) with no psychological treatment. A = control, B = psychological intervention. (Adapted from "Effect of Psychosocial Treatment on Survival of Patients with Metastatic Breast Cancer," by D. Spiegel, J. R. Bloom, H. C. Kramer, and E. Gotheil, 1989, *Lancet*, 14, 888–891. Copyright © 1989 by The Lancet Ltd. Reprinted by permission.)

survival-enhancing effects of treatment (Goodwin et al., 2001). Thus, it is safe to say that the jury is still out on a specific survival-enhancing effect of these treatments.

The initial success of these treatments in at least some studies has generated a great deal of interest in exactly how they might work (Anderson & Baum, 2001). Possibilities include better health habits, closer adherence to medical treatment, and improved endocrine functioning and response to stress, all of which may improve immune function (Classen, Diamond, & Spiegel, 1998). Andersen, Kiecolt-Glaser, and Glaser (1994) have suggested similar factors as important but also stress the benefits of enhanced social adjustment and coping. Nezu et al. (1999) demonstrated that problem-solving skills reduced cancer-related distress substantially. There is even preliminary evidence that psychological factors may contribute not only to the *course* but also to the *development* of cancer and other diseases (e.g., Stam & Steggles, 1987). Perceived lack of control, inadequate coping responses, overwhelmingly stressful life events, or the use of inappropriate coping responses (such as denial) may all contribute to the development of cancer (Schneiderman, Antoni, Ironson, LaPerriere, & Fletcher, 1992; Williams & Schneiderman, 2002). However, most studies on which these conclusions are based involve retrospective psychological tests of people who have cancer; much stronger evidence is required to demonstrate that psychological factors may contribute to the onset of cancer.

Psychological factors are also prominent in treatment and recovery from cancer in children (Koocher, 1996). Many types of cancer require invasive and painful medical procedures (Courneya et al., 2003); the suffering can be difficult to bear, not only for the children but also for the parents and health-care providers. Children usually struggle and cry hysterically, so to complete many of the procedures they must be physically restrained. Not only does their behaviour interfere with successful completion, but the stress and anxiety associated with repeated painful procedures may have their own detrimental effect on the disease process.

Research by pediatric psychologists has shown that when children are coping with the pain of medical procedures and surgery, some coping strategies are better than others (e.g., Bennett-Branson & Craig, 1993; Reid, Chambers, McGrath, & Finley, 1997). For example, a study by Graeme Reid of the University of Western Ontario and his colleagues (1997) showed that children who reported that they used distraction as a way of coping experienced less pain and distress following surgery. In contrast, children who used emotion-focused avoidance (i.e., the free expression of emotion without efforts to regulate feelings when in pain) experienced more pain and distress following surgery (Reid et al., 1997). Psychological procedures designed to reduce pain and stress in children undergoing surgery include breathing exercises, watching films of exactly what happens to take the uncertainty out of the procedure, and rehearsal of the procedure with dolls, all of which make the interventions much more tolerable and therefore more successful for young patients (Hubert, Jay, Saltoun, & Hayes, 1988; McGrath & DeVeber, 1986). These procedures are used more routinely today for children about to undergo surgery or painful medical procedures. Pediatric psychologist Patrick McGrath at Dalhousie University and his colleagues have also developed a handbook for parents outlining ways to help make cancer treatments less painful for children (e.g., McGrath, Finley, & Turner, 1992).

## *Cardiovascular Problems*

The *cardiovascular system* comprises the heart, blood vessels, and complex control mechanisms for regulating their function. Many things can go wrong with this system and lead to **cardiovascular disease.** For example, many individuals, particularly older individuals, suffer **strokes,** also called *cerebral vascular accidents,* which are temporary blockages of blood vessels leading to the brain or a rupture of blood vessels in the brain that results in temporary or permanent brain damage and loss of functioning. People with Raynaud's disease lose circulation to peripheral parts of their bodies such as their fingers and toes, suffering some pain and continual sensations of cold in their hands and feet. The cardiovascular problems receiving the most

Psychological preparation reduces suffering and facilitates recovery in children who undergo surgery.

© Royalty-Free/CORBIS

attention these days are hypertension and coronary heart disease, and we look at both. First, let's consider the case of John.

## John
### The Human Volcano

John is a 55-year-old business executive, married, with two teenage children. For most of his adult life, John has smoked about a pack of cigarettes each day. Although he maintains a busy and active schedule, John is mildly obese, partly from regular meals with business partners and colleagues. He has been taking several medications for high blood pressure since age 42. John's doctor has warned him repeatedly to cut down on his smoking and to exercise more frequently, especially because John's father died of a heart attack. Although John has episodes of chest pain, he continues his busy and stressful lifestyle. It is difficult for John to slow down, because his business has been doing extremely well during the past 10 years.

Moreover, John believes that life is too short, that there is no time to slow down. He sees relatively little of his family and works late most evenings. Even when he's at home, John typically works into the night. It is difficult for him to relax; he feels a constant urgency to get as many things done as possible and prefers to work on several tasks simultaneously. For instance, John often proofreads a document, engages in a phone conversation, and eats lunch all at the same time. He attributes much of the success of his business to his working style. Despite his success, John is not well liked by his peers. His co-workers and employees often find him to be overbearing, easily frustrated, and, at times, even hostile. His subordinates in particular claim he is overly impatient and critical of their performance.

**cardiovascular disease** Afflictions in the mechanisms, including the heart, blood vessels, and their controllers, that are responsible for transporting blood to the body's tissues and organs. Psychological factors may play important roles in such diseases and their treatments.

**stroke** Temporary blockage of blood vessels supplying the brain, or a rupture of vessels in the brain, resulting in temporary or permanent loss of brain functioning. Also known as *cerebral vascular accident.*

Do you think John has a problem? Most people would recognize that his behaviours and attitudes make his life unpleasant and possibly lethal. Some of these behaviours and attitudes appear to operate directly on the cardiovascular system and may result in hypertension and coronary heart disease.

## Hypertension

**Hypertension** (high blood pressure) is a major risk factor not only for stroke and heart disease but also for kidney disease. This makes hypertension an extremely serious medical condition. Blood pressure increases when the blood vessels leading to organs and peripheral areas constrict (become narrower), forcing more and more blood to muscles in central parts of the body. Because so many blood vessels have constricted, the heart muscles must work much harder to force the blood to all parts of the body, which causes the increased pressure. These factors produce wear and tear on the ever-shrinking blood vessels and lead to cardiovascular disease. A small percentage of cases of hypertension can be traced to specific physical abnormalities such as kidney disease or tumours on the adrenal glands (Papillo & Shapiro, 1990), but the overwhelming

In both Canada and the United States, Black people suffer from hypertension in disproportionately high numbers.

Charles Thatcher/Stone/Getty Images

majority have no specific verifiable physical cause and are considered **essential hypertension.** In blood pressure readings, the first value is called the *systolic blood pressure*, the pressure when the heart is pumping blood. The second value is the *diastolic blood pressure*, the pressure between beats when the heart is at rest. Generally, elevations in diastolic pressure seem to be more worrisome in terms of risk of disease.

Previously, blood pressure was defined as high by the World Health Organization if it exceeded 160/95 (Papillo & Shapiro, 1990), although measures of 140/90 or higher were considered "borderline" and cause for concern (Wolf-Maier et al., 2003). The new guidelines, released by the U.S. Joint National Committee on Prevention, Detection, Evaluation, and Treatment of High Blood Pressure, are a bit different. The new guidelines change the former blood pressure definitions to (1) normal: less than 120/less than 80; (2) prehypertension: 120–139/80–89; (3) stage 1 hypertension: 140–159/90–99; and (4) stage 2 hypertension: at or greater than 160/at or greater than 100. So 140/90 is no longer considered "borderline"—it is hypertension and should be treated with lifestyle changes to avoid medication (Tyler, 2003). According to the latest comprehensive survey, 26.7% of individuals between age 35 and age 64 suffer from hypertension in North America, with a corresponding and shocking figure of 44.2% in six European countries. These data are presented in Figure 7.7. These are extraordinary numbers when you consider that hypertension, contributing to as many fatal diseases as it does, has been called the "silent killer." The relationship of hypertension to risk of death from stroke in each country is presented in Figure 7.7 and illustrates that hypertension is associated with premature mortality. Even more striking is the fact that in both Canada and the United States, Black people are much more likely to develop hypertension and to have hypertensive vascular diseases than White people (Brannon & Feist, 1997; Yan et al., 2003). This makes hypertension a principal disorder of concern among Black people (International Interdisciplinary Conference on Hypertension in Blacks, 1999). Saab and colleagues (1992) demonstrated that during laboratory stress tests, Blacks without high blood pressure show greater vascular responsiveness, including heightened blood pressure. Thus, Blacks in general may be at greater risk to develop hypertension.

**hypertension** Also known as high blood pressure; a major risk factor for stroke and heart and kidney disease that is intimately related to psychological factors.

**essential hypertension** High blood pressure with no verifiable physical cause, which makes up the overwhelming majority of high blood pressure cases.

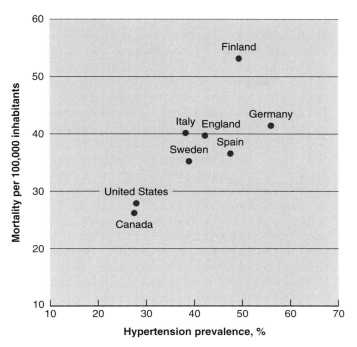

**Figure 7.7** ■ Prevalence of hypertension versus stroke mortality in six European and two North American countries in men and women 35 to 64 years old, age adjusted. (From "Hypertension Prevalence and Blood Pressure Levels in 6 European Countries, Canada, and the United States," by K. Wolf-Maier, et al., *Journal of the American Medical Association*, 289(14):2367 (Figure 4). Copyright © 2003 by the American Medical Association. Reprinted with permission.)

You will not be surprised to learn there are biological, psychological, and social contributions to the development of this potentially deadly condition. As noted by Karina Davidson and her colleagues, it has been clear since the 1930s that an elevated cardiovascular response to stress is associated with hypertension (Gerin et al., 2000; Linden, Gerin, & Davidson, 2003). It has also long been clear that hypertension runs in families and likely is subject to marked genetic influences (Papillo & Shapiro, 1990; Williams, Marchuk, & Gadde, 2001). As established by the work of Blaine Ditto and his colleagues (e.g., Adler, Ditto, France, & France, 1994), when stressed in the laboratory, even individuals with *normal* blood pressure show greater reactivity in their blood pressure if their parents have high blood pressure than individuals with normal blood pressure whose parents also had normal blood pressure (see also Clark, 2003; Fredrikson & Matthews, 1990). Thus, it doesn't take much to activate an inherited vulnerability to hypertension. In fact, the offspring of parents with hypertension are at twice the risk of developing hypertension as children of parents with normal blood pressure (Brannon & Feist, 1997; Kaplan, 1980).

Donald Meichenbaum, Myles Genest and their colleagues report that elevated blood pressure is evident even during the first few weeks of life in babies of hypertensive parents (Turk, Meichenbaum, & Genest, 1983). Studies examining neurobiological causes of hypertension have centred on two factors central to the regulation of blood pressure: autonomic nervous system activity and mechanisms regulating sodium in the kidneys. When the sympathetic branch of the autonomic nervous system becomes active, one consequence is the constriction of blood vessels, which produces greater resistance against circulation; that is, blood pressure is elevated (Guyton, 1981). Because the sympathetic nervous system is very responsive to stress, many investigators have long assumed that stress is a major contributor to essential hypertension. Sodium and water regulation, one of the functions of the kidneys, is also important in regulating blood pressure. Retaining too much salt increases blood volume and heightens blood pressure. This is one reason that people with hypertension are often told to restrict their intake of salt.

Psychological factors, such as personality, coping style, and, again, level of stress, have been used to explain individual differences in blood pressure (Winters & Schneiderman, 2000). For example, in a review of 28 studies, Uchino et al. (1996) found a strong relationship between levels of social support and blood pressure. Loneliness, depression, and uncontrollability are psychological mechanisms that may contribute to the association between hypertension and social support. But a more recently completed long-term study identifies two psychological factors, each of which almost doubles the risk of hypertension: hostility, particularly in interpersonal relations, and a sense of time urgency or impatience. To reach this conclusion, more than 5000 Black and White adults were followed for 15 years (Yan et al., 2003). It is likely that the combination of these two factors is an even more powerful risk factor. Also, both anger and hostility have been associated with increases in blood pressure in the laboratory setting (Jamner, Shapiro, Goldstein, & Hug, 1991; Miller, Smith, Turner, Guijarro, & Hallet, 1996).

The notion that hostility or repressed hostility predicts hypertension (and other cardiovascular problems) can be traced back to Alexander (1939), who suggested that an inability to express anger could result in hypertension and other cardiovascular problems. What may be more important is not whether anger is suppressed but rather how frequently anger and hostility are experienced and expressed to others (Brondolo et al., 2003; Winters & Schneiderman, 2000).

Let's return to the case of John for a moment. John clearly suffered from hypertension. Do you detect any anger in John's case study? John's hypertension may be related to his stressful lifestyle, frustration levels, and hostility. In fact, work conducted at Dalhousie University by Karina Davidson and her colleagues has shown that the ability to control anger by expressing these feelings constructively is associated with markedly lower blood pressure in the population (Davidson, MacGregor, Stuhr, Dixon, & MacLean, 2000), suggesting it might help patients, too. General stress management interventions also appear effective in helping control high blood pressure in hypertensive patients, as identified in a comprehensive review of the literature by University of British Columbia health psychologist Wolfgang Linden and his colleagues (Spence, Barnett, Linden, Ramsden, & Taenzer, 1999).

## Coronary Heart Disease

It may not surprise you that psychological and social factors contribute to high blood pressure, but can changes in behaviour and attitudes prevent heart attacks? The answers are still not entirely clear, but increasing evidence indicates that psychological and social factors are implicated in coronary heart disease (Winters & Schneiderman, 2000). Why is this important? Heart disease is the number one cause of death in Western countries, including Canada (see Table 7.1).

**Coronary heart disease (CHD),** quite simply, is a blockage of the arteries supplying blood to the heart muscle (the *myocardium*). A number of terms describe heart disease. Chest pain resulting from partial obstruction of the arteries is called *angina pectoris* or, usually, just *angina*. *Atherosclerosis* occurs when a fatty substance or plaque builds up inside the arteries and causes an obstruction. *Ischemia* is the name for deficiency of blood to a body part caused by the narrowing of the arteries by too much plaque. And *myocardial infarction*, or *heart attack*, is the death of heart tissue when a specific artery becomes completely clogged with plaque. Arteries can constrict or become blocked for a variety of reasons other than plaque. For example, a blood clot might lodge in the artery.

It seems clear that we inherit a vulnerability to CHD (and to many other physical disorders) and that other factors such as diet, exercise, and culture make important contributions to our cardiovascular status (Thoresen & Powell, 1992). But what sort of psychological factors contribute to CHD?

A variety of studies suggest strongly that stress, anxiety, and anger, combined with poor coping skills and low social support, are implicated in CHD (Johnston, 1997; Winters & Schneiderman, 2000). Some studies indicate that even healthy men who experience stress are later more likely to experience

CHD than low-stress groups (Rosengren, Tibblin, & Wilhelmsen, 1991). For such individuals, stress-reduction procedures may prove to be an important preventive technique. There is a great deal of evidence on the value of stress-reduction procedures in preventing future heart attacks (Williams & Schneiderman, 2002). One report from researchers in the Netherlands summarized results from 37 studies, using analytic procedures that combine the results from these studies. The effects of stress-reduction programs on CHD were apparent. Specifically, these studies in the aggregate yielded a 34% reduction in death from heart attacks, a 29% reduction in the recurrence of heart attacks, and a significant positive effect on blood pressure, cholesterol levels, body weight, and other risk factors for CHD (Dusseldorp, van Elderen, Maes, Meulman, & Kraaij, 1999). This brings us to an important question: Can we identify, before an attack, people who are under a great deal of stress that might make them susceptible to a first heart attack? The answer seems to be "yes," but the answer is more complex than we first thought.

Clinical investigators reported several decades ago that certain groups of people engage in a cluster of behaviours in stressful situations that seem to put them at considerable risk for CHD. These behaviours include excessive competitive drive, a sense of always being pressured for time, impatience, incredible amounts of energy that may show up in accelerated speech and motor activity, and angry outbursts. This set of behaviours, which came to be called the **type A behaviour pattern,** was first identified by two cardiologists (Friedman & Rosenman, 1959, 1974). The **type B behaviour pattern,** also described by these clinicians, applies to people who basically do not have type A attributes. In other words, the type B individual is more relaxed, less concerned about deadlines, and seldom feels the pressure or, perhaps, the excitement of challenges or overriding ambition.

The concept of the type A personality or behaviour pattern is widely accepted in our hard-driving, goal-oriented culture. Indeed, some early studies

---

**coronary heart disease (CHD)** Blockage of the arteries supplying blood to the heart muscle, a major cause of death in Western culture, with social and psychological factors involved.

**type A behaviour pattern** Cluster of behaviours including excessive competitiveness, time-pressured impatience, accelerated speech, and anger; originally thought to promote high risk for heart disease.

**type B behaviour pattern** Cluster of behaviours including a relaxed attitude, indifference to time pressure, and less forceful ambition; originally thought to cause low risk for heart disease.

Both type A behaviour and coronary heart disease seem to be culturally determined.

supported the concept of type A behaviour as putting people at risk for CHD (Friedman & Rosenman, 1974). But the most convincing evidence came from two large prospective studies that followed thousands of patients over a long period to determine the relationship of their behaviour to heart disease. The first study was the Western Collaborative Group Study. In this project, 3154 healthy men, aged 39 to 59, were interviewed at the beginning of the study to determine their typical behavioural patterns. They were then followed for 8 years. The basic finding was that the men who displayed a type A behaviour pattern at the beginning of the study were at least twice as likely to develop CHD as the men with a type B behaviour pattern. When the investigators analyzed the data for the younger men in the study (aged 39 to 49), the results were even more striking, with CHD developing approximately six times more frequently in the type A group than in the type B group (Rosenman et al., 1975).

A second major study is the Framingham Heart Study that has been ongoing for more than 40 years (Haynes, Feinleib, & Kannel, 1980) and has taught us much of what we know about the development and course of CHD. In this study, 1674 healthy men and women were categorized by type A or type B behaviour pattern and followed for 8 years. Again, both men and women with a type A pattern were more than twice as likely to develop CHD as their type B counterparts (in men, the risk was nearly three times as great). But, in the male group, the results were evident only in those individuals in higher-status white-collar occupations, not in individuals with blue-collar socioeconomic status and occupations. For women, the results were strongest for those with a low level of education (Eaker,

Pinsky, & Castelli, 1992). Therefore, it is possible that stress differentially affects men with higher socioeconomic status and women with lower socioeconomic status.

Population-based studies in Europe essentially replicated these results (DeBacker, Kittel, Kornitzer, & Dramaix, 1983; French-Belgian Collaborative Group, 1982). It is interesting that a large study of Japanese men conducted in Hawaii *did not* replicate these findings (Cohen & Reed, 1985). The prevalence of type A behaviour among Japanese men is much lower than among men in North America (18.7% versus approximately 50%). Similarly, the prevalence of CHD is equally low (Japanese men 4%, North American men 13%; Haynes & Matthews, 1988). In a study that illustrates the effects of culture more dramatically, 3809 North Americans of Japanese descent were classified into groups according to how "traditionally Japanese" they were (in other words, did they speak Japanese at home, retain traditional Japanese values and behaviours, and so on). Those who were the "most Japanese" had the lowest incidence of CHD, not significantly different from Japanese men in Japan. In contrast, the group that was the "least Japanese" had a three to five times greater incidence of CHD (Marmot & Syme, 1976; Matsumoto, 1996). Clearly, sociocultural differences are important (Baker, Richter, & Anand, 2001).

Despite these positive results, at least in Western cultures, the type A concept has proved much more complex and elusive than scientists had hoped. First, it is difficult to determine whether someone is type A from structured interviews, questionnaires, or other measures of this construct, because the measures often do not agree with one another. Many people have *some* of the characteristics of type A but not all of them, and others present with a mixture of types A and B. The notion that we can divide the world into two types of people—an assumption underlying the early work in this area—has long since been discarded. As a result, more recent studies have not necessarily supported the relationship of type A behaviour to CHD (Dembroski & Costa, 1987; Hollis, Connett, Stevens, & Greenlick, 1990).

## The Role of Chronic Negative Emotions

At this point, investigators decided that something might be wrong with the type A construct itself (Matthews, 1988; Rodin & Salovey, 1989). A general consensus developed that some behaviours and emotions representative of the type A personality might be important in the development of CHD, but not all of them. The primary factor that seems to be responsible for much of the relationship is anger (Miller et al., 1996). Ironson and colleagues (1992) found that anger impaired the pumping efficiency of the heart in individuals with heart disease, putting them at risk for dangerous disturbances in heart rhythm (arrhythmias). This study confirms earlier findings relating the frequent experience of anger to later CHD (Houston, Chesney, Black, Cates, & Hecker, 1992; T. W. Smith, 1992). Results from an important study strengthen this conclusion. Iribarren et al. (2000) evaluated 374 young, healthy adults, both White and Black, over 10 years. Those with high hostility and anger showed evidence of coronary artery calcification, an early sign of CHD.

Is type A irrelevant to the development of heart disease? Most investigators conclude that some components of the type A construct are important determinants of CHD, with a chronically high level of negative affect, such as anger, one of the prime candidates, and the time urgency/impatience factor another (Williams, Barefoot, & Schneiderman, 2003; Winters & Schneiderman, 2000). Recall again the case of John, who had all the type A behaviours, including time urgency, but also had frequent angry outbursts. John was clearly high in a personality trait referred to as hostility. A study conducted at Dalhousie University by Karina Davidson and her colleagues suggests that an intervention focusing on reducing hostility may be very useful for men with CHD (Gidron, Davidson, & Bata, 1999). A group of men with CHD who were high in hostility were randomly assigned to a hostility intervention or to an information-control group. Immediately following the intervention and 2 months later, the men who had received the active intervention reported less hostility and were observed to be less hostile. Moreover, the men who had received the active intervention showed lower diastolic blood pressure at follow-up. These results are very promising and support the important role of anger and hostility in CHD. Whether a hostility-reduction intervention can prevent future heart attacks in CHD men remains to be determined (Gidron et al., 1999).

But what about people who experience closely related varieties of negative affect on a chronic basis? Look back to Figure 7.2 and notice the close relationship among stress, anxiety, and depression. Some evidence indicates that the physiological components of these emotions and their effects on the cardiovascular system may be similar. We also know that the emotion of anger, so commonly associated with stress, is closely related to the emotion of fear, as evidenced in the fight/flight syndrome.

Fight is the typical behavioural action tendency associated with anger, and flight or escape is associated with fear. But our bodily alarm response, activated by an immediate danger or threat, is associated with both emotions.

Some investigators, after reviewing the literature, have concluded that anxiety and depression are as important as anger in the development of CHD (e.g., Brannon & Feist, 1997; Williams et al., 2003), while others have cautioned that the role of negative emotions other than anger as risk factors for CHD remains somewhat controversial (e.g., Baker et al., 2001). In a study of 896 people who had endured heart attacks, Frasure-Smith, Lesperance, Juneau, Talajic, and Bourassa (1999) found that patients who were depressed were three times more likely to die in the year following their heart attacks than those who were not depressed, regardless of how severe their initial heart disease was. Thus, it may be that the chronic experience of the negative emotions of stress (anger), anxiety (fear), and depression (ongoing) and the neurobiological activation that accompanies these emotions provide the most important psychological contributions to CHD and perhaps to other physical disorders. On the other hand, in the Ironson et al. (1992) study, participants who were asked to imagine being in situations producing performance anxiety (having to give a speech or take a difficult test) *did not* experience the same effect on their hearts as those who imagined anger—at least, not in those individuals with existing CHD. As has been cautiously noted by Brian Baker of the University of Toronto, we still have much to learn about these relationships (Baker et al., 2001).

## Chronic Pain

Pain is not in itself a disorder, yet for most of us it is the fundamental signal of injury, illness, or disease. The importance of pain in our lives cannot be underestimated. Without low levels of pain providing feedback on the functioning of the body and its various systems, we would incur substantially more injuries. For example, you might lie out in the hot sun a lot longer. You might not roll over while sleeping or shift your posture while sitting, thereby affecting your circulation in a way that might be harmful. Reactions to this kind of pain are mostly automatic; that is, we are not aware of the discomfort. When pain crosses the threshold of awareness, which varies a great deal from one person to another, we are forced to take action. If we can't relieve the pain ourselves or we are not sure of its cause, we usually seek medical help. The cost of chronic pain in Canada, including medical expenses, lost productivity, and lost income (but not including the social costs) is estimated to exceed $10 billion annually (Chronic Pain Association of Canada [CPAC], 2003). In fact, 80% of all visits to physicians are due to pain (Turk & Gatchel, 2002).

There are two kinds of clinical pain: acute and chronic. **Acute pain** typically follows an injury and disappears once the injury heals or is effectively treated, often within a month (Philips & Grant, 1991). **Chronic pain,** by contrast, may begin with an acute episode but *does not decrease* over time, even when the injury has healed or effective treatments have been administered. Typically, chronic pain is in the muscles, joints, or tendons, particularly in the lower back. Vascular pain caused by enlarged blood vessels may be chronic, as may headaches; pain caused by the slow degeneration of tissue, as in some terminal diseases; and pain caused by the growth of cancerous tumours that impinge on pain receptors (Melzack & Wall, 1982; S. Taylor, 1999). Surveys indicate that more than 18% of Canadians endure severe chronic pain (CPAC, 2003). Thus, in Canada alone, millions of people experience chronic pain, yet most researchers now agree that the causes of chronic pain and the resulting enormous drain on our health-care system *are substantially psychological and social* (Dersh, Polatin, & Gatchel, 2002; Turk & Monarch, 2002). Consider the case of Preepi, described by Christine Korol and Kenneth Craig (2001) of the University of British Columbia.

## Preepi
### Resigned to Pain

Preepi was injured when she slipped on a wet floor while she was carrying a stack of dishes in the restaurant where she worked 2 years ago. She has been unable to work since her injury and complains of severe low back pain and numbness down her right leg. She was 52 at the time she was first assessed in a multidisciplinary pain program and presented as having a severe disability (e.g., she was only able to stand or sit for 5 minutes at a time, had severely decreased range of motion and little strength, and relied primarily on her family to help her with her activities of daily living). She reported through a Punjabi interpreter to the psychologist on the team that her mother-in-law and her two teenage children took care of household chores for her and that her husband was very helpful because he would rub her back and bring her pain medication.

Despite support from her family, Preepi felt guilty about not being able to care for her family, reported that it was God's will that she suffer, and was resigned to the fact that, after 2 years, she would probably always suffer. On careful assessment, Preepi was diagnosed as depressed with occasional suicidal ideation. She was admitted to the chronic pain management program in the clinic, and the treatment team noted that they would have to pay special attention to the many factors contributing to her continued disability (e.g., family solicitousness, resignation and helplessness, depressed mood, and sedentary lifestyle). (From Korol & Craig, 2001, pp. 260–261.)

To better understand the experience of pain, clinicians and researchers generally make a clear distinction between the subjective experience termed *pain*, reported by the patient, and the overt manifestations of this experience, termed *pain behaviours*. Pain behaviours include changing the way the person sits or walks, continually complaining about pain to others, grimacing, and, most important, avoiding various activities, particularly those involving work or leisure. Finally, an emotional component of pain called *suffering* sometimes accompanies pain and sometimes does not (Fordyce, 1988; Liebeskind, 1991). Because they are so important, we first review psychological and social contributions to pain.

### Psychological and Social Aspects

In mild forms, chronic pain can be an annoyance that eventually wears you down and takes the pleasure out of your life. Severe chronic pain may cause you to lose your job, withdraw from your family, give up the fun in your life, and focus your entire awareness on seeking relief. What is interesting for our purposes is that the *severity* of the pain does not seem to predict the *reaction* to it. Some individuals experience intense pain frequently and yet continue to work productively, rarely seek out medical services, and lead reasonably normal lives; others become invalids. These differences appear to be primarily because of psychological factors (Dersh

**acute pain**   Pain that typically follows an injury and disappears once the injury heals or is effectively treated.

**chronic pain**   Enduring pain that does not decrease over time; may occur in muscles, joints, and the lower back; and may be due to enlarged blood vessels or degenerating or cancerous tissue. Other significant factors are social and psychological.

et al., 2002; Turk & Monarch, 2002). It will come as no surprise that these factors are the same as those implicated in the stress response and other negative emotional states, such as anxiety and depression (Ohayon & Schatzberg, 2003; see Chapters 4 and 6).

The determining factor seems to be the individual's general sense of control over the situation: whether or not he or she can deal with the pain and its consequences in an effective and meaningful way. Recall Preepi's feelings of hopelessness and resignation toward her pain; these psychological factors likely contributed to her distress and pain-related disability as much as the original work-related injury itself. As observed by researchers Bandura, O'Leary, Taylor, Gauthier, and Gossard (1987), when a positive sense of control is combined with a generally optimistic outlook about the future, there is substantially less distress and disability (see also Gatchel & Turk, 1999; Keefe & France, 1999). Positive psychological factors are also associated with active attempts to cope, such as exercise and other regimens, as opposed to suffering passively as Preepi did (Strahl, Kleinknecht, & Dinnel, 2000; Turk & Gatchel, 2002).

To take one example, H. Clare Philips at the University of British Columbia studied 117 patients who suffered from back and neck pain after an injury (Philips & Grant, 1991). Almost all were expected to recover quickly, but fully 40% of them still reported substantial pain after 6 months, thereby qualifying for "chronic pain" status. Of the 60% who reported no pain at the 6-month point, most had been pain free since approximately 1 month after the accident. Furthermore, Philips and Grant report that the relationship between the experience of pain and the subsequent disability was not as strongly related to the intensity of the pain as other factors, such as personality and socioeconomic differences and whether the person planned to initiate a lawsuit concerning the injury. Generally, a profile of negative emotion such as anxiety and depression, poor coping skills, low social support, and the possibility of being compensated for pain through disability claims predict most types of chronic pain (Dersh et al., 2002; Gatchel & Dersh, 2002).

Canadian research groups have been at the forefront of research on the involvement of anxiety-related factors in explaining chronic pain. For example, the research of Gordon Asmundson and colleagues suggests that the fear of pain could predispose a person to the development of chronic pain following a physical injury. The idea is that people who fear pain will tend to avoid activity following an injury because of concerns that they may reinjure themselves or experience uncontrollable pain. This avoidance of activity reduces their anxiety in the short term but can contribute to maintaining pain in the long term, because their bodies become deconditioned due to lack of exercise (Asmundson, Jacobson, Allerdings, & Norton, 1996; Stewart & Asmundson, 2006). Recall Preepi's sedentary lifestyle following her injury. In the short term, her avoidance of the movement involved in household chores might have helped her avoid unpleasant back pain sensations. But in the longer term, Preepi's inactivity probably led to deconditioning, which may have maintained or even exacerbated her pain.

Another important psychological factor is *pain catastrophizing*. Canada Research Chair Michael Sullivan at McGill University defines pain catastrophizing as "an exaggerated negative response brought to bear during actual or anticipated painful experience" (Sullivan et al., 2001). A catastrophizer might think or feel the following things when experiencing pain: "I can't stop thinking of how much it hurts" (rumination), "I worry that something serious might happen" (magnification), and "There is nothing I can do to reduce the intensity of the pain" (helplessness; see Sullivan, Bishop, & Pivik, 1995). For example, Preepi appeared to believe she was helpless in controlling the pain, which led to her feeling resigned to

Some people with chronic pain or disability cope extremely well and become high achievers.

Larry Dale Gordon/Image Bank/Getty Images

suffer. Pain catastrophizing may be a risk factor for chronic pain and disability (Sullivan et al., 2001). Indeed, some preliminary results from recent intervention research suggest that an early treatment emphasis on reducing pain catastrophizing following injury may prevent acute pain from becoming chronic (Sullivan & Stanish, 2003).

That the experience of pain can be largely disconnected from disease or injury is perhaps best exemplified by *phantom limb pain*—a phenomenon that has been described and investigated extensively by Canada Research Chair recipient Joel Katz at York University (e.g., Katz & Gagliese, 1999). In this condition, people who have lost an arm or leg feel excruciating pain in the limb that is no longer there. Furthermore, they can describe in exquisite detail the exact location of the pain and its type, such as a dull ache or a sharp, cutting pain. That they are fully aware the limb is amputated does nothing to relieve the pain. Evidence suggests that changes in the sensory cortex of the brain may contribute to this phenomenon (Flor et al., 1995; Katz & Gagliese, 1999). Generally, someone who thinks pain is disastrous, uncontrollable, or reflective of personal failure experiences more intense pain and greater psychological distress than someone who does not feel this way (Gil, Williams, Keefe, & Beckham, 1990; Turk & Gatchel, 2002). Thus, treatment programs for chronic pain concentrate on psychological factors.

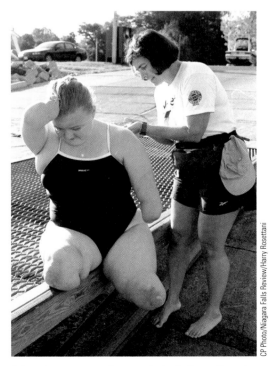

It is not uncommon for people to feel specific pain in limbs that are no longer part of them.

Other examples of psychological influences on the experience of pain are encountered every day. Athletes with significant tissue damage frequently continue to perform and report relatively little pain. In an important study, 65% of war veterans wounded in combat reported feeling no pain when they were injured. Presumably, their attention was focused externally on what they had to do to survive rather than internally on the experience of pain (Melzack & Wall, 1982).

Social factors also influence how we experience pain. Fordyce (1976, 1988; see also Kearns, Otis, & Wise, 2002) has studied social forms of pain behaviour such as verbal complaints, facial expressions, and obvious limps or other symptoms that may reflect strong social contingencies. For example, family members who were formerly critical and demanding may become caring and sympathetic (Kearns et al., 2002; Romano, Jensen, Turner, Good, & Hops, 2000). Recall the behaviour of Preepi's family members. Although they likely meant well, their sympathy and helpfulness may actually have helped maintain Preepi's chronic pain. This phenomenon is referred to as *operant* control of pain behaviour because the behaviour clearly seems under the control of social consequences. But these consequences have an uncertain relation to the amount of pain being experienced.

By contrast, a strong network of social support may reduce pain. Jamison and Virts (1990) studied 521 chronic pain patients (with back, abdominal, and chest conditions) and discovered that those who lacked social support from their families reported more pain sites and showed more pain behaviour, such as staying in bed. These patients also exhibited more emotional distress *without* rating their pain as any more intense than patients with strong socially supportive families. The patients with strong support returned to work earlier, showed less reliance on medications, and increased their activity levels more quickly than the others.

Although these results may seem to contradict studies on the operant control of pain, different mechanisms may be at work. General social support may reduce the stress associated with pain and injury and promote more adaptive coping procedures and control. However, specifically reinforcing pain behaviours, particularly in the absence of social supports, may powerfully increase such behaviour. These complex issues have not yet been entirely sorted out.

## Biological Aspects

No one thinks pain is entirely psychological, just as no one thinks it is entirely physical. As with other disorders, we must consider how they interact.

**Gate Control Theory** The *gate control theory* developed by international pain expert Ronald Melzack at McGill University (Melzack & Wall, 1965, 1982) accommodates both psychological and physical factors. According to this theory, nerve impulses from painful stimuli make their way to the spinal column and from there to the brain. An area called the *dorsal horns of the spinal column* acts as a "gate" and may open and transmit sensations of pain if the stimulation is sufficiently intense. Specific nerve fibres referred to as *small fibres* (A-delta and C fibres) and *large fibers* (A-beta fibres) determine the pattern and the intensity of the stimulation. Small fibres tend to open the gate, thereby increasing the transmission of painful stimuli, whereas large fibres tend to close the gate.

Most important for our purpose is that the brain sends signals back down the spinal cord that may affect the gating mechanism. For example, a person with negative emotions such as fear or anxiety may experience pain more intensely because the basic message from the brain is to be vigilant against possible danger or threat. Then again, in a person whose emotions are more positive or who is totally absorbed in an activity (such as a runner intent on finishing a long race), the brain sends down an inhibitory signal that closes the gate. Although many think that the gate control theory is overly simplistic—and it has recently been updated (Melzack, 1999)—research findings continue to support its basic elements, particularly as it describes the complex interaction of psychological and biological factors in the experience of pain (Gatchel & Turk, 1999; Turk & Monarch, 2002).

**Endogenous Opioids** The neurochemical means by which the brain inhibits pain is an important discovery. Drugs such as heroin and morphine are manufactured from opioid substances. It now turns out that **endogenous** (natural) **opioids** exist within the body. Called *endorphins* or *enkephalins*, they act much like neurotransmitters. The brain uses them to shut down pain, even in the presence of marked tissue damage or injury. Because endogenous opioids are distributed widely throughout the body, they may be implicated in a variety of psychopathological conditions, including eating disorders and, more commonly, the "runners' high" that accompanies the release of endogenous opioids after intense (and sometimes painful) physical activity. Albert Bandura, Janel Gauthier, and their colleagues (1987) found that people with a greater sense of self-efficacy and control had a higher tolerance for pain than individuals with low self-efficacy and that they increased their production of endogenous opioids when they were confronted with a painful stimulus.

### Gender Differences in Pain

Most animal and human studies have been conducted on males to avoid the complications of hormonal variation. But men and women seem to experience different types of pain. On the one hand, in addition to menstrual cramps and labour pains, women suffer more frequently than men from migraine headaches, arthritis, carpal tunnel syndrome, and temporomandibular joint pain (Lipchik, Holroyd, & Nash, 2002; Miaskowski, 1999). Men, on the other hand, have more cardiac pain and backache. Men and women also seem to have somewhat different pain-regulating mechanisms. Although both males and females have endogenous opioid systems, this system may be more powerful in men. In contrast, the female neurochemistry may be based on an estrogen-dependent neuronal system that may have evolved to cope with the pain associated with reproductive activity (Mogil, Sternberg, Kest, Marek, & Liebeskind, 1993). It is an "extra" pain-regulating pathway in females that, if taken away by removing hormones, has no implications for the remaining pathways, which continue to work. One implication of this finding is that males and females may benefit from different kinds of drugs, different kinds of psychological interventions, or unique combinations of these treatments to best manage and control pain.

## *Chronic Fatigue Syndrome*

In the mid-19th century, a rapidly growing number of patients suffered from lack of energy, marked fatigue, a variety of aches and pains, and, on occasion, low-grade fever. No physical pathology could be discovered, and Beard (1869) labelled the condition *neurasthenia*, literally, lack of nerve strength (Abbey & Garfinkel, 1991; Costa e Silva & DeGirolamo, 1990). The disease was attributed to the demands of the time, including a preoccupation with material success, a strong emphasis on hard work, and the changing role of women. Neurasthenia disappeared in the early 20th century in Western cultures but remains one of the most common psychological diagnoses in China (Good & Kleinman, 1985; Kleinman, 1986). Now **chronic fatigue syndrome (CFS)** is spreading rapidly throughout the Western

**endogenous opioids** Substances occurring naturally throughout the body that function like neurotransmitters to shut down pain sensation even in the presence of marked tissue damage. These may contribute to psychological problems such as eating disorders. Also known as endorphins or enkephalins.

**chronic fatigue syndrome (CFS)** Incapacitating exhaustion following only minimal exertion, accompanied by fever, headaches, muscle and joint pain, depression, and anxiety.

world (Jason, Fennell, & Taylor, 2003). The symptoms of CFS, listed in Table 7.2, are almost identical to those of neurasthenia and, until recently, were attributed to viral infection, specifically the Epstein-Barr virus (Straus et al., 1985); immune system dysfunction (Straus, 1988); exposure to toxins; or clinical depression (Chalder, Cleare, & Wessely, 2000; Costa e Silva & DiGirolamo, 1990). No evidence has yet to support any of these hypothetical physical causes (Chalder et al., 2000; Jason et al., 2003).

People with CFS suffer considerably and often must give up their careers. In a group of 100 patients followed for 18 months, chronic fatigue symptoms did not decrease significantly in fully 79% of cases. Better mental health to begin with, as well as less use of sedating medications and a more "psychological" as opposed to medical attribution for causes, led to better outcomes (Schmaling, Fiedelak, Katon, Bader, & Buchwald, 2003). As pointed out by leading CFS researcher Susan Abbey at the Centre for Addiction and Mental Health in Toronto, both neurasthenia in the 19th century and CFS in the present century have been attributed to an extremely stressful environment, the changing role of women, and the rapid dissemination of new technology and information (Abbey & Garfinkel, 1991). Both disorders are most common in women. It is possible that a virus or a specific immune system dysfunction will be found to account for CFS. Another possibility suggested by Abbey and Garfinkel (1991) is that the condition represents a rather non-specific response to stress. But it is not clear why certain individuals respond with chronic fatigue instead of some other psychological or physical disorder.

| **TABLE 7.2** Definition of Chronic Fatigue Syndrome |
| --- |
| **Inclusion Criteria** |
| 1. Clinically evaluated, medically unexplained fatigue of at least 6 months duration that is: <ul><li>of new onset (not lifelong)</li><li>not resulting from ongoing exertion</li><li>not substantially alleviated by rest</li><li>a substantial reduction in previous level of activities</li></ul> |
| 2. The occurrence of four or more of the following symptoms: <ul><li>Subjective memory impairment</li><li>Sore throat</li><li>Tender lymph nodes</li><li>Muscle pain</li><li>Joint pain</li><li>Headache</li><li>Unrefreshing sleep</li><li>Postexertional malaise lasting more than 24 hours</li></ul> |

*Source:* Adapted from Fukuda et al., 1994.

Sharpe (1997) has developed one of the first models of the causes of CFS that accounts for all of its features (see Figure 7.8). Sharpe theorizes that individuals with particularly achievement-oriented lifestyles (driven, perhaps, by a basic sense of inadequacy) undergo a period of extreme stress or acute illness. They misinterpret the lingering

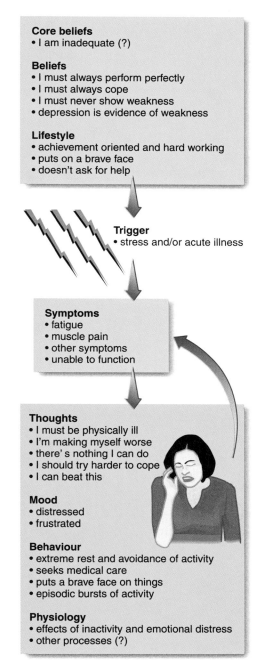

**Figure 7.8** ■ A complex specific model of chronic fatigue syndrome. (From "Chronic Fatigue Syndrome," by M. Sharpe, in *Science and Practice of Cognitive Behaviour Therapy*, edited by D. M. Clark and C. G. Fairburn, pp. 381–414. Copyright © 1997 by Oxford University Press. Adapted with permission.)

symptoms of fatigue, pain, and inability to function at their usual high levels as a continuing disease that is worsened by activity and improved by rest. This results in behavioural avoidance, helplessness, depression, and frustration. They think they should be able to conquer the problem and cope with its symptoms. Chronic inactivity, of course, leads to lack of stamina, weakness, and increased feelings of depression and helplessness that in turn result in episodic bursts of long activity followed by further fatigue.

Pharmacological treatment has not proven effective for CFS (Afari & Buchwald, 2003; Chalder et al., 2000), but Sharpe in Oxford has developed a cognitive-behavioural program that includes procedures to increase activity, regulate periods of rest, and direct cognitive therapy at the cognitions specified in Figure 7.8. This treatment also includes relaxation, breathing exercises, and general stress-reduction procedures, interventions we describe in the next section (Sharpe, 1992, 1993, 1997). Time will tell if Sharpe's approach to CFS is correct in whole or in part, but it is the first comprehensive model and it does have treatment implications. In an early controlled trial evaluating this approach, 60 patients were assigned to the cognitive-behavioural treatment or to treatment as usual. Seventy-three percent of the patients in the cognitive-behavioural treatment group improved on measures of fatigue, disability, and illness belief, a result far superior to the control group (Sharpe et al., 1996). In a second, more sophisticated large-scale evaluation of a similar cognitive-behavioural approach to CFS (Deale, Chalder, Marks, & Wessely, 1997), 60 patients with CFS were randomly assigned to cognitive-behavioural therapy or relaxation exercises alone. The results indicated that fatigue diminished and overall functioning improved significantly more in the group that received cognitive-behavioural therapy. Seventy percent of individuals who completed cognitive-behavioural therapy achieved substantial improvement in physical functioning at a 6-month

follow-up compared with only 19% of those in the relaxation-only group. A 5-year follow-up indicates the gains were largely maintained (Deale, Husain, Chalder, & Wessely, 2001). These results are encouraging and have been widely noted as one of the best treatment options to date (Bleijenberg, Prins, & Bazelmans, 2003; Whiting et al., 2001).

## Concept Check 7.2

Answer the following questions about the psychosocial effects on physical disorders.

1. Which of the following is not considered a part of the experience of pain?
   a. The subjective impression of pain as reported by the patient
   b. Pain behaviours or overt manifestations of pain
   c. Cuts, bruises, and other injuries
   d. An emotional component called suffering
2. Some evidence shows that psychological factors may contribute to both the course and the _____ of cancer, AIDS, and other diseases, as well as to treatment and recovery.
3. Psychosocial and biological factors contribute to the development of this potentially deadly condition of high blood pressure, _____, and to the development of _____, the blockage of arteries supplying blood to heart muscle.
4. Psychologists identified two types of behaviour patterns one of which they alleged contributes to the development of coronary heart disease. What types were developed?
5. No evidence exists to show that there is a physical cause for the disease of _____ that often causes individuals to give up their careers and suffer considerably.

# Psychological Treatment of Physical Disorders

- *Describe the use of biofeedback and progressive muscle relaxation as treatments for stress-related disorders.*

- *Identify some procedures and strategies used in stress management and in prevention and intervention programs.*

Certain experiments suggest that pain is not only bad for you but also may kill you. It has been shown that postsurgical pain in rats doubles the rate at

which a certain cancer metastasizes (spreads) to the lungs (Page, Ben-Eliyahu, Yirmiya, & Liebeskind, 1993). Rats undergoing abdominal surgery *without* morphine developed twice the number of lung metastases as rats who were given morphine for the same surgery. The rats undergoing surgery with the pain-killing drug had even lower rates of metastases than rats that did not have surgery.

This effect may result from the interaction of pain with the immune system. Pain may reduce the number of killer T cells in the immune system, perhaps because of the general stress reaction to the pain. Thus, if a rat is in *extreme* pain, the associated stress may further enhance the pain, completing a vicious circle. If this result is found to apply to humans, it is important because the general consensus is that we are reluctant to use pain-killing medication in chronic diseases such as cancer. Some estimates suggest that fewer than half of all cancer patients receive sufficient pain relief. Direct evidence is available on the benefits of early pain relief in patients undergoing surgery. Findings from Joel Katz, Anthony Vaccarino, Ronald Melzack and their colleagues, along with Chris France and his colleagues, have shown that patients receiving pain medication before surgery reported less pain after surgery and requested less pain medication (Coderre, Katz, Vaccarino, & Melzack, 1993; Keefe & France, 1999). Adequate pain-management procedures, either medical or psychological, are an essential part of the management of chronic disease.

A variety of psychological treatments have been developed for physical disorders and pain, including biofeedback, relaxation procedures, and hypnosis (Turk & Gatchel, 2002). But because of the overriding role of stress in the etiology and maintenance of many physical disorders, comprehensive stress-management programs are increasingly incorporated into medical centres where such disorders are treated. We briefly review specific psychological approaches to physical disorders and describe a typical comprehensive stress-management program.

## Biofeedback

**Biofeedback** is a process of making patients aware of specific physiological functions that, ordinarily, they would not notice consciously, such as heart rate, blood pressure, muscle tension in specific areas of the body, EEG rhythms (brain waves), and patterns of blood flow (Andrasik, 2000; Schwartz & Andrasik, 2003). Conscious awareness is the first step, but the second step is more remarkable. In the 1960s, Neal Miller reported that rats could *learn to directly control* many of these responses. He used a

© Cindy Charles/PhotoEdit

In biofeedback, the patient learns to control physiological responses that are visible on a screen.

variation of operant conditioning procedures in which the animals were reinforced for increases or decreases in their physiological responses (Miller, 1969). Although it was subsequently difficult to replicate these findings with animals, clinicians applied the procedures with some success to humans who suffered from various physical disorders or stress-related conditions, such as hypertension and headache.

Clinicians use physiological monitoring equipment to make the response, such as heart rate, visible or audible to the patient. The patient then works with the therapist to learn to control the response. A successful response produces some type of signal. For example, if the patient is successful in lowering his or her blood pressure by a certain amount, the pressure reading will be visible on a gauge and a tone will sound. It wasn't long before researchers discovered that humans could discriminate changes in autonomic nervous system activity with a high degree of accuracy (Blanchard & Epstein, 1977).

One goal of biofeedback has been to reduce tension in the muscles of the head and scalp, thereby relieving headaches. Pioneers in this field found that biofeedback was successful in this area (Holroyd, Andrasik, & Noble, 1980), although no more successful than deep muscle relaxation procedures (Andrasik, 2000; Holroyd & Penzien,

---

**biofeedback** Use of physiological monitoring equipment to make individuals aware of their own bodily functions, such as blood pressure or brain waves, that they cannot normally access, with the purpose of controlling these functions.

1986). Because of these results, some have thought that biofeedback might achieve its effects with tension headaches by simply teaching people to relax. However, Holroyd and colleagues (1984) concluded instead that the success of biofeedback, at least for headaches, may depend not on reducing tension but on the extent to which the procedures instill a sense of *control* over the pain. (How do you think this relates to the study of stress in baboons described in the beginning of the chapter?) Whatever the mechanism, biofeedback and relaxation are more effective treatments than, for example, placebo medication interventions, and the results of these two treatments are not altogether interchangeable, in that some people benefit more from biofeedback and others benefit from relaxation procedures. For this reason, applying both treatments is a safe strategy (Andrasik, 2000; Schwartz & Andrasik, 2003). Several reviews have found that 38% to 63% of patients undergoing relaxation or biofeedback achieve significant reductions in headaches compared with approximately 35% who receive placebo medication (Blanchard, 1992; Holroyd & Penzien, 1986). Furthermore, the effects of biofeedback and relaxation seem to be long lasting (Andrasik, 2000; Lisspers & Öst, 1990).

## Relaxation and Meditation

Various types of relaxation and meditation procedures have been used, either alone or with other procedures, to treat physical disorder and pain patients. In *progressive muscle relaxation*, devised by Edmund Jacobson in 1938, people become acutely aware of any tension in their bodies and counteract it by relaxing specific muscle groups. In Jacobson's original conception, learning the art of relaxation was a structured procedure that took months or even years to master. In most clinics today, however, the procedure is usually taught in weeks, and it is seldom used as the sole treatment (Bernstein & Borkovec, 1973; Bernstein, Borkovec, & Hazlett-Stevens, 2000). A number of procedures focus attention either on a specific part of the body or on a single thought or image. This attentional focus is often accompanied by regular slowed breathing. In *transcendental meditation*, attention is focused solely on a repeated syllable, or the *mantra*.

Herbert Benson stripped transcendental meditation of what he considered its nonessentials and developed a brief procedure he calls the **relaxation response,** in which a person silently repeats a mantra to minimize distraction by closing the mind to intruding thoughts. Although Benson suggested focusing on the word *one*, any neutral word or phrase would do. Individuals who meditate for 10 or 20 minutes a day report feeling calmer or more relaxed throughout the day. These brief, simple procedures can be powerful in reducing the flow of certain neurotransmitters and stress hormones, an effect that may be mediated by an increased sense of control and mastery (Benson, 1975, 1984). Benson's ideas are popular and are now taught in many medical schools and offered by many major hospitals (Roush, 1997). Relaxation has generally positive effects on headaches, hypertension, and acute and chronic pain, although the results are sometimes relatively modest (S. E. Taylor, 1999). Nonetheless, relaxation and meditation are almost always part of a comprehensive pain-management program.

## A Comprehensive Stress- and Pain-Reduction Program

In our own stress-management program (Barlow, Rapee, & Reisner, 2001), individuals practise a variety of stress-management procedures presented to them in a workbook. First, they learn to monitor their stress closely and to identify the stressful events in their daily lives. (Samples of a stressful events record and a daily stress record are in Figure 7.9.) Note that clients are taught to be specific about recording the times they experience stress, the intensity of the stress, and what seems to trigger the stress. They also note the somatic symptoms and thoughts that occur when they are stressed. All this monitoring becomes important in carrying through with the program, but it can be helpful in itself because it reveals precise patterns and causes of stress and helps clients learn what changes to make to cope better.

After learning to monitor stress, clients are taught deep muscle relaxation, which involves, first, tensing various muscles to identify the location of different muscle groups. (Instructions for tensing specific muscle groups are included in Table 7.3.) Clients are then systematically taught to relax the muscle groups beyond the point of inactivity, that is, to actively let go of the muscle so that no tension remains in it.

Appraisals and attitudes are an important part of stress, and clients learn how they exaggerate the negative impact of events in their day-to-day lives. In the program, the therapist and client use cognitive therapy to develop more realistic appraisals and attitudes, as exemplified in the case of Sally.

**relaxation response** Active components of meditation methods, including repetitive thoughts of a sound to reduce distracting thoughts and closing the mind to other intruding thoughts, that decrease the flow of stress hormones and neurotransmitters and cause a feeling of calm.

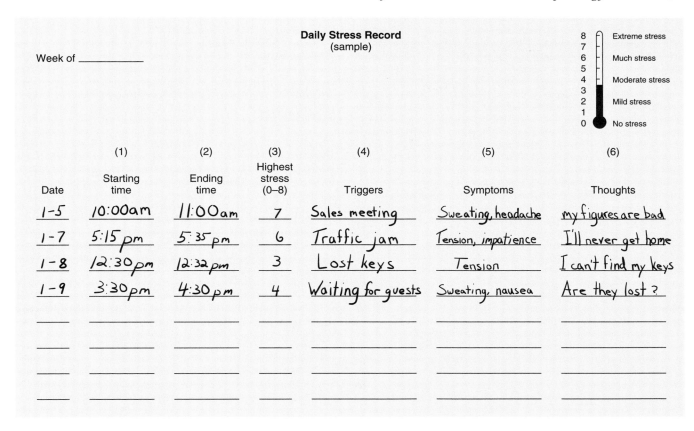

**Daily Stress Record**
(sample)

| | 8 | Extreme stress |
| | 7 | |
| | 6 | Much stress |
| | 5 | |
| | 4 | Moderate stress |
| | 3 | |
| | 2 | Mild stress |
| | 1 | |
| | 0 | No stress |

Week of _____

| | (1) | (2) | (3) | (4) | (5) | (6) |
|---|---|---|---|---|---|---|
| Date | Starting time | Ending time | Highest stress (0–8) | Triggers | Symptoms | Thoughts |
| 1-5 | 10:00am | 11:00am | 7 | Sales meeting | Sweating, headache | my figures are bad |
| 1-7 | 5:15pm | 5:35pm | 6 | Traffic jam | Tension, impatience | I'll never get home |
| 1-8 | 12:30pm | 12:32pm | 3 | Lost keys | Tension | I can't find my keys |
| 1-9 | 3:30pm | 4:30pm | 4 | Waiting for guests | Sweating, nausea | Are they lost? |

**Figure 7.9** ■ Methods for monitoring stress. (From *Mastering Stress 2001: A Lifestyle Approach*, by D. H. Barlow, R. M. Rapee, and L. C. Reisner, 2001, p. 28. Copyright © 2001 by American Health Publishing Co. Adapted with permission.)

# Sally
## Improving Her Perception

(Sally is a 40-year-old real estate agent.)

**SALLY:** My mother is always calling just when I'm in the middle of doing something important and it makes me so angry, I find that I get short with her.

**THERAPIST:** Let's try and look at what you just said in another way. When you say that she *always* phones in the middle of something, it implies 100% of the time. Is that true? How likely is it really that she will call when you are doing something important?

**SALLY:** Well, I suppose that when I think back over the last 10 times she's called, most of the times I was just watching TV or reading. There was once when I was making dinner and it burned because she interrupted me. Another time, I was busy with some work I had brought home from the office, and she called. I guess that makes it 20% of the time.

**THERAPIST:** OK, great; now let's go a bit further. So what if she calls at an inconvenient time?

**SALLY:** Well, I know that one of my first thoughts is that she doesn't think anything I do is important. But before you say anything, I know that is a major overestimation since she obviously doesn't know what I'm doing when she calls. However, I suppose I also think that it's a major interruption and inconvenience to have to stop at that point.

**THERAPIST:** Go on. What is the chance that it is a major inconvenience?

**SALLY:** When I was doing my work, I forgot what I was up to and it took me 10 minutes to work it out again. I guess that's not so bad; it's only 10 minutes. And when the dinner burned, it was really not too bad, just a little burned. Part of that was my fault anyway, because I could have turned the stove down before I went to the phone.

**THERAPIST:** So, it sounds like quite a small chance that it would be a major inconvenience, even if your mother does interrupt you.

**SALLY:** True. And I know what you are going to say next. Even if it is a major inconvenience, it's not the end of the world. I have handled plenty of bigger problems than this at work.

**TABLE 7.3** Suggestions for Tensing Muscles

| Large Muscle Groups | Instructions for Tensing Muscles |
|---|---|
| Lower arm | Make fist, palm down, and pull wrist toward upper arm. |
| Upper arm | Tense biceps; with arms by side, pull upper arm toward side without touching. (Try not to tense lower arm while doing this; let lower arm hang loosely.) |
| Lower leg and foot | Point toes upward to knees. |
| Thighs | Push feet hard against floor. |
| Abdomen | Pull in stomach toward back. |
| Chest and breathing | Take a deep breath and hold it about 10 seconds, then release. |
| Shoulders and lower neck | Shrug shoulders, bringing shoulders up until they almost touch ears. |
| Back of neck | Put head back and press against back of chair. |
| Lips | Press lips together; don't clench teeth or jaw. |
| Eyes | Close eyes tightly but don't close too hard (be careful if you have contacts). |
| Lower forehead | Pull eyebrows down and in (try to get them to meet). |
| Upper forehead | Raise eyebrows and wrinkle your forehead. |

*Source:* From *Mastering Stress 2001: A Lifestyle Approach,* by D. H. Barlow, R. M. Rapee, and L. C. Reisner, 2001 pp. 113–114. Copyright © 2001 by the American Health Publishing Co. Adapted with permission.

In this program, individuals work hard to identify unrealistic negative thoughts and to develop new appraisals and attitudes almost instantaneously when negative thoughts occur. Such assessment is often the most difficult part of the program. After the session just related, Sally began using what she had learned in cognitive therapy to reappraise stressful situations. Finally, clients in *stress-reduction* programs develop new coping strategies, such as *time management* and *assertiveness training.* During time-management training, patients are taught to prioritize their activities and pay less attention to nonessential demands. During assertiveness training, they learn to stand up for themselves in an appropriate way. Clients also learn other procedures for managing everyday problems.

A number of studies have evaluated some version of this comprehensive program. The results suggest that it is generally more effective than individual components alone, such as relaxation or biofeedback, for chronic pain (Keefe, Dunsmore, & Burnett, 1992; Turk, 2002), CFS (Deale et al., 1997), tension headaches (Blanchard et al., 1990; Lipchik

et al., 2002), hypertension (Ward, Swan, & Chesney, 1987), and cancer pain (Crichton & Moorey, 2003; Fawzy, Cousins, et al., 1990).

## Drugs and Stress-Reduction Programs

We have already noted the enormous nationwide reliance on over-the-counter analgesic medication for pain, particularly headaches. Some evidence suggests that *chronic* reliance on these medications lessens the efficacy of comprehensive programs in the treatment of headache and may make headaches worse because patients experience *increased* headache pain every time the medication wears off or is stopped (rebound headaches; Capobianco, Swanson, & Dodick, 2001).

Holroyd, Nash, Pingel, Cordingley, and Jerome (1991) compared a comprehensive cognitive-behavioural treatment with an antidepressant drug, amitriptyline, in the treatment of tension headaches. The psychological treatment produced at least a 50% reduction in headache activity in 56% of the patients, whereas the drug produced a comparable reduction in only 27% of users. Grazzi et al. (2002) treated 61 patients with migraine headaches and analgesic overuse by withdrawing the patients from analgesics and then starting them on a more comprehensive but non-addicting medication regimen, either combined with biofeedback and relaxation or not (drugs only). After 3 years, significantly more individuals in the medication-only condition had relapsed by resuming analgesic use and were experiencing more headache pain. It is important that psychological treatment also seems to reduce drug consumption fairly consistently (Radnitz, Appelbaum, Blanchard, Elliott, & Andrasik, 1988), as it did in the Grazzi et al. (2002) study, not only for headaches but also for severe hypertension.

## Denial as a Means of Coping

We have emphasized the importance of confronting and working through our feelings, particularly after stressful or traumatic events. Beginning with Freud, mental health professionals have recognized the importance of reliving or processing intense emotional experiences to put them behind us and to develop better coping responses. For example, individuals undergoing coronary artery bypass surgery who were optimistic recovered more quickly, returned to normal activities more rapidly, and reported a stronger quality of life 6 months after surgery than those who were not optimistic (Scheier et al., 1989). People cope with the stress of health problems and medical procedures in a variety of different ways, some of which are more helpful, or more harmful, than others (Endler, Parker, & Summerfeldt,

1998). Scheier et al. (1989) also discovered a link between optimism and the coping styles that patients use to deal with severe stressors such as bypass surgery. They found that optimistic people are less likely to use denial as a means of coping with their surgery. Most mental health professionals work to eliminate denial because it has many negative effects. For example, people who deny the severe pain connected with disease may not notice meaningful variations in their symptoms, and they typically avoid treatment regimens or rehabilitation programs.

But is denial always harmful? Most individuals who are functioning well deny the implications of a potentially serious condition, at least initially (S. E. Taylor, 1999). A common reaction is to assume that what they have is not serious or it will go away quickly. Most people with serious diseases react this way, including those with cancer (Meyerowitz, 1983) and CHD (Krantz & Deckel, 1983). Several groups of investigators (e.g., Hackett & Cassem, 1973; Meyerowitz, 1983) have found that during that extremely stressful period when a person is first diagnosed, denial of the general implications and of anxiety and depression may help the patient endure the shock more easily. He or she is then more able to develop coping responses later. In one study, high initial denial resulted in less time in the intensive care section of the hospital (Levine et al., 1988), although, after discharge, the same patients were not as good at doing what they had to do to enhance their rehabilitation. Other studies show lower levels of corticosteroids and other stress-related responses among deniers during the most stressful phase of the illness (Katz, Weiner, Gallagher, & Hellman, 1970). Thus, the value of denial as a coping mechanism may depend more on timing than on anything else. In the long run, though, all the evidence indicates that at some point we must face the situation, process our emotions, and come to terms with what is happening.

## Modifying Behaviours to Promote Health

In the beginning of the chapter, we talked of psychological and social factors influencing health and physical problems in two distinct ways: by directly affecting biological processes and through unhealthy lifestyles. In this section, we consider the effects of an unhealthy lifestyle.

Research is teaching us that many common diseases can be prevented and others can be postponed or controlled simply by making positive lifestyle changes. Unhealthy eating habits, lack of exercise, and smoking are three of the most common behaviours that put us at risk in the long term for a number of physical disorders. High-risk behaviours

and conditions are listed in Table 7.4. Many of these behaviours contribute to diseases and physical disorders that are among the leading causes of death, including not only CHD and cancer but also accidents of various kinds (related to consumption of alcohol and the non-use of safety restraints), cirrhosis of the liver (related to excessive consumption of alcohol), and a variety of respiratory diseases, including influenza and pneumonia (related to smoking and stress; Sexton, 1979).

Behavioural self-care is also very important in the management of diabetes: The patient must regularly administer and adjust insulin and medications, self-test blood glucose levels, and manage his or her diet and exercise levels (Vallis et al., 2003). Considerable work is ongoing to develop effective behaviour modification procedures to improve diet, increase adherence to drug and medical treatment programs, and develop optimal exercise programs. Often the health psychologist using these behaviour modification procedures with a client with a stress-related physical disorder must begin by helping the patient enhance his or her motivation to change unhealthy behaviours (Vallis et al., 2003). Here we review briefly three areas of interest: injury control, the prevention of AIDS, and efforts to reduce smoking in China.

---

**TABLE 7.4** Areas for Health-Risk Behaviour Modification

- Smoking
- Hyperlipidemia
- High blood pressure
- Dietary habits related to disease:
  *High sodium; low calcium, magnesium, potassium*—High blood pressure
  *High fat*—Cardiovascular disease and cancer of the prostate, breast, colon, and pancreas
  *High simple carbohydrates*—Diabetes mellitus
  *Low fibre*—Diabetes mellitus, digestive diseases, cardiovascular disease, colon cancer
  *Low intake of vitamins A and C*—Cancer
- Sedentary lifestyle
- Obesity
- Substance abuse (alcohol and drug)
- Non-use of seat belts
- High-risk sexual behaviour
- Nonadherence to recommended immunization and screening procedures
- High stress levels and type A personality
- High-risk situations for childhood accidents, neglect, abuse
- Poor dental hygiene/infrequent care
- Sun exposure
- Poor quality relationships/supports
- Occupational risks

*Source:* Reprinted from "Primary Care and Health Promotion: A Model for Preventive Medicine" by M.B. Johns et al., 1987, *The American Journal of Preventive Medicine*, 3 (6): 351. © 1987, with permission from Elsevier.

## Injury Prevention

Injuries are the fourth-leading cause of death in Canada across all age ranges (see Table 7.1) and the top cause of death for younger people age 1 to 45. Furthermore, the loss of productivity to the individual and society from injuries is far greater than from other leading causes of death: heart disease, cancer, and stroke (Rice & MacKenzie, 1989). For this reason, methods for reducing injury have become a major focus within the areas of health psychology and behavioural medicine. Spielberger and Frank (1992) point out that psychological variables are crucial in mediating virtually all the factors that lead to injury. The psychological contributors have been understudied until recently, but they are now beginning to receive attention. A good example is the work being done on preventing accidents in children (e.g., Peterson & Roberts, 1992). Injuries kill more children than the next six causes of childhood death combined (Dershewitz & Williamson, 1977; Scheidt et al., 1995), yet most people, including parents, don't think too much about prevention, even in their own children, because they usually consider injuries to be fated and, therefore, out of their hands (Peterson, Farmer, & Kashani, 1990; Peterson & Roberts, 1992).

However, a variety of programs focusing on behaviour change have proved effective for preventing injuries in children (Sleet, Hammond, Jones, Thomas, & Whitt, 2003). For example, children have been systematically and successfully taught to escape fires (Jones & Haney, 1984), identify and report emergencies (Jones & Ollendick, 2002; Jones & Kazdin, 1980), safely cross streets (Yeaton & Bailey, 1978), ride bicycles safely, and deal with injuries such as serious cuts (Peterson & Thiele, 1988). In many of these programs, the participating children maintained the safety skills they had learned for months after the intervention—as long as assessments were continued, in most cases. Because little evidence indicates that repeated warnings are effective in preventing injuries, programmatic efforts to change behaviour are important, yet such programs are non-existent in most communities.

## AIDS Prevention

Earlier we documented the horrifying spread of AIDS, particularly in developing countries. In developed countries like Canada and the United States, AIDS is most commonly accounted for by high-risk sexual contact among male homosexuals or bisexuals or those with a history of injection drug use (Centers for Disease Control, 1994). According to the Canadian Youth, Sexual Health, and AIDS study conducted at Queen's University, Acadia University, the University of Laval, and the University of Alberta (Boyle, Doherty, Fortin, & MacKinnon, 2002), Canadian youth are another population that is highly vulnerable to HIV infection due to the high prevalence of risky behaviours and attitudes. These risk factors include high rates of risky sexual behaviour, substance use including injection drug use, and beliefs that HIV is not a threat to them. Although existing data suggest that HIV prevalence is currently low among Canadian youth (Health Canada, 2002), the high levels of risky attitudes and behaviours in this group show that the potential for HIV to spread certainly exists among young Canadians (Boyle et al., 2002). In developing countries, like Africa, for instance, AIDS is almost exclusively linked to heterosexual intercourse with an infected partner (Centers for Disease Control, 1994; World Health Organization, 2000). There is no vaccine for the disease. *Changing high-risk behaviour is the only effective prevention strategy* (Catania et al., 2000).

Comprehensive programs are particularly important because testing alone to learn whether a person is HIV-positive or HIV-negative does little to change behaviour (e.g., Landis, Earp, & Koch, 1992). Even educating at-risk individuals is generally ineffective in changing high-risk behaviour (Helweg-Larsen & Collins, 1997). A successful comprehensive behaviour-change program focusing on high-risk youth was conducted by William Fisher of the University of Western Ontario and his colleagues (Fisher, Fisher, Bryan, & Misovich, 2002). This study assessed the effects of three school-based HIV prevention interventions on urban, minority high school students' levels of HIV prevention knowledge, motivation, and behavioural skills (e.g., around condom use). These outcomes were assessed at 1 month, 3 months, and 1 year following the interventions. The three interventions were classroom-based, peer-based, and a combined

The prevalence of AIDS is high in Africa, where these women are taking part in a memorial ceremony for those who have died of the disease.

treatment. Each was compared with a "standard of care" control condition (i.e., the school's standard HIV/AIDS curriculum, which consisted largely of brief HIV prevention education delivered in health classes).

In the classroom-based intervention, teachers taught five classes focusing on (1) factual information about HIV transmission and prevention and dispelling myths (e.g., that there are "safe" partners); (2) changing students' attitudes and social norms about HIV risk and prevention; (3) enhancing students' motivation to engage in HIV prevention; (4) training in behavioural skills for abstinence from sex and for acquiring and using condoms; and (5) training in effectively communicating about safer sex. In the peer-based intervention, the same material was presented but by popular peers through informal contacts with same-sex friends and acquaintances. The combined treatment involved both the classroom-based and the peer-based interventions described above.

Some of the results are presented in Table 7.5 for sexually inexperienced students (top panel) and for sexually experienced students (bottom panel); these results show levels of knowledge, motivation, and behavioural skills in adolescents in the four conditions at pretreatment and again at 1 month following the treatment. Each of the active interventions was better than the control treatment on some of the outcomes at the 1-month follow-up. The combined treatment proved effective relative to the control treatment on *all* outcome measures across both sexually inexperienced and sexually experienced students. These findings are very promising and point to the importance of adding psychological techniques (motivational enhancement, behavioural skills training) to educational efforts in preventing HIV in youth. Incorporating more effective prevention programs like this one (Fisher et al., 2002) into Canadian schools, could help bridge the current gaps in HIV prevention for youth identified in a recent Canadian government report (Health Canada, 1999).

### Smoking in China

Despite efforts by the government to reduce smoking among its citizens, China has one of the most tobacco-addicted populations in the world. Approximately 250 million people in China, 90% of them male, are habitual smokers. China consumes 33% of all cigarettes in the world, and smoking is projected to kill 100 million Chinese people in the next 50 years (Lam, Ho, Hedley, Mak, & Peto, 2001).

In one early attempt to reach these individuals, health professionals took advantage of the strong family ties in China and decided to persuade the

**TABLE 7.5** Results of the HIV Prevention Program for High-Risk Adolescents

| Measure | Classroom | Peer | Combined | Control |
|---|---|---|---|---|
| **Sexually Inexperienced Participants** (*n* = 777) | | | | |
| Knowledge | | | | |
| Pretreatment | 13.07 | 13.72 | 13.57 | 12.51 |
| Posttreatment | 15.61* | 14.35 | 16.58* | 13.01 |
| Motivation | | | | |
| Pretreatment | 3.97 | 4.08 | 4.09 | 3.93 |
| Posttreatment | 4.17* | 4.16 | 4.30* | 3.95 |
| Behavioural Skills | | | | |
| Pretreatment | 3.68 | 3.84 | 3.82 | 3.68 |
| Posttreatment | 3.85 | 3.82 | 4.04* | 3.69 |
| **Sexually Experienced Participants** (*n* = 755) | | | | |
| Knowledge | | | | |
| Pretreatment | 12.91 | 13.50 | 13.95 | 13.00 |
| Posttreatment | 15.03* | 14.94* | 16.19* | 13.38 |
| Motivation | | | | |
| Pretreatment | 4.30 | 4.27 | 4.42 | 4.23 |
| Posttreatment | 4.20 | 4.37* | 4.46* | 4.10 |
| Behavioural Skills | | | | |
| Pretreatment | 3.96 | 4.11 | 4.11 | 4.09 |
| Posttreatment | 3.98 | 4.10 | 4.19* | 3.98 |

Note: Significant pretreatment to posttreatment increase relative to standard-of-care control is indicated via an asterisk (*).

*Source:* From Fisher, J.D., Fisher, W.A., Bryan, A.D., and Misovich, S.J. Information-Motivation-Behavioral Skills Model—Based HIV Risk Behavior Change Intervention for Inner-City High School Youth. *Health Psychology* 2002, 21(2), 177-186, Table 2, p.182. Copyright © 2002 by the American Psychological Association. Adapted with permission.

*children* of smokers to intervene with their fathers. In so doing, they conducted the largest study yet reported of attempted behaviour modification to promote health. In 1989, the Chinese government developed an antismoking campaign in 23 primary schools in Hangzhou, capital of Zhejiang province. Children took home antismoking literature and questionnaires to almost 10 000 fathers. They then wrote letters to their fathers asking them to quit smoking, and they submitted monthly reports on their fathers' smoking habits to the schools. Approximately 9 months later, the results were assessed. Indeed, the children's intervention had some effect. Almost 12% of the fathers in the intervention group had quit smoking for at least 6 months. By contrast, in a control group of another 10 000 males, the quit rate was only 0.2%.

Since then, the Chinese government has become more involved in smoking prevention efforts. One notable example is the Wuhan smoking prevention trial. Investigators from North America and China are collaborating to prevent smoking by more than 5000 adolescents in both locations. Unger et al. (2002) found that smoking by peers and availability of cigarettes were equally strong risk factors for smoking in adolescents in both China and North America. This will be one major target for the prevention program.

Approximately 250 million people in China are habitual smokers, 90% of them male. Thus, Chinese men are at very high risk of smoking-related diseases such as cardiovascular disease and lung cancer.

## Summary

Large-scale health behaviour modification programs, such as those described in this section, cost money. Nonetheless, results show that efforts like these are worthwhile to individuals, to the community, and to public health officials. Many lives will be saved and disability leave will be decreased to an extent that will more than cover the original costs of the programs. Unfortunately, we still have a ways to go, since implementation of this type of program is not widespread, at present.

## Concept Check 7.3

Check your understanding of psychological treatment by matching the treatments to the correct scenarios or statements: (a) biofeedback, (b) meditation and relaxation, (c) cognitive coping procedure, (d) denial, (e) modifying behaviours to promote health

1. Mary is often upset by stupid things other people are always doing. Her doctor wants her to realize her exaggeration of these events. _____
2. Karl can't seem to focus on anything at work. He feels too stressed. He needs a way of minimizing intruding thoughts that he can use at work in a short amount of time. _____
3. Harry's blood pressure soars when he feels stressed. His doctor showed him how to become aware of his body processes to control them better. _____
4. At a world conference, leaders met to discuss how to reduce the risk of childhood injuries, AIDS risks, and the number of smoking-related diseases. Professionals suggested programs involving teaching individuals about _____.
5. Initially strong _____ can help a patient endure the shock of bad news; however, later it can inhibit or prevent the healing process.

# Summary

## Psychological and Social Factors That Influence Health

- Psychological and social factors play a major role in developing and maintaining a number of physical disorders.
- Two fields of study have emerged as a result of a growing interest in psychological factors contributing to illness. *Behavioural medicine* involves the application of behavioural science techniques to prevent, diagnose, and treat medical problems. *Health psychology* is a subfield that focuses on psychological factors involved in the promotion of health and well-being.

- Psychological and social factors may contribute directly to illness and disease through the psychological effects of stress on the immune system and other physical functioning. If the immune system is compromised, it may no longer be able to attack and eliminate antigens from the body effectively, or it may begin to attack the body's normal tissue instead, a process known as *autoimmune disease*.
- Growing awareness of the many connections between the nervous system and the immune system has resulted in the new field of *psychoneuroimmunology*.
- Diseases that may be related in part to the effects of stress on the immune system include AIDS, rheumatoid arthritis, and cancer.

## Psychosocial Effects on Physical Disorders

- Long-standing patterns of behaviour or lifestyle may put people at risk for developing certain physical disorders. For example, unhealthy sexual practices can lead to AIDS and other sexually transmitted diseases, and unhealthy behavioural patterns, such as poor eating habits, lack of exercise, or type A behaviour patterns, may contribute to cardiovascular diseases such as stroke, hypertension, and coronary heart disease.
- Of the leading causes of death in Canada, about half of these deaths can be traced to lifestyle behaviours.
- Psychological and social factors also contribute to chronic pain. The brain inhibits pain through naturally occurring endogenous opioids, which may also be implicated in a variety of psychological disorders.
- Chronic fatigue syndrome is a relatively new disorder that is attributed at least in part to stress but that may also have a viral or immune system dysfunction component.

## Psychosocial Treatment of Physical Disorders

- A variety of psychosocial treatments have been developed with the goal of either treating or preventing physical disorders. Among these are *biofeedback* and the *relaxation response*.
- Comprehensive stress- and pain-reduction programs include not only relaxation and related techniques but also new methods to encourage effective coping, including stress management, realistic appraisals, and improved attitudes through cognitive therapy.
- Comprehensive programs are generally more effective than individual components delivered singly.
- Other interventions aim to modify such behaviours as unsafe sexual practices, smoking, and unhealthy dietary habits. Such efforts have been made in a variety of areas, including injury control, AIDS prevention, and smoking cessation campaigns in China.

## Key Terms

behavioural medicine, 272
health psychology, 272
general adaptation syndrome (GAS), 273
stress, 273
self-efficacy, 276
immune system, 276
antigens, 277
autoimmune disease, 278

rheumatoid arthritis, 278
psychoneuro-immunology (PNI), 278
AIDS-related complex (ARC), 279
cancer, 281
psycho-oncology, 281
cardiovascular disease, 283

stroke, 283
hypertension, 284
essential hypertension, 284
coronary heart disease (CHD), 286
type A behaviour pattern, 286
type B behaviour pattern, 286

acute pain, 289
chronic pain, 289
endogenous opioids, 292
chronic fatigue syndrome (CFS), 292
biofeedback, 295
relaxation response, 296

## Answers to Concept Checks

**7.1** 1. c  2. b  3. a  4. e  5. d

**7.2** 1. c  2. development  3. hypertension, coronary heart disease  4. type A (hard-driving, impatient), type B (relaxed, less concerned)  5. chronic fatigue syndrome

**7.3** 1. c  2. b  3. a  4. e  5. d

### InfoTrac College Edition

If your instructor ordered your book with InfoTrac College Edition, please explore this online library for additional readings, review, and a handy resource for short assignments.

Go to **http://infotrac.thomsonlearning.com**

Enter these search terms: biofeedback training, stress (physiology), self-efficacy (psychology), chronic fatigue syndrome, intractable pain, acute pain, coronary heart disease, hypertension, cardiovascular disease, nursing, cancer, stroke (disease), rheumatoid arthritis, autoimmune disease, immune disease

 ### The Abnormal Psychology Book Companion Website

Go to **www.essentialsabnormalpsych.nelson.com** for practice quiz questions, Internet links, critical thinking exercises, and more.

### Abnormal Psychology Live CD-ROM

- **Orel, Social Support/HIV:** A North American Black client demonstrates the power of strong social support from family and friends and the pursuit of personal interests such as art to deal with the ongoing struggles of being an HIV/AIDS patient.
- **Studying the Effects of Emotions on Physical Health:** This video illustrates recent findings on how emotional experiences—such as stress, loneliness, and sociability—affect physical health.
- **Breast Cancer Support and Education:** This clip investigates whether providing group *support* or group *education* is more helpful to women who are facing breast cancer.
- **Research on Exercise and Weight Control:** This video examines a program designed to determine the most successful ways to control weight. The study followed 200 women over the course of one year, teaching them behaviour modification skills, giving them low fat/low calorie diets to follow, and assigning them exercise programs. A key question for the study was to discover if intensity of exercise makes a difference in weight loss.

**Thomson NOW!** **http://hed.nelson.com** Go to this site for the link to ThomsonNow™, your one-stop study shop. Take a Pretest for this chapter and ThomsonNow™ will generate a personalized Study Plan based on your test results! The Study Plan will identify the topics you need to review and direct you to online resources to help you master those topics. You can then take a Posttest to help you determine the concepts you have mastered and what you still need work on.

## Video Concept Review

For challenging concepts that typically need more than one explanation, Mark Durand provides a video review via ThomsonNow™ of the following topic:

- The reciprocal nature of psychosocial factors and physical disorders.

# Chapter Quiz

1. Which of the following is an interdisciplinary field that applies knowledge about human thoughts, emotions, and activities to prevent, diagnose, and treat medical problems?
   a. behavioural medicine
   b. endogenous medicine
   c. health psychology
   d. medical psychology

2. The general adaptation syndrome describes several stages people experience in response to sustained stress. These stages occur in which order?
   a. alarm, resistance, exhaustion
   b. resistance, alarm, exhaustion
   c. resistance, exhaustion, alarm
   d. exhaustion, alarm, resistance

3. Cortisol is:
   a. a neurotransmitter that reduces anxiety.
   b. a neurohormone whose chronic secretion enhances hippocampal and immune functioning.
   c. a portion of the brain that stimulates the HPA axis in response to stress.
   d. a hormone that stimulates the hippocampus to turn off the stress response.

4. Next month Shanti has to take an important college entrance exam. Which factor is most likely to influence whether her response to the exam is positive or negative?
   a. the genetic vulnerability to stress that Shanti has inherited from her parents
   b. whether Shanti will be taking the exam in a room by herself or with other students
   c. Shanti's beliefs about how much control she has over the situation
   d. how much time Shanti has to study before the exam

5. Joan has been living with HIV for 3 years and has just started participating in a stress-management support group. Based on previous research, what might Joan expect from her participation?
   a. an increase in the activity of T helper and natural killer cells
   b. an increase in the amount of antigens in her system
   c. an increase in depression as she discusses her illness
   d. an increase in immune functioning, but only for the first few weeks of the group

6. The study of how psychosocial factors influence cancer is known as:
   a. psychopathology.
   b. psychopharmacology.
   c. psycho-oncology.
   d. oncosociology.

7. Which of the following is a risk factor for coronary heart disease?
   a anger that is part of the type A behaviour pattern
   b. belligerence that is part of the type B behaviour pattern
   c. competitive drive that is part of the type B behaviour pattern
   d. carefree disregard for deadlines that is part of the type A behaviour pattern

8. Biofeedback can be used to teach people how to:
   a. reduce their competitive drive and sense of urgency.
   b. consciously control physiological functions that are outside awareness.
   c. develop more supportive social support networks.
   d. control their facial expressions to control their mood.

9. Which of the following accurately characterizes the effects of denial as a coping strategy?
   a. Individuals who undergo coronary artery bypass surgery return to normal activities more rapidly if they deny their pain.
   b. Denial may have damaging short-term consequences in terms of the stress response, but it seems to be helpful to rehabilitation in the long term.
   c. People who deny their disease may not notice meaningful variations in their symptoms.
   d. Denial appears to have exclusively negative consequences on health and adaptation.

10. Which three behaviours, all of which can be modified, put people at the most risk for physical problems?
    a. unhealthy diet, lack of exercise, smoking
    b. pollution, unhealthy diet, lack of exercise
    c. lack of exercise, smoking, reckless driving
    d. smoking, alcohol use, "road rage"

*(See the Appendix on page 601 for answers.)*

# Exploring Physical Disorders and Health Psychology

Psychological and behavioural factors are major contributors to illness and death.

- Behavioural medicine applies behavioural science to medical problems.
- Health psychology focuses on psychological influences on health and improving health care.

## PSYCHOLOGICAL AND SOCIAL FACTORS INFLUENCE BIOLOGY

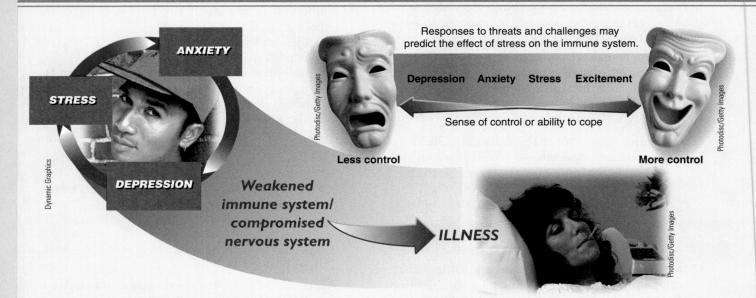

ANXIETY

STRESS

DEPRESSION

Dynamic Graphics

Weakened immune system/ compromised nervous system

ILLNESS

Responses to threats and challenges may predict the effect of stress on the immune system.

Depression    Anxiety    Stress    Excitement

Sense of control or ability to cope

**Less control**

**More control**

Photodisc/Getty Images

---

### AIDS (Acquired Immune Deficiency Syndrome)

- The human immunodeficiency virus (HIV) attacks the immune system and opportunistic infections develop uncontrollably.
- Psychological treatments focus on strengthening the immune system and gaining a sense of control.
- Although drug therapy may control the virus, there is so far no biological means of prevention and the disease is still always fatal.

### Cardiovascular Problems

- The heart and blood vessels can be damaged by
  - *Stroke*: blockage or rupture of blood vessels in the brain;
  - *Hypertension:* constriction of blood vessels at organs and extremities puts extra pressure on the heart, which eventually weakens;
  - *Coronary heart disease*: blockage of arteries supplying blood to the heart.
- Biological, psychological, and social factors contribute to all these conditions and are addressed in treatment.

### Chronic Pain

- May begin with an acute episode but does not diminish when injury heals.
- Typically involves joints, muscles, and tendons; may result from enlarged blood vessels, tissue degeneration, or cancerous tumors.
- Psychological and social influences may cause and maintain chronic pain to a significant degree.

### Cancer

- Abnormal cell growth produces malignant tumors.
- Psychosocial treatments may prolong life, alleviate symptoms, and reduce depression and pain.
- Different cancers have different rates of recovery and mortality.
- *Psycho-oncology* is the study of psychosocial factors involved in the course and treatment of cancer.

# PSYCHOSOCIAL TREATMENTS FOR PHYSICAL DISORDERS

The stress reaction associated with pain may reduce the number of natural killer (NK) cells in the immune system.

**EXTREME PAIN**

**DISEASE OR INJURY; ENHANCED DISEASE OR INJURY**

**STRESS**

Photodisc/Getty Images

## BIOFEEDBACK

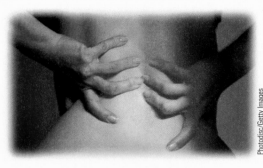

- Electronic monitors make physiological responses such as heart beat visible on a computer screen.
- Patient learns to increase or decrease the response, thereby improving functioning (decreasing tension).
  —Developing a sense of control may be therapeutic.

Photodisc/Getty Images

## RELAXATION AND MEDITATION

- *Progressive muscle relaxation:* Person learns to locate physical tension and to counteract it by relaxing a specific muscle group.
- *Meditation:* Focusing attention on a specific body part or process or on an affirming thought or image; in some forms, focusing on a single silently repeated syllable (mantra) "empties" the mind. Meditation is accompanied by slow, regular breathing.
  – Meditating daily for at least 10 to 20 minutes imparts calm and relaxation by reducing certain neurotransmitters and stress hormones and increasing a sense of control.

# BEHAVIOUR MODIFICATION TO PROMOTE HEALTH

Many injuries and diseases can be prevented or controlled through lifestyle changes involving diet, substance use, exercise, and safety precautions.

## INJURY CONTROL

Photodisc/Getty Images

- Injuries are the leading cause of death for people age 1 to 45, especially children.

  - Most people consider injuries to be out of their control and therefore do not change high-risk behaviours.
  - In children, prevention focuses on
    – escaping fires
    – crossing streets
    – using car seats, seat belts, and bicycle helmets
    – first aid

## AIDS PREVENTION

- Changing high-risk behaviour through individual and community education is the only effective strategy.
  – Eliminate unsafe sexual practices through cognitive-behavioural self-management training and social support networks.
  – Show drug abusers how to clean needles and make safe injections.
- Target minorities and women, groups that do not perceive themselves to be at risk.
  – Media coverage focuses on gay white males.
  – More women are infected through heterosexual interactions than by IV drug use.

Photodisc/Getty Images

# 8 Eating and Sleep Disorders

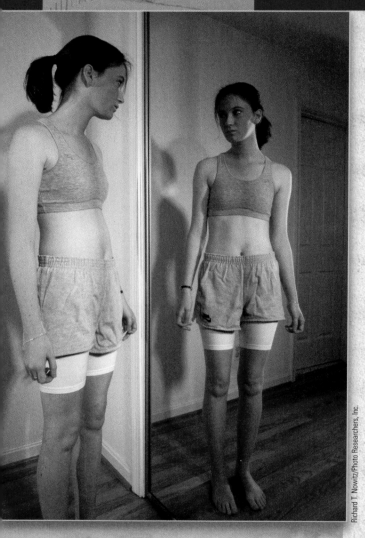

Richard T. Nowitz/Photo Researchers, Inc.

**Major Types of Eating Disorders**
 Bulimia Nervosa
 Anorexia Nervosa
 Binge-Eating Disorder
 Statistics

**Causes of Eating Disorders**
 Social Dimensions
 Biological Dimensions
 Psychological Dimensions
 An Integrative Model

**Treatment of Eating Disorders**
 Drug Treatments
 Psychological Treatments
 Preventing Eating Disorders

**Sleep Disorders: The Major Dyssomnias and Parasomnias**
 An Overview of Sleep Disorders
 Primary Insomnia
 Primary Hypersomnia
 Narcolepsy
 Breathing-Related Sleep Disorders
 Circadian Rhythm Sleep Disorders

**Treatment of Sleep Disorders**
 Medical Treatments
 Environmental Treatments
 Psychological Treatments
 Preventing Sleep Disorders
 Parasomnias and Their Treatment

**Visual Summaries: Exploring Eating Disorders
Exploring Sleep Disorders**

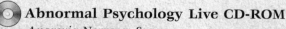 **Abnormal Psychology Live CD-ROM**
 Anorexia Nervosa: Susan
 Anorexia Nervosa/Bulimia: Twins
 Sleep Cycle

We now continue our discussion of the interaction of psychological and social factors and physical functioning. Most of us take our bodies for granted. We wake up in the morning assuming we will be alert enough to handle our required daily activities; we eat two or three meals a day and perhaps some snacks in between; we may engage in some vigorous exercise and, on some days, in sexual activity. We don't focus on our functioning to any great degree unless it is disrupted by illness or disease. And yet, psychological and social factors can significantly disrupt these "activities of survival."

In this chapter we examine psychological disruptions of two of our relatively automatic behaviours, eating and sleeping, which have substantial impact on the rest of our behaviour.

# Major Types of Eating Disorders

- ■ *Describe the defining features and clinical manifestations of bulimia nervosa.*

- ■ *Describe the clinical manifestations and medical complications associated with anorexia nervosa.*

- ■ *Compare the symptoms and psychological features of binge-eating disorder and bulimia.*

Although some of the disorders we discuss in this chapter can be deadly, many of us are not aware that they are widespread among us. They began to increase during the 1950s and 1960s and have spread insidiously over the ensuing decades. In **bulimia nervosa**, out-of-control eating episodes, or **binges**, are followed by self-induced vomiting, excessive use of laxatives, or other attempts to "purge" (get rid of) the food. In **anorexia nervosa**, the person eats nothing beyond minimal amounts of food, so body weight sometimes drops dangerously. The chief characteristic of these related disorders is an overwhelming, all-encompassing drive to be thin. In fact, a study of 176 patients receiving treatment for an eating disorder in Pisa, Italy, and Toronto, a full 83% evidenced extremely high levels of drive for thinness (Ramacciotti et al., 2002). Work by Toronto-based researchers has shown that patients with bulimia nervosa do not differ from those with anorexia nervosa in terms of drive to be thin (Garner, Olmsted, & Polivy, 1983). Of the people with anorexia nervosa who are followed over a sufficient period, up to 20% die as a result of their disorder, with slightly more than 5% dying within 10 years (e.g., Keel et al., 2003; Ratnasuriya, Eisler, Szmuhter, & Russell, 1991; Sullivan, 1995; Theander, 1985; Zipfel, Lowe, Deter, & Herzog, 2000). As many as half the deaths are suicides (Agras, 2001; Keel et al., 2003; Thompson & Kinder, 2003).

A growing number of studies in different countries indicate that eating disorders are widespread and that they increased dramatically in Western countries from about 1960 to 1995, according to the most recent data we have (Hoek, 2002). In Switzerland, from 1956 to 1958 the number of new cases of anorexia nervosa under treatment among females between age 12 and age 25 was 3.98 per 100 000. There were 16.76 new cases per 100 000 during the 1973 to 1975 period, a fourfold increase (Willi & Grossman, 1983). Similar results were found in Scotland by Eagles, Johnston, Hunter, Lobban, and Millar (1995) between 1965 and 1991; by Lucas, Beard, O'Fallon, and Kurlan (1991) in North America over a 50-year period; and by Moller-Madsen and Nystrup (1992) in Denmark between 1970 and 1989. Eagles et al. (1995) documented a steady increase of more than 5% per year in Scotland.

Even more dramatic are the data for bulimia nervosa. Garner and Fairburn (1988) reviewed rates of referral to a major eating disorder centre in Toronto. Between 1975 and 1986, the referral rates for anorexia rose slowly, but the rates for bulimia rose dramatically—from virtually none to more than 140 per year. Similar findings have been reported from other parts of the world (Hay & Hall, 1991; Lacey, 1992). The reason for this increase is not

---

**bulimia nervosa** Eating disorder involving recurrent episodes of uncontrolled excessive (binge) eating followed by compensatory actions to remove the food (e.g., deliberate vomiting, laxative abuse, excessive exercise).

**binge** Relatively brief episode of uncontrolled, excessive consumption, usually of food or alcohol.

**anorexia nervosa** Eating disorder characterized by recurrent food refusal leading to dangerously low body weight.

known. Toronto researchers Paul Garfinkel and Barbara Dorian (2001) have suggested that it may relate to the increased prevalence of dieting and pre-occupation with the body among young women who are simultaneously being exposed to social pressures toward consumption and incredible food availability.

Other studies estimate a sixfold increase in death rates among those with eating disorders compared with the normal population (Crisp, Callender, Halek, & Hsu, 1992; Patton, 1988). The mortality rate from eating disorders, particularly anorexia, is the highest for any psychological disorder, even depression (Harris & Barraclough, 1998; Keel et al., 2003; Vitiello & Lederhendler, 2000).

Although reports of cases of eating disorders are documented throughout history, eating problems were not recognized as psychological disorders until relatively recently. In 1872 Sir William Withey Gull, a British physician, was the first to use the term *anorexia nervosa*. According to psychiatrists Sidney Kennedy and David Goldbloom (1996), the first Canadian description of anorexia nervosa appeared in the *Maritime Medical Journal* in 1895. The recognition of bulimia nervosa as a separate entity did not occur until much later, when the condition was described in the 1970s (e.g., Russell, 1979). Eating disorders were included for the first time as a separate group of disorders in DSM-IV; before then, they had been classified as one of the disorders usually diagnosed in infancy, childhood, or adolescence (see Chapter 13) because of their typical onset in adolescence.

What makes this increase in eating disorders even more intriguing is that the increase tends to be culturally specific. Until recently, eating disorders were not found in developing countries, where access to sufficient food is so often a daily struggle; only in the West, where food is generally plentiful, have they been rampant. Now this is changing; evidence suggests that eating disorders are going global. Unsystematic interviews with health professionals in Asia (Efon, 1997), as well as more formal studies (Lee, 1993), show estimates of prevalence in those countries, particularly Japan and Hong Kong, are approaching those in Canada, the United States, and other Western countries. Not everyone in the world is at risk. Eating disorders tend to occur in a relatively small segment of the population. More than 90% of the severe cases are young females, mostly in families with upper-middle and upper-class socioeconomic status, who live in a socially competitive environment. Perhaps the most visible example is the late Diana, Princess of Wales, who recounted her 7-year battle with bulimia (Morton, 1992). She reported bingeing and vomiting four or more times a day during her honeymoon.

The specificity of these disorders in terms of sex, age, and social class is unparalleled and makes

The late Princess of Wales spoke candidly about her battle against bulimia.

the search for causes all the more interesting. In these disorders, unlike most others, the strongest contributions to etiology seem to be sociocultural rather than psychological or biological factors. We begin by examining bulimia nervosa and anorexia nervosa in some detail. We then briefly consider a further category under consideration for inclusion in the DSM called *binge-eating disorder*.

## Bulimia Nervosa

You are probably familiar with bulimia nervosa from your own experience or a friend's. It is one of the most common psychological disorders on university campuses. Consider the case of Phoebe.

## Phoebe
### Apparently Perfect

Phoebe was a popular, attractive, intelligent, and talented teenager. By the time she was finishing high school, she had accomplished a great deal. She was on the student council throughout her high school years and she dated the captain of the football team. Phoebe had many talents, among them a beautiful singing voice and marked ability in ballet. Each year at Christmastime, her ballet company performed the *Nutcracker Suite*, and Phoebe attracted much attention with her poised performance in a lead role. She played on several of the school athletic teams. Phoebe maintained an A-minus average, was considered a model student, and was headed for a top-ranked university.

But Phoebe had a secret: She was haunted by her belief that she was fat and ugly. Every single bite of food that she put in her mouth was, in her mind, another step down the inexorable path that led to the end of her success and popularity. Phoebe had been concerned about her weight since she was 11. Ever the perfectionist, she began regulating her eating in junior high school. She would skip breakfast (over the protestations of her mother), eat a small bowl of pretzels at noon, and allow herself one-half of whatever she was served for dinner.

This behaviour continued into high school, as Phoebe struggled to restrict her eating to occasional binges on junk food. Sometimes she stuck her fingers down her throat after a binge (she even tried a toothbrush once), but this tactic was unsuccessful. In grade 10, Phoebe reached her full adult height of 157 centimetres (5 feet 2 inches) and weighed 50 kilograms (110 pounds); she continued to fluctuate between 48 and 50 kilograms (105 and 110 pounds) throughout high school. By the time she was in grade 12, Phoebe was obsessed with what she would eat and when. She used every bit of her willpower attempting to restrict her eating, but occasionally she failed.

One day during the fall of grade 12, she came home after school, and alone in front of the TV, she ate two big boxes of candy. Depressed, guilty, and desperate, she went to the bathroom and stuck her fingers further down her throat than she had ever before dared. She vomited. And she kept vomiting. Although so physically exhausted that she had to lie down for half an hour, Phoebe had never felt such an overwhelming sense of relief from the anxiety, guilt, and tension that always accompanied her binges. She realized that she had gotten to eat all that candy and now her stomach was empty. It was the perfect solution to her problems.

Phoebe learned quickly what foods she could easily vomit. And she always drank lots of water. She began to restrict her eating even more. She ate almost nothing until after school, but then the results of her dreaming and scheming and planning all morning would be realized. Although the food sometimes varied, the routine did not. She might pick up a dozen doughnuts and a box of cookies. When she got home, she might make a bowl of popcorn.

And then she ate and ate, forcing down the doughnuts, cookies, and popcorn until her stomach hurt. Finally, with a mixture of revulsion and relief, she purged, forcing herself to vomit. When she was done, she stepped on the scale to make sure she had not gained any weight and then collapsed into bed and slept for about half an hour.

This routine went on for about 6 months, until April of that same academic year. By this time Phoebe had lost much of her energy, and her schoolwork was deteriorating. Her teachers noticed this and saw that she looked bad. She was continually tired, her skin was broken out, and her face puffed up, particularly around her mouth. Her teachers and mother suspected that she might have an eating problem. When they confronted her, she was relieved her problem was finally out in the open.

In an effort to eliminate opportunities to binge and purge, her mother rearranged her schedule to be home in the afternoon when Phoebe got there; in general, her parents minimized the occasions when Phoebe was left alone, particularly after eating. This tactic worked for about a month. Mortally afraid of gaining weight and losing her popularity, Phoebe resumed her pattern, but she was now much better at hiding it. For 6 months, Phoebe binged and purged approximately 15 times a week.

When Phoebe went away to university that fall, things became more difficult. Now she had a roommate in residence to contend with, and she was more determined than ever to keep her problem a secret. Although the student health service offered workshops and seminars on eating disorders for first-year university students, Phoebe knew that she could not break her cycle without the risk of gaining weight. To avoid the communal bathroom in residence, she went to a deserted place behind a nearby building to vomit. Social life at university often involved drinking beer and eating fattening foods, so she vomited more often. Nevertheless, she gained 5 kilograms (10 pounds) and weighed 55 kilograms (120 pounds). Gaining weight is common among first-year university students, but her mother commented without thinking one day that Phoebe seemed to be putting on weight. This remark was devastating to Phoebe.

She kept her secret until the beginning of her second year in university, when her world fell apart. One night, after drinking a lot of beer at a party, Phoebe and her friends went to Kentucky Fried Chicken. Although Phoebe did not truly binge because she was with friends, she did eat a lot of fried chicken, the most forbidden food on her list. Her guilt, anxiety, and tension increased to new heights. Her stomach throbbed with pain, but when she tried to vomit, her gag reflex seemed to be gone. Breaking into hysterics, she called her boyfriend and told him she was ready to kill herself. Her loud sobbing and crying attracted the attention of her friends in her residence, who attempted to comfort her. She confessed her problem to them. She also called her parents. At this point, Phoebe realized that her life was out of control and that she needed professional help.

## Clinical Description

The hallmark of bulimia nervosa is eating a larger amount of food—typically, more junk food than fruits and vegetables—than most people would eat under similar circumstances (Fairburn & Cooper, 1993; Wilson & Pike, 2001). Patients with bulimia readily identify with this description, even though the actual caloric intake for binges varies significantly from person to person (Franko, Wonderlich, Little, & Herzog, 2004). Just as important as the *amount* of food eaten is that the eating is experienced as *out of control* (Fairburn, Cooper, & Cooper, 1986), a criterion that is an integral part of the definition of binge eating. Both criteria characterized Phoebe.

Another important criterion is that the individual attempts to *compensate* for the binge eating and potential weight gain, almost always by **purging techniques.** Techniques include self-induced vomiting immediately after eating, as in the case of Phoebe, and using laxatives (drugs that relieve constipation) and diuretics (drugs that result in loss of fluids through greatly increased frequency of urination). Some people use both methods; others attempt to compensate in other ways. Some fast for long periods between binges. Others exercise excessively. However, rigorous exercising is more usually a characteristic of anorexia nervosa. Caroline Davis and her colleagues at York University (Davis et al., 1997) found that fully 81% of a group of patients with anorexia nervosa exercised excessively, compared with 57% of a group of patients with bulimia nervosa.

Bulimia nervosa is subtyped in DSM-IV-TR into *purging type* and *non-purging type* (exercise or fasting). But the non-purging type has turned out to be rare, accounting for only 6% to 8% of patients with bulimia (Hay & Fairburn, 1998; Striegel-Moore et al., 2001). A study by Paul Garfinkel and his colleagues compared purging versus non-purging bulimics (Garfinkel et al., 1996). In comparison with non-purging bulimics, those who purged developed their eating disorder at a

younger age and had higher rates of comorbid depression, anxiety disorders, and alcohol abuse, as well as higher rates of earlier sexual abuse (Garfinkel et al., 1996). However, other studies have found little evidence of any differences between purging and non-purging types of bulimia in severity of psychopathology, frequency of binge episodes, or prevalence of major depression or panic disorder, leading some to question whether this is a useful subtype (Franko et al., 2004; Tobin, Griffing, & Griffing, 1997).

Purging is not a particularly efficient method of reducing caloric intake. Vomiting reduces approximately 50% of the calories just consumed, less if it is delayed (Kaye, Weltzin, Hsu, McConaha, & Bolton, 1993); laxatives and related procedures have little effect, acting, as they do, so long after the binge.

One of the more important additions to the DSM-IV-TR criteria is the specification of a psychological characteristic clearly present in Phoebe. Despite her accomplishments and success, she felt her continuing popularity and self-esteem would largely be determined by the weight and shape of her body. Paul Garfinkel (1992) noted that, of 107 women seeking treatment for bulimia nervosa, only 3% did not share this attitude. Recent investigations confirm the construct validity of the diagnostic category of bulimia nervosa, suggesting that the major features of the disorder (bingeing, purging, overconcern with body shape, etc.) "cluster together" in someone with this problem (Bulik, Sullivan, & Kendler, 2000; Fairburn et al., 2003; Franko et al., 2004; Gleaves, Lowe, Snow, Green, & Murphy-Eberenz, 2000; Keel, Mitchell, Miller, Davis, & Crow, 2000).

## Medical Consequences

Chronic bulimia with purging has a number of medical consequences (Pomeroy, 2004). One is salivary gland enlargement caused by repeated vomiting, which gives the face a chubby appearance. This was noticeable with Phoebe. Repeated vomiting also may erode the dental enamel on the inner surface of the front teeth. More important, continued vomiting may upset the chemical balance of bodily fluids, including sodium and potassium levels. This condition, called an *electrolyte imbalance*, can result in serious medical complications if unattended, including cardiac arrhythmia (disrupted heartbeat), seizures, and renal (kidney) failure, all of which can be fatal. Normalization of eating habits will quickly

---

**purging techniques**   In the eating disorder bulimia nervosa, the self-induced vomiting or laxative abuse used to compensate for excessive food ingestion.

reverse the imbalance. Intestinal problems resulting from laxative abuse are also potentially serious; they can include severe constipation or permanent colon damage. Finally, some individuals with bulimia have marked calluses on their fingers or the backs of their hands caused by the friction of contact with the teeth and throat when repeatedly sticking their fingers down their throats to stimulate the gag reflex.

## Disorder Criteria Summary
Bulimia Nervosa

Features of bulimia nervosa include:
- Recurrent episodes of binge eating, characterized by an abnormally large intake of food within a 2-hour period, combined with a sense of lack of control over eating during these episodes
- Recurrent, inappropriate compensatory behaviour to prevent weight gain, such as self-induced vomiting; misuse of laxatives; fasting; or excessive exercising
- On average, bingeing and inappropriate compensatory behaviour occur at least twice a week for at least 3 months
- Excessive preoccupation with body shape and weight

*Source:* Based on DSM-IV-TR. Used with permission from the *Diagnostic and Statistical Manual of Mental Disorders,* Fourth Edition, Text Revision. Copyright 2000. American Psychiatric Association.

### Associated Psychological Disorders

An individual with bulimia usually presents with additional psychological disorders, particularly anxiety and mood disorders (see review by O'Brien & Vincent, 2003). One of the authors of this text and his colleagues compared 20 patients with bulimia nervosa to 20 individuals with panic disorder and to another 20 with social phobia (Schwalburg, Barlow, Alger, & Howard, 1992). The most striking finding was that fully 75% of the patients with bulimia also presented with an anxiety disorder such as social phobia or generalized anxiety disorder; patients with anxiety disorders, on the other hand, did not necessarily have an elevated rate of eating disorders. Mood disorders, particularly depression, also commonly co-occur with bulimia, with about 20% of bulimic patients meeting criteria for a mood disorder when interviewed and close to 50% at some point during the course of their disorder (Agras, 2001). For years, one prominent theory suggested that eating disorders are simply a way of expressing depression. But most evidence indicates that depression *follows* bulimia and may be a reaction to it (Brownell & Fairburn, 1995; Hsu, 1990). Some

research suggests a high prevalence of borderline personality disorder in patients with bulimia (e.g., Kennedy, McVey, & Katz, 1990). Finally, substance abuse commonly accompanies bulimia nervosa and vice versa (see review by Stewart & Brown, in press). For example, Keel et al. (2003) reported that 33% of their combined sample of individuals with either bulimia or anorexia or with both also met criteria for substance abuse, including both alcohol and drugs. As another example, Stewart, Brown, Devoulyte, Theakston, and Larsen (2006) studied 58 women in treatment for alcoholism through Addiction Prevention and Treatment Services in the Capital District Health Authority in Nova Scotia. A full 71% of the women alcoholics reported binge eating, with 91% of those displaying binge-eating patterns that clinicians would consider severe. In a study by Kristin von Ranson at the University of Calgary and her colleagues, eating disorders were associated with nicotine dependence in adolescent girls and with alcohol abuse in adult women (von Ranson, Iacono, & McGue, 2002). Recent work by Eliott Goldner and colleagues in Vancouver suggests that bulimia may also be related to behaviours suggesting poor impulse control, such as compulsive shoplifting (Goldner, Geller, Birmingham, & Remick, 2000). In summary, bulimia seems related to anxiety disorders, mood disorders, substance use disorders, borderline personality, and impulse control disorders.

## *Anorexia Nervosa*

Like Phoebe, the overwhelming majority of individuals with bulimia are within 10% of their normal weight (Hsu, 1990). In contrast, individuals with anorexia nervosa (which literally means a "nervous loss of appetite," an incorrect definition because appetite often remains healthy) differ in one important way from individuals with bulimia. They are so successful at losing weight that they put their lives in considerable danger. Both anorexia and bulimia are characterized by a morbid fear of gaining weight and losing control over eating. The major difference seems to be whether the individual is successful at losing weight. People with anorexia are proud of both their diets and their extraordinary control, and they usually do not see themselves as having an illness. People with bulimia are ashamed of both the problem itself and their lack of control, and they tend to be secretive about their bulimic symptoms (Brownell & Fairburn, 1995). The denial of illness in anorexia and the shame and secrecy in bulimia mean that people with eating disorders do not seek treatment as early as they should (Kaplan & Garfinkel, 1999). Consider the case of Julie.

## Julie
### The Thinner the Better

Julie was 17 years old when she first came for help. If you looked hard enough past her sunken eyes and pasty skin, you could see that she had once been attractive. But at present, she looked emaciated and unwell. Eighteen months earlier she had been overweight, weighing almost 65 kilograms (140 pounds) at 155 centimetres (5 feet 1 inch). Her mother, a well-meaning but overbearing and demanding woman, nagged Julie incessantly about her appearance. Her friends were kinder but no less relentless. Julie, who had never had a date, was told by a friend she was really cute and would have no trouble getting dates if she lost some weight. So she did! After many previous unsuccessful attempts, she was determined to succeed this time.

After several weeks on a strict diet, Julie noticed she was losing weight. She felt a control and mastery that she had never known before. It wasn't long before she received positive comments, not only from her friends but from her mother. Julie began to feel good about herself. The difficulty was that she was losing weight too fast. She stopped menstruating. But now nothing could stop her from dieting. By the time she reached our clinic, she weighed 35 kilograms (75 pounds) but she thought she looked fine and, perhaps, could even stand to lose a bit more weight. Her parents had just begun to worry about her. In fact, Julie did not initially seek treatment for her eating behaviour. Rather, she had developed a numbness in her left lower leg and a left foot drop that a neurologist determined was caused by peritoneal nerve paralysis believed to be related to inadequate nutrition. The neurologist referred her to our clinic.

Like most people with anorexia, Julie said she probably should put on a little weight, but she didn't mean it. She thought she looked fine but she had "lost all taste for food," a report that may not have been true because most people with anorexia crave food at least some of the time but control their cravings. Nevertheless, she was participating in most of her usual activities and continued to do extremely well in school and in her extracurricular pursuits. Her parents were happy to buy her most of the workout videotapes available, and she began doing one every day, and then two. When her

parents suggested she was exercising enough, perhaps too much, she worked out when no one was around. After every meal, she exercised with a workout tape until, in her mind, she burned up all the calories she had just taken in.

Responses to the current physical fitness and exercise craze can become extreme for female athletes (Davis & Strachan, 2001). Perhaps one of the best-known examples is the world-class gymnast Christy Henrich, who died of kidney failure at the age of 22. Christy weighed approximately 43 kilograms (about 95 pounds) at the peak of her career. Later, during repeated hospitalizations for anorexia, Christy had to be physically restrained to prevent excessive exercise; like Julie, she exercised to the point of exhaustion if given half a chance. When she died in 1994, Christy weighed 30 kilograms (64 pounds). Another well-known example is accomplished athlete Elaine Tanner, who represented Canada in swimming at the Commonwealth Games, the Pan-Am Games, and the Olympics in the 1960s, winning 15 medals and setting new records. Tanner developed anorexia after competing in the Olympics at age 17 (Bornath, 2002). She was finally able to overcome the disorder, but it took 19 years!

## Clinical Description

Anorexia nervosa is less common than bulimia, but there is a great deal of overlap. For example, many individuals with bulimia have a history of anorexia; that is, they once used fasting to reduce their body weight below desirable levels (Fairburn, Welch, Doll, Davies, & O'Connor, 1997; Mitchell & Pyle, 1988).

Although decreased body weight is the most notable feature of anorexia nervosa, it is not the core of the disorder. Many people lose weight because of a medical condition, but people with anorexia have an intense fear of obesity and relentlessly pursue thinness (Bruch, 1986; Garfinkel & Garner, 1982; Hsu, 1990; Schlundt & Johnson, 1990; Stice, Cameron, Killen, Hayward, & Taylor, 1999). As with Julie, the disorder most commonly begins in an adolescent who is overweight or who perceives herself to be. She then starts a diet that escalates into an obsessive preoccupation with being thin. She continues to see herself as overweight despite her weight loss. In fact, a recent study by Randi McCabe at McMaster University showed that patients with anorexia nervosa have a tendency to overreport their body weight (McCabe, McFarlane, Polivy, & Olmsted, 2001). As we noted earlier, the work of

Caroline Davis and her colleagues (1997) indicates that severe, almost punishing exercise is common, as with Julie. Dramatic weight loss is achieved through severe caloric restriction or by combining caloric restriction and purging.

Based largely on the work of Paul Garfinkel and his colleagues, DSM-IV-TR specifies two subtypes of anorexia nervosa. In the *restricting type,* individuals diet to limit caloric intake; in the *binge-eating–purging type,* they rely on purging. Unlike individuals with bulimia, the binge-eating–purging anorexic binges on relatively small amounts of food and purges more consistently, in some cases each time she eats. Approximately half the individuals who meet criteria for anorexia engage in binge eating and purging (Agras, 1987; Garfinkel, Moldofsky, & Garner, 1979). Some research has shown that binge-purge anorexics engage in such impulsive behaviour as stealing, alcohol and drug abuse, and self-mutilation more than restricting anorexics, and their moods are more variable (labile); in this way they resemble normal-weight bulimics (Garner, Garfinkel, & O'Shaughnessy, 1985). However, other prospective data collected over 8 years on 136 individuals with anorexia reveal few differences between these two subtypes in severity of symptoms or personality (Eddy et al., 2002). Over time, fully 62% of the restrictive subtype had begun bingeing or purging. Thus, subtyping may not be useful in predicting the future course of the disorder but, rather, may reflect a certain phase or stage of anorexia.

An individual with anorexia is never satisfied with his or her weight loss. Staying the same weight from one day to the next or gaining any weight is likely to cause intense panic, anxiety, and depression. Only continued weight loss every day for weeks on end is satisfactory. Although DSM-IV-TR criteria specify body weight 15% below that expected, the average is approximately 25% to 30% below normal by the time treatment is sought (Hsu, 1990). Another key criterion of anorexia is a marked disturbance in body image. When Julie looked at herself in the mirror, she saw something very different from what others saw. They saw an emaciated, sickly, frail girl in the throes of semi-starvation. Julie saw a girl who needed to lose at least a few kilograms from some parts of her body. For Julie, her face and buttocks were the problems. Other girls might focus on other parts, such as the arms or legs or stomach.

After seeing numerous doctors, people like Julie become good at mouthing what others expect to hear. They may agree they are underweight and need to gain a few kilograms—but they don't believe it. Question further and they will tell you the girl in the mirror is fat. For this reason, individuals with anorexia seldom seek treatment on their own. Usually pressure from somebody in the family leads to the initial visit, as in Julie's case (Agras, 1987; Sibley & Blinder, 1988). Perhaps as a demonstration of absolute control over their eating, some anorexic individuals show increased interest in cooking and food. Some have become expert chefs, preparing all the food for the family. Others hoard food in their rooms, looking at it from time to time. We review research that seems to explain these curious behaviours.

## Medical Consequences

One common medical complication of anorexia nervosa is cessation of menstruation (amenorrhea), which also occurs relatively frequently in bulimia (Crow, Thuras, Keel, & Mitchell, 2002). This defining feature can be an objective physical index of the degree of food restriction (Franko et al., 2004). Although some studies have demonstrated a strong correlation between ovulation and resulting menstruation and weight (Fairburn, Cooper, Doll, & Welch, 1999a; Pirke, Schweiger, & Fichter, 1987), overwhelming evidence indicates that alterations in endocrine levels resulting in amenorrhea are a consequence of semi-starvation rather than a cause.

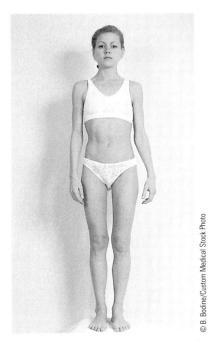
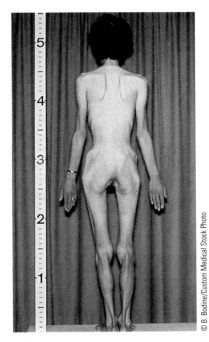

These women are at different stages of anorexia.

© B. Bodine/Custom Medical Stock Photo

Although amenorrhea is currently required for a diagnosis of anorexia nervosa in females, Paul Garfinkel and Barbara Dorian (2001) have expressed concern about the decision to include this criterion in the DSM-IV. An epidemiological study by Garfinkel's group showed that there were no differences in eating disorder severity, comorbidity, or family history of eating disorders between patients with anorexia who did and did not display amenorrhea (Garfinkel et al., 1996). An additional challenge with this criterion appears when considering a diagnosis of anorexia nervosa for girls who have not yet started to menstruate. The DSM-IV-TR only requires the amenorrhea for women who have already started to menstruate. However, it is possible that an adolescent who is delayed in reaching puberty and in beginning to menstruate may be delayed because of the presence of anorexia nervosa.

Other medical signs and symptoms of anorexia include dry skin, brittle hair or nails, and sensitivity to or intolerance of cold temperatures. Also, it is relatively common to see *lanugo*, downy hair on the limbs and cheeks. Cardiovascular problems, such as chronically low blood pressure and heart rate, can also result. If vomiting is part of the anorexia, electrolyte imbalance and resulting cardiac and kidney problems can result, as in bulimia. Two characteristic features of anorexia nervosa (i.e., low body weight and amenorrhea) are important risk factors for the development of osteoporosis. In fact, several studies have documented the presence of severe osteoporosis and bone fractures in anorexic patients (see review by Garfinkel, 2002).

### Associated Psychological Disorders

As with bulimia nervosa, anxiety disorders and mood disorders are often present in individuals with anorexia (Agras, 2001; Garfinkel et al., 1996; Kaye et al., 1993; O'Brien & Vincent, 2003; Vitiello & Lederhendler, 2000), with Agras noting current depression in 33% of the cases and rates of depression occurring at some point during their lives in as many as 60% of cases. Interestingly, one anxiety disorder that seems to co-occur frequently with anorexia is obsessive-compulsive disorder (OCD; see Chapter 4). In anorexia, unpleasant thoughts are focused on gaining weight, and individuals engage in a variety of behaviours, some of them ritualistic, to rid themselves of such thoughts. Future research will determine whether anorexia and OCD are truly similar or simply resemble each other. Substance abuse is also common in individuals with anorexia nervosa, but only in the binge-purge subtype (see reviews in Keel et al., 2003; Stewart & Brown, in press; Wilson, 1993). Co-occurring substance abuse is a strong predictor of mortality, particularly by suicide.

**Disorder Criteria Summary**
Anorexia Nervosa

Features of anorexia nervosa include:
- Refusal to maintain body weight at or above a minimally normal level
- Intense fear of gaining weight
- Inappropriate evaluation of one's weight or shape, or denial of the seriousness of the current low body weight
- Amenorrhea

*Source:* Based on DSM-IV-TR. Used with permission from the *Diagnostic and Statistical Manual of Mental Disorders,* Fourth Edition, Text Revision. Copyright 2000. American Psychiatric Association.

## Binge-Eating Disorder

Recent research has focused on a group of individuals who experience marked distress because of binge eating but do *not* engage in extreme compensatory behaviours and therefore cannot be diagnosed with bulimia (Castonguay, Eldredge, & Agras, 1995; Fairburn et al., 1998; Spitzer et al., 1991). These individuals have **binge-eating disorder (BED).** Currently, BED is in the appendix of DSM-IV-TR as a potential new disorder requiring further study. Many investigators are beginning to conclude that it should be included as a full-fledged disorder in future editions of the DSM, or at least combined with existing disorders. Bulik et al. (2000) studied anorectic and bulimic behaviour in 2163 female twins. They suggested there is enough evidence to support BED as a disorder in the next revision of the DSM. Castonguay et al. (1995), on the other hand, suggest that bulimia and BED could be combined, because bingeing is a prominent feature of both disorders; individuals could then be subtyped as to whether they purge or not and whether they are obese or not.

A study by Keri Sullivan at the University of Calgary found that individuals with BED are distinguishable from those with bulimia nervosa in that those with BED have higher rates of obesity and lower levels of eating concern and dietary restraint; however, the two groups showed similar elevations on shape and weight concerns (Sullivan, 2001). Further research will determine whether the BED designation would be useful (Fairburn, Hay, & Welch,

**binge-eating disorder (BED)**  Pattern of eating involving distress-inducing binges not followed by purging behaviours; being considered as a new DSM diagnostic category.

1993; Fairburn & Wilson, 1993; Garfinkel, Kennedy, & Kaplan, 1995; Steiger, Bruce, & Israel, 2003).

The general consensus is that about 20% of obese individuals in weight-loss programs engage in binge eating, with the number rising to approximately 50% among candidates for bariatric surgery (surgery to correct severe or morbid obesity). Fairburn, Cooper, Doll, Norman, and O'Connor (2000), in a notable study, identified 48 individuals with BED and were able to prospectively follow 40 of them for 5 years. The prognosis was relatively good for this group, with only 18% retaining the full diagnostic criteria for BED at a 5-year follow-up. The percentage of this group who were obese, however, increased from 21% to 39%.

About half try dieting before bingeing, and half start with bingeing and then attempt to diet (Abbott et al., 1998); those who begin bingeing first become more severely affected and more likely to have additional disorders (Spurrell, Wilfley, Tanofsky, & Brownell, 1997). It's also increasingly clear that individuals with BED have some of the same concerns about shape and weight as people with anorexia and bulimia (Eldredge & Agras, 1996; Fairburn et al., 1998; Wilfley, Schwartz, Spurrell, & Fairburn, 2000). Also, it seems that approximately 33% binge to alleviate "bad moods" or negative affect (e.g., Grilo, Masheb, & Wilson, 2001; Stice, Akutagawa, Gaggar, & Agras, 2000; Stice et al., 2001) and that negative affect or feeling down can trigger bingeing (e.g., Davis, Freeman, & Garner, 1988; Polivy & Herman, 1993). These individuals are more psychologically disturbed than the 67% who represent a pure dieting subtype and do not use bingeing to regulate mood (Grilo et al., 2001).

## Statistics

Clear cases of bulimia have been described for thousands of years (Parry-Jones & Parry-Jones, 2002), but bulimia nervosa was recognized as a distinct psychological disorder only in the 1970s (Boskind-Lodahl, 1976; Russell, 1979). Therefore, information on prevalence has been acquired relatively recently.

We have already noted that the overwhelming majority (90% to 95%) of individuals with bulimia are women; most are white and middle to upper-middle class. The 5% to 10% of cases who are male have a slightly later age of onset, and a large minority are homosexual or bisexual (Rothblum, 2002). For example, Carlat, Camargo, and Herzog (1997) accumulated information on 135 male patients with eating disorders who were seen over 13 years and found that 42% were either homosexual or bisexual. Recent research by D. Blake Woodside and colleagues in Toronto indicates that men with eating disorders are similar in most respects to women with eating disorders (Woodside, Garfinkel, Lin, Goering, & Kaplan, 2001). Male athletes in sports that require weight regulation, such as wrestling, are another large group of males with eating disorders. During 1998, stories were widely published about the deaths of three wrestlers from complications of eating disorders. Interestingly, the gender imbalance in bulimia was not always present. Historians of psychopathology note that for hundreds of years the vast majority of (unsystematically) recorded cases were male (Parry-Jones & Parry-Jones, 1994, 2002). Because women with bulimia are overwhelmingly preponderant today, most of our examples are women.

Age of onset is typically 16 to 19 years (Fairburn et al., 1997; Garfinkel et al., 1995; Mitchell & Pyle, 1988), although signs of impending bulimic behaviour can occur much earlier, as in Phoebe's case. Schlundt and Johnson (1990), summarizing a large number of surveys, suggest that between 6% and 8% of young women, especially on university campuses, meet criteria for bulimia nervosa. Gross and Rosen (1988) reported that as many as 9% of high school girls would meet criteria, although only about 2% were purging at that age. Most people who seek treatment are in the purging subtype.

A somewhat different view of the prevalence of bulimia comes from studies of the population as a whole rather than of specific groups of adolescents. In one of the better studies, sampling more than 8000 individuals in Ontario, the lifetime prevalence was 1.1% for females and 0.1% for males (Garfinkel et al., 1995). Another 2.3% of females showed partial syndromes in which they displayed some of the symptoms of bulimia nervosa but not enough to meet the full DSM-IV-TR diagnostic criteria (Garfinkel et al., 1995). The low prevalence rate observed for males is consistent with earlier reports (Carlat & Camargo, 1991). In a careful study in New Zealand (Bushnell, Wells, Hornblow, Oakley-Browne, & Joyce, 1990), the lifetime prevalence of bulimia nervosa among women age 18 to 44 years was 1.6%. However, the rate was substantially higher among younger women. For instance, among women age 18 to 24, the prevalence was 4.5%. Among women age 25 to 44, the prevalence was 2%, but it was only 0.4% among women age 45 to 64. Numbers seem to be highest in urban areas (Hoek et al., 1995).

In an important prevalence study reported by Kendler and colleagues (1991), 2163 twins (more than 1000 sets of twins), from whom some results were reported earlier, were interviewed, and the lifetime prevalence of bulimia nervosa was found to be 2.8%, increasing to 5.3% when marked bulimic symptoms that did not meet full criteria for the disorder were included. Once again, the prevalence was greatest in younger women. As is evident in Figure 8.1, the risk was much higher for females born from 1960 onward than for females born before 1960. Nevertheless, as pointed out by Fairburn and his colleagues (Fairburn & Beglin, 1990; Fairburn, Hay, & Welch, 1993), estimates are probably low, because many individuals with eating disorders refuse to participate in studies. Therefore, the percentages represent only those individuals who consented to participate in the survey.

Once bulimia develops, it tends to be chronic if untreated (Fairburn, Cooper, Doll, Norman, & O'Connor, 2000; Fairburn et al., 2003; Keel & Mitchell, 1997); one study by Todd Heatherton and colleagues shows the "drive for thinness" and accompanying symptoms were still present in a group of women 10 years after diagnosis (Joiner, Heatherton, & Keel, 1997). In an important study of the course of bulimia, referred to earlier, Fairburn et al. (2000) identified a group of 102 females with bulimia nervosa and followed 92 of them prospectively for 5 years. About one-third improved to the point where they no longer met diagnostic criteria each year, but another third who had improved previously relapsed. Between 50% and 67% exhibited serious eating disorder symptoms at the end of each

year of the 5-year study, indicating this disorder has a relatively poor prognosis. In a follow-up study, Fairburn et al. (2003) reported that the strongest predictors of persistence were a history of childhood obesity and a continuing overemphasis on the importance of being thin. In addition, individuals tend to retain their bulimic symptoms, instead of shifting to symptoms of other eating disorders, providing further validation for bulimia nervosa as a diagnostic category (Keel et al., 2000).

The same high percentage (90% to 95%) of individuals with anorexia are female, with onset also in adolescence, usually around the age of 13 (Fairburn et al., 1999a; Herzog, 1988). Studies cited in the beginning of this chapter noted the increase in rates of anorexia beginning in the 1960s and 1970s. Walters and Kendler (1995) have now analyzed data from the same 2163 twins mentioned previously to determine the prevalence of anorexia nervosa. The results indicate that 1.62% met criteria for lifetime prevalence, and this figure increased to 3.70% with the inclusion of marked anorexic symptoms that did not meet full criteria for the disorder, suggesting that bulimia is somewhat more common than anorexia (see also Garner & Fairburn, 1988). Once anorexia develops, its course seems more chronic than even bulimia, and it is more resistant to treatment (Garfinkel, 2002; Herzog et al., 1999; Vitiello & Lederhendler, 2000).

### Cross-Cultural Considerations

We have already discussed the highly culturally specific nature of anorexia and bulimia. A particularly striking finding is that these disorders develop in immigrants who have recently moved to Western countries (Nasser, 1988). One of the more interesting studies is Nasser's (1986) survey of 50 Egyptian women in London universities and 60 Egyptian women in Cairo universities. There were no instances of eating disorders in Cairo, but 12% of the Egyptian women in England had developed eating disorders. Mumford, Whitehouse, and Platts (1991) found the same result with Asian women living in North America. The prevalence of eating disorders varies among most North American minority populations. The prevalence of eating disorders among Black and Asian North American females is lower than among Caucasians, but they are more frequent among Aboriginal women (Crago, Shisslak, & Estes, 1997). Generally, surveys reveal that Black adolescent girls have less body dissatisfaction, fewer weight concerns, and a more positive self-image, and perceive themselves to be thinner than they actually are compared with Caucasian adolescent girls (Celio, Zabinski, & Wilfley, 2002). Major risk factors for eating disorders in all groups include being overweight, being in a higher social

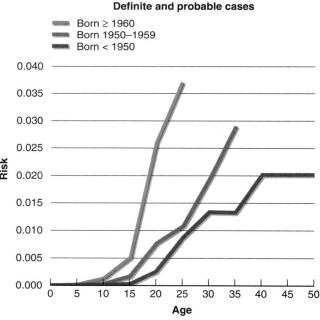

**Figure 8.1** ▪ Lifetime prevalence of bulimia among female twins. (From "The Genetic Epidemiology of Bulimia Nervosa," by G. S. Kendler, C. MacLean, M. Neale, R. Kessler, A. Heath, and L. Evans *American Journal of Psychiatry*, 148(12), 1627–1637. Copyright © 1991 by the American Psychiatric Association. Reprinted by permission.)

class, and acculturating to the Western majority (Crago et al., 1997; Raich et al., 1992; Smith & Krejci, 1991; Wilfley & Rodin, 1995).

One culturally determined difference in criteria for eating disorders has been reported by Lee, Leung, Wing, Chiu, and Chen (1991). In traditional Chinese cultures, it has been widely assumed that being slightly plump is highly valued, with ideals of beauty focused on the face rather than the body. Therefore, in this group, acne was more often reported as a precipitant for anorexia nervosa than was a fear of being fat, and body image disturbance was rare (Lee, Hsu, & Wing, 1992). Patients said they refused to eat because of feelings of fullness or pain, although it is possible they related food intake to their skin conditions. Beyond that, they met all criteria for anorexia. More recent studies, however, call into question this ideal (Kawamura, 2002). Leung, Lam, and Sze (2001) analyzed data from the Miss Hong Kong Beauty Pageant from 1975 to 1999 and found that winners were taller and thinner than the average Chinese women, with a "curvaceous" narrow waist and full-hip body shape. They note that this ideal matches depictions of beauty in classical Chinese literature, and it challenges the notion that plumpness is valued, at least in Hong Kong.

In Japan, the prevalence of anorexia nervosa among teenage girls is still lower than the rate in North America, but, as mentioned previously, it seems to be increasing. The need to be thin or the fear of becoming overweight has not been as important in Japanese culture as it is in North America, although this may be changing as cultures around the world become more Westernized (Kawamura, 2002). Body image distortion and denial that a problem exists are clearly present in patients who have the disorder (Ritenbaugh, Shisstak, Teufel, Leonard-Green, & Prince, 1994).

An interesting recent study by Madjulika Gupta and her colleagues at the University of Western Ontario compared weight-related body image concerns in young women aged 18 to 24 years in Canada and India (Gupta, Chaturvedi, Chandarana, & Johnson, 2001). This cross-cultural study found that women's overall levels of the core eating disorder features of drive for thinness and body dissatisfaction did not differ between the two cultures. However, body image concerns presented slightly differently in the two samples. In the Canadian women, body dissatisfaction was related to concerns about the weight of the abdomen, hips, thighs, and legs. In the Indian women, in contrast, body dissatisfaction was related to concerns about the weight of the face, neck, shoulders, and chest (i.e., upper torso).

In conclusion, anorexia and bulimia are relatively homogeneous and, until recently, overwhelmingly associated with Western cultures. In addition, the frequency and pattern of occurrence among minority Western cultures differs somewhat but is associated with closer identification with Caucasian middle-class values.

## Developmental Considerations

Because the overwhelming majority of cases begin in adolescence, it is clear that anorexia and bulimia are strongly related to development (McVey, Pepler, Davis, Flett, & Abdolell, 2002; Polivy, Herman, Mills, & Brock, 2003). As pointed out by Striegel-Moore, Silberstein, and Rodin (1986) and Attie and Brooks-Gunn (1995), differential patterns of physical development in girls and boys interact with cultural influences to create eating disorders. After puberty, girls gain weight primarily in fat tissue, whereas boys develop muscle and lean tissue. As the ideal look in Western countries is tall and muscular for men and thin and prepubertal for women, physical development brings boys closer to the ideal and takes girls further away.

## Concept Check 8.1

Check your understanding of eating disorders by identifying the proper disorder in the following scenarios: (a) bulimia nervosa, (b) anorexia nervosa, (c) binge-eating disorder.

1. Jason has been having episodes lately when he eats prodigious amounts of food. He's been putting on a lot of weight because of it. _____

2. I noticed Elena eating a whole pie, a cake, and two bags of potato chips the other day when she didn't know I was there. She ran to the bathroom when she was finished and it sounded like she was vomiting. This disorder can lead to an electrolyte imbalance, resulting in serious medical problems. _____

3. Pam eats large quantities of food in a short time. She then takes laxatives and exercises for long periods to prevent weight gain. She has been doing this almost daily for several months and feels she will become worthless and ugly if she gains even an ounce. _____

4. Kirsten has lost several kilos and now weighs less than 40 kilograms (90 pounds). She eats only a small portion of the food her mother serves her and fears that intake above her current 500 calories daily will make her fat. Since losing the weight, Kirsten has stopped having periods. She sees a fat person in the mirror. _____

# Causes of Eating Disorders

■ *Describe the possible social, psychological, and neurobiological causes of eating disorders.*

As with all the disorders discussed in this book, biological, psychological, and social factors contribute to the development of these serious eating disorders, but the evidence is increasingly clear that the most dramatic factors are social and cultural.

## Social Dimensions

Remember that anorexia and bulimia are the most culturally specific psychological disorders yet identified. What drives so many young people into a punishing and life-threatening routine of semi-starvation or purging? For many young Western women, looking good is more important than being healthy. For young females in middle- to upper-class competitive environments, self-worth, happiness, and success are determined largely by body measurements and percentage of body fat, factors that have little or no correlation with personal happiness and success in the long run. The cultural imperative for thinness directly results in dieting, the first dangerous step down the slippery slope to anorexia and bulimia (Polivy & Herman, 1993).

What makes the modern emphasis on thinness in women even more puzzling is that standards of desirable body sizes change much like fashion styles in clothes, if not as quickly (Cash & Pruzinsky, 2002). Several groups of investigators have documented this phenomenon in some interesting ways over the years. Garner, Garfinkel, Schwartz, and Thompson (1980) collected data from *Playboy* magazine centrefolds and from contestants in major

*The Three Graces* by Peter Paul Rubens/Museo del Prado, Madrid/SuperStock
© Vauthey Pierre/Corbis Sygma

Changing concepts of ideal weight are evident in a 17th-century painting by Peter Paul Rubens and in a photograph of a current fashion model.

beauty pageants from 1959 to 1978. During this period, both *Playboy* centrefolds and the beauty pageant contestants became significantly thinner. Bust and hip measurements became smaller, although waists became somewhat larger, suggesting a change in what is considered desirable in the *shape* of the body in addition to weight. The preferred shape during the 1960s and 1970s was thinner and more tubular than before (Agras & Kirkley, 1986). Wiseman, Gray, Mosimann, and Ahrens (1992) updated the research, collecting data from 1979 to 1988, and reported that 69% of the *Playboy* centrefolds and 60% of the beauty pageant contestants weighed 15% or more below normal for their age and height, meeting one of the criteria for anorexia. More recently, Rubinstein and Caballero (2000) compiled data on weight and height from beauty pageant winners from 1922 through 1999. They found that since the 1970s most of these winners would be considered undernourished. Just as important, when Wiseman and colleagues (1992) counted diet and exercise articles in six women's magazines from 1959 to 1988, they found a significant increase in both, with articles on exercise increasing dramatically during the 1980s, surpassing the number on diet.

Levine and Smolak (1996) refer to "the glorification of slenderness" in magazines and on television, where the vast majority of females are thinner than average North American women. Because overweight men are two to five times more common as television characters than overweight women, the message from the media to be thin is clearly aimed at women (Fouts & Burggraf, 2000). Stice, Schupak-Neuberg, Shaw, and Stein (1994) established a strong relationship between amount of media exposure and symptoms of eating disorder in university women. In another study, girls who watched 8 or more hours of TV per week reported significantly greater body dissatisfaction than girls who watched less TV (Gonzalez-Lavin & Smolak, 1995; Levine & Smolak, 1996). An analysis of prime-time situation comedies revealed that 12% of female characters were dieting, and many were making disparaging comments about their body image (Tiggermann, 2002). Finally, Thompson and Stice (2001) found that risk for developing eating disorders was directly related to the extent to which women internalize or "buy in" to the media messages and images glorifying thinness.

During the 1920s, the ideal female body was similar in shape to the ideal today (Agras & Kirkley, 1986); however, this shape was achieved through fashion (e.g., through use of girdles) rather than dieting. No diet articles appeared in the magazines of the period that were sampled, whereas today we see what Brownell and Rodin (1994) have called

***Anorexia Nervosa: Susan***
*"Basically ... I don't want to eat because it seems like, as soon as I eat, I just gain weight, get fat.... There are some times when I can't stop it, I just have to, and then, once I eat, there is a strong urge to either purge or take a laxative.... It never stops.... It becomes very obsessive, where you're getting on the scales ten times a day.... I weigh 96 pounds [43 kilograms] now."*

Thomson Learning

"the dieting maelstrom," in which health professionals, the media, and a powerful diet and food industry all have stakes.

The problem with today's standards is that they are increasingly difficult to achieve, because the size and weight of the average woman has increased over the years with improved nutrition; there is also a general increase in size throughout history (Brownell, 1991; Brownell & Rodin, 1994). Whatever the cause, the collision between our culture and our physiology (Brownell, 1991; Brownell & Fairburn, 1995) has had some negative effects, one of which is that women are no longer satisfied with their bodies.

A second clear effect is the dramatic increase, especially among women, in dieting and exercise to achieve what may be an impossible goal. Look at the increase in dieting since the 1950s. Dwyer, Feldman, Seltzer, and Mayer reported in 1969 that more than 80% of female high school students in grade 12 wished to lose weight and that 30% were dieting. Among their male counterparts, fewer than 20% wished to lose weight and only 6% were dieting. More recently, Hunnicut and Newman (1993) surveyed a sample of 3632 students in grade 8 and grade 10 and found that 60.6% of females and 28.4% of males were dieting. Although these studies are not directly comparable, younger girls typically diet less than older girls, which suggests the increase in dieting is even more dramatic.

Fallon and Rozin (1985), studying male and female undergraduates, found that men rated their current size, their ideal size, and the size they figured would be most attractive to the opposite sex as approximately equal; indeed, they rated their ideal body weight as *heavier* than the weight females thought most attractive in men (see Figure 8.2). Women, however, rated their current figures as much heavier than what they judged the most attractive, which in turn, was rated as heavier than what they thought was ideal.

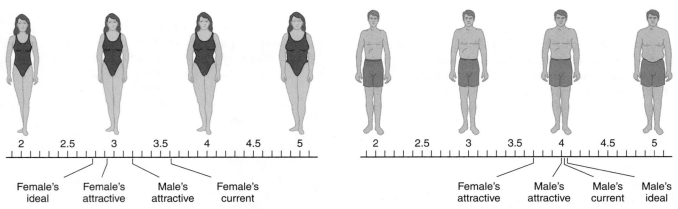

**Figure 8.2** ■ Male and female ratings of body size. (Based on Stunkard, Sorensen, & Schulsinger, 1980.)

A recent study by Forestell, Humphrey, and Stewart (2004) at Dalhousie University, using figures similar to those displayed in Figure 8.2, showed that undergraduate women are particularly critical of women's hip size when making evaluations of physical attractiveness. An additional interesting finding from the Fallon and Rozin (1985) study was that women's judgment of ideal female body weight was less than the weight that men thought was most attractive. This conflict between reality and fashion seems most closely related to the current epidemic of eating disorders. The efforts of some people to maintain thin, athletic shapes are almost superhuman. Major beauty pageant contestants work out an average of 14 hours per week, with some exercising 35 hours per week (Trebbe, 1979).

Now we have some more specific information on how these attitudes about body image are socially transmitted in adolescent girls. Paxton, Schutz, Wertheim, and Muir (1999) explored the influence of close friendship groups on attitudes concerning body image, dietary restraint, and extreme weight-loss behaviours. In a clever experiment, the authors identified 79 different friendship cliques in a group of 523 adolescent girls. They found that these friendship cliques tended to share the same attitudes toward body image, dietary restraint, and the importance of attempts to lose weight. It was also clear from the study that these friendship cliques contributed significantly to the formation of individual body image concerns and eating behaviours. In other words, if your friends tend to use extreme dieting or other weight-loss techniques, there is a greater chance that you will, too (Field et al., 2001; Vanderwal & Thelen, 2000).

Most people who diet don't develop eating disorders, but Patton, Johnson-Sabine, Wood, Mann, and Wakeling (1990) determined in a prospective study that adolescent girls who dieted were eight times more likely to develop an eating disorder 1 year later than those who weren't dieting. Telch

and Agras (1993) noted marked increases in bingeing during and after rigorous dieting in 201 obese women. Stice, Cameron, Killen, Hayward, and Taylor (1999) demonstrated that one reason attempts to lose weight may lead to eating disorders is that weight reduction efforts in adolescent girls are more likely to result in weight *gain* than weight loss! To establish this finding, 692 girls, initially the same weight, were followed for 4 years. Girls who attempted dieting faced more than 300% greater risk of obesity than those who did not diet. Results are presented in Figure 8.3.

It is not yet entirely clear why dieting leads to bingeing in some people but not all (Polivy & Herman, 1993), but the relationship is strong (Davis et al., 1988). For example, a recent daily diary study by Howard Steiger and his colleagues at the Douglas Hospital Eating Disorders Unit in Montreal showed that attempts to limit and control their dietary intake precipitated binge eating episodes in most bulimics (Steiger, Lehoux, & Gauvin, 1999).

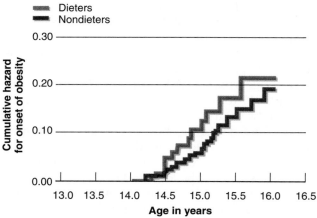

**Figure 8.3** ■ The onset of obesity over 4 years for self-labelled dieters versus self-labelled nondieters. (From Stice et al., 1999.)

The work of Janet Polivy and C. Peter Herman at the University of Toronto has contributed much to our understanding of the negative consequences of chronic dieting. Their early lab-based work showed how a broken diet can readily lead to a binge in women who chronically restrict their diets (e.g., Polivy & Herman, 1985). In a more recent study, Urbszat, Herman, and Polivy (2002) told 46 undergraduates that they would either be dieting for a week (Group 1) or not (Group 2) and then presented them with food under the pretext of giving them a taste test. But investigators were really looking at how much they ate during the test, not their ratings of taste. People who expected to go on a diet ate more than the group that didn't but *only* if they were "restrained eaters" who were continually attempting to restrict their intake of food, particularly fattening food. Thus, attempts to restrict intake may put people at risk for bingeing. Polivy and Herman's most recent work focuses on the more general negative psychological impacts of dieting, such as low self-esteem, food preoccupation, and negative mood—a phenomenon they have labelled the "false hope syndrome" (e.g., Polivy, 2001; Polivy & Herman, 2002b). In brief, this perspective asserts that people's false hopes about self-change attempts are initially strongly reinforced. Recall the praise that Julie received from her friends and her mother when she first started to lose weight. Unfortunately, the positive feelings and sense of control that people feel with their initial successes at self-change lead them to continue to pursue unrealistic or even impossible goals for weight loss that ultimately result in extreme disappointment and a decline in self-esteem.

The conflict over body image would be bad enough if size were infinitely malleable, but it is not. Increasing evidence indicates a strong genetic contribution to body size (e.g., Rutherford, McGuffin, Katz, & Murray, 1993); that is, some of us are born to be heavier than others, and we are all shaped differently. Although most of us can be physically fit, few can achieve the levels of fitness and shape so highly valued today. It is biologically nearly impossible (Brownell, 1991; Brownell & Fairburn, 2002). Nevertheless, many young people in our society fight biology to the point of starvation. In adolescence, cultural standards are often experienced as peer pressure and are much more influential than reason and fact. The high number of males who are homosexual among the relatively small numbers of males with eating disorders has also been attributed to pressures in the gay culture to be physically trim (Carlat et al., 1997). Conversely, pressure to appear more fit and muscular are also apparent for a substantial proportion of men (Pope et al., 2000).

## Dietary Restraint

As mentioned previously, those with eating disorders tend to display a strong preoccupation with food. We have known since the 1950s that long-term dieting can cause preoccupation with food (e.g., hoarding food, collecting recipes; see Keys, Brozek, Henschel, Michelson, & Taylor, 1950). More recent studies using experimental cognitive tasks have confirmed this relationship of dieting to food preoccupations. Several studies have shown that chronic dieters pay more attention to information about food than to other types of information (e.g., Francis, Stewart, & Hounsell, 1997; Stewart & Samoluk, 1997). Chronic dieters also appear to remember information better when it pertains to food (Israeli & Stewart, 2001). These attentional and memory biases favouring information about food are consistent with the possibility that chronic dieting causes a preoccupation with food and eating, which in turn could contribute to binge eating.

If cultural pressures to be thin are as important as they seem to be in triggering eating disorders, then such disorders would be expected to occur where these pressures are particularly severe, which is just what happens to ballet dancers, who are under extraordinary pressures to be thin. In an important study, Garner, Garfinkel, Rockert, and Olmsted (1987) followed a group of 11- to 14-year-old female students in an internationally acclaimed ballet school in Toronto. Their conservative estimate was that at least 25% of these girls developed eating disorders during the 2 years of the study. In another study, Szmukler, Eisler, Gillis, and Haywood (1985) examined 100 adolescent female ballet students in London, England. Fully 7% were diagnosed with anorexia nervosa, and an additional 3% were borderline cases. Another 20% had lost a significant amount of weight, and 30% were clearly afraid of becoming fat, although they were below normal weight (Garner & Garfinkel, 1985). All these figures are much higher than in the population as a whole.

Similar results are apparent among athletes, particularly females, such as gymnasts, figure skaters, and tennis players (Davis & Strachan, 2001). For example, in a recent study of 41 female Canadian competitive figure skaters, Gail Taylor and Diane Ste-Marie (2001) of the University of Ottawa found that all of the figure skaters had used weight control measures at some point in their lives. About 93% reported that they perceived weight-loss pressures to be associated with the sport of figure skating (Taylor & Ste-Marie, 2001).

The case of Canadian female tennis player Carling Bassett illustrates how weight-loss pressures in competitive athletics can serve as triggers for an eating disorder. Bassett was Canada's leading female tennis player in the 1980s and was inducted into Canada's Sports Hall of Fame. She experienced a 3-year bout of bulimia, which she developed as a teenager while she was competing professionally. "At 15, I wasn't heavy by any means," she told a reporter, "but I gained a lot of weight; I went from 111 to 126 [pounds; 51 to 57 kilograms]. At 14, 15, 16…you want to look good all the time. You start feeling pressure" (Neill & Sider, 1992).

Bassett was introduced to self-induced vomiting as a weight control strategy at age 16 by an older female tennis player. She said about purging: "It's so easy to get into and so hard to get out of. I hated myself that I couldn't stop." Her mother recalls the negative impact the eating disorder had on Bassett and her family: "She became skeletal. You'd try to force food on her, and she'd just throw up. We screamed and yelled." Bassett kept her eating disorder hidden from other tennis players, even from her husband, tennis star Robert Seguso, until her symptoms because so disruptive that she attempted recovery with Seguso's help (Neill & Sider, 1992).

What goes on in ballet classes or competitive sports that has such a devastating effect on girls? Consider the case of Phoebe again.

## Phoebe
### Dancing to Destruction

Phoebe remembered clearly that during her early years in ballet the older girls talked incessantly about their weight. Phoebe performed very well and looked forward to the rare compliment. In fact, the ballet mistress seemed to comment more on weight than on dance technique, often remarking, "You'd dance better if you lost weight." If one little girl managed to lose a kilogram through heroic dieting, the instructor always pointed it out: "You've done well working on your weight; the rest of you had better follow this example." One day, without warning, the instructor said to Phoebe, "You need to lose 3 kilograms before the next class." At that time Phoebe was 157 centimetres (5 feet 2 inches) tall and weighed 44 kilograms (98 pounds). The next class was in 2 days. After one of these admonitions and several days of restrictive eating, Phoebe experienced her first uncontrollable binge.

Early in high school, Phoebe gave up the rigours of ballet to pursue a variety of other interests. She did not forget the glory of her starring roles as a young dancer or how to perform the steps. She still danced from time to time by herself and retained the grace that

serious dancers effortlessly display. But in university, as she stuck her head in the toilet bowl, vomiting her guts out for perhaps the third time that day, she realized there was one lesson she had learned in ballet class more deeply and thoroughly than any other—the life-or-death importance of being thin at all costs.

As Phoebe's case shows, dieting is one factor that can contribute to eating disorders (Polivy & Herman, 2002a).

### Family Influences

Much has been made of the possible significance of family interaction patterns in cases of eating disorders. A number of investigators (e.g., Attie & Brooks-Gunn, 1995; Bruch, 1985; Humphrey, 1986, 1988, 1989; Minuchin, Rosman, & Baker, 1978) have found that the "typical" family of someone with anorexia is successful, hard-driving, concerned about external appearances, and eager to maintain harmony. To accomplish these goals, family members often deny or ignore conflicts or negative feelings and tend to attribute their problems to other people at the expense of frank communication among themselves (Fairburn et al., 1999a; Hsu, 1990).

Pike and Rodin (1991) confirmed the differences in interactions within the families of girls with disordered eating in comparison with control families. Basically, mothers of girls with disordered eating seemed to act as "society's messengers" in wanting their daughters to be thin (Steinberg & Phares, 2001). They were likely to be dieting themselves and, generally, were more perfectionistic than control mothers in that they were less satisfied with their families and family cohesion (Fairburn et al., 1997, 1999a). A study by D. Blake Woodside and his colleagues (2002) reported similar findings from data collected in the international Price Foundation family study of eating disorders. Participants were recruited from London, Los Angeles, Munich, New York, Philadelphia, Pittsburgh, and Toronto. Mothers of those girls with eating disorders showed elevated levels of perfectionism and more concerns about weight and shape than did the controls (Woodside et al., 2002). Other family studies by Howard Steiger and colleagues demonstrated that a link exists between the abnormal eating attitudes of daughters and their mothers (Steiger, Stotland, Trottier, & Ghadirian, 1996) and that family preoccupation with appearance had a direct influence on body dissatisfaction and eating disorder symptoms (Leung, Schwartzman, & Steiger, 1996).

Lynn Carpenter is the mother of the late Sheena Carpenter—a young anorexic woman who died of starvation in Toronto at age 22. Lynn has candidly spoken about the role of parents' attitudes toward weight and shape inadvertently triggering eating disorder behaviours in their children. Sheena had wanted to be a model or an actress. When she died, she weighed only 23 kilograms (50 pounds). In an interview, Lynn talked about the role she believes she had in initiating her daughter's illness: "Sheena didn't stand a chance. I always had body issues, so she grew up with me always griping about my cellulite. Always negative." These messages about the importance of being thin reportedly had an effect on Sheena quite early in life. Lynn recalled an event that took place when Sheena was only 6 years old. On a hot summer day, Lynn found Sheena dressed in a snowsuit and doing jumping jacks. "Look Mom," Sheena said, "This way I won't put on any weight" (Strobel, 2002). But Lynn Carpenter was not the sole messenger in relaying society's message about the importance of low body weight to her daughter. Apparently when Sheena was 14 years old, a modelling agency told her a thinner face would make her more photogenic. Sheena Carpenter's tragic story led to her mother establishing a refuge in Toronto called Sheena's Place, which offers support programs and group sessions to women with eating disorders. Canadian singer Anne Murray, whose daughter, Dawn Langstroth, has also struggled with anorexia, is the honorary director of Sheena's Place (Strobel, 2002).

Whatever the preexisting relationships, after the onset of an eating disorder, particularly anorexia, family relationships can deteriorate quickly. Nothing is more frustrating than watching your daughter starve herself at a dinner table where food is plentiful. Educated and knowledgeable parents, including psychologists and psychiatrists with full understanding of the disorder at hand, have reported resorting to physical violence (e.g., hitting or slapping) in moments of extreme frustration, in a vain attempt to get their daughters to put some food, however little, in their mouths. The parents' guilt and anguish, so evident in the interview with Lynn Carpenter (Strobel, 2002), often exceed the levels of anxiety and depression present in the children with the disorder.

## Biological Dimensions

Like most psychological disorders, eating disorders run in families and thus seem to have a genetic component (Strober, 2002). Although completed studies are only preliminary, they suggest that relatives of patients with eating disorders are four to five times more likely than the general population to develop eating disorders themselves, with the risks for female relatives of patients with anorexia a bit higher (e.g., Hudson, Pope, Jonas, & Yurgelun-Todd,

1983; Strober, Freeman, Lampert, Diamond, & Kaye, 2000; Strober & Humphrey, 1987). In important twin studies of bulimia by Kendler and colleagues (1991) and of anorexia by Walters and Kendler (1995), researchers used structured interviews to ascertain the prevalence of the disorders among 2163 female twins. In 23% of identical twin pairs, both twins had bulimia, as compared with 9% of fraternal twins. Because no adoption studies have yet been reported, strong sociocultural influences cannot be ruled out, and other studies have produced inconsistent results (Fairburn, Cowen, & Harrison, 1999b). For anorexia, numbers were too small for precise estimates, but the disorder in one twin did seem to confer a significant risk for both anorexia and bulimia in the co-twin.

An emerging consensus is that genetic makeup is about half of the equation among causes of anorexia and bulimia (Klump, Kaye, & Strober, 2001; Wade, Bulik, Neale, & Kendler, 2000; Strober, 2002). Again, there is no clear agreement on just *what* is inherited (Fairburn et al., 1999b). Hsu (1990) speculates that non-specific personality traits such as emotional instability and, perhaps, poor impulse control might be inherited. In other words, a person might inherit a tendency to be emotionally responsive to stressful life events and, as one consequence, might eat impulsively in an attempt to relieve stress and anxiety (Strober, 2002). Data from Kendler et al. (1995) would support this interpretation. Klump et al. (2001) mention perfectionist traits with negative affect. This biological vulnerability might then interact with social and psychological factors to produce an eating disorder.

A twin study by Toronto-based psychologist Randy Katz and his colleagues in London, England, suggests that some symptoms of eating disorders may themselves have a partially genetic basis. In a community-recruited sample of 147 identical and 99 fraternal female twin pairs, they estimated that body dissatisfaction is 52% heritable, drive for thinness is 44% heritable, and dieting tendencies are 42% heritable. The rest of the variance in these eating disordered behaviours and attitudes is attributable to environmental influences (Rutherford et al., 1993).

Obviously, biological processes are active in the regulation of eating and thus of eating disorders, and substantial evidence points to the hypothalamus as playing an important role. Investigators have studied the hypothalamus and the major neurotransmitter systems—including norepinephrine, dopamine, and, particularly, serotonin—that pass through it to determine whether something is malfunctioning when eating disorders occur (Vitiella & Lederhendler, 2000). Low levels of serotonergic activity are associated with impulsivity in general and binge eating specifically (see Chapter 2). Thus, most drugs currently under study as treatments for bulimia target the serotonin system (e.g., de Zwaan, Roerig, & Mitchell, 2004; Garfinkel, 2002; Kaye et al., 1998; Walsh et al., 1997).

Some interesting research also points to the role of exercise in causing or maintaining anorexia nervosa. Recall the case of Julie, who also reported having "lost all taste for food." According to the work of John Pinel and his colleagues at the University of British Columbia, Julie and other anorexics differ from most people who are starving because food lacks "positive incentive value" for them in terms of their desire to actually eat it (Pinel, Assanand, & Lehman, 2000). According to W. Frank Epling and W. David Pierce, Julie's reported loss of positive incentive to eat can be explained by the fact that she was exercising excessively—completing a workout videotape after every meal. These researchers describe a phenomenon they refer to as "activity anorexia" (see Chapter 3), where excessive physical activity can paradoxically cause a loss of appetite (Epling & Pierce, 1992; Pierce & Epling, 1996) for reasons that are not yet well understood.

If investigators find a strong association between neurobiological functions and eating disorders, the question of cause or effect remains. At present, the consensus is that some neurobiological abnormalities exist in people with eating disorders, but they are a *result* of semistarvation or a binge–purge cycle rather than a cause, although they may contribute to the *maintenance* of the disorder once it is established.

## Psychological Dimensions

Clinical observations indicate that many young women with eating disorders have a diminished sense of personal control and confidence in their own abilities and talents (Bruch, 1973, 1985; Striegel-Moore, Silberstein, & Rodin, 1993; Walters & Kendler, 1995). This may be manifested as strikingly low self-esteem (Fairburn, Cooper, & Shafran, 2003). They also display more perfectionistic attitudes, learned, perhaps, from their families, which may reflect attempts to exert control over important events in their lives (Fairburn et al., 1997, 1999a; Joiner, Heatherton, & Keel, 1997; Woodside et al., 2002). Canadian psychologist Todd Heatherton and his colleagues have noted that people with anorexia nervosa and bulimia nervosa share perfectionistic traits, and those traits likely play a crucial role in their eating disorder (Heatherton & Baumeister, 1991; see also Davis, 1997; Goldner, Cockell, & Srikameswaran, 2002; Hewitt, Flett, & Ediger, 1995; Pliner & Haddock, 1996). However, perfectionism alone is only weakly associated with the development of an eating disorder, because individuals must

first consider themselves overweight and manifest low self-esteem before the trait of perfectionism makes a contribution (Vohs, Bardone, Joiner, Abramson, & Heatherton, 1999). But when perfectionism is directed to distorted perception of body image, a powerful engine to drive eating disorder behaviour is in place (Shafran, Cooper, & Fairburn, 2002). Women with eating disorders are intensely preoccupied with how they appear to others (Fairburn, et al., 2003). They also perceive themselves as frauds, considering false any impressions they make of being adequate, self-sufficient, or worthwhile. In this sense they feel like impostors in their social groups and experience heightened levels of social anxiety (Smolak & Levine, 1996). Striegel-Moore and colleagues (1993) suggest these social self-deficits are likely to increase as a consequence of the eating disorder, further isolating the woman from the social world.

Specific distortions in perception of body shape change frequently, depending on day-to-day experience. McKenzie, Williamson, and Cubic (1993) found that bulimic women judged their body size to be larger and their ideal weight to be less than same-size controls. Indeed, women with bulimia judged that their bodies were larger after they ate a candy bar and drank a soft drink, whereas the judgments of women in control groups were unaffected by snacks. Thus, rather minor events related to eating may activate fear of gaining weight, further distortions in body image, and corrective schemes such as purging.

Rosen and Leitenberg (1985) observed substantial anxiety before and during snacks, which they theorized is *relieved* by purging. They suggested the state of relief strongly reinforces the purging, in that we tend to repeat behaviour that gives us pleasure or relief from anxiety. This seemed to be true for Phoebe. One method of reducing the anxiety associated with eating that motivates purging is binge exposure with response prevention. In this treatment the client who has an eating disorder is repeatedly exposed to her preferred binge food (e.g., chips, ice cream) and each time she is prevented from binge eating and purging. This technique has been shown to be successful in reducing urges to binge, lack of control, feelings of guilt, and feelings of anxiety for women with bulimia nervosa and anorexia nervosa, binge-purge subtype (Kennedy, Katz, Neitzert, Ralevski, & Medlowitz, 1995). However, other evidence suggests that in treating bulimia, reducing the anxiety associated with eating is less important than countering the tendency to overly restrict food intake and the associated negative attitudes about body image that lead to bingeing and purging (e.g., Agras, Schneider, Arnow, Raeburn, & Telch, 1989; Fairburn, Agras, & Wilson, 1992; Wilson & Pike, 2001).

## An Integrative Model

Although the three major eating disorders are identifiable by their unique characteristics, and the specific diagnoses have some validity, it is becoming increasingly clear that all eating disorders have much in common in terms of causal factors. It may be more useful to lump the eating disorders into one diagnostic category, simply noting which specific features such as dietary restraint, bingeing, or purging occur. Recently, Fairburn and colleagues have attempted to develop this approach (e.g., Fairburn et al., 2003). Thus, we have integrated a discussion of the causes of eating disorders.

In putting together what we know about eating disorders, it is important to remember, once again,

that no one factor seems sufficient to cause them (see Figure 8.4). Individuals with eating disorders may have some of the same biological vulnerabilities (such as being highly responsive to stressful life events) as individuals with anxiety disorders (Kendler et al., 1995). Anxiety and mood disorders are also common in the families of individuals with eating disorders (Schwalberg et al., 1992), and negative emotions and "mood intolerance" seem to trigger binge eating in many patients (Davis et al., 1988; Polivy & Herman, 1993). In addition, as we will see, drug and psychological treatments with proven effectiveness for anxiety disorders are the treatments of choice for eating disorders. Indeed, we could conceptualize eating disorders as anxiety disorders focused exclusively on a fear of becoming overweight.

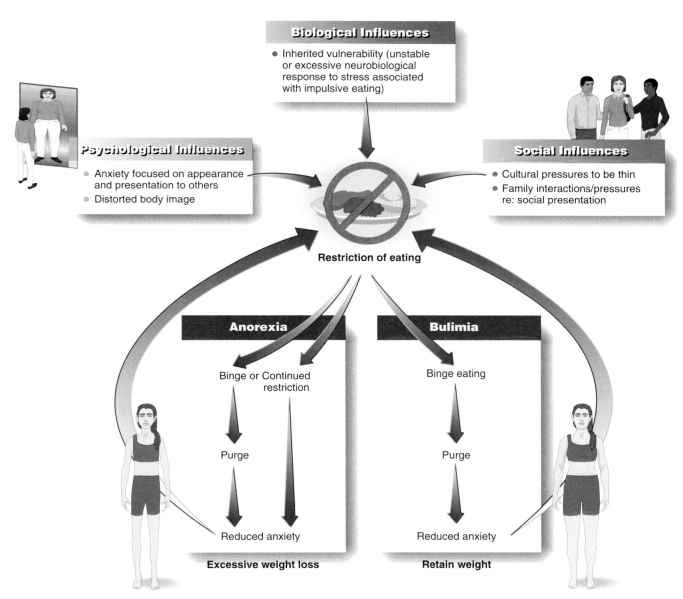

**Figure 8.4** ▪ An integrative causal model of eating disorders.

In any case, it is clear that social and cultural pressures to be thin motivate significant restriction of eating, usually through severe dieting. Remember, however, that many people go on strict diets, including adolescent females, but only a small minority develop eating disorders, so dieting alone does not account for the disorders. It is also important to note that the interactions in high-income, high-achieving families may be a factor. An emphasis on looks and achievement, and perfectionistic tendencies, may help establish strong attitudes about the overriding importance of physical appearance to popularity and success. These attitudes result in an exaggerated focus on body shape and weight. Finally, there is the question of why a small minority of individuals with eating disorders can successfully control their intake through dietary restraint, resulting in alarming weight loss (anorexia), whereas the majority are unsuccessful at losing weight and compensate in a cycle of bingeing and purging (bulimia), although most individuals with anorexia go on to bingeing and purging at some point (Eddy et al., 2002). These differences, at least initially, may be determined by biology or physiology, such as a genetically determined disposition to be somewhat thinner to begin with. Then again, perhaps pre-existing personality characteristics, such as a tendency to be overcontrolling or to act impulsively, are important determinants of which disorder a girl develops—anorexia nervosa or bulimia nervosa, respectively (Goldner, Srikameswaran, Schroeder, Livesly, & Birmingham, 1999; Polivy & Herman, 2002a).

# Treatment of Eating Disorders

■ *Compare the use of medications with psychological therapies for the treatment of eating disorders.*

Only since the 1980s have there been treatments for bulimia; treatments for anorexia have been around much longer but were poorly developed. Rapidly accumulating evidence indicates that at least one, and possibly two, psychological treatments are effective, particularly for bulimia nervosa. Certain drugs may also help, although the evidence is not so strong.

## Drug Treatments

At present, drug treatments have not been found to be effective in the treatment of anorexia nervosa (e.g., Attia, Haiman, Walsh, & Flater, 1998; de Zwann et al., 2004; Garner & Needleman, 1996; Kruger & Kennedy, 2000; Vitiello & Lederhendler, 2000; Wilson & Fairburn, 2002), although one small study suggested that Prozac might be effective in preventing relapse after weight has been restored (Kaye et al., 2001). On the other hand, there is some evidence that drugs may be useful in some cases of bulimia. The drugs generally considered the most effective for bulimia are the same antidepressant medications proven effective for mood disorders and anxiety disorders (Kaye, Strober, Stein, & Gendall, 1999; Walsh et al., 1997; Wilson et al., 1999; Wilson & Fairburn, 2002). The U.S. Food and Drug Administration in 1996 approved Prozac as effective for eating disorders. Effectiveness is usually measured by reductions in the frequency of binge eating and by the percentage of patients who stop binge eating and purging, at least for a period of time. In two studies, one of tricyclic antidepressant drugs and the other of fluoxetine (Prozac), researchers found the average *reduction* in binge eating and purging was, respectively, 47% and 65% (Walsh, 1991; Walsh, Hadigan, Devlin, Gladis, & Roose, 1991). However, although antidepressants are more effective than placebo in the short term, the available evidence suggests that, pending further evaluation, antidepressant drugs alone do not have substantial long-lasting effects on bulimia nervosa (Walsh, 1995; Wilson & Fairburn, 2002). Nonetheless, research by Maureen Whittal at the University of British Columbia, and her colleagues, suggests that antidepressants show promise in enhancing the effects of psychological treatment (Whittal, Agras, & Gould, 1999).

## Psychological Treatments

Until the 1980s, psychological treatments were directed at the patient's low self-esteem and difficulties in developing an individual identity. Disordered patterns of family interaction and communication were also targeted for treatment. However, these treatments alone did not have the effectiveness that clinicians hoped they might (e.g., Minuchin et al., 1978; Russell, Szmukler, Dare, & Eisler, 1987). Short-term cognitive-behavioural treatments target

nd associated attitudes
...ce and significance of
...these strategies have
...e for bulimia (Wilson
... & Loeb, 2004).

...treatment approach
...ologist Christopher
...age is teaching the
...nces of binge eating
...effectiveness of vom-
...weight control. The
...e also described, and
...t small, manageable
...imes per day with no
...between any planned
...inates the alternating
...ary restriction that are
...er stages of treatment,
...altering dysfunctional
...t body shape, weight,
...gies for resisting the
...ge are also developed,
...s so that the individual
...after eating during the
...(Fairburn, Marcus, &
...irburn, & Davis, 1987;
...aluations of short-term
...s) cognitive-behavioural
...ave been good, showing
...le alternative treatments
...purging but also for dis-
...companying depression.
...s seem to last (Whittal et
...itousek, Wilson, & Bauer,
...r, Glass, & Westen, 2003),
...number of patients who
...r do not benefit.
...refully conducted study,
...er, Hope, and O'Connor
...ee different treatments.
...*herapy* (CBT) focused on
...*nd* changing attitudes about
...*aviour therapy* (BT) focused
...g habits; and *interpersonal*
...used on improving interper-
...patients receiving CBT, both
...g declined by more than 90%
...addition, 36% of the patients
...ating and purging; the others
...des. Attitudes toward body
...improved. These results were
...an the results from BT. Even
...he finding that IPT did as well
...follow-up, although CBT was
...assessment immediately after

treatment was completed. This result indicates that IPT caught up with CBT in terms of effectiveness by the end of the 1-year follow-up. This is particularly interesting because IPT does not concentrate directly on disordered eating patterns or dysfunctional attitudes about eating but rather on improving interpersonal functioning and reducing interpersonal conflict, a focus that may, in turn, promote changes in eating habits and attitudes. Both treatments were more effective than BT. Patients in the two effective treatments had retained their gains at a 6-year follow-up (Fairburn et al., 1995; see Figure 8.5). Very similar results were found in a study by Agras, Walsh, Fairburn, Wilson, and Kraemer (2000), comparing the effectiveness of CBT and IPT in the treatment of bulimia nervosa.

The investigators conclude that CBT is the preferred psychological treatment for bulimia nervosa because it works significantly faster. Nevertheless, it is intriguing that IPT was almost as effective after 1 year even though this treatment does not concentrate directly on the disordered eating patterns but rather on the interpersonal relationships of the patient. Clearly, we need to understand much more about how to improve such treatments to deal more

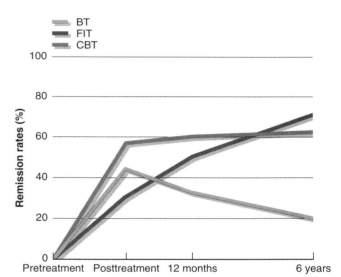

**Figure 8.5** ■ Remission rates (i.e., proportion not meeting DSM-IV criteria for eating disorder) in patients who received cognitive-behavioural therapy (CBT) (*n* = 35), behaviour therapy (BT) (*n* = 22), or focal interpersonal therapy (FIT) (*n* = 32). Mean (±SD) length of follow-up was 5.8 ± 2.0 years. (From "Psychotherapy and Bulimia Nervosa: The Longer-Term Effects of Interpersonal Psychotherapy, Behaviour Therapy and Cognitive Behaviour Therapy," by C. G. Fairburn, R. Jones, R. C. Peveler, R. A. Hope, and M. O'Connor, 1993, *Archives of General Psychiatry, 50,* 419–428. Copyright © 1993 by the American Medical Association. Reprinted by permission.)

successfully with the growing number of patients with eating disorders.

Many programs for eating disorders in Canada (e.g., Toronto, Halifax) rely on both CBT and IPT techniques. In fact, not only is integration of these two treatment modalities quite commonplace, but data also support the effectiveness of combined CBT and IPT in the treatment of women with eating problems. For example, a study conducted in Australia in two clinical settings showed that women with eating disorders who completed a 10-week integrated CBT/IPT program were significantly improved on most measures of eating pathology and general psychopathology at the end of treatment and at follow-up, relative to those women on a waiting list (Crafti, 2002).

## Phoebe
### Taking Control

During her second year in university, Phoebe entered a short-term CBT program. She made good progress during the first several months and worked carefully to eat regularly and gain control over her eating. She also made sure that she was with somebody during her high-risk times and planned alternative activities that would reduce her temptation to purge if she felt she had eaten too much at a restaurant or drunk too much beer at a party. During the first 2 months Phoebe had three slips, and she and her therapist discussed what led to her temporary relapse. Much to Phoebe's surprise, she did not gain weight on this program, even though she did not have time to increase her exercise. Nevertheless, she still was preoccupied with food, was concerned about her weight and appearance, and had strong urges to vomit if she thought she had overeaten the slightest amount.

During the 9 months following treatment, Phoebe reported that her urges seemed to decrease somewhat, although she had one major slip after eating a big pizza and drinking a lot of beer. She reported that she was thoroughly disgusted with herself for purging, and she was careful to return to her program after this episode. Two years after finishing treatment, Phoebe reported that her urges to vomit had disappeared, a report confirmed by her parents. All that remained of her problem were some bad but increasingly vague and distant memories.

Another variant of CBT, developed by Ron Davis of Lakehead University and his colleagues in Toronto, is brief group psychoeducation for bulimia nervosa. The main goal of psychoeducation is to help bulimic individuals normalize their eating and reduce their body image disturbance. This goal is achieved through providing them with information relevant to bulimia nervosa and with useful strategies such as meal planning, problem solving, and self-monitoring. The main differences from CBT are that psychoeducation is briefer, is delivered in a lecture-type format, and is not tailored to the unique needs of individual patients (Davis & Olmsted, 1992). Research has shown this approach to be better than a wait-list control in helping bulimic individuals reduce their symptoms (Davis, Olmsted, & Rockert, 1990). The intervention is particularly effective for those with less severe bulimia (Davis, Olmsted, & Rockert, 1992). Nonetheless, improvements in bulimia are even better when the psychoeducation approach is followed by 16 weeks of CBT than when patients receive the psychoeducation alone (Davis, McVey, Heinmaa, Rockert, & Kennedy, 1999).

Short-term treatments for eating disorders, although clearly effective for many, are no panacea. Indeed, some people do not benefit at all from either brief psychoeducation or short-term CBT. Evidence now suggests that combining drugs with psychosocial treatments might boost the overall outcome, at least in the short term (Whittal et al., 1999; Wilson et al., 1999). In the largest study to date (Walsh et al., 1997), CBT was significantly superior to supportive psychotherapy (in which the therapist is understanding and sympathetic and encourages patients to achieve their goals) in the treatment of bulimia nervosa; adding two antidepressant medications to CBT, including an SSRI, modestly increased the benefit of CBT. But CBT remains the preferred treatment for bulimia, and it is superior to medication alone (Wilson & Fairburn, 2002). There is also evidence that people who do not respond to CBT might benefit from IPT methods (Fairburn, Jones, et al., 1993; Klerman, Weissman, Rounsaville, & Chevron, 1984) or from antidepressant medication (Walsh et al., 2000).

Both private and public eating disorder treatment centres and clinics can be found across Canada (e.g., Halifax, Montreal, Toronto, Vancouver). Programs at many of these centres and clinics are world renowned for the quality of services they provide as well as for the important research they contribute in terms of understanding, preventing, and treating eating disorders. Most of these centres and clinics provide combinations of psychoeducation, psychotherapy (e.g., CBT and IPT), and

their clients with
are staffed by multi-
ychologists, psychia-
upational therapists,
om has unique skills
le with eating disor-

92) adapted CBTs for
, and the preliminary
their study, the fre-
educed by an average
tients abstinent from
atment. Agras, Telch,
rnell (1997) followed
D for 1 year and found
nent, 41% of the partic-
ng and 72% binged less
e eating was reduced by
p remained abstinent.
d stopped binge eating
weight loss of approxi-
nds) over the follow-up
nued to binge gained
(8 pounds). Thus, stop-
cal to sustaining weight
finding consistent with
oss procedures (Marcus,
Iarcus et al., 1990; Telch,
n contrast to results with
PT is as effective as CBT
et al., 2002). Finally, one
hat an antiobesity drug,
that reduces feelings of
ive than placebo for BED

rs that self-help procedures
atment of BED (e.g., Loeb,
uvie, 2000; Peterson et al.,
er of the Toronto Hospital
opher Fairburn to conduct
of this approach (Carter &
andomly assigned 72 females
-help group in which partic-
uiled their manual, a guided
rapists would meet with the
s they read the manual, or a
. Fifty percent of the guided
% of the pure self-help group
ng versus 8% of the wait-list
e improvements were main-
follow-up. If further studies
gs, then a self-help approach
e first treatment offered before
xpensive and time-consuming
nts.

## Anorexia Nervosa

In anorexia, of course, the most important initial goal is to restore the patient's weight to a point that is at least within the low-normal range (American Psychiatric Association, 1993). If body weight is below 70% of the average or if weight has been lost very rapidly, inpatient treatment would be recommended (American Psychiatric Association, 1993; Casper, 1982) because severe medical complications, particularly acute cardiac failure, could occur if weight restoration is not begun immediately. If the weight loss has been more gradual and seems to have stabilized, weight restoration can be accomplished on an outpatient basis.

Restoring weight is probably the easiest part of treatment. Clinicians who treat patients in different settings, as reported in a variety of studies, find that at least 85% will be able to gain weight. The gain is often as much as one-quarter to half a kilogram (a half-pound to a pound) a day until weight is within the normal range. Typical strategies used with inpatients are outlined in Table 8.1. Knowing they can leave the hospital when their weight gain is adequate is often sufficient to motivate young women

---

**TABLE 8.1** Strategies to Attain Weight Gain

1. Weight restoration occurs with other treatments, such as individual and family therapy, so that the patient does not feel that eating and weight gain are the only goals of treatment.
2. The patient trusts the treatment team and believes that she will not be allowed to become overweight.
3. The patient's fear of loss of control is contained; this may be accomplished by having her eat frequent, smaller meals (e.g., four to six times per day, with 400 to 500 calories per meal) to produce a gradual but steady weight gain (e.g., an average of 0.2 kg/day).
4. A member of the nursing staff is present during mealtimes to encourage the patient to eat and to discuss her fears and anxiety about eating and weight gain.
5. Gradual weight gain rather than the amount of food eaten is regularly monitored, and the result is made known to the patient; thus, the patient should be weighed at regular intervals, and she should know whether she has gained or lost weight.
6. Some negative and positive reinforcements exist, such as the use of graduated level of activity and bed rest, whether or not these reinforcements are formally conceptualized as behaviour modification techniques, so that the patient may thereby learn that she can control not only her behaviour but also the consequence of her behaviour.
7. The patient's self-defeating behaviour, such as surreptitious vomiting or purging, is confronted and controlled.
8. The dysfunctional conflict between the patient and the family about eating and food is not reenacted in the hospital; if the pattern is to be reenacted in a therapeutic lunch session, the purpose is clearly defined.

*Source:* From L. K. G. Hsu, *Eating disorders,* 136. Copyright © 1990 by Guilford Press. Reprinted by permission.

(Agras, Barlow, Chapin, Abel, & Leitenberg, 1974). Julie gained about 18 pounds during her 5-week hospital stay.

Then the difficult stage begins. As Hsu (1988) and others have demonstrated, initial weight gain is a poor predictor of long-term outcome in anorexia. Without attention to the patient's underlying dysfunctional attitudes about body shape and interpersonal disruptions in her life, she will almost always relapse. For restricting anorexics, the focus of treatment must shift to their marked anxiety over becoming obese and losing control of eating, as well as to their undue emphasis on thinness as a determinant of self-worth, happiness, and success. In this regard, effective treatments for restricting anorexics are similar to those for patients with bulimia nervosa (Fairburn, Shafran, & Cooper, 1999; Pike, Loeb, & Vitousek, 1996; Vitousek, Watson, & Wilson, 1998). In a recent study (Pike et al., 2003) extended (1-year) outpatient CBT was significantly better than continued nutritional counselling, with only 22% failing (relapsing or dropping out) with CBT versus 73% failing with nutritional counselling.

Recent research highlights the importance of assessing clients with eating disorders' readiness for change since patients with anorexia nervosa are often difficult to treat (Goldner, 1989). New interventions derived from those used in the treatment of substance use disorders (see Chapter 10), are being developed that focus on enhancing the patient's motivation to change (see Kaplan & Garfinkel, 1999). For example, a study by Joanne Gusella and her colleagues at the IWK Health Centre in Halifax administered a motivational measure to 34 adolescents with eating disorders before the commencement of an eating disorders group. Those girls who reported being more ready to change at treatment outset showed greater improvements in their eating disorders symptoms over the course of the group. The group also assisted the girls in earlier stages of change to be more ready to change by the end of the group (Gusella, Butler, Nichols, & Bird, 2003). A similar study by Josie Geller at the St. Paul's Hospital Eating Disorders Program in Vancouver examined motivation to change in 56 adult women with anorexia. Like the findings in Gusella's study, Geller (2002) found that anorexic patients who were at a more advanced stage of readiness to change were more likely to complete assigned behavioural recovery activities (e.g., increasing caloric intake) and to accept intensive treatment for their anorexia. Given the clear importance of motivation to change in recovery from anorexia, new treatments that target motivational enhancement are promising innovations in eating disorders treatment (Kaplan & Garfinkel, 1999).

In addition, every effort is made to include the family to accomplish two goals. First, the negative and dysfunctional communication regarding food and eating must be eliminated and meals must be made more structured and reinforcing. Second, attitudes toward body shape and image distortion are discussed at some length in family sessions. Unless the therapist attends to these attitudes, individuals with anorexia are likely to face a lifetime preoccupation with weight and body shape, struggle to maintain marginal weight and social adjustment, and be subject to repeated hospitalization. Family therapy seems effective, particularly with young girls (younger than 19 years of age) with a short history of the disorder (Eisler et al., 1997). Recent research by a team at the Hospital for Sick Children in Toronto showed that a substantially less costly family group psychoeducation approach was just as effective as a more traditional family therapy approach in assisting hospitalized adolescents with anorexia and their families, at least in the short term (Geist, Heinmaa, Stephens, Davis, & Katzman, 2000). Nevertheless, the long-term results of treatment for anorexia are more discouraging than for bulimia, with substantially lower rates of full recovery than for bulimia over a 7.5-year period (Herzog et al., 1999).

Probably one of the most talked-about stories of the treatment of anorexia nervosa in Canadian history involves the Montreux clinic—an expensive and exclusive private clinic for women and adolescents with anorexia nervosa in Victoria, British Columbia. Montreux was directed by Peggy Claude-Pierre, a mother who had helped her own two teenage daughters overcome eating disorders. Claude-Pierre received a good deal of media attention, including interviews by Oprah Winfrey and Pamela Wallin, given her claims of a striking 90% recovery rate for clinic patients and the message of hope contained in her reported treatment philosophy of unconditional love.

The clinic came under investigation when a former employee made allegations that the staff was inadequately trained and the clients not properly screened. More serious allegations were made that the clients were being force-fed and held against their will. Although, as we mentioned earlier, it is essential for very emaciated patients with anorexia to be hospitalized to prevent potentially severe medical complications, these clients were admitted to Montreux with no medical supervision. In fact, the director, Claude-Pierre, did not have a graduate degree in psychology or any medical training. In spite of strong protests from her supporters, the residential clinic was eventually closed in December 1999 on the order of the local health officer (Dineen, 2002; McLintock, 2002).

## Preventing Eating Disorders

Attempts are being made to prevent the development of eating disorders. If successful methods are confirmed, they will be important because many cases of eating disorders are resistant to treatment and most individuals who do not receive treatment suffer for many years, in some cases all of their lives (Keel, Mitchell, Miller, Davis, & Crow, 1999; Killen, 1996; Herzog et al., 1999). The development of eating disorders during adolescence is a risk factor for a variety of additional disorders during adulthood, including cardiovascular symptoms, chronic fatigue and infectious diseases, and anxiety and mood disorders (Johnson, Cohen, Kasen, & Brook, 2002). Before implementing a prevention program, however, it is necessary to target specific behaviours to change. Killen et al. (1994) conducted a prospective analysis of a sample of 887 young adolescent girls. Over a 3-year interval, 32 girls, or 3.6% of the sample, developed symptoms of eating disorders.

Early concern about being overweight was the most powerful predictive factor of later symptoms. The instrument used to measure weight concerns is presented in Table 8.2. Girls who scored high on this scale (an average score of 58) were at substantial risk for developing serious symptoms. Killen et al. (1996) then evaluated a prevention program on 967 girls from 11 to 13 years of age in grade 6 and grade 7. Half the girls were put on the intervention program and the other half were not. The program emphasized that female weight gain after puberty is normal and that excessive caloric restriction could actually cause increased gain. The interesting results were that the intervention had relatively little effect on the treatment group as a whole compared with the control group. But for those girls at high risk for developing eating disorders (as reflected by a high score on the scale in Table 8.2), the program significantly reduced weight concerns (Killen, 1996; Killen et al., 1994). The authors conclude from this preliminary study that the most cost-effective preventive approach would be to carefully screen 11- and 12-year-old girls who are at high risk for developing eating disorders and to apply the program selectively to them (Killen, 1996). Our best hope for dealing effectively with eating disorders may lie with preventive approaches such as this.

In Canada, Gail McVey and Ron Davis have examined the effectiveness of a program aimed at girls in grade 6 that is designed to promote a healthy body image and ultimately prevent the development of eating disorders. The program was tested on 263 girls, half of whom were assigned to the intervention and the other half to a control group. The intervention was six sessions long and

| **TABLE 8.2** | Instrument to Measure Weight Concerns in 8- to 11-Year-Old Girls |
| --- | --- |

1. How much *more* or *less* do you feel you worry about your weight and body shape than other girls your age?
   1. I worry a lot less than other girls (4)*
   2. I worry a little less than other girls (8)
   3. I worry about the same as other girls (12)
   4. I worry a little more than other girls (16)
   5. I worry a lot more than other girls (20)
2. How afraid are you of gaining 3 pounds?
   1. Not afraid of gaining (4)
   2. Slightly afraid of gaining (8)
   3. Moderately afraid of gaining (12)
   4. Very afraid of gaining (16)
   5. Terrified of gaining (20)
3. When was the last time you went on a diet?
   1. I've never been on a diet (3)
   2. I was on a diet about 1 year ago (6)
   3. I was on a diet about 6 months ago (9)
   4. I was on a diet about 3 months ago (12)
   5. I was on a diet about 1 month ago (15)
   6. I was on a diet less than 1 month ago (18)
   7. I'm now on a diet (21)
4. How important is your weight to you?
   1. My weight is not important compared with other things in my life (5)
   2. My weight is a little more important than some other things (10)
   3. My weight is more important than most, but not all, things in my life (15)
   4. My weight is the most important thing in my life (20)
5. Do you ever feel fat?
   1. Never (4)
   2. Rarely (8)
   3. Sometimes (12)
   4. Often (16)
   5. Always (20)

*Value assigned to each answer is in parentheses. Thus, if you chose an answer worth 12 in questions 1, 2, 3, and 5, and an answer worth 10 in question 4, your score would be 58. (Remember that the prediction from this scale worked for girls aged 11–13 but hasn't been evaluated in university students.)

*Source:* Killen, 1996.

focused on countering the effects of media portrayals of the desirability of being thin as well as training the girls in self-esteem enhancement, stress management, and peer relationship skills. Body image satisfaction increased and eating problems decreased from pretreatment to posttreatment. But these effects were not specific to the girls who had received the intervention—they were also seen in the girls in the control group (McVey & Davis, 2002). Might the presence of the program in the school have changed the school climate, promoting improved body image for girls in the school regardless of whether they took part in the intervention?

Niva Piran of the Ontario Institute for Studies in Education ran a prevention program for young women that emphasized changes in the school culture at a well-known ballet school in Toronto (Piran, 1998). In focus groups, students explored their experiences of body image dissatisfaction at the school and outside the school. They each formed an action plan to implement changes in the school culture (Piran, 2001). Specific changes included moving away from a focus on body shape and toward an increased focus on body conditioning and physical stamina, and not permitting teachers to make comments about students' body shape (recall the impact of Phoebe's experiences with her ballet instructor's comments about her body weight and shape). This prevention program has been very successful: Abnormal eating attitudes have decreased among girls in the school as have rates of bingeing, vomiting, and laxative abuse (Piran, 1999). In view of the severity and chronicity of eating disorders, preventing these disorders through widespread educational and intervention efforts would be clearly preferable to waiting until the disorders develop (Piran, 1997).

## Concept Check

Mark the following statement
and treatment of eating disor
(T) or False (F).

1. Many young women with
   have a diminished sense o
   and confidence in their o
   talents, are perfectionis
   intensely preoccupied with
   to others. _____

2. Biological factors and the s
   to use diet and exercise to
   impossible weight goals co
   high numbers of people wit
   vosa and bulimia nervosa. _

3. One study showed that ma
   much smaller female body s
   attractive than women do. _

4. Antidepressants help individ
   anorexia nervosa but have
   bulimia nervosa. _____

5. Cognitive-behavioural therap
   interpersonal psychotherapy (
   successful treatments for buli
   although CBT is the prefer
   _____

6. Attention must be focused on
   dysfunctional attitudes about b
   the individual will most likely
   treatment. _____

# Sleep Disorders: The Major Dyssomnias an Parasomnias

- *Identify the critical diagnostic features of each of the major sleep disorders.*

- *Describe the nature of REM and non-REM periods of sleep and how they relate to the parasomnias.*

- *Define circadian rhythms and explain their relation to the sleep-wake cycle.*

- *Describe the medical and psychological treatments used for the treatment of sleep disorders.*

We spend about one-third of our lives asleep. That means most of us sleep nearly 3000 hours per *year.* For many of us, sleep is energizing, both mentally and physically. Unfortunately, most people do not get enough sleep, and one out of every four North

Americans reports getting less than 7 hou daily during the work week—which wo about an hour and a half less than a ce (National Sleep Foundation, 2002). M know what it's like to have a bad night's s

d as the day wears on
rch tells us that even
ly a few days impedes
an Dongen, Maislin,
Now imagine, if you
ce you've had a good
suffer, it is difficult to
efficiency and produc-
l. Lack of sleep also
d by sleep researcher
University, people who
more health problems
upfer, 2003) and are
people who sleep nor-
ng to the research of
of the University of
Chronobiology, and his
h problems are linked
ems, digestive and res-
llergies, and rheumatic
& Badley, 2001). Why
l to sleep problems?
system functioning is
n a few hours of sleep
000; Savard, Laroche,
). Sleep problems are a
ng in substantial annual
ker productivity, absen-
es (Chilcott & Shapiro,
Ivers, 2003; Walsh &

urself how sleep disor-
abnormal psychology.
rbed sleep clearly have
refore could be consid-
ns. However, like other
problems interact in
ological factors.

consider the various
le can experience, we
rmal stages of sleep and
ween these stages during
better understand how
terrupted in abnormal
by University of British
anley Coren in his pop-
(1996), sleep can be
tates: (1) the slow-wave
sleeps deeply, and (2) the
**(REM)** state in which
s awake and in which the
ms. Between these two
transition stages. Sleep
refer to four numbered
er in the depth of sleep
the person transitions
to drowsiness and then
the person drifts in and

out of awareness of his or her surroundings. In Stage 2, the person is truly sleeping, yet the sleep is light (i.e., the sleeper can easily be aroused). When awoken from this stage of sleep, 70% of people report that they didn't think they were asleep, but were just "dozing and thinking" (Coren, 1996). Stages 3 and 4 make up deep, slow-wave sleep. Stage 3 involves moderately deep sleep and Stage 4 very deep sleep. Not only are people hard to awaken when in Stage 4 sleep, but when awoken, they may appear disoriented for a few minutes (Coren, 1996).

Throughout the night, we experience 90-minute cycles of sleep, progressing from light sleep to deeper sleep, then back to light sleep and ending with REM sleep and dreaming. When we awaken in the morning, we typically awaken out of REM sleep during a dream. Normal sleepers spend about 20% of their sleep time in deep sleep, 30% dreaming, and 50% in light sleep (Coren, 1996).

Now that we have reviewed the normal stages of sleep and the normal sleep cycle, let us turn our attention to a consideration of the various sleep disorders.

## An Overview of Sleep Disorders

The study of sleep has long influenced concepts of abnormal psychology. Moral treatment, used in the 19th century for people with severe mental illness, included encouraging patients to get adequate amounts of sleep as part of therapy (Armstrong, 1993). Freud greatly emphasized dreams and discussed them with patients as a way of better understanding their emotional lives (Antrobus, 2000). Researchers who prevented people from sleeping for prolonged periods found that chronic sleep deprivation often had profound effects. An early study in this area looked at the effects of keeping 350 volunteers awake for 112 hours (Tyler, 1955). Seven volunteers engaged in bizarre behaviour that seemed psychotic. Subsequent research suggested that interfering with the sleep of people with preexisting psychological problems can create these disturbing results (Brauchi & West, 1959). A number of the disorders covered in this book are frequently associated with sleep complaints, including schizophrenia, major depression, bipolar disorder, and anxiety-related disorders. Individuals with a range of developmental disorders (see Chapter 13) are also at greater risk for having sleep disorders (Durand, 1998). For example, Penny Corkum of

---

**rapid eye movement (REM) sleep** Periodic intervals of sleep during which the eyes move rapidly from side to side, and dreams occur, but the body is inactive.

Dalhousie University and her colleagues note that reports of sleep problems in children with attention deficit/hyperactivity disorder (ADHD) are prevalent, although the exact nature of sleep problems in children with ADHD remain to be determined (Corkum, Tannock, & Moldofsky, 1998; see also Gruber, Sadeh, & Raviv, 2000). You may think at first that a sleep problem is the result of a psychological disorder. For example, how often have you been anxious about a future event (an upcoming exam, perhaps) and not been able to fall asleep? However, the relationship between sleep disturbances and mental health is more complex. Sleep problems may cause the difficulties people experience in everyday life (Bonnet, 2000), or they may result from some disturbance common to a psychological disorder.

In Chapter 4 we explained how a brain circuit in the limbic system may be involved with anxiety. We know that this region of the brain is also involved with our dream sleep (i.e., REM sleep; Verrier, Harper, & Hobson, 2000). This mutual neurobiological connection suggests that anxiety and sleep may be interrelated in important ways, although the exact nature of the relationship is still unknown. Similarly, REM sleep seems related to depression, as noted in Chapter 6 (Emslie, Rush, Weinberg, Rintelmann, & Roffwarg, 1994). In one study, researchers found that cognitive-behavioural therapy improved depression symptoms among a group of depressed men and normalized their REM sleep patterns (Nofzinger et al., 1994). Furthermore, sleep deprivation has temporary antidepressant effects on some people (Hillman, Kripke, & Gillin, 1990), although in people who are not already depressed sleep deprivation may bring on a depressed mood (Boivin et al., 1997).

In yet another example of the relation of sleep problems to psychological disorders, sleep difficulties are commonly reported by people with schizophrenia in the prodromal phase (i.e., just before the onset of the psychotic episode; see Chapter 12 and Herz, 1985). For example, in a study conducted at four sites in Canada and the United States, Miller et al. (2002) found that sleep disturbances were experienced by 37% of the patients with schizophrenia just before the onset of their psychotic episode. We do not fully understand how psychological disorders are related to sleep, yet accumulating research points to the importance of understanding sleep if we are to complete the broader picture of abnormal behaviour.

Sleep disorders are divided into two major categories: **dyssomnias** and **parasomnias** (see Table 8.3).

**dyssomnias**   Problems in getting to sleep or in obtaining sufficient quality sleep.

**parasomnias**   Abnormal behaviours such as nightmares or sleepwalking that occur during sleep.

---

**TABLE 8.3**   DSM-IV-TR Sleep Disorders

| | Sleep Disorder | Description |
|---|---|---|
| Dyssomnias | (Disturbances in the amount, timing, or quality of sleep.) | |
| | Primary Insomnia | Difficulty initiating or maintaining sleep, or sleep that is not restorative (person not feeling rested even after normal amounts of sleep). |
| | Primary Hypersomnia | Complaint of excessive sleepiness that is displayed as either prolonged sleep episodes or daytime sleep episodes. |
| | Narcolepsy | Irresistible attacks of refreshing sleep occurring daily, accompanied by episodes of brief loss of muscle tone (cataplexy). |
| | Breathing-Related Sleep Disorder | Sleep disruption leading to excessive sleepiness or insomnia caused by sleep-related breathing difficulties. |
| | Circadian Rhythm Sleep Disorder (Sleep-Wake Schedule Disorder) | Persistent or recurrent sleep disruption leading to excessive sleepiness or insomnia caused by a mismatch between the sleep-wake schedule required by a person's environment and his or her circadian sleep-wake pattern. |
| Parasomnias | (Disturbances in arousal and sleep stage transition that intrude into the sleep process.) | |
| | Nightmare Disorder (Dream Anxiety Disorder) | Repeated awakenings with detailed recall of extended and extremely frightening dreams, usually involving threats to survival, security, or self-esteem. The awakenings generally occur during the second half of the sleep period. |
| | Sleep Terror Disorder | Recurrent episodes of abrupt awakening from sleep, usually occurring during the first third of the major sleep episode and beginning with a panicky scream. |
| | Sleepwalking Disorder | Repeated episodes of arising from bed during sleep and walking about, usually occurring during the first third of the major sleep episode. |

*Source:* From *Diagnostic and Statistical Manual of Mental Disorders*, Fourth Edition, Text Revision. Copyright © 2000 American Psychiatric Association. Reprinted with permission.

s in getting
th sleeping
able to fall
ave a 9 a.m.
he quality of
reshed even
le night. The
terized by
physiological
eep, such as

mprehensive
can be deter-
**raphic (PSG)**
s one or more
oratory, being
measures that
n desaturation
vements; brain
by an *electro-*
nts, measured
cle movements,
*raph;* and heart activity,
*ogram.* Daytime behav-
rns are also noted, for
uses drugs or alcohol,
nterpersonal problems,
as a psychological dis-
ta can be both time con-
important to ensure an
tment plan. One alterna-
ssessment of sleep is to
called an *actigraph.* This
mber of arm movements,
oaded into a computer to
quality of sleep (Monk,

s and researchers find it
age number of hours the
lay, taking into account
percentage of time actu-
t lying in bed trying to
y dividing the amount of
unt of time in bed. An SE
fall asleep as soon as your
do not wake up during the
of 50% would mean half
t trying to fall asleep; that
time. Such measurements
mine objectively how well

ne whether a person has a
observe his or her *daytime*
hile awake. For example, if
s to fall asleep at night but
and you feel rested during
t have a problem. A friend

© Charles Gupton/CORBIS

This person is participating in a polysomnograph, an overnight electronic evaluation of sleep patterns.

who also takes 90 minutes to fall asleep but finds this delay anxiety provoking and is fatigued the next day might be considered to have a sleep problem.

## Primary Insomnia

Insomnia is one of the most common sleep disorders. You may picture someone with insomnia as being awake all the time. However, it isn't possible to go completely without sleep. For example, after being awake for about 40 hours, a person begins having **microsleeps** that last several seconds or longer (Roehrs, Carskadon, Dement, & Roth, 2000). In the rare occurrences of *fatal familial insomnia* (a degenerative brain disorder), total lack of sleep eventually leads to death (Fiorino, 1996). Despite the common use of the term *insomnia* to mean "not sleeping," it applies to a number of complaints (Savard et al., 2003). People are considered to have insomnia if they have trouble falling asleep at night (difficulty initiating sleep), if they wake up frequently or too early and can't go back to sleep (difficulty maintaining sleep), or even if they sleep a reasonable number of hours but are still not rested the next day (non-restorative sleep). Consider the case of Sonja.

**polysomnographic (PSG) evaluation** Assessment of sleep disorders in which a client sleeping in the lab is monitored for heart, muscle, respiration, brain wave, and other functions.

**sleep efficiency (SE)** Percentage of time actually spent sleeping of the total time spent in bed.

**microsleeps** Short, seconds-long periods of sleep that occur in people who have been deprived of sleep.

## Sonja
### School on Her Mind

Sonja was a 23-year-old law student with a history of sleep problems. She reported that she never really slept well, both having trouble falling asleep at night and usually awakening again in the early morning. She had been using the nighttime cold medication Nyquil several times per week over the past few years to help her fall asleep. Unfortunately, since she started law school last year, her sleep problems had grown even worse. She would lie in bed awake until the early morning hours thinking about school, getting only 3–4 hours of sleep on a typical night. In the morning she had a great deal of difficulty getting out of bed and was frequently late for her early morning class.

Sonja's sleep problems and their interference with her schoolwork were causing her to experience increasingly severe depression. In addition, she recently reported having a severe anxiety attack that woke her in the middle of the night. All of these difficulties caused her to be increasingly isolated from family and friends, who finally convinced her to seek help.

We return to Sonja later in this chapter.

### Clinical Description

Sonja's symptoms meet the DSM-IV-TR criteria for **primary insomnia,** with *primary* indicating that the complaint is not related to other medical or psychiatric problems.

Sonja's is a typical case of insomnia. She had trouble both initiating and maintaining sleep. Other people sleep all night but still feel as if they've been awake for hours. Although most people can carry out necessary day-to-day activities, their inability to concentrate can have serious consequences, such as debilitating accidents when they attempt to drive long distances (like bus drivers) or handle dangerous material (like electricians). Students with insomnia like Sonja's may do poorly in school because of difficulty concentrating.

### Statistics

Almost a third of the general population report some symptoms of insomnia during any given year (National Sleep Foundation, 2002), and 17% indicate their problems with sleeping are severe (Gillin, 1993). One study suggests that nearly one-quarter of Canadians report insomnia (Sutton et al., 2001). In another study 31% of the people who expressed concern about sleep continued to experience difficulties a year later (Ford & Kamerow, 1989), a result showing that sleep problems may become chronic. For many of these individuals, sleep difficulties are a lifetime affliction (Neylan et al., 2003). Approximately 35% of elderly people report excessive daytime sleepiness (Blazer, 1999; Whitney et al., 1998).

A number of psychological disorders are associated with insomnia (Benca, Obermeyer, Thisted, & Gillin, 1992; Buysse, Morin, & Reynolds, 2001; Okuji et al., 2002). Total sleep time often decreases with depression, substance use disorders, anxiety disorders, and dementia of the Alzheimer's type. The interrelationship between alcohol use and sleep disorders can be particularly troubling. Alcohol is often used to initiate sleep (Gillin, 1993; Neylan, et al., 2003). In small amounts it helps make people drowsy, but it also interrupts ongoing sleep. Interrupted sleep causes anxiety, which often leads to repeated alcohol use and an obviously vicious cycle (Stewart, 1996).

Women report insomnia twice as often as men (Sutton et al., 2001). Does this mean that men sleep better than women? Not necessarily. Remember, a sleep problem is considered a disorder *only if you experience discomfort* about it. Women may be more frequently diagnosed as having insomnia because they more often report the problem, not necessarily because their sleep is disrupted more. Women may be more aware of their sleep patterns than men or may be more comfortable acknowledging and seeking help for problems.

Just as normal sleep needs change over time, complaints of insomnia differ in frequency among people of different ages. Estimates of insomnia among young children range from 25% to more than 40% (Anders, 2001). As children move into adolescence, their biologically determined sleep schedules shift toward a later bedtime (Sadeh, Raviv, & Gruber, 2000). However, at least in North America, children are still expected to rise early for school, causing chronic sleep deprivation.

The percentage of individuals who complain of sleep problems increases as they become older adults. This higher rate in reports of sleeping problems among older people makes sense when you remember that the number of hours we sleep decreases as we age. It is not uncommon for someone over 65 to sleep fewer than 6 hours and wake up several times each night.

**primary insomnia** Difficulty in initiating, maintaining, or gaining from sleep; not related to other medical or psychological problems.

medical and psycho-
in and physical dis-
during the day, and

related to problems
its control of temper-
an acute increase in
which normally falls
ak, 2000). People who
have a delayed temper-
mperature doesn't drop
sy until later at night
90). As a group, people
higher body tempera-
d their body tempera-
lack of fluctuation may
& Moline, 1989).
logical stresses can dis-
993). Poll your friends
ms to see how many of
alling asleep or are not
The stress you experience
erfere with your sleep, at
study by Sutton and col-
having a very stressful life
est predictors of insomnia
nt study by Morin et al.
duals with insomnia to 27
that those with insomnia
of day-to-day minor stres-
sity of major negative life
eepers. Not only did the
r lives to be more stressful,
er levels of arousal before
eepers (Morin et al., 2003).

Research by Charles Morin and his colleagues also shows that people with insomnia may have unrealistic expectations about how much sleep they need ("I need a full 8 hours") and about how disruptive disturbed sleep will be ("I won't be able to think or do my job if I sleep for only 5 hours"; Morin, Stone, Trinkle, Mercer, & Remsberg, 1993). It is important to recognize the role of cognition in insomnia; our thoughts alone may disrupt our sleep.

Is poor sleeping a learned behaviour? It is generally accepted that people suffering from sleep problems associate the bedroom and bed with the frustration and anxiety that go with insomnia. Eventually, the arrival of bedtime may cause anxiety (Bootzin & Nicassio, 1978). Interactions associated with sleep may contribute to children's sleep problems. For example, one study found that when a parent was present when the child fell asleep, the child was more likely to wake during the night (Adair, Bauchner, Philipp, Levenson, & Zuckerman, 1991). Researchers think that some children learn to fall asleep only with a parent present; if they wake up at night, they are frightened at finding themselves alone and their sleep is disrupted. Despite widespread acceptance of the role of learning in insomnia, relatively little research has been done on this phenomenon, perhaps in part because this type of research would involve going into homes and bedrooms at an especially private time.

Cross-cultural sleep research has focused primarily on children. In the predominant culture in North America, infants are expected to sleep on their own, in a separate bed, and, if possible, in a separate room. However, in many other cultures as diverse as rural Guatemala and Korea and urban Japan, the child spends the first few years of life in the same room and sometimes the same bed as the

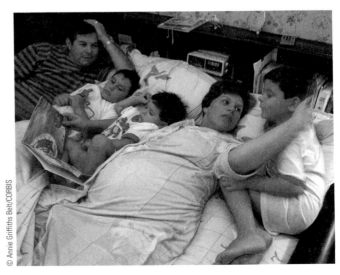

usually sleep alone (left). In many cultures, all family members share the same bed (right).

mother (Mosko, Richard, & McKenna, 1997). In many cultures mothers report that they do not ignore the cries of their children (K. Lee, 1992; Morelli, Rogoff, Oppenheim, & Goldsmith, 1992), in stark contrast to North America, where most pediatricians recommend that parents ignore the cries of their infants at night (Ferber, 1985). One conclusion from this research is that sleep can be negatively affected by cultural norms, as in North America. Unmet demands can result in stress that negatively affects the ultimate sleep outcome for children (Durand, Mindell, Mapstone, & Gernert-Dott, 1998).

An integrative view of sleep disorders includes several assumptions. The first is that at some level, both *biological and psychological factors* are present in most cases. A second assumption is that these multiple factors are *reciprocally related*. For example, Adair and colleagues (1991) observed that children who woke frequently at night often fell asleep in the presence of parents. However, they also noted that child temperament (or personality) may have played a role in this arrangement, because these children had comparatively difficult temperaments, and their parents were presumably present to attend to sleep initiation difficulties. In other words, personality characteristics, sleep difficulties, and parental reaction interact in a reciprocal manner to produce and maintain sleep problems.

People may be biologically vulnerable to disturbed sleep. This vulnerability differs from person to person and can range from mild to more severe disturbances. For example, a person may be a light sleeper (easily aroused at night) or have a family history of insomnia, narcolepsy, or obstructed breathing. All these factors can lead to eventual sleeping problems. Such influences have been referred to as *predisposing conditions* (Spielman & Glovinsky, 1991); they may not, by themselves, always cause problems, but they may combine with other factors to interfere with sleep (see Figure 8.6).

### An Integrative Model

Biological vulnerability may in turn interact with *sleep stress* (Durand et al., 1995), which includes a number of events that can negatively affect sleep. For example, poor bedtime habits (such as having too much alcohol or caffeine) can interfere with falling asleep (Hauri, 1991; Petit, Azad, Byszewski, Sarazan, & Power, 2003). Note that biological vulnerability and sleep stress influence each other (Figure 8.6). Although we may intuitively assume that biological factors come first, extrinsic influences such as poor sleep hygiene (the daily activities that affect how we sleep) can affect the physiological activity of sleep. One of the most striking examples of this phenomenon is jet lag, in which people's sleep patterns are disrupted, sometimes seriously, when they fly across

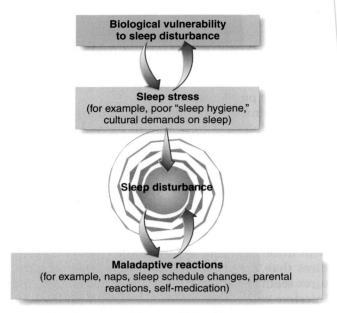

**Figure 8.6** ■ An integrative multidimensional model of sleep disturbance.

several time zones. Whether disturbances continue or become more severe may depend on how they are managed. For example, many people react to disrupted sleep by taking over-the-counter sleeping pills. Unfortunately, most people are not aware that **rebound insomnia**—where sleep problems reappear, sometimes worse—may occur when the medication is withdrawn. This rebound leads people to think they still have a sleep problem, re-administer the medicine, and go through the cycle repeatedly. In other words, taking sleep aids can perpetuate sleep problems (Westra & Stewart, 2002).

Other ways of reacting to poor sleep can also prolong problems. It seems reasonable that a person who hasn't had enough sleep can make up for this loss by napping during the day. Unfortunately, naps that alleviate fatigue during the day can also disrupt sleep the next night. Anxiety can also extend the problem, as demonstrated by the research of Charles Morin. Lying in bed worrying about school, family problems, or even about not being able to sleep will interfere with your sleep (Morin, 1993).

### *Primary Hypersomnia*

*Insomnia* involves not getting enough sleep (the prefix *in* means "lacking" or "without"), and **hypersomnia** is a problem of sleeping too much

---

**rebound insomnia** In a person with insomnia, the worsened sleep problems that can occur when medications are used to treat insomnia and then withdrawn.

**hypersomnia** Abnormally excessive sleep; a person with this condition will fall asleep several times a day.

ount or abnormal
leep all night find
eral times the next

ame to my office to
ss. We talked about
ot wrong on the last
ut to leave she said
uring my class. This
ut I thanked her for
d, "you don't under-
in *all* of my classes,
I didn't quite under-
to tell me and joked
ofessors more care-
probably true. But I
h sleeping too much."
riously, Ann told me
been a problem since
ions that were monot-
she couldn't be active,
happen several times a
e was doing. Recently,
d become a problem
rticularly interesting or
vision and driving long
ematic.
er father had a similar
y been diagnosed with
iscuss next) and was
inic. Both she and her
sed with hypersomnia.
d Ritalin (a stimulant
ars ago and said that it
fective in keeping her
he said the drug helped
s but did not eliminate

gnostic criteria for hyper-
y the excessive sleepiness
also the subjective impres-
(American Psychiatric
Remember that whether
depends on how it affects
y. Ann found her disorder
terfered with driving and
s. Hypersomnia caused her
cademically and upset her

Excessive sleepiness can be very disruptive.

personally, both of which are defining features of this disorder. She slept approximately 8 hours each night, so her daytime sleepiness couldn't be attributed to insufficient sleep.

Several factors that can cause excessive sleepiness would not be considered hypersomnia. For example, people with insomnia (who get inadequate amounts of sleep) often report being tired during the day. In contrast, people with hypersomnia sleep through the night and appear rested upon awakening, but they still complain of being excessively tired throughout the day. Another sleep problem that can cause a similar excessive sleepiness is a breathing-related sleep disorder called **sleep apnea.** People with this problem have difficulty breathing at night. They often snore loudly, pause between breaths, and wake in the morning with a dry mouth and headache. In identifying hypersomnia, you need to rule out insomnia, sleep apnea, or other reasons for sleepiness during the day (American Psychiatric Association, 2000a).

We are just beginning to understand the nature of hypersomnia, so relatively little research has been done on its causes. Genetic influences seem to be involved in a portion of cases, because 39% of people with hypersomnia have a family history of the disorder (Guilleminault & Pelayo, 2000; Parkes & Block, 1989). A significant subgroup of people diagnosed with hypersomnia previously were exposed to a viral infection such as mononucleosis,

**sleep apnea** Disorder involving brief periods when breathing ceases during sleep.

hepatitis, and viral pneumonia, which suggests there may be more than one cause (Guilleminault & Pelayo, 2000).

## Narcolepsy

Ann described her father as having **narcolepsy,** a different form of the sleeping problem she and her brother shared (Mukai, Uchid, Miyazaki, Nishihara, & Honda, 2003). In addition to daytime sleepiness, people with narcolepsy experience *cataplexy*, a sudden loss of muscle tone. Cataplexy occurs while the person is awake and can range from slight weakness in the facial muscles to complete physical collapse. Cataplexy lasts from several seconds to several minutes; it is usually preceded by strong emotion such as anger or happiness. Imagine that while cheering for your favourite team, you suddenly fall asleep; while arguing with a friend, you collapse to the floor in a sound sleep. You can imagine how disruptive this disorder can be!

Cataplexy appears to result from a sudden onset of REM sleep. Instead of falling asleep normally and going through the four non-REM stages that typically precede REM sleep (see Coren, 1996), people with narcolepsy periodically progress right to this dream sleep stage almost directly from the state of being awake. One outcome of REM sleep is the inhibition of input to the muscles, and this seems to be the process that leads to cataplexy.

Two other characteristics distinguish people who have narcolepsy (Mukai et al., 2003) both of which were discussed earlier in Chapter 4 in the context of Newfoundlanders' experience of the "Old Hag." First, narcoleptics commonly report *sleep paralysis,* a brief period after awakening when they can't move or speak that is often frightening to those who go through it. Second, narcoleptics often experience *hypnagogic hallucinations*, vivid and often terrifying experiences that begin at the start of sleep and are said to be unbelievably realistic because they include not only visual aspects but also touch, hearing, and even the sensation of body movement. Examples of hypnagogic hallucinations, which, like sleep paralysis, can be terrifying, include the vivid illusion of being caught in a fire or flying through the air.

Narcolepsy is relatively rare, occurring in 0.03% to 0.16% of the population, with the numbers approximately equal among males and females. The problems associated with narcolepsy usually are first seen during the teenage years. Fortunately, the cataplexy, hypnagogic hallucinations, and sleep paralysis often decrease in frequency over time, although sleepiness during the day does not seem to diminish with age.

Sleep paralysis and hypnagogic hallucinations may serve a role in explaining a most unusual phenomenon—UFO experiences. Each year numerous people report sighting unidentified flying objects—UFOs—and some even tell of visiting with inhabitants of other planets (Sheaffer, 1986). A group of scientists led by the late Nicholas Spanos, whose research was first discussed in Chapter 5, examined people who had had such experiences, separating them into those who had non-intense experiences (seeing only lights and shapes in the sky) and those with intense experiences (seeing and communicating with aliens; Spanos, Cross, Dickson, & DuBreuil, 1993). They found that a majority of the reported UFO incidents occurred at night and that 60% of the intense UFO stories were associated with sleep episodes. Specifically, the reports of these intense accounts were often described in ways that resembled accounts of people experiencing a frightening episode of sleep paralysis and hypnagogic hallucination, as illustrated by the following account:

> I was lying in bed facing the wall, and suddenly my heart started to race. I could feel the presence of three entities standing beside me. I was unable to move my body but could move my eyes. One of the entities, a male, was laughing at me, not verbally but with his mind. He made me feel stupid. He told me telepathically, "Don't you know by now that you can't do anything unless we let you?" (Spanos et al., 1993, p. 627)

Specific genetic models of narcolepsy are now being articulated (Wieczorek et al., 2003). Previous research with Doberman pinschers and Labrador retrievers, who also inherit this disorder, suggests that narcolepsy is associated with a cluster of genes on chromosome 6, and it may be an autosomal recessive trait. Advances in understanding the etiology and treatment of such disorders can be credited to the help of "man's best friend."

## Breathing-Related Sleep Disorders

For some people, sleepiness during the day or disrupted sleep at night has a physical origin, namely, problems with breathing while asleep. In DSM-IV-TR these problems are diagnosed as **breathing-related sleep disorders.** People whose breathing is interrupted during their sleep experience numerous brief arousals throughout the night and do not feel rested even after 8 or 9 hours asleep (Bootzin, Manber, Perlis, Salvio, & Wyatt, 1993). For all of us,

---

**narcolepsy** Sleep disorder involving sudden and irresistible sleep attacks.

**breathing-related sleep disorders** Sleep disruption leading to excessive sleepiness or insomnia, caused by a breathing problem such as interrupted (apnea) or laboured (hypoventilation) breathing.

relax during sleep,
newhat and making
. For some, unfortu-
d a great deal and
*ion);* in the extreme,
to 30 seconds) when
r, called *sleep apnea.*
nly minimally aware
doesn't attribute the
ning. However, a bed
snoring (which is one
l have noticed fright-
ted breathing. Other
athing difficulties are
the night, morning
falling asleep during
no resulting feeling of
2003).

common in males and
20% of the population
ere are three types of
t causes, daytime com-
bstructive, central, and
*uctive sleep apnea* (OSA)
tops despite continued
tory system (Bassiri &
esity is sometimes associ-
, as is increasing age.
lves the complete cessa-
ty for brief periods and is
certain central nervous
cerebral vascular disease,
nerative disorders (White,
al sleep apnea tend not to
e sleepiness. Because of the
ms, people tend not to seek
w relatively little about its
*Mixed sleep apnea,* is a com-
structive and central sleep
athing difficulties interrupt
mptoms similar to those of

### hm Sleep Disorders

ack": Many Canadians use this
remind themselves to turn the
in the spring and back again 1
ost of us consider the shift to
e a minor inconvenience and
to see how disruptive this time
at least a day or two, we may
e day and have difficulty falling
most as if we had jet lag. The
do with how our biological
his change in time. Convention
at this new time, but our brains
thing different. If the struggle

continues for any length of time, you may have
what is called a **circadian rhythm sleep disorder.**
This disorder is characterized by disturbed sleep
(either insomnia or excessive sleepiness during the
day) brought on by the brain's inability to synchronize its sleep patterns with the current patterns of
day and night.

In the 1960s, German and French scientists identified several bodily rhythms that seem to persist
without cues from the environment, rhythms that
are self-regulated (Aschoff & Wever, 1962; Siffre,
1964). Because these rhythms don't exactly match
our 24-hour day, they are called "circadian" (from
*circa* meaning "about" and *dian* meaning "day"). If
our circadian rhythms don't match the 24-hour day,
why isn't our sleep completely disrupted over time?

Fortunately, our brains have a mechanism that
keeps us in sync with the outside world. Our biological clock is in the *suprachiasmatic nucleus* in
the hypothalamus (Coren, 1996). Connected to the
suprachiasmatic nucleus is a pathway that comes
from our eyes. The light we see in the morning and
the decreasing light at night signal the brain to
reset the biological clock each day. Unfortunately,
some people have trouble sleeping when they want
to because of problems with their circadian
rhythms. The causes may be outside the person
(e.g., crossing several time zones in a short amount
of time) or internal.

Not being synchronized with the normal wake
and sleep cycles causes people's sleep to be interrupted when they do try to sleep and to be tired
during the day. There are several types of circadian
rhythm sleep disorders. *Jet lag type* is, as its name
implies, caused by rapidly crossing multiple time
zones (Arendt, Stone, & Skene, 2000). People with
jet lag usually report difficulty going to sleep at the
proper time and feeling fatigued during the day.
Interestingly, older people, introverts (loners), and
early risers (morning people) are most likely to be
negatively affected by these time zone changes
(Gillin, 1993). *Shift work type* sleep problems are
associated with work schedules (Monk, 2000).
Many people, such as hospital employees, police, or
emergency personnel, work at night or must work
irregular hours; as a result, they may have problems
sleeping or experience excessive sleepiness during
waking hours (Boivin et al., 1997). Almost two-
thirds of all workers on rotating shifts complain of
poor sleep (Neylan et al., 2003).

In contrast with jet lag and shift-work sleep-
related problems, which have external causes such

**circadian rhythm sleep disorder**  Sleep disturbance
resulting in sleepiness or insomnia, caused by the body's
inability to synchronize its sleep patterns with the current
pattern of day and night.

as long-distance travel and job selection, several circadian rhythm sleep disorders seem to arise from within the person experiencing the problems. Extreme night owls, people who stay up late and sleep late, may have a problem known as *delayed sleep phase type*. Sleep is delayed or later than normal bedtime. At the other extreme, people with an *advanced sleep phase type* of circadian rhythm disorder are "early to bed and early to rise." Here, sleep is advanced or earlier than normal bedtime. In part because of our general lack of knowledge about them, DSM-IV-TR does not include the advanced sleep phase type as a circadian rhythm sleep disorder.

Research on why our sleep rhythms are disrupted is advancing at a great pace, and we are now beginning to understand the circadian rhythm process. Scientists believe the hormone *melatonin* contributes to the setting of our biological clocks that tell us when to sleep. This hormone is produced by the pineal gland, in the centre of the brain. Melatonin (don't confuse with *melanin*, the chemical that determines skin colour) has been nicknamed the "Dracula hormone" because its production is stimulated by darkness and ceases in daylight. When our eyes see that it is nighttime, this information is passed on to the pineal gland, which, in turn, begins producing melatonin. Researchers believe that both light and melatonin help set the biological clock.

## Concept Check 8.3

Match the following descriptions of sleeping problems with the correct term: (a) cataplexy, (b) primary hypersomnia, (c) primary insomnia, (d) sleep apnea, (e) sleep paralysis, (f) narcolepsy, (g) circadian rhythm sleep disorder, (h) breathing-related sleep disorder.

1. Sometimes when Trudy awakens, she cannot move or speak. This is terrifying. _____
2. Susan's husband is extremely overweight. He snores every night and often wakes up exhausted as though he never slept. Susan suspects that he may be suffering from _____.
3. Suzy can hardly make it through a full day of work if she doesn't take a nap during her lunch hour. No matter how early she goes to bed in the evening, she still sleeps as late as possible in the morning. _____
4. Jerod wakes up several times each night because he feels he is about to hyperventilate. He can't seem to get enough air, and often his wife will wake him to tell him to quit snoring. _____
5. Charlie has had considerable trouble sleeping since he started a new job that requires him to change shifts every 3 weeks. Sometime he works during the day and sleeps at night, and other times he works at night and sleeps during the day. _____
6. Jill has problems staying awake throughout the day. Even while talking on the phone or riding the bus across town, she often loses muscle tone and falls asleep for a while. _____

# Treatment of Sleep Disorders

■ *Describe the uses and limitations of medical treatments for chronic sleep problems.*

■ *Match the nature of sleep problems (e.g., intrusive thoughts) with the specific treatment recommendation.*

When we can't fall asleep or we awaken frequently, or when sleep does not restore our energy and vitality, we need help. A number of biological and psychological interventions have been designed and evaluated to help people regain the benefits of normal sleep.

## Medical Treatments

Perhaps the most common treatments for insomnia are medical. People who complain of insomnia to a medical professional are likely prescribed one of several *benzodiazepine* or related medications,

gs such as triazolam
oien) and the long-
m (Dalmane). Short-
nly brief drowsiness)
g-acting drugs some-
morning, and people
ess. The long-acting
s preferred when neg-
nxiety are observed in
g drugs (Gillin, 1993).
most likely to use med-
. A study by Keith
at Lakehead University
vere significantly more
to be prescribed benzo-
ownlee et al., 2002).
backs to medical treat-
fett-Jerrott & Stewart,
00; Stewart & Westra,
2002). First, benzodi-
use excessive sleepiness
rments such as memory
eep-promoting medica-
n how much they cause
ns et al., 1995). Second,
dependent on them and
m, deliberately or not.
are meant for short-term
commended for use longer
se can cause dependence
Therefore, although med-
or sleep problems that will
hort period (e.g., insomnia
o hospitalization), they are
problems.

hypersomnia or narcolepsy,
scribe a stimulant such as
in, the medication Ann was
or modafinil (Guilleminault
aplexy, or loss of muscle tone,
with antidepressant medica-
eople with narcolepsy are
se antidepressants suppress
eep. Cataplexy seems to be
onset of REM sleep; therefore,
nedication can be helpful in
s.

athing-related sleep disorders
he person breathe better during
s means recommending weight
who are obese, the neck's soft
he airways. Unfortunately, this
proved successful for most
eep disorders (Guilleminault &

derate cases of obstructive sleep
ually involves either a medication

or a mechanical device that improves breathing. Medications include those that help stimulate respiration (e.g., medroxyprogesterone) or the tricyclic antidepressants, which are thought to act on the locus ceruleus that affects REM sleep. These latter drugs seem to reduce the muscle tone loss usually seen during REM sleep, which means the respiratory muscles do not relax as much as usual at this time, thereby improving the person's breathing (Kryger, 2000). Certain mechanical devices—such as the continuous positive air pressure machine—have also been used to reposition either the tongue or the jaw during sleep to help improve breathing, but people tend to resist them because of discomfort. Severe breathing problems may require surgery to help remove blockages in parts of the airways.

## Environmental Treatments

Because medication as a primary treatment isn't usually recommended (Doghramji, 2000; Roehrs & Roth, 2000), other ways of getting people back in step with their sleep rhythms are usually tried. One general principle for treating circadian rhythm disorders is that *phase delays* (moving bedtime later) are easier than *phase advances* (moving bedtime earlier). In other words, it is easier to stay up several hours later than usual than to force yourself to go to sleep several hours earlier. Scheduling shift changes in a clockwise direction (going from day to evening schedule) seems to help workers adjust better. People can best readjust their sleep patterns by going to bed several hours later each night until bedtime is at the desired hour (Czeisler et al., 1981). A drawback of this approach is that it requires the person to sleep during the day for several days, which is obviously difficult for people with regularly scheduled responsibilities.

Another recent effort to help people with sleep problems involves using bright light to trick the brain into readjusting the biological clock. (In Chapter 6 we described the pioneering work of Raymond Lam with light therapy for *seasonal affective disorder*.) Very bright light may help people with circadian rhythm problems readjust their sleep patterns (Terman & Terman, 2000). People typically sit in front of a bank of fluorescent lamps that generate light greater than 2500 lux, an amount significantly different from normal indoor light (250 lux). Several hours of exposure to this bright light have successfully reset the circadian rhythms of a number of individuals (Czeisler & Allan, 1989). Although this type of treatment is still new and relatively untested, it provides some hope for people with sleep problems.

Pascal Goetgheluck/Science Photo Library

Bright light therapy can help people with circadian rhythm sleep disorders readjust their sleep patterns.

## *Psychological Treatments*

As you can imagine, the limitations of using drugs to help people sleep better has led to the development of psychological treatments. Table 8.4 lists and briefly describes some of the psychological approaches to insomnia. Different treatments are used to help people with different kinds of sleep problems. For example, relaxation treatments reduce the physical tension that seems to prevent some people from falling asleep at night. Some people report that their anxiety about work, relationships, or other situations prevents them from sleeping or wakes them up in the middle of the night. To address this problem, cognitive treatments are used.

Given the links of anxiety to insomnia, Viens, De Koninck, Mercier, St-Onge, and Lorrain (2003) from the University of Ottawa compared progressive relaxation with a treatment they referred to as anxiety management training (which basically combined progressive relaxation with cognitive relaxation techniques). Both groups were able to get to sleep more quickly following therapy, and lab-based sleep evaluations showed that their slow-wave sleep and sleep satisfaction increased. Both groups also showed decreases in anxiety and depression. Finally, the treatments were equally effective (Viens et al., 2003).

Other research shows that some psychological treatments for insomnia may be more effective than others. For adult sleep problems, *stimulus control* may be recommended. People are instructed to use the bedroom only for sleeping and for sex and *not* for work or other anxiety-provoking activities (e.g., watching the news on television). The work of Charles Morin and colleagues suggests that *progressive relaxation* or *sleep hygiene* (changing daily habits that may interfere with sleep) alone may not be as effective as stimulus control alone for some people (Lacks & Morin, 1992).

Sonja—the law student we profiled earlier—was helped with her sleep problems using several techniques. She was instructed to limit her time in bed to about 4 hours of sleep time (*sleep restriction*), about the amount of time she actually slept each night. The period was lengthened when she began to sleep through the night. Sonja was also asked not to do any schoolwork while in bed and to get out of bed if she couldn't fall asleep within 15 minutes (stimulus control). Finally, therapy involved confronting her unrealistic expectations about how much sleep was enough for a person of her age (cognitive therapy). Within about 3 weeks of treatment, Sonja was

### TABLE 8.4  Psychological Treatments For Insomnia

| Sleep Treatment | Description |
|---|---|
| Cognitive | This approach focuses on changing the sleepers' unrealistic expectations and beliefs about sleep ("I must have 8 hours of sleep each night"; "If I get less than 8 hours of sleep it will make me ill"). Therapist attempts to alter beliefs and attitudes about sleeping by providing information on topics such as normal amounts of sleep and a person's ability to compensate for lost sleep. |
| Cognitive relaxation | Because some people become anxious when they have difficulty sleeping, this approach uses meditation or imagery to help with relaxation at bedtime or after a night waking. |
| Graduated extinction | Used for children who have tantrums at bedtime or wake up crying at night, this treatment instructs the parent to check on the child after progressively longer periods of time until the child falls asleep on his or her own. |
| Paradoxical intention | This technique involves instructing individuals in the opposite behaviour from the desired outcome. Telling poor sleepers to lie in bed and try to stay awake as long as they can is used to try to relieve the performance anxiety surrounding efforts to try to fall asleep. |
| Progressive relaxation | This technique involves relaxing the muscles of the body in an effort to introduce drowsiness. |

r night as opposed to
d fewer interruptions
ore refreshed in the
rgy during the day.
f studies by Charles
combined treatments
ith insomnia (Morin,
93; see also Petit et al.,
randomized placebo-
h medical and psycho-
tive in improving the
Colecchi, Stone, Sood,
term, however, the psy-
er able to maintain its
p (see also review by

e of the cognitive treat-
Instead, treatment often
routines such as a bath,
ng a story, to help chil-
. Graduated extinction
as been used with some
lems and for waking at
, 1990; Mindell, 1999).
and behavioural treat-
mportant for insomnia.
ort-term use of medica-
terventions may prove to
treatment for insomnia
it et al., 2003).
ent research for the other
nonexistent. For the most
ort groups assist in man-
and social effects of dis-
are especially helpful for
feelings of low self-esteem
et al., 1993).

*Disorders*

erally agree that a significant
roblems people experience
d by following a few steps
ed to as *sleep hygiene*, these
be relatively simple to follow
oblems such as insomnia for
al., 2003). Some of the sleep
ations rely on allowing the
r sleep to take over, replacing
ce on our activities that inter-
ample, setting a regular time to
each day can help make falling
Avoiding the use of caffeine and
both stimulants—can also help
uch as nighttime awakening.
a number of the sleep hygiene
for preventing sleep problems.
e controlled prospective research

## TABLE 8.5 Good Sleep Habits

Establish a set bedtime routine.

Develop a regular bedtime and a regular time to awaken.

Eliminate all foods and drink that contain caffeine 6 hours before bedtime.

Limit any use of alcohol or tobacco.

Try drinking milk before bedtime.

Eat a balanced diet, limiting fat.

Go to bed only when sleepy and get out of bed if you are unable to fall asleep or back to sleep after 15 minutes.

Do not exercise or participate in vigorous activities in the hours before bedtime.

Do include a weekly program of exercise during the day.

Restrict activities in bed to those that help induce sleep.

Reduce noise and light in the bedroom.

Increase exposure to natural and bright light during the day.

Avoid extreme temperature changes in the bedroom (i.e., too hot or too cold).

*Source:* From "Good Sleep Habits," by V. M. Durand, in *Sleep Better! A Guide to Improving Sleep for Children with Special Needs*, by V. M. Durand, 1998, Baltimore: Paul H. Brookes Publishing Co., p. 60. Adapted with permission.

on preventing sleep disorders, this approach appears to be among the most promising techniques currently available.

## *Parasomnias and Their Treatment*

Have you ever been told that you walk in your sleep? Talk in your sleep? Have you ever had troublesome nightmares? Do you grind your teeth in your sleep? If you answered "yes" to one or more of these questions (and it's likely you did), you have experienced sleep problems in the category of parasomnia. Parasomnias are not problems with sleep itself but abnormal events that occur either during sleep or during that twilight time between sleeping and waking. Some events associated with parasomnia are not unusual if they happen while you are awake (walking to the kitchen to look into the refrigerator) but can be distressing if they take place while you are sleeping.

Parasomnias are of two types: those that occur during rapid eye movement (REM) sleep, and those that occur during non-rapid eye movement sleep (NREM). As you might have guessed, **nightmares** occur during REM or dream sleep. About 10% to 50% of children and 5% to 10% of adults experience them (Neylan et al., 2003). To qualify as a nightmare

**nightmares** Frightening and anxiety-producing dreams occurring during rapid eye movement (REM) sleep. The individual recalls the bad dreams and recovers alertness and orientation quickly.

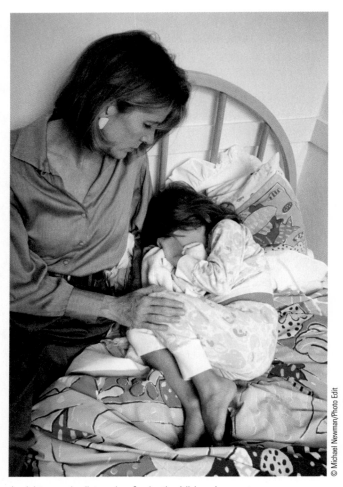

A nightmare is distressing for both child and parent.

disorder, according to DSM-IV-TR criteria, these experiences must be so distressful that they impair a person's ability to carry on normal activities. Some researchers distinguish nightmares from *bad dreams* by whether or not you wake up as a result. Nightmares are defined as disturbing dreams that awaken the sleeper; bad dreams are those that do not awaken the person experiencing them. Using this definition, Montreal researchers Antonio Zadra and Don Donderi (2000) have shown that university students report an average of 30 bad dreams and 10 nightmares per year. Because nightmares are so common, you would expect that a great deal of research would have focused on their causes and treatment. Unfortunately, this is not so, and we still know little about why people have nightmares and how to treat them. Fortunately, they tend to decrease with age.

**Sleep terrors,** which most commonly afflict children, usually begin with a piercing scream. The child is extremely upset, is often sweating, and frequently has a rapid heartbeat. On the surface, sleep terrors appear to resemble nightmares—the child cries and appears frightened—but they occur during NREM sleep and therefore are not caused by frightening dreams. During sleep terrors children cannot be easily awakened and comforted, as they can during a nightmare. Children do not remember sleep terrors, despite their often dramatic effect on the observer. Approximately 5% of children (more boys than girls) may experience sleep terrors; for adults, the prevalence rate is less than 1% (Buysse, Reynolds, & Kupfer, 1993). As with nightmares, we know relatively little about sleep terrors, although several theories have been proposed, including the possibility of a genetic component because the disorder tends to occur in families (Mindell, 1993). Treatment for sleep terrors usually begins with a recommendation to wait and see whether they disappear on their own. If the problem is frequent or continues a long time, sometimes antidepressants (imipramine) or benzodiazepines are recommended, although their effectiveness has not yet been clearly demonstrated (Mindell, 1993).

One approach to reducing chronic sleep terrors is the use of *scheduled awakenings*. In the first controlled study of its kind, Durand and Mindell (1999) instructed parents of children who were experiencing almost nightly sleep terrors to awaken their child briefly approximately 30 minutes before a typical episode. This simple technique, which was faded out over several weeks, was successful in almost completely eliminating these disturbing events.

It might surprise you to learn that **sleepwalking** (also called *somnambulism*) occurs during NREM sleep (Broughton, 2000). This means that when people walk in their sleep they are probably not acting out a dream. This parasomnia typically occurs during the first few hours while a person is in the deep stages of sleep. The DSM-IV-TR criteria for sleepwalking require that the person leave the bed, although less active episodes can involve small motor behaviours such as sitting up in bed and picking at the blanket or gesturing. Because sleepwalking occurs during the deepest stages of sleep, waking someone during an episode is difficult; if the person is wakened, he or she typically will not remember what has happened. It is not true, however, that waking a sleepwalker is somehow dangerous.

Sleepwalking is primarily a problem during childhood, although a small proportion of adults are affected. A relatively large number of children—from 15% to 30%—have at least one episode of

**sleep terrors** Episodes of apparent awakening from sleep, accompanied by signs of panic, followed by disorientation and amnesia for the incident. These occur during NREM sleep, so they do not involve frightening dreams.

**sleepwalking** A parasomnia that involves leaving the bed during NREM—deep, non-dreaming—sleep.

eported to have mul-
l., 2003; Thorpy &
t part, the course of
people over the age
parasomnia.

derstand why some
ctors such as extreme
ation, use of sedative
have been implicated
alsh, 1988). On occa-
have been associated
ling homicide and sui-
2000). In one case in
Kenneth Parks, drove
his mother-in-law, and
-law. He was acquitted
ng sleepwalking as his
Billings, & Cartwright,
controversial, although
itimacy of some violent
sleepwalking episodes.
genetic component to
er incidence observed
and within families
ted disorder, *nocturnal*
individuals rise from
gh they are still asleep,
an previously thought,
% of individuals in one
ecause of insomnia com-
artara, 1997).

ck 8.4

blems of the cases below
ing: (a) nocturnal eating
rors, and (c) nightmares.
from her bed nearly every
rush to comfort her, but

she doesn't respond. Her heart rate is elevated during these episodes, and her pyjamas are soaked in sweat. The next day Ashley has no memory of the experience. _____

2. Rick has been dieting for more than a month but continues to gain weight. He has noticed that food is missing from the refrigerator, but he has no memory of eating. _____

3. Eddie occasionally cries out from his bedroom at night. His parents take turns going into his room during these episodes and are eventually able to calm him down. He usually tells them that he was being chased by a big green monster and that he almost was caught. His parents noticed that these nighttime events may have started after he watched television at a friend's house. _____

**Part B**

Fill in the blanks to make the following statements correct about the treatment of sleep disorders.

4. After Shirley's husband died at the age of 70, she could not sleep. For her insomnia, Shirley's family doctor prescribed enough _____ medications to get her through the hardest first week.

5. Dominic expressed concern to his doctor about developing a sleep disorder. His doctor suggested some relatively simple lifestyle changes otherwise known as good _____.

6. Ashley wakes up screaming every night, disregarding her parents' efforts to comfort her. Her heart rate is elevated in these episodes, and her pyjamas are soaked in sweat. The next day, she has no memory of the experience. To help reduce these episodes, Ashley's pediatrician used _____.

---

ating Disorders

ting disorders has increased
half century. As a result, they
parate group of disorders in

valent eating disorders. In
ting results in out-of-control
s that are often followed by
through vomiting or other

means. Anorexia nervosa, in which food intake is cut down dramatically, results in substantial weight loss and sometimes dangerously low body weight.

- In binge-eating disorder, a pattern of binge eating is *not* followed by purging.
- Bulimia nervosa and anorexia nervosa are largely confined to young, middle- to upper-class women in Western cultures who are pursuing a thin body

shape that is culturally mandated and biologically inappropriate, making it extremely difficult to achieve.

- Without treatment, eating disorders become chronic and can, on occasion, result in death.

## Causes of Eating Disorders

- In addition to sociocultural pressures, causal factors include possible biological and genetic vulnerabilities (the disorders tend to run in families), psychological factors (low self-esteem), social anxiety (fears of rejection), and distorted body image (relatively normal-weight individuals view themselves as fat and ugly).

## Treatment of Eating Disorders

- Several psychosocial treatments are effective, including cognitive-behavioural approaches combined with family therapy and interpersonal psychotherapy. Drug treatments are less effective.

## Sleep Disorders: The Major Dyssomnias

- Sleep disorders are highly prevalent in the general population and are of two types: dyssomnias (disturbances of sleep) and parasomnias (abnormal events such as nightmares and sleepwalking that occur during sleep).
- Of the dyssomnias, the most common disorder, primary insomnia, involves the inability to initiate sleep, problems maintaining sleep, or failure

to feel refreshed after a full night's sleep. Other dyssomnias include primary hypersomnia (excessive sleep), narcolepsy (sudden and irresistible sleep attacks), circadian rhythm sleep disorders (sleepiness or insomnia caused by the body's inability to synchronize its sleep patterns with day and night), and breathing-related sleep disorders (disruptions that have a physical origin, such as sleep apnea, that leads to excessive sleepiness or insomnia).

- The formal assessment of sleep disorders, a polysomnographic evaluation, is typically done by monitoring the heart, muscles, respiration, brain waves, and other functions of a sleeping client in the lab. In addition to such monitoring, it is helpful to determine the individual's sleep efficiency, a percentage based on the time the individual actually sleeps as opposed to time spent in bed trying to sleep.
- Parasomnias such as nightmares occur during REM (or dream) sleep, and sleep terrors and sleepwalking occur during NREM sleep.

## Treatment of Sleep Disorders

- Benzodiazepine medications have been helpful for short-term treatment of many of the dyssomnias, but they must be used carefully or they might cause rebound insomnia, a withdrawal experience that can cause worse sleep problems after the medication is stopped. Any long-term treatment of sleep problems should include psychological interventions such as stimulus control and sleep hygiene.

## Key Terms

| | | | |
|---|---|---|---|
| bulimia nervosa, 309 | dyssomnias, 336 | rebound insomnia, 340 | circadian rhythm sleep |
| binge, 309 | parasomnias, 336 | hypersomnia, 340 | disorders, 343 |
| anorexia nervosa, 309 | polysomnographic (PSG) | sleep apnea, 341 | nightmares, 347 |
| purging techniques, 312 | evaluation, 337 | narcolepsy, 342 | sleep terrors, 348 |
| binge-eating disorder | sleep efficiency (SE), 337 | breathing-related sleep | sleepwalking, 348 |
| (BED), 316 | microsleeps, 337 | disorders, 342 | |
| rapid eye movement | primary insomnia, 338 | | |
| (REM) sleep, 335 | | | |

## Answers to Concept Checks

**8.1**  1. c  2. a  3. a  4. b

**8.2**  1. T  2. T  3. F (females find a smaller size more attractive than men)  4. F (they help with bulimia nervosa, not anorexia)  5. T  6. T

**8.3**  1. e  2. d  3. b  4. h  5. g  6. f

**8.4**  **Part A**  1. b  2. a  3. c

**Part B**  4. benzodiazepine  5. sleep hygiene  6. scheduled awakenings

**dition**

book with InfoTrac
this online library
iew, and a handy
. Go to:

**ing.com**

orexia nervosa, body
eating, eating disor-
a syndromes, sleep-
nt, insomnia, obesity,
thrive

**Psychology**
**n Website**

**malpsych.nelson.com**
Internet links, critical

**hology**

**osa:** An example of
talks about her fears
enough" to be seen as a
the disorder!

- **Twins, Anorexia Nervosa/Bulimia:** Two twins talk about their battle with food.
- **Sleep Cycle:** This clip describes the normal cycle of REM and NREM sleep throughout the night—a cycle that may be altered in sleep disorders.

**Thomson NOW!** **http://hed.nelson.com** Go to this site for the link to ThomsonNow™, your one-stop study shop. Take a Pretest for this chapter and ThomsonNow™ will generate a personalized Study Plan based on your test results! The Study Plan will identify the topics you need to review and direct you to online resources to help you master those topics. You can then take a Posttest to help you determine the concepts you have mastered and what you still need work on.

## Video Concept Review

For challenging concepts that typically need more than one explanation, Mark Durand provides a video review via ThomsonNow™ of the following topic:

- Why obesity is not included in the DSM-IV-TR.

# Chapter Quiz

1. It is estimated that _____ of individuals with eating disorders die as a result of the disorder, with as many as 50% of those deaths coming from _____.
   a. 20%; homicide
   b. 20%; suicide
   c. 50%; homicide
   d. 50%; suicide

2. Dr. Thompson sees a patient with a chubby face, calluses on her fingers, and small scars on the back of her hand. Tests indicate that the patient is slightly over her expected weight and that she has an electrolyte imbalance. The patient reports that she is having persistent constipation and that she feels as if her heart has been skipping beats. These symptoms are consistent with:
   a. depression.
   b. anxiety.
   c. anorexia nervosa.
   d. bulimia nervosa.

3. Research on bulimia nervosa suggests that it most often co-occurs with:
   a. anxiety disorders.
   b. mood disorders.
   c. psychotic disorders.
   d. substance use disorders.

4. The typical age of onset for anorexia nervosa is _____, whereas the typical age range of onset for bulimia nervosa is _____.
   a. 20; younger
   b. 20; older
   c. 13; younger
   d. 13; older

5. In a study by Fallon and Rozin, female undergraduates:
   a. rated their current body size the same as the ideal body size.
   b. rated the ideal body size smaller than the attractive body size.
   c. rated the ideal body size heavier than the attractive body size.
   d. rated their current body size smaller than the ideal body size.

6. Which of the following statements is true of cognitive-behavioural therapy (CBT) and interpersonal therapy (IPT) in the treatment of bulimia?
   a. CBT appears to work faster than IPT, but they both seem to have the same positive effect at a 1-year follow-up.
   b. CBT and IPT appear to have the same impact in both the short term and the long term.
   c. IPT appears to work faster than CBT, but they both seem to have the same positive effect at a 1-year follow-up.
   d. Neither CBT nor IPT appears to be effective in the treatment of bulimia.

7. Which of the following is used to measure arm movements as an indicator of sleep activity and sleep quality?
   a. electrocardiogram
   b. electromyograph
   c. electroencephalograph
   d. actigraph

8. While sleeping, Michael, a 55-year-old overweight male, experiences a cessation in his breathing for short periods. Michael's wife reports that he snores continuously and never feels rested. Michael's symptoms are consistent with:
   a. narcolepsy.
   b. sleep apnea.
   c. sleep-wake schedule disorder.
   d. cataplexy.

9. Mr. Dunn has been experiencing insomnia for several weeks. His doctor recommends that he only lie in bed for 3 hours, the amount of time that he actually sleeps each night. The amount of time Mr. Dunn lies in bed is then increased as he begins to sleep more. This treatment is known as:
   a. sleep hygiene.
   b. sleep restriction.
   c. phase delay.
   d. progressive relaxation.

10. The primary difference between sleep terrors and nightmares is:
    a. sleep terrors usually begin with a scream.
    b. children do not remember nightmares.
    c. sleep terrors occur during NREM sleep.
    d. sleep terrors are more prevalent in the population.

*(See the Appendix on page 601 for answers.)*

# E... ating Disorders

Indi... ...s:
- Fe... ...sing drive to be thin
- Ar... ...ales from middle- to-upper-class families, wh... ...e environments
- L... ...es until recently

*EAT...*

...amounts of mostly

...vomiting

...s exercise

...causing
...nd
...h

*Social*—Cultural and social emphasis on slender ideal, leading to body dissatisfaction and preoccupation with food and eating.

*...hological—*
...hished sense of
...onal control and
...confidence, causing
...elf-esteem. Distorted
...y image.

Photodisc/
Getty Images

*CAUSES*

*Biological*—Possible genetic tendency to poor impulse control, emotional instability, and perfectionistic traits

## ANOREXIA NERVOSA

### Characteristics

- Intense fear of obesity and persistent pursuit of thinness; perpetual dissatisfaction with weight loss
- Severe caloric restriction, often with excessive exercise and sometimes with purging, to the point of semi-starvation
- Severely limiting caloric intake may cause cessation of menstruation, downy hair on limbs and cheeks, dry skin, brittle hair or nails, sensitivity to cold, and danger of acute cardiac or kidney failure
- Weight at least 15% below normal
- Average age of onset is about 13 years of age

### Treatment

- Hospitalization (at 70% below normal weight)
- Outpatient treatment to restore weight and correct dysfunctional attitudes on eating and body shape
- Family therapy
- Tends to be chronic if left untreated; more resistant to treatment than bulimia

Photodisc/Getty Images

## ...E-EATING DISORDER

### ...racteristics

- ...imilar to bulimia with
- ...ut-of-control food binges, but
- ...o attempt to purge the food (vomiting, laxative, diuretics) or compensate ...or excessive intake
- ...Marked physical and emotional stress; some sufferers binge to alleviate ...bad moods
- ...Binge eaters share same concerns about weight and body shape as individuals with anorexia and bulimia
- ...Tends to affect more older people than either bulimia or anorexia

### ...reatment

- Short-term CBT to address behaviour and attitudes on eating and body shape
- IPT to improve interpersonal functioning
- Drug treatments that reduce feelings of hunger
- Self-help approaches

# Exploring Sleep Disorders

Characterized by extreme disruption in the everyday lives of affected individuals, and are an important factor in many psychological disorders.

## SLEEP DISORDERS

### DYSSOMNIAS

Disturbances in the timing, amount, or quality of sleep.

#### Primary Insomnia

- Characteristics include difficulty initiating sleep, difficulty maintaining sleep, or nonrestorative sleep.
- Causes include pain, insufficient exercise, drug use, environmental influences, anxiety, respiratory problems, and biological vulnerability.
- Treatment may be medical (benzodiazepines) or psychological (anxiety reduction, improved sleep hygiene); combined approach is usually most effective.

#### Narcolepsy

- Characteristics include sudden daytime onset of REM sleep combined with cataplexy, a rapid loss of muscle tone that can be quite mild or result in complete collapse. Often accompanied by sleep paralysis and/or hypnagogic hallucinations.
- Causes are likely to be genetic.
- Treatment is medical (stimulant drugs).

#### Primary Hypersomnia

- Characteristics include abnormally excessive sleep and sleepiness, and involuntary daytime sleeping. Classified as a disorder only when it's subjectively perceived as disruptive.
- Causes may involve genetic link and/or excess serotonin.
- Treatment is usually medical (stimulant drugs).

#### Breathing-Related Sleep Disorder

- Characteristics include disturbed sleep and daytime fatigue resulting from hypoventilation (labored breathing) or sleep apnea (suspended breathing).
- Causes may include narrow or obstructed airway, obesity, and increasing age.
- Treatments to improve breathing are medical or mechanical.

#### Circadian Rhythm Sleep Disorder

- Characteristics include sleepiness or insomnia.
- Caused by inability to synchronize sleep patterns with current pattern of day and night due to jet lag, shift work, delayed sleep, or advanced sleep (going to bed earlier than normal bedtime).
- Treatment includes phase delays to adjust bedtime and bright light to readjust biological clock.

### DIAGNOSING SLEEP DISORDERS

A polysomnographic (PSG) evaluation assesses an individual's sleep habits with various electronic tests to measure airflow, brain activity, eye movements, muscle movements, and heart activity. Results are weighed with a measure of sleep efficiency (SE), the percentage of bed time spent asleep.

### PARASOMNIAS

Abnormal behaviours that occur during sleep.

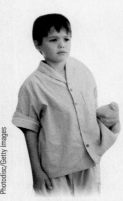

#### Nightmares

Frightening REM dreams that awaken the sleeper. Nightmares qualify as nightmare disorder when they are stressful enough to impair normal functioning. Causes are unknown, but they tend to decrease with age.

#### Sleep Terrors

Occur during non-REM (nondreaming) sleep and most commonly afflict children. Sleeping child screams, cries, sweats, sometimes walks, has rapid heartbeat, and cannot easily be awakened or comforted. More common in boys than girls, and possible genetic link since tend to run in families. May subside with time.

#### Sleepwalking

Occurs at least once during non-REM sleep in 15% to 30% of children under age 15. Causes may include extreme fatigue, sleep deprivation, sedative or hypnotic drugs, and stress. Adult sleepwalking is usually associated with other psychological disorders. May have a genetic link.

# Sexual and Gender Identity Disorders

**What Is Normal Sexuality?**
*Gender Differences*
*Cultural Differences*
*The Development of Sexual Orientation*

**Gender Identity Disorder**
*Defining Gender Identity Disorder*
*Causes*
*Treatment*

**Overview of Sexual Dysfunctions**
*Sexual Desire Disorders*
*Sexual Arousal Disorders*
*Orgasm Disorders*
*Sexual Pain Disorders*
*Assessing Sexual Behaviour*

**Causes and Treatment of Sexual Dysfunction**
*Causes of Sexual Dysfunction*
*Treatment of Sexual Dysfunction*

**Paraphilia: Clinical Descriptions**
*Fetishism*
*Voyeurism and Exhibitionism*
*Transvestic Fetishism*
*Sexual Sadism and Sexual Masochism*
*Pedophilia and Incest*
*Paraphilia in Women*
*Causes of Paraphilia*

**Assessing and Treating Paraphilia**
*Psychological Treatment*
*Drug Treatments*
*Summary*

**Visual Summary: Exploring Sexual and Gender Identity Disorders**

 **Abnormal Psychology Live CD-ROM**
*Erectile Dysfunction: Clark*
*Changing Over: Jessica*

Earl and Nazima Kowall/Corbis

# What Is Normal Sexuality?

■ *Describe how sociocultural factors influence what are considered "normal" sexual behaviours.*

You have all read magazine surveys reporting sensational information on sexual practices. According to one, men can reach orgasm 15 or more times a day (in reality, such ability is very rare) and women fantasize about being raped (this is even rarer). Surveys like this fail us on two counts: First, they claim to reveal sexual norms when they are really, for the most part, distorted half-truths. Second, the facts they present typically are not based on any scientific methodology that would make them reliable, although they do sell magazines.

What is normal sexual behaviour? As we will see, it depends. More to the point, when is sexual behaviour that is somewhat different from the norm a disorder? Again, it depends. Current views tend to be quite tolerant of a variety of sexual expressions, even if they are unusual, unless the behaviour is associated with a substantial impairment in functioning. Three kinds of sexual behaviour meet this definition. In *gender identity disorders*, there is psychological dissatisfaction with one's biological sex. The disorder is not specifically sexual but rather a disturbance in the person's sense of identity as a male or a female. But these disorders are often grouped with sexual disorders, as in DSM-IV-TR. Individuals with *sexual dysfunction* find it difficult to function adequately while having sex; for example, they may not become aroused or achieve orgasm. *Paraphilia*, the relatively new term for sexual deviation, includes disorders in which sexual arousal occurs primarily in the context of inappropriate objects or individuals. *Philia* means a strong attraction or liking, and *para* indicates the attraction is abnormal. Paraphilic arousal patterns tend to be focused rather narrowly, often precluding mutually consenting adult patterns, even if desired. Before describing these three types of disorders, we return to our initial question, "What is normal sexual behaviour?" to gain an important perspective.

Determining the prevalence of sexual practices accurately requires careful surveys sampling specific populations. For more than 40 years, sex researchers and public health officials have relied on the comprehensive survey of sexual behaviours and attitudes by a pioneer investigator into sexual behaviour, Alfred Kinsey (e.g., Kinsey, Pomeroy, & Martin, 1948; Kinsey, Pomeroy, Martin, & Gebhard, 1953). But more recent surveys are updating our knowledge on what is currently "normal" sexual behaviour in our culture. Some such studies have focused on rates of sexual risk taking and some on

issues such as gender differences in different aspects of sexual behaviours.

As we discussed briefly in Chapter 7, the sexual risks taken by university students, other young adults, and adolescents remain alarmingly high despite the well-publicized AIDS epidemic and the recent increase in other sexually transmitted diseases (STDs; Maticka-Tyndale, 2001). For example, a study by DeBuono, Zinner, Daamen, and McCormack (1990) showed that although condom use in university women increased from 12% in 1975 to 41% in 1989, more than half the sexually active university women still practised unprotected sex!

According to Eleanor Maticka-Tyndale at the University of Windsor, other areas of concern from the perspective of AIDS and STD prevention are the number of sexual partners that young people have and the seeming casualness of these encounters (Maticka-Tyndale, 2001). Youth most commonly move through a pattern of serial monogamy—they are with one partner for a time and then move on to another exclusive partner when that relationship ends. But some youth engage in sex outside a primary relationship (e.g., when travelling or when away from a primary partner, or in a casual sexual encounter). Three Canadian surveys suggest that about one-third of adolescent males and about one-quarter of adolescent females report two or more sexual partners in a year (see Table 9.1). The cumulative number of sexual

| **TABLE 9.1** Proportion of Male and Female Adolescents with Multiple Intercourse Partners in Past Year | | |
|---|---|---|
| | Males | Females |
| National Population Health Survey, 1996[a] | | |
| 15–17 years, >1 partner | 31% | 24% |
| 18–19 years, >1 partner | 38% | 24% |
| Nova Scotia, 1996 (Grades 10–12)[b] | 20% | 17% |
| 15–18 years, >2 partners | 20% | 17% |
| Quebec, 1998[c] | | |
| 15–19 years, >1 partner | 32% | 33% |

[a] Maticka-Tyndale, McKay, & Barrett, 2001
[b] Langille, 2000
[c] Institute de la statistique du Quebec, 2001

*Source:* Maticka-Tyndale, E. Sexual Health and Canadian Youth: How Do We Measure Up? *Canadian Journal of Human Sexuality* Spring 2001; 10, 1–2; pp. 1–17.

...thus add up over the ... risk for AIDS/STDs

...men tend toward a ...ttern of sexual rela-...in sexual behaviour ...amatic. One common ...is that a much higher ...report that they mas-...asm; Oliver & Hyde, ...indy Meston and her ...ts at the University of ...gs supported this dif-...only 48% of women

reported masturbating alone (Meston, Trapnell, & Gorzalka, 1996). The results of this survey are shown in Table 9.2. Among those who did masturbate, the frequency of masturbation was also greater for men than for women (see right side of Table 9.2). Thus, gender differences in masturbation appear to persist today even when other long-standing gender differences in sexual behaviour, such as the probability of engaging in premarital intercourse, have virtually disappeared (Clement, 1990; Meston et al., 1996; see left side of Table 9.2).

Meston and colleagues' study (1996) also revealed that endorsement of many types of sexual fantasy was significantly higher for men than women (e.g., intercourse, oral-genital sex, sadism, and promiscuity fantasies). The only fantasy endorsed more often by

## ...ges of University Men and Women Who Participated in Various ...onal and Intrapersonal Sexual Behaviours

| Men (n = 275) | Women (n = 427) | Intrapersonal Sexual Behaviours | Men (n = 275) | Women (n = 427) |
|---|---|---|---|---|
| | | Fantasy total | 33 | 25* |
| 80 | 81 | **Gender Orientation Fantasies** | | |
| 73 | 74 | Homosexual fantasies | 11 | 18 |
| 72 | 71 | Fantasizing you are of opposite sex | 14 | 11 |
| 68 | 72 | Dressing in clothes of opposite sex | 13 | 11 |
| 73 | 70 | **Intercourse Fantasies** | | |
| 75 | 73 | Having intercourse in unusual positions | 84 | 53* |
| | | Anal intercourse | 34 | 10* |
| 67 | 65 | Sexual intercourse | 93 | 81* |
| 67 | 64 | **Masochism Fantasies** | | |
| 68 | 68 | Being tied up or bound during sex | 40 | 35 |
| 63 | 62 | Being forced to submit to sex | 29 | 35 |
| 69 | 68 | Being sexually degraded | 6 | 9 |
| 25 | 32 | **Sadism Fantasies** | | |
| 29 | 26 | Whipping or beating sexual partner | 11 | 4 |
| 41 | 41 | Degrading sexual partner | 9 | 3* |
| | | Forcing partner to submit to sex | 29 | 13* |
| 44 | 46 | **Promiscuity Fantasies** | | |
| 51 | 53 | Mate swapping fantasies | 17 | 8* |
| 55 | 50 | Forbidden lover in sexual adventures | 44 | 36 |
| | | Being a prostitute | 9 | 16 |
| 50 | 52 | Having >1 partner simultaneously | 71 | 31* |
| 47 | 49 | **Miscellaneous Fantasies** | | |
| 36 | 40 | Sexual relations with animals | 3 | 4 |
| 28 | 34 | Using artificial devices for stimulation | 32 | 23 |
| 35 | 42 | Dressing in erotic garments | 34 | 51* |
| 5 | 11 | Oral-genital sex | 76 | 47* |
| 5.40 | 5.37 | *Frequency of fantasies (0–8 scale)* | 4.63 | 2.92* |
| 61 | 57 | *Masturbating alone (% of sample)* | 80 | 48* |
| 17.29 | 17.50 | *Masturbation frequency (masturbators only; 0–8)* | 3.81 | 2.46* |
| 2.65 | 3.01 | *Age of first interest in sex (in years)* | 13.50 | 15.00* |
| | | *Ideal frequency of sexual intercourse (0–8)* | 4.43 | 3.85* |

...s indicated via asterisks (*).

...ferences in sexuality: Variations in sexual behavior between Asian and Non-Asian university students" by C. M. Meston, ...6, *Archives of Sexual Behavior*, 25(1), 44–49. Reprinted with kind permission of Springer Science and Business Media.

women involved dressing in erotic garments (see right side of Table 9.2). Men also reported fantasizing more frequently than women (Meston et al., 1996).

Another continuing gender difference is reflected in attitudes toward *casual* premarital sex, with men expressing a far more permissive attitude than women, although this gap is becoming much smaller. In comparison with undergraduate women, Meston et al. (1996) found that undergraduate males reported having experienced a greater number of one-night stands, predicted a greater number of sexual partners in the next 5 years, and reported more frequent fantasies about having sex with someone other than their steady dating partner. By contrast, no significant mean differences existed between males and females in self-reported number of lifetime or past year sexual partners (Meston et al., 1996).

There also appear to be gender differences in "sexual self-schemas"—basic or core beliefs about sexual aspects of ourselves. Women tend to report the experience of passionate and romantic feelings and an openness to sexual experience as integral parts of their sexuality. However, a substantial number of women also hold an embarrassed, conservative, or self-conscious schema that sometimes conflicts with more positive aspects of their sexual attitudes. Men, on the other hand, evidence a strong component of feeling powerful, independent, and aggressive as part of their sexuality in addition to being passionate, loving, and open to experience. Also, men do not generally possess negative core beliefs reflecting self-consciousness, embarrassment, or feeling behaviourally inhibited (e.g., Andersen, Cyranowski, & Espindle, 1999; Cyranowski, Aarestad, & Andersen, 1999).

## Cultural Differences

What is normal in 2006 in Western countries like Canada and the United States may not necessarily be normal in other parts of the world. For example, in about half of more than 100 societies surveyed worldwide, premarital sexual behaviour is culturally accepted and encouraged; in the remaining half, premarital sex is unacceptable and discouraged (Bancroft, 1989; Broude & Greene, 1980). Thus, what is normal sexual behaviour in one culture is not necessarily normal in another, and the wide range of sexual expression must be considered in diagnosing the presence of a disorder.

## The Development of Sexual Orientation

Reports suggest that **homosexuality** runs in families (Bailey & Benishay, 1993), and concordance for homosexuality is more common among identical twins than among fraternal twins or natural siblings (Bailey, Pillard, Neale, & Agyei, 1993; Whitnam, Diamond, & Martin, 1993). A recent review by Martin Lalumière, Ray Blanchard, and Kenneth Zucker (2000) at the Centre for Addiction and Mental Health in Toronto also shows that homosexuals have a 39% greater chance of being non-right-handed (left handed or mixed handed) than heterosexuals (Lalumière, Blanchard, & Zucker, 2000) consistent with the possibility that the actual structure of the brain might be different in homosexuals and heterosexuals (Allen & Gorski, 1992; Byne et al., 2000). Another report suggests a possible gene (or genes) for homosexuality on the X chromosome (Hamer, Hu, Magnuson, Hu, & Pattatucci, 1993).

The principal conclusion drawn in the media is that sexual orientation has a biological cause. Gay rights activists are decidedly split on the significance of these findings. Some are pleased with the biological interpretation, because people can no longer assume homosexuals have made a morally depraved choice of supposedly deviant arousal patterns. Others, however, note how quickly the public has pounced on the implication that something is biologically wrong with individuals with homosexual arousal patterns, assuming that someday the abnormality will be detected in the fetus and prevented, perhaps through genetic engineering.

Do such arguments over biological causes sound familiar? Think back to studies described in Chapter 2 that attempted to link complex behaviour to particular genes. In almost every case, these studies could not be replicated, and investigators fell back on a model in which genetic contributions to behavioural traits and psychological disorders come from many genes, each making a relatively small contribution to a *vulnerability*. This generalized biological vulnerability then interacts in a complex way with various environmental conditions, personality traits, and other contributors to determine behavioural patterns.

The same thing is now happening with sexual orientation. For example, neither Bailey et al. (1999) nor Rice, Anderson, Risch, and Ebers (1999), in later studies, could replicate the report suggesting a specific gene for homosexuality (Hamer et al., 1993). Most theoretical models outlining these complex interactions for sexual orientation imply that there may be many pathways to the development of heterosexuality or homosexuality and that no one factor—biological or psychological—can predict the outcome (Bancroft, 1994; Byne & Parsons, 1993).

Bem (1996) refers to his model of the development of sexual orientation as "exotic becomes erotic," a phrase that summarizes the principles of

---

**homosexuality** Sexual attraction to members of the same sex.

the theory nicely. Bem proposes that we inherit a temperament to behave in certain ways that later interacts with environmental factors to produce sexual orientation (see Figure 9.1). For example, if a boy prefers active and aggressive or "boy typical" behaviours, he will feel similar to his same-sex peers. A young boy who feels less aggressive may avoid rough-and-tumble play in favour of "girl typical" activities. Their activities, whether typical or atypical, lead children to feel different from either their opposite or their same-sex peers. A young boy with boy-typical activities will feel more different from girls than he does from boys, making the opposite sex more "exotic." Sexual attraction in later years will be to the group of more exotic individuals. A young boy who engages in girl-typical activities is likely to feel more different from other boys than he does from girls. Therefore, what is exotic to this boy is other boys. Sexual attraction later follows.

One of the more intriguing findings from the twin studies of Bailey and Pillard (1991) is that approximately 50% of the identical twins with the *same genetic structure* and the *same environment* (growing up in the same house) *did not* have the same sexual orientation. Also intriguing is the finding in a study of 302 homosexual men conducted by Ray Blanchard and colleagues (Blanchard & Bogaert, 1998; Cantor, Blanchard, Paterson, & Bogaert, 2002) that males growing up with older brothers are more likely to be homosexual, whereas having older sisters, or younger brothers or sisters, is not correlated with later sexual orientation. This may suggest the importance of environmental influences, although the mechanism has not been identified.

In any case, the simple one-dimensional claims that homosexuality is caused by a gene or that heterosexuality is caused by healthy early developmental experiences will continue to appeal to the general population. Although we could be wrong, neither explanation is likely to be proved correct. Almost certainly, biology sets certain limits within which social and psychological factors affect development (Diamond, 1995).

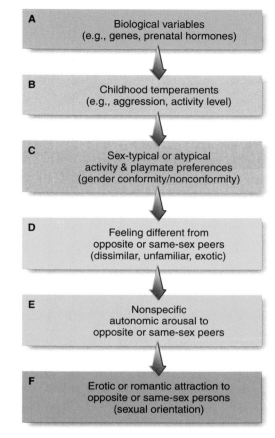

**Figure 9.1** ■ The sequence of events leading to sexual orientation for most men and women in a gender-polarizing culture. (From Bem, D.J. (1996) Exotic becomes erotic: A developmental theory of sexual orientation. *Psychological Review*, 103, 320–335.)

# Gender Identity Disorder

■ *Describe the defining clinical features, causes, and treatments of gender identity disorder, and distinguish gender identity disorder from transvestic fetishism.*

What is it that makes you think you are a man? Or a woman? Clearly, it's more than your sexual arousal patterns or your anatomy. It's also more than the reactions and experiences of your family and of society. The essence of your masculinity or femininity is a deep-seated personal sense called *gender identity*. This sense of the self as male or female is typically consolidated by age 3 or 4 (Bradley & Zucker, 1997). **Gender identity disorder** is present if a person's physical gender is not consistent with

**gender identity disorder** Psychological dissatisfaction with one's own biological gender, a disturbance in the sense of one's identity as a male or female. The primary goal is not sexual arousal but rather to live the life of the opposite gender.

that person's sense of identity. People with this disorder feel trapped in a body of the wrong sex. Consider the case of Joe.

## Joe
### Trapped in the Wrong Body

Joe was a 17-year-old male and the last of five children. Although his mother had wanted a girl, he became her favourite child. His father worked long hours and had little contact with the boy. For as long as Joe could remember, he had thought of himself as a girl. He began dressing in girls' clothes of his own accord before he was 5 years old and continued cross-dressing into junior high school. He developed interests in cooking, knitting, crocheting, and embroidering, skills he acquired by reading an encyclopedia. His older brother often scorned him for his distaste of such "masculine" activities as hunting.

Joe associated mostly with girls during this period, although he remembered being strongly attached to a boy in grade 1. In his sexual fantasies, which developed around 12 years of age, he pictured himself as a female having intercourse with a male. His extremely effeminate behaviour made him the object of scorn and ridicule when he entered high school at age 15. Usually passive and unassertive, he ran away from home and attempted suicide. Unable to continue in high school, he attended secretarial school, where he was the only boy in his class. During his first interview with a therapist he reported, "I am a woman trapped in a man's body and I would like to have surgery to become a woman."

We return to Joe in our discussion of treatment.

## *Defining Gender Identity Disorder*

Gender identity disorder (or *transsexualism*, as it used to be called) must be distinguished from *transvestic fetishism*, a paraphilic disorder (discussed later) in which individuals, usually males, are sexually aroused by wearing articles of clothing associated with the opposite sex. The primary purpose of cross-dressing is sexual gratification. In the case of gender identity disorder, in contrast, the primary goal is not sexual but rather the desire to live life openly in a manner consistent with that of the other gender.

Gender identity disorder must also be distinguished from *intersexed individuals (hermaphrodites)*, who are born with ambiguous genitalia associated with documented hormonal or other physical abnormalities. Depending on their particular mix of characteristics, they are usually "assigned" a specific sex at birth, sometimes undergoing surgery and hormonal treatments to alter their sexual anatomy. Individuals with gender identity disorder, by contrast, have no demonstrated physical abnormalities.

Finally, gender identity disorder must be distinguished from the homosexual arousal patterns of a male who sometimes behaves effeminately or a woman with homosexual arousal patterns and masculine mannerisms. Such an individual does not feel like a woman trapped in a man's body or have any desire to be a woman (or vice versa). Note also, as the DSM-IV-TR criteria do, that gender identity is *independent* of sexual arousal patterns. For example, a male-to-female transsexual (a male with a feminine gender identity) may be sexually attracted to females, which, technically, makes his arousal homosexual. Coleman, Bockting, and Gooren (1993) reported on nine female-to-male individuals who were sexually attracted to men. Thus, heterosexual women before surgery were gay men after surgery. Chivers and Bailey (2000) compared a group possessing this attribute with a group of female-to-male individuals who were attracted to women both before and after surgery, and they found the groups did not differ in the strength of their gender identity (as males), although the latter group was more sexually assertive and, understandably, more interested in surgery to create an artificial penis.

Gender identity disorder is relatively rare. The estimated incidence based on studies in several countries is 1 in 37 000 in Sweden, 1 in 24 000 in Australia, and 1 in 11 000 in the Netherlands for biological males, compared with 1 in 103 000, 1 in 150 000, and 1 in 30 000, respectively, for biological females (Baker, van Kesteren, Gooren, & Bezemer, 1993; Ross, Walinder, Lundstrom, & Thuwe, 1981). Many countries now allow a series of legal steps to change gender identity. In Germany, between 2.1 and 2.4 per 100 000 in the population took at least the first legal steps of changing their first names. Again, the male–female ratio is 2.3:1 (Weitze & Osburg, 1996).

Probably the best-known case of male-to-female transsexualism in Canada is Enza Anderson, who gained international attention when she ran for mayor of Toronto in 2000 and came in third. Enza always felt she was female and started dressing as a girl secretly as a teenager, borrowing clothes from her mother. Enza takes estrogen and has had electrolysis hair-removal treatments; she would like to receive breast implants and is considering sex reassignment surgery (which we describe later). Enza trained as a civil engineer but is not working in that field because she cannot easily dress as a woman and be herself. You can visit her website at http://tgmedia.enacre.net/lorna_lynne/enza.html.

In some cultures individuals with mistaken gender identity (i.e., those who would be considered to have gender identity disorder in Western culture) are often accorded the status of "shaman" or "seer" and treated as wisdom figures (Carmody & Carmody, 1993). Stoller (1976) reported on two contemporary feminized Native North American men who were not only accepted but also esteemed by their tribes for their expertise in healing rituals. It was when the White settlers started to colonize North America that the oppression of such people began. Such individuals were labelled "berdache" (Herdt, 1987). Williams (1986) has argued that individuals with mistaken gender identity should be considered a third gender (i.e., an alternative or intermediate gender), since berdaches appear to be accepted by their societies as distinct from both men and women. Contrary to the respect accorded these individuals in some cultures, social tolerance for them is relatively low in Western cultures.

Enza Anderson is a transsexual activist living in Toronto. She gained international attention when she ran for mayor of Toronto in 2000.

## Causes

Research has yet to uncover any specific biological contributions to gender identity disorder, although it seems likely that a biological predisposition will be discovered. Early research suggests that, as with sexual orientation, slightly higher levels of testosterone or estrogen at certain critical periods of development might masculinize a female fetus or feminize a male fetus (e.g., Gladue, Green, & Hellman, 1984; Imperato-McGinley, Peterson, Gautier, & Sturla, 1979). Variations in hormonal levels could occur naturally or because of medication that a pregnant mother is taking. However, scientists have yet to establish a link between prenatal hormonal influence and later gender identity, although it is still possible that one exists. Structural differences in the area of the brain that controls male sex hormones have been observed in individuals with male-to-female gender identity disorder (Zhou, Hofman, Gooren, & Swaab, 1995) with the result that the brains are comparatively more feminine. But it isn't clear whether this is a cause or an effect.

### Disorder Criteria Summary
Gender Identity Disorder

Features of gender Identity disorder include:
- Strong and persistent cross-gender identification, unrelated to any perceived cultural advantage of being the other sex
- Persistent discomfort with her or his sex, or sense of inappropriateness of gender roles of that sex
- Preoccupation with getting rid of primary and secondary sex characteristics, or belief that he or she was born the wrong sex
- Feelings are not caused by a physical intersex condition
- Clinically significant distress or impairment in functioning

*Source:* Based on DSM-IV-TR. Used with permission from the *Diagnostic and Statistical Manual of Mental Disorders,* Fourth Edition, Text Revision. Copyright 2000. American Psychiatric Association.

At least some evidence suggests that gender identity firms up between 18 months and 3 years of age (Ehrhardt & Meyer-Bahlburg, 1981; Money & Ehrhardt, 1972) and is relatively fixed after that. But newer studies suggest that preexisting biological factors have already had their impact. One interesting and tragic case illustrating this phenomenon was originally reported by Green and Money (1969), who described the sequence of events that occurred in the case of David/Brenda (originally referred to in Chapter 3 of this text).

## David/Brenda
### Nature over Nurture

A set of male identical twins was born into a well-adjusted family in Winnipeg. Several weeks later, an unfortunate accident occurred. Although circumcision went routinely for one boy, the physician's hand slipped so that the electric current in the device burned off the penis of the second boy. The parents consulted specialists in children with intersexual problems and were faced with a choice. The specialists suggested that the easiest solution would be to reassign their son as a girl, and the parents agreed. At the age of several months, David became "Brenda." The parents purchased a new wardrobe and treated the child in every way possible as a girl. These twins were followed through childhood and, upon reaching puberty, the young girl was given hormonal replacement therapy.

After 6 years the doctors lost track of the case but assumed Brenda had adjusted well. In fact, she endured almost intolerable inner turmoil. We know this because two clinical scientists found the family and reported a long-term follow-up (Diamond & Sigmundson, 1997) and because this person, whose real name was David/Brenda Reimer, told the story from his own point of view as an adult in a book called *As Nature Made Him* (Colapinto, 2000) and on *Oprah*. Brenda never adjusted to her assigned gender. As a child she preferred rough and tumble play and resisted wearing girls' clothes. In public bathrooms she often insisted on urinating while standing up, which usually made a mess. By early adolescence Brenda was pretty sure she was a boy, but her doctors pressed her to act more feminine.

When she was 14 she confronted her parents, telling them she was so miserable she was considering suicide. At that point they told her the true story and the muddy waters of her mind began to clear. Shortly thereafter, Brenda had additional surgery changing her back to David. Although David married and adopted three children, his life was tortured by his early experiences and he eventually committed suicide in 2004 (Canadian Press, 2004).

It certainly seems that biology expressed itself in David/Brenda's case. However, other case studies of children whose genders were similarly reassigned very early in life show that the children adapted successfully (e.g., Bradley, Oliver, Chernick, & Zucker, 1998; Gearhart, 1989).

Kenneth Zucker and Susan Bradley in Toronto have studied boys who behave in effeminate ways, investigating what makes them that way and following what happens to them. Research from their clinic led to the discovery that when most young boys spontaneously display "feminine" interests and behaviours, they are typically discouraged by most families and these behaviours usually cease. However, boys who consistently display these behaviours are not discouraged, and are sometimes encouraged, as seemed to be the case with Joe (Zucker & Bradley, 1995; see also Green, 1987). It has also been suggested that a parent's preference for a girl or a boy might influence how a child is raised within the family with respect to encouragement or discouragement of gender-stereotypic behaviours in the child (Bradley & Zucker, 1997). In fact, evidence from the Toronto clinic does suggest that, at least for some mothers of boys with gender identity disorder, the mother's difficulty in dealing with her disappointment about not having a girl does indeed have an impact on the way in which she relates to her son (Zucker & Bradley, 1995; Zucker, Bradley, & Ipp, 1993). Girls with gender identity disorder have been less systematically studied with respect to the role of family factors (Bradley & Zucker, 1997).

Other factors, such as excessive attention and physical contact on the part of the mother, *may* also play some role, as may a lack of male playmates during the early years of socialization (Green, 1987). These are just some of the factors identified as characteristic of effeminate boys. Remember that as-yet-undiscovered biological factors may also contribute to the spontaneous display of cross-gender behaviours and interests. However, in follow-ups of these boys, few seem to develop the "wrong" gender identity (Green, 1987), although we are not sure how many do so because follow-up studies are continuing. The most likely adult outcome is the development of homosexual preferences, but even this particular sexual arousal pattern seems to occur exclusively in only approximately 40% of the feminine boys. Another 32% show some degree of *bisexuality,* sexual attraction to both their own and the opposite sex. Looking at it from the other side, 60% were functioning heterosexually (Green, 1987). We can safely say that the causes of mistaken gender identity are still something of a mystery.

### Treatment

Treatment is available for gender identity disorder in a few specialty clinics around the world, although much controversy surrounds treatment (Carroll, 2000). At present, the most common decision is to alter the anatomy physically to be consistent with the identity through **sex reassignment surgery.** Recently, psychosocial treatments to directly alter mistaken gender identity itself have been attempted in a few cases.

## Sex Reassignment Surgery

To qualify for surgery at a reputable clinic, individuals must live in the opposite-sex role for 1 to 2 years so that they can be sure they want to change sex. They also must be stable psychologically, financially, and socially (Blanchard & Steiner, 1990). In male-to-female candidates, hormones are administered to promote *gynecomastia* (the growth of breasts) and the development of other secondary sex characteristics. Facial hair is typically removed through electrolysis. If the individual is satisfied with the events of the trial period, the genitals are removed and a vagina is constructed.

For female-to-male transsexuals, an artificial penis is typically constructed through plastic surgery, using sections of skin and muscle from elsewhere in the body, such as the thigh. Breasts are surgically removed. Genital surgery is more difficult and complex in biological females. Estimates of transsexuals' satisfaction with surgery indicate predominantly successful adjustment (approximately 75% improved) among those who could be reached for follow-ups, with female-to-male conversions adjusting better than male to female (Bodlund & Kullgren, 1996; Carroll, 2000). However, many people were lost to follow-up. Approximately 7% of sex reassignment cases later regret surgery (Bancroft, 1989; Lundstrom, Pauly, & Walinder, 1984). This is unfortunate, because the surgery is irreversible. Also, as many as 2% attempt suicide after surgery, a rate much higher than for the general population. One problem may be incorrect diagnosis and assessment. These assessments are complex and should always be done at highly specialized gender identity clinics. Nevertheless, surgery has made life worth living for some people who suffered the effects of existing in what they felt to be the wrong body.

A controversial issue in Canada has been whether sex reassignment surgery should be a publicly funded medical procedure. The treatment of this issue varies by province and territory. Alberta, British Columbia, and Saskatchewan are the only provinces that currently fund sex reassignment surgery. The procedure was funded in Ontario for 30 years. The high cost of the procedure, and efforts to cut costs in health care spending, led the Ontario government to delist this surgery as eligible for medicare coverage in 1998. However, advocacy groups argue that transgendered people's dignity is being harmed by the change in access to this surgery. In fact, four transsexual individuals took the Ontario government to task in September 2003, in an important human rights hearing (Egale Canada, 2003). In November 2005, the Human Rights Tribunal ruled that the province should pay for sex reassignment surgery for three of the four complainants. However, the tribunal stopped short of requiring the Ontario government to relist this procedure as an eligible expense under the province's public health insurance plan (CUPE, 2005).

## Treatment of Intersexuality

As we noted, surgery and hormonal replacement therapy has been standard treatment for many intersexed individuals (hermaphrodites) who may be born with physical characteristics of both sexes. Recently, this group of individuals has been the subject of more careful evaluation, resulting in some new ideas and new approaches to treatment (Fausto-Sterling, 2000a, 2000b). Specifically, Fausto-Sterling suggested previously that there are five sexes: males; females; "herms," who are named after true hermaphrodites, or people born with both testes and ovaries; "merms," who are anatomically more male than female but possess some aspect of female genitalia; and "ferms," who have ovaries but possess some aspect of male genitalia. She estimates, based on the best evidence available, that for every 1000 children born, 17, or 1.7%, may be intersexual in some form. What Fausto-Sterling (2000b) and others have noted is that individuals in this group are often dissatisfied with surgery, much as David/Brenda was in the case we described. There have been instances in which doctors, upon observing anatomical sexual ambiguity after birth, treat it as an emergency and immediately perform surgery.

Fausto-Sterling suggests that an increasing number of pediatric endocrinologists, urologists, and psychologists are beginning to examine the wisdom of early genital surgery that results in an irreversible gender assignment. Instead, health professionals may want to examine closely the precise nature of the intersexed condition and consider surgery only as a last resort, and only when they are sure the particular condition will lead to a specific psychological gender identity. Otherwise, psychological treatments to help individuals adapt to their particular sexual anatomy, or their emerging gender identity, might be more appropriate.

---

**sex reassignment surgery**　Surgical procedures to alter a person's physical anatomy to conform to that person's psychological gender identity.

## Psychosocial Treatment

In some clinics, therapists, in cooperation with their clients, attempt to change gender identity before considering surgery. Most adult clients cannot conceive of changing their basic identity. However, some individuals request psychological treatment before embarking on a treatment course leading to surgery, usually because they are in great psychological distress or because surgery is immediately unavailable. The first successful effort to change gender identity was reported from our sexuality clinic (Barlow, Reynolds, & Agras, 1973). Joe, described earlier, was extremely depressed and suicidal; because surgery was not possible at his age without parental consent, which was not forthcoming, he agreed to a course of psychological treatment.

Joe's greatest difficulty was the ridicule and scorn heaped on him for his extremely effeminate gestures. We developed a behavioural rating scale for gender-specific motor behaviour (Barlow et al., 1979; Beck & Barlow, 1984) to help Joe identify the precise ways he sat, stood, and walked that were stereotypically masculine or feminine. Through behavioural rehearsal and modelling, he learned to act in a more typically masculine manner when he so chose. Soon he reported enormous satisfaction in avoiding ridicule by simply choosing to behave differently in some situations. What followed was more extensive role playing and rehearsal for social skills as he learned to make better eye contact and converse more positively and confidently. After this phase of therapy he was better adjusted, but he still felt he was really a woman and he was strongly sexually attracted to males.

During the next phase, a female therapist worked directly on his fantasies, encouraging him to imagine himself in sexual situations with a woman and to generate more characteristically masculine fantasies as he went about his day-to-day business. After several months of intensive training, Joe's gender identity began to change. At the end of this phase, much to his delight, he reported that he now felt like a 17-year-old boy in addition to behaving like one, although he was still sexually attracted to males. Because he expressed a strong desire to become sexually attracted to females, procedures were implemented to alter his patterns of sexual arousal, and at a 5-year follow-up Joe had made a successful adjustment.

Two additional cases were treated in a similar fashion (Barlow, Abel, & Blanchard, 1979) and also resulted in altered gender identity. These two individuals, who were somewhat older than Joe, wished to retain their homosexual arousal patterns, and they were assisted in adjusting to a standard homosexual lifestyle without the burden of mistaken gender identity. Similar efforts to treat gender identity disturbance in prepubescent boys have been successful in a number of cases with follow-ups of 4 years or more (Rekers, Kilgus, & Rosen, 1990).

The issue of whether gender identity disorder in children should be treated has been hotly debated. On one side of the issue are researchers and theorists such as Nancy Bartlett of Mount Saint Vincent's University and her colleagues. They argue against the placement of gender identity disorder of childhood in the DSM system, on the basis of an extensive literature review. They believe that children who experience discomfort with the socially prescribed gender role behaviours of their sex, but who do not experience discomfort with their biological sex, should not be labelled with gender identity disorder and certainly should not be treated. They express concern that considering gender identity disorder in children a mental disorder may contribute to social stigmatization of these children (Bartlett, Vasey, & Bukowski, 2000).

On the other side of the argument are researchers such as Kenneth Zucker and his colleagues, who argue that psychological interventions should be initiated for those children evidencing symptoms of gender identity disorder (e.g., Stein, Zucker, & Dixon, 2001). They argue that without treatment, these children are socially ostracized. They argue against the common conception among pediatricians that children "grow out of" this pattern of behaviour. They also point out that gender identity problems appear easier to resolve if they are treated in childhood as opposed to in adolescence or adulthood (Stein et al., 2001). Psychological treatment at the Gender Identity Clinic in Toronto combines the involvement of parents in treatment, the discouragement of the child's cross-gender behaviour, and the promotion of opportunities for the child to develop same-sex friendships and skills (Bradley & Zucker, 1997).

## Concept Check 9.1

Answer the following questions about normal sexuality and gender identity disorder.

1. What gender differences exist in both sexual attitudes and sexual behaviour? _____
2. How does sexual orientation develop? _____
3. Charlie always felt out of place with the boys. At a young age, he preferred to play with girls and insisted that his parents call him "Charlene." He later claimed that he felt like a woman trapped in a man's body. What disorder could Charlie have? _____
4. What could be the cause of Charlie's disorder? _____
5. What treatments could be given to Charlie? _____

# Overview of Sexual Dysfunctions

- ■ *Define sexual dysfunction.*

- ■ *Describe how sexual dysfunctions are organized around the sexual response cycle.*

Before describing **sexual dysfunctions,** note that the problems that arise in the context of sexual interactions may occur in both heterosexual and homosexual relationships. Inability to become aroused or reach orgasm seems to be as common in homosexual as in heterosexual relationships, but we discuss them in the context of heterosexual relationships, which are the majority of cases we see in our clinics. The three main stages of the sexual response cycle—desire, arousal, and orgasm (see Figure 9.2)—are each associated with specific sexual dysfunctions. In addition, pain can become associated with sexual functioning, which leads to additional dysfunctions.

An overview of the DSM-IV-TR categories of the sexual dysfunctions we examine is in Table 9.3. As you can see, both males and females can experience parallel versions of most disorders, which take on specific forms determined by anatomy and other gender-specific characteristics. However, two disorders are sex specific: Premature ejaculation obviously occurs only in males, and vaginismus—painful contractions or spasms of the vagina during attempted penetration—appears only in females. Sexual dysfunctions can be either lifelong or acquired. *Lifelong* refers to a chronic condition that is present during a person's entire sexual life; *acquired* refers to a disorder that begins after sexual activity has been relatively normal. In addition, disorders can be either *generalized*, occurring every time the individual attempts sex, or *situational*, occurring only with some partners or at certain times but not with other partners or at other times. Finally, sexual dysfunctions are further specified as

---

**sexual dysfunction** Sexual disorder in which the client finds it difficult to function adequately while having sex.

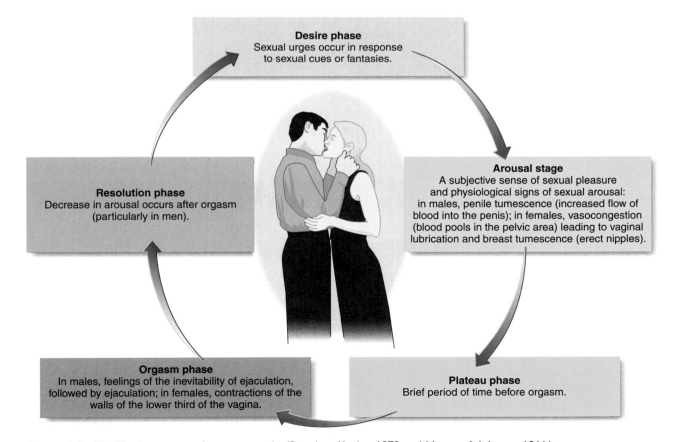

**Figure 9.2** ■ The human sexual response cycle. (Based on Kaplan, 1979, and Masters & Johnson, 1966.)

(1) due to psychological factors or (2) due to psychological factors combined with a general medical condition. The latter specification occurs when there is a demonstrable vascular, hormonal, or associated physical condition known to contribute to the sexual dysfunction.

We learned much about the prevalence of the various sexual dysfunctions in North America from a large and particularly well-done probability sample of 1749 women and 1410 men aged 18 to 59 years (Laumann, Paik, & Rosen, 1999). The surprising estimates of prevalence of sexual dysfunctions are presented and discussed in the context of each disorder. But in the aggregate, fully 43% of all women and 31% of men experience sexual dysfunction, making this class of disorder the most prevalent of any psychological or physical disorder.

Before we describe the prevalence of specific sexual dysfunctions, we need to note an important study in which 100 well-educated, happily married couples who were not seeking treatment were carefully interviewed (Frank, Anderson, & Rubinstein, 1978). More than 80% of these couples reported that their marital and sexual relations were happy and satisfying. Surprisingly, 40% of the men reported occasional erectile and ejaculatory difficulties and 63% of the women reported occasional dysfunctions of arousal or orgasm. But the crucial finding was that these dysfunctions did not detract from the respondents' overall sexual satisfaction. In another study, only 45% of women experiencing difficulties with orgasm reported the issue as problematic (Fugl-Meyer & Sjogren Fugl-Meyer, 1999). Bancroft, Loftus, and Long (2003) have extended this analysis in a survey of close to 1000 women involved in a heterosexual relationship for at least 6 months. The interesting results indicate that although 44.3% met objective criteria for one of the disorders in Table 9.3, only 24.4% were distressed about it! These studies indicate that sexual satisfaction and occasional sexual dysfunction are not mutually exclusive categories. In the context of a healthy relationship, occasional or partial sexual dysfunctions are easily accommodated.

## Sexual Desire Disorders

Two disorders reflect problems with the desire phase of the sexual response cycle. Each of these disorders is characterized by little or no interest in sex that is causing problems in a relationship.

### Hypoactive Sexual Desire Disorder

A person with **hypoactive sexual desire disorder** has little or no interest in any type of sexual activity. It is difficult to assess low sexual desire, and a great deal of clinical judgment is required (Bach, Wincze, & Barlow, 2001; Pridal & LoPiccolo, 2000). You might gauge it by frequency of sexual activity—say, less than twice a month for a married couple. Or you might determine whether someone ever *thinks* about sex or has sexual fantasies. Then there is the person who has sex twice a week but really doesn't want to and thinks about it only because his wife wants to have sex more often. This individual might have no desire despite having frequent sex. Consider the case of Mr. and Mrs. C.

**hypoactive sexual desire disorder** Apparent lack of interest in sexual activity or fantasy that would be expected considering the person's age and life situation.

**TABLE 9.3** Categories of Sexual Dysfunction among Men and Women

| Type of Disorder | Sexual Dysfunction | |
| --- | --- | --- |
| | Men | Women |
| Desire | Hypoactive sexual desire disorder (little or no desire to have sex) | Hypoactive sexual desire disorder (little or no desire to have sex) |
| | Sexual aversion disorder (aversion to and avoidance of sex) | Sexual aversion disorder (aversion to and avoidance of sex) |
| Arousal | Male erectile disorder (difficulty attaining or maintaining erections) | Female sexual arousal disorder (difficulty attaining or maintaining lubrication or swelling response) |
| Orgasm | Inhibited male orgasm | Inhibited female orgasm |
| | Premature ejaculation | |
| Pain | Dyspareunia (pain associated with sexual activity) | Dyspareunia (pain associated with sexual activity) |
| | | Vaginismus (muscle spasms in the vagina that interfere with penetration) |

*Source: From Sexual Dysfunction: A Guide for Assessment and Treatment, by J. P. Wincze and M. P. Carey, 1991. Copyright © 1991 by Guilford Press. Reprinted by permission.*

## Mr. and Mrs. C.
### Getting Started

Mrs. C., a 31-year-old successful business-woman, was married to a 32-year-old lawyer. They had two children, ages 2 and 5, and had been married 8 years when they entered therapy. The presenting problem was Mrs. C.'s lack of sexual desire. Mr. and Mrs. C. were interviewed separately during the initial assessment and both professed attraction to and love for their partner. Mrs. C. reported that she could enjoy sex once she got involved and usually was orgasmic. The problem was her total lack of desire to get involved in the first place. She avoided her husband's sexual advances and looked on his affection and romanticism with great skepticism and, usually, anger and tears. Mrs. C. was raised in an upper-middle-class family that was supportive and loving. However, from age 6 to age 12 she had been repeatedly pressured into sexual activity by a male cousin who was 5 years her senior. This sexual activity was always initiated by the cousin, always against her will. She did not tell her parents because she felt guilty, as the boy did not use physical force to make her comply. It appeared that romantic advances by Mr. C. triggered memories of abuse by her cousin.

The treatment of Mr. and Mrs. C. is discussed later in this chapter.

Problems of hypoactive sexual desire disorder used to be presented as marital rather than sexual difficulties. Since the recognition in the late 1980s of hypoactive sexual desire as a distinct disorder, however, couples increasingly present to sex therapy clinics with one of the partners reporting this problem (Hawton, 1995; Pridal & LoPiccolo, 2000). Best estimates suggest that more than 50% of patients who come to sexuality clinics for help complain of hypoactive sexual desire (Kaplan, 1979; Pridal & LoPiccolo, 2000). In many clinics it is the most frequent presenting complaint of women; men present more often with erectile dysfunction (Hawton, 1995). Earlier studies (e.g., Frank et al., 1978) suggested that approximately 25% of individuals might have hypoactive sexual desire. The North American survey mentioned earlier confirmed that 22% of women and 5% of men have the disorder. For men, the prevalence increases with age; for women, it decreases with age (Laumann et al., 1999). Schreiner-Engel and Schiavi (1986) noted that patients with this disorder rarely have sexual fantasies, seldom masturbate (in their sample, 35% of the women and 52% of the men never masturbated, and most of the rest masturbated no more than once a month), and attempt intercourse once a month or less.

---

### Disorder Criteria Summary
#### Hypoactive Sexual Desire Disorder

Features of hypoactive sexual desire disorder include:
- Persistent or recurrent disinterest in sexual fantasies and lack of desire for sexual activity
- Significant distress or interpersonal difficulty because of this lack of desire
- Lack of desire not better accounted for as part of another disorder (e.g., mood, anxiety, somatoform) and not because of the physiological effects of medication or a drug of abuse

*Source:* Based on DSM-IV-TR. Used with permission from the *Diagnostic and Statistical Manual of Mental Disorders,* Fourth Edition, Text Revision. Copyright 2000. American Psychiatric Association.

### Sexual Aversion Disorder

On a continuum with hypoactive sexual desire disorder is **sexual aversion disorder,** in which even the thought of sex or a brief casual touch may evoke fear, panic, or disgust (Kaplan, 1987). In some cases, the principal problem might be panic disorder (see Chapter 4), in which the fear or alarm response is associated with the physical sensations of sex. In other cases, sexual acts and fantasies may trigger traumatic images or memories similar to but perhaps not as severe as those experienced by people with posttraumatic stress disorder (see Chapter 4). Consider the case of Lisa from one of our clinics.

## Lisa
### The Terror of Sex

Lisa was 36, had been married for 3 years, and was a full-time student. She had been married once before. Lisa reported that sexual problems had begun 9 months earlier. She complained of poor lubrication during intercourse and of having "anxiety attacks" during sex. She had not attempted intercourse in 2 months and had tried only intermittently during the past 9 months. Despite their sexual difficulties, Lisa had a loving and close relationship with her husband.

---

**sexual aversion disorder** Extreme and persistent dislike of sexual contact or similar activities.

She could not remember precisely what happened 9 months ago except that she had been under a great deal of stress and experienced an anxiety attack during sex. Even her husband's touch was becoming increasingly intolerable because she was afraid it might bring on the scary feelings again. Her primary fear was of having a heart attack and dying during sex.

Among male patients presenting for sexual aversion disorder, 10% experienced panic attacks during attempted sexual activity. Kaplan (1987) reports that 25% of 106 patients presenting with sexual aversion disorder also met criteria for panic disorder. In such cases, treating the panic may be a necessary first step.

## Sexual Arousal Disorders

Disorders of arousal are called **male erectile disorder** and **female sexual arousal disorder.** The problem here is not desire. Many individuals with arousal disorders have frequent sexual urges and fantasies and a strong desire to have sex. Their problem is in becoming physically aroused: A male has difficulty achieving or maintaining an erection, and a female cannot achieve or maintain adequate lubrication (Bach et al., 2001; Segraves & Althof, 1998). Consider the case of Bill.

### Bill
#### Long Marriage, New Problem

Bill, a 58-year-old White man, was referred to our clinic by his urologist. He was a retired accountant who had been married for 29 years to his 57-year-old wife, a retired nutritionist. They had no children. For the past several years, Bill had had difficulties obtaining and maintaining an erection. He reported a rather rigid routine he and his wife had developed to deal with the problem. They scheduled sex for Sunday mornings. However, Bill had to do a number of chores first, including letting the dog out, washing the dishes, and shaving. The couple's current behaviour consisted of mutual hand stimulation. Bill was "not allowed" to attempt insertion until after his wife had climaxed. Bill's wife was adamant that she was not going to change her sexual behaviour and "become a whore," as she put it. This included refusing to try K-Y jelly as a

lubricant appropriate to her postmenopausal decrease in lubrication. She described their behaviour as "lesbian sex."

Bill and his wife agreed that despite marital problems over the years, they had always maintained a good sexual relationship until the onset of the current problem and that sex had kept them together during their earlier difficulties. Useful information was obtained in separate interviews. Bill masturbated on Saturday night in an attempt to control his erection the following morning; his wife was unaware of this. In addition, he quickly and easily achieved a full erection when viewing erotica in the privacy of the sexuality clinic laboratory (surprising the assessor). Bill's wife privately acknowledged being angry at her husband for an affair that he had had 20 years earlier.

At the final session, three specific recommendations were made: for Bill to cease masturbating the evening before sex, for the couple to use a lubricant, and for them to delay the morning routine until after they had had sexual relations. The couple called back 1 month later to report that their sexual activity was much improved.

The old and somewhat derogatory terms for male erectile disorder and female arousal disorder are *impotence* and *frigidity*, but these are imprecise labels that do not identify the specific phase of the sexual response where the problems are localized. The man typically feels more impaired by his problem than the woman does by her own. Inability to achieve and maintain an erection makes intercourse difficult or impossible. Women who are unable to achieve vaginal lubrication, however, may be able to compensate by using a commercial lubricant (Schover & Jensen, 1988; Wincze & Barlow, 1997). In women, arousal and lubrication may decrease at any time but, as in men, such problems tend to accompany aging (Bartlik & Goldberg, 2000; Rosen, 2000). In addition, until relatively recently, some women were not as concerned as men about experiencing intense pleasure during sex as long as they could

**male erectile disorder**   Recurring inability in some men to attain or maintain adequate penile erection until completion of sexual activity.

**female sexual arousal disorder**   Recurrent inability in some women to attain or maintain adequate lubrication and swelling sexual excitement responses until completion of sexual activity.

consummate the act; this is generally no longer the case (Morokoff, 1993; Wincze & Carey, 2001). It is unusual for a man to be completely unable to achieve an erection. More typical is a situation like Bill's, where full erections are possible during masturbation and partial erections during attempted intercourse, but with insufficient rigidity to allow penetration.

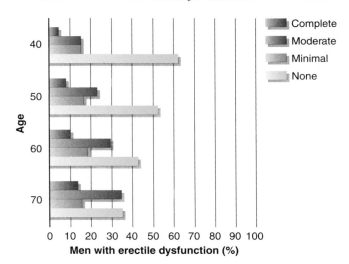

Figure 9.3 ■ Estimated prevalence and severity of erectile dysfunction in a sample of 1290 men between 40 and 70 years of age. (Adapted from "Impotence and Its Medical and Physiological Correlates: Results of the Massachusetts Male Aging Study," by H. A. Feldman, I. Goldstein, D. G. Hatzichristou, R. J. Krane, and J. B. McKunlay, 1994, *Journal of Urology*, 151, pp. 54–61. Copyright © 1994 by the American Urological Association.)

## Disorder Criteria Summary
### Sexual Arousal Disorder

Features of sexual arousal disorder in females include:
- Persistent or recurrent inability to attain, or to maintain, an adequate lubrication-swelling response of sexual excitement during sexual activity
- Significant distress or interpersonal difficulty because of this inability
- Inability not better accounted for as part of another disorder (e.g., mood, anxiety, cognitive) and not caused by the physiological effects of medication or a drug of abuse

Features of sexual arousal disorder in males include:
- Persistent and recurrent inability to attain or to maintain an adequate erection during sexual activity
- Significant distress or interpersonal difficulty because of this inability
- Inability is not better accounted for as part of another disorder and not caused by the physiological effects of a medication or a drug of abuse

*Source:* Based on DSM-IV-TR. Used with permission from the *Diagnostic and Statistical Manual of Mental Disorders*, Fourth Edition, Text Revision. Copyright 2000. American Psychiatric Association.

The prevalence of erectile dysfunction is startlingly high and increases with age. Data from the North American survey indicate that 5% of men between 18 and 59 fully meet a stringent set of criteria for erectile dysfunction (Laumann et al., 1999). But this figure most certainly underestimates the prevalence because erectile dysfunction increases rapidly in men after age 60. Data from another study (shown in Figure 9.3) suggest that at least some impairment is present in approximately 40% of men in their 40s and 70% of men in their 70s (Feldman, Goldstein, Hatzichristou, Krane, & McKunlay, 1994; Kim & Lipshultz, 1997); incidence (new cases) increases dramatically with age to 46 new cases each year per 1000 men in their 60s (Johannes et al., 2000). Male erectile disorder is easily the most common problem for which men seek help, accounting for 50% or more of the men referred to specialists for sexual problems (Hawton, 1995). The prevalence of female arousal

disorders is somewhat more difficult to estimate because many women still do not consider absence of arousal to be a problem, let alone a disorder. The Laumann et al. (1999) survey reports a prevalence of 14% of females experiencing an arousal disorder. Because disorders of desire, arousal, and orgasm often overlap, it is difficult to estimate precisely how many women with specific arousal disorders present to sex clinics (Segraves & Althof, 1998; Wincze & Carey, 2001).

## Orgasm Disorders

The orgasm phase of the sexual response cycle can also become disrupted in one of several ways. The orgasm either occurs at an inappropriate time or not at all.

### Inhibited Orgasm

An inability to achieve an orgasm despite adequate sexual desire and arousal is commonly seen in women (Stock, 1993; Wincze & Barlow, 1997), but **inhibited orgasm** is relatively rare in men. Consider the case of Greta and Will.

---

**inhibited orgasm** Inability to achieve orgasm despite adequate sexual desire and arousal; commonly seen in women but relatively rare in men.

## Greta and Will
### Loving Disunion

Greta, a teacher, and Will, an engineer, were an attractive couple who came together to the first interview and entered the office clearly showing affection for each other. They had been married for 5 years and were in their late 20s. When asked about the problems that had brought them to the office, Greta quickly reported that she didn't think she had ever had an orgasm—"didn't think" because she wasn't really sure what an orgasm was! She loved Will very much and on occasion would initiate lovemaking, although with decreased frequency over the past several years.

Will certainly didn't think Greta was reaching orgasm. In any case, he reported, they were clearly going in "different directions" sexually, in that Greta was less and less interested. She had progressed from initiating sex occasionally early in their marriage to almost never doing so, except for an occasional spurt every 6 months or so, when she would initiate two or three times in a week. But Greta noted that it was the physical closeness she wanted most during these times rather than sexual pleasure. Further inquiry revealed that she did become sexually aroused on occasion but had never in her life reached orgasm, even during several attempts at masturbation mostly before her marriage. Both Greta and Will reported that the sexual problem was a concern to them because everything else about their marriage was positive.

Greta had been brought up in a strict but loving and supportive Catholic family that more or less ignored sexuality. The parents were always careful not to display their affections in front of Greta, and when her mother caught Greta touching her genital area, she was cautioned rather severely to avoid that kind of activity.

We discuss Greta and Will's treatment later.

An inability to reach orgasm is the most common complaint among women who seek therapy for sexual problems. Although the North American survey mentioned earlier did not estimate the prevalence of **female orgasmic disorder** specifically, approximately 25% of women report significant difficulty reaching orgasm (Heiman, 2000). The problem is equally present in different age groups, and unmarried women were 1.5 times more likely than married women to experience orgasmic disorder. In diagnosing this problem, it is necessary to determine that the women "never or almost never" reach orgasm (Wincze & Carey, 2001). This distinction is important because only approximately 50% of all women experience reasonably regular orgasms during sexual intercourse (LoPiccolo & Stock, 1987). Therefore, approximately 50% do not achieve orgasm with every sexual encounter, unlike most men, who tend to experience orgasm more consistently. Thus, the "never or almost never" inquiry is important, along with establishing the extent of the couple's distress, in diagnosing orgasmic dysfunction.

In the North American survey, approximately 8% of men report having delayed orgasms or none during sexual interactions (Laumann et al., 1999). Men seldom seek treatment for this condition. It is possible that in many cases some men reach climax through alternative forms of stimulation and that male orgasmic disorder is accommodated by the couple (Apfelbaum, 2000).

Some men who are unable to ejaculate with their partners can obtain an erection and ejaculate during masturbation. In the most usual pattern ejaculation is delayed; this is called *retarded ejaculation*. Occasionally men suffer from *retrograde ejaculation*, in which ejaculatory fluids travel backward into the bladder rather than forward. This phenomenon is usually due to the effects of certain drugs or a coexisting medical condition and should not be confused with **male orgasmic disorder.**

---

### Disorder Criteria Summary
#### Orgasmic Disorder

Features of orgasmic disorder include:
- Persistent or recurrent delay in, or absence of, orgasm following a normal sexual excitement phase
- Significant distress or interpersonal difficulty because of this absence or delay
- Condition is not better accounted for by another disorder (e.g., mood, anxiety, cognitive), and is not caused by the physiological effects of medication or a drug of abuse

*Source:* Based on DSM-IV-TR. Used with permission from the *Diagnostic and Statistical Manual of Mental Disorders,* Fourth Edition, Text Revision. Copyright 2000. American Psychiatric Association.

---

**female orgasmic disorder**   Recurring delay or absence of orgasm in some women following a normal sexual excitement phase, relative to their prior experience and current stimulation. Also known as *inhibited (female) orgasm.*

**male orgasmic disorder**   Recurring delay in or absence of orgasm in some men following a normal sexual excitement phase, relative to age and current stimulation. Also known as *inhibited (male) orgasm.*

## Premature Ejaculation

A far more common male orgasmic disorder is **premature ejaculation,** ejaculation that occurs well before the man and his partner wish it to (Polonsky, 2000; Weiner, 1996). Consider the rather typical case of Gary.

### Gary
#### Running Scared

Gary, a 31-year-old salesman, engaged in sexual activity with his wife three or four times a month. He noted that he would have liked to have had sex more often but his busy schedule kept him working about 80 hours a week. His primary difficulty was an inability to control the timing of his ejaculation. Approximately 70% to 80% of the time he ejaculated within seconds of penetration. This pattern had been constant since he met his wife approximately 13 years earlier. Previous experience with other women, although limited, was not characterized by premature ejaculation. In an attempt to delay his ejaculation, Gary distracted himself by thinking of nonsexual things (scores of ball games or work-related issues) and sometimes attempted sex soon after a previous attempt because he seemed not to climax as quickly under these circumstances. Gary reported masturbating seldom (three or four times a year at most). When he did masturbate, he usually attempted to reach orgasm quickly, a habit he acquired during his teens to avoid being caught by a family member.

One of his greatest concerns was that he was not pleasing his wife, and under no circumstances did he want her told that he was seeking treatment. Further inquiry revealed that he made many extravagant purchases at his wife's request, even though it strained their finances, because he wished to please her. He felt that if they had met recently, his wife probably would not even accept a date with him because he had lost much of his hair and she had lost weight and was more attractive than she used to be.

Treatment for Gary and his wife is described shortly.

The frequency of premature ejaculation seems to be quite high. In the Laumann et al. (1999) survey, 21% of all men met criteria for premature ejaculation, making it the most frequent male sexual dysfunction. Similarly, 23% of a sample of male university alumni self-identified with premature ejaculation in a study conducted by researchers at the University of New Brunswick (Grenier & Byers, 2001). This difficulty is also a presenting complaint in as many as 60% of men who seek treatment for sexual dysfunction (Malatesta & Adams, 1984; Polonsky, 2000). (But many of these men also present with erectile dysfunction as their major problem.) In one clinic, premature ejaculation was the principal complaint of 16% of men seeking treatment (Hawton, 1995).

It is difficult to define "premature." An adequate length of time before ejaculation varies from individual to individual. Some surveys indicate that men who complain of premature ejaculation typically climax no more than 1 or 2 minutes after penetration, compared with 7 to 10 minutes in individuals without this complaint (Strassberg, Kelly, Carroll, & Kircher, 1987). A perception of lack of control over orgasm, however, may be the more important psychological determinant of this complaint. Three components seem to be involved in men's self-identification of premature ejaculation complaints: a behavioural component (i.e., the regularity of their rapid ejaculation experience), an emotional component (i.e., worry or concern about ejaculating too early), and an efficiency component (i.e., perceiving that they have little control over the timing of their ejaculation; Grenier & Byers, 2001).

Although occasional early ejaculation is normal, serious and consistent premature ejaculation appears to occur primarily in inexperienced men with less education (Laumann et al., 1999). Grenier and Byers (2001) found the only predictor of premature ejaculation in their sample was a lower frequency of intercourse. The contrast in ages between men with erectile disorder and those complaining of premature ejaculation is striking. Although premature ejaculation is typically seen in young men (DSM-IV-TR; APA, 2004), the majority of men consulting physicians about erectile disorder are between 40 and 64 years of age (IMS Health Canada, 2004a).

## Sexual Pain Disorders

In the **sexual pain disorders,** intercourse is associated with marked pain. For some men and women, sexual desire is present, and arousal and orgasm are

---

**premature ejaculation** Recurring ejaculation before the person wishes it, with minimal sexual stimulation.

**sexual pain disorder** Recurring genital pain in either males or females before, during, or after sexual intercourse.

easily attained, but the pain of intercourse is so severe that sexual behaviour is disrupted. This subtype is named **dyspareunia,** which, in its original Greek, means "unhappily mated as bedfellows" (Wincze & Carey, 2001). Obviously this is not an accurate or descriptive name, but it has been used for decades and is accepted. Dyspareunia is diagnosed only if no medical reasons for pain can be found. It can be tricky to make this assessment (Binik, Bergeron, & Khalifé, 2000). Several years ago a patient of ours described having sharp pains in his head like a migraine headache that began during ejaculation and lasted for several minutes. This man, in his 50s at the time, had had a healthy sexual relationship with his wife until a severe fall approximately 2 years earlier that left him partially disabled and with a severe limp. The pain during ejaculation developed shortly thereafter. Extensive medical examination from a number of specialists revealed no physical reason for the pain. Thus, he met the criteria for dyspareunia, and psychological interventions were administered—in this case, without benefit. He subsequently engaged in manual stimulation of his wife and, occasionally, intercourse, but he avoided ejaculation.

Dyspareunia is rarely seen in clinics, with estimates ranging from 1% to 5% of men (Bancroft, 1989; Spector & Carey, 1990) and a more substantial 10% to 15% of women (Hawton, 1995; Rosen & Leiblum, 1995). Glatt, Zinner, and McCormack (1990) report that many women experience pain occasionally, but it either resolves or is not sufficient to motivate them to seek treatment. Dyspareunia in women has been associated with depressive and anxious symptoms and with marital adjustment problems (Meana, Binik, Kahlife, & Cohen, 1998). When those with dyspareunia do seek treatment, Lori Brotto of the University of British Columbia recommends that such cases should be approached from a pain-management perspective. In particular, she recommends focusing on the patient's chronic pain, the impact of the dyspareunia on the couple's relationship, and any associated psychological effects (Graziottin & Brotto, 2004).

A more common problem is **vaginismus,** in which the pelvic muscles in the outer third of the vagina undergo involuntary spasms when intercourse is attempted (Leiblum, 2000; Reissing, Binik, & Samir, 1999). The spasm reaction of vaginismus may occur during any attempted penetration, including a gynecological exam or insertion of a tampon (Beck, 1993; Reissing et al., 1999). Women report sensations of "ripping, burning, or tearing during attempted intercourse" (Beck, 1993, p. 384). Although vaginismus is considered a sexual pain disorder, the experience of pain is not necessary for a DSM-IV-TR diagnosis (Reissing et al., 1999). Consider the case of Jill.

## Jill
### Sex and Spasms

Jill was referred to our clinic by another therapist because she had not consummated her marriage of 1 year. At 23 years of age, she was an attractive and loving wife who managed a motel; her husband worked as an accountant. Despite numerous attempts in a variety of positions to engage in intercourse, Jill's severe vaginal spasms prevented penetration of any kind. Jill was also unable to use tampons. With great reluctance, she submitted to gynecological exams at infrequent intervals. Sexual behaviour with her husband consisted of mutual masturbation or, on occasion, Jill had him rub his penis against her breasts to the point of ejaculation. She refused to engage in oral sex. Jill, an anxious young woman, came from a family in which sexual matters were seldom discussed and sexual contact between the parents had ceased some years before. Although she enjoyed petting, Jill's general attitude was that intercourse was disgusting. Furthermore, she expressed some fears of becoming pregnant despite taking adequate contraceptive measures. She also thought that she would perform poorly when she did engage in intercourse, therefore embarrassing herself with her new husband.

Although we have no data on the prevalence of vaginismus in community samples, best estimates are that it affects well over 5% of women who seek treatment in North America and 10% to 15% in Britain (Beck, 1993; Hawton, 1995). The prevalence of this condition in cultures with very conservative views of sexuality, such as Ireland, may be much higher—as high as 42% to 55% in at least two clinic samples (Barnes, Bowman, & Cullen, 1984; O'Sullivan, 1979). (Of course, results from any one clinic may not be applicable even to other clinics, let alone to the population of Ireland.) Results from the North American survey indicate that approximately 7% of women suffer from one or the other types of sexual pain disorder, with higher proportions of younger and less educated women reporting this problem (Laumann et al., 1999).

---

**dyspareunia**  Pain or discomfort during sexual intercourse.

**vaginismus**  Recurring involuntary muscle spasms in the outer third of the vagina that interfere with sexual intercourse.

## Disorder Criteria Summary
### Sexual Pain Disorders

Features of dyspareunia include:
- Recurrent or persistent genital pain associated with sexual intercourse in either male or female
- Significant distress or interpersonal difficulty due to this pain
- Pain is not caused exclusively by vaginismus or lack of lubrication, is not better accounted for by another disorder (e.g., mood, anxiety, cognitive), and is not due to the physiological effects of medication or a drug of abuse

Features of vaginismus include:
- Recurrent or persistent involuntary spasm of the musculature of the outer third of the vagina that interferes with sexual intercourse
- Significant distress or interpersonal difficulty due to these spasms
- Spasms not due to another disorder (e.g., somatization disorder), and are not due exclusively to the physiological effects of a general medical condition

*Source:* Based on DSM-IV-TR. Used with permission from the *Diagnostic and Statistical Manual of Mental Disorders,* Fourth Edition, Text Revision. Copyright 2000. American Psychiatric Association.

## Assessing Sexual Behaviour

There are three major aspects to the assessment of sexual behaviour (Wiegel, Wincze, & Barlow, 2002):

1. *Interviewing,* usually supported by numerous questionnaires because patients may provide more information on paper than in a verbal interview
2. *A thorough medical evaluation,* to rule out the variety of medical conditions that can contribute to sexual problems
3. *Psychophysiological assessment,* to directly measure the physiological aspects of sexual arousal

Many clinicians assess the ability of individuals to become sexually aroused under a variety of conditions by taking psychophysiological measurements while the patient is either awake or asleep. In men, penile erection is measured directly, using, for example, a *penile strain gauge* developed in one of our clinics (Barlow, Becker, Leitenberg, & Agras, 1970; see also Kuban, Barbaree, & Blanchard, 1999). As the penis expands, the strain gauge picks up the changes and records them on a polygraph. Note that subjects are often not aware of these more objective measures of their arousal; their awareness differs as a function of the type of problem they have. Penile rigidity is also important to measure in

cases of erectile dysfunction, because large erections with insufficient rigidity will not be adequate for intercourse (Wiegel et al., 2002).

The comparable device for women is a *vaginal photoplethysmograph* (Everaerd, Laan, Roth, & van der Velde, 2000; Rosen & Beck, 1988). This device, which is smaller than a tampon, is inserted by the woman into her vagina. A light source at the tip of the instrument and two light-sensitive photoreceptors on the sides of the instrument measure the amount of light reflected back from the vaginal walls. Because blood flows to the vaginal walls during arousal, the amount of light passing through them decreases with increasing arousal. Cindy Meston and Boris Gorzalka have used this device to study normal and abnormal sexual arousal in women, in their research (e.g., Meston & Gorzalka, 1996; Meston, 2000).

Typically, individuals undergoing physiological assessment view an erotic videotape for 2 to 5 minutes or, on occasion, listen to an erotic audiotape (e.g., Bach, Brown, & Barlow, 1999; Weisburg, Brown, Wincze, & Barlow, 2001). The patient's sexual responsivity during this time is assessed psychophysiologically. Patients also report subjectively on the amount of sexual arousal they experience. This assessment allows the clinician to carefully observe the conditions under which arousal is possible for the patient. For example, many individuals with psychologically based sexual dysfunctions may achieve strong arousal in a laboratory but be unable to become aroused with a partner (Bancroft, 1997; Sakheim, Barlow, Abrahamson, & Beck, 1987).

Because erections most often occur during REM sleep in physically healthy men, psychophysiological measurement of *nocturnal penile tumescence* (NPT) was in the past used frequently to determine a man's ability to obtain normal erectile response. If he could attain normal erections while he was asleep, the reasoning went, then the causes of his dysfunction were psychological. An inexpensive way to monitor nocturnal erections is for the clinician to provide a simple "snap gauge" that the patient fastens around his penis each night before he goes to sleep. If the snap gauge has come undone he has probably had a nocturnal erection. But this is a crude and often inaccurate screening device that should never supplant medical and psychological evaluation (Carey, Wincze, & Meisler, 1993; Wiegel et al., 2002). Finally, we now know that lack of NPT could also be due to psychological problems, such as depression, or to a variety of medical difficulties that have nothing to do with physiological problems preventing erections (Rosen, 2000; Wiegel et al., 2002).

## Concept Check 9.2

Diagnose the following sexual dysfunctions.

1. Kay is in a serious sexual relationship and is quite content. Lately though, the thought of her boyfriend's touch disgusts her. Kay has no idea what is causing this. She could be suffering from (a) panic disorder, (b) sexual arousal disorder, (c) sexual aversion disorder, or (d) both a and b. _____

2. After Bob was injured playing football, he started having pain in his arm during sex. All medical reasons for the pain have been ruled out. Bob is probably displaying (a) dyspareunia, (b) vaginismus, (c) penile strain gauge, or (d) male orgasmic disorder. _____

3. Kelly has no real desire for sex. She has sex only because she feels that otherwise her husband may leave her. Kelly suffers from (a) sexual aversion disorder, (b) hypoactive sexual desire disorder, (c) boredom, or (d) female sexual arousal disorder. _____

4. Bill lacks the ability to control ejaculation. The majority of the time he ejaculates within seconds of penetration. He suffers from (a) male erectile disorder, (b) stress, (c) premature ejaculation, or (d) both a and b. _____

5. Samantha came into the office because she is unable to orgasm. She loves her husband but stopped initiating sex. She is most likely suffering from (a) female orgasmic disorder, (b) female sexual arousal disorder, (c) vaginismus, or (d) dislike for her husband. _____

# Causes and Treatment of Sexual Dysfunction

■ *Describe the defining clinical features and known causes of sexual dysfunctions, including important gender differences.*

■ *Describe the psychosocial and medical treatments for sexual dysfunctions, including what is known about their relative effectiveness.*

As with most disorders, biological, psychological, and social factors contribute to the development of sexual dysfunction. And these problems can be treated either psychologically or medically.

## Causes of Sexual Dysfunction

Individual sexual dysfunctions seldom present in isolation. Usually a patient referred to a sexuality clinic complains of an assortment of sexual problems, although one may be of most concern (Hawton, 1995; Wincze & Barlow, 1997). A 45-year-old man recently referred to our clinic had been free of problems until 10 years earlier, when he was under a great deal of pressure at work and was preparing to take a major career-related licensing examination. He began experiencing erectile dysfunction about 50% of the time, a condition that had now progressed to approximately 80% of the time. In addition, he reported that he had no control over ejaculation, often ejaculating before penetration with only a semierect penis. Over the past 5 years, he had lost most interest in sex and was

coming to treatment only at his wife's insistence. Thus, this man suffered simultaneously from erectile dysfunction, premature ejaculation, and low sexual desire.

Because of the frequency of such combinations, we discuss the causes of various sexual dysfunctions together, reviewing briefly the biological, psychological, and social contributions and specifying causal factors thought to be associated exclusively and specifically with one or another dysfunction.

### Biological Contributions

A number of physical and medical conditions contribute to sexual dysfunction (Wiegel et al., 2002; Wincze & Carey, 2001). Although this is not surprising, most patients, and even many health professionals, are, unfortunately, unaware of the connection. Neurological diseases and other conditions that affect the nervous system, such as diabetes and kidney disease, may directly interfere with sexual functioning by reducing sensitivity in the genital area, and they are a common cause of erectile dysfunction in males (Schover & Jensen, 1988; Wincze & Barlow, 1997). Feldman et al. (1994) reported that 28% of men with diabetes experienced complete erectile failure. *Vascular disease* is a major cause of erectile difficulties. The two relevant vascular problems are *arterial insufficiency* (constricted arteries), which makes it difficult for blood to reach the penis, and *venous leakage* (blood flows out too quickly for an erection to be maintained) (Wincze & Carey, 2001).

*Chronic illness* can also indirectly affect sexual functioning. For example, it is not uncommon for individuals who have had heart attacks to be wary of the physical exercise involved in sexual activity to the point of preoccupation. They often become unable to achieve arousal despite being assured by their physicians that sexual activity is safe for them (Cooper, 1988).

A major physical cause of sexual dysfunction is *prescription medication*. Drug treatments for high blood pressure, called antihypertensive medications, in the class known as beta-blockers including propranolol, may contribute to sexual dysfunction. Tricyclic antidepressant medications and other antidepressant and antianxiety drugs may also interfere with sexual desire and arousal in both men and women (Segraves & Althof, 1998). A number of these drugs, particularly the psychoactive drugs, may dampen sexual desire and arousal by altering levels of serotonin in the brain. Sexual dysfunction—specifically low sexual desire and arousal difficulties—is the most widespread side effect of the antidepressant drugs SSRIs, such as Prozac (see Chapter 6), and as many as 75% of individuals who take these medications experience some degree of sexual dysfunction (Montejo-Gonzalez et al., 1997). Some people are aware that *alcohol* suppresses sexual arousal, but they may not know that most *other drugs of abuse* such as cocaine and heroin also produce widespread sexual dysfunction in frequent users and abusers, both male and female. Cocores, Miller, Pottash, and Gold (1988) and Macdonald, Waldorf, Reinarman, and Murphy (1988) reported that more than 60% of a large number of cocaine users had a sexual dysfunction. In the Cocores group's study, some of the patients also abused alcohol.

There is also the misconception that alcohol facilitates sexual arousal and behaviour. What actually happens is that alcohol at low and moderate levels reduces social inhibitions so people feel more like having sex (and perhaps are more willing to request it; Crowe & George, 1989; Wiegel et al., 2002). People's expectation that arousal will increase when they drink alcohol may have more effect than any disinhibition that does occur because of the effects of the alcohol itself, at least at

### Erectile Dysfunction: Clark

*"In the process of becoming aroused, all of a sudden it would be over. And I didn't understand that at all. So then everything is coupled with a bunch of depressing thoughts, like fear of failure. And so I begin to say, is this happening to me because I'm afraid I'm going to fail, and I don't want to be embarrassed by that? It's really very difficult to deal with emotionally.... The worse I feel about myself, the slower I am sexually, and sometimes I describe it as the fear of losing masculinity."*

Thomson Learning

low doses (Roehrich & Kinder, 1991; Wilson, 1977). Physically, alcohol is a central nervous system *suppressant*, and for men to achieve erection and women to achieve lubrication, it is much more difficult when the central nervous system is suppressed (Schiavi, 1990). Chronic alcohol abuse may cause permanent neurological damage and may virtually eliminate the sexual response cycle. Such abuse may lead to liver and testicular damage, resulting in decreased testosterone levels and related decreases in sexual desire and arousal.

Chronic alcoholism can also cause fertility problems in both men and women (Malatesta & Adams, 2001). Fahrner (1987) examined the prevalence of sexual dysfunction among male alcoholics and found that 75% had erectile dysfunction, low sexual desire, and premature or delayed ejaculation.

Many people report that cocaine or marijuana enhances sexual pleasure. Although little is known about the effects of marijuana across the range of use, it is unlikely that chemical effects increase pleasure. Rather, in those individuals who report some enhancement of sexual pleasure (and many don't), the effect may be psychological in that their attention is focused more completely and fully on sensory stimulation (Buffum, 1982), a factor that seems to be an important part of healthy sexual functioning. If so, imagery and attentional focus can be enhanced with non-drug procedures such as meditation, in which a person practises concentrating on something with as few distractions as possible. Finally, a report from Mannino, Klevens, and Flanders (1994), studying more than 4000 armed forces veterans, suggests that cigarette smoking contributes to erectile dysfunction.

### Psychological Contributions

A recent study by Rosemary Basson (2001) of the Vancouver Hospital Centre for Sexuality, Gender Identity, and Reproductive Health investigated the contributing factors to low sexual desire in women. Study participants were a sample of 47 women referred to the clinic for this problem. Identified contributing factors are summarized in Table 9.4. As can be seen in the table, psychological factors that decreased arousability were the most common contributing variable, being relevant in 85% of the cases (Basson, 2001).

| TABLE 9.4 Contributing Factors to Low Sexual Desire in a Clinic-Referred Sample of Women ($n = 47$) | |
|---|---|
| **Contributing Factor** | **% of Cases Where Relevant** |
| Psychological factors decreasing arousability | 85 |
| Minimal sexual stimuli or context | 53 |
| Emotional intimacy lacking | 50 |
| Depression | 43 |
| Androgen deficiency | 25 |

Source: Basson, 2001.

But psychological contributing factors obviously comprise a broad category of influences.

How do we account for sexual dysfunction from a psychological perspective? Basically, we have to break the concept of performance anxiety into several components. One component is *arousal*, another is *cognitive processes*, and a third is *negative affect*.

When confronted with the possibility of having sexual relations, individuals who are dysfunctional tend to expect the worst and find the situation to be relatively negative and unpleasant (Weisberg et al., 2001). As far as possible, they avoid becoming aware of any sexual cues (and therefore are not aware of how aroused they are physically, thus underreporting their arousal). They also may distract themselves with negative thoughts, such as, "I'm going to make a fool of myself; I'll never be able to get aroused; she [or he] will think I'm stupid," (Renaud & Byers, 2001). We know that as arousal increases, a person's attention focuses more intently and consistently. But the person who is focusing on negative thoughts will find it impossible to become sexually aroused.

People with normal sexual functioning react to a sexual situation positively. They focus their attention on the erotic cues and do not become distracted. When they become aroused, they focus even more strongly on the sexual and erotic cues, allowing themselves to become increasingly sexually aroused. The model presented in Figure 9.4 illustrates both functional and dysfunctional sexual arousal (Barlow, 1986, 2002). Experiments demonstrate that sexual arousal is strongly determined by

psychological factors, particularly cognitive and emotional factors, that are powerful enough to determine whether blood flows to the appropriate areas of the body, such as the genitals, confirming again the strong interaction of psychological and biological factors in most of our functioning.

In summary, normally functioning men show increased sexual arousal during "performance demand" conditions, experience positive affect, are distracted by nonsexual stimuli, and have a pretty good idea of how aroused they are. Men with sexual problems such as erectile dysfunction show decreased arousal during performance demand, experience negative affect, are not distracted by nonsexual stimuli, and *do not* have an accurate sense of how aroused they are. This process seems to apply to most sexual dysfunctions, which, you will remember, tend to occur together, but it is particularly applicable to sexual arousal disorders (Wiegel, Scepkowski, & Barlow, in press).

We know little about the psychological (or biological) factors associated with premature ejaculation (Ertekin, Colakoglu, & Altay, 1995; Weiner, 1996). We do know that the condition is most prevalent in young men and that excessive physiological arousal in the sympathetic nervous system may lead to rapid ejaculation. These observations suggest some men may have a naturally lower threshold for ejaculation; that is, they require less stimulation and arousal to ejaculate. Unfortunately, the psychological factor of anxiety also increases sympathetic arousal. Thus, when a man becomes anxiously aroused about ejaculating too quickly, his concern only makes the problem worse. We return to the role of anxiety in sexual dysfunctions later.

### Social and Cultural Contributions

The model of sexual dysfunction displayed in Figure 9.4 helps explain why some individuals may be dysfunctional *at the present time* but not how they *became* that way. Although we do not know for sure why some people develop problems, many people learn early that sexuality can be negative and somewhat threatening, and the responses they develop reflect this belief. This negative cognitive set has been termed *erotophobia*, which is presumably learned early in childhood from families, religious authorities, or others. Erotophobia seems to predict sexual difficulties later in life (Byrne & Schulte, 1990). Thus, for some individuals, sexual cues become associated early with negative affect. In other cases, both men and women may experience specific negative or traumatic events after a period of relatively well-adjusted sexuality. These negative events might include sudden failure to become aroused or actual sexual trauma such as rape. We have already spoken about the potentially

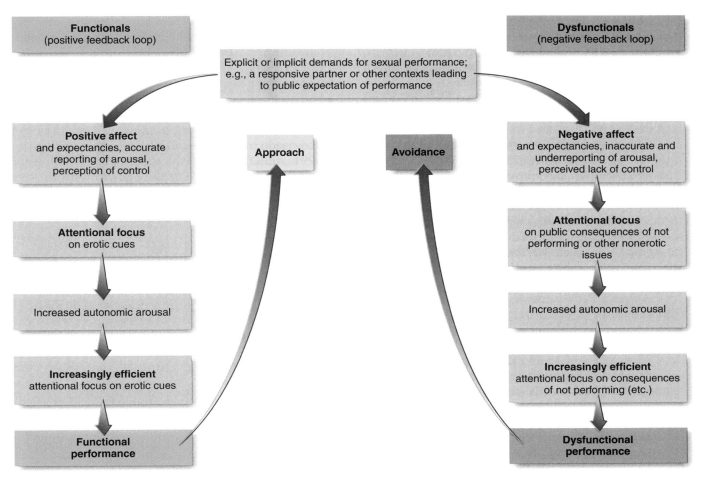

**Figure 9.4** ■ A model of functional and dysfunctional sexual arousal. (Adapted from Barlow, DH, Causes of Sexual Dysfunction: The Role of Anxiety and Cognitive Interference, *Journal of Consulting and Clinical Psychology*, 1986, 54:140–148. © 1986 American Psychological Association.)

tragic effects on sexual functioning of early sexual abuse. Recently, Meston and her colleagues have shown that childhood sexual abuse may exert its negative effects on adult sexual functioning by way of its impact on the meanings that women attribute to many sexually relevant concepts (Meston & Heiman, 2000). For example, a woman who was sexually abused as a child may think of concepts pertaining to sex as bad or dirty, which in turn would have a negative impact on her ability to function sexually.

Laumann et al. (1999), in the North American sex survey, found a substantial impact of early traumatic sexual events on later sexual functioning. For example, if women were sexually victimized by an adult before puberty, or were forced to have sexual contact of some kind, they were approximately twice as likely to have orgasmic dysfunction as women who had not been touched before puberty or forced to have sex at any time. For male victims of adult-child contact, the probability of experiencing erectile dysfunction is over 3 times greater than if they had

not had the contact. Thus, traumatic sexual acts of all kinds have long-lasting effects on subsequent sexual functioning, in both men and women, sometimes lasting decades beyond the original event. Such stressful events may initiate negative affect, in which individuals experience a loss of control over their sexual response cycle, throwing them into the kind of dysfunctional pattern depicted in Figure 9.4. It is common for people who experience erectile failure during a particularly stressful time to continue sexual dysfunction long after the stressful situation has ended.

In addition to generally negative attitudes or experiences associated with sexual interactions, a number of other factors may contribute to sexual dysfunction. Among these, the most common is a marked deterioration in close interpersonal relationships. It is difficult to have a satisfactory sexual relationship in the context of growing dislike for one's partner. Occasionally, the partner may no longer seem physically attractive. Kelly, Strassberg, and Kircher (1990) found that anorgasmic women, in addition to displaying more negative attitudes toward masturbation, greater sex guilt, and greater endorsement of sex myths, reported discomfort in telling their partners what sexual activities might increase their arousal or lead to orgasm, such as direct clitoral stimulation. Poor sexual skills might also lead to frequent sexual failure and, ultimately, lack of desire.

Thus, social and cultural factors seem to affect later sexual functioning. Researchers studying this phenomenon have constructed an important concept called *script theory* of sexual functioning. According to this theory, we all operate according to "scripts" that reflect social and cultural expectations and guide our behaviour (Gagnon, 1990; Laumann, Gagnon, Michael, & Michaels, 1994). Discovering these scripts, both in individuals and across cultures, will tell us much about sexual functioning. For example, a person who learns that sexuality is potentially dangerous, dirty, or forbidden is more vulnerable to developing sexual dysfunction later in life. This pattern is most evident in cultures with restrictive attitudes toward sex (Meston, Trapnell, & Gorzalka, 1998). For example, vaginismus is relatively rare in North America but is the most common cause of unconsummated marriages in Ireland (Barnes, 1981; O'Sullivan, 1979).

Cultural scripts may also contribute to the type of sexual dysfunction reported. In India, for example, Verma, Khaitan, and Singh (1998) reported that 77% of a large number of male patients in a sexuality clinic reported difficulties with premature ejaculation. In addition, 71% of male patients complained of being extremely concerned about nocturnal emissions associated with erotic dreams. The authors note that this focus on problems with ejaculation is most likely caused by a strong culturally held belief in India that loss of semen causes depletion of physical and mental energy. It is also interesting that out of 1000 patients presenting to this clinic only 36 were female, most likely reflecting the devaluation of sexual experiences for females because of religious and social reasons in India.

Even in Canadian culture, certain socially communicated expectations and attitudes may stay with us despite our relatively enlightened and permissive attitude toward sex. Cyranowski and colleagues (1999) have demonstrated that a negative sexual self-schema (being emotional and self-conscious about sex) and a concept similar to Byrne's erotophobia and Gagnon's scripts, may later lead to sexual difficulties under stressful situations. Zilbergeld (1992) has elaborated a number of myths about sex believed by many men, and Heiman and LoPiccolo (1988) have done the same for women. Some examples of these common

myths of male and female sexuality are, respectively, that "A man should be able to make the earth move for his partner, or at least knock her socks off" and that "Normal women have an orgasm every time they have sex." Baker and DeSilva (1988) converted an earlier version of Zilbergeld's male myths into a questionnaire and presented it to groups of sexually functional and dysfunctional men. Men with dysfunctions showed significantly greater belief in the myths than did men who were sexually functional. We explore such myths further in our discussion of treatment.

### The Interaction of Psychological and Physical Factors

Having reviewed the various causes, we must now say that seldom is any sexual dysfunction associated exclusively with either psychological or physical factors (Leiblum & Rosen, 2000; Wiegel et al., in press). More often there is a subtle combination of factors. To take a typical example, a young man, vulnerable to developing anxiety and holding to a certain number of sexual myths (the social contribution), may experience erectile failure unexpectedly after using drugs or alcohol, as many men do (the biological contribution). He will anticipate the next sexual encounter with anxiety, wondering if the failure might happen again. This combination of experience and apprehension activates the psychological sequence depicted in Figure 9.4, regardless of whether he's had a few drinks.

In summary, socially transmitted negative attitudes about sex may interact with a person's relationship difficulties and predispositions to develop performance anxiety and, ultimately, lead to sexual dysfunction. From a psychological point of view, we don't know why some individuals develop one dysfunction and not another, although it is common for several dysfunctions to occur in the same patient. Possibly, an individual's specific biological predispositions interact with psychological factors to produce a specific sexual dysfunction.

## Treatment of Sexual Dysfunction

Unlike most other disorders discussed in this book, one surprisingly simple treatment is effective for a large number of individuals who experience sexual dysfunction: education. Ignorance of the most basic aspects of the sexual response cycle and intercourse often leads to long-lasting dysfunctions (Bach et al., 2001; Wincze & Carey, 2001). Consider the case of Carl, who recently came to one of our clinics.

## Carl
### Never Too Late

Carl, a 55-year-old White man, was referred to one of our clinics by his urologist because Carl had difficulty maintaining an erection. Although he had never been married, he was at present involved in an intimate relationship with a 50-year-old woman. This was only his second sexual relationship. He was reluctant to ask his partner to come to the clinic because of his embarrassment in discussing sexual issues. A careful interview revealed that Carl engaged in sex twice a week, but requests by the clinician for a step-by-step description of his sexual activities revealed an unusual pattern: Carl skipped foreplay and immediately proceeded to intercourse! Unfortunately, because his partner was not aroused and lubricated, he was unable to penetrate her. His valiant efforts sometimes resulted in painful abrasions for both of them. Two sessions of extensive sex education, including specific step-by-step instructions for carrying out foreplay, provided Carl with a new outlook on sex. For the first time in his life he had successful, satisfying intercourse, much to his delight and his partner's.

---

In the case of hypoactive sexual desire disorder, one common presentation is a marked difference *within* a couple that leads to one partner's being labelled as having low desire. For example, if one partner is quite happy with sexual relations once a week but the other partner desires sex every day, the latter partner may accuse the former of having low desire and, unfortunately, the former partner might agree. Facilitating better conditions often resolves these misunderstandings. Fortunately, for people with this and more complex sexual dysfunctions, treatments are now available, both psychosocial and biological (medical). Advances in medical treatments, particularly for erectile dysfunction, have been dramatic in just the last few years. We look first at psychosocial treatments; then we examine the latest medical procedures.

### Psychosocial Treatments

Among the many advances in our knowledge of sexual behaviour, none was more dramatic than the publication in 1970 by William Masters and Virginia Johnson of *Human Sexual Inadequacy*. The procedures outlined in this book literally revolutionized sex therapy by providing a brief, direct, and reasonably successful therapeutic program for sexual dysfunctions. Underscoring again the common basis of most sexual dysfunctions, a similar approach to therapy is taken with all patients, male and female, with some slight variations depending on the specific sexual problem (e.g., premature ejaculation or orgasmic disorder). This intensive program involves a male and a female therapist to facilitate communication between the dysfunctional partners. (Masters and Johnson were the original male and female therapists.) Therapy is conducted daily over a 2-week period.

The actual program is straightforward. In addition to providing basic education about sexual functioning, altering deep-seated myths, and increasing communication, the clinicians' primary goal is to eliminate psychologically based performance anxiety (refer back to Figure 9.4). To accomplish this, Masters and Johnson introduced *sensate focus* and *non-demand pleasuring*. In this exercise, couples are instructed to refrain from intercourse or genital caressing and simply to explore and enjoy each other's body through touching, kissing, hugging, massaging, or similar kinds of behaviour. In the first phase, *non-genital pleasuring*, breasts and genitals are excluded from the exercises. After successfully accomplishing this phase, the couple moves to genital pleasuring but with a ban on orgasm and intercourse and clear instructions to the man that achieving an erection is not the goal.

At this point, arousal should be reestablished and the couple should be ready to attempt intercourse. So as not to proceed too quickly, this stage is also broken into parts. For example, a couple might be instructed to attempt *the beginnings* of penetration; that is, the depth of penetration and the time it lasts are only gradually built up, and both genital and non-genital pleasuring continue. Eventually, full intercourse and thrusting are accomplished. After this 2-week intensive program, recovery was reported by Masters and Johnson for the vast majority of more than 790 sexually dysfunctional patients, with some differences in the rate of recovery depending on the disorder. Close to 100% of individuals with premature ejaculation recovered, whereas the rate for more difficult cases of lifelong generalized erectile dysfunction was closer to 60%.

Specialty sexuality clinics based on the pioneering work of Masters and Johnson were established to administer these new treatment techniques. Subsequent research revealed that many of the structural aspects of the program did not seem necessary. For example, one therapist seems to be as effective as two (LoPiccolo, Heiman, Hogan, & Roberts, 1985), and seeing patients once a week seems to be as effective as seeing them every day (Heiman & LoPiccolo,

1983). It has also become clear in the succeeding decades that the results achieved by Masters and Johnson were much better than those achieved in clinics around the world using similar procedures. Reasons for this difference are not entirely clear. One possibility is that because patients had to take at least 2 weeks off and fly to St. Louis to meet with Masters and Johnson, they may have been highly motivated to begin with.

Sex therapists have expanded on and modified these procedures over the years to take advantage of recent advances in knowledge (e.g., Bach et al., 2001; Leiblum & Rosen, 2000). Results with sex therapy for erectile dysfunction indicate that as many as 60% to 70% of the cases show a positive treatment outcome for at least several years, although there may be some slipping after that (Sarwer & Durlak, 1997; Segraves & Althof, 1998). For better treatment of *specific* sexual dysfunctions, sex therapists integrate specific procedures into the context of general sex therapy.

For example, to treat premature ejaculation, most sex therapists use a procedure developed by Semans (1956), sometimes called the *squeeze* technique, in which the penis is stimulated, usually by the partner, to nearly full erection. At this point the partner firmly squeezes the penis near the top where the head of the penis joins the shaft, which quickly reduces arousal. These steps are repeated until (for heterosexual partners) eventually the penis is briefly inserted in the vagina without thrusting. If arousal occurs too quickly, the penis is withdrawn and the squeeze technique is employed again. In this way the man develops a sense of control over arousal and ejaculation. Reports of success with this approach over the past 20 years suggest that 60% to 90% of men benefit, but the success rates drop to about 25% after 3 years or more of follow-up (Polonsky, 2000; Segraves & Althof, 1998). Gary, the 31-year-old salesman, was treated with this method, and his wife was cooperative

during the procedures. Brief marital therapy also persuaded Gary that his insecurity over his perception that his wife no longer found him attractive was unfounded. After treatment, he reduced his work hours somewhat, and the couple's marital and sexual relations improved.

Lifelong female orgasmic disorder may be treated with explicit training in masturbatory procedures. For example, Greta was still unable to achieve orgasm with manual stimulation by her husband, even after proceeding through the basic steps of sex therapy. At this point, following certain standardized treatment programs for this problem (e.g., Heiman, 2000; Heiman & LoPiccolo, 1988), Greta and Will purchased a vibrator and Greta was taught to let go of her inhibitions by talking out loud about how she felt during sexual arousal, even shouting or screaming if she wanted to. In the context of appropriate genital pleasuring and disinhibition exercises, the vibrator brought on Greta's first orgasm. With practice and good communication, the couple eventually learned how to bring on Greta's orgasm without the vibrator. Although Will and Greta were both delighted with her progress, Will was concerned that Greta's screams during orgasm would attract the attention of the neighbours. Summaries of results from a number of studies, including work by Meston and her colleagues, suggest 70% to 90% of women will benefit from treatment, and these gains are stable and even improve over time (Heiman, 2000; Heiman & Meston, 1997).

To treat vaginismus, the woman and, eventually, the partner gradually insert larger and larger dilators at the woman's own pace. After the woman (and then the partner) can insert the largest dilator, in a heterosexual couple the woman gradually inserts the man's penis. These exercises are carried out in the context of genital and non-genital pleasuring to retain arousal. Close attention must be accorded to any increased fear and anxiety that may be associated with the process, which may trigger memories of early sexual abuse that may have contributed to the onset of the condition. These procedures are highly successful, with a large majority of women (80% to 100%) overcoming vaginismus in a relatively short period (Leiblum, 2000; Segraves & Althof, 1998).

However, Elke Reissing, Irv Binik, and Samir Khalifé (1999) in Montreal have been critical of this literature's focus on the achievement of penile–vaginal intercourse as the indicator of therapy "success." These researchers argue that additional relevant outcomes that should be (but rarely are) assessed are (1) whether the vaginal muscle spasm has in fact been resolved, (2) whether interference with intercourse has been decreased, (3) whether intercourse is less painful or more pleasurable, and (4) whether the couple is experiencing greater sexual satisfaction (Reissing et al., 1999).

A therapist usually treats a dysfunction in one partner by seeing the couple together.

A variety of treatment procedures have also been developed for low sexual desire (e.g., Pridal & LoPiccolo, 2000; Wincze & Carey, 2001). At the heart of these treatments are the standard reeducation and communication phases of traditional sex therapy with, possibly, the addition of masturbatory training and exposure to erotic material. Each case may require individual strategies. Remember Mrs. C., who was sexually abused by her cousin? Therapy involved helping the couple understand the impact of the repeated, unwanted sexual experiences in Mrs. C.'s past and to approach sex so Mrs. C. was much more comfortable with foreplay. She gradually lost the idea that once sex was started she had no control. She and her husband worked on starting and stopping sexual encounters. Cognitive restructuring was used to help Mrs. C. interpret her husband's amorousness in a positive rather than a skeptical light. In general, approximately 50% to 70% of individuals with low sexual desire benefit from sex therapy, at least initially (Hawton, 1995; Segraves & Althof, 1998).

Gilles Trudel, Andre Marchand, and their colleagues (2001) at the University of Quebec at Montreal recently conducted the first extensive controlled study on the treatment of hypoactive sexual desire disorder with a novel, short-term, cognitive-behavioural group treatment program. Seventy-four couples (aged 20 to 55 years) in which the woman had low sexual desire participated in the treatment. Results showed that the treatment decreased symptoms of the disorder and also improved overall cognitive, behavioural, and marital functioning in these couples (Trudel et al., 2001).

## Medical Treatments

A variety of pharmacological and surgical techniques have been developed in recent years to treat sexual dysfunction, almost all focusing on male erectile disorder. But the introduction of the drug Viagra in Canada in March 1999 and similar drugs such as Levitra and Cialis, introduced subsequently, are the best known. We look at the four most popular procedures: oral medication, injection of vasoactive substances directly into the penis, surgery, and vacuum device therapy. Before we begin, note that it is important to combine any medical treatment with a comprehensive educational and sex therapy program to ensure maximum benefit.

Several so-called wonder drugs for various disorders have been introduced with a flourish, including Prozac for depression and Redux for obesity. As noted in Chapter 2, the usual course is initial overwhelming enthusiasm that the drug is a cure-all followed by a period of profound disappointment as people realize the drug is not what it's promised to be and may even be harmful in some cases. Finally, rationality sets in and the drug, if it has been proven effective in a number of studies, usually is found to be of moderate benefit to some people and becomes a useful part of a treatment plan.

The wonder drug of 1999 was sildenafil (trade-name Viagra) for erectile dysfunction. Guy Lafleur, from the Montreal Canadiens hockey team, was the spokesman in the initial marketing campaign for Viagra in Canada. Results from several clinical trials suggested that between 50% and 80% of a large number of men benefit from this treatment (Conti, Pepine, & Sweeney, 1999; Goldstein et al., 1998) in that erections become sufficient for intercourse. However, as many as 30% may suffer severe headaches as a side effect, particularly at higher doses (Rosen, 2000; Virag, 1999), and reports of sexual satisfaction are not optimal. Only time will tell how effective the treatment really is, but its reception is following the same course as other wonder drugs. For example, in 1999 (the year Viagra was introduced in this country), prescriptions dispensed in Canada for erectile dysfunction climbed to 655 000—almost quadrupling the previous market (IMS Health Canada, 2004a)! Today, Viagra is by far the most common treatment for erectile disorder, representing 90% of the 1.3 million prescriptions dispensed for erectile disorder in Canada in 2003 (IMS Health Canada, 2004a), despite a cost of between $12 and $13 a pill (IMS Health Canada, 2004b).

For some time, yohimbine (Carey & Johnson, 1996) and testosterone (Schiavi, White, Mandeli, & Levine, 1997) have been used to treat erectile dysfunction. But although they are safe and have relatively few side effects, only negligible effects on erectile dysfunction have been reported (Mann et al., 1996). Recently, Meston and her colleagues have produced results suggesting that yohimbine when combined with another drug, L-arginine glutamate, is superior to placebo in increasing vaginal responses to erotic stimuli among women with sexual arousal disorder (Meston & Worcel, 2002). Future research still needs to establish the utility of this drug combination in treating symptoms of the disorder outside the laboratory.

Some urologists teach patients to inject vasodilating drugs such as *papaverine* or *prostaglandin* directly into the penis when they want to have sexual intercourse. These drugs dilate the blood vessels, allowing blood to flow to the penis and thereby producing an erection within 15 minutes that can last from 1 to 4 hours (Rosen, 2000; Segraves & Althof, 1998). Because this procedure is a bit painful (although not as much as you might think), a substantial number of men, usually 50% to 60%, stop using it after a short time. In one study, 50 of 100 patients discontinued papaverine for various reasons (Lakin et al., 1990; Segraves & Althof, 1998). Side effects include bruising and, with repeated injections, the development of fibrosis nodules in the penis (Gregoire, 1992; Rosen, 2000). Although some patients have found papaverine helpful, it needs more study, and scientists are attempting to develop more palatable ways to deliver the drug. A soft capsule that contains the drug, called MUSE, can be inserted directly into the urethra, but this is somewhat painful, is less effective than injections, and remains awkward and artificial enough to most likely preclude wide acceptance (Delizonna, Wincze, Litz, Brown, & Barlow, 2001).

Insertion of *penile prostheses* or implants has been a surgical option for almost 100 years; only recently are they good enough to approximate normal sexual functioning. One procedure involves implanting a semirigid silicone rod that can be bent by the male into correct position for intercourse and manoeuvred out of the way at other times. In a more popular procedure, the male squeezes a small pump that is surgically implanted into the scrotum, forcing fluid into an inflatable cylinder and thus producing an erection. The newest model of penile prosthetic device is an inflatable rod that contains the pumping device, which is more convenient than having the pump outside the rod. However, surgical implants fall short of restoring presurgical sexual functioning or assuring satisfaction in most patients (Gregoire, 1992; Kim & Lipshultz, 1997), and they are now generally used only if other approaches don't work. On the other hand, this procedure has proved useful for men who must have a cancerous prostate removed, which most often causes erectile

dysfunction (Ramsawh, Morgantaler, Covino, Barlow, & DeWolfe, 2005). *Vascular surgery* to correct arterial or venous malfunctions has also been attempted (e.g., Bennett, 1988). Although the initial results are often successful, follow-up evaluations reveal a high failure rate.

Another approach is *vacuum device therapy*, which works by creating a vacuum in a cylinder placed over the penis. The vacuum draws blood into the penis, which is then trapped by a specially designed ring placed around the base of the penis. Although using the vacuum device is rather awkward, between 70% and 100% of users report satisfactory erections, particularly if psychological sex therapy is ineffective (Segraves & Althof, 1998; Witherington, 1988). The procedure is less intrusive than surgery or injections, but it remains awkward and artificial enough to, most likely, preclude wide acceptance (Delizonna et al., 2001).

## Summary

Treatment programs, both psychosocial and medical, offer hope to most people who have sexual dysfunctions. Unfortunately, such programs are not readily available in many locations because few health and mental health professionals are trained to apply them, although the availability of Viagra for male erectile dysfunction is widespread. Psychological treatment of sexual arousal disorders requires further improvement, and treatments for low sexual desire are largely untested. New medical developments appear yearly, but most are still intrusive and clumsy. New drugs such as Viagra and Levitra exhibit some success for erectile dysfunction, and many more such drugs are in development (Rosen, 2000).

Unfortunately, most health professionals tend to ignore the issue of sexuality in the aging. Along with the usual emphasis on communication, education, and sensate focus, appropriate lubricants for women and a discussion of methods to maximize the erectile response in men should be a part of any sexual counselling for older couples. More important, even with reduced physical capabilities, continued sexual relations, not necessarily including intercourse, should be an enjoyable and important part of an aging couple's relationship. Further research and development in the treatment of sexual dysfunction must address all these issues. Nevertheless, the overwhelming consensus is that a combination of psychological and drug treatment, when indicated, will continue to be the treatment strategy of choice.

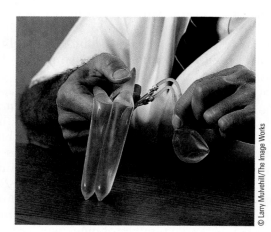

© Larry Mulvehill/The Image Works

An inflatable penile implant may be used for men with inadequate sexual functioning.

Sexual behaviour often continues well into old age.

© Photos.com

# Paraphilia: Clinical Descriptions

■ *Identify the common clinical features of each of the major paraphilias.*

■ *Explain what is known about the causes of paraphilias.*

If you are like most people, your sexual interest is directed to other physically mature adults (or late adolescents), all of whom are capable of freely offering or withholding their consent. But what if you are sexually attracted to something or somebody other than another adult, such as animals (particularly horses and dogs [Williams & Weinberg, 2003]), or to a vacuum cleaner? (Yes, it does happen!) Or what if your only means of obtaining sexual satisfaction is to commit a brutal murder? Such patterns of sexual arousal and countless others exist in a large number of individuals, causing untold human suffering both for them and, if their behaviour involves other people, for their victims. As noted in the beginning of the chapter, these disorders of sexual arousal are called **paraphilias.**

Over the years, we have assessed and treated a large number of these individuals, ranging from the slightly eccentric and sometimes pitiful case to some of the most dangerous killer-rapists encountered anywhere. We begin by describing briefly the major types of paraphilia, using in all instances cases from our own files. As with sexual dysfunctions, it is unusual for an individual to have just one paraphilic pattern of sexual arousal. Many of our cases may present with two, three, or more patterns, although one is usually dominant (Abel et al., 1987; Abel, Becker, Cunningham-Rathner, Mittelman, & Rouleau, 1988). Furthermore, it is not uncommon for individuals with paraphilia to also have comorbid mood, anxiety, and substance use disorders (Raymond, Coleman, Ohlerking, Christenson, & Miner, 1999).

Although paraphilias are not widely prevalent and estimates of their frequency are hard to come by, some disorders, such as transvestic fetishism, seem relatively common (Bancroft, 1989; Mason, 1997). You may have been the victim of *frotteurism* in a large city, typically on a crowded subway or bus. In this situation women have been known to

**paraphilias** Sexual disorders and deviations in which sexual arousal occurs almost exclusively in the context of inappropriate objects or individuals.

experience more than the usual jostling and pushing from behind. What they discover, much to their horror, is a male with a frotteuristic arousal pattern rubbing against them until he is stimulated to the point of ejaculation. Because the victims cannot escape easily, the frotteuristic act is usually successful.

## Fetishism

In **fetishism**, a person is sexually attracted to non-living objects. There are almost as many different types of fetishes as there are objects, although women's undergarments and shoes are popular. Fetishistic arousal is associated with two different classes of objects or activities: (1) an inanimate object or (2) a source of specific tactile stimulation, such as rubber, particularly clothing made out of rubber. Shiny black plastic is also used (Bancroft, 1989; Junginger, 1997). Most, if not all, of the person's sexual fantasies, urges, and desires focus on this object. A third source of attraction (sometimes called *partialism*) is a part of the body, such as the foot, buttocks, or hair, but this attraction is no longer technically classified as a fetish because distinguishing it from more normal patterns of arousal is often difficult.

For a period of several months, bras hung on a woman's backyard clothesline disappeared. The women in the neighbourhood soon began talking to each other and discovered that bras were missing from every clothesline for blocks around. A police stakeout caught the perpetrator, who turned out to have a strong fetish for brassieres.

---

### Disorder Criteria Summary
Fetishism

Features of fetishism include:
- Over a period of at least 6 months, recurrent, intense, sexually arousing fantasies, urges, or behaviours involving the use of non-living objects
- Sexual fantasies, urges, or behaviours cause significant distress or impairment in daily functioning
- Fetish objects are not limited to articles specific to cross-dressing (as in transvestic fetishism) or devices designed for tactile genital stimulation (e.g., a vibrator)

*Source:* Based on DSM-IV-TR. Used with permission from the *Diagnostic and Statistical Manual of Mental Disorders*, Fourth Edition, Text Revision. Copyright 2000. American Psychiatric Association.

---

## Voyeurism and Exhibitionism

**Voyeurism** is the practice of observing an unsuspecting individual undressing or naked to become aroused. **Exhibitionism,** by contrast, is achieving sexual arousal and gratification by exposing one's genitals to unsuspecting strangers. Consider the case of Robert.

### Robert
#### Outside the Curtains

Robert, a 31-year-old married blue-collar worker, reported that he first started "peeping" into windows when he was 14. He rode around the neighbourhood on his bike at night, and when he spotted a female through a window he stopped and watched. During one of these episodes, he felt the first pangs of sexual arousal. Eventually he began masturbating while watching, thereby exposing his genitals, although out of sight. When he was older, he drove around until he spotted some prepubescent girls. He parked his car near them, unzipped his fly, called them over, and attempted to carry on a nonsexual conversation. Later he was sometimes able to talk a girl into mutual masturbation and fellatio. Although he was arrested several times, paradoxically the threat of arrest increased his arousal (Barlow & Wincze, 1980).

---

Remember that anxiety actually *increases* arousal under some circumstances. Many voyeurs just don't get the same satisfaction from attending readily available strip shows at a local bar. Although paraphilias may occur separately, it is not unusual to find them co-occurring.

---

**fetishism** Long-term, recurring, intense sexually arousing urges, fantasies, or behaviour involving the use of non-living, unusual objects, which cause distress or impairment in life functioning.

**voyeurism** Paraphilia in which sexual arousal is derived from observing unsuspecting individuals undressing or naked.

**exhibitionism** Sexual gratification attained by exposing one's genitals to unsuspecting strangers.

## Disorder Criteria Summary
Voyeurism and Exhibitionism

Features of voyeurism include:

- Over a period of at least 6 months, recurrent, intense, sexually arousing fantasies, urges, or behaviours that involve observing an unsuspecting person who is naked, disrobing, or engaging in sexual activity
- Person has acted on these sexual urges, or the sexual fantasies, urges, or behaviours cause significant distress or impairment in daily functioning

Features of exhibitionism include:

- Over a period of at least 6 months, recurrent, intense, sexually arousing fantasies, urges, or behaviours involving the exposure of one's genitals to an unsuspecting stranger
- Person has acted on these sexual urges, or the sexual fantasies, urges, or behaviours cause significant distress or impairment in daily functioning

*Source:* Based on DSM-IV-TR. Used with permission from the *Diagnostic and Statistical Manual of Mental Disorders,* Fourth Edition, Text Revision. Copyright 2000. American Psychiatric Association.

## Transvestic Fetishism

In **transvestic fetishism,** sexual arousal is strongly associated with the act of dressing in clothes of the opposite sex, or *cross-dressing.* Consider the case of Mr. M.

## Mr. M.
### Strong Man in a Dress

Mr. M., a 31-year-old married police officer, came to one of our clinics seeking treatment for uncontrollable urges to dress in women's clothing and appear in public. He had been doing this for 16 years and had been discharged from the Armed Forces for cross-dressing. Since then, he had risked public disclosure on several occasions. Mr. M.'s wife had threatened to divorce him because of the cross-dressing, and yet she frequently purchased women's clothing for him and was "compassionate" while he wore them.

Note that Mr. M. was in the Armed Forces before he joined the police. It is not unusual for males who are strongly inclined to dress in female clothes to compensate by associating with so-called macho organizations. Some of our cross-dressing patients have been associated with various paramilitary organizations.

Nevertheless, most individuals with this disorder do not seem to display compensatory behaviours.

Interestingly, the wives of many men who cross-dress have accepted their husbands' behaviour and can be supportive if it is a private matter between them. Docter and Prince (1997) reported that 60% of more than 1000 cases of transvestic fetishism were married at the time of the survey. Some people, both married and single, join cross-dressing clubs that meet periodically or subscribe to newsletters devoted to the topic. Research by Kurt Freund and his colleagues at the Centre for Addiction and Mental Health in Toronto suggests that transvestic fetishism is indistinguishable from other fetishes in most respects (Freund, Seto, & Kuban, 1996).

## Sexual Sadism and Sexual Masochism

Both **sexual sadism** and **sexual masochism** are associated with either inflicting pain or humiliation (sadism) or suffering pain or humiliation (masochism). Although Mr. M. was extremely concerned about his cross-dressing, he was also disturbed by another problem. To maximize his sexual pleasure during intercourse with his wife, he had her wear a collar and leash, tied her to the bed, and handcuffed her. He sometimes tied himself with ropes, chains, handcuffs, and wires, all while he was cross-dressed. Mr. M. was concerned he might injure himself seriously. As a member of the police force he had heard of cases and even investigated one himself in which an individual was found dead, tightly and completely bound in harnesses, handcuffs, and ropes. In many such cases something goes wrong and the individual accidentally hangs himself or herself, an event that should be distinguished from the closely related condition called *hypoxiphilia,* which involves self-strangulation to reduce the flow of oxygen to the brain and enhance the sensation of orgasm. It may seem paradoxical that a person has to either inflict or receive pain to become sexually aroused, but these types of cases are not uncommon. On many occasions, the behaviours are mild and harmless, but they can become dangerous and costly. It was not unusual that Mr. M. presented with three different patterns of deviant arousal, in his case sexual masochism, sexual sadism, and transvestic fetishism.

**transvestic fetishism** Paraphilia in which individuals, usually males, are sexually aroused or receive gratification by wearing clothing of the opposite sex.

**sexual sadism** Paraphilia in which sexual arousal is associated with inflicting pain or humiliation.

**sexual masochism** Paraphilia in which sexual arousal is associated with experiencing pain or humiliation.

Belts, chains, and handcuffs may increase sexual arousal in individuals with sadistic or masochistic tendencies.

Murderer Paul Bernardo obtained sexual gratification from inflicting pain and humiliation upon his victims (i.e., sadism).

### Sadistic Rape

After murder, rape is the most devastating assault one person can make on another. It is not classified as a paraphilia because most instances of rape are better characterized as an assault by a male (or, rarely, a female) whose patterns of sexual arousal are not paraphilic. Instead, many rapists meet criteria for antisocial personality disorder (see Chapter 11) and may engage in a variety of antisocial and aggressive acts. Many rapes could be described as opportunistic, in that an aggressive or antisocial individual with a marked lack of empathy and disregard for inflicting pain on others (Bernat, Calhoun, & Adams, 1999) spontaneously took advantage of a vulnerable and unsuspecting person. These unplanned assaults often occur during robberies or other criminal events. Knight and Prentky (1990) describe rapes motivated by anger and vindictiveness against specific women and that may have been planned in advance (Hucker, 1997).

Several years ago, it was determined in one of our clinics that certain rapists do fit definitions of paraphilia closely and could probably better be described as *sadists*. Two audiotapes were constructed on which were described (1) mutually enjoyable sexual intercourse and (2) sexual intercourse involving force on the part of the male (rape). Each tape was played twice for selected listeners. The non-rapists became sexually aroused to descriptions of mutually consenting intercourse, but not to those involving force. Rapists, however, became aroused to both types of descriptions (Abel, Barlow, Blanchard, & Guild, 1977). Paul Bernardo would be an example of this type of sadistic rapist. Bernardo and his wife, Karla Homolka, were involved in the rape and murder of two teenage girls in St. Catharines, Ontario, as well as in the rape and death of Karla's younger sister, Tammy. Bernardo also turned out to be the "Scarborough Rapist" who terrorized and raped more than 20 women in the Toronto area.

### Disorder Criteria Summary
Sexual Sadism and Sexual Masochism

Features of sexual sadism include:
- Over a period of at least 6 months, recurrent, intense, sexually arousing sexual fantasies, urges, or behaviours involving acts in which the suffering of another offers sexual excitement
- Person has acted on these sexual urges with a non-consenting person, or the fantasies, urges, or behaviours cause significant distress or impairment

Features of sexual masochism include:
- Over a period of at least 6 months, recurrent, intense, sexually arousing fantasies, urges, or behaviours involving the act of being humiliated, beaten, bound, or otherwise made to suffer
- Fantasies, urges, or behaviours cause significant distress or impairment

*Source:* Based on DSM-IV-TR. Used with permission from the *Diagnostic and Statistical Manual of Mental Disorders*, Fourth Edition, Text Revision. Copyright 2000. American Psychiatric Association.

## Pedophilia and Incest

Perhaps the most tragic sexual deviance is a sexual attraction to children (or very young adolescents), called **pedophilia.** Individuals with this pattern of arousal may be attracted to male children, female children, or both. In one survey, as many as 12% of men and 17% of women reported being touched inappropriately by adults when they were children (Fagan, Wise, Schmidt, & Berlin, 2002). Approximately 90% of abusers are male and 10% female (Fagan et al., 2002).

If the children are the person's relatives, the pedophilia takes the form of **incest.** Although pedophilia and incest have much in common, victims of pedophilia tend to be young children and victims of incest tend to be girls who are beginning to mature physically (Rice & Harris, 2002). William Marshall at Queen's University demonstrated by using penile strain gauge measures that incestuous males are, in general, more aroused to adult women than are males with pedophilia, who tend to focus exclusively on children (Marshall, 1997; Marshall, Barbaree, & Christophe, 1986). Thus, incestuous relations may have more to do with availability and interpersonal issues ongoing in the family than pedophilia, as in the case of Tony.

### Tony
### More and Less a Father

Tony, a 52-year-old married television repairman, came in depressed. About 10 years earlier he had begun sexual activity with his 12-year-old daughter. Light kissing and some fondling gradually escalated to heavy petting and, finally, mutual masturbation. When his daughter was 16 years old, his wife discovered the ongoing incestuous relationship. She separated from her husband and eventually divorced him, taking her daughter with her. Soon, Tony remarried. Just before his initial visit to one of our clinics, Tony visited his daughter, then 22 years old, who was living alone in a different city. They had not seen each other for 5 years. A second visit, shortly after the first, led to a recurrence of the incestuous behaviour. At this point, Tony became extremely depressed and told his new wife the whole story. She contacted one of our clinics with his full cooperation while his daughter sought treatment in her own city.

We return to the case of Tony later, but several features are worth noting. First, Tony loved his daughter very much and was bitterly disappointed

and depressed over his behaviour. On occasion, a child molester is abusive and aggressive, sometimes killing the victims; in these cases, the disorder is often both sexual sadism and pedophilia. A recent study by Philip Firestone and colleagues of the University of Ottawa showed that child molesters who kill or attempt to kill their victims can be differentiated from child molesters who are not physically abusive and from controls in terms of their sexual arousal response to sexual vignettes (Firestone, Bradford, Greenberg, & Nunes, 2000). These researchers had these three groups of men listen to three types of vignettes describing three types of scenes (i.e., sex with a consenting adult, sex with a "consenting" child, and assault involving a child victim) and measured their sexual arousal responses. Study results are displayed in Figure 9.5. It was found that a greater proportion of both types of child molesters showed enhanced arousal responses to the vignette describing sex with a "consenting" child relative to men in the control group (see Figure 9.5, left panel). However, the homicidal child molesters showed increased sexual arousal to the vignette describing the assault on the child victim relative to the men in both other groups (see Figure 9.5, right panel).

A recent example of a homicidal child molester is the case of 36-year-old Michael Briere. The Montreal native pled guilty to the murder of 10-year-old Holly Jones in Toronto. Jones was abducted while walking home from a friend's house in May 2003. Her dismembered body was found a day later. Briere was arrested a month later and charged with her murder. Briere had abducted Jones off the street after viewing child pornography obtained via the Internet. He sexually assaulted the little girl, strangled her, and then dismembered her body to dispose of it. Briere pled guilty and was sentenced to life in prison in June 2004 (CBC News Online, 2004a; "Briere Pleads Guilty," 2004). The horrors of such cases appearing all too often in the media might make people think that most child molesters are physically violent toward their victims.

But, in fact, most child molesters are *not* physically abusive. Rarely is a child physically forced or injured. In the Firestone et al. (2000) study, only 27 men qualified for the homicidal child molesters group as compared with 189 men in the non-homicidal child molesters group. For the more usual case of a non-homicidal child molester, from the molester's perspective, no harm is done because there is no physical force or threats. In fact, child molesters

**pedophilia** Paraphilia (sexual deviation) involving strong sexual attraction toward children.

**incest** Deviant sexual attraction directed toward one's own family member; often the attraction of a father toward a daughter who is maturing physically.

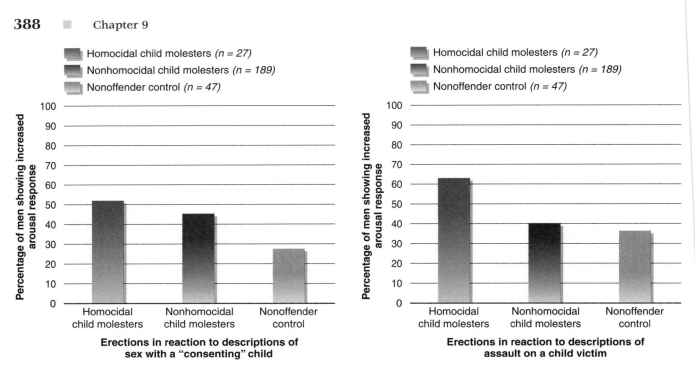

**Figure 9.5** ■ Erectile arousal differences between homicidal and non-homicidal child molesters and normal control males. Both types of child molesters became aroused to descriptions of sex with a "consenting" child (Figure 9.5a), while only the homicidal child molesters became aroused to descriptions of assault on a child (Figure 9.5b). Note: Percentages reflect the proportion of men in each group who showed a larger arousal response to the vignette in question relative to their arousal response to descriptions of sex with a consenting adult. (Adapted from Firestone, P., Bradford, J.M., Greenberg, D.M., & Nunes, K.L. (2000). Differentiation of homicidal child molesters, nonhomicidal child molesters, and nonoffenders by phallometry. *American Journal of Psychiatry,* 157:1847–1850.)

often rationalize their behaviour as "loving" the child or teaching the child useful lessons about sexuality. The child molester almost never considers the psychological damage the victim suffers, yet these interactions often destroy the child's trust and ability to share intimacy. For example, male victims of the molestations by Catholic priests at the Mount Cashel orphanage in Newfoundland in the 1970s reported long-term negative consequences of these interactions in their adult lives including flashbacks of the abuse experience, difficulties

forming relationships with women, and a lack of trust ("Newfoundland Brother Gets 4 Years," 1992). Child molesters rarely gauge their power over the children, who may participate in the molestation without protest yet be frightened and unwilling. Often children feel responsible for the abuse because no outward force or threat was used by the adult, and only after the abused children grow up are they able to understand they were powerless to protect themselves and not responsible for what was done to them.

Mount Cashel Orphanage in Newfoundland was the site of a set of well-known cases of pedophilia in which many young male victims were molested by Catholic priests at the orphanage in the 1970s. The victims suffered adverse psychological consequences of these molestation experiences into adulthood.

### Disorder Criteria Summary
Pedophilia

Features of pedophilia include:
- Over a period of at least 6 months, recurrent, intense, sexually arousing fantasies, urges, or behaviours involving sexual activity with children (generally aged 13 and under)
- Person has acted on these sexual urges, or the fantasies, urges, or behaviours cause significant distress or impairment in daily functioning
- The person is at least 16 years old and at least 5 years older than the child or children

*Source:* Based on DSM-IV-TR. Used with permission from the *Diagnostic and Statistical Manual of Mental Disorders,* Fourth Edition, Text Revision. Copyright 2000. American Psychiatric Association.

## Paraphilia in Women

Paraphilia is seldom seen in women and was thought to be absent in women for many years, with the possible exception of sadomasochistic practices. But in recent years several reports have appeared describing individual cases or small series of cases. For example, J. Paul Fedoroff and his colleagues at the forensic service of the Centre for Addiction and Mental Health in Toronto have reported what seems to be the largest series of cases of women with paraphilia, 12 cases seen in their clinic (Fedoroff, Fishell, & Fedoroff, 1999). Although some women had more than one paraphilia, 5 of the 12 presented with pedophilia, 4 of the 12 presented with exhibitionism, and 3 presented with sadomasochistic tendencies.

To take several examples, one heterosexual woman had been convicted of sexually molesting an unrelated 9-year-old boy while she was babysitting. It seems she had touched the boy's penis and asked him to masturbate in front of her while she watched religious programs on television. It is not unusual for individuals with paraphilia to rationalize their behaviour by engaging in some other practices that they consider to be morally correct or uplifting at the same time. Yet another woman came to treatment because of her "uncontrollable" rituals of undressing in front of her apartment window and masturbating approximately five times a month. In addition she would, on occasion, drive her truck through the neighbourhood where she would attempt to befriend cats and dogs by offering them food. She would then place honey or other food substances on her genital area so the animals would lick her. As with most paraphilias, the woman herself was horrified by this activity and was seeking treatment to eliminate it, although she found it highly sexually arousing.

## Causes of Paraphilia

Although no substitute for scientific inquiry, case histories often provide hypotheses that can then be tested by controlled scientific observations. Let's return to the cases of Robert and Tony to see if their histories contain any clues.

### Robert
#### Revenge on Repression

Robert (who sought help for exhibitionism) was raised by a stern authoritarian father and a passive mother in a small town in British Columbia. His father, who was a firm believer in Fundamentalist Christian religion, often preached the evils of sexual intercourse to his family. Robert learned little about sex from his father except that it was bad, so he suppressed any emerging heterosexual urges and fantasies and as an adolescent felt very uneasy around girls his own age. By accident, he discovered a private source of sexual gratification: staring at attractive and unsuspecting females through the window. This led to his first masturbatory experience.

Robert reported in retrospect that being arrested was not so bad because it disgraced his father, which was his only way of getting back at him. The courts treated him lightly (which is not unusual), and his father was publicly humiliated, forcing the family to move from their small town (Barlow & Wincze, 1980).

### Tony
#### Trained Too Young

Tony, who sought help because of an incestuous relationship with his daughter, reported an early sexual history that contained a number of interesting events. Although he was brought up in a reasonably loving and outwardly normal Catholic family, he had an uncle who did not fit the family pattern. When he was 9 or 10, Tony was encouraged by his uncle to observe a game of strip poker that the uncle was playing with a neighbour's wife. During this period, he also observed his uncle fondling a waitress at a drive-in restaurant and shortly thereafter was instructed by his uncle to fondle his young female cousin. Thus, he had an early model for mutual fondling and masturbation and obtained some pleasure from interacting in this way with young girls. Although the uncle never touched Tony, his behaviour was clearly abusive. When Tony was about 13, he engaged in mutual manipulation with a sister and her girlfriend, which he remembers as pleasurable. Later, when Tony was 18, a brother-in-law took him to a prostitute and he first experienced sexual intercourse. He remembered this visit as unsatisfactory because, on that and subsequent visits to prostitutes, he ejaculated prematurely—a sharp contrast to his early experience with young girls. Other experiences with adult women were also unsatisfactory. When he joined the armed forces and was sent overseas, he sought prostitutes who were often as young as 12.

These cases remind us that deviant patterns of sexual arousal often occur in the context of other sexual and social problems. Undesired kinds of arousal may be associated with deficiencies in levels of "desired" arousal with consensual adults; this was certainly true for both Tony and Robert, whose sexual relationships with adults were incomplete. As William Marshall has pointed out, in many cases, an inability to develop adequate social relations with the appropriate people for sexual relationships seems to be associated with a developing of inappropriate sexual outlets (Marshall, 1997; see also Barlow & Wincze, 1980). However, many people with deficient sexual and social skills do *not* develop deviant patterns of arousal.

Early experience seems to have an effect that may be accidental. Tony's early sexual experiences just happened to be of the type he later found sexually arousing. Many pedophiles also report being abused themselves as children, which turns out to be a strong predictor of later sexual abuse by the victim (Fagan et al., 2002). Robert's first erotic experience occurred while he was "peeping." But many of us do not find our early experiences reflected in our sexual patterns.

Another factor may be the nature of the person's early sexual fantasies. For example, in a famous study, Stanley J. Rachman demonstrated that sexual arousal could become associated with a neutral object—a boot, for example—if the boot was repeatedly presented while the individual was sexually aroused (Rachman & Hodgson, 1968; see also Bancroft, 1989). One of the most powerful engines for the development of unwanted arousal may be *early sexual fantasies that are repeatedly reinforced through the strong sexual pleasure associated with masturbation.* Before a pedophile or sadist ever acts on his behaviour, he may fantasize about it thousands of times while masturbating. Expressed as a clinical or operant conditioning paradigm, this is another example of a learning process in which a behaviour (sexual arousal to a specific object or activity) is repeatedly reinforced through association with a pleasurable consequence (orgasm). This mechanism may explain why paraphilias are almost exclusively male disorders. The basic differences in frequency of masturbation between men and women that exist across cultures may contribute to the differential development of paraphilias. As we have seen, on rare occasions, cases of women with paraphilia do turn up (Fedoroff et al., 1999; Hunter & Mathews, 1997), and a comprehensive study of 100 female child sexual abusers is under way (Wiegel, 2004).

However, if early experiences contribute strongly to later sexual arousal patterns, then what about the Sambia males who practise exclusive homosexual behaviour during childhood and early adolescence and yet are exclusively heterosexual as adults? In such cohesive societies, the social demands or "scripts" for sexual interactions are much stronger and more rigid than in our culture and thus may override the effects of early experiences (Baldwin & Baldwin, 1989).

In addition, therapists and sex researchers who work with paraphilics have observed what seems to be an incredibly strong sex drive. It is not uncommon for some paraphilics to masturbate three or four times a day. In a case seen in one of our clinics, a sadistic rapist masturbated approximately every half hour all day long, just as often as it was physiologically possible. We have speculated elsewhere that activity this consuming may be related to the obsessional processes of obsessive-compulsive disorder (Barlow, 2002). In both instances, the very act of trying to suppress unwanted emotionally charged thoughts and fantasies seems to have the paradoxical effect of *increasing* their frequency and intensity (see Chapter 4). This process is also ongoing in eating disorders and addictions, when attempts to restrict strong addictive cravings lead to uncontrollable *increases* in the undesired behaviours. (Recall Polivy and Herman's work on the causal role of dietary restraint in explaining binge eating, discussed in Chapter 8.) Psychopathologists are becoming interested in the phenomenon of weak inhibitory control across these disorders, which may indicate a weak biologically based behavioural inhibition system (BIS) in the brain (Fowles, 1993; Kafka, 1997) that might repress serotonergic functioning. (You may remember from Chapter 4 that the BIS is a brain circuit associated with anxiety and inhibition.)

The model shown in Figure 9.6 incorporates the factors thought to contribute to the development of paraphilia. Nevertheless, all speculations, including

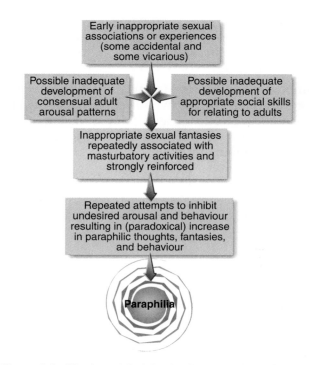

**Figure 9.6**  ■  A model of the development of paraphilia.

the hypotheses we have described, have little scientific support at this time. For example, this model does not include the biological dimension. Excess arousal in paraphilics could be biologically based. Before we can make any steadfast conclusions here, more research is needed.

# Assessing and Treating Paraphilia

■ *Describe available psychosocial and drug treatments for paraphilias, including what is known about their relative effectiveness.*

In recent years we have developed sophisticated methods for assessing specific patterns of sexual arousal (Looman & Marshall, 2001; Maletzky, 1998). This development is important in studying paraphilia because sometimes even the individual presenting with the problem is not fully aware of what caused arousal. An individual once came in complaining of uncontrollable arousal to open-toed white sandals worn by women. He noted that he was irresistably drawn to any woman wearing such sandals and would follow her for kilometres. These urges occupied much of his summer. Subsequent assessment revealed that the sandal itself had no erotic value for this individual; rather, he had a strong sexual attraction to women's feet, particularly moving in a certain way.

Using the model of paraphilia described previously, we assess each patient not only for the presence of deviant arousal but also for levels of appropriate arousal to adults, for social skills, and for the ability to form relationships. Tony had no problems with social skills: He was 52 years old, reasonably happily married, and generally compatible with his second wife. His major difficulty was his continuing strong incestuous attraction to his daughter. Nevertheless, he loved his daughter very much and wished strongly to interact in a normal fatherly way with her.

## Psychological Treatment

A number of treatment procedures are available for decreasing unwanted arousal. Most are behaviour therapy procedures directed at changing the associations and context from arousing and pleasurable to neutral. One procedure, carried out entirely in the imagination of the patient, called **covert sensitization,** was first described by Cautela (1967; see also Barlow, 1993). Sexually arousing images are associated with the very consequences of the behaviour that bring the patient to treatment. The notion here is that the patient's arousal patterns are undesirable because of their long-term consequences, but the immediate pleasure and thus strong reinforcement they provide more than overcome any thoughts of possible

harm or danger that might arise in the future. This model also applies to much unwanted addictive behaviour, as we will discuss in Chapter 11.

In imagination, harmful or dangerous consequences can be associated directly with the unwanted behaviour and arousal in a powerful and emotionally meaningful way. One of the most powerful negative aspects of Tony's behaviour was his embarrassment over the thought of being discovered by his current wife, other family members, or, most important, the family priest. Therefore, he was guided through the fantasy described here.

## Tony
### Imagining the Worst

You are alone with your daughter in your trailer. You realize that you want to caress her breasts. So you put your arm around her, slip your hand inside her blouse, and begin to caress her breasts. Unexpectedly the door to the trailer opens and in walks your wife with Father X. Your daughter immediately jumps up and runs out the door. Your wife follows her. You are left alone with Father X. He is looking at you as if waiting for an explanation of what he has just seen. Seconds pass, but they seem like hours. You know what Father X must be thinking as he stands there staring at you. You are very embarrassed and want to say something, but you can't seem to find the right words. You realize that Father X can no longer respect you as he once did. Father X finally says, "I don't understand this; this is not like you." You both begin to cry. You realize that you may have lost the love and

---

**covert sensitization** Cognitive-behavioural intervention to reduce unwanted behaviours by having clients imagine the extremely aversive consequences of the behaviours and establish negative rather than positive associations with them.

respect of both Father X and your wife, who are important to you. Father X asks, "Do you realize what this has done to your daughter?" You think about this and you hear your daughter crying; she is hysterical. You want to run, but you can't. You are miserable and disgusted with yourself. You don't know if you will ever regain the love and respect of your wife and Father X.

*Source:* From "Measurement and Modification of Incestuous Behavior: A Case Study," by T. L. Harbert, D. H. Barlow, M. Hersen, and J. B. Austin, 1974, *Psychological Reports, 34,* 79–86. Copyright © Psychological Reports, Reproduced with permission of the authors and publisher.

During 6 or 8 sessions, the therapist narrates such scenes dramatically, and the patient is then instructed to imagine them on a daily basis until all arousal disappears. The results of Tony's treatment are presented in Figure 9.7. "Card-sort scores" are a measure of how much Tony wanted sexual interactions with his daughter in comparison with his wish for nonsexual fatherly interactions. His incestuous arousal was largely eliminated after 3 to 4 weeks, but the treatment did not affect his desire to interact with his daughter in a healthier manner. These results were confirmed by psychophysiological measurement of his arousal response. A return of some arousal at a 3-month follow-up prompted us to ask Tony if anything unusual was happening in his life. He confessed that his marriage had taken a turn for the worse and sexual relations with his wife had all but ceased. A period of marital therapy restored the therapeutic gains (see Figure 9.7). Several years later, after his daughter's therapist decided she was ready, she and Tony resumed a nonsexual relationship, which they both wanted.

Two major areas in Tony's life needed treatment: deviant (incestuous) sexual arousal and marital problems. As noted by Howard Barbaree at the Centre for Addiction and Mental Health in Toronto, most individuals with paraphilic arousal patterns need help in the areas of family and interpersonal functioning (Barbaree & Seto, 1997; see also Rice & Harris, 2002). In addition, many require intervention to help strengthen appropriate patterns of arousal. In **orgasmic reconditioning,** patients are instructed to masturbate to their usual fantasies but to substitute more desirable ones just before ejaculation. With repeated practice, patients should be able to begin the desired fantasy earlier in the masturbatory process and still retain their arousal. This technique, first described by Davison (1968), has been used with some success in a variety of settings (Brownell, Hayes, & Barlow, 1977; Maletzky, 1998). Finally, as with most strongly pleasurable but undesirable behaviours (including addiction), care must be taken to provide the patient with coping skills to

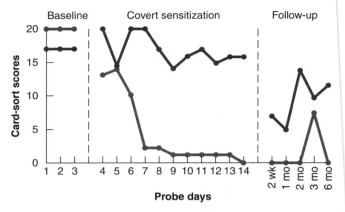

**Figure 9.7** ■ Ratings of Tony's incestuous urges (deviant) and desire for normal interactions with daughter (non-deviant) during covert desensitization treatment. (Reproduced with permission of the authors and publisher from Harbert, T.L., Barlow, D.H., Hersen, M., & Austin, J.B. Measurement and Modification of Incestuous Behavior: A Case Study. *Psychological Reports* 1974, 34, 79–86. © Psychological Reports, 1974.)

prevent slips or relapses (see Chapter 11). **Relapse prevention** treatment created for addictions (Laws, 1989; Laws & O'Donohue, 1997) does just that. Patients are taught to recognize the early signs of temptation and to institute a variety of self-control procedures before their urges become too strong.

The success of treatment with this rich array of procedures is surprisingly high when carried out by an experienced professional. Maletzky and colleagues reported on the treatment over 17 years of some 7000 sexual offenders of numerous types. A variety of procedures were used in a program of 3 to 4 months in a clinic devoted exclusively to this type of treatment. The numbers of people successfully treated are presented by category in Table 9.5 (Maletzky, 1998). These are truly astounding numbers. What makes them even more impressive is that Maletzky collected objective physiological outcome measures on almost every case, in addition to patients' reports of progress. In many cases, he also obtained corroborating information from families and legal authorities.

**orgasmic reconditioning** Learning procedure to help clients strengthen appropriate patterns of sexual arousal by pairing appropriate stimuli with the pleasurable sensations of masturbation.

**relapse prevention** Extending therapeutic progress by teaching the client how to cope with future troubling situations.

| TABLE **9.5** | Treatment Outcome for Paraphilias | |
|---|---|---|

| Category | N | Percentage Meeting Criteria for Success[a] |
|---|---|---|
| Situational pedophilia, heterosexual | 3012 | 95.6 |
| Predatory pedophilia, heterosexual | 864 | 88.3 |
| Situational pedophilia, homosexual | 717 | 91.8 |
| Predatory pedophilia, homosexual | 596 | 80.1 |
| Exhibitionism | 1130 | 95.4 |
| Rape | 543 | 75.5 |
| Voyeurism | 83 | 93.9 |
| Public masturbation | 77 | 94.8 |
| Frotteurism | 65 | 89.3 |
| Fetishism | 33 | 94.0 |
| Transvestic fetishism | 14 | 78.6 |
| Telephone scatologia | 29 | 93.1 |
| Zoophilia | 23 | 95.6 |

[a]A treatment success was defined as an offender who:
1. Completed all treatment sessions.*
2. Reported no covert or overt deviant sexual behaviour at the end of treatment or at any follow-up session.†
3. Demonstrated no deviant sexual arousal, defined as greater than 20% on the penile plethysmograph, at the end of treatment or at any follow-up session.†
4. Had no repeat legal charges for any sexual crime at the end of treatment or at any follow-up session.†
*Any offender who dropped out of treatment, even if the offender met other criteria for success, was counted as a treatment failure.
†Follow-up sessions occurred at 6, 12, 24, 36, 48, and 60 months after the end of active treatment.

*Source:* From Maletzky, 1998.

Although these results are extremely good overall, men who rape have the lowest success rate among all offenders with a single diagnosis, and individuals with multiple paraphilias have the lowest success rate of any group. Maletzky also examined factors associated with failure. Among the strongest predictors were a history of unstable social relationships, an unstable employment history, strong denial the problem exists, a history of multiple victims, and a situation in which the offender continues to live with a victim (as might be typical in cases of incest). Despite these encouraging statistics, we must continue to incorporate effective treatments into our correctional system and to develop improved treatments that focus on relapse prevention, given the high rates of sexual offenders (e.g., pedophiles) and the fact that so many who have been incarcerated show up in the correctional system again as reoffenders.

Other groups using similar treatment procedures have achieved comparable success rates (Becker, 1990; Fagan et al., 2002). In general, results are less satisfactory when general summaries of the outcomes from all studies are evaluated, including programs that do not always incorporate these approaches (e.g., Nagayama Hall, 1995; Quinsey, Khanna, & Malcolm, 1998). Thus, therapist knowledge and expertise seem to be important.

William Marshall and his colleagues have been studying empathy deficits in specific groups of sexual offenders. Their research has shown that both child molesters and rapists suppress empathy toward their victims, failing to consider the psychological or physical damage the woman or child is experiencing (e.g., Fernandez & Marshall, 2003; Marshall & Moulden, 2001). Thus, many therapy programs for rapists and child molesters now include techniques designed to increase the perpetrators' empathy with their victims (Marshall, 1999).

## Drug Treatments

The most popular drug used to treat paraphilics (Bradford, 1997) is an antiandrogen called *cyproterone acetate.* This drug eliminates sexual desire and fantasy by reducing testosterone levels dramatically, but fantasies and arousal return as soon as the drug is removed. This is the "chemical castration" treatment you may have read about in the news. A second drug is *medroxyprogesterone acetate* (Depo-Provera is the injectable form), a hormonal agent that reduces testosterone (Fagan et al., 2002). These drugs may be useful for dangerous sexual offenders who do not respond to alternative treatments or to temporarily suppress sexual arousal in patients who require it, but it is not always successful. In an earlier report (Maletzky, 1991), it was necessary to administer the drug to only 8 of approximately 5000 patients. More recently, Rösler and Witztum (1998) of Hadassah University Hospital in Jerusalem report successful "chemical castration" of 30 men with severe long-standing paraphilia using triptorelin, which inhibits gonadotropin secretion in men. This drug appears to be somewhat more effective than the other drugs mentioned here with fewer side effects, based on this one study.

## Summary

Based on evidence from a number of clinics, the psychosocial treatment of paraphilia is surprisingly effective. Success rates ranging from 70% to 100% with follow-ups for longer than 10 years in some cases seem to make this one of the more treatable psychological disorders. However, most results are uncontrolled observations from a small number of clinical research centres, and it seems that results are not as good in other clinics and offices. In any case, like treatment for sexual dysfunctions, psychosocial approaches to paraphilia are not readily available outside of specialized treatment centres. In the meantime, the outlook for most individuals with this disorder is bleak because paraphilias run a chronic course and recurrence is common.

## Concept Check 9.4

Check your understanding of sexual paraphilias by matching the scenarios with the correct label: (a) exhibitionism, (b) voyeurism, (c) fetishism, (d) sexual masochism.

1. Jane enjoys being slapped with leather whips during foreplay. Without such stimulation, she is unable to achieve orgasm during sex. _____
2. Michael has a collection of women's panties that arouse him. He loves to look at, collect, and wear them. _____
3. Sam finds arousal in walking up to strangers in the park and showing them his genitals. _____
4. Peeping Tom loves to look through Susie's bedroom window and watch her undress. He gets extremely excited as she disrobes. He is practising _____
5. What Peeping Tom does not realize is that Susie knows that he is watching. She is aroused by slowly undressing while others are watching, and she fantasizes about what they are thinking. Susie's behaviour is called _____.
6. What Peeping Tom will be shocked to find out is that "Susie" is actually Scott, a man who can become aroused only if he wears feminine clothing. Scott's behaviour is _____.

# Summary

## What Is Normal Sexuality?

- Patterns of sexual behaviour, both heterosexual and homosexual, vary around the world in terms of both behaviour and risks. Approximately 20% of individuals who have been surveyed engage in sex with numerous partners, which puts them at risk for sexually transmitted diseases such as AIDS. Recent surveys also suggest that as many as 60% of North American university women practise unsafe sex by not using appropriate condoms.
- Three different types of disorders are associated with sexual functioning and gender identity: gender identity disorder, sexual dysfunctions, and paraphilias.

## Gender Identity Disorder

- Gender identify disorder is a dissatisfaction with one's biological sex and the sense that one is really the opposite gender (e.g., a woman trapped in a man's body). A person develops gender identity between 18 months and 3 years of age, and it seems that both appropriate gender identity and mistaken gender identity have biological roots influenced by learning.

- Treatment includes both psychosocial approaches, which have been attempted on only a few cases thus far, and sex reassignment surgery.

## Overview of Sexual Dysfunctions

- Sexual dysfunction includes a variety of disorders in which people find it difficult to function adequately during sexual relations.
- Specific sexual dysfunctions include disorders of sexual desire—hypoactive sexual desire disorder and sexual aversion disorder—in which interest in sexual relations is extremely low or nonexistent; disorders of sexual arousal—male erectile disorder and female sexual arousal disorder—in which achieving or maintaining adequate penile erection or vaginal lubrication is problematic; and orgasmic disorders—female orgasmic disorder and male orgasmic disorder—in which orgasm occurs too quickly or not at all. The most common disorder in this category is premature ejaculation, which occurs in males; inhibited orgasm is commonly seen in females.
- Sexual pain disorders, in which unbearable pain is associated with sexual relations, include dyspareunia and vaginismus.

- The three components of assessment are interviewing, a complete medical evaluation, and psychophysiological assessment.

## Causes and Treatment of Sexual Dysfunctions

- Sexual dysfunction is associated with socially transmitted negative attitudes about sex, interacting with current relationship difficulties, and anxiety focused on sexual activity.
- Psychological treatment of sexual dysfunctions is generally successful but not readily available. In recent years, various medical approaches have become available, including the drug Viagra. These treatments focus mostly on male erectile dysfunction and are promising.

## Paraphilia: Clinical Descriptions

- Paraphilia is sexual attraction to inappropriate people, such as children, or to inappropriate objects, such as articles of clothing.
- The paraphilias include fetishism, in which sexual arousal occurs almost exclusively in the context of inappropriate objects or individuals; exhibitionism, in which sexual gratification is attained by exposing one's genitals to unsuspecting strangers; voyeurism, in which sexual arousal is derived from observing unsuspecting individuals undressing or naked; transvestic fetishism, in which individuals are sexually aroused by wearing clothing of the opposite sex; sexual sadism, in which sexual arousal is associated with inflicting pain or humiliation; sexual masochism, in which sexual arousal is associated with experiencing pain or humiliation; and pedophilia, in which there is a strong sexual attraction toward children. Incest is a type of pedophilia in which the victim is related to the perpetrator, often a son or daughter.

## Causes and Treatment of Paraphilia

- The development of paraphilia is associated with deficiencies in consensual adult sexual arousal, deficiencies in consensual adult social skills, deviant sexual fantasies that may develop before or during puberty, and attempts by the individual to suppress thoughts associated with these arousal patterns.
- Psychological treatments of paraphilia, including covert sensitization, orgasmic reconditioning, and relapse prevention, seem highly successful but are available only in specialized clinics.

## Key Terms

homosexuality, 358
gender identity
    disorder, 359
sex reassignment
    surgery, 363
sexual dysfunction, 365
hypoactive sexual desire
    disorder, 366
sexual aversion
    disorder, 367

male erectile
    disorder, 368
female sexual arousal
    disorder, 368
inhibited orgasm, 369
female orgasmic
    disorder, 370
male orgasmic
    disorder, 370

premature
    ejaculation, 371
sexual pain disorder, 371
dyspareunia, 372
vaginismus, 372
paraphilias, 383
fetishism, 384
voyeurism, 384
exhibitionism, 384

transvestic fetishism, 385
sexual sadism, 385
sexual masochism, 385
pedophilia, 387
incest, 387
covert sensitization, 391
orgasmic
    reconditioning, 392
relapse prevention, 392

## Answers to Concept Checks

**9.1**  1. more men masturbate and do it more often; men are more permissive about casual sex, etc.

2. both genetics and psychological influences appear to be involved in the development of sexual orientation

3. gender identity disorder

4. abnormal hormone levels during development, social/parental influences

5. sex reassignment surgery, psychosocial treatment to adjust to either gender

**9.2**  1. c  2. a  3. b  4. c  5. a

**9.3**  1. T  2. F (sometimes increases arousal)
3. T  4. T 5. F (e.g., non-demand pleasuring, squeeze technique, etc.) 6. T

**9.4**  1. d  2. c  3. a  4. b  5. a  6. c

 **InfoTrac College Edition**

If your instructor ordered your book with InfoTrac College Edition, please explore this online library for additional readings, review, and a handy resource for short assignments. Go to:

**http://infotrac.thomsonlearning.com**

Enter these search terms: sexual disorders, erectile dysfunction, psychosexual therapy, sensate focus, premature ejaculation, paraphilia, fetishism, exhibitionism, pedophilia, child sexual abuse, incest, sex psychology, sadomasochism

## The Abnormal Psychology Book Companion Website

Go to **www.essentialsabnormalpsych.nelson.com** for practice quiz questions, Internet links, critical thinking exercises, and more.

## Abnormal Psychology Live CD-ROM

- **Erectile Dysfunction: Clark,** an example of a man with erectile dysfunction, is a rather complicated case in which depression, physical symptoms, and cultural expectations all seem to play a role in his problem.
- **Changing Over: Jessica** discusses her life as a transsexual, both before and after her sex reassignment surgery.

**Thomson NOW!** **http://hed.nelson.com** Go to this site for the link to ThomsonNow™, your one-stop study shop. Take a Pretest for this chapter and ThomsonNow™ will generate a personalized Study Plan based on your test results! The Study Plan will identify the topics you need to review and direct you to online resources to help you master those topics. You can then take a Posttest to help you determine the concepts you have mastered and what you still need work on.

## Video Concept Review

For challenging concepts that typically need more than one explanation, Mark Durand provides a video review via ThomsonNow™ of the following topic:

- The differences among gender identity disorder (transsexualism), transvestic fetishism, and being transgendered.

# Chapter Quiz

1. Which of the following statements is NOT true about current sex differences in sexual attitudes and behaviour:

   a. more men than women report that they masturbate.

   b. men are much more likely to engage in pre-marital intercourse than women.

   c. among those who masturbate, men masturbate more frequently than women.

   d. men fantasize more frequently than women.

2. Research evidence on the origins of homosexuality has suggested a possible role for all of the following EXCEPT:

   a. genetic or chromosomal influences.

   b. emotionally distant fathers.

   c. size or function of brain structures.

   d. exposure to hormones.

3. The most common form of treatment for gender identity disorder is:

   a. exposure therapy.

   b. antidepressant medication.

   c. cognitive-behavioural therapy.

   d. sexual reassignment surgery.

4. In which phase of the sexual response cycle can men experience difficulty attaining or maintaining erections?

   a. resolution

   b. orgasm

   c. arousal

   d. plateau

5. Simone and her partner have sexual intercourse about once a month. Simone says she wants to have sex but can't seem to achieve adequate lubrication to make sex enjoyable. Simone's symptoms are most consistent with:

   a. impotence.

   b. sexual aversion disorder.

   c. sexual arousal disorder.

   d. vaginismus.

6. Which component is essential to the diagnosis of female orgasmic disorder?

   a. orgasms occur less frequently than desired

   b. a 20% to 30% reduction in the frequency of orgasms in the last 6 months

   c. a 70% to 80% reduction in the frequency of orgasms in the last year

   d. orgasm never or almost never occurs

7. The overarching goal of Masters and Johnson's psychological treatment for sexual dysfunction was:

   a. reducing or eliminating psychologically based performance anxiety.

   b. helping couples to increase the frequency of their sexual encounters to normalize sexual experiences.

   c. encouraging couples to be more willing to try medical treatments, despite their potential side effects.

   d. helping both individuals in a couple to understand past parental influences on contemporary sexual relations within the couple.

8. A disorder in which an inappropriate, inanimate object is the source of sexual arousal is known as a:

   a. parapathology.

   b. paranormality.

   c. paraphilia.

   d. paraphasia.

9. Which of the following statements is an accurate characterization of pedophilia?

   a. It involves an attraction to male children more often than female children.

   b. It is most commonly directed at girls who are beginning to mature physically.

   c. It is often rationalized by the perpetrator as an acceptable way to teach children about sexuality.

   d. It involves the use of physical force to get a child to perform sexual acts.

10. Shane is being treated for a paraphilia by imagining harmful consequences occurring in response to his unwanted behaviour and arousal. Shane is receiving what kind of treatment?

    a. covert sensitization

    b. marital therapy

    c. relapse prevention

    d. orgasmic reconditioning

*(See the Appendix on page 601 for answers.)*

# Exploring Sexual and Gender Identity Disorders

- Sexual behaviour is considered normal in our culture unless it is associated with one of three kinds of impaired functioning—gender identity disorder, sexual dysfunction, or paraphilia.
- Sexual orientation probably has a strong biological basis that is influenced by environmental and social factors.

## GENDER IDENTITY DISORDERS

Present when a person feels trapped in a body that is the "wrong" sex, that does not match his or her innate sense of personal identity. (Gender identity is independent of sexual arousal patterns.) Relatively rare.

### Biological Influences

- Not yet confirmed, although likely to involve prenatal exposure to hormones.
  - Hormonal variations may be natural or result from medication.

Photodisc/Getty Images

### Psychosocial Influences

- Gender identity develops between 1 1/2 and 3 years of age.
  - "Masculine" behaviours in girls and "feminine" behaviours in boys evoke different responses in different families.

### Treatment

- Sex reassignment surgery: removal of breasts or penis; genital reconstruction
  - Requires rigorous psychological preparation and financial and social stability
- Psychosocial intervention to change gender identity
  - Usually unsuccessful except as temporary relief until surgery

## PARAPHILIAS

Sexual arousal occurs almost exclusively in the context of inappropriate objects or individuals.

### Causes

- Preexisting deficiencies
  - In levels of arousal with consensual adults
  - In consensual adult social skills
- Treatment received from adults during childhood
- Early sexual fantasies reinforced by masturbation
- Extremely strong sex drive combined with uncontrollable thought processes

Gazelle Technologies

### Treatment

- *Covert sensitization:* Repeated mental reviewing of aversive consequences to establish negative associations with behaviour
- *Relapse prevention:* Therapeutic preparation for coping with future situations
- *Orgasmic reconditioning:* Pairing appropriate stimuli with masturbation to create positive arousal patterns
- *Medical:* Drugs that reduce testosterone to suppress sexual desire. Fantasies and arousal return when drugs are stopped.

### Types of Paraphilias

*Fetishism:* Sexual attraction to nonliving objects

*Voyeurism:* Sexual arousal achieved by viewing unsuspecting person undressing or naked

*Exhibitionism:* Sexual gratification from exposing one's genitals to unsuspecting strangers

*Transvestite fetishism:* Sexual arousal from wearing opposite-sex clothing (cross-dressing)

*Sexual sadism:* Sexual arousal associated with inflicting pain or humiliation

*Sexual masochism:* Sexual arousal associated with experiencing pain or humiliation

*Pedophilia:* Strong sexual attraction to children

Photodisc/Getty Images

*Incest:* Sexual attraction to family member

# SEXUAL DYSFUNCTIONS

Sexual dysfunctions can be
- **Lifelong:** Present during entire sexual history
- **Acquired:** Interrupts normal sexual pattern
- **Generalized:** Present in every encounter
- **Situational:** Present only with certain partners or at certain times

## Types of Sexual Dysfunctions

*Sexual Desire Disorders*

**Hypoactive sexual desire disorder:** Apparent lack of interest in sexual activity or fantasy

**Sexual aversion disorder:** Extreme persistent dislike of sexual contact

*Sexual Arousal Disorders*

**Male erectile disorder:** Recurring inability to achieve or maintain adequate erection

**Female sexual arousal disorder:** Recurring inability to achieve or maintain adequate lubrication

*Orgasm Disorders*

**Inhibited orgasm:** Inability to achieve orgasm despite adequate desire and arousal

**Premature ejaculation:** Ejaculation before it is desired, with minimal stimulation

*Sexual Pain Disorders*

**Dyspareunia:** Marked pain associated with intercourse for which there is no medical cause. Occurs in males and females.

**Vaginismus:** Involuntary muscle spasms in the front of the vagina that prevent or interfere with intercourse

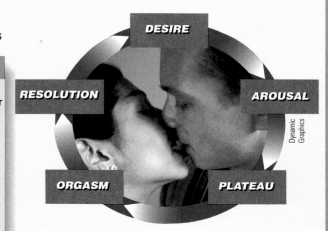

Dynamic Graphics

DESIRE · AROUSAL · PLATEAU · ORGASM · RESOLUTION

**THE HUMAN SEXUAL RESPONSE CYCLE**
A dysfunction is an impairment in one of the sexual response stages.

## CAUSES

### Psychological Contributions
- Distraction
- Underestimates of arousal
- Negative thought processes

Photodisc/Getty Images

### Psychological and Physical Interactions
- A combination of influences is almost always present.
  - Specific biological predisposition *and* psychological factors may produce a particular disorder.

### Sociocultural Contributions
- Erotophobia, caused by formative experiences of sexual cues as alarming
- Negative experiences, such as rape
- Deterioration of relationship

### Biological Contributions
- Neurological or other nervous system problems
- Vascular disease
- Chronic illness
- Prescription medication
- Drugs of abuse, including alcohol

### Treatment

**Psychosocial:** Therapeutic program to facilitate communication, improve sexual education, and eliminate anxiety. Both partners participate fully.

**Medical:** Almost all interventions focus on male erectile disorder, including drugs, prostheses, and surgery. Medical treatment is combined with sexual education and therapy to achieve maximum benefit.

# 10 Substance-Related Disorders

© David Young-Wolff/PhotoEdit

## Perspectives on Substance-Related Disorders
*Levels of Involvement*
*Diagnostic Issues*

## Depressants
*Alcohol Use Disorders*
*Sedative, Hypnotic, or Anxiolytic Substance Use Disorders*

## Stimulants
*Amphetamine Use Disorders*
*Cocaine Use Disorders*
*Nicotine Use Disorders*
*Caffeine Use Disorders*

## Opioids

## Hallucinogens
*Marijuana*
*LSD and Other Hallucinogens*

## Other Drugs of Abuse

## Causes of Substance-Related Disorders
*Biological Dimensions*
*Psychological Dimensions*
*Cognitive and Learning Factors*
*Social Dimensions*
*Cultural Dimensions*
*An Integrative Model*

## Treatment of Substance-Related Disorders
*Biological Treatments*
*Psychosocial Treatments*
*Prevention*

## Visual Summary: Exploring Substance-Related Disorders

 ## Abnormal Psychology Live CD-ROM
*Substance Use Disorder: Tim*
*Nicotine Dependence*

Would you be surprised if we told you that a group of psychological disorders costs Canadian citizens nearly 20 billion dollars each year, kills nearly 50 000 Canadians annually, and is implicated in street crime, homelessness, and interpersonal violence? Would you be even more surprised to learn that most of us have behaved in ways characteristic of these disorders at some point in our lives? You shouldn't. Smoking cigarettes, drinking alcohol, and using illegal drugs are all related to these disorders, and

they are responsible for astronomical financial costs and the tragic waste of tens of thousands of human lives each year (Single, Robson, Rehm, & Xie, 1996). In this chapter we explore the **substance-related disorders,** which are associated with the abuse of drugs such as alcohol, cocaine, and heroin and with a variety of other substances people take to alter the way they think, feel, and behave. These disorders represent a problem that has cursed us for millennia and continues to affect how we live, work, and play.

# Perspectives on Substance-Related Disorders

■ *Describe the nature of substance-related disorders.*

■ *Distinguish among substance use, substance intoxication, substance abuse, and substance dependence.*

The cost in lives, money, and emotional turmoil has made the issue of drug abuse a major concern worldwide. The Roman Catholic Church issued a universal catechism in 1992 that officially declared drug abuse and drunk driving to be sins (Riding, 1992). Yet from the well-known heavy drug use of music legend Neil Young in his early career and the death of two of his close friends from drug overdoses (McDonough, 2002) to the boozing and drug involvement of Montreal-born singer and songwriter Leonard Cohen (Walsh, 2001), illicit drug use and heavy drinking occupy the lives of many. Consider the public controversies surrounding Alberta Premier Ralph Klein's intoxicated behaviour while visiting a homeless shelter in 2001 and British Columbia Premier Gordon Campbell's embarrassing driving-while-intoxicated charge in Hawaii in 2003. Both Canadian politicians have since quit drinking alcohol (O'Malley & Missio, 2003). Stories such as these not only are told about the rich and famous, but also are retold in every corner of our society.

Consider the case of Danny, who has the disturbing but common habit of **polysubstance use,** using multiple substances. (We cover this issue in more detail later in the chapter.)

## Danny
### Multiple Dependencies

At the age of 35, Danny was in jail, awaiting trial on charges that he broke into a gas station and stole money. Danny's story illustrates the lifelong pattern that characterizes the behaviour of

many people who are affected by substance-related disorders.

Danny grew up in the suburbs. He was well liked in school and an average student. Like many of his friends, he smoked cigarettes in his early teens and drank beer with his friends at night behind his high school. Unlike most of his friends, however, Danny almost always drank until he was obviously drunk; he also experimented with many other drugs, including cocaine, heroin, "speed" (amphetamines), and "downers" (barbiturates).

After high school, Danny attended a local community college for one semester, but he dropped out after failing most of his courses. His dismal performance seemed to be related to his missing most classes. He had difficulty getting up for classes after partying most of the night. His moods were highly variable, and he was often unpleasant. Danny's family knew he occasionally drank too much, but they didn't know (or didn't want to know) about his other drug use. He had for years forbidden anyone to go into his room, after his mother found little packets of white powder (probably cocaine) in his sock drawer. He said he was keeping them for a friend and that he would return them immediately. Money was sometimes missing

---

**substance-related disorders** Range of problems associated with the use and abuse of drugs such as alcohol, cocaine, heroin, and other substances people use to alter the way they think, feel, and behave. These are extremely costly in human and financial terms.

**polysubstance use** Use of multiple mood- and behaviour-altering substances, such as drugs.

from the house, and once some stereo equipment "disappeared," but if anyone in his family suspected Danny they never admitted it.

After high school, Danny held a series of low-paying jobs, and when he was working his family reassured themselves that he was back on track and things would be fine. Unfortunately, he rarely held a job for more than a few months. He was usually fired for poor job attendance and performance. Because he continued to live at home, Danny could survive despite frequent periods of unemployment. When he was in his late 20s, Danny announced that he needed help and planned to check into an alcohol rehabilitation centre; he still would not admit to using other drugs. His family's joy and relief were overwhelming, and no one questioned his request for several thousand dollars to help pay for the private program he said he wanted to attend. Danny disappeared for several weeks, presumably because he was in the rehabilitation program. However, a call from the local police station put an end to this fantasy: Danny had been found quite high, living in an abandoned building. Danny had spent his family's money on drugs and had a 3-week binge with some friends. Danny's deceptiveness and financial irresponsibility greatly strained his relationship with his family. He was allowed to continue living at home, but his parents and siblings excluded him from their emotional lives. Danny seemed to straighten out, and he held a job at a gas station for almost 2 years. He became friendly with the station owner and his son. However, without any obvious warning, Danny resumed drinking and using drugs and was arrested for robbing the very place that had kept him employed for many months.

Why did Danny become dependent on drugs when many of his friends and siblings did not? Why did he steal from his family and friends? What ultimately became of him? We return to Danny's frustrating story later when we look at the causes and treatment of substance-related disorders.

## Levels of Involvement

Although each drug described in this chapter has unique effects, there are similarities in the ways they are used and how people who abuse them are treated. We first survey some concepts that apply to substance-related disorders in general, noting important terminology and addressing several diagnostic issues.

Can you use drugs and not abuse them? Can you abuse drugs and not become addicted to them? To answer these important questions, we first need to outline what we mean by *substance use, substance intoxication, substance abuse,* and *dependence.* The term *substance* refers to chemical compounds that are ingested to alter mood or behaviour. Although you might first think of drugs such as cocaine and heroin, this definition also includes more commonplace legal drugs such as alcohol, the nicotine found in tobacco, and the caffeine in coffee, tea, soft drinks, and chocolate. As we will see, these so-called safe drugs also affect mood and behaviour, they can be addictive, and they account for more health problems and mortality than all illegal drugs combined. You could make a good argument for directing drug abuse prevention efforts toward cigarette smoking (nicotine use) because of its addictive properties and negative health consequences.

To understand substance-related disorders, we must first know what it means to ingest **psychoactive substances**—which alter mood and/or behaviour—to become intoxicated or high, to abuse these substances, and to become dependent on or addicted to them.

### Substance Use

Substance use is the ingestion of psychoactive substances in moderate amounts that does not significantly interfere with social, educational, or occupational functioning. Most of you reading this chapter probably use some sort of psychoactive substance on occasion. Drinking a cup of coffee in the morning to wake up or smoking a cigarette and having a drink with a friend to relax are examples of substance use, as is the occasional ingestion of illegal drugs such as marijuana, cocaine, amphetamines, or barbiturates.

### Intoxication

Our physiological reaction to ingested substances—drunkenness or getting high—is referred to as **substance intoxication.** For a person to become intoxicated depends on which drug he or she takes, how much is ingested, and the person's individual biological reaction. For many of the substances we discuss here, intoxication is experienced as impaired judgment, mood changes, and lowered motor ability (e.g., problems walking or talking).

---

**psychoactive substances**   Substances, such as drugs, that alter mood or behaviour.

**substance intoxication**   Physiological reactions, such as impaired judgment and motor ability, and mood changes resulting from the ingestion of psychoactive substances.

## Disorder Criteria Summary
### Substance Intoxication

Features of substance intoxication include:
- Development of a reversible, substance-specific syndrome because of recent ingestion of (or exposure to) a substance
- Clinically significant maladaptive behaviour or psychological changes, such as belligerence, cognitive impairment, and impaired functioning, that develops during or shortly after use of the substance

*Source:* Based on DSM-IV-TR. Used with permission from the *Diagnostic and Statistical Manual of Mental Disorders*, Fourth Edition, Text Revision. Copyright 2000. American Psychiatric Association.

### Substance Abuse

Defining **substance abuse** by how much of a substance is ingested is problematic. For example, is drinking two glasses of wine in an hour abuse? Three glasses? Six? Is taking one injection of heroin considered abuse? DSM-IV-TR (American Psychiatric Association, 2000a) defines substance abuse in terms of how significantly it interferes with the user's life. If substances disrupt your education, job, or relationships with others, and put you in physically dangerous situations (e.g., while driving), and if you have related legal problems, you would be considered a drug abuser.

Danny seems to fit this definition of abuse. His inability to complete a semester of community college was a direct result of drug use. Danny often drove while drunk or under the influence of other drugs, and he had already been arrested twice. In fact, Danny's use of multiple substances was so relentless and pervasive that he would probably be diagnosed as drug dependent, which indicates a severe form of the disorder.

### Substance Dependence

Drug dependence is usually described as addiction. Although we use the term *addiction* routinely when we describe people who seem to be under the control of drugs, there is some disagreement about how to define addiction, or **substance dependence** (Woody & Cacciola, 1997). In one definition, the person is physiologically dependent on the drug or drugs, requires increasingly greater amounts of the drug to experience the same effect **(tolerance),** and will respond physically in a negative way when the substance is no longer ingested (**withdrawal;** Franklin & Frances, 1999). Tolerance and withdrawal are physiological reactions to the chemicals being ingested. How many of you have experienced a headache when you didn't get your morning coffee? You were probably going through caffeine withdrawal. In a more extreme example, withdrawal from alcohol can cause

## Disorder Criteria Summary
### Substance Abuse

Substance abuse involves a maladaptive pattern of substance use, although not outright dependence, leading to clinically significant impairment or distress as evidenced by one or more of the following during a 1-year period:
- Recurrent substance use causing a failure to fulfill work, school, or family obligations
- Recurrent substance use in situations where it is physically hazardous (e.g., driving)
- Recurrent legal problems related to substance use
- Continued substance use despite having persistent or recurring social or interpersonal problems caused or made worse by the use of the substance

*Source:* Based on DSM-IV-TR. Used with permission from the *Diagnostic and Statistical Manual of Mental Disorders*, Fourth Edition, Text Revision. Copyright 2000. American Psychiatric Association.

*alcohol withdrawal delirium* (or *delirium tremens—* the *DTs*), in which a person can experience frightening hallucinations and body tremors. Withdrawal from many substances can bring on chills, fever, diarrhea, nausea and vomiting, and aches and pains. However, not all substances are physiologically addicting. For example, you do not go through severe physical withdrawal when you stop taking LSD or marijuana. Cocaine withdrawal has a pattern that includes anxiety, lack of motivation, and boredom (Mack, Franklin, & Frances, 2003). We return to the ways drugs act on our bodies when we examine the causes of abuse and dependence.

Another view of substance dependence uses the *drug-seeking behaviours* themselves as a measure of dependence. The repeated use of a drug, a desperate need to ingest more of the substance (stealing money to buy drugs, standing outside in the cold to smoke), and the likelihood that use will resume after a period of abstinence are behaviours that define the extent of drug dependence. Such behavioural reactions are different

**substance abuse** Pattern of psychoactive substance use leading to significant distress or impairment in social and occupational roles and in hazardous situations.

**substance dependence** Maladaptive pattern of substance use characterized by the need for increased amounts to achieve the desired effect, negative physical effects when the substance is withdrawn, unsuccessful efforts to control its use, and substantial effort expended to seek it or recover from its effects.

**tolerance** Need for increased amounts of a substance to achieve the desired effect, and a diminished effect with continued use of the same amount.

**withdrawal** Severely negative physiological reaction to removal of a psychoactive substance, which can be alleviated by the same or a similar substance.

from the physiological responses to drugs we described before and are sometimes referred to in terms of *psychological dependence*. The DSM-IV-TR definition of substance dependence combines the physiological aspects of tolerance and withdrawal with the behavioural and psychological aspects (American Psychiatric Association, 2000a).

This definition of dependence must be seen as a "work in progress." By these criteria, many people can be considered dependent on such activities as sex, work, or even eating chocolate. Figure 10.1 shows the results of applying the DSM-IV-TR definition of dependence to a variety of daily activities, including substance use (Franklin, 1990). Is your own behaviour on this list? Obviously, what most people consider serious addiction to drugs is qualitatively different from dependence on shopping or television. But some have argued that problematic forms of gambling behaviour (see Figure 10.1), now classified as "pathological gambling" in the **"Impulse Control Disorders"** section of the DSM-IV-TR (see Langewisch & Frisch, 1998), share much in common with substance dependence and should be recategorized as an "addiction without the drug" (Potenza, 2001).

When we compare the DSM-IV-TR criteria for pathological gambling with those for substance dependence, we see some strong parallels. The pathological gambling criterion involving the need to gamble increasing amounts of money over time suggests tolerance like that seen in substance dependence. And the pathological gambling criterion involving restlessness and irritability when attempting to stop gambling suggests withdrawal symptoms like those seen in substance dependence, even though no substance has been ingested. As noted by pathological gambling expert Robert

Ladouceur (1996), as opportunities for legal gambling have increased in recent years, pathological gambling has become a prevalent problem in both Canada and in the United States. A review by David Hodgins and his colleagues at the University of Calgary concluded that the Aboriginal population has a particularly high rate of gambling problems (Wardman, el-Guebaly, & Hodgins, 2001). Studies of pathological gambling's similarities to and overlap with substance dependence could help immensely in improving treatments for problem gamblers (Stewart & Kushner, 2003). For example, if pathological gambling is a form of dependence similar to dependence on alcohol or cocaine, then interventions that have proven effective in the treatment of substance dependence may also prove useful in the treatment of pathological gambling.

### Disorder Criteria Summary
#### Substance Dependence

Substance dependence involves a maladaptive pattern of substance use, leading to clinically significant impairment or distress, as evidenced by three or more of the following within a 1-year period:

- Increased tolerance for the substance, evidenced either by a need for larger amounts to achieve the same effect or by a diminished effect using the same amount
- Withdrawal symptoms or continued use of the substance to avoid withdrawal symptoms
- Substance is frequently taken in larger amounts or for a longer time than was intended
- Persistent desire or unsuccessful attempts to control use of the substance
- Obtaining or using the substance, or recovering from its effects, takes up a good deal of time
- Significant social, work-related, or recreational activities are reduced or avoided because of substance use
- Substance use continues despite the knowledge that it is causing physiological or psychological problems

*Source:* Based on DSM-IV-TR. Used with permission from the *Diagnostic and Statistical Manual of Mental Disorders,* Fourth Edition, Text Revision. Copyright 2000. American Psychiatric Association.

Let's go back to the questions we started with: "Can you use drugs and not abuse them?" "Can you abuse drugs and not become addicted to or dependent on them?" The answer to the first question is yes. Obviously, some people drink wine or beer on a regular basis without drinking to excess. Although it is not commonly believed, some people

AP Wide World Photos/David Duprey

As the options for people to legally gamble increase, we can expect more and more individuals with symptoms of pathological gambling.

**impulse control disorders** Disorders that deprive a person of the ability to resist acting on a drive or temptation. Pathological gambling is one example.

ACCORDING TO THE STANDARD psychiatric definition, any drug user who passes three of the nine tests below is hooked. Several researchers were asked to apply the tests not only to drugs but also to other substances and activities—chocolate, sex, shopping. Their responses show it's possible to become addicted to all sorts of things. For example, serious runners could pass three of the tests by spending more time running than originally intended, covering increasing distances, and experiencing withdrawal symptoms (a devoted runner forced to stop because of an injury, say, might become anxious and irritable). Of course, that sort of dependency isn't necessarily destructive. Conversely, a drug that fails the addictiveness test—LSD, for instance—may be harmful just the same. That so many things are potentially addictive suggests the addiction's cause is not confined to the substance or activity—our culture may play a large role too.

| | Nicotine | Alcohol | Caffeine | Cocaine | Crack | Heroin | Ice* | LSD | Marijuana | PCP | Valium, Xanax, etc.† | Steroids | Chocolate | Running | Gambling | Shopping | Sex | Work | Driving | Television | Mountain climbing |
|---|---|---|---|---|---|---|---|---|---|---|---|---|---|---|---|---|---|---|---|---|---|
| **TAKES** substance or does activity more than originally intended | ✓ | ✓ | ✓ | ✓ | ✓ | ✓ | ✓ | | ✓ | ✓ | ✓ | ✓ | ✓ | ✓ | ✓ | ✓ | ✓ | ✓ | | ✓ | ✓ |
| **WANTS** to cut back or has tried to cut back but failed | ✓ | ✓ | ✓ | ✓ | ✓ | ✓ | ✓ | | ✓ | ✓ | ✓ | ✓ | ✓ | ✓ | ✓ | ✓ | ✓ | ✓ | | ✓ | ✓ |
| **SPENDS** lots of time trying to get substance or set up activity, taking substance or doing activity, or recovering | ✓ | ✓ | | ✓ | ✓ | ✓ | ✓ | ✓ | ✓ | ✓ | ✓ | | | ✓ | ✓ | ✓ | ✓ | ✓ | | ✓ | ✓ |
| **IS OFTEN** intoxicated or suffers withdrawal symptoms when expected to fulfill obligations at work, school, or home | | ✓ | | ✓ | ✓ | ✓ | ✓ | | ✓ | ✓ | ✓ | | | | | | | | | | |
| **CURTAILS** or gives up important social, occupational, or recreational activities because of substance or activity | | ✓ | | ✓ | ✓ | ✓ | ✓ | | ✓ | ✓ | ✓ | | | ✓ | ✓ | ✓ | ✓ | ✓ | | ✓ | ✓ |
| **USES** substance or does activity despite persistent social, psychological, or physical problems caused by substance or activity | ✓ | ✓ | ✓ | ✓ | ✓ | ✓ | ✓ | ✓ | ✓ | ✓ | ✓ | ✓ | ✓ | ✓ | ✓ | ✓ | ✓ | ✓ | | ✓ | ✓ |
| **NEEDS** more and more of substance or activity to achieve the same effect (tolerance) | ✓ | ✓ | ✓ | ✓ | ✓ | ✓ | ✓ | | | | ✓ | | | | ? | | | | | | |
| **SUFFERS** characteristic withdrawal symptoms when activity or substance is discontinued (cravings, anxiety, depression, jitters) | ✓ | ✓ | ✓ | ✓ | ✓ | ✓ | ✓ | | ✓ | | | | ✓ | ✓ | ? | ✓ | ✓ | ✓ | | ✓ | ✓ |
| **TAKES** substance or does activity to relieve or avoid withdrawal symptoms | ✓ | ✓ | ✓ | ✓ | ✓ | ✓ | ✓ | | | | ✓ | | | | | | | | | | |

* Methamphetamine
† Benzodiazepines

Research by Valerie Fahey

**Figure 10.1** ■ Ice, LSD, chocolate, TV: Is everything addictive? (From the sidebar "Is Everything Addictive?" *In Health*, January/February 1990. Adapted from *In Health*, © 1990 by permission. For subscriptions, please call 1-800-274-2522.)

use drugs such as heroin, cocaine, or crack (a form of cocaine) occasionally (i.e., several times a year) without abusing them (Goldman & Rather, 1993). What is disturbing is that we do not know ahead of time who is likely to become dependent with even a passing use of a substance.

It may seem counterintuitive, but dependence can be present without abuse. For example, cancer patients who take morphine for pain may become dependent on the drug—build up a tolerance and go through withdrawal if it is stopped—without abusing it (Portenoy & Payne, 1997). Later in this chapter we

## Disorder Criteria Summary
### Pathological Gambling

The person displays persistent and recurrent maladaptive gambling behaviour as indicated by 5 or more of the following:

- Preoccupation with gambling
- Needs to gamble with increasing amounts of money to achieved desired excitement
- Repeated unsuccessful efforts to control, cut back, or stop gambling
- Restlessness or irritability when attempting to cut down or stop gambling
- Gambling as a way to escape from problems or relieve negative mood
- Chasing gambling losses
- Lying to conceal extent of involvement in gambling
- Committing illegal acts to finance gambling
- Jeapordizing relationships, job or educational/career opportunity because of gambling
- Reliance on others for money to deal with gambling debts

*Source:* Based on DSM-IV-TR. Used with permission from the *Diagnostic and Statistical Manual of Mental Disorders,* Fourth Edition, Text Revision. Copyright 2000. American Psychiatric Association.

discuss biological and psychosocial theories of the causes of substance-related disorders and of why we have individualized reactions to these substances.

Expert professionals in the substance use field were asked about the relative "addictiveness" of various drugs (Franklin, 1990). The survey results are shown in Figure 10.2. You may be surprised to see nicotine placed just ahead of methamphetamine and crack cocaine as the most addictive of drugs. Although this is only a subjective rating by these experts, it shows that our society sanctions or proscribes drugs based on factors other than their addictiveness.

## Diagnostic Issues

In early editions of the DSM, alcoholism and drug abuse weren't treated as disorders in and of themselves. Instead, they were categorized as *sociopathic personality disturbances* (a forerunner of the current *antisocial personality disorder,* which we discuss in Chapter 11), because substance use was seen as a symptom of other problems. It was considered a sign of moral weakness, and the influence of genetics and biology was hardly acknowledged. A separate category was created in DSM-III, in 1980, and since then we have acknowledged the complex biological and psychological nature of the problem.

The DSM-IV-TR term *substance-related disorders* indicates several subtypes of diagnoses for each substance, including dependence, abuse, intoxication, and/or withdrawal. These distinctions help clarify the problem and focus treatment on the appropriate aspect of the disorder. Danny received the diagnosis "cocaine dependence" because of the tolerance he showed for the drug, his use of larger amounts than he intended, his unsuccessful attempts to stop using it, and the activities he gave up to buy it. His pattern of use was more pervasive than simple abuse, and the diagnosis of dependence provided a clear picture of his need for help.

Substance use.

Substance abuse.

Substance dependence.

Intoxication.

TO RANK today's commonly used drugs by their addictiveness, experts were asked to consider two questions: How easy is it to get hooked on these substances, and how hard is it to stop using them? Although a person's vulnerability to a drug also depends on individual traits—physiology, psychology, and social and economic pressures—these rankings reflect only the addictive potential inherent in the drug. The numbers are relative rankings, based on the experts' scores for each substance.

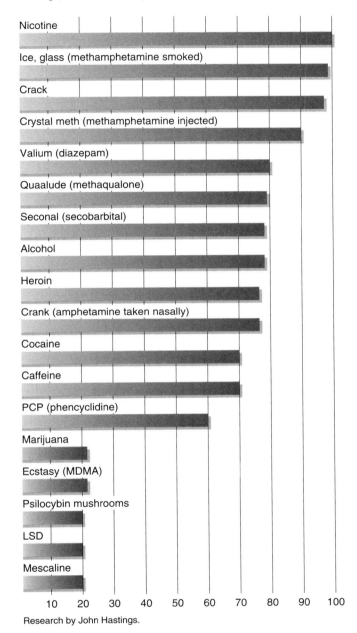

Research by John Hastings.

**Figure 10.2** ■ Easy to get hooked on, hard to get off. (From "Easy to Get Hooked On, Hard to Get Off," In Health, November/December 1990, p. 37. Reprinted from In Health, © 1990 by permission. For subscriptions, please call 1-800-274-2522.)

Symptoms of other disorders can complicate the substance abuse picture significantly. For example, do some people drink to excess because they are

depressed, or do drinking and its consequences (e.g., loss of friends, job) create depression? Researchers estimate that almost three-quarters of the people with alcohol disorders have an additional psychiatric disorder, such as major depression, antisocial personality disorder, or bipolar disorder (Compton, Cottler, Jacobs, Ben-Abdallah, & Spitznagel, 2003; Conrod & Stewart, 2005). For example, in an epidemiological study of six countries, including Canada, alcohol disorders were found to be highly comorbid with mood and anxiety disorders (Merikangas et al., 1998). As another example, in reviews of the literature by Canadian researchers (Crockford & el-Guebaly, 1998; Stewart & Kushner, 2003), alcohol disorders were shown to be highly comorbid with pathological gambling.

Substance use disorder might occur concurrently with other disorders for several reasons (Grant & Dawson, 1999; Stewart, 1996). First, substance-related disorders and anxiety and mood disorders are highly prevalent in our society and may occur together so often just by chance. Second, drug intoxication and withdrawal can cause symptoms of anxiety, depression, and psychosis, and can increase risk taking. For example, analyses of data collected in the Canadian National Population Health Survey have shown that those who have been drinking in the past year (particularly heavy drinkers) are at increased risk for clinical depression (Patten & Charney, 1998; Wang & Patten, 2002). As another example, a laboratory-based study by Ellery, Stewart, and Loba (2005) showed that ingestion of alcohol led to increased risk taking among regular gamblers when they were using a video lottery terminal (VLT) relative to gamblers ingesting a nonalcoholic control beverage. This finding suggests that alcohol's effects in increasing risk taking may contribute to the high co-occurrence of alcohol and gambling disorders. A third explanation for the high comorbidity of substance use disorders with other mental health problems is that the mental health disorder causes the substance use disorder. For example, people with anxiety disorders like posttraumatic stress disorder may self-medicate with substances for their anxiety symptoms, resulting in a substance use disorder (Stewart, 1996).

Because substance-related disorders can be so complicated, the DSM-IV-TR tries to define when a symptom is a result of substance use and when it is not. Basically, if symptoms seen in schizophrenia or in extreme states of anxiety appear during intoxication or within 6 weeks after withdrawal from drugs, they aren't considered signs of a separate psychiatric disorder. So, for example, individuals who show signs of severe depression just after they have stopped taking heavy doses of stimulants would not be diagnosed with a major mood disorder. However, individuals who were severely depressed before they used stimulants and those whose symptoms persist more than 6 weeks after they stop might have a separate disorder (Mack et al., 2003).

We now turn to the individual substances themselves, their effects on our brains and bodies, and how they are used in our society. We have grouped the substances into five general categories.

- **Depressants:** These substances result in behavioural sedation and can induce relaxation. They include alcohol (ethyl alcohol) and the sedative, hypnotic, and anxiolytic drugs in the families of barbiturates (e.g., Seconal) and benzodiazepines (e.g., Valium, Halcion).
- **Stimulants:** These substances cause us to be more active and alert and can elevate mood. Included in this group are amphetamines, cocaine, nicotine, and caffeine.

- **Opioids:** The major effect of these substances is to produce analgesia (reduce pain) and euphoria. Heroin, opium, codeine, morphine, and oxycodone are included in this group.
- **Hallucinogens:** These substances alter sensory perception and can produce delusions, paranoia, and hallucinations. Marijuana and LSD are included in this category.
- **Other drugs of abuse:** Other substances that are abused but do not fit neatly into one of the categories here include inhalants (e.g., airplane glue), anabolic steroids, and other over-the-counter and prescription medications (e.g., nitrous oxide). These substances produce a variety of psychoactive effects that are characteristic of the substances described in the previous categories.

# Depressants

- *Describe the physiological and psychological effects of alcohol.*

- *Identify what is known about the prevalence, course, and cultural and social factors related to alcohol use and abuse.*

- *Describe the physiological and psychological effects of sedative, hypnotic, or anxiolytic substance use disorders.*

The depressants primarily *decrease* central nervous system activity. Their principal effect is to reduce our levels of physiological arousal and help us relax. Included in this group are alcohol and the sedative, hypnotic, and anxiolytic drugs such as those prescribed for insomnia (see Chapter 8). These substances are among those most likely to produce symptoms of physical dependence, tolerance, and withdrawal. We first look at the most commonly used of these substances—alcohol—and the **alcohol use disorders** that can result.

## Alcohol Use Disorders

Danny's substance abuse began when he drank beer with friends, a rite of passage for many teenagers. Alcohol has been widely used throughout history. Recently, for example, scientists found evidence of wine or beer in pottery jars at the site of a Sumerian trading post in western Iran that dates back 6000 years (Goodwin & Gabrielli, 1997). For hundreds of years, Europeans drank large amounts of beer, wine, and hard liquor. When they came to North America in the early 1600s, they brought their considerable thirst for alcohol with them. Alcohol was not a problem for Native Canadians until the French introduced brandy and the British introduced rum (Smart, 1985; Stewart, 2002).

Reports of the early missionaries contain many descriptions of intoxication among Natives and early settlers (e.g., Dailey, 1968); government control activities and antidrinking movements quickly followed (Smart, 1985; Stewart, 2002). For example, the Temperance Movement allowed for the benefits of moderate drinking while morally condemning the heavy use of spirits (Stewart, 2002; Vallee, 1998). The Women's Christian Temperance Union tried to have alcohol education courses introduced into schools and was successful in several Canadian provinces (Smart, 1985; Stewart, 2002). The work of Temperance Movement proponents

**depressants** Psychoactive substances that result in behavioural sedation, including alcohol and the sedative, hypnotic, and anxiolytic drugs.

**stimulants** Psychoactive substances that elevate mood, activity, and alertness, including amphetamines, caffeine, cocaine, and nicotine.

**opioids** Addictive psychoactive substances such as heroin, opium, and morphine that cause temporary euphoria and analgesia (pain reduction).

**hallucinogen** Any psychoactive substance such as LSD or marijuana that can produce delusions, hallucinations, paranoia, and altered sensory perception.

**alcohol use disorders** Cognitive, biological, behavioural, and social problems associated with alcohol use and abuse.

paved the way for the American prohibition (1919–1933). Although prohibition did reduce overall levels of use in the United States, it had some unintended side effects, such as increases in organized crime and bootlegging, some of which originated in Canada (Stewart, 2002). These problems led to the repeal of Prohibition near the beginning of the Depression.

### Disorder Criteria Summary
Alcohol Intoxication

Features of alcohol intoxication include:
- Significant maladaptive behavioural or psychological changes because of alcohol ingestion
- Signs of one or more of the following: slurred speech, incoordination, unsteady gait, nystagmus, attention or memory impairment, stupor or coma

*Source:* Based on DSM-IV-TR. Used with permission from the *Diagnostic and Statistical Manual of Mental Disorders,* Fourth Edition, Text Revision. Copyright 2000. American Psychiatric Association.

## Clinical Description

Although alcohol is a depressant, its initial effect is an apparent stimulation. We generally experience a feeling of well-being, our inhibitions are reduced, and we become more outgoing. This is because what is initially depressed—or slowed—are the inhibitory centres in the brain. With continued drinking, however, alcohol depresses more areas of the brain, which impedes the ability to function properly. Motor coordination is impaired (staggering, slurred speech), reaction time is slowed, we become confused, our ability to make judgments is reduced, even vision and hearing can be negatively affected, all of which help to explain why driving while intoxicated is clearly dangerous.

## Effects

Alcohol affects many parts of the body (see Figure 10.3). After it is ingested, it passes through the esophagus (1) and into the stomach (2), where small amounts are absorbed. From there most of it travels to the small intestine (3), where it is easily absorbed into the bloodstream. The circulatory system distributes the alcohol throughout the body, where it contacts every major organ, including the heart (4). Some of the alcohol goes to the lungs, where it vaporizes and is exhaled, a phenomenon that is the basis for the *breath analyzer* test that measures levels of intoxication. As alcohol passes through the liver (5), it is broken down or metabolized into carbon dioxide and water by enzymes (Maher, 1997). An average-size person is able to metabolize about 7 to 10 grams of alcohol per hour, an amount comparable to about one beer, one glass

***Substance Use Disorder: Tim***
*"When I drink, I don't care about anything, as long as I'm drinking. Nothing bothers me. The world doesn't bother me. So when I'm not drinking, the problems come back, so you drink again. The problems will always be there. You just don't realize it when you're drinking. That's why people tend to drink a lot."*

Thomson Learning

of wine, or 1 ounce of 90-proof spirits (Moak & Anton, 1999).

Most of the substances we describe in this chapter, including marijuana, the opiates, and tranquillizers, interact with specific receptors in the brain cells. The effects of alcohol, however, are much more complex. Alcohol influences a number of different neuroreceptor systems, which makes it difficult to study. For example, the *gamma-aminobutyric acid (GABA) system,* which we discussed in Chapter 2 and Chapter 4, seems to be particularly sensitive to alcohol. GABA, as you will recall, is an inhibitory neurotransmitter. Its major role is to interfere with the firing of the neuron it attaches to. When GABA attaches to its receptor, chloride ions enter the

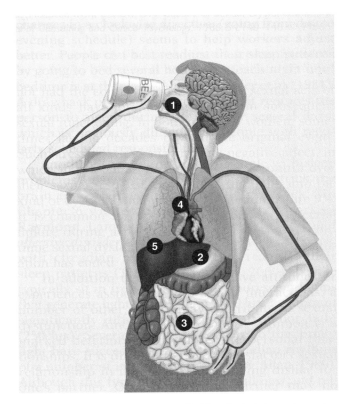

**Figure 10.3** ■ The path travelled by alcohol throughout the body (see text for complete description).

cell and make it less sensitive to the effects of other neurotransmitters. Alcohol seems to reinforce the movement of these chloride ions; as a result, the neurons have difficulty firing. In other words, although alcohol seems to loosen our tongues and make us more sociable, it makes it difficult for neurons to communicate with each other (Oscar-Berman, Shagrin, Evert, & Epstein, 1997). Because the GABA system seems to act on our feelings of anxiety, alcohol's antianxiety properties may result from its interaction with the GABA system (Conrod, Pihl, Stewart, & Dongier, 2000a).

The *glutamate system* is under study for its role in the effects of alcohol. In contrast to the GABA system, the glutamate system is excitatory, helping neurons to fire. It is suspected to be involved in learning and memory, and it may be the avenue through which alcohol affects our cognitive abilities. Blackouts, the loss of memory for what happens during intoxication, may result from the interaction of alcohol with the glutamate system. The *serotonin system* also appears to be sensitive to alcohol. This neurotransmitter system affects mood, sleep, and eating behaviour and is thought to be responsible for alcoholic cravings (Oscar-Berman et al., 1997). Alcohol also exerts effects on the dopamine reward system, and these effects may be responsible for the pleasurable feelings people experience when drinking alcohol (Conrod, Peterson, Pihl, & Mankowski, 1997). Finally, as noted by Christina Gianolakis of McGill University, at certain doses, alcohol also results in release of endogenous opioids—our bodies' naturally occurring analgesics—which may explain why alcohol has pain-numbing effects (Gianolakis, 2001; Peterson et al., 1996). Because alcohol affects so many neurotransmitter systems, we should not be surprised that it has such widespread and complex effects.

The long-term effects of heavy drinking are often severe. Withdrawal from chronic alcohol use typically includes hand tremors and, within several hours, nausea or vomiting, anxiety, transient hallucinations, agitation, insomnia, and, at its most extreme, **withdrawal delirium** (or *delirium tremens*—the *DTs*), a condition that can produce frightening hallucinations and body tremors. The devastating experience of DTs can be reduced with adequate medical treatment (Gallant, 1999).

Whether alcohol will cause organic damage depends on genetic vulnerability, frequency of use, the length of drinking binges, the blood alcohol levels attained during the drinking periods, and whether the body is given time to recover between binges (Mack et al., 2003). Consequences of long-term excessive drinking include liver disease, pancreatitis, cardiovascular disorders, and brain damage (see Figures 10.4 and 10.5).

Part of the folklore concerning alcohol is that it permanently kills brain cells (neurons). As we see later, this may not be true. Some evidence for brain damage comes from the experiences of people who are alcohol dependent and have blackouts, seizures, and hallucinations. Memory and the ability to perform certain tasks may also be impaired. More seriously, two types of organic brain syndromes may result from long-term heavy alcohol use: dementia and Wernicke's disease. *Dementia*, which we discuss more fully in Chapter 13, involves the general loss of intellectual abilities and can be a direct result of neurotoxicity or "poisoning of the brain" by excessive amounts of alcohol (Moak & Anton, 1999). *Wernicke's disease* results in confusion, loss of muscle coordination, and unintelligible speech (Gallant, 1999); it is believed to be caused by a deficiency of thiamine, a vitamin metabolized poorly by heavy drinkers.

---

**withdrawal delirium**   Frightening hallucinations and body tremors that result when a heavy drinker withdraws from alcohol. Also known as *delirium tremens (DTs)*.

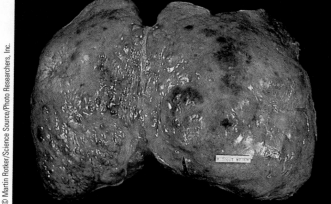

**Figure 10.4** ■   A healthy liver (left) and a cirrhotic liver scarred by years of alcohol abuse (right).

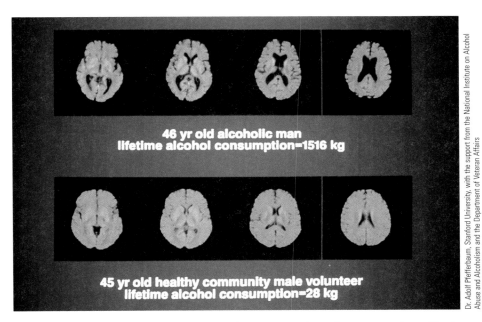

46 yr old alcoholic man
lifetime alcohol consumption=1516 kg

45 yr old healthy community male volunteer
lifetime alcohol consumption=28 kg

Dr. Adolf Pfefferbaum, Stanford University, with the support from the National Institute on Alcohol Abuse and Alcoholism and the Department of Veteran Affairs

**Figure 10.5** ■ The dark areas in the top brain images show the extensive loss of brain tissue that results from heavy alcohol use.

The effects of alcohol abuse extend beyond the health and well-being of the drinker. Although alcohol was suspected for years to negatively affect prenatal development, this connection has been studied in earnest only a short time (Jones & Smith, 1973; Lemoine, Harousseau, Borteyru, & Menuet, 1968). **Fetal alcohol syndrome (FAS)** is now generally recognized as a combination of problems that can occur in a child whose mother drank while she was pregnant. These problems include fetal growth retardation, cognitive deficits, behaviour problems, and learning difficulties (Barr & Streissguth, 2001; Hamilton, Kodituwakku,

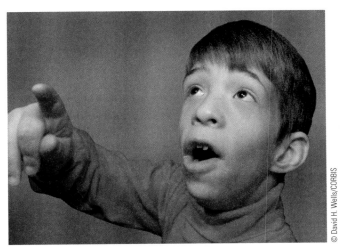

© David H. Wells/CORBIS

Physical characteristics of fetal alcohol syndrome include skin folds at the corners of the eyes, low nasal bridge, short nose, groove between nose and upper lip, small head circumference, small eye opening, small midface, and thin upper lip.

Sutherland, & Savage, 2003). In addition, children with FAS often have characteristic facial features.

### Statistics on Use

Because alcohol consumption is legal in North America, we know more about it than about most of the other psychoactive substances we discuss in this chapter (with the possible exception of nicotine and caffeine, also legal here). Despite a national history of heavy alcohol use, most adults in Canada drink in moderation. For example, a study by Adlaf, Ivis, and Smart (1994) surveyed the alcohol consumption practices of a large sample of the Ontario population. Their findings suggest that 20% of the Ontario population is at moderate to high risk for alcohol dependence based on their alcohol intake levels. Alcohol use in Canada has diminished during the past 20 years (see CCSA, 1999); this decline is paralleled in many other major industrialized countries, including the United States. Figure 10.6 shows that change in alcohol consumption in 25 countries between 1979 and 1984. Reduced consumption may reflect increased public awareness of the health risks associated with alcohol use and abuse. A change in the demographics may also partly account for the decline, because the proportion of the over-60 population in Canada has increased, and alcohol use among people in this age group is historically low (Stewart, 2002).

Men are more likely than women to drink alcohol and are also more likely to drink heavily (Statistics Canada, 2003). For example, in a 1998–1999 Canadian population survey, it was found that 16% of adult men were classified as heavy drinkers as compared with only 4% of adult women. Drinking practices also vary across societies even in Westernized countries. For example, a comparison of the results of the 1998 Canadian Campus Survey conducted with undergraduates at 16 universities across Canada, with the 1999 College Alcohol Study of students at 119 colleges and universities in the United States, revealed that a higher proportion of Canadian than

**fetal alcohol syndrome (FAS)** Pattern of problems including learning difficulties, behaviour deficits, and characteristic physical flaws, resulting from heavy drinking by the victim's mother when she was pregnant with the victim.

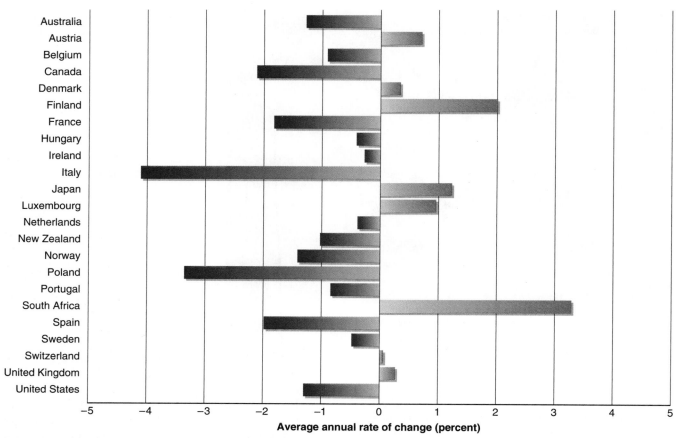

**Figure 10.6** ■ Average annual rate of change (percent) in per capita alcohol consumption for 25 countries, 1979–1984. (From *Alcoholic Beverage Taxation and Control Policies* (8th ed.), by Ron Brazeau and Nancy Burr, 1992. © Brewers Association of Canada. Reprinted by permission.)

American students drink alcohol, but that a higher proportion of American students are binge drinkers (episodic heavy drinkers; Kuo et al., 2002, 2003).

### Statistics on Abuse and Dependence

Our everyday experience tells us that not everyone who drinks becomes dependent on alcohol or abuses it. However, researchers estimate that about 10% of Canadian drinkers experience some level of problems with alcohol (CCSA, 1999), with about 3% of Canadian adults thought to be alcohol dependent in any given year (Statistics Canada, 2002a). For example, in the 1993 General Social Survey of Canadians, 5% of current drinkers admitted to experiencing physical health problems as a consequence of their drinking, and 5% reported financial problems related to their alcohol use (CCSA, 1999).

Outside Canada, rates of alcohol abuse and dependence vary widely. Compared with the Canadian average of 3% (Satistics Canada, 2002a), the prevalence of alcohol dependence in Peru is about 35%; in South Korea it is approximately 22%. It is about 3.5% in Taipei and as low as 0.45% in Shanghai (Helzer & Canino, 1992; Yamamoto, Silva, Sasao, Wang, & Nguyen, 1993). Such cultural differences can be accounted for by different attitudes toward

drinking, the availability of alcohol, physiological reactions, and family norms and patterns. For example, the high drinking rates in Korea may reflect the cultural expectation that men drink heavily on some social occasions (C. K. Lee, 1992).

### Progression

Remember that Danny went through periods of heavy alcohol and drug use but also had times when he was relatively "straight" and did not use drugs. Similarly, many people who abuse alcohol or are dependent on it fluctuate between drinking heavily, drinking "socially" without negative effects, and being abstinent, not drinking at all (Schuckit, Smith, Anthenelli, & Irwin, 1993; Vaillant, 1983). It seems that about 20% of people with severe alcohol dependence have a spontaneous remission and do not re-experience problems with drinking (Ludwig, 1985; Vaillant, 1983).

Alcohol researchers Linda and Mark Sobell, who worked at the Addiction Research Foundation in Toronto in the 1980s and 1990s, noted that it used to be thought that once problems arose with drinking they would become steadily worse, following a predictable downward pattern as long as the person kept drinking (Sobell & Sobell, 1993). In other words, like a disease that isn't treated properly, alcoholism will get progressively worse if left unchecked. First championed by Jellinek more than 60 years ago, this view continues to influence the way people view and treat the disorder (Jellinek, 1946, 1952, 1960). Unfortunately, Jellinek based his model of the progression of alcohol use on a now famous but faulty study (Jellinek, 1946).

It appears instead that the course of *alcohol dependence* may be progressive for most people, although the course of *alcohol abuse* may be more variable. For example, early use of alcohol may predict later abuse. A study of almost 6000 lifetime drinkers by David DeWitt and his colleagues at the Centre for Addiction and Mental Health in Ontario found that drinking at an early age—from ages 11 to 14—was predictive of later alcohol use disorders (DeWitt, Adlaf, Offord, & Ogborne, 2000). A second study followed 636 male inpatients in an alcohol rehabilitation centre (Schuckit et al., 1993). Among these chronically alcohol-dependent men, a general progression of alcohol-related life problems did emerge, although not in the specific pattern proposed by Jellinek. Three-quarters of the men reported moderate consequences of their drinking, such as demotions at work, in their 20s. During their 30s, the men had more serious problems, such as regular blackouts and signs of alcohol withdrawal. By their late 30s and early 40s, these men demonstrated long-term serious consequences of their drinking, which included hallucinations, withdrawal convulsions, and hepatitis or pancreatitis. This study suggests a common pattern among people with chronic alcohol abuse and dependence, one with increasingly severe consequences. This progressive pattern is not inevitable for everyone who abuses alcohol, although we do not as yet understand what distinguishes those who are and those who are not susceptible (Sobell & Sobell, 1993; Vaillant & Hiller-Sturmhöfel, 1997).

Finally, statistics frequently link alcohol with violent behaviour (Nestor, 2002). A review of numerous studies conducted by Robert Pihl and his colleagues at McGill University have found that many people who commit such violent acts as murder, rape, and assault are intoxicated at the time of the crime (Murdoch, Pihl, & Ross, 1990). We hope you are skeptical of this type of correlation. Just because drunkenness and violence overlap does not mean that alcohol will necessarily make you violent. Laboratory studies show that alcohol does make subjects more aggressive (Bushman, 1993; see also review by Hoaken & Stewart, 2003). However, whether a person behaves aggressively outside the laboratory probably involves a number of interrelated factors, such as the quantity and timing of alcohol consumed, the person's history of violence,

© Michael Newman/Photo Edit

Intoxication is often involved in cases of domestic violence.

his or her expectations about drinking, and what happens to the individual while intoxicated. Alcohol does not *cause* aggression, but it may increase a person's likelihood of engaging in impulsive acts, and it may impair the ability to consider the consequences of acting impulsively (Nestor, 2002; Pihl, Peterson, & Lau, 1993).

## Sedative, Hypnotic, or Anxiolytic Substance Use Disorders

The general group of depressants also includes *sedative* (calming), *hypnotic* (sleep-inducing), and *anxiolytic* (anxiety-reducing) drugs (Mack et al., 2003). These drugs include the barbiturates and the benzodiazepines. **Barbiturates** (which include Amytal, Seconal, and Nembutal) are a family of sedative drugs first synthesized in Germany in 1882 (McKim, 1991). They were prescribed to help people sleep and

---

**barbiturates**  Sedative (and addictive) drugs including Amytal, Seconal, and Nembutal that are used as sleep aids.

replaced such drugs as alcohol and opium. Barbiturates were widely prescribed by physicians during the 1930s and 1940s, before their addictive properties were fully understood. By the 1950s they were among the drugs most abused by adults in North America (Franklin & Frances, 1999).

The **benzodiazepines** (which today include Valium, Xanax, Rohypnol, and Halcion) have been used since the 1960s, primarily to reduce anxiety. These drugs were originally touted as a miracle cure for the anxieties of living in our highly pressured technological society. Although it has been known since the 1980s that they are not appropriate for reducing the tension and anxiety resulting from everyday stresses and strains (Cooperstock & Hill, 1982), billions of doses of benzodiazepines are consumed by North Americans each year (Shabecoff, 1987). Sixteen million prescriptions of benzodiazepines were made to Canadians in 2000 alone (Gadsby, 2001). In general, benzodiazepines are considered much safer than barbiturates, with less risk of abuse and dependence (Warneke, 1991). Nonetheless, as noted by clinical psychologist Henny Westra at York University, the potential for developing dependence on benzodiazepines for those using them in the treatment of anxiety or sleep disorders should not be minimized (e.g., Westra & Stewart, 1998). The potential for benzodiazepine dependence resulting from prescriptions originally intended to be therapeutic was recognized as early as the 1970s, as is illustrated in a case report by Agrawal (1978) in the *Canadian Psychiatric Association Journal* of a 30-year-old woman who became dependent on the benzodiazepine Diazepam after having been prescribed it originally for a backache.

In addition to the potential for dependence with the anxiolytics, reports on the misuse of Rohypnol also show how dangerous these drugs can be. Rohypnol (otherwise known as "roofies" and the "date rape drug") gained a following among teenagers in the 1990s because it has the same effect as alcohol without the telltale odour. However, there are disturbing reports of men giving the drug to women without their knowledge, making it easier for them to engage in date rape (Smith & Wesson, 1999).

### Clinical Description

At low doses, barbiturates relax the muscles and can produce a mild feeling of well-being. However, larger doses can have results similar to those of heavy drinking: slurred speech and problems walking, concentrating, and working. At extremely high doses the diaphragm muscles can relax so much that they cause death by suffocation. Overdosing on barbiturates is a common means of suicide.

Like barbiturates, benzodiazepines are used to calm an individual and induce sleep. In addition, drugs in this class are prescribed as muscle relaxants and anticonvulsants (antiseizure medications; Smith & Wesson, 1999). People who use them for non-medical reasons report first feeling a pleasant high and a reduction of inhibition, similar to the effects of drinking alcohol. However, with continued use, tolerance and dependence can develop. Users who try to stop taking the drug experience symptoms like those of alcohol withdrawal (anxiety, insomnia, tremors, and delirium; Westra & Stewart, 1998).

The DSM-IV-TR criteria for sedative, hypnotic, and anxiolytic drug use disorders do not differ substantially from those for alcohol disorders. Both include maladaptive behavioural changes such as inappropriate sexual or aggressive behaviour, variable moods, impaired judgment, impaired social or occupational functioning, slurred speech, motor coordination problems, and unsteady gait.

### Disorder Criteria Summary
**Sedative, Hypnotic, or Anxiolytic Intoxication**

Features of sedative, hypnotic, or anxiolytic intoxication include:
- Significant maladaptive behaviour or psychological change during or after use of the drug
- Signs of one or more of the following: slurred speech, incoordination, unsteady gait, nystagmus, attention or memory impairment, stupor or coma

*Source:* Based on DSM-IV-TR. Used with permission from the *Diagnostic and Statistical Manual of Mental Disorders,* Fourth Edition, Text Revision. Copyright 2000. American Psychiatric Association.

Like alcohol, sedative, hypnotic, and anxiolytic drugs affect the brain by impacting the GABA neurotransmitter system (Gardner, 1997); as a result, when people combine alcohol with any of these drugs, there can be synergistic effects (Fils-Aime, 1993). In other words, if you drink alcohol after taking a benzodiazepine or barbiturate, the total effects can reach dangerous levels. One theory about actress Marilyn Monroe's death in 1962 is that she combined alcohol with too many barbiturates and unintentionally killed herself.

---

**benzodiazepines** Antianxiety drugs including Valium, Xanax, Dalmane, and Halcion also used to treat insomnia. Effective against anxiety (and, at high potency, panic disorder), they show some side effects, such as some cognitive and motor impairment, and may result in dependence and addiction. Relapse rates are extremely high when the drug is discontinued.

## Statistics

Barbiturate use has declined and benzodiazepine use has increased since 1960 (Warneke, 1991). A study by Ruiz, Offermans, Lanctot, and Busto (1993) compared rates of benzodiazepine prescriptions in Canada (a developed country) and Chile (a developing country) over 5 years. Total benzodiazepine use was similar in the two countries, but the patterns of use of specific benzodiazepines differed substantially. For example, over the 5 years, a substantial increase in rapidly eliminated benzodiazepines (like Halcion) was observed in Canada, whereas a substantial increase in slowly eliminated benzodiazepines (like Valium) was observed in Chile. This difference is significant because the slowly eliminated benzodiazepines are associated with a greater risk of falls (Ray, Thapa, & Gideon, 2000).

## Concept Check 10.1

### Part A

Check your understanding of substance-related definitions by stating whether the following case summaries describe (a) use, (b) intoxication, (c) abuse, or (d) dependence.

1. Joe is a member of the high school football team and is out celebrating a big win. Joe doesn't believe in drinking alcohol, but he doesn't mind taking a hit of marijuana every now and then. Because Joe had such a good game, he decides to smoke marijuana to celebrate. Despite his great performance in the game, Joe is easily irritated, laughing one minute and yelling the next. The more Joe boasts about his stats, the more difficult it is to understand him. _____
2. Jill routinely drinks diet cola. Instead of having coffee in the morning, she heads for the fridge. Another habit of Jill's is having a cigarette immediately after dinner. If for some reason Jill is unable to have her diet cola in the morning or her cigarette in the evening, she is not dependent on them and can still function normally. _____
3. Steve is a 23-year-old college student who started drinking heavily when he was 16. Instead of getting drunk at weekend parties, Steve drinks a moderate amount every night. In high school Steve would become drunk after about six beers; now his tolerance has more than doubled. Steve claims alcohol relieves the pressures of college life. He once attempted to quit drinking, but he had chills, fever, diarrhea, nausea and vomiting, and body aches and pains. _____
4. Jan is 32 and has just been fired from her third job in 1 year. She has been absent from work 2 days a week for the past 3 weeks. Not only did her boss telephone her and find her speech slurred, but she was also seen at a local pub in a drunken state during regular office hours. During her previous job, she came to work with alcohol on her breath and was unable to conduct herself in an orderly fashion. When confronted about her problems, Jan went home and tried to forget the situation by drinking more. _____

### Part B

Match the following disorders with their corresponding effects: (a) substance-related disorder, (b) dementia, (c) impulse-control disorder, (d) alcohol use disorders, (e) Wernicke's disease.

1. Disorders in which the effects of the drug impede the ability to function properly by affecting vision, motor control, reaction time, memory, and hearing. _____
2. Disorders that deprive a person of the ability to resist acting on a drive or temptation. _____
3. Disorders affecting the way people think, feel, and behave. _____
4. Disorder involving the decline of intellectual abilities through, for example, excess consumption of alcohol. _____

# Stimulants

■ *Describe the physiological and psychological effects of stimulants.*

Of all the psychoactive drugs used in Canada, the most commonly consumed are the stimulants. Included in this group are caffeine (in coffee, chocolate, and many soft drinks), nicotine (in tobacco products such as cigarettes), amphetamines, and cocaine. You probably used caffeine when you got up this morning. In contrast to the depressant drugs, stimulants—as their name suggests—make you more alert and energetic. They have a long history of use. Chinese physicians, for example, have used an amphetamine compound called *Ma-huang* for more than 5000 years (King & Ellinwood, 1997). Ma-huang (or ephedra) was marketed in North America in health food stores as a dietary supplement and weight loss aid. Ma-huang made the news when its manufacture and sale was banned, given its links to serious health problems (e.g., it can cause a serious rise in blood pressure) and even deaths (Canadian Press, 2003). The case of Ma-huang provides an important illustration of how natural compounds can be just as dangerous as manufactured drugs. We describe several stimulants and their effects on behaviour, mood, and cognition.

## Amphetamine Use Disorders

At low doses, amphetamines can induce feelings of elation and vigour and can reduce fatigue. You literally feel "up." However, after a period of elevation you come back down and "crash," feeling depressed or tired. In sufficient quantities, stimulants can lead to **amphetamine use disorders.**

Amphetamines are manufactured in the laboratory; they were first synthesized in 1887 and later used as a treatment for asthma and as a nasal decongestant (King & Ellinwood, 1997). Because amphetamines also reduce appetite, some people take them to lose weight. Long-haul truck drivers, pilots, and some university students trying to "pull all-nighters" use amphetamines to get that extra energy boost and stay awake. In fact, the use of amphetamines by two U.S. pilots to stay awake has been implicated in the "friendly fire" death of four Canadian soldiers in Afghanistan in 2002. The case increased awareness of how common amphetamine use is among pilots and has raised consciousness of possible negative consequences of this practice such as impaired judgment (Campbell, 2003). Amphetamines are prescribed for people with *narcolepsy*, a sleep disorder characterized by excessive sleepiness (see Chapter 8). Some of these drugs (Ritalin) are even given to children with *attention deficit/hyperactivity disorder* (discussed in Chapter 13), although these too are being abused for their psychostimulant effects.

DSM-IV-TR diagnostic criteria for amphetamine intoxication include significant behavioural symptoms, such as euphoria or affective blunting, changes in sociability, interpersonal sensitivity, anxiety, tension, anger, stereotyped behaviours, impaired judgment, and impaired social or occupational functioning. In addition, physiological symptoms occur during or shortly after amphetamine or related substances are ingested and can include heart rate or blood pressure changes, perspiration or chills, nausea or vomiting, weight loss, muscular weakness, respiratory depression, chest pain, seizures, or coma. The danger in using amphetamines and the other stimulants is their negative effects, like those experienced

by the pilots involved in the friendly fire incident in Afghanistan mentioned earlier. Severe intoxication or overdose can cause hallucinations, panic, agitation, and paranoid delusions (Mack et al., 2003). Amphetamine tolerance builds quickly, making it doubly dangerous. Withdrawal often results in apathy, prolonged periods of sleep, irritability, and depression.

### Disorder Criteria Summary
#### Amphetamine Intoxication

Features of amphetamine (or related substance) intoxication include:
- Significant maladaptive behaviour or psychological changes (e.g., euphoria, hypervigilance, impaired judgment, impaired functioning) during or shortly after use of amphetamine
- Two or more of the following signs: increased or decreased heart rate, dilation of pupils, elevated or lowered blood pressure, nausea, evidence of weight loss, psychomotor agitation or retardation, muscular weakness, confusion, seizures or coma

*Source:* Based on DSM-IV-TR. Used with permission from the *Diagnostic and Statistical Manual of Mental Disorders,* Fourth Edition, Text Revision. Copyright 2000. American Psychiatric Association.

Periodically, certain "designer drugs" appear in local mini-epidemics. An amphetamine called methylene-dioxymethamphetamine (MDMA), first synthesized in 1912 in Germany, was used as an appetite suppressant (Grob & Poland, 1997). Recreational use of this drug, now commonly called Ecstasy, rose sharply in the late 1980s. Among Toronto students surveyed in 1999, past-year use of Ecstacy was 7%, the highest rate observed in a gradual upward trend since 1991 (Bernstein, Adlaf, & Paglia, 2002). The effects of this drug are best described by a user: "just like speed but without the comedown, and you feel warm and trippy like acid, but without the possibility of a major freak-out" (O'Hagan, 1992, p. 10). A purified crystallized form of amphetamine, called "ice," is ingested through smoking. This drug causes marked aggressive tendencies and stays in the system longer than cocaine, making it particularly dangerous (Stein & Ellinwood, 1993). However enjoyable these new amphetamines may be in the short term, the potential for users to become dependent on them is extremely high, with great risk for long-term difficulties. Moreover, death can result: in 1999, there were nine MDMA-related deaths in Ontario (Bernstein et al., 2002).

**amphetamine use disorders** Psychological, biological, behavioural, and social problems associated with amphetamine use and abuse.

Designer drugs, especially Ecstasy, are popular among young people.

Amphetamines stimulate the central nervous system by enhancing the activity of norepinephrine and dopamine. Specifically, amphetamines help the release of these neurotransmitters and block their reuptake, thereby making more of them available throughout the system (Stein & Ellinwood, 1993). Too much amphetamine—and therefore too much dopamine and norepinephrine—can lead to hallucinations and delusions. As we see in Chapter 12, this effect has stimulated theories on the causes of schizophrenia, which can also include hallucinations and delusions.

## Cocaine Use Disorders

The use and misuse of drugs, such as those leading to **cocaine use disorders,** wax and wane according to societal fashion, moods, and sanctions (Uddo, Malow, & Sutker, 1993). Cocaine replaced amphetamines as the stimulant of choice in the 1970s (Stein & Ellinwood, 1993). Cocaine is derived from the leaves of the coca plant, a flowering bush indigenous to South America.

Latin Americans have chewed coca leaves for centuries to get relief from hunger and fatigue (Musto, 1992). Cocaine was introduced into North America in the late 19th century; it was widely used

from then until the 1920s. In 1885, Parke, Davis & Co. manufactured coca and cocaine in 15 different forms, including coca-leaf cigarettes and cigars, inhalants, and crystals. For people who couldn't afford these products, a cheaper way to get cocaine was in Coca-Cola, which up until 1903 contained 60 mg of cocaine per 240 ml (8-ounce) serving (Gold, 1997; Mack et al., 2003).

### Clinical Description

Like the amphetamines, in small amounts cocaine increases alertness, produces euphoria, increases blood pressure and pulse, and causes insomnia and loss of appetite. Remember that Danny snorted (inhaled) cocaine when he partied through the night with his friends. He later said the drug made him feel powerful and invincible—the only way he really felt self-confident. The effects of cocaine are

For centuries, Latin Americans have chewed coca leaves to get relief from hunger and fatigue.

**cocaine use disorders**   Cognitive, biological, behavioural, and social problems associated with the use and abuse of cocaine.

short lived; for Danny they lasted less than an hour, and he had to snort repeatedly to keep himself up. During these binges he often became paranoid, experiencing exaggerated fears that he would be caught or that someone would steal his cocaine. Such paranoia is common among cocaine abusers, occurring in two-thirds or more (Mack et al., 2003; Satel, 1992). Cocaine also makes the heart beat more rapidly and irregularly, and it can have fatal consequences, depending on a person's physical condition and the amount of the drug ingested.

We saw that alcohol can damage the developing fetus. It has also been suspected that the use of cocaine (especially crack) by pregnant women may adversely affect their babies. Susan Potter of Acadia University, Philip Zelazo of McGill University, and their colleagues (Potter, Zelazo, Stack, & Papageorgiou, 2000) conducted a carefully controlled study of the cognitive effects of cocaine exposure on the developing fetus. They found subtle deficits in auditory information processing among the cocaine-exposed infants that may help explain the growing evidence that fetal cocaine exposure is associated with subsequent language deficits among children exposed to this drug while still developing in the mother's uterus (Potter et al., 2000).

## Statistics

Cocaine use across most age groups in Canada has decreased during the past 15 years. Surveys continue to indicate low levels of past-year cocaine use in the general population in Canada. For example, Toronto surveys in 1998–1999 indicate that about 1% of adults and about 6% of students used cocaine in the past year (Bernstein et al., 2002). Cocaine is most often snorted through the nose, but it may also be injected. In Vancouver, 80% of needle exchange clients inject cocaine (Strathdee et al., 1997). In Montreal, this figure is 70% (Hankins, 1997), and in Halifax it is 52% (Grandy, 1995). Crack cocaine is a crystallized form of cocaine that is smoked rather than snorted or injected (Closser, 1992). Recent surveys in Toronto indicate that use of crack cocaine is reported by fewer than 1% of adults and by about 2% of students (Bernstein et al., 2002).

Cocaine is in the same group of stimulants as amphetamines because it has similar effects on the brain. The "up" seems to come primarily from the effect of cocaine on the dopamine system. Cocaine enters the bloodstream and is carried to the brain. There the cocaine molecules block the reuptake of dopamine. As you know, neurotransmitters released at the synapse stimulate the next neuron and then are recycled back to the original neuron. Cocaine seems to bind to places where dopamine neurotransmitters reenter their home neuron, blocking

**Disorder Criteria Summary**
Cocaine Intoxication

Features of cocaine intoxication include:
- Significant maladaptive behaviour or psychological changes impairing function because of use of cocaine
- Two or more of the following: increased or decreased heart rate, dilation of pupils, elevated or lowered blood pressure, perspiration or chills, nausea, evidence of weight loss, psychomotor agitation or retardation, muscular weakness, confusion, seizures or coma

*Source:* Based on DSM-IV-TR. Used with permission from the *Diagnostic and Statistical Manual of Mental Disorders,* Fourth Edition, Text Revision. Copyright 2000. American Psychiatric Association.

their reuptake by the neuron. The dopamine that cannot be taken in by the neuron remains in the synapse, causing repeated stimulation of the next neuron. This stimulation of the dopamine neurons in the "pleasure pathway" (the site in the brain that seems to be involved in the experience of pleasure) causes the high associated with cocaine use.

As late as the 1980s, many felt cocaine was a wonder drug that produced feelings of euphoria without being addictive (Franklin & Frances, 1999). Cocaine fooled us. Dependence does not resemble that of many other drugs early on, and typically people only find that they have a growing inability to resist taking more (Mack et al., 2003). Few negative effects are noted at first; however, with continued use, sleep is disrupted, increased tolerance causes a need for higher doses, paranoia and other negative symptoms set in, and the cocaine user gradually becomes socially isolated.

Again, Danny's case illustrates this pattern. He was a social user for a number of years, using cocaine only with friends and only occasionally. Eventually he had more frequent episodes of excessive use or binges, and he found himself increasingly craving the drug between binges. After the binges, Danny would crash and sleep. Cocaine withdrawal isn't like that of alcohol. Instead of rapid heartbeat, tremors, or nausea, withdrawal from cocaine produces pronounced feelings of apathy and boredom. Think for a minute how dangerous this type of withdrawal is. First, you're bored with everything and find little pleasure from the everyday activities of work or relationships. The one thing that can "bring you back to life" is cocaine. As you can imagine, a particularly vicious cycle develops: Cocaine is abused, withdrawal causes apathy, cocaine abuse resumes. The atypical withdrawal pattern misled people into believing that cocaine was not addictive. We now know that cocaine abusers go through

CP Photo/Calgary Herald/Dean Bicknell

Canadian equestrian star Eric Lemaze was not allowed to compete in the 2000 Sydney Olympics because of a relapse to cocaine abuse.

The tobacco plant is indigenous to North America, and First Nations people cultivated and smoked the leaves centuries ago. Today, almost a quarter of all Canadians smoke, which is down from the 49.5% who were smokers in 1965 (Physicians for a Smoke Free Canada, 2002).

DSM-IV-TR does not describe an intoxication pattern for nicotine. Rather, it lists withdrawal symptoms, which include depressed mood, insomnia, irritability, anxiety, difficulty concentrating, restlessness, and increased appetite and weight gain. Nicotine in small doses stimulates the central nervous system; it can relieve stress and improve mood. But it can also cause high blood pressure and increase the risk of heart disease and cancer (Slade, 1999). High doses can blur your vision, cause confusion, lead to convulsions, and sometimes even cause death. Once smokers are dependent on nicotine, going without it causes withdrawal symptoms (Slade, 1999). If you doubt the addictive power of nicotine, consider that the rate of relapse among people trying to give up drugs is equivalent among those using alcohol, heroin, and cigarettes (see Figure 10.7).

Nicotine is inhaled into the lungs, where it enters the bloodstream. Only 7 to 19 seconds after a person inhales the smoke, the nicotine reaches the brain (Benowitz, 1996). Nicotine appears to stimulate

patterns of tolerance and withdrawal comparable to those experienced by abusers of other psychoactive drugs (Mack et al., 2003).

## Nicotine Use Disorders

When you think of addicts, what image comes to mind? Do you see dirty and dishevelled people huddled on an old mattress in an abandoned building, waiting for the next fix? Do you picture businesspeople huddled outside a city building on a rainy afternoon furtively smoking cigarettes? Both these images are accurate, because the nicotine in tobacco is a psychoactive substance that produces patterns of dependence, tolerance, and withdrawal—**nicotine use disorders**—comparable to the other drugs we have discussed so far (Schmitz, Schneider, & Jarvik, 1997). In 1942, the Scottish physician Lennox Johnson "shot up" nicotine extract and found after 80 injections that he liked it more than cigarettes and felt deprived without it (Kanigel, 1988). This colourless, oily liquid is what gives smoking its pleasurable qualities.

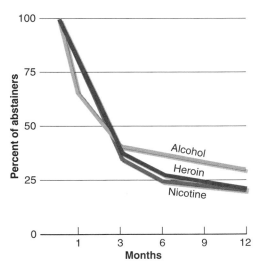

**Figure 10.7** ■ Relapse rates for nicotine compared with alcohol and heroin. Smokers trying to give up cigarettes backslide about as frequently as alcoholics and heroin addicts. (Adapted from "Nicotine Becomes Addictive," by R. Kanigel, 1988, *Science Illustrated*, October/November, 12–14, 19–21. Copyright © 1988 by Science Illustrated. Reprinted with permission.)

**nicotine use disorders** Cognitive, biological, behavioural, and social problems associated with the use and abuse of nicotine.

***Nicotine Dependence***

*"You can't simply focus on nicotine itself. Many of the medications do that—they focus on replacing the nicotine, such as nicotine gum or the patch—and that's very valuable, but you really have to focus on all the triggers, the cues, and the environment."*

Thomson Learning

specific receptors—*nicotinic acetylcholine receptors*—in the midbrain reticular formation and the limbic system, the site of the "pleasure pathway" mentioned before (McGehee, Heath, Gelber, Devay, & Role, 1995). Some evidence also points to how nicotine may affect the fetal brain, possibly increasing the likelihood that children of mothers who smoke during pregnancy will smoke later in life (Kandel, Wu, & Davies, 1994). Smokers dose themselves throughout the day in an effort to keep nicotine at a steady level in the bloodstream (10 to 50 nanograms per millilitre; Dalack, Glassman, & Covey, 1993).

Smoking has been linked with signs of negative affect, such as depression, anxiety, and anger (Hall, Muñoz, Reus, & Sees, 1993; Zvolensky, Schmidt, & Stewart, 2003). Many people who quit smoking but later resume report that feelings of depression or anxiety were responsible for the relapse (Slade, 1999). This finding suggests that nicotine may help improve mood. However, there is a complex relationship between cigarette smoking and negative affect. For example, severe depression is found to occur significantly more often among people with nicotine dependence (Breslau, Kilbey, & Andreski, 1993).

stimulant" because it is thought to be the least harmful of all the addictive drugs, caffeine can still lead to **caffeine use disorders.** This drug is found in tea, coffee, many of the cola drinks sold today, and cocoa products.

As most of you have experienced firsthand, caffeine in small doses can elevate your mood and decrease fatigue. In larger doses, it can make you feel jittery and can cause insomnia. Because caffeine takes a relatively long time to leave our bodies (it has a blood half-life of about 6 hours), sleep can be disturbed if the caffeine is ingested in the hours close to bedtime (Bootzin, Manber, Perlis, Salvio, & Wyatt, 1993). As with the other psychoactive drugs, people react variously to caffeine; some are sensitive to it and others can consume relatively large amounts with little effect. Research suggests that moderate use of caffeine (a cup of coffee per day) by pregnant women does not harm the developing fetus (Mills et al., 1993).

As with other stimulants, regular caffeine use can result in tolerance and dependence on the drug (Strain, Mumford, Silverman, & Griffiths, 1994). Those of you who have experienced headaches, drowsiness, and a generally unpleasant mood when denied your morning coffee have had the withdrawal symptoms characteristic of this drug (Silverman, Evans, Strain, & Griffiths, 1992). Caffeine's effect on the brain seems to involve the neurotransmitters *adenosine* and, to a lesser extent, *serotonin* (Greden & Walters, 1997). Caffeine seems to block adenosine reuptake. However, we do not yet know the role of adenosine in brain function or whether the interruption of the adenosine system is responsible for the elation and increased energy that come with caffeine use.

---

### Disorder Criteria Summary
#### Nicotine Withdrawal

Features of nicotine withdrawal include:
- Daily use of nicotine for several weeks or more
- Abrupt cessation or reduction in nicotine use resulting in four or more of the following: dysphoric or depressed mood, insomnia, irritability or anger, anxiety, difficulty concentrating, restlessness, decreased heart rate, increased appetite or weight gain
- Significant distress or impairment in functioning

*Source:* Based on DSM-IV-TR. Used with permission from the *Diagnostic and Statistical Manual of Mental Disorders,* Fourth Edition, Text Revision. Copyright 2000. American Psychiatric Association.

### Disorder Criteria Summary
#### Caffeine Intoxication

Features of caffeine intoxication include:
- Recent consumption of caffeine, usually in excess of 250 mg
- Five or more of the following signs: restlessness, nervousness, excitement, insomnia, flushed face, diuresis, gastrointestinal disturbance, muscle twitching, rambling flow of thought or speech, increased heart rate or cardiac arrhythmia, periods of inexhaustibility, psychomotor agitation
- Significant distress or impairment in functioning

*Source:* Based on DSM-IV-TR. Used with permission from the *Diagnostic and Statistical Manual of Mental Disorders,* Fourth Edition, Text Revision. Copyright 2000. American Psychiatric Association.

## Caffeine Use Disorders

Caffeine is the most common of the psychoactive substances, used regularly by 90% of all North Americans (Goldstein, 1994). Called the "gentle

**caffeine use disorders**   Cognitive, biological, behavioural, and social problems associated with the use and abuse of caffeine.

# Opioids

■ *Distinguish opioids from hallucinogens, and describe their psychological and physiological effects.*

The word *opiate* refers to the natural chemicals in the opium poppy that have a narcotic effect (they relieve pain and induce sleep). In some circumstances they can cause **opioid use disorders.** The broader term *opioids* refers to the family of substances that includes natural opiates, synthetic variations (methadone, pethidine), and the comparable substances that occur naturally in the brain (enkephalins, beta-endorphins, and dynorphins; Mack et al., 2003). In *The Wizard of Oz,* the Wicked Witch of the West puts Dorothy, Toto, and their companions to sleep by making them walk through a field of poppies, a literary allusion to the opium poppies used to produce morphine, codeine, and heroin.

Just as the poppies lull Dorothy, the Cowardly Lion, and Toto, opiates induce euphoria, drowsiness, and slowed breathing. High doses can lead to death if respiration is completely depressed. Opiates are also *analgesics,* substances that help relieve pain. People are sometimes given morphine before and after surgery to calm them and help block pain. A newer prescription opiate drug used in the treatment of pain is oxycodone (OxyContin). This drug appears to be of increasing concern in terms of its potential for abuse and for lethal overdose. Oxycodone has featured prominently in the news on the east coast, particularly in Cape Breton, Nova Scotia, where it is the number one street drug. Along with other prescription narcotics, oxycodone was linked to the death of 12 residents in 2003–2004. Although controversy continues about the degree to which these statistics represent cause for particular concern, the Nova Scotia College of Physicians and Surgeons sent out a letter to its members, providing practice guidelines to minimize

inappropriate prescribing of oxycodone and thus minimize its abuse potential (Moulton, 2004).

Withdrawal from opioids can be so unpleasant that people may continue to use these drugs despite a sincere desire to stop. However, barbiturate and alcohol withdrawal can be even more distressing. The perception among many people that opioid withdrawal can be life threatening stems from the experiences of heroin addicts in the 1920s and 1930s. These users had access to cheaper and purer forms of the drug than are available today and withdrawal had more serious side effects than withdrawal from the weaker versions currently in use (McKim, 1991). Even so, people who cease or reduce their opioid intake begin to experience symptoms within 6 to 12 hours; these include excessive yawning, nausea and vomiting, chills, muscle aches, diarrhea, and insomnia—temporarily disrupting work, school, and social relationships. The symptoms can persist for 1 to 3 days, and the withdrawal process is completed in about a week.

Because opiate users tend to be secretive, estimates of the exact number of people who use, abuse, or are dependent on these drugs are difficult to come by. Emergency room admissions over the period between 1995 and 2002 indicate a 34.5% increase resulting from the most commonly abused opiate— heroin (Substance Abuse and Mental Health Services Administration, 2003). People who use opiates face risks beyond addiction and the threat of overdose. Because these drugs are usually injected intravenously, users are at increased risk for HIV infection and therefore AIDS. In fact, HIV among injection drug users is increasing dramatically, with Vancouver now having the highest rate in North America (Strathdee et al., 1997).

The life of an opiate addict is bleak. Results from a 24-year follow-up study of more than 500 addicts in California highlight a pessimistic view of their lives (Hser, Anglin, & Powers, 1993). At the follow-up in 1985–1986, 27.7% of addicts had died, and the mean age at death was only about 40 years. Almost half the deaths were the results of homicide, suicide, or accident, and about a third were from drug overdose. There was a fairly stable pattern of daily narcotic use in 7% to 8% of the group.

© Dan Gair/Index Stock Imagery

Opium poppies.

**opioid use disorders** Cognitive, biological, behavioural, and social problems associated with the use and abuse of opiates and their synthetic variants.

The high or "rush" experienced by users comes from activation of the body's natural opioid system. In other words, the brain already has its own opioids—called enkephalins and endorphins—that provide narcotic effects (Mack et al., 2003; Simon, 1997). Heroin, opium, morphine, and other opiates activate this system (just as does alcohol at certain doses; Gianolakis, 2001; Peterson et al., 1996). The discovery of the natural opioid system was a major breakthrough in the field of psychopharmacology: Not only does it allow us to study the effects of addictive drugs on the brain, but it has also led to important discoveries that may help us treat people dependent on these drugs.

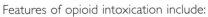

**Disorder Criteria Summary**
Opioid Intoxication

Features of opioid intoxication include:
- Significant maladaptive behaviour or psychological changes as a result of opioid use
- Pupillary constriction (or dilation) and one or more of the following: drowsiness or coma, slurred speech, impairment in attention or memory

*Source:* Based on DSM-IV-TR. Used with permission from the *Diagnostic and Statistical Manual of Mental Disorders,* Fourth Edition, Text Revision. Copyright 2000. American Psychiatric Association.

# Hallucinogens

■ *Describe the physiological and psychological effects of the hallucinogens.*

The substances we have examined so far affect people by making them feel "up" if they are stimulants such as cocaine, caffeine, and nicotine, or "calmed down" if they are depressants such as alcohol and the barbiturates. Next we explore the substances that can lead to **hallucinogen use disorder.** They essentially change the way the user perceives the world. Sight, sound, feelings, taste, and even smell are distorted, sometimes in dramatic ways, when a person is under the influence of drugs such as marijuana and LSD.

## Marijuana

**Marijuana** was the drug of choice in the 1960s and early 1970s. Although it has decreased in popularity, it is still the most routinely used illegal substance in Canada, with 10% of Toronto adults reporting marijuana use in a recent survey (Bernstein et al., 2002). Marijuana is the name given to the dried parts of the *cannabis* or hemp plant (its full scientific name is *cannabis sativa;* Iversen, 2000). Cannabis grows wild throughout the tropical and temperate regions of the world, which accounts for one of its nicknames, "weed."

Reactions to marijuana usually include mood swings. Otherwise normal experiences seem extremely funny, or the person might enter a dreamlike state where time seems to stand still. Users often report heightened sensory experiences, seeing vivid colours, or appreciating the subtleties of music. Perhaps more than any other drug, however, marijuana can produce very different reactions in people. It is not uncommon for someone to report having no reaction to the first use of the drug; it also

Marijuana.

appears that people can "turn off" the high if they are sufficiently motivated (Iversen, 2000). The feelings of well-being produced by small doses can change to paranoia, hallucinations, and dizziness

**hallucinogen use disorders** Cognitive, biological, behavioural, and social problems associated with the use and abuse of hallucinogenic substances.

**marijuana** *(cannabis sativa)* Dried part of the hemp plant, a hallucinogen that is the most widely used illegal substance.

when larger doses are taken. Research on frequent marijuana users suggests that impairments of memory, concentration, motivation, self-esteem, relationships with others, and employment are common negative outcomes of long-term use (Haas & Hendin, 1987; Roffman & Barnhart, 1987). The impairment in motivation—apathy, or unwillingness to carry out long-term plans—has sometimes been called *amotivational syndrome,* although how prevalent this problem is remains unclear (Iversen, 2000).

The evidence for marijuana tolerance is contradictory. Chronic and heavy users report tolerance, especially to the euphoric high (Johnson, 1991); they are unable to reach the levels of pleasure they experienced earlier. However, evidence also indicates "reverse tolerance," when regular users experience more pleasure from the drug after repeated use. Major signs of withdrawal do not usually occur with marijuana. Chronic users who stop taking the drug report a period of irritability, restlessness, appetite loss, nausea, and difficulty sleeping (Johnson, 1991); but no evidence suggests they go through the craving and psychological dependence characteristic of other substances (Grinspoon & Bakalar, 1997).

Controversy surrounds the use of marijuana for medicinal purposes. In the United States, the popular media frequently describe individuals who illegally use marijuana to help ward off the nausea associated with chemotherapy or to ease the symptoms of other illnesses such as glaucoma, and the medical benefits of this drug may be promising (Grinspoon & Bakalar, 1997). Unfortunately, marijuana smoke may contain as many carcinogens as tobacco smoke, and long-term use may contribute to diseases such as lung cancer. This potential health risk should be weighed against the benefits of using marijuana under certain medical circumstances. In 1999, Health Canada began giving exemptions on compassionate grounds to certain seriously ill patients, allowing them to legally use marijuana for medicinal purposes if they are not benefiting from traditional medications (Pearson, 2002).

Most marijuana users inhale the drug by smoking the dried leaves in marijuana cigarettes; others use preparations such as hashish, which is the dried form of the resin in the leaves of the female plant. Marijuana contains more than 80 varieties of the chemicals called *cannabinoids,* which are believed to alter mood and behaviour. The most common of these chemicals includes the *tetrahydrocannabinols,* otherwise known as THC. An exciting finding in the area of marijuana research is that the brain makes its own version of THC, a neurochemical called *anandamide* after the Sanskrit word *ananda,* which means "bliss" (Fackelmann, 1993). Because work in this area is so new, scientists are only beginning to explore how this neurochemical affects the brain and our behaviour.

## Disorder Criteria Summary
### Cannabis Intoxication

Features of cannabis intoxication include:
- Significant maladaptive behaviour or psychological changes (e.g., euphoria, anxiety, impaired judgment) because of cannabis use
- Two or more of the following: bloodshot eyes, increased appetite, dry mouth, increased heart rate

*Source:* Based on DSM-IV-TR. Used with permission from the *Diagnostic and Statistical Manual of Mental Disorders,* Fourth Edition, Text Revision. Copyright 2000. American Psychiatric Association.

## LSD and Other Hallucinogens

On a Monday afternoon in April 1943, Albert Hoffmann, a scientist at a large Swiss chemical company, prepared to test a newly synthesized compound. He had been studying derivatives of ergot, a fungus that grows on diseased kernels of grain, and sensed that he had missed something important in the 25th compound of the lysergic acid series. Ingesting what he thought was an infinitesimally small amount of this drug, which he referred to in his notes as LSD-25, he waited to see what subtle changes might come over him as a result. Thirty minutes later he reported no change; but some 40 minutes after taking the drug he began to feel dizzy and had a noticeable desire to laugh. Riding his bicycle home, he hallucinated that the buildings he passed were moving and melting. By the time he arrived home, he was terrified he was losing his mind. Hoffmann was experiencing the first recorded "trip" on LSD (Stevens, 1987).

**LSD (*d*-lysergic acid diethylamide)** is the most common hallucinogenic drug. It is produced synthetically in laboratories, although naturally occurring derivatives of this grain fungus (ergot) have been found historically. In Europe during the Middle Ages, an outbreak of illnesses occurred as a result of people's eating grain that was infected with the fungus. One version of this illness—later called ergotism—constricted the flow of blood to the arms or legs and eventually resulted in gangrene and the loss of limbs. Another type of illness resulted in convulsions, delirium, and hallucinations. Years later, scientists connected ergot with the illnesses and began studying versions of this fungus for possible benefits. This is the type of work Hoffmann was engaged in when he discovered LSD's hallucinogenic properties.

**LSD (*d*-lysergic acid diethylamide)**   Most common hallucinogenic drug; a synthetic version of the grain fungus ergot.

LSD remained in the laboratory until the 1960s, when it was first produced illegally for recreational use. The mind-altering effects of the drug suited the social effort to reject established culture and enhanced the search for enlightenment that characterized the mood and behaviour of many people during the decade. The late Timothy Leary, at the time a Harvard research professor, first used LSD in 1961 and immediately began a movement to have every child and adult try the drug and "turn on, tune in, and drop out."

During this time, LSD was also being experimented with in the context of therapy. For example, in the 1950s, Dr. Humphrey Osmond performed an experiment to test the theory that the spiritual aspect of the LSD trip could be used to assist in recovery from alcoholism. Participants were 1000 patients with a history of severe alcoholism who were receiving treatment at the Weyburn Hospital in Saskatchewan. They were administered a single high dose of LSD. Osmond reported that 50% did not drink alcohol again, leading him to argue strongly for the efficacy of this approach (Lee & Shlain, 1985). In fact, William (Bill) Wilson, co-founder of Alcoholics Anonymous (AA), is known to have experimented with and advocated this controversial approach to the treatment of alcoholism (Roberts & Hruby, 1984).

There are a number of other hallucinogens, some occurring naturally in a variety of plants: *psilocybin* (found in certain species of mushrooms); *lysergic acid amide* (found in the seeds of the morning glory plant); *dimethyltryptamine* (DMT; found in the bark of the Virola tree, which grows in South and Central America); and *mescaline* (found in the peyote cactus plant).

The DSM-IV-TR diagnostic criteria for hallucinogen intoxication are similar to those for marijuana: perceptual changes such as the subjective intensification of perceptions, depersonalization, and hallucinations. Physical symptoms include pupillary dilation, rapid heartbeat, sweating, and blurred vision (American Psychiatric Association, 2000a). Many users have written about hallucinogens, and they describe a variety of experiences. The kinds of sensory distortions reported by Hoffmann are characteristic reactions. People tell of watching intently as a friend's ear grows and bends in beautiful spirals or of looking at the bark of a tree and seeing little civilizations living there. These people will tell you that they usually know what they are seeing isn't real but that it looks as real as anything they have ever seen. But many also recount experiences that are more intense than hallucinations, with an emotional content that sometimes takes on religious proportions.

Tolerance develops quickly to a number of the hallucinogens, including LSD, psilocybin, and mescaline (Pechnick & Ungerleider, 1997). If taken repeatedly over a period of days, these drugs completely lose their effectiveness. However, sensitivity returns after about a week of abstinence. For most of the hallucinogens, no withdrawal symptoms are reported. Even so, a number of concerns have been expressed about their use. One is the possibility of psychotic reactions. Stories in the popular press about people who jumped out of windows because they believed they could fly or who stepped into moving traffic with the mistaken idea that they couldn't be hurt have provided for sensational reading, but little evidence suggests that using hallucinogens produces a greater risk than being drunk or under the influence of any other drug. People do report having "bad trips"; these are the sort of frightening episodes in which clouds turn into threatening monsters or deep feelings of paranoia take over. Usually someone on a bad trip can be "talked down" by supportive people who provide constant reassurance that the experience is the temporary effect of the drug and it will wear off in a few hours.

© Ted Streshinsky/CORBIS

The psychedelic art of the 1960s reflects the visual distortions that result from taking hallucinogens.

We still do not fully understand how LSD and the other hallucinogens affect the brain. Most of these drugs bear some resemblance to neurotransmitters; LSD, psilocybin, lysergic acid amide, and DMT are chemically similar to serotonin; mescaline resembles norepinephrine; and a number of other hallucinogens we have not discussed are similar to acetylcholine. However, the mechanisms responsible for the hallucinations and other perceptual changes that users experience remain unknown.

### Disorder Criteria Summary
Hallucinogen Intoxication

Features of hallucinogen intoxication include:
- Significant maladaptive behaviour or psychological changes because of hallucinogen use
- Perceptual changes while awake and alert such as subjective intensification of perceptions, hallucinations, feelings of depersonalization, and illusions, following hallucination use
- Two or more of the following signs: dilation of pupils, increased heart rate, sweating, palpitations, blurring of vision, tremors, incoordination

*Source:* Based on DSM-IV-TR. Used with permission from the *Diagnostic and Statistical Manual of Mental Disorders,* Fourth Edition, Text Revision. Copyright 2000. American Psychiatric Association.

# Other Drugs of Abuse

- *Identify drugs of abuse other than those described thus far, which are also used to alter sensory experiences.*

- *Describe the physiological and psychological effects of inhalants, steroids, and designer drugs.*

A number of other substances are used by individuals to alter sensory experiences. These drugs do not fit neatly into the classes of substances we just described but are nonetheless of great concern because they can be physically damaging to those who ingest them. We briefly describe *inhalants, steroids,* and a group of drugs commonly referred to as *designer drugs.*

*Inhalants* include a variety of substances found in volatile solvents—making them available to breathe into the lungs directly. Among the more common inhalants used for abuse include spray paint, hair spray, paint thinner, gasoline, amyl nitrate, nitrous oxide ("laughing gas"), nail polish remover, felt-tipped markers, airplane glue, contact cement, dry-cleaning fluid, and spot remover (Pandina & Hendren, 1999). Inhalant use is most commonly observed among young males (age 13–15 years) who are economically disadvantaged (Franklin & Frances, 1999). In Canada, inhalant use is a particular problem among Aboriginal youth (Coleman, Charles, & Collins, 2001). These drugs are rapidly absorbed into the bloodstream through the lungs by inhaling them from containers or on a cloth held up to the mouth and nose. The high associated with the use of inhalants resembles that of alcohol intoxication and usually includes dizziness, slurred speech, incoordination, euphoria, and lethargy (American Psychiatric Association, 2000a). Users build up a tolerance to the drugs, and withdrawal—which involves sleep disturbance, tremors, irritability, and nausea—can last from 2 to 5 days. Unfortunately, use can also increase aggressive and antisocial behaviour, and long-term use can damage bone marrow, kidneys, liver, and the brain (Franklin & Frances, 1999).

*Anabolic-androgenic steroids* (more commonly referred to as steroids or "roids") are derived from or are a synthesized form of the hormone testosterone (Pandina & Hendren, 1999). The legitimate medical uses of these drugs focus on people with asthma, anemia, breast cancer, and males with inadequate sexual development. However, the anabolic action of these drugs (that can produce increased body mass) has resulted in their illicit use by those wishing to bulk up and improve their physical abilities. Steroids can be taken orally or through injection, and some estimates suggest that approximately 2% of males will use the drug illegally at some point in their lives (Pandina & Hendren, 1999). Users sometimes administer the drug on a schedule of several weeks or months followed by a break from its use—called "cycling"—or combine several types of steroids—called "stacking." Steroid use differs from other drug use because the substance does not produce a desirable high but instead is used to enhance performance and body size. Dependence on the substance therefore seems to involve the desire to maintain the performance gains obtained rather than a need to re-experience an altered emotional or physical state. Research on the long-term effects of steroid use seems to suggest that mood disturbances are common (e.g., depression, anxiety, and panic attacks; Pandina & Hendren, 1999), and there is a concern that more serious physical consequences may result from its regular use.

The term *designer drugs* is shorthand for a growing group of drugs developed by pharmaceutical companies to target specific diseases and disorders. It was only a matter of time before some would use the developing technology to design "recreational drugs." We have already described one of the more common illicit designer drugs—MDMA, or Ecstasy—in the section on stimulants.

In 1998, Canadian sprinter Ben Johnson won the 100 metre dash at the Seoul Olympic Games. He was later stripped of his gold medal after officials found he had taken anabolic steroids to enhance his performance (BBC, 2004).

This amphetamine is one of a small but feared growing list of related substances that includes 3,4 methelenedioxyethamphetamine (MDEA or Eve), and 2-(4-Bromo-2,5-dimethoxy-phenyl)-ethylamine (BDMPEA or Nexus). Their ability to heighten a person's auditory and visual perception, as well as the senses of taste and touch, have led to these drugs being incorporated into the activities of those who attend nightclubs, all-night dance parties (raves), or large social gatherings of primarily gay men (circuit parties; McDowell, 1999). Phencyclidine (or PCP) is snorted, smoked, or injected intravenously and causes impulsivity and aggressiveness.

A drug that is related to phencyclidine and is associated with the "drug club" scene is ketamine (street names include K, Special K, and Cat Valium), a dissociative anesthetic that produces a sense of detachment with a reduced awareness of pain (McDowell, 1999). Gamma hydroxybutyrate (GHB, or liquid Ecstasy) is a central nervous system depressant that was marketed in health food stores in the 1980s as a means of stimulating muscle growth. Users report that, at low doses, it can produce a state of relaxation and increased tendency to verbalize, but at higher doses or with alcohol or other drugs it can result in seizures, severe respiratory depression, and coma. Use of all these drugs can result in tolerance and dependence, and their increasing popularity among adolescents and young adults raises significant public health concerns.

## Concept Check 10.2

Determine whether the following statements about stimulants are True (T) or False (F).

1. _____  Amphetamines have been used as appetite suppressants.
2. _____  Use of crack cocaine by pregnant mothers adversely affects all their babies.
3. _____  Stimulants have been used for more than 5000 years.
4. _____  Regular use of stimulants can result in tolerance and dependence on the drugs.
5. _____  Amphetamines are naturally occurring drugs that induce feelings of elation and vigour and can reduce fatigue.
6. _____  Compared with all other drugs, caffeine can produce the most variable reactions in people.
7. _____  An ingredient of the beverage Coca-Cola in the 1800s was cocaine.

# Causes of Substance-Related Disorders

■ *Describe the psychological and physiological processes involved in substance dependence, including the role of positive and negative reinforcement, expectancies, and social and cultural factors.*

■ *Identify the genetic contribution to substance-related disorders, with particular emphasis on alcoholism.*

■ *Describe the main features of the integrative model of substance-related disorders.*

People continue to use psychoactive drugs for their effects on mood, perception, and behaviour despite the obvious negative consequences of abuse and dependence. We saw that despite his clear potential as an individual, Danny continued to use drugs to his detriment. Various factors help explain why people like Danny persist in using drugs. Drug abuse and dependence, once thought to be the result of moral weakness, are now believed to be influenced by a combination of biological and psychosocial factors.

Why do some people use psychoactive drugs without abusing or becoming dependent on them? Why do some people stop using these drugs or use them in moderate amounts after being dependent on them and others continue a lifelong pattern of dependence despite their efforts to stop? These questions continue to occupy the time and attention of numerous researchers throughout the world.

## Biological Dimensions

### Familial and Genetic Influences

As you already have seen throughout this book, many of the psychological disorders are influenced in important ways by genetics. Mounting evidence indicates that drug abuse in general, and alcohol abuse specifically, follows this pattern. A great deal of animal research confirms the importance of genetic influences on substance abuse (Crabbe, Belknap, & Buck, 1994). In work with humans, twin, family, and adoption studies indicate that certain people may be genetically vulnerable to drug abuse (Anthenelli & Schuckit, 1997; Gordis, 2000c; McGue, 1999). Twin studies of smoking, for example, find a moderate genetic influence (Lerman et al., 1999). However, most genetic data on substance abuse come from research on alcoholism, which is widely studied because alcohol use is legal and many people are dependent on it (Gordis, 2000c; Lerman et al., 1999). Among men, both twin and adoption studies suggest genetic factors play a role in alcoholism (McGue, 1999). The research on women, however, is

sometimes contradictory. Several studies suggest that genetics has relatively little influence on alcoholism in women (e.g., McGue, Pickens, & Svikis, 1992), and others suggest the disorder may be inherited in some form (e.g., Pickens et al., 1991).

A group of researchers—referred to as the Collaborative Study on the Genetics of Alcoholism—have worked together to search for the genes that may influence alcoholism. Two studies have pointed to genes that may influence alcoholism on chromosomes 1, 2, 7, and 11, plus a finding that a gene on chromosome 4 may protect people from becoming dependent (Long et al., 1998; Reich et al., 1998). As the search for the genes responsible for alcoholism continues, the next obvious question is how these genes work to influence addiction—a field of research called *functional genomics.*

Genetic research to date tells us that substance abuse in general is affected by our genes, but no one gene causes substance abuse or dependence. Research suggests that genetic factors may affect how people experience certain drugs, which in turn may partly determine who will or will not become abusers.

### Neurobiological Influences

The pleasurable experiences reported by people who use psychoactive substances partly explain why people continue to use them (Gardner, 1997). In behavioural terms, people are *positively reinforced* for using drugs. But what mechanism is responsible for such experiences? Complex and fascinating studies indicate the brain appears to have a natural "pleasure pathway" that mediates our experience of reward. All abused substances seem to affect this internal reward centre. In other words, what psychoactive drugs may have in common is their ability to activate this reward centre and provide the user with a pleasurable experience, at least for a time.

The pleasure centre was discovered 50 years ago by James Olds and Peter Milner at McGill University, who studied the effects of electrical stimulation of rat brains (Olds, 1956; Olds & Milner,

1954). If certain areas were stimulated with very small amounts of electricity, the rats behaved as if they had received something pleasant, such as food. The exact location of the area in the human brain is still subject to debate, although it is believed to include the *dopaminergic system* and its *opioid-releasing neurons*, which begin in the midbrain ventral tegmental area and then work their way forward through the nucleus accumbens and on to the frontal cortex (Korenman & Barchas, 1993).

How do different drugs that affect different neurotransmitter systems all converge to activate the pleasure pathway, which is primarily made up of dopamine-sensitive neurons? Researchers are only beginning to sort out the answers to this question, but some surprising findings have emerged in recent years. For example, we know that amphetamines and cocaine act directly on the dopamine system. Other drugs, however, appear to increase the availability of dopamine in more roundabout and intricate ways.

This complicated picture is far from complete. Other pleasure pathways may exist in the brain (Wise, 1988). The coming years should yield even more interesting insights into the interaction of drugs and the brain. One aspect that awaits explanation is how drugs not only provide pleasurable experiences (positive reinforcement) but also help remove unpleasant experiences such as pain, feelings of illness, or anxiety (negative reinforcement). Aspirin is a negative reinforcer: We take it not because it makes us feel good but because it stops us from feeling bad. In much the same way, one property of the psychoactive drugs is that they stop people from feeling bad, an effect as powerful as making them feel good.

With several drugs, negative reinforcement is related to the anxiolytic effect, the ability to reduce anxiety (discussed briefly in the section on the sedative, hypnotic, and anxiolytic drugs). Alcohol has an anxiolytic effect. The neurobiology of how these drugs reduce anxiety seems to involve the septal/hippocampal system (Gray, 1987), which includes a large number of GABA-sensitive neurons. As noted by Robert Pihl and his colleagues (1993), certain drugs may reduce anxiety by enhancing the activity of GABA in this region, thereby inhibiting the brain's normal reaction (anxiety/fear) to anxiety-producing situations.

Researchers have identified individual differences in the way people respond to alcohol. Understanding these response differences is important because they may help explain why some people continue to use drugs until they acquire a dependence on them, whereas others stop before this happens. A number of studies compare individuals with and without a family history of alcoholism. For example, research by Robert Pihl, Jordan Peterson, and their colleagues suggests that individuals at high familial genetic risk for alcoholism may experience more of a pleasurable response to alcohol ingestion than do others. This pleasurable response is indexed through heart rate increases to alcohol and degree of beta-endorphin release to alcohol ingestion (Peterson, Pihl, Seguin, Finn, & Stewart, 1993; Peterson et al., 1996; Stewart, Finn, & Pihl, 1992). Thus, this laboratory-based research on the effects of alcohol suggests that what may be inherited among those genetically vulnerable to alcoholism is a propensity to experience the pleasurable consequences of drinking to a greater extent than others.

## Psychological Dimensions

We have shown that the substances people use to alter mood and behaviour have unique effects. The high from heroin differs substantially from the experience of smoking a cigarette, which in turn differs from the effects of amphetamines or LSD. Nevertheless, it is important to point out the similarities in the way people react to most of these substances.

### Positive Reinforcement

The feelings that result from using psychoactive substances are pleasurable in some way, and people will continue to take the drugs to recapture the pleasure. Research shows clearly that many of the drugs used and abused by humans also seem to be pleasurable to animals (Young & Herling, 1986). Laboratory animals will work to have injected into their bodies drugs such as cocaine, amphetamines, opiates, sedatives, and alcohol, which demonstrates that even without social and cultural influences these drugs are pleasurable. Human research also indicates that to some extent all the psychoactive drugs provide a pleasurable experience (Goldstein, 1994; Gordis, 2000a).

### Negative Reinforcement

Most researchers have looked at how drugs help reduce unpleasant feelings through negative reinforcement. Many people are likely to initiate and continue drug use to escape unpleasantness in their lives. In addition to the initial euphoria, many drugs provide escape from physical pain (opiates), from stress (alcohol), or from panic and anxiety (benzodiazepines). This phenomenon has been explored under a number of different names, including *tension reduction, negative affect,* and *self-medication,* each of which has a somewhat different focus (Cappell & Greeley, 1987).

Basic to many views of abuse and dependence is the premise that substance use becomes a way for users to cope with the unpleasant feelings that go along with life circumstances (Cooper, Russell, &

George, 1988; Zack, Toneatto, & MacLeod, 1999). Drug use by soldiers in Vietnam is one tragic example of this phenomenon. Almost 42% of these mostly young men experimented with heroin, half of whom became dependent, because the drug was readily available and because of the extreme stress of the war (Jaffe, Knapp, & Ciraulo, 1997). It is interesting that only 12% of these soldiers were still using heroin 3 years after their return home (Robins, Helzer, & Davis, 1975), which suggests that once the stressors were removed they no longer needed the drug to relieve their pain. People who experience trauma such as sexual abuse are more likely to abuse alcohol (Stewart, 1996). These observations emphasize the important role played by each aspect of abuse and dependence—biological, psychological, social, and cultural—in determining who will and who will not have difficulties with these substances. Recent findings that adolescents tend to use drugs as a way to cope with unpleasant feelings (Chassin, Pillow, Curran, Molina, & Barrera, 1993) suggest that to prevent people from using drugs we may need to address influences such as stress and anxiety, a strategy we discuss in our section on treatment.

Many people who use psychoactive substances experience a crash after being high. So why don't they just stop taking drugs? One explanation involves an interesting integration of both the positive and negative reinforcement processes (Solomon, 1980; Solomon & Corbit, 1974). The *opponent-process theory* holds that an increase in positive feelings will be followed by an increase in negative feelings a short time later. Similarly, an increase in negative feelings will be followed by a period of positive feelings. Athletes often report feeling depressed after finally attaining a long-sought goal. The opponent-process theory claims that this mechanism is strengthened with use and weakened by disuse. So a person who has been using a drug for some time will need more of it to achieve the same results (tolerance). At the same time, the negative feelings that follow drug use tend to intensify. For many people, this is the point at which the motivation for drug taking shifts from desiring the euphoric high to alleviating the increasingly unpleasant crash. Unfortunately, the best remedy is more of the same drug. People who are hung over after drinking too much alcohol are often advised to have "the hair of the dog that bit you." The sad irony here is that the very drug that can make you feel so bad is also the one thing that can take away your pain. You can see why people can become enslaved by this insidious cycle.

Researchers have also looked at substance abuse as a way of self-medicating for other problems (Conrod et al., 2000a). If people have difficulties with anxiety, for example, they may be attracted to barbiturates or alcohol because of their anxiety-reducing qualities. In one study, researchers were successful in treating a small group of cocaine addicts who had ADHD with methylphenidate (Ritalin; Khantzian, Gawin, Kleber, & Riordan, 1984). They had hypothesized that these individuals used cocaine to help focus their attention. Once their ability to concentrate improved with the methylphenidate, the users stopped ingesting cocaine. Research is just beginning to outline the complex interplay among stressors, negative feelings, other psychological disorders, and negative reactions to the drugs themselves as causative factors in psychoactive drug use.

## Cognitive and Learning Factors

What people expect to experience when they use drugs influences how they react to them (Goldman, Del Boca, & Darkes, 1999). A person who expects to be less inhibited when she drinks alcohol will act less inhibited whether she drinks alcohol or a placebo she thinks is alcohol (Cooper, Russell, Skinner, Frone, & Mudar, 1992; Wilson, 1987). This observation about the influence of how we think about drug use has been labelled an *expectancy effect* and has received considerable research attention.

Expectancies develop before people use drugs, perhaps as a result of parents' and peers' drug use, advertising, and media figures who model drug use (Miller, Smith, & Goldman, 1990). In one study, a large group of students in grades 7 and 8 were given questionnaires that focused on their expectations about drinking. The researchers reexamined the students 1 year later to see how their expectancies predicted their later drinking (Christiansen, Smith, Roehling, & Goldman, 1989). One surprising finding was the marked increase in drinking among the students only 1 year later. When researchers first questioned them, about 10% of the students reported getting drunk two to four times per year. This number had risen to 25% by the next year. The students' expectations of drinking did predict who would later have drinking problems. Students who thought that drinking would improve their social behaviour and their cognitive and motor abilities (despite all evidence to the contrary) were more likely to have drinking problems 1 year later. These results suggest that children may begin drinking partly because they believe drinking will have positive effects.

Expectations appear to change as people have more experience with drugs, although their expectations are similar for alcohol, nicotine (Brandon & Baker, 1992; Wetter et al., 1994), marijuana, and cocaine (Schafer & Brown, 1991). Some evidence from the laboratory of Peter Finn, a clinical psychologist from Montreal, points to positive expectancies—believing you will feel good if you take a drug—as an indirect influence on drug problems. In other words, what these beliefs may do is to increase the likelihood you will take certain drugs, which in turn will increase the likelihood that problems will arise (Finn, Sharkansky, Brandt, & Turcotte, 2000).

Once people stop taking drugs after prolonged or repeated use, powerful urges called *cravings* can interfere with efforts to remain off these drugs (Anton, 1999; Breiner, Stritzke, & Lang, 1999; Tiffany, 1999). If you've ever tried to give up ice cream and then found yourself compelled to have some, you have a limited idea of what it might be like to crave a drug. These urges seem to be triggered by factors such as the availability of the drug, contact with things associated with drug taking (e.g., sitting in a bar), specific moods (e.g., being depressed), or having a small dose of the drug. For example, the sight and smell of beer will increase the likelihood of a drinker consuming even more beer (Perkins, Ciccocioppo, Jacobs, & Doyle, 2003). Research is under way to determine how cravings may work in the brain (Hommer, 1999) and whether certain medications can be used to reduce these urges and help supplement treatment (Swift, 1999).

Important research by Shep Siegel, Marvin Krank, and Riley Hinson at McMaster University in the 1980s examined the role of conditioning in accounting for important aspects of addiction such as craving. If a particular stimulus (e.g., a needle in the case of an injection drug user) is repeatedly paired with drug taking and consequent unconditioned drug effects (e.g., the euphoric effects of the drug), then that stimulus can become a conditioned stimulus signalling that the drug effect is coming (Siegel, 1982). According to the research of Seigel and of many others since, with repeated learning opportunities involving pairing of the conditioned stimulus with drug taking, the drug taker will develop conditioned compensatory responses that are in the opposite direction to the drug's original (unconditioned) effect. For example, if decreased heart rate is the unconditioned drug effect, a conditioned compensatory response could involve increased heart rate. This conditioned compensatory response is initiated when the drug taker is exposed to the cues (conditioned stimulus such as the needle) associated with drug taking.

This phenomenon can explain many aspects of addiction including tolerance, craving, and overdose. For example, with respect to tolerance, as the conditioned compensatory response develops, it works against (in the opposite direction to) the unconditioned drug effect, reducing the subjective experience of the drug effect for the user. With respect to overdose, heroin users are more likely to overdose when injecting in an unfamiliar environment, even when using their usual dose of heroin. From the perspective of conditioning theory, this happens because the usual drug cues are not present to initiate the conditioned compensatory response. Thus, the user experiences the full unconditioned effect of the drug, resulting in an overdose (Siegel, Hinson, Krank, & McCully, 1982). Although much of this research was conducted with animals, it has had important implications for the treatment of people with substance dependence.

## Social Dimensions

Previously we pointed out the importance of exposure to psychoactive substances as a necessary prerequisite to their use and possible abuse. You could probably list a number of ways people are exposed to these substances—through friends, through the media, and so on. For example, research on the consequences of cigarette advertising suggests the effects of media exposure may be more influential than peer pressure in determining whether teens smoke (Pierce & Gilpin, 1995). Research such as this has led to increasing restrictions by the Canadian government on how and where cigarette companies can advertise their product (Canadian Council on Smoking & Health and Physicians for a Smoke Free Canada, 2003).

Research suggests that drug-addicted parents spend less time monitoring their children than parents without drug problems (Dishion, Patterson, & Reid, 1988) and that this is an important contribution to early adolescent substance use (Chassin et al., 1993). When parents did not provide appropriate supervision, their children developed friendships with peers who supported drug use. But recent research by Alberta psychologist Nancy Galambos suggests that parenting can exert an important influence on teenagers' use of alcohol and drugs, even in the face of potentially negative peer influences. Specifically, parents who use firm behavioural control were able to stop the upward spiral of externalizing behaviours (including substance abuse) among those teens who were affiliating with deviant peers (Galambos, Barker, & Almeida, 2003).

How does our society view people who are dependent on drugs? This issue is of tremendous importance because it affects efforts to legislate the sale, manufacture, possession, and use of these substances. It also dictates how drug-dependent individuals are treated. Two views of substance abuse and dependence characterize contemporary thought: *moral weakness* and the *disease model of dependence*. According to the moral weakness view, drug use is seen as a failure of self-control in the face of temptation; this is a psychosocial perspective.

Drug users lack the character or moral fibre to resist the lure of drugs. We saw earlier, for example, that the Catholic Church made drug abuse an official sin—an indication of its disdain. The disease model, in contrast, assumes that drug dependence is caused by an underlying physiological disorder; this is a biological perspective. Just as diabetes or asthma can't be blamed on the afflicted individuals, neither should drug dependence. As noted by Canadian clinical psychologist G. Alan Marlatt (1995), Alcoholics Anonymous and similar organizations see drug dependence as an incurable disease over which the addict has no control.

Neither perspective in itself does justice to the complex interrelationship between the psychosocial and the biological influences that affect substance disorders. Viewing drug use as moral weakness leads to punishing those afflicted with the disorder, whereas a disease model includes seeking treatment for a medical problem. On the other hand, people certainly help determine the outcome of treatment for drug abuse and dependence, and messages that the disorder is out of their control can at times be counterproductive. A comprehensive view of substance-related disorders that includes both psychosocial and biological influences is needed for this important societal concern to be addressed adequately.

## Cultural Dimensions

When we examine a behaviour as it appears in different cultures, it is necessary to reexamine what is considered abnormal (Matsumoto, 1994). Each culture has its own preferences for psychoactive drugs and its own proscriptions for substances it finds unacceptable. Keep in mind that in addition to defining what is or is not acceptable, cultural norms affect the rates of substance abuse and dependence in important ways. For example, in certain cultures, including Korea, members are expected to drink alcohol heavily on certain social occasions (C. K. Lee, 1992). As we have seen before, exposure to these substances in addition to social pressure for heavy and frequent use may facilitate their abuse, and this may explain the high abuse rates in countries such as Korea. On the other hand, poor economic conditions in certain parts of the world limit the availability of drugs, which appears in part to account for the relatively low prevalence of substance abuse in Mexico and Brazil (de Almeidia-Filho, Santana, Pinto, & de Carvalho-Neto, 1991; Ortiz & Medicna-Mora, 1988).

As yet we do not know whether biological differences across cultures contribute to the varying use and abuse rates. Looking ahead to what we may find through future research, it is important for us to consider that biological factors may interact with

Photodisc

In many cultures, alcohol is used ceremonially.

cultural norms in a complex way. For example, it seems logical that cultural norms may develop over time as a consequence of biological differences. Certain cultures may adapt their drug use (e.g., condoning substance use only in "safe" social surroundings) to ethnically idiosyncratic reactions (e.g., a tendency to react aggressively). On the other hand, we have seen in looking at other disorders that behaviour can also affect biology, and we may discover that the norms established by a society affect the biology of its people. Research on the cultural dimensions of substance abuse is in its infancy, but it holds great promise for helping unravel the mysteries of this disorder.

## An Integrative Model

Any explanation of substance use, abuse, and dependence must account for the basic issue raised earlier in this chapter: "Why do some people use drugs but not abuse them or become dependent?" Figure 10.8 illustrates how the multiple influences we have discussed may interact to account for this process. Access to a drug is a necessary but obviously not sufficient condition for abuse or dependence. Exposure has many sources, including the media, parents, peers, and, indirectly, lack of supervision. Whether people use a drug depends also on social and cultural expectations, some encouraging and some discouraging, such as laws against possession or sale of the drug.

The path from drug use to abuse and dependence is more complicated (see Figure 10.8). As major stressors aggravate many of the disorders we have discussed, so do they increase the risk of abuse and dependence on psychoactive substances. Genetic influences may be of several different types. Some individuals may inherit a greater sensitivity to the positively reinforcing effects of certain drugs and others to the negatively reinforcing effects (anxiolytic or analgesic) of certain drugs. Other psychiatric conditions may indirectly put someone at risk for substance abuse. For example, antisocial personality disorder, characterized by the frequent violation of social norms (see Chapter 11), is thought to include a lowered rate of arousal; this may account for the increased prevalence of substance abuse in this group.

Equifinality, the concept that a particular disorder may arise from multiple and different paths, is particularly appropriate to substance disorders. It is clear that abuse and dependence cannot be predicted from one factor, be it genetic, neurobiological, psychological, or cultural. For example, some people with the genes common to many with substance abuse problems do not become abusers. Many people who experience the most crushing stressors, such as abject poverty or bigotry and violence, cope without resorting to drug use. There are different pathways to abuse, and we are only now beginning to identify their basic outlines.

Once a drug has been used repeatedly, biology and cognition conspire to create dependence. Continual use of most drugs causes tolerance, which requires the user to ingest more of the drug to produce the same effect. Conditioning is also a factor. If pleasurable drug experiences are associated with certain settings, a return to such a setting will later cause urges to develop, even if the drugs themselves are not available.

This obviously complex picture still does not convey the intricate lives of people who develop substance-related disorders (Wills, Vaccaro, McNamara, & Hirky, 1996). Each person has his or her own story and path to abuse and dependence. We have only begun to discover the commonalities of substance disorders; we need to understand a great deal more about how all the factors interact to produce them.

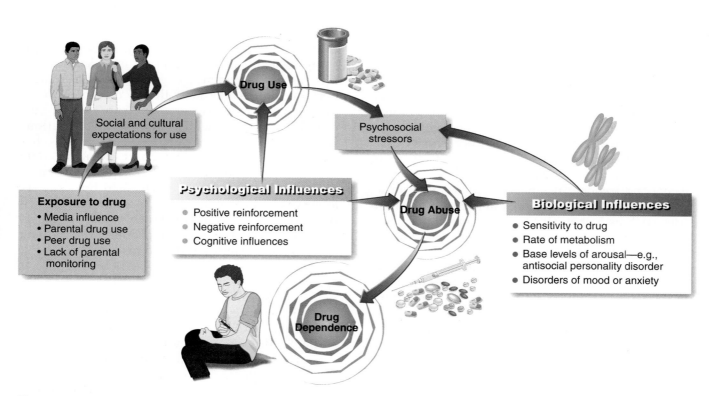

**Figure 10.8** ■ An integrative model of substance-related disorders.

## Concept Check 10.3

### Part A

Match the following descriptions with their corresponding substances: (a) opioids, (b) amphetamines, (c) cocaine, (d) hallucinogens, (e) nicotine, (f) caffeine.

1. These drugs, including LSD, influence perception and distort feelings, sights, sounds, and smells. _____
2. These create feelings of elation and vigour and reduce fatigue. They are prescribed to people with narcolepsy and ADHD. _____
3. These lead to euphoria, drowsiness, and slowed breathing. These substances are analgesics, relieving pain. Users tend to be secretive, preventing a great deal of research in this area. _____
4. This substance causes euphoria, appetite loss, and increased alertness. Dependence appears after years of use. Mothers addicted to this have the potential to give birth to irritable babies. _____
5. This is the most common psychoactive substance because it is legal, elevates mood, and decreases fatigue. It's readily available in many beverages. _____
6. This substance stimulates the nervous system and relieves stress. The DSM-IV-TR describes withdrawal symptoms instead of an intoxication pattern. _____

### Part B

Indicate whether these statements about the causes of substance-related disorders are True (T) or False (F).

1. Research with both animals and humans indicates that substance abuse in general is affected by our genes, though not one particular gene. _____
2. To some extent, all psychoactive drugs provide a pleasurable experience, creating positive reinforcement. _____
3. Negative reinforcement is involved in the continuance of drug use because drugs often provide escape from pain, stress, panic, etc. _____
4. The expectancy effect is illustrated when a person who expects to be less inhibited when drinking alcohol is given a placebo and acts/feels normally. _____
5. The media and parental influences have no effect on adolescent drug use; it is solely a peer pressure factor. _____

# Treatment of Substance-Related Disorders

■ *Describe various psychological and medical treatments for addictions.*

■ *Identify the role of early prevention and relapse prevention programs, including what is known about their relative effectiveness.*

When we left Danny, he was in jail, awaiting the legal outcome of being arrested for robbery. At this point in his life Danny needs more than legal help; he needs to free himself from his addiction to alcohol and cocaine. And the first step in his recovery has to come from him. Danny must admit he needs help, that he does have a problem with drugs, and that he needs others to help him overcome his chronic dependence. The personal motivation to work on a drug problem appears to be essential in the treatment of substance abuse (W. R. Miller, 1985). A therapist cannot help someone who doesn't want to change, and this can be a problem in treating substance abuse just as it is for people with disorders such as anorexia nervosa and antisocial personality disorder. Fortunately (and at last), Danny's arrest seemed to shock him into realizing how serious his problems had become, and he was now ready to confront them head-on.

Treating people who have substance-related disorders is a difficult task. Perhaps because of the combination of influences that often work together to keep people hooked, the outlook for those who are dependent on drugs is often not positive. We will see in the case of heroin dependence, for example, that a best-case scenario is often just trading one addiction (heroin) for another (methadone). And even people who successfully cease taking drugs may feel the urge to resume drug use all their lives.

Treatment for substance-related disorders focuses on several areas. Sometimes the first step is to help someone through the withdrawal process, and for some, the ultimate goal is abstinence. In other situations the goal is to get a person to maintain a less harmful, more moderate level of drug use without escalating its intake, and sometimes it is geared toward preventing exposure to drugs.

We discuss the treatment of substance-related disorders as a group because treatments have so much in common. For example, many programs that treat people for dependence on a variety of substances also teach skills for coping with life stressors. Some biological treatments focus on how to mask the effects of the ingested substances. We discuss the obvious differences among substances as they arise.

## Biological Treatments

There have been a variety of biologically based approaches designed primarily to change the way substances are experienced. In other words, scientists are trying to find ways to prevent people from experiencing the pleasant highs associated with drug use or to find alternative substances that have some of the positive effects (e.g., reducing anxiety) without their addictive properties.

### Agonist Substitution

Increased knowledge about how psychoactive drugs work on the brain has led researchers to explore ways of changing how they are experienced by people who are dependent on them. One method, **agonist substitution,** involves providing the person with a safer drug that has a chemical makeup similar to the addictive drug (therefore the name *agonist*). *Methadone* is an opiate agonist that is often given as a heroin substitute (Kleber, 1999). Methadone is a synthetic narcotic developed in Germany during World War II when morphine was not available for pain control; it was originally called *adolphine* after Adolph Hitler (Bellis, 1981). Although it does not give the quick high of heroin, methadone initially provides the same analgesic (pain reducing) and sedative effects. However, when users develop a tolerance for methadone it loses its analgesic and sedative qualities. Because heroin and methadone are *cross-tolerant*, acting on the same neurotransmitter receptors, a heroin addict who takes methadone may become addicted to the methadone instead (O'Brien, 1996). Research suggests that when addicts combine methadone with counselling, many reduce their use of heroin and engage in less criminal activity (Ball & Ross, 1991). The news is not all good, however. A proportion of people under methadone treatment continue to abuse other substances such as cocaine (Condelli, Fairbank, Dennis, & Rachal, 1991) and benzodiazepines (Iguchi et al., 1990). Research suggests that some people who use methadone as a substitute for heroin benefit significantly, but they may be dependent on methadone for the rest of their lives (O'Brien, 1996).

Addiction to cigarette smoking is also treated by a substitution process. The drug is provided to smokers in the form of nicotine gum or a nicotine patch, which lack the carcinogens included in cigarette smoke; the dose is later tapered off to lessen withdrawal from the drug. In general, nicotine gum has been successful in helping people stop smoking, although it works best in combination with supportive psychological therapy (Cepeda-Benito, 1993; Hall et al., 1996; Hughes, 1993). People must be taught how to use the gum properly, and about 20% of people who successfully quit smoking become dependent on the gum itself (Hughes, Gust, Skoog, Keenan, & Fenwick, 1991). The nicotine patch, which requires less effort and provides a steadier nicotine replacement, may be somewhat more effective in helping people quit smoking (Hatsukami et al., 2000; Hughes, 1993; Tiffany, Cox, & Elash, 2000). However, if either treatment is used without a comprehensive psychological treatment program (see later), a substantial number of smokers relapse after they stop using the gum or patch (Cepeda-Benito, 1993).

### Antagonist Treatments

We described how many of the psychoactive drugs produce euphoric effects through their interaction with the neurotransmitter systems in the brain. What would happen if the effects of these drugs were blocked so that the drugs no longer produced the pleasant results? Would people stop using the drugs? **Antagonist drugs** block or counteract the effects of psychoactive drugs, and a variety of drugs that seem to cancel out the effects of opiates have been used with people dependent on a variety of substances (O'Brien & Cornish, 1999). The most often prescribed opiate-antagonist drug, *naltrexone*, has had only limited success with individuals who are not simultaneously participating in a structured treatment program (Goldstein, 1994). When it is given to a person who is dependent on opiates, it produces immediate withdrawal symptoms, an extremely unpleasant effect. A person must be withdrawn from the opiate completely before starting naltrexone, and because it removes the euphoric effects of the opiates, the user must be highly motivated to continue treatment.

Naltrexone has also been evaluated as a treatment for alcohol dependence because it prevents alcohol reinforcement by inhibiting dopamine release in the nucleus accumbens (O'Malley, 1996; Stewart, Collins, Blackburn, Ellery, & Klein, 2005). Results suggest that naltrexone may enhance an overall treatment approach that includes psychotherapy (O'Malley et al., 1992).

---

**agonist substitution** Replacement of a drug on which a person is dependent with one having a similar chemical makeup, an *agonist*. Used as a treatment for substance dependence.

**antagonist drugs** Medications that block or counteract the effects of psychoactive drugs.

University of Calgary psychiatrists David Crockford and Nady el-Guebaly (1998) have described the results of a case study of a 49-year-old man with comorbid alcohol dependence and pathological gambling who was effectively treated for both disorders with naltrexone. The naltrexone was particularly beneficial in helping reduce this patient's cravings (Crockford & el-Guebaly, 1998). Other drugs are now being studied to see whether they can help improve the outcomes of people who wish to reduce their drug use. For example, a relatively new drug—*ondansetron*—is being studied and may be particularly helpful for people who developed alcoholism at or before their early 20s (B. A. Johnson et al., 2000; Kranzler, 2000). Overall, naltrexone or the other drugs being explored are not the magic bullets that would shut off the addict's response to psychoactive drugs and put an end to dependence. They do appear to help some drug abusers handle withdrawal symptoms and the craving that accompanies attempts to abstain from drug use; antagonists may therefore be a useful addition to other therapeutic efforts.

### Aversive Treatment

In addition to looking for ways to block the euphoric effects of psychoactive drugs, workers in this area may prescribe drugs that make ingesting the abused substances extremely unpleasant. The expectation is that a person who associates the drug with feelings of illness will avoid using the drug. The most commonly known aversive treatment uses *disulfiram* (Antabuse) with people who are alcohol dependent (Gallant, 1999). Antabuse prevents the breakdown of acetaldehyde, a by-product of alcohol, and the resulting buildup of acetaldehyde causes feelings of illness. People who drink alcohol after taking Antabuse experience nausea, vomiting, and elevated heart rate and respiration. Ideally, Antabuse is taken each morning, before the desire to drink wins out (Nathan, 1993). Unfortunately, non-compliance is a major concern, and a person who skips the Antabuse for a few days is able to resume drinking. In Canada, the supplier of brand-name disulfiram (i.e., Antabuse) discontinued this product in 2001 (Pharmacists.ca, 2003). However, this medication is still available in Canada in non-brand-name (generic) form (i.e., as disulfiram).

Efforts to make smoking aversive have included the use of *silver nitrate* in lozenges or gum. This chemical combines with the saliva of a smoker to produce a bad taste in the mouth. Research has not shown it to be particularly effective (E. J. Jensen, Schmidt, Pedersen, & Dahl, 1991). Both Antabuse for alcohol abuse and silver nitrate for cigarette smoking have generally been less than successful as treatment strategies on their own, primarily because they require that people be extremely motivated to continue taking them outside the supervision of a mental health professional (Leccese, 1991).

### Other Biological Treatments

Medication is frequently prescribed to help people deal with the often very disturbing symptoms of withdrawal. *Clonidine*, developed to treat hypertension, has been given to people withdrawing from opiates. Because withdrawal from certain prescribed medications such as the sedatives can cause cardiac arrest or seizures, these drugs are gradually tapered off to minimize dangerous reactions. In addition, sedative drugs (benzodiazepines) are often prescribed to help minimize discomfort for people withdrawing from other drugs such as alcohol (McCreery & Walker, 1993).

One of the few controlled studies of the use of medication to treat cocaine abuse (Gawin et al., 1989) found that *desipramine*, one of the antidepressant drugs, was more effective in increasing abstinence rates among cocaine users than lithium or a placebo. However, 41% of those receiving the medication were unable to achieve even a month of continuous cocaine abstinence, suggesting it may not be helpful for a large subgroup of users. Other medications—such as *acamprostate* (which affects the glutamate and GABA neurotransmitter systems) and several SSRIs (including Zoloft and Prozac)—are now being tested for their potential therapeutic properties, especially for alcohol dependence (Gordis, 2000c).

## *Psychosocial Treatments*

Most of the biological treatments for substance abuse show some promise with people who are trying to eliminate their drug habit. However, none of these treatments alone is successful for most people (American Psychiatric Association, 2000c). Most research indicates a need for social support or therapeutic intervention. Because so many people need help to overcome their substance disorder, a number of models and programs have been developed. Unfortunately, in no other area of psychology have unvalidated and untested methods of treatment been so widely accepted. A reminder: The fact that a program has not been subject to the scrutiny of research does not mean it doesn't work, but the sheer number of people receiving services of unknown value is cause for concern. We next review several therapeutic approaches that *have* been evaluated.

### Inpatient Facilities

Inpatient treatment facilities are designed to help people get through the initial withdrawal period and to provide supportive therapy so that they can go back to their communities (Morgan, 1981). Inpatient care can be extremely expensive (Miller & Hester, 1986). The question arises, then, as to how effective this type of care is compared with outpatient therapy that can cost 90% less. Research suggests there may be no difference between intensive residential setting programs and quality outpatient care in the outcomes for alcoholic patients (Miller & Hester, 1986) or for drug treatment in general (Guydish, Sorensen, Chan, Werdegar, & Acampora, 1999; Smith, Kraemer, Miller, DeBusk, & Taylor, 1999). Although some people improve as inpatients, they may not need this expensive care.

## Alcoholics Anonymous and Its Variations

Without question, the most popular model for the treatment of substance abuse is a variation of the Twelve Step program first developed by Alcoholics Anonymous (AA). Established in 1935 by two alcoholic professionals, William "Bill W." Wilson and Robert "Dr. Bob" Holbrook Smith, the foundation of AA is the notion that alcoholism is a disease and alcoholics must acknowledge their addiction to alcohol and its destructive power over them. The addiction is seen as more powerful than any individual; therefore, they must look to a higher power to help them overcome their shortcomings. Central to the design of AA is its independence from the established medical community and the freedom it offers from the stigmatization of alcoholism (Denzin, 1987; Robertson, 1988). An important component is the social support it provides through group meetings.

Since 1935, AA has steadily expanded to include almost 97 000 groups in more than 100 countries (Emrick, 1999). In one survey conducted by researcher Robin Room, formerly of the Addiction Research Foundation in Toronto, more than 3% of the adult population reported they had at one time attended an AA meeting (Room, 1993). The Twelve Steps of AA are the basis of its philosophy (see Table 10.1). In them you can see the reliance on prayer and a belief in God.

Reaction is rarely neutral to AA and similar organizations, such as Cocaine Anonymous and Narcotics Anonymous (N. S. Miller, Gold, & Pottash, 1989). Many people credit the approach with saving their lives, whereas others object that its reliance on spirituality and adoption of a disease model foster dependence. Because participants attend meetings anonymously and only when they feel the need to, conducting systematic research on its effectiveness has been unusually difficult (W. R. Miller & McCrady, 1993). There have been numerous attempts, however, to evaluate AA's effect on alcoholism (Emrick, Tonigan, Montgomery, & Little, 1993). Although there are not enough data to show what percentage of people abstain from using alcohol as a result of participating in AA, Emrick and his colleagues found that those people who regularly participate in AA activities and follow its guidelines carefully are more likely to have a positive outcome. Other studies suggest that people who fully participate in AA do as well as those receiving cognitive-behavioural treatments (Ouimette, Finney, & Moos, 1997). On the other hand, a large number of people who initially contact AA for their drinking problems seem to drop out, 50% after 4 months and 75% after 12 months (Alcoholics Anonymous, 1990). AA is clearly an effective treatment for *some* people with alcohol dependence. We do not yet know, however, who is likely to succeed and who is likely to fail in AA. Other treatments are needed for the large numbers of people who do not respond to AA's approach.

## Controlled Use

One of the tenets of AA is total abstinence; recovering alcoholics who have just one sip of alcohol are believed to have "slipped" until they again achieve abstinence. However, some researchers question this assumption and believe at least a portion of abusers of several substances (notably alcohol and nicotine) may be capable of becoming social users without resuming their abuse of these drugs. Some people who smoke only occasionally are thought to react differently to nicotine than heavy users (Goldstein, 1994).

In the alcoholism treatment field, the notion of teaching people **controlled drinking** is extremely controversial. Mark and Linda Sobell conducted an important study showing partial success in

Well-known Canadian comedian Mary Walsh has struggled with an alcohol use disorder and has publicly acknowledged being a member of Alcoholics Anonymous (AA).

CP Photo/Charlottetown Guardian/Brian McInnis

**controlled drinking** A controversial treatment approach to alcohol dependence in which severe abusers are taught to drink in moderation.

## TABLE 10.1 Twelve Suggested Steps of Alcoholics Anonymous

1. We admitted we were powerless over alcohol—that our lives had become unmanageable.
2. Came to believe that a power greater than ourselves could restore us to sanity.
3. Made a decision to turn our will and our lives over to the care of God *as we understood Him.*
4. Made a searching and fearless moral inventory of ourselves.
5. Admitted to God, to ourselves, and to another human being the exact nature of our wrongs.
6. Were entirely ready to have God remove all these defects of character.
7. Humbly asked Him to remove our shortcomings.
8. Made a list of all persons we had harmed, and became willing to make amends to them all.
9. Made direct amends to such people wherever possible, except when to do so would injure them or others.
10. Continued to take personal inventory and, when we were wrong, promptly admitted it.
11. Sought through prayer and meditation to improve our conscious contact with God as we understood Him, praying only for knowledge of His will for us and the power to carry that out.
12. Having had a spiritual awakening as the result of these steps, we tried to carry this message to alcoholics and to practice these principles in all our affairs.

*Source:* The Twelve Steps are reprinted with permission of Alcoholics Anonymous World Services, Inc. (A.A.W.S.). Permission to reprint the Twelve Steps does not mean that A.A.W.S. has reviewed or approved the contents of this publication, or that A.A.W.S. necessarily agrees with the views expressed herein. A.A. is a program of recovery from alcoholism only—use of the Twelve Steps in connection with programs and activities which are patterned after A.A., but which address other problems, or in any other non-A.A. context, does not imply otherwise.

teaching severe abusers to drink in a limited way (Sobell & Sobell, 1978). Forty male alcoholics were assigned either to a program that taught them how to drink in moderation or to a group that was abstinence oriented. The Sobells followed the men for more than 2 years, maintaining contact with 98% of them. At the 2-year follow-up, those who participated in the controlled drinking group were functioning well 85% of the time, whereas the men in the abstinence group were functioning well only 42% of the time. Nonetheless, some of the men in both groups suffered serious relapses and required rehospitalization, and some were incarcerated. Thus, controlled drinking may be a viable alternative to abstinence for some alcohol abusers, although it clearly isn't a cure.

The controversy over this study began with a paper published by Pendery, Maltzman, and West (1982). The authors had contacted the men in the Sobell study after 10 years and found that only 1 of the 20 men in the experimental group maintained a pattern of controlled drinking. Although this reevaluation made headlines, it had a number of flaws as pointed out by Alan Marlatt and his colleagues (Marlatt, Larimer, Baer, & Quigley, 1993). Most serious was the lack of data on the abstinence group over the same 10-year follow-up period.

The controversy over the Sobell study still had a chilling effect on controlled drinking as a treatment of alcohol abuse in the United States. In contrast, controlled drinking is widely accepted as a treatment for alcoholism in the United Kingdom (Rosenberg, 1993). This approach is more widely accepted in Canada than in the United States but less so than in the United Kingdom. Research on this approach in the ensuing years (Marlatt et al., 1993) seems to show that controlled drinking is at least as effective as abstinence, but that neither treatment is successful for 70% to 80% of patients over the long term—a rather bleak outlook for people with alcohol dependence.

### Component Treatment

Most comprehensive treatment programs aimed at helping people with substance abuse and dependence problems have a number of components thought to boost the effectiveness of the "treatment package." We saw in our review of biological treatments that their effectiveness is increased when psychologically based therapy is added. In *aversion therapy*, which uses a conditioning model, substance use is paired with something extremely unpleasant, such as a brief electric shock or feelings of nausea. For example, a person might be offered a drink of alcohol and receive a painful shock when the glass reaches his or her lips. The goal is to counteract the positive associations with substance use with the negative associations. The negative associations can also be made by imagining unpleasant scenes in a technique called *covert sensitization* (Cautela, 1966); the person might picture himself or herself beginning to snort cocaine and be interrupted with visions of herself becoming violently ill.

One component that seems to be a valuable part of therapy for substance use is *contingency management* (Higgins & Petry, 1999; Petry, Martin, Cooney, & Kranzler, 2000). Here, the clinician and client together select the behaviours that the client needs to change and decide on the reinforcers that will reward reaching certain goals, perhaps money or small retail items such as CDs. In a study of cocaine abusers, clients received things like lottery tickets for having cocaine-negative urine specimens (Higgins et al., 1993). This study found greater abstinence rates among cocaine-dependent users with the contingency management approach and other skills training than among users in a more traditional counselling program that included a Twelve Step approach to treatment.

Another package of treatments is the *community reinforcement approach* (Miller, Meyers, & Hiller-Sturmhöfel, 1999; Meyers, Villanueva, & Smith, 2005). Several different facets of the drug problem are addressed to help identify and correct aspects of the person's life that might contribute to substance use or interfere with efforts to abstain. First, a spouse, friend, or relative who is not a substance user is recruited to participate in relationship therapy to help the abuser improve his or her relationships with other important people. Second, clients are taught how to identify the antecedents and consequences that influence their drug taking. For example, if they are likely to use cocaine with certain friends, clients are taught to recognize the relationship and encouraged to avoid the associations. Third, clients are given assistance with employment, education, finances, or other social service areas that may help reduce their stress. Fourth, new recreational options help the person replace substance use with new activities. Preliminary studies of the community reinforcement approach with alcohol and cocaine abusers appear encouraging, although more research is needed to assess its long-term effectiveness.

Attempts to match treatments to the particular needs of individual clients (treatment matching) has received increased attention from workers in the area of substance abuse. For example, the U.S. National Institute on Alcohol Abuse and Alcoholism initiated Project MATCH (Matching Alcoholism Treatment to Client Heterogeneity) to assess whether people with differing characteristics (having little hope for improvement versus searching for spiritual meaning) would respond better or worse to different treatments (Project MATCH Research Group, 1993). Findings suggest that well-run programs of various types can be effective with a range of people with substance use problems (Project MATCH Research Group, 1997). Although few specific matches were recommended on the basis of the Project MATCH findings, research is ongoing to help clinicians tailor their treatments to the particular needs of their substance-abusing clients (Jaffe et al., 1996; Project MATCH Research Group, 1998).

Recent research by Patricia Conrod and her colleagues in Montreal suggests that matching on the basis of substance-abusing clients' personality and motivations for substance use improves outcomes for substance-abusing women (Conrod et al., 2000b). In Conrod et al.'s study, female substance abusers recruited from the community were randomly assigned to receive one of three brief interventions: (1) a motivation-matched intervention

involving personality-specific motivational and coping skills training; (2) a motivational control intervention involving a film about substance abuse and a supportive discussion with a therapist; and (3) a motivation-mismatched intervention targeting a theoretically different personality profile. The personality profiles targeted were: (1) anxiety sensitivity (associated with benzodiazepine dependence and comorbid anxiety disorders); (2) hopelessness (associated with opioid analgesic dependence and comorbid depression); (3) impulsivity (associated with cocaine and alcohol dependence and comorbid antisocial personality disorder); and (4) sensation seeking (associated with exclusive alcohol dependence). Assessment at 6-months post-intervention indicated that only the matched intervention was superior to the motivational control intervention in reducing the severity and frequency of problematic substance abuse and in prevention the use of multiple medical services (see Figure 10.9 for sample study results). These findings indicate promise for client-treatment matching approaches that match at the level of motivations or substance abuse.

### Relapse Prevention

Another kind of treatment directly addresses the problem of relapse. The **relapse prevention** treatment model developed by Alan Marlatt looks at the learned aspects of dependence and sees relapse as a failure of

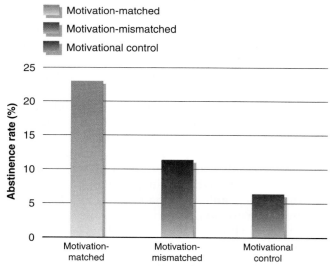

**Figure 10.9** ■ Abstinence rates from alcohol following treatment in three groups: motivation-matched, motivation-mismatched, and motivational control intervention. Only the motivation-matched intervention resulted in an abstinence rate that was significantly higher than the motivational control intervention. (Adapted from Conrod, P.J., Stewart, S.H., Pihl, R.O., Cote, S., Fontaine, V., & Dongier, M. (2000) Efficacy of brief coping skills interventions that match different personality profiles of female substance abusers. *Psychology of Addictive Behaviors*, 14, 231–242.)

cognitive and behavioural coping skills (Marlatt & Gordon, 1985). Therapy involves helping people remove any ambivalence about stopping their drug use by examining their beliefs about the positive aspects of the drug ("There's nothing like a cocaine high") and confronting the negative consequences of its use ("I fight with my wife when I'm high"). High-risk situations are identified ("having extra money in my pocket") and strategies are developed to deal with potentially problematic situations and with the craving that arises from abstinence. Incidents of relapse are dealt with as occurrences from which the person can recover; instead of looking on these episodes as inevitably leading to more drug use, people in treatment are encouraged to see them as episodes brought on by temporary stress or a situation that can be changed. Research on this technique suggests that it may be particularly effective for alcohol problems (Irvin, Bowers, Dunn, & Wang, 1999), marijuana dependence (Stephens, Roffman, & Simpson, 1994), smoking (Gruder et al., 1993; Shiffman et al., 1996), and cocaine abuse (Carroll, 1992).

## Harm Reduction

In direct contrast to the current zero tolerance, "Just say no to drugs" approach taken by the United States government to combat substance abuse and dependence, a very different approach is currently predominant in Europe and elsewhere around the world (Marlatt, 1998). This approach is known as **harm reduction**—an approach also championed by Alan Marlatt (e.g., Roberts & Marlatt, 1999). The harm reduction approach recognizes that substance use occurs in society and seeks to minimize the harm associated with substance use as its primary goal. Abstinence can be the final goal of a substance-abusing client within a harm reduction approach, but it does not have to be. Thus, the controlled drinking interventions developed by the Sobells represent an example of the harm reduction approach.

Another example of the harm reduction approach is the establishment of safer injection sites (SISs) for injection drug users. In fact, Canada's first such facility opened in Vancouver in September 2003 (Follman, 2003). Injection drug use represents a growing health problem in Canada—increasing the risk for overdose and HIV/AIDS and hepatitis C infections. At SISs, it is legal for drug users to inject their drug using clean equipment, under medical supervision. SISs minimize the risk of overdose, disease, and other negative health effects that can result from using unclean equipment and unsafe injecting practices. SISs also direct substance-dependent clients to treatment programs and operate as primary health care units (Elliott, Malkin, & Gold, 2002).

The establishment of the Vancouver SIS has been widely criticized by conservative politicians within Canada and by the U.S. government (Follman, 2003). Opponents argue that SISs condone or encourage drug use and that a strict abstinence-oriented approach would better contain drug use (Elliott et al., 2002). Proponents argue that SISs offer a safer, hygienic place to inject, with access to medical intervention and other health and social services, providing a positive message of concern for the drug user's health and well-being. Proponents argue that SISs can benefit the broader community as well, by reducing the public nuisance associated with drug taking in the streets of the community (e.g., discarded needles).

Scientific evidence lends support to the use of SISs. The experiences of countries such as Switzerland, Germany, the Netherlands, and Australia suggest that including SISs as a part of a broader government drug policy benefit both drug users and communities (Elliott et al., 2002). Given that the Vancouver facility is relatively new, researchers are still evaluating its health impact. After the pilot project ends at the end of 2007, the accumulated evidence will be reviewed, and the Canadian government will make decisions about whether to continue operation of the Vancouver SIS and whether to open additional SIS facilities in other jurisdictions. Results available thus far appear favourable (e.g., Wood et al., 2004, 2006). For example, studies have shown that the presence of the SIS has led to an increased uptake of clients into detoxification programs and addiction treatment, to a reduction in public drug injection, and to a decrease in the amount of injection-related litter in the Vancouver downtown eastside area (Wood et al., 2004, 2006). Moreover, the negative effects projected by critics do not appear to have materialized. The presence of the SIS in Vancouver has not led to an increase in drug-related crime, rates of arrest for drug trafficking, assaults, or robbery. In fact, rates of vehicle break-ins and theft have decreased in the area since the opening of the SIS (Wood et al., 2004). For more information on the Vancouver SIS, see http://www.vch.ca/sis.

## *Prevention*

In education-based programs, harm reduction approaches to prevention and early intervention (e.g., Conrod, Stewart, Comeau, & Maclean, 2006; Dimeff, Baer, Kivlahan, & Marlatt, 2002) appear more promising than programs encouraging a "no drug use" message (Pentz, 1999). And fortunately,

---

**relapse prevention** Using cognitive and behavioural skills to avoid a recurrence of substance dependence, such as by avoiding or anticipating high-risk situations.

**harm reduction** Approach to substance abuse prevention and treatment that seeks to minimize the harm associated with substance use as its primary goal (e.g., controlled drinking interventions, safe injection sites for injection drug users).

more comprehensive programs that involve skills training to avoid or resist social pressures (such as peers) and environmental pressures (such as media portrayals of drug use) can be effective in preventing drug abuse among some (Dimeff et al., 2002). Similarly, skills-based early interventions targeted to those teens at high risk for substance misuse appear promising (Conrod et al., 2006).

Over the past few years, the strategies for preventing substance abuse and dependence have shifted from education-based approaches to more wide-ranging approaches including the use of community-based interventions (Gordis, 2000b). For example, community-based intervention strategies to reduce binge drinking and alcohol-related injuries (e.g., car crashes, assaults) can involve mobilizing communities to encourage responsible beverage service (i.e., not serving too much alcohol to bar patrons), limiting alcohol access to underage drinkers, increasing local enforcement of drinking and driving laws, and using zoning laws to limit access to alcohol (Holder et al., 2000). But implementing this sort of intervention is obviously beyond the scope of one research investigator or even a consortium of researchers collaborating across many sites. It requires the cooperation of governmental, educational, and even religious institutions. We may need to rethink our approach to preventing drug use and abuse.

## Concept Check 10.4

Determine whether you understand how treatments for substance-related disorders work by matching the examples with the following terms: (a) dependent, (b) cross-tolerant, (c) agonist substitution, (d) antagonist, (e) relapse prevention, (f) controlled drinking, (g) aversion therapy, (h) covert sensitization, (i) contingency management, (j) anonymous.

1. Methadone is used to help heroin addicts kick their habit in a method called _____.
2. Heroin and methadone are _____, which means they affect the same neurotransmitter receptors.
3. Unfortunately, the heroin addict may become permanently _____ on methadone.
4. _____ drugs block or counteract the effects of psychoactive drugs and are sometimes effective in treating addicts.
5. This controversial treatment for alcoholism, _____, involves drinking in moderation.
6. In _____, substance use is paired with something extremely unpleasant (like alcohol and vomiting with Antabuse).
7. The _____ model involves therapy that helps individuals remove ambivalence about stopping their drug use by examining their beliefs about the positive and negative aspects of drug use.
8. By imagining unpleasant scenes, the technique of _____ helps the person associate the negative effects of the drug with drug use.
9. It has been difficult to evaluate rigorously the effectiveness of AA because the participants are _____.
10. _____ is a controversial treatment for alcohol abuse because of a negative but flawed experimental finding, but also because it conflicts with the belief in total abstinence.
11. In _____, the clinician and client work together to decide which behaviours the client needs to change and which reinforcers will be used as rewards for reaching set goals.

# Summary

## Perspectives on Substance-Related Disorders

- In DSM-IV-TR, substance-related disorders are divided into depressants (alcohol, barbiturates, and benzodiazepines), stimulants (amphetamine, cocaine, nicotine, and caffeine), opiates (heroin, codeine, and morphine), and hallucinogens (marijuana and LSD).
- Specific diagnoses are further categorized as substance dependence, substance abuse, substance intoxication, and substance withdrawal.
- Non-medical drug use continues to cost Canadians billions of dollars and seriously impairs the lives of millions of Canadians each year.

## Depressants

- Depressants are a group of drugs that decrease central nervous system activity. The primary effect is to reduce our levels of physiological arousal and help us relax. Included in this group are alcohol and sedative, hypnotic, and anxiolytic drugs, such as those prescribed for insomnia.

## Stimulants

- Stimulants, the most commonly consumed psychoactive drugs, include caffeine (in coffee, chocolate, and many soft drinks), nicotine (in tobacco products such as cigarettes), amphetamines, and cocaine. In contrast to the depressant drugs, stimulants make us more alert and energetic.

## Opioids

- Opiates include opium, morphine, codeine, and heroin; they have a narcotic effect—relieving pain and inducing sleep. The broader term *opioids* is used to refer to the family of substances that includes these opiates and to the synthetic variations created by chemists (methadone, pethidine) and the similarly acting substances that occur naturally in our brains (enkephalins, beta-endorphins, and dynorphins).

## Hallucinogens

- Hallucinogens essentially change the way the user perceives the world. Sight, sound, feelings, and even smell are distorted, sometimes in dramatic ways, in a person under the influence of drugs such as marijuana and LSD.

## Causes of Substance-Related Disorders

- Most psychotropic drugs seem to produce positive effects by acting directly or indirectly on the dopaminergic mesolimbic system (the pleasure pathway). In addition, psychosocial factors such as expectations, stress, and cultural practices interact with the biological factors to influence drug use.

## Treatment of Substance-Related Disorders

- Substance dependence is treated successfully only in a minority of those affected, and the best results reflect the motivation of the drug user and a combination of biological and psychosocial treatments.
- Programs aimed at preventing drug abuse may have the greatest chance of significantly affecting the drug problem.

## Key Terms

substance-related disorders, 401
polysubstance use, 401
psychoactive substances, 402
substance intoxication, 402
substance abuse, 403
substance dependence, 403
tolerance, 403
withdrawal, 403

impulse control disorders, 404
depressants, 408
stimulants, 408
opioids, 408
hallucinogen, 408
alcohol use disorders, 408
withdrawal delirium, 410
fetal alcohol syndrome (FAS), 411

barbiturates, 413
benzodiazepines, 414
amphetamine use disorders, 416
cocaine use disorders, 417
nicotine use disorders, 419
caffeine use disorders, 420
opioid use disorders, 421

hallucinogen use disorders, 422
marijuana, 422
LSD (*d*-lysergic acid diethylamide), 423
agonist substitution, 434
antagonist drugs, 434
controlled drinking, 436
relapse prevention, 439
harm reduction, 439

## Answers to Concept Checks

**10.1 Part A**  1. b  2. a  3. d  4. c

  **Part B**  1. d  2. c  3. a  4. b

**10.2** 1. T

  2. F (the use of crack by pregnant mothers adversely affects some babies but not all)

  3. T

  4. T

  5. F (amphetamines are produced in the lab)

  6. F (marijuana produces the most variable reactions in people)

  7. T

**10.3 Part A**  1. d  2. b  3. a  4. c  5. f  6. e

  **Part B**  1. T  2. T  3. T  4. F (they would still act uninhibited)  5. F (all have an effect)

**10.4**  1. c  2. b  3. a  4. d  5. f  6. g  7. e  8. h  9. j  10. f  11. i

## InfoTrac College Edition

If your instructor ordered your book with InfoTrac College Edition, please explore this online library for additional readings, review, and a handy resource for short assignments. Go to:

**http://infotrac.thomsonlearning.com**

Enter these search terms: drug abuse, drug addicts, drug withdrawal symptoms, substance abuse, substance dependence, stimulants, narcotics, alcohol use diorders, fetal alcohol syndrome, marijuana

 ## The Abnormal Psychology Book Companion Website

Go to **www.essentialsabnormalpsych.nelson.com** for practice quiz questions, Internet links, critical thinking exercises, and more.

## Abnormal Psychology Live CD-ROM

- **Substance Use Disorder:** Tim describes the key criteria and shows how the disorder has had an impact on his life.
- **Nicotine Dependence:** Learn how nicotine increases the power of cues associated with smoking and how this research might aid the design of more effective programs to help people quit tobacco.

**Thomson NOW!** **http://hed.nelson.com** Go to this site for the link to ThomsonNow™, your one-stop study shop. Take a Pretest for this chapter and ThomsonNow™ will generate a personalized Study Plan based on your test results! The Study Plan will identify the topics you need to review and direct you to online resources to help you master those topics. You can then take a Posttest to help you determine the concepts you have mastered and what you still need work on.

## Video Concept Review

For challenging concepts that typically need more than one explanation, Mark Durand provides a video review via ThomsonNow™ of the following topic:

- The similarities between substance-related disorders and impulse-control disorders like pathological gambling.

# Chapter Quiz

1. The definition of substance abuse according to the DSM-IV-TR is based on:
   a. how much of the substance is consumed per day.
   b. how much of the substance is consumed per week.
   c. how significantly the substance interferes with the user's life.
   d. the type of substance used.

2. _____ is the need for greater amounts of a drug to experience the same effect, whereas _____ is the negative physical response that occurs when a drug is not taken.
   a. Tolerance; withdrawal
   b. Delirium; withdrawal
   c. Dependence; tolerance
   d. Accommodation; abuse

3. Which of the following statements most accurately describes the relationship between gender and alcohol consumption?
   a. Women are more likely to use alcohol, but men are more likely to be heavy drinkers.
   b. Men are more likely to use alcohol, but women are more likely to be heavy drinkers.
   c. Women are more likely to use alcohol and be heavy drinkers.
   d. Men are more likely to use alcohol and be heavy drinkers.

4. Dr. Myers prescribes medication to help control a patient's seizures. The patient reports that the medication also makes her feel calm and helps her sleep. Dr. Myers most likely prescribed a(n):
   a. hallucinogen.
   b. opiate.
   c. benzodiazepine.
   d. amphetamine.

5. The primary neurotransmitter affected by cocaine is _____, whereas one of the primary neurotransmitters affected by caffeine is _____.
   a. serotonin; norepinephrine
   b. acetylcholine; serotonin
   c. norepinephrine; dopamine
   d. dopamine; serotonin

6. For marijuana users, "reverse tolerance" occurs when:
   a. chronic use renders the user unable to feel high.
   b. a first-time user does not feel high.
   c. more pleasure from the drug is reported after repeated use.
   d. a chronic user experiences withdrawal symptoms.

7. Gino is a recovering alcoholic. To help with his treatment, Gino's physician prescribed a drug that causes Gino to experience shortness of breath and severe vomiting if he drinks. What drug has the physician prescribed?
   a. Antabuse
   b. MDMA
   c. amyl nitrate
   d. PCP

8. One psychological component of addiction may involve taking a drug to avoid negative feelings associated with coming down from a high. What theory describes this use of substances to avoid worsening lows?
   a. tolerance theory
   b. substance cycle theory
   c. opponent-process theory
   d. polydependence theory

9. Research shows that the way individuals think about a drug influences the way they act when using the drug. This phenomenon is known as the:
   a. tolerance paradigm.
   b. expectancy effect.
   c. dependency model.
   d. opponent-process theory.

10. Carlos's psychiatrist treats him for cocaine abuse by delivering a shock when Carlos attempts to use cocaine, a treatment known as _____. In contrast, Lisa's therapist has her imagine having painful seizures at the same time that Lisa is thinking about using cocaine, a treatment known as _____.
    a. aversion therapy; covert sensitization
    b. contingency management; relapse prevention
    c. narcotics anonymous; controlled use
    d. agonist substitution; aversive treatment

*(See the Appendix on page 601 for answers.)*

# Exploring Substance-Related Disorders

- Many kinds of problems can develop when people use and abuse substances that alter the way they think, feel, and behave.
- Once seen as due to personal weakness, drug abuse and dependence are now thought to be influenced by both biological and psychosocial factors.

## Social Influences

- Exposure to drug—through media, peers, parents, or lack of parental monitoring—versus no exposure to drug
- Social expectations and cultural norms for use
- Family, culture/society, and peers (all or some) supportive versus unsupportive of drug use

Brand X Pictures/Getty Images

## Psychological Influences

### Not to use
- Fear of effects of drug use
- Decision not to use drugs
- Feeling of confidence and self-esteem without drug use

### To use
- Drug use for pleasure; association with "feeling good" (positive reinforcement)
- Drug use to avoid pain and escape unpleasantness by "numbing out" (negative reinforcement)
- Feeling of being in control when on drug
- Positive expectations/urges about what drug use will be like
- Avoidance of withdrawal symptoms
- Presence of other psychological disorders: mood, anxiety, etc.

## CAUSES OF DRUG USE AND DRUG ABUSE

Photodisc/Getty Images

## Biological Influences

- Inherited genetic vulnerability affects
  —body's sensitivity to drug
  —body's ability to metabolize drug
- Drugs activate natural reward center ("pleasure pathway") in brain

## TREATMENT
Best to use multiple approaches

### Psychosocial Treatments

- Aversion therapy—to create negative associations with drug use (shocks with drinking, imagining nausea with cocaine use)
- Contingency management to change behaviours by rewarding chosen behaviours
- Alcoholics Anonymous and its variations
- Inpatient hospital treatment (can be expensive)
- Controlled use
- Community reinforcement
- Relapse prevention

### Biological Treatments

- Agonist substitution
  —replacing one drug with a similar one (methadone for heroin, nicotine gum and patches for cigarettes)
- Antagonist substitution
  —blocking one drug's effect with another drug (naltrexone for opiates and alcohol)
- Aversive treatments
  —making drug ingestion very unpleasant (using Antabuse, which causes nausea and vomiting when mixed with alcohol, to treat alcoholism)
- Drugs to help recovering person deal with withdrawal symptoms (clonidine for opiate withdrawal, sedatives for alcohol, etc.)

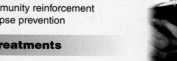

Photodisc/Getty Images

## Types of Drugs

### Depressants
**Examples:**
Alcohol, Barbiturates (sedatives: Amytal, Seconal, Nembutal), Benzodiazepines (antianxiety: Valium, Xanax, Halcion)

**Effects:**
- Decreased central nervous system activity
- Reduced levels of body arousal
- Relaxation

### Stimulants
**Examples:**
Amphetamines, Cocaine, Nicotine, Caffeine

**Effects:**
- Increased physical arousal
- User feels more alert and energetic

### Opiates
**Examples:**
Heroin, Morphine, Codeine

**Effects:**
- Narcotic—reduce pain and induce sleep and euphoria by mirroring opiates in the brain (endorphins, etc.)

### Hallucinogens
**Examples:**
Marijuana, LSD

**Effects:**
- Altered mental and emotional perception
- Distortion (sometimes dramatic) of sensory perceptions

Photodisc/Getty Images

# 11 Personality Disorders

**An Overview of Personality Disorders**
*Aspects of Personality Disorders*
*Categorical and Dimensional Models*
*Personality Disorder Clusters*
*Statistics and Development*
*Gender Differences*
*Comorbidity*

**Cluster A Personality Disorders**
*Paranoid Personality Disorder*
*Schizoid Personality Disorder*
*Schizotypal Personality Disorder*

**Cluster B Personality Disorders**
*Antisocial Personality Disorder*
*Borderline Personality Disorder*
*Histrionic Personality Disorder*
*Narcissistic Personality Disorder*

**Cluster C Personality Disorders**
*Avoidant Personality Disorder*
*Dependent Personality Disorder*
*Obsessive-Compulsive Personality Disorder*

**Personality Disorders Under Study**

**Visual Summary: Exploring Personality Disorders**

 **Abnormal Psychology Live CD-ROM**
*Antisocial Personality Disorder: George*
*Borderline Personality Disorders*

© Shutterstock

# An Overview of Personality Disorders

■ *Describe the essential features of personality disorders according to DSM-IV-TR and why they are listed on Axis II.*

According to DSM-IV-TR, **personality disorders** are "enduring patterns of perceiving, relating to, and thinking about the environment and oneself that are exhibited in a wide range of social and personal contexts," and "are inflexible and maladaptive, and cause significant functional impairment or subjective distress" (American Psychiatric Association, 2000a, p. 686). Now that you have taken out your yellow marker and highlighted this definition of personality disorders, what do you think it means?

We all think we know what a "personality" is. It's all the characteristic ways a person *behaves* and *thinks*: "Michael tends to be shy"; "Mindy likes to be very dramatic"; "Juan is always suspicious of others"; "Annette is very outgoing"; "Bruce seems to be very sensitive and gets upset very easily over minor things"; "Sean has the personality of an eggplant!" We tend to type people as behaving in one way in many different situations. For example, like Michael, many of us are shy with people we don't know, but we aren't shy around our friends. A truly shy person is shy even among people he or she has known for some time. The shyness is part of the way the person behaves in most situations. We have all probably behaved in all the ways noted here (dramatic, suspicious, outgoing, easily upset). However, we usually consider a way of behaving part of a person's personality only if it occurs many times and in many places. In this chapter we look at characteristic ways of behaving in relation to personality disorders. First we examine in some detail how we conceptualize personality disorders and the issues related to them; then we describe the disorders themselves.

## Aspects of Personality Disorders

What if a person's characteristic ways of thinking and behaving cause significant distress to the self or others? What if the person can't seem to change this way of relating to the world and is unhappy? We might consider this person to have a *personality disorder*. The DSM-IV-TR definition notes that these personality characteristics are "inflexible and maladaptive, and cause significant functional impairment or subjective distress." Unlike many of the disorders we have already discussed, personality disorders are chronic; they do not come and go but originate in childhood and continue throughout adulthood. Because they affect personality, these chronic problems pervade every aspect of a person's life. If a man

is overly suspicious, for example (a sign of a possible paranoid personality disorder), this trait will affect almost everything he does, including his employment (he may have to change jobs frequently if he believes co-workers conspire against him), his relationships (he may not be able to sustain a lasting relationship if he can't trust anyone), and even where he lives (he may have to move often if he suspects his landlord is out to get him).

DSM-IV-TR notes that having a personality disorder *may* distress the affected person. However, individuals with personality disorders may not feel any subjective distress; indeed, it may be acutely felt by others because of the actions of the person with the disorder. As noted by forensic psychologist Robert Hare at the University of British Columbia, this is particularly common with antisocial personality disorder, because the individual may show a blatant disregard for the rights of others yet exhibit no remorse (Hare, 1993). In certain cases, someone other than the person with the personality disorder must decide whether the disorder is causing significant functional impairment, because the affected person often cannot make such a judgment.

DSM-IV-TR lists 10 specific personality disorders and several others that are being studied for future consideration; we review them all. Unfortunately, as we see later, many people who have personality disorders in addition to other psychological problems tend to do poorly in treatment. Data from several studies show that people who are depressed have a worse outcome in treatment if they also have a personality disorder (Sanderson & Clarkin, 1994; Shea et al., 1990). Nonetheless, the prospects for treatment success for people who have personality disorders may be more optimistic than previously thought (Howes & Vallis, 1996; Perry, Banon, & Ianni, 1999). For example, Michael Vallis and his colleagues have suggested that there are grounds to be cautiously optimistic about the potential uses of cognitive therapy in individuals with personality disorders (Vallis, Howes, & Standage, 2000).

Most disorders we discuss in this book are in Axis I of DSM-IV-TR, which includes the standard

---

**personality disorders**  Enduring maladaptive patterns of relating to the environment and oneself, exhibited in a wide range of contexts that cause significant functional impairment or subjective distress.

traditional disorders. The personality disorders are included in a separate axis, Axis II, because as a group they are distinct. The characteristic traits are more ingrained and inflexible in people who have personality disorders, and the disorders themselves are less likely to be successfully modified.

Having personality disorders on a separate axis requires the clinician to consider in each assessment whether the person has a personality disorder. In the axis system, a patient can receive a diagnosis on only Axis I, only Axis II, or on both axes. A diagnosis on both Axis I and Axis II indicates that a person has both a current disorder (Axis I) and a more chronic problem (e.g., personality disorder). As you will see, it is not unusual for one person to be diagnosed on both axes.

You may be surprised to learn that the category of personality disorders is controversial, because it involves a number of unresolved issues. Examining these issues can help us understand all the disorders described in this book.

## *Categorical and Dimensional Models*

Most of us are sometimes suspicious of others and a little paranoid, overly dramatic, too self-involved, or reclusive. Fortunately, these characteristics have not lasted too long or been overly intense, and they haven't significantly impaired how we live and work. People with personality disorders, however, display problem characteristics over extended periods and in many situations, which can cause great emotional pain for themselves and/or others. Their difficulty, then, can be seen as one of *degree* rather than *kind;* in other words, the problems of people with personality disorders may just be extreme versions of the problems many of us experience on a temporary basis, such as being shy or suspicious.

The distinction between problems of *degree* and problems of *kind* is usually described in terms of *dimensions* instead of *categories*. The issue that continues to be debated in the field is whether personality disorders are extreme versions of otherwise normal personality variations (dimensions) or ways of relating that are different from psychologically healthy behaviour (categories; Costa & Widiger, 1994; Gunderson, 1992). For example, John Livesley and his colleagues have been strongly advocating for a change from the current categorical approach to personality disorders used in the DSM-IV-TR to a dimensional-based approach (e.g., Livesley, Schroeder, Jackson, & Jang, 1994). We can see the difference between dimensions and categories in everyday life. For example, we often label people's size categorically, as tall, medium, or short. But height can also be viewed dimensionally, in inches or centimetres.

Most people in the field see personality disorders as extremes on one or more personality dimensions. Yet because of the way people are diagnosed with the DSM, the personality disorders—like most other disorders—end up being viewed in categories. You have two choices—either you do (yes) or you do not (no) have a disorder. For example, either you have antisocial personality disorder or you don't. The DSM doesn't rate how dependent you are; if you meet the criteria, you are labelled as having dependent personality disorder. There is no in between when it comes to personality disorders.

There are advantages to using categorical models of behaviour, the most important being their convenience. With simplification, however, comes problems. One is that the mere act of using categories leads clinicians to *reify* them; that is, to view disorders as real "things," comparable to the realness of an infection or a broken arm. Some argue that personality disorders are not things that exist but points at which society decides a particular way of relating to the world has become a problem. There is the important unresolved issue again: Are personality disorders just an extreme variant of normal personality, or are they distinctly different disorders?

Many researchers believe that many or all personality disorders represent extremes on one or more personality dimensions. Consequently, some have proposed that the DSM-IV-TR personality disorders section be replaced or at least supplemented by a dimensional model (Livesley & Jang, 2000; Widiger, 1991) in which individuals not only would be given categorical diagnoses but also would be rated on a series of personality dimensions. Widiger (1991) believes such a system would have at least three advantages over a purely categorical system: (1) It would retain more information about each individual, (2) it would be more flexible because it would permit both categorical and dimensional differentiations among individuals, and (3) it would avoid the often arbitrary decisions involved in assigning a person to a diagnostic category.

Although no general consensus exists about what the basic personality dimensions might be, there are several contenders (Eysenck & Eysenck, 1975; Tellegen, 1978; Watson, Clark, & Harkness, 1994). One of the more widely accepted is called the *five-factor model*, or the "Big Five," and is taken from work on normal personality (Costa & McCrae, 1990; Goldberg, 1993; Stewart & Devine, 2000). In this model, people can be rated on a series of personality dimensions, and the combination of five components describes why people are so different. The five factors or dimensions are *extraversion* (talkative, assertive, and active versus silent, passive, and reserved), *agreeableness* (kind, trusting, and warm versus hostile, selfish, and mistrustful), *conscientiousness* (organized, thorough, and reliable versus careless, negligent, and unreliable), *neuroticism* (nervous, moody, and temperamental versus even-tempered), and *openness to experience* (imaginative, curious, and creative versus shallow and imperceptive; Goldberg, 1993). On each dimension, people are rated high, low, or somewhere between.

Cross-cultural research establishes the universal nature of the five dimensions. In German, Portuguese, Hebrew, Chinese, Korean, and Japanese samples, individuals have personality trait structures similar to North American samples (McCrae & Costa, 1997). A number of researchers, including John Livesley and his colleagues, are trying to determine whether people with personality disorders can also be rated in a meaningful way along the dimensions identified in the five-factor model and whether the system will help us better understand these disorders (Krueger, Caspi, Moffitt, Silva, & McGee, 1996; Schroeder, Wormworth, & Livesley, 1993).

## Personality Disorder Clusters

DSM-IV-TR divides the personality disorders into three groups, or *clusters;* this will probably continue until a strong scientific basis is established for viewing them differently (American Psychiatric Association,

2000a). The cluster division (see Table 11.1) is based on resemblance. Cluster A is called the odd or eccentric cluster; it includes paranoid, schizoid, and schizotypal personality disorders. Cluster B is the dramatic, emotional, or erratic cluster; it consists of antisocial, borderline, histrionic, and narcissistic personality disorders. Montreal researchers Karl Looper and Joel Paris (2000) have found that all four disorders in this cluster are characterized by elevated impulsivity. Cluster C is the anxious or fearful cluster; it includes avoidant, dependent, and obsessive-compulsive personality disorders. Michael Bagby and his colleagues at the Centre for Addiction and Mental Health in Toronto have obtained some research support for the existence of these three clusters (Bagby, Joffe, Parker, & Schuller, 1993). We follow this order in our review.

## Statistics and Development

Canadian data on the prevalence of personality disorders are generally lacking, save in the case of antisocial personality disorder (Health Canada, 2002). However, American studies indicate that personality disorders are found in 0.5% to 2.5% of the general population, 10% to 30% of all individuals served in inpatient settings, and in 2% to 10% of those individuals in outpatient settings (American

**TABLE 11.1** DSM-IV-TR Personality Disorders

| Personality Disorder | Description |
|---|---|
| **Cluster A—Odd or Eccentric Disorders** | |
| Paranoid personality disorder | A pervasive distrust and suspiciousness of others such that their motives are interpreted as malevolent. |
| Schizoid personality disorder | A pervasive pattern of detachment from social relationships and a restricted range of expression of emotions in interpersonal settings. |
| Schizotypal personality disorder | A pervasive pattern of social and interpersonal deficits marked by acute discomfort with and reduced capacity for close relationships and by cognitive or perceptual distortions and eccentricities of behaviour. |
| **Cluster B—Dramatic, Emotional, or Erratic Disorders** | |
| Antisocial personality disorder | A pervasive pattern of disregard for and violation of the rights of others. |
| Borderline personality disorder | A pervasive pattern of instability of interpersonal relationships, self-image, affect, and control over impulses. |
| Histrionic personality disorder | A pervasive pattern of excessive emotion and attention seeking. |
| Narcissistic personality disorder | A pervasive pattern of grandiosity (in fantasy or behaviour), need for admiration, and lack of empathy. |
| **Cluster C—Anxious or Fearful Disorders** | |
| Avoidant personality disorder | A pervasive pattern of social inhibition, feelings of inadequacy, and hypersensitivity to negative evaluation. |
| Dependent personality disorder | A pervasive and excessive need to be taken care of, which leads to submissive and clinging behaviour and fears of separation. |
| Obsessive-compulsive personality disorder | A pervasive pattern of preoccupation with orderliness, perfectionism, and mental and interpersonal control at the expense of flexibility, openness, and efficiency. |

*Source:* From *Diagnostic and Statistical Manual of Mental Disorders,* Fourth Edition, Text Revision. Copyright © 2000 American Psychiatric Association. Reprinted with permission.

Personality disorders originate in childhood or adolescence.

© Paula Lerner/Woodfin Camp

Psychiatric Association, 2000a), which makes them relatively common. As you can see from Table 11.2, schizoid, narcissistic, and avoidant personality disorders are relatively rare, occurring in less than 1% of the general population. Paranoid, schizotypal, antisocial, borderline, histrionic, dependent, and obsessive-compulsive personality disorders are found in 1% to 4% of the general population.

Personality disorders are thought to originate in childhood or adolescence and continue into the adult years (Phillips, Yen, & Gunderson, 2003) and to be so ingrained that an onset is difficult to pinpoint. Maladaptive personality characteristics develop over time into the maladaptive behaviour patterns that create distress for the affected person and draw the attention of others. Our relative lack of information about such important features of personality disorders as their developmental course is a repeating theme. The gaps in our knowledge of the course of about half these disorders are visible in Table 11.2. One reason for this dearth of research is that many individuals seek treatment not in the early developmental phases of their disorder but only after years of distress. This delay makes it difficult to study people with personality disorders from the beginning, although a few research studies have helped us understand the development of several disorders.

People with borderline personality disorder are characterized by their volatile and unstable relationships; they tend to have persistent problems in early adulthood, with frequent hospitalizations, unstable personal relationships, severe depression, and suicidal gestures. Approximately 6% succeed in their suicidal attempts (J. C. Perry, 1993; Stone, 1989). On the bright side, their symptoms gradually improve if they survive into their 30s (Dulit, Marin, & Frances, 1993), although elderly individuals may have difficulty making plans and may be disruptive in nursing

## TABLE 11.2  Statistics and Development of Personality Disorders

| Disorder | Prevalence | Gender Differences | Course |
|---|---|---|---|
| Paranoid personality disorder | 1% to 3% (Bernstein, Useda, & Siever, 1993) | More common in males (O'Brien, Trestman, & Siever, 1993) | Insufficient information |
| Schizoid personality disorder | Less than 1% in United States, Canada, New Zealand, Taiwan (Weissman, 1993) | More common in males (O'Brien et al., 1993) | Insufficient information |
| Schizotypal personality disorder | 3% to 5% (Weissman, 1993) | More common in males (Kotsaftis & Neale, 1993) | Chronic: some go on to develop schizophrenia |
| Antisocial personality disorder | 3% in males; less than 1% in females (Sutker, Bugg, & West, 1993) | More common in males (Dulit, Marin, & Frances, 1993) | Dissipates after age 40 (Hare, McPherson, & Forth, 1988) |
| Borderline personality disorder | 1% to 3% (Widiger & Weissman, 1991) | Females make up 75% of cases (Dulit et al., 1993) | Symptoms gradually improve if individuals survive into their 30s (Dulit et al., 1993). Approximately 6% die by suicide (J. C. Perry, 1993). |
| Histrionic personality disorder | 2% (Nestadt et al., 1990) | Equal numbers of males and females (Nestadt et al., 1990) | Chronic |
| Narcissistic personality disorder | Less than 1% (Zimmerman & Coryell, 1990) | More prevalent among men | May improve over time (Cooper & Ronningstam, 1992; Gunderson, Ronningstam, & Smith, 1991) |
| Avoidant personality disorder | Less than 1% (Reich, Yates, & Nduaguba, 1989; Zimmerman & Coryell, 1990) | Equal numbers of males and females (Millon, 1986) | Insufficient information |
| Dependent personality disorder | 2% (Zimmerman & Coryell, 1989) | May be equal numbers of male and females (Reich, 1987) | Insufficient information |
| Obsessive-compulsive personality disorder | 4% (Weissman, 1993) | More common in males (Stone, 1993) | Insufficient information |

homes (Rosowsky & Gurian, 1992). People with antisocial personality disorder display a characteristic disregard for the rights and feelings of others; they tend to continue their destructive behaviours of lying and manipulation through adulthood. Fortunately, as indicated by the research of Robert Hare, Leslie McPherson, and Adelle Forth (1988), some tend to burn out after the age of 40 and engage in fewer criminal activities. As a group, however, the problems of people with personality disorders continue, as shown when researchers follow their progress over the years (Phillips & Gunderson, 2000).

## Gender Differences

Borderline personality disorder is diagnosed much more frequently in females, who make up about 75% of the identified cases (Dulit et al., 1993; see Table 11.2). Historically, histrionic and dependent personality disorders were identified by clinicians more often in women (Dulit et al., 1993; Stone, 1993), but according to more recent studies of their prevalence in the general population, equal numbers of males and females may have histrionic and dependent personality disorders (Lilienfeld, Van Valkenburg, Larntz, & Akiskal, 1986; Nestadt et al., 1990; Reich, 1987). If this observation holds up in future studies, why have these disorders been predominantly diagnosed among females in general clinical practice and in other studies (Dulit et al., 1993)?

Do the disparities indicate differences between men and women in basic genetic makeup and/or sociocultural experiences, or do they represent biases on the part of the clinicians who make the diagnoses? Take, for example, a study by Ford and Widiger (1989), who sent fictitious case histories to clinical psychologists for diagnosis. One case described a person with *antisocial personality disorder*, which is characterized by irresponsible and reckless behaviour and usually diagnosed in males; the other case described a person with *histrionic personality disorder*, which is characterized by excessive emotionality and attention seeking and more often diagnosed in females. The patient was identified as male in some versions of each case and as female in others, although everything else was identical. As the graph in Figure 11.1 shows, when the antisocial personality disorder case was labelled male, most psychologists gave the correct diagnosis. However, when the same case was labelled female, most psychologists diagnosed it as histrionic personality disorder rather than antisocial personality disorder. This finding of an underdiagnosis of antisocial personality disorder in female clients was replicated in a similar study conducted in Toronto with psychiatry residents (Belitsky et al., 1996). In the original Ford and Widiger (1989) study, being labelled a

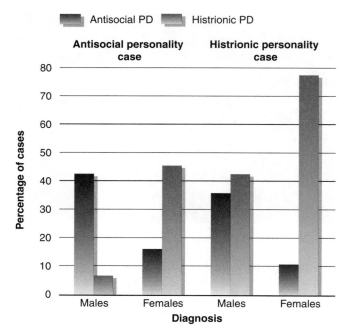

**Figure 11.1**  ■  Gender bias in diagnosing personality disorders (PDs). Data are shown for the percentage of cases clinicians rated as antisocial personality disorder or histrionic personality disorder, depending on whether the case was described as a male or a female. (From Ford & Widiger, 1989.)

woman increased the likelihood of a diagnosis of histrionic personality disorder. The authors concluded that the psychologists incorrectly diagnosed more women as having histrionic personality disorder (Ford & Widiger, 1989).

Such gender differences in diagnoses have been criticized by several authors. For example, some have argued that histrionic personality disorder, like several of the other personality disorders, is biased against females. Many of the features of histrionic personality disorder, such as overdramatization, vanity, seductiveness, and overconcern with physical appearance, are characteristic of the Western "stereotypical female" (Kaplan, 1983). This disorder may simply be the embodiment of extremely "feminine" traits (Chodoff, 1982); branding such an individual mentally ill, according to Kaplan, reflects society's inherent bias against females. Interestingly, the "macho" personality (Mosher & Sirkin, 1984), in which the individual possesses stereotypically masculine traits, is nowhere to be found in the DSM (see also Pantony & Caplan, 1991). What do you think the sex ratio would be for people diagnosed with this "personality disorder"?

Remember, however, that just because certain disorders are observed more in men or in women doesn't necessarily indicate bias (Lilienfeld et al., 1986). And when it is present, bias can occur at different stages of the diagnostic process. The criteria for the disorder may themselves be biased *(criterion gender bias)*, or the assessment measures and the way they are used may be biased *(assessment gender bias;* Widiger & Spitzer, 1991). For example, Westen (1997) found that although clinicians use the behaviours outlined in DSM-IV-TR for Axis I disorders, for the personality disorders in Axis II they tend to use subjective impressions based on their interpersonal interactions with the client. This difference may well allow more bias, including gender bias, to influence diagnoses of personality disorders.

## Comorbidity

Looking at Table 11.2 and adding up the prevalence rates across the personality disorders, you might conclude that between 20% and 30% of all people are affected. In fact, the percentage of people in the general population with a personality disorder is estimated to be between 0.5% and 2.5% (American Psychiatric Association, 2000a). What accounts for this discrepancy? A major concern with the personality disorders is that people tend to be diagnosed with more than one. The term *comorbidity* historically describes the condition in which a person has multiple diseases (Caron & Rutter, 1991). A fair amount of disagreement is ongoing about whether the term should be used with psychological disorders because of the frequent overlap of different disorders (e.g., Nurnberg et al., 1991). In just one example, Morey (1988) conducted a study of 291 people who were diagnosed with personality disorder and found considerable overlap (see Table 11.3). In the far left column of Table 11.3 is the primary diagnosis, and across the table are the percentages of people who also meet the criteria for other disorders. For

Gender bias may affect the diagnosis of clinicians who associate certain behavioural characteristics with one sex or the other.

example, a person identified with borderline personality disorder also has a 32% likelihood (i.e., a one in three chance) of fitting the definition of another supposedly different disorder—paranoid personality disorder (Grove & Tellegen, 1991).

Do people really tend to have more than one personality disorder? Are the ways we define these

**TABLE 11.3**   Diagnostic Overlap Of Personality Disorders

Percentage of People Qualifying for Other Personality Disorder Diagnoses

| Diagnosis | Paranoid | Schizoid | Schizotypal | Antisocial | Borderline | Histrionic | Narcissistic | Avoidant | Dependent | Obsessive-compulsive |
|---|---|---|---|---|---|---|---|---|---|---|
| Paranoid | | 23.4 | 25.0 | 7.8 | 48.4 | 28.1 | 35.9 | 48.4 | 29.7 | 7.8 |
| Schizoid | 46.9 | | 37.5 | 3.1 | 18.8 | 9.4 | 28.1 | 53.1 | 18.8 | 15.6 |
| Schizotypal | 59.3 | 44.4 | | 3.7 | 33.3 | 18.5 | 33.3 | 59.3 | 29.6 | 11.1 |
| Antisocial | 27.8 | 5.6 | 5.6 | | 44.4 | 33.3 | 55.6 | 16.7 | 11.1 | 0.0 |
| Borderline | 32.0 | 6.2 | 9.3 | 8.2 | | 36.1 | 30.9 | 36.1 | 34.0 | 2.1 |
| Histrionic | 28.6 | 4.8 | 7.9 | 9.5 | 55.6 | | 54.0 | 31.7 | 30.2 | 4.8 |
| Narcissistic | 35.9 | 14.1 | 14.1 | 15.6 | 46.9 | 53.1 | | 35.9 | 26.6 | 10.9 |
| Avoidant | 39.2 | 21.5 | 20.3 | 3.8 | 44.3 | 25.3 | 29.1 | | 40.5 | 16.5 |
| Dependent | 29.2 | 9.2 | 12.3 | 3.1 | 50.8 | 29.2 | 26.2 | 49.2 | | 9.2 |
| Obsessive-compulsive | 21.7 | 21.7 | 13.0 | 0.0 | 8.7 | 13.0 | 30.4 | 56.5 | 26.1 | |

*Source:* "Personality disorders in DSM-III and DSM-III-R," by Lesley C. Morey, 1988, *American Journal of Psychiatry,* 145, 537–577. Copyright © 1988 by the American Psychiatric Association. Reprinted with permission.

disorders inaccurate, and do we need to improve our definitions so that they do not overlap? Or did we divide the disorders in the wrong way to begin with, and do we need to rethink the categories? Such questions about comorbidity are just a few of the important issues faced by researchers who study personality disorders.

**Specific Personality Disorders**   We now review the personality disorders currently in DSM-IV-TR, 10 in all, and look briefly at a few categories being considered for inclusion.

## Concept Check 11.1

Fill in the blanks to complete the following statements about personality disorders.

1. Unlike many disorders, personality disorders are _____; they originate in childhood and continue throughout adulthood.

2. Personality disorders as a group are distinct and therefore placed on a separate axis, _____.

3. It's debated whether personality disorders are extreme versions of otherwise normal personality variations (therefore classified as dimensions) or ways of relating that are different from psychologically healthy behaviour (classified as _____).

4. Personality disorders are divided into three clusters or groups: _____ contains the odd or eccentric disorders; _____ the dramatic, emotional, and erratic disorders; and _____ the anxious and fearful disorders.

5. Gender differences are evident in the research of personality disorders, although some differences in the findings may be because of _____.

6. People with personality disorders are often diagnosed with other disorders, a phenomenon called _____.

# Cluster A Personality Disorders

■ *Describe the essential characteristics of each of the Cluster A (odd/eccentric) personality disorders, including information pertaining to etiology and treatment.*

Three personality disorders—paranoid, schizoid, and schizotypal—share common features that resemble some of the psychotic symptoms seen in schizophrenia. These "odd" or "eccentric" personality disorders are described next.

## Paranoid Personality Disorder

Although it is probably adaptive to be a little wary of other people and their motives, being too distrustful can interfere with making friends, working with others, and, in general, getting through daily interactions in a functional way. People with **paranoid personality disorder** are excessively mistrustful and suspicious of others without justification. They assume other people are out to harm or trick them; therefore, they tend not to confide in others. Consider the case of Jake.

### Jake
#### Victim of Conspiracy?

Jake grew up in a middle-class neighbourhood, and although he never got in serious trouble, he had a reputation in high school for arguing with teachers and classmates. After high school he enrolled in the local community college, but he flunked out after the first year. Jake's lack of

**paranoid personality disorder**   Cluster A (odd or eccentric) personality disorder involving pervasive distrust and suspiciousness of others such that their motives are interpreted as malevolent.

success in school was in part attributable to his failure to take responsibility for his poor grades. He began to develop conspiracy theories about fellow students and professors, believing they worked together to see him fail. Jake bounced from job to job, each time complaining that his employer was spying on him. His parents brought him to a psychologist, and he was diagnosed with paranoid personality disorder.

## Clinical Description

The defining characteristic of people with paranoid personality disorder is a pervasive unjustified distrust (American Psychiatric Association, 2000a). Certainly there may be times when someone is deceitful and "out to get you"; however, people with paranoid personality disorder are suspicious in situations where most other people would agree their suspicions are unfounded. Even events that have nothing to do with them are interpreted as personal attacks (Phillips & Gunderson, 2000). These people would view a neighbour's barking dog or a delayed airline flight as a deliberate attempt to annoy them. Unfortunately, such mistrust often extends to people close to them and makes meaningful relationships very difficult. Imagine what a lonely existence this must be! Suspiciousness and mistrust can show themselves in a number of ways. People with paranoid personality disorder may be argumentative, may complain, or may be quiet, but they are obviously hostile toward others. They often appear tense and are "ready to pounce" when they think they've been slighted by someone. These individuals are very sensitive to criticism and have an excessive need for autonomy (Bernstein, Useda, & Siever, 1993).

## Causes

Evidence for biological contributions to paranoid personality disorder is limited. Some research suggests the disorder may be slightly more common among the relatives of people who have schizophrenia, although the association does not seem to be strong (Bernstein et al., 1993; Coryell & Zimmerman, 1989; Kendler & Gruenberg, 1982). In other words, relatives of individuals with schizophrenia *may* be more likely to have paranoid personality disorder than people who do not have a relative with schizophrenia. As we see later with the other odd or eccentric personality disorders in Cluster A, there seems to be some relationship with schizophrenia, although its exact nature is not yet clear (Siever, 1992).

Psychological contributions to this disorder are even less certain, although some interesting

### Disorder Criteria Summary
#### Paranoid Personality Disorder

Features of paranoid personality disorder include:
- Pervasive distrust and suspiciousness of others
- Suspicion that others are exploiting, harming, or deceiving the person
- Preoccupation with unjustified doubts about the loyalty of friends or associates
- Tendency to read hidden demeaning or threatening meanings into benign remarks
- Bearing persistent grudges over insults, injuries, or slights
- Person perceives attack on his or her character or reputation that are not apparent to others
- Recurrent suspicions, without justification, regarding the fidelity of spouse or sexual partner
- Does not occur exclusively with schizophrenia, a mood disorder with psychotic features, or another psychotic disorder

*Source:* Based on DSM-IV-TR. Used with permission from the *Diagnostic and Statistical Manual of Mental Disorders*, Fourth Edition, Text Revision. Copyright 2000. American Psychiatric Association.

speculations have been made. Some psychologists point directly to the thoughts of people with paranoid personality disorder as a way of explaining their behaviour. One view is that people with this disorder have the following basic mistaken assumptions about others: "People are malevolent and deceptive," "They'll attack you if they get the chance," and "You can be OK only if you stay on your toes" (Freeman, Pretzer, Fleming, & Simon, 1990). This is a maladaptive way to view the world, yet it seems to pervade every aspect of the lives of these individuals. Although we don't know why they develop these perceptions, some speculation is that the roots are in their early upbringing. Their parents may teach them to be careful about making mistakes and to impress on them that they are different from other people (Turkat & Maisto, 1985). This vigilance causes them to see signs that other people are deceptive and malicious (Beck & Freeman, 1990). It is certainly true that people are not always benevolent and sincere, and our interactions are sometimes ambiguous enough to make other people's intentions unclear. Looking too closely at what other people say and do can sometimes lead you to misinterpret them.

Cultural factors have also been implicated in paranoid personality disorder. Certain groups of people, such as prisoners, refugees, people with hearing impairments, and the elderly, are thought to be particularly susceptible because of their unique experiences (Christenson & Blazer, 1984; O'Brien, Trestman, & Siever, 1993). Imagine how

People with paranoid personality disorder often believe that impersonal situations exist specifically to annoy or otherwise disturb them.

you might view other people if you were an immigrant who had difficulty with the language and the customs of your new culture. Such innocuous things as other people laughing or talking quietly might be interpreted as somehow directed at you.

We have seen how someone could misinterpret ambiguous situations as malevolent. Therefore, cognitive and cultural factors may interact to produce the suspiciousness observed in some people with paranoid personality disorder.

### Treatment

Because people with paranoid personality disorder are mistrustful of everyone, they are unlikely to seek professional help when they need it, and they also have difficulty developing the trusting relationships necessary for successful therapy (Phillips & Gunderson, 2000). When these individuals finally do seek therapy, the trigger is usually a crisis in their lives or other problems such as anxiety or depression and not necessarily their personality disorder.

Therapists try to provide an atmosphere conducive to developing a sense of trust (Freeman et al., 1990). They often use cognitive therapy to counter the person's mistaken assumptions about others, focusing on changing the person's beliefs that all people are malevolent and most people cannot be trusted (Tyrer & Davidson, 2000). Be forewarned, however, that to date there are no confirmed demonstrations that any form of treatment can significantly improve the lives of people with paranoid personality disorder. Nonetheless, a review of the literature by Quebec researchers Stephane Bouchard and his colleagues concluded that cognitive restructuring can be helpful in reducing paranoid beliefs (Bouchard, Vallieres, Roy, & Maziade, 1996). Unfortunately, an Australian survey of mental health professionals indicated that only 11% of therapists who treat paranoid personality disorder thought these individuals would continue in therapy long enough to be helped (Quality Assurance Project, 1990).

## Schizoid Personality Disorder

Do you know someone who is a "loner"? Someone who would choose a solitary walk over an invitation to a party? A person who comes to class alone, sits alone, and leaves alone? Now, magnify this preference for isolation many times over and you can begin to grasp the impact of **schizoid personality disorder** (Kalus, Bernstein, & Siever, 1995). People with this personality disorder show a pattern of detachment from social relationships and a very limited range of emotions in interpersonal situations (Phillips & Gunderson, 2000). They seem "aloof," "cold," and "indifferent" to other people. The term *schizoid* is relatively old, having been used by Bleuler (1924) to describe people who have a tendency to turn inward and away from the outside world. These people were said to lack emotional expressiveness and pursued vague interests. Consider the case of Mr. Z.

### Mr. Z.
#### All on His Own

A 39-year-old scientist was referred after his return from being stationed in Baffin Island where he had stopped cooperating with others, withdrawn to his room, and begun drinking on his own. Mr. Z. was orphaned at 4 years old, raised by an aunt until 9, and subsequently looked after by an aloof housekeeper. At university he excelled at physics, but chess was his only contact with others. Throughout his subsequent life he made no close friends and engaged primarily in solitary activities. Until his move to Baffin Island, he had been quite successful in his research work in physics. He was now, some months after his return, drinking at least a bottle of Schnapps each day and his work had continued to deteriorate. He presented as self-contained and unobtrusive, and he was difficult to engage effectively. He was at a loss to explain his colleagues' anger at his aloofness in Baffin Island and appeared indifferent to their opinion of him.

**schizoid personality disorder** Cluster A (odd or eccentric) personality disorder featuring a pervasive pattern of detachment from social relationships and a restricted range of expression of emotions.

He did not appear to require any interpersonal relations.

(Case excerpt from "Treatment Outlines for Paranoid, Schizotypal and Schizoid Personality Disorders," by the Quality Assurance Project, 1990, *Australian and New Zealand Journal of Psychiatry*, 24, 339–350. Reprinted with permission of the Royal Australian and New Zealand College of Psychiatrists.)

## Clinical Description

Individuals with schizoid personality disorder seem neither to desire nor to enjoy closeness with others, including romantic or sexual relationships. As a result they appear cold and detached and do not seem affected by praise or criticism. Unfortunately, homelessness appears to be prevalent among people with this personality disorder, perhaps as a result of their lack of close friendships and lack of dissatisfaction about not having a sexual relationship with another person (Rouff, 2000).

### Disorder Criteria Summary
Schizoid Personality Disorder

Features of schizoid personality disorder include:

- Pervasive pattern of detachment from social relationships and a restricted range of expression of emotions, beginning by early adulthood
- Lack of desire for or enjoyment of close relationships, including family relationships
- Almost always chooses solitary activities
- Little if any interest in sexual experiences with another person
- Takes pleasure in few, if any, activities
- Lacks close friends or confidantes other than first-degree relatives
- Appears indifferent to praise or criticism from others
- Shows emotional coldness or detachment
- Does not occur exclusively with schizophrenia or another disorder

*Source:* Based on DSM-IV-TR. Used with permission from the *Diagnostic and Statistical Manual of Mental Disorders*, Fourth Edition, Text Revision. Copyright 2000. American Psychiatric Association.

The social deficiencies of people with schizoid personality disorder are similar to those of people with paranoid personality disorder, although they are more extreme. As Beck and Freeman (1990) put it, they "consider themselves to be observers rather than participants in the world around them" (p. 125). They do not seem to have the very unusual thought processes that characterize the other disorders in Cluster A (Kalus, Bernstein, & Siever, 1993;

see Table 11.4). For example, people with paranoid and schizotypal personality disorders often have ideas of reference, mistaken beliefs that meaningless events relate just to them. In contrast, those with schizoid personality disorder share the social isolation, poor rapport, and constricted affect (showing neither positive nor negative emotion) seen in people with paranoid personality disorder. We see in Chapter 12 that this distinction among psychotic-like symptoms is important to understanding people with schizophrenia, some of whom show the "positive" symptoms (actively unusual behaviours such as ideas of reference) and others only the "negative" symptoms (the more passive manifestations of social isolation or poor rapport with others).

| **TABLE 11.4** | Grouping Schema for Cluster A Disorders | |
|---|---|---|
| **Psychotic-like Symptoms** | | |
| Cluster A Personality Disorder | "Positive" (e.g., ideas of reference, magical thinking, and perceptual distortions) | "Negative" (e.g., social isolation, poor rapport, and constricted affect) |
| Paranoid | Yes | Yes |
| Schizoid | No | Yes |
| Schizotypal | Yes | No |

*Source:* Adapted from "Schizophrenia Spectrum Personality Disorders," by L. J. Siever, in *Review of Psychiatry*, Vol. 11, A. Tasman and M. B. Riba (eds.), 1992, pp. 25–42. Copyright © 1992, the American Psychiatric Press.

## Causes and Treatment

Research on the genetic, neurobiological, and psychosocial contributions to schizoid personality disorder remains to be conducted (Phillips et al., 2003). Childhood shyness is reported as a precursor to later adult schizoid personality disorder. It may be that this personality trait is inherited and serves as an important determinant in the development of this disorder. Research over the past several decades has pointed to biological causes of the childhood disorder of autism (see Chapter 13)—a disorder characterized by pervasive impairments in social interactions. It is possible that a similar biological dysfunction combines with early learning or early problems with interpersonal relationships to produce the social deficits that define schizoid personality disorder (Wolff, 2000). For example, research on the neurochemical dopamine suggests that people with a lower density of dopamine receptors scored higher on a measure of "detachment" (Farde, Gustavsson, & Jonsson, 1997). It may be that dopamine (which seems to be involved with schizophrenia as well) may contribute to the social aloofness of people with schizoid personality disorder.

It is rare for a person with this disorder to request treatment except in response to a crisis such as extreme depression or losing a job (Kalus et al., 1995). Therapists often begin treatment by pointing out the value in social relationships. The person with the disorder may even need to be taught the emotions felt by others to learn empathy (Beck & Freeman, 1990). Because their social skills were never established or have atrophied through lack of use, people with schizoid personality disorder often receive social skills training. The therapist takes the part of a friend or significant other in a technique known as *role-playing* and helps the patient practise establishing and maintaining social relationships (Beck & Freeman, 1990). This type of social skills training is helped by identifying a social network—a person or people who will be supportive (Stone, 2001). Outcome research on this type of approach is unfortunately quite limited, so we must be cautious in evaluating the effectiveness of treatment for people with schizoid personality disorder.

## Schizotypal Personality Disorder

People with **schizotypal personality disorder** are typically socially isolated, like those with schizoid personality disorder. In addition, they behave in ways that would seem unusual to many of us (Siever, Bernstein, & Silverman, 1995), and they tend to be suspicious and to have odd beliefs (Kotsaftis & Neale, 1993). Consider the case of Mr. S.

## Mr. S.
### Man with a Mission

Mr. S. was a 35-year-old chronically unemployed man who had been referred by a physician because of a vitamin deficiency. This problem was thought to have arisen because Mr. S. avoided any foods that "could have been contaminated by machine." He had begun to develop alternative ideas about diet in his 20s, and he soon left his family and began to study an Eastern religion. "It opened my third eye; corruption is all about," he said.

He now lived by himself on a small farm in British Columbia, attempting to grow his own food and bartering for items he could not grow himself. He spent his days and evenings researching the origins and mechanisms of food contamination and, because of this knowledge, had developed a small band who followed his ideas. He had never married and maintained little contact with his family: "I've never been close to my father. I'm a vegetarian."

He said he intended to take a herbalism course to improve his diet before returning to his life on the farm. He had refused medication from the physician and became uneasy when the facts of his deficiency were discussed with him.

(Case excerpt from "Treatment Outlines for Paranoid, Schizotypal and Schizoid Personality Disorders," by the Quality Assurance Project, 1990, *Australian and New Zealand Journal of Psychiatry, 24,* 339–350. Reprinted with permission of the Royal Australian and New Zealand College of Psychiatrists.)

### Clinical Description

People given a diagnosis of schizotypal personality disorder are often considered "odd" or "bizarre" because of how they relate to other people, how they think and behave, and even how they dress. They have *ideas of reference,* which means they think insignificant events relate directly to them. For example, they may believe that somehow everyone on a passing city bus is talking about them, yet they may be able to acknowledge this is unlikely. Again, as we see in Chapter 12, some people with schizophrenia also have ideas of reference, but they are usually not able to "test reality" or see the illogic of their ideas.

Individuals with schizotypal personality disorder also have odd beliefs or engage in "magical thinking," believing, for example, that they are clairvoyant or telepathic. In addition, they report unusual perceptual experiences, including such *illusions* as feeling the presence of another person when they are alone. Notice the subtle but important difference between the *feeling* as if someone else is in the room and the more extreme perceptual distortion in people with schizophrenia who might report there *is* someone else in the room when there isn't. Only a small proportion of individuals with schizotypal personality disorder go on to develop schizophrenia (Wolff, Townshed, McGuire, & Weeks, 1991). Unlike people who simply have unusual interests or beliefs, those with schizotypal personality disorder tend to be suspicious and have paranoid thoughts, express little emotion, and may dress or behave in unusual ways (e.g., wear many

---

**schizotypal personality disorder** Cluster A (odd or eccentric) personality disorder involving a pervasive pattern of interpersonal deficits featuring acute discomfort with, and reduced capacity for, close relationships, as well as by cognitive or perceptual distortions and eccentricities of behaviour.

layers of clothing in the summertime or mumble to themselves; Siever, Bernstein, & Silverman, 1991). Prospective research on children who later develop schizotypal personality disorder found that they tend to be passive and unengaged and are hypersensitive to criticism (Olin et al., 1997).

Clinicians have to be warned that different cultural beliefs or practices may lead to a mistaken diagnosis of schizotypal personality disorder. For example, some people who practise certain religious rituals—such as speaking in tongues, practising voodoo, or mind reading—may do so with such obsessiveness as to make them seem extremely unusual, thus leading to a misdiagnosis (American Psychiatric Association, 2000a). Mental health workers have to be particularly sensitive to cultural practices that may differ from their own and can distort their view of certain seemingly unusual behaviours.

## Disorder Criteria Summary
### Schizotypal Personality Disorder

Features of schizotypal personality disorder include:
- Pervasive pattern of social and interpersonal deficits marked by acute discomfort with close relationships, cognitive (or perceptual) distortions, and eccentricities of behaviour, beginning by early adulthood
- Incorrect interpretations of casual incidents and external events as having a particular or unusual meaning specifically for the person
- Odd beliefs or magical thinking that influences behaviour and is inconsistent with subcultural norms
- Unusual perceptual experiences, including bodily illusions
- Odd thinking and speech (e.g., vague, overelaborate, stereotyped)
- Suspiciousness or paranoid ideation
- Inappropriate or constricted affect
- Behaviour or appearance that is odd, eccentric, or peculiar
- Lack of close friends or confidantes other than first-degree relatives
- Excessive social anxiety associated with paranoid fears rather than negative judgments about self
- Does not occur exclusively with schizophrenia or another disorder

*Source:* Based on DSM-IV-TR. Used with permission from the *Diagnostic and Statistical Manual of Mental Disorders,* Fourth Edition, Text Revision. Copyright 2000. American Psychiatric Association.

## Causes

Historically, the word *schizotype* was used to describe people who were predisposed to develop schizophrenia (Meehl, 1962; Rado, 1962). Schizotypal personality disorder is viewed by some to be one phenotype of a schizophrenia genotype. Recall that a *phenotype* is the way a person's genetics is expressed. Your genotype is the gene or genes that make up a particular disorder. However, depending on a variety of other influences, the way you turn out—your phenotype—may vary from other people's phenotype, even if they have a similar genetic makeup to yours. Some people are thought to have "schizophrenia genes" (the genotype) and yet, because of the relative lack of biological influences (e.g., prenatal illnesses) or environmental stresses (e.g., poverty), some will have the less severe schizotypal personality disorder (the phenotype).

The idea of a relationship between schizotypal personality disorder and schizophrenia arises in part from the way people with the two disorders behave. Many characteristics of schizotypal personality disorder, including ideas of reference, illusions, and paranoid thinking, are similar but milder forms of behaviours observed among people with schizophrenia. Genetic research also seems to support a relationship. Family, twin, and adoption studies, largely conducted in Norway, have shown an increased prevalence of schizotypal personality disorder among relatives of people with schizophrenia who do not also have schizophrenia themselves (Dahl, 1993; Torgersen, Onstad, Skre, Edvardsen, & Kringlen, 1993). However, these studies also tell us that the environment can strongly influence schizotypal personality disorder. For example, research from Britain suggests a woman's exposure to influenza in pregnancy may increase the chance of schizotypal personality disorder in her children (Venables, 1996). It may be that a subgroup of people with schizotypal personality disorder has a similar genetic makeup when compared with people with schizophrenia.

Biological theories of schizotypal personality disorder are receiving empirical support. For example, cognitive assessment of people with this disorder point to mild to moderate decrements in their ability to perform on tests involving memory and learning, suggesting some damage in the left hemisphere (Voglmaier et al., 2000). Research by Roger Graves and his colleagues at the University of Victoria suggests that abnormalities in semantic association abilities may contribute to the thinking oddities displayed by schizotypal individuals. They examined people with high levels of magical ideation (MI)—a thinking style similar to that of schizotypal patients. High-MI participants were found to consider unrelated words as more closely associated than low-MI participants. Thus, for schizotypal people, "loose associations" may not be loose after all (Mohr, Graves, Gianotti, Pizzagalli, & Brugger, 2001). Other research using magnetic resonance imaging (MRI) points to generalized brain abnormalities in patients with schizotypal personality disorder (Dickey et al., 2000).

## Treatment

Some estimate that between 30% and 50% of the people with this disorder who request clinical help also meet the criteria for major depressive disorder. Treatment will obviously include some of the medical and psychological treatments for depression (Goldberg, Schultz, Resnick, Hamer, & Schultz, 1987; Stone, 2001).

Controlled studies of attempts to treat groups of people with schizotypal personality disorder are few, and, unfortunately, the results are modest at best. One general approach has been to teach social skills to help them reduce their isolation from and suspicion of others (O'Brien et al., 1993; Stone, 2001). A rather unusual tactic used by some therapists is not to encourage major changes at all; instead, the goal is to help the person accept and adjust to a solitary lifestyle (Stone, 1983).

Not surprisingly, medical treatment has been similar to that for people who have schizophrenia. In one study, haloperidol, often used with schizophrenia, was given to 17 people with schizotypal personality disorder (Hymowitz, Frances, Jacobsberg, Sickles, & Hoyt, 1986). There were some improvements in the group, especially with ideas of reference, odd communication, and social isolation. Unfortunately, because of the negative side effects of the medication, including drowsiness, many stopped taking their medication and dropped out of the study. About half the participants persevered through treatment but showed only mild improvement.

Further research on the treatment of people with this disorder is important for a variety of reasons. They tend not to improve over time, and some evidence indicates that some will go on to develop the more severe characteristics of schizophrenia.

### Concept Check 11.2

Which personality disorders are described below?

1. Carlos, who seems eccentric, never shows much emotion. He has always sought solitary activities in school and at home. He has no close friends. At birthday parties during his adolescence, he would take his gifts to a corner to play. Carlos appears indifferent to what others say, has never had a girlfriend, and expresses no desire to have sex. He is meeting with a therapist only because his family tricked him into going. _____

2. Paul trusts no one and incorrectly believes other people want to harm him or cheat him out of his life earnings. He is sure his wife is having an affair although he has no proof. He no longer confides in friends or divulges any information to co-workers for fear that it will be used against him. He dwells for hours on harmless comments by family members. _____

3. Alison lives alone out in the country and has little contact with relatives or any other individuals in a nearby town. She is extremely concerned with pollution, fearing that harmful chemicals are in the air and water around her. If it is necessary for her to go outside, she covers her body with excessive clothing and wears a face mask to avoid the contaminated air. She has developed her own water purification system and makes her own clothes. _____

# Cluster B Personality Disorders

■ *Describe the essential characteristics of each of the Cluster B (dramatic/erratic) personality disorders.*

■ *Identify the differences between psychopathy and antisocial personality disorder.*

People diagnosed with the next four personality disorders we highlight—antisocial, borderline, histrionic, and narcissistic—all have behaviours that have been described as "dramatic," "emotional," or "erratic." These personality disorders with exaggerated presentations are described next.

## Antisocial Personality Disorder

People with **antisocial personality disorder** are among the most dramatic of the individuals a clinician will see in a practice and are characterized as having a history of failing to comply with social norms. They perform actions most of us would find unacceptable, such as stealing from friends and family. They also tend to be irresponsible, impulsive, and deceitful (Widiger & Corbitt, 1995). Robert Hare describes them as "social predators who charm, manipulate, and ruthlessly plow their way through life, leaving a broad trail of broken hearts, shattered expectations, and empty wallets. Completely lacking in conscience and empathy, they selfishly take what they want and do as they please, violating social norms and expectations without the slightest sense of guilt or regret" (Hare, 1993, p. xi). An epidemiological study conducted with individuals in Edmonton shows that about 3% of adults meet criteria for antisocial personality disorder (Swanson, Bland, & Newman, 1994). Just who are these people with antisocial personality disorder? Consider the case of Ryan.

### Ryan
The Thrill Seeker

I first met Ryan on his 17th birthday. Unfortunately, he was celebrating the event in a psychiatric hospital. He had been truant from school for several months and had gotten into some trouble; the local judge who heard his case had recommended psychiatric evaluation one more time, though Ryan had been hospitalized six previous times, all for problems related to drug use and truancy. He was a veteran of the system and already knew most of the staff. I interviewed him to assess why he was admitted this time and to recommend treatment.

My first impression was that Ryan was cooperative and pleasant. He pointed out a tattoo on his arm that he had made himself, saying that it was a "stupid" thing to have done and that he now regretted it. In fact, he regretted many things and was looking forward to moving on with his life. I later found out that he was never truly remorseful for anything.

Our second interview was quite different. During those 48 hours, Ryan had done a number of things that showed why he needed a great deal of help. The most serious incident involved a 15-year-old girl named Ann who attended class with Ryan in the hospital school. Ryan had told her that he was going to get himself discharged, get in trouble, and be sent to the same correctional facility Ann's father was in, where he would rape her father. Ryan's threat so upset Ann that she hit her teacher and several of the staff. When I spoke to Ryan about this, he smiled slightly and said he was bored and that it was fun to upset Ann. When I asked whether it bothered him that his behaviour might extend her stay in the hospital, he looked puzzled and said, "Why should it bother me? She's the one who'll have to stay in this hellhole!"

Just before Ryan's admittance, a teenager in his town was murdered. A group of teens went to the local cemetery at night to perform satanic rituals, and a young man was stabbed to death, apparently over a drug purchase. Ryan was in the group, although he did not stab the boy. He told me that they occasionally dug up graves to get skulls for their parties; not because they really believed in the devil, but because it was fun and it scared the younger kids. I asked, "What if this were the grave of someone you knew, a relative or a friend? Would it bother you that strangers were digging up the remains?" He shook his head. "They're dead, man; they don't care. Why should I?"

Ryan told me he loved PCP, or "angel dust," and that he would rather be "dusted" than anything else. He routinely made the 2-hour trip to Toronto to buy drugs in a particularly dangerous neighbourhood. He denied that he was ever nervous. This wasn't machismo; he really seemed unconcerned.

Ryan made little progress. I discussed his future in family therapy sessions, and we talked about his pattern of showing supposed regret and remorse and then stealing money from his parents and going back onto the street. In fact, most of our discussions centred on trying to give his parents the courage to say no to him and not to believe his lies.

One evening, after many sessions, Ryan said he had seen the "error of his ways" and that he felt bad he had hurt his parents. If they would only take him home this one last time, he would be the son he should have been all these years. His speech moved his parents to tears, and they looked at me gratefully as if to thank me for

---

**antisocial personality disorder** Cluster B (dramatic, emotional, or erratic) personality disorder involving a pervasive pattern of disregard for and violation of the rights of others. Similar to the non-DSM label *psychopathy* but with greater emphasis on overt behaviour rather than personality traits.

curing their son. When Ryan finished talking, I smiled, applauded, told him it was the best performance I had ever seen. His parents turned on me in anger. Ryan paused for a second, then he too smiled and said, "It was worth a shot!" Ryan's parents were astounded that he had once again tricked them into believing him; he hadn't meant a word of what he had just said. Ryan was eventually discharged to a drug rehabilitation program. Within 4 weeks, he had convinced his parents to take him home, and within 2 days he had stolen all their cash and disappeared; he apparently went back to his friends and to drugs.

When he was in his 20s, after one of his many arrests for theft, he was diagnosed as having antisocial personality disorder. His parents never summoned the courage to turn him out or refuse him money, and he continues to con them into providing him with a means of buying more drugs.

## Clinical Description

Individuals with antisocial personality disorder tend to have long histories of violating the rights of others (Widiger & Corbitt, 1995). They are often described as being aggressive because they take what they want and are indifferent to the concerns of other people. Lying and cheating seem to be second nature to them, and often they appear unable to tell the difference between the truth and the lies they make up to further their own goals (Hare, Forth, & Hart, 1989). They show no remorse or concern over the sometimes devastating effects of their actions. Substance abuse is common, occurring in 83% of people with antisocial personality disorder (Dulit et al., 1993; Smith & Newman, 1990), and appears to be a lifelong pattern among these individuals (Mailloux, Forth, & Kroner, 1997; Skodol, Oldham, & Gallaher, 1999). The long-term outcome for people with antisocial personality disorder is often poor, regardless of gender (Pajer, 1998). One longitudinal study, for example, found that antisocial boys were more than twice as likely to die an unnatural death (e.g., accident, suicide, homicide) as their non-antisocial peers, which may be attributed to factors such as alcohol abuse and poor self-care (e.g., reckless behaviour; Laub & Vaillant, 2000).

Antisocial personality disorder has had a number of names over the years. Philippe Pinel (1801/1962) identified what he called *manie sans délire* (mania without delirium) to describe people with unusual emotional responses and impulsive rages but no deficits in reasoning ability (Sutker, Bugg, & West, 1993). Other labels have included "moral insanity,"

"egopathy," "sociopathy," and "psychopathy." A great deal has been written about these labels; we focus on the two that have figured most prominently in psychological research: **psychopathy** and DSM-IV-TR's antisocial personality disorder. As you will see, there are important differences between the two.

**Defining Criteria**  Hervey Cleckley (1941/1982), a psychiatrist who spent much of his career working with the "psychopathic personality," identified a constellation of 16 major characteristics, most of which are personality traits and are sometimes referred to as the "Cleckley criteria." They include superficial charm and good intelligence; absence of delusions and other signs of irrational thinking; absence of "nervousness" and other psychoneurotic manifestations; unreliability; untruthfulness and insincerity; lack of remorse or shame; inadequately motivated antisocial behaviour; poor judgment and failure to learn by experience; pathologic egocentricity and incapacity for love; general poverty in major affective reactions; specific loss of insight; unresponsiveness in general interpersonal relations; fantastic and uninviting behaviour, with drink and without; suicide rarely carried out; sex life impersonal, trivial, and poorly integrated; and failure to follow any life plan (Cleckley, 1982, p. 204).

Robert Hare and his colleagues, building on the descriptive work of Cleckley, researched the nature of psychopathy (e.g., Hare, 1970; Harpur, Hare, & Hakstian, 1989) and developed a 20-item checklist that serves as an assessment tool. Six of the criteria that Hare (1991) includes in his Revised Psychopathy Checklist (PCL-R) are as follows:

1. Glibness/superficial charm
2. Grandiose sense of self-worth
3. Proneness to boredom/need for stimulation
4. Pathological lying
5. Conning/manipulative
6. Lack of remorse

With some training, clinicians are able to gather information from interviews with a person, along with material from significant others or institutional files (e.g., prison records), and assign the person scores on the checklist, with high scores indicating psychopathy (Hare, 1991).

The DSM-IV-TR criteria for antisocial personality disorder focus almost entirely on observable *behaviours* (e.g., "impulsively and repeatedly changes employment, residence, or sexual partners"). In contrast, the Cleckley/Hare criteria focus

---

**psychopathy**  Non-DSM category similar to antisocial personality disorder but with less emphasis on overt behaviour; indicators include superficial charm, lack of remorse, and other personality characteristics.

primarily on underlying *personality traits* (e.g., being self-centred or manipulative). DSM-IV-TR and previous versions chose to use only observable behaviours so that clinicians could reliably agree on a diagnosis. The framers of the criteria felt that trying to assess a personality trait—for example, whether someone was manipulative—would be more difficult than determining whether the person engaged in certain behaviours, such as repeated fighting.

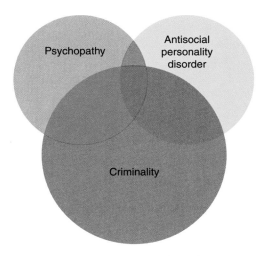

**Figure 11.2** ■ Overlap and lack of overlap among antisocial personality disorder, psychopathy, and criminality.

---

**Disorder Criteria Summary**
Antisocial Personality Disorder

Features of antisocial personality disorder include:
- Person at least 18 years of age who has shown a pervasive pattern of disregard for and violation of the rights of others since age 15
- Failure to conform to social norms, as evidenced by repeatedly breaking the law
- Deceitfulness, including lying, using aliases, or conning others for profit or pleasure
- Impulsivity or failure to plan ahead
- Irritability or aggressiveness, as indicated by frequent fights or assaults
- Reckless disregard for safety of others
- Consistent irresponsibility with employment or paying bills
- Lack of remorse at harming others
- Evidence of conduct disorder with onset before age 15
- Does not occur exclusively during the course of schizophrenia or a manic episode

*Source:* Based on DSM-IV-TR. Used with permission from the *Diagnostic and Statistical Manual of Mental Disorders,* Fourth Edition, Text Revision. Copyright 2000. American Psychiatric Association.

---

**Antisocial Personality, Psychopathy, and Criminality**
Although Cleckley did not deny that many psychopaths are at greatly elevated risk for criminal and antisocial behaviours, he did emphasize that some have few or no legal or interpersonal difficulties. In other words, some psychopaths are not criminals and some do not display the aggressiveness that is a DSM-IV-TR criterion for antisocial personality disorder. Although the relationship between psychopathic personality and antisocial personality disorder is uncertain, the two syndromes clearly do not overlap perfectly (Hare, 1983). Figure 11.2 illustrates the relative overlap among the characteristics of *psychopathy* as described by Cleckley and Hare, *antisocial personality disorder* as outlined in DSM-IV-TR, and *criminality,* which includes all people who get into trouble with the law. Despite much debate as to whether psychopathy or antisocial personality disorder is a more useful construct, a recent study with incarcerated Canadian offenders showed that measures of psychopathy and of antisocial personality

disorder were similarly useful in identifying persistently antisocial offenders: violent reoffending was significantly predicted (and to the same degree) by the two measures (Skilling, Harris, Rice, & Quinsey, 2002).

Although psychopathy and antisocial personality disorder are both related to criminality, as you can see in Figure 11.2, not everyone who has psychopathy or antisocial personality disorder becomes involved with the legal system. What separates many in this group from those who get into trouble with the law may be IQ. In a prospective, longitudinal study, White, Moffit, and Silva (1989) followed almost 1000 children, beginning at age 5, to see what predicted antisocial behaviour at age 15. They found that, of the 5-year-olds determined to be at high risk for later delinquent behaviour, 16% did indeed have run-ins with the law by the age of 15 and 84% did not. What distinguished these two groups? In general, the at-risk children with lower IQs were the ones who got in trouble. Thus, having a higher IQ may help protect some people from developing more serious problems or may at least prevent them from getting caught! Some psychopaths function quite successfully in certain segments of society (e.g., politics, business, entertainment). Because of the difficulty in identifying these people, such "successful" or "subclinical" psychopaths (who meet some but not all the criteria for psychopathy) have not been the focus of much research. In a clever exception, Widom (1977) recruited a sample of subclinical psychopaths through advertisements in underground newspapers that invited many of the major personality characteristics of psychopathy. For example, one of the advertisements read as follows:

> Wanted: charming, aggressive, carefree people who are impulsively irresponsible but are good at handling people and at looking after number one.

Widom found that her sample appeared to possess many of the same characteristics as imprisoned psychopaths; for example, a large percentage of them received low scores on questionnaire measures of empathy and socialization and their parents tended to have higher rates of psychopathology, including alcoholism. Moreover, many of these individuals had stable occupations and had managed to stay out of prison. Widom's study, although lacking a comparison group, shows that at least some individuals with psychopathic personality traits avoid repeated contact with the legal system and may even function successfully in society.

Identifying psychopaths among the criminal population seems to have important implications for predicting their future criminal behaviour (Hare, 1999). One study conducted in British Columbia by forensic psychologist James Ogloff and his colleagues found that criminals who scored high on Hare's PCL-R put in less effort and showed fewer improvements in a therapy program than did criminals who were not psychopaths (Ogloff, Wong, & Greenwood, 1990). Other studies, such as one by Marnie Rice, Grant Harris, and Vernon Quinsey of the Penetanguishine Mental Health Centre in Ontario and Queen's University have shown that psychopathic criminals are more likely than non-psychopathic criminals to repeat their criminal offences, especially those that are violent and/or sexual in nature (Rice, Harris, & Quinsey, 1990).

Michael Woodworth and Stephen Porter examined characteristics of criminal homicides as a function of the offender's level of psychopathy. They ranked each offender's homicide on a scale ranging from purely instrumental (planned out) to purely reactive (spontaneous). This distinction is one of the most relevant in assessing risk for future violence and for predicting treatment outcome for criminal

offenders (Eaves, Douglas, Webster, Ogloff, & Hart, 2000). Psychopaths rarely committed spontaneous "hot-blooded" murders. Rather, their murders were usually planned with a selfish goal in mind. This finding was intriguing because it contrasts with the common view of psychopaths as highly impulsive (Woodworth & Porter, 2002). This finding is corroborated by the results of a study by Brown and Forth (1997): Psychopathy was associated with less (rather than more) intense negative emotions experienced before sexual offending among 60 incarcerated rapists. The rapes and homicides of children and young women by infamous criminals Paul Bernardo, Karla Homolka, and Clifford Olson exemplify the planning involved in the cold-blooded types of murders committed by psychopathic offenders.

As we review the literature on antisocial personality disorder, note that the people included in the research may be members of only one of the three groups we have described. For example, genetic research is usually conducted with criminals because they and their families are easier to identify than members of the other groups. As you now know, the criminal group may include people other than those with antisocial personality disorder or psychopathy. Keep this in mind as you read on.

**Conduct Disorder**    Before we discuss causal factors, it is important to note the developmental nature of antisocial behaviour. DSM-IV-TR provides a separate diagnosis for children who engage in behaviours that violate society's norms: *conduct disorder*. Many children with conduct disorder become juvenile offenders (Eppright, Kashani, Robison, & Reid, 1993) and tend to become involved with drugs (VanKammen, Loeber, & Stouthamer-Loeber, 1991). Ryan fit into this category. More important, the research of Richard Tremblay and his colleagues supports a stable, lifelong pattern of antisocial behaviour in a subgroup of antisocial children. Specifically, a group of young children who display antisocial behaviour has been shown to be likely to continue these behaviours as the members grow older, while many others desist (Charlebois, LeBlanc, Gagnon, Larivée, & Tremblay, 1993). Data from long-term follow-up research indicate that many adults with antisocial personality disorder or psychopathy had conduct disorder as children (Robins, 1978); the likelihood increases if the child has both conduct disorder and attention deficit/hyperactivity disorder (Lynam, 1996).

There is a tremendous amount of interest in studying a group that causes a great deal of harm to society. Research has been conducted for a number of years, so we know a great deal more about antisocial personality disorder than about the other personality disorders.

***Antisocial Personality Disorder: George***
*"I have hatred inside me. I don't care how much I beat somebody.... The more I hear somebody, the more anger I get inside me.... I used drugs when I was ... probably 9 or 10 years old ... smoked marijuana.... First time I drank some alcohol I think I was probably about 3 years old.... I assaulted a woman.... I had so much anger.... I was just like a bomb ... it's just ticking ... and the way I'm going, that bomb was going to blow up in me. I wouldn't be able to get away from it ... going to be a lot of people hurt.... I'm not going out without taking somebody with me."*

Thomson Learning

## Genetic Influences

Family, twin, and adoption studies all suggest a genetic influence on both antisocial personality disorder and criminality (Bock & Goode, 1996; DiLalla & Gottesman, 1991). For example, Crowe (1974) examined children of mothers who were felons who were later adopted by other families and compared them with adopted children of normal mothers. All were separated from their mothers as newborns, minimizing the possibility that environmental factors from their biological families were responsible for the results. Crowe found that the adopted offspring of felons had significantly higher rates of arrests, conviction, and antisocial personality than did the adopted offspring of normal mothers, which suggests at least some genetic influence on criminality and antisocial behaviour.

However, Crowe also found something else interesting: The adopted children of felons who themselves later became criminals had spent more time in interim orphanages than either the adopted children of felons who did not become criminals or the adopted children of normal mothers. As Crowe points out, this suggests a *gene–environment interaction;* in other words, genetic factors may be important only in the presence of certain environmental influences (alternatively, certain environmental influences are important *only* in the presence of certain genetic predispositions). Genetic factors may present a vulnerability, but actual development of criminality may require environmental factors, such as a deficit in early, high-quality contact with parents or parent-surrogates.

This gene–environment interaction was demonstrated most clearly by Cadoret, Yates, Troughton, Woodworth, and Stewart (1995), who studied adopted children and their likelihood of developing conduct problems. If the children's biological parents had a history of antisocial personality disorder *and* their adoptive families exposed them to chronic stress through marital, legal, or psychiatric problems, the children were at greater risk for conduct problems. Again, research shows that genetic influence does not necessarily mean certain disorders are inevitable.

Data from twin studies generally support those of adoption studies. Twin researchers Kerry Jang, John Livesley, and Philip Vernon have shown that a personality characteristic called *dyssocial behaviour* (similar to the traits displayed by those with antisocial personality disorder) has a large genetic component (Jang, Vernon, & Livesley, 2001; Livesley, Jang, & Vernon, 1998). In a review of the major twin studies of criminality, Eysenck and Eysenck (1978) found that the average concordance rate for criminality among monozygotic twins was 55%, whereas among dizygotic twins it was only 13%, again suggesting a large genetic component. We must remember several limitations when we interpret findings on the genetics of criminality. First, "criminality" is an extremely heterogeneous category that includes people with and without antisocial personality disorder and psychopathy. Genetics may influence one or more subtypes of criminality. Second, it is clear that environmental factors play a substantial role in many, if not all, cases of criminality. In the studies reviewed by Eysenck and Eysenck (1978), for example, the concordance rate of criminality among identical twins would be 100% if criminality were caused entirely by genetic factors. Finally, the interaction between genes and environment may be important in the genesis of criminality (see Crowe, 1974, for example). Genetic factors may substantially contribute to criminal behaviour only in the presence of certain environmental factors (Rutter, 1997). Large-scale research on twins with conduct disorder supports the role of genetic and environmental influences on this disorder as well (Slutske et al., 1997, 1998).

## Neurobiological Influences

A great deal of research has focused on neurobiological influences that may be specific to antisocial personality disorder. One thing seems clear: General brain damage does not explain why some people become psychopaths or criminals; as noted by Simon Fraser University psychologist Stephen Hart and his colleagues, psychopaths appear to score as well on neuropsychological tests as the rest of us (Hart, Forth, & Hare, 1990). However, such tests are designed to detect significant damage in the brain and will not pick up subtle changes in chemistry or structure that could affect behaviour. Two major theories have attracted a great deal of attention: (1) the *underarousal hypothesis* and (2) the *fearlessness hypothesis.*

**The Underarousal Hypothesis** According to the underarousal hypothesis, psychopaths have abnormally low levels of *cortical arousal* (Quay, 1965).

Many prisons allow visits between inmates and their children, in part to help reduce later problems in those children.

There appears to be an inverted U-shaped relation between arousal and performance. The *Yerkes-Dodson curve* suggests that people with *either* very high or very low levels of arousal tend to experience negative affect and perform poorly in many situations, whereas individuals with intermediate levels of arousal tend to be relatively content and perform satisfactorily in most situations.

According to the underarousal hypothesis, the abnormally low levels of cortical arousal characteristic of psychopaths are the primary cause of their antisocial and risk-taking behaviours; they seek stimulation to boost their chronically low levels of arousal. This means that Ryan lied, took drugs, and dug up graves to achieve the same level of arousal we might get from talking on the phone with a good friend or watching television.

Low-frequency *theta waves* are found in brain wave measures of children and largely disappear in adulthood; their specific purpose is yet unknown. Evidence suggests that many psychopaths have excessive theta waves when they are awake. This finding led Robert Hare to generate another theory related to arousal levels, sometimes referred to as the *cortical immaturity hypothesis* of psychopathy (Hare, 1970). Hare's theory holds that the cerebral cortex of psychopaths is at a relatively primitive stage of development. This hypothesis may help explain why the behaviour of psychopaths is often childlike and impulsive: Their cerebral cortices, which play such a key role in the inhibition and control of impulses, may be insufficiently developed. But remember that many psychopaths are not impulsive, as indicated by the recent research of investigators like Adelle Forth and Stephen Porter discussed earlier (e.g., Brown & Forth, 1997; Woodworth & Porter, 2002).

The data on theta waves are open to an alternative and perhaps simpler explanation. Because theta waves also indicate states such as drowsiness or boredom, psychopaths' higher levels of theta waves may simply reflect their relative lack of concern regarding being hooked up to psychophysiological equipment! Picture yourself having your brain waves measured. You sit next to the intimidating polygraph machine, attached to a number of electrodes and wires. How will you react? As a non-psychopath, you will probably feel anxiety and apprehension. In contrast, a psychopath, who is low in anxiety, will probably be bored, apathetic, and unresponsive. The excessive theta waves of psychopaths may simply reflect their relative absence of anxiety.

**The Fearlessness Hypothesis**   According to the fearlessness hypothesis, psychopaths possess a higher threshold for experiencing fear than most other individuals (Lykken, 1957, 1982). In other words, things that greatly frighten the rest of us have little or no effect on the psychopath. Remember that Ryan was unafraid of going alone to dangerous neighbourhoods to buy drugs. According to proponents of this hypothesis, the fearlessness of the psychopath gives rise to all other major features of the syndrome.

**The Brain and Psychopathy**   Theorists have tried to connect what we know about the workings of the brain with clinical observations of people with antisocial personality disorder, especially those with psychopathy. Several theorists have applied the late British researcher Jeffrey Gray's (1987) model of brain functioning to this population (Fowles, 1988; Quay, 1993). According to Gray, three major brain systems influence learning and emotional behaviour: the behavioural inhibition system (BIS), the reward system (REW), and the fight/flight system. The BIS is responsible for our ability to stop or slow down when we are faced with impending punishment, non-reward, or novel situations, which leads to anxiety and frustration. The BIS is thought to be located in the septal-hippocampal area of the brain and involves the noradrenergic and serotonergic neurotransmitter systems. The REW system is responsible for our approach behaviour—in particular, our approach to positive rewards—and is associated with hope and relief. This system probably involves the dopaminergic neurotransmitter system in the mesolimbic area of the brain, which we previously noted as the pleasure pathway for its role in substance use and abuse (Chapter 10).

If you think about the behaviour of psychopaths, the possible malfunctioning of these systems is clear. An imbalance between the BIS and the REW may make the fear and anxiety produced by the BIS less apparent and the positive feelings associated with the REW more prominent (Levenston, Patrick, Bradley, & Lang, 2000; Quay, 1993). Theorists have proposed that this type of neurobiological dysfunction may explain why psychopaths aren't anxious about committing the antisocial acts that characterize their disorder.

## Psychological and Social Dimensions

What goes on in the mind of a psychopath? In one of several studies of how psychopaths process reward and punishment, Newman, Patterson, and Kosson (1987) set up a card-playing task on a computer; they provided five-cent rewards and fines for correct and incorrect answers to psychopathic and non-psychopathic criminal offenders. The game was constructed so that at first they were rewarded about 90% of the time and fined only about 10% of the time. Gradually, the odds changed until the probability of getting a reward was 0%. Despite feedback that reward was no longer forthcoming, the psychopaths continued to play and lose. As a result of this and other studies, the researchers hypothesized that once psychopaths set their sights on a reward goal, they are less likely than non-psychopaths to be deterred despite signs the goal is no longer achievable (Newman & Wallace, 1993). Again, considering the reckless and daring behaviour of some psychopaths (robbing banks without a mask and getting caught immediately), failure to abandon an unattainable goal fits the overall picture.

Studies of aggressive children, who may develop antisocial personality disorder or psychopathy, suggests that aggression in such children may escalate, in part as a result of their interactions with their parents (Patterson, 1982; Robins, 1978). Patterson found that the parents often give in to the problem behaviours displayed by their children. For example, parents ask their son to make his bed and he refuses. One parent yells at the boy. He yells back and becomes abusive. At some point his interchange becomes so aversive that the parent stops fighting and walks away, thereby ending the fight but also letting the son not make his bed. Giving in to these problems results in short-term gains for both the parent (calm is restored in the house) and the child (he gets what he wants), but it results in continuing problems. The child has learned to continue fighting and not give up, and the parent learns that the only way to "win" is to withdraw all demands. This "coercive family process" combines with other factors, such as parents' inept monitoring of their child's activities and less parental involvement, to help maintain the aggressive behaviours (Patterson, DeBaryshe, & Ramsey, 1989; Sansbury & Wahler, 1992).

Although little is known about which environmental factors play a direct role in causing antisocial personality disorder and psychopathy (as opposed to childhood conduct disorders), evidence from adoption studies strongly suggests that shared environmental factors—that tend to make family members similar—are important to the etiology of criminality and perhaps antisocial personality disorder. For example, in the Swedish adoption study by Sigvardsson, Cloninger, Bohman, and von-Knorring (1982), low social status of the adoptive parents increased the risk of nonviolent criminality among females. Like children with conduct disorders, individuals with antisocial personality disorder come from homes with inconsistent parental discipline (e.g., Robins, 1966). It is not known for certain, however, whether inconsistent discipline directly causes antisocial personality disorder; it is conceivable, for example, that parents have a genetic vulnerability to antisocial personality disorder that they pass on to their children but that also causes them to be inadequate parents.

One interesting study looked at the social environment and attitudes of neighbourhoods and their effect on violent crime. Sampson, Raudenbush, and Earls (1997) asked residents of city neighbourhoods questions about the willingness of local residents to intervene for the common good; for example, whether neighbours would intervene if children were skipping school and hanging out on the street. The researchers found that the degree of mutual trust and solidarity in a neighbourhood was inversely related to violent crime. This study points out that factors outside the family can influence behaviours associated with antisocial personality disorder.

A final factor that has been implicated in antisocial personality disorder is the role of stress. One study found that trauma associated with combat may increase the likelihood of antisocial behaviour. Barrett and colleagues studied more than 2000 army veterans of the Vietnam War (Barrett et al., 1996). Even after adjusting for histories of childhood problems, the researchers found that those who had been exposed to the most traumatic events were most likely to engage in violence, illegal activities, lying, and using aliases.

## Developmental Influences

The forms that antisocial behaviours take change as children move into adulthood, from truancy and stealing from friends to extortion, assaults, armed robbery, or other crimes (Forth & Mailloux, 2000; Hare, Forth, & Strachan, 1992). Fortunately, clinical lore and scattered empirical reports (Robins, 1966) suggest that rates of antisocial behaviour begin to decline rather markedly around the age of 40. Hare et al. (1988) provided empirical support for this phenomenon. They examined the conviction rates of male psychopaths and male non-psychopaths who had been incarcerated for a variety of crimes. The researchers found that between age 16 and age 45 the conviction rates of non-psychopaths remained relatively constant. In contrast, the conviction rates of psychopaths remained relatively constant until about 40, at which time they decreased markedly (see Figure 11.3). Why antisocial behaviour often declines around middle age remains unanswered.

## An Integrative Model

How can we put all this information together to get a better understanding of people with antisocial personality disorder? Remember that research in each area may involve people labelled as having antisocial personality disorder, people labelled as psychopathic, or criminals. Whatever the label, it appears these people have a genetic vulnerability to antisocial behaviours and personality traits. Perhaps this vulnerability results in underarousal and/or fearlessness. The genetic inheritance might be the propensity for weak BIS and overactive REW that could partially account for the differences in cognitive set (Newman & Wallace, 1993).

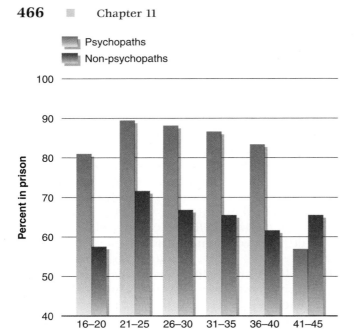

Legend:
- Psychopaths
- Non-psychophaths

**Figure 11.3** ▪ Lifetime course of criminal behaviour in psychopaths and non-psychopaths. (Based on Hare, McPherson, & Forth, 1988.)

In a family that may already be under stress because of divorce or substance abuse (Hetherington, Stanley-Hagan, & Anderson, 1989; Patterson et al., 1989), there may be an interaction style that actually encourages antisocial behaviour on the part of the child (Wootton, Frick, Shelton, & Silverthorn, 1997). The child's antisocial and impulsive behaviour alienates other children who might be good role models and attracts others who encourage antisocial behaviour (Vuchinich, Bank, & Patterson, 1992). These behaviours may also result in the child's dropping out of school and a poor occupational history in adulthood, which help create increasingly frustrating life circumstances that further incite acts against society (Caspi, Elder, & Bem, 1987).

Children with conduct disorder may become adults with antisocial personality disorder.

This is, admittedly, an abbreviated version of a complex scenario. The important element is that in this integrative model of antisocial behaviour, biological, psychological, and cultural factors combine in intricate ways to create someone like Ryan.

### Treatment

One of the major problems with treating people in this group is typical of numerous personality disorders: They rarely identify themselves as needing treatment. Because of this, and because they can be very manipulative even with their therapists, most clinicians are pessimistic about the outcome of treatment for adults who have antisocial personality disorder, and there are few documented success stories (Meloy, 2001). Antisocial behaviour is predictive of poor prognosis even in childhood (Kazdin & Mazurick, 1994). In general, therapists agree with incarcerating these people to deter future antisocial acts. Clinicians encourage identification of high-risk children so that treatment can be attempted before they become adults (Patterson, 1982).

The most common treatment strategy for children involves parent training (Patterson, 1986; Sanders, 1992). Parents are taught how to recognize behaviour problems early and how to use praise and privileges to reduce problem behaviour and encourage prosocial behaviours. Treatment studies typically show that these types of programs can significantly improve the behaviours of many children who display antisocial behaviours (Patterson, Chamberlain, & Reid, 1982; Webster-Stratton & Hammond, 1997). A number of factors, however, put families at risk either for not succeeding in treatment or for dropping out early; these include cases with a high degree of family dysfunction, socioeconomic disadvantage, high family stress, parent's history of antisocial behaviour, and severe conduct disorder on the part of the child (Dumas & Wahler, 1983; Kazdin, Mazurick, & Bass, 1993).

Some researchers are now examining how a multifaceted approach to treatment can help reduce delinquent behaviour on the part of juvenile offenders. Programs that combine the behavioural approaches just described with efforts to improve family relationships and provide services to the families in their communities are reporting some success. One study treating 155 violent and chronic juvenile offenders observed that improving family relations and decreasing the child's associations with delinquent peers resulted in significant reductions in delinquent behaviour (Huey, Henggeler, Brondino, & Pickrel, 2000).

### Prevention

We have seen a dramatic increase in the amount of research on prevention strategies focused on children at risk for later antisocial personality disorder.

The aggressive behaviour of young children is remarkably stable, meaning that children who hit, insult, and threaten others are likely to continue as they grow older. Unfortunately, these behaviours become more serious over time and are the early signs of the homicides and assaults seen among some adults (Eron & Huesmann, 1990; Singer & Flannery, 2000).

Approaches to change this aggressive course are being implemented mainly in school and preschool settings and emphasize behavioural supports for good behaviour and skills training to improve social competence (Flannery et al., 2003). A number of types of these programs are under evaluation, and the results look promising. Aggression can be reduced and social competence (e.g., making friends, sharing) can be improved among young children, and these results generally maintain over a few years (Flannery et al., 2003). It is too soon to assess the success of such programs in preventing adult antisocial behaviours typically observed among people with this personality disorder. However, given the ineffectiveness of treatment for adults, prevention may be the best approach to this problem.

## Borderline Personality Disorder

People with **borderline personality disorder** lead tumultuous lives. Their moods and relationships are unstable, and usually they have a poor self-image. These people often feel empty and are at great risk of dying by their own hands. Consider the case of Claire.

### Claire
#### A Stranger Among Us

I have known Claire for over 30 years and have watched her through the good but mostly bad times of her often shaky and erratic life as a person with borderline personality disorder. Claire and I went to school together from grade 8 through high school, and we've kept in touch periodically. My earliest memory of her is of her hair, which was cut short and rather unevenly. She told me that when things were not going well she cut her own hair severely, which helped to "fill the void." I later found out that the long sleeves she usually wore hid scars and cuts that she had made herself.

Claire was the first of our friends to smoke. What was unusual about this and her later drug use was not that they occurred (this was in the 1960s!) or that they began early; it was that she didn't seem to use them to get attention, like everyone else. Claire was also one of the first whose parents divorced, and both of them seemed to abandon her emotionally. She later told me that her father was an alcoholic who had regularly beaten her and her mother. She did poorly in school and had a very low opinion of herself. She frequently said she was stupid and ugly, yet she was obviously neither.

Throughout our school years, Claire left town periodically, without any explanation. I learned many years later that she was in psychiatric facilities to get help with her suicidal depression. She often threatened to kill herself, although we didn't guess that she was serious.

In our later teens we all drifted away from Claire. She had become more and more unpredictable, sometimes berating us for a perceived slight ("You're walking too fast. You don't want to be seen with me!") and at other times desperate to be around us. We were obviously confused by her behaviour. With some people, emotional outbursts can bring you closer together. Unfortunately for Claire, these incidents and her overall demeanour made us feel that we didn't know her at all. As we all grew older, the "void" she described in herself became overwhelming and eventually shut us all out.

Claire married twice, and both times had very passionate but stormy relationships interrupted by hospitalizations. She tried to stab her first husband during a particularly violent rage. She tried a number of drugs, but mainly used alcohol to "deaden the pain."

Now, in her mid-40s, things have calmed down some, although she says she is rarely happy. Claire does feel a little better about herself and is doing well as a travel agent. Although she is seeing someone, she is reluctant to become very involved because of her personal history. Claire was ultimately diagnosed with depression and borderline personality disorder.

### Clinical Description

Borderline personality disorder is one of the most common personality disorders; it is observed in every culture and is seen in 2% to 3% of the general population (Gunderson, 2001). Claire's life illustrates the

**borderline personality disorder** Cluster B (dramatic, emotional, or erratic) personality disorder involving a pervasive pattern of instability of interpersonal relationships, self-image, affect, and control over impulses.

instability characteristic of people with borderline personality disorder. They tend to have turbulent relationships, fearing abandonment but lacking control over their emotions (Phillips et al., 2003). They frequently engage in suicidal and/or self-mutilative behaviours, cutting, burning, or punching themselves. Claire sometimes used her cigarette to burn her palm or forearm, and she carved her initials in her arm. A significant proportion—about 6%—succeed at suicide (Stone, 1989; Widiger & Trull, 1993).

People with this personality disorder are often very intense, going from anger to deep depression in a short time. They also are characterized by impulsivity; Paul Links and his colleagues at Saint Michael's Hospital in Toronto have argued that impulsivity is the core aspect of borderline personality disorder (Links, Heslegrave, & van Reekum, 1999). This impulsiveness can be seen in their drug abuse and self-mutilation. Although not so obvious as to why, the self-injurious behaviours such as cutting sometimes are described as tension reducing by people who engage in these behaviours (Bohus et al., 2000). Claire's empty feeling is also common; these people are sometimes described as chronically bored and have difficulties with their own identities (Wilkinson-Ryan & Westen, 2000). The mood disorders we discussed in Chapter 6 are common among people with borderline personality disorder, with 24% to 74% having major depression and 4% to 20% having bipolar disorder (Widiger & Rogers, 1989). Eating disorders are also common, particularly bulimia (see Chapter 8): Almost 25% of bulimics also have borderline personality disorder (Levin & Hyler, 1986). Up to 67% of the people with this disorder are also diagnosed with at least one substance use disorder (Dulit et al., 1993; Skodol et al., 1999). As with antisocial personality disorder, people with borderline personality disorder tend to improve during their 30s and 40s, although they

may continue to have difficulties into old age (Rosowsky & Gurian, 1992). Unfortunately, longitudinal research suggests a poor prognosis for people with borderline personality disorder. Patients were followed for several years; about half of them still had the disorder 7 years later (Links, Heslegrave, & van Reekum, 1998).

> ### Disorder Criteria Summary
> #### Borderline Personality Disorder
>
> Features of borderline personality disorder include:
> - Pervasive pattern of instability in interpersonal relationships, self-image, and affect, and marked impulsivity beginning by early adulthood
> - Frantic efforts to avoid real or imagined abandonment
> - Pattern of unstable and intense interpersonal relationships characterized by alternating between extremes of idealization and devaluation
> - Persistently unstable self-image or sense of self
> - Self-dangerous impulsivity (e.g., sex, substance abuse, reckless driving)
> - Recurrent suicidal behaviour, gestures, threats, or self-mutilation
> - Intense episodes of dysphoria, irritability, or anxiety, usually lasting a few hours
> - Chronic feelings of emptiness
> - Inappropriate, intense anger or difficulty controlling anger
> - Transient, stress-related paranoid ideation or severe dissociative symptoms

*Source:* Based on DSM-IV-TR. Used with permission from the *Diagnostic and Statistical Manual of Mental Disorders,* Fourth Edition, Text Revision. Copyright 2000. American Psychiatric Association.

## Causes

The results from almost 20 family studies suggest that borderline personality disorder is more prevalent in families with the disorder and somehow linked with mood disorders (e.g., Baron, Gruen, Asnis, & Lord, 1985; Zanarini, Gunderson, Marino, Schwartz, & Frankenburg, 1988). One such study was conducted by Paul Links and his colleagues (Links, Steiner, & Huxley, 1988). Just as schizotypal personality disorder seems to share a familial association with schizophrenia, borderline personality disorder may have a similar connection to mood disorders (Widiger & Trull, 1993). Although some traits may be inherited (e.g., impulsivity), there appears to be a great deal of room for environmental influences.

Cognitive factors in borderline personality disorder are just beginning to be explored. Here the question is, just how do people with this disorder process information, and does this contribute to their difficulties? One study that took a look at the thought processes of these individuals asked people

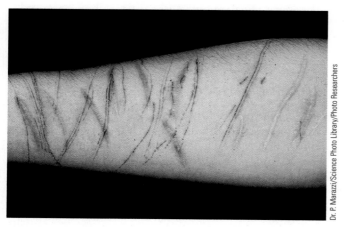

Borderline personality disorder is often accompanied by self-mutilation.

with and without borderline personality disorder to look at words projected on a computer screen and try to remember some of the words and try to forget others (Korfine & Hooley, 2000). When the words were not related to the symptoms of borderline personality disorder—for example, "celebrate," "charming," "collect"—both groups performed equally well. However, when they were presented with words that might be relevant to the disorder—for example, "abandon," "suicidal," "emptiness"—individuals with borderline personality disorder remembered more of these words despite being instructed to forget them. This preliminary evidence for a memory bias may hold clues to the nature of this disorder and may someday be helpful in designing more effective treatment.

One psychosocial influence that has received a great deal of attention is the possible contribution of early trauma, especially sexual and physical abuse (Links & van Reekum, 1993). Several studies have shown that people with this disorder are more likely to report abuse than are individuals with other psychiatric conditions (e.g., Goldman, D'Angelo, DeMaso, & Mezzacappa, 1992; Ogata et al., 1990). Wagner and Linehan (1994) found that among women with both borderline personality disorder and parasuicidal behaviour (which includes both serious and minor suicide attempts), 76% reported some type of childhood sexual abuse and had made the most serious attempts to commit suicide. In a large study, researchers found an even higher rate of abuse histories in individuals with borderline personality disorder, with 91% reporting abuse and 92% reporting being neglected before the age of 18 (Zanarini et al., 1997). Although we do not know whether abuse and neglect cause later borderline personality disorder (data are based on recollection and a correlation between the two phenomena), they may be predisposing factors in at least some cases. If childhood abuse or neglect does lead to most cases of borderline personality disorder, the connection may explain why women are affected more often than men. Girls are two or three times more likely to be sexually abused than boys (Herman, Perry, & van der Kolk, 1989). Moreover, the work of Harriet MacMillan at McMaster University has shown that the association between a history of abuse in childhood and psychopathology in adulthood (including personality disorders) is stronger for women than for men (MacMillan et al., 2001).

Building on the possible link to abuse, Gunderson and Sabo (1993) argued that borderline personality disorder is similar to posttraumatic stress disorder (PTSD); they see many resemblances in the two behaviour patterns. Herman et al. (1989) have drawn similar parallels; for example, difficulties in the regulation of mood, impulse control, and interpersonal relationships. This discussion about borderline personality disorder and PTSD can be viewed from a political perspective. Some writers argue that what the mental health profession calls borderline personality disorder is simply a case of PTSD among women, and a diagnosis of PTSD puts the emphasis on the victimization of women rather than on their mental illness. This distinction in assigning a diagnosis is an important one and represents a debate that will continue for some time (Becker, 2000). These observations all seem to support the hypothesis that borderline personality disorder may be caused by early trauma. It is important to remember, however, that not all cases of borderline personality disorder resemble PTSD (Zanarini et al., 1998).

Borderline personality disorder has been observed among people who have gone through rapid cultural changes. The problems of identity, emptiness, fears of abandonment, and low anxiety threshold have been found in child and adult immigrants (Laxenaire, Ganne-Vevonec, & Streiff, 1982; Skhiri, Annabi, Bi, & Allani, 1982). These observations further support the possibility that early trauma may, in some individuals, lead to borderline personality disorder.

Remember, however, that a history of childhood trauma, including sexual and physical abuse, occurs in a number of other disorders, such as somatoform disorder, panic disorder, and dissociative identity disorder. In addition, a portion of individuals with borderline personality disorder have no apparent history of such abuse (Gunderson & Sabo, 1993). Although childhood sexual and physical abuse seems to play some role in the etiology of borderline personality disorder, neither appears to be necessary or sufficient to produce the syndrome. Zanarini and Frankenberg (1997) attempt to integrate the different aspects of etiology in borderline personality disorder. They suggest that childhood trauma combines with a predisposing temperament or personality and a stressful triggering event causes the unstable behaviours. The individuals abused as children who do not develop the disorder may lack the biological predisposition that, in this case, may be a volatile or impulsive personality style (Figueroa & Silk, 1997).

### Treatment

In contrast to the extensive research on the nature of borderline personality disorder, relatively few studies have examined the effects of treatment. Many people appear to respond positively to a variety of medications, including tricyclic antidepressants (Soloff et al., 1989; Stone, 1986) and lithium (Links, Steiner, Boiago, & Irwin, 1990). However, efforts to provide successful treatment are complicated by problems with drug abuse, non-compliance with treatment, and suicide attempts. As a result, many clinicians are reluctant to work with people who have borderline personality disorder.

Research on psychological treatment is growing (Gunderson, 2001; Gunderson & Links, 2001). One of the most thoroughly researched treatments was developed by Linehan (1987, 1993). This approach—which she calls *dialectical behaviour therapy* (DBT)—involves helping people cope with the stressors that seem to trigger suicidal behaviours. Weekly individual sessions provide support, and patients are taught how to identify and regulate their emotions (McMain, Korman, & Dimeff, 2001). Problem solving is emphasized so that they can handle difficulties more effectively. In addition, they receive treatment similar to that used for people with PTSD, in which prior traumatic events are re-experienced to help extinguish the fear associated with them (see Chapter 4). In the final stage of therapy, clients learn to trust their own responses rather than depend on the validation of others, sometimes by visualizing themselves not reacting to criticism.

Preliminary results suggest that DBT may help reduce suicide attempts, dropouts from treatment, and hospitalizations (Linehan, Armstrong, Suarez, Allmon, & Heard, 1991; Linehan, Heard, & Armstrong, 1992). A follow-up of 39 women who received either DBT or general therapeutic support (called "treatment as usual") for 1 year showed that, during the first 6 months of follow-up, the women in the DBT group were less suicidal, less angry, and better adjusted socially (Linehan & Kehrer, 1993). Another study examined how treating these individuals with DBT in an inpatient setting—psychiatric hospital—for approximately 3 months before discharge to home would improve their outcomes (Bohus et al., 2000). The participants improved in a number of areas such as with a reduction in self-injury (e.g., cutting themselves), depression, and anxiety. Additional work remains to be done on validating this approach to treatment, including more follow-up data on long-term outcomes (Westen, 2000) and reducing the feelings of hopelessness experienced by people with this disorder (Scheel, 2000); nevertheless, the results so far make this type of treatment promising.

## Histrionic Personality Disorder

Individuals with **histrionic personality disorder** tend to be overly dramatic and often seem almost to be acting, which is why the term *histrionic*, which means theatrical in manner, is used. Consider the case of Pat.

### Pat
#### Always Onstage

When we first met, Pat seemed to radiate enjoyment of life. She was single, in her mid-30s, and was going to university part-time for her master's degree. She often dressed flamboyantly. During the day she taught children with disabilities, and when she didn't have class in the evening she was often out late on a date. When I first spoke with her, she enthusiastically told me how impressed she was with my work in the field of developmental disabilities and that she had been extremely successful in using some of my techniques with her students. She was clearly overdoing the praise, but who wouldn't appreciate such flattering comments?

Because some of our research included children in her classroom, I saw Pat frequently. Over a period of weeks, however, our interactions grew strained. She frequently complained of various illnesses and injuries (falling in the parking lot, twisting her neck looking out a window) that interfered with her work. She was very disorganized, often leaving to the last minute tasks that required considerable planning. Pat made promises to other people that were impossible to keep but seemed to be aimed at winning their approval; when she broke the promise, she usually made up a story designed to elicit sympathy and compassion. For example, she promised the mother of one of her students that she would put on a "massive and unique" birthday party for her daughter but completely forgot about it until the mother showed up with cake and juice. Upon seeing her, Pat flew into a rage and blamed the principal for keeping her late after school, although there was no truth to this accusation.

Pat often interrupted meetings about research to talk about her latest boyfriend. The boyfriends changed almost weekly, but her enthusiasm ("Like no other man I have ever met!") and optimism about the future ("He's the guy I want to spend the rest of my life with!") remained high for each of them. Wedding plans were seriously discussed

**histrionic personality disorder** Cluster B (dramatic, emotional, or erratic) personality disorder involving a pervasive pattern of excessive emotionality and attention seeking.

with almost every one, despite their brief acquaintance. Pat was ingratiating, especially to the male teachers, who often helped her out of trouble she got into because of her disorganization.

When it became clear that she would probably lose her teaching job because of her poor performance, Pat managed to manipulate several of the male teachers and the assistant principal into recommending her for a new job in a nearby school district. A year later she was still at the new school but had been moved twice to different classrooms. According to teachers she worked with, Pat still lacked close interpersonal relationships, although she described her current relationship as "deeply involved." After a rather long period of depression, Pat sought help from a psychologist, who diagnosed her as also having histrionic personality disorder.

## Clinical Description

People with histrionic personality disorder are inclined to express their emotions in an exaggerated fashion, for example, hugging someone they have just met or crying uncontrollably during a sad movie (Pfohl, 1995). They also tend to be vain, self-centred, and uncomfortable when they are not in the limelight. They are often seductive in appearance and behaviour, and they are typically very concerned about their looks. Pat, for example, spent a great deal of money on unusual jewellery and was sure to point it out to anyone who would listen. In addition, people with histrionic personality disorder seek reassurance and approval constantly and may become upset or angry when others do not attend to them or praise them. People with histrionic personality disorder also tend to be impulsive and have great difficulty delaying gratification.

People with histrionic personality disorder tend to be vain, extravagant, and seductive.

The cognitive style associated with histrionic personality disorder is impressionistic (Shapiro, 1965), characterized by a tendency to view situations in global, black-and-white terms. Speech is often vague, lacking in detail, and characterized by hyperbole (Pfohl, 1991). For example, when Pat was asked about a date she had had the night before, she might say it was "way cool" but fail to provide more detailed information.

The high rate of this diagnosis among women versus men raises questions about the nature of the disorder and its diagnostic criteria. As we first discussed in the beginning of this chapter, there is some thought that the features of histrionic personality disorder, such as overdramatization, vanity, seductiveness, and overconcern with physical appearance, are characteristic of the Western stereotypical female and may lead to an overdiagnosis among women. Sprock (2000) examined this important question and found some evidence for a bias among psychologists and psychiatrists to associate the diagnosis with women rather than men.

**Disorder Criteria Summary**
Histrionic Personality Disorder

Features of histrionic personality disorder include:
- Pervasive pattern of excessive emotionality and attention seeking, beginning by early adulthood and present in a variety of contexts
- Discomfort in situations in which he or she is not the centre of attention
- Interaction with others often characterized by inappropriate sexually seductive or provocative behaviour
- Displays rapidly shifting and shallow expressions of emotion
- Consistently uses physical appearance to draw attention
- Style of speech that is excessively impressionistic and lacks details
- Is easily influenced by others or circumstances
- Considers relationships to be more intimate than they actually are

*Source:* Based on DSM-IV-TR. Used with permission from the *Diagnostic and Statistical Manual of Mental Disorders*, Fourth Edition, Text Revision. Copyright 2000. American Psychiatric Association.

## Causes

Despite its long history, little research has been done on the causes or treatment of histrionic personality disorder. One hypothesis involves a possible relationship with antisocial personality disorder. Evidence suggests that histrionic personality and antisocial personality co-occur much more often than chance would account for. Lilienfeld and his colleagues (1986), for example, found that roughly two-thirds of people with histrionic personality also met criteria for antisocial personality disorder. The evidence for this association has led to the suggestion (e.g., Cloninger, 1978; Lilienfeld, 1992) that histrionic personality and antisocial personality may be sex-typed alternative expressions of the same unidentified underlying condition. Females with the underlying condition may be predisposed to exhibit a predominantly histrionic pattern, whereas males with the underlying condition may be predisposed to exhibit a predominantly antisocial pattern.

### Treatment

Although a great deal has been written about ways of helping people with this disorder, little research demonstrates success (Dulit et al., 1993; Horowitz, 2001). Some therapists have tried to modify the attention-getting behaviour. Kass, Silvers, and Abrams (1972) worked with five women, four of whom had been hospitalized for suicide attempts and all of whom were later diagnosed with histrionic personality disorder. The women were rewarded for appropriate interactions and fined for attention-getting behaviour. The therapists noted improvement after an 18-month follow-up, but they did not collect scientific data to confirm their observation.

A large part of therapy for these individuals usually focuses on the problematic interpersonal relationships. They often manipulate others through emotional crises, using charm, sex, seductiveness, or complaining (Beck & Freeman, 1990). People with histrionic personality disorder often need to be shown how the short-term gains derived from this interactional style result in long-term costs, and they need to be taught more appropriate ways of negotiating their wants and needs.

## Narcissistic Personality Disorder

We all know people who think highly of themselves—perhaps exaggerating their real abilities. They consider themselves somehow different from others and deserving of special treatment. In **narcissistic personality disorder,** this tendency is taken to its extreme. In Greek mythology, Narcissus was a youth who spurned the love of Echo. So enamoured was he of his own beauty, that he spent his days admiring his own image reflected in a pool of water. Psychoanalysts, including Freud, used the term *narcissistic* to describe people who show an exaggerated sense of self-importance and are preoccupied with receiving attention (Cooper & Ronningstam, 1992). Consider the case of Willie.

### Willie
#### It's All About Me

Willie was an office assistant in a small attorney's office. Now in his early 30s, Willie had an extremely poor job history. He never stayed employed at the same place for more than 2 years, and spent considerable time working through temporary employment agencies. Your first encounter, though, would make you believe that he was extremely competent and that he ran the office. If you entered the waiting room you were greeted by Willie, even though he wasn't the receptionist. He would be extremely solicitous, asking how he could be of assistance, offer you coffee, and ask you to make yourself comfortable in "his" reception area. Willie liked to talk, and any conversation was quickly redirected in a way that kept him the centre of attention.

This type of ingratiating manner was welcomed at first but soon annoyed other staff. This was especially true when he referred to the other workers in the office as his staff, even though he was not responsible for supervising any of them. The conversations with visitors and staff often consumed a great deal of his time and the time of other staff, and this was becoming a problem.

He quickly became controlling in his job—a pattern that was revealed in his other positions—eagerly taking charge of duties that were assigned to others. Unfortunately, he did not complete these tasks well, and this created a great deal of friction.

When confronted with any of these difficulties, Willie would first blame others. Ultimately, though, it would become clear that Willie's self-centredness and controlling nature were at the root of many of the office inefficiencies. During a disciplinary meeting with all of the law firm's partners, an unusual step, Willie became explosively abusive and blamed them for being out to get him. He insisted that his performance was exceptional at all of his previous positions—something that was contradicted by his previous employers—and that they were at fault. After calming down, he revealed a previous drinking problem, a history of depression, and multiple family problems, all of which he believed contributed to any difficulties he experienced.

**narcissistic personality disorder** Cluster B (dramatic, emotional, or erratic) personality disorder involving a pervasive pattern of grandiosity in fantasy or behaviour; need for admiration, and lack of empathy.

The firm recommended he be seen at a university clinic as a condition of his continued employment, where he was diagnosed with major depression and narcissistic personality disorder.

## Clinical Description

People with narcissistic personality disorder have an unreasonable sense of self-importance and are so preoccupied with themselves that they lack sensitivity and compassion for other people (Gunderson, Ronningstam, & Smith, 1995). They aren't comfortable unless someone is admiring them. Their exaggerated feelings and their fantasies of greatness, called *grandiosity*, create a number of negative attributes. They require and expect a great deal of special attention—the best table in the restaurant, the illegal parking space in front of the movie theatre. They also tend to use or exploit others for their own interests and show little empathy. When confronted with other successful people, they can be extremely envious and arrogant. And because they often fail to live up to their own expectations, they are frequently depressed.

## Disorder Criteria Summary
### Narcissistic Personality Disorder

Features of narcissistic personality disorder include:

- Pervasive pattern of grandiosity and need for admiration and empathy, beginning by early adulthood
- Grandiose sense of self-importance (e.g., exaggerates talents)
- Preoccupation with fantasies of unlimited success, power, brilliance, beauty, or ideal love
- Belief that he or she is "special" and can only be understood by, or should associate with, other special or high-status people
- Requests excessive admiration
- Attitude of entitlement toward fulfilling expectations
- Exploits others to achieve ends
- Lacks empathy
- Is often envious of others or believes that others are envious
- Arrogant manner

*Source:* Based on DSM-IV-TR. Used with permission from the *Diagnostic and Statistical Manual of Mental Disorders*, Fourth Edition, Text Revision. Copyright 2000, American Psychiatric Association.

## Causes and Treatment

We start out as infants being self-centred and demanding, which is part of our struggle for survival. However, part of the socialization process involves teaching children empathy and altruism.

Some writers, including Austrian native Heinz Kohut (1971, 1977), believe that narcissistic personality disorder arises largely from a profound failure of modelling empathy by the parents early in a child's development. As a consequence, the child remains fixated at a self-centred, grandiose stage of development. In addition, the child (and later the adult) becomes involved in an essentially endless and fruitless search for the ideal person who will meet his or her unfulfilled empathic needs.

In a sociological view, Lasch (1978) wrote in his popular book *The Culture of Narcissism* that this personality disorder is increasing in prevalence in most Western societies, primarily as a consequence of large-scale social changes, including greater emphasis on short-term hedonism, individualism, competitiveness, and success. According to Lasch, the "me generation" has produced more than its share of individuals with narcissistic personality disorder. Indeed, reports confirm that narcissistic personality disorder is increasing in prevalence (Cooper & Ronningstam, 1992). However, this apparent rise may be a consequence of increased interest in and research on the disorder.

Some have questioned whether narcissism and psychopathy are redundant concepts. A study by Delroy Paulhus and his colleague at the University of British Columbia addressed this issue (Paulhus & Williams, 2002). They administered measures of psychopathy and narcissism to 245 students along with other measures including a measure of the five-factor model of personality. Although psychopaths and narcissists were found to share elevated disagreeableness on the five-factor measure and a tendency to be self-enhancers, they did not share any other features. The authors thus concluded that narcissism and psychopathy are overlapping but distinct traits.

Treatment research is extremely limited in both number of studies and reports of success (Groopman & Cooper, 2001). When therapy is attempted with these individuals it often focuses on their grandiosity, their hypersensitivity to evaluation, and their lack of empathy toward others (Beck & Freeman, 1990). Cognitive therapy aims at replacing their fantasies with a focus on the day-to-day pleasurable experiences that are truly attainable. Coping strategies such as relaxation training are used to help them face and accept criticism. Helping them focus on the feelings of others is also a goal. Because individuals with this disorder are vulnerable to severe depressive episodes, particularly in middle age, treatment is often initiated for the depression. However, it is impossible to draw any conclusions about the impact of such treatment on the actual narcissistic personality disorder.

Correctly identify the type of personality disorder described below.

1. Matt is 19 and has been in trouble with the law since he was 14. He lies to his parents, vandalizes buildings in the community, and, when caught, shows no remorse. He frequently fights with others and doesn't care whom he injures. _____

2. Alan is involved in drugs and has casual sexual encounters. He feels empty unless he does dangerous and exciting things. He threatens to commit suicide if his girlfriend suggests getting help or if she talks about leaving him. He alternates between loving her and hating her. He has low self-esteem and has recently experienced high levels of stress. _____

3. The therapist immediately notices that Joan displays extreme emotional behaviour a great deal when she speaks, so much so that she seems to be acting. _____

4. Katherine thinks she is the best candidate for any job, thinks her performance is always excellent, and looks for admiration from others. _____

# Cluster C Personality Disorders

■ *Describe the essential characteristics of each of the Cluster C (anxious/fearful) personality disorders, including information pertaining to etiology and treatment.*

People diagnosed with the next three personality disorders we highlight—avoidant, dependent, and obsessive-compulsive—share common features with people who have anxiety disorders. These "anxious" or "fearful" personality disorders are described next.

## Avoidant Personality Disorder

As the name suggests, people with **avoidant personality disorder** are extremely sensitive to the opinions of others and therefore avoid most relationships. Their extremely low self-esteem, coupled with a fear of rejection, causes them to be limited in their friendships and very dependent on those they feel comfortable with. Consider the case of Jane.

### Jane
#### Not Worth Noticing

Jane was raised by an alcoholic mother who had borderline personality disorder and who abused her verbally and physically. As a child she made sense of her mother's abusive treatment by believing that she (Jane) must be an intrinsically unworthy person to be treated so badly. As an adult in her late 20s, Jane still expected to be rejected when others found out that she was inherently unworthy and bad.

Jane was highly self-critical and predicted that she would not be accepted. She thought that people would not like her, that they would see she was a loser, and that she would not have anything to say. She became upset if she perceived that someone in even the most fleeting encounter was reacting negatively or neutrally. If a newspaper vendor failed to smile at her or a sales clerk was slightly curt, Jane automatically thought it must be because she (Jane) was somehow unworthy or unlikable. She then felt quite sad. Even when she was receiving positive feedback from a friend, she discounted it. As a result, Jane had few friends and certainly no close ones.

(Case excerpt from *Cognitive Therapy of Personality Disorders*, by A. T. Beck and A. Freeman, 1990. Copyright © 1990 by Guilford Press. Reprinted with permission.)

### Clinical Description

Millon (1981), who initially proposed this diagnosis, notes that it is important to distinguish between individuals who are asocial because they are apathetic, affectively flat, and relatively uninterested in

**avoidant personality disorder**  Cluster C (anxious or fearful) personality disorder featuring a pervasive pattern of social inhibition, feelings of inadequacy, and hypersensitivity to criticism.

interpersonal relationships (comparable to what DSM-IV-TR terms *schizoid personality disorder*) and individuals who are asocial because they are interpersonally anxious and fearful of rejection. It is the latter who fit the criteria of avoidant personality disorder (Millon & Martinez, 1995). These individuals feel chronically rejected by others and are pessimistic about their future.

## Causes

A number of theories have been proposed that integrate biological and psychosocial influences as the cause of avoidant personality disorder. Millon (1981), for example, suggests that these individuals may be born with a difficult temperament or personality characteristics. As a result, their parents may reject them or at least not provide them with enough early, uncritical love. This rejection, in turn, may result in low self-esteem and social alienation, conditions that persist into adulthood. Limited support does exist for psychosocial influences. Stravynski, Elie, and Franche (1989) questioned a group of people with avoidant personality disorder and a group of healthy controls about their early treatment by their parents. Those with the disorder remembered their parents as more rejecting, more guilt engendering, and less affectionate than the control group. Meyer and Carver (2000) found that these individuals were more likely to report childhood experiences of isolation, rejection, and conflict with others.

In interpreting the results of these studies some caution is in order. You probably noticed that these are *retrospective studies,* relying on the participants' memories for a report of what had happened. The differences in the reports could be a consequence of differences in their ability to remember their childhoods rather than actual differences in the ways they were treated. Also, it could be that people with avoidant personality disorder are more sensitive to the way they are treated; therefore, their memories are different from what actually happened. The findings are intriguing nonetheless and should be followed up as a possible contributor to our understanding of this disorder.

## Treatment

In contrast to the scarcity of research into most of the other personality disorders, there are a number of well-controlled studies on approaches to therapy for people with avoidant personality disorder (Sutherland, 2001). Lynn Alden and her colleagues have been at the forefront of the field in developing effective approaches for treating individuals with avoidant personality disorder. Behavioural intervention techniques for anxiety and social skills

## Disorder Criteria Summary
### Avoidant Personality Disorder

Features of avoidant personality disorder include:
- Pervasive pattern of social inhibition, feelings of inadequacy, and hypersensitivity to negative evaluation, beginning by early adulthood
- Avoidance of occupational activities that involve significant interpersonal contact because of fears of criticism or rejection
- Unwillingness to get involved with people unless certain of being liked
- Restraint with intimate relationships because of fear of being shamed or ridiculed
- Preoccupation with being criticized or rejected in social situations
- Inhibited in new interpersonal situations because of feelings of inadequacy
- Views self as socially inept, unappealing, or inferior
- Unusual reluctance to take personal risks or to engage in new activities for fear they may prove embarrassing

*Source:* Based on DSM-IV-TR. Used with permission from the *Diagnostic and Statistical Manual of Mental Disorders,* Fourth Edition, Text Revision. Copyright 2000. American Psychiatric Association.

problems have had some success (Alden, 1989; Alden & Capreol, 1993; Renneberg, Goldstein, Phillips, & Chambless, 1990; Stravynski, Lesage, Marcouiller, & Elie, 1989). In particular, Alden's work shows that social skills training within a support group can help people with avoidant personality disorder become more assertive (e.g., Alden, 1989). Because the problems experienced by people with avoidant personality disorder resemble those of people with social phobia, many of the same treatments are used for both groups (see Chapter 4).

Renneberg et al. (1990) identified areas that caused anxiety in a group of 17 people with avoidant personality disorder, including a fear of rejection, a fear of criticism, and anxiety about their appearance. In groups of 5 or 6 patients, they used *systematic desensitization,* which involves relaxing in the presence of feared situations (e.g., "You speak to a group of people at work, and you realize that your voice is not powerful enough. Your voice is childish"), and *behavioural rehearsal,* in which patients act out situations that cause anxiety. As a group, these people improved in such areas as fear of negative evaluation and social avoidance and distress. The improvements tended to be modest, although, given the usually poor outcomes found among people with personality disorders, even moderate improvement is encouraging.

## *Dependent Personality Disorder*

We all know what it means to be dependent on another person. People with **dependent personality disorder,** however, rely on others to make ordinary decisions as well as important ones, which results in an unreasonable fear of abandonment. Consider the case of Karen.

### Karen
#### Whatever You Say

Karen was a 45-year-old married woman who was referred for treatment by her physician for problems with panic attacks. During the evaluation, she appeared to be very worried, sensitive, and naive. She was easily overcome with emotion and cried on and off throughout the session. She was self-critical at every opportunity throughout the evaluation. For example, when asked how she got along with other people, she reported that "others think I'm dumb and inadequate," although she could give no evidence as to what made her think that. She reported that she didn't like school because "I was dumb," and that she always felt that she was not good enough.

Karen described staying in her first marriage for 10 years, even though "it was hell." Her husband had affairs with many other women and was verbally abusive. She tried to leave him many times but gave in to his repeated requests to return. She was finally able to divorce him, and shortly afterward she met and married her current husband, whom she described as kind, sensitive, and supportive. Karen stated that she preferred to have others make important decisions and agreed with other people in order to avoid conflict. She worried about being left alone without anyone to take care of her and reported feeling lost without other people's reassurance. She also reported that her feelings were easily hurt, so she worked hard not to do anything that might lead to criticism.

(Case excerpt from *Cognitive Therapy of Personality Disorders,* by A. T. Beck and A. Freeman, 1990. Copyright © 1990 by Guilford Press. Reprinted with permission.)

### Clinical Description

Dependent personality disorder belongs in the anxious/fearful cluster of DSM-IV-TR personality disorders because the interpersonally dependent behaviour is motivated by anxiety (Stewart,

Knize, & Pihl, 1992). Individuals with dependent personality disorder sometimes agree with other people when their own opinion differs to avoid being rejected (Hirschfeld, Shea, & Weise, 1995). Their desire to obtain and maintain supportive and nurturant relationships may lead to their other behavioural characteristics (Bornstein, 1997), including submissiveness, timidity, and passivity. People with this disorder are similar to those with *avoidant personality disorder* in their feelings of inadequacy, sensitivity to criticism, and need for reassurance. However, people with avoidant personality disorder respond to these feelings by avoiding relationships, whereas those with dependent personality disorder respond by clinging to relationships (Hirschfeld, Shea, & Weise, 1991).

### Causes and Treatment

We are all born dependent on other people for food, physical protection, and nurturance. Part of the socialization process involves helping us live independently (Bornstein, 1992). It is thought such disruptions as the early death of a parent or neglect or rejection by caregivers may cause people to grow up fearing abandonment (Stone, 1993). This view comes from work in child development on "attachment," or how children learn to bond with their parents and other people who are important in their lives (Bowlby, 1977). If early bonding is interrupted, individuals may be constantly anxious that they will lose people close to them.

Research by David A. Clark and his colleagues suggests that certain personality traits may be relevant to the etiology of dependent personality disorder, as well. In particular, these researchers have been investigating the role of the personality constructs of sociotropy and autonomy. *Sociotropy* refers to a personality orientation involving a strong investment in positive social interactions, whereas *autonomy* refers to a personality style involving a strong investment in independence from others, mobility, and freedom of choice (Beck, 1983, 1987). Clark, Steer, Haslam, Beck, and Brown (1997) found that a sample of 2000 psychiatric patients was characterized by four clusters in terms of patients' responses to a sociotropy–autonomy measure: an autonomous group, a sociotropic group, an individualistic achievement group, and a group of low-scoring patients. Diagnoses of dependent personality disorder were significantly more common in the

---

**dependent personality disorder**  Cluster C (anxious or fearful) personality disorder characterized by a person's pervasive and excessive need to be taken care of, a condition that leads to submissive and clinging behaviour and fears of separation.

sociotropic group, and significantly less common in the individualistic achievement group, compared with the other groups (Clark et al., 1997).

**Disorder Criteria Summary**
Dependent Personality Disorder

Features of dependent personality disorder include:
- Pervasive and excessive need to be taken care of that leads to submissive and clinging behaviour and fears of separation, beginning by early adulthood
- Difficulty in making everyday decisions without advice and reassurance from others
- Relies on others to assume responsibility for most major areas of her or his life
- Difficulty expressing disagreement with others for fear of loss of support or because of lack of self-confidence
- Difficulty in initiating projects or doing things alone because of lack of self-confidence
- Goes to excessive lengths to obtain nurturing and support from others
- Feels uncomfortable or helpless when alone
- Urgently seeks another relationship as a source of care and support when a close relationship ends
- Unreasonably preoccupied with fears of being left to take care of self

*Source:* Based on DSM-IV-TR. Used with permission from the *Diagnostic and Statistical Manual of Mental Disorders,* Fourth Edition, Text Revision. Copyright 2000. American Psychiatric Association.

The treatment literature for this disorder is mostly descriptive; very little research exists to show whether a particular treatment is effective (Perry, 2001). On the surface, because of their attentiveness and eagerness to give responsibility for their problems to the therapist, people with dependent personality disorder can appear to be ideal patients. However, their submissiveness negates one of the major goals of therapy, which is to make the person more independent and personally responsible. Therapy therefore progresses gradually, as the patient develops confidence in his or her ability to make decisions independently (Beck & Freeman, 1990). There is a particular need for care that the patient does not become overly dependent on the therapist.

## Obsessive-Compulsive Personality Disorder

People who have **obsessive-compulsive personality disorder** are characterized by a fixation on things being done "the right way." Although many might envy their persistence and dedication, this preoccupation with details prevents them from completing much of anything. Consider the case of Daniel.

## Daniel
### Getting It Exactly Right

Each day at exactly 8 a.m., Daniel arrived at his office at the university where he was a graduate student in psychology. On his way, he always stopped at Tim Hortons to buy coffee. After arriving at his office, he drank his coffee and read *The Globe and Mail* from 8 to 9:15 a.m. At 9:15 he reorganized the files that held the hundreds of papers related to his doctoral dissertation, now several years overdue. From 10 a.m. until noon he read one of these papers, highlighting relevant passages. Then he took the paper bag that held his lunch (always a peanut butter and jelly sandwich and an apple) and went to the cafeteria to purchase a soft drink and eat by himself. From 1 p.m. until 5 p.m. he held meetings, organized his desk, made lists of things to do, and entered his references into a new database program on his computer. At home, Daniel had dinner with his wife, then worked on his dissertation until after 11 p.m., although much of the time was spent trying out new features of his home computer.

Daniel was no closer to completing his dissertation than he had been four and a half years ago. His wife was threatening to leave him because he was equally rigid about everything at home and she didn't want to remain in this limbo of graduate school forever. When Daniel eventually sought help from a therapist for his anxiety over his deteriorating marriage, he was diagnosed as having obsessive-compulsive personality disorder.

## Clinical Description

Like many with this personality disorder, Daniel is work oriented, spending little time going to movies or parties or doing anything that isn't related to psychology. Because of their general rigidity, these people tend to have poor interpersonal relationships (Pfohl & Blum, 1995).

This personality disorder seems to be only distantly related to obsessive-compulsive disorder (OCD), one of the anxiety disorders we described

**obsessive-compulsive personality disorder** Cluster C (anxious or fearful) personality disorder featuring a pervasive pattern of preoccupation with orderliness, perfectionism, and mental and interpersonal control at the expense of flexibility, openness, and efficiency.

People with obsessive-compulsive personality disorder are preoccupied with doing things "the right way."

**Disorder Criteria Summary**
Obsessive-Compulsive Personality Disorder

Features of obsessive-compulsive personality disorder include:

- Pervasive pattern of preoccupation with orderliness, perfectionism, and mental and interpersonal control, at the expense of flexibility, openness, and efficiency, beginning by early adulthood
- Preoccupation with details, rules, lists, order, organization, or schedules to the extent that the major point of the activity is lost
- Perfectionism that interferes with task completion
- Excessively devoted to work and productivity to the exclusion of leisure activities and friendships
- Overly conscientious, scrupulous, and inflexible about matters of morality, ethics, or values
- Inability to discard worn-out or worthless objects even with no sentimental value
- Reluctance to delegate tasks or to work with others unless they submit to exactly his or her way of doing things
- Adopts a miserly spending style toward both self and others, largely out of fear of future catastrophes
- Rigidity and stubbornness

*Source:* Based on DSM-IV-TR. Used with permission from the *Diagnostic and Statistical Manual of Mental Disorders,* Fourth Edition, Text Revision. Copyright 2000. American Psychiatric Association.

in Chapter 4. People like Daniel tend not to have the obsessive thoughts and the compulsive behaviours seen in the like-named OCD. Although people with the anxiety disorder sometimes show characteristics of the personality disorder, they also show the characteristics of other personality disorders as well (e.g., avoidant, histrionic, dependent; Stone, 1993).

An intriguing theory suggests that the psychological profiles of many serial killers point to the role of obsessive-compulsive personality disorder. Ferreira (2000) notes that these individuals do not often fit the definition of someone with a severe mental illness—such as schizophrenia—but are "masters of control" in manipulating their victims. Their need to control all aspects of the crime fits the pattern of people with obsessive-compulsive personality disorder, and some combination of this disorder and unfortunate childhood experiences may lead to this disturbing behaviour pattern. At the other end of the behavioural spectrum, it is common to find obsessive-compulsive personality disorder among gifted children, whose quest for perfectionism can be debilitating (Nugent, 2000).

Causes and Treatment

There seems to be a weak genetic contribution to this disorder (McKeon & Murray, 1987; Stone, 1993). Some people may be predisposed to favour structure in their lives, but to reach the level it did in Daniel may require parental reinforcement of conformity and neatness.

We do not have much information on the successful treatment of individuals with this disorder (McCullough & Maltsberger, 2001). Therapy often attacks the fears that seem to underlie the need for orderliness. These individuals are often afraid that what they do will be inadequate, so they procrastinate and excessively ruminate about important issues and minor details alike. Therapists help the individual relax or use distraction techniques to redirect the compulsive thoughts. Research by Alberta investigators Kirsten Ferguson and Margaret Rodway (1994) indicates that cognitive behaviour therapy can be effective in treating one important aspect of obsessive compulsive personality disorder—namely perfectionism.

**Concept Check 11.4**

Match the following scenarios with the correct personality disorder.

1. Lynn is afraid to be alone and seeks constant reassurance from her family and friends. Only 1 month after her first abusive marriage ended, she jumped into another marriage with a man she hardly knew. She thinks that if she shows any resolve or initiative she will be abandoned and will have to take care of herself. Lynn is self-critical and claims she is unintelligent and has no skills. _____

2. The therapist discovers that Tim has yet to fill out the information form, although he was given at least 15 minutes. Tim says he first had to resharpen the pencil, clean it of debris, and then he noticed the pencil sharpener wasn't clean. The paper also wasn't properly placed on the clipboard. _____

3. Jeffery is especially anxious at even the thought of social interaction. He disregards compliments and reacts excessively to criticism, which only feeds his pervasive feelings of inadequacy. Jeffery takes everything personally, assuming that neighbors don't say hello because he is a nuisance to live by. _____

# Personality Disorders Under Study

■ *Describe some "personality disorders" that have been proposed for inclusion in the DSM categorization (e.g., depressive personality disorder, negativistic personality disorder).*

We started this chapter by noting difficulties in categorizing personality disorders. For example, the high overlap between categories suggests there may be other ways to arrange these pervasive difficulties of character. It shouldn't surprise you to learn that other personality disorders have been proposed for inclusion in the DSM—for example, sadistic personality disorder, which includes people who receive pleasure by inflicting pain on others (Fiester & Gay, 1995), and self-defeating personality disorder, which includes people who are overly passive and accept the pain and suffering imposed by others (Fiester, 1995). However, few studies supported the existence of these disorders, so they were not included in DSM-IV-TR

(Pfohl, 1993). Two new categories of personality disorder are under study. *Depressive personality disorder* includes self-criticism, dejection, a judgmental stance toward others, and a tendency to feel guilt. Some evidence indicates this may indeed be a personality disorder distinct from dysthymic disorder (the chronic mood disorder described in Chapter 6); research is continuing in this area (Phillips et al., 1998). *Negativistic personality disorder* is characterized by passive aggression in which people adopt a negativistic attitude to resist routine demands and expectations (Fossati et al., 2000). Neither category has yet had enough research support to warrant inclusion as additional personality disorders in the DSM.

# Summary

## An Overview of Personality Disorders

• The personality disorders represent long-standing and ingrained ways of thinking, feeling, and behaving that can cause significant distress. Because people may display two or more of these maladaptive ways of interacting with the world, considerable disagreement remains over how to categorize the personality disorders.

• DSM-IV-TR includes 10 personality disorders that are divided into three clusters: Cluster A ("odd or eccentric") includes paranoid, schizoid, and schizotypal personality disorders; Cluster B ("dramatic, emotional, or erratic") includes antisocial, borderline, histrionic, and narcissistic personality disorders; Cluster C ("anxious or fearful") includes avoidant, dependent, and obsessive-compulsive personality disorders.

## Cluster A Personality Disorders

• People with paranoid personality disorder are excessively mistrustful and suspicious of other people without justification. They tend not to confide in others and expect other people to do them harm.

• People with schizoid personality disorder show a pattern of detachment from social relationships and a very limited range of emotions in interpersonal situations. They seem aloof, cold, and indifferent to other people.

• People with schizotypal personality disorder are typically socially isolated and behave in ways that would seem unusual to most of us. In addition, they tend to be suspicious and have odd beliefs about the world.

## Cluster B Personality Disorders

- People with antisocial personality disorder have a history of failing to comply with social norms. They perform actions most of us would find unacceptable, such as stealing from friends and family. They also tend to be irresponsible, impulsive, and deceitful.
- In contrast to the DSM-IV-TR criteria for antisocial personality, which focuses almost entirely on observable behaviours (e.g., impulsively and repeatedly changing employment, residence, or sexual partners), the related concept of psychopathy primarily reflects underlying personality traits (e.g., self-centredness and manipulativeness).
- People with borderline personality disorder lack stability in their moods and in their relationships with other people, and they usually have poor self-esteem. These individuals often feel empty and are at great risk of suicide.
- Individuals with histrionic personality disorder tend to be overly dramatic and often appear almost to be acting.
- People with narcissistic personality disorder think highly of themselves—beyond their real abilities. They consider themselves somehow different from others and deserving of special treatment.

## Cluster C Personality Disorders

- People with avoidant personality disorder are extremely sensitive to the opinions of others and therefore avoid social relationships. Their extremely low self-esteem, coupled with a fear of rejection, causes them to reject the attention others desire.
- Individuals with dependent personality disorder rely on others to the extent of letting them make everyday decisions and major ones; this results in an unreasonable fear of being abandoned.
- People who have obsessive-compulsive personality disorder are characterized by a fixation on things being done "the right way." This preoccupation with details prevents them from completing much of anything.

## Treatment

- Treating people with personality disorders is often difficult because they usually do not see that their difficulties are a result of the way they relate to others.
- Personality disorders are important for the clinician to consider because they may interfere with efforts to treat more specific problems such as anxiety, depression, or substance abuse. Unfortunately, the presence of one or more personality disorders is associated with a poor treatment outcome and a generally negative prognosis.

## Key Terms

personality disorders, 446
paranoid personality
    disorder, 452
schizoid personality
    disorder, 454

schizotypal personality
    disorder, 456
antisocial personality
    disorder, 459
psychopathy, 460

borderline personality
    disorder, 467
histrionic personality
    disorder, 470
narcissistic personality
    disorder, 472

avoidant personality
    disorder, 474
dependent personality
    disorder, 476
obsessive-compulsive
    personality
    disorder, 477

## Answers to Concept Checks

**11.1**  1. chronic   2. Axis II   3. categories
    4. Cluster A, Cluster B, Cluster C   5. bias
    6. comorbidity

**11.2**  1. schizoid   2. paranoid   3. schizotypal

**11.3**  1. antisocial   2. borderline   3. histrionic
    4. narcissistic

**11.4**  1. dependent   2. obsessive-compulsive
    3. avoidant

 **InfoTrac College Edition**

If your instructor ordered your book with InfoTrac College Edition, please explore this online library for additional readings, review, and a handy resource for short assignments. Go to:

**http://infotrac.thomsonlearning.com**

Enter these search terms: personality disorder, psychopathy

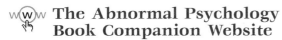 **The Abnormal Psychology Book Companion Website**

Go to **www.essentialsabnormalpsych.nelson.com** for practice quiz questions, Internet links, critical thinking exercises, and more.

 **Abnormal Psychology Live CD-ROM**

- **Antisocial Personality Disorder:** George describes his long history of violating people's rights.
- **Borderline Personality Disorders:** These women discuss the most troubling symptoms of their disorder.

**Thomson NOW!** **http://hed.nelson.com** Go to this site for the link to ThomsonNow™, your one-stop study shop. Take a Pretest for this chapter and ThomsonNow™ will generate a personalized Study Plan based on your test results! The Study Plan will identify the topics you need to review and direct you to online resources to help you master those topics. You can then take a Posttest to help you determine the concepts you have mastered and what you still need work on.

## Video Concept Review

For challenging concepts that typically need more than one explanation, Mark Durand provides a video review via ThomsonNow™ of the following topic:

- The differences between narcissistic personality disorder and histrionic personality disorder.

# Chapter Quiz

1. The dimensional versus categorical debate over the nature of personality disorders can also be described as a debate between _____ and _____.
   a. diagnosis; prognosis
   b. state; trait
   c. degree; kind
   d. qualitative; quantitative

2. Some personality disorders are diagnosed more frequently in men than in women. One explanation for this difference is that:
   a. symptoms are interpreted by clinicians in different ways depending on the gender of the person with the symptoms.
   b. men are more likely to seek help from mental health professionals than women.
   c. most clinicians are men, and they tend to see psychopathology more often in patients of the same gender as themselves.
   d. because of hormonal differences, women are more likely to have acute disorders and men are more likely to have chronic personality disorders.

3. Genetic research and an overlap in symptoms suggests a common relationship between schizophrenia and _____.
   a. borderline personality disorder
   b. schizotypal personality disorder
   c. schizoid personality disorder
   d. antisocial personality disorder

4. Criteria for psychopathy emphasize _____, and criteria for antisocial personality disorder emphasize _____.
   a. behaviour; personality
   b. personality; behaviour
   c. criminal conduct; social isolation
   d. social isolation; criminal conduct

5. Which symptom is characteristic of persons with borderline personality disorder?
   a. impulsivity
   b. hebephrenia
   c. mania
   d. grandiosity

6. Which theory suggests psychopaths may engage in antisocial and risk-taking behaviour to stimulate their cortical system?
   a. equifinality hypothesis
   b. transcortical magnetic stimulation hypothesis
   c. underarousal hypothesis
   d. equipotential hypothesis

7. Greeting a new acquaintance with effusive familiarity, crying uncontrollably during a movie, and trying to be the centre of attention at a party are typical behaviours of someone with:
   a. borderline personality disorder.
   b. narcissistic personality disorder.
   c. histrionic personality disorder.
   d. paranoid personality disorder.

8. Which of the following statements is most true about borderline personality disorder?
   a. Childhood abuse is rare in people with borderline personality disorder.
   b. Borderline personality disorder is more frequently diagnosed in men than in women.
   c. Behaviours in borderline personality disorder overlap those seen in posttraumatic stress disorder.
   d. Borderline personality disorder is seldom accompanied by self-mutilation.

9. People with which personality disorder often exhibit childlike, egocentric behaviours?
   a. paranoid
   b. antisocial
   c. schizotypal
   d. narcissistic

10. An individual who is preoccupied with details, rules, organization, and scheduling to the extent that it interferes with daily functioning may have:
    a. obsessive-compulsive personality disorder.
    b. narcissistic personality disorder.
    c. antisocial personality disorder.
    d. schizoid personality disorder.

*(See the Appendix on page 601 for answers.)*

# Exploring Personality Disorders

- People with personality disorders think and behave in ways that cause distress to themselves and/or the people who care about them.
- There are three main groups, or clusters, of personality disorders, which usually begin in childhood.

## HISTRIONIC
### excessively emotional

**Biological Influences**
- Possible link to antisocial disorder — women histrionic/men antisocial

**Psychological Influences**
- Vain and self-centred
- Easily upset if ignored
- Vague and hyperbolic
- Impulsive; difficulty delaying gratification

**CAUSES**

**Social/Cultural Influences**
- Overly dramatic behaviour attracts attention
- Seductive
- Approval-seeking

**Treatment**
- Little evidence of success
- Rewards and fines
- Focus on interpersonal relations

## PARANOID
### extreme suspicion

**Biological Influences**
- Possible but unclear link with schizophrenia

**Psychological Influences**
- Thoughts that people are malicious, deceptive, and threatening
- Behaviour based on mistaken assumptions about others

**CAUSES**

**Social/Cultural Influences**
- "Outsiders" may be susceptible because of unique experiences (e.g., prisoners, refugees, people with hearing impairments, and the elderly)
- Parents' early teaching may influence

**Treatment**
- Difficult because of client's mistrust and suspicion
- Cognitive work to change thoughts
- Low success rate

## CLUSTER A
### ODD OR ECCENTRIC

## CLUSTER B
### DRAMATIC, EMOTIONAL, OR ERRATIC

## NARCISSISTIC
### exaggerated self-importance

**Biological Influences**
- overlapping with, but distinct from, psychopathy

**Psychological Influences**
- pervasive grandiosity
- need for admiration
- lack of empathy

**CAUSES**

**Social/Cultural Influences**
- failure of parents to model empathy to young child
- increasing in prevalence in Western societies
- cultural emphasis on individualism and success

**Treatment**
- little research
- focuses on grandiosity, hypersensitivity to criticism, and lack of empathy
- often treatment for comorbid depression

*Gazelle Technologies*

## SCHIZOID
### social isolation

**Biological Influences**
- May be associated with lower density of dopamine receptors

**Psychological Influences**
- Very limited range of emotions
- Apparently cold and unconnected
- Unaffected by praise or criticism

**CAUSES**

**Social/Cultural Influences**
- Preference for social isolation
- Lack of social skills
- Lack of interest in close relationships, including romantic or sexual

**Treatment**
- Learning value of social relationships
- Social skills training with role playing

## SCHIZOTYPAL
### suspicion and odd behaviour

**Biological Influences**
- Genetic vulnerability for schizophrenia but without the biological or environmental stresses present in that disorder

**Psychological Influences**
- Unusual beliefs, behaviour, or dress
- Suspiciousness
- Believing insignificant events are personally relevant (ideas of reference)
- Expressing little emotion
- Symptoms of major depressive disorder

**CAUSES**

**Social/Cultural Influences**
- Preference for social isolation
- Excessive social anxiety
- Lack of social skills

**Treatment**
- Teaching social skills to reduce isolation and suspicion
- Medication (haloperidol) to reduce ideas of reference, odd communication, and isolation
- Low success rate

## ANTISOCIAL
*violation of others' rights*

### Biological Influences
- Genetic vulnerability combined with environmental influences
- Abnormally low cortical arousal
- High fear threshold

### Psychological Influences
- Difficulty learning to avoid punishment
- Indifferent to concerns of others

**Treatment**
- Seldom successful (incarceration instead)
- Parent training if problems are caught early
- Prevention through preschool programs

*CAUSES*

### Social/Cultural Influences
- Criminality
- Stress/exposure to trauma
- Inconsistent parental discipline
- Socioeconomic disadvantage

## CLUSTER B
### DRAMATIC, EMOTIONAL, OR ERRATIC

ThinkStock/Getty Images

## BORDERLINE
*tumultuous instability*

### Biological Influences
- Familial link to mood disorders
- Possibly inherited tendencies (impulsivity or volatility)

### Psychological Influences
- Suicidal
- Erratic moods
- Impulsivity

**Treatment**
- Dialectical behaviour therapy
- Medication
  — tricyclic antidepressants
  — minor tranquilizers
  — lithium

*CAUSES*

### Social/Cultural Influences
- Early trauma, especially sexual/physical abuse
- Rapid cultural changes (immigration) may trigger symptoms

---

## DEPENDENT
*pervasive need to be taken care of*

### Psychological Influences
- Early "loss" of caretaker (death, rejection, or neglect) leads to fear of abandonment
- Timidity and passivity

**Treatment**
- Little research
- Appear as ideal clients
- Submissiveness negates independence

## CLUSTER C
### ANXIOUS OR FEARFUL

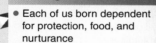

### Biological Influences
- Each of us born dependent for protection, food, and nurturance

*CAUSES*

### Social/Cultural Influences
- Agreement to avoid conflict
- Similar to avoidant in
  — inadequacy
  — sensitivity to criticism
  — need for reassurance
  **BUT**
  for those same shared reasons
  — avoidants withdraw
  — dependents cling

Photodisc/
Getty Images

## OBSESSIVE-COMPULSIVE
*fixation on details*

### Biological Influences
- Distant relation to OCD
- Probable weak genetic role
  — predisposition to structure combined with parental reinforcement

### Psychological Influences
- Generally rigid
- Dependent on routines
- Procrastinating

**Treatment**
- Little information
- Therapy
  — attack fears behind need
  — relaxation or distraction techniques redirect compulsion to order

*CAUSES*

### Social/Cultural Influences
- Work oriented
- Poor interpersonal relationships

## AVOIDANT
*inhibition*

### Biological Influences
- Innate characteristics may cause rejection

### Psychological Influences
- Low self-esteem
- Fear of rejection/criticism leads to fear of attention
- Extreme sensitivity
- Resembles social phobia

*CAUSES*

### Social/Cultural Influences
- Insufficient parental affection

**Treatment**
- Behavioural intervention techniques sometimes successful
  — systematic desensitization
  — behavioural rehearsal
- Improvements usually modest

# 12 Schizophrenia and Other Psychotic Disorders

Robert Daly/Stone/Getty Images

**Perspectives on Schizophrenia**
*Early Figures in Diagnosing Schizophrenia*
*Identifying Symptoms*

**Clinical Description, Symptoms, and Subtypes**
*Positive Symptoms*
*Negative Symptoms*
*Disorganized Symptoms*
*Schizophrenia Subtypes*
*Other Psychotic Disorders*

**Prevalence and Causes of Schizophrenia**
*Statistics*
*Development*
*Cultural Factors*
*Genetic Influences*
*Neurobiological Influences*
*Psychological and Social Influences*

**Treatment of Schizophrenia**
*Biological Interventions*
*Psychosocial Interventions*
*Treatment across Cultures*
*Prevention*

**Visual Summary: Exploring Schizophrenia**

 **Abnormal Psychology Live CD-ROM**
*Schizophrenia: Etta*
*Positive versus Negative Symptoms*
*Common Symptoms of Schizophrenia*

# Perspectives on Schizophrenia

■ *Define schizophrenia and describe the different symptoms included in this diagnosis.*

■ *Trace the history of schizophrenia research, including the contributions of Kraepelin and Bleuler.*

A middle-aged man walks the streets of Toronto with aluminum foil on the inside of his hat so Martians can't read his mind. A young woman sits in her college classroom and hears the voice of God telling her she is a vile and disgusting person. You try to strike up a conversation with the supermarket bagger, but he stares at you vacantly and will say only one or two words in a flat, toneless voice. Each of these people may have **schizophrenia,** the startling disorder characterized by a broad spectrum of cognitive and emotional dysfunctions including delusions and hallucinations, disorganized speech and behaviour, and inappropriate emotions.

Schizophrenia is a complex syndrome that inevitably has a devastating effect on the lives of the person affected and on those of family members. This disorder can disrupt a person's perception, thought, speech, and movement: almost every aspect of daily functioning. Society often devalues these individuals. For example, people with these severe mental health problems are twice as likely to be harassed in public as people without schizophrenia (Berzins, Petch, & Atkinson, 2003). And despite important advances in treatment, complete recovery from schizophrenia is rare. This catastrophic disorder takes a tremendous emotional toll on everyone involved. In addition to the emotional costs, the financial drain is considerable. The annual cost to Canadian society is in the billions of dollars when factors such as hospitalization, disability payments, welfare payments, and lost wages are considered (British Columbia Schizophrenia Society, 2001). Because schizophrenia is so widespread, affecting approximately 1 out of every 100 people at some point in their lives, and because its consequences are so severe, research on its causes and treatment has spread rapidly. Given the attention it has received, you would think the question, "What is schizophrenia?" would by now be answered easily. It is not.

In this chapter we explore this intriguing disorder and review efforts to determine whether schizophrenia is distinct in itself, or a combination of disorders. As noted by Walter Heinrichs and his colleagues at York University, the search is complicated by the presence of subtypes with different presentations and combinations of symptoms such as hallucinations, delusions, and disorders of speech, emotion, and socialization (Heinrichs, 1993; Heinrichs & Awad, 1993; Heinrichs, Ruttan, Zakzanis, & Case, 1997). After discussing the characteristics of people with schizophrenia, we describe research into its causes and treatment.

## Early Figures in Diagnosing Schizophrenia

Toward the end of the 19th century, the German psychiatrist Emil Kraepelin (1899) provided what stands today as the most enduring description and categorization of schizophrenia. Two of Kraepelin's accomplishments are especially important. First, he combined several symptoms of insanity that had usually been viewed as reflecting separate and distinct disorders: **catatonia** (alternating immobility and excited agitation), **hebephrenia** (silly and immature emotionality), and **paranoia** (delusions of grandeur or persecution). Kraepelin thought these symptoms shared similar underlying features and included them under the Latin term **dementia praecox.** Although the clinical manifestation might differ from person to person, Kraepelin believed an early onset at the heart of each disorder ultimately develops into "mental weakness."

In a second important contribution, Kraepelin (1898) distinguished dementia praecox from manic-depressive illness (bipolar disorder). For people with dementia praecox, an early age of onset and a poor outcome were characteristic; in contrast, these patterns were not essential to manic depression

**schizophrenia** Devastating psychotic disorder that may involve characteristic disturbances in thinking (delusions), perception (hallucinations), speech, emotions, and behaviour.

**catatonia** Disorder of movement involving immobility or excited agitation.

**hebephrenia** Silly and immature emotionality, a characteristic of some types of schizophrenia.

**paranoia** Person's irrational beliefs that he or she is especially important (delusions of grandeur) or that other people are seeking to do him or her harm.

**dementia praecox** Latin term meaning "premature loss of mind," an early label for what is now called schizophrenia, emphasizing the disorder's frequent appearance during adolescence.

(Peters, 1991). Kraepelin also noted the numerous symptoms in people with dementia praecox, including hallucinations, delusions, negativism, and stereotyped behaviour.

A second major figure in the history of schizophrenia was Kraeplin's contemporary, Eugen Bleuler, a Swiss psychiatrist who introduced the term *schizophrenia* (1908). The label was significant because it signalled Bleuler's departure from Kraepelin on what he thought was the core problem. *Schizophrenia*, which comes from the combination of the Greek words for split (*skhizein*) and mind (*phren*), reflected Bleuler's belief that underlying all the unusual behaviours shown by people with this disorder was an **associative splitting** of the basic functions of personality. This concept emphasized the "breaking of associative threads," or the destruction of the forces that connect one function to the next. Furthermore, Bleuler believed that a difficulty with keeping a consistent train of thought characteristic of all people with this disorder led to the many and diverse symptoms they displayed. Whereas Kraepelin focused on early onset and poor outcomes, Bleuler highlighted what he believed to be the universal underlying problem. Unfortunately, the concept of "split mind" inspired the common but incorrect use of the term *schizophrenia* to mean split or multiple personality.

## Identifying Symptoms

It is not easy to point to one thing that makes a person "schizophrenic." As you read about different disorders in this book, you have learned that a particular behaviour, way of thinking, or emotion usually defines or is characteristic of each disorder. For example, depression always includes feelings of sadness, and panic disorder is always accompanied by intense feelings of anxiety. Surprisingly, this isn't the case for schizophrenia. Schizophrenia is actually a number of behaviours or symptoms that aren't necessarily shared by all the people who are given this diagnosis.

Despite significant variations, researchers have identified clusters of symptoms that make up the disorder of schizophrenia. Later we describe these dramatic symptoms, such as seeing or hearing things

Eugen Bleuler (1857–1939), a Swiss psychiatrist, introduced the term *schizophrenia* and was a pioneer in the field.

## Arthur
### Saving the Children

We first met 22-year-old Arthur at an outpatient clinic in a psychiatric hospital. Arthur's family was extremely concerned and upset by his unusual behaviour and was desperately seeking help for him. They said that he was "sick" and "talking like a crazy man," and they were afraid he might harm himself.

Arthur had a normal childhood in a middle-class suburban neighbourhood. His parents had been happily married until his father's death several years earlier. Arthur was an average student throughout school and had received a college diploma. His family seemed to think he regretted not continuing on to receive a bachelor's degree at university. Arthur had worked in a series of temporary jobs, and his mother reported that he seemed satisfied with what he was doing. He lived and worked in a major city, some 15 minutes from his mother and his married brother and sister.

Arthur's family said that about 3 weeks before he came to the clinic he had started speaking strangely. He had been laid off from his job a few days before because of cutbacks and hadn't communicated with any of his family members for several days. When they next spoke with him, his behaviour startled them. Although he had always been idealistic and anxious to help other people, he now talked about saving all the starving children in the world with his "secret plan." At first his family assumed this was just an example of Arthur's sarcastic wit, but his demeanour changed to one of extreme concern, and he spoke nonstop about his plans. He began carrying several spiral notebooks that he claimed contained his scheme for helping starving children; he said he would reveal it only at the right time to the right person. Suspecting that Arthur might be taking drugs, which could explain the sudden and dramatic change in his behaviour, his family searched his

that others do not (hallucinations) or having beliefs that are unrealistic, bizarre, and not shared by others in the same culture (delusions). But first, consider the case of an individual who had an intense but relatively rare short-term episode of psychotic behaviour.

---

**associative splitting** Separation among basic functions of human personality (e.g., cognition, emotion, perception) that was seen by some as the defining characteristics of schizophrenia.

apartment. Although they didn't find any evidence of drug use, they did find his chequebook and noticed a number of strange entries. Over the past several weeks, Arthur's handwriting had deteriorated, and he had written notes instead of the usual cheque information ("Start to begin now"; "This is important!"; "They must be saved"). He had also made unusual notes in several of his most prized books, a particularly alarming development given his reverence for these books.

As the days went on, Arthur showed dramatic changes in emotion, often crying and acting apprehensive. He stopped wearing socks and underwear and, despite the extremely cold weather, wouldn't wear a jacket when he went outdoors. At the family's insistence, he moved into his mother's apartment. He slept little and kept the family up until the early morning. His mother said it was like being in a living nightmare. Each morning she would wake up with a knot in her stomach, not wanting to get out of bed because she felt so helpless to do anything to rescue Arthur from his obvious distress.

The family's sense of alarm grew as Arthur revealed more details of his plan. He said that he was going to the German embassy because that was the only place people would listen to him. He would climb the fence at night when everyone was asleep and present his plan to the German ambassador. Fearing that Arthur would be hurt trying to enter the embassy grounds, his family contacted a local psychiatric hospital, described Arthur's condition, and asked that he be admitted. Much to their surprise and disappointment, they were told that Arthur could commit himself but that they couldn't bring him in involuntarily unless he was in danger of doing harm to himself or others. The fear that Arthur might be harmed wasn't sufficient reason to admit him involuntarily.

His family finally talked Arthur into meeting the staff at the outpatient clinic. In our interview, it was clear he was delusional, firmly believing in his ability to help all starving children. After some cajoling, I finally convinced him to let me see his books. He had written random thoughts (e.g., "The poor, starving souls"; "The moon is the only place") and made drawings of rocket ships. Parts of his plan involved building a rocket ship that would go to the moon, where he would create a community for all malnourished children, a place where they could live and be helped. After a few brief comments on his plan, I began to ask him about his health.

"You look tired; are you getting enough sleep?"

"Sleep isn't really needed," he noted. "My plans will take me through, and then they can all rest."

"Your family is worried about you," I said. "Do you understand their concern?"

"It's important for all concerned to get together, to join together," he replied.

With that, he got up and walked out of the room and out of the building, after telling his family that he would be right back. After 5 minutes they went to look for him, but he had disappeared. He was missing for 2 days, which caused his family a great deal of concern about his health and safety. In an almost miraculous sequence of events, they found him walking the streets of the city. He acted as if nothing had happened. Gone were his notebooks and the talk of his secret plan.

What caused Arthur to act so strangely? Was it being fired from his job? Was it the death of his father? Was it a genetic predisposition to have schizophrenia or another disorder that kicked in during a period of stress? Unfortunately, we will never know exactly what happened to Arthur to make him behave so bizarrely and then recover so quickly and completely. However, the research that we discuss next may shed some light on schizophrenia and related disorders and may potentially help other Arthurs and their families.

# Clinical Description, Symptoms, and Subtypes

- ■ *Distinguish among positive, negative, and disorganized symptoms of schizophrenia.*

- ■ *Describe the clinical characteristics and major subtypes of schizophrenia and other psychotic disorders.*

The case of Arthur shows the range of problems experienced by people with schizophrenia or other psychotic disorders. The term *psychotic* has been used to characterize many unusual behaviours, although in its strictest sense it usually involves delusions (irrational beliefs) and/or hallucinations (sensory experiences in the absence of external events). Schizophrenia is one of the disorders that involve **psychotic behaviour;** we describe others in more detail later.

Schizophrenia can affect all the functions we rely on each day. Before we describe the symptoms, it is important to look carefully at the specific characteristics of people who exhibit these behaviours, partly because we constantly see distorted images of people with schizophrenia. Headlines such as "Ex-Mental Patient Kills Family" falsely imply that everyone with schizophrenia is dangerous and violent. A recent Quebec survey found that the majority of respondents thought that people with schizophrenia were dangerous or violent (Stip, Caron, & Lane, 2001). But statistics show otherwise. Another Canadian study examined nearly 700 cases from a forensic hospital and found that people with a schizophrenia diagnosis were far less likely to commit future violent crimes than those with a history of violent crime but no schizophrenia diagnosis (Noonan, 2003). Nonetheless, media portrayals continue to frequently depict people with schizophrenia as violent (Noonan, 2003). Like mistakenly assuming that "schizophrenia" means "split personality," the popular press misrepresents abnormal psychology to the detriment of people who experience these debilitating disorders.

DSM-IV-TR has a multiple-part process for determining whether someone has schizophrenia. Later we discuss the symptoms the person experiences during the disorder (*active phase symptoms*), the course of the disorder, and the subtypes of schizophrenia in use.

Mental health workers typically distinguish between *positive* and *negative* symptoms of schizophrenia. A third dimension, *disorganized* symptoms, also appears to be an important aspect of the disorder (Black & Andreasen, 1999; Ho, Black, & Andreasen, 2003). There is not yet universal agreement about which symptoms should be included in these categories. Positive symptoms generally include the more active manifestations of abnormal behaviour or an excess or distortion of normal behaviour; these include delusions and hallucinations (American Psychiatric Association, 2000a). Negative symptoms involve deficits in normal behaviour in areas such as speech and motivation (Carpenter, 1994; Earnst & Kring, 1997). Disorganized symptoms include rambling speech, erratic behaviour, and inappropriate affect (Ho et al., 2003). A diagnosis of schizophrenia requires that two or more positive, negative, and/or disorganized symptoms be present for at least 1 month. A great deal of research has focused on the different symptoms of schizophrenia, each of which is described here in some detail.

---

**Disorder Criteria Summary**
Schizophrenia

Features of schizophrenia include (to different degrees, depending on subtype):
- Delusions
- Hallucinations
- Disorganized speech
- Grossly disorganized or catatonic behaviour
- Negative symptoms such as affective flattening, alogia, or avolition
- Social and occupational dysfunction
- Neglected self-care
- Persistence for at least 6 months

*Source:* Based on DSM-IV-TR. Used with permission from the *Diagnostic and Statistical Manual of Mental Disorders,* Fourth Edition, Text Revision. Copyright 2000. American Psychiatric Association.

## *Positive Symptoms*

We next describe the **"positive" symptoms** of schizophrenia, which are the more obvious signs of psychosis. These include the disturbing experiences of delusions and hallucinations.

### Delusions

A belief that would be seen by most members of a society as a misrepresentation of reality is called a *disorder of thought content,* or a **delusion.** Because of its importance in schizophrenia, delusion has been called "the basic characteristic of madness" (Jaspers, 1963). If, for example, you believe that squirrels are aliens sent to Earth on a reconnaissance mission, you would be considered delusional. The media often portray people with schizophrenia as believing they are famous or important people (such as Napoleon or Jesus Christ). Arthur's belief that he could end starvation for all of the world's children is also a *delusion of grandeur.*

A common delusion in people with schizophrenia is that others are "out to get them." Called *delusions of persecution,* these beliefs can be most disturbing. One of us worked with a world-class cyclist who was on her way to making the Olympic team. Tragically, however, she developed a belief that other competitors were determined to sabotage her

---

**psychotic behaviour**   Severe psychological disorder characterized by hallucinations and loss of contact with reality.

**positive symptoms**   More overt symptoms, such as delusions and hallucinations, displayed by some people with schizophrenia.

**delusion**   Psychotic symptom involving disorder of thought content and presence of strong beliefs that are misrepresentations of reality.

efforts, which forced her to stop riding for years. She believed opponents would spray her bicycle with chemicals that would take her strength away, and they would slow her down by putting small pebbles in the road that only she would ride over. These thoughts created a great deal of anxiety, and she refused even to go near her bicycle for some time.

Other more unusual delusions include *Capgras syndrome,* in which the person believes someone he or she knows has been replaced by a double, and *Cotard's syndrome,* in which the person believes a part of his or her body (e.g., the brain) has changed in some impossible way (Black & Andreasen, 1999).

An intriguing possibility is that delusions may serve a purpose for people with schizophrenia who are otherwise quite upset by the changes taking place within themselves. For example, G. A. Roberts (1991) studied 17 people who had elaborate delusions about themselves and the world and compared them with a matched group of people who previously had delusions but were now improving. The "deluded" individuals expressed a much stronger sense of purpose and meaning in life *and less depression,* all of which seemed related to their delusional belief systems. Compare this with the opposite situation we discussed in Chapter 6, where we found that people who were depressed seemed sadder but wiser. That delusions may serve an adaptive function is at present just a theory with little support, but it may help us understand the phenomenon and its effect on those who experience it.

### Hallucinations

Did you ever think someone called your name, only to discover that no one was there? Did you ever think you saw something move by you, yet nothing did? We all have fleeting moments when we think we see or hear something that isn't there. However, for many people with schizophrenia, these perceptions are very real and occur regularly. The experience of sensory events without input from the surrounding environment is called an **hallucination.** The case of David illustrates the phenomena of hallucinations and other disorders of thought that are common among people with schizophrenia.

## David
### Missing Uncle Bill

David was 25 years old when I met him; he had been living in a psychiatric hospital for about 3 years. He was a little overweight and of average height; he typically dressed in a T-shirt and jeans and tended to be active. I first encountered him

while I was talking to another man who lived on the same floor. David interrupted us by pulling on my shoulder. "My Uncle Bill is a good man. He treats me well." Not wanting to be impolite, I said, "I'm sure he is. Maybe after I've finished talking to Michael here, we can talk about your uncle." David persisted, "He can kill fish with a knife. Things can get awfully sharp in your mind, when you go down the river. I could kill you with my bare hands—taking things into my own hands.... I know you know!" He was now speaking very quickly and had gained emotionality, along with speed, as he spoke. I talked to him quietly until he calmed down for the moment. Later I looked into David's file for some information about his background.

David was brought up on a farm by his Aunt Katie and Uncle Bill. His father's identity is unknown and his mother, who had mental retardation, couldn't care for him. David, too, was diagnosed as having mental retardation, although his functioning was only mildly impaired, and he attended school. The year David's Uncle Bill died, his high school teachers first reported unusual behaviour. David occasionally talked to his deceased Uncle Bill in class. Later, he became increasingly agitated and verbally aggressive toward others and was diagnosed as having schizophrenia. He managed to graduate from high school but never obtained a job after that; he lived at home with his aunt for several years. Although his aunt sincerely wanted him to stay with her, his threatening behaviour escalated to the point that she requested he be seen at the local psychiatric hospital.

I spoke with David again and had a chance to ask him a few questions. "Why are you here in the hospital, David?" "I really don't want to be here," he told me. "I've got other things to do. The time is right, and you know, when opportunity knocks ..." He continued for a few minutes until I interrupted him. "I was sorry to hear that your Uncle Bill died a few years ago. How are you feeling about him these days?" "Yes, he died. He was sick and now he's gone. He likes to fish with me, down at the river. He's going to take me hunting. I have guns. I can shoot you and you'd be dead in a minute."

David's conversational speech resembled a ball rolling down a rocky hill. Like an accelerating object, his speech gained momentum the longer he went on and, as if bouncing off obstacles, the topics almost always went in

---

**hallucination**  Psychotic symptom of perceptual disturbance in which things are seen, heard, or otherwise sensed although they are not real or actually present.

unpredictable directions. If he continued for too long, he often became agitated and spoke of harming others. David also told me that his uncle's voice spoke to him repeatedly. He heard other voices also, but he couldn't identify them or tell me what they said. We return to David's case later in this chapter when we discuss causes and treatments.

Hallucinations can involve any of the senses, although hearing things that aren't there, or *auditory hallucination*, is the most common form experienced by people with schizophrenia. David had frequent auditory hallucinations, usually of his uncle's voice. When David heard a voice that belonged to his Uncle Bill, he often couldn't understand what his uncle was saying; on other occasions the voice was clearer. "He told me to turn off the TV. He said, 'It's too damn loud, turn it down, turn it down.' Other times he talks about fishing. 'Good day for fishing. Got to go fishing.'" You could tell when David was hearing voices. He was usually unoccupied, and he sat and smiled as if listening to someone next to him, but no one was there. This behaviour is consistent with research, which suggests that people tend to experience hallucinations more frequently when they are unoccupied or restricted from sensory input (e.g., Margo, Hemsley, & Slade, 1981).

Exciting research on hallucinations uses sophisticated brain-imaging techniques to try to localize these phenomena in the brain. Using single photon emission computed tomography (SPECT) to study the cerebral blood flow of men with schizophrenia who also had auditory hallucinations, researchers in London, England, made a surprising discovery (McGuire, Shah, & Murray, 1993). The researchers used the brain-imaging technique while the men were experiencing hallucinations and while they were not, and they found that the part of the brain most active during hallucinations was *Broca's area* (see Figure 12.1). This finding is surprising because Broca's area is known to be involved in speech production. Because auditory hallucinations usually involve understanding the "speech" of others, you might expect more activity in *Wernicke's area*, which involves language comprehension. However, this study supports an earlier finding by a different group of researchers who also found that Broca's area was more active than Wernicke's area during hallucinations (Cleghorn et al., 1992). These observations support a theory that people who are hallucinating are *not* hearing the voices of others but are listening to their own thoughts or their own voices and cannot recognize the difference. They may have deficits in speech processing that result in these distortions (Hoffman, Rapoport, Mazure, & Quinlan, 1999).

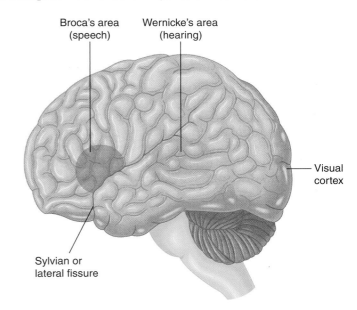

**Figure 12.1** ■ Major areas of functioning of the cerebral cortex. In most people, only the left hemisphere is specialized for language.

More advanced imaging technology is allowing researchers to get a better view of just what is going on inside the brain during hallucinations, and it should help them identify the role of the brain in the symptoms observed among people with schizophrenia (e.g., Silbersweig et al., 1995).

## Negative Symptoms

In contrast to the active presentations that characterize the positive symptoms of schizophrenia, the **negative symptoms** usually indicate the absence or insufficiency of normal behaviour. They include emotional and social withdrawal, apathy, and poverty of thought or speech. Approximately 25% of people with schizophrenia display these symptoms (Ho et al., 2003; Malla et al., 2002).

### Avolition

Combining the prefix *a*, meaning "without," and *volition*, which means "an act of willing, choosing, or deciding," **avolition** is the inability to initiate and persist in activities. People with this symptom (also referred to as *apathy*) show little interest in performing even the most basic day-to-day functions, including those associated with personal hygiene.

A recent study by researchers at the Centre for Addiction and Mental Health in Toronto examined

**negative symptoms** Symptoms involving deficits in normal behaviour, such as flat affect and poverty of speech, displayed by some people with schizophrenia.

**avolition** Apathy, or the inability to initiate or persist in important activities.

the level of avolition in 28 patients with schizophrenia and its relationship to other symptoms of schizophrenia and to treatment outcome. As expected, avolition was not related to positive symptoms of schizophrenia. Unexpectedly though, avolition was not related to negative symptoms of schizophrenia other than emotional withdrawal. Finally, avolition was more highly associated with poor treatment outcome than were other schizophrenia symptoms—positive or negative (Kiang, Christensen, Remington, & Kapur, 2003).

### Alogia

Derived from the combination of *a* ("without") and *logos* ("words"), **alogia** refers to the relative absence of speech. A person with alogia may respond to questions with brief replies that have little content and may appear uninterested in the conversation. For example, to the question, "Do you have any children?" most parents might reply, "Oh yes, I have two beautiful children, a boy and a girl. My son is 6 and my daughter is 12." In the following exchange, someone with alogia responds to the same question:

**Interviewer:** Do you have any children?
**Client:** Yes.
**Interviewer:** How many children do you have?
**Client:** Two.
**Interviewer:** How old are they?
**Client:** Six and twelve.

Such deficiency in communication is believed to reflect a negative thought disorder rather than inadequate communication skills. Some researchers, for example, suggest that people with alogia may have trouble finding the right words to formulate their thoughts (Alpert, Clark, & Pouget, 1994). Sometimes alogia takes the form of delayed comments or slow responses to questions. Talking with individuals who manifest this symptom can be extremely frustrating, making you feel as if you are "pulling teeth" to get them to respond.

### Anhedonia

A related symptom is called **anhedonia,** which derives from the word *hedonic,* pertaining to pleasure. Anhedonia is the presumed lack of pleasure experienced by some people with schizophrenia. Like some mood disorders, anhedonia signals an indifference to activities that would typically be considered pleasurable, including eating, social interactions, and sexual relations. Given the similarities of the negative schizophrenia symptom of anhedonia to symptoms of depression, some have questioned the distinctiveness of anhedonia and the mood disorders (e.g., Candido & Romney, 2002; Romney & Candido, 2001). For example, University of Calgary researcher David

Romney and his associate Carmie Candido administered measures of depression, positive symptoms, negative symptoms, and anhedonia to a sample of 27 patients with major depression and a sample of 54 patients with schizophrenia. They found support for the idea that anhedonia is better conceptualized as a symptom of depression than as a negative symptom of schizophrenia.

### Affective Flattening

Imagine that people wore masks at all times: You could communicate with them but you wouldn't be able to see their emotional reactions. Approximately one-quarter of the people with schizophrenia exhibit what is called **flat affect** (Malla et al., 2002). They are similar to people wearing masks because they do not show emotions when you would normally expect them to. They may stare at you vacantly, speak in a flat and toneless manner, and seem unaffected by things going on around them. However, although they do not react openly to emotional situations, they may be responding on the inside.

Berenbaum and Oltmanns (1992) compared people with schizophrenia who had flat (or "blunted") affect with those who did not. The two groups were shown clips from films selected to create emotional reactions in the viewer. Berenbaum and Oltmanns found that the people with flat affect showed little change in facial expression, although they reported experiencing the appropriate emotions.

***Schizophrenia: Etta***
*"If anyone gets into the house, they say I'd get shot.... [Who said?] That's the eagle.... The eagle works through General Motors. They have something to do with my General Motors cheque I get every month ... when you do the 25 of the clock, it means that you leave the house 25 after 1 to mail letters so that they can check on you ... and they know where you're at. That's the eagle.... If you don't do something they tell you to do, Jesus makes the shotgun sound, and then ... not to answer the phone or the doorbell ... because you'd get shot [by the] eagle."*

Thomson Learning

**alogia** Deficiency in the amount or content of speech, a disturbance often seen in people with schizophrenia.

**anhedonia** Inability to experience pleasure, associated with some mood and schizophrenic disorders.

**flat affect** Apparently emotionless demeanour (including toneless speech and vacant gaze) when a reaction would be expected.

The authors concluded that the flat affect in schizophrenia may represent difficulty expressing emotion, not a lack of feeling. In a replication of this type of research, Kring and Neale (1996) also observed people with flat affect who reported appropriate emotional reactions, and they confirmed the emotional responses through physiological recordings.

The expression of affect—or the lack of this expression—may be an important symptom of the development of schizophrenia. In a creative research study, Walker and colleagues examined the facial expressions of children who later developed schizophrenia and compared them with the expressions of brothers and sisters who did not develop the disorder (Walker, Grimes, Davis, & Smith, 1993). They identified adults who already showed other signs of schizophrenia and looked at home movies taken when they were children. The researchers were able to show that children who later went on to develop schizophrenia typically displayed less positive and more negative affect than their siblings. This suggests that emotional expression may be one way to identify potential schizophrenia in children.

### Asociality

The severe deficits in social relationships, such as having few friendships, little interest in socializing, and poor social skills, shown by some people with schizophrenia are referred to collectively as asociality. A study by researchers Joel Goldberg and Louis Schmidt (2001) at McMaster University compared 23 patients with schizophrenia with 23 controls without schizophrenia on measures of current sociability and shyness as well as childhood inhibition. Patients were higher on all of these characteristics than were the controls. Moreover, levels of asociality were associated with greater levels of other types of negative symptoms, supporting the grouping of asociality in this dimension of schizophrenia symptoms.

## *Disorganized Symptoms*

Perhaps the least studied and therefore the least understood of the symptoms of schizophrenia are referred to as the *disorganized symptoms*. These include a variety of erratic behaviours that affect speech, motor behaviour, and emotional reactions.

### Disorganized Speech

A conversation with someone who has schizophrenia can be particularly frustrating. If you want to understand what is bothering or upsetting this person, eliciting relevant information is especially difficult. For one thing, people with schizophrenia often lack *insight*, an awareness that they have a problem. In addition, they experience "associative splitting" (Bleuler, 1908) and "cognitive slippage" (Meehl, 1962). These phrases help describe the speech problems of people with schizophrenia: Sometimes they jump from topic to topic and at other times they talk illogically. DSM-IV-TR uses the term **disorganized speech** to describe such communication problems. Let's go back to our conversation with David to demonstrate the symptom.

**VMD:** Why are you here in the hospital, David?

**DAVID:** I really don't want to be here. I've got other things to do. The time is right, and you know, when opportunity knocks …

David didn't really answer the question he was asked. This type of response is called *tangentiality*— that is, going off on a tangent instead of answering a specific question (Andreasen, 1979). David also abruptly changed the topic of conversation to unrelated areas, a behaviour that has variously been called *loose association* or *derailment* (Cutting, 1985).

**VMD:** I was sorry to hear that your Uncle Bill died a few years ago. How are you feeling about him these days?

**DAVID:** Yes, he died. He was sick, and now he's gone. He likes to fish with me, down at the river. He's going to take me hunting. I have guns. I can shoot you and you'd be dead in a minute.

Photodisc

Negative symptoms of schizophrenia include social withdrawal and apathy.

---

**disorganized speech** Style of talking often seen in people with schizophrenia, involving incoherence and a lack of typical logic patterns.

Again, David didn't answer the question. The therapist could not tell whether he didn't understand the question, couldn't focus his attention, or found it too difficult to talk about his uncle. You can see why people spend a great deal of time trying to interpret all the hidden meanings behind this type of conversation. Unfortunately, such analyses have yet to provide us with useful information about the nature of schizophrenia or its treatment.

### Inappropriate Affect and Catatonic Behaviour

Occasionally, people with schizophrenia display **inappropriate affect,** laughing or crying at improper times. Sometimes they exhibit bizarre behaviours such as hoarding objects or acting in unusual ways in public. People with schizophrenia engage in a number of other "active" behaviours that are usually viewed as unusual. For example, catatonia is one of the most curious symptoms in some individuals with schizophrenia; it involves motor dysfunctions that range from wild agitation to immobility. On the active side of the continuum, some people pace excitedly or move their fingers or arms in stereotyped ways. At the other end of the extreme, people hold unusual postures, as if they were fearful of something terrible happening if they move (**catatonic immobility**). This manifestation can also involve *waxy flexibility*, or the tendency to keep their bodies and limbs in the position they are put in by someone else.

Again, to receive a diagnosis of schizophrenia, a person must display two or more positive, negative, and/or disorganized symptoms for a major portion of at least 1 month. Depending on the combination of symptoms displayed, two people could receive the same diagnosis but behave very differently, one having marked hallucinations and delusions and the other displaying disorganized speech and some of the negative symptoms. Proper treatment depends on differentiating individuals in terms of their varying symptoms.

## Schizophrenia Subtypes

As we noted earlier, the search for subtypes of schizophrenia began before Kraepelin described his concept of schizophrenia. Three divisions have persisted: *paranoid* (delusions of grandeur or persecution), *disorganized* (or *hebephrenic;* silly and immature emotionality), and *catatonic* (alternate immobility and excited agitation). Research supports dividing schizophrenia into these categories, because differences among them are identifiable (Ho et al., 2003). For example, the prognosis for individuals with the disorganized subtype is more pessimistic than for people with the other subtypes. People with the catatonic subtype have a distinctive course and treatment

response. Because of their usefulness, DSM-IV-TR has integrated all three subtypes into its revised classification system for schizophrenia.

### Paranoid Type

People with the **paranoid type of schizophrenia** stand out because of their delusions or hallucinations; at the same time, their cognitive skills and affect are relatively intact. They generally do not have disorganized speech or flat affect, and they typically have a better prognosis than people with other forms of schizophrenia. The delusions and hallucinations usually have a theme, such as grandeur or persecution. The DSM-IV-TR criteria

Homeless people who suffer from paranoid schizophrenia often bear the additional burden of persecutory delusions, which interfere with outside efforts to help.

**inappropriate affect** Emotional displays that do not match the situation.

**catatonic immobility** Disturbance of motor behaviour in which the person remains motionless, sometimes in an awkward posture, for extended periods.

**paranoid type of schizophrenia** Type of schizophrenia in which symptoms primarily involve delusions and hallucinations; speech and motor and emotional behaviour are relatively intact.

for inclusion in this subtype specify preoccupation with one or more delusions or frequent auditory hallucinations but without a marked display of disorganized speech, disorganized or catatonic behaviour, or flat or inappropriate affect (American Psychiatric Association, 2000a).

### Disorganized Type

In contrast to the paranoid type of schizophrenia, people with the **disorganized type of schizophrenia** show marked disruption in their speech and behaviour; they also show flat or inappropriate affect, such as laughing in a silly way at the wrong times (American Psychiatric Association, 2000a). They also seem unusually self-absorbed and may spend considerable amounts of time looking at themselves in the mirror (Ho et al., 2003). If delusions or hallucinations are present, they tend not to be organized around a central theme, as in the paranoid type, but are more fragmented. This subtype was previously called *hebephrenic*. Individuals with this diagnosis tend to show signs of difficulty early, and their problems are often chronic, lacking the remissions (improvement of symptoms) that characterize other forms of the disorder (Hardy-Bayle, Sarfati, & Passerieu, 2003).

### Catatonic Type

In addition to the unusual motor responses of remaining in fixed positions (waxy flexibility), engaging in excessive activity, and being oppositional by remaining rigid, individuals with the **catatonic type of schizophrenia** sometimes display odd mannerisms with their bodies and faces, including grimacing (American Psychiatric Association, 2000a). They often repeat or mimic the words of others (*echolalia*) or the movements of others (*echopraxia*). This cluster of behaviours is relatively rare, and there is some debate about whether it should remain classified as a separate subtype of schizophrenia (McGlashan & Fenton, 1991). Its infrequency may be partly the result of the success of neuroleptic medications.

### Undifferentiated Type

People who do not fit neatly into these subtypes are classified as having an **undifferentiated type of schizophrenia;** they include people who have the major symptoms of schizophrenia but who do not meet the criteria for paranoid, disorganized, or catatonic types.

### Residual Type

People who have had at least one episode of schizophrenia but who no longer manifest major symptoms are diagnosed as having the **residual type of schizophrenia.** Although they may not experience bizarre delusions or hallucinations, they may display residual or "leftover" symptoms, such as negative symptoms, or they may still have unusual ideas that are not fully delusional. Residual symptoms can include social withdrawal, bizarre thoughts, inactivity, and flat affect.

Research suggests that the paranoid subtype may have a stronger familial link than the others and that these people may function better before and after episodes of schizophrenia than people diagnosed with other subtypes (Ho et al., 2003). More work will determine whether dividing schizophrenia into five subtypes helps us understand and treat people.

An alternative system for subtyping schizophrenia, introduced in the mid-1970s by Strauss, Carpenter, and Bartko (1974), emphasizes the positive, negative, and, more recently, disorganized symptoms. Crow elaborated on this approach, suggesting that schizophrenia can be dichotomized into two types (Crow, 1980, 1985), based on a variety of characteristics, including symptoms, response to medication, outcome, and the presence or absence of intellectual impairment. Type I is associated with the positive symptoms of hallucinations and delusions, a good response to medication, an optimistic prognosis, and the absence of intellectual impairment. In contrast, Type II includes people with the negative symptoms of flat affect and poverty of speech who show a poor response to medication, a pessimistic prognosis, and intellectual impairments. Although not without its critics (Andreasen & Carpenter, 1993), Crow's model has influenced current thinking regarding the nature of schizophrenia.

Several other disorders also characterized by psychotic behaviours such as hallucinations and delusions do not manifest in the same way as schizophrenia. In the next section we distinguish them from schizophrenia and describe them in greater detail.

## *Other Psychotic Disorders*

The psychotic behaviours of some individuals do not fit neatly under the heading of schizophrenia as we have just described. Several other categories of disorders depict these significant variations.

---

**disorganized type of schizophrenia**   Type of schizophrenia featuring disrupted speech and behaviour, disjointed delusions and hallucinations, and flat or silly affect.

**catatonic type of schizophrenia**   Type of schizophrenia in which motor disturbances (rigidity, agitation, odd mannerisms) predominate.

**undifferentiated type of schizophrenia**   Category for individuals who meet the criteria for schizophrenia but not for one of the defined subtypes.

**residual type of schizophrenia**   Diagnostic category for people who have experienced at least one episode of schizophrenia and who no longer display its major symptoms but still show some bizarre thoughts or social withdrawal.

## Schizophreniform Disorder

Some people experience the symptoms of schizophrenia for a few months only; they can usually resume normal lives. The symptoms sometimes disappear as the result of successful treatment, but often for reasons unknown. The label **schizophreniform disorder** classifies these symptoms, but because relatively few studies are available on this disorder, data on important aspects of it are sparse. It appears, however, that the lifetime prevalence is approximately 0.2% (American Psychiatric Association, 2000a). The DSM-IV-TR diagnostic criteria for schizophreniform disorder include onset of psychotic symptoms within 4 weeks of the first noticeable change in usual behaviour, confusion at the height of the psychotic episode, good *premorbid* social and occupational functioning (i.e., functioning before the psychotic episode), and the absence of blunted or flat affect (American Psychiatric Association, 2000a).

**Disorder Criteria Summary**
Schizophreniform Disorder

Features of schizophreniform disorder include:
- At least two of these symptoms: delusions, hallucinations, disorganized speech, grossly disorganized or catatonic behaviour, negative symptoms (affective flattening, alogia, avolition)
- Persistence of symptoms for at least 1 month but less than 6 months

*Source:* Based on DSM-IV-TR. Used with permission from the *Diagnostic and Statistical Manual of Mental Disorders*, Fourth Edition, Text Revision. Copyright 2000. American Psychiatric Association.

## Schizoaffective Disorder

Historically, people who had symptoms of schizophrenia and who exhibited the characteristics of mood disorders (e.g., depression or bipolar affective disorder) were lumped in the category of schizophrenia (Siris, 2000). Now, however, this mixed bag of problems is diagnosed as **schizoaffective disorder** (Ho et al., 2003). The prognosis is similar to the prognosis for people with schizophrenia—that is, individuals tend not to get better on their own and are likely to continue experiencing major life difficulties for years. DSM-IV-TR criteria for schizoaffective disorder require that in addition to the presence of a mood disorder there have been delusions or hallucinations for at least 2 weeks in the absence of prominent mood symptoms (American Psychiatric Association, 2000a).

## Delusional Disorder

Delusions are beliefs that are not generally held by other members of a society. The major feature of **delusional disorder** is a persistent belief that is

**Disorder Criteria Summary**
Delusional Disorder

Features of delusional disorder include:
- Non-bizarre delusions for 1 month or longer
- Functioning is not markedly impaired apart from the delusions
- Any mood episodes that have occurred at the same time have been brief relative to the delusional periods
- The disturbance is not because of the direct physiological effects of a medical condition, medication, or abuse of a drug

*Source:* Based on DSM-IV-TR. Used with permission from the *Diagnostic and Statistical Manual of Mental Disorders*, Fourth Edition, Text Revision. Copyright 2000. American Psychiatric Association.

contrary to reality in the absence of other characteristics of schizophrenia. For example, a woman who believes without evidence that co-workers are tormenting her by putting poison in her food and spraying her apartment with harmful gases has a delusional disorder. This disorder is characterized by a persistent delusion that is not the result of an organic factor such as brain seizures or of any severe psychosis. Individuals tend not to have flat affect, anhedonia, or other negative symptoms of schizophrenia; importantly, however, they may become socially isolated because they are suspicious of others. The delusions are often long standing, sometimes persisting several years (Ho et al., 2003).

DSM-IV-TR recognizes the following delusional subtypes: *erotomanic, grandiose, jealous, persecutory,* and *somatic.* An erotomanic delusion is the irrational belief that the individual is loved by another person, usually of higher status. Some individuals who stalk celebrities appear to have erotomanic delusional disorder. For example, Vancouver-based singer and songwriter Sarah McLachlan was pursued in the early 1990s by a computer programmer from Ottawa named Uwe Vandrei. He sent her flowers and hundreds of disturbing letters, and even made some comments to her in person. Vandrei took his own life in 1994, after he was unsuccessful in suing McLachlan for

---

**schizophreniform disorder**  Psychotic disorder involving the symptoms of schizophrenia but lasting less than 6 months.

**schizoaffective disorder**  Psychotic disorder featuring symptoms of both schizophrenia and major mood disorder.

**delusional disorder**  Psychotic disorder featuring a persistent belief contrary to reality (delusion) but no other symptoms of schizophrenia.

allegedly using his letters as the basis for her song "Possession" on her 1993 CD *Fumbling Towards Ecstasy* (Fitzgerald, 2000).

The grandiose type of delusion involves believing in one's inflated worth, power, knowledge, identity, or special relationship to a deity or famous person. A person with the jealous type of delusion believes the sexual partner is unfaithful. The persecutory type of delusion involves believing oneself (or someone close) is being malevolently treated in some way. Finally, with the somatic type of delusion, the person feels afflicted by a physical defect or general medical condition. These delusions differ from the more bizarre types often found in people with schizophrenia because in delusional disorder *the imagined events could be happening but aren't* (e.g., mistakenly believing you are being followed); in schizophrenia, however, *the imagined events aren't possible* (e.g., believing your brain waves broadcast your thoughts to other people around the world).

Delusional disorder seems to be relatively rare, affecting 24 to 30 people out of every 100 000 in the general population. Among those people with identified psychological disorders, between 1% and 4% are thought to have delusional disorder (Ho et al., 2003). Researchers can't be confident about the percentages because they know that many of these individuals have no contact with the mental health system.

The onset of delusional disorder is relatively late: The average age of first admission to a psychiatric facility is between 40 and 49 (Munro, 1999). However, because many people with this disorder can lead relatively normal lives, they may not seek treatment until their symptoms become most disruptive. Delusional disorder seems to afflict more females than males (55% and 45%, respectively, of the affected population).

We know relatively little about either the biological or the psychosocial influences on delusional disorder (Munro, 1999). Research on families by Winokur (1985) suggests that the characteristics of suspiciousness, jealousy, and secretiveness may occur more often among the relatives of people with delusional disorder than among the population at large, suggesting some aspect of this disorder may be inherited.

A number of other disorders can cause delusions, and their presence should be ruled out before diagnosing delusional disorder. For example, abuse of amphetamines, alcohol, and cocaine can cause delusions, as can brain tumours, Huntington's disease, and Alzheimer's disease (Breier, 1993).

## Brief Psychotic Disorder

Recall the puzzling case of Arthur, who suddenly experienced the delusion that he could save the world and whose intense emotional swings lasted only a few days. He would receive the DSM-IV-TR diagnosis of **brief psychotic disorder,** which is characterized by the presence of one or more positive symptoms such as delusions, hallucinations, or disorganized speech or behaviour lasting 1 month or less. Individuals like Arthur regain their previous ability to function well in day-to-day activities. Brief psychotic disorder is often precipitated by extremely stressful situations.

## Shared Psychotic Disorder (Folie à Deux)

Relatively little is known about **shared psychotic disorder (folie à deux),** the condition in which an individual develops delusions simply as a result of a close relationship with a delusional individual. The content and nature of the delusion originate with the partner and can range from the relatively bizarre, such as believing enemies are sending harmful gamma rays through your house, to the fairly ordinary, such as believing you are about to receive a major promotion despite evidence to the contrary. Jose Silveira and Mary Seeman (1995) of the Hospital for Sick Children in Toronto reviewed 61 published case studies of individuals with shared psychotic disorder. On the basis of their review, they suggested that shared psychotic disorder occurs in predisposed individuals who become socially isolated with a psychotic person (Silveira & Seeman, 1995).

*Schizotypal personality disorder,* discussed in Chapter 11, is a related psychotic disorder. As you may recall, the characteristics are similar to those experienced by people with schizophrenia but are less severe. Some evidence also suggests that schizophrenia and schizotypal personality disorder may be genetically related as part of a "schizophrenia spectrum."

Remember that although people with related psychotic disorders display many of the characteristics of schizophrenia, these disorders differ significantly. Next, we examine the nature of schizophrenia and learn how researchers have attempted to understand and treat people who have it.

---

**brief psychotic disorder** Psychotic disturbance involving delusions, hallucinations, or disorganized speech or behaviour but lasting less than 1 month; often occurs in reaction to a stressor.

**shared psychotic disorder (folie à deux)** Psychotic disturbance in which an individual develops a delusion similar to that of a person with whom he or she shares a close relationship.

## Concept Check 12.1

**Part A** Determine which subtype of schizophrenia is described in each scenario.

1. Gary often has delusions and hallucinations that convince him enemies are out to persecute him. _____
2. Sabine displays motor immobility, and she often repeats words said by others around her. _____
3. Carrie had an episode of schizophrenia in the past, but she no longer displays the major symptoms of the disorder. She does, however, still have some negative, unusual ideas and displays flat affect on occasion. _____
4. Tram suffers from a type of schizophrenia that is identified by disruption and incoherence in his speech and behaviour. He also shows inappropriate affect, often laughing in sad or upsetting situations. _____
5. You sit down next to a gentleman who suddenly giggles. When you ask what he's laughing at, he answers, but you can't make sense of what he says. _____

**Part B** Diagnose the type of psychotic disorders described in each of the following. Choose from: (a) schizophreniform disorder, (b) schizoaffective disorder, (c) delusional disorder, (d) shared psychotic disorder.

6. Carol reveals to her therapist that she hears numerous voices talking to her and giving her orders. For the past month or so, these voices have been commenting on her everyday behaviour. Her doctor has just sent her to this therapist for what he believes to be a major depressive episode. She had begun to sleep all the time and contemplated suicide often. _____
7. Scott believes his wife is unfaithful and has been this way for years. He has no proof. A private investigator was hired, and he claimed Scott's wife is loving and devoted. Scott disregarded this and considered the possibility that the investigator was one of his wife's lovers. _____
8. Sarah believes the federal government is out to get her. She thinks agents follow her daily, monitor her calls, and read her mail. Her roommate Courtney tried to convince her otherwise. However, after a year of this, Courtney began to believe Sarah was correct and the government was out to get her, too. _____
9. If Brooke's schizophrenic symptoms disappeared after about 4 months and she returned to her normal life, what diagnosis might she have received? _____

# Prevalence and Causes of Schizophrenia

- ■ *Describe the prevalence of schizophrenia in society.*
- ■ *Identify the potential genetic, neurobiological, developmental, and psychosocial contributions and risk factors for schizophrenia.*
- ■ *Describe what is known about abnormalities in neurocognitive and biological functioning and their relation to the various types of schizophrenia.*

Studying schizophrenia reveals the many levels on which we must decipher what makes us behave the way we do. To uncover the causes of this disorder, researchers look in several areas: (1) the possible genes involved in schizophrenia, (2) the chemical action of the drugs that help many people with this disorder, and (3) abnormalities in the working of the brains of people with schizophrenia (Sawa & Snyder, 2002). As we survey the work of many specialists, we examine many state-of-the-art techniques for studying both biological and psychosocial influences, a process that may be slow going at times but will bring new insight to your understanding of psychopathology.

## Statistics

Schizophrenia sometimes defies our desire for simplicity. We have seen how very different symptoms can be displayed by individuals who would all be considered to have the disorder; in some people they develop slowly, and in others they occur suddenly.

Schizophrenia is generally chronic, and most people with the disorder have a very difficult time functioning in society. This is especially true of their ability to relate to others; they tend not to establish or maintain significant relationships, and therefore, many people with schizophrenia never marry or have children. Unlike the delusions of people with other psychotic disorders, the delusions of people with schizophrenia are likely to be outside the realm of possibility. Finally, even when individuals with schizophrenia improve with treatment, they are likely to experience difficulties throughout their lives.

Worldwide, the lifetime prevalence rate of schizophrenia is roughly equivalent for men and women, and it is estimated at 0.2% to 1.5% in the general population (Ho et al., 2003), which means the disorder will affect around 1% of the population at some point. A recent study by Simon Fraser University researcher Elliot Goldner and his colleagues suggests that 1-year prevalence of schizophrenic disorders in the British Columbia population was 0.4% (Goldner, Jones, & Waraich, 2003). Life expectancy is slightly less than average, partly because of the higher rate of suicide and accidents among people with schizophrenia (Ho et al., 2003). Although there is some disagreement about the distribution of schizophrenia between men and women, the difference between the sexes in age of onset is clear. For men, the likelihood of onset diminishes with age, but it can still first occur after the age of 75. The onset for women is lower than for men until age 36, when the relative risk for onset switches, with more women than men being affected later in life (Howard, Castle, Wessely, & Murray, 1993). Women appear to have more favourable outcomes than men (Ho et al., 2003).

## Development

Increasing attention has been paid to the developmental course of schizophrenia (Asarnow, 1994; Walker, 1991), which may shed some light on its causes. Research suggests that children who later develop schizophrenia show some abnormal signs before they display the characteristic symptoms (Fish, 1987). Their emotional reactions may be abnormal, with less positive and more negative affect than their unaffected siblings (Walker et al., 1993). Remember that although the age of onset varies, schizophrenia is generally seen by early adulthood. If the causative factors are present early on, why does the disorder show itself only later in life?

It may be that brain damage early in the developmental period causes later schizophrenia (McNeil, Cantor-Graae, & Weinberger, 2001). However, instead of resulting in an immediate progressive deterioration, the damage may lie dormant until later in development, when the signs of schizophrenia first appear. Some research finds that people with schizophrenia

who demonstrate early signs of abnormality at birth and during early childhood tend to fare better than people who do not (Torrey, Bowler, Taylor, & Gottesman, 1994). One interpretation of these results is that the earlier the damage occurs, the more time the brain has to compensate for it, which results in milder symptoms.

A life-span perspective may at least partly reveal the development of schizophrenia (Belitsky & McGlashan, 1993). In one of the few studies that have followed people with schizophrenia into late life, Winokur, Pfohl, and Tsuang (1987) tracked 52 people over a 40-year period. Their general finding was that older adults tended to display fewer positive symptoms, such as delusions and hallucinations, and more negative symptoms, such as speech and cognitive difficulties.

The relapse rate must also be considered in discussing the course of schizophrenia. Unfortunately, a great many people who improve after an episode of schizophrenia later experience the symptoms again. Most people with schizophrenia fluctuate between severe and moderate levels of impairment throughout their lives (Harrow, Sands, Silverstein, & Goldberg, 1997). Figure 12.2 illustrates the data from one study that show the course of schizophrenia among four prototypical groups (Shepherd, Watt, Falloon, & Smeeton, 1989). As you can see, about

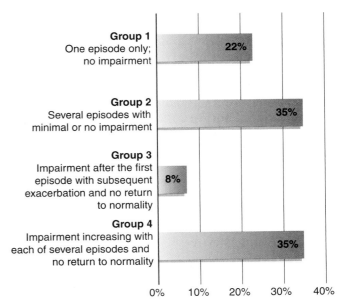

**Figure 12.2** ■ The natural history of schizophrenia: A 5-year follow-up. (From "The Natural History of Schizophrenia: A Five-Year Follow-Up Study of Outcome and Prediction in a Representative Sample of Schizophrenia," by M. Shepherd, D. Watt, I. Falloon, & N. Smeeton, 1989, *Psychological Medicine, 46* (Suppl. 15). Copyright © 1989 by Cambridge University Press. Reprinted with the permission of Cambridge University Press.)

22% of the group had one episode of schizophrenia and improved without lasting impairment. However, the remaining 78% experienced several episodes, with differing degrees of impairment between them. Relapses are an important subject in the field of schizophrenia; we return to this phenomenon when we discuss causes and treatment.

## Cultural Factors

Because schizophrenia is so complex, the diagnosis can be controversial. Some have argued that "schizophrenia" does not really exist but is a derogatory label for people who behave in ways outside the cultural norm (e.g., Laing, 1967; Szasz, 1961). Although the idea that schizophrenia exists only in the minds of mental health professionals is certainly provocative, this extreme view is contradicted by experience. As clinicians, we have had a great deal of contact with people who have this disorder and with their families and friends, and the tremendous amount of emotional pain resulting from schizophrenia gives definite credence to its existence. In addition, many people in extremely diverse cultures have the symptoms of schizophrenia, which supports the notion that it is a reality for many people worldwide (Ihara, Berrios, & McKenna, 2003; Patel & Andrade, 2003). Schizophrenia is thus universal, affecting all racial and cultural groups studied so far.

However, the course and outcome of schizophrenia vary from culture to culture. For example, in Colombia, India, and Nigeria, more people improve significantly or recover than in other countries (Leff, Sartorius, Jablensky, Korten, & Ernberg, 1992). These differences may be because of cultural variations or prevalent biological influences such as immunization, but we cannot yet explain these differences in outcomes.

In North America, proportionately more Blacks receive the diagnosis of schizophrenia than do Whites (Lindsey & Paul, 1989). Research from England suggests that people from devalued ethnic minority groups (e.g., Afro-Caribbeans) may be victims of bias and stereotyping (Lewis, Croft-Jeffreys, & Anthony, 1990); in other words, they may be more likely to receive a diagnosis of schizophrenia than members of a dominant group. One prospective study of schizophrenia among different ethnic groups in London found that although the outcomes of schizophrenia appear similar across these groups, Blacks were more likely to be detained against their will, brought to the hospital by police, and given emergency injections (Goater et al., 1999). The differing rates of schizophrenia, therefore, may to be because of *misdiagnosis* rather than to any real cultural distinctions. However, an additional factor contributing to this imbalance is being revealed in our advancing knowledge of genetics. There may be genetic variants unique to certain racial groups that contribute to the development of schizophrenia (Glatt, Tampilic, Christie, DeYoung, & Freimer, 2004), a factor we explore in more detail next.

## Genetic Influences

We could argue that no other area of abnormal psychology so clearly illustrates the enormous complexity and intriguing mystery of genetic influences on behaviour as does the phenomenon of schizophrenia (Bassett, Chow, Waterworth, & Brzustowicz, 2001). Despite the possibility that schizophrenia may be several different disorders, we can safely make one generalization: *Genes are responsible for making some individuals vulnerable to schizophrenia.* We will look at a range of research findings from family, twin, adoptee, offspring of twins, and linkage and association studies (Faraone, Tsuang, & Tsuang, 1999). We conclude by discussing the compelling reasons that no one gene is responsible for schizophrenia; rather, multiple genes combine to produce vulnerability. Gottesman (1991) has produced a detailed but highly readable discussion of this research in his book *Schizophrenia Genesis: The Origins of Madness.*

### Family Studies

In 1938, German researcher Franz Kallmann published a major study of the families of people with schizophrenia (Kallmann, 1938). Kallmann examined family members of more than 1000 people diagnosed with schizophrenia in a Berlin psychiatric hospital. Several of his observations continue to guide research on schizophrenia. Kallmann showed that the severity of the parent's disorder influenced the likelihood of the child having schizophrenia: The more severe the parent's schizophrenia, the more likely the children were to develop it. Another observation was important: All forms of schizophrenia (e.g., catatonic, paranoid) were seen within the families. In other words, it does not appear that you inherit a predisposition for, say, paranoid schizophrenia. Instead, you may inherit a general predisposition for schizophrenia that manifests in the same form or differently from that of your parent. More recent research from Ireland confirms this observation and suggests that families that have a member with schizophrenia are at risk not just for schizophrenia alone or for all psychological disorders; instead, there appears to be some familial risk for a spectrum of psychotic disorders related to schizophrenia (Kendler et al., 1993).

Gottesman (1991) summarized the data from about 40 studies of schizophrenia, as shown in Figure 12.3. The most striking feature of this graph is its orderly demonstration that the risk of having schizophrenia varies according to how many genes

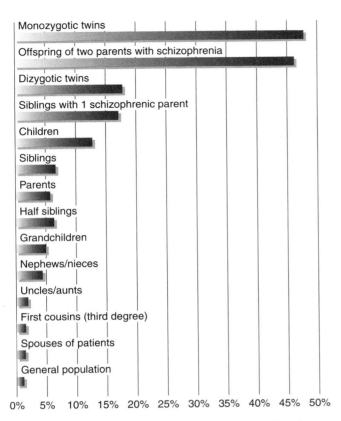

| | |
|---|---|
| Monozygotic twins | |
| Offspring of two parents with schizophrenia | |
| Dizygotic twins | |
| Siblings with 1 schizophrenic parent | |
| Children | |
| Siblings | |
| Parents | |
| Half siblings | |
| Grandchildren | |
| Nephews/nieces | |
| Uncles/aunts | |
| First cousins (third degree) | |
| Spouses of patients | |
| General population | |

0%  5%  10%  15%  20%  25%  30%  35%  40%  45%  50%

**Figure 12.3** ■ Risk of developing schizophrenia. (Based on Gottesman, 1991.)

an individual shares with someone who has the disorder. For example, you have the greatest chance (approximately 48%) of having schizophrenia if it has affected your identical (monozygotic) twin, a person who shares 100% of your genetic information. Your risk drops to about 17% with a fraternal (dizygotic) twin, who shares about 50% of your genetic information. And having any relative with schizophrenia makes you more likely to have the disorder than someone in the general population without such a relative (about 1%). Because family studies can't separate genetic influence from the impact of the environment, we use twin and adoption studies to help us evaluate the role of shared experiences in the cause of schizophrenia.

Twin Studies

If they are raised together, identical twins share 100% of their genes and 100% of their environment, whereas fraternal twins share only about 50% of their genes and 100% of their environment. If the environment is solely responsible for schizophrenia, we would expect little difference between identical and fraternal twins with regard to this disorder. If only genetic factors are relevant, both identical twins would always have schizophrenia (be concordant) and the fraternal twins would both have it about 50% of the time. Research from twin studies indicates

that the truth is somewhere in the middle (e.g., Kendler & Diehl, 1993; Sherman et al., 1997).

In one of the most fascinating of "nature's experiments," identical quadruplets, all of whom have schizophrenia, have been studied extensively. Nicknamed the "Genain" quadruplets (from the Greek, meaning "dreadful gene"), these women have been followed by researchers for years (e.g., Mirsky et al., 2000; Rosenthal, 1963). In a sense, the women represent the complex interaction between genetics and environment. All four shared the same genetic predisposition, and all were brought up in the same particularly dysfunctional household; yet the time of onset for schizophrenia, the symptoms and diagnoses, the course of the disorder, and, ultimately, their outcomes, differed significantly from sister to sister.

The case of the Genain quadruplets reveals an important consideration in studying genetic influences on behaviour—*unshared environments* (Plomin, 1990). We tend to think that siblings, and especially identical multiples, are brought up the same way. The impression is that "good" parents expose their children to favourable environments and "bad" parents give them unstable experiences. However, even identical siblings can have different prenatal and family experiences and therefore be exposed to varying degrees of biological and environmental stress. For example, Hester, one of the Genain sisters, was described by her disturbed parents as a habitual masturbator, and she had more social problems than her sisters as she grew up. Hester was the first to experience severe symptoms of schizophrenia, at age 18, but her sister Myra was not hospitalized until 6 years later. This unusual case demonstrates that even siblings who are very close in every aspect of their lives can have considerably different experiences physically and socially as they grow up, which may result in vastly different outcomes.

The Genain quadruplets all had schizophrenia but exhibited different symptoms over the years.

## Adoption Studies

Several adoption studies have distinguished the roles of the environment and genetics as they affect schizophrenia. These studies often span many years; because people often do not show the first signs of schizophrenia until middle age, researchers need to be sure all the offspring reach that point before drawing conclusions. Many schizophrenia studies are conducted in Europe, primarily because of the extensive and comprehensive records kept in many of these countries.

The largest adoption study is being conducted in Finland (Tienari, 1991). From a sample of almost 20 000 women with schizophrenia, the researchers found 190 children who had been given up for adoption. The data from this study support the idea that schizophrenia represents a "spectrum" of related disorders, all of which overlap genetically. If an adopted child had a biological mother with schizophrenia, he or she had about a 5% chance of having the disorder (compared with about only 1% in the general population). However, if the biological mother had schizophrenia or one of the related psychotic disorders (e.g., delusional disorder, schizophreniform disorder) the risk that the adopted child would have one of these disorders rose to about 22% (Tienari et al., 2003). Even when raised away from their biological parents, children of parents with schizophrenia have a much higher chance of having the disorder themselves. Something other than living in the home of a person with schizophrenia must account for this disorder.

## The Offspring of Twins

Twin and adoption studies strongly suggest a genetic component for schizophrenia, but what about children who develop schizophrenia even though their parents do not? For example, the study by Tienari and colleagues (2003) we just discussed found that 1.7% of the children with non-schizophrenic parents developed schizophrenia. Does this mean you can develop schizophrenia without "schizophrenic genes"? Or are some people carriers, having the genes for schizophrenia but for some reason not showing the disorder themselves? An important clue to this question comes from research on the children of twins with schizophrenia.

In a study begun in 1971, 21 identical twin pairs and 41 fraternal twin pairs with a history of schizophrenia were identified, along with their children (Fischer, 1971; Gottesman & Bertelsen, 1989). The researchers wanted to determine the relative likelihood that a child would have schizophrenia if his or her parent did and if the parent's twin had schizophrenia but the parent did not. Figure 12.4 illustrates the findings from this study. For example, if your parent is an identical (monozygotic) twin with

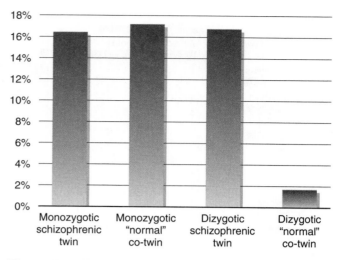

**Figure 12.4** ■ Risk for schizophrenia among children of twins. (Gottesman & Bertelsen, 1989.)

schizophrenia, you have about a 17% chance of having the disorder yourself, a figure that holds if you are the child of an unaffected identical twin whose co-twin has the disorder.

On the other hand, look at the risks for the child of a fraternal (dizygotic) twin. If your parent is the twin with schizophrenia, you have about a 17% chance of having schizophrenia yourself. However, if your parent does not have schizophrenia but your parent's fraternal twin does, your risk is only about 2%. The only way to explain this finding is through genetics. The data clearly indicate that you can have genes that predispose you to schizophrenia, not show the disorder yourself, but still pass on the genes to your children. In other words, you can be a "carrier" for schizophrenia. This is some of the strongest evidence yet that people are genetically vulnerable to schizophrenia. Remember, however, there is only a 17% chance of inheritance, meaning that other factors help determine who will have this disorder.

## Linkage and Association Studies

Genetic linkage and association studies rely on traits such as blood types (whose exact location on the chromosome is already known) that are inherited in families with the disorder you are looking for—in this case, schizophrenia. Because we know the location of the genes for these traits (called *marker genes*), we can make a rough guess about the location of the disorder genes inherited with them. To date, researchers have looked at several sites for genes that may be responsible for schizophrenia. For example, regions of chromosomes 1, 6, 8, 10, 13, 18, and 22 are implicated in this disorder (Sawa & Snyder, 2002), and a particular genetic deficit (22q11 deletion syndrome) is being explored as the cause of a subtype of schizophrenia (Bassett et al., 2001; Hodgkinson, Murphy, O'Neill, Brzustowicz, & Bassett, 2001).

## The Search for Markers

In the search for markers, researchers look for common traits other than the symptoms of the disorder. If some people have the positive symptoms of schizophrenia, others have the negative symptoms, and still others have a mixture of these symptoms, yet they all have a particular problem completing a certain task, the skill deficit would be useful for identifying what else these people may have in common.

Several potential markers for schizophrenia have been studied over the years. As noted by McGill University psychologist Gillian O'Driscoll and her colleagues, one of the more highly researched is called *smooth-pursuit eye movement* or eye-tracking (O'Driscoll, Lenzenweger, & Holzman, 1998). While keeping your head still, you must be able to track a moving pendulum, back and forth, with your eyes. The ability to track objects smoothly across the visual field is deficient in many people who have schizophrenia (e.g., Clementz & Sweeney, 1990); it does not appear to be the result of drug treatment or institutionalization (Lieberman et al., 1993). It also seems to be a problem for relatives of these people and is observed more frequently among people with schizophrenia than in others who do not have the disorder (Thaker & Avila, 2003). Figure 12.5 shows the decreasing likelihood of observing this abnormal eye-tracking ability the further a person is genetically from someone with schizophrenia. When all these observations are combined, they suggest an eye-tracking deficit may be a marker for schizophrenia that could be used in further study (O'Driscoll et al., 1998).

## Evidence for Multiple Genes

As we have seen, schizophrenia involves more than one gene, a phenomenon referred to as *quantitative trait loci* (Levinson et al., 1998; Plomin, Owen, & McGuffin, 1994). The schizophrenia we see most often is probably caused by several genes located at different sites throughout the chromosomes. This model would also clarify why there can be gradations of severity in people with the disorder (from mild to severe) and why the risk of having schizophrenia increases with the number of affected relatives in the family.

## *Neurobiological Influences*

The belief that schizophrenia involves a malfunctioning brain goes back as far as the writings of Emil Kraepelin (1856–1926). It is therefore not surprising that a great deal of research has focused on the brain. Before we discuss some of this work, however, be forewarned: To study abnormalities in the brain for clues to the cause of schizophrenia is to face all the classic problems of doing correlational research we discussed in Chapter 3. For example, if a person has schizophrenia and too much of a neurotransmitter, (1) does too much neurotransmitter cause schizophrenia, (2) does schizophrenia create too much of the neurotransmitter, or (3) does something else cause both the schizophrenia and the chemical imbalance? Keep this caveat in mind as you review the following research.

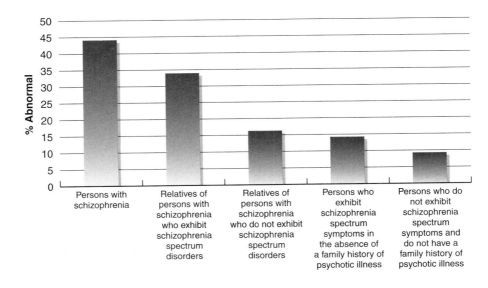

**Figure 12.5** ■ Abnormal smooth-pursuit eye movements and schizophrenia. (From "Schizophrenia, V: Risk Markers," by G. K. Thaker and M. Avila, *American Journal of Psychiatry, 160*, 1578. Copyright © 2003 by American Psychiatric Association. Adapted with permission.)

## Dopamine

One of the most enduring yet still controversial theories of the cause of schizophrenia involves the neurotransmitter *dopamine* (Carlsson, 1995; Maas et al., 1997). Before we consider the research, however, let's review briefly how neurotransmitters operate in the brain and how they are affected by neuroleptic medications. In Chapter 2 we discussed the sensitivity of specific neurons to specific neurotransmitters and described how they cluster throughout the brain. The top of Figure 12.6 shows two neurons and the important synaptic gap that separates them. Neurotransmitters are released from the storage vessels (synaptic vesicles) at the end of the axon, cross the gap, and are taken up by receptors in the dendrite of the next axon. Chemical "messages" are transported in this way from neuron to neuron throughout the brain.

This process can be influenced in a number of ways, and the rest of Figure 12.6 illustrates some of them. The chemical messages can be increased by agonistic agents or decreased by antagonistic agents.

(Remember that the word *antagonistic* means hostile or unfriendly; in some way, this is the effect of antagonistic agents on the chemical messenger service.) *Antagonistic effects* slow down or stop messages from being transmitted by preventing the release of the neurotransmitter, blocking uptake at the level of the dendrite, or causing leaks that reduce the amount of neurotransmitter ultimately released. On the other hand, *agonistic effects* assist with the transference of chemical messages and, if extreme, can produce too much neurotransmitter activity by increasing production or release of the neurotransmitter and by affecting more receptors at the dendrites.

What we've learned about antipsychotic medications points to the possibility that the dopamine system is too active in people with schizophrenia. The simplified picture in Figure 12.6 does not show that there are actually different receptor sites and that a chemical such as dopamine produces different results depending on which of those sites it affects. In schizophrenia, attention has focused on several dopamine sites, in particular those referred to simply as $D_1$ and $D_2$.

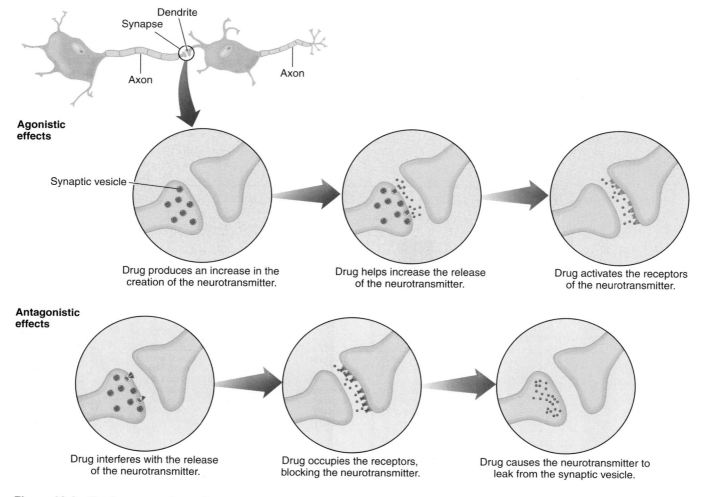

**Agonistic effects**

Drug produces an increase in the creation of the neurotransmitter.

Drug helps increase the release of the neurotransmitter.

Drug activates the receptors of the neurotransmitter.

**Antagonistic effects**

Drug interferes with the release of the neurotransmitter.

Drug occupies the receptors, blocking the neurotransmitter.

Drug causes the neurotransmitter to leak from the synaptic vesicle.

**Figure 12.6** ■ Some ways drugs affect neurotransmission.

In a story that resembles a mystery plot, several pieces of "circumstantial evidence" are clues to the role of dopamine in schizophrenia:

1. Antipsychotic drugs (*neuroleptics*) that are often effective in treating people with schizophrenia are dopamine antagonists, partially blocking the brain's use of dopamine (Creese, Burt, & Snyder, 1976; Seeman, Lee, Chau Wong, & Wong, 1976).
2. These drugs can produce negative side effects similar to those in Parkinson's disease, a disorder known to be caused by insufficient dopamine.
3. The drug L-dopa, a dopamine agonist used to treat people with Parkinson's disease, produces schizophrenia-like symptoms in some people (Davidson et al., 1987).
4. Amphetamines, which also activate dopamine, can make psychotic symptoms worse in some people with schizophrenia (van Kammen, Docherty, & Bunney, 1982).

In other words, when drugs are administered that are known to increase dopamine (agonists), there is an increase in schizophrenic behaviour; when drugs that are known to decrease dopamine activity (antagonists) are used, schizophrenic symptoms tend to diminish. Taking these observations together, researchers theorized that schizophrenia in some people was attributable to excessive dopamine activity.

Despite these observations, some evidence contradicts the dopamine theory (Carson & Sanislow, 1993; Davis, Kahn, Ko, & Davidson, 1991):

1. A significant number of people with schizophrenia are not helped by the use of dopamine antagonists.
2. Although the neuroleptics block the reception of dopamine quickly, the relevant symptoms subside only after several days or weeks, much more slowly than researchers would expect.
3. These drugs are only partly helpful in reducing the negative symptoms (e.g., flat affect, anhedonia) of schizophrenia.

In addition to these concerns, there is evidence of a "double-edged sword" with respect to schizophrenia. A medication called *clozapine*—along with a family of similar drugs—is effective with many people who were not helped with traditional neuroleptic medications (Wahlbeck, Cheine, Essali, & Adams, 1999). That's the good news. But as pointed out by Shitj Kapur and his colleagues in Toronto, the bad news for the dopamine theory is that clozapine and these other new medications are weak dopamine antagonists, much less able to block the dopamine sites than other drugs (Kapur, Zipursky, & Remington, 1999). Why would a medication inefficient at blocking dopamine be effective as a treatment for schizophrenia if schizophrenia is caused by excessive dopamine activity?

The answer may be that although dopamine is involved in the symptoms of schizophrenia, the relationship is more complicated than we once thought (Potter & Manji, 1993). Current thinking points to *at least three specific neurochemical abnormalities* simultaneously at play in the brains of people with schizophrenia.

Strong evidence now leads us to believe that schizophrenia is partially the result of *excessive stimulation of striatal dopamine $D_2$ receptors* (Laruelle, Kegeles, & Abi-Darham, 2003). Recall that the striatum is part of the basal ganglia found deep within the brain. These cells control movement, balance, and walking, and they rely on dopamine to function. Huntington's disease (which involves problems in motor function) involves deterioration in this brain area. How do we know that excessive stimulation of $D_2$ receptors is involved in schizophrenia? One clue is that the most effective antipsychotic drugs all share dopamine $D_2$ receptor antagonism (Ho et al., 2003)—meaning they help block the stimulation of the $D_2$ receptors.

A second area of interest to scientists investigating the cause of schizophrenia is the observation of *a deficiency in the stimulation of prefrontal $D_1$ receptors* (Koh, Bergson, Undie, Goldman-Rakic, & Lidow, 2003). Therefore, although some dopamine sites may be overactive (e.g., striatal $D_2$), a second type of dopamine site in the part of the brain that we use for planning and organizing (prefrontal $D_1$ receptors) appears to be less active and may account for negative symptoms of schizophrenia such as avolition. As we will discuss later in this chapter, lower prefrontal activity in people with schizophrenia is referred to as *hypofrontality*.

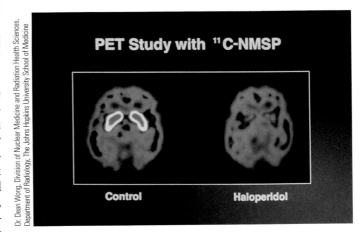

These PET images show the brain of a man with schizophrenia who had never been medicated (left) and after he received haloperidol (right). The red and yellow areas indicate activity in the $D_2$ receptors; haloperidol evidently reduced dopamine activity.

Finally, a third and more recent area of neurochemical interest involves research on *alterations in prefrontal activity involving glutamate transmission* (Goff & Coyle, 2001). Glutamate is an excitatory neurotransmitter that is found in all areas of the brain and is only now being studied in earnest. Like dopamine, glutamate has different types of receptors. The ones being studied for their role in schizophrenia are the N-methyl-d-aspartate (NMDA) receptors. The effects of certain drugs that affect NMDA receptors point to clues to schizophrenia. Two recreational drugs described in Chapter 10—phencyclidine (PCP) and ketamine—can result in psychotic-like behaviour in people without schizophrenia and can exacerbate psychotic symptoms in those with schizophrenia. Both PCP and ketamine are NMDA antagonists, suggesting that a deficit in glutamate or blocking of NMDA sites may be involved in some of the symptoms of schizophrenia (Goff & Coyle, 2001).

You can see that research on these two neurotransmitters is complex and awaits further clarification. However, advances in technology are leading us closer to the clues behind this enigmatic disorder and closer still to better treatments.

### Brain Structure

Evidence for neurological damage in people with schizophrenia comes from a number of observations (Ho et al., 2003). A child with a parent who has the disorder, and who is thus at risk, tends to show subtle but observable neurological problems such as abnormal reflexes and inattentiveness (Fish, 1977; Hans & Marcus, 1991). These difficulties are persistent: Adults who have schizophrenia show deficits in their ability to perform certain tasks and to attend during reaction time exercises (Cleghorn & Albert, 1990). Such findings suggest that brain damage or dysfunction may cause or accompany schizophrenia, although no single site is probably responsible for the whole range of symptoms (Ho et al., 2003).

One of the most reliable observations about the brain in people with schizophrenia involves the size of the ventricles (see Figure 12.7). As early as 1927, researchers noted that these liquid-filled cavities showed enlargement in some brains examined in people with schizophrenia (Jacobi & Winkler, 1927). Since then, more sophisticated techniques have been developed for observing the brain, and in the almost 50 studies conducted on ventricle size, the great majority show abnormally large lateral ventricles in people with schizophrenia (Pahl, Swayze, & Andreasen, 1990). Ventricle size in itself may not be a problem, but the dilation (enlargement) of the ventricles indicates that adjacent parts of the brain either have not developed fully or have

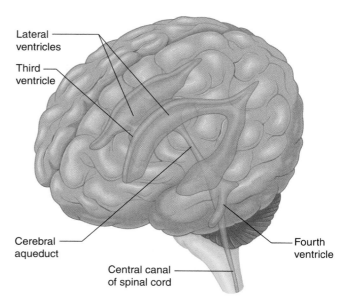

**Figure 12.7**   ■   Location of the cerebrospinal fluid in the human brain. This extracellular fluid surrounds and cushions the brain and spinal cord. It also fills the four interconnected cavities (cerebral ventricles) within the brain and the central canal of the spinal cord.

atrophied, thus allowing the ventricles to become larger.

Ventricle enlargement is not seen in everyone who has schizophrenia. Several factors seem to be associated with this finding. For example, enlarged ventricles are observed more often in men than in women (Goldstein & Lewine, 2000). Also, ventricles seem to enlarge in proportion to age and to the duration of the schizophrenia. One study found that individuals with schizophrenia who were exposed to influenza prenatally may be more likely to have enlarged ventricles (Takei, Lewis, Jones, Harvey, & Murray, 1996). (We describe the possible role of prenatal exposure to influenza and schizophrenia in the next section.)

In a study of ventricle size, researchers investigated the possible role of genetics (Staal et al., 2000). Using the brain-imaging technique, magnetic resonance imaging (MRI), investigators compared brain structure among people with schizophrenia, their same-sex siblings who did not have schizophrenia, and healthy volunteers. Both the people with schizophrenia and their otherwise unaffected siblings had enlargement of the third ventricle compared with the volunteers. This suggests that the enlargement of ventricles may be related to susceptibility to schizophrenia.

We touched on the concept of unshared environments in the section on genetics (Plomin, 1990). Although twins are identical genetically, they can experience a number of environmental differences, even before they are born. For instance, in the intrauterine environment twins must compete for nutrients, and they may not be equally successful. In addition, birth complications, such as the loss of oxygen (anoxia), could affect only one of the twins (Carson & Sanislow, 1993). Obstetrical complications appear often among twins with schizophrenia in discordant identical pairs, and among the more severely affected if both twins have schizophrenia (McNeil, 1987). Different experiences by twins who are already predisposed to the disorder could damage the brain and cause the types of symptoms we associate with schizophrenia.

The frontal lobes of the brain have also interested people looking for structural problems associated with schizophrenia (Gur & Pearlson, 1993). This area may be less active in people with schizophrenia than in people without the disorder, a phenomenon sometimes known as *hypofrontality* (*hypo* means less active or deficient). Neuropsychological research by several Canadian teams has shown that patients with schizophrenia perform poorly relative to comparison groups on cognitive tasks known to be related to functioning of the frontal lobes (e.g., Zakzanis, Troyer, Rich, & Heinrichs, 2000). For example, James Everett and colleagues at Laval University showed that patients with schizophrenia performed more poorly than healthy controls on a task called the Wisconsin Card Sorting Task—a test requiring planning and organizational abilities subserved by the frontal lobes (Everett, Lavoie, Gagnon, & Gosselin, 2001). Further research suggests that deficient activity in a particular area of the frontal lobes, the dorsolateral prefrontal cortex (DLPFC), may be implicated in schizophrenia (e.g., Berman & Weinberger, 1990). When people with and without schizophrenia are given tasks that involve the DLPFC, less activity (measured by cerebral blood flow) is recorded in the brains of those with schizophrenia. A recent large scale review showed that hypofrontality distinguishes about half of schizophrenia patients from non-schizophrenic people (Davidson & Heinrichs, 2003). Hypofrontality also seems to be associated with the negative symptoms of schizophrenia (Andreasen et al., 1992) and with the eye-tracking deficits mentioned earlier (O'Driscoll et al., 1999).

It appears that several brain sites are implicated in the cognitive dysfunction observed among people with schizophrenia, especially the prefrontal cortex, various other related cortical regions, and subcortical circuits including the thalmus and the stratum (Ho et al., 2003). Remember that this dysfunction seems to occur *before the onset* of schizophrenia. In other words, brain damage may develop progressively, beginning before the symptoms of the disorder are apparent, perhaps prenatally (Weinberger, 1995).

## Viral Infection

A curious fact about schizophrenia is that, according to some authors, no adequate descriptions of people having this disorder appear earlier than about 1800 (e.g., Gottesman, 1991). If you look at historic records or read ancient literature, you can find people with disorders such as mental retardation, mania, depression, and senile dementia. Even William Shakespeare, who describes most human conditions, mentions nothing that resembles our current image of schizophrenia. Historically, such an obvious aberration of behaviour is puzzlingly absent. (However, there is now some evidence that at least a few cases of schizophrenia-like disorder may have existed as early as the 14th century (Heinrichs, 2003).)

One intriguing hypothesis is that schizophrenia is a recent phenomenon, appearing only during the past 200 years and that, like AIDS, it may involve some newly introduced virus (Gottesman, 1991). In other words, a "schizo-virus" could have caused some cases of this debilitating disorder (Torrey, 1988b). Whether or not this disorder is a recent phenomenon, there is evidence that a virus-like disease may account for some cases (Kirch, 1993). The higher prevalence of schizophrenia among men living in urban areas (Lewis, David, Andreasson, & Allbeck, 1992) implies that they are more likely to have been exposed to infectious agents than their peers in less populated areas.

Several studies have shown that schizophrenia may be associated with prenatal exposure to influenza. For example, Mednick and colleagues followed a large number of people after a severe Type A2 influenza epidemic in Helsinki, Finland, and found that those whose mothers were exposed to influenza during the second trimester of pregnancy were much more likely to have schizophrenia than others (Cannon, Barr, & Mednick, 1991). This observation has been confirmed by some researchers (e.g., O'Callaghan, Sham, Takei, Glover, & Murray, 1991; Venables, 1996) but not by others (e.g., Torrey, Rawlings, & Waldman, 1988).

Evidence that second-trimester developmental problems may be associated with schizophrenia has led researchers to look further into this area. Among the types of cells that normally migrate to the cortex during this period are the fingertip dermal cells, which are responsible for the number of fingerprint ridges. Although there is no such thing as an abnormal number of ridges, identical twins generally have the same number. However, if some interruption in second-trimester fetal development resulted in schizophrenia (when, according to the viral theory, a virus may have its effect), it would also affect the fingertip dermal cells. Researchers compared the fingerprint ridges of identical twins who were discordant for schizophrenia with those of identical twins without schizophrenia (Bracha, Torrey, Gottesman, Bigelow, & Cunniff, 1992). They found that the number of ridges on the fingertips of the twins without schizophrenia differed very little from each other; however, they differed a great deal among about one-third of the twin pairs who were discordant for schizophrenia. This study suggests that ridge count may be a marker of prenatal brain damage. Although there is no characteristic fingerprint for schizophrenia, this physical sign may add to our understanding of the second-trimester conditions that can trigger the genetic predisposition for schizophrenia (Weinberger, 1995).

The indications that virus-like diseases may cause damage to the fetal brain, which later may cause the symptoms of schizophrenia, are suggestive and may help explain why some people with schizophrenia behave the way they do (Mednick et al., 1998). However, there is not yet enough evidence to prove the existence of a "schizo-virus."

## Psychological and Social Influences

That one identical twin may develop schizophrenia and the other may not suggests that schizophrenia involves something in addition to genes. We know that early brain trauma, perhaps resulting from a second-trimester virus-like attack or obstetrical complications, may generate physical stress that contributes to schizophrenia. All these observations show clearly that schizophrenia does not fall neatly into a few simple causal packages. For instance, not all people with schizophrenia have enlarged ventricles, nor do they all have a hypofrontality or excessive activity in their dopamine systems. The causal picture may be further complicated by psychological and social factors. We next look at research into psychosocial factors. Do emotional stressors or family interaction patterns *initiate* the symptoms of schizophrenia? And how might those factors cause people to relapse after a period of improvement?

### Stress

It is important to learn how much and what kind of stress makes a person with a predisposition for schizophrenia develop the disorder. Think back to the two cases we presented at the beginning of this chapter. Did you notice any precipitating events? Arthur's father had died several years earlier, and Arthur was laid off from his job around the time his symptoms first appeared. David's uncle had died the same year he began acting strangely. Were these stressful events just coincidences, or did they contribute to the men's later problems?

Researchers have studied the effects of a variety of stressors on schizophrenia. Dohrenwend and Egri (1981), for instance, observed that otherwise healthy

people who engage in combat during a war often display temporary symptoms that resemble those of schizophrenia. In an early study, Brown and Birley (1968; Birley & Brown, 1970) examined people whose onset of schizophrenia could be dated within a week. These individuals had experienced a high number of stressful life events in the 3 weeks just before they started showing signs of the disorder. In a large-scale study sponsored by the World Health Organization, researchers also looked at the role of life events in the onset of schizophrenia (Day et al., 1987). This cross-national study confirmed the findings of Brown and Birley across eight different research centres.

The *retrospective* nature of such research creates problems. Each study relies on after-the-fact reports, collected after the person showed signs of schizophrenia. We always wonder whether such reports are biased in some way and therefore misleading (Hirsch, Cramer, & Bowen, 1992). One study used a *prospective* approach to examine the impact of stress on relapse.

Ventura, Nuechterlein, Lukoff, and Hardesty (1989) identified 30 people with recent-onset schizophrenia and followed them for a 1-year period. The researchers interviewed the subjects every 2 weeks to learn whether they had experienced any stressful life events and whether their symptoms had changed. Notice that, unlike the previous studies, this research examines the factors that predict the recurrence of schizophrenic symptoms after a period of improvement. During the 1-year assessment period, 11 of the 30 people had a significant relapse, that is, their symptoms returned or worsened. Like Brown and Birley, Ventura et al. found that relapses occurred when stressful life events increased during the previous month. Other research demonstrates that stressful life events can increase depression among people with schizophrenia, which in turn may contribute to relapse (Ventura, Nuechterlein, Subotnik, Hardesty, & Mintz, 2000). An important finding from the first study is that, although the people experienced more stressful events *as a group* just before their relapse, 55% of those suffering a relapse *did not* have a major life event during the previous month. Other factors must account for the return of symptoms among these people (Bebbington et al., 1993; Ventura, Nuechterlein, Hardesty, & Gitlin, 1992).

In Chapters 6 and 7, we examined how social support can exert a moderating influence in reducing the negative impact of stress in both mental health and physical disorders (i.e., mood disorders and chronic pain, respectively). Some recent Canadian research supports the important role of social support in schizophrenia as well. A longitudinal study by David Erickson and Morton Beiser at the University of Ottawa and the Centre for

Addiction and Mental Health showed that higher levels of social support from non-family members in the social network predicted better outcomes 5 years later among patients experiencing their first episode of schizophrenia (Erickson, Beiser, & Iacono, 1998). But what of the role of family members? We look at this important influence next.

### Families and Relapse

A great deal of research has studied how interactions within the family affect people who have schizophrenia. For example, the term **schizophrenogenic mother** was used for a time to describe a mother whose cold, dominant, and rejecting nature was thought to cause schizophrenia in her children (Fromm-Reichmann, 1948). In addition, the term **double bind communication** was used to portray a communication style that produced conflicting messages, which, in turn, caused schizophrenia to develop (Bateson, 1959). Here, the parent presumably communicates messages that have two conflicting meanings; for example, a mother responds coolly to her child's embrace but says, "Don't you love me anymore?" when the child withdraws. Although these theories are no longer supported, they have been—and in some cases continue to be—destructive, producing guilt in parents who are persuaded that their early mistakes caused devastating consequences.

Recent work has focused more on how family interactions contribute not to the onset of schizophrenia but to relapse after initial symptoms are observed. Research has focused on a particular emotional communication style known as **expressed emotion.** This communication style is characterized by intrusiveness, high levels of emotional response, a negative attitude toward the illness on the part of family members, and low tolerance and unrealistic expectations of the patient (Cole & Kazarian, 1988). The expressed emotion concept was formulated by Brown and colleagues in London, England. Following a sample of people who had been discharged from the hospital after an episode of schizophrenic symptoms, they found that former patients who had limited contact with relatives did better than patients who spent longer periods with their families (Brown, 1959). Additional research results indicated that if the level of *criticism* (disapproval), *hostility* (animosity), and *emotional overinvolvement* (intrusiveness) expressed by the families was high, patients tended to relapse (Brown, Monck, Carstairs, & Wing, 1962).

Other researchers, including John Cole of the London Psychiatric Hospital and Shahe Kazarian of the University of Western Ontario, have since found that ratings of high expressed emotion in a family are a good predictor of relapse among people with chronic schizophrenia (Bebbington, Bowen, Hirsch, & Kuipers, 1995; Kazarian, Malla, Cole, & Baker,

1990). If you have schizophrenia and live in a family with high expressed emotion, you are 3.7 times more likely to relapse than if you lived in a family with low expressed emotion (Kavanagh, 1992; Parker & Hadzi-Pavlovic, 1990). Here are examples of interviews that show how families of people with schizophrenia might communicate expressed emotion (Hooley, 1985, pp. 148–149).

### High Expressed Emotion

- I always say, "Why don't you pick up a book, do a crossword or something like that to keep your mind off it." That's even too much trouble.
- I've tried to jolly him out of it and pestered him into doing things. Maybe I've overdone it, I don't know.

### Low Expressed Emotion

- I know it's better for her to be on her own, to get away from me and try to do things on her own.
- Whatever she does suits me.
- I just tend to let it go because I know that when she wants to speak she will speak.

The literature on expressed emotion is valuable to our understanding of why symptoms of schizophrenia recur. It may also show us how to treat people with this disorder so that they do not experience further psychotic episodes (Mueser et al., 1993).

An interesting issue that arises when studying family influences is whether what we see is unique to our culture or is universal. Looking at expressed emotion across different cultures may help us learn whether it is a *cause* of schizophrenia. Remember that schizophrenia is observed with about the same rate worldwide, with a prevalence of about 1% in the global population. If a factor such as high expressed emotion in families is a causal agent, we should see the same rates in families across cultures; in fact, however, they differ, as you can see in Figure 12.8. These data come from an analysis of the concept of expressed emotion in several studies, from India, Mexico, Great Britain, and North America (Jenkins & Karno, 1992). The differences suggest that there are cultural variations in how families react to someone with schizophrenia and that their reactions do not cause the disorder (Weisman, 1997; Weisman & Lopez, 1997). However, critical and hostile

---

**schizophrenogenic mother** According to an obsolete, unsupported theory, a cold, dominating, and rejecting parent who was thought to cause schizophrenia in her offspring.

**double bind communication** According to an obsolete, unsupported theory, the practice of transmitting conflicting messages that was thought to cause schizophrenia.

**expressed emotion** The hostility, criticism, and overinvolvement demonstrated by some families toward a family member with a psychological disorder; this can often contribute to the person's relapse.

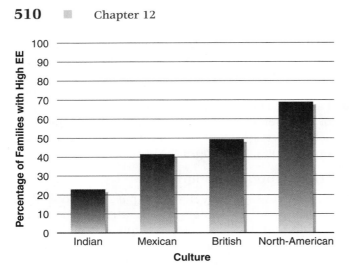

**Figure 12.8** ■ Cultural differences in expressed emotion (EE). (Jenkins & Karno, 1992.)

environments clearly provide additional stressors that can in turn lead to more relapses. It is also very important to consider the possibility that critical comments and emotional overinvolvement may be family responses to a schizophrenic patient's unusual and disturbing behaviours, as suggested by the research of Suzanne King (2000) at the Douglas Hospital in Montreal. In fact, recent evidence gathered by Laval University researchers Helene Provencher and Frank Fincham (2000) demonstrates that, unfortunately, it is common for family members to see a schizophrenic patient's symptoms as being intentional; this interpretation may help to explain why certain patient behaviours can evoke hostility in family members. Overall,

the relation between the behaviour of patients with schizophrenia and expressed emotion in family members appears to be a reciprocal process.

## Concept Check 12.2

Check your understanding of genetic vulnerability by filling in the blanks of the statements associated with family, twin, and adoption studies. Choose from: (a) higher, (b) lower, (c) equal, (d) severity, (e) type, (f) identical twin, (g) specific, (h) fraternal twin, (i) general.

1. The likelihood of a child's having schizophrenia is influenced by the _____ of the parent's disorder. The child may inherit a(n) _____ predisposition for schizophrenia that is the same or different from that of the parent.
2. The greatest risk of having schizophrenia is in those who have a(n) _____ with schizophrenia. Any relative with schizophrenia will make those individuals chances _____ than/to the general population.
3. Raised in a home other than that of their biological parents, adopted children of parents with schizophrenia have a(n) _____ chance of having the disorder themselves. Children of people with schizophrenia adopted into families without schizophrenia have a(n) _____ than average chance of having schizophrenia.

# Treatment of Schizophrenia

■ *Describe biological and psychosocial treatments for schizophrenia and the general goals of therapy.*

If you remember our descriptions of Arthur and David, you will recall their families' concern for them. Arthur's mother spoke of the "living nightmare" and David's aunt expressed concern for both her safety and David's. In each case the family was desperate to help, but what do you do for someone who has delusions, hears his dead uncle's voice, or can't communicate complete thoughts? The search for help has taken many paths, sometimes down some disturbing roads; for example, in the 1500s primitive surgery was conducted to remove the "stone of madness," which was thought to cause disturbed behaviour. As barbaric as this practice may seem today, it is not very different from the prefrontal lobotomies performed

on people with schizophrenia as late as the 1950s. This procedure severed the frontal lobes from the lower portion of the brain, which sometimes calmed the patient but also caused cognitive and emotional deficits. Even today, some societies use crude surgical procedures to eliminate the symptoms of schizophrenia. In Kenya, for instance, Kisii tribal doctors listen to their patients to find the location of the noises in the patients' heads (hallucinations), then get them drunk, cut out a piece of scalp, and scrape the skull in the area of the voices (Mustafa, 1990).

In the Western world today, treatment usually begins with one of the neuroleptic drugs that are invaluable in reducing the symptoms of schizophrenia

An early 16th-century painting of psychosurgery, in which part of the brain is removed to treat mental illness.

*The Surgeon by Jan Sanders van Hemessen/© Bridgeman Art Library/SuperStock*

for many people. They are typically used in combination with a variety of psychosocial treatments to reduce relapse, compensate for skills deficits, and improve cooperation for taking the medications (American Psychiatric Association, 2000b).

## *Biological Interventions*

Researchers have assumed for more than 100 years that schizophrenia requires some form of biological intervention. Emil Kraepelin, who so eloquently described dementia praecox in the late 19th century, saw the disorder as a brain disease. Lacking a biological treatment, he routinely recommended that the physician use "good patience, kindly disposition, and self-control" to calm excited patients (Nagel, 1991). This approach was seen as only a temporary way of helping the person through disturbing times and was not thought to be an actual treatment.

During the 1930s, several novel biological treatments were tried. One approach was to inject massive doses of insulin—the drug that given in smaller doses is used to treat diabetes—to induce comas in people suffering from schizophrenia. *Insulin coma therapy* was thought for a time to be helpful, but closer examination showed it carried great risk of serious illness and death. During this time *psychosurgery*, including prefrontal lobotomies, was introduced; and in the late 1930s, electroconvulsive therapy (ECT) was advanced as a treatment for schizophrenia. As with earlier drastic treatments, initial enthusiasm for ECT faded because it was found not to be beneficial for most people with schizophrenia—although it is still used with a limited number of people today (Fink & Sackeim,

1996). As we explained in Chapter 6, ECT is sometimes recommended for people who experience severe episodes of depression.

### Antipsychotic Medications

A breakthrough in the treatment of schizophrenia came during the 1950s with the introduction of several drugs that relieved symptoms in many people (Lehmann & Ban, 1997; Potkin, Albers, & Richmond, 1993). Called *neuroleptics* (meaning "taking hold of the nerves"), these medications provided the first real hope that help was available for people with schizophrenia. The late psychiatrist Heinz Lehmann of McGill University is credited by many (e.g., Dongier, 1999) with introducing neuroleptic medications for the treatment of schizophrenia to North America (see Lehmann & Hanrahan, 1954, for an early study). When they are effective, neuroleptics help people think more clearly and reduce or eliminate hallucinations and delusions. They work by affecting the positive symptoms (delusions, hallucinations, agitation) and to a lesser extent the negative and disorganized ones, such as social deficits. Table 12.1 shows the classes of these drugs (based on their chemical structure) and their trade names (Potkin et al., 1993).

Recall from our discussion of the dopamine theory of schizophrenia that the neuroleptics are dopamine antagonists. One of their major actions

| **TABLE 12.1** | **Commonly Used Antipsychotic Medications** | |
|---|---|---|
| Class | Example* | Degree of Extrapyramidal Side Effects |
| Phenothiazines | Chlorpromazine/*Thorazine* | moderate |
| | Fluphenazine/*Prolixin* | high |
| | Mesoridazine/*Serentil* | low |
| | Perphenazine/*Trilafon* | high |
| | Thioridazine/*Mellaril* | low |
| | Trifluoperazine/*Stelazine* | high |
| Butyrophenone | Haloperidol/*Haldol* | high |
| Others | Loxapine/*Loxitane* | high |
| | Molindone/*Moban* | low |
| | Thiothixene/*Navane* | high |
| Second-generation agents | Aripiprazole/*Abilify* | low |
| | Clozapine/*Clozaril* | low |
| | Olanzapine/*Zyprexa* | low |
| | Quetiapine/*Seroquel* | low |
| | Risperidone/*Risperdal* | low |
| | Ziprasidone/*Geodon* | low |

*The trade name is in italics.

*Source:* Adapted from "Practice Guidelines for the Treatment of Patients with Schizophrenia," Second Edition by the American Psychiatric Association, 2004, *American Journal of Psychiatry, 161* (suppl), 1–56.

in the brain is to interfere with the dopamine neurotransmitter system. However, they can also affect other systems, such as the serotonergic and glutamate system. We are just beginning to understand the mechanisms by which these drugs work.

In general, each drug is effective with some people and not with others. Clinicians and patients often must go through a trial-and-error process to find the medication that works best, and some individuals do not benefit significantly from any of them. The earliest neuroleptic drugs, called conventional antipsychotics, are effective for approximately 60% of people who try them (American Psychiatric Association, 2000b). However, many people are not helped by antipsychotics or experience unpleasant side effects. Fortunately, some people respond well to newer medications; the most common are clozapine, risperidone, and olanzapine. First marketed in 1990, clozapine is now used widely, and resperidone and other newer drugs hold promise for helping patients who were previously unresponsive to medications (American Psychiatric Association, 2004; Wahlbeck et al., 1999). These medications tend to have fewer serious side effects than the conventional antipsychotics (Davis, Chen, & Glick, 2003). Moreover, recent research by Kimberly Good and colleagues at Dalhousie University provides preliminary evidence that the newer medications may be helpful in improving cognitive functioning, at least among patients experiencing their first psychotic episode (Good et al., 2002).

## Non-Compliance with Medication: Why?

Despite the optimism generated by the effectiveness of antipsychotics, they work only when they are taken properly, and many people with schizophrenia do not routinely take their medication. David frequently "cheeked" the Haldol pills that were helpful in reducing his hallucinations, holding them in his mouth until he was alone, then spitting them out. Approximately 7% of the people prescribed antipsychotic medication refuse to take it at all (Hoge et al., 1990). Research on the prevalence of occasional non-compliance suggests that a majority of people with schizophrenia stop taking their medication from time to time. A follow-up study, for example, found that over a 2-year period, three out of four patients studied refused to take their antipsychotic medication for at least 1 week (Weiden et al., 1991).

A number of factors seem to be related to patients' non-compliance with a medication regimen, including negative doctor–patient relationships, cost of the medication, and poor social support (Weiden et al., 1991). Not surprisingly, negative side effects are a major factor in patient refusal. Antipsychotics can produce a number of unwanted physical symptoms, such as grogginess, blurred vision, and dryness of the mouth. Because the drugs affect neurotransmitter systems, more serious side effects, called *extrapyramidal symptoms*, can also result (Umbricht & Kane, 1996). These symptoms include the motor difficulties similar to those experienced by people with Parkinson's disease, sometimes called parkinsonian symptoms. *Akinesia* is one of the most common; it includes an expressionless face, slow motor activity, and monotonous speech (Blanchard & Neale, 1992). Another extrapyramidal symptom is *tardive dyskinesia*, which involves involuntary movements of the tongue, face, mouth, or jaw and can include protrusions of the tongue, puffing of the cheeks, puckering of the mouth, and chewing movements. Tardive dyskinesia seems to result from long-term use of high doses of antipsychotic medication, is often irreversible, and may occur in as many as 20% of people who take the medications over long periods (Morgenstern & Glazer, 1993). These serious negative side effects have justifiably concerned people who otherwise benefit from the drugs.

To learn what patients themselves say, Windgassen (1992) questioned 61 people who had had recent onsets of schizophrenia. About half reported the feeling of sedation or grogginess as an unpleasant side effect: "I always have to fight to keep my eyes open," "I felt as though I was on drugs ... drowsy, and yet really wound up" (p. 407). Other complaints included deterioration in the ability to think or concentrate (18%), problems with salivation (16%), and blurred vision (16%). Although a third of the patients felt the medications were beneficial, about 25% had a negative attitude toward them. A significant proportion of people who could benefit from antipsychotic medications find them unacceptable as a treatment, which may explain the relatively high rates of refusal and non-compliance.

Researchers have made this a major treatment issue in schizophrenia, realizing that medications can't be successful if they aren't taken regularly. Clinicians hoped that the new antipsychotics such as clozapine, which produce fewer negative side effects, would allay some legitimate concerns. However, even clozapine produces undesirable effects, and its use must be monitored closely to avoid rare effects that are potentially life threatening (Umbricht & Kane, 1996). Researchers hoped compliance rates would improve with the introduction of injectable medications. Instead of taking an oral antipsychotic every day, patients can have their medications injected every few weeks. Unfortunately, non-compliance remains an issue, primarily because patients do not return to the hospital or clinic for repeated doses (Weiden et al., 1991). Psychosocial interventions are now used not only to treat schizophrenia but also to increase medication-taking compliance by helping patients communicate better with professionals about their concerns.

Family members of persons with schizophrenia are also seriously impacted by the disorder. Here a mother comforts her daughter who has just returned from a psychiatric facility, but also worries about the future.

© Ghislain & Marie David de Lossy/Getty Images

## Psychosocial Interventions

Historically, a number of psychosocial treatments have been tried for schizophrenia, reflecting the belief that the disorder results from problems in adapting to the world because of early experiences (Nagel, 1991). Many therapists have thought that individuals who could achieve insight into the presumed role of their personal histories could be safely led to deal with their current situations. Although clinicians who take a psychodynamic or psychoanalytic approach to therapy continue to use this type of treatment, research suggests that their efforts at best may not be beneficial and at worst may be harmful (Mueser & Berenbaum, 1990; Scott & Dixon, 1995b).

Today, few believe that psychological factors alone cause people to have schizophrenia or that traditional psychotherapeutic approaches will cure them. We will see, however, that psychological methods do have an important role (American Psychiatric Association, 2004). Despite the great promise of drug treatment, the problems with ineffectiveness, inconsistent use, and relapse suggest that by themselves drugs may not be effective with many people. As with a number of the disorders discussed in this text, recent work in the area of psychosocial intervention has suggested the value of an approach that uses both kinds of treatment (Tarrier et al., 1999, 2000).

Until relatively recently, most people with severe and chronic cases of schizophrenia were treated in hospital settings. During the 19th century, inpatient care involved "moral treatment," which emphasized improving patients' socialization, helping them establish routines for self-control, and showing them the value of work and religion (Armstrong, 1993). Various types of such "milieu"

treatment have been popular, but, with one important exception, none seems to have helped people with schizophrenia (Tucker, Ferrell, & Price, 1984).

In the 1970s, Paul and Lentz (1977) conducted pioneering work that borrowed from the behavioural approaches used by Ayllon and Azrin (1968). Paul and Lentz designed an environment for inpatients that encouraged appropriate socialization, participation in group sessions, and self-care such as bed making, while discouraging violent outbursts. They set up an elaborate **token economy,** in which residents could earn access to meals and small luxuries by behaving appropriately. A patient could, for example, buy cigarettes with the tokens earned for keeping his or her room neat. On the other hand, a patient would be fined (lose tokens) for being disruptive or otherwise acting inappropriately. This incentive system was combined with a full schedule of daily activities. Paul and Lentz compared the effectiveness of applied behavioural (or *social learning*) principles with traditional inpatient environments. In general, they found that patients who went through their program did better than others on social, self-care, and vocational skills, and more of them could be discharged from the hospital. This study was one of the first to show that people experiencing the debilitating effects of schizophrenia can learn to perform some skills they need to live more independently.

Since 1955, many efforts have combined to halt the routine institutionalization of people with schizophrenia in both Canada and the United States (Talbott, 1990). This trend has occurred in part because of court rulings that limit involuntary hospitalization (as we saw in Arthur's case), in part because of the relative success of antipsychotic medication, and in part because of fiscal crisis and ensuing cutbacks in health care (Hanna, 2001). In Canada, provincial mental hospitals released thousands of patients and closed down more than 32 500 beds between 1960 and 1976; this trend continues to the present day (Nichols, 1995). The bad news is that policies of deinstitutionalization have often been ill conceived, so that the process has sometimes resulted in problems (Barnes & Toews, 1983). For example, as a consequence of deinstitutionalization, many people who have schizophrenia are homeless (e.g., Stuart & Arboleda-Florez, 2000). See Chapter 14 for a more in-depth discussion of the problem of homelessness in Canada and of the relation of deinstitutionalization to homelessness. The good news is that more attention is being focused on supporting these people in their

---

**token economy** Behaviour modification system in which individuals earn items they can exchange for desired rewards by displaying appropriate behaviours.

communities, among their friends and families. The trend is away from creating better hospital environments and toward the perhaps more difficult task of addressing complex problems in the less predictable and insecure world outside.

One of the more insidious effects of schizophrenia is its negative impact on a person's ability to relate to other people. Although not as dramatic as hallucinations and delusions, this problem can be the most visible impairment displayed by people with schizophrenia and can prevent them from getting and keeping jobs and making friends. In social skills training, clinicians attempt to reteach social skills such as basic conversation, assertiveness, and relationship building to people with schizophrenia (Dobson, McDougall, Busheikin, & Aldous, 1995; Smith, Bellack, & Liberman, 1996).

Therapists divide complex social skills into their component parts, which they model. Then the clients role-play and ultimately practise their new skills in the "real world," all while receiving feedback and encouragement at signs of progress. This isn't as easy as it may sound. For example, how would you teach someone to make a friend? Many skills are involved, such as maintaining eye contact when you talk to someone and providing the prospective friend with some (but not too much!) positive feedback on his or her own behaviour ("I really enjoy talking to you").

Such individual skills are practised and then combined until they can be used naturally (Liberman, DeRisi, & Mueser, 1989). Basic skills can be taught to people with schizophrenia, but there is some disagreement about how ultimately successful the treatment is (Bellack & Mueser, 1992; Hogarty et al., 1992). The problem is that the positive results of social skills training may fade after the training is over (Scott & Dixon, 1995b). The challenge of teaching social skills, as with all therapies, is to maintain the effects over a long period.

In addition to social skills, programs often teach a range of ways people can adapt to their disorder yet still live in the community. In the Independent Living Skills Program developed by Ekman and colleagues (1992), the focus is on helping people take charge of their own care by such methods as identifying signs that warn of a relapse and learning how to manage their medication (see Table 12.2; Corrigan, Wallace, Schade, & Green, 1994; Eckman et al., 1992). Preliminary evidence indicates that this type of training may help prevent relapses by people with schizophrenia, although longer-term outcome research is needed to see how long the effects last. To address some of the obstacles to this much desired maintenance, such programs combine skills training with the support of a multidisciplinary team that provides services directly in the community, which

**TABLE 12.2  Independent Living Skills Program**

| Module | Skill Areas | Learning Objectives |
|---|---|---|
| Symptom management | Identifying warning signs of relapse | To identify personal warning signs<br>To monitor personal warning signs with assistance from other people |
| | Managing warning signs | To obtain assistance from health-care providers in differentiating personal warning signs from persistent symptoms, medication side effects, and variations in mood; to develop an emergency plan for responding to warning signs |
| | Coping with persistent symptoms | To recognize and monitor persistent personal symptoms; to obtain assistance from health-care providers in differentiating persistent symptoms from warning signs, medication side effects, and variations in mood; to use specific techniques for coping with persistent symptoms<br>To monitor persistent symptoms daily |
| | Avoiding alcohol and street drugs | To identify the adverse effects of alcohol and illicit drugs and the benefits of avoiding them; to refuse offers of alcohol and street drugs; to know how to resist using these substances in coping with anxiety, low self-esteem, or depression; to discuss openly use of alcohol and drugs with health-care providers |
| Medication management | Obtaining information about anti-psychotic medication | To understand how these drugs work, why maintenance drug therapy is used, and the benefits of taking medication |
| | Knowing correct self-administration and evaluation | To follow the appropriate procedures for taking medication; to evaluate responses to medication daily |
| | Identifying side effects of medication | To know the specific side effects that sometimes result from taking medication and what to do when these problems occur |
| | Negotiating medication issues with health-care providers | To practice ways of obtaining assistance when problems occur with medication |

*Source:* From "Techniques for Training Schizophrenic Patients in Illness Self-Management: A Controlled Trial," by T. A. Eckman, W. C. Wirshing, S. R. Marder, R. P. Liberman, K. Johnston-Cronk, K. Zimmermann, and J. Mintz, *American Journal of Psychiatry*, 149, 1549–1555. Copyright © 1992 by the American Psychiatric Association. Reprinted by permission.

seems to reduce hospitalization (Scott & Dixon, 1995a). The more time and effort given to these services, the more likely the improvement (Brekke, Long, Nesbitt, & Sobell, 1997).

In our discussion of the psychosocial influences on schizophrenia we reviewed some of the work linking the person's social and emotional environments to the recurrence of schizophrenic episodes (e.g., Bebbington et al., 1995). It is logical to ask whether families could be helped by learning to reduce their level of expressed emotion and whether this would result in fewer relapses and better overall functioning for people with schizophrenia. Several studies have addressed these issues in a variety of ways (e.g., Hogarty et al., 1986, 1991), and behavioural family therapy has been used to teach the families of people with schizophrenia to be more supportive (Dixon & Lehman, 1995; Mueser, Liberman, & Glynn, 1990). Research on professionals who provide care for people who have schizophrenia, and who may also display high levels of expressed emotion, is also an active area of study (Barrowclough & Tarrier, 1998; Tattan & Tarrier, 2000).

In contrast to traditional therapy, behavioural family therapy resembles classroom education (Falloon et al., 1985). Family members are informed about schizophrenia and its treatment, relieved of the myth that they caused the disorder, and taught practical facts about antipsychotic medications and their side effects. They are also helped with communication skills so that they can become more empathic listeners, and they learn constructive ways of expressing negative feelings to replace the harsh criticism that characterizes some family interactions. In addition, they learn problem-solving skills to help them resolve conflicts that arise. Like the research on social skills training, outcome research suggests that the effects of behavioural family therapy are significant during the first year but less robust 2 years after intervention (Hogarty et al., 1991). This type of therapy, therefore, must be ongoing if patients and their families are to benefit from it (Mueser et al., 2001).

Adults with schizophrenia face great obstacles to maintaining gainful employment. Their social skills deficits make reliable job performance and adequate employee relationships a struggle. To address these difficulties, some programs focus on vocational rehabilitation, such as supportive employment (Bustillo, Lauriello, Horan, & Keith, 2001). Providing coaches who give on-the-job training may help some people with schizophrenia maintain meaningful jobs (Bond, Drake, Mueser, & Becker, 1997; Drake, McHugo, Becker, Anthony, & Clark, 1996; Lehman, 1995).

Social skills training, family therapy, and vocational rehabilitation may be helpful additions to biological treatment for schizophrenia. Significant relapses may be avoided or delayed by such psychosocial interventions. A review by Falloon,

Brooker, and Graham-Hole (1992) showed that multilevel treatments reduce the number of relapses among people receiving drug therapy in comparison with simple social support or educational efforts.

A general trend in the treatment of schizophrenia today is toward early intervention. Research has shown that getting patients onto the right medications and into effective psychotherapy as soon as possible, and providing information and support to affected families right away, can actually reduce the severity of future relapses (e.g., Drury, Birchwood, Cochrane, & MacMillan, 1996). Early psychosis intervention programs have now been developed in several major centres across Canada (e.g., Halifax, Toronto, London, Hamilton, and Calgary; Nichols, 1995). Many of these programs are designed to meet the needs of individuals experiencing a first episode of psychosis.

A relatively newer approach to the treatment of schizophrenia that has been applied over the last decade is cognitive behavioural therapy (CBT; see reviews by Bouchard, Vallieres, Roy, & Maziade, 1996; Norman & Townsend, 1999; Rector & Beck, 2001). CBT has typically been applied to auditory hallucinations and delusions (i.e., positive symptoms; Norman & Townsend, 1999), although CBT strategies have been developed to treat both positive and negative symptoms (Beck & Rector, 2000). Despite a good deal of initial skepticism as to whether symptoms of a disorder with such a strong physiological basis could be amenable to "talk therapy" (e.g., Patience, 1994, versus John, Turkington, & Kingdon, 1994), more recent reviews of the literature are unanimous in supporting the potential of this approach in the treatment of patients with schizophrenia. For example, in a review of the literature conducted with CBT developer Aaron Beck, University of Toronto psychologist Neil Rector found that CBT produces large clinical effects on both positive and negative symptoms of schizophrenia (Rector & Beck, 2001). Thus, CBT appears a promising approach in a set of treatments we now have available for intervening with people diagnosed with schizophrenia.

The locus of treatment has expanded over the years from locked wards in large mental hospitals to family homes in local communities. In addition, the services have expanded to include self-advocacy and self-help groups. Former patients have organized programs to provide mutual support (Beard, Propst, & Malamud, 1982). Psychosocial clubs have differing models, but all are "person centred" and focus on obtaining positive experiences through employment opportunities, friendship, and empowerment. Some research indicates that participation may help reduce relapses (Beard, Malamud, & Rossman, 1978), but because it is possible that those who participate may be a special group of individuals, it is difficult to interpret improvements (Mueser et al., 1990).

## Treatment across Cultures

Treatment of schizophrenia and its delivery differ from one country to another and across cultures within countries (Carter & Neufeld, 1998). In China, for example, the most frequently used treatment is antipsychotic medication, although 7% to 9% of patients also receive traditional herbal medicine and acupuncture (Mingdao & Zhenyi, 1990). In many countries in Africa, people with schizophrenia are kept in prisons, primarily because of the lack of adequate alternatives (Mustafa, 1990). Generally, the movement away from housing people in large institutional settings to community care is ongoing in most Western countries.

## Prevention

One strategy for preventing a disorder such as schizophrenia—which typically first shows itself in early adulthood—is to identify and treat children who may be at risk for developing the disorder later in life. In our discussion of genetics, we noted that approximately 13% of the children born to parents who have schizophrenia are likely themselves to develop the disorder. These high-risk children have been the focus of several studies, both *prospective* (before and during an expected situation) and *longitudinal* (over long periods).

A classic at-risk study was initiated in the 1960s by Mednick and Schulsinger in Denmark (Mednick & Schulsinger, 1965, 1968). They identified 207 Danish children of mothers who had severe cases of schizophrenia and 104 control children born to mothers who had no history of the disorder. The average age of these children was about 15 when they were first identified, and the researchers followed them for 10 years to determine whether any factors had predicted who would and would not develop schizophrenia. Mednick and Schulsinger identified *instability of early family rearing environment*, which suggests that environmental influences may trigger the onset of schizophrenia (Cannon et al., 1991). Poor parenting may place additional strain on a vulnerable person who is already at risk. When the at-risk children in the Danish study enter middle age, we will know the eventual outcomes for all of them; until then, we cannot draw strong conclusions from the study (Mirsky, 1995).

As we await the outcomes of these long-term studies, other approaches may prove valuable for reducing the rates of this disorder. For example, we have seen that factors such as birth complications and certain early illnesses (e.g., viruses) may trigger the onset of schizophrenia, especially among those individuals who are genetically predisposed. Therefore, interventions such as vaccinations against viruses for women of childbearing age may be effective preventive measures (McGrath, 2000).

## Concept Check 12.3

Read the descriptions and then match them to the following words: (a) clozapine, (b) extrapyramidal symptoms, (c) glutamate, (d) dopamine, (e) metabolites, (f) token economy, (g) vocational rehabilitation, (h) social skills training, (i) family therapy.

1. Recent studies sometimes indicate that deficits or irregularities in two neurotransmitter systems, specifically _____ and _____, may explain some of the symptoms of schizophrenia.
2. Setting up an elaborate _____ in which patients are fined for disruptive or inappropriate behaviour and rewarded for appropriate behaviour is beneficial in hospitals.
3. Difficult cases of schizophrenia seem to improve with a newer antipsychotic medication called _____.
4. In _____, clinicians attempt to reteach behaviours such as basic conversation, assertiveness, and relationship building to people with schizophrenia.
5. Because antipsychotic medications may cause serious side effects, some patients stop taking them. One serious side effect is called _____, which may include parkinsonian symptoms.
6. Aside from social skills training, two psychosocial treatments for schizophrenia, _____ (teaching family members to be supportive) and _____ (teaching meaningful jobs), may be helpful.

# Summary

## Clinical Description, Symptoms, and Subtypes

- Schizophrenia is characterized by a broad spectrum of cognitive and emotional dysfunctions that include delusions and hallucinations, disorganized speech and behaviour, and inappropriate emotions.

- The symptoms of schizophrenia can be divided into positive, negative, and disorganized. Positive symptoms are active manifestations of abnormal behaviour, or an excess or distortion of normal behaviour, and include delusions and hallucinations. Negative symptoms involve deficits in normal behaviour on such dimensions as affect, speech, and motivation.

Disorganized symptoms include rambling speech, erratic behaviour, and inappropriate affect.

- DSM-IV-TR divides schizophrenia into five subtypes. People with the paranoid type of schizophrenia have prominent delusions or hallucinations even as their cognitive skills and affect remain relatively intact. People with the disorganized type of schizophrenia tend to show marked disruption in their speech and behaviour; they also show flat or inappropriate affect. People with the catatonic type of schizophrenia have unusual motor responses, such as remaining in fixed positions (waxy flexibility), engaging in excessive activity, and being oppositional by remaining rigid. In addition, they display odd mannerisms with their bodies and faces, including grimacing. People who do not fit neatly into these subtypes are classified as having an undifferentiated type of schizophrenia. Some people who have had at least one episode of schizophrenia but who no longer have major symptoms are diagnosed as having the residual type of schizophrenia.
- Several other disorders are characterized by psychotic behaviours such as hallucinations and delusions; these include schizophreniform disorder (which includes people who experience the symptoms of schizophrenia for less than 6 months); schizoaffective disorder (which includes people who have symptoms of schizophrenia and exhibit the characteristics of mood disorders such as depression and bipolar affective disorder); delusional disorder (which includes people with a persistent belief that is contrary to reality, in the absence of the other characteristics of schizophrenia); brief psychotic disorder (which includes people with one or more positive symptoms such as delusions, hallucinations, or disorganized speech or behaviour over the course of less than a month); and shared psychotic disorder (which includes individuals who develop delusions simply as a result of a close relationship with a delusional individual).

## Prevalence and Causes of Schizophrenia

- A number of causative factors have been implicated for schizophrenia, including genetic influences, neurotransmitter imbalances, structural damage to the brain caused by a prenatal viral infection or birth injury, and psychological stressors.
- Relapse appears to be triggered by hostile and critical family environments characterized by high expressed emotion.

## Treatment of Schizophrenia

- Successful treatment for people with schizophrenia rarely includes complete recovery. However, the quality of life for these individuals can be meaningfully affected by combining antipsychotic medications with psychosocial approaches, employment support, and community-based and family interventions.
- Treatment typically involves antipsychotic drugs that are usually administered with a variety of psychosocial treatments with the goal of reducing relapse and improving skills in deficits and compliance in taking the medications. The effectiveness of treatment is limited because schizophrenia is typically a chronic disorder.

## Key Terms

| | | | |
|---|---|---|---|
| schizophrenia, 486 | avolition, 491 | catatonic type of schizophrenia, 495 | brief psychotic disorder, 497 |
| catatonia, 486 | alogia, 492 | undifferentiated type of schizophrenia, 495 | shared psychotic disorder (folie à deux), 497 |
| hebephrenia, 486 | anhedonia, 492 | residual type of schizophrenia, 495 | schizophrenogenic mother, 509 |
| paranoia, 486 | flat affect, 492 | | |
| dementia praecox, 486 | disorganized speech, 493 | | |
| associative splitting, 487 | inappropriate affect, 494 | schizophreniform disorder, 496 | double bind communication, 509 |
| psychotic behaviour, 489 | catatonic immobility, 494 | schizoaffective disorder, 496 | expressed emotion, 509 |
| positive symptoms, 489 | paranoid type of schizophrenia, 494 | delusional disorder, 496 | token economy, 513 |
| delusion, 489 | disorganized type of schizophrenia, 495 | | |
| hallucination, 490 | | | |
| negative symptoms, 491 | | | |

## Answers to Concept Checks

**12.1 Part A**  1. paranoid  2. catatonic  3. residual  4. disorganized  5. disorganized

   **Part B**  6. b  7. c  8. d  9. a

**12.2**  1. d, i  2. f, a  3. a, a

**12.3**  1. d, c  2. f  3. a  4. h  5. b  6. i, g

## InfoTrac College Edition

If your instructor ordered your book with InfoTrac College Edition, please explore this online library for additional readings, review, and a handy resource for short assignments. Go to:

**http://infotrac.thomsonlearning.com**

Enter these search terms: schizophrenia, paranoia, psychoses, dementia praecox, hallucinations, delusions

## w(w)w The Abnormal Psychology Book Companion Website

Go to **www.essentialsabnormalpsych.nelson.com** for practice quiz questions, Internet links, critical thinking exercises, and more.

## Abnormal Psychology Live CD-ROM

- **Etta:** An example of a lower-functioning patient with schizophrenia.
- **Positive versus Negative Symptoms:** A team of clinicians describe the differences between positive and negative symptoms.

- **Common Symptoms of Schizophrenia:** A clinician reviews the most common psychotic symptoms in schizophrenia, and his discussion is interspersed with patients who exemplify these symptoms.

**Thomson NOW!** **http://hed.nelson.com** Go to this site for the link to ThomsonNow™, your one-stop study shop. Take a Pretest for this chapter and ThomsonNow™ will generate a personalized Study Plan based on your test results! The Study Plan will identify the topics you need to review and direct you to online resources to help you master those topics. You can then take a Posttest to help you determine the concepts you have mastered and what you still need work on.

## Video Concept Review

For challenging concepts that typically need more than one explanation, Mark Durand provides a video review via ThomsonNow™ of the following topic:

- The relevance of psychologists and psychological treatments for psychotic disorders.

# Chapter Quiz

1. One distinction used to characterize symptoms of schizophrenia divides them into what two broad categories?

   a. paranoid and catatonic

   b. episodic and chronic

   c. psychiatric and somatic

   d. positive and negative

2. Emotional and social withdrawal, apathy, and poverty of speech and thought are examples of what type of symptoms in schizophrenia?

   a. psychotic

   b. negative

   c. disorganized

   d. positive

3. Rhonda fears that her employer is trying to poison her with gas emitted from the overhead lights in her office. Given what you know about Rhonda's thoughts, what subtype of schizophrenia is she most likely to have?

   a. catatonic

   b. disorganized

   c. paranoid

   d. undifferentiated

4. Which disorder is characterized by symptoms similar to those seen in schizophrenia but of shorter duration, often with successful remission of symptoms?

   a. schizophreniform disorder

   b. delusional disorder

   c. schizoaffective disorder

   d. bipolar disorder

5. Most people with schizophrenia:

   a. have multiple episodes that get progressively worse.

   b. have only one episode with full recovery after it.

   c. have episodes of alternating positive and negative symptoms.

   d. have multiple episodes, with different degrees of impairment between episodes.

6. Research on cultural factors and schizophrenia suggests that Blacks:

   a. may have higher rates than other ethnic groups because of misdiagnosis.

   b. may have higher rates than other ethnic groups because they are exposed to more prejudice and bias.

   c. may be more vulnerable to schizophrenia because of chromosomal differences.

   d. with schizophrenia are more likely to experience negative symptoms than positive symptoms.

7. Which sibling of an individual with schizophrenia is most likely to develop schizophrenia?

   a. monozygotic twin raised in the same home

   b. monozygotic twin raised in a different home

   c. dizygotic twin raised in the same home

   d. dizygotic twin raised in a different home

8. Which statement is true about antipsychotic medications and the treatment of schizophrenia?

   a. Antipsychotic medications are not as effective as psychosocial treatments.

   b. Different medications are effective with different people and to a different degree.

   c. All antipsychotic medications appear to be equally effective for all patients.

   d. Most patients go through a trial-and-error period to determine whether antipsychotic, antidepressant, or antianxiety medications are most effective for them.

9. Which type of psychosocial treatment has been most effective for treating the behavioural problems seen in schizophrenia?

   a. psychodynamic psychotherapy

   b. moral treatment

   c. psychosurgery

   d. token economies

10. Which two psychosocial interventions appear to be most helpful for people with schizophrenia?

    a. hypnosis and psychosurgery

    b. ECT and social skills training

    c. psychoanalytic psychotherapy and expressed emotion management

    d. family therapy and vocational rehabilitation

*(See the Appendix on page 601 for answers.)*

# Exploring Schizophrenia

- Schizophrenia disrupts perception of the world, thought, speech, movement, and almost every other aspect of daily functioning.
- Usually chronic with a high relapse rate, complete recovery from schizophrenia is rare.

## TRIGGER

- Stressful, traumatic life event
- High expressed emotion (family criticism, hostility, and/or intrusion)
- Sometimes there is no obvious trigger.

### Biological Influences

- Inherited tendency (multiple genes) to develop disease
- Prenatal/birth complications— viral infection during pregnancy or birth injury affect child's brain cells
- Brain chemistry (abnormalities in the dopamine and glutamate systems)
- Brain structure (enlarged ventricles)

### Social Influences

- Environment (early family experiences) can trigger onset
- Culture influences interpretation of disease/symptoms (hallucinations, delusions)

## CAUSES

### Behavioural Influences

- **Positive symptoms:**
  — active manifestations of abnormal behaviour (delusions, hallucinations, disorganized speech, odd body movements, catatonia)
- **Negative symptoms:**
  — flat affect (lack of emotional expression)
  — avolition (lack of initiative, apathy)
  — alogia (relative absence in amount or content of speech)

### Emotional and Cognitive Influences

- Interaction styles that are high in criticism, hostility, and emotional overinvolvement can trigger a relapse

## TREATMENT OF SCHIZOPHRENIA

### Individual, Group, and Family Therapy

- Can help patient and family understand the disease and symptom triggers.
- Teaches families communication skills.
- Provides resources for dealing with emotional and practical challenges.

### Social Skills Training

- Can occur in hospital or community settings.
- Teaches the person with schizophrenia social, self-care, and vocational skills.

### Medications

- Taking neuroleptic medications may help people with schizophrenia to:
  — clarify thinking and perceptions of reality
  — reduce hallucinations and delusions
- Drug treatment must be consistent to be effective. Inconsistent dosage may aggravate existing symptoms or create new ones.

# SYMPTOMS OF SCHIZOPHRENIA

People with schizophrenia do not all show the same kinds of symptoms. Symptoms vary from person to person and may be cyclical. Common symptoms include:

## DELUSIONS

- Unrealistic and bizarre beliefs not shared by others in the culture
- May be delusions of grandeur (that you are really Mother Teresa or Napoleon) or delusions of persecution (the cyclist who believed her competitors were sabotaging her by putting pebbles in the road)

© Ron Chapple/Thinkstock/Jupiter Images

## HALLUCINATIONS

- Sensory events that aren't based on any external event (hearing voices, seeing people who have died)
- Many have auditory hallucinations (David hears his dead uncle talking to him)

## DISORGANIZED SPEECH

- Jumping from topic to topic
- Talking illogically (not answering direct questions, going off on tangents)
- Speaking in unintelligible words and sentences

## BEHAVIOURAL PROBLEMS

- Pacing excitably, wild agitation
- Catatonic immobility
- Waxy flexibility (keeping body parts in the same position when they are moved by someone else)
- Inappropriate dress (coats in the summer, shorts in the winter)
- Inappropriate affect
- Ignoring personal hygiene

© Royalty-Free/Corbis

© Luba V. Nel/Shutterstock

## WITHDRAWAL

- Lack of emotional response (flat speech, little change in facial expressions)
- Apathy (little interest in day-to-day activities)
- Delayed and brief responses in conversation
- Loss of enjoyment in pleasurable activities (eating, socializing, sex)

### Types of Schizophrenia

*Paranoid*
- Delusions of grandeur or persecution
- Hallucinations (especially auditory)
- Higher level of functioning between episodes
- May have stronger familial link than other types

Photodisc/Getty Images

*Disorganized*
- Disorganized speech and/or behavior
- Immature emotionality (inappropriate affect)
- Chronic and lacking in remissions

*Catatonic*
- Alternating immobility and excited agitation
- Unusual motor responses (waxy flexibility, rigidity)
- Odd facial or body mannerisms (often mimicking others)
- Rare

*Residual*
- Person has had at least one schizophrenic episode but no longer shows major symptoms
- Still shows "leftover" symptoms (social withdrawal, bizarre thoughts, inactivity, flat affect)

*Undifferentiated*
- Symptoms of several types that taken together do not neatly fall into one specific category

Photodisc/Getty Images

# 13

# Developmental and Cognitive Disorders

© Ellen B. Senisi/The Image Works

## Common Developmental Disorders
*Attention Deficit/Hyperactivity Disorder*
*Learning Disorders*

## Pervasive Developmental Disorders
*Autistic Disorder*
*Treatment of Pervasive Developmental Disorders*

## Mental Retardation
*Clinical Description*
*Statistics*
*Causes*
*Treatment of Mental Retardation*
*Prevention of Developmental Disorders*

## Cognitive Disorders
*Delirium*
*Dementia*
*Amnestic Disorder*

## Visual Summaries: Exploring Developmental Disorders, Exploring Cognitive Disorders, Dementia

 ## Abnormal Psychology Live CD-ROM
*Edward: ADHD in a Gifted Student*
*ADHD: Sean*
*Autism: Christina*
*Rebecca: A First-Grader with Autistic Disorder*
*Lauren: A Kindergartner with Down Syndrome*
*Computer Simulations and Senile Dementia*
*Amnestic Disorder: Mike*
*Life Skills Training*
*Bullying Prevention*
*Autism: The Nature of the Disorder*
*Alzheimer's: Tom*

# Common Developmental Disorders

■ *Describe the central defining features of ADHD.*

■ *Identify the main features and types of learning disorders, and explain how they are typically treated.*

Almost all of the disorders described in this book are developmental disorders in the sense that they change over time. Most disorders originate in childhood, although the full presentation of the problem may not manifest itself until much later. Disorders that show themselves early in life often persist as the person grows older, so the term *childhood disorder* may be misleading. In the first part of this chapter we cover those disorders that are revealed in a clinically significant way during a child's developing years and are of concern to families and the educational system (Mash & Wolfe, 2003). Remember, however, that these difficulties often persist through adulthood and are typically lifelong problems, not ones unique to children.

Again, a number of difficulties and, indeed, distinct disorders begin in childhood. In certain disorders, some children are fine except for difficulties with talking. Others have problems relating to their peers. Still other children have a combination of conditions that significantly hinder their development.

Before we discuss specific disorders, we need to address the broad topic of development in relation to disorders usually first diagnosed in infancy, childhood, or adolescence. Does it matter when in the developmental period certain problems arise? Are disruptions in development permanent, thus making any hope for treatment doubtful?

Recall that in Chapter 2 we described developmental psychopathology as the study of how disorders arise and how they change with time. Childhood is considered particularly important because the brain changes significantly for several years after birth; this is also when critical developments occur in social, emotional, cognitive, and other important competency areas. For the most part, these changes follow a pattern: The child develops one skill before acquiring the next. Although this pattern of change is only one aspect of development, it is an important concept for us at this point because it implies that any disruption in the development of early skills will, by the very nature of this sequential process, disrupt the development of later skills. For example, some researchers believe that people with autism suffer from a disruption in early social development, which prevents them from developing important social relationships, even with their parents. From a developmental perspective, the absence of early and

meaningful social relationships has serious consequences. Children whose motivation to interact with others is disrupted may have a more difficult time learning to communicate; that is, they may not want to learn to speak if other people are not important to them. We don't know whether a disruption in communication skills is a direct outcome of the disorder or a by-product of disrupted early social development.

Understanding this type of developmental relationship is important for several reasons. Knowing what processes are disrupted will help us understand the disorder better and may lead to more appropriate intervention strategies. It may be important to identify children with attention deficit/hyperactivity disorder, for example, because their problems with impulsivity may interfere with their ability to create and maintain friendships, an important developmental consideration. Similarly, identifying a disorder such as autism at an early age is important for these children so that their social deficits can be addressed before they affect other skill domains, such as language and communication. Too often, people see early and pervasive disruptions in developmental skills and expect a negative prognosis, with the problems predetermined and permanent. Remember that biological and psychosocial influences continuously interact with each other. Therefore, even for disorders such as attention deficit/hyperactivity disorder and autism that have clear biological bases, the presentation of the disorder is different for each individual. Changes at the biological or the psychosocial level may reduce the impact of the disorder.

One note of caution is appropriate here. There is real concern in the profession, especially among developmental psychologists, that some workers in the field may view aspects of normal development as symptoms of abnormality. For example, *echolalia*, which involves repeating the speech of others, was once thought to be a sign of autism. However, when we study the development of speech in children without disorders, we find that repeating what someone else says is an intermediate step in language development. In children with autism, therefore, echolalia is just a sign of relatively delayed language skills and not a symptom of their disorder (Durand, 2004). Here again, as noted by developmental psychologist and autism expert Jacob Burack from McGill University, knowledge of normal development is important for understanding the nature of childhood psychological disorders (Burack, Iarocci, Bowler, & Mottron, 2002). With that caveat in mind, we now examine several of the disorders usually diagnosed first in infancy, childhood, or adolescence, including *attention deficit/hyperactivity disorder,* which involves characteristics of inattention or hyperactivity and impulsivity, and *learning disorders,* which are characterized by one or more difficulties in areas such as reading and writing. We then focus on *autism,* a more severe disability, in which the child shows significant impairment in social interactions and communication and restricted patterns of behaviour, interest, and activities. Finally, we examine *mental retardation,* which involves significant deficits in cognitive abilities.

## Attention Deficit/Hyperactivity Disorder

Do you know people who flit from activity to activity, who start many tasks but seldom finish one, who have trouble concentrating, and who don't seem to pay attention when others speak? These people may have **attention deficit/hyperactivity disorder (ADHD),** one of the most common reasons children are referred for mental health services (Popper, Gammon, West, & Bailey, 2003). The primary characteristics of such people include a pattern of inattention, such as not paying attention to school- or work-related tasks, or of hyperactivity and impulsivity. These deficits can significantly disrupt academic efforts and social relationships. Consider the case of Danny.

### Danny
The Boy Who Couldn't Sit Still

Danny, a handsome 9-year-old boy, was referred to one of us because of the significant difficulties he was experiencing at school and at home. Danny had a great deal of energy and loved playing most sports, especially baseball. Academically, he was experiencing substantial difficulties with his grades. His teacher reported that Danny's performance was diminishing and she believed he would do better if he paid more attention in class. Danny rarely spent more than a few minutes on a task without some interruption: He would get up out of his seat, rifle through his desk, or constantly ask questions. His peers were frustrated with him because he was equally impulsive during their interactions: He never

finished a game, and in sports he tried to play all the positions simultaneously.

At home, Danny was considered a handful. His room was in a constant mess because he became engaged in a game or activity only to drop it and initiate something else. Danny's parents reported that they often scolded him for not carrying out some task, although the reason seemed to be that he forgot what he was doing rather than that he deliberately tried to defy them. They also said that, out of their own frustration, they sometimes grabbed him by the shoulders and yelled "Slow down!" because his hyperactivity drove them crazy.

### Clinical Description

Danny has many of the characteristics of ADHD. Like Danny, people with this disorder have a great deal of difficulty sustaining their attention on a task or an activity (Popper et al., 2003). As a result, their tasks are frequently unfinished and they often seem not to be listening when someone else is speaking. In addition to this serious disruption in attention, some people with ADHD display motor hyperactivity (American Academy of Pediatrics, 2000; Mariani & Barkley, 1997). Children with this disorder are often described as fidgety in school, unable to sit still for more than a few minutes. Danny's restlessness in his classroom was a considerable source of concern for his teacher and peers, who were frustrated by his impatience. In addition to hyperactivity and problems sustaining attention, impulsivity—acting apparently without thinking—is a common complaint made about people with ADHD. For instance, during meetings of his baseball team, Danny often shouted responses to the coach's questions even before the coach had finished his sentence.

For ADHD, DSM-IV-TR differentiates two types of symptoms. The first includes problems of *inattention.* People may appear not to listen to others; they may lose necessary school assignments, books, or tools; and they may not pay enough attention to details, making careless mistakes. The second type of symptom includes *hyperactivity,* which includes fidgeting, having trouble sitting for any length of time, always being on the go, and *impulsivity,* which includes blurting out answers before questions have been completed and having trouble waiting turns. Either the first (inattention) or the second (hyperactivity and impulsivity) domains of symptoms must

---

**attention deficit/hyperactivity disorder (ADHD)**
Developmental disorder featuring maladaptive levels of inattention, excessive activity, and impulsiveness.

***Edward: ADHD in a Gifted Student***
*"He's very, very intelligent; his grades don't reflect that because he will just neglect to do a 240-point assign-ment if somebody doesn't stay behind it ... What I try to do with him is come in and cut it down to 'this is what I want by tomorrow, this is what I want day after tomorrow.'"*

Thomson Learning

be present for someone to be diagnosed with ADHD. The work of clinical psychologist Virginia Douglas at McGill University was largely responsible for recognition that problems of inattention often accompany symptoms of hyperactivity (Douglas, 1972). Her work led to changes in the conceptualization of and diagnostic criteria for this disorder, which used to be called "hyperactive child syndrome."

Inattention, hyperactivity, and impulsivity often cause other problems that appear secondary to ADHD. Academic performance tends to suffer, especially as the child progresses in school. The cause of this poor performance is not known. It could be a result of the problems with attention and impulsivity characteristic of ADHD, or it might be caused by factors such as brain impairment that may be responsible for the disorder itself (Frick, Strauss, Lahey, & Christ, 1993). Children with ADHD are likely to be unpopular and rejected by their peers (Erhardt & Hinshaw, 1994). Here, however, the difficulty appears to be directly related to the behaviours symptomatic of ADHD, because inattention, impulsivity, and hyperactivity get in the way of establishing and maintaining friendships. Research by University of British Columbia clinical psychologist Charlotte Johnston and her colleagues indicates that problems with peers combined with frequent negative feedback from parents and teachers often result in low self-esteem among these children (Johnston, Pelham, & Murphy, 1985).

### Statistics

ADHD is estimated to occur in about 6% of school-aged children, with boys outnumbering girls roughly four to one (Popper et al., 2003). The reason for this large gender difference is unknown. It may be that adults are more tolerant of hyperactivity among girls with ADHD, who tend to be less active than boys with ADHD. Whether ADHD has a different presentation in girls is as yet unknown, but this may account for the different prevalence rates for girls and boys. Outcomes may also be different for boys and girls. For example, research by Herrero, Hechtman, and Weiss (1994) at the Montreal Children's Hospital and McGill University

## Disorder Criteria Summary
### Attention Deficit/Hyperactivity Disorder (ADHD)

Features of ADHD include:

- Six or more symptoms of inattention, persisting 6 months or more, such as careless mistakes in school, difficulty sustaining attention in tasks or at play, often appearing not to listen when spoken to, failure to follow through with schoolwork or chores, frequent difficulty organizing tasks and activities, avoids/dislikes tasks that require sustained mental effort, often loses things necessary for tasks or activities, easily distracted, often forgetful
- Six or more symptoms of hyperactivity and impulsivity, persisting 6 months or more, such as frequent fidgeting with hands or feet or squirming in seat, often leaves seat in classroom, often running or climbing at inappropriate times, difficulty engaging quietly in leisure activities, excessive talking, blurting out answers before questions are posed, difficulty awaiting turn, often interrupts or intrudes on others
- Inattention, hyperactivity, and impulsivity are maladaptive and inconsistent with developmental level
- Some of symptoms present before age 7
- Some impairment from symptoms is present in two or more settings
- Significant impairment in functioning

*Source:* Based on DSM-IV-TR. Used with permission from the *Diagnostic and Statistical Manual of Mental Disorders,* Fourth Edition, Text Revision. Copyright 2000. American Psychiatric Association.

suggests that ADHD is a risk factor for antisocial outcomes in boys but not in girls. Children with ADHD are first identified as different from their peers around age 3 or 4; their parents describe them as very active, mischievous, slow to toilet train, and oppositional (Conners, March, Frances, Wells, & Ross, 2001). The symptoms of inattention, impulsivity, and hyperactivity become increasingly obvious during the school years. Despite the perception that children grow out of ADHD, their problems usually continue: 68% of children with ADHD have ongoing difficulties through adulthood (Faraone, 2000). Over time, children with ADHD seem to be less impulsive, although inattention persists (Hart, Lahey, Loeber, Applegate, & Frick, 1995). Research shows that adults with ADHD were more likely than individuals without ADHD to have driving difficulties such as crashes, and they are more likely to be cited for speeding and have their licenses suspended (Barkley, Murphy, & Kwasnik, 1996; Faraone et al., 2000). In short, although the manifestations of ADHD change as people grow older, many of their problems persist.

In addition to the gender differences among children with ADHD, children are more likely to receive the label of ADHD in North America than anywhere else in the world (Popper et al., 2003). However, with improvements in diagnosis worldwide, countries that previously reported lower rates of ADHD are finding similar numbers of these children being brought to the attention of helping professionals (Montiel-Nava, Pena, & Montiel-Barbero, 2003). This change suggests that the disorder may not simply be a reflection of a "lack of tolerance" on the part of teachers or parents in North America for active or impulsive children but rather an indication that ADHD is a disorder that affects a significant number of children all over the world.

### ADHD: Sean

*"[He] would never think before he did stuff. And actually, the thing that really made me go, 'Something is desperately wrong here'—we had a little puppy. Real tiny little dog. And Sean was upstairs playing with it. And my daughter had gone upstairs, and went, 'Mom, something's wrong with the dog's paw.' And I looked and this poor little dog had a broken paw. Sean had dropped her. But—didn't say anything to anyone. Just left the poor little dog sitting there. And I thought, 'Wow. This is just not normal.'"*

Thomson Learning

## Causes

As with many other disorders, we are at a period when important information about the genetics of ADHD is beginning to be uncovered. We have known for some time that ADHD is more common in families with one person having the disorder. For example, the relatives of children with ADHD have been found to be more likely to have ADHD themselves than would be expected in the general population (Biederman et al., 1992). Importantly, these families display an increase in psychopathology in general, including conduct disorder, mood disorders, anxiety disorders, and substance abuse (Faraone et al., 2000). This suggests that some shared genetic deficits may contribute to the problems experienced by individuals with these disorders (Faraone, 2003).

Once again, researchers are finding that more than one gene is probably responsible for ADHD (Sprich, Biederman, & Crawford, 2000). Research in this area is following the same progression as for other disorders and involves large collaborative studies across many laboratories worldwide (Faraone, 2003). Most attention to date has focused on genes associated with the neurochemical dopamine, although norepinephrine, serotonin, and GABA are also implicated in the cause of ADHD (Popper et al., 2003). More specifically, there is strong evidence that ADHD is associated with the dopamine $D_4$ receptor gene, the dopamine transporter gene, and the dopamine $D_5$ receptor gene. However, it should be pointed out that each of these genes on its own puts a person at a relatively small additional risk to ADHD. Research over the next few years should yield exciting new insights into the origins of ADHD.

For several decades, ADHD has been thought to involve brain damage, and this notion is reflected in the previous use of labels such as "minimal brain damage" or "minimal brain dysfunction" (Ross & Pelham, 1981). In recent years, scanning technology has permitted a sophisticated assessment of the validity of this assumption. One thing is clear—there are likely several different brain mechanisms that can lead to the attention deficits, along with the impulsivity and hyperactivity seen in individuals with ADHD. A general finding from brain-imaging studies of those with and without ADHD is that although no major damage is found in the brains of those with ADHD, there are subtle differences. One of the more reliable findings is that the volume (or overall size) of the brain is smaller in children with ADHD (Castellanos et al., 2003; Hill et al., 2003). Three areas of the brain appear smaller than is typical—the frontal cortex (in the outer portion of the brain), the basal ganglia (deep within the brain), and the cerebellar vermis (part of the cerebellum in the back of the brain; Popper et al., 2003). This smaller volume seems to occur early in the development of the brain, meaning that general progressive damage is not occurring in these individuals. Researchers are actively engaged in narrowing down just what parts of the brain are involved and how they may contribute to the symptoms we see in ADHD.

A variety of such toxins as allergens and food additives have been considered as possible causes of ADHD over the years, although little evidence supports the association. The theory that food additives such as artificial colours, flavourings, and preservatives are responsible for the symptoms of ADHD has had a substantial impact. Feingold (1975) presented this view along with recommendations for eliminating these substances as a treatment for ADHD. Hundreds of thousands of families have put their children on the Feingold diet, despite evidence that it has little or no effect on the symptoms of ADHD (Barkley, 1990). In fact, a review of the research literature, conducted by Daniel Waschbusch while at Dalhousie University, concludes that dietary management is simply not an effective treatment for ADHD (Waschbusch & Hill, 2001, 2003).

One of the more consistent findings among children with ADHD involves its association with maternal smoking. Mothers who smoke during pregnancy may be up to three times more likely to have a child with ADHD than mothers who do not smoke (Linnet et al., 2003). It is not yet clear if it is the toxic effect of smoking itself that causes ADHD or some associated process.

Psychological and social dimensions of ADHD further influence the disorder. Negative responses by parents, teachers, and peers to the affected child's impulsivity and hyperactivity may contribute to his or her feelings of low self-esteem (Barkley, 1989). Years of constant reminders by teachers and parents to behave, sit quietly, and pay attention may create a negative self-image in these children, which, in turn, can have a negative impact on their ability to make friends. Thus, the possible biological influences on impulsivity, hyperactivity, and attention, combined with attempts to control these children, may lead to their being rejected and to consequent poor self-image. An integration of the biological and psychological influences on ADHD suggests that both need to be addressed when designing effective treatments (Rapport, 2001).

## Treatment

Treatment for ADHD has proceeded on two fronts: biological and psychosocial interventions (Biederman, Spencer, Wilens, & Greene, 2001). Typically, the goal of biological treatments is to reduce the children's impulsivity and hyperactivity and to improve their attentional skills. Psychosocial treatments generally focus on broader issues such as improving academic performance, decreasing disruptive behaviour, and improving social skills. Although these two kinds of approaches have typically developed independently, recent efforts combine them to have a broader impact on people with ADHD.

Since the use of stimulant medication with children with ADHD was first described (Bradley, 1937), hundreds of studies have documented the effectiveness of this kind of medication in reducing the core symptoms of the disorder. Drugs such as methylphenidate (Ritalin, Metadate, Concerta), D-amphetamine (Dexedrine, Dextrostat), and pemoline (Cylert) have proved helpful for approximately 70% of cases in at least temporarily reducing hyperactivity and impulsivity and improving concentration on tasks (Berman, Douglas, & Barr, 1999; Brodeur & Pond, 2001). Cylert has a greater likelihood of negative side effects, so it is currently discouraged from use on a routine basis. Adderall, which is a longer-acting version of these psychostimulants, reduces the need for multiple doses for children during the day but has similar positive effects (Grcevich, Rowane, Marcellino, & Sullivan-Hurst, 2001).

Research suggests that other drugs, such as certain antidepressants (bupropion, imipramine) and a drug used for treating high blood pressure (clonidine), may have similar effects on people with ADHD (Popper et al., 2003). All these drugs seem to improve compliance and decrease negative behaviours in many children, but they do not appear to produce substantial improvement in learning and academic performance, and their effects do not usually last over the long term when the drugs are discontinued.

Originally, it seemed paradoxical or contrary to expectation that children would calm down after taking a stimulant. However, on the same low doses, children and adults with and without ADHD react in the same way. It appears that stimulant medications reinforce the brain's ability to focus attention during problem-solving tasks (Volkow & Swanson, 2003). Without stimulant medications, children with ADHD perform more poorly on a variety of cognitive tasks than do children with other disorders, including anxiety or mood disorders (Szatmari, Offord, Siegel, Finlayson, & Tuff, 1990). Although the use of stimulant medications remains controversial, especially for children, most clinicians recommend them temporarily, in combination with psychosocial interventions, to help improve children's social and academic skills (e.g., Douglas, Barr, Desilets, & Sherman, 1995).

There are two main concerns about the use of stimulant medications in the treatment of children with ADHD. The first concern pertains to stimulant drugs' potential for abuse. We saw in Chapter 10 that drugs such as Ritalin are sometimes abused for their ability to create elation and reduce fatigue (Volkow & Swanson, 2003). This is of particular concern for children with ADHD because they are at increased risk for later substance abuse (Molina & Pelham, 2003). A second concern is that these medications may be overprescribed and their long-term effects not well understood (Evenson, 2001). A recent study by Elisa Romano and her colleagues

A child with ADHD is likely to behave inappropriately regardless of the setting.

at the University of Montreal found that methylphenidate (Ritalin) use increased 36% among Canadian children over a 2-year period (Romano, Baillargeon, Wu, Robaey, & Tremblay, 2002). A concern related to overprescription is about the side effects commonly associated with stimulant medications such as insomnia, drowsiness, irritability, and appetite suppression (Schachter, Pham, King, Langford, & Moher, 2001).

In addition to these concerns, some portion of children with ADHD do not respond to medications, and most children who do respond do not show gains in the important areas of academics and social skills (Biederman et al., 2001; Pelham, Waschbusch, Hoza, Pillow, & Gnagy, 2001). Because of these findings, researchers have applied various behavioural interventions to help these children at home and in school (Fiore, Becker, & Nero, 1993; Garber, Garber, & Spizman, 1996). In general, the programs set such goals as increasing the amount of time the child remains seated, the number of math papers completed, or appropriate play with peers. Reinforcement programs reward the child for improvements and, at times, punish misbehaviour with loss of rewards (Braswell & Bloomquist, 1994). Other programs incorporate parent training to teach families how to respond constructively to their child's behaviours and how to structure the child's day to help prevent difficulties (Sonuga-Barke, Daley, Thompson, Laver-Bradbury, & Weeks, 2001). Although many children have benefited from these types of programs, others have not, and there is no way to predict which children will respond positively (Fiore et al., 1993). In sum, both medication and behavioural interventions have shortcomings. Most clinicians typically recommend a combination of approaches designed to individualize treatments for children with ADHD (e.g., Waschbusch, Kipp, & Pelham, 1998), targeting both short-term management issues (decreasing hyperactivity and impulsivity) and long-term concerns (preventing and reversing academic decline and improving social skills).

To determine whether a combined approach to treatment is the most effective, a large-scale study was conducted by six teams of researchers (Jensen et al., 2001). Labelled the Multimodal Treatment of Attention-Deficit Hyperactivity Disorder Study, this project included 579 children who were randomly assigned to one of four groups. One group of the children received routine care without medication or specific behavioural interventions (community care, or CC). The three treatment groups consisted of medication management (usually methylphenidate; MedMgt), intensive behavioural treatment (Beh), and the combination (Comb), and the study lasted 14 months. Initial reports from the study suggested that Comb and MedMgt alone were superior to Beh alone and CC interventions for ADHD symptoms.

For problems that went beyond the specific symptoms of ADHD, such as social skills, academics, parent–child relations, oppositional behaviour, and anxiety or depression (see Schachar et al., 2002), results suggested advantages of Comb over single treatments (MedMgt, Beh) and CC.

Some controversy surrounds the interpretation of these findings; specifically, whether or not Comb is superior to MedMgt alone (Biederman et al., 2001; Pelham, 1999). Practically speaking, if there is no difference between these two treatments, most parents and therapists would opt for simply providing medication for these children. As we mentioned previously, behavioural interventions have the added benefit of improving aspects of the child and family that are not directly affected by medication. Reinterpretations of the data from this large-scale study continue, and more research likely will be needed to clarify the combined and separate effects of these two approaches to treatment (Conners et al., 2001). Despite these advances, however, children with ADHD continue to pose a considerable challenge to their families and to the educational system.

## Learning Disorders

Academic achievement is highly valued in our society. Because parents often invest a great deal of time and emotional energy to ensure their children's academic success, it can be extremely upsetting when a child with no obvious intellectual deficits does not achieve as expected. In this section we describe **learning disorders** in reading, mathematics, and written expression—all characterized by performance that is substantially below what would be expected given the person's age, IQ, and education. We also look briefly at disorders that involve how we communicate. Consider the case of Alice.

### Alice
#### Taking a Reading Disorder to College

Alice, a 20-year-old college student, sought help because of her difficulty in several of her classes. She reported that she had enjoyed school and had been a good student up until about grade 6, when her grades suffered significantly. Her teacher informed her parents that she wasn't working up to her potential and she needed to be better motivated. Alice had always worked hard in school but promised to try harder. However,

**learning disorders** Reading, mathematics, or written expression performance substantially below levels expected relative to the person's age, IQ, and education.

with each report card her mediocre grades made her feel worse about herself. She managed to graduate from high school, but by that time she felt she was not as bright as her friends.

Alice enrolled in the local community college and again found herself struggling with the work. Over the years, she had learned several tricks that seemed to help her study and at least get passing grades. She read the material in her textbooks aloud to herself; she had earlier discovered that she could recall the material much better this way than if she just read silently to herself. Reading silently, she could barely remember any of the details just minutes later.

After her second year in community college, Alice transferred to the university, which she found even more demanding and where she failed most of her classes. After our first meeting, I suggested that she be formally assessed to identify the source of her difficulty. As suspected, Alice had a learning disability.

Scores from an IQ test placed her above average, but she was also found to have significant difficulties with reading. Her comprehension was poor, and she could not remember most of the content of what she read. We recommended that she continue with her trick of reading aloud, because her comprehension for what she heard was adequate. In addition, Alice was taught how to analyze her reading—that is, how to outline and take notes. She was even encouraged to audiotape her lectures and play them back to herself as she drove around in her car. Although Alice did not become an A student, she was able to graduate from the university, and she now works with young children who have learning disabilities.

## Clinical Description

According to DSM-IV-TR criteria, Alice would be diagnosed as having a **reading disorder,** which is defined as a significant discrepancy between a person's reading achievement and what would be expected for someone of the same age (American Psychiatric Association, 2000a). This particular learning disorder is also known as dyslexia. More specifically, the criteria require that the person read at a level significantly below that of a typical person of the same age, cognitive ability (as measured on an IQ test), and educational background. In addition, this disability cannot be caused by a sensory difficulty such as trouble with sight or hearing. Similarly, DSM-IV-TR defines a **mathematics disorder** as achievement below expected performance in mathematics and a **disorder of written expression** as achievement

below expected performance in writing. In each of these disorders, the difficulties are sufficient to interfere with the students' academic achievement and to disrupt their daily activities.

**Disorder Criteria Summary**
Learning Disorders

Features of learning disorders include the following:
- Performance in reading, math, or writing at level substantially below the person's chronological age, measured intelligence, and education
- Disturbance significantly interferes with academic achievement or activities of daily life requiring these skills
- If sensory deficit is present, learning difficulties are in excess of those associated with it

*Source:* Based on DSM-IV-TR. Used with permission from the *Diagnostic and Statistical Manual of Mental Disorders,* Fourth Edition, Text Revision. Copyright 2000. American Psychiatric Association.

## Statistics

Estimates of how prevalent learning disorders are range from 5% to 10% (Young & Beitchman, 2001), although the frequency of this diagnosis appears to increase in wealthier regions. According to school principals who participated in the National Longitudinal Survey of Children and Youth, an average of 12% of children in their schools had a learning disability (Statistics Canada, 1996b). According to Statistics Canada's Health and Activity Limitation Survey, learning disability is the most common long-term condition suffered by children up to 14 years of age (Statistics Canada, 1991). In fact, more than half of all Canadian school children classified as having a disability have a learning disability (Statistics Canada, 1996b; see Figure 13.1).

Difficulties with reading are the most common of the learning disorders and occur in some form in approximately 5% to 15% of the general population (Beitchman & Young, 1997; Popper et al., 2003). Scottish inventor Alexander Graham Bell, most famous for inventing the telephone, reportedly suffered from dyslexia. Mathematics disorder appears in approximately 6% of the population (Gross-Tsur, Manor, & Shalev, 1996), but we have limited information about the prevalence of disorders of written expression among children and adults. Early studies suggested that boys were more likely to have a reading disorder than girls, although more contemporary

**reading disorder**   Reading performance is significantly below age norms.

**mathematics disorder**   Mathematics performance is significantly below age norms.

**disorder of written expression**   Writing performance is significantly below age norms.

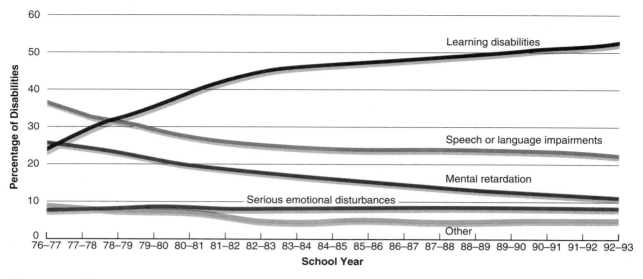

**Figure 13.1** ■ More than half of all schoolchildren classified as having a disability have learning disabilities (Statistics Canada, 1996b); 30 years ago, the proportion was around 25%.

research indicates that boys and girls may be equally affected by this disorder (Wadsworth, DeFries, Stevenson, Gilger, & Pennington, 1992).

A learning disorder can lead to a number of different outcomes, depending on the extent of the disability and the extent of available support. One study found that about 32% of students with learning disabilities dropped out of school (Wagner, 1990). In addition, employment rates for students with learning disorders tend to be discouragingly low, ranging from 60% to 70% (Shapiro & Lentz, 1991). The low figure may be partly because of the students' low expectations; one study reported that only 50% of high school students with learning disabilities had post-graduation plans (Shapiro & Lentz, 1991). The low figure may also be due in part to difficulties these individuals have in holding a job. According to the Handicapped Employment Program of the Ontario Ministry of Labour, adults with learning disabilities who have not received appropriate education or training typically hold a job for only 3 months. Additionally, learning disorders may be related to the later development of other mental health problems. For example, a study by Toronto-based researcher Joseph Beitchman and his colleagues suggests that adolescents with learning disorders are at increased risk for substance use disorders (Beitchman, Wilson, Douglas, Young, & Adlaf, 2001).

Some individuals with learning disorders do attain their education or career goals; however, this appears to be more difficult for people with severe learning disorders (Spreen, 1988). Psychologist Maggie Bruck notes that individuals with reading disorders can succeed in college or university if they are provided with instructional supports such as tutors, tape-recorded lectures, and tests without time limits (Bruck, 1987). Unfortunately though, interviews with adults who have learning disabilities reveal that their school experiences were generally negative and that

the effects often lasted beyond graduation. One man who did not have special assistance during school reports the following:

> I faked my way through school because I was very bright. I resent most that no one picked up my weaknesses. Essentially I judge myself on my failures.... [I] have always had low self-esteem. In hindsight I feel that I had low self-esteem in college.... I was afraid to know myself. A blow to my self-esteem when I was in school was that I could not write a poem or a story.... I could not write with a pen or pencil. The computer has changed my life. I do everything on my computer. It acts as my memory. I use it to structure my life and for all of my writing since my handwriting and written expression has always been so poor. (Polloway, Schewel, & Patton, 1992, p. 521)

A group of disorders loosely identified as verbal or communication disorders seem closely related to learning disorders. These disorders can appear deceptively benign, yet their presence early in life can cause wide-ranging problems later on. For a brief overview of these disorders, which include **stuttering, expressive language disorder, selective mutism,** and **tic disorder,** see Box 13.1.

**stuttering**  Disturbance in the fluency and time patterning of speech (e.g., sound and syllable repetitions or prolongations).

**expressive language disorder**  An individual's problem with spoken communication, as measured by significantly low scores on standardized tests of expressive language relative to nonverbal intelligence test scores. Symptoms may include a markedly limited vocabulary or errors in verb tense.

**selective mutism**  Developmental disorder characterized by the individual's consistent failure to speak in specific social situations despite speaking in other situations.

**tic disorder**  Disruption in early development involving involuntary motor movements or vocalizations.

## BOX 13.1 Communication and Related Disorders

### Stuttering

#### Clinical Description

A disturbance in speech fluency that includes a number of problems with speech, such as repeating syllables or words, prolonging certain sounds, making obvious pauses, or substituting words to replace ones that are difficult to articulate.

#### Statistics

Occurs twice as frequently among boys as among girls; begins most often in children under the age of 3 (Yairi & Ambrose, 1992); 98% of cases occur before the age of 10 (Mahr & Leith, 1992); approximately 80% of children who stutter before they enter school will no longer stutter after they have been in school a year or so (Yairi & Ambrose, 1992).

#### Causes

Rather than anxiety causing stuttering, stuttering makes people anxious (Miller & Watson, 1992); multiple brain pathways appear to be involved (Fox et al., 1996); genetic influences also may be a factor (Andrews, Morris-Yates, Howie, & Martin, 1991).

#### Treatment

*Psychological:* Parents are counselled about how to talk to their children; as noted by Mireielle Gagnon and Robert Ladouceur, the *regulated-breathing method* is a promising behavioural treatment in which the person is instructed to stop speaking when a stuttering episode occurs and then to take a deep breath (exhale, then inhale) before proceeding (Gagnon & Ladouceur, 1992).

*Pharmacological:* The serious side effects of haloperidol outweigh any benefit it may offer; verapamil may decrease the severity of stuttering in some individuals (Brady, 1991).

### Expressive Language Disorders

#### Clinical Description

Limited speech in *all* situations; expressive language (what is said) is significantly below their usually average *receptive language* (what is understood).

#### Statistics

2.2% of 3-year-olds experience this disorder (Silva, 1980); boys are almost five times as likely as girls to be affected (Whitehurst et al., 1988).

#### Causes

An unfounded psychological explanation is that the children's parents may not speak to them enough; a biological theory is that middle ear infection is a contributory cause.

#### Treatment

May be self-correcting and may not require special intervention.

### Selective Mutism

#### Clinical Description

Persistent failure to speak in specific situations—such as school—despite the ability to do so.

#### Statistics

Less than 1% of children; more prevalent among girls than boys; most often between the ages of 5 and 7.

#### Causes

Not much is known; anxiety is one possible cause (Kristensen, 2000).

#### Treatment

Contingency management: giving children praise and reinforcers for speaking while ignoring their attempts to communicate in other ways.

### Tic Disorder

#### Clinical Description

Involuntary motor movements (*tics*), such as head twitching, or vocalizations, such as grunts, that often occur in rapid succession, come on suddenly, and happen in idiosyncratic or stereotyped ways. In one type, *Tourette's disorder*, vocal tics often include the involuntary repetition of obscenities.

#### Statistics

Of all children, 12% to 24% show some tics during their growing years (Ollendick & Ollendick, 1990); 2 to 8 children out of every 10 000 have Tourette's disorder (Leckman et al., 1997b); usually develops before the age of 14; high comorbidity with obsessive-compulsive behaviour.

#### Causes

Inheritance may be through a dominant gene or genes (Bowman & Nurnberger, 1993; Wolf et al., 1996).

#### Treatment

*Psychological:* Self-monitoring, relaxation training, and habit reversal.
*Pharmacological:* Haloperidol and more recently pimozide and clonidine.

---

### Causes

Theories about the etiology of learning disorders assume a diverse and complex origin and include genetic, neurobiological, and environmental factors. For example, some disorders of reading may have a genetic basis; the parents and siblings of people with reading disorders are more likely to display these disorders than are relatives of people without reading problems (Popper et al., 2003). When identical twins are studied, if one twin receives a diagnosis of reading disorder, there appears to be an almost 100% chance that the second twin will receive the same diagnosis (100%

concordance), further supporting a genetic influence (Vandenberg, Singer, & Pauls, 1986). As we saw with ADHD, the genetics of disorders of reading are complex, and genes on chromosomes 2, 3, 6, 15, and 18 have all been repeatedly linked to these difficulties (Kaminen et al., 2003). Remember, however, that problems in learning are extremely diverse and undoubtedly are influenced by multiple biological and psychosocial influences.

Various forms of subtle brain damage have also been thought responsible for learning disabilities; some of the earliest theories involve a neurological explanation (Hinshelwood, 1896). Studies show a link between phonological processing problems and reading disabilities in both children and adults (e.g., Bruck, 1992; Stringer & Stanovich, 2000). Research suggests structural and functional differences in the brains of people with learning disabilities. For example, one study looked at children who are delayed in mastering language or reading skills because they are not able to distinguish certain sounds (e.g., the difference between "da" and "ga"; Kraus et al., 1996). The researchers found that the children's brains simply did not register the difference between the sounds. The research of John Connolly and his colleagues at Dalhousie University similarly shows weaker and delayed neural responses during reading of sentences among dyslexic readers compared with controls (Helenius, Salmelin, Service, & Connolly, 1999). Such findings imply a neuropsychological deficit that interferes with the processing of certain essential language information. Such physiological deficits are not consistent across individuals, however (Hynd & Semrud-Clikeman, 1989), which is not surprising, given that people with learning disorders display different types of cognitive problems and therefore probably represent a number of etiological subgroups (Beitchman & Young, 1997; Popper et al., 2003).

We saw that Alice persisted despite the obstacles caused by her learning disorder, as well as by the reactions of teachers and others. What helped her continue toward her goal when others choose, instead, to drop out of school? Psychological and motivational factors that have been reinforced by others seem to play an important role in the eventual outcome of people with learning disorders. Factors such as socioeconomic status, cultural expectations, parental interactions and expectations, and child management practices, together with existing neurological deficits and the types of support provided in the school, seem to determine outcome (Young & Beitchman, 2001).

## Treatment of Learning Disorders

As we will see in the case of mental retardation, learning disorders primarily require educational intervention. Biological treatment is typically restricted to those individuals who may also have ADHD, which we have seen involves impulsivity and an inability to sustain attention, and can be helped with certain stimulant medications such as methylphenidate (Ritalin). Educational efforts can be broadly categorized into (1) efforts to remediate directly the underlying basic *processing* of problems (e.g., by teaching students visual and auditory perception skills); (2) efforts to improve *cognitive* skills through general instruction in listening, comprehension, and memory; and (3) targeting the *behavioural* skills needed to compensate for specific problems the student may have with reading, mathematics, or written expression—such as those we discussed in the case of Alice (Reeve & Kauffman, 1988). For example, Alice's reading disorder was helped by the behavioural skill of reading aloud (Hinchley & Levy, 1988).

For children with learning disorders who have difficulties processing language, treatment using exercises such as specially designed computer games that help children distinguish sounds appears to be helpful (Merzenich et al., 1996). Considerable research supports the usefulness of teaching the behavioural skills necessary to improve academic skills (Young & Beitchman, 2001).

PATTERN    MOTION

CONTROLS

V1/V2                V5/MT

DYSLEXICS

V1/V2

Courtesy National Institute of Mental Health

These functional MRI scans of composite data from six dyslexic adults and eight controls show a horizontal slice through the brain, with the face at the top. Imaging shows atypical brain activity associated with dyslexia. The scans were performed while subjects tracked a pattern of moving dots on a computer screen. A brain area (V5/MT) normally active during such motion tasks did not switch on in dyslexic subjects (right). Their brain activity was more similar to that of controls during a pattern recognition task (left).

© Larry Williams/Corbis

Specially designed computer games may help children with learning disorders improve their language skills.

## Concept Check 13.1

Assign a label of (a) ADHD, (b) selective mutism, (c) Tourette's disorder, or (d) reading disorder to each of the following cases.

1. Ten-year-old Michael is frequently off-task at school. He often forgets to bring his homework to school and typically comes home without an important book. He works quickly and makes careless mistakes. _____

2. Jan was a good student until grade 5. She studied a great deal, but her grades continued to drop. Now, in the final year of high school and concerned about graduation, Jan has sought help. She places above average on an IQ test but shows significant problems with reading and comprehension. _____

3. Nine-year-old Evan can be frustrating to his parents, teachers, and friends. He often calls out answers in school, sometimes before the complete question is asked. He has trouble waiting his turn during games and does things seemingly without thinking. _____

4. Nine-year-old Cathy is described by everyone as a "handful." She fidgets constantly in class, drumming her fingers on the desk, squirming in her chair, and getting up and sitting down. She has trouble waiting her turn at work or at play, and she sometimes has violent outbursts. _____

5. At home, 8-year-old Hanna has been excitedly telling her cousins about a recent trip to a theme park. This would surprise her teachers, who have never heard her speak. _____

# Pervasive Developmental Disorders

■ *Define pervasive developmental disorders, and describe the three main symptom clusters of autistic disorder.*

People with **pervasive developmental disorders** all experience problems with language, socialization, and cognition (Durand & Mapstone, 1999). The word *pervasive* means that these problems are not relatively minor but significantly affect individuals throughout their lives. Included under the heading of pervasive developmental disorders are **autistic disorder** (or **autism**), **Asperger's disorder, Rett's disorder, childhood disintegrative disorder,** and **pervasive developmental disorder—not otherwise specified.** We focus on one of the more prevalent pervasive developmental disorders— autistic disorder—with the other disorders highlighted in Box 13.2. There is general agreement that children with a pervasive developmental disorder can be identified fairly easily because of the delays in their daily functioning. However, as noted by autism expert Peter Szatmari from McMaster University, what is not so easily agreed on is how we should define specific subdivisions of the general category of pervasive developmental disorders (Szatmari, 2000).

## Autistic Disorder

*Autistic disorder,* or *autism,* is a childhood disorder characterized by significant impairment in social interactions and communication and by restricted patterns of behaviour, interest, and activities (Durand, 2004). Individuals have a puzzling array of symptoms.

## Clinical Description

Three major characteristics of autism are expressed in DSM-IV-TR: impairment in social interactions, impairment in communication, and restricted behaviour, interests, and activities (American Psychiatric Association, 2000a). Consider the case of Amy.

---

**pervasive developmental disorders** Wide-ranging, significant, and long-lasting dysfunctions that appear before the age of 18.

**autistic disorder (autism)** Pervasive developmental disorder characterized by significant impairment in social interactions and communication and by restricted patterns of behaviour, interest, and activity.

**Asperger's disorder** Pervasive developmental disorder characterized by impairments in social relationships and restricted or unusual behaviours but without the language delays seen in autism.

**Rett's disorder** Progressive neurological developmental disorder featuring constant hand-wringing, mental retardation, and impaired motor skills.

**childhood disintegrative disorder** Pervasive developmental disorder involving severe regression in language, adaptive behaviour, and motor skills after a 2- to 4-year period of normal development.

**pervasive developmental disorder—not otherwise specified** Severe and pervasive impairments in social interactions, but the disorder does not meet all of the criteria for autistic disorder.

## Developmental Disorders

### Asperger's Disorder

#### Clinical Description

Impaired social relationships and restricted or unusual behaviours or activities, but without the language delays associated with autism; few severe cognitive impairments; IQ usually in the average range; often exhibit clumsiness and poor coordination; some researchers think it may be a mild form of autism.

#### Statistics

Prevalence uncertain; estimated at between 1 and 36 per 10 000 (Volkmar & Klin, 2000); believed to occur more often in boys than girls (Volkmar & Cohen, 1991).

#### Causes

Limited causal research conducted to date; some evidence suggests that it runs in families so a genetic contribution is suspected (Folstein & Santangelo, 2000).

#### Treatment

Similar to that for autism; less need to work on communication and academic skills.

### Rett's Disorder

#### Clinical Description

A progressive neurological disorder that primarily affects girls. It is characterized by constant hand-wringing, increasingly severe mental retardation, and impaired motor skills, all of which appear *after* an apparently normal start in development (Van Acker, 1991). Motor skills seem to deteriorate progressively over time; social skills, however, develop normally at first, decline between age 1 and age 3, and then partially improve.

#### Statistics

Rett's disorder is relatively rare, occurring in approximately 1 per 12 000 to 15 000 live female births.

#### Causes

It is unlikely that psychological factors play a role in causation; more likely, it is a genetic disorder involving the X chromosome.

#### Treatment

Focuses on teaching self-help and communication skills and on efforts to reduce problem behaviours.

### Childhood Disintegrative Disorder

#### Clinical Description

Involves severe regression in language, adaptive behaviour, and motor skills after a 2- to 4-year period of normal development (Malhotra & Gupta, 1999).

#### Statistics

Rare, occurring once in approximately every 100 000 births (Kurita, Kita, & Miyake, 1992).

#### Causes

Although no specific cause has been identified, several factors suggest a neurological origin, with abnormal brain activity in almost half the cases; incidence of seizures is about 10% and may rise to nearly 25% in teenagers (Hill & Rosenbloom, 1986).

#### Treatment

Typically involves behavioural interventions to regain lost skills and behavioural and pharmacological treatments to help reduce behavioural problems.

### Pervasive Developmental Disorder—Not Otherwise Specified

#### Clinical Description

Severe and pervasive impairments in social interactions but does not meet all of the criteria for autistic disorder. These individuals may not display the early avoidance of social interaction but still may exhibit significant social problems. Their problems may become more obvious later than 3 years of age.

#### Statistics

Little good evidence for prevalence at this time.

#### Causes

It is likely that some of the same genetic influences (Chudley, Gutierrez, Jocelyn, & Chodirker, 1998) and neurobiological impairments common in autism are involved in these individuals (Juul-Dam, Townsend, & Courchesne, 2001).

#### Treatment

Focuses on teaching socialization and communication skills and on efforts to reduce problem behaviours.

## Amy
### In Her Own World

Amy, 3 years old, spends much of her day picking up pieces of lint. She drops the lint in the air and then watches intently as it falls to the floor. She also licks the back of her hands and stares at the saliva. She hasn't spoken yet and can't feed or dress herself. Several times a day she screams so loudly that the neighbours at first thought she was being abused. She doesn't seem to be interested in her mother's love and affection but will take her mother's hand to lead her to the refrigerator. Amy likes to eat butter—whole pats of it, several at a time. Her mother uses the pats of butter that you get at some restaurants to help Amy learn and to keep her well behaved. If Amy helps with dressing herself, or if she sits quietly for several minutes, her mother gives her some butter. Amy's mother knows that the butter isn't good for her, but it is the only thing that seems to get through to the child. The family's pediatrician has been concerned about Amy's developmental delays for some time and has recently suggested that she be evaluated by specialists. The pediatrician thinks Amy may have autism and the child and her family will probably need extensive support.

**Impairment in Social Interactions**   One of the defining characteristics of people with autistic disorder is that they do not develop the types of social relationships expected for their age (Durand, 2004). Amy never made any friends among her peers and often limited her contact with adults to using them as tools—for example, taking the adult's hand to reach for something she wanted. For young children, the signs of social problems usually include a failure to engage in skills such as joint attention (Dawson et al., 2004). When sitting with a parent in front of a favourite toy, young children will typically look back and forth between the parent and the toy, smiling, in an attempt to engage the parent with the toy. However, this skill in joint attention is noticeably absent in children with autism.

One current view on the social deficits of people with autism is that they lack a theory of mind (i.e., the ability to appreciate that others have a point of reference that differs from their own; Baron-Cohen, Tager-Flusberg, & Cohen, 1994). More recently though, Philip Zelazo, Jr., of the University of Toronto and Sophie Jacques of Dalhousie University have argued that autistic individuals' poor performance on theory of mind tasks may instead be attributed to more general difficulties with "executive functioning" (i.e., planning, organizing, sequencing, abstracting; e.g., Zelazo, Burack, Boseovski, Jacques, & Frye, 2001; Zelazo, Jacques, Burack, & Frye, 2002).

**Impairment in Communication**   People with autism nearly always have severe problems with communicating (Mundy, Sigman, & Kasari, 1990). About 50% never acquire useful speech (Rutter, 1978; Volkmar et al., 1994). In those with some speech, much of their communication is unusual. Some repeat the speech of others, a pattern called *echolalia* we referred to before as a sign of delayed speech development. If you say, "My name is Eileen, what's yours?" they will repeat all or part of what you said: "Eileen, what's yours?" Often, not only are your words repeated but so is your intonation. Some who can speak are unable or unwilling to carry on conversations with others. Another aspect of the communication deficits of autistic children is a lack of spontaneous pretend play or social imitative play appropriate to the child's developmental level (Rutherford & Rogers, 2003).

*Autism: Christina*
*"Last year she used (the communication book) a lot more in communicating with us. We have different pictures in the book. They're called picture symbols to represent what she might want, what she might need, what she's asking of us."*

**Restricted Behaviour, Interests, and Activities**   The more striking characteristics of autism include restricted patterns of behaviour, interests, and activities. Amy appeared to like things to stay the same: She became extremely upset if even a small change was introduced (such as moving her toys in her room). This intense preference for the status quo has been called *maintenance of sameness*. Often, people with autism spend countless hours in *stereotyped and ritualistic behaviours,* making such stereotyped movements as spinning around in circles, waving their hands in front of their eyes with their heads cocked to one side, or biting their hands.

### Statistics

Autism was once thought to be a rare disorder, although more recent estimates of its occurrence seem to show an increase in its prevalence (Bryson & Smith, 1998). Previous estimates placed the rate at about 2 to 20 per 10 000 people, although it is now believed to be as high a 1 in every 166 births, especially when the estimates are combined with the other pervasive developmental disorders (Chakrabarti & Fombonne, 2001; Fombonne, 2003a, 2003b). Gender differences for autism vary depending on the IQ level of the person affected. For people with IQs under 35, autism is more prevalent among females; in the higher IQ range, it is more prevalent among males. We do not know the reason for these differences (Volkmar, Szatmari, & Sparrow, 1993). Autistic disorder appears to be a universal phenomenon, identified in every part of the world including Sweden (Gillberg, 1984), Japan (Sugiyama & Abe, 1989), Russia (Lebedinskaya & Nikolskaya, 1993), and China (Chung, Luk, & Lee, 1990). The vast majority of people with autism develop the associated symptoms before the age 3 (American Psychiatric Association, 2000a).

There are people with autism along the continuum of IQ scores. Almost half are in the severe to profound range of mental retardation (IQ less than 50), about a quarter test in the mild to moderate range (IQ of 50 to 70), and the remaining

## Disorder Criteria Summary
### Autistic Disorder

Features of autistic disorder include:

- Impairment in social interaction, evidenced by a variety of nonverbal behaviours such as lack of eye-to-eye gaze, facial expression, body postures; failure to develop peer relationships; lack of interest in sharing enjoyment or achievements with others; lack of social or emotional reciprocity
- Impairment in communication, such as: delay in development of spoken language, impairment in inability to initiate or sustain a conversation with others, stereotyped and repetitive use of language or idiosyncratic language, lack of make-believe or imitative play appropriate to developmental level
- Restricted repetitive and stereotyped patterns of behaviour, such as unusual preoccupation that is abnormal in either its intensity or its focus, inflexible adherence to routines or rituals, stereotyped and repetitive motor mannerisms, persistent preoccupation with parts of objects
- Onset of delays or abnormal functioning before age 3

*Source:* Based on DSM-IV-TR. Used with permission from the *Diagnostic and Statistical Manual of Mental Disorders,* Fourth Edition, Text Revision. Copyright 2000. American Psychiatric Association.

people display abilities in the borderline to average range (IQ greater than 70; Fombonne, 1999; Waterhouse, Wing, & Fein, 1989).

IQ measures are used to determine prognosis: The higher children score on IQ tests, the less likely they are to need extensive support by family members or people in the helping professions.

Former Canadian Football League quarterback Doug Flutie has a son with autistic disorder. In 2001, he and his wife started the Doug Flutie, Jr., Foundation for Autism to honour their son and to help other families facing childhood autism through support and education.

Conversely, young children with autistic disorder who score poorly on IQ tests are more likely to be severely delayed in acquiring communication skills and to need a great deal of educational and social support as they grow older. Usually, language abilities and IQ scores are reliable predictors of how children with autistic disorder will fare later in life: The better the language skills and IQ test performance, the better the prognosis.

### Causes: Psychological and Social Dimensions

Autism is a puzzling condition, so we should not be surprised to find numerous theories of why it develops. One generalization is that autistic disorder probably does not have a single cause (Rutter, 1978; Szatmari, 2003). Instead, a number of biological contributions may combine with psychosocial influences to result in the unusual behaviours of people with autism. Because historical context is important to research, it is helpful to examine past and more recent theories of autism. Historically, autistic disorder was seen as the result of failed parenting (Bettelheim, 1967; Ferster, 1961). Mothers and fathers of children with autism were characterized as perfectionistic, cold, and aloof (Kanner, 1949), with relatively high socioeconomic status (Allen, DeMyer, Norton, Pontius, & Yang, 1971; Cox, Rutter, Newman, & Bartak, 1975) and higher IQs than the general population (Kanner, 1943). Descriptions such as these have inspired theories holding parents responsible for their children's unusual behaviours. These views were devastating to a generation of parents, who felt guilty and responsible for their children's problems. Imagine being accused of such coldness toward your own child as to cause serious and permanent disabilities! Later research contradicts these studies, suggesting that on a variety of personality measures the parents of individuals with autism may not differ substantially from parents of children without disabilities (Koegel, Schreibman, O'Neill, & Burke, 1983; McAdoo & DeMyer, 1978).

Other theories about the origins of autism were based on the unusual speech patterns of some individuals—namely, their tendency to avoid first-person pronouns such as *I* and *me* and to use *he* and *she* instead. For example, if you ask a child with autism, "Do you want something to drink?" he might say, "He wants something to drink" (meaning "I want something to drink"). This observation led some theorists to wonder whether autism involves a lack of self-awareness (Goldfarb, 1963; Mahler, 1952). Imagine, if you can, not understanding that your existence is distinct. There is no "you," only "them"! Such a debilitating view of the world was used to explain the unusual ways people with

Courtesy Lee-Yun Chu

Timothy plays violin and piano as well as baseball. Autistic disorder occurs in all cultures and races.

Thomson Learning

**Rebecca: A First-Grader with Autistic Disorder**
"*Getting her out of her routine is something that sets her off.... Routine is extremely, extremely important with her.*"

autism behaved. Theorists suggested that the withdrawal seen among people with autistic disorder reflected a lack of awareness of their own existence.

However, later research has shown that some people with autistic disorder seem to have self-awareness (Dawson & McKissick, 1984; Spiker & Ricks, 1984) and it follows a developmental progression. Just like children without a disability, those with cognitive abilities below the level expected for a child of 18 to 24 months show little or no self-recognition, but people with more advanced abilities demonstrate self-awareness. Self-concept may be lacking when people with autism also have cognitive disabilities or delays and not because of autism itself.

The phenomenon of *echolalia*, repeating a word or phrase spoken by another person, was once believed to be an unusual characteristic of this disorder. Subsequent work in developmental psychopathology, however, has demonstrated that repeating the speech of others is part of the normally developing language skills observed in most young children (Koegel, 1995; Prizant & Wetherby, 1989). Even a behaviour as disturbing as the self-injurious behaviour sometimes seen in people with autism is observed in milder forms, such as head banging, among typically developing infants (de Lissovoy, 1961). This type of research has helped workers isolate the facts from the myths about autism and clarify the role of development in the

disorder. Primarily, it appears that what clearly distinguish people with autism from others are social deficiencies.

At present, few workers in the field of autism believe that psychological or social influences play a major role in the development of this disorder. To the relief of many families, it is now clear that poor parenting is not responsible for autism. Deficits in such skills as socialization and communication appear to be biological in origin. Biological theories about the origins of autism, examined next, have received much empirical support.

## Causes: Biological Dimensions

A number of different medical conditions have been associated with autism, including congenital rubella (German measles), and difficulties during pregnancy and labour. However, although a small percentage of mothers exposed to the rubella virus have children with autism, most often no autism is present. We still don't know why certain conditions sometimes result in autism.

**Genetic Influences**  It is now clear that autism has a genetic component (Cook, 2001). We know that families that have one child with autism have a 3% to 5% risk of having another child with the disorder. When compared with the incidence rate of less than 0.5% in the general population, this rate is evidence of a genetic component in the disorder. The exact genes involved in the development of autism remain elusive. There is evidence for some involvement with chromosome 15 (Cook et al., 1998), although there may be as many as 10 genes involved in this complex disorder (Halsey & Hyman, 2001).

**Neurobiological Influences**  Evidence that autism is associated with some form of organic (brain) damage comes most obviously from the prevalence data showing that three of every four people with autism also have some level of mental retardation. In addition, it has been estimated that between 30% and 75% of these people display some neurological abnormality such as clumsiness and abnormal posture or gait (Tsai & Ghaziuddin, 1992). These observations provide suggestive but only correlational evidence that autism is physical in origin. With

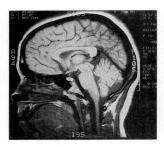
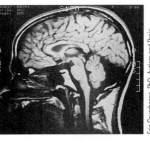

Eric Courchesne, PhD, Autism and Brain
Development Research Laboratory, La Jolla, CA

MRIs of two different brains: The person on the left has no neurological disorders, and the person on the right has autism. Note (lower right) that the cerebellum is smaller in the person with autism.

modern brain-imaging and scanning technologies, a clearer picture is evolving of the possible neurological dysfunctions in people with autism (Peterson, 1995). Researchers using CT and MRI technologies have found abnormalities of the cerebellum, including reduced size, among people with autism. Courchesne and colleagues examined the brain of a 21-year-old man who had a diagnosis of autism but no other neurological disorders and a tested IQ score in the average range (Courchesne, Hesselink, Jernigan, & Yeung-Courchesne, 1987). He was selected as a participant because he did not have the severe cognitive deficits seen in three-quarters of people with autism. Hence, the researchers could presume that he was free of any brain damage associated with mental retardation but not necessarily with autism. After obtaining the informed consent of this man and his parents, they conducted an MRI scan of his brain. As seen in the photo on this page, the most striking finding was that the cerebellum of the participant was abnormally small compared with that of a person without autism. Although this kind of abnormality has not been found in every study using brain imaging, it appears to be one of the more reliable findings of brain involvement in autism to date (Courchesne, 1991) and it may point out an important subtype of people with autism.

The study of autism is a relatively young field and still awaits an integrative theory. It is likely, however, that further research will identify the biological mechanisms that may ultimately explain the social aversion experienced by many people with the disorder. Also to be outlined are the psychological and social factors that interact early with the biological influences, producing the deficits in socialization and communication and the characteristic unusual behaviours of individuals with autism.

## Treatment of Pervasive Developmental Disorders

Most treatment research has focused on children with autism, so we primarily discuss treatment research for these individuals. However, because treatment for all pervasive developmental disorders relies on a similar approach, this research should be relevant across disorders. One generalization that can be made about autism and the other pervasive developmental disorders is that no completely effective treatment exists. We have not been successful in eliminating the social problems experienced by these individuals. Rather, like the approach to individuals with mental retardation, most efforts at treating people with pervasive developmental disorders focus on enhancing their communication and daily living skills and on reducing problem behaviours such as tantrums and self-injury (Durand, 1999b). We describe some of these approaches next, including work on early intervention for young children with autism.

### Psychosocial Treatments

Early psychodynamic treatments were based on the belief that autism is the result of improper parenting, and these treatments encouraged ego development (Bettelheim, 1967). Given our current understanding about the nature of the disorder, we should not be surprised to learn that treatments based solely on ego development have not had a positive impact on the lives of people with autism (Kanner & Eisenberg, 1955). Greater success has been achieved with behavioural approaches that focus on skill building and behavioural treatment of problem behaviours. This approach is based on the early work of Ferster and Lovaas. Although the work of these researchers has been greatly refined over the past 30 years, the basic premise—that people with autism can learn and that they can be taught some of the skills they lack—remains central. There is a great deal of overlap between the treatment of autism and the treatment of mental retardation. With that in mind, we highlight several treatment areas that are particularly important for people with autism, including communication and socialization.

**Communication** Problems with communication and language are among the defining characteristics of this disorder. People with autism often do not acquire meaningful speech; they tend to either have limited speech or use unusual speech such as echolalia. Teaching people to speak in a useful way is difficult. Think about how we teach languages: It mostly involves imitation. Imagine how you would teach a young girl to say the word *spaghetti*. You could wait several days until she said a word that sounded something like "spaghetti" (maybe "confetti"), then reinforce her. You could then spend several weeks trying to shape "confetti" into something closer to "spaghetti." Or you could just prompt, "Say 'spaghetti.'" Fortunately, most children can imitate and learn to communicate efficiently. But a child who has autism can't or won't imitate.

The communication deficits typical of autism often lead to social isolation.

In the mid-1960s, Lovaas and colleagues took a monumental first step toward addressing the difficulty of getting children with autism to respond. They used the basic behavioural procedures of *shaping* and *discrimination training* to teach these non-speaking children to imitate others verbally (Lovaas, Berberich, Perloff, & Schaeffer, 1966). The first skill the researchers taught them was to imitate other people's speech. They began by reinforcing a child with food and praise for making any sound while watching the teacher. After the child mastered that step, they reinforced the child only if she or he made a sound after the teacher made a request—such as the phrase, "Say 'ball'" (a procedure known as *discrimination training*). Once the child reliably made some sound after the teacher's request, the teacher used shaping to reinforce only approximations of the requested sound, such as the sound of the letter "b." Sometimes the teacher helped the child with physical prompting—in this case, by gently holding the lips together to help the child make the sound of "b." Once the child responded successfully, a second word was introduced—such as "mama"—and the procedure was repeated. This continued until the child could correctly respond to multiple requests, demonstrating imitation by copying the words or phrases made by the teacher. Once the children could imitate, speech was easier, and progress was made in teaching some of them to use labels, plurals, sentences, and other more complex forms of language (Lovaas, 1977). Despite the success of some children in learning speech, other children do not respond to this training, and workers sometimes use alternatives to vocal speech such as sign language and devices that have vocal output and can literally "speak" for the child (Johnson, Baumgart, Helmstetter, & Curry, 1996).

**Socialization** One of the most striking features of people with autism is their unusual reactions to other people. One study compared rates of adolescent interaction among children with autism, those with Down syndrome, and those developing normally; the adolescents with autism showed significantly fewer interactions with their peers (Attwood, Frith, & Hermelin, 1988). Although social deficits are among the more obvious problems experienced by people with autism, limited progress has been achieved toward developing social skills. Behavioural procedures have increased behaviours such as playing with toys or with peers, although the *quality* of these interactions appears to remain limited (Durand & Carr, 1988). In other words, behavioural clinicians have not found a way of teaching people with autism the subtle social skills that are important for interactions with peers—including how to initiate and maintain social interactions that lead to meaningful friendships.

**Timing and Settings for Treatment** Lovaas (1987) used intensive behavioural treatment for communication and social skills problems for 40 hours or more per week, in early intervention efforts with very young children. Such intensive treatment seemed to improve intellectual and educational functioning; these improvements appear to be long lasting (McEachin, Smith, & Lovaas, 1993).

Lovaas found that the children who improved most had been placed in regular classrooms, and children who did not do well were placed in separate special education classes. As we will see in our discussion of mental retardation, children with even the most severe disabilities are now being taught in regular classrooms. In addition, *inclusion*—helping children fully participate in the social and academic life of their peers—applies not only to school but to all aspects of life. Many different models are being used to integrate people with autism to normalize their experiences (Durand, 1999b). For instance, community homes are being recommended over separate residential settings, including special foster care programs (M. D. Smith, 1992), and supported employment options are being tested that would let individuals with autism have regular jobs. The behavioural interventions discussed are essential to easing this transition to fully integrated settings.

### Biological Treatment

No one medical treatment has been found to cure autism. In fact, medical intervention has had little success. A variety of pharmacological treatments have been tried, and some medical treatments have been heralded as effective before research has validated them. Although vitamins and dietary changes have been promoted as one approach to treating autism and initial reports were optimistic, research to date has found little support that they significantly help children with autism (Holm & Varley, 1989).

Because autism may result from a variety of different deficits, it is unlikely that one drug will work for everyone with this disorder. Much current work is focused on finding pharmacological treatments for specific behaviours or symptoms.

### Integrating Treatments

The treatment of choice for people with pervasive developmental disorder combines various approaches to the many facets of this disorder. For children, most therapy consists of school education combined with special psychological supports for problems with communication and socialization. Behavioural approaches have been most clearly documented as benefiting children in this area. Pharmacological treatments can help some of them on a temporary basis. Parents also need support because of the great demands and stressors involved in living with and caring for such children. As children with autism grow older, intervention focuses on efforts to integrate them into the community, often with supported living arrangements and work settings. Because the range of abilities of people with autism is so great, however, these efforts differ dramatically. Some people are able to live in their own apartments with only minimal support from family members. Others, with more severe forms of mental retardation, require more extensive efforts to support them in their communities.

## Concept Check 13.2

Determine how well you are able to diagnose the disorder in each of the following situations by labelling them autistic disorder, Asperger's disorder, Rett's disorder, childhood disintegrative disorder, or pervasive developmental disorder—not otherwise specified.

1. Once Kevin turned 4, his parents noticed that his motor skills and language abilities were beginning to regress dramatically. _____
2. Six-year-old Megan doesn't entirely avoid social interactions, but she experiences many problems in communicating and dealing with people. _____
3. Five-year-old Sharmila has a low IQ and enjoys sitting in the corner by herself, where she arranges her blocks in little lines or watches the pump bubble in the fish tank. She cannot communicate verbally, but she throws temper tantrums when her parents try to get her to do something she doesn't want to do. _____
4. Three-year-old Abby has severe mental retardation and trouble walking on her own. One of the characteristics of her disorder is constant hand-wringing. _____
5. Brad's parents first noticed when he was an infant that he did not like to play with other children or to be touched or held. He spent most of his time in his playpen by himself. His speech development, however, was not delayed. _____

# Mental Retardation

- *Define mental retardation, including the main DSM-IV-TR categories used to classify people with mental retardation.*

- *Describe what is known about the incidence and prevalence of mental retardation.*

**Mental retardation** is a disorder evident in childhood as significantly below-average intellectual and adaptive functioning (Luckasson et al., 1992). People with mental retardation experience difficulties with day-to-day activities to an extent that reflects both the severity of their cognitive deficits and the type and amount of assistance they receive. Perhaps more than any other group we have studied, people with mental retardation have throughout history received treatment that can best be described as shameful (Scheerenberger, 1983).

With notable exceptions, societies throughout the ages have devalued individuals whose intellectual abilities are deemed less than adequate.

The field of mental retardation has undergone dramatic and fundamental changes during the past decade. What it means to have mental retardation,

**mental retardation** Significantly below-average intellectual functioning paired with deficits in adaptive functioning such as self-care or occupational activities, appearing before age 18.

The colourful tapestries of Canadian artist Jane Cameron, who has Down syndrome, hang in galleries all over the world. She has flourished both as an artist and as a swimmer in the Special Olympics.

how to define it, and how people with this disorder are treated have been scrutinized, debated, and fought over by a variety of concerned groups. We describe the disorder in the context of these important changes, explaining both the status of people who have mental retardation and our current understanding of how best to understand its causes and treatment.

The manifestations of mental retardation are varied. Some individuals function quite well, even independently, in our complex society, such as Calgarian Jane Cameron, whose tapestries are found in galleries around the world. Others with mental retardation have significant cognitive and physical impairments and require considerable assistance to carry on day-to-day activities. Consider the case of James.

## James
### Up to the Challenge

James's mother contacted us because he was disruptive at school and at work. James was 17 and attended the local high school. He had Down syndrome and was described as very likable and, at times, mischievous. He enjoyed skiing, bike riding, and many other activities common among teenage boys. In fact, his desire to participate was a source of some conflict between him and his mother: He wanted to take the driver's education course at school, which his mother felt would set him up for failure; and he had a girlfriend he wanted to date, a prospect that also caused his mother concern.

School administrators complained because James didn't participate in activities such as physical education, and at the work site that was part of his school program he was often sullen, sometimes lashing out at the supervisors. They were considering moving him to a program with more supervision and less independence.

James's family had moved frequently during his youth, and they experienced striking differences in the way each community responded to James and his mental retardation. In some school districts, he was immediately placed in classes with other children his age and his teachers were provided with additional assistance and consultation. In others, it was just as quickly recommended that he be taught separately. Sometimes the school district had a special classroom in the local school for children with mental retardation. Other districts had programs in other towns, and James would have to travel an hour to and from school each day. Every time he was assessed in a new school, the evaluation was similar to earlier ones. He received scores on his IQ tests in the range of 40 to 50, which placed him in the moderate range of mental retardation. Each school gave him the same diagnosis: Down syndrome with moderate mental retardation. At each school, the teachers and other professionals were competent and caring individuals who wanted the best for James and his mother. Yet some believed that to learn skills James needed a separate program with specialized staff. Others felt they could provide a comparable education in a regular classroom and that to have peers without disabilities would be an added benefit.

In high school, James had several academic classes in a separate classroom for adolescents with learning problems, but he participated in some classes, such as gym, with students who did not have mental retardation. His current difficulties in gym (not participating) and at work (being oppositional) were jeopardizing his placement in both programs. When I spoke with

James's mother, she expressed frustration that the work program was beneath him because he was asked to do boring, repetitive work such as folding paper. James expressed a similar frustration, saying that he was treated like a baby. He could communicate fairly well when he wanted to, although he sometimes would get confused about what he wanted to say, and it was difficult to understand everything he tried to articulate. On observing him at school and at work, and after speaking with his teachers, we realized that a common paradox had developed. James resisted work he thought was too easy. His teachers interpreted his resistance to mean that the work was too hard for him, and they gave him even simpler tasks. He resisted or protested more vigorously, and they responded with even more supervision and structure.

Later, when we discuss treatment, we return to James, showing how we intervened at school and work to help him progress and become more independent.

## Clinical Description

People with mental retardation display a broad range of abilities and personalities. Individuals like James, who have mild or moderate impairments, can, with proper preparation, carry out most of the day-to-day activities expected of any of us. Many can learn to use mass transportation, purchase groceries, and hold a variety of jobs. Those with more severe impairments may need help to eat, bathe, and dress themselves, although with proper training and support they can achieve a degree of independence. These individuals experience impairments that affect most areas of functioning. Language and communication skills are often the most obvious. James was only mildly impaired in this area, needing help with articulation. In contrast, people with more severe forms of mental retardation may never learn to use speech as a form of communication, requiring alternatives such as sign language or special communication devices to express even their most basic needs. Because many cognitive processes are adversely affected, individuals with mental retardation have difficulty learning, but the level of challenge depends on how extensive the cognitive disability is.

Before examining the specific criteria for mental retardation, note that, like the personality disorders we described in Chapter 11, mental retardation is included on Axis II of DSM-IV-TR. Remember that separating disorders by axes serves two purposes: first, indicating that disorders on Axis II tend to be more chronic and less amenable to treatment, and second, reminding clinicians to consider whether these disorders, if present, are affecting an Axis I disorder. People can be diagnosed on both Axis I (e.g., generalized anxiety disorder) and Axis II (e.g., mild mental retardation). Also note that although the DSM-IV-TR retains the term mental retardation to describe the deficits in intellectual functioning, in Canada individuals with this pattern of deficits are often referred to as "intellectually handicapped" or as "developmentally delayed" by the public and media.

The DSM-IV-TR criteria for mental retardation are in three groups. First, a person must have *significantly subaverage intellectual functioning*, a determination made with one of several IQ tests with the cutoff score set by the DSM-IV-TR at approximately 70 or below. Roughly 2% to 3% of the population score at 70 or below on these tests. The American Association on Mental Retardation (AAMR)—a worldwide organization with chapters in several Canadian provinces—has its own, similar definition of mental retardation (i.e., a cutoff score of approximately 70 to 75 or below; Luckasson et al., 1992).

The second criterion of both the DSM-IV-TR and AAMR definitions for mental retardation calls for *concurrent deficits or impairments in adaptive functioning*. In other words, scoring "approximately 70 or below" on an IQ test is not sufficient for a diagnosis of mental retardation; a person must also have significant difficulty in at least two of the following areas: communication, self-care, home living, social and interpersonal skills, use of community resources, self-direction, functional academic skills, work, leisure, health, and safety. To illustrate, although James had many strengths, such as his ability to communicate and his social and interpersonal skills (he had several good friends), he was not as proficient as other teenagers at caring for himself in areas such as home living, health, and safety or in academic areas. This aspect of the definition is important because it excludes people who can function well in society but for various reasons do poorly on IQ tests. For instance, someone whose primary language is not English may do poorly on an IQ test but may still function at a level comparable to his or her peers. This person would not be considered to have mental retardation even if he or she scored below 70 on the IQ test.

The final criterion for mental retardation is the *age of onset*. The characteristic below-average intellectual and adaptive abilities must be evident before the person is 18. This cutoff is designed to identify affected individuals during the developmental period, when the brain is developing and therefore when any problems should become evident. The age criterion rules out the diagnosis of mental retardation for adults who suffer from brain trauma or forms of dementia that impair their abilities. The age of 18 is somewhat arbitrary, but it is the age at which most children leave school, when our society considers a person an adult.

## Disorder Criteria Summary
### Mental Retardation

Features of mental retardation include:
- Intellectual functioning significantly below average, with a measurement of approximately 70 or below on an IQ test
- Deficits or impairments in adaptive functioning in areas such as communication, self-care, home living, interpersonal skills, use of community resources, functional-academic skills, safety
- Onset before age 18

*Source:* Based on DSM-IV-TR. Used with permission from the *Diagnostic and Statistical Manual of Mental Disorders,* Fourth Edition, Text Revision. Copyright 2000. American Psychiatric Association.

The imprecise definition of mental retardation points to an important issue: Mental retardation, perhaps more than any other disorder, is defined by society. The cutoff score of 70 or 75 is based on a statistical concept (two or more standard deviations from the mean) and not on qualities inherent in people who supposedly have mental retardation. There is little disagreement about the diagnosis for people with the most severe disabilities; however, the majority of people diagnosed with mental retardation are in the mild range of cognitive impairment. They need some support and assistance, but remember that the criteria for using the label "mental retardation" are based partly on a somewhat arbitrary cutoff score for IQ that can (and does) change with changing social expectations.

People with mental retardation differ significantly in their degree of disability. Almost all classification systems have differentiated these individuals in terms of their ability or on the etiology of the mental retardation (Hodapp & Dykens, 1994). Traditionally (and still evident in the DSM-IV-TR), classification systems have identified four levels of mental retardation: *mild,* which is identified by an IQ score between 50 or 55 and 70; *moderate,* with a range of 35–40 to 50–55; *severe,* ranging from 20–25 up to 35–40; and *profound,* which includes people with IQ scores below 20–25. It is difficult to categorize each level of mental retardation according to "average" individual achievements by people at each level. A person with severe or profound mental retardation tends to have extremely limited formal communication skills (no spoken speech or only one or two words) and may require great or even total assistance in dressing, bathing, and eating. Yet people with these diagnoses have a wide range of skills that depend on training and the availability of other supports. Similarly, people like James, who have mild or moderate mental retardation, should be able to live independently or with minimal supervision; again, however, their achievement depends in part on their education and the community support available to them.

Perhaps the most controversial change in the AAMR definition of mental retardation is its description of different levels of this disorder, which are based on the level of support or assistance people need: *intermittent, limited, extensive,* or *pervasive* (Luckasson et al., 1992). You may recognize parallels with the DSM-IV-TR levels of mental retardation, including the use of four categories. Thus, someone who needs only intermittent support in AAMR terms is similar to a person labelled by DSM-IV-TR as having mild mental retardation. Similarly, the categories of limited, extensive, and pervasive support may be analogous to the levels of moderate, severe, and profound mental retardation, respectively. The important difference is that the AAMR system identifies the role of "needed supports" in determining level of functioning, whereas DSM-IV-TR implies that the ability of the person is the sole determining factor. The AAMR system focuses on the specific areas of assistance a person needs that can then be translated into training goals. Whereas his DSM-IV-TR diagnosis might be "moderate mental retardation," James might receive the following AAMR diagnosis: "a person with mental retardation who needs limited supports in home living, health and safety, and in academic skills." The AAMR definition emphasizes the types of support James and others require, and it highlights the need to identify what assistance is available when considering a person's abilities and potential. However, at this writing, the AAMR system has not been assessed empirically to determine whether it has greater value than traditional systems.

An additional method of classification has been used in the educational system to identify the abilities

Mental retardation can be defined in terms of the level of support people need.

of students with mental retardation. It relies on three categories: *educable mental retardation* (based on an IQ of 50 to approximately 70–75), *trainable mental retardation* (IQ of 30 to 50), and *severe mental retardation* (IQ below 30; Cipani, 1991). The assumption is that students with educable mental retardation (comparable to mild mental retardation) could learn basic academic skills; students with trainable mental retardation (comparable to moderate mental retardation) could not master academic skills but could learn rudimentary vocational skills; and students with severe mental retardation (comparable to severe and profound mental retardation) would not benefit from academic or vocational instruction. Built into this categorization system is the automatic negative assumption that certain individuals cannot benefit from certain types of training. This system and the potentially stigmatizing and limiting DSM-IV-TR categories (mild, moderate, severe, and profound mental retardation) inspired the AAMR categorization of needed supports. Current trends are away from the educational system of classification, because it inappropriately creates negative expectations in teachers. Clinicians continue to use the DSM-IV-TR system; we have yet to see whether the AAMR categories will be widely adopted.

### Lauren: A Kindergartner with Down Syndrome

*"The speech has been the most difficult ... and communication naturally just causes tremendous behaviour difficulties.... If there is not a way for her to communicate to us what her needs are and how she's feeling ... it really causes a lot of actual shutdowns with Lauren.... She knows exactly what she wants and she is going to let you know even though she can't verbalize it."*

Thomson Learning

## Statistics

Approximately 90% of people with mental retardation fall under the label of mild mental retardation (IQ of 50 to 70; Popper & West, 1999), and when you add individuals with moderate, severe, and profound mental retardation (IQ below 50) they represent 1% to 3% of the general population (Larson et al., 2001). In Canada, current statistics suggest that 70 babies a week are born with mental retardation (Goldner, 2003).

The course of mental retardation is chronic, meaning that people do not recover. However, the prognosis for people with this disorder varies considerably. Given appropriate training and support,

individuals with less severe forms can live relatively independent and productive lives. People with more severe impairments require more assistance to participate in work and community life. Mental retardation is observed more often among males, with a male-to-female ratio of about 1.6 to 1 (Laxova, Ridler, & Bowen-Bravery, 1977). This difference may be present mainly among people with mild mental retardation; no gender differences are found among people with severe forms (Richardson, Katz, & Koller, 1986).

## Causes

There are literally hundreds of known causes of mental retardation, including the following:

- *Environmental:* for example, deprivation, abuse, and neglect
- *Prenatal:* for instance, exposure to disease or drugs while still in the womb
- *Perinatal:* such as difficulties during labor and delivery
- *Postnatal:* for example, infections or head injury

As we mentioned in Chapter 10, heavy use of alcohol among pregnant women can produce a disorder in their children called *fetal alcohol syndrome,* a condition that can lead to severe learning disabilities. Other prenatal factors that can produce mental retardation include the pregnant woman's exposure to disease and chemicals and poor nutrition. In addition, lack of oxygen (anoxia) during birth, and malnutrition and head injuries during the developmental period can lead to severe cognitive impairments. Despite the rather large number of known causes of mental retardation, keep one fact in mind: Nearly 75% of cases either cannot be attributed to any known cause or are thought to be the result of social and environmental influences (Zigler &

© Bob Daemmrich/Stock Boston

Although she cannot speak, this girl is learning to communicate with an eye-gaze board, pointing to or simply looking at the image that conveys her message.

Hodapp, 1986). Most affected individuals have mild mental retardation and are sometimes referred to as having cultural-familial mental retardation.

## Biological Dimensions

A majority of the research on the causes of mental retardation focuses on biological influences. We next look at biological dimensions that appear responsible for the more common forms of mental retardation.

**Genetic Influences**   Most researchers believe that people with mental retardation probably are affected by multiple gene disorders in addition to environmental influences (Abuelo, 1991). However, a portion of the people with more severe mental retardation have identifiable single-gene disorders, involving a gene that is *dominant* (expresses itself when paired with a normal gene), *recessive* (expresses itself only when paired with another copy of itself), or *X linked* (present on the X or sex chromosome).

Only a few dominant genes result in mental retardation, probably as a result of natural selection: Someone who carries a dominant gene that results in mental retardation is less likely to have children and thus less likely to pass the gene to offspring. Therefore, this gene becomes less likely to continue in the population. However, some people, especially those with mild mental retardation, marry and have children, thus passing on their genes. One example of a dominant gene disorder, *tuberous sclerosis*, is relatively rare, occurring in 1 of approximately every 30 000 births. About 60% of the people with this disorder have mental retardation (Vinken & Bruyn, 1972), and most have seizures (uncontrolled electrical discharges in the brain) and characteristic bumps on their skin that during adolescence resemble acne.

A recessive disorder called *phenylketonuria,* or PKU, affects 1 of every 14 000 newborns and is characterized by an inability to break down a chemical in our diets called phenylalanine. For example, diet soft drinks contain phenylalanine. Until the mid-1960s, the majority of people with PKU had mental retardation, seizures, and behaviour problems, resulting from high levels of this chemical. However, researchers developed a screening technique that identifies the existence of PKU; infants are now routinely tested at birth, and any individuals identified with PKU can be successfully treated with a special diet that avoids the chemical phenylalanine. This is a rare example of the successful prevention of one form of mental retardation.

Ironically, successful early identification and treatment of people with PKU during the past 3 decades has some worried that an outbreak of PKU-related mental retardation will recur. The special diet to prevent symptoms is necessary only until the person reaches age 6 or 7. At this point, people tend to become lax and eat a regular diet—fortunately, with no harmful consequences for themselves. Because untreated maternal PKU can harm the developing fetus (Lenke & Levy, 1980), there is concern now that women with PKU who are of childbearing age may not stick to their diets and inadvertently cause PKU-related mental retardation in their children before birth. Many physicians now recommend dietary restriction through the childbearing period (Hellekson, 2001).

*Lesch-Nyhan syndrome,* an X-linked disorder, is characterized by mental retardation, signs of cerebral palsy (spasticity or tightening of the muscles), and self-injurious behaviour, including finger and lip biting (Nyhan, 1978). Only males are affected, because a recessive gene is responsible; when it is on the X chromosome in males it does not have a normal gene to balance it because males do not have a second X chromosome. Women with this gene are carriers and do not show any of the symptoms.

As our ability to detect genetic defects improves, more disorders will be identified genetically. The hope is that our increased knowledge will be accompanied by improvements in our ability to treat or, as in the case of PKU, prevent mental retardation and other negative outcomes.

**Chromosomal Influences**   It was only about 50 years ago that the number of chromosomes—46—was correctly identified in human cells (Tjio & Levan, 1956). Three years later, researchers found that people with Down syndrome (the disorder James displayed) had an additional small chromosome (Lejeune, Gauthier, & Turpin, 1959). Since that time, a number of other chromosomal aberrations that result in mental retardation have been identified. We describe Down syndrome and fragile X syndrome in some detail, but there are hundreds of other ways in which abnormalities among the chromosomes can lead to mental retardation.

**Down syndrome,** the most common chromosomal form of mental retardation, was first identified by the British physician Langdon Down in 1866. Down had tried to develop a classification system for people with mental retardation based on their resemblance to people of other races; he described individuals with this particular disorder as "mongoloid" because they resembled people from Mongolia (Scheerenberger, 1983). The term *mongoloidism* was used for some time but has been replaced with the term *Down syndrome.* The disorder is caused by the

---

**Down syndrome**   Type of mental retardation caused by a chromosomal aberration (chromosome 21) and involving characteristic physical appearance.

presence of an extra 21st chromosome and is therefore sometimes referred to as *trisomy 21*. For reasons we don't completely understand, during cell division two of the 21st chromosomes stick together (a condition called *nondisjunction*), creating one cell with one copy that dies and one cell with three copies that divide to create a person with Down syndrome.

People with Down syndrome have characteristic facial features, including folds in the corners of their upwardly slanting eyes, a flat nose, and a small mouth with a flat roof that makes the tongue protrude somewhat. Like James, they tend to have congenital heart malformations. Tragically, nearly *all* adults with Down syndrome past the age of 40 show signs of dementia of the Alzheimer's type, a degenerative brain disorder that causes impairments in memory and other cognitive disorders (Visser et al., 1997). This disorder among people with Down syndrome occurs earlier than usual (sometimes in their early 20s) and has led to the finding that at least one form of Alzheimer's disease is attributable to a gene on the 21st chromosome.

In 1999, 366 babies in Canada were born with Down syndrome, making its incidence about 1 in 900 births (Canadian Down Syndrome Society, 2000). The incidence of children born with Down syndrome has been tied to maternal age: As the age of the mother increases, so does her chance of having a child with this disorder (Figure 13.2). A woman at age 20 has a 1 in 2000 chance of having a child with Down syndrome; at the age of 35 this risk increases to 1 in 500, and at the age of 45 it increases again to 1 in 18 births (Evans & Hammerton, 1985; Hook, 1982).

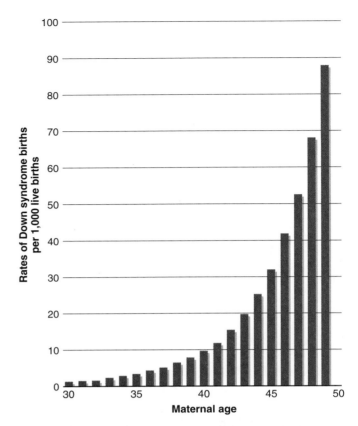

**Figure 13.2**  ■  The increasing likelihood of Down syndrome with maternal age. (Based on data from Hook, 1982).

Despite these numbers, many more children with Down syndrome are born to younger mothers because, as women get older, they tend to have fewer children. The reason for the rise in incidence with maternal age is not clear. Some suggest that because a woman's ova (eggs) are all produced in youth, the older ones have been exposed to toxins, radiation, and other harmful substances over longer periods. This exposure may interfere with the normal meiosis (division) of the chromosomes, creating an extra 21st chromosome (Pueschel & Goldstein, 1991). Others believe the hormonal changes that occur as women age are responsible for this error in cell division (Crowley, Hayden, & Gulati, 1982).

For some time it has been possible to detect the presence of Down syndrome—but not the degree of mental retardation—through *amniocentesis*, a procedure that involves removing and testing a sample of the fluid that surrounds the fetus in the amniotic sac. A number of other disorders can also be detected through amniocentesis.

**Fragile X syndrome** is a second common chromosomally related cause of mental retardation

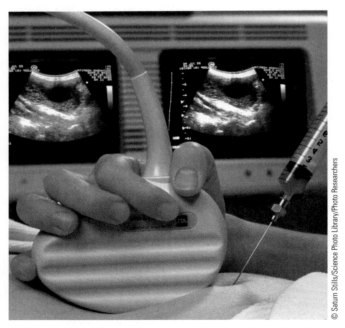

Amniocentesis can detect the presence of Down syndrome in a fetus. Guided by an ultrasound image, the doctor withdraws amniotic fluid for analysis.

**fragile X syndrome**  Pattern of abnormality caused by a defect in the X chromosome resulting in mental retardation, learning problems, and unusual physical characteristics.

(Dykens, Leckman, Paul, & Watson, 1988). As its name suggests, this disorder is caused by an abnormality on the X chromosome, a mutation that makes the tip of the chromosome look as though it were hanging from a thread, giving it the appearance of fragility (Sutherland & Richards, 1994). As with Lesch-Nyhan syndrome, which also involves the X chromosome, fragile X primarily affects males because they do not have a second X chromosome with a normal gene to balance out the mutation. Unlike Lesch-Nyhan carriers, however, women who carry fragile X syndrome commonly display mild to severe learning disabilities (Smith, 1993). Men with the disorder display moderate to severe levels of mental retardation and also have higher rates of hyperactivity, short attention spans, gaze avoidance, and perseverative speech. In addition, such physical characteristics as large ears, testicles, and head circumference are also common. Estimates are that 1 of every 2000 males is born with fragile X syndrome (Dykens et al., 1988).

## Psychological and Social Dimensions

**Cultural-familial retardation** is the presumed cause of up to 75% of the cases of mental retardation and is perhaps the least understood (Popper & West, 1999). Individuals with cultural-familial retardation tend to score in the mild mental retardation range on IQ tests and have relatively good adaptive skills (Zigler & Cascione, 1984). Their mental retardation is thought to result from a combination of psychosocial and biological influences, although the specific mechanisms that lead to this type of mental retardation are not yet understood. The cultural influences that may contribute to this condition include abuse, neglect, and social deprivation.

It is sometimes useful to consider people with mental retardation in two distinct groups: those with cultural-familial retardation and those with biological (or "organic") forms of mental retardation. People in the latter group have more severe forms of mental retardation that are usually traceable to known causes such as fragile X syndrome. Figure 13.3 shows that the cultural-familial group is composed primarily of individuals at the lower end of the IQ continuum, whereas in the organic group genetic, chromosomal, and other factors affect intellectual performance. The organic group increases the number of people at the lower end of the IQ continuum so that it exceeds the expected rate for a normal distribution (Zigler & Hodapp, 1986).

Two views of cultural-familial retardation further our understanding of this phenomenon. The *difference view* holds that those with cultural-familial retardation have a subset of deficits, such as attentional (Fisher & Zeaman, 1973) or memory problems (Ellis, 1970), that represents a limited portion of the

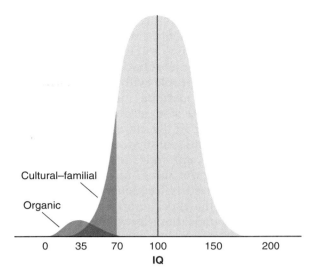

**Figure 13.3** ■ The actual distribution of IQ scores for individuals with cultural-familial retardation and organic retardation. Note that the cultural-familial group represents the normal expected lower end of the continuum but that the organic group is a separate and overlapping group. (Adapted from *Understanding Mental Retardation*, by E. Zigler and R. M. Hodapp. Copyright © 1986 by Cambridge University Press. Reprinted with permission.)

larger set of deficiencies experienced by people with more severe forms of mental retardation. In other words, these individuals *differ* from people without mental retardation in terms of specific damage, and they are similar to people with more severe retardation. In contrast, the *developmental view* sees the mild mental retardation of people with cultural-familial retardation as simply a difference in the rate and ultimate ceiling of an otherwise normal developmental sequence (Zigler & Balla, 1982). Put another way, as children these individuals go through the same developmental stages as people without mental retardation, but they do so at a slower pace and do not attain all the skills they probably would have if they had developed in a more supportive environment (Zigler & Stevenson, 1993). Support is mixed for both of these views of the nature of cultural-familial retardation. Much is still not understood about people with cultural-familial retardation; future work may reveal important subgroups among them.

## Treatment of Mental Retardation

Direct biological treatment of mental retardation is currently not a viable option. Generally, the treatment of individuals with mental retardation parallels

---

**cultural-familial retardation**  Mild mental retardation that may be caused largely by environmental influences.

that of people with pervasive developmental disorders, attempting to teach them the skills they need to become more productive and independent. For individuals with mild mental retardation, intervention is similar to that for people with learning disorders. Specific learning deficits are identified and addressed to help the student improve such skills as reading and writing. At the same time, these individuals often need additional support to live in the community. For people with more severe disabilities, the general goals are the same; however, the level of assistance they need is frequently more extensive. Remember that the expectation for all people with mental retardation is that they will in some way participate in community life, attend school and later hold a job, and have the opportunity for meaningful social relationships. Advances in electronic and educational technologies have made this goal realistic even for people with profound mental retardation.

People with mental retardation can acquire skills through the many behavioural innovations first introduced in the early 1960s to teach such basic self-care as dressing, bathing, feeding, and toileting to people with even the most severe disabilities (Reid, Wilson, & Faw, 1991). The skill is broken into its component parts (a procedure called a *task analysis*) and the person is taught each part in succession until he or she can perform the whole skill. Performance on each step is encouraged by praise and by access to objects or activities the person desires (reinforcers). Success in teaching these skills is usually measured by the level of independence the person can attain by using them. Typically, most individuals, regardless of their disability, can be taught to perform some skills.

Communication training is very important for people with mental retardation. Making their needs

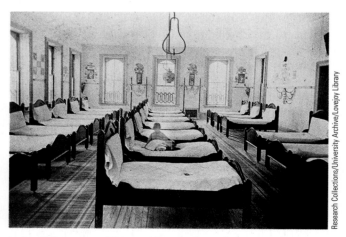

In the 19th century, children with mental retardation were housed in asylums for the "feeble-minded" like the one illustrated here. Today, great efforts are made to keep children with mental retardation in their homes and communities.

and wants known is essential for personal satisfaction and for participation in most social activities. The goals of communication training differ, depending on the existing skills. For people with mild levels of mental retardation, the goals may be relatively minor (e.g., improving articulation) or more extensive (e.g., organizing a conversation; Abbeduto & Rosenberg, 1992). Some, like James, have communication skills that are already adequate for day-to-day needs.

For individuals with the most severe disabilities, this type of training can be particularly challenging, because they may have multiple physical or cognitive deficits that make spoken communication difficult or impossible (Warren & Reichle, 1992). Creative researchers, however, use alternative systems that may be easier for these individuals, including the sign language used primarily by people with hearing disabilities and *augmentative communication strategies*. Augmentative strategies may use picture books, teaching the person to make a request by pointing to a picture—for instance, pointing to a picture of a cup to request a drink (Reichle, Mirenda, Locke, Piche, & Johnston, 1992). A variety of computer-assisted devices can be programmed so that the individual presses a button to produce complete spoken sentences (e.g., "Would you come here? I need your help."). People with limited communication skills can be taught to use these devices, which helps them reduce the frustration of not being able to relate their feelings and experiences to other people (Durand, 1993).

Concern is often expressed by parents, teachers, and employers that some people with mental retardation can be physically or verbally aggressive or may hurt themselves. Considerable debate has ensued over the proper way to reduce these behaviour problems; the most heated discussions involve whether to use painful punishers (Repp & Singh, 1990). Alternatives to punishment that may be equally effective in reducing behaviour problems such as aggression and self-injury (Durand, 1999a) include teaching people how to communicate their need or desire for such things as attention that they seem to be getting with their problem behaviours. To date, however, no treatment or treatment package has proved successful in all cases, although important advances are being made in significantly reducing even severe behaviour problems for some people.

In addition to ensuring that people with mental retardation are taught specific skills, caretakers also focus on the important task of supporting them in their communities. *Supported employment* involves helping an individual find and participate satisfactorily in a competitive job (Bellamy, Rhodes, Mank, & Albin, 1988). Research has shown that not only can people with mental retardation be placed in meaningful jobs, but also that despite the costs associated with supported employment, it can ultimately be cost effective (McCaughrin, 1988). The benefits to people who achieve the satisfaction of being a productive part of society are incalculable.

There is general agreement about *what* should be taught to people with mental retardation. The controversy in recent years has been over *where* this teaching should take place. Should people with mental retardation, especially the severe forms, be taught in specially designed separate classrooms or workshops, or should they attend their neighbourhood public schools and work at local businesses? Increasingly, teaching strategies to help these students learn are being used in regular classrooms and in preparing them to work at jobs in the community (Meyer, Peck, & Brown, 1991). There is at present no cure for mental retardation, but the current prevention and treatment efforts suggest that meaningful changes can be achieved in the lives of these people.

## *Prevention of Developmental Disorders*

Unfortunately, Canada has a rather dark history in terms of the types of efforts that were undertaken to prevent certain developmental disorders. In particular, "eugenics" advocates argued for the prevention of mental retardation through sexual sterilization of individuals with mental retardation. Eugenics was a movement involving applications of genetics knowledge at the time, for which the goal was to improve the human race through better breeding. In the 1920s and 1930s, British Columbia and Alberta introduced legislation allowing for sterilization of the "feeble-minded" without the patient's consent, to improve the gene pool by preventing mental retardation. Sterilizations were performed in other Canadian provinces as well, despite the absence of similar legislation. Provincial sterilization laws were repealed in the 1970s, and today, the rights of individuals with mental retardation are protected under the Charter of Rights and Freedoms (McLaren, 1990).

Current efforts to prevent developmental disorders are in their early stages. One such effort—early intervention—has been described for pervasive developmental disorders and appears to hold considerable promise for some children. In addition, early intervention combining educational, medical, and social supports can target and assist children who, because of inadequate environments, are at risk for developing cultural-familial retardation (Fewell & Glick, 1996; Ramey & Ramey, 1992). One such effort at early intervention identified a group of children shortly after birth and provided them with an intensive preschool program and medical and nutritional supports. This intervention continued until the children began formal education (Martin, Ramey, & Ramey, 1990). The authors of this study found that for all but one of the children in a control group who received medical and nutritional support but not the intensive educational experiences, each had IQ scores below 85 at age 3. But the 3-year-olds in the experimental group all tested above 85. Such findings are important because they show the potential for creating a lasting impact on the lives of these children and their families.

Although it does appear that many children can make significant progress if interventions are initiated early in life (Ramey & Ramey, 1998), a number of important questions remain regarding early intervention efforts. Not all children, for example, benefit significantly from such efforts, and future research will need to resolve a number of lingering concerns. For example, we need to determine how best to identify children and families who will benefit from such programs, how early in the child's development it is important to begin programs, and how long to continue them to produce desirable outcomes (Ramey & Ramey, 1994).

Given recent advances in genetic screening and technology, it may someday be possible to detect and ultimately correct genetic and chromosomal abnormalities—research that could fundamentally change our approach to children with developmental disorders. For example, one study used mice with a disease similar to an inherited enzyme deficiency (Sly disease) found in some individuals with mental retardation. Researchers found that they could transplant healthy brain cells into the diseased young mice to correct the disease (Snyder, Taylor, & Wolfe, 1995). Someday it may be possible for similar research to be performed prenatally on children identified as having syndromes associated with mental retardation (Simonoff, Bolton, & Rutter, 1996). For example, it may soon be possible to conduct *prenatal gene therapy*, where a developing fetus that has been screened for a genetic disorder may be the target of intervention before birth (Ye, Mitchell, Newman, & Batshaw, 2001). This prospect is not without its difficulties, however (Durand, 2001).

One cause of concern is the reliability of gene therapy. This technology is not sufficiently advanced to produce intended results consistently. Currently, any such intervention may cause unwanted mutations or other complications, which in turn could be fatal to the fetus. For example, a study using a mouse model of PKU—the recessive gene disorder we discussed earlier that results in mental retardation—used a specific technique to modify the gene responsible for this disorder (Nagasaki et al., 1999). Despite results suggesting that some of the signs of the disorder could be reversed, the technique also provoked a host immune response against the added material. As a consequence, the biochemical changes lasted for only 10 days and they failed to reduce the serum phenylalanine concentration responsible for the cognitive delays observed among PKU patients. So, although there remains optimism that future advances will prove helpful in treating and preventing certain forms of developmental disorders, the medical advances are not sufficiently refined to be useful today.

Psychosocial interventions will need to parallel the advances in biomedical technology to ensure proper implementation. For example, biological risk factors for several of the developmental disorders include malnutrition and exposure to toxins including lead and alcohol (Bryant & Maxwell, 1999). Although medical researchers can identify the role of these biological events in cognitive development, psychologists will need to support these efforts. Behavioural intervention for safety training (e.g., involving lead-based paints in older homes), substance-use treatment and prevention, and behavioural medicine (e.g., "wellness" efforts) are examples of crucial roles played by psychologists that may contribute to preventing certain forms of developmental disorders.

## Concept Check 13.3

In the following situations, label each level of mental retardation as mild, moderate, severe, or profound. Also label the corresponding levels of necessary support: intermittent, limited, extensive, or pervasive.

1. Bobby received an IQ score of 45. He lives in a fully staffed group home and needs a great deal of help with many tasks. He is beginning to receive training for a job in the community. _____/_____
2. James received an IQ score of 20. He needs help with all his basic needs, including dressing, bathing, and eating. _____/_____
3. Komar received an IQ score of 65. He lives at home, goes to school, and is preparing to work when he is finished with school. _____/_____
4. Katie received an IQ score of 30. She lives in a fully staffed group home where she is trained in basic adaptive skills and communication. She is improving over time and can communicate by pointing or using her eye-gaze board. _____/_____

# Cognitive Disorders

- ▪ *Describe the symptoms of delirium and dementia, including what is known about their prevalence, causes, and treatment.*
- ▪ *Identify the principal causes of and treatments for amnestic disorders.*

Research on the brain and its role in psychopathology has increased at a rapid pace, and we have described many of the latest advances throughout this book. All the disorders we have reviewed are in some way influenced by the brain. We have seen, for example, that relatively subtle changes in neurotransmitter systems can significantly affect mood, cognition, and behaviour. Unfortunately, the brain is sometimes affected profoundly, and, when this happens, drastic changes occur. Remember, neurons do not regenerate when they are injured and die. Any such damage is as yet irreversible, usually accumulating until certain symptoms appear. In this section we examine the brain disorders that affect cognitive processes such as learning, memory, and consciousness.

Whereas mental retardation and other learning disorders are believed to be present from birth, most cognitive disorders develop much later in life. In this section we review three classes of cognitive disorders: *delirium*, an often temporary condition displayed as confusion and disorientation; *dementia*, a progressive condition marked by gradual deterioration of a broad range of cognitive abilities; and *amnestic disorders*, dysfunctions of memory caused by a medical condition or a drug or toxin.

The DSM-IV-TR label "cognitive disorders" reflects a shift in the way these disorders are viewed (Weiner, 2003). In previous editions of the DSM they were defined as "organic mental disorders," along with mood, anxiety, personality, hallucinosis, and delusional disorders. The word *organic* indicated that brain damage or dysfunction was believed to be involved. Although brain dysfunction is still thought to be the primary cause, we now know that some dysfunction in the brain is involved in most disorders described in DSM-IV-TR (American Psychiatric Association, 2000a).

We have repeatedly emphasized the complex relationship between neurological and psychosocial influences in many, if not all, psychological disorders. Few people would disagree, for example, that schizophrenia involves some damage to the brain. In one sense, then, most disorders are "organic." This fundamental shift in perspective immediately affected the categorizing of disorders. The term *organic mental disorders* covered so many as to make any distinction meaningless. Consequently, the traditional organic disorders—delirium, dementia, and amnestic disorders—were kept together, and the others—organic mood, anxiety, personality, hallucinosis, and delusional disorders—were categorized with disorders that shared their symptoms (such as anxiety and mood disorders).

Once the term *organic* was dropped, attention moved to developing a better label for delirium, dementia, and the amnestic disorders. The term *cognitive disorders* signifies that their predominant feature is the impairment of such cognitive abilities as memory, attention, perception, and thinking. Although disorders such as schizophrenia and depression also involve cognitive problems, they are not believed to be primary characteristics (Weiner, 2003). Problems still exist with this term, however, because although the cognitive disorders usually first appear in older adults, mental retardation and learning disorders, which are apparent early, also have cognitive impairment as a predominant characteristic. Forthcoming research may provide a more useful way of distinguishing among disorders. Figure 13.4 illustrates how the incidence of disability

due to cognitive functions (memory and speech) rise with increasing age, with rates being highest for these types of disability in those aged 65 and older. In contrast, the prevalence of disability due to psychological problems does not follow this age pattern and rates decline after age 65 (Statistics Canada, 2001b). As our life expectancy increases, cognitive disorders become more prevalent and have emerged as a major concern for mental health professionals.

As with certain other disorders, it may be useful to clarify why cognitive disorders are discussed in a textbook on abnormal psychology. Because they so clearly have organic causes, we could argue that they are purely medical concerns. We will see, however, that the consequences of a cognitive disorder often include profound changes in a person's behaviour and personality. Intense anxiety and/or depression are common, especially among people with dementia. In addition, paranoia is frequently reported, as are extreme agitation and aggression. Families and friends are also profoundly affected by such changes. Imagine your emotional distress as a loved one is transformed into a different person, often one who no longer remembers who you are or your history together. The deterioration of cognitive ability, behaviour, and personality and the effects on others are a major concern for mental health professionals.

## *Delirium*

The disorder known as **delirium** is characterized by impaired consciousness and cognition during the course of several hours or days (Conn & Lieff, 2001; Rahkonen et al., 2000). Delirium is one of the earliest-recognized mental disorders: Descriptions of people with these symptoms were written more than 2500 years ago (Lipowski, 1990). Consider the case of Mr. J.

### Mr. J.
#### Sudden Distress

Mr. J., an older gentleman, was brought to the hospital emergency room. He didn't know his own name and at times he didn't seem to recognize his daughter, who was with him. Mr. J. appeared confused, disoriented, and a little agitated. He had difficulty speaking clearly and could not focus his attention to answer even the most basic questions. Mr. J.'s daughter reported that he had begun acting this way the night

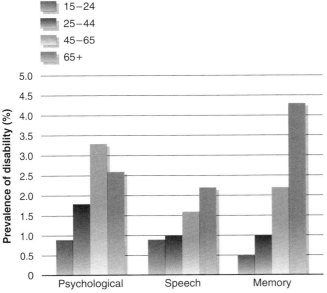

**Figure 13.4** ■ Rates for disability among Canadians aged 15 years and over, specific for age and source of disability: psychological, memory, or speech. (Adapted from the Statistics Canada, *A Profile of Disability in Canada, 2001*, Catalogue 89-577, December 2002.)

---

**delirium** Rapid-onset reduced clarity of consciousness and cognition, with confusion, disorientation, and deficits in memory and language.

before, had been awake most of the time since then, was frightened, and seemed even more confused today. She told the nurse that this behaviour was not normal for him and she was worried that he was becoming senile. She mentioned that his doctor had just changed his hypertension medication and wondered whether the new medication could be causing her father's distress. Mr. J. was ultimately diagnosed as having substance-induced delirium (a reaction to his new medication); once the medication was stopped, he improved significantly over the next 2 days. This scenario is played out daily in most major metropolitan hospital emergency rooms.

## Clinical Description and Statistics

People with delirium appear confused, disoriented, and out of touch with their surroundings. They cannot focus and sustain their attention on even the simplest tasks. There are marked impairments in memory and language. Mr. J. had trouble speaking; he was not only confused but also couldn't remember basic facts such as his own name. As we saw, the symptoms of delirium do not come on gradually but develop over hours or a few days, and they can vary over the course of a day.

Delirium is estimated to be present in as many as 10% to 30% of the people who come into acute care facilities such as emergency rooms (American Psychiatric Association, 2000a). A study by Michel Elie and his colleagues at McGill University determined the prevalence of delirium in emergency department patients aged 65 years and above to be about 10% (Elie et al., 2000). It is most prevalent among older adults, people undergoing medical procedures, cancer patients, and people with acquired immune deficiency syndrome (AIDS; Bourgeois, Seaman, & Servis, 2003). According to a review of the literature by Elie and his colleagues, the five most common risk factors for delirium are dementia (a cognitive disorder to be discussed in the next section of this chapter), medication, medical illness, older age, and male gender (Elie, Cole, Primeau, & Bellavance, 1998). Delirium subsides relatively quickly, with full recovery expected in most cases within several weeks. A minority of individuals continue to have problems on and off; some even lapse into a coma and may die. In fact, the symptoms of delirium are often present during the last several hours of life among terminally ill patients (Rockwood & Lindesay, 2002).

Many medical conditions that impair brain function have been linked to delirium, including intoxication by drugs and poisons; withdrawal from drugs such as alcohol and sedative, hypnotic, and anxiolytic

drugs; infections; head injury; and various other types of brain trauma (Bourgeois et al., 2003). DSM-IV-TR recognizes several causes of delirium among its subtypes. The criteria for *delirium due to a general medical condition* include a disturbance of consciousness (reduced awareness of the environment) and a change in cognitive abilities such as memory and language skills, occurring over a short period and brought about by a general medical condition. Other subtypes include the diagnosis received by Mr. J.—*substance-induced delirium—delirium due to multiple etiologies,* and *delirium not otherwise specified.* The last two categories indicate the often complex nature of delirium.

## Disorder Criteria Summary
### Delirium

Features of delirium include:
- Disturbance of consciousness with reduced ability to focus, sustain, or shift attention
- A change in cognition (such as a memory deficit or disorientation) that is not accounted for by dementia
- Disturbance develops over a short period and fluctuates during the course of the day
- Evidence of a physiological basis

*Source:* Based on DSM-IV-TR. Used with permission from the *Diagnostic and Statistical Manual of Mental Disorders,* Fourth Edition, Text Revision. Copyright 2000. American Psychiatric Association.

That delirium can be brought on by the improper use of medication can be a particular problem for older adults, because they tend to use prescription medications more than any other age group (Cole, 2004). Moreover, the elderly also tend to be multiple medication users (Millar, 1998), putting them at risk for adverse drug interactions. The risk of problems among the elderly is increased further because they tend to eliminate drugs from their systems less efficiently than younger individuals. It is not surprising, then, that adverse drug reactions resulting in hospitalization are almost six times higher among elderly people than in other age groups (Col, Fanale, & Kronholm, 1990). And it is believed that delirium brought on by improper use of medications contributes to the very large number of hip fractures that result annually from falls by older adults (Ray, Griffin, Schaffner, Baugh, & Melton, 1987) and the many serious car accidents that occur each year among elderly drivers (Ray, Fought, & Decker, 1992). Although there has been some improvement in the use of medication among older adults, improper use continues to produce serious side effects, including symptoms of delirium (Cole, 2004). Because possible combinations of illnesses and medications are so numerous, determining the cause of delirium is extremely difficult (Bourgeois et al., 2003).

Delirium may be experienced by children who have high fevers or who are taking certain medications and is often mistaken for non-compliance (Turkel & Tavaré, 2003). It often occurs during the course of dementia; as many as 44% of people with dementia suffer at least one episode of delirium (Bourgeois et al., 2003). Because many of the primary medical conditions can be treated, delirium is often reversed within a relatively short time.

Factors other than medical conditions can trigger delirium. Older adults are more susceptible to developing delirium as a result of mild infections or medication changes (American Psychiatric Association, 2000c). Sleep deprivation, immobility, and excessive stress can also cause delirium (Sandberg, Franklin, Bucht, & Gustafson, 2001).

### Treatment

Acute delirium and delirium brought on by withdrawal from alcohol or other drugs is usually treated with haloperidol or other antipsychotic medications, which help calm the individual (Brown, 2001; Wise, Hilty, & Cerda, 2001). Infections, brain injury, and tumours are given the necessary and appropriate medical intervention.

Psychosocial interventions may also be beneficial (American Psychiatric Association, 2000c). The goal of non-medical treatment is to reassure the person to help him or her deal with the agitation, anxiety, and hallucinations of delirium. A person in the hospital may be comforted by familiar personal belongings such as family photographs (Gleason, 2003). Also, a patient who is included in all treatment decisions retains a sense of control (Katz, 1993). This type of psychosocial treatment can help the person manage during this disruptive period until the medical causes are identified and addressed. Some evidence suggests that this type of support can also delay institutionalization for elderly patients (Rahkonen et al., 2001).

### Prevention

Preventive efforts may be most successful in assisting people who are susceptible to delirium. Proper medical care for illnesses and therapeutic drug monitoring can play a significant role in preventing delirium.

## Concept Check 13.4

Match the terms with the following descriptions of delirium: (a) elderly, (b) counselling, (c) trauma, (d) memory, (e) confused, (f) cause

1. Various types of brain _____, such as head injury or infection, have been linked to delirium.
2. Delirium severely affects people's _____, making tasks such as recalling one's own name difficult.
3. Treatment of delirium depends upon the _____ of the episode and can include medications and/or psychosocial intervention.
4. People who suffer from delirium appear to be _____ or out of touch with their surroundings.
5. The _____ population is at the greatest risk of experiencing delirium because of improper use of medications.

## *Dementia*

Few things are more frightening than the possibility that you will one day not recognize those you love, that you will not be able to perform the most basic of tasks, and, worse yet, that you will be acutely aware of this failure of your mind. When family members show these signs, adult children often deny any difficulty, coming up with excuses ("I forget things, too") for their parents' failing abilities. **Dementia** is the cognitive disorder that makes these fears real: a gradual deterioration of brain functioning that affects judgment, memory, language, and other advanced cognitive processes. Dementia is caused by several medical conditions and by the abuse of drugs or alcohol that cause negative changes in cognitive functioning. Some of these conditions—for instance, infection or depression—can cause dementia, although it is often reversible through treatment of the primary condition. Some forms of the disorder, such as Alzheimer's disease, are at present irreversible. Although delirium and dementia can occur together, dementia has a gradual progression as opposed to delirium's acute onset; people with dementia are not disoriented or confused in the early stages, unlike people with delirium. Like delirium, however, dementia has many causes, including a variety of traumas to the brain such as stroke (which destroys blood vessels), the infectious diseases of syphilis and HIV, severe head injury, the introduction of certain toxic or poisonous substances, and diseases such as Parkinson's, Huntington's and the most common cause of dementia, Alzheimer's disease. Consider the rare personal account by Diana, a woman who poignantly writes of her experiences with this disorder (McGowin, 1993).

**dementia** Gradual-onset deterioration of brain functioning involving memory loss, inability to recognize objects or faces, and problems in planning and abstract reasoning. These are associated with frustration and discouragement.

## Diana
### Humiliation and Fear

At the age of 45, Diana Friel McGowin was a successful legal assistant, wife, and mother, but she was beginning to experience "lapses." She writes about developing these problems just before the party she was planning for her family.

*Nervously, I checked off the table appointments on a list retrieved from my jumpsuit pocket. Such a list had never been necessary before, but lately I noticed frequent little episodes of confusion and memory lapses.*

*I had decided to "cheat" on this family buffet and have the meal prepared on a carry-out basis. Cooking was also becoming increasingly difficult, due to what my children and my husband Jack teasingly referred to as my "absentmindedness" (pp. 1–2).*

In addition to memory difficulties, other problems began at this time, including brief dizzy spells. Diana wrote of her family's growing awareness of the additional symptoms.

*Shaun walked past me on his way to the kitchen, and paused. "Mom, what's up? You look ragged," he commented sleepily. "Late night last night, plenty of excitement, and then up early to get your father off to work," I answered. Shaun laughed disconcertingly. I glanced up at him ruefully. "What is so funny?" I demanded. "You, Mom! You are talking as though you are drunk or something! You must really be tired!" (pp. 4–5).*

In the early stages of her dementia, Diana tended to explain these changes in herself as temporary, with such causes as tension at work. However, the extent of her dysfunction continued to increase, and she had more frightening experiences. In one episode, she describes an attempt to drive home from a brief errand.

*Suddenly, I was aware of car horns blowing. Glancing around, nothing was familiar. I was stopped at an intersection and the traffic light was green. Cars honked impatiently, so I pulled straight ahead, trying to get my bearings. I could not read the street sign, but there was another sign ahead; perhaps it would shed some light on my location. A few yards ahead, there was a park ranger building. Trembling, I wiped my eyes, and breathing deeply, tried to calm myself. Finally, feeling ready to speak, I started the car again and approached the ranger station. The guard smiled and inquired how he could assist me. "I appear to be lost," I began, making a great effort to keep my voice level, despite my emotional state. "Where do you need to go?" the guard asked politely. A cold chill enveloped me as I realized I could not remember the name of my street. Tears began to flow down my cheeks. I did not know where I wanted to go (pp. 7–8).*

Diana's difficulties continued. She sometimes forgot the names of her children and once astounded her nephew when she didn't recognize him. If she left home, she almost invariably got lost. She learned to introduce herself as a tourist from out of town, because people would give her better directions. She felt as if there "was less of me every day than there was the day before."

During initial medical examinations, Diana didn't recall this type of problem in her family history. However, a look through some of her late mother's belongings revealed that she was not the first to experience symptoms of dementia.

*Then I noticed the maps. After mother's death I had found mysterious hand drawn maps and bits of directions scribbled on note papers all over her home. They were in her purses, in bureau drawers, in the desks, seemingly everywhere. Too distraught at the time to figure out their purpose, I simply packed them all away with other articles in the box. Now I smoothed out each map and scrawled note, and placed them side by side. They covered the bedroom floor. There were maps to every place my mother went about town, even to my home and my brother's home. As I deciphered each note and map, I began recollecting my mother's other eccentric habits. She would not drive out of her neighborhood. She would not drive at night. She was teased by both myself and my brother about "memory goofs" and would become irate with both of her children over their loving teasing.*

*Then with a chill, I recalled one day when I approached my mother to tell her something, and she did not recognize me (p. 52).*

After several evaluations, which included an MRI showing some damage in several parts of her brain, Diana's neurologist concluded that she had dementia. The cause could be a stroke she had several years before that damaged several small areas of her brain by breaking or blocking several blood vessels. The dementia could also indicate Alzheimer's disease. People at the same stage of decline as Diana Friel McGowin will continue to deteriorate and eventually may die from complications of their disorder.

## Clinical Description and Statistics

Depending on the individual and the cause of the disorder, the gradual progression of dementia may have somewhat different symptoms, although all aspects of cognitive functioning are eventually affected. In the initial stages, memory impairment is typically seen as an inability to register ongoing events. In other words, a person can remember how to talk, and may remember events from many years ago, but have trouble remembering what happened in the past hour. For example, Diana still knew how to use the stove but couldn't remember whether she had turned it on or off.

Diana couldn't find her way home because visuospatial skills are impaired among people with dementia. **Agnosia,** the inability to recognize and name objects, is one of the most familiar symptoms. **Facial agnosia,** the inability to recognize even familiar faces, can be extremely distressing to family members. Diana failed to recognize not only her nephew but also co-workers whom she had seen every day for years. A general deterioration of intellectual function results from impairment in memory, planning, and abstract reasoning.

Perhaps because victims of dementia are aware that they are deteriorating mentally, emotional changes often occur as well. Common side effects are delusions (irrational beliefs), depression, agitation, aggression, and apathy (Lyketsos et al., 2000). Again, it is difficult to establish the cause-and-effect relationship. We don't know how much behavioural change is caused by progressive brain deterioration directly and how much is a result of the frustration and discouragement that inevitably accompany the loss of function and the isolation of "losing" loved ones. Cognitive functioning continues to deteriorate until the person requires almost total support to carry out day-to-day activities. Ultimately, death

occurs as the result of inactivity combined with the onset of other illnesses such as pneumonia.

Dementia can occur at almost any age, although dementia of the Alzheimer's type rarely occurs in people under 45 years of age (American Psychiatric Association, 2000d). The incidence of dementia is highest in older adults. According to the Canadian Study of Health and Aging (Rockwood, Wolfson, & McDowell, 2001), about 8% of Canadians over 65 are affected by Alzheimer's disease and related dementias (Canadian Study of Health and Aging Working Group, 1994). This study found a prevalence of 2% in people between 65 and 74; this rate increased to a little over 10% in those aged 75 to 84 and to more than 30% in people aged 85 and older (see Figure 13.5; Canadian Study of Health and Aging Working Group, 1994).

The actual rate may be considerably higher, however, especially among older adults. Evans and colleagues (1989) estimated that 47% of adults over the age of 85 may have dementia of the Alzheimer's type and a study of centenarians (people 100 years and older) found that almost 90% showed signs of dementia (Blansjaar, Thomassen, & Van Schaick, 2000). Thus, prevalence rates have varied considerably across studies. This discrepancy in estimates may result from several factors. For example, using data from the Canadian Study of Health and Aging, researchers at the University of Western Ontario and the London Health Sciences Centre have demonstrated how the use of different diagnostic

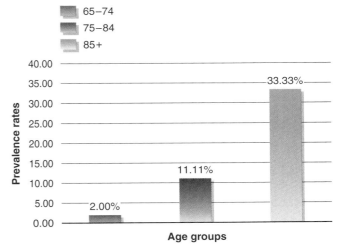

**Figure 13.5** ■ Prevalence of dementia in three age groups of elderly Canadians. (Adapted from Canadian Study of Health and Aging Working Group: Canadian Study of Health and Aging: Study methods and prevalence of dementia. *CMAJ* 1994; 150: 899–913.)

People with facial agnosia, a common symptom of dementia, are unable to recognize faces, even those of their closest friends and relatives.

**agnosia** Inability to recognize and name objects; may be a symptom of dementia or other brain disorders.

**facial agnosia** Type of agnosia characterized by a person's inability to recognize even familiar faces.

criteria can dramatically affect prevalence estimates for dementia (Erkinjuntti, Ostbye, Steenhuis, & Hachinski, 1997).

An additional problem with confirming prevalence figures for dementia is that survival rates alter the outcomes. Incidence studies, which count the number of new cases in a year, may thus be the most reliable method for assessing the frequency of dementia, especially among the elderly. In one study, the annual incidence rates for dementia were 2.3% for people 75 to 79 years of age, 4.6% for people 80 to 84 years of age, and 8.5% for those 85 and older (Paykel et al., 1994). The research showed that the rate for new cases doubled with every 5 years of age. In addition, the rate for dementia was comparable for men and women and was equivalent across educational level and social class. Many other studies, however, find greater increases of dementia among women (e.g., Canadian Study of Health and Aging Working Group, 2000), although this may be because of the tendency of women to live longer. Dementia of the Alzheimer's type may, as we discuss later, be more prevalent among women. Together, results suggest that dementia is a relatively common disorder among older adults, and the chances of developing it increase rapidly after the age of 75.

In addition to the human costs of dementia, the medical costs are staggering. But medical costs are only a fraction of the total financial burden of caring for a person with dementia. Yearly nursing home costs are astounding. Many times family members care for an afflicted person around the clock, which is an inestimable personal and financial commitment (Bourgeois et al., 2003). In a review of the literature, a team of researchers in Hong Kong found that the economic costs associated with the care of individuals with dementia of the Alzheimer's type were highly variable across studies. This variation was mostly due to differences in the methods that researchers used to calculate economic costs and to variations in care patterns in different areas of the world. The researchers concluded, however, that there is little doubt that the economic impact of dementia is substantial (Leung, Yeung, Chi, & Chu, 2003). Authors of a recent Canadian review drew similar conclusions and warned that the economic impact of dementia is likely to worsen worldwide as a greater proportion of the world's population becomes elderly (Alloul et al., 1998).

The statistics on prevalence and incidence cover dementias that arise from a variety of etiologies. DSM-IV-TR groups are based on presumed cause, but determining the cause of dementia is an inexact process. Sometimes, as with dementia of the Alzheimer's type, clinicians rely on ruling out alternative explanations—identifying all the things that are not the cause—instead of determining the precise origin.

Five classes of dementia based on etiology have been identified: (1) dementia of the Alzheimer's type, (2) vascular dementia, (3) dementia due to other general medical conditions, (4) substance-induced persisting dementia, and (5) dementia due to multiple etiologies. A sixth, dementia not otherwise specified, is included when etiology cannot be determined. We emphasize dementia of the Alzheimer's type because of its prevalence (almost half of those with dementia exhibit this type) and the relatively large amount of research conducted on its etiology and treatment.

## Dementia of the Alzheimer's Type

The German psychiatrist Alois Alzheimer first described the disorder that bears his name in 1906. He wrote of a 51-year-old woman who had a "strange disease of the cerebral cortex" that manifested as a progressive memory impairment and other behavioural and cognitive problems including suspiciousness (Weiner, 2003). He called the disorder an "atypical form of senile dementia;" thereafter, it was referred to as **Alzheimer's disease.**

The DSM-IV-TR diagnostic criteria for **dementia of the Alzheimer's type** include multiple cognitive deficits that develop gradually and steadily. Predominant is the impairment of memory, orientation, judgment, and reasoning. The inability to integrate new information results in failure to learn new associations. Individuals with Alzheimer's disease forget important events and lose objects. Their interest in non-routine activities narrows. They tend to lose interest in others and, as a result, become more socially isolated. As the disorder progresses, they can become agitated, confused, depressed, anxious, or even combative. Many of these difficulties become more pronounced late in the day—in a phenomenon referred to as *sundowner syndrome*—perhaps as a result of fatigue or a disturbance in the brain's biological clock (Weiner, 2003).

As noted in a review by University of Western Ontario researchers Edward Helmes and Truls Ostbye (2002), people with dementia of the Alzheimer's type also display one or more other cognitive disturbances,

---

**Alzheimer's disease**   The "strange disease of the cerebral cortex" that causes an "atypical form of senile dementia," discovered in 1906 by the German psychiatrist Alois Alzheimer.

**dementia of the Alzheimer's type**   Gradual onset of cognitive deficits caused by Alzheimer's disease, principally identified by a person's inability to recall newly or previously learned material. The most common form of dementia.

including **aphasia** (difficulty with language), *apraxia* (impaired motor functioning), *agnosia* (failure to recognize objects), or difficulty with activities such as planning, organizing, sequencing, or abstracting information. One example of the language difficulties experienced by people with Alzheimer's disease is *anomia* (problems with naming objects; Auchterlonie, Phillips, & Chertkow, 2002). These cognitive impairments also have a serious negative impact on social and occupational functioning and represent a significant decline from previous abilities.

---

### Disorder Criteria Summary
#### Alzheimer's Disease

Features of dementia of the Alzheimer's type include:
- Multiple cognitive deficits, including memory impairment, and at least one of the following disturbances: aphasia, apraxia, agnosia, or disturbance in executive functioning (e.g., planning, sequencing)
- Significant impairment in functioning, involving a decline from previous level
- Gradual onset and continuing cognitive decline

*Source:* Based on DSM-IV-TR. Used with permission from the *Diagnostic and Statistical Manual of Mental Disorders*, Fourth Edition, Text Revision. Copyright 2000. American Psychiatric Association.

---

A definitive diagnosis of Alzheimer's disease can be made only after an autopsy determines that certain characteristic types of damage are present in the brain, although clinicians are accurate in identifying this condition in living patients 70% to 90% of the time (Bourgeois et al., 2003). To make a diagnosis without direct examination of the brain, a simplified version of a mental status exam is used to assess language and memory problems (see Table 13.1).

In an interesting, somewhat controversial study, the writings of a group of Catholic nuns collected over several decades appeared to indicate early in life which women were most likely to develop Alzheimer's disease later (Massie et al., 1996). Researchers observed that samples from the nuns' journals over the years differed in the number of ideas each contained, which the scientists called "idea density." Some sisters described events in their lives simply: "I was born in Eau Claire, Wis, on May 24, 1913 and was baptized in St. James Church." Others were more elaborate: "The happiest day of my life so far was my First Communion Day, which was in June nineteen hundred and twenty when I was but eight years of age, and four years later in the same month I was confirmed by Bishop D. D. McGavich." When autopsy findings on 14 of the nuns were correlated with idea density, the simple writing (low idea density) occurred among all five of the nuns with Alzheimer's disease (Massie et al., 1996). This

---

**aphasia** Impairment or loss of language skills resulting from brain damage caused by stroke, Alzheimer's disease, or other illness or trauma.

---

## TABLE 13.1 Testing For Dementia Of The Alzheimer's Type

**One part of the diagnosis of the dementia of Alzheimer's disease uses a relatively simple test of the patient's mental state and abilities like this one, called the Mini Mental State Inpatient Consultation Form. A low score on such a test does not necessarily indicate a medical diagnosis of dementia.**

| Type* | Maximum Score† | Question |
|---|---|---|
| Orientation | 5 | What is the (year) (season) (date) (day) (month)? |
| | 5 | Where are we (province or territory) (country) (town) (hospital) (floor)? |
| Registration | 3 | Name three objects, using 1 second to say each. Then ask the patient all three after you have said them. Give one point for each correct answer. Then repeat them until the patient learns all three. Count and record the number of trials. |
| Attention and Calculation | 5 | Count backward from given number (like 100) by subtracting 7s. (Give one point for each correct answer; stop after five answers.) Alternatively, spell "world" backward. |
| Recall | 3 | Name the three objects learned above. (Give one point for each correct answer.) |
| Language | 9 | Have a patient name a pencil and a watch. (1 point) |
| | | Repeat the following: "No ifs, ands, or buts." (1 point) |
| | | Follow a three-stage command: "Take a piece of paper in your right hand, fold it in half, and put it on the floor." (3 points) |
| | | Read and obey the following: "Close your eyes." (1 point) |
| | | Write a sentence. (1 point) |
| | | Copy this design. (1 point) |

*The examination also includes an assessment of the patient's level of consciousness:   Alert   Drowsy   Stupor   Coma.
†Total maximum score is 30.

*Source:* Adapted from the Mini Mental State examination form, Folstein, Folstein, & McHugh, 1975.

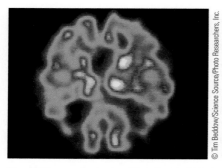 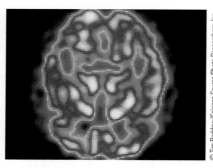

The PET scan of a brain afflicted with Alzheimer's disease (left) shows significant tissue deterioration in comparison with a normal brain (right).

is an elegant research study because the daily lives of the nuns were similar on a day-to-day basis, which ruled out many other possible causes. However, we must be cautious in depending on this study, because only a small number of people were examined. It is not yet clear that dementia of the Alzheimer's type has such early signs, but research continues in the hope of early detection so that early intervention can be developed.

One encouraging recent finding by Holly Tuokko at the University of Victoria suggests that elderly people's performance on a drawing test, often used to supplement the mental status exam described earlier, can be useful in identifying which elderly individuals will develop dementia in the future (O'Rourke, Tuokko, Hayden, & Beattie, 1997). The drawing test is a subtest of the Clock Test (Tuokko, Hadjistavropoulos, Rae, & O'Rourke, 2000). The patient is asked to place numbers on a drawing of a circle to make it into a clock, and to place the clock's hands in the position to indicate the time as 11:10. Errors are scored. This test is already established as helpful in identifying patients with Alzheimer's disease (Shulman, Shedletsky, & Silver, 1986). The more recent longitudinal research suggests that the clock drawing test may also prove to be a useful tool for early detection (O'Rourke et al., 1997).

Cognitive deterioration of the Alzheimer's type is slow during the early and later stages but more rapid during the middle stages (Stern et al., 1994). Although it was once thought that the average survival time was about 8 years (Report of the Advisory Panel on Alzheimer's Disease, 1995), recent Canadian data suggest that the survival time may be much shorter. Christina Wolfson of McGill University and her colleagues made use of data from the Canadian Study of Health and Aging and found that the median survival time after the onset of Alzheimer's disease was only 3 years (Wolfson et al., 2001). In some forms, the disease can occur relatively early, during the 40s or 50s (sometimes referred to as presenile dementia), but it usually appears during the 60s or 70s (Wise, Gray, & Seltzer, 1999). Approximately 50% of the cases of

dementia are ultimately found to be the result of Alzheimer's disease, which is believed to afflict more than 238 000 Canadians over age 65 and many millions more worldwide (Canadian Study on Health and Aging Working Group, 2001).

Some research on prevalence suggests that Alzheimer's disease may occur most often in people who are poorly educated (Fratiglioni et al., 1991; Korczyn, Kahana, & Galper, 1991). Greater impairment among uneducated people might indicate a much earlier onset, suggesting that Alzheimer's disease causes intellectual dysfunction that in turn hampers educational efforts. Or there could be something about intellectual achievement that prevents or delays the onset or symptoms of the disorder. To address these issues, Stern and colleagues (1994) examined the incidence of Alzheimer's type dementia to learn whether educational levels affected who would and who would not later be diagnosed with the disorder. They found that those with the least amount of formal education were more likely to develop dementia than those with more education. It is important that the researchers were able to study living individuals before they could be identified as having dementia; such a prospective study rules out many alternative explanations for the results. Stern and his colleagues concluded that educational attainment may somehow create a mental "reserve," involving a learned set of skills that help a person cope longer with the cognitive deterioration that marks the beginning of dementia. Like Diana's mother, who made copious notes and maps to help her function despite her cognitive deterioration, some people may adapt more successfully than others and thus escape detection longer. Brain deterioration may thus be comparable for both groups, but better educated individuals may be able to function successfully on a day-to-day basis for a longer period. This tentative hypothesis may prove useful in designing treatment strategies, especially during the early stages of the disorder.

A biological version of this theory—called the *cerebral reserve hypothesis*—suggests that the more synapses a person develops throughout life, the more neuronal death must take place before the signs of dementia are obvious (Bourgeois et al., 2003; Tanzi & Parson, 2000). Mental activity that occurs with education presumably builds up this reserve of synapses and serves as a protective factor in the development of the disorder. It is likely that both skill development and the changes in the brain with education may contribute to how quickly the disorder progresses.

Research suggests that Alzheimer's disease may be more prevalent among women (Alzheimer's Society of Canada, 2004; Garre-Olmo et al., 2004), even when women's higher survival rate is factored into the statistics. In other words, because women live longer than men on average, they are more likely to experience Alzheimer's and other diseases, but longevity alone does not account for the higher prevalence of the disorder among women. A tentative explanation involves the hormone estrogen. Women lose estrogen as they grow older, so perhaps it is protective against the disease. Research supporting this hypothesis found that women who participate in estrogen replacement therapy after menopause may have a later onset or reduced incidence of Alzheimer's disease (Lambert, Coyle, & Lendon, 2004; Shepherd, 2001).

Finally, there appear to be questions about the prevalence of Alzheimer's disease according to racial identity. Early research seemed to suggest that certain populations (such as those with Japanese, Nigerian, certain Native American, and Amish backgrounds) were less likely to be affected (e.g., Pericak-Vance et al., 1996; Rosenberg et al., 1996). However, more recent work indicates that some of these differences may have been the result of differences in who seeks assistance (which is seen as unacceptable in some cultural groups) and differences in education (which we saw may delay the onset of obvious symptoms; Fitzpatrick et al., 2004). Findings such as these help bring us closer to understanding the causes of this devastating disease.

## Vascular Dementia

Each year, 500 000 people die from strokes (any diseases or traumas to the brain that result in restriction or cessation of blood flow). Although stroke is one of the top causes of death in Canadian seniors (Stokes & Lindsay, 1996), many people survive, but one potential long-term consequence can be severely debilitating. According to University of Toronto neuropsychologist Donald Stuss, **vascular dementia** is a progressive brain disorder that is second only to Alzheimer's disease as a cause of dementia (Stuss & Cummings, 1990). The word *vascular* refers to blood vessels. When the blood vessels in the brain are blocked or damaged and no longer carry oxygen and other nutrients to certain areas of brain tissue, damage results. MRI scans of Diana Friel McGowin's brain showed a number of damaged areas, or multiple infarctions, left by a stroke several years earlier; this was one probable cause of her dementia. Because multiple sites in the brain can be damaged, the profile of degeneration—the particular skills that are impaired—differs from person to person. DSM-IV-TR lists as criteria for

vascular dementia the memory and other cognitive disturbances that are identical to those for dementia of the Alzheimer's type. However, certain neurological signs of brain tissue damage, such as abnormalities in walking and weakness in the limbs, are observed in many people with vascular dementia but not in people in the early stages of dementia of the Alzheimer's type.

In comparison with research on dementia of the Alzheimer's type, there are fewer studies on vascular dementia, perhaps because of its lower incidence rates. One study, of people living in a Swedish city, suggests that the lifetime risk of having vascular dementia is 4.7% among men and 3.8% among women (Hagnell et al., 1992). The higher risk for men is typical for this disorder, in contrast with the higher risk among women for Alzheimer's type dementia (Alzheimer's Society of Canada, 2004). The relatively high rate of cardiovascular disease among men in general may account for their increased risk of vascular dementia. The onset of vascular dementia is typically more sudden than for the Alzheimer's type, probably because the disorder is the result of stroke, which inflicts brain damage immediately. The outcome, however, is similar for people with both types: Ultimately, they will require formal nursing care until they succumb to an infectious disease such as pneumonia.

## Dementia Due to Other General Medical Conditions

In addition to Alzheimer's disease and vascular damage, a number of other neurological and biochemical processes can lead to dementia. DSM-IV-TR lists several other types with specific causes, including *dementia due to HIV disease, dementia due to head trauma, dementia due to Parkinson's disease, dementia due to Huntington's disease, dementia due to Pick's disease,* and *dementia due to Creutzfeldt-Jakob disease.* Each of these is discussed here. Other medical conditions that can lead to dementia include normal pressure hydrocephalus (excessive water in the cranium because of brain shrinkage), hypothyroidism (an underactive thyroid gland), brain tumour, and vitamin B12 deficiency. In their effect on cognitive ability, these disorders are comparable to the other forms of dementia we have discussed so far.

---

**vascular dementia** Progressive brain disorder involving loss of cognitive functioning caused by blockage of blood flow to the brain. Appears concurrently with other neurological signs and symptoms.

The human immunodeficiency virus-type-1, which causes acquired immune deficiency syndrome (AIDS), can also cause dementia (i.e., **HIV-1 disease;** S. Perry, 1993; Robinson & Qaqish, 2002). This impairment seems to be independent of the other infections that accompany HIV; in other words, the HIV infection itself seems to be responsible for the neurological impairment (Bourgeois et al., 2003). The early symptoms of dementia due to HIV are cognitive slowness, impaired attention, and forgetfulness. Affected individuals also tend to be clumsy, to show repetitive movements such as tremors and leg weakness, and to become apathetic and socially withdrawn (Navia, 1990).

People with HIV seem particularly susceptible to cognitive impairments in the later stages of HIV infection, although significant impairment of cognitive abilities may occur earlier (Heaton et al., 1994). Cognitive impairments are observed in 29% to 87% of people with AIDS (Lipton & Weiner, 2003), and approximately one-third of the infected people ultimately meet the criteria for dementia due to HIV disease (Day et al., 1992; Price & Brew, 1988). HIV disease accounts for a relatively small percentage of people with dementia compared with Alzheimer's disease and vascular causes, but its presence complicates an already devastating and ultimately fatal set of conditions.

Like dementia from Parkinson's disease, Huntington's disease, and several other causes, dementia resulting from HIV is sometimes referred to as *subcortical dementia*, because it affects primarily the inner areas of the brain, below the outer layer called the *cortex* (Bourgeois et al., 2003). The distinction between "cortical" (including dementia of the Alzheimer's type) and "subcortical" is important because of the different expressions of dementia in these two categories (see Table 13.2). *Aphasia*, which involves impaired language skills, occurs among people with dementia of the Alzheimer's type but not among people with subcortical dementia. In contrast, people with subcortical dementia are more likely to experience severe depression and anxiety than those with dementia of the Alzheimer's type. In general, motor skills including speed and coordination are impaired early on among those with subcortical dementia. The differing patterns of impairment can be attributed to the different areas of the brain affected by the disorders.

**Head trauma,** injury to the head and therefore to the brain, is typically caused by accidents and can lead to cognitive impairments in both children and adults. Memory loss is the most common symptom (Lipton & Weiner, 2003).

**Parkinson's disease** is a degenerative brain disorder that affects about 1 out of every 1000 people worldwide (Freedman, 1990). Nearly 100 000 people

**TABLE 13.2** Characteristics of Dementias

| Characteristic | Dementia of the Alzheimer's Type | Subcortical Dementias |
|---|---|---|
| Language | Aphasia (difficulties with articulating speech) | No aphasia |
| Memory | Both recall and recognition are impaired | Impaired recall; normal or less impaired recognition |
| Visuospatial skills | Impaired | Impaired |
| Mood | Less severe depression and anxiety | More severe depression and anxiety |
| Motor speed | Normal | Slowed |
| Coordination | Normal until late in the progression | Impaired |

*Source:* From Table I-2: "Contrasting Characteristics of Cortical and Subcortical Dementia Syndromes" p. 7, adapted from *Subcortical Dementia*, edited by Jeffrey L. Cummings. Copyright © 1990 by Jeffrey L. Cummings. Used by permission of Oxford University Press.

in Canada have Parkinson's (Parkinson Society of Canada, 2002). Movie and television star Michael J. Fox has this progressive disorder. Motor problems are characteristic among people with Parkinson's disease, who tend to have stooped posture, slow body movements (called *bradykinesia*), tremors, and jerkiness in walking. The voice is also affected; afflicted individuals speak in a soft monotone. The changes in motor movements are the result of damage to dopamine pathways. Because dopamine is involved in complex movement, a reduction in this neurotransmitter makes affected individuals increasingly unable to control their muscle movements, which leads to tremors and muscle weakness.

Some people with Parkinson's develop dementia (La Rue, 1992); conservative estimates place the rate at twice that found in the general population (Gibb, 1989). The pattern of impairments for these individuals fits the general pattern of subcortical dementia (Table 13.2).

**Huntington's disease** is a genetic disorder that initially affects motor movements, typically in the form of *chorea*, involuntary limb movements

---

**HIV-1 disease** Human immunodeficiency virus-type-1 that causes AIDS and can cause dementia.

**head trauma** Injury to the head and therefore to the brain, typically caused by accidents; can lead to cognitive impairments, including memory loss.

**Parkinson's disease** Degenerative brain disorder principally affecting motor performance (e.g., tremors, stooped posture) associated with reduction in dopamine. Dementia may be a result as well.

**Huntington's disease** Genetic disorder marked by involuntary limb movements and progressing to dementia.

AP/Wide World Photos

Edmonton native Michael J. Fox provides his time and celebrity status to efforts to cure Parkinson's disease, a degenerative disease that is severely affecting his life.

(Folstein, Brandt, & Folstein, 1990). People with Huntington's can live for 20 years after the first signs of the disease appear, although skilled nursing care is often required during the last stages. Just as with Parkinson's disease, only a portion of people with Huntington's disease go on to display dementia—somewhere between 20% and 80%—although some researchers believe that all Huntington's patients would eventually display dementia if they lived long enough (Edwards, 1994). Dementia due to Huntington's disease also follows the subcortical pattern.

The search for the gene responsible for Huntington's disease is like a detective story. For some time researchers have known that the disease is inherited as an autosomal dominant disorder, meaning that approximately 50% of the offspring of an adult with Huntington's will develop the disease. Since 1979, Wexler and colleagues (e.g., Wexler et al., 2004) have been studying the largest known extended family in the world afflicted by Huntington's disease, in small villages in Venezuela. The villagers have cooperated with the research, in part because Wexler herself lost her mother, three uncles, and her maternal grandfather to Huntington's, and she too may have the disorder (Turkington, 1994). Using genetic linkage analysis techniques (see Chapter 3), these researchers first mapped the deficit to an area on chromosome 4 (Gusella et al., 1983) and then identified the elusive

gene (Huntington's Disease Collaborative Research Group, 1993). Finding that one gene causes a disease is exceptional; research on other inherited mental disorders typically points to multiple gene (polygenic) influences.

**Pick's disease** is a rare neurological condition that produces a cortical dementia similar to that of Alzheimer's disease. The course of this disease is believed to last from 5 to 10 years, although its cause is as yet unknown (McDaniel, 1990). Like Huntington's disease, Pick's disease usually occurs relatively early in life—during a person's 40s or 50s—and is therefore considered an example of presenile dementia. An even rarer condition, **Creutzfeldt-Jakob disease,** is believed to affect only one in every million individuals (Edwards, 1994). An alarming development in the study of Creutzfeldt-Jakob disease is the finding of 10 cases of a new variant that may be linked to bovine spongiform encephalopathy (BSE), more commonly referred to as "mad cow disease" (Smith & Cousens, 1996). This discovery led to a ban on exporting beef from the United Kingdom because the disease might be transmitted from infected cattle to humans. More recently, we experienced similar problems in Canada. In May 2003, veterinary officials in Alberta identified a single sick cow. This announcement led the United States and Mexico to institute a ban on Canadian beef which resulted in a severe slump in the Canadian beef industry (CBC News Online, 2004b). We do not yet have definitive information about the link between mad cow disease and the new form of Creutzfeldt-Jakob disease.

## Substance-Induced Persisting Dementia

Prolonged drug use, especially in combination with poor diet, can damage the brain and, in some circumstances, can also lead to dementia. As many as 7% of individuals who are dependent on alcohol meet the criteria for dementia (Oslin & Cary, 2003). DSM-IV-TR identifies several drugs that can lead to symptoms of dementia, including alcohol, inhalants such as glue or gasoline (which some people inhale for the euphoric feeling they produce), and the sedative, hypnotic, and anxiolytic drugs (see Chapter 10). These drugs pose a threat because they create dependence, making it difficult for a user to stop ingesting them. The resulting brain damage can be permanent and can cause the same symptoms seen in dementia of the Alzheimer's type

**Pick's disease** Rare neurological disorder that results in presenile (early onset) dementia.

**Creutzfeldt-Jakob disease** Extremely rare condition that causes dementia.

(Parsons & Nixon, 1993). The DSM-IV-TR criteria for substance-induced persisting dementia are essentially the same as for the other forms of dementia; they include memory impairment and at least one of the following cognitive disturbances: aphasia (language disturbance), apraxia (inability to carry out motor activities despite intact motor function), agnosia (failure to recognize or identify objects despite intact sensory function), or a disturbance in executive functioning (such as planning, organizing, sequencing, and abstracting).

## Causes of Dementia

As our technology for studying the brain advances, so does our understanding of the many and varied causes of dementia. A complete description of what we know about the origins of this type of brain impairment is beyond the scope of this book, but we next highlight some of the insights available for more common forms of dementia.

**Biological Influences** Cognitive abilities can be adversely compromised in many ways. As we have seen, dementia can be caused by a number of processes: Alzheimer's disease, Huntington's disease, Parkinson's disease, head trauma, substance abuse, and others. The most common cause of dementia, Alzheimer's disease, is also the most mysterious. Because of its prevalence and our relative ignorance about the factors responsible for it, Alzheimer's disease has held the attention of a great many researchers who are trying to find the cause and ultimately a treatment or cure for this devastating condition.

Findings from Alzheimer's research seem to appear almost daily. We should be cautious when interpreting the output of this fast-paced and competitive field; too often, as we have seen in other areas, findings are heralded prematurely as conclusive and important. Remember that "discoveries" of a single gene for bipolar disorder, schizophrenia, and alcoholism were later shown to be based on overly simplistic accounts. Similarly, findings from Alzheimer's research are sometimes too quickly sanctioned as accepted truths before they have been replicated, an essential validation process.

One lesson in scientific caution comes from research that demonstrates a negative correlation between cigarette smoking and Alzheimer's disease (Brenner et al., 1993). In other words, the study found that smokers are less likely than nonsmokers to develop Alzheimer's disease. Does this mean smoking has a protective effect, shielding a person against the development of this disease? On close examination, the finding may instead be the result of the differential survival rates of those who smoke and those who do not. In general, nonsmokers tend to live longer and are thereby more likely to develop Alzheimer's disease, which appears later in life. Some believe the relative inability of cells to repair themselves, a factor that may be more pronounced among people with Alzheimer's disease, may interact with cigarette smoking to shorten the lives of smokers who are at risk for Alzheimer's (Riggs, 1993). Put another way, smoking may exacerbate the degenerative process of Alzheimer's disease, causing people with the disease who also smoke to die much earlier than nonsmokers who have Alzheimer's. These types of studies and the conclusions drawn from them should make us sensitive to the complicated nature of the disorders we study.

Another theory about Alzheimer's disease that remains largely unsubstantiated is the aluminum hypothesis, which asserts that exposure to aluminum (e.g., through occupational exposure) is involved in causing Alzheimer's disease. However, many studies, such as the large-scale Canadian Study of Health and Aging, have failed to support a strong role of aluminum exposure as a risk factor (Canadian Study of Health and Aging Working Group, 1994). Most scientists now conclude that if aluminum exposure plays any role in Alzheimer's disease, the role is small (Alzheimer's Association, 2004).

What do we know about Alzheimer's disease, the most common cause of dementia? After the death of the patient he described as having a "strange disease of the cerebral cortex," Alois Alzheimer performed an autopsy. He found that the brain contained large numbers of tangled, strand-like filaments (referred to as *neurofibrillary tangles*). This type of damage occurs in everyone with Alzheimer's disease, although we do not know what causes it. A second type of degeneration results from gummy protein deposits—called *amyloid plaques* (also referred to as *senile* or *neuritic plaques*)—that accumulate in the brains of people with this disorder. Amyloid plaques are also found in older adults who do not have symptoms of dementia, but they have far fewer of them than individuals with Alzheimer's disease (Bourgeois et al., 2003). Both forms of damage—neurofibrillary tangles and amyloid plaques—accumulate over the years and are believed to produce the characteristic cognitive disorders we have been describing.

These two types of degeneration affect extremely small areas and can be detected only by a microscopic examination of the brain. Even sophisticated brain-scan techniques are not yet powerful enough to observe these changes in the living brain, which is why a definitive diagnosis of Alzheimer's disease requires an autopsy. In addition to having neurofibrillary tangles and amyloid plaques, over time the brains of many people with Alzheimer's disease atrophy (shrink) to a greater extent than would be expected through normal aging (Bourgeois et al., 2003). Because brain shrinkage has many causes, however, only by observing the tangles and plaques can a diagnosis of Alzheimer's be properly made.

Rapid advances are being made toward uncovering the genetic bases of Alzheimer's disease (Merikangas & Risch, 2003). Because important discoveries happen almost daily, we cannot speak conclusively; however, certain overall themes have arisen from genetic research. As with most other behavioural disorders we have examined, multiple genes seem to be involved in the development of Alzheimer's disease. Table 13.3 illustrates what we know so far. Genes on chromosomes 21, 19, 14, 12, and 1 have all been linked to certain forms of Alzheimer's disease (Marx, 1998). The link to chromosome 21 was discovered first and resulted from the unfortunate observation that individuals with Down syndrome, who have three copies of chromosome 21 instead of the usual two, developed the disease at an unusually high rate (Report of the Advisory Panel on Alzheimer's Disease, 1995). More recent work has located relevant genes on other chromosomes. These discoveries indicate that there is more than one genetic cause of Alzheimer's disease. Some forms, including the one associated with chromosome 14, have an early onset. A team of researchers at the University of Toronto headed by geneticist and neurologist Peter St. George-Hyslop were the first to uncover gene mutations on chromosome 14 in the early-onset familial form of Alzheimer's disease (Jeffrey, 1995; Sherrington et al., 1995). Diana Friel McGowin may have an early-onset form, because she started noting symptoms at the age of 45. In contrast, Alzheimer's disease associated with chromosome 19 seems to be a late-onset form of the disease that has an effect only after about age 60.

Some of the genes that are now identified are *deterministic,* meaning that if you have one of these genes you have a nearly 100% chance of developing Alzheimer's (Merikangas & Risch, 2003). Deterministic genes such as the β-amyloid precursor gene and the Presenilin-1 and Presenilin-2 genes will inevitably lead to Alzheimer's, but, fortunately, these genes are rare in the general population. For treatment purposes, this means that even if we can find a way to prevent these genes from leading to Alzheimer's, it will only help a relatively small number of people. On the other hand, some genes—including the apolipoprotein-E 4 (ApoE4) gene—are known as *susceptibility* genes. These genes only slightly increase your risk of developing Alzheimer's, but in contrast to the deterministic genes, these are more common in the general population (Merikangas & Risch, 2003). If future research can find ways to interfere with the ApoE4 gene, many people will be helped.

Although closing in on the genetic origins of Alzheimer's has not brought immediate treatment implications, researchers are nearer to understanding how the disease develops, which may result in improved medical interventions in the future. Genetic research has advanced our knowledge of how the amyloid plaques develop in the brains of people with Alzheimer's disease, and this knowledge may hold a clue to the disease's origins. In the core of the plaques is a solid, waxy substance called *amyloid protein.* Just as cholesterol buildup on the walls of blood vessels chokes the blood supply, deposits of amyloid proteins are believed by some researchers to cause the cell death associated with Alzheimer's (Bourgeois et al., 2003).

For all of the disorders described in this book, we have identified the role of biological and/or psychological stressors as partially responsible for the onset of the disorder. Does dementia of the Alzheimer's type—which appears to be a strictly biological event—follow the same pattern? One of the leading candidates for an external contributor to this disorder is head trauma. It appears that repeated blows to the head can bring on *dementia pugilistica,* named after the boxers who suffer from this type of dementia. Fighters who carry the ApoE4 gene may be at greater risk for developing dementia attributed to head trauma (Jordan et al., 1997). Head trauma may be one stressor that initiates the onset of dementias of varying types. As with each of the disorders discussed, psychological and biological stressors may interact with physiological processes to produce Alzheimer's disease.

**Psychological and Social Influences**   Research has mostly focused on the biological conditions that produce dementia. Although few would claim that psychosocial influences directly cause the type of brain deterioration seen in people with dementia, they may help determine onset and course. For example, a person's lifestyle may involve contact with factors that can cause dementia. We saw, for instance, that substance abuse can lead to dementia

| **TABLE 13.3** | Genetic Factors in Alzheimer's Disease | |
|---|---|---|
| Gene | Chromosome | Age of Onset |
| APP | 21 | 45 to 66 |
| Presenilin 1 | 14 | 28 to 62 |
| Presenilin 2 | 1 | 40 to 85 |
| ApoE4 | 19 | 60 |
| A2M | 12 | 70 |

*Source:* "New Gene Tied to Common Form of Alzheimer's," by J. Marx, *Science,* 291, 507–509. Copyright © 1998 AAAS. Adapted with permission.

and, as we discussed previously (see Chapter 10), whether a person abuses drugs is determined by a combination of biological and psychosocial factors. In the case of vascular dementia, a person's biological vulnerability to vascular disease will influence the chances of strokes that can lead to this form of dementia. Lifestyle issues such as diet, exercise, and stress influence cardiovascular disease and therefore help determine who ultimately experiences vascular dementia.

Cultural factors may also affect this process. For example, hypertension and strokes are prevalent among Blacks and those of Asian heritage (Cruickshank & Beevers, 1989), which may explain why vascular dementia is more often observed in members of these groups (de la Monte, Hutchins, & Moore, 1989). In an extreme example, exposure to a viral infection can lead to dementia similar in form to Creutzfeldt-Jakob disease and to mad cow disease (both of which were discussed earlier in the chapter) through a condition known as *kuru*. Kuru is a fatal disease of the nervous system that is caused by a slow-acting virus. This virus is passed through a ritual form of cannibalism practised in Papua New Guinea as a part of mourning (Gajdusek, 1977). In yet another example of how cultural factors may play a role, dementia caused by head trauma and malnutrition are relatively prevalent in preindustrial rural societies (Lin, 1986; Westermeyer, 1989), which suggests that social engineering in the form of occupational safety and economic conditions influencing diet also affect the prevalence of certain forms of dementia. It is apparent that psychosocial factors help influence who does and who does not develop certain forms of dementia. Brain deterioration is a biological process but, as we have seen throughout this text, even biological processes are influenced by psychosocial factors.

Psychosocial factors also influence the course of dementia. Recall that educational attainment may affect the onset of dementia (Fratiglioni et al., 1991; Korczyn et al., 1991). Having certain skills may help some people cope better than others with the early stages of dementia. As we saw earlier, Diana Friel McGowin's mother was able to carry on her day-to-day activities by making maps and using other tricks to help compensate for her failing abilities. The early stages of confusion and memory loss may be better tolerated in cultures with lowered expectations of older adults. In certain cultures, including the Chinese, younger people are expected to take the demands of work and care from older adults after a certain age (Ikels, 1991). Dementia may go undetected for years in these societies.

Much remains to be learned about the cause and course of most types of dementia. As we saw in Alzheimer's and Huntington's disease, certain genetic factors make some individuals vulnerable to progressive cognitive deterioration. In addition, brain trauma, some diseases, and exposure to certain drugs such as alcohol, inhalants, and the sedative, hypnotic, and anxiolytic drugs can cause the characteristic decline in cognitive abilities. We also noticed that psychosocial factors can help determine who is subject to these causes and how they cope with the condition. Looking at dementia from this integrative perspective should help us view treatment approaches in a more optimistic light. It may be possible to protect people from conditions that lead to dementia and to support them in dealing with the devastating consequences of having it. We next review attempts to help from both biological and psychosocial perspectives.

## Treatment

For many of the disorders we have considered, treatment prospects are fairly good. Clinicians can combine various strategies to reduce suffering significantly. Even when treatment does not bring expected improvements, mental health professionals have usually been able to stop problems from progressing. This is not the case in the treatment of dementia.

One factor preventing major advances in the treatment of dementia is the nature of the damage caused by this disorder. The brain contains billions of neurons, many more than are used. Damage to some can be compensated for by others because of plasticity. However, there is a limit to where and how many neurons can be destroyed before vital functioning is disrupted. Neurons are currently irreplaceable, although researchers are closing in on this previously insurmountable obstacle (Kirschenbaum et al., 1994). Therefore, with extensive brain damage, no known treatment can restore lost abilities. The goals of treatment therefore become (1) trying to prevent certain conditions, such as substance abuse, that may bring on dementia; (2) trying to stop the brain damage from spreading and becoming worse; and (3) attempting to help these individuals and their caregivers cope with the advancing deterioration. Most efforts in treating dementia have focused on the second and third goals, with biological treatments aimed at stopping the cerebral deterioration and psychosocial treatments directed at helping patients and caregivers cope.

A troubling statistic further clouds the tragic circumstances of dementia: More than half the caregivers of people with dementia—usually relatives—eventually become clinically depressed (Burns, 2000; Clyburn, Stones, Hadjistavropoulos, & Tuokko, 2000). Compared with the general public, these caregivers are twice as likely to develop depression (Canadian Study of Health and Aging

Working Group, 1994), and they use more psychotropic medications and report stress symptoms at three times the normal rate (George, 1984). Caring for people with dementia, especially in its later stages, is clearly an especially trying experience (O'Rourke & Cappeliez, 2002). As a result, clinicians are becoming increasingly sensitive to the needs of these caregivers and research is exploring interventions to assist them to care for people with dementia (Gottlieb & Johnson, 2000; Hepburn, Tornatore, Center, & Ostwald, 2001).

**Biological Treatments** Dementia due to known infectious diseases, nutritional deficiencies, and depression can be treated if it is caught early. Unfortunately, however, no known treatment exists for most types of dementia responsible for the vast majority of cases. Dementia due to stroke, HIV, Parkinson's disease, and Huntington's disease is not currently treatable because there is no effective treatment for the primary disorder. However, exciting research in several related areas has brought us closer to helping individuals with these forms of dementia. Substances that may help preserve and perhaps restore neurons—called *glial cell-derived neurotrophic factor*—may someday be used to help reduce or reverse the progression of degenerative brain diseases (Tomac et al., 1995). Researchers are also looking into the possible benefits of transplanting fetal brain tissue (taken from aborted fetuses) into the brains of people with such diseases. Preliminary results from these studies appear promising (e.g., Kopyov, Jacques, Lieberman, Duma, & Rogers, 1996). Dementia brought on by strokes may now be more preventable by new drugs that help prevent much of the damage inflicted by the blood clots that are characteristic of stroke (Bourgeois et al., 2003). Most current attention is on a treatment for dementia of the Alzheimer's type, because it affects so many people. Here, too, success has been modest at best.

Much work has been directed at developing drugs that will enhance the cognitive abilities of people with dementia of the Alzheimer's type (Rockwood & Joffres, 2002). Many seem to be effective initially, but long-term improvements have not been observed in placebo-controlled studies (Bourgeois et al., 2003). Several drugs that have had a modest impact on cognitive abilities in some patients include tacrine hydrochloride (Cognex), donepezil (Aricept), rivastigmine (Exelon), and galantamine (Reminyl; Weiner & Schneider, 2003). These drugs prevent the breakdown of the neurotransmitter acetylcholine, which is deficient in people with Alzheimer's disease, thus making more acetylcholine available to the brain. Research suggests that people's cognitive abilities improve to the point where they were 6 months earlier (Rogers &

Friedhoff, 1996; Samuels & Davis, 1997). But the gain is not permanent. Even people who respond positively do not stabilize but continue to experience the cognitive decline associated with Alzheimer's disease. In addition, if they stop taking the drug—as almost three-quarters of the patients do because of negative side effects such as liver damage and nausea—they lose even that 6-month gain (Winker, 1994). The drugs and required testing are quite costly, so the affected person and the family must decide whether the cost is worth the temporary benefit.

Several other medical approaches appear to hold promise in slowing the course of Alzheimer's disease. For example, most of you have heard of using *Ginkgo biloba* (maidenhair) to improve memory. Several studies suggest that this herbal remedy may produce modest improvements in the memory of people with Alzheimer's disease (Weiner & Schneider, 2003). Similarly, the effects of vitamin E have been evaluated. One large study found that among individuals with moderately severe impairment, high doses of the vitamin (2000 IU per day) delayed progression compared with a placebo (Sano et al., 1997). Several findings point to the beneficial effects of estrogen replacement therapy (prescribed for some women following menopause) on Alzheimer's disease (e.g., Tang et al., 1996). Finally, aspirin and other nonsteroidal anti-inflammatory drugs have also been demonstrated to be helpful in slowing the onset of the disease (Stewart, Kawas, Corrada, & Metter, 1997). To date, however, no drugs are available that directly treat and therefore completely stop the progression of the conditions that cause the cerebral damage in Alzheimer's disease.

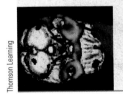

***Computer Simulations and Senile Dementia***
*"Our cognitive activity arises from the neural networks in the brain. Whenever you lose an individual neuron, you're not losing an idea, you're just losing a tiny bit of the resolution, or the crispness, of that idea."*

Thomson Learning

**Psychosocial Treatments** Psychosocial treatments focus on enhancing the lives of people with dementia and their families. People with dementia can be taught skills to compensate for their lost abilities. Recall that Diana's mother learned on her own to make maps to help her get from place to place. Diana herself began making lists so that she would not forget important things. Some researchers have evaluated more formal adaptations to help people in the early stages of dementia. Bourgeois (1992, 1993) created "memory wallets" to help people with dementia carry on conversations. On white index cards inserted into a plastic wallet are printed declarative statements such as "My husband John and I have 3 children," or "I was born on January 6, 1921, in Winnipeg." In one study, Bourgeois (1992) found that six adults with dementia could, with minimal training, use this memory aid to improve their conversations with others. Three of the adults used their memory wallets with people who had initially not been involved in the training, such as children and grandchildren. (One participant withdrew from the training after several weeks, which seemed to coincide with a substantial decline in her cognitive abilities during that time.) Other researchers have used similar devices to help people orient themselves in time and place, another ability disrupted by dementia (Hanley, 1986; Hanley & Lusty, 1984). Adaptations such as these help people communicate with others and remain aware of their surroundings, and these can also reduce the frustration that accompanies the awareness of their own decline.

Individuals with advanced dementia are not able to feed, bathe, or dress themselves. They cannot communicate with or recognize even familiar family members. They may wander from home and become lost. Because they are no longer aware of social stigma, they may engage in public displays of sexual behaviour such as masturbation. They may be frequently agitated or even physically violent. To help both the person with dementia and the caregiver, researchers have explored interventions for dealing with these consequences of the disorder (Fisher & Carstensen, 1990). For example, some research indicates that a combination of exercise for patients and teaching caregivers how to

handle their behaviour problems can improve the overall health and the depression in people with Alzheimer's (Teri et al., 2003).

Of great concern is the tendency of people with dementia to wander. Sometimes they wind up in places or situations that may be dangerous (e.g., stairwells, the street). Often, the person with dementia is tied to a chair or bed, or sedated, to prevent roaming. Unfortunately, physical and medical restraint has its own risks, including additional medical complications; it also adds greatly to the loss of control and independence that already plague the person with dementia. Psychological treatment as an alternative to restraint sometimes involves providing cues for people to help them safely navigate around their home or other areas (Hussian & Brown, 1987). Coloured arrows and grids on the floor indicate "safe" and "dangerous" areas, allowing people more freedom to be mobile; they also relieve caregivers of the necessity of constant monitoring.

Someone with dementia can become agitated and sometimes be verbally and physically aggressive. This behaviour is understandably very stressful for people trying to provide care. In these situations, medical intervention is often used, although frequently with only modest results (Loebel, Dager, & Kitchell, 1993). Caregivers are often given assertiveness training to help them deal with hostile behaviours. Otherwise, caregivers may either passively accept all the criticism inflicted by the person with dementia, which increases stress, or become angry and aggressive in return. This last response is of particular concern because of the potential for *elder abuse*. Four percent or approximately 100 000 elderly people living in private dwellings in Canada have recently suffered elder abuse (Alberta Family and Social Services, 1990). Withholding food or medication or inflicting physical abuse is most common among caregivers of elderly people who have cognitive deficits (Sachs & Cassel, 1989). It is important to teach caregivers how to handle stressful circumstances so that they do not escalate into abusive situations. Little objective evidence supports the usefulness of assertiveness training for reducing caregiver stress, and we await research to guide future efforts.

In general, families of people with dementia can benefit from supportive counselling to help them cope with the frustration, depression, guilt, and loss that take a heavy emotional toll. One group, which conducted a large-scale study of 555 principal caregivers over a 3-year period, identified a number of steps that can be taken to support caregivers through this difficult time (Aneshensel, Pearlin, Mullan, Zarit, & Whitlatch, 1995). Early on, caregivers need basic information on the causes and treatment of dementia, as well as on financial and

© John Livzey

Simple signs and labels can help people with memory loss.

legal issues, and on locating help for the patient and the family. As the dementia progresses, and the affected person increasingly requires assistance, caregivers will need help managing behavioural difficulties (wandering away, violent outbursts) and developing effective ways to communicate with the patient. Clinicians also assist the family with decisions about hospitalizations and, finally, help them adjust during bereavement (Martin-Cook, Svetlik, & Weiner, 2003).

Overall, the outlook for stopping the cognitive decline characteristic of dementia is not good, and we have no sense that a research breakthrough is imminent. The best available medications provide some recovery of function, but they do not stop the progressive deterioration. Psychological interventions may help people cope more effectively with the loss of cognitive abilities, especially in the earlier stages of this disorder, but for now the emphasis is on helping caregivers—the other victims of dementia—as the person they care for continues to decline.

### Prevention

Several avenues are now being explored as potential opportunities to prevent dementia in older adults (Black, Patterson, & Feightner, 2001). Estrogen replacement therapy, for example, appears to be related to decreased risk of dementia of the Alzheimer's type among women (Shepherd, 2001), although there is, in turn, an increased risk of breast cancer. Preliminary research indicates that proper treatment of systolic hypertension may also cut the risk of dementia (Clarke, 1999). Because of the possible role in the development of dementia, proper treatment and prevention of stroke should reduce dementia related to cerebrovascular disease. Safety measures that result in a widespread reduction in head trauma and reduced exposure to neurotoxins may also aid this effort. The judicious use of non-steroidal anti-inflammatory medication also appears to decrease the relative risk of developing dementia of the Alzheimer's type (Black et al., 2001). There appear to be many potentially fruitful research areas that may lead to the successful prevention of this devastating disorder.

## Concept Check 13.5

**Part A** Identify the following symptoms of dementia from the given descriptions: (a) facial agnosia, (b) agnosia, (c) aphasia.

1. Your elderly Aunt Bessie can no longer form complete, coherent sentences. _____
2. She does not recognize her own home any longer. _____

3. Aunt Bessie no longer recognizes you when you visit, even though you are her favourite niece. _____

**Part B** Identify the cognitive disorders described.

4. A decline in cognitive functioning that is gradual and continuous and has been associated with neurofibrillary tangles and amyloid plaques. _____
5. Grandpa has suffered from a number of strokes but can still care for himself. However, his ability to remember important things has been declining steadily for the past few years. _____

## *Amnestic Disorder*

Say these three words to yourself: *apple, bird, roof*. Try to remember them, and then count backward from 100 by 3s. After about 15 seconds of counting, can you still recall the three words? Probably so. However, people with *amnestic disorder* will not remember them, even after such a short period (Bourgeois et al., 2003). The loss of this type of memory, which we described as a primary characteristic of dementia, can occur without the loss of other high-level cognitive functions. The main deficit of **amnestic disorder** appears to be the inability to transfer information like the list we just described into long-term memory, which can cover minutes, hours, or years. This disturbance in memory is caused by either the physiological effects of a medical condition, such as head trauma, or the long-term effects of a drug. Consider the case of S.T.

### S.T.
#### Remembering Fragments

S.T., a 67-year-old White woman, suddenly fell, without loss of consciousness. She appeared bewildered and anxious but oriented to person and place yet not to time. Language functioning was normal. She was unable to recall her birthplace, the ages of her children, or any recent Canadian prime ministers. She could not remember three objects for 1 minute, nor recall what she had eaten for her last meal. She could not name the colour of any object shown to her

---

**amnestic disorder** Deterioration in the ability to transfer information from short- to long-term memory in the absence of other dementia symptoms, as a result of head trauma or drug abuse.

but could correctly name the colour related to certain words—for example, "grass," "sky." Object naming was normal. Examined 1 year later, she could repeat five digits forward and backward but could not recall her wedding day, the cause of her husband's death, or her children's ages. She did not know her current address or phone number and remembered zero out of three objects after 5 minutes. While she was described by her family as extremely hard-working prior to her illness, after hospitalization she spent most of her time sitting and watching television. She was fully oriented, displayed normal language function, and performed simple calculations without error (Cole, Winkelman, Morris, Simon, & Boyd, 1992, pp. 63–64).

The DSM-IV-TR criteria for amnestic disorder describe the inability to learn new information or to recall previously learned information. As with all cognitive disorders, memory disturbance causes significant impairment in social and occupational functioning. The woman we just described (S.T.) was diagnosed with a type of amnestic disorder called *Wernicke-Korsakoff syndrome*, which is caused by damage to the thalamus, a small region deep inside the brain that acts as a relay station for information from many other parts of the brain. In her case, the damage to the thalamus was believed to be the result of a stroke that caused vascular damage. Another common cause of the Wernicke-Korsakoff syndrome is chronic heavy alcohol use. As you saw, S.T. had

pronounced difficulty recalling information presented just minutes before. Although she could repeat a series of numbers, she couldn't remember three objects that were presented to her moments earlier. As with other people with amnestic disorder, despite these obvious deficits with her memory, her language command was fine and she could perform simple chores. Yet these individuals are often significantly impaired in social or vocational functioning because of the importance of memory to such activities.

As we saw with the other cognitive impairments, a range of traumas to the brain can cause permanent amnestic disorders. Research has focused on attempting to prevent the damage associated with Wernicke-Korsakoff syndrome. Specifically, a deficiency in thiamine (vitamin B1) because of alcohol abuse in people developing Wernicke-Korsakoff syndrome is leading researchers to try supplementing this vitamin, especially for very heavy drinkers (e.g., Bowden, Bardenhagen, Ambrose, & Whelan, 1994; Martin, Pekovich, McCool, Whetsell, & Singleton, 1994). To date, however, there is little research pointing to successful long-term assistance in treating people with amnestic disorders (Burke & Bohac, 2001).

---

## Disorder Criteria Summary
### Amnestic Disorder

Features of amnestic disorder include:
- Development of memory impairment such as inability to learn new information or inability to recall previously learned information
- Significant impairment in functioning, representing a decline from previous level
- Disturbance does not occur exclusively during the course of delirium or dementia
- Evidence of a physiological basis, such as head trauma

*Source:* Based on DSM-IV-TR. Used with permission from the *Diagnostic and Statistical Manual of Mental Disorders*, Fourth Edition, Text Revision. Copyright 2000. American Psychiatric Association.

---

### Amnestic Disorder: Mike

*"I still have a pretty major memory problem, which has since brought about a divorce and which I now have a new girlfriend, which helps very much. I even call her … my new brain or my new memory.… If I want to know something, besides on relying on this so-called memory notebook, which I jot notes down in constantly and have it every day dated, so I know what's coming up or what's for that day. She also helps me very much with the memory. My mother types up the pages for this notebook, which has each half hour down and the date, the day and the date, which anything coming within an hour or two or the next day or the next week, I can make a note of it so that when that morning comes, and I wake up, I right away, one of the first things, is look at the notebook. What have I got to do today?"*

Thomson Learning

---

## Concept Check 13.6

Insert either a T for true or F for false for statements pertaining to amnestic disorder.

1. The abuse of alcohol and trauma to the brain can cause amnestic disorders. _____
2. Ginkgo biloba has been found to be effective in treating amnestic disorders. _____
3. Amnestic disorder refers to the inability to learn new information or to recall previously learned information. _____

# Summary

## Common Developmental Disorders

- Developmental psychopathology is the study of how disorders arise and change with time. These changes usually follow a pattern, with the child mastering one skill before acquiring the next. This aspect of development is important because it implies that any disruption in the acquisition of early skills will, by the very nature of the developmental process, also disrupt the development of later skills.

- The primary characteristics of people with attention deficit/hyperactivity disorder are a pattern of inattention (such as not paying attention to school- or work-related tasks), or hyperactivity-impulsivity, or both. These deficits can significantly disrupt academic efforts and social relationships.

- DSM-IV-TR groups the learning disorders as reading disorder, mathematics disorder, and disorder of written expression. All are defined by performance that falls far short of expectations based on intelligence and school preparation.

- Verbal or communication disorders seem closely related to learning disorders. They include stuttering, a disturbance in speech fluency; expressive language disorder, very limited speech in all situations but without the types of cognitive deficits that lead to language problems in people with mental retardation or one of the pervasive developmental disorders; selective mutism, refusal to speak despite having the ability to do so; and tic disorder, which includes involuntary motor movements such as head twitching and vocalizations such as grunts that occur suddenly, in rapid succession, and in idiosyncratic or stereotyped ways.

## Pervasive Developmental Disorders

- People with pervasive developmental disorders all experience trouble progressing in language, socialization, and cognition. The use of the word *pervasive* means these are not relatively minor problems (like learning disabilities) but conditions that significantly affect how individuals live. Included in this group are autistic disorder, Rett's disorder, Asperger's disorder, and childhood disintegrative disorder.

- Autistic disorder, or autism, is a childhood disorder characterized by significant impairment in social interactions, gross and significant impairment in communication, and restricted patterns of behaviour, interest, and activities. It probably does not have a single cause; instead, a number of biological conditions may contribute, and these, in combination with psychosocial influences, result in the unusual behaviours displayed by people with autism.

## Mental Retardation

- The definition of mental retardation has three parts: significantly subaverage intellectual functioning, concurrent deficits or impairments in present adaptive functioning, and an onset before the age of 18.

- Down syndrome is a type of mental retardation caused by the presence of an extra 21st chromosome. It is possible to detect the presence of Down syndrome in utero through a process known as amniocentesis.

- Two other types of mental retardation are common: fragile X syndrome, which is caused by a chromosomal abnormality of the tip of the X chromosome, and cultural-familial retardation, the presumed cause of up to 75% of mental retardation cases, which is thought to be caused by a combination of psychosocial and biological factors.

## Delirium

- Delirium is a temporary state of confusion and disorientation that can be caused by brain trauma, intoxication by drugs or poisons, surgery, and a variety of other stressful conditions, especially among older adults.

## Dementia

- Dementia is a progressive and degenerative condition marked by gradual deterioration of a broad range of cognitive abilities including memory, language, and planning, organizing, sequencing, and abstracting information.

- Alzheimer's disease is the leading cause of dementia; there is currently no known cause or cure.

- To date, there is no effective treatment for the irreversible dementias caused by Alzheimer's disease, Parkinson's disease, Huntington's disease, and the various other less common conditions that produce this progressive cognitive impairment. Treatment often focuses on helping the patient cope with the continuing loss of cognitive skills and helping caregivers deal with the stress of caring for the affected individuals.

## Amnestic Disorder

- Amnestic disorders involve a dysfunction in the ability to recall recent and past events. The most common is Wernicke-Korsakoff syndrome, a memory disorder usually associated with chronic alcohol abuse.

## Key Terms

attention deficit/ hyperactivity disorder (ADHD), 524
learning disorders, 528
reading disorder, 529
mathematics disorder, 529
disorder of written expression, 529
stuttering, 530
expressive language disorder, 530
selective mutism, 530

tic disorder, 530
pervasive developmental disorders, 533
autistic disorder (autism), 533
Asperger's disorder, 533
Rett's disorder, 533
childhood disintegrative disorder, 533
pervasive developmental disorder—not otherwise specified, 533

mental retardation, 540
Down syndrome, 545
fragile X syndrome, 546
cultural-familial retardation, 547
delirium, 551
dementia, 553
agnosia, 555
facial agnosia, 555
Alzheimer's disease, 556
dementia of the Alzheimer's type, 556

aphasia, 557
vascular dementia, 559
HIV-1 disease, 560
head trauma, 560
Parkinson's disease, 560
Huntington's disease, 560
Pick's disease, 561
Creutzfeldt-Jakob disease, 561
amnestic disorder, 567

## Answers to Concept Checks

**13.1** 1. a  2. d  3. a  4. a  5. b

**13.2** 1. childhood disintegrative disorder
2. pervasive developmental disorder—not otherwise specified  3. autistic disorder
4. Rett's disorder  5. Asperger's disorder

**13.3** 1. moderate/limited support  2. profound/ pervasive support  3. mild/intermittent support  4. severe/extensive support

**13.4** 1. c  2. d  3. f  4. e  5. a

**13.5 Part A**  1. c  2. b  3. a

**Part B**  4. dementia of the Alzheimer's type
5. vascular dementia

**13.6** 1. T  2. F  3. T

## InfoTrac College Edition

If your instructor ordered your book with InfoTrac College Edition, please explore this online library for additional readings, review, and a handy resource for short assignments. Go to:

**http://infotrac.thomsonlearning.com**

Enter these search terms: attention-deficit hyperactivity disorder, language acquisition, language disorders in children, pervasive developmental disorder, mental retardation, Down syndrome, behaviour disorders in children, autism, autistic children, Asperger's syndrome, prenatal screening, learning disabilities, delirium, dementia, Alzheimer's disease, head trauma, Parkinson's disease, Huntington's chorea, Creutzfeldt-Jakob disease

## The Abnormal Psychology Book Companion Website

Go to **www.essentialsabnormalpsych.nelson.com** for practice quiz questions, Internet links, critical thinking exercises, and more.

## Abnormal Psychology Live CD-ROM

- **Edward:** This segment shows interviews with Edward, who suffers from ADHD, and his teacher, who describes Edward's struggles in school and the various strategies to help his grades reflect his high level of intelligence.
- **Sean:** This child's mother and psychologists describe and discuss Sean's behaviour before his treatment with a behaviour modification program at school and at home. Clinician Dr. Jim Swanson also discusses what we believe is involved in ADHD.
- **Christina:** This clip shows Christina's school, where we see how she spends a typical day in a mainstreamed classroom. There are interviews with her teacher's aide and a background interview

with Dr. Mark Durand to describe functional communication issues and other cutting-edge research trends in autism.

- **Rebecca:** This segment shows an autistic child in a mainstreamed grade 1 classroom and interviews her teachers about what strategies work best in helping Rebecca learn and control her behaviour.
- **Lauren:** The teacher and mother of a kindergartner with Down syndrome are interviewed to discuss strategies for teaching her new skills and managing her behaviour difficulties.
- **Neural Networks—Cognition and Dementia:** In this clip, Dr. James McClelland proposes that computer simulations of the brain's neural networks can reveal how human cognition works— and even how cognition fails in dementia.
- **Mike, an Amnestic Patient:** Following an accident, Mike struggles with memory problems that affect his employment, his relationship, and his sense of self. You'll notice how he expresses himself both in his language and the flatness of his emotion.
- **Life Skills:** This segment shows an empirically validated program that teaches anger management to reduce violence in school-aged and adolescent students.
- **Bullying Prevention:** This segment features an empirically validated program that shows how to teach students specific strategies for dealing with bullying behaviours in school.

- **Nature of the Disorder—Autism:** Dr. Mark Durand's research program deals with the motivation behind problem behaviours and how communication training can be used to lessen such behaviours.
- **Tom, a Patient with Alzheimer's:** This is a rather moving clip in which Tom's family talks about him, and we see a surprising example of memory that still works.

**Thomson NOW!** **http://hed.nelson.com** Go to this site for the link to ThomsonNow™, your one-stop study shop. Take a Pretest for this chapter and ThomsonNow™ will generate a personalized Study Plan based on your test results! The Study Plan will identify the topics you need to review and direct you to online resources to help you master those topics. You can then take a Posttest to help you determine the concepts you have mastered and what you still need work on.

## Video Concept Review

For challenging concepts that typically need more than one explanation, Mark Durand provides a video review via ThomsonNow™ of the following topic:

- The difference between delirium and dementia.

# Chapter Quiz

1. According to the DSM-IV-TR, the two symptoms that are characteristic of ADHD are:

   a. inattention and hyperactivity.
   b. echolalia and impulsivity.
   c. hallucinations and delusions.
   d. obsessions and compulsions.

2. Echolalia is characterized by which of the following behaviours?

   a. continuously reading the same sentence or words
   b. repeating the speech of others
   c. mimicking the movements of others
   d. staring ahead without blinking for long periods

3. Behavioural techniques are often used to address communication problems that occur with autism. _____ involves rewarding the child for progressive approximations of speech, and _____ involves rewarding the child for making sounds that the teacher requests.

   a. Shaping; discrimination training
   b. Modelling; syntax training
   c. Imitating; expression training
   d. Processing; academic training

4. Research has shown that ADHD in children is associated with:

   a. chronic neglect.
   b. having an alcoholic father.
   c. maternal smoking during pregnancy.
   d. death of a parent in early childhood.

5. The regulated breathing method, a behavioural technique used to reduce _____, involves taking a deep breath when an episode occurs before continuing.

   a. motor tics
   b. stuttering
   c. mutism
   d. impulsivity

6. _____ is a form of mental retardation caused by the presence of an extra 21st chromosome.

   a. Down syndrome
   b. Fragile X syndrome
   c. PKU syndrome
   d. Fetal alcohol syndrome

7. Joe has mild mental retardation. His therapist is teaching him a skill by breaking it down into its component parts. Joe's therapist is implementing what technique?

   a. skills treatment
   b. biofeedback
   c. component processing
   d. task analysis

8. _____ is characterized by acute confusion and disorientation; whereas _____ is marked by deterioration in a broad range of cognitive abilities.

   a. Delirium; amnesia
   b. Amnesia; delirium
   c. Dementia; delirium
   d. Delirium; dementia

9. Which disorder can be diagnosed definitively only at autopsy by the presence of large numbers of amyloid plaques and neurofibrillary tangles?

   a. vascular dementia
   b. dementia of the Alzheimer's type
   c. delirium
   d. Parkinson's disease

10. Psychological and social influences are important to consider when studying dementia because they:

   a. can accelerate the type of brain damage seen in this disease.
   b. provide a rationale for psychopharmacological intervention.
   c. may help determine the time of onset and course of dementia.
   d. can be used to reverse the progression of Alzheimer's disease.

*(See the Appendix on page 601 for answers.)*

# Exploring Developmental Disorders

Disorders that appear early in life and disrupt the normal course of development.

- Interrupting or preventing the development of one skill impedes mastery of the skill that is normally acquired next.
- Knowing what skills are disrupted by a particular disorder is essential to developing appropriate intervention strategies.

**COGNITION**
**LANGUAGE**
**SOCIALIZATION**

## TYPES OF DEVELOPMENTAL DISORDERS

### ATTENTION DEFICIT/HYPERACTIVITY DISORDER

**Description:**
- Inattentive, overactive, and impulsive behaviour
- Disrupted schooling and relationships
- Symptoms may change with maturity, but problems persist
- More prevalent in boys than girls

**Causes**
- Research suggests hereditary factor
- Abnormal neurology
- Possible link with maternal smoking
- Negative responses by others create low self-esteem

**Treatment**
- Biological (medication)
  - improves compliance
  - decreases negative behaviours
  - effects not long term
- Psychological (behavioural)
  - goal setting and reinforcement

### LEARNING DISORDERS

**Description:**
- Reading, math, and written expression fall behind IQ, age, and education
- May also be accompanied by ADHD

**Causes**
- Theories assume genetic, neurobiological, and environmental factors

**Treatment**
- Education intervention
  - basic processing
  - cognitive and behavioural skills

Photodisc/Getty Images

### COMMUNICATION DISORDERS

Closely related to learning disorders, but comparatively benign. Early appearance, wide range of problems later in life.

#### Types of Communication Disorders

**STUTTERING**
**Description:**
Disturbance in speech fluency (repeating words, prolonging sounds, extended pauses)
**Treatment:**
- Psychological
- Pharmacological

**EXPRESSIVE LANGUAGE DISORDERS**
**Description:**
Limited speech in all situations
**Treatment:**
- May be self-correcting

**SELECTIVE MUTISM**
**Description:**
Failure to speak in specific situations (e.g., school)
**Treatment:**
- Contingency management

**TIC DISORDER**
**Description:**
Involuntary motor movements (tics), such as physical twitches or vocalizations
**Treatment:**
- Psychological
- Pharmacological

Photodisc/Getty Images

**Infancy**

**Childhood**

**Adolescence**

# PERVASIVE DEVELOPMENTAL DISORDERS

## AUTISTIC DISORDER

*Description:*
- Severely impaired socialization and communication
- Restricted behaviour, interests, and activities
  — echolalia
  — maintenance of sameness
  — stereotyped, ritualistic behaviours
- Symptoms almost always develop before 36 months of age

### Causes

- Little conclusive data
- Numerous biological factors
  — clear genetic component
  — evidence of brain damage (cognitive deficits) combined with psychosocial influences

### Treatment

- Behavioural focus
  — communication
  — socialization
  — living skills
- Inclusive schooling
- Temporary benefits from medication

## ASPERGER'S DISORDER

*Description:*
Impaired socialization and restricted/unusual behaviours, but without language delays
- Few cognitive impairments (average IQ)
- May be mild autism, not separate disorder

## RETT'S DISORDER

*Description:*
Progressive neurological disorder after apparently normal early development
- Primarily affects girls
- Mental retardation
- Deteriorating motor skills
- Constant hand-wringing

## CHILDHOOD DISINTEGRATIVE DISORDER

*Description:*
Severe regression after 2–4 years of normal development
- Affects language, adaptive behaviour, and motor skills
- Evidence of neurological origin

# MENTAL RETARDATION

*Description:*
- Adaptive and intellectual functioning significantly below average
  — language and communication impairments
- Wide range of impairment—from mild to profound—in daily activities (90% of affected individuals have mild impairments)

### Causes

- Hundreds of identified factors
  — genetic
  — prenatal
  — perinatal
  — postnatal
  — environmental
- Nearly 75% of cases cannot be attributed to any known cause

### Treatment

- No biological intervention
- Behavioural focus similar to that for autism
- Prevention
  — genetic counseling
  — biological screening
  — maternal care

# Exploring Cognitive Disorders

- When the brain is damaged, the effects are irreversible, accumulating until learning, memory, or consciousness are obviously impaired.
- Cognitive disorders develop much later than mental retardation and other learning disorders, which are believed to be present at birth.

## TYPES OF COGNITIVE DISORDERS

### DELIRIUM

Photodisc/Getty Images

**Description**
- Impaired consciousness and cognition for several hours or days
  — confusion, disorientation, inability to focus
- Most prevalent among older adults, people with AIDS, and patients on medication

**Causes (subtypes)**
- Delirium due to a general medical condition
- Substance-induced delirium
- Delirium due to multiple etiologies
- Delirium not otherwise specified

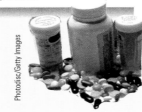

Photodisc/Getty Images

**Treatment**
- Pharmacological
  — benzodiazepines
  — antipsychotics
- Psychosocial
  — reassurance
  — presence of personal objects
  — inclusion in treatment decisions

### AMNESTIC DISORDER

**Description**
- Permanent short-term memory loss without impairment of other cognitive functions
  — inability to learn new information or recall previously learned information
  — significant impairment in social and occupational functioning

Photodisc/Getty Images

**Causes**
- Medical condition such as head trauma
- Lasting effects of a drug, even after the substance is no longer ingested

**Treatment**
- Prevention: proper medical care and drug monitoring
- No long-term success at combating damage

**Subtype: Wernicke/Korsakoff Syndrome**
- Caused by damage to the thalamus from injury (stroke) or chronic heavy alcohol use (thiamine depletion)

# Dementia

- Gradual deterioration of brain functioning that affects judgment, memory, language, and other advanced cognitive processes.
- Caused by medical condition or drug abuse.
- Some forms are irreversible; some are resolved by treatment of primary condition.

## TYPES OF DEMENTIA

### DEMENTIA OF THE ALZHEIMER'S TYPE

**Description**
- Increasing memory impairment and other multiple behavioural and cognitive deficits, affecting language, motor functioning, ability to recognize people or things, and/or planning
- Most prevalent dementia
- Subject of most research

Photodisc/Getty Images

#### Causes
- Progressive brain damage, evident in neurofibrillary tangles and neuritic plaque, confirmed by autopsy but assessed by simplified mental status exam
- Involves multiple genes

#### Treatment
- No cure so far, but hope lies in genetic research and amyloid protein in neuritic plaques
- Management may include lists, maps, and notes to help maintain orientation
- New medications that prevent acetylocholine breakdown and vitamin therapy show promise

### SUBSTANCE-INDUCED PERSISTING DEMENTIA

Photodisc/Getty Images

- Caused by brain damage due to prolonged drug use, especially in combination with poor diet, as in alcohol dependency; other substances may include inhalants, and the sedative, hypnotic, and anxiolytic drugs
- Treatment focuses on prevention

### VASCULAR DEMENTIA

Photodisc/Getty Images

- Permanent deterioration due to blocked or damaged blood vessels in the brain (stroke)
- Symptoms identical to Alzheimer's and may also include problems with walking and weakness of limbs
- Treatment focuses on coping

### DEMENTIA DUE TO OTHER GENERAL MEDICAL CONDITIONS

- Similar in effect to other cognitive disorders, but caused by:
  —head trauma
  —HIV, Parkinson's, Huntington's, Pick's, or Creutzfeldt-Jakob disease
  —hydrocephalus, hypothyroidism, brain tumor, and vitamin B12 deficiency
- Treatment of primary condition is sometimes possible

# 14 Mental Health Services: Legal and Ethical Issues

**Civil Commitment**
  *Criteria for Civil Commitment*
  *Defining Mental Illness*
  *Dangerousness*
  *Deinstitutionalization and Homelessness*
  *An Overview of Civil Commitment*

**Criminal Commitment**
  *The Insanity Defence*
  *Reactions to the Insanity Defence*
  *Fitness to Stand Trial*
  *Duty to Warn*
  *Mental Health Professionals as Expert Witnesses*

**Patients' Rights and Clinical Practice Guidelines**
  *The Right to Treatment*
  *The Right to Refuse Treatment*
  *Ethics of Research Involving Human Participants*
  *Clinical Practice Guidelines*

**Conclusions**

 **Abnormal Psychology Live CD-ROM**
  *False Memories*

We begin this chapter with a return to Arthur, whom we described in Chapter 12 as having psychotic symptoms. Revisiting the case from his family's perspective reveals the complexities of mental health law and the ethical aspects of working with people who have psychological disorders.

## Arthur
### A Family's Dilemma

As you remember, Arthur's family members brought him to one of our clinics because he was speaking and acting strangely. He talked incessantly about his "secret plan" to save all the starving children in the world. His family's concern intensified when Arthur said he was planning to break into the German embassy and present his plan to the German ambassador. Alarmed by his increasingly inappropriate behaviour and fearing he would be hurt, the family was astounded to learn they could not force him into a psychiatric hospital. Arthur could admit himself—which was not likely, given his belief that nothing was wrong with him—but they had no power to admit him involuntarily unless he was in danger of doing harm to himself or others. The family coped with this emergency as best they could for several weeks until the worst of Arthur's behaviours began to diminish.

Arthur experienced what is known as brief psychotic disorder (see Chapter 12). Fortunately for him, this is one of the few psychotic disorders that is not chronic. What is important here is to see how the mental health system responded. Because Arthur had not hurt himself or someone else, he had to seek help on his own before the hospital would assist him, even though everyone involved realized that such action on his part was very unlikely. This response by the mental health system added one more layer of helplessness to the family's already desperate emotional state. Why wouldn't the mental health facility admit Arthur, who was clearly out of touch with reality and in need of help? Why couldn't his own family authorize the mental health facility to act? What would have happened if Arthur had entered the German embassy and hurt or, worse, killed someone? Would he have gone to jail, or would he have finally received help from the mental health community? Would Arthur have been held responsible if he hurt other people while he was delusional? These are just a few of the many issues that surface when we try to balance the rights of people who have psychological disorders with the responsibilities of society to provide care.

Mental health professionals daily face such questions. They must both diagnose and treat people and also consider individual and societal rights and responsibilities. As we describe how systems of ethics and legal concepts have developed, remember they change with time and with shifting societal and political perspectives on mental illness. How we treat people with psychological disorders is in part a function of how society views them. For example, do people with mental illness need help and protection, or does society need protection from them? As public opinion of people with mental illness changes, so do the laws affecting them, and legal and ethical issues have an effect on both research and practice. As you will see, the issues affecting research and practice are often complementary. For one example, confidentiality (i.e., that no information will be released to a third party) is required to protect the identity of a participant in a research study and of a patient seeking help for a psychological disorder. Because people who receive mental health services often simultaneously participate in research studies, we must consider the concerns of both constituencies.

# Civil Commitment

- *Differentiate the legal concept of mental illness from a clinically diagnosed psychological disorder.*

- *Discuss the relation between dangerousness and mental illness.*

- *Describe the relations among mental illness, deinstitutionalization, and homelessness.*

The legal system exercises significant influence over the mental health system, for better or for worse. Laws have been designed to protect people who display abnormal behaviour and society. Often, achieving this protection is a delicate balancing act, with the scales sometimes thought to be tipped in favour of the rights of individuals and at other times in favour of society as a whole. For example, each province and territory has **civil commitment laws** under the provincial or territorial Mental Health Acts that detail when a person can be legally detained in a psychiatric institution—even against his or her will (Douglas & Koch, 2001). When Arthur's family tried to have him involuntarily committed to a mental health facility, hospital officials decided that because he was not in imminent danger of hurting himself or others he could not be committed against his will. In this case, the laws of his provincial Mental Health Act protected Arthur from involuntary commitment, but they also put him and others at potential risk by not compelling him to get help. In civil commitment law, the rights of people are pitted against the responsibility of the government (in this case the provinces and territories) to care for its citizens (Douglas & Koch, 2001).

## Criteria for Civil Commitment

Although there is variability across provinces, as outlined in Table 14.1, most provincial legislation permits commitment when the following three conditions have been met: (1) The person has a "mental disorder"; (2) the person is dangerous to himself or herself or others; and (3) the person is in need of treatment (Douglas & Koch, 2001). All Canadian jurisdictions require the first two of these three criteria, and some, but not all, also require the third (see Table 14.1). Although every Canadian jurisdiction requires that a person be mentally ill before he or she can be detained under civil commitment legislation, the definition of "mental illness" differs across jurisdictions, as we will see in the next section of this chapter. Similarly, although every Canadian jurisdiction also requires that a person be a danger to self or others, or that the person needs to be hospitalized for his or her safety or protection or for the safety and protection of others, the provinces vary considerably in how they define "safety" or "protection" (Douglas & Koch, 2001). For example, British Columbia defines these terms very broadly (i.e., the person requiring hospitalization for his or her own protection or the protection of others). Broad definitions such as this one can require a great deal of subjective judgment from the court and from mental health professionals. In contrast, Ontario defines these terms much more strictly (i.e., requiring that the person's mental disorder will likely result in serious bodily harm or imminent and serious physical impairment to himself or herself or another person; see Douglas & Koch, 2001). With these differences across jurisdictions

in how strictly defined dangerousness is, you can see how it would have been easier for Arthur to have been committed under the legislation in British Columbia than under the legislation in Ontario.

The Canadian jurisdictions also differ in terms of several other issues surrounding civil commitment. For example, the jurisdictions vary in terms of whether the patient has the right to refuse treatment, the right to be informed of the reasons for his or her hospital detention, the right to apply to a review panel that can grant a discharge from the hospital, and the specified right to legal counsel. These safeguards are built into the civil commitment process to guarantee the rights of the person being examined and to ensure that no one is involuntarily committed to a psychiatric facility for other than legitimate reasons. The legislations relevant to civil commitment across Canada also vary in terms of whether they allow peace officers to apprehend persons with apparent mental disorder, and in how long a person can be detained (see Table 14.1).

How the conditions for civil commitment are interpreted has varied over the years and has always been controversial. It is important to see that the government justifies its right to act against the wishes of an individual—in this case, to commit someone to a mental health facility—under two types of authority: police power and *parens patriae* ("state as the parent") power. Under police power, the government takes responsibility for protecting public health, safety, and welfare and can create laws and regulations to ensure this protection. Criminal offenders are held in custody if they are a threat to society. This first rationale for civil commitment has a long history under Canadian law. Even as Europeans were settling Canada, people with mental illness could be detained in order to prevent them from harming others. The provinces and territories apply the second rationale for civil commitment—*parens patriae* power—in circumstances in which citizens are not likely to act in their own best interest. For example, it is used to commit individuals with severe mental illness to mental health facilities when it is believed that they might be harmed because they are unable to secure the basic necessities of life, such as food and shelter, or because they do not recognize their need for treatment (Perlin, 2000). Under *parens patriae* power, the government acts as a surrogate parent, presumably in the best interests of a person who needs help.

---

**civil commitment laws** Legal proceedings that determine a person has a mental illness and may be hospitalized, even involuntarily.

## TABLE 14.1 A Comparison of Civil Commitment Legislation across Canadian Jurisdictions

| Specified statutory factors | B.C. | Yukon | Alta. | NWT | Sask. | Man. | Ont. | Que. | N.B. | N.S. | P.E.I. | Nfld. |
|---|---|---|---|---|---|---|---|---|---|---|---|---|
| Requirement of mental disorder | Yes | Yes | Yes | Yes | Yes | Yes | Yes | Yes | Yes | Yes | Yes | Yes |
| Functional definition of mental illness | Yes | Yes | Yes | Yes | Yes | Yes | No | No | Yes | No | Yes | No |
| Requirement of danger to self or others | Yes | Yes | Yes | Yes | Yes | Yes | Yes | Yes | Yes | Yes | Yes | Yes |
| Strict definition of danger | No | Yes | Yes | Yes | No | Yes | Yes | No | No | No | No | No |
| Requirement of need for treatment | Yes | No | No | No | Yes | Yes | No | Yes | No | Yes | No | No |
| Right to refuse/consent to treatment | No | No | No | No | No | Yes | Yes | No | No | Yes | No | No |
| Right to be informed of reasons for detention | Yes | Yes | Yes | Yes | Yes | Yes | Yes | Yes | Yes | No | Yes | No |
| Right to apply for review panel | Yes | Yes | Yes | No | Yes | Yes | Yes | Yes* | Yes | Yes | Yes | Yes |
| Specified right to legal counsel | Yes | Yes | No | Yes | No | Yes | Yes | No | Yes | Yes | Yes | No |
| Provision for apprehension by peace officer | Yes | Yes | Yes | Yes | Yes | Yes | Yes | No | Yes | Yes | Yes | Yes |
| Length of short-term commitment order | 48 h. | 24 h. | 24 h. | 48 h. | 24 h. | 72 h. | 72 h. | 48 h. | 72 h. | 48 h. | 72 h. | 15 day |
| Length of initial commitment certificate | 1 mo. | 21 day | 1 mo. | 14 day | 21 day | 3 wks. | 2 wks. | 21 day | 1 mo. | 7 day | 30 day | 1 mo. |
| Length of second commitment certificate | 1 mo. | 21 day | 1 mo. | 1 mo. | 21 day | 3 mo. | 1 mo. | 3 mo. | 2 mo. | 1 mo. | 90 day | 2 mo. |
| Length of further commitment certificate | 3,6 mo. | 21 day | 1,6 mo. | 3,6 mo. | 21 day, 1 y | 3 mo. | 2,3 mo. | 6 mo. | 3 mo. | 3,6mo. | 12 mo. | 3,6 mo., 1 y |
| Discharge criteria specified | Yes | No | Yes | Yes | Yes | Yes | Yes | No | Yes | No | Yes | No |
| Statutory presence of review panel | Yes | Yes | Yes | No | Yes | Yes | Yes | Yes* | Yes | Yes | Yes | Yes |
| Director may give treatment consent | Yes | Yes | Yes | Yes | Yes | Yes | Yes | Yes | Yes | Yes | Yes | Yes |
| Specified right to appeal to court | Yes | Yes | Yes | Yes | Yes | Yes | Yes | No | No | Yes | No | Yes |
| Any person may bring issue before court | Yes | Yes | Yes | Yes | Yes | Yes | Yes | Yes | Yes | Yes | Yes | Yes |

Notes:

Statutes are as amended by annual provincial amending legislation.

The Manitoba legislature assented to Bill 35 (a new Mental Health Act) in June 1998.

* In the Quebec legislation, the Commission des affaires sociales seems to be the functional equivalent of statutorily created Review Panels in other provinces' schemes. As such, while Quebec does not have a statutory Review Panel per se, it has a body that serves some of the same purposes (e.g., to review the legitimacy of detention).

Statutes: B.C. – Mental Health Act, R.S.B.C. 1996, C. 288; Yukon – Mental Health Act, S.Y.T. 1989-90, C. 28; Alta. – Mental Health Act, S.A. 1988, c. M-31.1; NWT – Mental Health Act, R.S.N.W.T 1988, c. M-10; Sask. – Mental Health Services Act, S. S. 1984-85-86, c. M-13.1; Man. – Mental Health Act, C.C.S.M. 1998, c M110; Ont. – Mental Health Act, R.S.O. 1990, c.M.7; Que. – Mental Patients Protection Act, R.S.Q 1977, P-41; N.B. – An Act to Amend the Mental Health Act, S.N.B. 1989, c. 23; N.S. – Hospitals Act, R.S.N.S. 1989, c. 208; P.E.I. – Mental Health Act, S.P.E.I. 1994, c. 39; Nfld. – Mental Health Act, R.S.N. 1990, c. M-9.

*Source:* Adapted from Douglas & Koch, 2001, pp. 356–357. Updated to include information from the new Manitoba Mental Health Act that was unproclaimed at the time of writing of the original table.

A person in need of help can always voluntarily request admission to a mental health facility; after an evaluation by a mental health professional, he or she may be accepted for treatment. However, when an individual does not voluntarily seek help, but others feel that treatment or protection is necessary, the process of civil commitment may be initiated. The specifics of this process differ from province to province, but typically one or two physicians or psychiatrists must conduct an assessment and agree that the person meets the criteria for commitment outlined in the relevant jurisdiction's legislation (Douglas & Koch, 2001).

The government can exert *parens patriae* to protect people from hurting themselves.

## Defining Mental Illness

The concept of mental illness figures prominently in civil commitment, and it is important to understand how it is defined. **Mental illness** is a legal concept, typically meaning severe emotional or thought disturbances that negatively affect an individual's health and safety. As we mentioned earlier, each Canadian jurisdiction has its own definition. For example, in Saskatchewan, "mental illness" means "a disorder of thought, perceptions, feelings or behaviour that seriously impairs a person's judgement, capacity to recognize reality, ability to associate with others, or ability to meet the ordinary demands of life, in respect of which treatment is advisable" (Douglas & Koch, 2001, p. 355). Robertson (1994) refers to this type of definition of mental illness as a "functional definition" because it specifies the effect of the illness on the patient's thoughts and behaviour. In contrast, some other provinces like Newfoundland and Ontario (see Table 14.1) do not use a functional definition of mental illness and instead define mental disorder more traditionally as a "disease or disability of the mind" (Douglas & Koch, 2001, p. 355).

Mental illness is not synonymous with psychological disorder; in other words, receiving a DSM-IV-TR diagnosis does not necessarily mean that a person fits the legal definition of someone having a mental illness. Although the DSM is quite specific about criteria that must be met for diagnosis, considerable ambiguity exists about what constitutes a "disease or disability of the mind" or what are "adverse effects on his or her ability to function" as required in a functional definition of mental illness. This ambiguity allows for flexibility in making decisions about individual cases, but it also creates the possibility of subjective impression and bias influencing these decisions.

## Dangerousness

Assessing whether someone is a danger to himself, herself, or others is a critical determinant of the civil commitment process. **Dangerousness** is a particularly controversial concept for people with mental illnesses: Popular opinion tends to be that people who are mentally ill are more dangerous than those who are not. Though this conclusion is questionable, the belief is still widespread, in part because of sensational media reports. Such views are important to the process of civil commitment if they bias a determination of *dangerousness* and unfairly link it with severe mental illness.

The results of research on dangerousness and mental illness are mixed. Some studies show no unusual association between mental illness and violence (Steadman & Ribner, 1980; Teplin, 1985); others find a greater risk for violence among people with mental illness (Lindquist & Allebeck, 1990). A review of over 100 studies by researchers at Simon Fraser University showed that there was a link between risk for violence and certain forms of mental illness—specifically, psychotic disorders (Douglas & Hart, 1996). Thus, major mental illnesses such as bipolar disorder (manic phase) and schizophrenia do seem to elevate the odds of violence in comparison to other mental disorders and to individuals with no mental disorder. Douglas and Hart (1996) found that the psychotic symptoms of delusions and hallucinations were particularly strongly related to risk for violence. Even so, research clearly indicates that most (around 90%) of those with mental illness have no history of violence

---

**mental illness** Legal concept meaning severe emotional or thought disturbances that negatively affect an individual's health and safety.

**dangerousness** Tendency to violence that is more likely among those experiencing hallucinations and delusions.

(Monahan, 1992), so that the statistical association of mental illness to risk for violence observed in studies like the one by Douglas and Hart (1996) simply cannot translate into a policy of involuntary commitment for anyone with a mental disorder!

Unfortunately, the widely held misperception that people with mental illness in general are more dangerous may differentially affect ethnic minorities and women. Women, for example, are likely to be viewed as more dangerous than are men when they engage in similar aggressive behaviours (Coughlin, 1994). Homeless women are more likely to be involuntarily committed because they are perceived as less capable than men of caring for themselves, and thus at greater risk of harming themselves (Stefan, 1996). Black males are often perceived as dangerous, even when they don't exhibit any violent behaviour (Bond, DeCandia, & MacKinnon, 1988).

To return to the general issue, how do you determine whether a person is dangerous to others? How accurate are mental health professionals at predicting who will and who will not later be violent? The answers directly affect the process of civil commitment as well as the protection of society. If we can't accurately predict dangerousness, how can we justify involuntary commitment?

Early research on this issue suggested that psychologists were actually rather poor at predicting dangerousness (see reviews by Douglas & Webster, 1999; Webster, Douglas, Eaves, & Hart, 1997). However, more recent research has shown that accurate predictions of risk for violence are indeed possible (Douglas & Webster, 1999; Rice, 1997). Many of the advances in predicting dangerousness have been made by Canadian research teams, including the research conducted by Christopher Webster, an expert in risk for violence assessment at the University of Toronto.

Similarly, since risk for self-harm is one of the common criteria used for decisions about civil commitment, one might ask whether psychologists can accurately predict risk for suicidal behaviour. The job of assessing patients' risk for suicide and other self-harm is an important and common activity for many mental health professionals. A good deal of research, again much of which has been done by Canadian teams, shows that several important variables should be assessed in evaluating a patient's risk for self-injury. For example, a study done by forensic psychologist James Ogloff and his colleagues investigated nearly 300 psychiatric patients who had been involuntarily committed to the Riverview psychiatric hospital in British Columbia. These researchers investigated what variables predicted which patients would display self-injurious behaviour while in hospital. They found that those patients who reported suicidal thoughts while in

the hospital, those who showed verbal and physical aggression toward others in the hospital, those with a history of self-harm, and those who had engaged in a suicide attempt or other form of self-injurious behaviour within the two weeks before being committed to hospital were those most likely to harm themselves while in hospital (Jack, Nicholls, & Ogloff, 1998; Nicholls, Jack, & Ogloff, 1998). Research like this has led to guides to help clinicians with decision making about predicting self-harm that are more accurate than clinicians' global judgments and far better than chance (Douglas & Koch, 2001).

## Deinstitutionalization and Homelessness

Two trends have influenced the number of people in Canada who are involuntarily committed each year: (1) the increase in the number of people who were homeless, and (2) **deinstitutionalization,** the movement of people with severe mental illness out of institutions. Homelessness, although not exclusively a problem of the mentally ill, is largely determined by social views of people with mental illness. Estimates from social action agencies in the late 1980s placed the numbers of homeless people at between 100 000 and 250 000 in Canada alone (Hargrave, 1999). One night in January 1987, the Canadian Council on Social Development conducted a count of those who were using homeless shelters across Canada. They found that 7751 people sought shelter that night: 61% adult men, 27% adult women, and 12% children. Half of the people seeking shelter that night were receiving some form of social assistance; 33% abused alcohol; 15% abused other drugs; 20% were former psychiatric patients; and 3% were physically handicapped. More recent estimates provided by hostels, emergency shelters, advocacy groups, and government reports indicate that at least one in five homeless people in Canada have serious mental health or substance abuse problems (Social Worker Action Team, 2002). First Nations people, refugees, and ethnic minorities are over-represented among the Canadian homeless (Hargrave, 1999).

Information on the characteristics of people who are homeless is important because it provides us with clues about the reasons that people become homeless, and it dispels the notion that all homeless people have mental health problems. For a time, homelessness was blamed on strict civil commitment criteria and deinstitutionalization (Perlin,

---

**deinstitutionalization** Systematic removal of people with severe mental illness or mental retardation out of institutions like psychiatric hospitals.

People become homeless because of many factors, including economic conditions, mental health status, and alcohol or other drug abuse.

1996; Torrey, 1988a); that is, policies to severely limit who can be involuntarily committed, the limits placed on the stays of people with severe mental illness, and the concurrent closing of large psychiatric hospitals were held responsible for the substantial increase in homelessness during the 1980s. Although a sizable percentage of homeless people do have mental illness, the rise in homelessness is also due to such economic factors as increased unemployment and a shortage of low-income housing (Hargrave, 1999).

Deinstitutionalization—the closing of many large psychiatric hospitals—is one factor that many believe has contributed to increasing rates of homelessness in Canada (Turkheimer & Parry, 1992). Deinstitutionalization had two goals: (1) to downsize or even close the large provincial and territorial mental hospitals, and (2) to create a network of community mental health services where the released individuals could be treated. As noted by Douglas and Koch (2001), the deinstitutionalization movement led to the rapid downsizing of psychiatric facilities across Canada. In 1957, some 70 300 persons were detained in psychiatric institutions in

Canada (Dominion Bureau of Statistics, 1955–7). In 1975, this figure was down to 44 847 inpatients (Statistics Canada, 1975). Further decreases ensued. For example, in 1992–93 alone, 29 991 patients were discharged from psychiatric hospitals and the number detained was even lower (Douglas & Koch, 2001; Statistics Canada, 1995).

Thus, as we can see, the first goal of the deinstitutionalization movement appears to have been substantially accomplished. However, the second goal of providing alternative community care has not. Instead, there was **transinstitutionalization,** or the movement of people with severe mental illness from large psychiatric hospitals to nursing homes or other group residences, including jails and prisons, many of which provide only marginal services (Bachrach, 1987; Sharfstein, 1987). Because of the deterioration in care for many people who had previously been served by the provincial or territorial mental hospital system, deinstitutionalization is largely considered a failure. Although many praise the ideal of providing community care for people with severe mental illness, the support needed to provide this type of care has been severely deficient.

## An Overview of Civil Commitment

What should the criteria be for involuntarily committing someone with severe mental illness to a mental health facility? Should imminent danger to self or others be the only justification, or should society paternalistically coerce people who appear to be in distress and in need of asylum or safety? How do we address the concerns of families like Arthur's who see their loved ones overcome by psychological problems? And what of our need not to be harassed by homeless people with mental illness? When do these rights take precedence over the rights of an individual to be free from unwanted incarceration? It is clearly difficult to strike the appropriate balance between individual rights and the government's responsibility to care for its citizens. The mental health laws pertaining to civil commitment across Canadian jurisdictions have attempted to do just that. With high rates of Canadian people homeless due to factors such as strict civil commitment laws and the deinstitutionalization movement, it is tempting to conclude that the Canadian legal system has failed to strike this balance. However, the fact that laws can be changed should make us optimistic that the needs of individuals and of society can ultimately be addressed through the courts.

---

**transinstitutionalization** The movement of people with severe mental illness from large psychiatric hospitals to nursing homes, group residences, jails, and prisons, many of which provide only marginal services.

# Criminal Commitment

■ *Describe the specific legal standards for invoking the insanity defence in Canada and the issue of fitness to stand trial.*

What would have happened if Arthur had been arrested for trespassing on embassy grounds or, worse yet, if he had hurt or killed someone in his effort to present his plan for saving the world? Would he have been held responsible for his actions, given his obvious disturbed mental state? How would a jury have responded to him when he seemed fine just several days later? If he was not responsible for his behaviour then, why does he seem so normal now?

These questions are of enormous importance as we debate whether people should be held responsible for their criminal behaviour despite the possible presence of mental illness. For example, Nova Scotian Jane Hurshman admitted to shooting her common-law husband, Billy Stafford, to death but claimed she was driven to it by years of severe abuse perpetrated by Stafford (Valee, 1986). She was acquitted by a jury but on appeal, a new trial was ordered. Rather than go though another trial, Hurshman pleaded guilty to manslaughter and served a short jail term. Cases such

as this have ignited considerable controversy about the conditions under which people should be responsible for criminal behaviour. Jane Hurshman's experience and other similar cases (e.g., *Regina v. Lavallee*; see Regehr & Glancy, 1995) led to the recognition of battered woman syndrome in Canadian law (Schuller & Yarmey, 2001).

Battered woman syndrome is not recognized in the DSM-IV-TR. The term refers to a state of learned helplessness (see Chapter 6) that results from chronic abuse within a relationship such that a woman feels unable to leave (Walker, 1979). The Supreme Court of Canada has acknowledged that in certain extreme cases involving the battered woman syndrome, an accused may well be under a reasonable apprehension of death even though she is not in danger of "imminent or immediate harm" at the moment that force is used to protect herself. This is an expansion of the self-defence legal defence that is always available to any person accused of murder who reasonably believes that his or her life is in danger from an assault. A battered woman's apprehension about dying may be quite realistic; one study conducted in Ontario found that nearly 80% of female murder victims are killed by their spouses or intimate partners (Crawford & Gartner, 1992). Nonetheless, the battered woman syndrome defence has its critics, with some referring to it as the "abuse excuse" (e.g., Dershowitz, 1994).

**Criminal commitment** is the process by which people are held because (1) they have been accused of committing a crime and are detained in a mental health facility until they can be assessed as fit or unfit to participate in legal proceedings against them, or (2) they have been found not criminally responsible on account of a mental disorder (NCRMD).

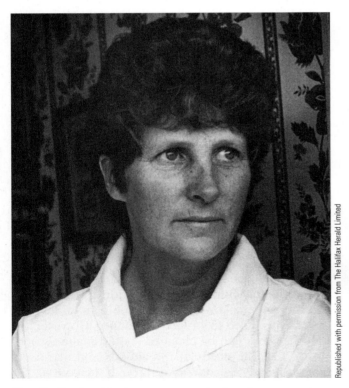

Nova Scotian Jane Hurshman was severely abused over a number of years by her common-law husband, Billy Stafford, whom she eventually killed. Cases like Hurshman's led to the acceptance of the "battered woman syndrome" as a murder defence in Canadian courts in 1990.

*Republished with permission from The Halifax Herald Limited*

## Concept Check 14.1

Commitment laws determine the conditions under which a person is certified to have a mental disorder and therefore placed in a hospital, sometimes in conflict with the person's

---

**criminal commitment**   Legal procedure by which a person is confined in a mental health facility because he or she has been accused of a crime but is not fit to stand trial, or because he or she has been found not criminally responsible on account of a mental disorder.

own wishes. The following paragraph is about civil commitment, criminal commitment, and the two types of authority by which the state takes control of its citizens. Check your understanding by filling in the blanks.

Several conditions must be met before the government is permitted to commit a person involuntarily: The person has a (1) _____; the person is considered (2) _____ to herself or himself or others, and the person is in need of (3) _____.

In the case of criminal commitment, people are held for two reasons: (4) _____ or (5) _____.

## The Insanity Defence

Not all people are punished for criminal behaviour. Why not? Because the law recognizes that, under certain circumstances, people are not responsible for their behaviour and it would be unfair and perhaps ineffective to punish them. Current views originate from a case recorded over 150 years ago in England. Daniel M'Naghten today might receive the diagnosis of paranoid schizophrenia (see Chapter 12). He held the delusion that the English Tory party was persecuting him, and he set out to kill the British prime minister. He mistook the man's secretary for the prime minister himself and killed the secretary instead. In what has become known as the M'Naghten rule, the English court decreed that people are not responsible for their criminal behaviour if they do not know what they are doing or if they don't know that what they are doing is wrong. An adaptation of this standard became part of Canadian law in 1894.

The M'Naghten rule was the most common insanity defence standard used in the last half of the 19th century and well into the 20th century. The requirements of the M'Naghten rule are still being used by numerous jurisdictions worldwide, including in Canada and many of the states in the United States (Ogloff & Whittemore, 2001). Other standards have been proposed in the United States to modify the M'Naghten rule because many critics feel that simply relying on an accused person's knowledge of right or wrong is too limiting and a broader definition is needed (Guttmacher & Weihofen, 1952). For example, a person with a compulsion may know what he or she is doing is considered wrong by society, and yet not be able to resist the compulsion. These proposed American alternatives to the M'Naghten rule are summarized in Table 14.2.

There have been changes to the insanity defence in Canada as well. Originally, under the 1985 Canadian Criminal Code, a person found not guilty by reason of insanity (NGRI) would be automatically detained in a psychiatric hospital until the mental disorder improved sufficiently to justify the patient's release. The purpose of this criminal commitment was to protect the public and to allow the patient to recover from his or her mental disorder. However, concerns were raised about whether patients detained under criminal commitment were actually receiving sufficient treatment. Concerns were also expressed that the detention periods in psychiatric facilities were often much longer than the prison sentence the person would have served if he or she had been convicted of the offence (Gelinas, 1994). Thus, in 1991, in the case of *Regina v. Swain* (1991), the Supreme Court ruled that this indeterminate detention infringed on the rights of the accused. There were also changes in the insanity defence. Specifically, the name of the defence was changed from not guilty by reason of insanity (NGRI) to not criminally responsible on account of mental

| **TABLE 14.2** | The M'Naghten Rule and Proposed Alternative Standards for the Insanity Defence | |
|---|---|
| **The M'Naghten Rule 1843** | It must be clearly proved that at the time of committing the act, the party accused was labouring under such a defect of reason, from disease of the mind, as not to know the nature and quality of the act he was doing; or if he did know it, that he did not know he was doing what was wrong. [101 Cl. & F. 200, 8 Eng. Rep. 718 (H.L. 1843)] |
| **The Durham Rule 1954** | An accused is not criminally responsible if his unlawful act was the product of mental disease or mental defect. [*Durham v. United States*, 214 F.2d 862, 876 (D.C. Cir. 1954)] |
| **American Law Institute (ALI) Rule 1962** | 1. A person is not responsible for criminal conduct if at the time of such conduct as a result of mental disease or defect he lacks substantial capacity either to appreciate the criminality (wrongfulness) of his conduct or to conform his conduct to the requirements of law.<br>2. As used in the Article, the terms "mental disease or defect" do not include an abnormality manifested only by repeated criminal or otherwise antisocial conduct. American Law Institute (1962). *Model penal code: Proposed official draft.* Philadelphia: Author. |

*Source:* Adapted from Ogloff & Whittemore (2001).

disorder (NCRMD). The wording of the standard was also revised, as follows:

> No person is criminally responsible for an act committed or an omission made while suffering from a mental disorder that rendered the person incapable of appreciating the nature and quality of the act or omission or of knowing that it was wrong. (Criminal Code of Canada, Section 16, 1992)

There are three main differences between the old NGRI and the newer NCRMD defences. First, the term "insanity" has been replaced by "mental disorder." Second, the defendant is now considered "not criminally responsible" as opposed to "not guilty." This difference may appear subtle but the change recognizes explicitly that the defendant did commit the crime as opposed to being "not guilty" of the crime. Finally, the meaning of "wrong" has changed from NGRI to NCRMD. Unlike NGRI, which was concerned only with legal wrongs, NCRMD judgments can be made if the person is incapable of knowing that his or her actions were either legally or morally wrong (Davis, 1993).

A well-known example of the successful use of the NCRMD defence in Canada is the case of André

In his 1995 trial for the attempted assassination of former Prime Minister Jean Chrétien, André Dallaire successfully used the NCRMD defence as he was suffering from paranoid schizophrenia at the time.

CP Photo/Fred Chartrand

Dallaire in 1995. In November of that year, Dallaire attempted to assassinate the Canadian prime minister at the time, Jean Chrétien. Dallaire broke into the prime minister's home armed with a knife, intending to slit Chrétien's throat. Chrétien and his wife were able to hide safely in a locked bedroom until the police came to arrest Dallaire. A psychiatric assessment revealed that Dallaire was suffering from a psychotic disorder, specifically paranoid schizophrenia (see Chapter 12). His hallucinations consisted of hearing voices that commanded him to kill the prime minister. He also displayed delusions of grandeur that he was a secret agent with a mission to avenge the outcome of the Quebec independence referendum (Fisher, 1996). Although Dallaire was found guilty of the crime of attempted murder of the prime minister, he was also found not to be criminally responsible for his actions because his intention to kill the prime minister was ruled to be the product of a mental disorder and because his mental disorder prevented him from comprehending the nature of his actions or the fact that his actions were wrong (Fisher, 1996). He was committed to the Royal Ottawa Hospital where he received treatment including antipsychotic medication. Once Dallaire was no longer delusional or hallucinating, he was conditionally released to a group home, and finally to the community with continued psychiatric care (Fisher, 1996).

Another example of the successful use of the NCRMD defense is described by James Ogloff and Karen Whittemore in the following case.

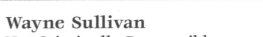

## Wayne Sullivan
### Not Criminally Responsible or "Getting Off Easy"?

On January 18, 1992, Mr. Wayne Sullivan, his wife, Maureen Sullivan, and a friend of Maureen's (Mrs. W.) were drinking at a pub in Prince George, British Columbia. Sometime after midnight, Mrs. W. drove the Sullivans home because the Sullivans were too drunk to drive. When they reached the Sullivans' home, Mrs. W. joined the Sullivans for a drink. Once they were all inside, Mr. Sullivan made several advances toward Mrs. W. when his wife was not there. Mr. Sullivan suggested that they have a "threesome." Mrs. W. declined. When Mrs. Sullivan rejoined them, she helped her husband to his room. The accused, Mr. Sullivan, claims that while in the bedroom his wife said that she no longer loved him and that she was in love with Mrs. W.

After Mr. Sullivan had been taken to his bedroom, the women had talked for a few minutes and then Mrs. W. decided to leave. As she gathered her belongings, she saw both of the Sullivans at the front door. Mrs. W. said that she saw a bright flash, heard a loud noise, and saw Mrs. Sullivan fall. Mr. Sullivan was standing over his wife and he had a gun in his hand. When Mrs. W asked Mr. Sullivan if he had shot Maureen, he replied that he had. Mr. Sullivan then pointed the gun at Mrs. W. and ordered her to go to the bedroom and disrobe. An argument ensued. Finally, Mr. Sullivan called 911.

At trial, Mr. Sullivan raised the defence of legal insanity—specifically, that he was not criminally responsible on account of mental disorder. A psychologist and a psychiatrist provided expert testimony for the defence that Mr. Sullivan was in a dissociative state (see Chapter 5) at the time of the shooting. The experts noted that while in this dissociative state, Mr. Sullivan would not have had the ability to appreciate the nature and consequences of his behaviour. In marked contrast, the psychiatrist called by the Crown stated that he doubted Mr. Sullivan had suffered dissociation. Instead, he testified that Mr. Sullivan's heavy drinking just before and at the time of the crime likely contributed to his behaviour.

At the completion of the trial, the jury found Mr. Sullivan not criminally responsible on account of mental disorder. Mr. Sullivan spent a short time in hospital and is now living in the community. (Adapted from Ogloff & Whittemore, 2001.)

## Reactions to the Insanity Defence

The NCRMD and the earlier NGRI legal defences represent an effort made by the legal system to focus on the needs of people with mental illness who also broke the law, providing mental health treatment instead of punishment. However, the successful use of concepts such as insanity or mental disorder in criminal cases have alarmed large segments of the population, just as have defences involving battered woman syndrome discussed earlier in this chapter. As noted by Ogloff and Whittemore (2001), when someone is found NCRMD, there is often a public outcry that the person has "got off" too easily. Research supports that the public often holds negative perceptions about the NCRMD defence. One telephone survey study found that 91% of people who responded agreed with the statement that "judges and juries have a hard time telling whether the defendants are really sane or insane"

(Hans, 1986). Almost 90% agreed the "insanity plea is a loophole that allows too many guilty people to go free." In a similar study, 90% of people agreed "the insanity plea is used too much. Too many people escape responsibilities for crimes by pleading insanity" (Pasewark & Seidenzahl, 1979). Do you think that either Dallaire or Sullivan "got off too easily"? Is there hard evidence that the insanity defence is used too often?

You will probably be surprised to learn that the old NGRI defence was used relatively infrequently in Canadian courts. For example, in 1991, only about 1000 individuals who had been found NGRI were being held in institutions across Canada (Roesch et al., 1997). Although the NCRMD defence is used somewhat more often, its use is still relatively uncommon (Roesch et al., 1997). For example, in British Columbia, in the 2 years following the legal change to the NCRMD defence, among those cases remanded for assessment of criminal responsibility, psychiatrists' recommendations favoured NCRMD only 28.6% of the time—a total of only 53 cases over two years. Moreover, individuals remanded for assessment of criminal responsibility in 1993–94 were more likely to be recommended NCRMD by the assessing psychiatrists than those remanded for assessment in 1992–93 (the year immediately after the change to the NCRMD defence). Together these findings show that although the use of this newer defence is increasing, it is still fairly uncommon (Roesch et al., 1997).

Negative public perceptions of the NCRMD defence also reflect a lack of appreciation by the public about just how serious the consequences are of using this defence (Ogloff & Whittemore, 2001). Although the NCRMD defence does not entail automatic detention in a psychiatric hospital, some defendants end up being incarcerated in psychiatric institutions for much longer periods of time than they would have been sentenced to prison if they had not employed this defence (Davis, 1994; Holley, Arboleda-Florez, & Crisanti, 1998). People with mental illness apparently do not often "beat the rap" as a result of being judged NCRMD.

A final issue relates to the legal concept of burden of proof, the weight of evidence needed to win a case. With respect to the defence of NCRMD, according to Canadian law, the defendant can raise the issue of NCRMD at any time. Recognizing the rights of the defendant, in contrast, the prosecution can only raise the possibility of NCRMD after the defendant has been found guilty or after the defence, for any reason, raises the issue of the defendant's mental state (Ogloff & Whittemore, 2001).

Society has long recognized the need to identify criminals who may not be in control of their behaviour and who may not benefit from simple incarceration. The challenge is in trying to do what may be impossible: determining whether the person knew what he or she was doing, knew right from wrong, and could control his or her behaviour. Mental health professionals cannot assess mental health retrospectively. An additional dilemma is the desire, on the one hand, to provide care to people with mental illness and, on the other, to treat them as responsible individuals. Finally, we must resolve the simultaneous and conflicting interests of wanting to assist people with mental illness and wanting to be protected from them. By evaluating the effects of various consequences, science may be able to help resolve some of these issues. We must reach a national consensus about the basic value of people with mental illness in order to decide how they should be dealt with legally. Concerns about law and order must be balanced with the rights of people with mental illness, providing adequate attention to both concerns.

## Fitness to Stand Trial

Before people can be tried for a criminal offence, they must be able to understand the charges against them and to assist with their own defence, criteria outlined by the Canadian Criminal Code in 1992. Thus, in addition to interpreting a person's state of mind during the criminal act, experts must also anticipate his or her state of mind during the subsequent legal proceedings. A person could be ruled not criminally responsible on account of mental disorder because of his or her mental illness at the time of the criminal act yet still be fit to stand trial.

The classic case for the determination of fitness in Canada is *Regina v. Pritchard* (1836). Lindsay (1977) describes three issues emerging from the criteria defined in the Pritchard ruling that need to be tapped in a fitness assessment: (1) is the accused able to assist in his or her defence? (2) does the accused understand his or her role in the proceedings? and (3) does the accused understand the nature or object of the proceedings? According to the Canadian Criminal Code: "Unfit to stand trial means ... in particular, unable on account of mental disorder to: (a) understand the nature or object of the proceedings, (b) understand the possible consequences of the proceedings, or (c) communicate with counsel" (as cited in Ogloff & Whittemore, 2001, p. 294).

A person determined to be unfit to stand trial typically loses the authority to make decisions and faces commitment. If the defendant is found to be unfit to stand trial, the court may decide the next step (e.g., detention in hospital) if it can do so readily, and if not, a review board must reach a decision in 45 days. The review board's three options are (1) conditionally discharge the accused; (2) detain the accused in hospital; or (3) order that the accused receive treatment (Ogloff & Whittemore, 2001).

Canadian researchers have contributed substantially to developing sound instruments and methods for assessing a defendant's **fitness to stand trial** (see review in Ogloff & Whittemore, 2001). For example, the Fitness Interview Test—Revised is a three-part instrument developed by Christopher Webster and his colleagues (Roesch, Zapf, Webster, & Eaves, 1999) that specifies the particular abilities required by an individual to demonstrate that he or she is fit to stand trial. In the first section, the individual's understanding of the nature and object of the proceedings is assessed (e.g., does the individual understand key components such as the arrest process, pleas available, and court procedures?). In the second section, the individual's understanding of the possible consequences of the proceedings is measured (e.g., the range of possible penalties, legal defences available). In the final section, the individual's capacity to contribute to his or her own defence is tapped (e.g., can he or she communicate with a lawyer and plan a legal strategy?). Research has shown that this test reliably screens out those individuals who are clearly fit to stand trial (Zapf & Roesch, 1997).

## Concept Check 14.2

The legal systems in both Canada and the United States have evolved to incorporate the idea that some people cannot be held responsible for their criminal actions due to mental disorder. Check your understanding of this idea by identifying the following concepts. Pick your answers from (a) fitness to stand trial, (b) American Law Institute rule, (c) the Durham rule, and (d) the M'Naughten rule.

1. The person could not distinguish between right and wrong at the time of the crime. _____
2. The person is not criminally responsible if the crime was due to "mental disease or mental defect." _____
3. The person is not responsible for the crime if he or she is not able to appreciate wrongfulness of behaviour due to mental disease or defect. _____
4. The defendant does not go to trial because he or she is unable to understand the proceedings and assist in the defence. _____

**fitness to stand trial**  Before people can be tried for a criminal offence, they must be determined able to understand the charges against them and able to assist with their own defence.

# Duty to Warn

Do mental health professionals have any responsibility for the actions of the people they serve? This question is especially important when we consider the dangerous behaviour exhibited by a minority of people with severe mental illness. What are the responsibilities of professionals who suspect that someone with whom they are working may hurt or even kill another person? Must they contact the appropriate authority or the person who may be harmed, or are they forbidden to discuss information disclosed during therapy sessions?

These issues are the subject of a tragic case in the United States known as *Tarasoff v. Regents of the University of California* (1974, 1976). In 1969, Prosenjit Poddar, a graduate student at the University of California, killed a fellow student, Tatiana Tarasoff, who had previously rejected his romantic advances. At the time of the murder he was being seen by two therapists at the University Health Center and had received a diagnosis of paranoid schizophrenia. At his last session, Poddar hinted that he was going to kill Tarasoff. His therapist believed this threat was serious and contacted the campus police, who investigated the allegation and received assurances from Poddar that he would leave Tarasoff alone. Weeks later, after repeated attempts to contact her, Poddar shot and stabbed Tarasoff until she died.

After learning of the therapists' role in the case, Tatiana Tarasoff's family sued the university, the therapists, and the university police, saying they should have warned Tatiana that she was in danger. The court agreed, and the Tarasoff case has been used ever since as a standard in the United States for therapists concerning their **duty to warn** a client's potential victims. Nonetheless, it is still difficult for therapists to know their exact responsibilities for protecting third parties from their clients. Good clinical practice dictates that any time they are in doubt they should consult with colleagues. A second opinion can be just as helpful to a therapist as to a client. We have not had a legal precedent in Canada like the ruling in the Tarasoff case in the United States (Birch, 1992). Nonetheless, the Alberta Court of Queen's Bench stated in *Wenden v. Trikha* (1991) that a duty to warn might be imposed for psychologists under some circumstances (Lyon, Hart, & Webster, 2001; Schuller & Ogloff, 2001).

In addition to this legal warning, the code of ethics of the Canadian Psychological Association (see Chapter 3) dictates how mental health practitioners should behave in such cases. The code is quite clear that psychologists have an ethical duty to warn a third party of impending danger from a client, very similar to the legal requirements imposed by the ruling in the Tarasoff case in the United States

(Ogloff & Olley, 1998). Specifically, the Canadian Psychological Association code requires that psychologists should do everything within reason to stop or offset the harmful or lethal consequences of other people's actions. The ethical response can include making a report to appropriate authorities (e.g., the police) or warning an intended victim. Moreover, the psychologist should take such actions even when a confidential relationship, like a patient–therapist relationship, is involved (Canadian Psychological Association [CPA], 2000).

Communications between a therapist and client are required to be held completely confidential, except in a very few exceptional situations (CPA, 2000). These exceptions are referred to as "limits to confidentiality." One such limit to confidentiality is when the psychologist must break confidentiality to allow for the protection of identifiable third parties at risk for harm (Schuller & Ogloff, 2001). Another such limit to confidentiality involves suspected cases of child abuse. In virtually every Canadian jurisdiction, psychologists have a duty to report suspected cases of child abuse, even when information pertaining to this suspicion was obtained within the otherwise confidential patient–therapist relationship (Schuller & Ogloff, 2001). A further situation where limits to confidentiality apply is when the psychologist judges the patient to be a risk to himself or herself (Schuller & Ogloff, 2001). The therapist may need to break confidentiality in order to arrange for proper care for a highly suicidal patient who does not wish to enter hospital, for example.

## Mental Health Professionals as Expert Witnesses

Judges and juries often have to rely on **expert witnesses,** individuals who have specialized knowledge, to assist them in making decisions (Melton, Petrila, Poythress, & Slobogin, 1987; O'Connor, Sales, & Shuman, 1996). The Canadian legal system has been relying more and more frequently on expert witness testimony in such areas as child custody disputes (Austin, Jaffe, & Friedman, 1994). We have alluded to several instances in which mental health professionals serve as experts, providing information about a person's dangerousness or ability to understand and participate in the defence. The public's perception of

---

**duty to warn**  Mental health professionals' responsibility to break confidentiality and notify the potential victim whom a client has specifically threatened.

**expert witness**  Person who because of special training and experience is allowed to offer opinion testimony in legal trials.

expert witnesses is characterized by ambivalence. On one hand, they see the value of persuasive expert testimony in educating a jury; on the other, they see expert witnesses as "hired guns" whose opinions suit the side that pays their bills (Hollien, 1990). How reliable are the judgments of mental health professionals who act as expert witnesses?

To take one example, in deciding whether someone should be civilly committed, the assessor must determine the person's potential for future violence. As we discussed earlier in this chapter, research suggests that mental health professionals can now make reliable predictions of dangerousness using appropriate tools (Douglas & Webster, 1999; Rice, 1997). A second area in which mental health professionals are frequently asked to provide consultation is in assigning a diagnosis. In Chapter 3, we discussed the development of systems to ensure the reliability of diagnoses. Recent revisions of diagnostic criteria, including the DSM-IV-TR, have addressed this issue directly, thus helping clinicians make diagnoses that are generally reliable. Remember, however, that the legal definition of mental illness is not matched by a comparable disorder in DSM-IV-TR. Therefore, statements about whether someone has a "mental illness" reflect determinations made by the court and not by mental health professionals.

Mental health professionals appear to have expertise in identifying malingering and in assessing

Dr. John Yuille, a forensic psychologist at the University of British Columbia and an expert in human memory, has provided a good deal of expert witness testimony in his areas of expertise. For example, he testified for the defence during the famous trial of the perpetration of multiple counts of alleged child abuse by a group of childcare workers in Martensville, Saskatchewan, in the early 1990s.

Courtesy of Dr. John C. Yuille

competence. Remember that to malinger is to fake or grossly exaggerate symptoms, usually in order to be absolved from blame (see Chapter 5). For example, a person might claim to have been actively hallucinating at the time of the crime and therefore not be responsible. Research suggests that malingering is readily detected using validated instruments like the Minnesota Multiphasic Personality Inventory (MMPI; e.g., Bagby, Nicholson, Bacchiochi, Ryder, & Bury, 2002; Bagby, Nicholson, & Buis, 1998). For example, research indicates that the MMPI is almost 90% accurate in revealing malingering in people claiming to have posttraumatic stress disorder (PTSD; McCaffrey & Bellamy-Campbell, 1989). However, recent work cautions that people who have knowledge about the MMPI validity scales (see Chapter 3) can be quite successful in avoiding detection that they are faking PTSD (Bury & Bagby, 2002). Mental health professionals also appear capable of providing reliable information about a person's competence, or ability to understand and assist with a defence (Melton et al., 1987). Overall, mental health professionals can provide judges and juries with reliable and useful information in certain specific areas (Gacano, 2000).

The research described here does not indicate how accurate expert testimony actually is under everyday conditions. In other words, under the right circumstances, experts can make accurate determinations of the short-term risks that a person will commit an act of violence, is faking certain symptoms, or is fit to stand trial, and of what diagnosis should be made. Yet other factors conspire to influence expert testimony. Personal and professional opinions that exceed the competence of the expert witness can influence what information is or is not presented, as well as how it is relayed to the court (Simon, 2003). For instance, if the expert witness believes in general that people should not be involuntarily committed to mental health facilities, this opinion will likely influence how the witness presents clinical information in civil commitment court proceedings.

# Patients' Rights and Clinical Practice Guidelines

■ *Define the concept of patient rights in the mental health system, including the right to treatment and the right to refuse treatment.*

Until about 20 years ago, people in mental health facilities were accorded few rights. What treatment they received, whether they could make phone calls, send and receive mail, or have visitors were typically decided by hospital personnel who rarely consulted with the patient. However, abuses of this

authority led to legal action and subsequent rulings by the courts concerning the rights of people in these facilities. Over the past 2 decades, constitutional protection of the rights of Canadian citizens have been explicitly extended to patients in psychiatric institutional settings (Olley & Ogloff, 1995).

## The Right to Treatment

One of the most fundamental rights of people in mental health facilities is, obviously, the right to treatment. For too many and for too long, conditions were poor and treatment was lacking in numerous large mental health facilities. In Canada, the rights to treatment of people with mental illness and mental retardation have been more explicitly recognized in Canadian law over the last two decades (Olley & Ogloff, 1995).

As noted by Maureen Olley and James Ogloff (1995), a related but separate right is the right to treatment in the least restrictive setting possible. For example, those with mental retardation should have a right to the least restrictive conditions necessary to achieve the purpose of habilitation. This right was established by a landmark case in the United States, *Wyatt v. Stickney* (1972). This case grew out of a lawsuit filed by the employees of large institutions in the state of Alabama who were fired because of funding difficulties. Among the standards set by the rulings in this case were minimum staff–patient ratios and physical requirements, such as a minimum number of showers and toilets per patient for a given number of residents. The case also mandated that facilities make positive efforts to attain treatment goals for their patients. To this end, it was ruled that institutions should make every attempt to move residents with mental retardation from (1) more to less structured living; (2) large to smaller facilities; (3) large to smaller living units; (4) group to individual residences; (5) segregated from the community to integrated into the community; and (6) dependent living to independent living. According to Olley and Ogloff (1995), in Canada, advocacy efforts and constitutional provisions (e.g., The Protection and Advocacy System for Persons with Developmental Disabilities, 1986; The Canadian Charter of Rights and Freedoms, 1982) protect the rights of mentally ill persons, such as the right to treatment in the least restrictive environment, and the right to refuse treatment, which we discuss next.

## The Right to Refuse Treatment

One of the most controversial issues in mental health today is the right of people, especially those with severe mental illness, to refuse treatment (Simon, 1999; Winick, 1997). Along with the development of the Canadian Charter of Rights and Freedoms in 1982, provinces like Manitoba and Ontario now explicitly recognize the right of involuntary but competent patients (e.g., someone who is involuntarily committed due to suicidality who nonetheless understands the risks and benefits of a proposed treatment) to refuse treatment (Gratzer & Matas, 1994). Some provinces such as British Columbia continue to fail to recognize this right and leave the decision

in the hands of individual physicians treating a given patient. It should be noted that this condition arises rarely: Fewer than 10% of involuntary patients persist in refusing treatment (Gratzer & Matas, 1994). Nonetheless, the issues involved can be quite complex when an involuntary patient does persist in refusing treatment, as is illustrated in the following case described by Douglas and Koch (2001):

## George Reid
### Asserting the Right to Refuse Treatment

In the early 1980s, George Reid committed a violent robbery, was arrested, and later was found not guilty by reason of insanity. He was held in a maximum security psychiatric facility, having been declared under the Ontario Mental Health Act to be an involuntary patient who was incompetent to make treatment decisions for himself. He was diagnosed with schizophreniform psychosis. His psychiatrist, Dr. Russell Fleming, proposed to treat him with psychotropic (antipsychotic) medication. Such medication usually has a beneficial effect on symptoms of psychosis, as well as restoring cognitive capacity to some extent. However, it also has side effects that many persons find highly undesirable. Under the legislation at the time, a "substitute decision maker" (in this case, a designate of the province) could provide consent to treatment on the behalf of an incompetent person. The psychiatrist applied to this person for consent to treat Mr. Reid. The substitute decision maker refused, as Mr. Reid had earlier expressed (when he was competent) that he did not want to take psychotropic medication. The psychiatrist appealed this decision to the psychiatric review board in Ontario, which granted consent to treatment. This decision was upheld by the Ontario District Court but later overturned by the Ontario Court of Appeal. The court of appeal held that treatment provided against the consent (even if given earlier) of a person is unconstitutional, violating the right of security of the person under section 7 of the Canadian Charter of Rights and Freedoms. This decision introduced a conundrum into the law: Although people could be admitted to hospital involuntarily, the mental illness that gave rise to their involuntary hospitalization could not be treated. Without treatment, patients' illnesses may not ever remit, and patients could then be hospitalized indefinitely. Although Ontario has dealt with this problem through revising its legislation, the Fleming case has dramatic implications for other provinces that may treat patients without their consent, or even against their express wishes. The inherent dilemma is that to provide treatment may be unconstitutional, but to withhold it may give rise to indefinite hospitalization, because the very basis for hospitalization—mental illness—may not remit without treatment (Douglas & Koch, 2001, pp. 353–354).

As illustrated in the case above, today, the argument about patients' rights to refuse treatment often centres on the use of antipsychotic medications. On one side of the issue is the mental health professional who believes that, under certain circumstances, people with severe mental illness are not capable of making a decision in their own best interest and that the clinician is therefore responsible for providing treatment despite the protestations of the affected person. On the other side, patients and their advocates argue that all people have a fundamental right to make decisions about their own treatment, even if doing so is not in their own best medical interests.

Although this controversy is not yet completely resolved, a related legal question is this: Can people be "forced" to become fit to stand trial? This is an interesting dilemma: If people facing criminal charges are delusional or have such frequent severe hallucinations that they cannot fully participate in the legal proceedings, can they be forced against their will to take medication to reduce these symptoms, thereby making them fit to stand trial?

## Ethics of Research Involving Human Participants

Throughout this text we have described research conducted worldwide with people who have psychological disorders, and we touched briefly in Chapter 3 on the issue of the ethical issues involved in conducting research with these individuals. In general, research involving human participants should be guided by the following ethical principles (Canadian Institutes of Health Research [CIHR], Natural Sciences and Engineering Research Council of Canada, Social Sciences and Humanities Research Council of Canada, 2003):

1. Respect for human dignity
2. Respect for free and informed consent
3. Respect for vulnerable persons
4. Respect for privacy and confidentiality
5. Respect for justice and inclusiveness
6. Balancing harm and benefits
7. Minimizing harm
8. Maximizing benefit

According to the principles outlined in the Tri-Council Policy Statement (CIHR et al., 2003), researchers must be respectful of the dignity of their research participants, as noted in principle 1. Protecting participants' dignity is particularly important for people with psychological disorders who may not be able to understand the research fully, as noted in principle 3. One of the most important concepts in research is that those who participate must be fully informed about the risks and benefits of the study, as noted in principle 2. Simple consent is not sufficient; it must be informed consent, or formal agreement by the individual to participate after being fully apprised of all important aspects of the study, including any possibility of harm (see Chapter 3).

Unfortunately, there are many examples in history where researchers have not followed ethical principles such as those outlined in the conduct of their research on various forms of abnormal behaviour. Take for example the brainwashing research of Dr. Ewan Cameron, which was conducted on psychiatric patients at the Allan Memorial Institute in Montreal in the 1950s and 1960s. Patients and their families were not asked for their consent to participate in Cameron's studies on experimental treatments for mental illness, nor were they adequately informed that his treatments were experimental and not standard practice. His treatments included multiple courses of shock treatment daily, and a technique called "psychic driving," which involved having patients listen to subliminal messages repeatedly while in a drug-induced coma. Although well-intentioned, these experimental procedures unfortunately resulted in horrific consequences for many, including patients being confused, unable to feed themselves, and unable to control their bladders (Collins, 1988). The ethical principles outlined in the Tri-Council policy statement (CIHR et al., 2003) help to ensure that this extreme type of tragic case does not happen in Canada again. However, a more recent case underlines the continued importance of these ethical principles such as the respect for free and informed consent and the sometimes grey areas that still exist in applied research today.

## Greg Aller
### Concerned about Rights

In 1988, 23-year-old Greg Aller signed a consent form agreeing to participate in a treatment study at a large university-affiliated psychiatric institute (Willwerth, 1993). Since the previous year, Greg had experienced vivid and frightening hallucinations and delusions about space aliens. His parents had contacted the university for assistance.

They learned that the university was initiating a new study to evaluate people in the early stages of schizophrenia and to assess the effects of the withdrawal of medication. If Greg participated he could receive extremely expensive drug therapy and counselling free. After taking the drug Prolixin for 3 months as part of the study, he improved dramatically; the hallucinations and delusions were gone. He was now able to enroll in university and he made the dean's list.

Although overjoyed with the results, Greg's parents were concerned about the second phase of the study, which involved taking him off the medication. They were reassured by the researchers that this was an important and normal part of treatment for people with schizophrenia and the potential for negative side effects of taking the drug for too long was great. They were also told the researchers would put Greg back on the medication if he grew considerably worse without it.

Toward the end of 1989, Greg was slowly taken off the drug, and he soon started having delusions about political figures and space aliens. Although his deterioration was obvious to his parents, Greg did not indicate to the researchers that he needed the medication or tell them of his now continuous hallucinations and delusions. Greg continued to deteriorate, at one point threatening to kill his parents. After several more months, Greg's parents persuaded him to ask for more medication. Although better than he was earlier, Greg has still not returned to the much-improved state he achieved following his first round of medication.

---

This case highlights the conflicts that can arise when researchers attempt to study important questions in psychopathology. Some have claimed that the researchers did not give Greg and his family all the information about the risks of treatment and the possibility of other approaches (Hilts, 1994). Critics claim that informed consent in this and similar situations is too often not fully met and that information is frequently coloured to ensure participation. However, the researchers note that what they did was no different from what would have happened outside the research study: They attempted to remove Greg from potentially dangerous antipsychotic medication. The controversy emerging from this case should be an added warning to researchers about their responsibilities to people who participate in their studies and their obligation to design added safeguards to protect the welfare of their study participants. Some are now exploring methods to assess formally whether participants with mental illness fully understand the

© Mojgan B. Azimi/Onyx

Greg Aller (right, with his parents) participated in a drug study at a university-affiliated psychiatric institute and suffered a severe relapse of psychotic symptoms when medication was withdrawn. He and his family subsequently raised the issue of informed consent for such research.

risks and benefits associated with these studies (Appelbaum, Grisso, Frank, O'Donnell, & Kupfer, 1999; Wirshing, Wirshing, Marder, Liberman, & Mintz, 1998).

## Concept Check 14.3

Psychological professionals assume many roles and responsibilities. Identify the following situations using one of these terms: (a) informed consent, (b) duty to warn, (c) expert witness, (d) deinstitutionalization, (e) malingering.

1. Dr. X testified in court that the defendant was faking and exaggerating symptoms to evade responsibility. Dr. X is acting as a(n) _____ and the defendant is _____.
2. The therapist has learned he is required to release more mentally ill patients from the hospital. He is worried that many of them will end up homeless and without continuing treatment as a result of _____.
3. One of my clients threatened his mother's life during his session today. Now I must decide whether I have a _____.
4. The clinical researcher knows the potential for harm of the participants is very slight, but is nevertheless careful to tell them about it and asks them whether they agree to give their _____.

## Clinical Practice Guidelines

Over the past decade, there have been attempts made to establish greater uniformity in the delivery of effective health and mental health care and to better communicate the latest developments in treating certain disorders effectively to practitioners. A greater emphasis has also been placed on research focused on improving systems for the delivery of health and mental health services.

To accomplish the above goals, some clinical practice guidelines have been published for specific disorders, including sickle cell disease, management of cancer pain, unstable angina, and depression in primary care settings. The hope is not only to reduce costs by eliminating unnecessary or ineffective treatments but also to facilitate the dissemination of effective interventions based on the latest research evidence. Treating people effectively—alleviating their pain and distress—is ultimately the most important way to reduce health care costs because these individuals will no longer request one treatment after another in an unending search for relief.

Recognizing the importance of this trend and the necessity that clinical practice guidelines be sound and valid, a task force of the American Psychological Association composed a template, or set, of principles for constructing and evaluating guidelines for clinical interventions for both psychological disorders and psychosocial aspects of physical disorders. These principles were published in 1995. They are necessary to ensure that future clinical practice guidelines will be comprehensive and consistent. As envisioned by the task force creating the template, the guidelines developed from it should help both the practitioner and the patient make decisions about appropriate treatment interventions for cognitive, emotional, and behavioural disorders and dysfunctions as well as psychosocial aspects of physical disorders. The guidelines will also ideally restrain administrators of health care plans in the United States from sacrificing or proscribing effective treatment, or limiting the amount of clinician time necessary to deliver treatment, in order to cut costs. The task force also felt that guidelines for psychosocial interventions could never be inflexible, since they must allow for the individual issues that arise in treating people with psychological disorders.

The Canadian Psychological Association (CPA) has been engaging in a similar exercise. Specifically, the Clinical Psychology section of the CPA has developed a task force on empirically supported treatments. They have developed recommendations for Canadian professional psychologists regarding the use of empirically supported treatments in psychology (see http://www.cpa.ca/documents/empiric_toc.html).

The APA task force decided that clinical practice guidelines for specific disorders should be constructed on the basis of two simultaneous considerations, or axes. The **clinical efficacy** axis is a thorough consideration of the scientific evidence to determine whether the intervention in question is effective. This evidence would answer the question, "Is the treatment effective when compared to an alternative treatment or to no treatment in a controlled clinical research context?" In Chapter 3, we briefly reviewed research strategies that are used to determine whether an intervention is effective. As you will remember, for many reasons a treatment might seem effective when it is not effective at all. For instance, if patients improve on their own while being treated simply because of the passage of time or the natural healing process, the treatment had little to do with the improvement. It is possible that non-specific effects of the treatment—perhaps just meeting with a caring health professional—are enough to make someone feel better without any contribution from the particular treatment technique.

To determine clinical efficacy, experiments must establish whether the intervention in question is better than no therapy, better than a non-specific therapy, or better than an alternative therapy. (The latter finding provides the highest level of evidence for a treatment's effectiveness.) We might also rely on information collected from various clinics where a large number of practitioners are treating the disorder in question. If these clinicians collect systematic data on the outcomes of their patients, they can ascertain how many are "cured," how many improve somewhat without recovering totally, and how many fail to respond to the intervention. Such data are referred to as quantified clinical observations or clinical replication series. Finally, a clinical consensus of leading experts is also a valuable source of information, although not as valuable as data from quantified clinical observations or randomized control trials.

The **clinical utility** axis is concerned with the effectiveness of the intervention in the practice setting in which it is to be applied, regardless of research evidence on its efficacy; in other words, will an intervention with proven efficacy in a research setting also be effective in the various frontline clinical settings in which it will be most frequently applied? For example, randomized controlled trials of therapy efficacy are often conducted with a very homogeneous group of patients who only have the disorder in question; those patients with comorbid disorders are typically excluded. But as we have discussed throughout this textbook, co-occurrence of more than one disorder

---

**clinical efficacy** One of a proposed set of guidelines for evaluating clinical interventions on the evidence of their effectiveness.

**clinical utility** One of a proposed set of guidelines for evaluating clinical interventions by whether they can be applied effectively and cost-effectively in real clinical settings.

(i.e., comorbidity) is a common phenomenon making it difficult to know if the results of the randomized controlled trial generalize to more complicated types of patients seen in frontline clinical settings. Also, is application of the intervention in the settings where it is needed feasible and cost-effective? This axis is concerned with external validity, the extent to which an internally valid intervention is effective in different settings or under different circumstances from those under which it was tested.

The first major issue to consider on the clinical utility axis is feasibility. Will patients accept the intervention and comply with its requirements, and is it relatively easy to administer? As noted in Chapter 6, electroconvulsive therapy (ECT) is an effective treatment for very severe depression in many cases, but it is extremely frightening to patients, many of whom refuse it. The treatment also requires sophisticated procedures and close

supervision by medical personnel, usually in a hospital setting. Therefore, it is not particularly feasible.

A second issue on the clinical utility axis is generalizability, which refers to the extent to which an intervention is effective with patients of differing backgrounds (ethnicity, age, sex) as well as in different settings (inpatient, outpatient, community) or with different therapists. Once again an intervention could be very effective in a research setting with one group of patients but generalize very poorly across different ethnic groups. For a summary of these two axes, see Table 14.3.

In reading the disorder chapters, you will have noted a number of effective treatments, both psychosocial and medical. However, most treatments are still in a preliminary stage of development. In the future, we will see a great deal of research to establish both the clinical efficacy and the clinical utility of various interventions for psychological disorders.

---

**TABLE 14.3    Overview of Template for Constructing Psychological Intervention Guidelines**

**Clinical Efficacy (Internal Validity)**

1. Better than alternative therapy (randomized controlled trials/RCTs)
2. Better than nonspecific therapy (RCTs)
3. Better than no therapy (RCTs)
4. Quantified clinical observations
5. Clinical consensus:
   Strongly positive
   Mixed
   Strongly negative
6. Contradictory evidence

Note: Confidence in treatment efficacy is based on both (a) the absolute and relative efficacy of the treatment and (b) the quality and replicability of the studies in which this judgment is made.

**Clinical Utility (External Validity)**

1. Feasibility
   A. Patient acceptability (cost, pain, duration, side effects, etc.)
   B. Patient choice in face of relatively equal efficacy
   C. Probability of compliance
   D. Ease of dissemination—number of practitioners with competence, requirements for training, opportunities for training, need for costly technologies or additional support personnel, etc.
2. Generalizability
   A. Patient characteristics
      (1) Cultural background issues
      (2) Gender issues
      (3) Developmental level issues
      (4) Other relevant patient characteristics
   B. Therapist characteristics
   C. Issues of robustness when applied in practice settings with different time frames, etc.
   D. Contextual factors regarding setting in which treatment is delivered
3. Costs and benefits
   A. Costs of delivering intervention to individual and society
   B. Costs to individual and society of withholding intervention

Note: Confidence in clinical utility as reflected on these three dimensions should be based on systematic and objective methods and strategies for assessing these characteristics of treatment as they are applied in actual practice. In some cases, randomized controlled trials will exist. More often, data will be in he form of quantified clinical observations (clinical replication series) or other strategies such as health economic calculations.

Source: From "Template for Developing Guidelines: Interventions for Mental Disorders and Psychosocial Aspects of Physical Disorders" by American Psychological Association Board of Professional Affairs Task Force on Psychological Intervention Guidelines, 1995. Approved by APA Council of Representatives, February 1995, Washington, D.C. Table 1, p.30. © 1995 by the American Psychological Association. Reprinted with permission.

In Chapter 1, we reviewed various activities that make up the role of scientist-practitioners in the mental health professions, who take a scientific approach to their clinical work in order to provide the most effective assessment procedures and interventions. Changes in the delivery of mental health services are likely to be accompanied by considerable disruption, because this is a major system that affects millions of people. But the change will also bring opportunities. Scientist-practitioners will contribute to the process of guidelines development in several ways. For example, as attempts are made to assess the clinical utility or external validity of interventions, the collected experience of thousands of mental health professionals will be immensely valuable. In fact, most of the information relevant to clinical utility or external validity will be collected by these clinicians in the course of their practice. Thus they will truly fulfill the scientist-practitioner role to the benefit of patients in our field.

# Conclusions

Therapy and scientific progress do not occur in a vacuum. People who study and treat abnormal behaviour are responsible not only for mastering the wealth of information we have only touched on in this book but also for understanding and appreciating their role in Canadian society and in the world at large. Every facet of life—from the biological to the social, political, and legal—interacts with every other; if we are to help people, we must appreciate this complexity.

We hope we have given you a good sense of the challenges faced by workers in the field of mental health and have spurred some of you to join us in this rewarding work.

# Summary

- Mental health law must balance a commitment to individual rights and fairness against majority concerns and a commitment to law and order.

## Civil Commitment

- Civil commitment laws determine the conditions under which a person may be certified legally to have a mental illness and therefore to be placed in a hospital, sometimes in conflict with the person's own wishes.
- Most Canadian jurisdictions permit commitment when several conditions have been met: (1) the person has a mental illness, (2) the person is dangerous to himself or herself or to others, or (3) the person is in need of treatment.
- "Mental illness" as used in legal system language is not synonymous with "psychological disorder"; each Canadian jurisdiction has its own definition of mental illness. Those provinces using functional definitions of mental illness include as "mentally ill" those people with very severe disturbances that negatively affect their health and safety.
- Having a severe mental illness seems to increase the likelihood of dangerousness, that is, that a person will commit violent acts in the future. In particular, having symptoms of hallucinations and delusions seems to indicate more risk for behaving violently.
- Strict civil commitment laws were designed to protect individual rights and freedoms. However, the combination of strict civil commitment laws and the lack of success with deinstitutionalization has resulted instead in transinstitutionalization and a rise in homelessness.

## Criminal Commitment

- Criminal commitment is the process by which people are held for one of two reasons: (1) they have been accused of committing a crime and are detained in a mental health facility until they can be determined as fit or unfit to participate in legal proceedings against them, or (2) they have been found not criminally responsible on account of a mental disorder (NCRMD).
- The insanity defence in Canada is currently the Not criminally responsible on account of a mental disorder (NCRMD) defence. It is primarily determined by a legal ruling from a historical case in England called the M'Naghten rule, which states that people are not responsible for criminal behaviour if they do not know what they are doing, or if they do know what they are doing but don't know it is wrong. Other rulings have influenced the insanity defence in the United States.
- A determination of fitness must be made before an individual can be tried for a criminal offence: To stand trial, people must be fit to do so—able to understand the charges against them and to assist with their own defence.

## Duty to Warn

- Duty to warn is an American legal standard and Canadian professional ethical standard that sets forth the responsibility of the therapist to warn potential victims that a client may attempt to hurt or kill them.

## Mental Health Professionals as Expert Witness

- Individuals who have specialized knowledge and who assist judges and juries in making decisions, especially about such issues as competence and malingering, are called expert witnesses.

## Patients' Rights

- One of the more fundamental rights of patients in mental facilities is their right to treatment; that is, they have a legal right to some sort of ongoing effort to both define and strive toward treatment goals. By contrast, a great deal of controversy exists over whether all patients are capable of

making a decision to refuse treatment. This is an especially difficult dilemma in the case of antipsychotic medications that may improve patients' symptoms but also bring with them severe negative side effects.

## Ethics of Research Involving Human Participants

- Those who participate in any research study must be fully informed of the risks and benefits and formally give their informed consent to participate.

## Clinical Practice Guidelines

- Clinical practice guidelines can play a major role in providing information about types of interventions likely to be effective for a specific disorder. Critical to such a determination are measures of clinical efficacy (internal validity) and clinical utility (external validity); in other words, the former is a measure of whether a treatment works and the latter is a measure of whether the treatment is effective in a variety of settings.

## Key Terms

| | | | |
|---|---|---|---|
| civil commitment laws, 579 | deinstitutionalization, 582 | criminal commitment, 584 | expert witnesses, 589 |
| mental illness, 581 | transinstitutionalization, 583 | fitness to stand trial, 588 | clinical efficacy, 594 |
| dangerousness, 581 | | duty to warn, 589 | clinical utility, 594 |

## Answers to Concept Checks

**14.1** 1. mental disorder  2. dangerous  3. treatment  4. They have been accused of committing crimes and they are waiting for their mental fitness to stand trial to be assessed  5. They have been found not criminally responsible on account of a mental disorder (NCRMD).

**14.2** 1. d  2. c  3. b  4. a

**14.3** 1. c, e  2. d  3. b  4. a

Enter these search terms: not criminally responsible on account of a mental disorder defense, mental illness, duty to warn (law)

 **The Abnormal Psychology Book Companion Website**

Go to **www.essentialsabnormalpsych.nelson.com** for practice quiz questions, Internet links, critical thinking exercises, and more.

 **InfoTrac College Edition**

If your instructor ordered your book with InfoTrac College Edition, please explore this online library for additional readings, review, and a handy resource for short assignments. Go to:

**http://infotrac.thomsonlearning.com**

 **Abnormal Psychology Live CD-ROM**

**False Memory Research:** Elizabeth Loftus is an American memory researcher who, like John Yuille, frequently serves as expert witness to the courts in areas pertaining to her research expertise. This clip of Elizabeth Loftus raises a host of questions about the use of expert witness testimony in trials related to child abuse that arise in therapy.

**Thomson NOW!** **http://hed.nelson.com** Go to this site for the link to ThomsonNow™, your one-stop study shop. Take a Pretest for this chapter and ThomsonNow™ will generate a personalized Study Plan based on your test results! The Study Plan will identify the topics you need to review and direct you to online resources to help you master

those topics. You can then take a Posttest to help you determine the concepts you have mastered and what you still need work on.

## Video Concept Review

For challenging concepts that typically need more than one explanation, Mark Durand provides a video review on the Abnormal Psychology Now site of the following topic:

- How can juries decide a person's sanity?

# Chapter Quiz

1. Concerning the insanity defence in Canada, an adaptation of which of the following standards became part of Canadian law in the late 1800s?

   a. the M'Naghten Rule
   b. the Durham Rule
   c. the American Law Institute Rule
   d. all of the above standards are included in Canadian law regarding the insanity defence

2. Sally has stopped eating because of her delusional belief that extraterrestrial aliens are trying to poison her. Because of her symptoms, Sally is placed in a psychiatric hospital involuntarily based on what civil authority?

   a. malingering
   b. uninformed consent
   c. police power
   d. *parens patriae*

3. Which statement is true regarding the relationship between mental illness and dangerousness?

   a. Men with mental illness who are of Asian ethnic background are more likely to be dangerous than men with mental illness from other ethnic groups.
   b. People with mental illness are more likely to be dangerous if they have been committed to a mental health facility against their will.
   c. Women with mental illness are more likely to be dangerous than women without mental illness.
   d. Having symptoms of hallucinations and delusions seems to indicate more risk for behaving violently.

4. One goal of taking people out of mental health facilities (deinstitutionalization) was to:

   a. create mental health centres in the community that could provide a network of supportive treatments.
   b. reduce the need for civil commitments, which had become too ethically complex.
   c. allow families to provide more intensive care in more familiar environments.
   d. test the effectiveness of new antipsychotic medications that had just been developed.

5. The *M'Naghten* rule incorporated what criterion to determine whether a person's mental state influenced guilt or innocence?

   a. Whether the act was within the individual's control.
   b. Whether an "average citizen" would excuse the act.
   c. Whether the individual knew that the act committed was wrong.
   d. Whether the individual felt remorse for the act.

6. The ruling in the Jane Hurshman case led to which change in the Canadian courts in the 1990s?

   a. the development of a legal standard on duty to warn
   b. the change in the name of the insanity defence from NGRI to NCRMD
   c. the acceptance of the "battered woman syndrome" as a murder defence
   d. legal ruling that mental health professionals must obtain informed consent for treatment from their patients

7. Research regarding use of the not criminally responsible on account of a mental disorder (NCRMD) defence has found that:

   a. the public underestimates how often people use the defence.
   b. the public overestimates how often people use this defence.
   c. the public underestimates how often people who use the defence are set free.
   d. the public overestimates how long people who are judged NCRMD are confined to a hospital.

8. Which of the following is not one of the three main differences between the Not guilty by reason of insanity (NGRI) defence and the Not criminally responsible on account of a mental disorder (NCRMD) defence?

   a. The term "insanity" has been replaced by "mental disorder."
   b. The change to NCRMD explicitly recognizes that the defendant did commit the crime as opposed to being "not guilty" of the crime.
   c. Only NCRMD judgments (but not NGRI judgments) can be made if the person is incapable of knowing that his or her actions were legally or morally wrong.
   d. People convicted of NCRMD (but not those convicted of NGRI) are detained in psychiatric hospitals, not prisons.

9. An individual who commits a crime but is judged not fit to stand trial may be:

   a. immediately released.
   b. sent to prison without a trial.
   c. committed to a mental health facility until he or she is fit to stand trial.
   d. committed to a mental health facility indefinitely.

10. According to the Tarasoff verdict in the United States, a therapist can release confidential information about a client when:
a. the therapist suspects the client may be dangerous, even though a threat has not been made.
b. the client has made a non-specific threat but the client has a history of violent behaviour.
c. the client poses a threat to the safety of a specific individual.
d. the client has made any threat of violence, even a non-specific threat.

*(See the Appendix on page 601 for answers.)*

# Answers to Chapter Quizzes

**Chapter 1 (page 33)**

1. b   2. c   3. d   4. a   5. d   6. b   7. b
8. c   9. d   10. c

**Chapter 2 (page 74)**

1. b   2. b   3. d   4. d   5. b   6. b   7. c
8. c   9. d   10. c

**Chapter 3 (page 125)**

1. c   2. b   3. a   4. d   5. a   6. d   7. b
8. c   9. a   10. c

**Chapter 4 (page 174)**

1. c   2. a   3. b   4. d   5. d   6. a   7. c
8. a   9. a   10. d

**Chapter 5 (page 212)**

1. d   2. a   3. c   4. d   5. b   6. b   7. b
8. a   9. d   10. d

**Chapter 6 (page 267)**

1. b   2. c   3. a   4. a   5. c   6. b   7. d
8. d   9. c   10. a

**Chapter 7 (page 305)**

1. a   2. a   3. d   4. c   5. a   6. c   7. a
8. b   9. c   10. a

**Chapter 8 (page 352)**

1. b   2. d   3. a   4. d   5. b   6. a   7. d
8. b   9. b   10. c

**Chapter 9 (page 397)**

1. b   2. b   3. d   4. c   5. c   6. d   7. a
8. c   9. c   10. a

**Chapter 10 (page 443)**

1. c   2. a   3. d   4. c   5. d   6. c   7. a
8. c   9. b   10. a

**Chapter 11 (page 482)**

1. c   2. a   3. b   4. b   5. a   6. c   7. c
8. c   9. d   10. a

**Chapter 12 (page 519)**

1. d   2. b   3. c   4. a   5. d   6. a   7. a
8. b   9. d   10. d

**Chapter 13 (page 572)**

1. a   2. b   3. a   4. c   5. b   6. a   7. d
8. d   9. b   10. c

**Chapter 14 (pages 599–600)**

1. a   2. d   3. d   4. a   5. c   6. c   7. b
8. d   9. c   10. c

# Glossary

**Note:** Many familiar words have specialized meanings and usage in psychology. A number of these, used in the text, are defined here.

**acute pain** Pain that typically follows an injury and disappears once the injury heals or is effectively treated.

**acute stress disorder** Severe reaction immediately following a terrifying event, often including amnesia about the event, emotional numbing, and derealization. Many victims later develop **posttraumatic stress disorder.**

**adoption studies** In genetics research, studies of first-degree relatives reared in different families and environments. If they share common characteristics, such as a disorder, this finding suggests that those characteristics have a genetic component.

**affect** Conscious, subjective aspect of an emotion that accompanies an action at a given time.

**agnosia** Inability to recognize and name objects; may be a symptom of **dementia** or other brain disorders.

**agonist** Chemical substance that effectively increases the activity of a **neurotransmitter** by imitating its effects.

**agonist substitution** Replacement of a drug on which a person is dependent with one having a similar chemical makeup, an **agonist.** Used as a treatment for substance dependence.

**agoraphobia** Anxiety about being in places or situations from which escape might be difficult.

**AIDS-related complex (ARC)** Group of minor health problems such as weight loss, fever, and night sweats that appears after HIV infection but before development of full-blown AIDS.

**alcohol use disorders** Cognitive, biological, behavioural, and social problems associated with alcohol use and abuse.

**alogia** Deficiency in the amount or content of speech, a disturbance often seen in people with **schizophrenia.**

**alters** Shorthand term for alter egos, the different personalities or identities in **dissociative identity disorder.**

**Alzheimer's disease** The "strange disease of the cerebral cortex" that causes an "atypical form of senile dementia," discovered in 1906 by the German psychiatrist Alois Alzheimer.

**amnestic disorder** Deterioration in the ability to transfer information from short- to long-term memory, in the absence of other **dementia** symptoms, as a result of **head trauma** or drug abuse.

**amphetamine use disorders** Psychological, biological, behavioural, and social problems associated with amphetamine use and abuse.

**analogue model** Approach to research employing participants who are similar to clinical clients, allowing replication of a clinical problem under controlled conditions.

**anhedonia** Inability to experience pleasure, associated with some mood and schizophrenic disorders.

**animal phobia** Unreasonable, enduring fear of animals or insects that usually develops early in life.

**anorexia nervosa** Eating disorder characterized by recurrent food refusal leading to dangerously low body weight.

**antagonist** Chemical substance that decreases or blocks the effects of a **neurotransmitter.**

**antagonist drugs** Medications that block or counteract the effects of psychoactive drugs.

**antigens** Foreign materials that enter the body, including bacteria and parasites.

**antisocial personality disorder** Cluster B (dramatic, emotional, or erratic) **personality disorder** involving a pervasive pattern of disregard for and violation of the rights of others. Similar to the non-DSM label **psychopathy** but with greater emphasis on overt behaviour rather than personality traits.

**anxiety** Mood state characterized by marked negative affect and bodily symptoms of tension in which a person apprehensively anticipates future danger or misfortune. Anxiety may involve feelings, behaviours, and physiological responses.

**aphasia** Impairment or loss of language skills resulting from brain damage caused by stroke, **Alzheimer's disease,** or other illness or trauma.

**Asperger's disorder** Pervasive developmental disorder characterized by impairments in social relationships and restricted or unusual behaviours but without the language delays seen in autism.

**association studies** Research strategies for comparing **genetic markers** in groups of people with and without a particular disorder.

**associative splitting** Separation among basic functions of human personality (e.g., cognition, emotion, perception) that was seen by some as the defining characteristic of **schizophrenia.**

**attention deficit/hyperactivity disorder (ADHD)** Developmental disorder featuring maladaptive levels of inattention, excessive activity, and impulsiveness.

**autistic disorder (autism)** Pervasive developmental disorder characterized by significant impairment in social interactions and communication and by restricted patterns of behaviour, interest, and activity.

**autoimmune disease** Condition in which the body's **immune system** attacks healthy tissue rather than antigens.

**avoidant personality disorder** Cluster C (anxious or fearful) **personality disorder** featuring a pervasive pattern of social inhibition, feelings of inadequacy, and hypersensitivity to criticism.

**avolition** Apathy, or the inability to initiate or persist in important activities.

**barbiturates** Sedative (and addictive) drugs including Amytal, Seconal, and Nembutal that are used as sleep aids.

**baseline** Measured rate of a behaviour before introduction of an intervention that allows comparison and assessment of the effects of the intervention.

**behavioural assessment** Measuring, observing, and systematically evaluating (rather than inferring) the client's thoughts, feelings, and behaviour in the actual problem situation or context.

**behavioural inhibition system (BIS)** Brain circuit in the limbic system that responds to threat signals by inhibiting activity and causing **anxiety.**

**behavioural medicine** Interdisciplinary approach applying behavioural science to the prevention, diagnosis, and treatment of medical problems.

**behavioural model** Explanation of human behaviour, including dysfunction, based on principles of learning and adaptation derived from experimental psychology.

**behaviourism** Explanation of human behaviour, including dysfunction, based on principles of learning and adaptation derived from experimental psychology.

**behaviour therapy** Array of therapy methods based on the principles of behavioural and **cognitive science,** as well as principles of learning as applied to clinical problems. It considers specific behaviours rather than inferred conflict as legitimate targets for change.

**benzodiazepines** Antianxiety drugs including Valium, Xanax, Dalmane, and Halcion also used to treat insomnia. Effective against **anxiety** (and, at high potency, **panic disorder**), they show some side effects, such as some cognitive and motor impairment, and may result in dependence and addiction. Relapse rates are extremely high when the drug is discontinued.

**binge** Relatively brief episode of uncontrolled, excessive consumption, usually of food or alcohol.

**binge-eating disorder (BED)** Pattern of eating involving distress-inducing binges not followed by purging behaviours; being considered as a new DSM diagnostic category.

**biofeedback** Use of physiological monitoring equipment to make individuals aware of their own bodily functions, such as blood pressure or brain waves, that they cannot normally access, with the purpose of controlling these functions.

**bipolar I disorder** The alternation of **major depressive episodes** with full manic episodes.

**bipolar II disorder** The alternation of **major depressive episodes** with hypomanic (not full manic) episodes.

**blood-injury-injection phobia** Unreasonable fear and avoidance of exposure to blood, injury, or the possibility of an injection. Victims often experience fainting and a drop in blood pressure.

**body dysmorphic disorder (BDD) Somatoform disorder** featuring a disruptive preoccupation with some imagined defect in appearance ("imagined ugliness").

**borderline personality disorder** Cluster B (dramatic, emotional, or erratic) **personality disorder** involving a pervasive pattern of instability of interpersonal relationships, self-image, affect, and control over impulses.

**brain circuits Neurotransmitter** currents or neural pathways in the brain.

**breathing-related sleep disorders** Sleep disruption leading to excessive sleepiness or insomnia, caused by a breathing problem such as interrupted (apnea) or laboured (hypoventilation) breathing.

**brief psychotic disorder** Psychotic disturbance involving **delusions, hallucinations,** or **disorganized speech** or behaviour, but lasting less than 1 month; often occurs in reaction to a stressor.

**bulimia nervosa** Eating disorder involving recurrent episodes of uncontrolled excessive **(binge)** eating followed by compensatory actions to remove the food (e.g., deliberate vomiting, laxative abuse, excessive exercise).

**caffeine use disorders** Cognitive, biological, behavioural, and social problems associated with the use of caffeine.

**cancer** Category of often-fatal medical conditions involving abnormal cell growth and malignancy.

**cardiovascular disease** Afflictions in the mechanisms, including the heart, blood vessels, and their controllers, that are responsible for transporting blood to the body's tissues and organs. Psychological factors may play important roles in such diseases and their treatments.

**case study method** Research procedure in which a single person or small group is studied in detail. The method does not allow conclusions about cause-and-effect relationships, and findings can be generalized only with great caution.

**catatonia** Disorder of movement involving immobility or excited agitation.

**catatonic immobility** Disturbance of motor behaviour in which the person remains motionless, sometimes in an awkward posture, for extended periods.

**catatonic type of schizophrenia** Type of **schizophrenia** in which motor disturbances (rigidity, agitation, odd mannerisms) predominate.

**catharsis** Rapid or sudden release of emotional tension thought to be an important factor in psychoanalytic therapy.

**childhood disintegrative disorder** Pervasive developmental disorder involving severe regression in language, adaptive behaviour, and motor skills after a 2- to 4-year period of normal development.

**chronic fatigue syndrome (CFS)** Incapacitating exhaustion following only minimal exertion, accompanied by fever, headaches, muscle and joint pain, depression, and **anxiety.**

**chronic pain** Enduring pain that does not decrease over time; may occur in muscles, joints, and the lower back; and may be due to enlarged blood vessels or degenerating or cancerous tissue. Other significant factors are social and psychological.

**circadian rhythm sleep disorder** Sleep disturbance resulting in sleepiness or insomnia, caused by the body's inability to synchronize its sleep patterns with the current pattern of day and night.

**civil commitment laws** Legal proceedings that determine a person has a mental illness and may be hospitalized, even involuntarily.

**classical categorical approach** Classification method founded on the assumption of clear-cut differences among disorders, each with a different known cause.

**classical conditioning** Fundamental learning process first described by Ivan Pavlov. An event that automatically elicits a response is paired with another stimulus event that does not (a neutral stimulus). After repeated pairings, the neutral stimulus becomes a conditioned stimulus that by itself can elicit the desired response.

**classification** Assignment of objects or people to categories on the basis of shared characteristics.

**clinical assessment** Systematic evaluation and measurement of psychological, biological, and social factors in a person presenting with a possible psychological disorder.

**clinical description** Details of the combination of behaviours, thoughts, and feelings of an individual that make up a particular disorder.

**clinical efficacy (axis)** One of a proposed set of guidelines for evaluating clinical interventions on the evidence of their effectiveness.

**clinical significance** Degree to which research findings have useful and meaningful applications to real problems.

**clinical utility (axis)** One of a proposed set of guidelines for evaluating clinical interventions by whether they can be applied effectively and cost effectively in real clinical settings.

**cocaine use disorders** Cognitive, biological, behavioural, and social problems associated with the use and abuse of cocaine.

**cognitive science** Field of study that examines how humans and other animals acquire, process, store, and retrieve information.

**cognitive-behavioural therapy (CBT)** Group of treatment procedures aimed at identifying and modifying faulty thought processes, attitudes and attributions, and problem behaviours; often used synonymously with **cognitive therapy.**

**cognitive therapy** Treatment approach that involves identifying and altering negative thinking styles related to psychological disorders such as depression and **anxiety** and replacing them with more positive beliefs and attitudes—and, ultimately, more adaptive behaviour and coping styles.

**cohort** Participants in each age group of a cross-sectional research study.

**cohort effect** Observation that people of different age groups also differ in their values and experiences.

**comorbidity** The presence of two or more disorders in an individual at the same time.

**comparative treatment research** Outcome research that contrasts two or more treatment methods to determine which is most effective.

**compulsions** Repetitive, ritualistic, time-consuming behaviours or mental acts a person feels driven to perform.

**confound** Any factor occurring in a research study that makes the results uninterpretable because its effects cannot be separated from those of the variables being studied.

**control group** Group of individuals in a research study who are similar to the experimental participants in every way but are not exposed to the treatment received by the experimental group; their presence allows a comparison of the differential effects of the treatment.

**controlled drinking** A controversial treatment approach to alcohol dependence in which abusers are taught to drink in moderation.

**conversion disorder** Physical malfunctioning, such as blindness or paralysis, suggesting neurological impairment but with no organic pathology to account for it.

**coronary heart disease (CHD)** Blockage of the arteries supplying blood to the heart muscle; a major cause of death in Western culture, with social and psychological factors involved.

**correlation** Degree to which two variables are associated.

**correlation coefficient** Computed statistic reflecting the strength and direction of any association between two variables. It can range from +1.00 through 0 (indicating no association) to –1.00, with the absolute value indicating the strength and the sign reflecting the direction.

**course** Pattern of development and change of a disorder over time.

**covert sensitization** Cognitive-behavioural intervention to reduce unwanted behaviours by having clients imagine the extremely aversive consequences of the behaviours and establish negative rather than positive associations with them.

**Creutzfeldt-Jakob disease** Extremely rare condition that causes **dementia.**

**criminal commitment** Legal procedure by which a person who is found not guilty of a crime by reason of insanity must be confined in a psychiatric hospital.

**cross-generational effect** Limit to the **generalizability** of longitudinal research because the group under study may differ from others in culture and experience.

**cross-sectional design** Methodology to examine a characteristic by comparing different individuals of different ages. Contrast with **longitudinal design.**

**cultural-familial retardation** Mild **mental retardation** that may be caused largely by environmental influences.

**cyclothymic disorder** Chronic (at least 2 years) **mood disorder** characterized by alternating **mood** elevation and depression levels that are not as severe as manic or **major depressive episodes.**

**dangerousness** Tendency to violence that, contrary to popular opinion, is generally not more likely among mental patients.

**defence mechanisms** Common patterns of behaviour, often adaptive coping styles when they occur in moderation, observed in response to particular situations. In **psychoanalysis,** these are thought to be unconscious processes originating in the **ego.**

**deinstitutionalization** Systematic removal of people with severe **mental illness** or **mental retardation** out of institutions like psychiatric hospitals.

**delirium** Rapid-onset reduced clarity of consciousness and cognition, with confusion, disorientation, and deficits in memory and language.

**delusion** Psychotic symptom involving disorder of thought content and presence of strong beliefs that are misrepresentations of reality.

**delusional disorder** Psychotic disorder featuring a persistent belief contrary to reality (**delusion**) but no other symptoms of **schizophrenia.**

**dementia** Gradual-onset deterioration of brain functioning involving memory loss, inability to recognize objects or faces, and problems in planning and abstract reasoning. These are associated with frustration and discouragement.

**dementia of the Alzheimer's type** Gradual onset of cognitive deficits caused by **Alzheimer's disease,** principally identified by person's inability to recall newly or previously learned material. The most common form of **dementia.**

**dementia praecox** Latin term meaning "premature loss of mind," an early label for what is now called **schizophrenia,** emphasizing the disorder's frequent appearance during adolescence.

**dependent personality disorder** Cluster C (anxious or fearful) **personality disorder** characterized by a person's pervasive and excessive need to be taken care of, a condition that leads to submissive and clinging behaviour and fears of separation.

**dependent variable** In an experimental research study, the phenomenon that is measured and expected to be influenced.

**depersonalization disorder Dissociative disorder** in which feelings of depersonalization are so severe they dominate the client's life and prevent normal functioning.

**depressants Psychoactive substances** that result in behavioural sedation, including alcohol and the sedative, hypnotic, and anxiolytic drugs.

**depressive cognitive triad** Thinking errors in depressed people negatively focused in three areas: themselves, their immediate world, and their future.

**derealization** Situation in which the individual loses his or her sense of the reality of the external world.

**diagnosis** Process of determining whether a presenting problem meets the established criteria for a specific **psychological disorder.**

**diathesis–stress model Hypothesis** that both an inherited tendency (a vulnerability) and specific stressful conditions are required to produce a disorder.

**dimensional approach** Method of categorizing characteristics on a continuum rather than on a binary, either-or, or all-or-none basis.

**directionality** Possibility that, when two variables, A and B, are correlated, variable A causes variable B or B causes A.

**disorder of written expression** Writing performance is significantly below age norms.

**disorganized speech** Style of talking often seen in people with **schizophrenia,** involving incoherence and a lack of typical logic patterns.

**disorganized type of schizophrenia** Type of **schizophrenia** featuring disrupted speech and behaviour, disjointed **delusions** and **hallucinations,** and flat or silly affect.

**dissociative amnesia Dissociative disorder** featuring the inability to recall personal information, usually of a stressful or traumatic nature.

**dissociative disorders** Disorders in which individuals feel detached from themselves or their surroundings, and reality, experience, and identity may disintegrate.

**dissociative fugue Dissociative disorder** featuring sudden, unexpected travel from home, along with an inability to recall one's past, sometimes with assumption of a new identity.

**dissociative identity disorder (DID)** Formerly known as *multiple personality disorder,* a disorder in which as many as 100 personalities or fragments of personalities coexist within one body and mind.

**dissociative trance disorder (DTD)** Altered state of consciousness in which the person believes firmly that he or she is possessed by spirits; considered a disorder only where there is distress and dysfunction.

**dopamine Neurotransmitter** whose generalized function is to activate other neurotransmitters and to aid in exploratory and pleasure-seeking behaviours (thus balancing **serotonin**). A relative excess of dopamine is implicated in **schizophrenia** (though contradictory evidence suggests the connection is not simple), and its deficit is involved in **Parkinson's disease.**

**double bind communication** According to an obsolete, unsupported theory, the practice of transmitting conflicting messages that was thought to cause **schizophrenia.**

**double-blind control** Procedure in outcome studies that prevents bias by ensuring that neither the participants nor the providers of the experimental treatment know who is receiving treatment and who is receiving placebo.

**double depression** Severe mood disorder typified by **major depressive episodes** superimposed over a background of **dysthymic disorder.**

**Down syndrome** Type of **mental retardation** caused by a chromosomal aberration (chromosome 21) and involving characteristic physical appearance.

**dream analysis** Psychoanalytic therapy method in which dream contents are examined as symbolic of **id** impulses and **intrapsychic conflicts.**

**duty to warn** Mental health professional's responsibility to break confidentiality and notify the potential victim whom a client has specifically threatened.

**dyspareunia** Pain or discomfort during sexual intercourse.

**dysphoric manic episode** See **mixed manic episode.**

**dyssomnias** Problems in getting to sleep or in obtaining sufficient quality sleep.

**dysthymic disorder Mood disorder** involving persistently depressed mood, with low self-esteem, withdrawal, pessimism, or despair, and present for at least 2 years with no absence of symptoms for more than 2 months.

**ego** In **psychoanalysis,** the psychic entity responsible for finding realistic and practical ways to satisfy **id** drives.

**ego psychology** Derived from **psychoanalysis,** this theory emphasizes the role of the **ego** in development and attributes **psychological disorders** to failure of the ego to manage impulses and internal conflicts.

**electroconvulsive therapy (ECT)** Biological treatment for severe, chronic depression involving the application of electrical impulses through the brain to produce seizures. The reasons for its effectiveness are unknown.

**electroencephalogram (EEG)** Measure of electrical activity patterns in the brain, taken through electrodes placed on the scalp.

**emotion** Pattern of action elicited by an external event and a feeling state, accompanied by a characteristic physiological response.

**endogenous opioids** Substances occurring naturally throughout the body that function like **neurotransmitters** to shut down pain sensation even in the presence of marked tissue damage. These may contribute to psychological problems such as eating disorders. Also known as endorphins or enkephalins.

**epidemiology Psychopathology** research method examining the **prevalence,** distribution, and consequences of disorders in populations.

**equifinality** Developmental **psychopathology** principle that a behaviour or disorder may have several different causes.

**essential hypertension** High blood pressure with no verifiable physical cause, which makes up the overwhelming majority of high blood pressure cases.

**etiology** Cause or source of a disorder.

**exhibitionism** Sexual gratification attained by exposing one's genitals to unsuspecting strangers.

**experiment** Research method that can establish causation by manipulating the variables in question and controlling for alternative explanations of any observed effects.

**expert witness** Person who because of special training and experience is allowed to offer opinion testimony in legal trials.

**expressed emotion** The hostility, criticism, and overinvolvement demonstrated by some families toward a family member with a **psychological disorder;** this can often contribute to the person's relapse.

**expressive language disorder** An individual's problems in spoken communication, as measured by significantly low scores on standardized tests of expressive language relative to nonverbal intelligence test scores. Symptoms may include a markedly limited vocabulary or errors in verb tense.

**external validity** Extent to which research study findings generalize, or apply, to people and settings not involved in the study.

**extinction** Learning process in which a response maintained by **reinforcement** in operant conditioning or pairing in **classical conditioning** decreases when that reinforcement or pairing is removed; also the procedure of removing that reinforcement or pairing.

**facial agnosia** Type of **agnosia** characterized by a person's inability to recognize even familiar faces.

**factitious disorder** Nonexistent physical or **psychological disorder** deliberately faked for no apparent gain except possibly sympathy and attention.

**false negative** Assessment error in which no pathology is noted (i.e., test results are negative) when it is actually present.

**false positive** Assessment error in which pathology is reported (i.e., test results are positive) when none is actually present.

**family studies** Genetic studies that examine patterns of traits and behaviours among relatives.

**fear** Emotional response consisting of an immediate alarm reaction to present danger or life-threatening emergencies.

**female orgasmic disorder** Recurring delay or absence of orgasm in some women following a normal sexual excitement phase, relative to their prior experience and current stimulation. Also known as **inhibited (female) orgasm.**

**female sexual arousal disorder** Recurrent inability in some women to attain or maintain adequate lubrication and swelling sexual excitement responses to allow for completion of sexual activity.

**fetal alcohol syndrome (FAS)** Pattern of problems including learning difficulties, behaviour deficits, and characteristic physical flaws, resulting from heavy drinking by the victim's mother when she was pregnant with the victim.

**fetishism** Long-term, recurring, intense sexually arousing urges, fantasies, or behaviour involving the use of nonliving, unusual objects, which cause distress or impairment in life functioning.

**fight/flight system (FFS)** Brain circuit in animals that when stimulated causes an immediate alarm and escape response resembling human panic.

**fight or flight response** Biological reaction to alarming stressors that musters the body's resources (e.g., blood flow, respiration) to resist or flee the threat.

**fitness to stand trial** Before people can be tried for a criminal offence, they must be determined able to understand the charges against them and able to assist with their own defence.

**flat affect** Apparently emotionless demeanour (including toneless speech and vacant gaze) when a reaction would be expected.

**fragile X syndrome** Pattern of abnormality caused by a defect in the X chromosome resulting in **mental retardation,** learning problems, and unusual physical characteristics.

**free association** Psychoanalytic therapy technique intended to explore threatening material repressed into the **unconscious.** The patient is instructed to say whatever comes to mind without censoring.

**gamma aminobutyric acid (GABA) Neurotransmitter** that reduces activity across the synapse and thus inhibits a range of behaviours and emotions, especially generalized anxiety.

**gender identity disorder** Psychological dissatisfaction with one's own biological gender, a disturbance in the sense of one's identity as a male or female. The primary goal is not sexual arousal but rather to live the life of the opposite gender.

**general adaptation syndrome (GAS)** Sequence of reactions to sustained **stress** described by Hans Selye. These stages are alarm, resistance, and exhaustion, which may lead to death.

**generalizability** Extent to which research results apply to a range of individuals not included in the study.

**generalized amnesia** Condition in which the person loses memory of all personal information, including his or her own identity.

**generalized anxiety disorder (GAD)** Anxiety disorder characterized by intense, uncontrollable, unfocused, chronic, and continuous worry that is distressing and unproductive accompanied by physical symptoms of tenseness, irritability, and restlessness.

**genes** Long deoxyribonucleic acid (DNA) molecules, the basic physical units of heredity that appear as locations on chromosomes.

**genetic linkage studies** Studies that seek to match the inheritance pattern of a disorder to that of a **genetic marker;** this helps researchers establish the location of the gene responsible for the disorder.

**genetic marker** Inherited characteristic for which the chromosomal location of the responsible gene is known.

**genotype** Specific genetic makeup of an individual.

**hallucination** Psychotic symptom of perceptual disturbance in which things are seen, heard, or otherwise sensed although they are not real or actually present.

**hallucinogen** Any **psychoactive substance** such as **LSD** or **marijuana** that can produce delusions, **hallucinations, paranoia,** and altered sensory perception.

**hallucinogen use disorders** Cognitive, biological, behavioural, and social problems associated with the use and abuse of hallucinogenic substances.

**harm reduction** Approach to **substance abuse** prevention and treatment that seeks to minimize the harm associated with substance use as its primary goal (e.g., controlled drinking interventions, safer injection sites for injection drug users).

**head trauma** Injury to the head and therefore to the brain, typically caused by accidents; can lead to cognitive impairments, including memory loss.

**health psychology** Subfield of **behavioural medicine** that studies psychological factors important in health promotion and maintenance.

**hebephrenia** Silly and immature emotionality, a characteristic of some types of **schizophrenia.**

**histrionic personality disorder** Cluster B (dramatic, emotional, or erratic) **personality disorder** involving a pervasive pattern of excessive emotionality and attention seeking.

**HIV-l disease** Human immunodeficiency virus-type-1 that causes AIDS and can cause **dementia.**

**homosexuality** Sexual attraction to members of the same sex.

**hormone** Chemical messenger produced by the endocrine glands.

**human genome project** Ongoing scientific attempt to develop a comprehensive map of all human genes.

**Huntington's disease** Genetic disorder marked by involuntary limb movements and progressing to **dementia.**

**hypersomnia** Abnormally excessive sleep; a person with this condition will fall asleep several times a day.

**hypertension** Also known as *high blood pressure;* a major risk factor for stroke and heart and kidney disease that is intimately related to psychological factors.

**hypoactive sexual desire disorder** Apparent lack of interest in sexual activity or fantasy that would not be expected considering the person's age and life situation.

**hypochondriasis** **Somatoform disorder** involving severe anxiety over the belief that one has a disease process without any evident physical cause.

**hypomanic episode** Less severe and less disruptive version of a **manic episode** that is one of the criteria for several **mood disorders.**

**hypothesis** Educated guess or statement to be tested by research.

**id** In **psychoanalysis,** the unconscious psychic entity present at birth representing basic drives.

**immune system** Body's means of identifying and eliminating any foreign materials (e.g., bacteria, parasites, even transplanted organs) that enter.

**implicit memory** Condition of memory in which a person cannot recall past events even though he or she acts in response to them.

**impulse control disorders** Disorders that deprive a person of the ability to resist acting on a drive or temptation. Pathological gambling is one example.

**inappropriate affect** Emotional displays that do not match the situation.

**incest** Deviant sexual attraction directed toward one's own family member; often the attraction of a father to a daughter who is maturing physically.

**incidence** Number of new cases of a disorder appearing during a specific time period (compare with **prevalence**).

**independent variable** Phenomenon that is manipulated by the experimenter in a research study and expected to influence the **dependent variable.**

**informed consent** Ethical requirement whereby research participants agree to participate in a research study only after they receive full disclosure about the nature of the study and their role in it.

**inhibited orgasm** Inability to achieve orgasm despite adequate sexual desire and arousal; commonly seen in women but relatively rare in men.

**intelligence quotient (IQ)** Score on an intelligence test estimating a person's deviation from average test performance.

**internal validity** Extent to which the results of a research study can be attributed to the **independent variable** after confounding alternative explanations have been ruled out.

**interpersonal psychotherapy (IPT)** Newer brief treatment approach that emphasizes resolution of interpersonal problems and stressors such as role disputes in marital conflict or forming relationships in marriage or a new job. It has demonstrated effectiveness for such problems as depression.

**intrapsychic conflicts** In **psychoanalysis,** the struggles among the **id, ego,** and **superego.**

**introspection** Early, non-scientific approach to the study of psychology involving systematic attempts to report thoughts and feelings that specific stimuli evoked.

**inverse agonist** Chemical substance that produces effects opposite those of a particular **neurotransmitter.**

**labelling** Applying a name to a phenomenon or a pattern of behaviour. The label may acquire negative connotations or be applied erroneously to the person rather than to his or her behaviours.

**learned helplessness theory of depression** Seligman's theory that people become anxious and depressed when they make an *attribution* that they have no control over the **stress** in their lives (whether in reality they do or not).

**learning disorders** Reading, mathematics, or written expression performance substantially below levels expected relative to the person's age, IQ, and education.

**level** The degree of behaviour change with different interventions (e.g., high or low).

**localized amnesia** Memory loss limited to specific times and events, particularly traumatic events. Also known as *selective amnesia.*

**longitudinal design** Systematic study of changes in the same individual or group examined over time.

**LSD (d-lysergic acid diethylamide)** Most common hallucinogenic drug; a synthetic version of the grain fungus ergot.

**maintenance treatment** Combination of continued **psychosocial treatment** and/or medication designed to prevent relapse following therapy.

**major depressive disorder, single or recurrent episode** Mood disorder involving one (*single episode*) or more (separated by at least 2 months without depression—*recurrent*) **major depressive episodes.**

**major depressive episode** Most common and severe experience of depression, including feelings of worthlessness, disturbances in bodily activities such as sleep, loss of interest, and the inability to experience pleasure, persisting at least 2 weeks.

**male erectile disorder** Recurring inability in some men to attain or maintain adequate penile erection until completion of sexual activity.

**male orgasmic disorder** Recurring delay in or absence of orgasm in some men following a normal sexual excitement phase, relative to age and current stimulation. Also known as **inhibited (male) orgasm.**

**malingering** Deliberate faking of a physical or **psychological disorder** motivated by gain.

**mania** Period of abnormally excessive elation or euphoria, associated with some **mood disorders.**

**marijuana (cannabis sativa)** Dried part of the hemp plant, a **hallucinogen** that is the most widely used illegal substance.

**mathematics disorder** Mathematics performance significantly below age norms.

**mental hygiene movement** Mid-19th-century effort to improve care of the mentally disordered by informing the public of their mistreatment.

**mental illness** Term formerly used to mean **psychological disorder** but less preferred because it implies that the causes of the disorder can be found in a medical disease process.

**mental retardation** Significantly below-average intellectual functioning paired with deficits in adaptive functioning such as self-care or occupational activities appearing before age 18.

**mental status exam** Relatively coarse preliminary test of a client's judgment, orientation to time and place, and emotional and mental state; typically conducted during an initial interview.

**microsleeps** Short, seconds-long periods of sleep that occur in people who have been deprived of sleep.

**mixed manic episode** Condition in which the individual experiences both elation and depression or **anxiety** at the same time. Also known as **dysphoric manic episode.**

**modelling** Learning through observation and imitation of the behaviour of other individuals and the consequences of that behaviour.

**mood** Enduring period of emotionality.

**mood disorders** Group of disorders involving severe and enduring disturbances in emotionality ranging from elation to severe depression.

**moral therapy** 19th-century psychosocial approach to treatment that involved treating patients as normally as possible in normal environments.

**multidimensional integrative approach** Approach to the study of **psychopathology,** which holds that **psychological**

**disorders** are always the products of multiple interacting causal factors.

**multiple baseline** **Single-case experimental research design** in which measures are taken on two or more behaviours or on a single behaviour in two or more situations. A particular intervention is introduced for each at different times. If behaviour change is coincident with each introduction, this is strong evidence that the intervention caused the change.

**narcissistic personality disorder** Cluster B (dramatic, emotional, or erratic) **personality disorder** involving a pervasive pattern of grandiosity in fantasy or behaviour, need for admiration, and lack of empathy.

**narcolepsy** Sleep disorder involving sudden and irresistible sleep attacks.

**natural environment phobia** Fear of situations or events in nature, especially heights, storms, and water.

**negative correlation** Association between two variables in which one increases as the other decreases.

**negative symptoms** Symptoms involving deficits in normal behaviour, such as **flat affect** and poverty of speech, displayed by some people with **schizophrenia.**

**neurohormones** Hormones that affect the brain and are increasingly the focus of study in **psychopathology.**

**neuroimaging** Sophisticated computer-aided procedures that allow non-intrusive examination of nervous system structure and function.

**neuron** Individual nerve cell responsible for transmitting information.

**neuropsychological testing** Assessment of brain and nervous system functioning by testing an individual's performance on behavioural tasks.

**neuroscience** Study of the nervous system and its role in behaviour, thoughts, and **emotions.**

**neurosis** Obsolete psychodynamic term for **psychological disorder** thought to result from unconscious conflicts and the **anxiety** they cause. Plural is *neuroses.*

**neurotransmitters** Chemicals that cross the **synaptic cleft** between nerve cells to transmit impulses from one **neuron** to the next. Their relative excess or deficiency is involved in several **psychological disorders.**

**nicotine use disorders** Cognitive, biological, behavioural, and social problems associated with the use of nicotine.

**nightmares** Frightening and anxiety-provoking dreams occurring during **rapid eye movement (REM) sleep.** The individual recalls the bad dreams and recovers alertness and orientation quickly.

**nomenclature** In a naming system or **nosology,** the actual labels or names that are applied. In **psychopathology,** these include **mood disorders** or eating disorders.

**norepinephrine (also noradrenaline) Neurotransmitter** that is active in the central and peripheral nervous systems, controlling heart rate, blood pressure, and respiration, among other functions. Because of its role in the body's alarm reaction, it may also contribute in general and indirectly to **panic attacks** and **anxiety** and **mood disorders.**

**nosology** Classification and naming system for medical and psychological phenomena.

**object relations** Modern development in psychodynamic theory involving the study of how children incorporate the memories and values of people who are close and important to them.

**obsessions** Recurrent intrusive thoughts or impulses the client seeks to suppress or neutralize while recognizing they are not imposed by outside forces.

**obsessive-compulsive disorder (OCD)** Anxiety disorder involving unwanted, persistent, intrusive thoughts and impulses as well as repetitive actions intended to suppress them.

**obsessive-compulsive personality disorder** Cluster C (anxious or fearful) **personality disorder** featuring a pervasive pattern of preoccupation with orderliness, perfectionism, and mental and interpersonal control at the expense of flexibility, openness, and efficiency.

**opioids** Addictive **psychoactive substances** such as heroin, opium, and morphine that cause temporary euphoria and analgesia (pain reduction).

**opioid use disorders** Cognitive, biological, behavioural, and social problems associated with the use and abuse of **opiates** and their synthetic variants.

**orgasmic reconditioning** Learning procedure to help clients strengthen appropriate patterns of sexual arousal by pairing appropriate stimuli with the pleasurable sensations of masturbation.

**pain disorder Somatoform disorder** featuring true pain but for which psychological factors play an important role in onset, severity, or maintenance.

**panic** Sudden overwhelming fright or terror.

**panic attack** Abrupt experience of intense fear or discomfort accompanied by a number of physical symptoms, such as dizziness or heart palpitations.

**panic control treatment (PCT)** Cognitive-behavioural treatment for **panic attacks,** involving gradual exposure to feared somatic sensations and modification of perceptions and attitudes about them.

**panic disorder with agoraphobia (PDA)** Fear and avoidance of situations the person believes might induce a dreaded **panic attack.**

**panic disorder without agoraphobia (PD)** **Panic attacks** experienced without development of **agoraphobia.**

**paranoia** Person's irrational belief that he or she is especially important (delusions of grandeur) or that other people are seeking to do him or her harm.

**paranoid personality disorder** Cluster A (odd or eccentric) **personality disorder** involving pervasive distrust and suspiciousness of others such that their motives are interpreted as malevolent.

**paranoid type of schizophrenia** Type of **schizophrenia** in which symptoms primarily involve **delusions** and **hallucinations;** speech and motor and emotional behaviour are relatively intact.

**paraphilias** Sexual disorders and deviations in which sexual arousal occurs almost exclusively in the context of inappropriate objects or individuals.

**parasomnias** Abnormal behaviours such as **nightmares** or **sleepwalking** that occur during sleep.

**Parkinson's disease** Degenerative brain disorder principally affecting motor performance (e.g., tremors, stooped posture) associated with reduction in **dopamine. Dementia** may be a result.

**pathological gambling** Persistent and recurrent maladaptive gambling behaviour.

**pathological** or **impacted grief reaction** Extreme reaction to the death of a loved one that involves psychotic features, **suicidal ideation,** or severe loss of weight or energy, or that persists more than 2 months.

**pedophilia Paraphilia** (sexual deviation) involving strong sexual attraction toward children.

**personality disorders** Enduring maladaptive patterns of relating to the environment and oneself, exhibited in a wide range of contexts that cause significant functional impairment or subjective distress.

**personality inventories** Self-report questionnaires that assess personal traits by asking respondents to identify descriptions that apply to them.

**person-centred therapy** Therapy method in which the client, rather than the counsellor, primarily directs the course of discussion, seeking self-discovery and self-responsibility.

**pervasive developmental disorders** Wide-ranging, significant, and long-lasting dysfunctions that appear before the age of 18.

**pervasive developmental disorder—not otherwise specified** Severe and pervasive impairments in social interactions, but does not meet all of the criteria for **autistic disorder.**

**phenotype** Observable characteristics or behaviours of an individual.

**phobia** Psychological disorder characterized by marked and persistent fear of an object or situation.

**Pick's disease** Rare neurological disorder that results in presenile (early onset) **dementia.**

**placebo control group** In an outcome experiment, a control group that does not receive the experimental manipulation but is given a similar procedure with an identical expectation of change, allowing the researcher to assess any **placebo effect.**

**placebo effect** Behaviour change resulting from the person's expectation of change rather than from the experimental manipulation.

**polysomnographic (PSG) evaluation** Assessment of sleep disorders in which a client sleeping in the lab is monitored for heart, muscle, respiration, brain wave, and other functions.

**polysubstance use** Use of multiple mood- and behaviour-altering substances, such as drugs.

**positive correlation** Association between two variables in which one increases as the other increases.

**positive symptoms** More overt symptoms, such as **delusions** and **hallucinations,** displayed by some people with **schizophrenia.**

**posttraumatic stress disorder (PTSD)** Enduring, distressing emotional disorder that follows exposure to a severe helplessness- or fear-inducing threat. The victim re-experiences the trauma, avoids stimuli associated with it, and develops a numbing of responsiveness and an increased vigilance and arousal.

**premature ejaculation** Recurring ejaculation before the person wishes it, with minimal sexual stimulation.

**prepared learning** Certain associations can be learned more readily than others because this ability has been adaptive for evolution.

**presenting problem** Original complaint reported by the client to the therapist. The actual treated problem may sometimes be a modification derived from the presenting problem.

**prevalence** Number of people displaying a disorder in the total population at any given time (compare with **incidence**).

**primary insomnia** Difficulty in initiating, maintaining, or gaining from sleep; not related to other medical or psychological problems.

**proband** In genetics research, the individual displaying the trait or characteristic being studied. Also known as **index case.**

**prognosis** Predicted future development of a disorder over time.

**projective tests** Psychoanalytically based measures that present ambiguous stimuli to clients on the assumption that their responses will reveal their unconscious conflicts. Such tests are inferential and lack high reliability and validity.

**prototypical approach** System for categorizing disorders using essential, defining characteristics and a range of variation on other characteristics.

**psychoactive substances** Substances, such as drugs, that alter mood or behaviour.

**psychoanalysis** Psychoanalytic assessment and therapy, which emphasizes exploration of, and insight into, unconscious processes and conflicts, pioneered by Sigmund Freud.

**psychoanalyst** Therapist who practises **psychoanalysis** after earning either an M.D. or a Ph.D. degree and receiving additional specialized postdoctoral training.

**psychoanalytic model** Complex and comprehensive theory originally advanced by Sigmund Freud that seeks to account for the development and structure of personality, as well as the origin of abnormal behaviour, based primarily on inferred inner entities and forces.

**psychodynamic psychotherapy** Contemporary version of **psychoanalysis** that still emphasizes unconscious processes and conflicts but is briefer and more focused on specific problems.

**psychological autopsy** Postmortem psychological profile of a suicide victim constructed from interviews with people who knew the person before death.

**psychological disorder** Psychological dysfunction associated with distress or impairment in functioning that is not a typical or culturally expected response.

**psychoneuroimmunology (PNI)** Study of psychological influences on the neurological responses involved in the body's immune response.

**psycho-oncology** Study of psychological factors involved in the course and treatment of **cancer.**

**psychopathology** Scientific study of **psychological disorders.**

**psychopathy** Non-DSM category similar to **antisocial personality disorder** but with less emphasis on overt behaviour; indicators include superficial charm, lack of remorse, and other personality characteristics.

**psychophysiological assessment** Measurement of changes in the nervous system reflecting psychological or emotional events such as **anxiety, stress,** and sexual arousal.

**psychosexual stages of development** In **psychoanalysis,** the sequence of phases a person passes through during development. Each stage is named for the location on the body where **id** gratification is maximal at that time.

**psychosocial treatment** Treatment practices that focus on social and cultural factors (such as family experience) and on psychological influences. These approaches include cognitive, behavioural, and interpersonal methods.

**psychotic behaviour** Severe **psychological disorder** category characterized by **hallucinations** and loss of contact with reality.

**purging techniques** In the eating disorder **bulimia nervosa,** the self-induced vomiting or laxative abuse used to compensate for excessive food ingestion.

**randomization** Method for placing individuals into research groups that assures each one of an equal chance of being assigned to any group, to eliminate any systematic differences across groups.

**rapid eye movement (REM) sleep** Periodic intervals of sleep during which the eyes move rapidly from side to side, and dreams occur, but the body is inactive.

**reading disorder** Reading performance significantly below age norms.

**rebound insomnia** In a person with insomnia, the worsened sleep problems that can occur when medications are used to treat insomnia and then withdrawn.

**reciprocal gene–environment model** **Hypothesis** that people with a genetic predisposition for a disorder may also have a genetic tendency to create environmental risk factors that promote the disorder.

**reinforcement** In operant conditioning, consequences for behaviour that strengthen it or increase its frequency. *Positive* reinforcement involves the contingent delivery of a desired consequence; *negative* reinforcement is the contingent escape from an aversive consequence. Unwanted behaviours may result from their reinforcement or the failure to reinforce desired behaviours.

**relapse prevention** Extending therapeutic progress by teaching the client how to cope with future troubling situations; using cognitive and behavioural skills to avoid a recurrence of substance dependence, such as by avoiding or anticipating high-risk situations.

**relaxation response** Active components of meditation methods, including repetitive thoughts of a sound to reduce distracting thoughts and closing the mind to other intruding thoughts, that decrease the flow of stress hormones and **neurotransmitters** and cause a feeling of calm.

**reliability** Degree to which a measurement is consistent—for example, over time or among different raters.

**research design** Plan of experimentation used to test a **hypothesis.**

**residual type of schizophrenia** Diagnostic category for people who have experienced at least one episode of **schizophrenia** and who no longer display its major symptoms but still show some bizarre thoughts or social withdrawal.

**retrospective information** Literally "the view back," data collected by examining records or recollections of the past. It is limited by the accuracy, validity, and thoroughness of the sources.

**Rett's disorder** Progressive neurological developmental disorder featuring constant hand-wringing, **mental retardation,** and impaired motor skills.

**reuptake** Action by which a **neurotransmitter** is quickly drawn back into the discharging **neuron** after being released into a **synaptic cleft.**

**reversal design** See **withdrawal design.**

**rheumatoid arthritis** Painful, degenerative disease in which the **immune system** essentially attacks itself, resulting in stiffness, swelling, and even destruction of the joints. Cognitive-behavioural treatments can help relieve pain and stiffness.

**schizoaffective disorder** Psychotic disorder featuring symptoms of both **schizophrenia** and major mood disorder.

**schizoid personality disorder** Cluster A (odd or eccentric) **personality disorder** featuring a pervasive pattern of detachment from social relationships and a restricted range of expression of **emotions.**

**schizophrenia** Devastating psychotic disorder that may involve characteristic disturbances in thinking **(delusions),** perception **(hallucinations),** speech, **emotions,** and behaviour.

**schizophreniform disorder** Psychotic disorder involving the symptoms of **schizophrenia** but lasting less than 6 months.

**schizophrenogenic mother** According to an obsolete, unsupported theory, a cold, dominating, and rejecting parent who was thought to cause **schizophrenia** in her offspring.

**schizotypal personality disorder** Cluster A (odd or eccentric) **personality disorder** involving a pervasive pattern of interpersonal deficits featuring acute discomfort with, and reduced capacity for, close relationships, as well as by cognitive or perceptual distortions and eccentricities of behaviour.

**scientist-practitioner model** Expectation that mental health professionals will apply scientific methods to their work. They must keep current in the latest research on diagnosis and treatment, they must evaluate their own methods for effectiveness, and they may generate their own research to discover new knowledge of disorders and their treatment.

**seasonal affective disorder (SAD) Mood disorder** involving a cycling of episodes corresponding to the seasons of the year, typically with depression occurring during the winter.

**selective mutism** Developmental disorder characterized by the individual's consistent failure to speak in specific social situations despite speaking in other situations.

**self-actualizing** Process emphasized in humanistic psychology in which people strive to achieve their highest potential against difficult life experiences.

**self-efficacy** Perception that one has the ability to cope with **stress** or challenges.

**separation anxiety disorder** Excessive, enduring fear in some children that harm will come to them or their parents while they are apart.

**sequential design** Combination of the **cross-sectional** and **longitudinal** research methods involving repeated study of different **cohorts** over time.

**serotonin** Neurotransmitter involved in information processing, coordination of movement, inhibition, and restraint; it also assists in the regulation of eating, sexual, and aggressive behaviours, all of which may be involved in different **psychological disorders.** Its interaction with **dopamine** is implicated in **schizophrenia.**

**sex reassignment surgery** Surgical procedures to alter a person's physical anatomy to conform to that person's psychological gender identity.

**sexual aversion disorder** Extreme and persistent dislike of sexual contact or similar activities.

**sexual dysfunction** Sexual disorder in which the client finds it difficult to function adequately while having sex.

**sexual masochism Paraphilia** in which sexual arousal is associated with experiencing pain or humiliation.

**sexual pain disorder** Recurring genital pain in either males or females before, during, or after sexual intercourse.

**sexual sadism Paraphilia** in which sexual arousal is associated with inflicting pain or humiliation.

**shaping** In operant conditioning, the development of a new response by reinforcing successively more similar versions of that response. Both desirable and undesirable behaviours may be learned in this manner.

**shared psychotic disorder (folie à deux)** Psychotic disturbance in which an individual develops a **delusion** similar to that of a person with whom he or she shares a close relationship.

**single-case experimental design** Research tactic in which an independent variable is manipulated for a single individual, allowing cause-and-effect conclusions but with limited **generalizability** (contrast with **case study method**).

**situational phobia** Fear of enclosed places (e.g., claustrophobia) or public transportation (e.g., fear of flying).

**sleep apnea** Disorder involving brief periods when breathing ceases during sleep.

**sleep efficiency (SE)** Percentage of time actually spent sleeping of the total time spent in bed.

**sleep terrors** Episodes of apparent awakening from sleep, accompanied by signs of **panic,** followed by disorientation and amnesia for the incident. These occur during NREM sleep, so they do not involve frightening dreams.

**sleepwalking** A **parasomnia** that involves leaving the bed during NREM—deep, non-dreaming—sleep.

**social phobia** Extreme, enduring, irrational fear and avoidance of social or performance situations.

**somatization disorder Somatoform disorder** involving extreme and long-lasting focus on multiple physical symptoms for which no medical cause is evident.

**somatoform disorders** Pathological concerns of individuals with the appearance or functioning of their bodies, usually in the absence of any identifiable medical condition.

**specific phobia** Unreasonable fear of a specific object or situation that markedly interferes with daily life functioning.

**standardization** Process of establishing specific norms and requirements for a measurement technique to ensure it is used consistently across measurement occasions. This includes instructions for administering the measure, evaluating its findings, and comparing these with data for large numbers of people.

**statistical significance** Probability that obtaining the observed research findings merely by chance is small.

**stimulants Psychoactive substances** that elevate **mood,** activity, and alertness, including amphetamines, caffeine, cocaine, and nicotine.

**stress** Body's physiological response to a stressor, which is any event or change that requires adaptation.

**stroke** Temporary blockage of blood vessels supplying the brain, or a rupture of vessels in the brain, resulting in temporary or permanent loss of brain functioning. Also known as *cerebral vascular accident.*

**stuttering** Disturbance in the fluency and time patterning of speech (e.g., sound and syllable repetitions or prolongations).

**substance abuse** Pattern of **psychoactive substance** use leading to significant distress or impairment in social and occupational roles and in hazardous situations.

**substance dependence** Maladaptive pattern of substance use characterized by the need for increased amounts to achieve the desired effect, negative physical effects when the substance is withdrawn, unsuccessful efforts to control its use, and substantial effort expended to seek it or recover from its effects.

**substance intoxication** Physiological reactions, such as impaired judgment and motor ability, and **mood** changes resulting from the ingestion of **psychoactive substances.**

**substance-related disorders** Range of problems associated with the use and abuse of drugs such as alcohol, cocaine, heroin, and other substances people use to alter the way they think, feel, and behave. These are extremely costly in human and financial terms.

**suicidal attempts** Efforts made to kill oneself.

**suicidal ideation** Serious thoughts about committing suicide.

**superego** In **psychoanalysis,** the psychic entity representing the internalized moral standards of parents and society.

**synaptic cleft** Space between nerve cells where chemical transmitters act to move impulses from one **neuron** to the next.

**systematic desensitization Behaviour therapy** technique to diminish excessive fears, involving gradual exposure to the feared stimulus paired with a positive coping experience, usually relaxation.

**taxonomy** System of naming and classification (e.g., of specimens) in science.

**testability** Ability of a **hypothesis,** for example, to be subjected to scientific scrutiny and to be accepted or rejected, a necessary condition for the hypothesis to be useful.

**tic disorder** Disruption in early development involving involuntary motor movements or vocalizations.

**token economy** Behaviour modification system in which individuals earn items they can exchange for desired rewards by displaying appropriate behaviours.

**tolerance** Need for increased amounts of a substance to achieve the desired effect, and a diminished effect with continued use of the same amount.

**transference** Psychoanalytic concept suggesting that clients may seek to relate to the therapist as they did to important authority figures, particularly their parents.

**transinstitutionalization** Movement of people with severe **psychological disorders** from large psychiatric hospitals to smaller group residences.

**transvestic fetishism Paraphilia** in which individuals, usually males, are sexually aroused or receive gratification by wearing clothing of the opposite sex.

**trend** The direction of change of a behaviour or behaviours (e.g., increasing or decreasing).

**twin studies** In genetics research, comparisons of twins with unrelated or less closely related individuals. If twins, particularly monozygotic twins who share identical **genotypes,** share common characteristics such as a disorder, even if they were reared in different environments, this is strong evidence of genetic involvement in those characteristics.

**type A behaviour pattern** Cluster of behaviours including excessive competitiveness, time-pressured impatience, accelerated speech, and anger; originally thought to promote high risk for heart disease.

**type B behaviour pattern** Cluster of behaviours including a relaxed attitude, indifference to time pressure, and less forceful ambition; originally thought to cause low risk for heart disease.

**unconditional positive regard** Acceptance by the counsellor of the client's feelings and actions without judgment or condemnation.

**unconscious** Part of the psychic makeup that is outside the awareness of the person.

**undifferentiated type of schizophrenia** Category for individuals who meet the criteria for **schizophrenia** but not for one of the defined subtypes.

**vaginismus** Recurring involuntary muscle spasms in the outer third of the vagina that interfere with sexual intercourse.

**validity** Degree to which a technique actually measures what it purports to measure.

**variability** Degree of change in a phenomenon over time.

**vascular dementia** Progressive brain disorder involving loss of cognitive functioning caused by blockage of blood flow to the brain. Appears concurrently with other neurological signs and symptoms.

**voyeurism Paraphilia** in which sexual arousal is derived from observing unsuspecting individuals undressing or naked.

**vulnerability** Susceptibility or tendency to develop a disorder.

**withdrawal** Severely negative physiological reaction to removal of a **psychoactive substance,** which can be alleviated by the same or a similar substance.

**withdrawal delirium** Frightening **hallucinations** and body tremors that result when a heavy drinker withdraws from alcohol. Also known as *delirium tremens (DTs).*

**withdrawal design** Removing a treatment to note whether it has been effective. In **single-case experimental designs,** a behaviour is measured **(baseline),** an **independent variable** is introduced *(intervention),* and then the intervention is withdrawn. Because the behaviour continues to be measured throughout *(repeated measurement),* any effects of the intervention can be noted. Also called **reversal design.**

# References

Abbeduto, L., & Rosenberg, S. (1992). Linguistic communication in persons with mental retardation. In S. F. Warren & J. Reichle (Eds.), *Causes and effects in communication and language intervention* (pp. 331–359). Baltimore: Paul H. Brookes.

Abbey, S. E., & Garfinkel, P. E. (1991). Neurasthenia and chronic fatigue syndrome: The role of culture in the making of a diagnosis. *American Journal of Psychiatry, 148*, 1638–1646.

Abbott, D. W., de Zwaan, M., Mussell, M. P., Raymond, N. C., Seim, H. C., Crow, S. J., et al. (1998). Onset of binge eating and dieting in overweight women: Implications for etiology, associated features and treatment. *Journal of Psychosomatic Research, 44*, 367–374.

Abel, G. G., Barlow, D. H., Blanchard, E. B., & Guild, D. (1977). The components of rapists' sexual arousal. *Archives of General Psychiatry, 34*, 895–903.

Abel, G. G., Becker, J. V., Cunningham-Rathner, J., Mittelman, M., & Rouleau, J. L. (1988). Multiple paraphilic diagnoses among sex offenders. *Bulletin of the American Academy of Psychiatry and Law, 16*, 153–168.

Abel, G. G., Becker, J. V., Mittelman, M., Cunningham-Rathner, J., Rouleau, J. L., & Murphy, W. E. (1987). Self-reported sex crimes of nonincarcerated paraphiliacs. *Journal of Interpersonal Violence, 2*, 3–25.

Abela, J. R. Z., & Sarin, S. (2002). Cognitive vulnerability to hopelessness depression: A chain is only as strong as its weakest link. *Cognitive Therapy & Research, 26*, 811–829.

Abramson, L. Y., Metalsky, G. I., & Alloy, L. B. (1989). Hopelessness depression: A theory-based subtype of depression. *Psychological Review, 96*(2), 358–372.

Abramson, L. Y., Seligman, M. E. P., & Teasdale, J. D. (1978). Learned helplessness in humans: Critique and reformulation. *Journal of Abnormal Psychology, 87*, 49–74.

Abuelo, D. N. (1991). Genetic disorders. In J. L. Matson & J. A. Mulick (Eds.), *Handbook of mental retardation* (2nd ed.) (pp. 97–114). Elmsford, NY: Pergamon Press.

Adair, J. G., Paivio, A. & Ritchie, P. (1996). Psychology in Canada. *Annual Review of Psychology, 47*, 341–370.

Adair, R., Bauchner, H., Philipp, B., Levenson, S., & Zuckerman, B. (1991). Night waking during infancy: Role of parent presence at bedtime. *Pediatrics, 87*, 500–504.

Adams, M., Kutcher, S., Antoniw, E., & Bird, D. (1996). Diagnostic utility of endocrine and neuroimaging screening tests in first-onset adolescent psychosis. *Journal of the American Academy of Child & Adolescent Psychiatry, 35*, 67–73.

Ader, R., & Cohen, N. (1975). Behaviorally conditioned immunosuppression. *Psychosomatic Medicine, 37*, 333–340.

Ader, R., & Cohen, N. (1993). Psycho-neuroimmunology: Conditioning and stress. *Annual Review of Psychology, 44*, 53–85.

Adlaf, E., Ivis, F. J., & Smart, R. (1994). *Alcohol and other drug use among Ontario adults in 1994 and changes since 1977.* Toronto: Addiction Research Foundation.

Adler, C. M., Côté, G., Barlow, D. H., & Hillhouse, J. J. (1994). *Phenomenological relationships between somatoform, anxiety, and psychophysiological disorders.* Unpublished manuscript.

Adler, P. S. J., Ditto, B., France, C., & France, J. (1994). Cardiovascular reactions to blood donation in offspring of hypertensives and normotensives. *Journal of Psychosomatic Research, 38*, 429–439.

Afari, N., & Buchwald, D. (2003). Chronic fatigue syndrome: A review. *American Journal of Psychiatry, 160*, 221–236.

Agras, W. S. (1987). *Eating disorders: Management of obesity, bulimia, and anorexia nervosa.* Elmsford, NY: Pergamon Press.

Agras, W. S. (2001). The consequences and costs of eating disorders. *Psychiatric Clinics of North America, 24*, 371–379.

Agras, W. S., Barlow, D. H., Chapin, H. N., Abel, G. G., & Leitenberg, H. (1974). Behavior modification of anorexia nervosa. *Archives of General Psychiatry, 30*, 279–286.

Agras, W. S., & Kirkley, B. G. (1986). Bulimia: Theories of etiology. In K. D. Brownell & J. P. Foreyt (Eds.), *Handbook of eating disorders: Physiology, psychology, and treatment of obesity, anorexia, and bulimia* (pp. 367–378). New York: Basic Books.

Agras, W. S., Schneider, J. A., Arnow, B., Raeburn, S. D., & Telch, C. F. (1989). Cognitive-behavioral and response-prevention treatments for bulimia nervosa. *Journal of Consulting and Clinical Psychology, 57*, 215–221.

Agras, W. S., Sylvester, D., & Oliveau, D. (1969). The epidemiology of common fears and phobia. *Comprehensive Psychiatry, 10*, 151–156.

Agras, W. S., Telch, C. F., Arnow, B., Eldredge, K., & Marnell, M. (1997). One year follow-up of cognitive-behavioral therapy of obese individuals with binge eating disorder. *Journal of Consulting and Clinical Psychology, 65*, 343–347.

Agras, W. S., Walsh, B. T., Fairburn, C. G., Wilson, G. T., & Kraemer, H. C. (2000). A multicenter comparison of cognitive-behavioral therapy and interpersonal psychotherapy for bulimia nervosa. *Archives of General Psychiatry, 57*, 459–466.

Agrawal, P. (1978). Diazepam addiction: A case report. *Canadian Psychiatric Association Journal, 23*, 35–37.

Aigner, M., & Bach, M. (1999). Clinical utility of DSM-IV pain disorder. *Comprehensive Psychiatry, 40*(5), 353–357.

Akiskal, H. S. (1997). Overview of chronic depressions and their clinical management. In H. S. Akiskal & G. B. Cassano (Eds.), *Dysthymia and the spectrum of chronic depressions* (pp. 1–34). New York: Guilford Press.

Akiskal, H. S., & Cassano, G. B. (Eds.). (1997). *Dysthymia and the spectrum of chronic depressions.* New York: Guilford Press.

Akiskal, H. S., & Pinto, O. (1999). The evolving spectrum: Prototypes I, II, III, and IV. *The Psychiatric Clinics of North America, 22*(3), 517–534.

Aktar, S., & Brenner, I. (1979). Differential diagnosis of fugue-like states. *Journal of Clinical Psychiatry, 40*, 381–385.

Albano, A. M., & Barlow, D. H. (1996). Breaking the vicious cycle: Cognitive-behavioral group treatment for socially anxious youth. In E. D. Hibbs & P. S. Jensen (Eds.), *Psychosocial treatment research and adolescent disorders* (pp. 43–62). Washington, DC: APA Press.

Albano, A. M., Chorpita, B. F., & Barlow, D. H. (1996). Childhood anxiety disorders. In E. J. Mash & R. A. Barkley (Eds.), *Child psychopathology* (pp. 196–241). New York: Guilford Press.

Albano, A. M., DiBartolo, P. M., Heimberg, R. G., & Barlow, D. H. (1995). Children and adolescents: Assessment and treatment. In R. G. Heimberg, M. R. Liebowitz, D. A. Hope, & F. Schneier (Eds.), *Social phobia: Diagnosis, assessment and treatment.* New York: Guilford Press.

Albano, A. M., Miller, P. P., Zarate, R., Côté, G., & Barlow, D. H. (1997). Behavioral assessment and treatment of PTSD in prepubertal children: Attention to development factors and innovative strategies in the case study of a family. *Cognitive and Behavioral Practice, 4*, 245–262.

Alberta Family and Social Services. (1990). *Elder abuse: What is it? What to do about it?* Retrieved November 24, 2003, from http://www.acjnet.org/docs/eldabpfv.html.

Albertini, R. S., & Phillips, K. A. (1999). Thirty-three cases of body dysmorphic disorder in children and adolescents. *Journal of the American Academy of Child and Adolescent Psychiatry, 38*(4), 453–459.

Alcoholics Anonymous. (1990). *Comments on A.A.'s triennial surveys.* New York: Alcoholics Anonymous World Services.

Alden, L. (1989). Short-term structured treatment for avoidant personality disorder. *Journal of Consulting and Clinical Psychology, 57*, 756–764.

Alden, L. E. (2001). Interpersonal perspectives on social phobia. In W. R. Crozier & L. E. Alden (Eds.), *International handbook of social anxiety: Research and interventions* (pp. 381–404). New York: Wiley.

Alden, L. E., & Capreol, M. J. (1993). Avoidant personality disorder: Interpersonal problems as predictors of treatment response. *Behavior Therapy, 24*, 357–376.

Alexander, F. (1950). *Psychosomatic medicine.* New York: Norton.

Alexander, F. G. (1939). Emotional factors in essential hypertension: Presentation of a tentative hypothesis. *Psychosomatic Medicine, 1*, 175–179.

Alexander, F. G., & Selesnick, S. T. (1966). *The history of psychiatry: An evaluation of psychiatric thought and practice from prehistoric times to the present.* New York: Harper & Row.

Allen, J. M., Lam, R. W., Remick, R. A., & Sadovnick, A. D. (1993). Depressive symptoms and family history in seasonal and nonseasonal mood disorders. *American Journal of Psychiatry, 150*(3), 443–448.

Allen, J., DeMyer, M., Norton, J., Pontius, W., & Yang, G. (1971). Intellectuality in parents of psychotic, subnormal, and normal children. *Journal of Autism and Childhood Schizophrenia, 1*, 311–326.

Allen, K., Bloscovitch, J., & Mendes, W. B. (2002). Cardiovascular reactivity in the presence of pets, friends, and spouses: The truth about cats and dogs. *Psychosomatic Medicine, 64*, 727–739.

Allen, L. S., & Gorski, R. A. (1992). Sexual orientation and the size of the anterior commissure in the human brain. *Proceedings of the National Academy of Science, 89*, 7199–7202.

Alloul, K., Sauriol, L., Kennedy, W., Laurier, C., Tessier, G., Novosel, S., & Contandriopoulos, A. (1998). Alzheimer's disease: A review of the disease, its epidemiology and economic impact. *Archives of Gerontology & Geriatrics, 27*, 189–221.

Alloy, L. B., Abramson, L. Y., Hogan, M. E., Whitehouse, W. G., Rose, D. T., Robinson, M. S., et al. (2000). The Temple-Wisconsin cognitive vulnerability to depression project: Lifetime history of axis I psychopathology in individuals at high and low cognitive risk for depression. *Journal of Abnormal Psychology, 109*, 403–418.

Alloy, L. B., Kelly, K. A., Mineka, S., & Clements, C. M. (1990). Comorbidity of anxiety and depressive disorders: A helplessness-hopelessness perspective. In J. D. Maser & C. R. Cloninger (Eds.), *Comorbidity of mood and anxiety disorders* (pp. 499–543). Washington, DC: American Psychiatric Press.

Alpert, M., Clark, A., & Pouget, E. R. (1994). The syntactic role of pauses in the speech of schizophrenic patients with alogia. *Journal of Abnormal Psychology, 103*, 750–757.

Altmuller, J., Palmer, L. J., Fischer, G., Scherb, H., & Wjst, M. (2001). Genome-wide scans of complex human diseases: True linkage is hard to find. *American Journal of Human Genetics, 69*, 936–950.

Alzheimer's Association. (2004). *Aluminum and Alzheimer: Does aluminum play a role in causing Alzheimer's disease?* Retrieved May 21, 2004, from http://www.corrosion-doctors.org/Pollution/Alumin-Alzheimer.htm.

Alzheimer's Society of Canada. (2004). *People with Alzheimer's disease and related dementias.* Retrieved August 17, 2004, from http://www.alzheimers.ca/english/disease/stats-people.htm.

American Academy of Pediatrics. (2000). Clinical practice guidelines: Diagnosis and evaluation of the child with attention-deficit/hyperactivity disorder. *Pediatrics, 105*, 1158–1170.

American Psychiatric Association. (1980). *Diagnostic and statistical manual of mental disorders* (3rd ed.). Washington, DC: Author.

American Psychiatric Association. (1990). *Benzodiazepine dependence, toxicity, and abuse: A task force report of the American Psychiatric Association.* Washington, DC: Author.

American Psychiatric Association. (1993). Practice guidelines for eating disorders. *American Journal of Psychiatry, 150*(2), 212–228.

American Psychiatric Association. (1994). *Diagnostic and statistical manual of mental disorders* (4th ed.). Washington, DC: Author.

American Psychiatric Association. (2000a). *Diagnostic and statistical manual of mental disorders* (4th ed.). (Text Revision). Washington, DC: Author.

American Psychiatric Association. (2000b). Schizophrenia. In *Practice guidelines for the treatment of psychiatric disorders: Compendium 2000* (pp. 200–412). Washington, DC: Author.

American Psychiatric Association. (2000c): *Practice guidelines for the treatment of patients with delirium: Compendium 2000* (pp. 31–68). Washington, DC: Author.

American Psychiatric Association. (2000d): *Practice guidelines for the treatment of patients with Alzheimer's disease and other dementias of late life: Compendium 2000* (pp. 69–137). Washington, DC: Author.

American Psychiatric Association. (2003). Practice guideline for the assessment and treatment of patients with suicidal behaviors. *American Journal of Psychiatry, 160* (Suppl.), 1–44.

American Psychiatric Association. (2004). Practice guideline for the treatment of patients with schizophrenia, second edition. *American Journal of Psychiatry, 161* (Suppl.), 1–56.

American Psychological Association. (1995). *Ethical conflicts in psychology.* Washington, DC: Author.

Amering, M., & Katschnig, H. (1990). Panic attacks and panic disorder in cross-cultural perspective. *Psychiatric Annals, 20*, 511–516.

Amir, N., Cashman, L., & Foa, E. B. (1997). Strategies of thought control and obsessive-compulsive disorder. *Behaviour Research and Therapy, 35*, 775–777.

Anastasi, A. (1988). *Psychological testing* (6th ed.). New York: Oxford University Press.

Anch, A. M., Browman, C. P., Mitler, M. M., & Walsh, J. K. (1988). *Sleep: A scientific perspective.* Englewood Cliffs, NJ: Prentice-Hall.

Ancoli-Israel, S. (2000). Insomnia in the elderly: A review for the primary care practitioner. *Sleep, 23* (Suppl. 1), S23–S30.

Anders, T. F. (2001). Childhood sleep disorders. In G. O. Gabbard (Ed.), *Treatment of psychiatric disorders* (Vol. 1) (3rd ed.) (pp. 359–380). Washington, DC: American Psychiatric Press.

Andersen, B. L., Cyranowski, J. M., & Espindle, D. (1999). Men's sexual self-schema. *Journal of Personality and Social Psychology, 76*(4), 645–661.

Andersen, B. L., Kiecolt-Glaser, J. K., & Glaser, R. (1994). A biobehavioral model of cancer stress and disease course. *American Psychologist, 49*, 389–404.

Anderson, B., & Baum, A. (2001). *Psychosocial interventions for cancer.* Washington, DC: American Psychological Association.

Anderson, D. J., Noyes, R., & Crowe, R. R. (1984). A comparison of panic disorder and generalized anxiety disorder. *American Journal of Psychiatry, 141*, 572–575.

Andrasik, F. (2000). Biofeedback. In D. I. Mostofsky & D. H. Barlow (Eds.), *The management of stress and anxiety in medical disorders* (pp. 66–83). Needham Heights, MA: Allyn & Bacon.

Andreasen, N. C. (1979). Thought, language, and communication disorders: I. Clinical assessment, definition of terms, and evaluation of their reliability. *Archives of General Psychiatry, 36*, 1315–1321.

Andreasen, N. C., & Bardach, J. (1977). Dysmorphophobia: Symptom or disease? *American Journal of Psychiatry, 134*, 673–676.

Andreasen, N. C., & Carpenter, W. T., Jr. (1993). Diagnosis and classification of schizophrenia. *Schizophrenia Bulletin, 19*(2), 199–214.

Andreasen, N. C., Rezai, K., Alliger, R., Swayze, V. W., Flaum, M., Kirchner, P., et al. (1992). Hypofrontality in neuroleptic-naive patients and in patients with chronic schizophrenia: Assessment with xenon 133 single-photon emission computed tomography with the Tower of London. *Archives of General Psychiatry, 49*, 943–958.

Andreasen, N. C., & Swayze, V. W. (1993). Neuroimaging. In J. A. Costa e Silva & C. C. Nadelson (Eds.), *International review of psychiatry* (Vol. 1). Washington, DC: American Psychiatric Press.

Andrews, G., Morris-Yates, A., Howie, P., & Martin, N. G. (1991). Genetic factors in stuttering confirmed. *Archives of General Psychiatry, 48*, 1034–1035.

Aneshensel, C. S., Pearlin, L. I., Mullan, J. T., Zarit, S. H., & Whitlatch, C. J. (1995). *Profiles in caregiving: The unexpected career.* San Diego, CA: Academic Press.

Angst, J. (1988). Clinical course of affective disorders. In T. Helgason & R. J. Daly (Eds.), *Depressive illness: Prediction of course and outcome* (pp. 1–44). Berlin: Springer-Verlag.

Angst, J., & Preizig, M. (1996). Course of a clinical cohort of unipolar, bipolar and schizoaffective patients: Results of a prospective study from 1959 to 1985. *Schweizer Archiv fur Neurologie und Psychiatrie, 146*, 1–16.

Angst, J., & Sellaro, R. (2000). Historical perspectives and natural history of bipolar disorder. *Biological Psychiatry, 48*(6), 445–457.

Anisman, H., Zaharia, M. D., Meaney, M. J., & Merali, Z. (1998). Do early life events permanently alter behavioral and hormonal responses to stressors? *International Journal of Developmental Neuroscience, 16*(3–4), 149–164.

Anthenelli, R. M., & Schuckit, M. A. (1997). Genetics. In J. H. Lowinson, P. Ruiz, R. B. Millman, & J. G. Langrod (Eds.), *Substance abuse: A comprehensive textbook* (pp. 41–51). Baltimore: Williams & Wilkins.

Anton, R. F. (1999). What is craving? Models and implications for treatment. *Alcohol Research & Health, 23*(3), 165–173.

Antoni, M. H., Baggett, L., Ironson, G., LaPerriere, A., August, S., Klimas, N., et al. (1991). Cognitive-behavioral stress management intervention buffers distress responses and immunologic changes following notification of HIV-1 seropositivity. *Journal of Consulting and Clinical Psychology, 59*(6), 906–915.

Antoni, M. H., Cruess, D. G., Cruess, S., Lutgendorf, S., Kumar, M., Ironson, G., et al. (2000). Cognitive-behavioral stress management intervention effects on anxiety, 24-hr urinary norepineph-rine output, and T-cytotoxic/suppressor cells over time among symptomatic HIV-infected gay men. *Journal of Consulting and Clinical Psychology, 68*, 31–45.

Antony, M. M., & Barlow, D. H. (2002). Specific phobias. In D. H. Barlow, *Anxiety and its disorders: The nature and treatment of anxiety and panic* (2nd ed.). New York: Guilford Press.

Antony, M. M., Brown, T. A., & Barlow, D. H. (1997a). Heterogeneity among specific phobia types in DSM-IV. *Behavior Research and Therapy, 35*, 1089–1100.

Antony, M. M., Brown, T. A., & Barlow, D. H. (1997b). Response to hyperventilation and 5.5% $CO_2$ inhalation of subjects with types of specific phobia, panic disorder, or no mental disorder. *American Journal of Psychiatry, 154*, 1089–1095.

Antony, M. M., Craske, M. G., & Barlow, D. H. (1995). *Mastery of your specific phobia, client workbook.* San Antonio, TX: Graywind Publications Incorporated/The Psychological Corporation.

Antony, M. M., McCabe, R. E., Leeuw, I., Sano, N., & Swinson, R. P. (2001). Effect of distraction and coping style on in vivo exposure for specific phobia of spiders. *Behaviour Research and Therapy, 39*, 1137–1150.

Antrobus, J. (2000). Theories of dreaming. In M. H. Kryger, T. Roth, and W. C. Dement (Eds.), *Principles and practice of sleep medicine* (3rd ed., pp. 472–481). Philadelphia: W. B. Saunders.

Apfelbaum, B. (2000). Retarded ejaculation: A much misunderstood syndrome. In

S. R. Leiblum & R C. Rosen (Eds.), *Principles and practice of sex therapy* (3rd ed., pp. 205–241). New York: Guilford Press.

Appelbaum, P. S., Grisso, T., Frank, E.,O'Donnell, S., & Kupfer, D. J. (1999). Competence of depressed patients for consent to research. *American Journal of Psychiatry, 156*, 1380–1384.

Appolinario, J. C., Bacaltchuk, J., Sichieri, R., Claudino, A. M., Godoy-Matos, A., Morgan, S., et al. (2003). A randomized, double-blind, placebo-controlled study of Sibutramine in the treatment of binge-eating disorder. *Archives of General Psychiatry, 60*, 1109–1116.

Archer, R. P., & Krishnamurthy, R. (1996). The Minnesota Multiphasic Personality Inventory-Adolescent (MMPI-A). In C. S. Newmark (Ed.), *Major psychological assessment instruments* (pp. 59–107). Boston: Allyn & Bacon.

Arendt, J., Stone, B., & Skene, D. (2000). Jet lag and sleep disruption. In M. H. Kryger, T. Roth, and W. C. Dement (Eds.), *Principles and practice of sleep medicine* (3rd ed., pp. 591–599). Philadelphia: W. B. Saunders.

Armstrong, H. E. (1993). Review of psychosocial treatments for schizophrenia. In D. L. Dunner (Ed.), *Current psychiatric therapy* (pp. 183–188). Philadelphia: W. B. Saunders.

Arrindell, W. A., Eisemann, M., Richter, J., Oei, T. P. S., Caballo, V. E., van der Ende, J., et al. (2003a). Masculinity-feminity as a national characteristic and its relationship with national agoraphobic fear levels: Fodor's sex role hypothesis revitalized. *Behaviour Research and Therapy, 41*, 795–807.

Arrindell, W. A., Eisemann, M., Richter, J., Oei, T. P. S., Caballo, V. E., van der Ende, J., et al. (2003b). Phobic anxiety in 11 nations. Part I: Dimensional constancy of the five-factor model. *Behaviour Research and Therapy, 41*, 461–479.

Asarnow, J. R. (1994). Annotation: Childhood-onset schizophrenia. *Journal of Child Psychology and Psychiatry, 35*, 1345–1371.

Asberg, M., Nordstrom, P., & Traskman-Bendz, L. (1986). Cerebrospinal fluid studies in suicide: An overview. *Annals of the American Academy of Science, 487*, 243–255.

Aschoff, J., & Wever, R. (1962). Spontanperiodik des Menschen die Ausschulus aller Zeitgeber. *Die Naturwissenschaften, 49*, 337–342.

Asmundson, G. J. G., Carleton, R. N., Wright, K. D., & Taylor, S. (2004). Psychological sequelae of remote exposure to the September 11th Terrorist Attacks in Canadians with and without panic. *Cognitive Behaviour Therapy, 33*, 51–59.

Asmundson, G. J. G., Jacobson, S. J., Allerdings, M. D., & Norton, G. R. (1996). Social phobia in disabled workers with chronic musculoskeletal pain. *Behaviour Research and Therapy, 34*, 939–943.

Asmundson, G. J. G., Norton, G. R., & Stein, M. B. (2002). *Clinical research in mental health: A practical guide.* Thousand Oaks, CA: Sage.

Asmundson, G. J. G., Taylor, S., & Cox, B. J. (Eds.). (2001). *Health anxiety: Clinical and research perspectives on hypochondriasis and related disorders.* New York: John Wiley & Sons.

Asmundson, G. J. G., Taylor, S., Sevgur, S., & Cox, B. J. (2001). Health anxiety: Conceptual, diagnostic, and epidemio-logical issues. In G. J. G. Asmundson, S. Taylor, & B. J. Cox (Eds.), *Health anxiety: Clinical and research perspectives on hypochondriasis and related disorders* (pp. 3–21). London: Wiley.

Attia, E., Haiman, C., Walsh, B. T., & Flater, S. R. (1998). Does fluoxetine augment the inpatient treatment of anorexia nervosa? *American Journal of Psychiatry, 155*(4), 548–551.

Attie, I., & Brooks-Gunn, J. (1995). The development of eating regulation across the life span. In D. Cicchetti & D. J. Cohen (Eds.), *Developmental psycho-pathology* (Vol. 2). New York: Wiley.

Attwood, A., Frith, U., & Hermelin, B. (1988). The understanding and use of interper-sonal gesture by autistic and Down's syn-drome children. *Journal of Autism and Developmental Disorders, 18*, 241–258.

Auchterlonie, S., Phillips, N. A., & Chertkow, H. (2002). Behavioral and electrical brain measures of semantic priming in patients with Alzheimer's disease: Implications for access failure versus deterioration hypotheses. *Brain and Cognition, 48*, 264–267.

Austin, G. W., Jaffe, P., & Friedman, B. (1994). Custody and access assessors: Effects of background and experience on analogue case judgement. *Canadian Journal of Behavioural Science, 26*, 463–475.

Ayllon, T., & Azrin, N. H. (1968). *The token economy: A motivational system for therapy and rehabilitation.* New York: Appleton-Century-Crofts.

Ayllon, T., & Michael, J. (1959). The psychi-atric nurse as a behavioral engineer. *Journal of the Experimental Analysis of Behavior, 2*, 323–334.

Azmitia, E. C. (1978). The serotonin-producing neurons of the midbrain median and dorsal raphe nuclei. In L. Iverson, S. Iverson, & S. Snyder (Eds.), *Handbook of psychopharmacology: Vol. 9. Chemical pathways in the brain* (pp. 233–314). New York: Plenum Press.

Baasher, T. A. (2001). Islam and mental health. *Eastern Mediterranean Health Journal, 7*, 372–376.

Bach, A. K., Brown, T. A., & Barlow, D. H. (1999). The effects of false negative feed-back on efficacy expectancies and sexual arousal in sexually functional males. *Behavior Therapy, 30*, 79–95.

Bach, A. K., Wincze, J. P., & Barlow, D. H. (2001). Sexual dysfunction. In D. H. Barlow (Ed.), *Clinical handbook of psychological disorders: A step-by-step treatment manual* (3rd ed.). New York: Guilford Press.

Bachrach, L. L. (1987). Deinstitutionalization in the United States: Promises and prospects. *New Directions for Mental Health Services, 35*, 75–90.

Baer, D. M., Wolf, M. M., & Risley, T. R. (1968). Some current dimensions of applied behavior analysis. *Journal of Applied Behavior Analysis, 1,* 91–97.

Bagby, R. M., Nicholson, R. A., Bacchiochi, J. R., Ryder, A. G., & Bury, A. S. (2002). The predictive capacity of the MMPI-2 and PAI validity scales and indexes to detect coached and uncoached feigning. *Journal of Personality Assessment, 78,* 69–86.

Bagby, R. M., Nicholson, R. A., & Buis, T. (1998). Utility of the Deceptive-Subtle items in the detection of malingering. *Journal of Personality Assessment, 70,* 405–415.

Bagby, R. M., Joffe, R. T., Parker, J. D. A., & Schuller, D. R. (1993). Re-examination of the evidence for the DSM-III personality disorder clusters. *Journal of Personality Disorders, 7,* 320–328.

Bagby, R. M., Ryder, A. G., & Cristi, C. (2002). Psychosocial and clinical predictors of response to pharmacotherapy for depression. *Journal of Psychiatry and Neuroscience, 27,* 250–257.

Bailey, J. M., & Benishay, D. S. (1993). Familial aggregation of female sexual orientation. *American Journal of Psychiatry, 150*(2), 272–277.

Bailey, J. M., & Pillard, R. C. (1991). A genetic study of male sexual orientation. *Archives of General Psychiatry, 48,* 1089–1096.

Bailey, J. M., Pillard, R. C., Dawood, K., Miller, M. B., Farrer, L. A., Trivedi, S., et al. (1999). A family history study of male sexual orientation using three independent samples. *Behavior Genetics, 29,* 79–86.

Bailey, J. M., Pillard, R. C., Neale, M. C., & Agyei, Y. (1993). Heritable factors influence sexual orientation in women. *Archives of General Psychiatry, 50,* 217–223.

Baker, A., van Kesteren, P. J., Gooren, L. J. G., & Bezemer, P. D. (1993). The prevalence of transsexualism in The Netherlands. *Acta Psychiatrica Scandinavica, 87,* 237–238.

Baker, B., Richter, A., & Anand, S. S. (2001). From the heartland: Culture, psychological factors, and coronary heart disease. In S. S. Kazarian & D. R. Evans (Eds.). *Handbook of cultural health psychology* (pp. 141–162), San Diego, CA: Academic Press.

Baker, C. D., & DeSilva, P. (1988). The relationship between male sexual dysfunction and belief in Zilbergeld's myths: An empirical investigation. *Sexual and Marital Therapy, 3*(2), 229–238.

Baldessarini, R. J. (1989). Current status of antidepressants: Clinical pharmacology and therapy. *Journal of Clinical Psychiatry, 50*(4), 117–126.

Baldwin, J. D., & Baldwin, J. I. (1989). The socialization of homosexuality and heterosexuality in a non-Western society. *Archives of Sexual Behavior, 18,* 13–29.

Ball, J. C., & Ross, A. (1991). *The effectiveness of methadone maintenance treatment.* New York: Springer-Verlag.

Ballenger, J. C., Burrows, G. D., DuPont, R. L., Lesser, I. M., Noyes, R., Pecknold, J. C., et al. (1988). Alprazolam in panic disorder and agoraphobia: Results from a multicenter trial: I. Efficacy in short-term treatment. *Archives of General Psychiatry, 45,* 413–422.

Bancroft, J. (1989). *Human sexuality and its problems* (2nd ed.). New York: Churchill Livingstone.

Bancroft, J. (1994). Homosexual orientation: The search for a biological basis. *British Journal of Psychiatry, 164,* 437–440.

Bancroft, J. (1997). Sexual problems. In D. M. Clark & C. G. Fairburn (Eds.), *Science and practice of cognitive behavior therapy* (pp. 243–257). New York: Oxford University Press.

Bancroft, J., Loftus, J., & Long, J. S. (2003). Distress about sex: A national survey of women in heterosexual relationships. *Archives of Sexual Behavior, 32,* 193–208.

Bandura, A. (1973). *Aggression: A social learning analysis.* Englewood Cliffs, NJ: Prentice-Hall.

Bandura, A. (1986). *Social foundations of thought and action: A social cognitive theory.* Englewood Cliffs, NJ: Prentice-Hall.

Bandura, A., Jeffery, R., & Bachicha, D. L. (1974). Analysis of memory codes and cumulative rehearsal in observational learning. *Journal of Research in Personality, 7,* 295–305.

Bandura, A., & McDonald, F. J. (1963). Influence of social reinforcement and the behavior of models in shaping children's moral judgment. *Journal of Abnormal and Social Psychology, 67,* 274–281.

Bandura, A., O'Leary, A., Taylor, C. B., Gauthier, J., & Gossard, D. (1987). Perceived self-efficacy and pain control: Opioid and nonopioid mechanisms. *Journal of Personality and Social Psychology, 53,* 563–571.

Bandura, A., Ross, D., & Ross, S. A. (1961). Transmission of aggression through imitation of aggressive models. *Journal of Abnormal and Social Psychology, 63,* 575–582.

Bandura, A., Ross, D., & Ross, S. A. (1963). Imitation of film-mediated aggressive models. *Journal of Abnormal and Social Psychology, 66,* 3–11.

Barbaree, H. E., & Seto, M. C. (1997). Pedophilia: Assessment and treatment. In D. R. Laws & W. O. O'Donohue (Eds.), *Sexual deviance: Theory, assesment, and treatment* (pp. 175–193). New York: Guilford Press.

Bargh, J. A., & Chartrand, T. L. (1999). The unbearable automaticity of being. *American Psychologist, 54,* 462–479.

Barinaga, M. (1997). New imaging methods provide a better view into the brain. *Science, 276,* 1974–1976.

Barkley, R. A. (1989). Attention deficit-hyperactivity disorder. In E. J. Mash & R. A. Barkley (Eds.), *Treatment of childhood disorders* (pp. 39–72). New York: Guilford Press.

Barkley, R. A. (1990). *Attention deficit hyperactivity disorder: A handbook for diagnosis and treatment.* New York: Guilford Press.

Barkley, R. A., Murphy, K. R., & Kwasnik, D. (1996). Motor vehicle driving competencies and risks in teens and young adults with attention deficit hyperactivity disorder. *Pediatrics, 98,* 1089–1095.

Barlow, D. H. (1986). Causes of sexual dysfunction: The role of anxiety and cognitive interference. *Journal of Consulting and Clinical Psychology, 54,* 140–148.

Barlow, D. H. (1988). *Anxiety and its disorders: The nature and treatment of anxiety and panic.* New York: Guilford Press.

Barlow, D. H. (1991). Disorders of emotion. *Psychological Inquiry, 2*(1), 58–71.

Barlow, D. H. (1993). Covert sensitization for paraphilia. In J. R. Cautela & A. J. Kearney (Eds.), *Covert conditioning casebook* (pp. 187–198). Pacific Grove, CA: Brooks/Cole.

Barlow, D. H. (2000). Unraveling the mysteries of anxiety and its disorders from the perspective of emotion theory. *American Psychologist, 55,* 1245–1263.

Barlow, D. H. (2002). *Anxiety and its disorders: The nature and treatment of anxiety and panic* (2nd ed.). New York: Guilford Press.

Barlow, D. H., Abel, G. G., & Blanchard, E. B. (1979). Gender identity change in transsexuals: Follow-up and replications. *Archives of General Psychiatry, 36,* 1001–1007.

Barlow, D. H., Becker, R., Leitenberg, H., & Agras, W. S. (1970). A mechanical strain gauge for recording penile circumference change. *Journal of Applied Behavior Analysis, 3,* 73–76.

Barlow, D. H., Brown, T. A., & Craske, M. G. (1994). Definitions of panic attacks and panic disorder in DSM-IV: Implications for research. *Journal of Abnormal Psychology, 103,* 553–554.

Barlow, D. H., Chorpita, B. F., & Turovsky, J. (1996). Fear, panic, anxiety, and disorders of emotion. In D. A. Hope (Ed.), *Perspectives on anxiety, panic and fear* (The 43rd Annual Nebraska Symposium on Motivation, pp. 251–328). Lincoln: Nebraska University Press.

Barlow, D. H., & Craske, M. G. (1989). *Mastery of your anxiety and panic.* Albany, NY: Graywind.

Barlow, D. H., & Craske, M. G. (2000). *Mastery of your anxiety and panic: Client workbook for anxiety and panic* (3rd ed.). Boulder, CO: Graywind Publications.

Barlow, D. H., Gorman, J. M., Shear, K. M., & Woods, S. W. (2000). Cognitive-behavioral therapy, imipramine, or their combination for panic disorder: A randomized controlled trial. *Journal of the American Medical Association, 283*(19), 2529–2536.

Barlow, D. H., Hayes, S. C., & Nelson, R. O. (1984). *The scientist practitioner: Research and accountability in clinical and educational settings.* Boston: Allyn & Bacon.

Barlow, D. H., Hayes, S. C., Nelson, R. O., Steele, D. L., Meeler, M. E., & Mills, J. R. (1979). Sex role motor behavior: A behavioral checklist. *Behavioral Assessment, 1,* 119–138.

Barlow, D. H., & Lehman, C. L. (1996). Advances in the psychosocial treatment of anxiety disorders: Implications for national health care. *Archives of General Psychiatry, 53,* 727–735.

Barlow, D. H., Levitt, J. T., & Bufka, L. F. (1999). The dissemination of empirically supported treatments: A view to the future. *Behaviour Research and Therapy, 37* (Suppl. 1), S147–162.

Barlow, D. H., & Liebowitz, M. R. (1995). Specific and social phobias. In

H. I. Kaplan & B. J. Sadock (Eds.), *Comprehensive textbook of psychiatry: VI* (pp. 1204–1217). Baltimore: Williams & Wilkins.

Barlow, D. H., Pincus, D. B., Heinrichs, N., & Choate, M. (2003). Anxiety disorders: A Lifespan developmental perspective. In I. Weiner (Ed.) *Comprehensive Handbook of Psychology* (Vol. 8). New York: John Wiley.

Barlow, D. H., Rapee, R. M., & Reisner, L. C. (2001). *Mastering stress 2001: A lifestyle approach.* Dallas, TX: American Health.

Barlow, D. H., Reynolds, E. J., & Agras, W. S. (1973). Gender identity change in a transsexual. *Archives of General Psychiatry, 28,* 569–576.

Barlow, D. H., & Wincze, J. P. (1980). Treatment of sexual deviations. In S. R. Leiblum & L. A. Pervin (Eds.), *Principles and practice of sex therapy* (pp. 347–375). New York: Guilford Press.

Barnard, A. (2000, September 12). When plastic surgeons should just say 'no.' *Boston Globe,* pp. E1, E3.

Barnes, G. E., & Toews, J. (1983). Deinstitutionalization of chronic mental patients in the Canadian context. *Canadian Psychology, 24,* 22–36.

Barnes, J. (1981). Non-consummation of marriage. *Irish Medical Journal, 74,* 19–21.

Barnes, J., Bowman, E. P., & Cullen, J. (1984). Biofeedback as an adjunct to psychotherapy in the treatment of vaginismus. *Biofeedback and Self-Regulation, 9,* 281–289.

Barnett, P. A., & Gotlib, I. H. (1988). Psychosocial functioning and depression: Distinguishing among antecedents, concomitants and consequences. *Psychological Bulletin, 104*(1), 97–126.

Baron, M., Gruen, R., Asnis, L., & Lord, S. (1985). Familial transmission of schizotypal and borderline personality disorders. *American Journal of Psychiatry, 142,* 927–934.

Baron-Cohen, S., Tager-Flusberg, H., & Cohen, D. J. (Eds.). (1994). *Understanding other minds: Perspectives from autism.* London: Oxford University Press.

Barr, H. M., & Streissguth, A. P. (2001). Identifying maternal self-reported alcohol use associated with fetal alcohol spectrum disorders. *Alcoholism: Clinical and Experimental Research, 25,* 283–287.

Barrett, D. H., Resnick, H. S., Foy, D. W., Dansky, B. S., Flanders, W. D., & Stroup, N. E. (1996). Combat exposure and adult psychosocial adjustment among U. S. Army veterans serving in Vietnam, 1965–1971. *Journal of Abnormal Psychology, 105,* 575–581.

Barrett, P. M., Dadds, M. R., & Rapee, R. M. (1996). Family treatment of childhood anxiety: A controlled trial. *Journal of Consulting and Clinical Psychology, 64,* 333–342.

Barrett, P. M., Duffy, A. L., Dadds, M. R., & Rapee, R. M. (2001). Cognitive-behavioral treatment of anxiety disorders in children: Long-term (6-year) follow-up. *Journal of Consulting and Clinical Psychology, 69,* 135–141.

Barrowclough, C., & Tarrier, N. (1998). The application of expressed emotion to clinical work in schizophrenia. *In Session: Psychotherapy in Practice, 4*(3), 7–23.

Barsky, A. J., Frank, C. B., Cleary, P. D., Wyshak, G., & Klerman, G. L. (1991). The relation between hypochondriasis and age. *American Journal of Psychiatry, 148,* 923–928.

Barsky, A. J., & Wyshak, G. (1990). Hypochondriasis and somatosensory amplification. *British Journal of Psychiatry, 157,* 404–409.

Barsky, A. J., Wyshak, G., & Klerman, G. L. (1986). Hypochondriasis: An evaluation of the DSM-III criteria in medical outpatients. *Archives of General Psychiatry, 43,* 493–500.

Barsky, A. J., Wyshak, G., Klerman, G. L., & Latham, K. S. (1990). The prevalence of hypochondriasis in medical outpatients. *Social Psychiatry and Psychiatric Epidemiology, 25,* 89–94.

Bartlett, N. H., Vasey, P. L., & Bukowski, W. M. (2000). Is gender identity disorder in children a mental disorder? *Sex Roles, 43,* 753–785.

Bartlik, B., & Goldberg, J. (2000). Female sexual arousal disorder. In S. R. Leiblum & R. C. Rosen (Eds.), *Principles and practice of sex therapy* (3rd ed., pp. 85–117). New York: Guilford Press.

Basoglu, M., Marks, I., Livanou, M., & Swinson, R. (1997). Double-blindness procedures, rater blindness, and ratings of outcome: Observations from a controlled trial. *Archives of General Psychiatry, 54,* 744–748.

Bassett, A. S., Chow, E. W., Waterworth, D. M., & Brzustowicz, L. (2001). Genetic insights into schizopherenia. *Canadian Journal of Psychiatry, 46*(2), 131–137.

Bassiri, A. G., & Guilleminault, C. (2000). Clinical features and evaluation of obstructive sleep apnea-hypopnea syndrome. In M. H. Kryger, T. Roth, and W. C. Dement (Eds.), *Principles and practice of sleep medicine* (3rd ed., pp. 869–878). Philadelphia: W. B. Saunders.

Basson, R. (2001). Using a different model for female sexual response to address women's problematic low sexual desire. *Journal of Sex and Marital Therapy, 27,* 395–403.

Bateson, G. (1959). Cultural problems posed by a study of schizophrenic process. In A. Auerbach (Ed.), *Schizophrenia: An integrated approach.* New York: Ronald Press.

Bauer, M. S., Calabrese, J., Dunner, D. L., Post, R., Whybrow, P. C., Gyulai, L., et al. (1994). Multisite data reanalysis of the validity of rapid cycling as a course modifier for bipolar disorder in DSM-IV. *American Journal of Psychiatry, 151,* 506–515.

Baxter, L. R., Guze, B. H., & Reynolds, C. A. (1993). Neuroimaging: Uses in psychiatry. In D. L. Dunner (Ed.), *Current psychiatric therapy.* Philadelphia: W. B. Saunders.

Baxter, L. R., Jr., Schwartz, J. M., Bergman, K. S., Szuba, M. P., Guze, B. H., Mazziotta, J. C., et al. (1992). Caudate glucose metabolic rate changes with both drug and behavior therapy for obsessive-compulsive disorder. *Archives of General Psychiatry, 49,* 681–689.

BBC. (2004). *1988:* Johnson stripped of Olympic gold. Retrieved August 17, 2004, from http://news.bbc.co.uk/onthisday/hi/dates/stories/september/27/newsid_2539000/2539525.stm.

Beach, S. R. H., Sandeen, E. E., & O'Leary, K. D. (1990). Depression in marriage: A model for etiology and treatment. In D. H. Barlow (Ed.), *Treatment manuals for practitioners.* New York: Guilford Press.

Beard, G. M. (1869). Neurasthenia or nervous exhaustion. *Boston Medical Surgical Journal, 3,* 217–221.

Beard, J. H., Malamud, T. J., & Rossman, E. (1978). Psychiatric rehabilitation and long-term rehospitalization rates: The findings of two research studies. *Schizophrenia Bulletin, 4,* 622–635.

Beard, J. H., Propst, R. N., & Malamud, T. J. (1982). The Fountain House model of psychiatric rehabilitation. *Psychosocial Rehabilitation Journal, 5,* 47–53.

Beardslee, W. R., Salt, P., Versage, E. M., Gladstone, T. R. G., Wright, E. J., & Rothberg, P. C. (1997). Sustained change in parents receiving preventive interventions for families with depression. *American Journal of Psychiatry, 154*(4), 510–515.

Bebbington, P. E., Bowen, J., Hirsch, S. R., & Kuipers, E. A. (1995). Schizophrenia and psychosocial stresses. In S. R. Hirsch and D. R. Weinberger (Eds.), *Schizophrenia* (pp. 587–604). Oxford, UK: Blackwell Science.

Bebbington, P. E., Brugha, T., MacCarthy, B., Potter, J., Sturt, E., Wykes, T., et al. (1988). The Camberwell Collaborative Depression Study: I. Depressed probands: Adversity and the form of depression. *British Journal of Psychiatry, 152,* 754–765.

Bebbington, P., Wilkins, S., Jones, P., Foerster, A., Murray, R., Toone, B., et al. (1993). Life events and psychosis: Initial results from the Camberwell Collaborative Psychosis Study. *British Journal of Psychiatry, 162,* 72–79.

Beck, A. T. (1967). *Depression: Clinical, experimental and theoretical aspects.* New York: Harper & Row.

Beck, A. T. (1976). *Cognitive therapy and the emotional disorders.* New York: International Universities Press.

Beck, A. T. (1983). Cognitive therapy of depression: New perspectives. In P. Clayton & J. E. Barrett (Eds.), *Treatment of depression: Old controversies and new approaches* (pp. 265–290). New York: Raven Press.

Beck, A. T. (1986). Hopelessness as a predictor of eventual suicide. *Annals of the New York Academy of Science, 487,* 90–96.

Beck, A. T. (1987). Cognitive models of depression. *Journal of Cognitive Psychotherapy, 1,* 5–37.

Beck, A. T., & Freeman, A. (1990). *Cognitive therapy of personality disorders.* New York: Guilford Press.

Beck, A. T., Hollon, S. D., Young, J. E., Bedrosian, R. C., & Budenz, D. (1985). Treatment of depression with cognitive therapy and amitriptyline. *Archives of General Psychiatry, 42,* 142–148.

Beck, A. T., & Rector, N. A. (2000). Cognitive therapy of schizophrenia: A new therapy for the new millennium.

*American Journal of Psychotherapy, 54,* 291–300.

Beck, A. T., Steer, R., Kovacs, M., & Garrison, B. (1985). Hopelessness and eventual suicide: A 10-year prospective study of patients hospitalized with suicidal ideation. *American Journal of Psychiatry, 142,* 559–563.

Beck, J. G. (1993). Vaginismus. In W. O'Donohue & J. H. Geer (Eds.), *Handbook of sexual dysfunctions: Assessment and treatment* (pp. 381–397). Boston: Allyn & Bacon.

Beck, J. G., & Barlow, D. H. (1984). Unraveling the nature of sex roles. In E. A. Blechman (Ed.), *Behavior modification with women* (pp. 34–59). New York: Guilford Press.

Beck, J. G., & Stanley, M. A. (1997). Anxiety disorders in the elderly: The emerging role of behavior therapy. *Behavior Therapy, 28,* 83–100.

Becker, D. (2000). When she was bad: Borderline personality disorder in a posttraumatic age. *American Journal of Orthopsychiatry, 70,* 422–432.

Becker, J. V. (1990). Treating adolescent sexual offenders. *Professional Psychology: Research and Practice, 21,* 362–365.

Beitchman, J. H., Wilson, B., Douglas, L., Young, A., & Adlaf, E. (2001). Substance use disorders in young adults with and without LD: Predictive and concurrent relationships. *Journal of Learning Disabilities, 34,* 317–332.

Beitchman, J. H., & Young, A. R. (1997). Learning disorders with a special emphasis on reading disorders: A review of the past 10 years. *Journal of the American Academy of Child and Adolescent Psychiatry, 36,* 1020–1032.

Belitsky, C. A., Toner, B. B., Ali, A., Yu, B., Osborne, S. L., & deRooy, E. (1996). Sex-role attitudes and clinical appraisal in psychiatry residents. *Canadian Journal of Psychiatry, 41,* 503–508.

Belitsky, R., & McGlashan, T. H. (1993). The manifestations of schizophrenia in late life: A dearth of data. *Schizophrenia Bulletin, 19,* 683–685.

Bell, C. C., Dixie-Bell, D. D., & Thompson, B. (1986). Further studies on the prevalence of isolated sleep paralysis in Black subjects. *Journal of the National Medical Association, 75,* 649–659.

Bell, I. R. (1994). Somatization disorder: Health care costs in the decade of the brain. *Biological Psychiatry, 35,* 81–83.

Bellack, A. S., & Mueser, K. T. (1992). Social skills training for schizophrenia? *Archives of General Psychiatry, 49,* 76.

Bellak, L. (1975). *The thematic apperception test, the children's apperception test, and the senior apperception technique in clinical use* (3rd ed.). New York: Grune & Stratton.

Bellamy, G. T., Rhodes, L. E., Mank, D. M., & Albin, J. M. (1988). *Supported employment: A community implementation guide.* Baltimore: Paul H. Brookes.

Bellis, D. J. (1981). *Heroin and politicians: The failure of public policy to control addiction in America.* Westport, CT: Greenwood Press.

Bem, D. J. (1996). Exotic becomes erotic: A developmental theory of sexual orientation. *Psychological Review, 103,* 320–335.

Benbadis, R. R., & Allen-Hauser, W. (2000). An estimate of the prevalence of psychogenic non-epileptic seizures. *Seizure, 9*(4), 280–281.

Benca, R. M., Obermeyer, W. H., Thisted, R. A., & Gillin, J. C. (1992). Sleep and psychiatric disorders: A meta-analysis. *Archives of General Psychiatry, 49,* 651–668.

Benedetti, A., Perugi, G., Toni, C., Simonetti, B., Mata, B., & Cassano, G. B. (1997). Hypochondriasis and illness phobia in panic-agoraphobic patients. *Comprehensive Psychiatry, 38*(2), 124–131.

Benkelfat, C., Ellenbogen, M. A., Dean, P., Palmour, R. M., & Young, S. N. (1994). Mood-lowering effect of tryptophan depletion: Enhanced susceptibility in young men at genetic risk for major affective disorders. *Archives of General Psychiatry, 51,* 687–697.

Bennett, A. H. (1988). Venous arterialization for erectile impotence. *Urologic Clinics of North America, 15,* 111–113.

Bennett-Branson, S. M., & Craig, K. D. (1993). Postoperative pain in children: Developmental and family influences on spontaneous coping strategies. *Canadian Journal of Behavioural Science, 25,* 355–383.

Benowitz, N. L. (1996). Pharmacology of nicotine: Addiction and therapeutics. *Annual Review of Pharmacology and Toxicology, 36,* 597–613.

Benson, H. (1975). *The relaxation response.* New York: William Morrow.

Benson, H. (1984). *Beyond the relaxation response.* New York: Times Books.

Berenbaum, H., & Oltmanns, T. F. (1992). Emotional experience and expression in schizophrenia and depression. *Journal of Abnormal Psychology, 101,* 37–44.

Berkman, L. F., & Syme, S. L. (1979). Social networks, host resistance, and mortality: A nine-year follow-up study of Alameda county residents. *American Journal of Epidemiology, 109,* 186.

Berman, A. L., & Jobes, D. A. (1991). *Adolescent suicide: Assessment and intervention.* Washington, DC: American Psychological Association.

Berman, K. F., & Weinberger, D. R. (1990). Lateralization of cortical function during cognitive tasks: Regional cerebral blood flow studies of normal individuals and patients with schizophrenia. *Journal of Neurology, Neurosurgery and Psychiatry, 53,* 150–160.

Berman, T., Douglas, V. I., & Barr, R. G. (1999). Effects of methylphenidate on complex cognitive processing in attention-deficit hyperactivity disorder. *Journal of Abnormal Psychology, 108,* 90–105.

Bernat, J. A., Calhoun, K. S., & Adams, H. E. (1999). Sexually aggressive and nonaggressive men: Sexual arousal and judgments in response to acquaintance rape and consensual analogues. *Journal of Abnormal Psychology, 108,* 662–673.

Bernstein, D. A., & Borkovec, T. D. (1973). *Progressive relaxation training: A manual for the helping professions.* Champaign, IL: Research Press.

Bernstein, D. A., Borkovec, T. D., & Hazlett-Stevens, H. (2000). *New directions in progressive relaxation training: A guidebook for helping professionals.* Westport, CT: Praeger.

Bernstein, D. P., Useda, D., & Siever, L. J. (1993). Paranoid personality disorder: Review of the literature and recommendations for DSM-IV. *Journal of Personality Disorders, 7,* 53–62.

Bernstein, J., Adlaf, E., & Paglia, A. (2002). Drug use in Toronto—2000. Retrieved October 25, 2003, from http://www.city .toronto.on.ca/drugcentre/rgdu00/rgdu1 .htm.

Berry, J. W. (2003). Origins of cross-cultural similarities and differences in human behavior: An ecocultural perspective. In A. Toomela (Ed.), *Cultural guidance in the development of the human mind* (pp. 97–109). Westport, CT: Ablex.

Bertelsen, B., Harvald, B., & Hauge, M. (1977). A Danish twin study of manic-depressive disorders. *British Journal of Psychiatry, 130,* 330–351.

Berzins, K. M., Petch, A., & Atkinson, J. M. (2003). Prevalence and experience of harassment of people with mental health problems living in the community. *British Journal of Psychiatry, 183,* 526–533.

Bettelheim, B. (1967). *The empty fortress.* New York: Free Press.

Bhagwanjee, A., Parekh, A., Paruk, Z., Petersen, I., & Subedar, H. (1998). Prevalence of minor psychiatric disorders in an adult African rural community in South Africa. *Psychological Medicine, 28,* 1137–1147.

Biederman, J., Faraone, S. V., Keenan, K., Benjamin, J., Krifcher, B., Moore, C., et al. (1992). Further evidence for family-genetic risk factors in attention deficit hyperactivity disorder: Patterns of comorbidity in probands and relatives in psychiatrically and pediatrically referred samples. *Archives of General Psychiatry, 49,* 728–738.

Biederman, J., Mick, E., Faraone, S. V., Spencer, T., Wilens, T. E., & Wozniak, J. (2000). Pediatric mania: A developmental subtype of bipolar disorder? *Biological Psychiatry, 48*(6), 458–466.

Biederman, J., Munir, K., Knee, D., Armentano, M., Autor, S., Waternaux, C., et al. (1987). High rate of affective disorders in probands with attention deficit disorder and in their relatives: A controlled family study. *American Journal of Psychiatry, 144*(3), 330–333.

Biederman, J., Rosenbaum, J. F., Hirshfeld, D. R., Farone, S. V., Bolduc, E. A., Gersten, M., et al. (1990). Psychiatric correlates of behavioral inhibition in young children of parents with and without psychiatric disorders. *Archives of General Psychiatry, 47,* 21–26.

Biederman, J., Spencer, T., Wilens, T., & Greene, R. (2001). Attention-deficit/ hyperactivity disorder. In G. O. Gabbard (Ed.), *Treatment of psychiatric disorders* (Vol. 1) (3rd ed.) (pp. 145–176). Washington, DC: American Psychiatric Press.

Bierut, L. J., Heath, A. C., Bucholz, K. K., Dinwiddie, S. H., Madden, P. A., Statham, D. J., et al. (1999). Major depressive disorder in a community-based twin sample: Are there different genetic and environmental contributions for men and women? *Archives of General Psychiatry, 56*(6), 557–563.

Biglan, A., Hops, H., Sherman, L., Friedman, L. S., Arthur, J., & Osteen, V. (1985). Problem solving interactions of depressed women and their husbands. *Behavior Therapy, 16*, 431–451.

Billingsley, R. L., McAndrews, M. P., & Smith, M. L. (2002). Intact perceptual and conceptual priming in temporal lobe epilepsy: Neuroanatomical and methodological implications. *Neuropsychology, 16*, 92–101.

Billingsley, R. L., Smith, M. L., & McAndrews, M. P. (2002). Developmental patterns in priming and familiarity in explicit recollection. *Journal of Experimental Child Psychology, 82*, 251–277.

Binik, Y. M., Bergeron, S., & Khalifé, S. (2000). Dyspareunia. In S. R. Leiblum & R. C. Rosen (Eds.), *Principles and practice of sex therapy* (3rd ed., pp. 154–180). New York: Guilford Press.

Binzer, M., Andersen, P. M., & Kullgren, G. (1997). Clinical characteristics of patients with motor disability due to conversion disorder: A prospective control group study. *Journal of Neurology, Neurosurgery, and Psychiatry, 63*(1), 83–88.

Birch, D. E. (1992). Duty to protect: Update and Canadian perspective. *Canadian Psychology, 33*, 94–104.

Birley, J., & Brown, G. W. (1970). Crisis and life changes preceding the onset or relapse of acute schizophrenia: Clinical aspects. *British Journal of Psychiatry, 16*, 327–333.

Biron, M., Risch, N., Hamburger, R., Mandel, B., Kushner, S., Newman, M., et al. (1987). Genetic linkage between X-chromosome markers and bipolar affective illness. *Nature, 326*, 289–292.

Bjorklund, D. F. (1989). *Children's thinking: Developmental function and individual differences.* Pacific Grove, CA: Brooks/Cole.

Black, D. W., & Andreasen, N. C. (1999). Schizophrenia, schizophreniform disorder, and delusional (paranoid) disorders. In R. E. Hales, S. C. Yudofsky, & J. A. Talbott (Eds.), *Textbook of psychiatry* (3rd ed., (pp. 425–477). Washington, DC: American Psychiatric Press.

Black, D. W., Monahan, P., Gable, J., Blum, N., Clancy, G., & Baker, P. (1998). Hoarding and treatment response in 38 nondepressed subjects with obsessive compulsive disorder. *Journal of Clinical Psychiatry, 5*, 420–425.

Black, D. W., Winokur, G., & Nasrallah, A. (1987). The treatment of depression: Electroconvulsive therapy vs. antidepressants: A naturalistic evaluation of 1,495 patients. *Comprehensive Psychiatry, 28*(2), 169–182.

Black, S. E., Patterson, C., & Feightner, J. (2001). Preventing dementia. *Canadian Journal of Neurological Science, 28* (Suppl. 1), S56.

Blackburn, I. M., & Moore, R. G. (1997). Controlled acute and follow-up trial of cognitive therapy and pharmacotherapy in out-patients with recurrent depression. *British Journal of Psychiatry, 171*, 328–334.

Blagys, M. D., & Hilsenroth, M. J. (2000). Distinctive features of short-term psychodynamic-interpersonal psychotherapy: A review of the comparative psychotherapy process literature. *Clinical Psychology: Science and Practice, 7*, 167–188.

Blanchard, C. G., Blanchard, E. B., & Becker, J. V. (1976). The young widow: Depressive symptomatology throughout the grief process. *Psychiatry, 39*, 394–399.

Blanchard, E. B. (1992). Psychological treatment of benign headache disorders. Special issue: Behavioral medicine: An update for the 1990s. *Journal of Consulting and Clinical Psychology, 60*(4), 537–551.

Blanchard, E. B., & Epstein, L. H. (1977). *A biofeedback primer.* Reading, MA: Addison-Wesley.

Blanchard, E. B., Appelbaum, K. A., Radnitz, C. L., Michultka, D., Morrill, B., Kirsh, C., et al. (1990). Placebocontrolled evaluation of abbreviated progressive muscle relaxation combined with cognitive therapy in the treatment of tension headache. *Journal of Consulting and Clinical Psychology, 58*(2), 210–215.

Blanchard, E. B., Kuhn, E., Rowell, D. L., Hickling, E. J., Wittrock, D., Rogers, R. L., et al. (2004). Studies of the vicarious traumatization of college students by the September llth attacks: Effects of proximity, exposure and connectedness. *Behaviour Research and Therapy, 42*, 191–205.

Blanchard, J. J., & Neale, J. M. (1992). Medication effects: Conceptual and methodological issues in schizophrenia research. *Clinical Psychology Review, 12*, 345–361.

Blanchard, R., & Bogaert, A. (1998). Birth order in homosexual versus heterosexual sex offenders against children, pubescents, and adults. *Archives of Sexual Behavior, 27*(6), 595–603.

Blanchard, R., & Steiner, B. W. (Eds.). (1990). *Clinical management of gender identity disorders in children and adults.* Washington, DC: American Psychiatric Press.

Bland, R. C. (1997). Epidemiology of affective disorders: A review. *Canadian Journal of Psychiatry, 42*, 367–377.

Bland, R. C., Orn, H., & Newman, S. C. (1988). Lifetime prevalence of psychiatric disorders in Edmonton. *Acta Psychiatrica Scandinavica, 77* (Suppl. 338), 24–32.

Blansjaar, B. A., Thomassen, R., & Van Schaick, H. W. (2000). Prevalence of dementia in centenarians. *International Journal of Geriatric Psychiatry, 15*(3), 219–225.

Blashfield, R. K., & Livesley, W. J. (1991). Metaphorical analysis of psychiatric classification as a psychological test. *Journal of Abnormal Psychology, 100*(3), 262–270.

Blazer, D. (1999). Geriatric psychiatry. In R. E. Hales, S. C. Yudofsky, & J. A. Talbot (Eds.), *Textbook of psychiatry* (3rd ed., pp. 1447–1462). Washington, DC: American Psychiatric Press.

Blazer, D. G. (1989). Current concepts: Depression in the elderly. *New England Journal of Medicine, 320*, 164–166.

Blazer, D. G., George, L., & Hughes, D. (1991). The epidemiology of anxiety disorders: An age comparison. In C. Salzman & B. Liebowitz (Eds.), *Anxiety disorders in the elderly* (pp. 17–30). New York: Springer.

Blazer, D. G., Hughes, D., George, L. K., Swartz, M., & Boyer, R. (1991). Generalized anxiety disorder. In L. N. Robins & D. A. Regier (Eds.), *Psychiatric disorders in America* (pp. 180–203). New York: Free Press.

Bleackley, C., Green, D., Lockshin, R. A., Melino, G., & Zakeri, Z. (2001). *Arnold H. Greenberg, 1941–2001.* Retrieved June 25, 2004, from http://www.celldeath-apoptosis .org/arnold_h.htm.

Blehar, M. C., & Rosenthal, N. E. (1989). Seasonal affective disorder and phototherapy. *Archives of General Psychiatry, 46*, 469–474.

Bleijenberg, G., Prins, J., & Bazelmans, E. (2003). Cognitive-behavioral therapies. In L. A. Jason, P. A. Fennell, & R. R. Taylor (Eds.), *Handbook of chronic fatigue syndrome.* Hoboken, NJ: John Wiley.

Bleuler, E. (1908). Die Prognose der Dementia praecox (Schizophreniegruppe). *Allgemeine Zeitschrift für Psychiatrie, 65*, 436–464.

Bleuler, E. (1924). *Textbook of psychiatry.* (A. A. Brill, Trans.) New York: Macmillan.

Bliss, E. L. (1984). A symptom profile of patients with multiple personalities including MMPI results. *Journal of Nervous and Mental Diseases, 172*, 197–211.

Bliss, E. L. (1986). *Multiple personality allied disorders and hypnosis.* New York: Oxford University Press.

Bloom, F. E., & Kupfer, D. J. (1995). *Psychopharmacology: The fourth generation of progress.* New York: Raven Press.

Bloom, F. E., Nelson, C. A., & Lazerson, A. (2001). *Brain, mind, & behavior* (3rd ed.). New York: Worth Publishers.

Blue, A. V., & Gaines, A. D. (1992). The ethnopsychiatric répertoire: A review and overview of ethnopsychiatric studies. In A. D. Gaines (Ed.), *Ethnopsychiatry: The cultural construction of professional and folk psychiatries* (pp. 397–484). Albany: State University of New York Press.

Blumenthal, S. J. (1990). An overview and synopsis of risk factors, assessment, and treatment of suicidal patients over the life cycle. In S. J. Blumenthal & D. J. Kupfer (Eds.), *Suicide over the life cycle: Risk factors, assessment and treatment of suicidal patients.* Washington, DC: American Psychiatric Press.

Blumenthal, S. J., & Kupfer, D. J. (Eds.) (1990). *Suicide over the life cycle: Risk factors, assessment, and treatment of suicidal patients.* Washington, DC: American Psychiatric Press.

Boag, T. (1970). Mental health of native peoples of the Arctic. *Canadian Psychiatric Association Journal, 15*, 115–120.

Bock, G. R., & Goode, J. A. (Eds.). (1996). *Genetics of criminal and antisocial behaviour* (Ciba Foundation, Vol. 194). Chichester, UK: Wiley.

Bockoven, J. S. (1963). *Moral treatment in American psychiatry.* New York: Springer.

Bodlund, O., & Kullgren, G. (1996). Transsexualism—general outcome and prognostic factors: A five-year follow-up study of nineteen transsexuals in the process of changing sex. *Archives of Sexual Behavior, 25,* 303–316.

Bohman, M., Cloninger, C. R., von Knorring, A. L., & Sigvardsson, S. (1984). An adoption study of somatoform disorders: III. Cross-fostering analysis and genetic relationship to alcoholism and criminality. *Archives of General Psychiatry, 41,* 872–878.

Bohus, M., Haaf, B., Stiglmayr, C., Pohl, U., Bohme, R., & Linehan, M. (2000). Evaluation of inpatient dialectical-behavioral therapy for borderline personality disorder—A prospective study. *Behavior Research and Therapy, 38*(9), 875–887.

Boivin, D. B., Czeisler, D. A., Dijk, D-J., Duffy, J. E., Folkard, S., Minors, D. S., et al. (1997). Complex interaction of the sleep-wake cycle and circadian phase modulates mood in healthy subjects. *Archives of General Psychiatry, 54,* 145–152.

Boll, T. J. (1985). Developing issues in clinical neuropsychology. *Journal of Clinical and Experimental Neuropsychology, 7*(5), 473–485.

Bonanno, G. A., & Kaltman, S. (1999). Toward an integrative perspective on bereavement. *Psychological Bulletin, 125*(6), 1004–1008.

Bond, A., & Lader, M. L. (1979). Benzodiazepines and aggression. In M. Sandler (Ed.), *Psychopharmacology of aggression.* New York: Raven Press.

Bond, C. F., DeCandia, C. G., & MacKinnon, J. (1988). Responses to race in a psychiatric setting: The role of patient's race. *Personality and Social Psychology Bulletin, 14,* 448–458.

Bond, G. R., Drake, R. E., Mueser, K. T., & Becker, D. R. (1997). An update on supported employment for people with severe mental illness. *Psychiatric Services, 48,* 335–346.

Bonnet, M. H. (2000). Sleep deprivation. In M. H. Kryger, T. Roth, & W. C. Dement (Eds.), *Principles and practice of sleep medicine* (3rd ed., pp. 53–71). Philadelphia: W. B. Saunders.

Boon, S., & Draijer, N. (1991). Diagnosing dissociative disorders in the Netherlands: A pilot study with the Structured Clinical Interview for DSM-III-R dissociative disorders. *American Journal of Psychiatry, 148,* 458–462.

Boon, S., & Draijer, N. (1993). Multiple personality disorder in the Netherlands: A clinical investigation of 71 cases. *American Journal of Psychiatry, 150,* 489–494.

Boothroyd, L. J., Kirmayer, L. J., Spreng, S., Malus, M., & Hodgins, S. (2001). Completed suicides among the Inuit of northern Quebec, 1982–1996: A case-control study. *Canadian Medical Association Journal, 165,* 749–755.

Bootzin, R. R., Engle-Friedman, M., & Hazelwood, L. (1983). Sleep disorders and the elderly. In P. M. Lewinson &

L. Teri (Eds.), *Clinical geropsychology: New directions in assessment and treatment.* Elmsford, NY: Pergamon Press.

Bootzin, R. R., Manber, R., Perlis, M. L., Salvio, M., & Wyatt, J. K. (1993). Sleep disorders. In P. B. Sutker & H. E. Adams (Eds.), *Comprehensive handbook of psychopathology* (2nd ed., pp. 531–561). New York: Plenum Press.

Bootzin, R. R., & Nicassio, P. M. (1978). Behavioral treatments of insomnia. In M. Hersen, R. Eisler, & P. M. Miller (Eds.), *Progress in behavior modification* (Vol. 6, pp. 1–45). New York: Academic Press.

Borkovec, T. D., & Costello, E. (1993). Efficacy of applied relaxation and cognitive-behavioral therapy in the treatment of generalized anxiety disorder. *Journal of Consulting and Clinical Psychology, 61*(4), 611–619.

Borkovec, T. D., & Hu, S. (1990) The effect of worry on cardiovascular response to phobic imagery. *Behaviour Research and Therapy, 28,* 69–73.

Borkovec, T. D., Newman, M. G., Pincus, A. L., & Lytle, R. (2002). A component analysis of cognitive-behavioral therapy for generalized anxiety disorder and the role of interpersonal problems. *Journal of Consulting and Clinical Psychology, 70,* 288–298.

Borkovec, T. D., & Ruscio, A. (2001). Psychotherapy for generalized anxiety disorder. *Journal of Clinical Psychiatry, 62,* 37–45.

Borkovec, T. D., & Whisman, M. A. (1996). Psychosocial treatment for generalized anxiety disorder. In M. R. Mavissakalian & R. F. Prien (Eds.), *Long-term treatments of anxiety disorders.* Washington, DC: American Psychiatric Press.

Bornath, L. M. (2002). *Elaine Tanner: Best female Canadian swimmer in the late 1960s.* Retrieved June 25, 2004, from http://www.almostfabulous.com/canadians/name/t/tannerelaine.php.

Bornstein, R. F. (1992). The dependent personality: Developmental, social, and clinical perspectives. *Psychological Bulletin, 112,* 3–23.

Bornstein, R. F. (1997). Dependent personality disorder in the DSM-IV and beyond. *Clinical Psychology: Science and Practice, 4,* 175–187.

Boskind-Lodahl, M. (1976). Cinderella's stepsisters: A feminist perspective on anorexia nervosa and bulimia. *Signs, 2,* 342–356.

Bouchard, S., Vallieres, A., Roy, M.-A., & Maziade, M. (1996). Cognitive restructuring in the treatment of psychotic symptoms in schizophrenia: A critical analysis. *Behavior Therapy, 27,* 257–277.

Bouchard, T. J., Jr., Lykken, D. T., McGue, M., Segal, N. L., & Tellegen, A. (1990). Sources of human psychological differences: The Minnesota study of twins reared apart. *Science, 250,* 223–228.

Bourgeois, J. A., Seaman, J. S., & Servis, M. E. (2003). Delirium, dementia, and amnestic disorders. In R. E. Hales & S. C. Yudofsky (Eds.), *Textbook of clinical psychiatry* (4th ed.) (pp. 259–308). Washington, DC: American Psychiatric Press.

Bourgeois, M. S. (1992). Evaluating memory wallets in conversations with persons with dementia. *Journal of Speech and Hearing Research, 35,* 1344–1357.

Bourgeois, M. S. (1993). Effects of memory aids on the dyadic conversations of individuals with dementia. *Journal of Applied Behavior Analysis, 26,* 77–87.

Bouton, M. E., Mineka, S., & Barlow, D. H. (2001). A modern learning-theory perspective on the etiology of panic disorder. *Psychological Review, 108,* 4–32.

Bowden, S., Bardenhagen, F., Ambrose, M., & Whelan, G. (1994). Alcohol, thiamin deficiency, and neuropsychological disorders. *Alcohol and Alcoholism Supplement, 2,* 267–272.

Bowlby, J. (1977). The making and breaking of affectionate bonds. *British Journal of Psychiatry, 130,* 201–210.

Bowman, E. S., & Coons, P. M. (2000). The differential diagnosis of epilepsy, pseudoseizures, dissociative identity disorder, and dissociative disorder not otherwise specified. *Bulletin of the Menninger Clinic, 64,* 164–180.

Bowman, E. S., & Nurnberger, J. I. (1993). Genetics of psychiatric diagnosis and treatment. In D. L. Dunner (Ed.), *Current psychiatric therapy* (pp. 46–53). Philadelphia: W. B. Saunders.

Bowman, M. (2000). The diversity of diversity: Canadian-American differences and their implications for clinical training and APA accreditation. *Canadian Psychology, 41,* 230–243.

Boyle, W., Doherty, M., Fortin, C., & MacKinnon, D. (2002). *Canadian youth, sexual health and AIDS study.* Toronto: Council Ministers of Education Canada.

Bracha, H. S., Torrey, E. F., Gottesman, I. I., Bigelow, L. B., & Cunniff, C. (1992). Second-trimester markers of fetal size in schizophrenia: A study of monozygotic twins. *American Journal of Psychiatry, 149,* 1355–1361.

Bradford, J. (1997). Medical interventions in sexual deviance. In D. R. Laws & W. O'Donohue (Eds.), *Sexual deviance: Theory, assessment and treatment* (pp. 449–464). New York: Guilford Press.

Bradley, B. P., & Mathews, A. (1988). Memory bias in recovered clinical depressives. Special issue: Information processing and the emotional disorders. *Cognition and Emotion, 2*(3), 235–245.

Bradley, B. P., Mogg, K., White, J., Groom, C., & de Bono, J. (1999). Attentional bias for emotional faces in generalized anxiety disorder. *British Journal of Clinical Psychology, 38,* 267–278.

Bradley, S. J., Oliver, G. D., Chernick, A. B., & Zucker, K. J. (1998). Experiment of nurture: Ablatio penis at 2 months, sex reassignment at 7 months, and a psychosexual follow-up in young adulthood. *Pediatrics, 102*(1), E9.

Bradley, S. J., & Zucker, K. J. (1997). Gender identity disorder: A review of the past 10 years. *Journal of the American Academy of Child and Adolescent Psychiatry, 36,* 872–880.

Bradley, W. (1937). The behavior of children receiving Benzedrine. *American Journal of Psychiatry, 94,* 577–585.

Brady, J. P. (1991). The pharmacology of stuttering: A critical review. *American Journal of Psychiatry, 148*, 1309–1316.

Brady, J. P., & Lind, D. L. (1961). Experimental analysis of hysterical blindness. *Archives of General Psychiatry, 4*, 331–339.

Brandon, S., Cowley, P., McDonald, C., Neville, P., Palmer, R., & Wellstood-Eason, S. (1984). Electroconvulsive therapy: Results in depressive illness from the Leicestershire trial. *British Medical Journal, 288*(6410), 22–25.

Brandon, T. H., & Baker, T. B. (1992). The Smoking Consequences Questionnaire: The subjective utility of smoking in college students. *Psychological Assessment, 3*, 484–491.

Brannon, L., & Feist, J. (1997). *Health psychology: An introduction to behavior and health.* Pacific Grove, CA: Brooks/Cole.

Braswell, L., & Bloomquist, M. (1994). *Cognitive behavior therapy of ADHD.* New York: Guilford Press.

Brauchi, J. T., & West, L. J. (1959). Sleep deprivation. *Journal of the American Medical Association, 171*, 11–14.

Brawman-Mintzer, O. (2001). Pharmacologic treatment of generalized anxiety disorder. *Psychiatric Clinics of North America, 24*, 119–137.

Brechtl, J. R., Breitbart, W., Galietta, M., Krivo, S., & Rosenfeld, B. (2001). The use of highly active antiretroviral therapy (HAART) in patients with advanced HIV infection: Impact on medical, palliative care, and quality of life outcomes. *Journal of Pain Symptom Management, 21*, 41–51.

Breier, A. (1993). Paranoid disorder: Clinical features and treatment. In D. L. Dunner (Ed.), *Current psychiatric therapy* (pp. 154–159). Philadelphia: W. B. Saunders.

Breiner, M. J., Stritzke, W. G. K., & Lang, A. R. (1999). Approaching avoidance: A step essential to the understanding of craving. *Alcohol Research and Health, 23*(3), 197–206.

Brekke, J. S., Long, J. D., Nesbitt, N., & Sobell, L. (1997). The impact of service characteristics on functional outcomes from community support programs for persons with schizophrenia: A growth curve analysis. *Journal of Consulting and Clinical Psychology, 65*, 464–475.

Bremner, J. D., Randall, P. R., Scott, T. M., Bronen, R. A., Seibyl, J. P., Southwick, S. M., et al. (1995). MRI-based measurement of hippocampal volume in patients with combat-related posttraumatic stress disorder. *American Journal of Psychiatry, 152*, 973–981.

Brener, N. D., Hassan, S. S., & Barrios, L. C. (1999). Suicidal ideation among college students in the United States. *Journal of Consulting and Clinical Psychology, 67*, 1004–1008.

Brenner, D. E., Kukull, W. A., van Belle, G., Bowen, J. D., McCormick, W. C., Teri, L., et al. (1993). Relationship between cigarette smoking and Alzheimer's disease in a population-based case-control study. *Neurology, 43*, 293–300.

Brent, D. A., & Kolko, D. J. (1990). The assessment and treatment of children and adolescents at risk for suicide. In S. J. Blumenthal & D. J. Kupfer (Eds.), *Suicide over the life cycle: Risk factors, assessment and treatment of suicidal patients.* Washington, DC: American Psychiatric Press.

Brent, D. A., Kerr, M. M., Goldstein, C., Bozigar, J., Wartella, M., & Allan, M. J. (1989). An outbreak of suicide and suicidal behavior in a high school. *Journal of the American Academy of Child and Adolescent Psychiatry, 28*(6), 918–924.

Brent, D. A., Perper, J. A., Goldstein, C. E., Kolko, D. J., Allan, M. J., Allman, C. J., et al. (1988). Risk factors for adolescent suicide: A comparison of adolescent suicide victims with suicidal inpatients. *Archives of General Psychiatry, 45*, 581–588.

Breslau, N., Kilbey, M. M., & Andreski, P. (1993). Nicotine dependence and major depression: New evidence from a prospective investigation. *Archives of General Psychiatry, 50*, 31–35.

Breslau, N., Schultz, L., & Peterson, E. (1995). Sex differences in depression: A role for preexisting anxiety. *Psychiatry Research, 58*, 112.

Breuer, J., & Freud, S. (1957). *Studies on hysteria.* New York: Basic Books (Original work published 1895).

Brewin, C. R., Andrews, B., & Gotlib, I. H. (1993). Psychopathology in early experience: A reappraisal of retrospective reports. *Psychological Bulletin, 113*, 82–98.

Briere pleads guilty to Holly Jones's murder. (2004, June 17). *The Globe and Mail.* Retrieved August 5, 2004, from http://www.theglobeandmail.com/servlet/story/RTGAM.20040617.wbrier0617B/BNStory/National.

British Columbia Schizophrenia Society. (2001). *Basic facts about schizophrenia.* Retrieved November 3, 2004, from http://www.mentalhealth.com/book/p40-sc02.html.

Broadhead, W. E., Kaplan, B. H., & James, S. A. (1983). The epidemiologic evidence for a relationship between social support and health. *American Journal of Epidemiology, 117*, 521–537.

Brodeur, D. A., & Pond, M. (2001). The development of selective attention in children with attention deficit hyperactivity disorder. *Journal of Abnormal Child Psychology, 29*, 229–239.

Brondolo, E., Rieppi, R., Erickson, S. A., Bagiella, E., Shapiro, P. A., McKinley, P., et al. (2003) Hostility, interpersonal interactions, and ambulatory blood pressure. *Psychosomatic Medicine, 65*, 1003–1011.

Broude, G. J., & Greene, S. J. (1980). Cross-cultural codes on 20 sexual attitudes and practices. In H. Barry, III, & A. Schlegel (Eds.), *Cross-cultural samples and codes* (pp. 313–333). Pittsburgh: University of Pittsburgh Press.

Broughton, R. J. (2000). NREM arousal parasomnias. In M. H. Kryger, T. Roth, & W. C. Dement (Eds.), *Principles and practice of sleep medicine* (3rd ed., pp. 693–706). Philadelphia: W.B. Saunders.

Broughton, R., Billings, R., & Cartwright, R. (1994). Homicidal somnambulism: A case report. *Sleep, 17*, 253–264.

Brown, G. K., Beck, A. T., Steer, R. A., & Grisham, J. R. (2000). Risk factors for suicide in psychiatric outpatients: A 20-year prospective study. *Journal of Consulting and Clinical Psychology, 63*(3), 371–377.

Brown, G. W. (1959). Experiences of discharged chronic schizophrenic mental hospital patients in various types of living groups. *Millbank Memorial Fund Quarterly, 37*, 105–131.

Brown, G. W. (1989). Depression. In G. W. Brown & T. O. Harris (Eds.), *Life events and illness* (pp. 49–93). New York: Guilford Press.

Brown, G. W., & Birley, J. L. T. (1968). Crisis and life change and the onset of schizophrenia. *Journal of Health and Social Behavior, 9*, 203–214.

Brown, G. W., & Harris, T. O. (1978). *Social origins of depression: A study of psychiatric disorder in women.* London UK: Tavistock.

Brown, G. W., Harris, T. O., & Hepworth, C. (1994). Life events and endogenous depression. *Archives of General Psychiatry, 51*, 525–534.

Brown, G. W., Monck, E. M., Carstairs, G. M., & Wing, J. K. (1962). Influence of family life on the course of schizophrenic illness. *British Journal of Preventive and Social Medicine, 16*, 55–68.

Brown, J., & Finn, P. (1982). Drinking to get drunk: Findings of a survey of junior and senior high school students. *Journal of Alcohol and Drug Education, 27*, 13–25.

Brown, R. E. (1994). *An introduction to neuroendocrinology.* Cambridge, UK: Cambridge University Press.

Brown, S. L., & Forth, A. E. (1997). Psychopathy and sexual assault: Static risk factors, emotional precursors, and rapist subtypes. *Journal of Consulting and Clinical Psychology, 65*, 848–857.

Brown, T. A., & Barlow, D. H. (2002). Classification of anxiety and mood disorders. In D. H. Barlow (Ed.), *Anxiety and its disorders: The nature and treatment of anxiety and panic.* (2nd ed.). New York: Guilford Press.

Brown, T. A., Barlow, D. H., & Liebowitz, M. R. (1994). The empirical basis of generalized anxiety disorder. *American Journal of Psychiatry, 15*(9), 1272–1280.

Brown, T. A., Campbell, L. A., Lehman, C. L., Grisham, J. R., & Mancill, R. B. (2001). Current and lifetime comorbidity of the DSM-IV anxiety and mood disorders in a large clinical sample. *Journal of Abnormal Psychology, 110*, 585–599.

Brown, T. A., Chorpita, B. F., & Barlow, D. H. (1998). Structural relationships among dimensions of the DSM-IV anxiety and mood disorders and dimensions of negative affect, positive affect, and autonomic arousal. *Journal of Abnormal Psychology, 107*(2), 179–192.

Brown, T. A., Marten, P. A., & Barlow, D. H. (1995). Discriminant validity of the symptoms comprising the DSM-III-R and DSM-IV associated symptom criterion of generalized anxiety disorder. *Journal of Anxiety Disorders, 9*, 317–328.

Brown, T. A., White, K. S., & Barlow, D. H. (2005). A psychometric reanalysis of the Albany panic and phobia questionnaire.

*Behaviour Research and Therapy, 43,* 337–355.

Brown, T. M. (2001). Substance-induced delirium and related encephalopathies. In G. O. Gabbard (Ed.), *Treatment of psychiatric disorders* (Vol. 1) (3rd ed.) (pp. 423–479). Washington, DC: American Psychiatric Press.

Brownell, K. D. (1991). Dieting and the search for the perfect body: Where physiology and culture collide. *Behavior Therapy, 22,* 1–12.

Brownell, K. D., & Fairburn, C. G. (Eds.). (1995). *Eating disorders and obesity: A comprehensive handbook.* New York: Guilford Press.

Brownell, K. D., & Fairburn, C. G. (2002). Eating disorders and obesity: A comprehensive handbook (2nd ed.). New York: Guilford Press.

Brownell, K. D., Hayes, S. C., & Barlow, D. H. (1977). Patterns of appropriate and deviant sexual arousal: The behavioral treatment of multiple sexual deviations. *Journal of Consulting and Clinical Psychology, 45*(6), 1144–1155.

Brownell, K. D., & Rodin, J. (1994). The dieting maelstrom: Is it possible and advisable to lose weight? *American Psychologist, 49*(9), 781–791.

Brownlee, K., Devins, G. M., Flanigan, M., Fleming, J. A. E., Morehouse, R., Moscovitch, A., et al. (2003). Are there gender differences in the prescribing of hypnotic medications for insomnia? *Human Psychopharmacology: Clinical and Experimental, 18,* 69–73.

Brownmiller, S. (1984). *Femininity.* New York: Ballantine Books.

Bruce, M. L., & Kim, K. M. (1992). Differences in the effects of divorce on major depression in men and women. *American Journal of Psychiatry, 149*(7), 914–917.

Bruch, H. (1973). *Eating disorders: Obesity, anorexia nervosa, and the person within.* New York: Basic Books.

Bruch, H. (1985). Four decades of eating disorders. In D. M. Garner & P. E. Garfinkel (Eds.), *Handbook of psychotherapy for anorexia nervosa and bulimia* (pp. 7–18). New York: Guilford Press.

Bruch, H. (1986). Anorexia nervosa: The therapeutic task. In K. D. Brownell & J. P. Foreyt (Eds.), *Handbook of eating disorders: Physiology, psychology, and treatment of obesity, anorexia, and bulimia* (pp. 328–332). New York: Basic Books.

Bruch, M. A., & Heimberg, R. G. (1994). Differences in perceptions of parental and personal characteristics between generalized and non-generalized social phobics. *Journal of Anxiety Disorders, 8,* 155–168.

Bruck, M. (1987). The adult outcomes of children with learning disabilities. *Annals of Dyslexia, 37,* 252–263.

Bruck, M. (1992). Persistence of dyslexics' phonological deficits. *Developmental Psychology, 28,* 874–886.

Bryant, D. M., & Maxwell, K. L. (1999). The environment and mental retardation. *International Review of Psychiatry, 11,* 56–67.

Bryson, S. E., & Smith, I. M. (1998). Epidemiology of autism: Prevalence, associated characteristics, and implications for research and service delivery. *Mental Retardation and Developmental Disabilities Research Reviews, 4,* 97–103.

Buda, M., & Tsuang, M. T. (1990). The epidemiology of suicide: Implications for clinical practice. In S. J. Blumenthal & D. J. Kupfer (Eds.), *Suicide over the life cycle: Risk factors, assessment and treatment of suicidal patients.* Washington, DC: American Psychiatric Press.

Buehler, R. E., Patterson, G. R., & Furniss, J. M. (1966). The reinforcement of behavior in institutional settings. *Behavior Research and Therapy, 4,* 157–167.

Buffett-Jerrott, S., & Stewart, S. H. (2002). Cognitive and sedative effects of benzodiazepine use. *Current Pharmaceutical Design, 8,* 45–58.

Buffett-Jerrott, S. E., Stewart, S. H., Bird, S., & Teehan, M. D. (1998). An examination of differences in the time course of oxazepam's effects on implicit vs. explicit memory. *Journal of Psychopharmacology, 12,* 338–347.

Buffett-Jerrott, S. E., Stewart, S. H., & Teehan, M. D. (1998). A further examination of the time-dependent effects of oxazepam and lorazepam on implicit and explicit memory. *Psychopharmacology, 138,* 344–353.

Buffum, J. (1982). Pharmacosexology: The effects of drugs on sexual function—A review. *Journal of Psychoactive Drugs, 14,* 5–44.

Bulik, C. M., Sullivan, P. F., & Kendler, K. S. (2000). An empirical study of the classification of eating disorders. *American Journal of Psychiatry, 157*(6), 886–895.

Burack, J. A., Iarocci, G., Bowler, D., & Mottron, L. (2002). Benefits and pitfalls in the merging of disciplines: The example of developmental psychopathology and the study of persons with autism. *Development and Psychopathology, 14,* 225–237.

Burke, K. C., Burke, J. D., Jr., Regier, D. A., & Rae, D. S. (1990). Age at onset of selected mental disorders in five community populations. *Archives of General Psychiatry, 47,* 511–518.

Burke, W. J., & Bohac, D. L. (2001). Amnestic disorder due to a general medical condition and amnestic disorder not otherwise specified. In G. O. Gabbard (Ed.), *Treatment of psychiatric disorders* (Vol. 1) (3rd ed.) (pp. 609–624). Washington, DC: American Psychiatric Press.

Burns, A. (2000). The burden of Alzheimer's disease. *International Journal of Neuropsychopharmacology, 3*(7), 31–38.

Burton, R. (1977). *Anatomy of melancholy.* (Reprint edition). New York: Random House (Original work published 1621).

Bury, A. S., & Bagby, R. M. (2002). The detection of feigned uncoached and coached post-traumatic stress disorder with MMPI-2 in a sample of workplace accident victims. *Psychological Assessment, 14,* 472–484.

Bushman, B. J. (1993). Human aggression while under the influence of alcohol and other drugs: An integrative research review. *Psychological Science, 2,* 148–152.

Bushnell, J. A., Wells, J. E., Hornblow, A. R., Oakley-Browne, M. A., & Joyce, P. (1990). Prevalence of three bulimia syndromes in the general population. *Psychological Medicine, 20,* 671–680.

Bustillo, J., Lauriello, J., Horan, W., & Keith, S. (2001). The psychosocial treatment of schizophrenia: An update. *American Journal of Psychiatry, 158*(2), 163–175.

Butcher, J. N. (2000). Revising psychological tests: Lessons learned from the revision of the MMPI. *Psychological Assessment, 12,* 263–271.

Butcher, J. N., Graham, J. R., Williams, C. L., & Ben-Porath, Y. S. (1990). *Development and use of the MMPI-2 content scales.* Minneapolis: University of Minnesota Press.

Butler, G., & Mathews, A. (1983). Cognitive processes in anxiety. *Advances in Behaviour Research and Therapy, 5,* 51–62.

Butler, L. D., Duran, R. E. F., Jasiukaitis, P., Koopman, C., & Spiegel, D. (1996). Hypnotizability and traumatic experience: A diathesis-stress model of dissociative symptomatology. *American Journal of Psychiatry, 153,* 42–63.

Buysse, D. J., Morin, C. M., & Reynolds, C. F., III. (2001). Sleep disorders. In G. O. Gabbard (Ed.), *Treatment of psychiatric disorders:* (Vol. 2) (3rd ed.) (pp. 2371–2431). Washington, DC: American Psychiatric Press.

Buysse, D. J., Reynolds, C. F., & Kupfer, D. J. (1993). Classification of sleep disorders: A preview of the DSM-IV. In D. L. Dunner (Ed.), *Current psychiatric therapy* (pp. 360–361). Philadelphia: W. B. Saunders.

Byne, W., & Parsons, B. (1993). Human sexual orientation: The biologic theories reappraised. *Archives of General Psychiatry, 50,* 228–239.

Byne, W., Lasco, M. S., Kemether, E., Edgar, M. A., Morgello, S., Jones, L. B., & Tobet, S. (2000). The interstitial nuclei of the human anterior hypothalamus: An investigation of sexual variation in volume and cell size, number and density. *Brain Research, 856,* 254–258.

Byrne, D., & Schulte, L. (1990). Personality dispositions as mediators of sexual responses. *Annual Review of Sex Research, 1,* 93–117.

Cadoret, R. J. (1978). Psychopathology in the adopted-away offspring of biologic parents with antisocial behavior. *Archives of General Psychiatry, 35,* 176–184.

Cadoret, R. J., Yates, W. R., Troughton, E., Woodworth, G., & Stewart, M. A. (1995). Genetic-environment interaction in the genesis of aggressivity and conduct disorders. *Archives of General Psychiatry, 52,* 916–924.

Cairney, J., Thorpe, C., Rietschlin, J., & Avison, W. R. (1999). 12-month prevalence of depression among single and married mothers in the 1994 National Population Health Survey. *Canadian Journal of Public Health, 90,* 320–324.

Campbell, D. (2003, January 15). Pep pills blamed in friendly fire case. *The Guardian.* Retrieved October 25, 2003, from http://www.guardian.co.uk/afghanistan/story/0,1284,874923,00.html.

Campo, J. V., & Negrini, B. J. (2000). Case study: Negative reinforcement and behavioral management of conversion disorder. *Journal of the American Academy of Child and Adolescent Psychiatry, 39*(6), 787–790.

Canadian Centre for Substance Abuse (1999). *Canadian Profile 1999. Alcohol: Highlights.* Retrieved November 15, 2002, from http://www.ccsa.ca/profile/cp99alc.htm.

Canadian Council on Smoking and Health and Physicians for a Smoke-Free Canada (2003). *Number of deaths in Canada caused by smoking.* Retrieved August 16, 2003, from http://www.media-awareness.ca/english/resources/educational/handouts/tobacco_advertising/number_of_deaths.cfm.

Canadian Down Syndrome Society (2000). New Down syndrome statistics. *CDSS Quarterly, 13.* Retrieved May 20, 2004, from http://www.cdss.ca/Newsletter%20Articles/medical%20and%20health/2000vol13-1, 8.html.

Canadian Institutes of Health Research, Natural Sciences and Engineering Research Council of Canada, Social Sciences and Humanities Research Council of Canada (2003). *Tri-council policy statement: Ethical conduct for research involving humans.* Ottawa, ON: Medical Research Council of Canada.

Canadian Press (2003, December 30). Questions about the herb ephedra and its ban by the FDA. Retrieved August 6, 2004, from http://www.medbroadcast.com/channel_health_news_details.asp?news_channel_id=1000&news_id=2957&channel_id=1012&relation_id=0.

Canadian Press (2004, May 11). Boy raised as girl has tragic demise: Doctor advised gender switch. *The Chronicle Herald, 56,* A1–A2.

Canadian Psychological Association (n.d.). *Empirically Supported Treatments in Psychology: Recommendations for Canadian Professional Psychology.* Retrieved February 18, 2004, from http://www.cpa.ca/documents/empiric_toc.html.

Canadian Psychological Association (2000). *Canadian code of ethics for psychologists* (3rd ed.). Ottawa, ON: Canadian Psychological Association.

Canadian Study of Health and Aging Working Group (1994). Canadian Study of Health and Aging: Study methods and prevalence of dementia. *Canadian Medical Association Journal, 150,* 899–913.

Canadian Study of Health and Aging Working Group (2000). The incidence of dementia in Canada. *Neurology, 55,* 66–73.

Canadian Study of Health and Aging Working Group (2001). Disability and frailty among elderly Canadians: A comparison of six surveys. *International Journal of Psychogeriatrics, 13* (Suppl. 1), 159–167.

Canadian Union of Public Employees (CUPE) (November 17, 2005). "Ontario tribunal rules on sex reassignment surgery." Retrieved November 22, 2006, from http://www.cupe.ca/www/news/stonehouse_tribunal.

Candido, C. L., & Romney, D. M. (2002). Depression in paranoid and nonparanoid schizophrenic patients compared with major depressive disorder. *Journal of Affective Disorders, 70,* 261–271.

Cannon, T. D., Barr, C. E., & Mednick, S. A. (1991). Genetic and perinatal factors in the etiology of schizophrenia. In E. F. Walker (Ed.), *Schizophrenia: A life-course developmental perspective* (pp. 9–31). New York: Academic Press.

Cannon, W. B. (1929). *Bodily changes in pain, hunger, fear and rage* (2nd ed.). New York: Appleton-Century-Crofts.

Cannon, W. B. (1942). Voodoo death. *American Anthropologist, 44,* 169–181.

Canter, A. (1996). The Bender-Gesalt Test (BGT). In C. S. Newmark (Ed.), *Major psychological assessment instruments* (pp. 400–430). Boston: Allyn & Bacon.

Canterbury Farms (1997). *The new wonder herb that has been around for 2,500 years!* Retrieved July 7, 2004, from http://www.nwgardening.com/stjohnswort.html.

Cantor, J. M., Blanchard, R., Paterson, A. D., & Bogaert, A. F. (2002). How many gay men owe their sexual orientation to fraternal birth order? *Archives of Sexual Behavior, 31,* 63–71.

Capobianco, D. J., Swanson, J. W., & Dodick, D. W. (2001). Medication–induced (analgesic rebound) headache: Historical aspects and initial descriptions of the North American experience. *Headache, 41,* 500–502.

Cappell, H., & Greeley, J. (1987). Alcohol and tension reduction: An update on research and theory. In H. T. Blane & K. E. Leonard (Eds.), *Psychological theories of drinking and alcoholism* (pp. 15–54). New York: Guilford Press.

Cardeña, E. A., & Gleaves, D. H. (2003). Dissociative disorders: Phantoms of the self. In M. Hersen & S. M. Turner (Eds.), *Adult psychopathology and diagnosis* (4th ed., pp. 476–505). New York: John Wiley.

Cardeña, E., Lewis-Fernandez, R., Bear, D., Pakianathan, I., & Spiegel, D. (1996). Dissociative disorders. In T. A. Widiger, A. J. Frances, H. A. Pincus, R. Ross, M. B. First, & W. W. Davis (Eds.), *DSM-IV sourcebook* (Vol. 2, pp. 973–1005). Washington, DC: American Psychiatric Press.

Carey, G. (1992). Twin imitation for antisocial behavior: Implications for genetic and family environment research. *Journal of Abnormal Psychology, 101,* 18–25.

Carey, M. P., & Johnson, B. T. (1996). Effectiveness of yohimbine in the treatment of erectile disorder: Four meta-analytic integrations. *Archives of Sexual Behavior, 25,* 341–360.

Carey, M. P., Wincze, J. P., & Meisler, A. W. (1993). Sexual dysfunction: Male erectile disorder. In D. H. Barlow (Ed.), *Clinical handbook of psychological disorders* (2nd ed., pp. 442–480). New York Guilford Press.

Carlat, D. J., & Camargo, C. A. (1991). Review of bulimia nervosa in males. *American Journal of Psychiatry, 148,* 831–843.

Carlat, D. J., & Camargo, C. A., Jr., & Herzog, D. B. (1997). Eating disorders in males: A report on 135 patients. *American Journal of Psychiatry, 154,* 1127–1132.

Carlson, G. A. (1990). Annotation: Child and adolescent mania—diagnostic considerations. *Journal of Child Psychology and Psychiatry, 31*(3), 331–341.

Carlson, G. A., & Kashani, J. H. (1988). Phenomenology of major depression from childhood through adulthood: Analysis of three studies. *American Journal of Psychiatry, 145*(10), 1222–1225.

Carlsson, A. (1995). The dopamine theory revisited. In S. R. Hirsch and D. R. Weinberger (Eds.), *Schizophrenia* (pp. 379–400). Oxford, England: Blackwell Science.

Carmody, D. L., & Carmody, J. T. (1993). *Native American Religions.* Mahwah, NJ: Paulist Press.

Caron, C., & Rutter, M. (1991). Comorbidity in childhood psychopathology: Concepts, issues, and research strategies. *Journal of Child Psychology and Psychiatry, 32,* 1063–1080.

Carpenter, W. T. (1994). The deficit syndrome. *American Journal of Psychiatry, 151,* 327–329.

Carpenter, W. T., Appelbaum, P. S., & Levine, R. J. (2003). The Declaration of Helsinki and clinical trials: A focus on placebo-controlled trials in schizophrenia. *American Journal of Psychiatry, 160,* 356–362.

Carrington, P. J. (1999). Gender, gun control, suicide and homicide in Canada. *Archives of Suicide Research, 5,* 71–75.

Carroll, B. J., Feinberg, M., Greden, J. F., Haskett, R. F., James, N. M., Steiner, M., et al. (1980). Diagnosis of endogenous depression: Comparison of clinical, research, and neuroendocrine criteria. *Journal of Affective Disorders, 2,* 177–194.

Carroll, B. J., Martin, F. I., & Davies, B. (1968). Resistance to suppression by dexamethasome of plasma 11-O.H.C.S. levels in severe depressive illness. *British Medical Journal, 3,* 285–287.

Carroll, E. M., Rueger, D. B., Foy, D. W., & Donahoe, C. P. (1985). Vietnam combat veterans with posttraumatic stress disorder: Analysis of marital and cohabitating adjustment. *Journal of Abnormal Psychology, 94,* 329–337.

Carroll, K. M. (1992). Psychotherapy for cocaine abuse: Approaches, evidence, and conceptual models. In T. R. Kosten & H. D. Kleber (Eds.), *Clinician's guide to cocaine addiction: Theory, research, and treatment* (pp. 290–313). New York: Guilford Press.

Carroll, R. A. (2000). Assessment and treatment of gender dysphoria. In S. R. Leiblum & R. C. Rosen (Eds.), *Principles and practice of sex therapy* (3rd ed., pp. 368–397). New York: Guilford Press.

Carson, R. C. (1991). Discussion: Dilemmas in the pathway of DSM-IV. *Journal of Abnormal Psychology, 100,* 302–307.

Carson, R. C. (1996). Aristotle, Galileo, and the *DSM* taxonomy: The case of schizophrenia. *Journal of Consulting and Clinical Psychology, 64*(6), 1133–1139.

Carson, R. C., & Sanislow, C. A. (1993). The schizophrenias. In P. B. Sutker & H. E. Adams (Eds.), *Comprehensive handbook of psychopathology* (pp. 295–333). New York: Plenum Press.

Cartensen, L. L., Charles, S. T., Isaacowitz, D., & Kennedy, Q. (2003). Life-span personality development and emotion. In R. J. Davidson, K. Scherer & H. H. Goldsmith (Eds.), *Handbook of affective sciences* (pp. 931–951). Oxford: Oxford University Press.

Carter, J. C., & Fairburn, C. G., (1998). Cognitive-behavioral self-help for binge eating disorder: A controlled effectiveness study. *Journal of Consulting and Clinical Psychology, 66,* 616–623.

Carter, J. R., & Neufeld, R. W. J. (1998). Cultural aspects of understanding people with schizophrenic disorders. In S. S. Kazarian & D. R. Evans (Eds.), *Cultural clinical psychology: Theory, research, and practice* (pp. 246–266). London UK: Oxford University Press.

Carter, R. M., Wittchen, H. U., Pfister, H., & Kessler, R. C. (2001). One-year prevalence of subthreshold and threshold DSM-IV generalized anxiety disorder in a nationally representative sample. *Depression and Anxiety, 13,* 78–88.

Caruso, J. C. (2001). Reliable component analysis of the Stanford-Binet: Fourth edition for 2- to 6-year-olds. *Psychological Assessment, 13,* 261–266.

Cash, T. F., & Pruzinsky, T. (2002). Understanding body images. In T. F. Cash & T. Pruzinsky (Eds.), *Body image: A handbook of theory, research and clinical practice* (pp. 3–12). New York: Guilford Press.

Casper, R. C. (1982). Treatment principles in anorexia nervosa. *Adolescent Psychiatry, 10,* 431–454.

Caspi, A., Elder, G. H., Jr., & Bem, D. L. (1987). Moving against the world: Life-course patterns of explosive children. *Developmental Psychology, 23,* 308–313.

Caspi, A., Sugden, K., Moffitt, T. E., Taylor, A., Craig, I. W., Harrington, H., et al. (2003). Influence of life stress on depression: Moderation by a polymorphism in the 5-HTT gene. *Science, 301,* 386–389.

Cassidy, F., Forest, K., Murry, E., & Carroll, B. J. (1998). A factor analysis of the signs and symptoms of mania. *Archives of General Psychiatry, 55,* 27–32.

Castellanos, F. X., Sharp, W. S., Gottesman, R. F., Greenstein, D. K., Giedd, J. N., & Rapoprt, J. L. (2003). Anatomic brain abnormalities in monozygotic twins discordant for attention deficit hyperactivity disorder. *American Journal of Psychiatry, 160,* 1693–1696.

Castonguay, L. G., Eldredge, K. L., & Agras, W. S. (1995). Binge eating disorder: Current state and directions. *Clinical Psychology Review, 15,* 815–890.

Catania, J. A., Morin, S. F., Canchola, J., Pollack, L., Chang, J., & Coates, T. J. (2000). U.S. priorities–HIV prevention. *Science, 290,* 717.

Cautela, J. R. (1966). Treatment of compulsive behavior by covert sensitization. *Psychological Record, 16,* 33–41.

Cautela, J. R. (1967). Covert sensitization. *Psychological Reports, 20,* 459–468.

CBC News Online (2004a, June 17). Killer of Holly Jones pleads guilty. Retrieved August 5, 2004, from http://www.cbc.ca/stories/2004/06/17/canada/holly040617.

CBC News Online (2004b, August 5). Timeline of BSE in Canada and the U.S. Retrieved August 11, 2004, from http://www.cbc.ca/news/background/madcow/timeline.html.

CBC Saskatchewan News Staff (2003, June 8). Possible Mackay forgets burning body: Expert. *CBC Saskatchewan,*. Retrieved June 10, 2004, from http://sask.cbc.ca/regional/servlet/View?filename=mackay020608.

Ceci, S. J. (2003). Cast in six ponds and you'll reel in something: Looking back on 25 years of research. *American Psychologist, 58,* 855–867.

Celio, A. A., Zabinski, M. F., & Wilfley, D. E. (2002). African American body images. In T. F. Cash & T. Pruzinsky (Eds.), *Body image: A handbook of theory, research and clinical practice* (pp. 234–242). New York: Guilford Press.

Centers for Disease Control (1994, September). *HIV/AIDS surveillance.* Atlanta: U.S. Department of Health and Human Services, Public Health Services.

Centers for Disease Control. (2003). Deaths, percent of total deaths, and death rates for the 15 leading causes of death in 5-year age groups, by race and sex: United States, 2000. Centers for Disease Control and National Center for Health Statistics, National Vital Statistics System.

Cepeda-Benito, A. (1993). Meta-analytical review of the efficacy of nicotine chewing gum in smoking treatment programs. *Journal of Consulting and Clinical Psychology, 61,* 822–830.

Chakrabarti, S., & Fombonne, E. (2001). Pervasive developmental disorders in preschool children. *Journal of the American Medical Association, 285,* 3093–3099.

Chalder, T., Cleare, A., & Wessely, S. (2000). The management of stress and anxiety in chronic fatigue syndrome. In D. I. Mostofsky & D. H. Barlow (Eds.), *The management of stress and anxiety in medical disorders* (pp. 160–179). Needham Heights, MA: Allyn & Bacon.

Chambless, D. L., Cherney, J., Caputo, G. C., & Rheinstein, B. J. G. (1987). Anxiety disorders and alcoholism: A study with inpatient alcoholics. *Journal of Anxiety Disorders, 1,* 29–40.

Chandler, M. J., & Lalonde, C. (1998). Cultural continuity as a hedge against suicide in Canada's First Nations. *Transcultural Psychiatry, 35,* 191–219.

Charbonneau, J., & O'Connor, K. (1999). Depersonalization in a non-clinical sample. *Behavioural and Cognitive Psychotherapy, 27,* 377–381.

Charlebois, P., LeBlanc, M., Gagnon, C., Larivée, S., & Tremblay, R. (1993). Age trends in early behavioral predictors of serious antisocial behaviors. *Journal of Psychopathology and Behavioral Assessment, 15,* 23–41.

Charney, D. S., & Drevets, W. C. (2002). Neurobiological basis of anxiety disorders. In K L. Davis, D. Charney, J T. Coyle & C. Nemeroff (Eds.) *Neuropsychopharmacology: The fifth generation of progress* (pp. 901–951). Philadelphia: Lippincott Williams & Wilkins.

Charney, D. S., Deutch, A. Y., Krystal, J. H., Southwick, S. M., & Davis, M. (1993). Psychobiological mechanisms of posttraumatic stress disorder. *Archives of General Psychiatry, 50,* 294–305.

Charney, D. S., Woods, S. W., Price, L. H., Goodman, W. K., Glazer, W. M., & Heninger, G. R. (1990). Noradrenergic dysregulation in panic disorder. In J. C. Ballenger (Ed.), *Neurobiology of panic disorder* (pp. 91–105). New York: Wiley-Liss.

Chassin, L., Pillow, D. R., Curran, P. J., Molina, B. S. G., & Barrera, M. (1993). Relation of parental alcoholism to early adolescent substance use: A test of three mediating mechanisms. *Journal of Abnormal Psychology, 102,* 3–19.

Chassin, L., Presson, C. C., Rose, J. S., & Sherman, S. J. (2001). From adolescence to adulthood: Age-related changes in beliefs about cigarette smoking in a midwestern community sample. *Health Psychology, 20,* 377–386.

Check, J. R. (1998). Munchausen syndrome by proxy: An atypical form of child abuse. *Journal of Practical Psychology and Behavioral Health, 4,* 340–345.

Chesney, M. A. (1986, November). *Type A behavior: The biobehavioral interface.* Keynote address presented at the annual meeting of the Association for Advancement of Behavior Therapy, Chicago.

Cheung, F. M. (1998). Cross-cultural psychopathology. *Comprehensive Clinical Psychology, 10,* 35–51.

Chilcott, L. A., & Shapiro, C. M. (1996). The socioeconomic impact of insomnia: An overview. *Pharmacoeconomics, 10,* 1–14.

China U.N. Theme Group on HIV/AIDS for the U.N. Country Team in China (2001). HIV/AIDS: China's titanic peril. In *2001 update of the AIDS situation and needs assessment report.* Beijing: UNAIDS.

Ching, S., Thoma, A., McCabe, R., & Antony, M. (2003). Measuring outcomes in aesthetic surgery: A comprehensive review of the literature. *Plastic and Reconstructive Surgery, 111*(4), 469–480.

Chivers, M. L., & Bailey, J. M. (2000). Sexual orientation of female-to-male transsexuals: A comparison of homosexual and nonhomosexual types. *Archives of Sexual Behavior, 29*(3), 259–279.

Chodoff, P. (1974). The diagnosis of hysteria: An overview. *American Journal of Psychiatry, 131,* 1073–1078.

Chodoff, P. (1982). Hysteria in women. *American Journal of Psychiatry, 139,* 545–551.

Chorpita, B. F., & Barlow, D. H. (1998). The development of anxiety: The role of control in the early environment. *Psychological Bulletin, 124*(1), 3–21.

Chorpita, B. F., Brown, T. A., & Barlow, D. H. (1998). Perceived control as a mediator of family environment in etiological models of childhood anxiety. *Behavior Therapy, 29,* 457–476.

Christenson, R., & Blazer, D. (1984). Epidemiology of persecutory ideation in an elderly population in the community.

*American Journal of Psychiatry, 141,* 1088–1091.

Christiansen, B. A., Smith, G. T., Roehling, P. V., & Goldman, M. S. (1989). Using alcohol expectancies to predict adolescent drinking behavior after one year. *Journal of Consulting and Clinical Psychology, 57,* 93–99.

Chronic Pain Association of Canada (2003). *Pain full facts.* Retrieved July 15, 2004, from http://ecn.ab.ca/cpac/page5.html.

Chudley, A. E., Gutierrez, E., Jocelyn, L. J., & Chodirker, B. N. (1998). Outcomes of genetic evaluation in children with pervasive developmental disorder. *Journal of Developmental and Behavioral Pediatrics, 19*(5), 321–325.

Chung, S. Y., Luk, S. L., & Lee, P. W. H. (1990). A follow-up study of infantile autism in Hong Kong. *Journal of Autism and Developmental Disorders, 20,* 221–232.

Cicchetti, D. (1991). A historical perspective on the discipline of developmental psychopathology. In J. Rolf, A. S. Masten, D. Cicchetti, K. H. Nuechterlein, & S. Weintraub (Eds.), *Risk and protective factors in the development of psychopathology* (pp. 2–28). New York: Cambridge University Press.

Cipani, E. (1991). Educational classification and placement. In J. L. Matson & J. A. Mulick (Eds.), *Handbook of mental retardation* (2nd ed., pp. 181–191). Elmsford, NY: Pergamon Press.

Clark, D. A., Beck, A. T., & Alford, B. A. (1999). *Scientific foundations of cognitive theory and therapy of depression.* New York: John Wiley.

Clark, D. A., & Purdon, C. L. (1995). The assessment of unwanted intrusive thoughts: A review and critique of the literature. *Behaviour Research and Therapy, 33,* 967–976.

Clark, D. A., Steer, R. A., Haslam, N., Beck, A. T., & Brown, G. K. (1997). Personality vulnerability, psychiatric diagnoses, and symptoms: Cluster analyses of the Sociotropy-Autonomy Subscales. *Cognitive Therapy and Research, 21,* 267–283.

Clark, D. M. (1986). A cognitive approach to panic. *Behaviour Research and Therapy, 24,* 461–470.

Clark, D. M. (1996). Panic disorder: From theory to therapy. In P. Salkovskis (Ed.), *Frontiers of cognitive therapy* (pp. 318–344). New York: Guilford Press.

Clark, D. M., Salkovskis, P. M. N., Hackmann, A., Wells, A., Fennell, M., Ludgate, S., et al. (1998). Two psychological treatments for hypochondriasis. *British Journal of Psychiatry, 173,* 218–225.

Clark, D. M., Salkovskis, P. M., Hackmann, A., Middleton, H., Anastasiades, P., & Gelder, M. (1994). A comparison of cognitive therapy, applied relaxation and imipramine in the treatment of panic disorder. *British Journal of Psychiatry, 164,* 759–69.

Clark, L. A. (1999). Introduction to the special section on the concept of disorder. *Journal of Abnormal Psychology, 108,* 371–373.

Clark, R. (2003). Parental history of hypertension and coping responses predict blood pressure changes in Black college volunteers undergoing a speaking task about perceptions of racism. *Psychosomatic Medicine, 65,* 1012–1019.

Clarke, C. E. (1999). Does the treatment of isolated systolic hypertension prevent dementia? *Journal of Human Hypertension, 13*(6), 357–358.

Clarkin, J. F., Carpenter, D., Hull, J., Wilner, P., & Glick, I. (1998). Effects of psychoeducational intervention for married patients with bipolar disorder and their spouses. *Psychiatric Services, 49*(4), 531–533.

Clarkin, J. F., Haas, G. L., & Glick, I. D. (1988). *Affective disorders in the family.* New York: Guilford Press.

Classen, C., Diamond, S., & Spiegel, D. (1998). Studies of life-extending psychosocial interventions. In J. Holland (Ed.), *Psycho-oncology.* Oxford: Oxford University Press.

Clayton, P. J., & Darvish, H. S. (1979). Course of depressive symptoms following the stress of bereavement. In J. E. Barrett (Ed.), *Stress and mental disorder.* New York: Raven.

Cleckley, H. M. (1982). *The mask of sanity* (6th ed.). St. Louis: Mosby (Original work published 1941).

Cleghorn, J. M., & Albert, M. L. (1990). Modular disjunction in schizophrenia: A framework for a pathological psychophysiology. In A. Kales, C. N. Stefanis, & J. A. Talbot (Eds.), *Recent advances in schizophrenia* (pp. 59–80). New York: Springer-Verlag.

Cleghorn, J. M., Franco, S., Szechtman, B., Kaplan, R. D., Szechtman, H., Brown, G. M., et al. (1992). Toward a brain map of auditory hallucinations. *American Journal of Psychiatry, 149,* 1062–1069.

Clement, U. (1990). Surveys of heterosexual behavior. *Annual Review of Sex Research, 1,* 45–74.

Clementz, B. A., & Sweeney, J. A. (1990). Is eye movement dysfunction a biological marker for schizophrenia? A methodological review. *Psychological Bulletin, 108,* 77–92.

Cloninger, C. R. (1978). The link between hysteria and sociopathy: An integrative model of pathogenesis based on clinical, genetic, and neurophysiological observations. In H. S. Akiskal & W. L. Webb (Eds.), *Psychiatric diagnosis: Exploration of biological predictors* (pp. 189–218). New York: Spectrum.

Cloninger, C. R. (1987). A systematic method for clinical description and classification of personality variants: A proposal. *Archives of General Psychiatry, 44,* 573–588.

Cloninger, C. R. (1989). Establishment of diagnostic validity in psychiatric illness: Robins and Guze's method revisited. In L. N. Robins & J. E. Barrett (Eds.), *The validity of psychiatric diagnosis* (pp. 9–16). New York: Raven Press.

Cloninger, C. R. (1996). Somatization disorder: Literature review for DSM-IV sourcebook. Washington, DC: American Psychiatric Press.

Closser, M. H. (1992). Cocaine epidemiology. In T. R. Kosten & H. D. Kleber (Eds.),

*Clinician's guide to cocaine addiction: Theory, research, and treatment* (pp. 225–240). New York: Guilford Press.

Clyburn, L. D., Stones, M. J., Hadjistavropoulos, T., & Tuokko, H. (2000). Predicting caregiver burden and depression in Alzheimer's disease. *Journals of Gerontology Series B: Psychological Sciences and Social Sciences, 55,* 2–13.

c-News News Staff (2003). Husband of 'missing' alderwoman disputes media claims. *CNEWS Canada,* May 12, 2003. Retrieved June 10, 2004, from http://cnews.canoe.ca/CNEWS/Canada/2003/05/09/83590-cp.html.

Coates, T. J., McKusick, L., Kuno, R., & Stites, D. P. (1989). Stress management training reduced number of sexual partners but did not improve immune function in men infected with HIV. *American Journal of Public Health, 79,* 885–887.

Cobb, S. (1976). Social support as a moderator of life stress. *Psychosomatic Medicine, 38,* 300.

Cochran, S. D. (1984). Preventing medical noncompliance in the outpatient treatment of bipolar affective disorders. *Journal of Consulting and Clinical Psychology, 52*(5), 873–878.

Cocores, J. A., Miller, N. S., Pottash, A. C., & Gold, M. S. (1988). Sexual dysfunction in abusers of cocaine and alcohol. *American Journal of Drug and Alcohol Abuse, 14,* 169–173.

Coderre, T. J., Katz, J., Vaccarino, A. L., & Melzack, R. (1993). Contribution of central neuroplasticity to pathological pain: Review of clinical and experimental evidence. *Pain, 52,* 259–285.

Cohen, J. (2002). Confronting the limits of success. *Science, 296,* 2320–2324.

Cohen, J. B., & Reed, D. (1985). Type A behavior and coronary heart disease among Japanese men in Hawaii. *Journal of Behavioral Medicine, 8,* 343–352.

Cohen, M. S., Rosen, B. R., & Brady, T. J. (1992). Ultrafast MRI permits expanded clinical role. *Magnetic Resonance, 2,* 26–37.

Cohen, S. (1996). Psychological stress, immunity, and upper respiratory infections. *Current Directions in Psychological Science, 5,* 86–90.

Cohen, S., & Herbert, T. B. (1996). Health psychology: Psychological factors and physical disease from the perspective of human psychoneuroimmunology. *Annual Review of Psychology, 47,* 113–142.

Cohen, S., Doyle, W. J., & Skoner, D. P. (1999). Psychological stress, cytokine production, and severity of upper respiratory illness. *Psychosomatic Medicine, 61,* 175–180.

Cohen, S., Doyle, W. J., Skoner, D. P., Fireman, P., Gwaltney, J. M., Jr., & Newsome, J. T. (1995). State and trait negative affect as predictors of objective and subjective symptoms of respiratory viral infections. *Journal of Personality and Social Psychology, 68,* 159–169.

Cohen, S., Doyle, W., Skoner, D. P., Rabin, B. S., & Gwaltney, J. M. (1997). Social ties and susceptibility to the common cold. *Journal of the American Medical Association, 277,* 1940–1944.

Cohen, S., Doyle, W. J., Turner, R., Alper, C. M., & Skoner, D. P. (2003). Sociability and susceptibility to the common cold. *Psychological Science, 14*(5), 389–395.

Col, N., Fanale, J. E., & Kronholm, P. (1990). The role of medical noncompliance and adverse drug reactions in hospitalizations of the elderly. *Archives of Internal Medicine, 150*, 841–845.

Colapinto, J. (2000). *As nature made him: The boy who was raised as a girl.* New York: HarperCollins.

Cole, J. D., & Kazarian, S. S. (1988). The Level of Expressed Emotion Scale: A new measure of expressed emotion. *Journal of Clinical Psychology, 44*, 392–397.

Cole, M. G. (2004). Delirium in elderly patients. *American Journal of Geriatric Psychiatry, 12*, 7–21.

Cole, M., Winkelman, M. D., Morris, J. C., Simon, J. E., & Boyd, T. A. (1992). Thalamic amnesia: Korsakoff syndrome due to left thalamic infarction. *Journal of the Neurological Sciences, 110*, 62–67.

Coleman, E., Bockting, W. O., & Gooren, L. (1993). Homosexual and bisexual identity in sex-reassigned female-to-male transsexuals. *Archives of Sexual Behavior, 22*, 37–50.

Coleman, H., Charles, G., & Collins, J. (2001). Inhalant use by Canadian aboriginal youth. *Journal of Child and Adolescent Substance Abuse, 10*(3), 1–20.

Collins, A. (1988). *In the sleep room: The story of the CIA brainwashing experiments in Canada.* Toronto: Lester and Orpen Dennys.

Collins, W. A., Maccoby, E. E., Steinberg, L., Hetherington, E. M., & Bornstein, M. H. (2000). Contemporary research on parenting: The case for nature and nurture. *American Psychologist, 55*, 218–232.

Comas-Diaz, L. (1981). Puerto Rican *espiritismo* and psychotherapy. *American Journal of Orthopsychiatry, 51*(4), 636–645.

Compas, B. E., Oppedisano, G., Connor, J. K., Gerhardt, C. A., Hinden, B. R., Achenbach, T. M., et al. (1997). Gender differences in depressive symptoms in adolescence: Comparison of national samples of clinically referred and nonreferred youths. *Journal of Consulting and Clinical Psychology, 65*, 617–626.

Compton, W. M., Cottler, L. B., Jacobs, J. L., Ben-Abdallah, A., & Spitznagel, E. L. (2003). The role of psychiatric disorders in predicting drug dependence treatment outcomes. *American Journal of Psychiatry, 160*, 890–895.

Condelli, W. S., Fairbank, J. A., Dennis, M. L., & Rachal, J. V. (1991). Cocaine use by clients in methadone programs: Significance, scope, and behavioral interventions. *Journal of Substance Abuse Treatment, 8*, 203–212.

Condon, W., Ogston, W., & Pacoe, L. (1969). Three faces of Eve revisited: A study of transient microstrabismus. *Journal of Abnormal Psychology, 74*, 618–620.

Conn, D. K., & Lieff, S. (2001). Diagnosing and managing delirium in the elderly. *Canadian Family Physician, 47*, 101–108.

Conners, C. K., Epstein, J. N., March, J. S., Angold, A., Wells, K. C., Klaric, J., et al. (2001). Multimodal treatment of ADHD in the MTA: An alternative outcome analysis. *Journal of the American Academy of Child and Adolescent Psychiatry, 40*(2), 159–167.

Conners, C. K., March, J. S., Frances, A., Wells, K. C., & Ross, R. (2001). Treatment of attention-deficit/hyperactivity disorder: Expert consensus guidelines. *Journal of Attention Disorders, 4* (Suppl. 1), 7–128.

Conrod, P. J., Peterson, J. B., Pihl, R. O., & Mankowski, S. (1997). Biphasic effects of alcohol on heart rate are influenced by alcoholic family history and rate of alcohol ingestion. *Alcoholism: Clinical and Experimental Research, 21*, 140–149.

Conrod, P. J., Pihl, R. O., Stewart, S. H., & Dongier, M. (2000). Validation of a system of classifying female substance abusers on the basis of personality and motivational risk factors for substance abuse. *Psychology of Addictive Behaviors, 14*, 243–256.

Conrod, P. J., & Stewart, S. H. (2005). A critical look at dual-focused cognitive-behavioural treatment for comorbid substance abuse and psychiatric disorders: Strengths, limitations and future directions. *Journal of Cognitive Psychotherapy, 19*, 265–289.

Conrod, P. J., Stewart, S. H., Comeau, M. N., & Maclean, M. (2006). Efficacy of cognitive behavioral interventions targeting personality risk factors for youth alcohol misuse. *Journal of Clinical Child and Adolescent Psychology, 35*, 550–563.

Conrod, P. J., Stewart, S. H., Pihl, R. O., Côté, S., Fontaine, V., & Dongier, M. (2000). Efficacy of brief coping skills interventions that match different personality profiles of female substance abusers. *Psychology of Addictive Behaviors, 14*, 231–242.

Conti, C. R., Pepine, C. J., & Sweeney, M. (1999). Efficacy and safety of sildenafil citrate in the treatment of erectile dysfunction in patients with ischemic heart disease. *American Journal of Cardiology, 83*, 29C–34C.

Conwell, Y., Duberstein, P. R., & Caine, E. D. (2002). Risk factors for suicide in later life. *Biological Psychiatry, 52*, 193–204.

Conwell, Y., Duberstein, P. R., Cox, C., Herrmann, J. H., Forbes, N. T., & Caine, E. D. (1996). Relationships of age and axis I diagnoses in victims of completed suicide: A psychological autopsy study. *American Journal of Psychiatry, 153*, 1001–1008.

Cook, E. H., Jr. (2001). Genetics of autism. *Child and Adolescent Psychiatric Clinics of North America, 10*(2), 333–350.

Cook, E. H., Jr., Courchesne, R. Y., Cox, N. J., Lord, C., Gonen, D., Guter, S. J., et al. (1998). Linkage-disequilibrium mapping of autistic disorder, with 15q11-13 markers. *American Journal of Human Genetics, 62*(5), 1077–1083.

Cook, E. W., III, Hodes, R. L., & Lang, P. J. (1986). Preparedness and phobia: Effects of stimulus content on human visceral conditioning. *Journal of Abnormal Psychology, 95*, 195–207.

Coons, P. M. (1986). Treatment progress in 20 patients with multiple personality disorder. *Journal of Nervous and Mental Disease, 174*, 715–721.

Coons, P. M. (1994). Confirmation of childhood abuse in child and adolescent cases of multiple personality disorder not otherwise specified. *Journal of Nervous and Mental Disease, 182*, 461–464.

Coons, P. M., Bowman, E. S., Kluft, R. P., & Milstein, V. (1991). The cross cultural occurrence of MPD: Additional cases from a recent survey. *Dissociation, 4*, 124–128.

Coons, W. H. (1957). Interaction and insight in group psychotherapy. *Canadian Journal of Psychology, 11*, 1–8.

Coons, W. H. (1967). The dynamics of change in psychotherapy. *Canadian Psychiatric Association Journal, 12*, 239–245.

Coons, W. H., & Peacock, E. P. (1970). Interpersonal interaction and personality change in group psychotherapy. *Canadian Psychiatric Association Journal, 15*, 347–355.

Cooper, A. J. (1988). Sexual dysfunction and cardiovascular disease. *Stress Medicine, 4*, 273–281.

Cooper, A. M., & Ronningstam, E. (1992). Narcissistic personality disorder. In A. Tasman & M. B. Riba (Eds.), *Review of psychiatry* (Vol. 11, pp. 80–97). Washington, DC: American Psychiatric Press.

Cooper, M., Corrado, R., Karlberg, A. M., & Adams, L. P. (1992). Aboriginal suicide in British Columbia: An overview. *Canada's Mental Health, 40*(3), 19–23.

Cooper, M. L., Russell, M., & George, W. H. (1988). Coping, expectancies, and alcohol abuse: A test of social learning formulations. *Journal of Abnormal Psychology, 97*, 218–230.

Cooper, M. L., Russell, M., Skinner, J. B., Frone, M. R., & Mudar, P. (1992). Stress and alcohol use: Moderating effects of gender, coping, and alcohol expectancies. *Journal of Abnormal Psychology, 101*, 139–152.

Cooperstock, R, & Hill, J. (1982). *The effects of tranquillization: Benzodiazepine use in Canada.* Ottawa, ON: Health Canada.

Coplan, J. D., Andrews, M. W., Rosenblum, L. A., Owens, M. J., Friedman, S., Gorman, J. M., et al. (1996). Persistent elevations of cerebrospinal fluid concentrations of corticotropin-releasing factor in adult nonhuman primates exposed to early life stressors: Implications for the pathophysiology of mood and anxiety disorders. *Proceedings of the National Academy of Sciences, 93*, 1619–1623.

Coplan, J. D., Trost, R. C., Owens, M. J., Cooper, T. B., Gorman, J. M., Nemeroff, C. B., et al. (1998). Cerebrospinal fluid concentrations of somatostatin and biogenic amines in grown primates reared by mothers exposed to manipulated foraging conditions. *Archives of General Psychiatry, 55*, 473–477.

Coren, S. (1996). *Sleep thieves: An eye-opening exploration into the science and mysteries of sleep.* New York: Free Press.

Corkum, P., Tannock, R., & Moldofsky, H. (1998). Sleep disturbances in children with attention-deficit/hyperactivity disorder. *Journal of the American Academy of Child and Adolescent Psychiatry, 37,* 637–646.

Corrigan, P. W., Wallace, C. J., Schade, M. L., & Green, M. F. (1994). Learning medication self-management skills in schizophrenia: Relationships with cognitive deficits and psychiatric symptoms. *Behavior Therapy, 25,* 5–15.

Coryell, W. H., & Zimmerman, M. (1989). Personality disorder in the families of depressed, schizophrenic, and never-ill probands. *American Journal of Psychiatry, 146,* 496–502.

Coryell, W., Endicott, J., & Keller, M. (1992). Rapid cycling affective disorder: Demographics, diagnosis, family history, and course. *Archives of General Psychiatry, 49,* 126–131.

Coryell, W., Endicott, J., Maser, J. D., Keller, M. B., Leon, A. C., & Akiskal, H. S. (1995). Long-term stability of polarity distinctions in the affective disorders. *American Journal of Psychiatry, 152,* 385–390.

Coryell, W., Solomon, D., Turvey, C., Keller, M., Leon, A. C., Endicott, J., et al. (2003). The long-term course of rapid-cycling bipolar disorder. *Archives of General Psychiatry, 60,* 914–920.

Costa e Silva, J. A., & DeGirolamo, G. (1990). Neurasthenia: History of a concept. In N. Sartorious, D. Goldberg, G. DeGirolamo, J. A. Costa e Silva, Y. Lecrubier, & U. Wittchen (Eds.), *Psychological disorders in general medical settings* (pp. 699–81). Toronto: Hogrefe and Huber.

Costa, E. (1985). Benzodiazepine-GABA interactions: A model to investigate the neurobiology of anxiety. In A. H. Tuma & J. D. Maser (Eds.), *Anxiety and the anxiety disorders.* Hillsdale, NJ: Erlbaum.

Costa, P. T., Jr., & McCrae, R. R. (1990). Personality disorders and the five-factor model of personality. *Journal of Personality Disorders, 4,* 362–371.

Costa, P. T., Jr., & Widiger, T. A. (Eds.). (1994). *Personality disorders and the five-factor model of personality.* Washington, DC: American Psychological Association.

Côté, G., O'Leary, T., Barlow, D. H., Strain, J. J., Salkovskis, P. M., Warwick, H. M. C., et al. (1996). Hypochondriasis. In T. A. Widiger, A. J. Frances, H. A. Pincus, R. Ross, M. B. First, & W. W. Davis (Eds.), *DSM-IV sourcebook* (Vol. 2, pp. 933–947). Washington, DC: American Psychiatric Press.

Côté, J. K., & Pepler, C. (2002). A randomized trial of a cognitive coping intervention for acutely ill HIV-positive men. *Nursing Research, 51*(4), 237–244.

Coughlin, A. M. (1994). Excusing women. *California Law Review, 82,* 1–93.

Courchesne, E. (1991). Neuroanatomic imaging in autism. *Pediatrics, 87,* 781–790.

Courchesne, E., Hesselink, J. R., Jernigan, T. L., & Yeung-Courchesne, R. (1987). Abnormal neuroanatomy in a non-retarded person with autism: Unusual findings with magnetic resonance imaging. *Archives of Neurology, 44,* 335–341.

Courneya, K. S., Friedenreich, C. M., Sela, R. A., Quinney, H. A., Rhodes, R. E., & Handman, M. (2003). The group psychotherapy and home-based physical exercise (group-hope) trial in cancer survivors: Physical fitness and quality of life outcomes. *Psycho-oncology, 12,* 357–374.

Cox, A., Rutter, M., Newman, S., & Bartak, L. (1975). A comparative study of infantile autism and specific developmental receptive language disorder: II. Parental characteristics. *British Journal of Psychiatry, 126,* 146–159.

Cox, B. J., Endler, N. S., & Norton, G. R. (1994). Levels of "nonclinical panic." *Journal of Behavior Therapy and Experimental Psychiatry, 25,* 35–40.

Cox, B. J., Endler, N. S., & Swinson, R. P. (1991). Clinical and nonclinical panic attacks: An empirical test of a panic-anxiety continuum. *Journal of Anxiety Disorders, 5,* 21–34.

Cox, B. J., Enns, M. W., Walker, J. R., Kjernisted, K., & Pidlubny, S. R. (2001). Psychological vulnerabilities in patients with major depression vs panic disorder. *Behaviour Research and Therapy, 39,* 567–573.

Cox, B. J., Norton, G. R., Swinson, R. P., & Endler, N. S. (1990). Substance abuse and panic related anxiety: A critical review. *Behaviour Research and Therapy, 28,* 385–393.

Cox, B. J., Swinson, R. P., Shulman, I. D., Kuch, K., & Reichman, J. T. (1993). Gender effects in alcohol use in panic disorder with agoraphobia. *Behaviour Research and Therapy, 31,* 413–416.

Cox, B. J., Walker, J. R., Enns, M. W., & Karpinski, D. C. (2002). Self-criticism in generalized social phobia and response to cognitive-behavioral treatment. *Behavior Therapy, 33,* 479–491.

Crabbe, J. C., Belknap, J. K., & Buck, K. J. (1994). Genetic animal models of alcohol and drug abuse. *Science, 264,* 1715–1723.

Craddock, N., & Jones, I. (2001). Molecular genetics of bipolar disorder. *British Journal of Psychiatry, 41,* 128–133.

Crafti, N. A. (2002). Integrating cognitive-behavioural and interpersonal approaches in a group program for the eating disorders: Measuring effectiveness in a naturalistic setting. *Behaviour Change, 19,* 22–38.

Crago, M., Shisslak, C. M., & Estes, L. S. (1997). Eating disturbances among American minority groups: A review. *The International Journal of Eating Disorders, 19,* 239–248.

Craighead, W. E., Hart, A. B., Craighead, L. W., & Ilardi, S. S. (2002). Psychosocial treatments for major depressive disorder. In P. E. Nathan & J. M. Gorman (Eds.), *A guide to treatments that work* (2nd ed., pp. 245–261). New York: Oxford University Press.

Craighead, W. E., Ilardi, S. S., Greenberg, M. P., & Craighead, L. W. (1997). Cognitive psychology: Basic theory and clinical implications. In A. Tasman, J. Key, & J. A. Lieberman (Eds.), *Psychiatry* (Vol. 1, pp. 350–368). Philadelphia: W. B. Saunders.

Craighead, W. E., Miklowitz, D. J., Frank, E., & Vajk, F. C. (2002). Psychosocial treatments for bipolar disorder. In P. E.

Nathan & J. M. Gorman (Eds.), *A guide to treatments that work* (2nd ed., pp. 263–275). New York: Oxford University Press.

Craske, M. G. (1999). *Anxiety disorders: Psychological approaches to theory and treatment.* Boulder, CO: Westview Press.

Craske, M. G., Antony, M. M., & Barlow, D. H. (1997). *Mastery of your specific phobia, therapist guide.* San Antonio, TX: Graywind Publications/The Psychological Corporation.

Craske, M. G., & Barlow, D. H. (1988). A review of the relationship between panic and avoidance. *Clinical Psychology Review, 8,* 667–685.

Craske, M. G., & Barlow, D. H. (2001). Panic disorder and agoraphobia. In D. H. Barlow (Ed.), *Clinical Handbook of Psychological Disorders.* (3rd ed.). New York: Guilford Press.

Craske, M. G., Barlow, D. H., Clark, D. M., Curtis, G. C., Hill, E. M., Himle, J. A., et al. (1996). Specific (simple) phobia. In T. A. Widiger, A. J. Frances, H. A. Pincus, R. Ross, M. B. First, & W. W. Davis (Eds.), *DSM-IV sourcebook* (Vol. 2, pp. 473–506). Washington, DC: American Psychiatric Press.

Craske, M. G., Barlow, D. H., & O'Leary, T. A. (1992). *Mastery of your anxiety and worry.* Albany, NY: Graywind Publications.

Craske, M. G., Brown, T. A., & Barlow, D. H. (1991). Behavioral treatment of panic disorder: A two-year follow-up. *Behavior Therapy, 22,* 289–304.

Craske, M. G., Lang, A. J., Rowe, M., DeCola, J. P., Simmons, J., Mann, C., et al. (2002). Presleep attributions about arousal during sleep: Nocturnal panic. *Journal of Abnormal Psychology, 111,* 52–62.

Craske, M. G., Rapee, R. M., & Barlow, D. H. (1988). The significance of panic expectancy for individual patterns of avoidance. *Behavior Therapy, 19,* 577–592.

Craske, M. G., & Rowe, M. K. (1997). Nocturnal panic. *Clinical Psychology: Science and Practice, 4,* 153–174.

Crawford, M. & Garnter, R. (1992). *Woman killing: Intimate femicide in Ontario, 1974–1990.* Toronto: Women We Honour Action Committee.

Creese, I., Burt, D. R., & Snyder, S. H. (1976). Dopamine receptor binding predicts clinical and pharmacological potencies of antischizophrenic drugs. *Science, 192,* 481–483.

Cremniter, D., Jamin, S., Kollenbach, K., Alvarez, J. C., Lecruibier, Y., Gilton, A., et al. (1999). CSF 5-HIAA levels are lower in impulsive as compared to nonimpulsive violent suicide attempts and control subjects. *Biological Psychiatry, 45*(12), 1572–1579.

Crichton, P., & Moorey, S. (2003). Treating pain in cancer patients. In D. C. Turk & R. J. Gatchel (Eds.), *Psychological approaches to pain management: A practitioner's handbook* (2nd ed.). New York: Guilford Press.

Crisp, A. H., Callender, J. S., Halek, C., & Hsu, L. K. G. (1992). Long-term mortality in anorexia nervosa: A 20-year follow-up of the St. George's and Aberdeen cohorts. *British Journal of Psychiatry, 161,* 104–107.

Crockford, D. N., & el-Guebaly, N. (1998). Psychiatric comorbidity in pathological gambling: A critical review. *Canadian Journal of Psychiatry, 43,* 43–50.

Cross-National Collaborative Group (1992). The changing rate of major depression: Cross-national comparisons. *Journal of the American Medical Association, 268,* 3098–3105.

Cross-National Collaborative Panic Study, Second Phase Investigators (1992). Drug treatment of panic disorder. Comparative efficacy of alprazolam, imipramine, and placebo. *British Journal of Psychiatry, 160,* 191–202.

Crow, S. J., Thuras, P., Keel, P. K., & Mitchell, J. E. (2002). Long-term menstrual and reproductive function in patients with bulimia nervosa. *American Journal of Psychiatry, 159,* 1048–1050.

Crow, T. J. (1980). Molecular pathology of schizophrenia: More than one dimension of pathology? *British Medical Journal, 280,* 66–68.

Crow, T. J. (1985). The two-syndrome concept: Origins and current status. *Schizophrenia Bulletin, 11,* 471–486.

Crowe, L. C., & George, W. H. (1989). Alcohol and human sexuality: Review and integration. *Psychological Bulletin, 105*(3), 374–386.

Crowe, R. R. (1974). An adoption study of antisocial personality. *Archives of General Psychiatry, 31,* 785–791.

Crowe, R. R. (1984). Electroconvulsive therapy: A current perspective. *New England Journal of Medicine, 311,* 163–167.

Crowley, P. H., Hayden, T. L., & Gulati, D. K. (1982). Etiology of Down syndrome. In S. M. Pueschel & J. E. Rynders (Eds.), *Down syndrome: Advances in biomedicine and behavioral sciences* (pp. 89–131). Cambridge, MA: Ware Press.

Cruickshank, J. K., & Beevers, D. G. (1989). *Ethnic factors in health and disease.* London UK: Wright.

CTV.ca News Staff (2003). Alderwoman to seek therapy to avoid charges. *CTV News, Shows and Sports,* May 21, 2003. Retrieved June 10, 2004, from http://www.ctv.ca/servlet/ArticleNews/story/CTVNews/1053451733897_24//.

Cummings, J. L. (1990). *Subcortical dementia.* New York: Oxford University Press.

Curtis, G. C., Hill, E. M., & Lewis, J. A. (1990). *Heterogeneity of DSM-III-R simple phobia and the simple phobia/agoraphobia boundary: Evidence from the ECA study.* Preliminary report to the Simple Phobia subcommittee of the DSM-IV Anxiety Disorders Work Group.

Cutting, J. (1985). *The psychology of schizophrenia.* New York: Churchill Livingstone.

Cyranowski, J. M., Aarestad, S. L., & Andersen, B. L. (1999). The role of sexual self-schema in a diathesis-stress model of sexual dysfunction. *Applied and Preventative Psychology, 8,* 217–228.

Cyranowski, J. M., Frank, E., Young, E. & Shear, M. K. (2000). Adolescent onset of the gender difference in lifetime rates of major depression. *Archives of General Psychiatry, 57,* 21–27.

Czeisler, C. A., & Allan, J. S. (1989). Pathologies of the sleep-wake schedule. In R. L. Williams, I. Karacan, & C. A. Morre (Eds.), *Sleep disorders: Diagnosis and treatment* (pp. 109–129). New York: John Wiley.

Czeisler, C. A., Richardson, G. S., Coleman, R. M., Zimmerman, J. C., Moore-Ede, M. C., Dement, W. C., et al. (1981). Chronotherapy: Resetting the circadian clocks of patients with delayed sleep phase insomnia. *Sleep, 4,* 1–21.

Dadds, M. R., Sanders, M. R., Morrison, M., & Rebgetz, M. (1992). Childhood depression and conduct disorder: II. An analysis of family interaction patterns in the home. *Journal of Abnormal Psychology, 101*(3), 505–513.

Dahl, A. A. (1993, Spring). The personality disorders: A critical review of family, twin, and adoption studies. *Journal of Personality Disorders,* Supplement, 86–99.

Dailey, R. C. (1968). The role of alcohol among North American Indian Tribes as reported in the Jesuit Relations. *Anthropologia, 10,* 45–49.

Dalack, G. W., Glassman, A. H., & Covey, L. S. (1993). Nicotine use. In D. L. Dunner (Ed.), *Current psychiatric therapy* (pp. 114–118). Philadelphia: W. B. Saunders.

Dana, R. H. (1996). The Thematic Apperception Test (TAT). In C. S. Newmark (Ed.), *Major psychological assessment instruments* (pp. 166–205). Boston: Allyn & Bacon.

Darwin, C. R. (1872). *The expression of emotions in man and animals.* London UK: John Murray.

Davidson, J., & Robertson, E. (1985). A follow-up study of postpartum illness, 1946–1978. *Acta Psychiatrica Scandinavica, 71*(15), 451–457.

Davidson, J., Swartz, M., Storck, M., Krishnan, R. R., & Hammett, E. (1985). A diagnostic and family study of post-traumatic stress disorder. *American Journal of Psychiatry, 142,* 90–93.

Davidson, J. R. T., Hughes, D. L., Blazer D. G., & George, L. K. (1991). Posttraumatic stress in the community: An epidemiological study. *Journal of Psychological Medicine, 21,* 713–721.

Davidson, K., MacGregor, M. W., Stuhr, J., Dixon, K., & MacLean, D. (2000). Constructive anger verbal behavior predicts blood pressure in a population-based sample. *Health Psychology, 19,* 55–64.

Davidson, L. L., & Heinrichs, R. W. (2003). Quantification of frontal and temporal lobe brain-imaging findings in schizophrenia: A meta-analysis. *Psychiatry Research: Neuroimaging, 122,* 69–87.

Davidson, M., Keefe, R. S. E., Mohs, R. C., Siever, L. J., Losonczy, M. F., Horvath, T. B., et al. (1987). L-Dopa challenge and relapse in schizophrenia. *American Journal of Psychiatry, 144,* 934–938.

Davidson, R. J. (1993). Cerebral asymmetry and emotion: Methodological conundrums. *Cognition and Emotion, 7,* 115–138.

Davis, C. (1997). Normal and neurotic perfectionism in eating disorders: An interactive model. *International Journal of Eating Disorders, 22,* 421–426.

Davis, C., Katzman, D. K., Kaptein, S., Kirsh, C., Brewer, H., Kalmbach, K., et al. (1997). The prevalence of high-level exercise in the eating disorders: Etiological implications. *Comprehensive Psychiatry, 38,* 321–326.

Davis, C., & Strachan, S. (2001). Elite female athletes with eating disorders: A study of psychopathological characteristics. *Journal of Sport and Exercise Psychology, 23,* 245–253.

Davis, J. M., Chen, N., & Glick, I. D. (2003). A meta-analysis of the efficacy of second-generation antipsychotics. *Archives of General Psychiatry, 60,* 553–564.

Davis, K. L., Kahn, R. S., Ko, G., & Davidson, M. (1991). Dopamine in schizophrenia: A review and reconceptualization. *American Journal of Psychiatry, 148,* 1474–1486.

Davis, M. (1992). The role of the amygdala in fear and anxiety. *Annual Review of Neuroscience, 15,* 353–375.

Davis, M. (2002). Neural circuitry of anxiety and stress disorders. In K. L. Davis, D. Charney, J. T. Coyle & C. Nemeroff (Eds.), *Neuropsychopharmacology: The fifth generation of progress* (pp. 901–930). Philadelphia: Lippincott Williams & Wilkins.

Davis, R., Freeman, R. J., & Garner, D. M. (1988). A naturalistic investigation of eating behavior in bulimia nervosa. *Journal of Consulting and Clinical Psychology, 56,* 273–279.

Davis, R., McVey, G., Heinmaa, M., Rockert, W., & Kennedy, S. (1999). Sequencing of cognitive-behavioral treatments for bulimia nervosa. *International Journal of Eating Disorders, 25,* 361–374.

Davis, R., & Olmsted, M. P. (1992). Cognitive-behavioral group treatment for bulimia nervosa: Integrating psychoeducation and psychotherapy. In H. Harper-Giuffre & K. R. MacKenzie (Eds.), *Group psychotherapy for eating disorders* (pp. 71–103). Washington, DC: American Psychiatric Press.

Davis, R., Olmsted, M. P., & Rockert, W. (1990). Brief group psychoeducation for bulimia nervosa: Assessing the clinical significance of change. *Journal of Consulting and Clinical Psychology, 58,* 882–885.

Davis, R., Olmsted, M. P., & Rockert, W. (1992). Brief group psychoeducation for bulimia nervosa: II. Prediction of clinical outcome. *International Journal of Eating Disorders, 11,* 205–211.

Davis, S. (1993). Changes to the Criminal Code provisions for mentally disordered offenders and their implications for Canadian psychiatry. *Canadian Journal of Psychiatry, 38,* 122–126.

Davis, S. (1994). Fitness to stand trial in Canada in light of the recent Criminal Code amendments. *International Journal of Law and Psychiatry, 17,* 319–329.

Davison, G. C. (1968). Elimination of a sadistic fantasy by a client-controlled counter-conditioning technique: A case study. *Journal of Abnormal Psychology, 73,* 91–99.

Dawson, G., & McKissick, F. C. (1984). Self-recognition in autistic children. *Journal of Autism and Developmental Disorders, 14*, 383–394.

Dawson, G., Toth, K., Abbott, R., Osterling, J., Munson, J., Estes, A., et al. (2004). Early social attention impairments in autism: Social orienting, joint attention, and attention to distress. *Developmental Psychology, 40*, 271–283.

Day, J., Grant, I., Atkinson, J. H., Brysk, L. T., McCutchan, J. A., Hesselink, J. R., et al. (1992). Incidence of AIDS dementia in a 2-year follow-up of AIDS and ARC patients on an initial phase II AZT placebo-controlled study: San Diego cohort. *Journal of Neuropsychiatry and Clinical Neuroscience, 4*, 15–20.

Day, R., Nielsen, J. A., Korten, A., Ernberg, G., Dube, K. C., Gebhart, J., et al. (1987). Stressful life events preceding the acute onset of schizophrenia: A cross-national study from the World Health Organization. *Cultural Medicine and Psychiatry, 11*, 123–205.

de Almeidia-Filho, N., Santana, V. S., Pinto, I. M., & de Carvalho-Neto, J. A. (1991). Is there an epidemic of drug misuse in Brazil? A review of the epidemiological evidence (1977–1988). *International Journal of the Addictions, 26*, 355–369.

de la Monte, S. M., Hutchins, G. M., & Moore, G. W. (1989). Racial differences in the etiology of dementia and frequency of Alzheimer lesions in the brain. *Journal of the National Medical Association, 81*, 644–652.

de Lissovoy, V. (1961). Head banging in early childhood. *Child Development, 33*, 43–56.

De Marco, R. R. (2000). The epidemiology of major depression: Implications of occurrence, recurrence, and stress in a Canadian community sample. *Canadian Journal of Psychiatry, 45*, 67–74.

de Zwaan, M., Roerig, J. L., & Mitchell, J. E. (2004). Pharmacological treatment of anorexia nervosa, bulimia nervosa and binge eating disorder. In J. K. Thompson (Ed.) *Handbook of eating disorders and obesity* (pp. 186–217). New York: John Wiley.

Deakin, J. F. W., & Graeff, F. G. (1991). Critique: 5-HT and mechanisms of defence. *Journal of Psychopharmacology, 5*(4), 305–315.

Deale, A., Chalder, T., Marks, I., & Wessely, S. (1997). Cognitive behavior therapy for chronic fatigue syndrome: A randomized controlled trial. *American Journal of Psychiatry, 154*, 408–414.

Deale, A., Husain, K., Chalder, T., & Wessely, S. (2001). Long-term outcome of cognitive behavioral therapy versus relaxation therapy for chronic fatigue syndrome: A 5-year follow-up study. *American Journal of Psychiatry, 158*, 2038–2042.

Dean, C., & Kendell, R. E. (1981). The symptomatology of postpartum illness. *British Journal of Psychiatry, 139*, 128–133.

Dean, R. R., Kelsey, J. E., Heller, M. R., & Ciaranello, R. D. (1993). Structural foundations of illness and treatment: Receptors. In D. L. Dunner (Ed.), *Current psychiatric therapy*. Philadelphia: W. B. Saunders.

DeBacker, G., Kittel, F., Kornitzer, M., & Dramaix, M. (1983). Behavior, stress, and psychosocial traits as risk factors. *Preventative Medicine, 12*, 32–36.

DeBuono, B. A., Zinner, S. H., Daamen, M., & McCormack, W. M. (1990). Sexual behavior of college women in 1975, 1986 and 1989. *New England Journal of Medicine, 322*(12), 821–825.

Delizonna, L. L., Wincze, J. P., Litz, B. T., Brown, T. A., & Barlow, D. H. (2001). A comparison of subjective and physiological measures of mechanically produced and erotically produced erections. (Or, is an erection an erection?) *Journal of Sex and Marital Therapy, 27*, 21–31.

Dell, P. F. (1998). Axis II pathology in outpatients with dissociative identity disorder. *Journal of Nervous and Mental Disease, 186*(6), 352–356.

Dembroski, T. M., & Costa, P. T., Jr. (1987). Coronary prone behavior: Components of the Type A pattern and hostility. *Journal of Personality, 55*(2), 211–235.

Denton, F. T., Feaver, C. H. & Spencer, B. G. (1998). The future population of Canada, its age distribution and dependency relations. *Canadian Journal on Aging, 17*, 83–109.

Denzin, N. K. (1987). *The recovering alcoholic*. Newbury Park, CA: Sage.

Depression Guideline Panel (1993, April). *Depression in primary care: Vol. 1. Detection and diagnosis* (AHCPR Publication No. 93–0550). Clinical practice guideline, No. 5. Rockville, MD: U.S. Department of Health and Human Services, Public Health Service, Agency for Health Care Policy and Research.

Deptula, D., & Pomara, N. (1990). Effects of antidepressants on human performance: A review. *Journal of Clinical Psychopharmacology, 10*, 105–111.

Depue, R. A., & Iacono, W. G. (1989). Neurobehavioral aspects of affective disorders. *Annual Review of Psychology, 40*, 457–492.

Depue, R. A., Luciana, M., Arbisi, P., Collins, P., & Leon, A. (1994). Dopamine and the structure of personality: Relation of agonist-induced dopamine activity to positive emotionality. *Journal of Personality and Social Psychology, 67*, 485–498.

Depue, R. A., Slater, J. F., Wolfstetter-Kausch, H., Klein, D., Goplerud, E., & Farr, D. (1981). A behavioral paradigm for identifying persons at risk for bipolar depressive disorder: A conceptual framework and five validation studies. *Journal of Abnormal Psychological Monographs, 90*, 381–437.

Depue, R. A., & Spoont, M. R. (1986). Conceptualizing a serotonin trait: A behavioral dimension of constraint. *Annals of the New York Academy of Sciences, 487*, 47–62.

Depue, R. A., & Zald, D. (1993). Biological and environmental processes in nonpsychotic psychopathology: A neurobehavioral system perspective. In C. Costello (Ed.), *Basic issues in psychopathology*. New York: Guilford Press.

Derry, P. A., & Kuiper, N. A. (1981). Schematic processing and self-reference in clinical depression. *Journal of Abnormal Psychology, 90*, 286–297.

Dersh, J., Polatin, P. B., & Gatchel, R. J. (2002). Chronic pain and psychopathology: Research findings and theoretical considerations. *Psychosomatic Medicine, 64*, 773–786.

Dershewitz, R. A., & Williamson, J. W. (1977). Prevention of childhood household injuries: A controlled clinical trial. *American Journal of Public Health, 67*, 1148–1153.

Dershowitz, A. (1994). *The abuse excuse and other cop-outs, sob stories, and evasions of responsibility*. Boston: Little Brown.

DeRubeis, R. J., Gelfand, L. A., Tang, T. Z., & Simons, A. D. (1999). Medications versus cognitive behavior therapy for severely depressed outpatients: Meta-analysis of four randomized comparisons. *American Journal of Psychiatry, 156*, 1007–1013.

Devins, G. M., Flanigan, M., Fleming, J. A. E., Morehouse, R., Moscovitch, A., Plamondon, J., et al. (1995). Differential illness intrusiveness associated with sleep-promoting medications. *European Psychiatry, 10* (Suppl. 3), 153–159.

Devinsky, O., Feldman, E., Burrowes, K., & Bromfield, E. (1989). Autoscopic phenomena with seizures. *Archives of Neurology, 46*(10), 1080–1088.

DeWitt, D. J., Adlaf, E. M., Offord, D. R., & Ogborne, A. C. (2000). Age at first alcohol use: A risk factor for the development of alcohol disorders. *American Journal of Psychiatry, 157*, 745–750.

Diamond, M. (1995). Biological aspects of sexual orientation and identity. In L. Diamant & R. D. McAnulty (Eds.), *The psychology of sexual orientation, behavior, and identity*. Westport, CT: Greenwood Press.

Diamond, M., & Sigmundson, K. (1997). Sex reassignment at birth: Long-term review and clinical implications. *Archives of Pediatric and Adolescent Medicine, 151*, 298–304.

DiBartolo, P. M., Brown, T. A., & Barlow, D. H. (1997). Effects of anxiety on attentional allocation and task performance: An information processing analysis. *Behaviour Research and Therapy, 35*, 1101–1111.

Dickey, C. C., Shenton, M. E., Hirayasu, Y., Fischer, I., Voglmaier, M. M., Niznikiewicz, M. A., et al. (2000). Large CSF volume is not attributable to ventricular volume in schizotypal personality disorder. *American Journal of Psychiatry, 157*, 48–54.

Diener, E. (2000). Subjective well-being: The science of happiness and a proposal for a national index. *American Psychologist, 55*, 34–43.

DiLalla, L. F., & Gottesman, I. I. (1991). Biological and genetic contributors to violence—Widom's untold tale. *Psychological Bulletin, 109*, 125–129.

Dimberg, U., & Öhman, A. (1983). The effects of directional facial cues on electrodermal conditioning to facial stimuli. *Psychophysiology, 20,* 160–167.

Dimeff, L. A., Baer, J. S., Kivlahan, D. R., & Marlatt, G. A. (2002). Brief alcohol screening and intervention for college students (BASICS): A harm reduction approach. *Journal of Psychiatry and Law, 30,* 275–278.

Dineen, T. (2002, August 15). Peggy Claude-Pierre: Angel for anorexics or misguided amateur? *The Vancouver Sun.* Retrieved June 24, 2004, from http://tanadineen.com/COLUMNIST/Columns/MontreuxClinic.htm.

Dishion, T. J., Patterson, G. R., & Reid, J. R. (1988). Parent and peer factors associated with drug sampling in early adolescence: Implications for treatment. In E. R. Rahdert & J. Gabowski (Eds.), *Adolescent drug abuse: Analyses of treatment research* (NIDA Research Monograph No. 77, DHHS Publication No. ADM88–1523, pp. 69–93). Rockville, MD: National Institute on Drug Abuse.

Ditto, B., Wilkins, J.-A., France, C. R., Lavoie, P., & Adler, P. S. (2003). On-site training in applied muscle tension to reduce vasovagal reactions to blood donation. *Journal of Behavioral Medicine, 26,* 53–65.

Dixon, J. C. (1963). Depersonalization phenomena in a sample population of college students. *British Journal of Psychiatry, 109,* 371–375.

Dixon, L. B., & Lehman, A. F. (1995). Family interventions for schizophrenia. *Schizophrenia Bulletin, 21,* 631–643.

Dobson, D. J. G., McDougall, G., Busheikin, J., & Aldous, J. (1995). Effects of social skills training and social milieu treatment on symptoms of schizophrenia. *Psychiatric Services, 46,* 376–380.

Dobson, K. (2003). *Frequently asked questions about clinical psychology.* Retrieved June 24, 2004, from University of Calgary Web site: http://www.psych.ucalgary.ca/students/careers/clinical_faq.html.

Dobson, K. S., & Shaw, B. F. (1987). Specificity and stability of self-referent encoding in clinical depression. *Journal of Abnormal Psychology, 96,* 34–40.

Docter, R. F., & Prince, V. (1997). Transvestism: A survey of 1032 crossdressers. *Archives of Sexual Behavior, 26,* 589–605.

Doghramji, K. (2000). The need for flexibility in dosing of hypnotic agents. *Sleep, 23* (Suppl. 1), S16–S20.

Dohrenwend, B. P., & Egri, G. (1981). Recent stressful life events and episodes of schizophrenia. *Schizophrenia Bulletin, 7,* 12–23.

Doidge, N., Simon, B., Brauer, L., Grant, D. C., First, M., Brunshaw, J., et al. (2002). Psychoanalytic patients in the U.S., Canada, and Australia: I. DSM-III-R disorders, indications, previous treatment, medications, and length of treatment. *Journal of the American Psychoanalytic Association, 50,* 575–614.

Dominion Bureau of Statistics (1955–57). *Mental health statistics: Patients in institutions.* Ottawa: Minister of Trade and Commerce.

Dongier, M. (1999). In memoriam – Heinz E. Lehmann, 1911–1999. *Journal of Psychiatry and Neuroscience, 24,* 362.

Douglas, K. S., & Hart, S. D. (1996, March). *Major mental disorder and violent behaviour: A meta-analysis of study characteristics and substantive factors influencing effect size.* Poster presented at the biennial conference of the American Psychology-Law Society, Hilton Head, South Carolina.

Douglas, K. S., & Koch, W. J. (2001). Civil commitment and civil competence: Psychological issues. In R. A. Schuller & J. R. P. Ogloff (Eds.), *Introduction to psychology and law: Canadian perspectives* (pp. 353–374). Toronto: University of Toronto Press.

Douglas, K. S., & Webster, C. D. (1999). Predicting violence in mentally and personality disordered individuals. In R. Roesch & S. D. Hart (Eds.), *Psychology and law: The state of the discipline* (pp. 175–239). Dordrecht, Netherlands: Kluwer.

Douglas, V. I. (1972). Stop, look and listen: The problem of sustained attention and impulse control in hyperactive and normal children. *Canadian Journal of Behavioural Science, 4,* 259-282.

Douglas, V. L., Barr, R. G., Desilets, J., & Sherman, E. (1995). Do high doses of stimulants impair flexible thinking in attention-deficit hyperactivity disorder? *Journal of the American Academy of Child and Adolescent Psychiatry, 34,* 877–885.

Draguns, J. G. (1990). Normal and abnormal behavior in cross-cultural perspective: Specifying the nature of their relationship. In J. Berman (Ed.), *Cross-Cultural Perspectives: Nebraska Symposium on Motivation 1989* (pp. 235–277). Lincoln: University of Nebraska Press.

Draguns, J. G. (1995). Cultural influences upon psychopathology: Clinical and practical implications. *Journal of Social Distress and the Homeless, 4,* 79–103.

Draguns, J. G., & Tanaka-Matsumi, J. (2003). Assessment of psychopathology across and within cultures: Issues and findings. *Behavior Research and Therapy, 41,* 755–776.

Drake, R. E., McHugo, G. J., Becker, D. R., Anthony, W. A., & Clark, R. E. (1996). The New Hampshire study of supported employment for people with severe mental illness. *Journal of Consulting and Clinical Psychology, 64,* 391–399.

Drury, V., Birchwood, M., Cochrane, R., & MacMillan, F. (1996). Cognitive therapy and recovery from acute psychosis: A controlled trial: II. Impact on recovery time. *British Journal of Psychiatry, 169,* 602–607.

Dubovsky, S. L. (1983). Psychiatry in Saudi Arabia. *American Journal of Psychiatry, 140,* 1455–1459.

Dugas, M. J., Gagnon, F., Ladouceur, R., & Freeston, M. H. (1998). Generalized anxiety disorder: A preliminary test of a conceptual model. *Behaviour Research and Therapy, 36,* 215–226.

Dugas, M. J., Ladouceur, R., Leger, E., Freeston, M. H., Langlois, F., Provencher, M., et al. (2003). Group cognitive-behavioral therapy for generalized anxiety disorder: Treatment outcome and long-term follow-up. *Journal of Consulting and Clinical Psycholology, 71,* 821–825.

Dulit, R. A., Marin, D. B., & Frances, A. J. (1993). Cluster B personality disorders. In D. L. Dunner (Ed.), *Current psychiatric therapy* (pp. 405–411). Philadelphia: W. B. Saunders.

Dumas, J., & Wahler, R. G. (1983). Predictors of treatment outcome in parent training: Mother insularity and socioeconomic disadvantage. *Behavioral Assessment, 5,* 301–313.

Durand, V. M. (1993). Functional communication training using assistive devices: Effects on challenging behavior and affect. *Augmentative and Alternative Communication, 9,* 168–176.

Durand, V. M. (1998). *Sleep better: A guide to improving the sleep of children with special needs.* Baltimore: Paul H. Brookes.

Durand, V. M. (1999a). Functional communication training using assistive devices: Recruiting natural communities of reinforcement. *Journal of Applied Behavior Analysis, 32,* 247–267.

Durand, V. M. (1999b). New directions in educational programming for students with autism. In D. Zager (Ed.), *Autism: Identification, education, and treatment* (2nd ed., pp. 323–343). Hillsdale, NJ: Erlbaum.

Durand, V. M. (2001). Future directions for children and adolescents with mental retardation. *Behavior Therapy.*

Durand, V. M. (2003). Functional communication training to treat challenging behavior. In W. O'Donohue, J. E. Fisher, and S. C. Hayes (Eds.), *Empirically supported techniques cognitive behavior therapy: Applying in your practice.* New York: John Wiley.

Durand, V. M. (2004). Past, present and emerging directions in education. In D. Zager (Ed.), *Autism: Identification, Education, and Treatment* (3rd ed.). Hillsdale, NJ: Erlbaum.

Durand, V. M., Blanchard, E. B., & Mindell, J. A. (1988). Training in projective testing: A survey of clinical training directors and internship directors. *Professional Psychology: Research and Practice, 19,* 236–238.

Durand, V. M., & Carr, E. G. (1988). Autism. In V. B. Van Hasselt, P. S. Strain, & M. Hersen (Eds.), *Handbook of developmental and physical disabilities* (pp. 195–214). New York: Pergamon Press.

Durand, V. M., & Mapstone, E. (1999). Pervasive developmental disorders. In W. K. Silverman & T. H. Ollendick (Eds.), *Developmental issues in the clinical treatment of children* (pp. 307–317). Needham Heights, MA: Allyn & Bacon.

Durand, V. M., & Mindell, J. A. (1990). Behavioral treatment of multiple childhood sleep disorders. *Behavior Modification, 14,* 37–49.

Durand, V. M., & Mindell, J. A. (1999). Behavioral intervention for childhood sleep terrors. *Behavior Therapy, 30,* 705–715.

Durand, V. M., Mindell, J., Mapstone, E., & Gernert-Dott, P. (1995). Treatment of multiple sleep disorders in children. In C. E. Schaefer (Ed.), *Clinical handbook of sleep disorders in children* (pp. 311–333). Northvale, NJ: Jason Aronson.

Durand, V. M., Mindell, J., Mapstone, E., & Gernert-Dott, P. (1998). Sleep problems. In T. S. Watson & F. M. Gresham (Eds.), *Handbook of child behavior therapy* (pp. 203–219). New York: Plenum Press.

*Durham v. United States.* (1954). 214 F.2d, 862, 874–875 (D.C. Cir.).

Durkheim, E. (1951). *Suicide: A study in sociology.* (J. A. Spaulding & G. Simpson, Trans.). New York: Free Press.

Dusseldorp, E., van Elderen, T., Maes, S., Meulman, J., & Kraaij, V. (1999). A meta-analysis of psychoeducational programs for coronary heart disease patients. *Health Psychology, 18,* 506–519.

Dwyer, E. (1992). Attendants and their world of work. In A. D. Gaines (Ed.), *Ethnopsychiatry: The cultural construction of professional and folk psychiatries* (pp. 291–305). Albany: State University of New York Press.

Dwyer, J. T., Feldman, J. J., Seltzer, C. C., & Mayer, J. (1969). Body image in adolescents: Attitudes toward weight and perception of appearance. *American Journal of Clinical Nutrition, 20,* 1045–1056.

Dyck, R. J., & White, J. (1998). Suicide prevention in Canada: Work in progress. In A. A. Leenars, S. Wenckstern, I. Sakinofsky, R. J. Dyck, M. J. Kral, & R. C. Bland (Eds.), *Suicide in Canada* (pp. 256–274). Toronto: University of Toronto Press.

Dykens, E., Leckman, J., Paul, R., & Watson, M. (1988). Cognitive, behavioral, and adaptive functioning in fragile X and non–fragile X retarded men. *Journal of Autism and Developmental Disorders, 18,* 41–52.

Eagles, J. M., Johnston, M. I., Hunter, D., Lobban, M., & Millar, H. R. (1995). Increasing incidence of anorexia nervosa in the female population of northeast Scotland. *American Journal of Psychiatry, 152,* 1266–1271.

Eaker, E. D., Pinsky, J., & Castelli, W. P. (1992). Myocardial infarction and coronary death among women: Psychosocial predictors from a 20-year follow-up of women in the Framingham study. *American Journal of Epidemiology, 135,* 854–864.

Earnst, K. S., & Kring, A. M. (1997). Construct validity of negative symptoms. *Clinical Psychology Review, 17,* 167–189.

Eaton, W. W., Anthony, J. C., Gallo, J., Cai, G., Tien, A., Romanoski, A., Lyketsos, C., et al. (1997). Natural history of diagnostic interview schedule/DSM-IV major depression: The Baltimore Epidemiologic Catchment Area follow-up. *Archives of General Psychiatry, 54,* 993–999.

Eaton, W. W., Kessler, R. C., Wittchen, H. U., & McGee, W. J. (1994). Panic and panic disorder in the United States. *American Journal of Psychiatry, 151,* 413–420.

Eaves, D., Douglas, K. S., Webster, C. D., Ogloff, J. R. P., & Hart, S. D. (2000). *Dangerous and long-term offenders: An assessment guide.* Burnaby, BC: Simon Fraser University, Mental Health, Law, and Policy Institute.

Ebigno, P. (1982). Development of a culture-specific screening scale of somatic complaints indicating psychiatric disturbance. *Culture, Medicine, and Psychiatry, 6,* 29–43.

Ebigno, P. O. (1986). A cross sectional study of somatic complaints of Nigerian females using the Enugu Somatization Scale. *Culture, Medicine, and Psychiatry, 10,* 167–186.

Eckman, T. A., Wirshing, W. C., Marder, S. R., Liberman, R. P., Johnston-Cronk, K., Zimmermann, K., et al. (1992). Techniques for training schizophrenic patients in illness self-management: A controlled trial. *American Journal of Psychiatry, 149,* 1549–1555.

Eddy, K. T., Keel, P. K., Dorer, D. J., Delinsky, S. S., Franko, D. L., & Herzog, D. B. (2002). A longitudinal comparison of anorexia nervosa subtypes. *International Journal of Eating Disorders, 31,* 191–201.

Edwards, A. J. (1994). *When memory fails: Helping the Alzheimer's and dementia patient.* New York: Plenum Press.

Efon, S. (1997, October 19). Tsunami of eating disorders sweeps across Asia. *San Francisco Examiner,* p. A27.

Egale Canada. (2003, September 26). *De-listing of Sex Reassignment Surgery (SRS) an injury to public health: Access to SRS by transsexuals is crucial to ensuring full dignity and participation.* Retrieved May 16, 2004, from http://www.egale.ca/index.asp?lang=E&menu=39&item=427.

Egeland, J. A., Gerhard, D. S., Pauls, D. L., Sussex, J. N., Kidd, K. K., Allen, C. R., et al. (1987). Bipolar affective disorders linked to DNA markers on chromosome 11. *Nature, 325*(6107), 783–787.

Ehrhardt, A. A., & Meyer-Bahlburg, H. F. L. (1981). Effects of prenatal sex hormones on gender-related behavior. *Science, 211,* 1312–1318.

Eich, E., Macaulay, D., Loewenstein, R. J., & Dihle, P. H. (1997a). Implicit memory, interpersonality amnesia, and dissociative identity disorder: Comparing patients with simulators. In D. Read & S. Lindsay (Eds.), *Recollections of Trauma* (pp. 469–474). New York: Plenum.

Eich, E., Macaulay, D., Loewenstein, R. J., & Dihle, P. H. (1997b). Memory, amnesia, and dissociative identity disorder. *Psychological Science, 8,* 417–422.

Eisen J., & Steketee, G. (1998). Course of illness in obsessive-compulsive disorder. In L. J. Dickstein, M. B. Riba, & J. M. Oldham (Eds.), *Review of psychiatry* (Vol. 16). Washington, DC: American Psychiatric Press.

Eisler, I., Dare, C., Russell, G. F. M., Szmukler, G., le Grange, D., & Dodge, E. (1997). Family and individual therapy in anorexia nervosa: A five-year follow-up. *Archives of General Psychiatry, 54,* 1025–1030.

Eldredge, K. L., & Agras, W. S. (1996). Weight and shape overconcern and emotional eating in binge eating disorder. *International Journal of Eating Disorders, 19,* 73–82.

Elie, M., Cole, M. G., Primeau, F. J., & Bellavance, F. (1998). Delirium risk factors in elderly hospitalized patients. *Journal of General Internal Medicine, 13,* 204–212.

Elie, M., Rousseau, F., Cole, M., Primeau, F., McCusker, J., & Bellavance, F. (2000). Prevalence and detection of delirium in elderly emergency department patients. *Canadian Medical Association Journal, 163,* 977–981.

Ellason, J. W., & Ross, C. A. (1997). Two-year follow up of inpatients with dissociative identity disorder. *American Journal of Psychiatry, 154,* 832–839.

Ellery, M., Stewart, S. H., & Loba, P. (2005). Alcohol's effects on risk-taking during Video Lottery Terminal (VLT) play among probable pathological and non-pathological gamblers. *Journal of Gambling Studies, 21,* 299–324.

Ellicott, A. G. (1988). *A prospective study of stressful life events and bipolar illness.* Unpublished doctoral dissertation, University of California, Los Angeles.

Elliot, D. M. (1997). Traumatic events: Prevalence and delayed recall in the general population. *Journal of Consulting and Clinical Psychology, 65,* 811–820.

Elliott, R., Malkin, I., & Gold, J. (2002). *Establishing safe injection sites in Canada: Legal and ethical issues.* Montreal: Canadian HIV/AIDS Legal Network.

Ellis, A. (1962). *Reason and emotion in psychotherapy.* Secaucus, NJ: Prentice-Hall.

Ellis, N. R. (1970). Memory processes in retardates and normals. In N. R. Ellis (Ed.), *International review of research in mental retardation* (Vol. 4, pp. 1–32). New York: Academic Press.

Emery, R. E. (1982). Interparental conflict and the children of discord and divorce. *Psychological Bulletin, 92,* 310–330.

Emrick, C. D. (1999). Alcoholics Anonymous and other 12-step groups. In M. Galanter & H. D. Kleber (Eds.), *Textbook of substance abuse treatment* (2nd ed., pp. 403–411). Washington, DC: American Psychiatric Press.

Emrick, C. D., Tonigan, J. S., Montgomery, H., & Little, L. (1993). Alcoholics Anonymous: What is currently known? In B. S. McCrady & W. R. Miller (Eds.), *Research on Alcoholics Anonymous: Opportunities and alternatives* (pp. 41–76). New Brunswick, NJ: Rutgers Center of Alcohol Studies.

Emslie, G. J., Rush, A. J., Weinberg, W. A., Rintelmann, J. W., & Roffwarg, H. P. (1994). Sleep EEG features of adolescents with major depression. *Biological Psychiatry, 36,* 573–581.

Endler, N. S. (1990). *Holiday of Darkness: A psychologist's personal journey out of his depression.* Toronto: Wall and Thompson.

Endler, N. S., & Flett, G. L. (2002). *Endler Multidimensional Anxiety Scales (EMAS) – Social Anxiety Scales (SAS): Manual.* Los Angeles: Western Psychological Services.

Endler, N. S., Parker, J. D. A., & Summerfeldt, L. J. (1998). Coping with health problems: Developing a reliable and valid multidimensional measure. *Psychological Assessment, 10,* 195–205.

Enns, M. W., Inayatulla, M., Cox, B., & Cheyne, L. (1997). Prediction of suicide intent in Aboriginal and non-Aboriginal adolescent inpatients: A research note. *Suicide and Life-Threatening Behavior, 27*, 218–224.

Enns, M. W., Kjernisted, K., & Lander, M. (2001). Pharmacological management of hypochondriasis and related disorders. In G. J. G. Asmundson, S. Taylor, & B. J. Cox (Eds.), *Health anxiety: Clinical and research perspectives on hypochondriasis and related conditions* (pp. 193–219). New York: Wiley.

Epling, W. F., & Pierce, W. D. (1992). *Solving the anorexia puzzle.* Toronto: Hogrefe & Huber.

Eppright, T. D., Kashani, J. H., Robison, B. D., & Reid, J. C. (1993). Comorbidity of conduct disorder and personality disorders in an incarcerated juvenile population. *American Journal of Psychiatry, 150*, 1233–1236.

Erdberg, P. (2000). Rorschach assessment. In G. Goldstein & M. Hersen (Eds.), *Handbook of psychological assessment* (pp. 437–449). New York: Pergamon Press.

Erhardt, D., & Hinshaw, S. P. (1994). Initial sociometric impressions of attention-deficit hyperactivity disorder and comparison boys: Predictions from social behaviors and from nonbehavioral variables. *Journal of Consulting and Clinical Psychology, 62*, 833–842.

Erickson, D. H., Beiser, M., & Iacono, W. G. (1998). Social support predicts 5-year outcome in 1st-episode schizophrenia. *Journal of Abnormal Psychology, 107*, 681–685.

Erikson, E. (1982). *The life cycle completed.* New York: Norton.

Erkinjuntti, T., Ostbye, T., Steenhuis, R., & Hachinski, V. (1997). The effect of different diagnostic criteria on the prevalence of dementia. *New England Journal of Medicine, 337*, 1667–1674.

Eron, L., & Huesmann, R. (1990). The stability of aggressive behavior—even unto the third generation. In. M. Lewis & S. Miller (eds.), *Handbook of developmental psychopathology* (pp. 147–156). New York: Plenum.

Ertekin, C., Colakoglu, Z., & Altay, B. (1995). Hand and genital sympathetic skin potentials in flaccid and erectile penile states in normal potent men and patients with premature ejaculation. *The Journal of Urology, 153*, 76–79.

Escobar, J. I., & Canino, G. (1989). Unexplained physical complaints: Psychopathology and epidemiological correlates. *British Journal of Psychiatry, 154*, 24–27.

Escobar, J. I., Gara, M., Waitzkin, H., Silver, R. C., Holman, A., & Compton, W. (1998). DSM-IV hypochondriasis in primary care. *General Hospital Psychiatry, 20*(3), 155–159.

Escobar, J. I., Waitzkin, H., Silver, R., Gara, M., & Holman, A. (1998). Abridged somatization: A study in primary care. *Psychosomatic Medicine, 60*, 466–472.

Esposito, C. L., & Clum, G. A. (2003). The relative contribution of diagnostic and psychosocial factors in the prediction of adolescent suicidal ideation. *Journal of Clinical Child and Adolescent Psychology, 32*, 386–395.

Esterling, B., Antoni, M., Schneiderman, N., LaPerriere, A., Ironson., G., Klimas, N., et al. (1992). Psychosocial modulation of antibody to Epstein-Barr viral capsid antigen and human herpes virus-Type 6 in HIV-1 infected and at-risk gay men. *Psychosomatic Medicine, 54*, 354–371.

Eth, S. (1990). Posttraumatic stress disorder in childhood. In M. Hersen & C. G. Last (Ed.), *Handbook of child and adult psychopathology: A longitudinal perspective.* Elmsford, NY: Pergamon Press.

Evans, D. A., Funkenstein, H. H., Albert, M. S., Scherr, P. A., Cook, N. R., Chonn, M. J., et al. (1989). Prevalence of Alzheimer's disease in a community population of older persons. *Journal of the American Medical Association, 262*, 2551–2556.

Evans, J. A., & Hammerton, J. L. (1985). Chromosomal anomalies. In A. M. Clarke, A. D. B. Clarke, & J. M. Berg (Eds.), *Mental deficiency: The changing outlook* (4th ed., pp. 213–266). New York: Free Press.

Evans, M. D., Hollon, S. D., DeRubeis, R. J., Pinsecki, J. M., Grove, W. M., Garvey, J. J., et al. (1992). Differential relapse following cognitive therapy and pharmacotherapy for depression. *Archives of General Psychiatry, 49*(10), 802–808.

Evenson, B. (2001, April 3). Scientology leads backlash. *National Post.* Retrieved May 20, 2004, from http://www.rickross.com/reference/scientology/scien300.html.

Everaerd, W., Laan, E. T. M., Roth, S., & van der Velde, J. (2000). Female sexuality. In L. T. Szuchman & F. Muscarella (Eds.), *Psychological perspectives on human sexuality* (pp. 101–146). New York: Wiley.

Everett, J., Lavoie, K., Gagnon, J.-F., & Gosselin, N. (2001). Performance of patients with schizophrenia on the Wisconsin Card Sorting Test (WCST). *Journal of Psychiatry and Neuroscience, 26*, 123–130.

Exner, J. E. (1974). *The Rorschach: A comprehensive system* (Vol. 1). New York: John Wiley.

Exner, J. E. (1978). *The Rorschach: A comprehensive system* (Vol. 2). *Current research and advanced interpretation.* New York: John Wiley.

Exner, J. E. (1986). *The Rorschach: A comprehensive system* (Vol. 1, 2nd ed.). New York: John Wiley.

Exner, J. E., & Weiner, I. B. (1982). *The Rorschach: A comprehensive system* (Vol. 3). *Assessment of children and adolescents.* New York: John Wiley.

Eysenck, H. J. (Ed.). (1967). *The biological basis of personality.* Springfield, IL: Charles C. Thomas.

Eysenck, H. J., & Eysenck, S. B. G. (1975). *Manual for the Eysenck Personality Questionnaire.* London UK: Hodder & Stoughton.

Eysenck, H. J., & Eysenck, S. B. G. (1978). Psychopathy, personality, and genetics. In R. D. Hare & D. Schalling (Eds.), *Psychopathic behaviour: Approaches to research* (pp. 197–223). Chichester, UK: John Wiley.

Ezzel, C. (1993). On borrowed time: Long-term survivors of HIV-l infection. *Journal of NIH Research, 5*, 77–82.

Fackelmann, K. A. (1993). Marijuana and the brain: Scientists discover the brain's own THC. *Science, 143*, 88–94.

Faden, R. R. (1987). Health psychology and public health. In G. L. Stone, S. M. Weiss, J. D. Matarazzo, N. E. Miller, J. Rodin, C. D. Belar, et al. (Eds.), *Health psychology: A discipline and a profession.* Chicago: University of Chicago Press.

Fagan, P. J., Wise, T. N., Schmidt, C. W., & Berlin, M. D. (2002). Pedophilia. *Journal of the American Medical Association, 288*, 2458–2465.

Fahrner, E. M. (1987). Sexual dysfunction in male alcohol addicts: Prevalence and treatment. *Archives of Sexual Behavior, 16*(3), 247–257.

Fairburn, C. G. (1985). Cognitive-behavioral treatment for bulimia. In D. M. Garner & P. E. Garfinkel (Eds.), *Handbook of psychotherapy for anorexia nervosa and bulimia* (pp. 160–192). New York: Guilford Press.

Fairburn, C. G., Agras, W. S., & Wilson, G. T. (1992). The research on the treatment of bulimia nervosa: Practical and theoretical implications. In G. H. Anderson & S. H. Kennedy (Eds.), *The biology of feast and famine: Relevance to eating disorders* (pp. 317–340). New York: Academic Press.

Fairburn, C. G., & Beglin, S. J. (1990). Studies of the epidemiology of bulimia nervosa. *American Journal of Psychiatry, 147*(4), 401–409.

Fairburn, C. G., & Cooper, Z. (1993). The Eating Disorder Examination. In C. G. Fairburn & G. T. Wilson (Eds.), *Binge eating: Nature, assessment, and treatment.* (pp. 317–360). New York: Guilford Press.

Fairburn, C. G., Cooper, Z., & Cooper, P. J. (1986). The clinical features and maintenance of bulimia nervosa. In K. D. Brownell & J. P. Foreyt (Eds.), *Handbook of eating disorders: Physiology, psychology, and treatment of obesity, anorexia, and bulimia* (pp. 389–404). New York: Basic Books.

Fairburn, C. G., Cooper, Z., & Shafran, R. (2003). Cognitive behavior therapy for eating disorders: A "transdiagnostic" theory and treatment. *Behaviour Research and Therapy, 41*, 509–528.

Fairburn, C. G., Cooper, Z., Doll, H. A., & Welch, S. L. (1999). Risk factors for anorexia nervosa: Three integrated case-control comparisons. *Archives of General Psychiatry, 56*, 468–476.

Fairburn, C. G., Cooper, Z., Doll, H. A., Norman, P., & O'Connor, M. (2000). The natural course of bulimia nervosa and binge eating disorder in young women. *Archives of General Psychiatry, 57*, 659–665.

Fairburn, C. G., Cowen, P. J., & Harrison, P. J. (1999). Twin studies and the etiology of eating disorders. *International Journal of Eating Disorders, 26*(4), 349–358.

Fairburn, C. G., Doll, H. A., Welch, S. L., Hay, P. J., Davies, B. A., & O'Connor, M. E. (1998). Risk factors for binge eating disorder. *Archives of General Psychiatry, 55*, 425–432.

Fairburn, C. G., Hay, P. J., & Welch, S. L. (1993). Binge eating and bulimia nervosa: Distribution and determinants. In C. G. Fairburn & G. T. Wilson (Eds.), *Binge eating: Nature, assessment, and treatment*. New York: Guilford Press.

Fairburn, C. G., Jones, R., Peveler, R. C., Hope, R. A., & O'Connor, M. (1993). Psychotherapy and bulimia nervosa: The longer-term effects of interpersonal psychotherapy, behaviour therapy and cognitive behaviour therapy. *Archives of General Psychiatry, 50*, 419–428.

Fairburn, C. G., Marcus, M. D., & Wilson, G. T. (1993). Cognitive behaviour therapy for binge eating and bulimia nervosa: A comprehensive treatment manual. In C. G. Fairburn & G. T. Wilson (Eds.), *Binge eating: Nature, assessment, and treatment*. New York: Guilford Press.

Fairburn, C. G., Norman, P. A., Welch, S. L., O'Connor, M. E., Doll, H., & Peveler, R. C. (1995). A prospective study of outcome in bulimia nervosa and the long-term effects of three psychological treatments. *Archives of General Psychiatry, 52*, 304–312.

Fairburn, C. G., Shafran, R., & Cooper, Z. (1999). A cognitive behavioural theory of anorexia nervosa. *Behaviour Research and Therapy, 37*, 1–13.

Fairburn, C. G., Stice, E., Cooper, Z., Doll, H. A., Norman, P. A., & O'Connor, M. E. (2003). Understanding persistence in bulimia nervosa: A 5-year naturalistic study. *Journal of Consulting and Clinical Psychology, 71*, 103–109.

Fairburn, C. G., Welch, S. L., Doll, S. A., Davies, B. A., & O'Connor, M. E. (1997). Risk factors for bulimia nervosa: A community-based case-control study. *Archives of General Psychiatry, 54*, 509–517.

Fairburn, C. G., & Wilson, G. T. (1993). Binge eating: Definition and classification. In C. G. Fairburn & G. T. Wilson (Eds.), *Binge eating: Nature, assessment, and treatment*. New York: Guilford Press.

Fallon, A. (1990). Culture in the mirror: Sociocultural determinants of body image. In T. F. Cash & T. Pruzinsky (Eds.), *Body images: Development, deviance, and change* (pp. 80–109). New York: Guilford Press.

Fallon, A. E., & Rozin, P. (1985). Sex differences in perceptions of desirable body shape. *Journal of Abnormal Psychology, 94*, 102–105.

Falloon, I. R. H., Boyd, J. L., McGill, C. W., Williamson, M., Razani, J., Moss, H. B., (1985). Family management in the prevention of morbidity of schizophrenia. *Archives of General Psychiatry, 42*, 887–896.

Falloon, I. R. H., Brooker, C., & Graham-Hole, V. (1992). Psychosocial interventions for schizophrenia. *Behaviour Change, 9*, 238–245.

Faraone, S. V. (2000). Attention deficit hyperactivity disorder in adults: Implications for theories of diagnosis. *Current Directions in Psychological Science, 9*, 33–36.

Faraone, S. V. (2003). Report from the 4th international meeting of the attention deficit hyperactivity disorder molecular genetics network. *American Journal of Medical Genetics, 121*, 55–59.

Faraone, S. V., Biederman, J., Mick, E., Williamson, S., Wilens, T., Spencer, T., et al. (2000). Family study of girls with attention deficit hyperactivity disorder. *American Journal of Psychiatry, 157*(7), 1077–1083.

Faraone, S. V., Biederman, J., Woznaik, J., Mundy, E., Mennin, D., & O'Donnell, D. (1997). Is comorbidity with ADHD a marker for juvenile onset mania? *Journal of the American Academy of Child and Adolescent Psychiatry, 36*(8), 1046–1055.

Faraone, S. V., Tsuang, M. T., & Tsuang, D. W. (1999). *Genetics of mental disorders: A guide for students, clinicians, and researchers*. Baltimore, MD: Guilford.

Farde, L., Gustavsson, J. P., & Jonsson, E. (1997). D2 dopamine receptors and personality traits. *Nature, 385*, 590.

Fausto-Sterling, A. (2000a). The five sexes, revisited. *The Sciences, 40*(4), 19–23.

Fausto-Sterling, A. (2000b). *Sexing the body*. New York: Basic.

Fava, G. A., Grandi, S., Zielezny, M., Rafanelli, C., & Canestrari, R. (1996). Four-year outcome for cognitive behavioral treatment of residual symptoms in major depression. *American Journal of Psychiatry, 153*, 945–947.

Fava, G. A., Rafanelli, C., Grandi, S., Conti, S., & Belluardo, P. (1998). Prevention of recurrent depression with cognitive behavioral therapy: Preliminary findings. *Archives of General Psychiatry, 55*(9), 816–820.

Fava, M., & Rosenbaum, J. F. (1991). Suicidality and fluoxetine: Is there a relationship? *Journal of Clinical Psychiatry, 52*(3), 108–111.

Fawzy, F. I., Cousins, N., Fawzy, N. W., Kemeny, M. E., Elashoff, R., & Morton, D. (1990). A structured psychiatric intervention for cancer patients: I. Changes over time in methods of coping and affective disturbance. *Archives of General Psychiatry, 47*, 720–728.

Fedoroff, I. C., & Taylor, S. (2001). Psychological and pharmacological treatments of social phobia: A meta-analysis. *Journal of Clinical Psychopharmacology, 21*, 311–324.

Fedoroff, J. P., Fishell, A., & Fedoroff, B., (1999). A case series of women evaluated for paraphilic sexual disorders. *Canadian Journal of Human Sexuality, 8*(2), 127–140.

Fein, G., & Callaway, E. (1993). Electroencephalograms and event-related potentials in clinical psychiatry. In D. L. Dunner (Ed.), *Current psychiatric therapy* (pp. 18–26). Philadelphia: W. B. Saunders.

Feinberg, M., & Carroll, B. J. (1984). Biological "markers" for endogenous depression: Effect of age, severity of illness, weight loss and polarity. *Archives of General Psychiatry, 41*, 1080–1085.

Feingold, B. F. (1975). *Why your child is hyperactive*. New York: Random House.

Feinstein, A., Stergiopoulos, V., Fine, J., & Lang, A. E. (2001). Psychiatric outcome in patients with a psychogenic movement disorder. *Neuropsychiatry, Neuropsychology, and Behavioral Neurology, 14*, 169–176.

Feldman, H. A., Goldstein, I., Hatzichristou, D. G., Krane, R. J., & McKunlay, J. B. (1994). Impotence and its medical and psychosocial correlates: Results of the Massachusetts Male Aging Study. *Journal of Urology, 151*, 54–61.

Ferber, R. (1985). *Solve your child's sleep problems*. New York: Simon & Schuster.

Ferguson, K. L., & Rodway, M. R. (1994). Cognitive behavioral treatment of perfectionism: Initial evaluation studies. *Research on Social Work Practice, 4*, 283–308.

Fernandez, F., Levy J. K., Lachar, B. L., & Small, G. W. (1995). The management of depression and anxiety in the elderly. *Journal of Clinical Psychiatry, 56* (Suppl. 2), 20–29.

Fernandez, Y. M., & Marshall, W. L. (2003). Victim empathy, social self-esteem, and psychopathy in rapists. *Sexual Abuse: Journal of Research and Treatment, 15*, 11–26.

Ferreira, C. (2000). Serial killers: Victims of compulsion or masters of control? In D. H. Fishbein (Ed.), *The science, treatment, and prevention of antisocial behaviors: Application to the criminal justice system* (pp. 15-1–15-18). Kingston, NJ: Civic Research Institute.

Ferster, C. B. (1961). Positive reinforcement and behavioral deficits of autistic children. *Child Development, 32*, 437–456.

Ferster, C. B., & Skinner, B. F. (1957). *Schedules of reinforcement*. New York: Appleton-Century-Crofts.

Feske, U., & Chambless, D. L. (1995). Cognitive behavioral versus exposure only treatment for social phobia: A meta-analysis. *Behavior Therapy, 26*, 695–720.

Fewell, R. R., & Glick, M. P. (1996). Program evaluation findings of an intensive early intervention program. *American Journal on Mental Retardation, 101*, 233–243.

Field, A. E., Camargo, C. A., Taylor, C. B., Bekey, C. S., Roberts, S. B., & Colditz, G. A. (2001). Peer, parent and media influences on the development of weight concerns and frequent dieting among preadolescent and adolescent girls and boys. *Pediatrics, 107*, 54–60.

Field, T., Healy, B., Goldstein, S., Perry, S., Bendell, D., Schanberg, S., et al. (1988). Infants of depressed mothers show "depressed" behavior even with nondepressed adults. *Child Development, 59*(6), 1569–1579.

Fiester, S. J. (1995). Self-defeating personality disorder. In W. J. Livesley (Ed.), *The DSM-IV personality disorders* (pp. 341–358). New York: Guilford Press.

Fiester, S. J., & Gay, M. (1995). Sadistic personality disorder. In W. J. Livesley (Ed.), *The DSM-IV personality disorders* (pp. 329–340). New York: Guilford Press.

Figueroa, E., & Silk, K. R. (1997). Biological implications of childhood sexual abuse in borderline personality disorder. *Journal of Personality Disorders, 11*, 71–92.

Fils-Aime, M. L. (1993). Sedative-hypnotic abuse. In D. L. Dunner (Ed.), *Current psychiatric therapy* (pp. 124–131). Philadelphia: W. B. Saunders.

Fincham, F. D., Beach, S. R. H., Harold, G. T., & Osborne, L. N. (1997). Marital satisfaction and depression: Different causal relationships for men and women? *Psychological Science, 8*(5), 351–357.

Fink, M., & Sackeim, H. A. (1996). Convulsive therapy in schizophrenia? *Schizophrenia Bulletin, 22,* 27–39.

Finn, P. R., Sharkansky, E. J., Brandt, K. M., & Turcotte, N. (2000). The effects of family risk, personality, and expectancies on alcohol use and abuse. *Journal of Abnormal Psychology, 109,* 122–133.

Finney, M. L., Stoney, C. M., & Engebretson, T. O. (2002). Hostility and anger expression in African-American and European American men is associated with cardiovascular and lipid reactivity. *Psychophysiology, 39,* 340–349.

Fiore, T. A., Becker, E. A., & Nero, R. C. (1993). Educational interventions for students with attention deficit disorder. *Exceptional Children, 60,* 163–173.

Fiorino, A. S. (1996). Sleep, genes and death: Fatal familial insomnia. *Brain Research Reviews, 22,* 258–264.

Firestone, P., Bradford, J. M., Greenberg, D. M., & Nunes, K. L. (2000). Differentiation of homicidal child molesters, nonhomicidal child molesters, and nonoffenders by phallometry. *American Journal of Psychiatry, 157,* 1847–1850.

First, M. B., Bell, C. C., Cuthbert, B., Krystal, J. H., Malison, R., Offord, D. R., et al. (2002). Personality disorders and relational disorders: A research agenda for addressing crucial gaps in DSM. In D. J. Kupfer, M. B. First & D. A. Regier (Eds.) *A research agenda for DSM-V* (pp. 123–199). Washington, DC: American Psychiatric Press.

Fischer, M. (1971). Psychoses in the offspring of schizophrenic monozygotic twins and their normal co-twins. *British Journal of Psychiatry, 118,* 43–52.

Fish, B. (1977). Neurobiological antecedents of schizophrenia in children: Evidence for an inherited, congenital, neurointegrative defect. *Archives of General Psychiatry, 34,* 1297–1313.

Fish, B. (1987). Infant predictors of the longitudinal course of schizophrenic development. *Schizophrenia Bulletin, 13,* 395–410.

Fisher, J. D., Fisher, W. A., Bryan, A. D., & Misovich, S. J. (2002). Information-motivation-behavioral skills model-based HIV risk behavior change intervention for inner-city high school youth. *Health Psychology, 21,* 177–186.

Fisher, J. E., & Carstensen, L. L. (1990). Behavior management of the dementias. *Clinical Psychology Review, 10,* 611–629.

Fisher, L. (1996, July 8). Bizarre right from Day 1. *Maclean's, 109,* 14.

Fisher, M., & Zeaman, D. (1973). An attention-retention theory of retardate discrimination learning. In N. R. Ellis (Ed.), *International review of research in mental retardation* (Vol. 6, pp. 169–256). New York: Academic Press.

Fitts, S. N., Gibson, P., Redding, C. A., & Deiter, P. J. (1989). Body dysmorphic disorder: Implications for its validity as a DSM-III-R clinical syndrome. *Psychological Reports, 64,* 655–658.

Fitzgerald, J. (2000). *Sarah McLachlan: Building a mystery.* Kingston, ON: Quarry Press.

Fitzgerald, P. B., Brown, T. L., Marston, N. A., Daskalakis, J., De Castella, A., & Kulkarni, J. (2003). Transcranial magnetic stimulation in the treatment of depression: A double-blind, placebo-controlled trial. *Archives of General Psychiatry, 60,* 1002–1008.

Fitzpatrick, A. L., Kuller, L. H., Ives, D. G., Lopez, O. L., Jagust, W., Breitner, J. C., et al. (2004). Incidence and prevalence of dementia in the cardiovascular health study. *Journal of the American Geriatric Society, 52,* 195–204.

Flannery, D. J., Liau, A. K., Powell, K. E., Vesterdal, W., Vazsonyi, A. T., Guo, S. et al. (2003). Initial behavior outcomes for the PeaceBuilders universal school-based violence prevention program. *Developmental Psychology, 39,* 292–308.

Fleming, J. E., Boyle, M. H., & Offord, D. R. (1993). The outcome of adolescent depression in the Ontario child health study follow-up. *Journal of the American Academy of Child and Adolescent Psychiatry, 32*(1), 28–33.

Flint, A. J. (1994). Epidemiology and co-morbidity of anxiety disorders in the elderly. *American Journal of Psychiatry, 151,* 640–649.

Flor, H., Elbert, T., Kenecht, S., Weinbruch, C., Pantev, C., Birbaumer, N., et al. (1995). Phantom limb pain as a perceptual correlate of corticol reorganization following arm amputation. *Nature, 375,* 482–484.

Foa, E. B., & Franklin, M. E. (2001). Obsessive compulsive disorder. In D. H. Barlow (Ed.), *Clinical Handbook of Psychological Disorders.* (3rd ed.). New York: Guilford Press.

Foa, E. B., & Meadows, E. A. (1997). Psychosocial treatments for posttraumatic stress disorder: A critical review. *Annual Review of Psychology, 48,* 449–480.

Foa, E. B., Jenike, M., Kozak, M. J., Joffe, R., Baer, L., Pauls, D., et al. (1996). Obsessive-compulsive disorder. In T. A. Widiger, A. J. Frances, H. A. Pincus, M. R. Ross, M. B. First, & W. W. Davis (Eds.), *DSM-IV sourcebook* (Vol. 2, pp. 549–576). Washington, DC: American Psychiatric Press.

Foley, D. J., Monjan, A. A., Simonsick, E. M., Wallace, R. B., & Blazer, D. G. (1999). Incidence and remission of insomnia among elderly adults: An epidemiologic study of 6,800 persons over three years. *Sleep, 22* (Suppl. 2), S366–S372.

Folks, D. G., Ford, C. U., & Regan, W. M. (1984). Conversion symptoms in a general hospital. *Psychosomatics, 25*(4), 285–295.

Follette, W. C., & Houts, A. C. (1996). Models of scientific progress and the role of theory in taxonomy development: A case study of the *DSM. Journal of Consulting and Clinical Psychology, 64*(6), 1120–1132.

Follman, M. (2003, September 8). Canada's safe haven for junkies. *Salon.com.* Retrieved October 27, 2003, from http://www.salon.com/news/feature/2003/09/08/vancouver/index_np.html.

Folstein, M. F., Folstein, S. E., & McHugh, P. R. (1975). Mini-mental state: A practical method for grading the cognitive state of patients for the clinician. *Journal of Psychiatric Research, 12,* 189–198.

Folstein, S. E., Brandt, J., & Folstein, M. F. (1990). Huntington's disease. In J. L. Cummings (Ed.), *Subcortical dementia* (pp. 87–107). New York: Oxford University Press.

Folstein, S. E., & Santangelo, S. L. (2000). Does Asperger syndrome aggregate in families? In A. Klin, F. R. Volkmar, & S. S. Sparrow (Eds.), *Asperger syndrome* (pp. 159–171). New York: Guilford Press.

Fombonne, E. (1999). The epidemiology of autism: A review. *Psychological Medicine, 29,* 769–786.

Fombonne, E. (2003a). Epidemiological surveys of autism and other pervasive developmental disorders: An update. *Journal of Autism and Developmental Disorders, 33,* 365–382.

Fombonne, E. (2003b). The prevalence of autism. *Journal of the American Medical Association, 289,* 87–89.

Ford, C. V. (1985). Conversion disorders: An overview. *Psychosomatics, 26,* 371–383.

Ford, D. E., & Kamerow, D. B. (1989). Epidemiologic study of sleep disturbances and psychiatric disorder: An opportunity for prevention? *Journal of the American Medical Association, 262,* 1479–1484.

Ford, M. R., & Widiger, T. A. (1989). Sex bias in the diagnosis of histrionic and antisocial personality disorders. *Journal of Consulting and Clinical Psychology, 57,* 301–305.

Fordyce, W. E. (1976). *Behavioral methods in chronic pain and illness.* St. Louis, MO: Mosby.

Fordyce, W. E. (1988). Pain and suffering: A reappraisal. *American Psychologist, 43*(4), 276–283.

Forestell, C. A., Humphrey, T. M., & Stewart, S. H. (2004). Involvement of body weight and shape factors in ratings of attractiveness by women: A replication and extension of Tassinary and Hansen (1998). *Personality and Individual Differences, 36,* 295–305.

Forth, A. E., & Mailloux, D. L. (2000). Psychopathy in youth: What do we know? In C. B. Gacono (Ed.), *Clinical and forensic assessment of psychopathy: A practitioner's guide* (pp. 25–54). Mahwah, NJ: Lawrence Erlbaum.

Fossati, A., Maffei, C., Bagnato, M., Donati, D., Donini, M., Fiorilli, M., et al. (2000). A psychometric study of DSM-IV passive-aggressive (negativistic) personality disorder criteria. *Journal of Personality Disorders, 14,* 72–83.

Foster, J. D. (2004, April 6). *Corson getting one more shot at the title.* Retrieved July 15, 2004, from http://www.dallasstars.com/news/newsDetail.jsp?id=2121.

Fouts, G., & Burggraf, K. (2000). Television situation comedies: Female weight, male negative comments, and audience reactions. *Sex Roles, 42*, 925–932.

Fowles, D. C. (1988). Psychophysiology and psychopathy: A motivational approach. *Psychophysiology, 25*, 373–391.

Fowles, D. C. (1993). A motivational theory of psychopathology. In W. Spaulding (Ed.), *Nebraska symposium on motivation: Integrated views of motivation, cognition, and emotion* (Vol. 41, pp. 181–238). Lincoln: University of Nebraska Press.

Fox, P. T., Ingham, R. J., Ingham, J. C., Hirsch, T. B., Downs, J. H., Martin, C., et al. (1996). A PET study of the neural systems of stuttering. *Nature, 382*, 158–161.

Foy, D. W., Resnick, H. S., Sipprelle, R. C., & Carroll, E. M. (1987). Premilitary, military and postmilitary factors in the development of combat related posttraumatic stress disorder. *The Behavior Therapist, 10*, 3–9.

Foy, D. W., Sipprelle, R. C., Rueger, D. B., & Carroll, E. M. (1984). Etiology of posttraumatic stress disorder in Vietnam veterans: Analysis of premilitary, military, and combat exposure influences. *Journal of Consulting and Clinical Psychology, 52*, 79–87.

Frances, A., & Blumenthal, S. J. (1989). Personality disorders and characteristics in youth suicide. In *Alcohol, drug abuse and mental health administration. Report of the secretary's task force on youth suicide: Vol. 12, risk factors for youth suicide* (DHHS Publication No. ADM89-1622, pp. 172–185). Washington, DC: U. S. Government Printing Office.

Francis, D., Diorio, J., Liu, D., & Meaney, M. J. (1999). Nongenomic transmission across generations of maternal behavior and stress responses in the rat. *Science, 286*, 1155–1158.

Francis, D. D., Diorio, J., Plotsky, P. M., Meaney, M. J. (2002). Environmental enrichment reverses the effects of maternal separation on stress reactivity. *Journal of Neuroscience, 22*, 7840–7843.

Frances, R., Franklin, J., & Flavin, D. (1986). Suicide and alcoholism. *Annals of the New York Academy of Science, 287*, 316–326.

Francis, G., & Hart, K. J. (1992). Depression and suicide. In V. B. Van Hasselt & D. J. Kolko (Eds.), *Inpatient behavior therapy for children and adolescents* (pp. 93–111). New York: Plenum Press.

Francis, J. A., Stewart, S. H., & Hounsell, S. Dietary Restraint and the Selective Processing of Forbidden and Nonforbidden Food Words. *Cognitive Therapy and Research*, v. 21 (6), 1997, pp. 633–646. © Plenum Publishing Corporation.

Frank, E., Anderson, C., & Rubinstein, D. (1978). Frequency of sexual dysfunction in "normal" couples. *New England Journal of Medicine, 299*, 111–115.

Frank, E., Cyranowski, J. M., Rucci, P., Shear, M. K., Fagiolini, A., Thase, M. E., et al. (2002). Clinical significance of lifetime panic spectrum symptoms in the treatment of patients with bipolar I disorder. *Archives of General Psychiatry. 59*, 905–911.

Frank, E., Hlastala, S., Ritenour, A., Houck, P., Tu, X. M., Monk, T. H., et al. (1997). Inducing lifestyle regularity in recovering bipolar disorder patients: Results from the Maintenance Therapies in Bipolar Disorder Protocol. *Biological Psychiatry, 41*, 1165–1173.

Frank, E., Kupfer, D. J., Perel, J. M., Cornes, C., Jarrett, D. B., Mallinger, A. G., et al. (1990). Three-year outcomes for maintenance therapies in recurrent depression. *Archives of General Psychiatry, 47*(12), 1093–1099.

Frank, E., Swartz, H. A., Mallinger, A. G., Thase, M. E., Weaver, E. V., & Kupfer, D. J. (1999). Adjunctive psychotherapy for bipolar disorder: Effects of changing treatment modality. *Journal of Abnormal Psychology, 108*(4), 579–587.

Franklin, D. (1990, November/December). Hooked-Not hooked: Why isn't everyone an addict? *Health*, pp. 39–52.

Franklin, J. E., & Frances, R. J. (1999). Alcohol and other psychoactive substance use disorders. In R. E. Hales, S. C. Yudofsky, & J. A. Talbott (Eds.), *Textbook of psychiatry* (3rd ed., pp. 363–423). Washington, DC: American Psychiatric Press.

Franko, D. L., Wonderlich, S. A., Little, D., & Herzog, D. B. (2004). Diagnosis and classification of eating disorders. In J. K. Thompson (Ed.) *Handbook of eating disorders and obesity* (pp. 58–80). New York: John Wiley.

Fraser, G. A. (1994). Dissociative phenomena and disorders: Clinical presentations. In R. M. Klein & B. K. Doane (Eds.), *Psychological concepts and dissociative disorders* (pp. 131–151). Hillside, NJ: Erlbaum.

Frasure-Smith, N., Lesperance, F., Juneau, M., Talajic, M., & Bourassa, M. G. (1999). Gender, depression, and one-year prognosis after myocardial infarction. *Psychosomatic Medicine, 61*, 26–37.

Fratiglioni, L., Grut, M., Forsell, Y., Viitanen, M., Grafstrom, M., Holmen, K., et al. (1991). Prevalence of Alzheimer's disease and other dementias in an elderly urban population: Relationship with age, sex and education. *Neurology, 41*, 1886–1892.

Fredrikson, M., Annas, P., & Wik, G. (1997). Parental history, aversive exposure and the development of snake and spider phobia in women. *Behavior Research and Therapy, 35*, 23–28.

Fredrikson, M., & Matthews, K. A. (1990). Cardiovascular responses to behavioral stress and hypertension: A meta-analytic review. *Annals of Behavioral Medicine, 12*(1), 30–39.

Freedman, M. (1990). Parkinson's disease. In J. L. Cummings (Ed.), *Subcortical dementia* (pp. 108–122). New York: Oxford University Press.

Freeman, A., Pretzer, J., Fleming, B., & Simon, K. M. (1990). *Clinical applications of cognitive therapy.* New York: Plenum Press.

Freeman, M. P., & McElroy, S. L. (1999). Clinical picture and etiological models of mixed states. *Psychiatric Clinics of North America, 22*(3), 535–546.

French-Belgian Collaborative Group (1982). Ischemic heart disease and psychological patterns: Prevalence and incidence studies in Belgium and France. *Advances in Cardiology, 29*, 25–31.

Freud, A. (1946). *Ego and the mechanisms of defense.* New York: International Universities Press.

Freud, S. (1957). Mourning and melancholia. In J. Strachey (Ed. and Trans.), *The standard edition of the complete psychological works of Sigmund Freud* (Vol. 14). London: Hogarth Press (Original work published 1917).

Freud, S. (1962). The neuro-psychoses of defence. In J. Strachey (Ed.), *The complete psychological works* (Vol. 3, pp. 45–62). London: Hogarth Press (Original work published 1894).

Freund, K., Seto, M. C., & Kuban, M. (1996). Two types of fetishism. *Behaviour Research and Therapy, 34*, 687–694.

Frick, P. J., Strauss, C. C., Lahey, B. B., & Christ, M. A. G. (1993). Behavior disorders of children. In P. B. Sutker & H. E. Adams (Eds.), *Comprehensive handbook of psychopathology* (pp. 765–789). New York: Plenum.

Friedl, M. C., & Draijer, N. (2000). Dissociative disorders in Dutch psychiatric inpatients. *American Journal of Psychiatry, 157*(6), 1012–1013.

Friedman, M., & Rosenman, R. H. (1959). Association of specific overt behavior pattern with blood and cardiovascular findings. *Journal of the American Medical Association, 169*, 1286.

Friedman, M., & Rosenman, R. H. (1974). *Type A behavior and your heart.* New York: Knopf.

Fromm-Reichmann, F. (1948). Notes on the development of treatment of schizophrenics by psychoanalytic psychotherapy. *Psychiatry, 11*, 263–273.

Frost, R. O., Sher, K. J., & Geen, T. (1986). Psychotherapy and personality characteristics of non-clinical compulsive checkers. *Behaviour Research and Therapy, 24*, 133–143.

Frost, R. O., Steketee, G., & Williams, L. (2002). Compulsive buying, compulsive hoarding, and obsessive-compulsive disorder. *Behavior Therapy, 33*, 201–214.

Fugl-Meyer, A. R., & Sjogren Fugl-Meyer, K. (1999). Sexual disabilities, problems, and satisfaction in 18–74 year old Swedes. *Scandinavian Journal of Sexology, 3*, 79–105.

Furer, P., Walker, J. R., Chartier, M., & Stein, M. B. (1997). Hypochondriacal concerns and somatization in panic disorder. *Depression and Anxiety, 6*, 78–85.

Furer, P., Walker, J. R., & Freeston, M. H. (2001). Approach to integrated cognitive-behavior therapy for intense illness worries. In G. J. G. Asmundson, S. Taylor, & B. J. Cox (Eds.), *Health anxiety: Clinical and research perspectives on hypochondriasis and related conditions* (pp. 161–192). New York: Wiley.

Fyer, A. J., Mannuzza, S., Chapman, T. F., Liebowitz, M. R., & Klein, D. F. (1993). A direct interview family study of social phobia. *Archives of General Psychiatry, 50*, 286–293.

Fyer, A. J., Mannuzza, S., Gallops, M. S., Martin, L. Y., Aaronson, C., Gorman, J. M., et al. (1990). Familial transmission of simple phobias and fears: A preliminary report. *Archives of General Psychiatry, 47*, 252–256.

Fyer, A., Liebowitz, M., Gorman, J., Compeas, R., Levin, A., Davies, S., et al. (1987). Discontinuation of alprazolam treatment in panic patients. *American Journal of Psychiatry, 144*, 303–308.

Gacono, C. B. (Ed.) (2000). *The clinical and forensic assessment of psychopathy: A practitioner's guide.* Mahwah, NJ: Erlbaum.

Gadsby, J. (2001, October 9). *Benzodiazepines: Responsible prescribing and informed use.* Retrieved August 17, 2004, from http://www.benzo.org.uk/jegres.htm.

Gagliese, L., & Katz, J. (2000). Medically unexplained pain is not caused by psychopathology. *Pain Research and Management, 5*, 251–257.

Gagnon, J. H. (1990). The explicit and implicit use of the scripting perspective in sex research. *Annual Review of Sex Research, 1*, 1–43.

Gagnon, M., & Ladouceur, R. (1992). Behavioral treatment of child stutterers: Replication and extension. *Behavior Therapy, 23*, 113–129.

Gajdusek, D. C. (1977). Unconventional viruses and the origin and disappearance of Kuru. *Science, 197*, 943.

Galambos, N. L., Barker, E. T., & Almeida, D. M. (2003). Parents do matter: Trajectories of change in externalizing and internalizing problems in early adolescence. *Child Development, 74*, 578–594.

Galambos, N. L., & Leadbeater, B. J. (2002). Transitions in adolescent research. In W. W. Hartup & R. K. Silbereisen (Eds.), *Growing Points in Developmental Science: An introduction* (pp. 287–306). Philadelphia: Psychology Press.

Gallagher-Thompson, D., & Osgood, N. J. (1997). Suicide later in life. *Behavior Therapy, 28*, 23–41.

Gallant, D. (1999). Alcohol. In M. Galanter & H. D. Kleber (Eds.), *Textbook of substance abuse treatment* (2nd ed., pp. 151–164). Washington, DC: American Psychiatric Press.

Garb, H. N., Wood, J. M., Nezworski, M. T., Grove, W. M., & Stejskal, W. J. (2001). Toward a resolution of the Rorschach controversy. *Psychological Assessment, 13*, 433–448.

Garber, S. W., Garber, M. D., & Spizman, R. F. (1996). *Beyond Ritalin: Facts about medication and other strategies for helping children, adolescents, and adults with attention deficit disorders.* New York: Villard.

Garcia, J., McGowan, B. K., & Green, K. F. (1972). Biological constraints on conditioning. In A. H. Black & W. F. Prokasy (Eds.), *Classical conditioning II: Current research and theory.* New York: Appleton-Century-Crofts.

Gardner, E. L. (1997). Brain reward mechanisms. In J. H. Lowinson, P. Ruiz, R. B. Millman, & J. G. Langrod (Eds.), *Substance abuse: A comprehensive textbook* (pp. 51–85). Baltimore: Williams & Wilkins.

Garfield, A. F., & Zigler, E. (1993). Adolescent suicide prevention: Current research and social policy implications. *American Psychologist, 48*(2), 169–182.

Garfinkel, P. E. (1992). Evidence in support of attitudes to shape and weight as a diagnostic criterion of bulimia nervosa. *International Journal of Eating Disorders, 11*(4), 321–325.

Garfinkel, P. E. (2002). Guest editorial: Eating disorders. *Canadian Journal of Psychiatry, 47*, 225–226.

Garfinkel, P. E., & Dorian, B. J. (2001). Improving understanding and care for the eating disorders. In R. H. Striegel-Moore & L. Smolak (Eds.), *Eating disorders: Innovative directions in research and practice* (pp. 9–26). Washington, DC: American Psychological Association.

Garfinkel, P. E., & Garner, D. M. (1982). *Anorexia nervosa: A multidimensional perspective.* New York: Brunner/Mazel.

Garfinkel, P. E., Kennedy, S. H., & Kaplan, A. S. (1995). Views on classification and diagnosis of eating disorders. *Canadian Journal of Psychiatry, 40*, 445–456.

Garfinkel, P. E., Lin, E., Goering P., Spegg, C., Goldbloom, D. S., Kennedy, S., et al. (1995). Bulimia nervosa in a Canadian community sample: Prevalence in comparison of subgroups. *American Journal of Psychiatry, 152*, 1052–1058.

Garfinkel, P. E., Lin, E., Goering, P., Spegg, C., Goldbloom, D. S., Kennedy, S., et al. (1996). Purging and nonpurging forms of bulimia nervosa in a community sample. *International Journal of Eating Disorders, 20*, 231–238.

Garfinkel, P. E., Moldofsky, H., & Garner, D. M. (1979). The heterogeneity of anorexia nervosa: Bulimia as a distinct subgroup. *Archives of General Psychiatry, 37*, 1036–1040.

Garland, A. F., & Zigler, E. (1993). Adolescent suicide prevention: Current research and social policy implications. *American Psychologist, 48*, 169–182.

Garlow, S. J., & Nemeroff, C. B. (2004). Neurochemistry of mood disorders: Clinical studies. In D. S. Charney & E. J. Nestler (Eds.), *The neurobiology of mental illness* (2nd ed.). New York: Oxford University Press.

Garmezy, N., & Rutter, M. (Eds.). (1983). *Stress, coping and development in children.* New York: McGraw-Hill.

Garner, D. M., & Fairburn, C. G. (1988). Relationship between anorexia nervosa and bulimia nervosa: Diagnostic implications. In D. M. Garner & P. E. Garfinkel (Eds.), *Diagnostic issues in anorexia nervosa and bulimia nervosa.* New York: Brunner/Mazel.

Garner, D. M., Fairburn, C. G., & Davis, R. (1987). Cognitive-behavioral treatment of bulimia nervosa: A critical appraisal. *Behavior Modification, 11*, 398–431.

Garner, D. M., & Garfinkel, P. E. (Eds.). (1985). *Handbook of psychotherapy for anorexia nervosa and bulimia.* New York: Guilford Press.

Garner, D. M., Garfinkel, P. E., & O'Shaughnessy, M. (1985). The validity of the distinction between bulimics with and without anorexia nervosa. *American Journal of Psychiatry, 142*, 581–587.

Garner, D. M., Garfinkel, P. E., Rockert, W., & Olmsted, M. P. (1987). A prospective study of eating disturbances in the ballet. *Psychotherapy and Psychosomatics, 48*, 170–175.

Garner, D. M., Garfinkel, P. E., Schwartz, D., & Thompson, M. (1980). Cultural expectation of thinness in women. *Psychological Reports, 47*, 483–491.

Garner, D. M., & Needleman, L. D. (1996). Step care and the decision-tree models for treating eating disorders. In J. K. Thompson (Ed.), *Body image, eating disorders and obesity* (pp. 225–252). Washington, DC: American Psychological Association.

Garner, D. M., Olmsted, M. P., & Polivy, J. (1983). Development and validation of a multidimensional Eating Disorder Inventory for anorexia nervosa and bulimia. *International Journal of Eating Disorders, 2*(2), 15–34.

Garre-Olmo, J., López-Pousa, S., Vilata-Franch, J., Turon-Estrada, A., Lozano-Gallego, M., Hernández-Ferràndiz, M., et al. (2004). Neuropsychological profile of Alzheimer's disease in women: Moderate and moderately severe cognitive decline. *Archives of Women's Mental Health, 7*, 27–36.

Gatchel, R. J., & Dersh, J. (2002). Psychological disorders and chronic pain: Are there cause-and-effect relationships? In D. C. Turk & R. J. Gatchel (Eds.), *Psychological approaches to pain management: A practitioner's handbook* (2nd ed.). New York: Guilford Press.

Gatchel, R. J., & Turk, D. C. (Eds.). (1999). *Psychosocial factors in pain: Critical perspectives.* New York: Guilford Press.

Gatz, M., & Smyer, M. A. (1992). The mental health system and older adults in the 1990s. *American Psychologist, 47*(6), 741–751.

Gawin, F. H., Kleber, H. D., Byck, R., Rounsaville, B. J., Kosten, T. R., Jatlow, P. I., et al. (1989). Desipramine facilitation of initial cocaine abstinence. *Archives of General Psychiatry, 46*, 117–121.

Gearhart, J. P. et al. (1989). Total ablation of the penis after circumcision electrocautery: A method of management and long term follow-up. *Journal of Urology, 42*, 789–801.

Geist, R., Heinmaa, M., Stephens, D., Davis, R., & Katzman, D. K. (2000). Comparison of family therapy and family group psychoeducation in adolescents with anorexia nervosa. *Canadian Journal of Psychiatry, 45*, 173–178.

Gelinas, L. (1994). The new rights of persons held in psychiatric institutions following the commission of a criminal offence: The Criminal Code revised and corrected. *Canada's Mental Health, 42*(1), 10–16.

Geller, B., Cooper, T. B., Graham, D. L., Fetner, H. M., Marsteller, F. A., & Wells,

J. M. (1992). Pharmacokinetically designed double-blind placebo-controlled study of nortriptyline in 6–12 year olds with major depressive disorder: *Journal of the American Academy of Child and Adolescent Psychiatry, 31*, 33–44.

Geller, J. (2002). Estimating readiness for change in anorexia nervosa: Comparing clients, clinicians and research assessors. *International Journal of Eating Disorders, 31*, 251–260.

George, L. K. (1984). *The burden of caregiving: Center reports of advances in research* (Vol. 8). Durham, NC: Duke University Center for the Study of Aging and Human Development.

George, M. S., Lisanby, S. H., & Sakheim, H. A. (1999). Transcranial magnetic stimulation. *Archives of General Psychiatry, 56*, 300–311.

Gerin, W., Pickering, T. G., Glynn, L., Christenfeld, N., Schwartz, A., Carroll, D., et al. (2000). An historical context for behavioral models of hypertension. *Journal of Psychosomatic Research, 48*, 369–377.

Gershon, E. S. (1990). Genetics. In F. K. Goodwin & K. R. Jamison (Eds.), *Manic-depressive illness* (pp. 373–401). New York: Oxford University Press.

Gershon, E. S., Kelsoe, J. R., Kendler, K. S., & Watson, J. D. (2001). It's time to search for susceptibility genes for major mental illnesses. *Science, 294*, 5.

Gianoulakis, C. (2001). Influence of the endogenous opioid system on high alcohol consumption and genetic predisposition to alcoholism. *Journal of Psychiatry and Neuroscience, 26*, 304–318.

Gibb, W. R. G. (1989). Dementia and Parkinson's disease. *British Journal of Psychiatry, 154*, 596–614.

Giedke, H., & Schwarzler, F. (2002). Therapeutic use of sleep deprivation in depression. *Sleep Medicine Reviews, 6*, 361–377.

Gieser, L., & Stein, M. I. (Eds.). (1999). *Evocative images: The Thematic Apperception Test and the art of projection.* Washington, DC: American Psychological Association.

Gil, K., Williams, D., Keefe, F., & Beckham, J. (1990). The relationship of negative thoughts to pain and psychological distress. *Behavior Therapy, 21*, 349–362.

Gilham, J. E., Reivich, K. J., Jaycox, L. H., & Seligman, M. E. P. (1995). Prevention of depressive symptoms in schoolchildren: Two-year follow-up. *Psychological Science, 6*(6), 343–351.

Gillberg, C. (1984). Infantile autism and other childhood psychoses in a Swedish urban region: Epidemiological aspects. *Journal of Child Psychology and Psychiatry, 25*, 35–43.

Gillies, L. (2001). Interpersonal psychotherapy for depression and other disorders. In D. H. Barlow (Ed.), *Clinical handbook of psychological disorders* (3rd ed., pp. 309–331). New York: Guilford Publications.

Gillin, J. C. (1993). Clinical sleep-wake disorders in psychiatric practice: Dyssomnias. In D. L. Dunner (Ed.), *Current psychiatric therapy* (pp. 373–380). Philadelphia: W. B. Saunders.

Gitlin, M. J., Swendsen, J., Heller, T. L., & Hammen, C. (1995). Relapse and impairment in bipolar disorder. *American Journal of Psychiatry, 152*, 1635–1640.

Gladue, B. A., Green, R., & Hellman, R. E. (1984). Neuroendocrine response to estrogen and sexual orientation. *Science, 225*, 1496–1499.

Glaser, R., Kennedy, S., Lafuse, W. P., Bonneau, R. H., Speicher, C. E., Hillhouse, J., et al. (1990). Psychological stress-induced modulation of IL-2 receptor gene expression and IL-2 production in peripheral blood leukocytes. *Archives of General Psychiatry, 47*, 707–712.

Glaser, R., Rice, J., Sheridan, J., Fertel, R., Stout, J., Speicher, C., et al. (1987). Stress-related immune suppression: Health implications. *Brain, Behavior, and Immunity, 1*, 7–20.

Glatt, A. E., Zinner, S. H., & McCormack, W. M. (1990). The prevalence of dyspareunia. *Obstetrics and Gynecology, 75*, 433–436.

Glatt, C. E., Tampilic, M., Christie, C., DeYoung, J., & Freimer, N. B. (2004). Re-screening serotonin receptors for genetic variants identifies population and molecular genetic complexity. *American Journal of Medical Genetics, 124*, 92–100.

Gleason, O. C. (2003). Delirium. *American Family Physician, 67*, 1027–1034.

Gleaves, D. H. (1996). The sociocognitive model of dissociative identity disorder: A reexamination of the evidence. *Psychological Bulletin, 120*, 42–59.

Gleaves, D. H., Lowe, M. R., Snow, A. C., Green, B. A., & Murphy-Eberenz, K. P. (2000). Continuity and discontinuity models of bulimia nervosa: A taxometric investigation. *Journal of Abnormal Psychology, 109*(1), 56–68.

Gleaves, D. H., Smith, S. M., Butler, L. D., & Spiegel, D. (2004). False and recovered memories in the laboratory and clinic: A review of experimental and clinical evidence. *Clinical Psychology: Science and Practice 11*, 3–28.

Goater, N., King, M., Cole, E. Leavey, G., Johnson-Sabine, E., Blizard, R., et al. (1999). Ethnicity and outcomes of psychosis. *British Journal of Psychiatry, 175*, 34–42.

Goering, P., Wasylenki, D., & Durbin, J. (2000). Canada's mental health system. *International Journal of Law and Psychiatry, 23*, 345–359.

Goff, D. C., & Coyle, J. T. (2001). The emerging role of glutamate in the pathophysiology and treatment of schizophrenia. *American Journal of Psychiatry, 158*, 1367–1377.

Gold, M. S. (1997). Cocaine (and crack): Clinical aspects. In J. H. Lowinson, P. Ruiz, R. B. Millman, & J. G. Langrod (Eds.), *Substance abuse: A comprehensive textbook* (pp. 181–199). Baltimore: Williams & Wilkins.

Gold, P. W., Goodwin, F. K., & Chrousos, G. P. (1988). Clinical and biochemical manifestations of depression: Relation to the neurobiology of stress. *New England Journal of Medicine, 319*, 348–353.

Goldapple, K., Segal, Z., Garson, C., Lau, M., Bieling, P., Kennedy, S., et al. (2004). Modulation of cortical-limbic pathways in major depression. *Archives of General Psychiatry, 61*, 34–41.

Goldberg, J. F., Harrow, M., & Grossman, L. S. (1995). Course and outcome in bipolar affective disorder: A longitudinal follow-up study. *American Journal of Psychiatry, 152*, 379–384.

Goldberg, J. O., & Schmidt, L. A. (2001). Shyness, sociability, and social dysfunction in schizophrenia. *Schizophrenia Research, 48*, 343–349.

Goldberg, L. (1993). The structure of phenotypic personality traits. *American Psychologist, 48*, 26–34.

Goldberg, S. C., Schultz, C., Resnick, R. J., Hamer, R. M., & Schultz, P. M. (1987). Differential prediction of response to thiothixene and placebo in borderline and schizotypal personality disorders. *Psychopharmacology Bulletin, 23*, 342–346.

Golden, C. J., Hammeke, T. A., & Purisch, A. D. (1980). *The Luria-Nebraska Battery manual.* Palo Alto, CA: Western Psychological Services.

Goldfarb, W. (1963). Self-awareness in schizophrenic children. *Archives of General Psychiatry, 8*, 63–76.

Goldman, M. S., & Rather, B. C. (1993). Substance use disorders: Cognitive models and architecture. In K. S. Dobson & P. C. Kendall (Eds.), *Psychopathology and cognition* (pp. 245–292). New York: Academic Press.

Goldman, M. S., Del Boca, F. K., & Darkes, J. (1999). Alcohol expectancy theory: The application of cognitive neuroscience. In H. Blane & K. Leonard (Eds.), *Psychological theories of drinking and alcoholism* (pp. 203–246). New York: Guilford Press.

Goldman, S. J., D'Angelo, E. J., DeMaso, D. R., & Mezzacappa, E. (1992). Physical and sexual abuse histories among children with borderline personality disorder. *American Journal of Psychiatry, 149*, 1723–1726.

Goldner, E. (1989). Treatment refusal in anorexia nervosa. *International Journal of Eating Disorders, 8*, 297–306.

Goldner, E. M., Cockell, S. J., & Srikameswaran, S. (2002). Perfectionism and eating disorders. In G. L. Flett & P. L. Hewitt (Eds.), *Perfectionism: Theory, research, and treatment* (pp. 319–340). Washington, DC: American Psychological Association.

Goldner, E. M., Geller, J., Birmingham, C. L., & Remick, R. A. (2000). Comparison of shoplifting behaviours in patients with eating disorders, psychiatric control subjects, and undergraduate control subjects. *Canadian Journal of Psychiatry, 45*, 471–475.

Goldner, E. M., Jones, W., & Waraich, P. (2003). Using administrative data to analyze the prevalence and distribution of schizophrenic disorders. *Psychiatric Services, 54*, 1017–1021.

Goldner, E. M., Srikameswaran, S., Schroeder, M. L., Livesley, W. J., & Birmingham, C. L. (1999). Dimensional assessment of personality pathology in patients with eating disorders. *Psychiatry Research, 85,* 151–159.

Goldner, V. (2003). Ironic gender/Authentic sex. *Studies in Gender and Sexuality, 4,* 113–139.

Goldstein, A. (1994). *Addiction: From biology to drug policy.* New York: W. H. Freeman.

Goldstein, B. (1994). *Psychology.* Belmont, CA, Thomson Brooks/Cole Publishing Co.

Goldstein, G. (2000). Comprehensive neuropsychological assessment batteries. In G. Goldstein & M. Hersen (Eds.), *Handbook of psychological assessment* (pp. 231–261). New York: Pergamon Press.

Goldstein, I., Lue, T. F., Padma-Nathan, H., Rosen, R. C., Steers, W. D., & Wicker, P. A., for the Sildenafil Study Group. (1998). Oral sildenafil in the treatment of erectile dysfunction. *New England Journal of Medicine, 338,* 1397–1404.

Goldstein, J. M., & Lewine, R. R. J. (2000). Overview of sex differences in schizophrenia: Where have we been and where do we go from here? In D. J. Castle, J. McGrath, & J. Kulkarni (Eds.), *Women and schizophrenia* (pp. 111–143). Cambridge: Cambridge University Press.

Gonzalez-Lavin, A., & Smolak, L. (1995, March). *Relationships between television and eating problems in middle school girls.* Paper presented at the meeting of the Society for Research in Child Development, Indianapolis, IN.

Good, B. J., & Kleinman, A. M. (1985). Culture and anxiety: Cross-cultural evidence for the patterning of anxiety disorders. In A. H. Tuma & J. D. Maser (Eds.), *Anxiety and the anxiety disorders.* Hillsdale, NJ: Erlbaum.

Good, K. P., Kiss, I., Buiteman, C., Woodley, H., Rui, Q., Whitehorn, D., et al. (2002). Improvement in cognitive functioning in patients with first-episode psychosis during treatment with quetiapine: An interim analysis. *British Journal of Psychiatry, 181* (Suppl. 43), 45–49.

Goodkin, K., Baldewicz, T. T., Asthana, D., Khamis, I., Blaney, N. T., Kumar, M., et al. (2001). A bereavement support group intervention affects plasma burden of human immunodeficiency virus type 1. Report of a randomized controlled trial. *Journal of Human Virology, 4,* 44–54.

Goodman, J. T. (2000). Three decades of professional psychology: Reflections and future challenges. *Canadian Psychology, 41,* 25–33.

Goodman, S. H., & Gotlib, I. H. (1999). Risk for psychopathology in the children of depressed mothers: A developmental model for understanding mechanisms of transmission. *Psychological Review, 106*(3), 458–490.

Goodwin, D. W., & Gabrielli, W. F. (1997). Alcohol: Clinical aspects. In J. H. Lowinson, P. Ruiz, R. B. Millman, & J. G. Langrod (Eds.), *Substance abuse: A comprehensive textbook* (pp. 142–148). Baltimore: Williams & Wilkins.

Goodwin, D. W., & Guze, S. B. (1984). *Psychiatric diagnosis* (3rd ed.). New York: Oxford University Press.

Goodwin, F. K. Fireman, B., Simon G. E., Hunkeler, E. M. Lee, J., & Revicki, D. (2003). Suicide risk in bipolar disorder during treatment with lithium and divalproex. *Journal of the American Medical Association, 290,* 1467–1473.

Goodwin, F. K., & Ghaemi, S. N. (1998). Understanding manic-depressive illness. *Archives of General Psychiatry, 55*(1), 23–25.

Goodwin, F. K., & Jamison, K. R. (1990). *Manic depressive illness.* New York: Oxford University Press.

Goodwin, P. J., Leszcz, M., Ennis, M., Koopmans, J., Vincent, L., Guther, H., et al. (2001). The effect of group psychosocial support on survival in metastatic breast cancer. *New England Journal of Medicine, 345,* 1719–1726.

Gordis, E. (2000a). Latest approaches to preventing alcohol abuse and alcoholism. *Alcohol Research and Health, 24*(1), 42–51.

Gordis, E. (2000b). Research refines alcohol treatment options. *Alcohol Research and Health, 24*(1) 53–61.

Gordis, E. (2000c). Why do some people drink too much? The role of genetic and psychosocial influences. *Alcohol Research and Health, 24*(1), 17–26.

Gorenstein, E. E., & Newman, J. P. (1980). Disinhibitory psychopathology: A new perspective and a model for research. *Psychological Review, 87,* 301–315.

Gotlib, I. H., & Abramson, L. Y. (1999). Atributional theories of emotion. In T. Dagleish & M. J. Power (Eds.), *Handbook of cognition and emotion.* Chichester, UK: John Wiley.

Gotlib, I. H., & Beach, S. R. H. (1995). A marital/family discord model of depression: Implications for therapeutic intervention. In N. S. Jacobson & A. S. Gurman (Eds.), *Clinical handbook of couple therapy* (pp. 411–436). New York: Guilford Press.

Gotlib, I. H., & Krasnoperova, E. (1998). Biased information processing as a vulnerability factor for depression. *Behavior Therapy, 29,* 603–617.

Gotlib, I. H., Kurtzman, H. S., & Blehar, M. C (1997). Cognition and depression: Issues and future directions. *Cognition and Emotion, 11,* 663–673.

Gotlib, I. H., & MacLeod, C. (1997). Information processing in anxiety and depression: A cognitive-developmental perspective. In J. Burack & J. Enns (Eds.), *Attention, development, and psychopathology* (pp. 350–378). New York: Guilford Press.

Gotlib, I. H., & Nolan, S. A. (2001). Depression. In A. S. Bellack & M. Hersen (Eds.), *Psychopathology in adulthood* (2nd ed.). Boston: Allyn & Bacon.

Gotlib, I. H., Ranganath, C., & Rosenfeld, J. P. (1998). Frontal EEG alpha asymmetry, depression, and cognitive functioning. *Cognition and Emotion, 12,* 449–478.

Gotlib, I. H., Roberts, J. E., & Gilboa, E. (1996). Cognitive interference in depression. In I. G. Sarason, G. R. Pierce, & B. R. Sarason (Eds.), *Cognitive interference: Theories, methods, and findings* (pp. 347–377). Mahwah, NJ: Erlbaum.

Gotlib, I. H., Whiffen, V. E., Wallace, P. M., & Mount, J. H. (1991). Prospective investigation of postpartum depression: Factors involved in onset and recovery. *Journal of Abnormal Psychology, 100*(2), 122–132.

Gotowiec, A., & Beiser, M. (1993–1994). Aboriginal children's mental health: Unique challenges. *Canada's Mental Health, 41*(4), 7–11.

Gottesman, I. I. (1991). *Schizophrenia genesis: The origins of madness.* New York: W. H. Freeman.

Gottesman, I. I. (1997). Twins: En route to QTLs for cognition. *Science, 276,* 1522–1523.

Gottesman, I. I., & Bertelsen, A. (1989). Dual mating studies in psychiatry—Offspring of inpatients with examples from reactive (psychogenic) psychoses. *International Review of Psychiatry, 1,* 287–296.

Gottlieb, B. H., & Johnson, J. (2000). Respite programs for caregivers of persons with dementia: A review with practice implications. *Aging and Mental Health, 4,* 119–129.

Gottlieb, G. (1998). Normally occurring environmental and behavioral influences on gene activity: From central dogma to probabilistic epigenesis. *Psychological Review, 105,* 492–802.

Gould, M. S. (1990). Suicide clusters and media exposure. In S. J. Blumenthal & D. J. Kupfer (Eds.), *Suicide over the life cycle: Risk factors, assessment and treatment of suicidal patients.* Washington, DC: American Psychiatric Press.

Gould, R. A., Buckminster, S., Pollack, M. H., Otto, M. W., & Yap, L. (1997). Cognitive-behavioral and pharmacological treatment for social phobia: A meta-analysis. *Clinical Psychology: Science and Practice, 4,* 291–306.

Gould, R. A., Otto, M. W., Pollack, M. H., & Yap, L. (1997). Cognitive behavioral and pharmacological treatment of generalized anxiety disorder: A preliminary meta-analysis. *Behavior Therapy, 28,* 285–305.

Gould, S. J. (1991). *Bully for brontosaurus: Reflections in natural history.* New York: W. W. Norton.

Grabe, H. J., Meyer, C., Hapke, U., Rumpf, H. J., Freyberger, H. J., Dilling, H., et al. (2003). Somatoform pain disorder in the general population. *Psychotherapy and Psychosomatics, 72,* 88–94.

Graeff, F. G. (1987). The anti-aversive action of drugs. In T. Thompson, P. B. Dews, & J. Barrett (Eds.), *Advances in behavioral pharmacology* (Vol. 6). Hillside, NJ: Erlbaum.

Graeff, F. G. (1993). Role of 5HT in defensive behavior and anxiety. *Review in the Neurosciences, 4,* 181–211.

Graf, P., Squire, L. R., & Mandler, G. (1984). The information that amnesic patients do not forget. *Journal of Experimental Psychology: Learning, Memory, and Cognition, 10,* 164–178.

Grandy, T. (1995). New occupational hazards of career addicts: Main Line Intravenous Needs Assessment (MINA). Document prepared by Main Line Needle Exchange with funding from Health Canada.

Grant, A. (1996). *No end of grief: Indian residential schools in Canada.* Winnipeg, MB: Pemmican.

Grant, B. F., & Dawson, D. A. (1999). Alcohol and drug use, abuse, and dependence: Classification, prevalence, and comorbidity. In B. S. McCrady & E. E. Epstein (Eds.), *Addictions: A comprehensive guidebook* (pp. 9–29). New York: Oxford University Press.

Grant, I., Patterson, T. L., & Yager, J. (1988). Social supports in relation to physical health and symptoms of depression in the elderly. *American Journal of Psychiatry, 145*(10), 1254–1258.

Gratzer, T. G., & Matas, M. (1994). The right to refuse treatment: Recent Canadian developments. *Bulletin of the American Academy of Psychiatry and the Law, 22,* 249–256.

Gray, J. A. (1982). *The neuropsychology of anxiety.* New York: Oxford University Press.

Gray, J. A. (1985). Issues in the neuropsychology of anxiety. In A. H. Tuma & J. D. Maser (Eds.), *Anxiety and the anxiety disorders* (pp. 5–25). Hillside, NJ: Erlbaum.

Gray, J. A. (1987). *The psychology of fear and stress* (2nd ed.). New York: Cambridge University Press.

Gray, J. A., & Buffery, A. W. H. (1971). Sex differences in emotional and cognitive behavior in mammals including man: Adaptive and neural bases. *Acta Psychologica, 35,* 89–111.

Gray, J. A., & McNaughton, N. (1996). The neuropsychology of anxiety: Reprise. In D. A. Hope (Ed.), *Perspectives on anxiety, panic and fear* (The 43rd Annual Nebraska Symposium on Motivation) (pp. 61–134). Lincoln: Nebraska University Press.

Graziottin, A., & Brotto, L. A. (2004). Vulvar vestibulitis syndrome: A clinical approach. *Journal of Sex and Marital Therapy, 30,* 125–139.

Grazzi, L., Andrasik, F., D'Amico, D., Leone, M., Usai, S., Kass, S. J., et al. (2002). Behavioral and pharmacologic treatment of transformed migraine with analgesic overuse: Outcome at 3 years. *Headache, 42,* 483–490.

Grcevich, S., Rowane, W. A., Marcellino, B., & Sullivan-Hurst, S. (2001). Retrospective comparison of Adderall and methylphenidate in the treatment of attention deficit hyperactivity disorder. *Journal of Child and Adolescent Psychopharmacology, 11*(1), 35–41.

Greden, J. F., & Walters, A. (1997). Caffeine. In J. H. Lowinson, P. Ruiz, R. B. Millman, & J. G. Langrod (Eds.), *Substance abuse: A comprehensive textbook* (pp. 294–307). Baltimore: Williams & Wilkins.

Green, B. L., Grace, M. C., Lindy, J. D., Titchener, J. L., & Lindy, J. G. (1983). Levels of functional impairment following a civilian disaster: The Beverly Hills Supper Club fire. *Journal of Consulting and Clinical Psychology, 51,* 573–580.

Green, R. (1987). *The "sissy boy syndrome" and the development of homosexuality.* New Haven: Yale University Press.

Green, R., & Money, J. (1969). *Transsexualism and sex reassignment.* Baltimore: Johns Hopkins Press.

Greenberg, A. H. (1994). The origins of the NK cell, or a Canadian in King Ivan's court. *Clinical and Investigative Medicine, 17,* 626–631.

Greenberg, L. S., & Paivio, S. C. (1997). *Working with emotions in psychotherapy.* New York: Guilford Press.

Greenberg, L. S., Watson, J. C., & Lietaer, G. (Eds.). (1998). *Handbook of experiential psychotherapy.* New York: Guilford Press.

Greenberg, M. S., & Beck, A. T. (1989). Depression versus anxiety: A test of the content specificity. *Journal of Abnormal Psychology, 98*(1), 9–13.

Greene, R. W., & Ollendick, T. H. (2000). Behavioral assessment of children. In G. Goldstein & M. Hersen (Eds.), *Handbook of psychological assessment* (pp. 453–470). New York: Pergamon Press.

Greenough, W. T., Withers, G. S., & Wallace, C. S. (1990). Morphological changes in the nervous system arising from behavioral experience: What is the evidence that they are involved in learning and memory? In L. R. Squire & E. Lindenlaub (Eds.), *The biology of memory, Symposia Medica Hoescht 23* (pp. 159–183). Stuttgart/New York: Schattauer Verlag.

Greer, S. (1999). Mind-body research in psychoncology. *Advances in Mind-Body Medicine, 15,* 236–244.

Gregoire, A. (1992). New treatments for erectile impotence. *British Journal of Psychiatry, 160,* 315–326.

Greist, J. H. (1990). Treatment of obsessive compulsive disorder: Psychotherapies, drugs, and other somatic treatments. *Journal of Clinical Psychiatry, 51,* 44–50.

Grenier, G., & Byers, E. S. (2001). Operationalizing premature or rapid ejaculation. *Journal of Sex Research, 38,* 369–378.

Griffin, J. (1989). *In search of sanity: A chronicle of the Canadian Mental Health Association, 1918–1988.* London, ON: Third Eye Publications.

Griffith, E. E. H., English, T., & Mayfield, U. (1980). Possession, prayer and testimony: Therapeutic aspects of the Wednesday night meeting in a Black church. *Psychiatry, 43*(5), 120–128.

Grilo, C. M., Masheb, R. M., & Wilson, G. T. (2001). Subtyping binge eating disorder. *Journal of Consulting and Clinical Psychology, 69,* 1066–1072.

Grinspoon, L., & Bakalar, J. B. (1997). Marijuana. In J. H. Lowinson, P. Ruiz, R. B. Millman, & J. G. Langrod (Eds.), *Substance abuse: A comprehensive textbook* (pp. 199–206). Baltimore: Williams & Wilkins.

Grissom, R. J., & Kim, J. J. (2001). Review of assumptions and problems in the appropriate conceptualization of effect size. *Psychological Methods, 6,* 135–146.

Grob, C. S., & Poland, R. E. (1997). MDMA. In J. H. Lowinson, P. Ruiz, R. B. Millman, & J. G. Langrod (Eds.), *Substance abuse: A comprehensive textbook* (pp. 269–275). Baltimore: Williams & Wilkins.

Groopman, L. C., & Cooper, A. M. (2001). Narcissistic personality disorder. In G. O. Gabbard (Ed.), *Treatment of psychiatric disorders* (Vol. 2) (3rd ed.) (pp. 2309–2326). Washington, DC: American Psychiatric Press.

Gross, J. J. (1999). Emotion and emotion regulation. In L. A. Pervin & O. P. John (Eds.), *Handbook of personality: Theory and research* (2nd ed., pp. 525–552). New York: Guilford Press.

Gross, J. J., & John, O. P. (2003). Individual differences in two emotion regulation processes: Implications for affect, relationships, and well-being. *Journal of Personality and Social Psychology, 85,* 348–362.

Gross, J. J., & Muñoz, R. F. (1995). Emotion regulation and mental health. *Clinical Psychology: Science and Practice, 2,* 151–164.

Gross, J., & Rosen, J. C. (1988). Bulimia in adolescents: Prevalence and psychosocial correlates. *International Journal of Eating Disorders, 7,* 51–61.

Gross-Tsur, V., Manor, O., & Shalev, R. S. (1996). Developmental dyscalcula: Prevalence and demographic features. *Developmental Medicine and Child Neurology, 38,* 25–33.

Grosz, H. J., & Zimmerman, J. (1965). Experimental analysis of hysterical blindness: A follow-up report and new experimental data. *Archives of General Psychiatry, 13,* 255–260.

Grosz, H. J., & Zimmerman, J. (1970). A second detailed case study of functional blindness: Further demonstration of the contribution of objective psychological laboratory data. *Behavior Therapy, 1,* 115–123.

Grove, W. M., & Tellegen, A. (1991). Problems in the classification of personality disorders. *Journal of Personality Disorders, 5,* 31–42.

Gruber, R., Sadeh, A., & Raviv, A. (2000). Instability of sleep patterns in children with attention-deficit/hyperactivity disorder. *Journal of the American Academy of Child and Adolescent Psychiatry, 39,* 495–501.

Gruder, C. L., Mermelstein, R. J., Kirkendol, S., Hedeker, D., Wong, S. C., Schreckengost, J., et al. (1993). Effects of social support and relapse prevention training as adjuncts to a televised smoking-cessation intervention. *Journal of Consulting and Clinical Psychology, 61,* 113–120.

Grunhaus, L., Schreiber, S., Dolberg, O. T., Polak, D., & Dannon, P. N. (2003). A randomized controlled comparison of electroconvulsive therapy and repetitive transcranial magnetic stimulation in severe and resistant nonpsychotic major depression. *Biological Psychiatry, 53,* 324–331.

Guilleminault, C., & Anagnos, A. (2000). Narcolepsy. In M. H. Kryger, T. Roth, and W. C. Dement (Eds.), *Principles and practice of sleep medicine* (3rd ed., pp. 676–686). Philadelphia: W. B. Saunders.

Guilleminault, C., & Dement, W. C. (1988). Sleep apnea syndromes and related sleep disorders. In R. L. Williams, I. Karacan, & C. A. Moore (Eds.), *Sleep disorders:*

*Diagnosis and treatment* (pp. 47–71). New York: John Wiley.

Guilleminault, C., & Pelayo, R. (2000). Idiopathic central nervous system hypersomnia. In M. H. Kryger, T. Roth, and W. C. Dement (Eds.), *Principles and practice of sleep medicine* (3rd ed., pp. 687–692). Philadelphia: W. B. Saunders.

Gündel, H., O'Connor, M. F., Littrell, L., Fort, C., & Lane, R. D. (2003). Functional neuroanatomy of grief: An FMRI study. *The American Journal of Psychiatry, 160,* 1946–1953.

Gunderson, J. G. (1992). Diagnostic controversies. In A. Tasman & M. B. Riba (Eds.), *Review of psychiatry* (Vol. 11, pp. 9–24). Washington, DC: American Psychiatric Press.

Gunderson, J. G. (2001). *Borderline personality disorder: A clinical guide.* Washington, DC: American Psychiatric Press.

Gunderson, J. G., & Links, P. S. (2001). Borderline personality disorder. In G. O. Gabbard (Ed.), *Treatment of psychiatric disorders* (Vol. 2) (3rd ed.) (pp. 2273–2291). Washington, DC: American Psychiatric Publishing.

Gunderson, J. G., Ronningstam, E., & Smith, L. E. (1991). Narcissistic personality disorder: A review of data on DSM-III-R descriptions. *Journal of Personality Disorders, 5,* 167–177.

Gunderson, J. G., Ronningstam, E., & Smith, L. E. (1995). Narcissistic personality disorder. In W. J. Livesley (Ed.), *The DSM-IV personality disorders* (pp. 201–212). New York: Guilford Press.

Gunderson, J. G., & Sabo, A. N. (1993). The phenomenological and conceptual interface between borderline personality disorder and PTSD. *American Journal of Psychiatry, 150,* 19–27.

Gupta, M. A., Chaturvedi, S. K., Chandarana, P. C., & Johnson, A. M. (2001). Weight-related body image concerns among 18–24-year-old women in Canada and India: An empirical comparative study. *Journal of Psychosomatic Research, 50,* 193–198.

Gur, R. E., & Pearlson, G. D. (1993). Neuroimaging in schizophrenia research. *Schizophrenia Bulletin, 19,* 337–353.

Guralnik, O., Schmeidler, J., & Simeon, D. (2000). Feeling unreal: Cognitive processes in depersonalization. *American Journal of Psychiatry, 157*(1), 103–109.

Gureje, O., Simon, G. E., Ustun, T. B., & Goldberg, D. P. (1997). Somatization in cross-cultural perspective: A World Health Organization study in primary care. *American Journal of Psychiatry, 154,* 989–995.

Gurvits, T. V., Shenton, M. E., Hokama, H., Ohta, H., Lasko, N. B., Gilbertson, M. W., et al. (1996). Magnetic resonance imaging study of hippocampal volume in chronic, combat-related posttraumatic stress disorder. *Biological Psychiatry, 40,* 1091–1099.

Gusella, J., Butler, G., Nichols, L., & Bird, D. (2003). A brief questionnaire to assess readiness to change in adolescents with eating disorders: Its application to group therapy. *European Eating Disorders Review, 11,* 58–71.

Gusella, J. F., Wexler, N. S., Conneally, P. M., Naylor, S. L., Anderson, M. A., Tanzi, R. E., et al. (1983). A polymorphic DNA marker genetically linked to Huntington's disease. *Nature, 306,* 234–239.

Guttmacher, M. S., & Weihofen, H. (1952). *Psychiatry and the law.* New York: Norton.

Guydish, J., Sorensen, J. L., Chan, M., Werdegar, D., & Acampora, A. (1999). A randomized trial comparing day and residential drug abuse treatment: 18-month outcomes. *Journal of Consulting and Clinical Psychology, 67*(3), 428–434.

Guyton, A. (1981). *Textbook of medical physiology.* Philadelphia: W. B. Saunders.

Guze, S. B., Cloninger, C. R., Martin, R. L., & Clayton, P. J. (1986). A follow-up and family study of Briquet's syndrome. *British Journal of Psychiatry, 149,* 17–23.

Haas, A. P., & Hendin, H. (1987). The meaning of chronic marijuana use among adults: A psychosocial perspective. *Journal of Drug Issues, 17,* 333–348.

Hackett, T. P., & Cassem, N. H. (1973). Psychological adaptation to convalescence in myocardial infarction patients. In J. P. Naughton, H. K. Hellerstein, & I. C. Mohler (Eds.), *Exercise testing and exercise training in coronary heart disease.* New York: Academic Press.

Haenen, M. A., de Jong, P. J., Schmidt, A. J. M., Stevens, S. & Visser, L. (2000). Hypochondriacs' estimation of negative outcomes: Domain-specificity and responsiveness to reassuring and alarming information. *Behaviour Research and Therapy, 38,* 819–833.

Hagnell, O., Franck, A., Grasbeck, A., Ohman, R., Ojesjo, L., Otterbeck, L., et al. (1992). Vascular dementia in the Lundby study: I. A prospective, epidemiological study of incidence and risk from 1957 to 1972. *Neuropsychobiology, 26,* 43–49.

Haig-Brown, C. (1988). *Resistance and Renewal: Surviving the Indian Residential School.* Vancouver, BC: Tillacum Library.

Hall, D. E., Eubanks, L., Meyyazhagan, S., Kenney, R. D., & Johnson, S. C. (2000). Evaluation of covert video surveillance in the diagnosis of Munchausen syndrome by proxy: Lessons from 41 cases. *Pediatrics, 6,* 1305–1312.

Hall, S. M., Muñoz, R. F., Reus, V. I., & Sees, K. L. (1993). Nicotine, negative affect, and depression. *Journal of Consulting and Clinical Psychology, 61,* 761–767.

Hall, S. M., Muñoz, R. F., Reus, V. I., Sees, K. L., Duncan, C., Humfleet, G. L., et al. (1996). Mood management and nicotine gum in smoking treatment: A therapeutic contact and placebo-controlled study. *Journal of Consulting and Clinical Psychology, 64,* 1003–1009.

Halsey, N. A., & Hyman, S. L. (2001). Measles-mumps-rubella vaccine and autistic spectrum disorder: Report from the new challenges in childhood immunizations conference convened in Oak Brook, Illinois, June 12–13, 2000. *Pediatrics, 107*(5), E84.

Hamer, D. H., Hu, S., Magnuson, V. L., Hu, N., & Pattatucci, A. M. (1993). A linkage between DNA markers on the X chromosome and male sexual orientation. *Science, 261,* 321–327.

Hamilton, D. A., Kodituwakku, P., Sutherland, R. J., & Savage, D. D. (2003). Children with Fetal Alcohol Syndrome are impaired at place learning but not cued-navigation in a virtual Morris water task. *Behavioural Brain Research, 143*(1), 85–94.

Hammen, C., & Brennan, P. A. (2001). Depressed adolescents of depressed and nondepressed mothers: Tests of an interpersonal impairment hypothesis. *Journal of Consulting and Clinical Psychology, 69,* 284–294.

Hammen, C., Burge, D., Burney, E., & Adrian, C. (1990). Longitudinal study of diagnoses in children of women with unipolar and bipolar affective disorder. *Archives of General Psychiatry, 47*(12), 1112–1117.

Hammen, C., Marks, T., Mayol, A., & DeMayo, R. (1985). Depressive self-schemas, life stress, and vulnerability to depression. *Journal of Abnormal Psychology, 94,* 308–319.

Hankin, B. L., & Abramson, L. Y. (2001). Development of gender differences in depression: An elaborated cognitive vulnerability-transactional stress theory. *Psychological Bulletin, 127,* 773–796.

Hankin, B. L., Abramson, L. Y. Moffitt, T. E., Silva, P. A., McGee, R., & Angell, K. E. (1998). Development of depression from preadolescence to young adulthood: Emerging gender differences in a 10-year longitudinal study. *Journal Abnormal Psychology, 107,* 128–140.

Hankins, C. (1997). Recognizing and countering the psychological and economic impact of HIV on women in developing countries. In J. Catalan & L. Sherr (Eds.), *Impact of AIDS: Psychological and social aspects of HIV infection* (pp. 127–135). Amsterdam: Harwood Academic Publishers.

Hanley, I. (1986). Reality orientation in the care of the elderly patient with dementia—Three case studies. In I. Hanley & M. Gilhooly (Eds.), *Psychological therapies for the elderly* (pp. 65–79). New York: New York University Press.

Hanley, I. G., & Lusty, K. (1984). Memory aids in reality orientation: A single-case study. *Behavior Research and Therapy, 22,* 709–712.

Hanna, G. L. (1995). Demographic and clinical features of obsessive-compulsive disorder in children and adolescents. *Journal of the American Academy of Child and Adolescent Psychiatry, 34,* 19–27.

Hanna, L. (2001). *Deinstitutionalization in Canada of the chronically mentally ill: Women as primary family caregivers and the governance of madness.* Retrieved November 6, 2003, from International Academy of Law and Mental Health Web site: http://www.ialmh.org/Montreal2001/sessions/governance_of_madness.htm.

Hans, S. L., & Marcus, J. (1991). Neurobehavioral development of infants at risk for schizophrenia: A review. In E. F. Walker (Ed.), *Schizophrenia: A life-course developmental perspective* (pp. 33–57). New York: Academic Press.

Hans, V. P. (1986). An analysis of public attitudes toward the insanity defense. *Criminology, 4,* 393–415.

Harbert, T. L., Barlow, D. H., Hersen, M., & Austin, J. B. (1974). Measurement and modification of incestuous behavior: A case study. *Psychological Reports, 34,* 79–86.

Hardy-Bayle, M. C., Sarfati, Y., & Passerieux, C. (2003). The cognitive basis of disorganization symptomatology in schizophrenia and its clinical correlates: Toward a pathogenetic approach to disorganization. *Schizophrenia Bulletin, 29,* 459–471.

Hare, R. D. (1970). *Psychopathy: Theory and research.* New York: John Wiley.

Hare, R. D. (1983). Diagnosis of antisocial personality disorder in two prison populations. *American Journal of Psychiatry, 140,* 887–890.

Hare, R. D. (1991). *Manual for the Revised Psychopathy Checklist.* Toronto: Multi-Health Systems.

Hare, R. D. (1993). *Without conscience: The disturbing world of the psychopaths among us.* New York: Pocket Books.

Hare, R. D. (1999). Psychopathy as a risk factor for violence. *Psychiatric Quarterly, 70,* 181–197.

Hare, R. D., Forth, A. E., & Hart, S. D. (1989). The psychopath as prototype for pathological lying and deception. In J. C. Yuille (Ed.), *Credibility assessment* (pp. 25–49). New York: Kluwer Academic/Plenum.

Hare, R. D., Forth, A. E., & Strachan, K. E. (1992). Psychopathy and crime across the life span. In R. D. Peters & R. J. McMahon (Eds.), *Aggression and violence throughout the life span* (pp. 285–300). Thousand Oaks, CA: Sage.

Hare, R. D., McPherson, L. M., & Forth, A. E. (1988). Male psychopaths and their criminal careers. *Journal of Consulting and Clinical Psychology, 56,* 710–714.

Hargrave, C. (1999). Homelessness in Canada: From housing to shelters to blankets. *Share International.* Retrieved February 14, 2004, from http://www .shareintl.org/archives/homelessness/ hl-ch_Canada.htm.

Hariri, A. R., Mattay, V. S., Tessitore, A., Kolachana, B., Fera, F., Goldman, D., et al. (2002). Serotonin transporter genetic variation and the response of the human amygdala. *Science, 297,* 400–402.

Harpur, T. J., Hare, R. D., & Hakstian, A. R. (1989). Two-factor conceptualization of psychopathy: Construct validity and assessment implications. *Psychological Assessment: 1,* 6–17.

Harrington, C. (2003). Great falls residents caught up in Heatherington story. *C-News,* May 8, 2003. Retrieved at http:// cnews.canoe.ca/CNEWS/Canada/2003/ 05/08/2654-cp.html.

Harris, E. C., & Barraclough, B. (1998). Excess mortality of mental disorder. *British Journal of Psychiatry, 173,* 11–53.

Harrist, A. W., & Ainslie, R. C. (1998). Marital discord and child behavior problems: Parent-child relationship quality and child interpersonal awareness as mediators. *Journal of Family Issues, 19,* 140–163.

Harrow, M., Sands, J. R., Silverstein, M. L., & Goldberg, J. F. (1997). Course and outcome for schizophrenia versus other psychotic patients: A longitudinal study. *Schizophrenia Bulletin, 23,* 287–303.

Hart, E. L., Lahey, B. B., Loeber, R., Applegate, B., & Frick, P. J. (1995). Developmental change in attention-deficit hyperactivity disorder in boys: A four-year longitudinal study. *Journal of Abnormal Child Psychology, 23,* 729–749.

Hart, S. D., Forth, A. E., & Hare, R. D. (1990). Performance of criminal psychopaths on selected neuropsychological tests. *Journal of Abnormal Psychology, 99,* 374–379.

Harvey, A. G., & Bryant, R. A. (1998). The relationship between acute stress disorder and posttraumatic stress disorder: A prospective evaluation of motor vehicle accident survivors. *Journal of Consulting and Clinical Psychology, 66,* 507–512.

Hathaway, S. R., & McKinley, J. C. (1943). *Manual for the Minnesota Multiphasic Personality Inventory.* New York: Psychological Corporation.

Hatsukami, D. K., Grillo, M., Boyle, R., Allen, S., Jensen, J., Bliss, R., et al. (2000). Treatment of spit tobacco users with transdermal nicotine system and mint snuff. *Journal of Consultling and Clinical Psychology, 68*(2), 241–249.

Hauri, P. J. (1991). Sleep hygiene, relaxation therapy, and cognitive interventions. In P. J. Hauri (Ed.), *Case studies in insomnia* (pp. 65–84). New York: Plenum Medical Books Company.

Hawkins, R. P. (1979). The functions of assessment: Implications for selection and development of devices for assessing repertoires in clinical, educational, and other settings. *Journal of Applied Behavior Analysis, 12,* 501–516.

Hawton, K. (1995). Treatment of sexual dysfunctions of sex therapy and other approaches. *British Journal of Psychiatry, 167,* 307–314.

Hawton, K., Houston, K., Haw, C., Townsend, E., & Harriss, L. (2003). Comorbidity of axis I and axis II disorders in patients who attempted suicide. *American Journal of Psychiatry, 160,* 1494–1500.

Hay, P., & Fairburn, C. (1998). The validity of the DSM-IV scheme for classifying bulimic eating disorders. *International Journal of Eating Disorders, 23,* 7–15.

Hay, P. J., & Hall, A. (1991). The prevalence of eating disorders in recently admitted psychiatric in-patients. *British Journal of Psychiatry, 159,* 562–565.

Hayes, S. C., Barlow, D. H., & Nelson-Gray, R. O. (1999). *The scientist-practitioner: Research and accountability in the age of managed care* (2nd ed.). Boston: Allyn & Bacon.

Haynes, S. G., Feinleib, M., & Kannel, W. B. (1980). The relationship of psychosocial factors to coronary heart disease in the Framingham study: III. Eight-year incidence of coronary heart disease. *American Journal of Epidemiology, 111,* 37–58.

Haynes, S. G., & Matthews, K. A. (1988). Area review: Coronary-prone behavior: Continuing evolution of the concept: Review and methodologic critique of recent studies on type A behavior and cardiovascular disease. *Annals of Behavioral Medicine, 10*(2), 47–59.

Haynes, S. N. (2000). Behavioral assessment of adults. In G. Goldstein & M. Hersen (Eds.), *Handbook of psychological assessment* (pp. 471–502). New York: Pergamon Press.

Hayward, G., Killen, J. D., Hammer, L. D., Litt, I. F., Wilson, D. M., Simmonds, B., et al. (1992). Pubertal stage and panic attack history in sixth- and seventh-grade girls. *American Journal of Psychiatry, 149,* 1239–1243.

Hazell P., O'Connell D., Heathcote D., Robertson J., & Henry D. (1995). Efficacy of tricyclic drugs in treating child and adolescent depression: A meta-analysis. *British Medical Journal, 8,* 897–901.

Health Canada. (1999). *New report highlights HIV prevention for youth.* News release #1999-94. Retrieved May 14, 2004, from http://www.hc-sc.gc.ca/english/ media/releases/1999/99_94e.htm.

Health Canada. (2000a). *Risk of important drug interactions between St. John's Wort and other prescription drugs.* Retrieved July 13, 2003, from http://www.hc-sc .gc.ca/hpfb-dgpsa/tpd-dpt/st_johns_ wort_e.html.

Health Canada. (2000b). *Leading causes of death and hospitalization in Canada.* Ottawa, ON: Population and Public Health Branch.

Health Canada. (2002). *HIV and AIDS in Canada: Surveillance report to June 30, 2002.* Ottawa, ON. Population and Public Health Branch: Division of HIV/AIDS Epidemiology and Surveillance, Centre for Infectious Disease Prevention and Control.

Heatherton, T. F., & Baumeister, R. F. (1991). Binge eating as escape from self-awareness. *Psychological Bulletin, 110,* 86–108.

Heaton, R. K., Velin, R. A., McCutchan, A., Gulevich, S. J., Atkinson, J. H., Waalace, M. R., et al. (1994). Neuropsychological impairment in human immunodeficiency virus-infection: Implications for employment. *Psychosomatic Medicine, 56,* 8–17.

Heim, C., & Nemeroff, C. B. (1999). The impact of early adverse experiences on brain systems involved in the pathophysiology of anxiety and affective disorders. *Biological Psychiatry, 46*(11), 1509–1522.

Heiman, J. R. (2000). Orgasmic disorders in women. In S. R. Leiblum & R. C. Rosen (Eds.), *Principles and practice of sex therapy* (3rd ed., pp. 118–153). New York: Guilford Press.

Heiman, J. R., & LoPiccolo, J. (1983). Clinical outcome of sex therapy: Effects of daily versus weekly treatment. *Archives of General Psychiatry, 40,* 443–449.

Heiman, J. R., & LoPiccolo, J. (1988). *Becoming orgasmic: A sexual and personal growth program for women* (rev. ed.). New York: Prentice Hall.

Heiman, J. R., & Meston, C. M. (1997). Empirically validated treatment for sexual dysfunction. *Annual Review of Sex Research, 8,* 148–195.

Heimberg, R. G., Dodge, C. S., Hope, D. A., Kennedy, C. R., Zollo, L., & Becker, R. E.

(1990). Cognitive behavioral group treatment for social phobia: Comparison to a credible placebo control. *Cognitive Therapy and Research, 14,* 1–23.

Heimberg, R. G., Klosko, J. S., Dodge, C. S., & Shadick, R. (1989). Anxiety disorders, depression and attributional style: A further test of the specificity of depressive attributions. *Cognitive Therapy and Research, 13*(1), 21–36.

Heimberg, R. G., Liebowitz, M. R., Hope, D. A., Schneier, F. R., Holt, C. S., Welkowitz, L. A., et al. (1998). Cognitive behavioral group therapy vs. phenelzine therapy for social phobia. *Archives of General Psychiatry, 55,* 1133–1141.

Heimberg, R. G., Salzman, D. G., Holt, C. S., & Blendell, K. A. (1993). Cognitive-behavioral group treatment for social phobia: Effectiveness at five-year follow-up. *Cognitive Therapy and Research, 17,* 325–339.

Heinrichs, R. W. (1993). Schizophrenia and the brain: Conditions for a neuropsychology of madness. *American Psychologist, 48,* 221–233.

Heinrichs, R. W. (2003). Historical origins of schizophrenia: Two early madmen and their illness. *Journal of the History of the Behavioral Sciences, 39,* 349–363.

Heinrichs, R. W., & Awad, A. G. (1993). Neurocognitive subtypes of chronic schizophrenia. *Schizophrenia Research, 9,* 49–58.

Heinrichs, R. W., Ruttan, L., Zakzanis, K. K., & Case, D. (1997). Parsing schizophrenia in neurocognitive tests: Evidence of stability and validity. *Brain and Cognition, 35,* 207–224.

Helenius, P., Salmelin, R., Service, E., & Connolly, J. F. (1999). Semantic cortical activation in dyslexic readers. *Journal of Cognitive Neuroscience, 11,* 535–550.

Hellekson, K. L. (2001). NIH consensus statement on phenylketonuria. *American Family Physician, 63*(7), 1430–1432.

Heller, W., & Nitschke, J. B. (1997). Regional brain activity in emotion: A framework for understanding cognition in depression. *Cognition and Emotion, 11*(5–6), 737–661.

Heller, W., Nitschke, J. B., & Miller, G. A. (1998). Lateralization in emotion and emotional disorders. *Current Directions in Psychological Science, 7*(1), 26–27.

Hellstrom, K., Fellenius, J., & Öst, L. G. (1996). One versus five sessions of applied tension in the treatment of blood phobia. *Behaviour Research and Therapy, 34,* 101–112.

Helmes, E., & Ostbye, T. (2002). Beyond memory impairment: Cognitive changes in Alzheimer's disease. *Archives of Clinical Neuropsychology, 17,* 179–193.

Helmes, E., & Reddon, J. R. (1993). A perspective on developments in assessing psychopathology: A critical review of the MMPI and MMPI-2. *Psychological Bulletin, 113,* 453–471.

Helweg-Larsen, M., & Collins, B. E. (1997). A social psychological perspective on the role of knowledge about AIDS in AIDS prevention. *Current Directions in Psychological Science, 6,* 23–26.

Helzer, J. E., & Canino, G. (1992). Comparative analyses of alcoholism in 10 cultural regions. In J. Helzer & G. Canino (Eds.), *Alcoholism—North America, Europe and Asia: A coordinated analysis of population data from ten regions* (pp. 131–155). London, UK: Oxford University Press.

Hepburn, K. W., Tornatore, J., Center, B., & Ostwald, S. W. (2001). Dementia family caregiver training: Affecting beliefs about caregiving and caregiver outcomes. *Journal of the American Geriatric Society, 49*(4), 450–457.

Herbert, T. B., & Cohen, S. (1993). Depression and immunity: A meta-analytic review. *Psychological Bulletin, 113*(3), 472–486.

Herdt, G. H. (1987). *The Sambia: Ritual and gender in New Guinea.* New York: Holt, Rinehart and Winston.

Herman, J. L., Perry, C., & van der Kolk, B. A. (1989). Childhood trauma in borderline personality disorder. *American Journal of Psychiatry, 146,* 490–495.

Herrero, M. E., Hechtman, L., & Weiss, G. (1994). Antisocial disorders in hyperactive subjects from childhood to adulthood: Predictive factors and characterization of subgroups. *American Journal of Orthopsychiatry, 64,* 510–521.

Herz, M. I. (1985). Prodromal symptoms and prevention of relapse in schizophrenia. *Journal of Clinical Psychiatry, 46*(11), 22–25.

Herzog, D. B. (1988). Eating disorders. In A. M. Nicoli, Jr. (Ed.), *The new Harvard guide to psychiatry* (pp. 434–445). Boston: Harvard University Press.

Herzog, D. B., Dorer, D. J., Keel, P. K., Selwyn, S. E., Ekeblad, E. R., Flores, A. T., et al. (1999). Recovery and relapse in anorexia and bulimia nervosa: A 7.5-year follow-up study. *Journal of the American Academy of Child and Adolescent Psychiatry, 38*(7), 829–837.

Hetherington, E. M., & Blechman, E. A. (Eds.). (1996). *Stress, coping and resiliency in children and families.* Mahwah, NJ: Erlbaum.

Hetherington, E. M., Stanley-Hagan, M., & Anderson, E. R. (1989). Marital transitions: A child's perspective. *American Psychologist, 44,* 303–312.

Hewitt, P. L., Flett, G. L., & Ediger, E. (1995). Perfectionism traits and perfectionistic self-presentation in eating disorder attitudes, characteristics, and symptoms. *International Journal of Eating Disorders, 18,* 317–326.

Higgins, S. T., & Petry, N. M. (1999). Contingency management: Incentives for sobriety. *Alcohol Research and Health, 23*(2), 122–127.

Higgins, S. T., Budney, A. J., Bickel, W. K., Hughes, J. R., Foerg, F., & Badger, G. (1993). Achieving cocaine abstinence with a behavioral approach. *American Journal of Psychiatry, 150,* 763–769.

Hilgard, E. R. (1992). Divided consciousness and dissociation. *Consciousness and Cognition, 1,* 16–31.

Hill, A. E., & Rosenbloom, L. (1986). Disintegrative psychosis of childhood: Teenage follow-up. *Developmental Medicine and Child Neurology, 28,* 34–40.

Hill, D. E., Yeo, R. A., Campbell, R. A., Hart, B., Vigil, J., & Brooks, W. (2003). Magnetic resonance imaging correlates of attention-deficit/hyperactivity disorder in children. *Neuropsychology, 17,* 496–506.

Hillman, E., Kripke, D. F., & Gillin, J. C. (1990). Sleep restriction, exercise, and bright lights: Alternate therapies for depression. In A. Tasman, C. Kaufman, & S. Goldfinger (Eds.), *American Psychiatric Press review of psychiatry: Section I: Treatment of refractory affective disorder.* (R. Post, section ed.) (Vol. 9, pp. 132–144). Washington, DC: American Psychiatric Press.

Hilts, P. J. (1994, March 10). Agency faults a U.C.L.A. study for suffering of mental patients. *New York Times,* p. A1.

Hinchley, J., & Levy, B. A. (1988). Developmental and individual differences in reading comprehension. *Cognition and Instruction, 5,* 3–47.

Hindmarch, I. (1986). The effects of psychoactive drugs on car handling and related psychomotor ability: A review. In J. F. O'Hanlon & J. J. Gier (Eds.), *Drugs and driving* (pp. 71–79). London: Taylor and Francis.

Hindmarch, I. (1990). Cognitive impairment with anti-anxiety agents: A solvable problem? In D. Wheatley (Ed.), *The anxiolytic jungle: Where, next?* (pp. 49–61). Chichester, UK: John Wiley.

Hinshelwood, J. A. (1896). A case of dyslexia: A peculiar form of word-blindness. *Lancet, 2,* 1451–1454.

Hirsch, S., Cramer, P., & Bowen, J. (1992). The triggering hypothesis of the role of life events in schizophrenia. *British Journal of Psychiatry, 161,* 84–87.

Hirschfeld, D. R., Rosenbaum, J. F., Biederman, J., Bolduc, E. A., Farone, S. V., Snidman, N., et al. (1992). Stable behavioral inhibition and its association with anxiety disorder. *Journal of the American Academy of Child and Adolescent Psychiatry, 31,* 103–111.

Hirschfeld, R. M. A., Keller, M. M., Panico, S., Arons, B. S., Barlow, D., Davidoff, F., et al. (1997). The National Depressive and Manic-Depressive Association consensus statement on the undertreatment of depression. *Journal of the American Medical Association, 277*(4), 333–340.

Hirschfeld, R. M., Shea, M. T., & Weise, R. E. et al. (1991). Dependent personality disorder: Perspectives for DSM-IV. *Journal of Personality Disorders, 5,* 135–149.

Hirschfeld, R. M. A., Shea, M. T., & Weise, R. (1995). Dependent personality disorder. In W. J. Livesley (Ed.), *The DSM-IV personality disorders* (pp. 239–256). New York: Guilford Press.

Hitchcock, P. B., & Mathews, A. (1992). Interpretation of bodily symptoms in hypochondriasis. *Behaviour Research and Therapy, 30*(3), 223–234.

Ho, B. C., Black, D. W., & Andreasen, N. C. (2003). Schizophrenia and other psychotic disorders. In R. E. Hales & S. C. Yudofsky (Eds.), *Textbook of clinical psychiatry* (4th ed.) (pp. 379–438). Washington, DC: American Psychiatric Press.

Hoaken, P. N. S., & Stewart, S. H. (2003). Drugs of abuse and the elicitation of human aggressive behavior. *Addictive Behaviors, 28*, 1533–1554.

Hockey Hall of Fame and Museum (2001). *Shayne Corson.* Retrieved July 15, 2004, from http://www.legendsofhockey.net:8080/LegendsOfHockey/jsp/SearchPlayer.jsp?player=10297.

Hodapp, R. M., & Dykens, E. M. (1994). Mental retardation's two cultures of behavioral research. *American Journal of Mental Retardation, 98*, 675–687.

Hodgkinson, K. A., Murphy, J. O'Neill, S., Brzustowicz, L., & Bassett, A. S. (2001). Genetic counselling for schizophrenia in the era of molecular genetics. *Canadian Journal of Psychiatry, 46* (2), 123–130.

Hoehn-Saric, R., McLeod, D. R., & Zimmerli, W. D. (1989). Somatic manifestations in women with generalized anxiety disorder: Psychophysiological responses to psychological stress. *Archives of General Psychiatry, 46*, 1113–1119.

Hoek, H. W. (2002). The distribution of eating disorders. In K. D. Brownell & C. G. Fairburn (Eds.), *Eating disorders and obesity: A comprehensive handbook* (2nd ed., pp. 207–211). New York: Guilford Press.

Hoek, H. W., Bartelds, A. I. M., Bosveld, J. J. F., van der Graaf, Y., Limpens, V. E. L., Maiwald, M., et al. (1995). Impact of urbanization on detection rates of eating disorders. *American Journal of Psychiatry, 152*, 1272–1278.

Hoffman, R. E., Rapaport, J., Mazure, C. M., & Quinlan, D. M. (1999). Selective speech perception alterations in schizophrenic patients reporting hallucinated "voices." *American Journal of Psychiatry, 156*, 393–399.

Hofmann, S. G. (2004). Cognitive mediation of treatment change in social phobia. *Journal of Consulting and Clinical Psychology, 72*, 393–399.

Hofmann, S. G., & Barlow, D. H. (2002). Social phobia (social anxiety disorder). In D. H. Barlow, *Anxiety and its disorders: The nature and treatment of anxiety and panic* (2nd ed.). New York: Guilford Press.

Hofmann, S. G., Lehman, C. L., & Barlow, D. H. (1997). How specific are specific phobias? *Journal of Behavior Therapy and Experimental Psychiatry, 28*, 233–240.

Hogarty, G. E., Anderson, C. M., Reiss, D. J., Kornblith, S. J., Greenwald, D. P., Javna, C. D., et al. (1986). Family psychoeducation, social skills training, and maintenance chemotherapy in the aftercare treatment of schizophrenia: I. One year effects of a controlled study on relapse and expressed emotion. *Archives of General Psychiatry, 43*, 633–642.

Hogarty, G. E., Anderson, C. M., Reiss, D. J., Kornblith, S. J., Greenwald, D. P., Ulrich, R. F., et al., and The Environmental-Personal Indicators in the Course of Schizophrenia (EPICS) Research Group. (1991). Family psychoeducation, social skills training, and maintenance chemotherapy in the aftercare treatment of schizophrenia. *Archives of General Psychiatry, 48*, 340–347.

Hogarty, G. E., Reis, D., Kornblith, S. J., Greenwald, D., Ulrich, R., & Carter, M. (1992). In reply. *Archives of General Psychiatry, 49*, 76–77.

Hoge, S. K., Appelbaum, P. S., Lawler, T., Beck, J. C., Litman, R., Greer, A., et al. (1990). A prospective, multicenter study of patients' refusal of antipsychotic medication. *Archives of General Psychiatry, 47*, 949–956.

Holder, H. D., Gruenewald, P. J., Ponicki, W. R., Treno, A. J., Grube, J. W., Saltz, R. F., et al. (2000). Effect of community-based interventions on high-risk drinking and alcohol-related injuries. *Journal of the American Medical Association, 284*, 2341–2347.

Hollander, E., Allen, A., Kwon, J., Aronwoitz, B., Schmeidler, J., Wong, C., et al. (1999). Clomipramine vs desipramine crossover trial in body dysmorphic disorder: Selective efficacy of a serotonin reuptake inhibitor in imagined ugliness. *Archives of General Psychiatry, 56*(11), 1033–1039.

Hollander, E., Liebowitz, M. R., Winchel, R., Klumker, A., & Klein, D. F. (1989). Treatment of body-dysmorphic disorder with serotonin reuptake blockers. *American Journal of Psychiatry, 146*, 768–770.

Hollender, E., Cohen, L. J., Simeon, D., & Rosen, J. (1994). Fluvoxamine treatment of body dysmorphic disorder. *Journal of Clinical Psychopharmacology, 14*, 75–77.

Holley, H., Arboleda-Florez, J., & Crisanti, A. (1998). Do forensic offenders receive harsher sentences? An examination of legal outcomes. *International Journal of Law and Psychiatry, 21*, 43–57.

Hollien, H. (1990). The expert witness: Ethics and responsibilities. *Journal of Forensic Sciences, 35*, 1414–1423.

Hollifield, M., Katon, W., Spain, D., & Pule, L. (1990). Anxiety and depression in a village in Lesotho, Africa: A comparison with the United States. *British Journal of Psychiatry, 156*, 343–350.

Hollis, J. F., Connett, J. E., Stevens, V. J., & Greenlick, M. R. (1990). Stressful life events, Type A behavior, and the prediction of cardiovascular and total mortality over six years. *Journal of Behavioral Medicine, 13*(3), 263–280.

Hollon, S. D., DeRubeis, R. J., Evans, M. D., Wiener, M. J., Garvey, M. J., Grose, W. M., et al. (1992). Cognitive therapy and pharmacotherapy for depression: Singly and in combination. *Archives of General Psychiatry, 49*(10), 772–781.

Hollon, S. D., Shelton, R. C., & Loosen, P. T. (1991). Cognitive therapy and pharmacotherapy for depression. *Journal of Consulting and Clinical Psychology, 59*(1), 88–99.

Holm, V. A., & Varley, C. K. (1989). Pharmacological treatment of autistic children. In G. Dawson (Ed.), *Autism: Nature, diagnosis, and treatment* (pp. 386–404). New York: Guilford Press.

Holroyd, K. A., Andrasik, F., & Noble, J. (1980). A comparison of EMG biofeedback and a credible pseudotherapy in treating tension headache. *Journal of Behavioral Medicine, 3*, 29–39.

Holroyd, K. A., Nash, J. M., Pingel, J. D., Cordingley, G. E., & Jerome, A. (1991). A comparison of pharmacological (amitriptyline HCL) and nonpharmacological (cognitive-behavioral) therapies for chronic tension headaches. *Journal of Consulting and Clinical Psychology, 59*(3), 387–393.

Holroyd, K. A., & Penzien, D. B. (1986). Client variables in the behavioral treatment of current tension headache: A meta-analytic review. *Journal of Behavioral Medicine, 9*, 515–536.

Holroyd, K. A., Penzien, D. B., Hursey, K. G., Tobin, D. L., Rogers, L., Holm, J. E., et al. (1984). Change mechanisms in EMG biofeedback training. Cognitive changes underlying improvements in tension headache. *Journal of Consulting and Clinical Psychology, 52*, 1039–1053.

Hommer, D. W. (1999). Functional imaging of craving. *Alcohol Research and Health, 23*(3), 187–196.

Hook, E. B. (1982). Epidemiology of Down syndrome. In S. M. Pueschel & J. E. Rynders (Eds.), *Down syndrome: Advances in biomedicine and the behavioral sciences* (pp. 11–88). Cambridge, MA: Ware Press.

Hooley, J. M. (1985). Expressed emotion: A review of the critical literature. *Clinical Psychology Review, 5*, 119–139.

Horen, S. A., Leichner, P. P., & Lawson, J. S. (1995). Prevalence of dissociative symptoms and disorders in an adult psychiatric inpatient population in Canada. *Canadian Journal of Psychiatry, 40*, 185–191.

Hornby, L. (Oct. 18, 2001). Panic hit Corson on Leaf's bench. *Toronto Sun.* Retrieved June 21, 2004, from http://www.canoe.ca/Health0110/18_corson-sun.html.

Horowitz, M. J. (2001). Histrionic personality disorder. In G. O. Gabbard (Ed.), *Treatment of psychiatric disorders* (Vol. 2) (3rd ed.) (pp. 2293–2307). Washington, DC: American Psychiatric Press.

Horowitz, M. J., Siegel, B., Holen, A., Bonanno, G. A., Milbrath, C., & Stinson, C. H. (1997). Diagnostic criteria for complicated grief disorder. *American Journal of Psychiatry, 154*, 904–910.

Horwath, E., & Weissman, M. (1997). Epidemiology of anxiety disorders across cultural groups. In S. Friedman (Ed.), *Cultural issues in the treatment of anxiety* (pp. 21–39). New York: Guilford Press.

House, J. S., Landis, K. R., & Umberson, D. (1988). Social relationships and health. *Science, 241*, 540–545.

House, J. S., Robbins, C., & Metzner, H. M. (1982). The association of social relationships and activities with mortality: Prospective evidence from the Tecumseh community health study. *American Journal of Epidemiology, 116*, 123.

Houston, B. K., Chesney, M. A., Black, G. W., Cates, D. S., & Hecker, M. H. L. (1992). Behavioral clusters and coronary heart disease risk. *Psychosomatic Medicine, 54*(4), 447–461.

Houts, A. C. (2001). The Diagnostic and Statistical Manual's new white coat and circularity of plausible dysfunctions: Response to Wakefield, *Part i. Behavior Research and Therapy, 39*, 315–345.

Howard, R., Castle, D., Wessely, S., & Murray, R. (1993). A comparative study of 470 cases of early-onset and late-onset schizophrenia. *British Journal of Psychiatry, 163,* 352–357.

Howes, J. L., & Vallis, T. M. (1996). Cognitive therapy with nontraditional populations: Application to post-traumatic stress disorder and personality disorders. In K. S. Dobson & K. D. Craig (Eds.), *Advances in cognitive-behavioral therapy* (Vol. 2., pp. 237–271). Thousand Oaks, CA: Sage.

Hser, Y., Anglin, M. D., & Powers, K. (1993). A 24-year follow-up of California narcotics addicts. *Archives of General Psychiatry, 50,* 577–584.

Hsu, L. K. G. (1988). The outcome of anorexia nervosa: A reappraisal. *Psychological Medicine, 18,* 807–812.

Hsu, L. K. G. (1990). *Eating disorders.* New York: Guilford Press.

Hubert, N. C., Jay, S. M., Saltoun, M., & Hayes, M. (1988). Approach-avoidance and distress in children undergoing preparation for painful medical procedures. *Journal of Clinical Child Psychology, 17,* 194–202.

Hucker, S. J. (1997). Sexual sadism: Psychopathology and theory. In D. R. Laws & W. T. O'Donohue (Eds.), *Sexual deviance: Theory, assessment, and treatment* (pp. 194–209). New York: Guilford Press.

Hudson, J. I., Mangweth, B., Pope, H. G. Jr., De Col, C., Hausmann, A., Gutweniger, S., et al. (2003). Family study of affective spectrum disorder. *Archives of General Psychiatry, 60,* 170–177.

Hudson, J., Pope, H., Jonas, J. M., & Yurgelun-Todd, D. (1983). Family history study of anorexia nervosa and bulimia. *British Journal of Psychiatry, 142,* 133–138.

Huey, S. J., Henggeler, S. W., Brondino, M. J., & Pickrel, S. G. (2000). Mechanisms of change in multisystemic therapy: Reducing delinquent behavior through therapist adherence and improved family and peer functioning. *Journal of Consulting and Clinical Psychology, 68,* 451–467.

Hufford, D. J. (1982). *The terror that comes in the night: An experience-centered study of supernatural assault traditions.* Philadelphia: University of Pennsylvania Press.

Hufford, M. R., Shields, A. L., Shiffman, S., Paty, J., & Balabanis, M. (2002). Reactivity to ecological momentary assessment: An example using undergraduate problem drinkers. *Psychology of Addictive Behaviors, 16,* 205–211.

Hughes, J. R. (1993). Pharmacotherapy for smoking cessation: Unvalidated assumptions, anomalies, and suggestions for future research. *Journal of Consulting and Clinical Psychology, 61,* 751–760.

Hughes, J. R., Gust, S. W., Skoog, K., Keenan, R. M., & Fenwick, J. W. (1991). Symptoms of tobacco withdrawal: A replication and extension. *Archives of General Psychiatry, 48,* 52–61.

Humphrey, L. L. (1986). Structural analysis of parent-child relationships in eating disorders. *Journal of Abnormal Psychology, 95,* 395–402.

Humphrey, L. L. (1988). Relationships within subtypes of anorexic, bulimic, and normal families. *Journal of the American Academy of Child and Adolescent Psychiatry, 27,* 544–551.

Humphrey, L. L. (1989). Observed family interactions among subtypes of eating disorders using structural analysis of social behavior. *Journal of Consulting and Clinical Psychology, 57,* 206–214.

Hunicutt, C. P., & Newman, I. A. (1993). Adolescent dieting practices and nutrition knowledge. *Health Values: The Journal of Health Behavior, Education and Promotion, 17*(4), 35–40.

Hunsley, J., & Bailey, J. M. (1999). The clinical utility of the Rorschach: Unfulfilled promises and an uncertain future. *Psychological Assessment, 11,* 266–277.

Hunsley, J., & Johnston, C. (2000). The role of empirically supported treatments in evidence-based psychological practice: A Canadian perspective. *Clinical Psychology: Science and Practice, 7,* 269–272.

Hunsley, J., Lee, C. M., & Aubry, T. (1999). Who uses psychological services in Canada? *Canadian Psychology, 40,* 232–240.

Hunt, W. A. (1980). History and classification. In A. E. Kazdin, A. S. Bellack, & M. Hersen (Eds.), *New perspectives in abnormal psychology.* New York: Oxford University Press.

Hunter, J. A., Jr., & Mathews, R. (1997). Sexual deviance in females. In D. R. Laws & W. T. O'Donohue (Eds.), *Sexual deviance: Theory, assessment, and treatment* (pp. 465–490). New York: Guilford Press.

Huntington's Disease Collaborative Research Group (1993). A novel gene containing a trinucleotide repeat that is expanded and unstable on Huntington's disease chromosomes. *Cell, 72,* 971–983.

Hurd, H. M., Drewry, W. F., Dewey, R., Pilgrim, C. W., Blumer, G. A., & Burgess, R. J. W. (1916). *The institutional care of the insane in the United States and Canada.* Oxford, UK: Johns Hopkins Press.

Hussian, R. A., & Brown, D. C. (1987). Use of two dimensional grid patterns to limit hazardous ambulation in demented patients. *Journal of Gerontology, 42,* 558–560.

Hyman, S. E., & Shore, D. (2000). An NIMH perspective on the use of placebos. *Biological Psychiatry, 47*(8), 689–691.

Hymowitz, P., Frances, A., Jacobsberg, L., Sickles, M., & Hoyt, M. (1986). Neuroleptic treatment of schizotypal personality disorder. *Comprehensive Psychiatry, 27,* 267–271.

Hynd, G. W., & Semrud-Clikeman, M. (1989). Dyslexia and brain morphology. *Psychological Bulletin, 106,* 447–482.

Hypericum Depression Trial Study Group (2002). Effect of hypericum perforatum (St. John's wort) in major depressive disorder: A randomized controlled trial. *Journal of the American Medical Association, 287,* 1853–1854.

Iguchi, M. Y., Griffiths, R. R., Bickel, W. K., Handelsman, L., Childress, A. R., & McLellan, A. T. (1990). Relative abuse liability of benzodiazepines in methadone maintenance populations in three cities. *Problems of drug dependence*

(pp. 364–365). (NIDA Publication No. ADM 90–1663). Washington, DC: U.S. Government Printing Office.

Ihara, H., Berrios, G. E., & McKenna, P. J. (2003). The association between negative and dysexecutive syndromes in schizophrenia: A cross-cultural study. *Behavioral Neurology, 14,* 63–74.

Ikels, C. (1991). Aging and disability in China: Cultural issues in measurement and interpretation. *Social Science Medicine, 32,* 649–665.

Imber, S. D., Glanz, L. M., Elkin, I., Sotsky, S. M., Boyer, J. L., & Leber, W. R. (1986). Ethical issues in psychotherapy research: Problems in a collaborative clinical trials study. *American Psychologist, 41,* 137–146.

Imperato-McGinley, J., Peterson, R. E., Gautier, T., & Sturla, E. (1979). Androgens and the evolution of male-gender identity among male pseudohermaphrodites with 5-alpha-reductase deficiency. *New England Journal of Medicine, 300,* 1233–1237.

IMS Health Canada (2004a). *A health information update from IMS health.* Retrieved August 5, 2004, from http://www.imshealthcanada.com/htmen/3_1_39.htm.

IMS Health Canada (2004b). *Early figures show Viagra expanding erectile dysfunction market.* Retrieved August 5, 2004, from http://www.imshealthcanada.com/htmen/4_2_1_13.htm.

Insel, T. R. (Ed.). (1984). *New findings in obsessive-compulsive disorder.* Washington, DC: American Psychiatric Press.

Insel, T. R., Scanlan, J., Champoux, M., & Suomi, S. J. (1988). Rearing paradigm in a nonhuman primate affects response to B-CCE challenge. *Psychopharmacology, 96,* 81–86.

Institute of Medicine. (2002). *Reducing Suicide: A National imperative.* Washington, DC: National Academic Press.

International Interdisciplinary Conference on Hypertension in Blacks (1999, July 9). *Linking race and genetics to cardiovascular disease for improved health among ethnic populations.* Retrieved July 15, 2004, from http://www.ishib.org/main/newsrel_lead_i99.htm.

Iribarren, C., Sidney, S., Bild, D. E., Liu, K., Markovitz, J. H., Roseman, J. M., et al. (2000). Association of hostility with coronary artery calcification in young adults. *Journal of the American Medicine Association, 283*(19), 2546–2551.

Ironson, G., Friedman, A., Klimas, N., Antoni, M., Fletcher, M. A., LaPerriere, A., et al. (1994). Distress, denial, and low adherence to behavioral interventions predict faster disease progression in gay men infected with human immunodeficiency virus. *International Journal of Behavioral Medicine, 1,* 90–105.

Ironson, G., Taylor, C. B., Boltwood, M., Bartzokis, T., Dennis, C., Chesney, M., et al. (1992). Effects of anger on left ventricular ejection fraction in coronary artery disease. *American Journal of Cardiology, 70,* 281–285.

Irvin, J. E., Bowers, C. A., Dunn, M. E., & Wang, M. C. (1999). Efficacy of relapse prevention: A meta-analytic review. *Journal of Consulting and Clinical Psychology, 67*(4), 563–570.

Irwin, M., Mascovich, A., Gillin, J. C., Willoughby, R., Pike, J., & Smith, T. L. (1994). Partial sleep deprivation reduces natural killer cell activity in humans. *Psychosomatic Medicine, 56,* 493–498.

Isaacowitz, D., Smith, T. T., & Carstensen, L. L. (2003). Socioemotional selectivity, positive bias, and mental health among trauma survivors in old age. *Ageing International, 28,* 181–199.

Israeli, A. L., & Stewart, S. H. (2001). Memory bias for forbidden food cues in restrained eaters. *Cognitive Therapy and Research, 25,* 37–47.

Iversen, L. L. (2000). *The science of marijuana.* New York: Oxford University Press.

Izard, C. E. (1992). Basic emotions, relations among emotions, and emotion-cognition relations. *Psychological Review, 99*(3), 561–565.

Jack, L., Nicholls, T., & Ogloff, J. R. P. (1998, March). *An investigation of inpatient self-injurious behavior among involuntarily hospitalized patients.* Poster presented at the Biennial Meeting of the American Psychology Law Society, Redondo Beach, CA.

Jacobi, W., & Winkler, H. (1927). Encephalographische Studien an chronischen Schizophrenen. *Arch. Psychiatr. Nervenk.r, 81,* 299–332.

Jacobs, S. (1993). *Pathologic grief: Maladaptation to loss.* Washington, DC: American Psychiatric Press.

Jacobs, S., Hansen, F., Berkman, L., Kasl, S., & Ostfeld, A. (1989). Depressions of bereavement. *Comprehensive Psychiatry, 30*(3), 218–224.

Jacobson, E. (1938). *Progressive relaxation.* Chicago: University of Chicago Press.

Jaffe, A. J., Rounsaville, B., Chang, G., Schottenfeld, R. S., Meyer, R. E., & O'Malley, S. O. (1996). Naltrexone, relapse prevention, and supportive therapy with alcoholics: An analysis of patient treatment matching. *Journal of Consulting and Clinical Psychology, 64,* 1044–1053.

Jaffe, J. H., Knapp, C. M., & Ciraulo, D. A. (1997). Opiates: Clinical aspects. In J. H. Lowinson, P. Ruiz, R. B. Millman, & J. G. Langrod (Eds.), *Substance abuse: A comprehensive textbook* (pp. 158–166). Baltimore: Williams & Wilkins.

Jaffe, S. E. (2000). Sleep and infectious disease. In M. H. Kryger, T. Roth, and W. C. Dement (Eds.), *Principles and practice of sleep medicine* (3rd ed., pp. 1093–1102). Philadelphia: W. B. Saunders.

Jaffee, S. R., Moffitt, T. E., Caspi, A., Fombonne, E., Poulton, R., & Martin, J. (2002). Differences in early childhood risk factors for juvenile-onset and adult-onset depression. *Archives of General Psychiatry, 59,* 215–222.

Jamison, K. R. (1989). Mood disorders and patterns of creativity in British writers and artists. *Psychiatry, 52,* 125–134.

Jamison, K. R. (1993). Touched with fire: Manic depressive illness and the artistic temperament. New York: Macmillan.

Jamison, R. N., & Virts, K. L. (1990). The influence of family support on chronic pain. *Behaviour Research and Therapy, 28*(4), 283–287.

Jamner, L. D., Shapiro, D., Goldstein, I. B., & Hug, R. (1991). Ambulatory blood pressure and heart rate in paramedics: Effects of cynical hostility and defensiveness. *Psychosomatic Medicine, 53,* 393–406.

Jang, K. L., Livesley, W. J., & Vernon, P. A. (1998). A twin study of genetic and environmental contributions to gender differences in traits delineating personality disorder. *European Journal of Personality, 12,* 331–344.

Jang, K. L., Paris, J., Zweig-Frank, H., & Livesley, W. J. (1998). Twin study of dissociative experience. *Journal of Nervous and Mental Disease, 186,* 345–351.

Jang, K. L., Vernon, P. A., & Livesley, W. J. (2001). Behavioural-genetic perspectives on personality function. *Canadian Journal of Psychiatry, 46,* 234–244.

Janicak, P. G., Dowd, S. M., Martis, B., Alam, D., Beedle, D., Krasuski, J., et al. (2002). Repetitive transcranial magnetic stimulation versus electroconvulsive therapy for major depression: Preliminary results of a randomized trial. *Biological Psychiatry,* 659–667.

Jason, L. A., Fennell, P. A., & Taylor, R. R. (2003). *Handbook of chronic fatigue syndrome.* Hoboken, NJ: John Wiley.

Jaspers, K. (1963). *General psychopathology* (J. Hoenig & M. W. Hamilton, Trans.). Manchester, UK: Manchester University Press.

Jeffrey, S. (1995, July 4). Toronto team uncovers Alzheimer's gene. *The Medical Post.* Retrieved May 21, 2004, from http://www.mentalhealth.com/mag1/p5m-alz1.html.

Jellinek, E. M. (1946). Phases in the drinking histories of alcoholics. *Quarterly Journal of Studies on Alcohol, 7,* 1–88.

Jellinek, E. M. (1952). Phases of alcohol addiction. *Quarterly Journal of Studies on Alcohol, 13,* 673–684.

Jellinek, E. M. (1960). *The disease concept of alcohol.* New Brunswick, NJ: Hillhouse Press.

Jenike, M. A., Baer, L., Ballantine, H. T., Martuza, R. L., Tynes, S., Giriunas, I., et al. (1991). Cingulotomy for refractory obsessive-compulsive disorder: A long-term follow-up of 33 patients. *Archives of General Psychiatry, 48,* 548–555.

Jenike, M. A., Baer, L., & Minichiello, W. E. (Eds.). (1986). *Obsessive-compulsive disorders: Theory and management.* Littleton, MA: PSG Publishing.

Jenkins, J. H., & Karno, M. (1992). The meaning of expressed emotion: Theoretical issues raised by cross-cultural research. *American Journal of Psychiatry, 149,* 9–21.

Jenkins, J. H., Kleinman, A., & Good, B. J. (1990). Cross-cultural studies of depression. In J. Becker & A. Kleinman (Eds.), *Psychosocial aspects of depression.* Hillsdale, NJ: Erlbaum.

Jensen, E. J., Schmidt, E., Pedersen, B., & Dahl, R. (1991). Effect on smoking cessation of silver acetate, nicotine and ordinary chewing gum. *Psychopharmacology, 104,* 470–474.

Jensen, P. S., Hinshaw, S. P., Swanson, J. M., Greenhill, L. L., Conners, C. K., Arnold, L. E., et al. (2001). Findings from the NIMH Multimodal Treatment Study of ADHD (MTA): Implications and applications for primary care providers. *Journal of Developmental and Behavioral Pediatrics, 22*(1), 60–73.

Jilek, W. G. (1982). Altered states of consciousness in North American Indian ceremonials. *Ethos, 10*(4), 326–343.

Jindal, R. D., Thase, M. E., Fasiczka, A. L., Friedman, E. S., Buysse, D. J., R. et al. (2002). Electroencephalographic sleep profiles in single-episode and recurrent unipolar forms of major depression: II. Comparison during remission. *Biological Psychiatry, 1,* 230–236.

Joffe, R., Segal, Z, & Singer, W. (1996). Change in thyroid hormone levels following response to cognitive therapy for major depression. *American Journal of Psychiatry, 153,* 411–413.

Johannes, C. B., Araujo, A. B., Feldman, H. A., Derby, C. A., Kleinman, K. P., & McKinlay, J. B. (2000). Incidence of erectile dysfunction in men 40 to 69 years old: Longitudinal results from the Massachusetts male aging study. *Journal of Urology, 163,* 460–463.

John, C., Turkington, D., & Kingdon, D. (1994). "Cognitive-behavioural therapy for schizophrenia": Reply. *British Journal of Psychiatry, 165,* 695.

Johnson, B. A. (1991). Cannabis. In I. B. Glass (Ed.), *International handbook of addiction behaviour* (pp. 69–76). London, UK: Tavistock/Routledge.

Johnson, B. A., Roache, J. D., Javors, M. A., DiClemente, C. C., Cloninger, C. R., Prihoda, T. J., et al. (2000). Ondansetron for reduction of drinking among biologically predisposed alcoholic patients. *Journal of the American Medical Association, 284*(8), 963–971.

Johnson, J. G., Cohen, P., Kasen, S., & Brook, J. S. (2002). Eating disorders during adolescence and the risk for physical and mental disorders during early adulthood. *Archives of General Psychiatry, 59,* 545–552.

Johnson, J. M., Baumgart, D., Helmstetter, E., & Curry, C. (1996). *Augmenting basic communication in natural contexts.* Baltimore, MD: Paul H. Brookes.

Johnson, S. L., & Miller, I. (1997). Negative life events and time to recovery from episodes of bipolar disorder. *Journal of Abnormal Psychology, 106*(3), 449–457.

Johnson, S. L., & Roberts, J. E. (1995). Life events and bipolar disorder: Implications from biological theories. *Psychological Bulletin, 117*(3), 434–449.

Johnson, S. L., Winett, C. A., Meyer, B., Greenhouse, W. J., & Miller, I. (1999). Social support and the course of bipolar disorder. *American Psychological Association, 180*(4), 558–566.

Johnston, C., Pelham, W. E., & Murphy, H. A. (1985). Peer relationships in ADHD and normal children: A developmental analysis of peer and teacher ratings. *Journal of Abnormal Child Psychology, 13,* 89–100.

Johnston, D. W. (1997). Cardiovascular disease. In D. M. Clark & C. G. Fairburn

(Eds.), *Science and practice of cognitive behaviour therapy* (pp. 341–358). Oxford, U. K.: Oxford University Press.

Joiner, T. E. (1997). Shyness and low social support as interactive diatheses, with loneliness as mediator: Testing an interpersonal-personality view of vulnerability to depressive symptoms. *Journal of Abnormal Psychology, 106*(3), 386–394.

Joiner, T. E., & Rudd, D. M. (1996). Toward a categorization of depression-related psychological constructs. *Cognitive Therapy and Research, 20*, 51–68.

Joiner, T. E., Jr. (1999). A test of interpersonal theory of depression in youth psychiatric inpatients. *Journal of Abnormal Child Psychology, 27*(1), 77–85.

Joiner, T. E., Jr., & Rudd, M. D. (2000). Intensity and duration of suicidal crises very as a function of previous suicide attempts and negative life events. *Journal of Consulting and Clinical Psychology, 68*(5), 909–916.

Joiner, T. F., Jr., Heatherton, T. F., & Keel, P. K. (1997). Ten year stability and predictive validity of five bulimia-related indicators. *American Journal of Psychiatry, 154*, 1133–1138.

Jones, J. C., & Barlow, D. H. (1990). The etiology of posttraumatic stress disorder. *Clinical Psychology Review, 10*, 299–328.

Jones, K. L., & Smith, D. W. (1973). Recognition of the fetal alcohol syndrome in early infancy. *Lancet, 2*, 999–1001.

Jones, M. C. (1924a). The elimination of children's fears. *Journal of Experimental Psychology, 7*, 383–390.

Jones, M. C. (1924b). A laboratory study of fear. The case of Peter. *Pedagogical Seminary, 31*, 308–315.

Jones, R. T., & Haney, J. I. (1984). A primary preventive approach to the acquisition and maintenance of fire emergency responding: Comparison of external and self-instruction strategies. *Journal of Community Psychology, 12*(2), 180–191.

Jones, R. T., & Kazdin, A. E. (1980). Teaching children how and when to make emergency telephone calls. *Behavior Therapy, 11*(4), 509–521.

Jones, R. T., & Ollendick, T. H. (2002). Residential fires. In A. M. La Greca, W. K. Silverman, E. Vernberg, & M. C. Roberts (Eds.), *Helping Children in disasters: Integrating research and practice.* Washington, DC: American Psychological Association.

Jordan, B. D., Relkin, N. R., Ravdin, L. D., Jacobs, A. R., Bennett, A., & Gandy, S. (1997). Apolipoprotein E Epsilon 4 associated with chronic traumatic brain injury in boxing. *Journal of the American Medical Association, 278*, 136–140.

Judd, L. L. (1997). The clinical course of unipolar major depressive disorders. *Archives of General Psychiatry, 54*, 989–991.

Judd, L. (2000). Course and chronicity of unipolar major depressive disorder: Commentary on Joiner. *Clinical Psychology: Science and Practice, 7*(2), 219–223.

Judd, L. L., Akiskal, H. S., Maser, J. D., Zeller, P. J., Endicott, J., Coryell, W., et al. (1998a). A prospective 12-year study of subsyndromal and syndromal depressive symptomatology in 431 patients with unipolar major depressive disorder. *Archives of General Psychiatry, 55*, 694–700.

Judd, L. L., Akiskal, H. S., Maser, J. D., Zeller, P. J., Endicott, J., Coryell, W., et al. (1998b). Major depressive disorder: A prospective study of residual subthreshold depressive symptoms as predictor of rapid relapse. *Journal of Affective Disorders, 50*, 97–108.

Junginger, J. (1997). Fetishism: Assessment and treatment. In D. R. Laws & W. O'Donohue (Eds.), *Sexual deviance: Theory, assessment and treatment* (pp. 92–110). New York: Guilford Press.

Juul-Dam, N., Townsend, J., & Courchesne, E. (2001). Prenatal, perinatal, and neonatal factors in autism, pervasive developmental disorder—not otherwise specified, and the general population. *Pediatrics, 107*(4), E63.

Kafka, M. P. (1997). A monoamine hypothesis for the pathophysiology of paraphilic disorders. *Archives of Sexual Behavior, 26*, 343–358.

Kagan, J. (1994). *Galen's prophesy.* New York: Basic Books.

Kagan, J. (1997). Temperament and the reactions to unfamiliarity. *Child Development, 68*, 139–143.

Kagan, J., Reznick, J. S., & Snidman, N. (1988). Biological bases of childhood shyness. *Science, 240*, 167–171.

Kagan, J., & Snidman, N. (1991). Infant predictors of inhibited and uninhibited profiles. *Psychological Science, 2*, 40–44.

Kagan, J., & Snidman, N. (1999). Early childhood predictors of adult anxiety disorders. *Biological Psychiatry, 46*, 1536–1541.

Kahn, S. (2001, May 15). Golden girl Uma admits to having body dysmorphic disorder (BDD). *Talk Surgery, Inc.* Retrieved June 10, 2004, from http://canoe.talksurgery.com/consumer/new/new00000056_1.html.

Kalat, J. W. (Ed.). (1998). *Biological psychology* (6th ed.). Pacific Grove, CA: Brooks/Cole.

Kallmann, F. J. (1938). *The genetics of schizophrenia.* New York: Augustin.

Kalus, O., Bernstein, D. P., & Siever, L. J. (1993). Schizoid personality disorder: A review of current status and implications for DSM-IV. *Journal of Personality Disorders, 7*, 43–52.

Kalus, O., Bernstein, D. P., & Siever, L. J. (1995). Paranoid personality disorder. In W. J. Livesley (Ed.), *The DSM-IV personality disorders* (pp. 58–70). New York: Guilford Press.

Kaminen, N., Hannula-Jouppi, K., Kestila, M., Lahermo, P., Muller, K., Kaaranen, M., et al. (2003). A genome scan for developmental dyslexia confirms linkage to chromosome 2p11 and suggests a new locus on 7q32. *Journal of Medical Genetics, 40*, 340–345.

Kandel, D. B., Wu, P., & Davies, M. (1994). Maternal smoking during pregnancy and smoking by adolescent daughters. *American Journal of Public Health, 84*, 1407–1413.

Kandel, E. R. (1983). From metapsychology to molecular biology: Explorations into the nature of anxiety. *American Journal of Psychiatry, 140*, 1277–1293.

Kandel, E. R., Jessell, T. M., & Schacter, S. (1991). Early experience and the fine tuning of synaptic connections. In E. R. Kandel, J. H. Schwartz, & T. M. Jessell, (Eds.), *Principles of neural science* (3rd ed., pp. 945–958). New York: Elsevier.

Kandel, E., Schwartz, J., & Jessell, T. (2000). *Principles of neural science* (4th ed.) New York: McGraw-Hill.

Kanigel, R. (1988, October/November). Nicotine becomes addictive. *Science Illustrated*, pp. 12–14, 19–21.

Kanner, L. (1943). Autistic disturbances of affective contact. *Nervous Child, 2*, 217–250.

Kanner, L. (1949). Problems of nosology and psychodynamics of early infantile autism. *American Journal of Orthopsychiatry, 19*, 416–426.

Kanner, L., & Eisenberg, L. (1955). Notes on the follow-up studies of autistic children. In P. Hoch & J. Zubin (Eds.), *Psychopathology of childhood* (pp. 227–239). New York: Grune & Stratton.

Kaplan, A. S., & Garfinkel, P E. (1999). Difficulties in treating patients with eating disorders: A review of patient and clinician variables. *Canadian Journal of Psychiatry, 44*, 665–670.

Kaplan, H. S. (1979). *Disorders of sexual desire.* New York: Brunner/Mazel.

Kaplan, H. S. (1987). *Sexual aversion, sexual phobias, and panic disorder.* New York: Brunner/Mazel.

Kaplan, M. (1983). A woman's view of DSM-III. *American Psychologist, 38*, 786–792.

Kaplan, N. M. (1980). The control of hypertension: A therapeutic breakthrough. *American Scientist, 68*, 537–545.

Kapur, S., Zipursky, R. B., & Remington, G. (1999). Clinical and theoretical implications of 5-HT2 and D2 receptor occupancy of clozapine, risperidone, and olanzapine in schizophrenia. *American Journal of Psychatry, 156*, 286–293.

Karno, M., & Golding, J. M. (1991). Obsessive-compulsive disorder. In L. N. Robins & D. A. Regier (Eds.), *Psychiatric disorders in America: The epidemiologic catchment area study* (pp. 204–219). New York: Free Press.

Karon, B. P. (2000). The clinical interpretation of the Thematic Apperception Test, Rorschach, and other clinical data: A reexamination of statistical versus clinical prediction. *Professional Psychology: Research and Practice, 31*, 230–233.

Kasch, K. L., Rottenberg, J., Arnow, B. A., & Gotlib, I. H. (2002). Behavioral activation and inhibition systems and the severity and course of depression. *Journal of Abnormal Psychology, 111*, 589–597.

Kashani, J. H., Hoeper, E. W., Beck, N. C., & Corcoran, C. M. (1987). Personality, psychiatric disorders, and parental attitude among a community sample of adolescents. *Journal of the American Academy of Child and Adolescent Psychiatry, 26*(6), 879–885.

Kashani, J. H., McGee, R. O., Clarkson, S. E. A., Walton, L. A., Williams, S., Silva, P. A., et al. (1983). Depression in a sample of 9-year-old children: Prevalence and associated characteristics. *Archives of General Psychiatry, 40,* 1217–1223.

Kass, D. J., Silvers, F. M., & Abrams, G. M. (1972). Behavioral group treatment of hysteria. *Archives of General Psychiatry, 26,* 42–50.

Katon, W. J. (2003). Clinical and health services relationships between major depression, depressive symptoms, and general medical illness. *Biological Psychiatry, 54,* 216–226.

Katon, W., Lin, E., Von Korff, M., Russo, J., Lipscomb, P., & Bush, T. (1991). Somatization: A spectrum of severity. *American Journal of Psychiatry, 148,* 34–40.

Katschnig, H., & Amering, M. (1990). Panic attacks and panic disorder in cross-cultural perspective. In J. C. Ballenger (Ed.), *Clinical aspects of panic disorder* (pp. 67–80). New York: Wiley.

Katz, I. R. (1993). Delirium. In D. L. Dunner (Ed.), *Current psychiatric therapy* (pp. 65–73). Philadelphia: W. B. Saunders.

Katz, I. R., Leshen, E., Kleban, M., & Jethanandani, V. (1989). Clinical features of depression in the nursing home. *International Psychogeriatrics, 1,* 5–15.

Katz, J., & Gagliese, L. (1999). Phantom limb pain: A continuing puzzle. In R. J. Gatchel & D. C. Turk (Eds.), *Psychosocial factors in pain: Critical perspectives* (pp. 284–300). New York: Guilford Press.

Katz, J. L., Weiner, H., Gallagher, T. F., & Hellman, I. (1970). Stress, distress, and ego defenses: Psychoendocrine response to impending breast tumor biopsy. *Archives of General Psychiatry, 23,* 131–142.

Katz, R., & McGuffin P. (1993). The genetics of affective disorders. *Progress in Experimental Personality and Psychopathology Research, 16,* 200–221.

Kavanagh, D. J. (1992). Recent developments in expressed emotion and schizophrenia. *British Journal of Psychiatry, 160,* 601–620.

Kawamura, K. Y. (2002). Asian American body images. In T. F. Cash & T. Pruzinsky (Eds.), *Body image: A handbook of theory, research and clinical practice* (pp. 243–249). New York: Guilford Press.

Kaye, W. H., Greeno, C. G., Moss, H., Fernstrom, J., Fernstrom, M., Lilenfeld, L. R., et al. (1998). Alterations in serotonin activity and psychiatric symptoms after recovery from bulimia nervosa. *Archives of General Psychiatry, 55,* 927–935.

Kaye, W. H., Nagata, T., Weltzin, T. E., Hsu, L. K., Sokol, M. S., McConaha, C., et al. (2001). Double-blind placebo-controlled administration of fluoxetine in restricting- and purging-type anorexia nervosa. *Biological Psychiatry, 49,* 644–652.

Kaye, W., Strober, M., Stein, D., & Gendall, K. (1999). New directions in treatment research of anorexia and bulimia nervosa. *Biological Psychiatry, 45,* 1285–1292.

Kaye, W. H., Weltzin, T. E., Hsu, L. K. G., McConaha, C. W., & Bolton, B. (1993). Amount of calories retained after binge eating and vomiting. *American Journal of Psychiatry, 150*(6), 969–971.

Kazarian, S. S., & Evans, D. R. (2001). Health psychology and culture: Embracing the 21st century. In S. S. Kazarian & D. R. Evans (Eds.), *Handbook of cultural health psychology* (pp. 3–43). San Diego, CA: Academic Press.

Kazarian, S. S., Malla, A. K., Cole, J. D., & Baker, B. (1990). Comparisons of two expressed emotion scales with the Camberwell Family Interview. *Journal of Clinical Psychology, 46,* 306–309.

Kazdin, A. E. (1979). Unobtrusive measures in behavioral assessment. *Journal of Applied Behavior Analysis, 12,* 713–724.

Kazdin, A. E. (1983). Hopelessness, depression, and suicidal intent among psychiatrically disturbed inpatient children. *Journal of Consulting and Clinical Psychology, 51*(4), 504–510.

Kazdin, A. E., & Mazurick, J. L. (1994). Dropping out of child psychotherapy: Distinguishing early and late dropouts over the course of treatment. *Journal of Consulting and Clinical Psychology, 62,* 1069–1074.

Kazdin, A. E., Mazurick, J. L., & Bass, D. (1993). Risk for attrition in treatment of antisocial children and families. *Journal of Child Clinical Psychology, 22,* 2–16.

Keane, T. M., & Barlow, D. H. (2002). Post traumatic stress disorder. In D. H. Barlow, *Anxiety and its disorders: The nature and treatment of anxiety and panic.* (2nd ed.). New York: Guilford Press.

Kearns, R. D., Otis, J. D., & Wise, E. A. (2002). Treating families of chronic pain patients: Application of a cognitive-behavioral transactional model. In D. C. Turk & R. J. Gatchel (Eds.), *Psychological approaches to pain management: A practioner's handbook* (2nd ed.). New York: Guilford Press.

Keck, P. E., & McElroy, S. L. (2002). Pharmacological treatments for bipolar disorder. In P. E. Nathan & J. M. Gorman (Eds.), *A guide to treatments that work* (2nd ed., pp. 277–299). New York: Oxford University Press.

Keefe, F. J., & France, C. R. (1999). Pain: Biopsychosocial mechanisms and management. *Current Directions in Psychological Science, 8,* 137–141.

Keefe, F. J., Dunsmore, J., & Burnett, R. (1992). Behavioral and cognitive-behavioral approaches to chronic pain: Recent advances and future directions. Special issue: Behavioral medicine: An update for the 1990s. *Journal of Consulting and Clinical Psychology, 60*(4), 528–536.

Keel, P. K., & Mitchell, J. E. (1997). Outcome in bulimia nervosa. *American Journal of Psychiatry, 154,* 313–321.

Keel, P. K., Dorer, D. J., Eddy, K. T., Franko, D. Charatan, D. L., & Herzog, D. B. (2003). Predictors of mortality in eating disorders. *Archives of General Psychiatry, 60,* 179–183.

Keel, P., Mitchell, J., Miller, K., Davis, T. L., & Crow, S. J. (1999). Long term outcome of bulimia nervosa. *Archives of General Psychiatry, 56,* 63–69.

Keel, P. K., Mitchell, J. E., Miller, K. B., Davis, T. L., & Crow, S. J. (2000). Predictive validity of bulimia nervosa as a diagnostic strategy. *American Journal of Psychiatry 157*(1), 136–138.

Keitner, G. I., Ryan, C. E., Miller, I. W., Kohn, R., Bishop, D. S., & Epstein, N. B. (1995). Role of the family in recovery and major depression. *American Journal of Psychiatry, 152,* 1002–1008.

Keller, M. B., Hirschfeld, R. M. A., & Hanks, D. L. (1997). Double depression: A distinctive subtype of unipolar depression. *Journal of Affective Disorders, 45,* 65–73.

Keller, M. B., Klein, D. N., Hirschfeld, R. M. A., Kocsis, J. H., McCullough, J. P., Miller, I., et al. (1995). Results of the DSM-IV mood disorders field trial. *American Journal of Psychiatry, 152,* 843–849.

Keller, M. B., Lavori, P. W., Endicott, J., Coryell, W., & Klerman, G. L. (1983). "Double depression": Two year follow-up. *American Journal of Psychiatry, 140*(6), 689–694.

Keller, M. B., Lavori, P. W., Mueller, T. I., Endicott, J., Coryell, W., Hirschfeld, R. M. A., et al. (1992). Time to recovery, chronicity, and levels of psychopathology in major depression. *Archives of General Psychiatry, 49,* 809–816.

Keller, M. B., McCollough, J. P., Klein, D. N., Arnow, B., Dunner, D. L., Gelenberg, A. J., et al. (2000). A comparison of nefazodone, the cognitive behavioral-analysis system of psychotherapy, and their combination for the treatment of chronic depression. *New England Journal of Medicine, 342*(20), 1462–1470.

Keller, M. B., & Wunder, J. (1990). Bipolar disorder in childhood. In M. Hersen & C. G. Last (Eds.), *Handbook of child and adult psychopathology: A longitudinal perspective.* Elmsford, NY: Pergamon Press.

Kellner, R. (1985). Functional somatic symptoms and hypochondriasis: A survey of empirical studies. *Archives of General Psychiatry, 42,* 821–833.

Kellner, R. (1986). *Somatization and hypochondriasis.* New York: Praeger-Greenwood.

Kellner, R., Hernandez, J., & Pathak, D. (1992). Hypochondriacal fears and beliefs, anxiety, and somatization. *British Journal of Psychiatry, 160,* 525–532.

Kelly, M. P., Strassberg, D. S., & Kircher, J. R. (1990). Attitudinal and experiential correlates of anorgasmia. *Archives of Sexual Behavior, 19*(2), 165–177.

Kemeny, M. E. (2003). The psychobiology of stress. *Current Directions in Psychological Science, 12*(4), 124–129.

Kemp, S. (1990). *Medieval psychology.* New York: Greenwood Press.

Kendler, K. S. (2001). Twin studies of psychiatric illness. *Achieves of General Psychiatry, 58,* 1005–1013.

Kendler, K. S., & Diehl, S. R. (1993). The genetics of schizophrenia: A current, genetic-epidemiologic perspective. *Schizophrenia Bulletin, 19,* 261–285.

Kendler, K. S., & Gruenberg, A. M. (1982). Genetic relationship between paranoid personality disorder and the "schizophrenic spectrum" disorders. *American Journal of Psychiatry, 139,* 1185–1186.

Kendler, K. S., Heath, A. C., Martin, N. G., & Eaves, L. J. (1987). Symptoms of anxiety and symptoms of depression: Same genes, different environments? *Archives of General Psychiatry, 44*(5), 451–457.

Kendler, K. S., Hettema, J. M., Butera, F., Gardner, C. O., & Prescott, C. A. (2003). Life event dimensions of loss, humiliation, entrapment, and danger in the prediction of onsets of major depression and generalized anxiety. *Archives of General Psychiatry, 60,* 789–796.

Kendler, K. S., Karkowski, L. M., & Prescott, C. A. (1999a). Fear and phobias: Reliability and heritability. *Psychological Medicine, 29,* 539–553.

Kendler, K. S., Karkowski, L. M., & Prescott, C. A. (1999b). Causal relationship between stressful life events and the onset of major depression. *American Journal of Psychiatry, 156*(6), 837–841.

Kendler, K. S., Kessler, R. C., Walters, E. E., MacLean, C., Neale, M. C., Heath, A. C., et al. (1995). Stressful life events, genetic liability, and onset of an episode of major depression in women. *American Journal of Psychiatry, 152,* 833–842.

Kendler, K. S., McGuire, M., Gruenberg, A. M., O'Hare, A., Spellman, M., & Walsh, D. (1993). The Roscommon Family Study: I. Methods, diagnosis of probands, and risk of schizophrenia in relatives. *Archives of General Psychiatry, 50,* 527–540.

Kendler, K. S., MacLean, C., Neale, M., Kessler, R., Heath, A., & Eaves, L. (1991). The genetic epidemiology of bulimia nervosa. *American Journal of Psychiatry, 148*(12), 1627–1637.

Kendler, K. S., Neale, M. C., Kessler, R. C., Heath, A. C., & Eaves, L. J. (1992). Generalized anxiety disorder in women: A population-based twin study. *Archives of General Psychiatry, 49,* 267–272.

Kendler, K. S., Neale, M. C., Kessler, R. C., Heath, A. C., & Eaves, L. J. (1993). A longitudinal twin study of 1-year prevalence of major depression in women. *Archives of General Psychiatry, 50,* 843–852.

Kennedy, K. (2001, October 22). Brotherly love. *Sports Illustrated.* Retrieved June 21, 2004, from http://www.macanxiety.com/corson.htm.

Kennedy, S. (2000). Psychological factors and immunity in HIV infection: Stress, coping, social support, and intervention outcomes. In D. I. Mostofsky & D. H. Barlow (Eds.), *The management of stress and anxiety in medical disorders* (pp. 194–205). Needham Heights, MA: Allyn & Bacon.

Kennedy, S. H., & Goldbloom, D. S. (1996). Eating disorders. In Q. Rae-Grant (Ed.), *Images in psychiatry: Canada* (pp. 229–234). Washington, DC: American Psychiatric Press.

Kennedy, S. H., Katz, R., Neitzert, C. S., Ralevski, E., & Mendlowitz, S. (1995). Exposure with response prevention treatment of anorexia nervosa-bulimic subtype and bulimia nervosa. *Behaviour Research and Therapy, 33,* 685–689.

Kennedy, S. H., McVey, G., & Katz, R. (1990). Personality disorders in anorexia nervosa and bulimia nervosa. *Journal of Psychiatric Research, 24,* 259–269.

Kertzner, R. M., & Gorman, J. M. (1992). Psychoneuroimmunology and HIV infection. In A. Tashan & M. B. Riba (Eds.), *Review of psychiatry* (Vol. 11). Washington, DC: American Psychiatric Press.

Kessler, R. C. (1997). The effects of stressful life events on depression. *Annual Review of Psychology, 48,* 191–214.

Kessler, R. C., Berglund, P., Demler, O., Jin, R., Koretz, D., Merikangas, K. R., et al. (2003). The epidemiology of major depressive disorder: Results from the National Comorbidity Survey Replication (NCS-R). *Journal of the American Medical Association, 289,* 3095–3105.

Kessler, R. C., McGonagle, K. A., Zhao, S., Nelson, C. B., Hughes, M., Eshleman, S., et al. (1994). Lifetime and 12-month prevalence of DSM-III-R psychiatric disorders among persons aged 15–54 in the United States: Results from the National Comorbidity Survey. *Archives of General Psychiatry 51,* 8–19.

Kessler, R. C., Nelson, C. B., McGonagle, K. A., Liu, J., Swartz, M., & Blazer, D. G. (1996). Comorbidity of DSM-III-R major depressive disorder in the general population: Results from the US National Comorbidity Survey. *British Journal of Psychiatry, 168*(Suppl. 30), 17–30.

Kessler, R. C., Sonnega, A., Bromet, E., Hughes, M., & Nelson, C. B. (1995). Posttraumatic stress disorder in the National Comorbidity Survey. *Archives of General Psychiatry, 52,* 1048–1060.

Kety, S. S. (1990). Genetic factors in suicide: Family, twin, and adoption studies. In S. J. Blumenthal & D. J. Kupfer (Eds.), *Suicide over the life cycle: Risk factors, assessment and treatment of suicidal patients* (pp. 127–133). Washington, DC: American Psychiatric Press.

Keys, A., Brozek, J., Henschel, A., Michelson, O., & Taylor, H. L. (1950). *The biology of human starvation* (Vol. 1). Minneapolis: University of Minnesota Press.

Khantzian, E. J., Gawin, F., Kleber, H. D., & Riordan, C. E. (1984). Methylphenidate (Ritalin) treatment of cocaine dependence: A preliminary report. *Journal of Substance Abuse Treatment, 1,* 107–112.

Kiang, M., Christensen, B. K., Remington, G., & Kapur, S. (2003). Apathy in schizophrenia: Clinical correlates and association with functional outcome. *Schizophrenia Research, 63,* 79–88.

Kiecolt-Glaser, J. K., & Glaser, R. (1987). Chronic stress and immunity in family caregivers of Alzheimer's disease victims. *Psychosomatic Medicine, 49*(5), 523–535.

Kiecolt-Glaser, J. K., & Glaser, R. (1992). Psychoneuroimmunology: Can psychological interventions modulate immunity? Special issue: Behavioral medicine: An update for the 1990s. *Journal of Consulting and Clinical Psychology, 60*(4), 569–575.

Kiecolt-Glaser, J. K., & Newton, T. L. (2001). Marriage and health: His and hers. *Psychological Bulletin, 127,* 475–503.

Kiehl, K. A., Smith, A. M., Hare, R. D., Mendrek, A., Forster, B. B., Brink, J. et al. (2001). Limbic abnormalities in affective processing by criminal psychopaths as revealed by functional magnetic resonance imaging. *Biological Psychiatry, 50,* 677–684.

Kiesler, D. J. (1966). Some myths of psychotherapy research and the search for a paradigm. *Psychological Bulletin, 65,* 110–136.

Kihlstrom, J. F. (1992). Dissociation and dissociations: A commentary on consciousness and cognition. *Consciousness and Cognition, 1,* 47–53.

Kihlstrom, J. F. (1994). One hundred years of hysteria. In S. J. Lynn & J. W. Rhue (Eds.), *Dissociation: Clinical and theoretical perspectives.* New York: Guilford Press.

Kihlstrom, J. F., Barnhardt, T. M., & Tataryn, D. J. (1992). The psychological unconscious: Found, lost, and regained. *American Psychologist, 47*(6), 788–791.

Kihlstrom, J. F., Glisky, M. L., Anguilo, M. J. (1994). Dissociative tendencies and dissociative disorders. *Journal of Abnormal Psychology, 103,* 117–124.

Killen, J. D. (1996). Development and evaluation of a school-based eating disorder symptoms prevention program. In L. Smolak, M. P. Levine, & R. Striegel-Moore (Eds.), *The developmental psychopathology of eating disorders: Implications for research, prevention, and treatment* (pp. 313–339). Mahwah, NJ: Erlbaum.

Killen, J. D., Taylor, C. B., Hayward, C., Haydel, F., Wilson, D. M., Hammer, L. D., et al. (1996). Weight concerns influence the development of eating disorders: A four-year prospective study. *Journal of Consulting and Clinical Psychology, 64,* 936–940.

Killen, J. D., Taylor, C. B., Hayward, C., Wilson, D. M., Hammer, L. D., Robinson, T. N., et al. (1994). The pursuit of thinness and onset of eating disorder symptoms in a community sample of adolescent girls: A three-year prospective analysis. *International Journal of Eating Disorders, 16,* 227–238.

Kilpatrick, D. G., Best, C. L., Veronen, L. J., Amick, A. E., Villeponteaux, L. A., & Ruff, G. A. (1985). Mental health correlates of criminal victimization: A random community survey. *Journal of Consulting and Clinical Psychology, 53,* 866–873.

Kilzieh, N., & Akiskal, H. S. (1999). Rapid-cycling bipolar disorder: An overview of research and clinical experience. *Psychiatric Clinics of North America, 22*(3), 585–607.

Kim, E. D., & Lipshultz, L. I. (1997, April 15). Advances in the treatment of organic erectile dysfunction. *Hospital Practice,* 101–120.

King, A. (1967). *The school at Mopass: A problem of identity.* San Francisco: Holt, Rinehart & Winston.

King, D. W., King, L. A., Foy, D. W., & Gudanowski, D. M. (1996). Prewar factors in combat related posttraumatic stress disorder: Structural equation modeling with a national sample of female and male Vietnam veterans.

*Journal of Consulting and Clinical Psychology, 64,* 520–531.

King, G. R., & Ellinwood, E. H. (1997). Amphetamines and other stimulants. In J. H. Lowinson, P. Ruiz, R. B. Millman, & J. G. Langrod (Eds.), *Substance abuse: A comprehensive textbook* (pp. 207–223). Baltimore: Williams & Wilkins.

King, N. J. (1993). Simple and social phobias. In T. H. Ollendick & R. J. Prinz (Eds.), *Advances in clinical child psychology* (Vol. 15, pp. 305–341). New York: Plenum Press.

King, S. (2000). Is expressed emotion cause or effect in the mothers of schizophrenic young adults? *Schizophrenia Research, 45,* 65–78.

King, S. A., & Strain, J. J. (1991). *Pain disorders: A proposed classification for DSM-IV.* Paper presented at the 144th annual meeting of the American Psychiatric Association, New Orleans.

Kinsey, A. C., Pomeroy, W. B., & Martin, C. E. (1948). *Sexual behavior in the human male.* Philadelphia: W. B. Saunders.

Kinsey, A. C., Pomeroy, W. B., Martin, C. E., & Gebhard, P. H. (1953). *Sexual behavior in the human female.* Philadelphia: W. B. Saunders.

Kinzie, J. D., Leung, P. K., Boehnlein, J., & Matsunaga, D. (1992). Psychiatric epidemiology of an Indian village: A 19-year replication study. *Journal of Nervous and Mental Disease, 180*(1), 33–39.

Kirch, D. G. (1993). Infection and autoimmunity as etiologic factors in schizophrenia: A review and reappraisal. *Schizophrenia Bulletin, 19,* 355–370.

Kirmayer, L. J. (1991). The place of culture in psychiatric nosology: Taijin kyofusho and DSM-III-R. *Journal of Nervous and Mental Disease, 179,* 19–28.

Kirmayer, L. J. (1994). Suicide among Canadian Aboriginal peoples. *Transcultural Psychiatric Research Review, 31,* 3–58.

Kirmayer, L. J. (2001). Cultural variations in the clinical presentation of depression and anxiety: Implications for diagnosis and treatment. *Journal of Clinical Psychiatry, 62* (Suppl. 13), 22–28.

Kirmayer, L. J., Boothroyd, L. J., Tanner, A., Adelson, N., & Robinson, E. (2000). Psychological distress among the Cree of James Bay. *Transcultural Psychiatry, 37,* 35–56.

Kirmayer, L. J., & Groleau, D. (2001). Affective disorders in cultural context. *Psychiatric Clinics of North America, 24,* 465–478.

Kirmayer, L. J., Looper, K. J., & Taillefer, S. (2003). Somatoform disorders. In M. Hersen & S. M. Turner (Eds.), *Adult psychopathology and diagnosis* (4th ed. pp. 420–475). New York: John Wiley.

Kirmayer, L. J., Malus, M., & Boothroyd, L. J. (1996). Suicide attempts among Inuit youth: A community survey of prevalence and risk factors. *Acta Psychiatrica Scandinavica, 94,* 8–17.

Kirmayer, L. J., & Robbins, J. M. (1991). Three forms of somatization in primary care: Prevalence, co-occurrence, and sociodemographic characteristics.

*Journal of Nervous and Mental Disease, 179,* 647–655.

Kirmayer, L. J., Robbins, J. M., & Paris, J. (1994). Somatoform disorders: Personality and the social matrix of somatic distress. *Journal of Abnormal Psychology, 103,* 125–136.

Kirmayer, L. J., & Weiss, M. (1993). *On cultural considerations for somatoform disorders in the DSM-IV.* In cultural proposals and supporting papers for DSM-IV. Submitted to the DSM-IV Task Force by the Steering Committee, NIMH-Sponsored Group on Culture and Diagnosis.

Kirschenbaum, B., Nedergaard, M., Preuss, A., Barami, K., Fraser, R. A., & Goldman, S. A. (1994). In vitro neuronal production and differentiation by precursor cells derived from the adult human forebrain. *Cerebral Cortex, 4,* 576–589.

Kleber, H. D. (1999). Opioids: Detoxification. In M. Galanter & H. D. Kleber (Eds.), *Textbook of substance abuse treatment* (2nd ed., pp. 251–279). Washington, DC: American Psychiatric Press.

Klein, D. N., Lewinsohn, P. M., & Seeley, J. R. (1997). Psychosocial characteristics of adolescents with a past history of dysthymic disorder: Comparison with adolescents with past histories of major depressive and non-affective disorders, and never mentally ill controls. *Journal of Affective Disorders, 42,* 127–135.

Klein, D. N., Lewinsohn, P. M., & Seeley, J. R. (2001). A family study of major depressive disorder in a community sample of adolescents. *Archives of General Psychiatry, 58*(1), 13–21.

Klein, D. N., Schwartz, J. E., Rose, S., & Leader, J. B. (2000). Five-year course and outcome of dysthymic disorder: A prospective, naturalistic follow-up study. *American Journal of Psychiatry, 157*(6), 931–939.

Klein, D. N., Taylor, E. B., Dickstein, S., & Harding, K. (1988). The early-late onset distinction in DSM-III-R dysthymia. *Journal of Affective Disorders, 14*(1), 25–33.

Klein, D. F. (1999). Harmful dysfunction, disorder, disease, illness, and evolution. *Journal of Abnormal Psychology, 108,* 421–429.

Klein, D. N., Lewinsohn, P. M., Rohde, P., Seeley, J. R., & Durbin, C. E. (2002). Clinical features of major depressive disorder in adolescents and their relatives: Impact on familial aggregation, implications for phenotype definition, and specificity of transmission. *Journal of Abnormal Psychology, 111,* 98–106.

Kleinknecht, R. A., Dinnel, D. L., Kleinknecht, E. E., Hiruma, N., & Harada, N. (1997). Cultural factors in social anxiety: A comparison of social phobia symptoms and *taijin kyofusho. Journal of Anxiety Disorders, 11,* 157–177.

Kleinman, A. (1982). Neurasthenia and depression: A study of somatization and culture in China. *Culture, Medicine, and Psychiatry, 6*(2), 117–190.

Kleinman, A. (1986). *Social origins of distress and disease: Depression, neurasthenia, and pain in modern China.* New Haven, CT: Yale University Press.

Klerman, G. L. (1988). Depression and related disorders of mood (affective disorders). In A. M. Nicholi, Jr. (Ed.), *The new Harvard guide to psychiatry.* Cambridge, MA: Harvard University Press.

Klerman, G. L., & Weissman, M. M. (1989). Increasing rates of depression. *Journal of the American Medical Association, 261,* 2229–2235.

Klerman, G. L., Weissman, M. M., Rounsaville, B. J., & Chevron, E. S. (1984). *Interpersonal psychotherapy of depression.* New York: Basic Books.

Klosko, J. S., Barlow, D. H., Tassinari, R., & Cerny, J. A. (1990). A comparison of alprazolam and behavior therapy in treatment of panic disorder. *Journal of Consulting and Clinical Psychology, 58,* 77–84.

Kluft, R. P. (1984). Treatment of multiple personality disorder. *Psychiatric Clinics of North America, 7,* 9–29.

Kluft, R. P. (1991). Multiple personality disorder. In A. Tasman & S. W. Goldinger (Eds.), *Review of psychiatry* (Vol. 10). Washington, DC: American Psychiatric Press.

Kluft, R. P. (1996). Treating the traumatic memories of patients with dissociative identity disorder. *American Journal of Psychiatry, 153,* 103–110.

Kluft, R. P. (1999). Current issues in dissociative identity disorder. *Journal of Practical Psychology and Behavioral Health, 5,* 3–19.

Klump, K. L., Kaye, W. H., & Strober, M. (2001). The evolving genetic foundations of eating disorders. *The Psychiatric Clinics of North America, 24,* 215–225.

Knight, R. A., & Prentky, R. A. (1990). Classifying sexual offenders: The development and corroboration of taxonomic models. In W. L. Marshall, D. R. Laws, & H. E. Barbaree (Eds.), *Handbook of sexual assault: Issues, theories and treatment of the offender* (pp. 23–52). New York: Plenum Press.

Koegel, L. K. (1995). Communication and language intervention. In R. L. Koegel & L. K. Koegel (Eds.), *Teaching children with autism: Strategies for initiating positive interactions and improving learning opportunities* (pp. 17–32). Baltimore, MD: Paul H. Brookes.

Koegel, R. L., Schreibman, L., O'Neill, R. E., & Burke, J. C. (1983). The personality and family interaction characteristics of parents of autistic children. *Journal of Consulting and Clinical Psychology, 51,* 683–692.

Koh, P. O., Bergson, C., Undie, A. S., Goldman-Rakic, P. S., & Lidow, M. S. (2003). Up-regulation of the D1 dopamine receptor–interacting protein, calcyon, in patients with schizophrenia. *Archives of General Psychiatry, 60,* 311–319.

Kohut, H. (1971). *The analysis of self.* New York: International Universities Press.

Kohut, H. (1977). *The restoration of the self.* New York: International Universities Press.

Kolb, B., Gibb, R., & Gorny, G. (2003). Experience-dependent changes in dendritic arbor and spine density in neocortex vary qualitatively with age and sex. *Neurobiology of Learning and Memory, 79*, 1–10.

Kolb, B., Gibb, R., & Robinson, T. E. (2003). Brain plasticity and behavior. *Current Directions in Psychological Science, 12*, 1–5.

Kolb, B., & Whishaw, I. Q. (1998). Possible regeneration of rat medial front cortex following neonatal frontal lesions. *Behavioral Brain Research, 91*, 127–141.

Kolb, B., & Whishaw, I. Q. (2003). *Fundamentals of human neuropsychology* (5th ed.). New York: Worth/Freeman.

Koocher, G. P. (1996). Pediatric oncology: Medical crisis intervention. In R. J. Resnick & R. H. Rozensky (Eds.), *Health psychology through the life span: Practice and research opportunities* (pp. 213–225). Washington, DC: American Psychological Association.

Kopyov, O. V., Jacques, D., Lieberman, A., Duma, C. M., & Rogers, R. L. (1996). Clinical study of fetal mesencephalic intracerebral transplants for the treatment of Parkinson's disease. *Cell Transplantation, 5*, 327–337.

Korczyn, A. D., Kahana, E., & Galper, Y. (1991). Epidemiology of dementia in Ashkelon, Israel. *Neuroepidemiology, 10*, 100.

Korenman, S. G., & Barchas, J. D. (1993). *Biological basis of substance abuse.* New York: Oxford University Press.

Korfine, L., & Hooley, J. M. (2000). Directed forgetting of emotional stimuli in borderline personality disorder. *Journal of Abnormal Psychology, 109*, 214–221.

Korol, C. T. & Craig, K. D. (2001). Pain from the perspectives of health psychology and culture. In S. S. Kazarian & D. R. Evans (Eds.), *Handbook of cultural health psychology* (pp. 241–265). San Diego, CA: Academic Press.

Kotsaftis, A., & Neale, J. M. (1993). Schizotypal personality disorder I: The clinical syndrome. *Clinical Psychology Review, 13*, 451–472.

Kovacs, M., Akiskal, H. S., Gatsonis, C., & Parrone, P. L. (1994). Childhood-onset dysthymic disorder. *Archives of General Psychiatry, 51*, 365–374.

Kovacs, M., Gatsonis, C., Paulauskas, S. L., & Richards, C. (1989). Depressive disorders in childhood: IV. A longitudinal study of comorbidity with and risk for anxiety disorders. *Archives of General Psychiatry, 46*(9), 776–782.

Kovacs, M., Goldston, D., & Gatsonis, C. (1993). Suicidal behaviors and childhood-onset depressive disorders: A longitudinal investigation. *Journal of the American Academy of Child and Adolescent Psychiatry, 32*, 8–20.

Kozak, J. M., Liebowitz, M. R., & Foa, E. B. (2000). Cognitive behavior therapy for obessesive-compulsive disorder: The NIMH sponsored collaborative study. In W. K. Goodman & M. V. Rudorfer (Eds.), *Obsessive-compulsive disorder: Contemporary issues in treatment. Personality and clinical psychology series* (pp. 501–530). Mahwah, NJ: Erlbaum.

Kraepelin, E. (1898). *The diagnosis and prognosis of dementia praecox.* Paper presented at the 29th Congress of Southwestern German Psychiatry, Heidelberg.

Kraepelin, E. (1899). *Kompendium der Psychiatrie* (6th ed.). Leipzig: Abel.

Kraepelin, E. (1913). *Psychiatry: A textbook for students and physicians.* Leipzig: Barth.

Krantz, D. S., & Deckel, A. W. (1983). Coping with coronary heart disease and stroke. In T. G. Burish & L. A. Bradley (Eds.), *Coping with chronic disease: Research and applications.* New York: Academic Press.

Kranzler, H. R. (2000). Medications for alcohol dependence: New vistas. *Journal of the American Medical Association, 284*(8), 1016–1017.

Kraus, N., McGee, T. J., Carrell, T. D., Zecker, S. G., Nicol, T. G., & Koch, D. B. (1996). Auditory neurophysiologic responses and discrimination deficits in children with learning problems. *Science, 273*, 971–973.

Kring, A. M., & Neale, J. M. (1996). Do schizophrenic patients show a disjunctive relationship among expressive, experiential, and psychophysiological components of emotion? *Journal of Abnormal Psychology, 105*, 249–257.

Krishnan, K. R., Doraiswamy, P. M., Venkataraman, S., Reed, D., & Richie, J. C. (1991). Current concepts in hypothalamo-pituitary-adrenal axis regulation. In J. A. McCubbin, P. G. Kaufmann, & C. B. Nemeroff (Eds.), *Stress, neuropeptides, and systemic disease* (pp. 19–35). San Diego: Academic Press.

Kristensen, H. (2000). Selective mutism and comorbidity with developmental disorder/delay, anxiety disorder, and elimination disorder. *Journal of the American Academy of Child and Adolescent Psychiatry, 39*, 249–256.

Kristiansen, C. M., Gareau, C., Mittlehold, J., DeCourville, N. H., & Hovdestad, W. E. (1999). The sociopolitical context of the delayed memory debate. In L. M. Williams & V. L. Banyard (Eds.), *Trauma and recovery* (pp. 331–347). Thousand Oaks, CA: Sage.

Krueger, R. F., Caspi, A., Moffitt, T. E., Silva, P. A., & McGee, R. (1996). Personality traits are differentially linked to mental disorders: A multitrait-multidiagnosis study of an adolescent birth cohort. *Journal of Abnormal Psychology, 105*, 299–312.

Krug, E. G., Kresnow, M. J., Peddicord, J. P., Dahlberg, L. L., Powell, K. E., Crosby, A. E., et al. (1998). Suicide after natural disasters. *New England Journal of Medicine, 338*(6), 373–378.

Kruger, S., & Kennedy, S. H. (2000). Psychopharmacotherapy of anorexia nervosa, bulimia nervosa and binge-eating disorder. *Journal of Psychiatry and Neuroscience, 25*, 497–508.

Kryger, M. H. (2000). Management of obstructive sleep apnea-hypoapnea syndrome: Overview. In M. H. Kryger, T. Roth, and W. C. Dement (Eds.), *Principles and practice of sleep medicine* (3rd ed., pp. 940–954). Philadelphia: W. B. Saunders.

Kuban, M., Barbaree, H. E., & Blanchard, R. (1999). A comparison of volume and circumference phallometry: Response magnitude and method agreement. *Archives of Sexual Behavior, 28*, 345–359.

Kuo, M., Adlaf, E. M., Lee, H., Gliksman, L., Demers, A., & Wechsler, H. (2002). More Canadian students drink but American students drink more: Comparing college alcohol use in two countries. *Addiction, 97*, 1583–1592.

Kuo, M., Adlaf, E. M., Lee, H., Gliksman, L., Demers, A., & Wechsler, H. (2003). More Canadian students drink but American students drink more: Comparing college alcohol use in two countries: Corrigendum. *Addiction, 98*, 373.

Kuo, W. H., Gallo, J. J., & Tien, A. Y. (2001). Incidence of suicide ideation and attempts in adults: The 13-year follow-up of a community sample in Baltimore, Maryland. *Psychological Medicine, 31*, 1181–91.

Kupfer, D. J. (1995). Sleep research in depressive illness: Clinical implications—A tasting menu. *Biological Psychiatry, 38*, 391–403.

Kupfer, D. J., First, M. B., & Regier, D. A. (2002). *A research agenda for DSM-V.* Washington, DC: American Psychiatric Press.

Kurita, H., Kita, M., & Miyake, Y. (1992). A comparative study of development and symptoms among disintegrative psychosis and infantile autism with and without speech loss. *Journal of Autism and Developmental Disorders, 22*, 175–188.

Kushner, M. G., Abrams, K., & Borchardt, C. (2000). The relationship between anxiety disorders and alcohol use disorders: A review of major perspectives and findings. *Clinical Psychology Review, 20*, 149–171.

Kushner, M. G., Sher, K. J., & Beitman, B. D. (1990). The relation between alcohol problems and the anxiety disorders. *American Journal of Psychiatry, 147*, 685–695.

La Greca, A. M., & Prinstein, M. J. (2002). Hurricanes and earthquakes. In A. N. La Greca, W. K. Silverman & M. C. Roberts (Eds.) *Helping Children Cope with Disasters and Terrorism* (Vol. 1, pp. 107–138). Washington, DC: American Psychological Association.

La Rue, A. (1992). *Aging and neuropsychological assessment.* New York: Plenum Press.

Lacey, J. H. (1992). The treatment demand for bulimia: A catchment area report of referral rates and demography. *Psychiatric Bulletin, 16*, 203–205.

Lachar, D., Bailley, S. E., Rhoades, H. M., Espadas, A., Aponte, M., Cowan, K. A., et al. (2001). New subscales for an anchored version of the Brief Psychiatric Rating Scale: Construction, reliability, and validity in acute psychiatric admissions. *Psychological Assessment, 13*, 384–395.

Lacks, P., & Morin, C. M. (1992). Recent advances in the assessment and treatment of insomnia. *Journal of Consulting and Clinical Psychology, 60*, 586–594.

Ladd, C. O., Huot, R. L., Thrivikraman, K. V., Nemeroff, C. B., Meaney, M. J., & Plotsky, P. M. (2000). Long-term behavioral and neuroendocrine adaptations to adverse early experience. In E. A. Mayer & C. B. Saper (Eds.), *Progress in brain research: The biological basis for mind body interactions*. (Vol. 122, pp. 81–103). Amsterdam: Elsevier.

Ladd, C. O., Owens, M. J., & Nemeroff, C. B. (1996). Persistent changes in corticotropin-releasing factor neuronal systems induced by maternal deprivation. *Endocrinology, 137*(4), 1212–1218.

Ladee, G. A. (1966). *Hypochondriacal syndromes*. New York: Elsevier.

Lader, M. H. (1975). *The psychophysiology of mental illness*. London: Routledge & Kegan Paul.

Lader, M., & Sartorius, N. (1968). Anxiety in patients with hysterical conversion symptoms. *Journal of Neurology, Neurosurgery, and Psychiatry, 31*, 490–495.

Lader, M. H., & Wing, L. (1964). Habituation of the psycho-galvanic reflex in patients with anxiety states and in normal subjects. *Journal of Neurology, Neurosurgery, and Psychiatry, 27*, 210–218.

Ladouceur, R. (1982). In vivo cognitive desensitization of flight phobia: A case study. *Psychological Reports, 50*, 459–462.

Ladouceur, R. (1996). The prevalence of pathological gambling in Canada. *Journal of Gambling Studies, 12*, 129–142.

Ladouceur, R., Dugas, M. J., Freeston, M. H., Rheaume, J., Blais, F., Gagnon, F., et al. (1999). Specificity of generalized anxiety disorder symptoms and processes. *Behavior Therapy, 30*, 191–207.

Ladouceur, R., Gosselin, P., & Dugas, M. J. (2000). Experimental manipulation of intolerance of uncertainty: A study of a theoretical model of worry. *Behaviour Research and Therapy, 38*, 933–941.

Laing, R. D. (1967). *The politics of experience*. New York: Pantheon.

Lakin, M. M., Montague, D. K., Vanderbrug Medendorp, S., Tesar, L., & Schover, L. R. (1990). Intracavernous injection therapy: Analysis of results and complications. *Journal of Urology, 143*, 1138–1141.

Lalonde, J. K., Hudson, J. I., Gigante, R. A., & Pope, H. G. (2001). Canadian and American psychiatrists' attitudes toward dissociative disorders diagnoses. *Canadian Journal of Psychiatry, 46*, 407–412.

Lalumière, M. L. Blanchard, R., & Zucker, K. J. (2000). Sexual orientation and handedness in men and women: A meta-analysis. *Psychological Bulletin, 126*, 575–592.

Lam, D. H., Watkins, E. R., Hayward, P., Bright, J., Wright, K., Kerr, N., et al. (2003). A randomized controlled study of cognitive therapy for relapse prevention for bipolar affective disorder: Outcome of the first year. *Archives of General Psychiatry, 60*, 145–152.

Lam, R. W. (1994). Morning light therapy for winter depression: Predictors of response. *Acta Psychiatrica Scandinavica, 89*, 97–101.

Lam, R. W., & Levitt, A. J. (1999). *Clinical guidelines for the treatment of seasonal affective disorder*. Vancouver, BC: Clinical & Academic Publishing.

Lam, R. W., Tam, E. M., Shiah, I.-S., Yatham, L. N., & Zis, A. P. (2000). Effects of light therapy on suicidal ideation in patients with winter depression. *Journal of Clinical Psychiatry, 61*, 30–32.

Lam, T. H., Ho, S. Y., Hedley, A. J., Mak, K. H., & Peto, R. (2001). Mortality and smoking in Hong Kong: Case-control study of all adult deaths in 1998. *British Medical Journal, 323*, 361–362.

Lambert, J. C., Coyle, N., & Lendon, C. (2004). The allelic modulation of apolipoprotein E expression by oestrogen: Potential relevance for Alzheimer's disease. *Journal of Medical Genetics, 41*, 104–112.

Lambert, M. C., Weisz, J. R., Knight, F., Desrosiers, M., Overly, K., & Thesiger, C. (1992). Jamaican and American adult perspectives on child psychopathology: Further explorations of the threshold model. *Journal of Consulting and Clinical Psychology, 60*, 146–149.

Lambert, M. J., Shapiro, D. A., & Bergin, A. E. (1986). The effectiveness of psychotherapy. In S. L. Garfield & A. E. Bergin (Eds.), *Handbook of psychotherapy and behavior change* (3rd ed.). New York: John Wiley.

Landis, S. E., Earp, J. L., & Koch, G. G. (1992). Impact of HIV testing and counseling on subsequent sexual behavior. *AIDS Education and Prevention, 4*(1), 61–70.

Lang, P. J. (1985). The cognitive psychophysiology of emotion: Fear and anxiety. In A. H. Tuma & J. D. Maser (Eds.), *Anxiety and the anxiety disorders*. Hillsdale, NJ: Erlbaum.

Lang, P. J. (1995). The emotion probe: Studies of motivation and attention. *American Psychologist, 50*, 372–385.

Lang, P. J., Bradley, M. M., & Cuthbert, B. N. (1998). Emotion, motivation, and anxiety: Brain mechanisms and psychophysiology. *Biological Psychiatry, 44*, 1248–1263.

Langewisch, M. W. J., & Frisch, G. R. (1998). Gambling behavior and pathology in relation to impulsivity, sensation seeking, and risk behavior in male college students. *Journal of Gambling Studies, 14*, 245–262.

Lapierre, Y. D. (1994). Pharmacological therapy of dysthymia. *Acta Psychiatrica Scandinavica Supplemental, 89*(383), 42–48.

Larson, S. A., Lakin, K. C., Anderson, L., Kwak, N., Lee, J. H., & Anderson, D. (2001). Prevalence of mental retardation and developmental disabilities: Estimates from the 1994/1995 National Health Interview Survey Disability Supplements. *American Journal on Mental Retardation, 106*, 231–252.

Laruelle, M., Kegeles, L. S., & Abi-Darham, A. (2003). Glutamate, dopamine, and schizophrenia: From pathophysiology to treatment. *Annals of the New York Academy of Sciences, 1003*, 138–158.

Lasch, C. (1978). *The culture of narcissism: American life in an age of diminishing expectations*. New York: W. W. Norton.

Lau, M. A., & Segal, Z. V. (2003). Depression in context: Strategies for guided action. *Journal of Cognitive Psychotherapy, 17*, 94–97.

Laub, J. H., & Vaillant, G. E. (2000). Delinquency and mortality: A 50-year follow-up study of 1,000 delinquent and nondelinquent boys. *American Journal of Psychiatry, 157*, 96–102.

Laumann, E., Gagnon, J., Michael, R., & Michaels, S. (1994). *The social organization of sexuality: Sexual practices in the United States*. Chicago: University of Chicago Press.

Laumann, E. O., Paik, A., & Rosen, R. C. (1999). Sexual dysfunction in the United States: Prevalence and predictors. *Journal of the American Medical Association, 281*, 537–544.

Lavallee, C., Robinson, E., & Laverdure, J. (1991). Description de la clientèle et des services de santé mentale au sein de la population crie du nord québécois. *Santé Culture Health, 8* (3), 265–284.

Laws, D. R. (Ed.). (1989). *Relapse prevention with sex offenders*. New York: Guilford Press.

Laws, D. R., & O'Donohue, W. (Eds.). (1997). *Sexual deviance: Theory, assessment and treatment*. New York: Guilford Press.

Laxenaire, M., Ganne-Vevonec, M. O., & Streiff, O. (1982). Les problèmes d'identité chez les enfants des migrants. *Annales Medico-Psychologiques, 140*, 602–605.

Laxova, R., Ridler, M. A. C., & Bowen-Bravery, M. (1977). An etiological survey of the severely retarded Hertfordshire children who were born between January 1, 1965 and December 31, 1967. *American Journal of Medical Genetics, 1*, 75–86.

Lazarus, R. S. (1968). Emotions and adaptation: Conceptual and empirical relations. In W. J. Arnold (Ed.), *Nebraska Symposium on Motivation* (Vol. 16). Lincoln: University of Nebraska Press.

Lazarus, R. S. (1991). Progress on a cognitive-motivational relational theory of emotion. *American Psychologist, 46*(8), 819–834.

Lazarus, R. S. (1995). Psychological stress in the workplace. In R. Crandall, P. L. Perrewe (Eds.), *Occupational stress: A handbook* (pp. 3–14). Philadelphia: Taylor & Francis.

Lebedinskaya, K. S., & Nikolskaya, O. S. (1993). Brief report: Analysis of autism and its treatment in modern Russian defectology. *Journal of Autism and Developmental Disorders, 23*, 675–697.

Leccese, A. P. (1991). *Drugs and society: Behavioral medicines and abusable drugs*. Englewood Cliffs, NJ: Prentice Hall.

Leckman, J. F., Grice, D. E., Boardman, J., Zhang, H., Vitali, A., Bondi, C., et al. (1997a). Symptoms of obsessive-compulsive disorder. *American Journal of Psychiatry, 154*, 911–917.

Leckman, J. F., Peterson, B. S., Anderson, G. M., Arnstein, A. F. T., Pauls, D. L., & Cohen, D. J. (1997b). Pathogenesis of Tourette's syndrome. *Journal of Child Psychology and Psychiatry, 38*, 119–142.

Lecrubier, Y., Bakker, A., Dunbar, G., & The Collaborative Paroxetine Panic Study Investigators. (1997). A comparison of paroxetine, clomipramine and placebo in the treatment of panic disorder. *Acta Psychiatrica Scandinavica, 95*, 145–152.

Lecrubier, Y., Judge, R., & The Collaborative Paroxetine Panic Study Investigators. (1997). Long term evaluation of paroxetine, clomipramine and placebo in panic disorder. *Acta Psychiatrica Scandinavica, 95*, 153–160.

LeDoux, J. E. (1995). In search of an emotional system in the brain: Leaping from fear to emotion to consciousness. In M. S. Gazzaniga (Ed.), *The cognitive neurosciences* (pp. 1049–1062). Cambridge, MA: MIT Press.

LeDoux, J. E. (1996). *The emotional brain: The mysterious underpinnings of emotional life.* New York: Simon & Schuster.

LeDoux, J. E. (2001). *Synaptic self.* New York: Viking.

Lee, C. K. (1992). Alcoholism in Korea. In J. Helzer & G. Canino (Eds.), *Alcoholism—North America, Europe and Asia: A coordinated analysis of population data from ten regions* (pp. 247–262). London, UK: Oxford University Press.

Lee, K. (1992). Pattern of night waking and crying of Korean infants from 3 months to 2 years old and its relation with various factors. *Journal of Developmental and Behavioral Pediatrics, 13,* 326–330.

Lee, K. K. (2000). *Urban poverty in Canada: A statistical profile.* Ottawa, ON: Canadian Council on Social Development.

Lee, M. A., & Shalin. (1985). *Acid dreams.* New York: Grove Weidenfeld.

Lee, S. (1993). How abnormal is the desire for slimness? A survey of eating attitudes and behavior among Chinese undergraduates in Hong Kong. *Psychological Medicines, 23,* 437–451.

Lee, S., Hsu, L. K. G., & Wing, Y. K. (1992). Bulimia nervosa in Hong Kong Chinese patients. *British Journal of Psychiatry, 161,* 545–551.

Lee, S., Leung, C. M., Wing, Y. K., Chiu, H. F., & Chen, C. N. (1991). Acne as a risk factor for anorexia nervosa in Chinese. *Australian and New Zealand Journal of Psychiatry, 25*(1), 134–137.

Lee, T. M., Chen, E. Y., Chan, C. C., Paterson, J. G., Janzen, H. L., & Blashko, C. A. (1998). Seasonal affective disorder. *Clinical Psychology: Science and Practice, 5,* 275–290.

Leenaars, A. A., & Lester, D. (1995). Impact of suicide prevention centres on suicide in Canada. *Crisis, 16,* 39.

Leff, J., Satorius, N., Jablensky, A., Korten, A., & Ernberg, G. (1992). The International Pilot Study of Schizophrenia: Five-year follow-up findings. *Psychological Medicine, 22,* 131–145.

Lehman, A. F. (1995). Vocational rehabilitation in schizophrenia. *Schizophrenia Bulletin, 21,* 645–656.

Lehmann, H. E., & Ban, T. A. (1997). The history of the psychopharmacology of schizophrenia. *Canadian Journal of Psychiatry, 42,* 152–162.

Lehmann, H. E., & Hanrahan, G. E. (1954). Chlorpromazine: New inhibiting agent for psychomotor excitement and manic states. *AMA Archives of Neurology and Psychiatry, 71,* 227–237.

Leiblum, S. R. (2000). Vaginismus: A most perplexing problem. In S. R. Leiblum & R. C. Rosen (Eds.), *Principles and practice of sex therapy* (3rd ed., pp. 181–202). New York: Guilford Press.

Leiblum, S. R., & Rosen, R. C. (Eds.). (2000). *Principles and practice of sex therapy* (3rd ed.). New York: Guilford Press.

Lejeune, J., Gauthier, M., & Turpin, R. (1959). Étude des chromosomes somatiques de neuf enfants mongoliens. *Comptes Rendus Hebdomadaires des Séances de l' Académie des Sciences. D: Sciences Naturelles (Paris), 248,* 1721–1722.

Lemoine, P., Harousseau, H., Borteyru, J. P., & Menuet, J. C. (1968). Les enfants de parents alcooliques: Anomalies observées. À propos de 127 cas [Children of alcoholic parents: Anomalies observed in 127 cases]. *Quest Medicine, 21,* 476–482.

Lenke, R. R., & Levy, H. (1980). Maternal phenylketonuria and hyperphenylalanemia: An international survey of the outcome of untreated and treated pregnancies. *New England Journal of Medicine, 303,* 1202–1208.

Lenze, E. J., Mulsant, B. H., Shear, K. M., Schulberg, H. C., Dew, M. A., Begley, A. E., et al. (2000). Comorbid anxiety disorders in depressed elderly patients. *American Journal of Psychiatry, 157*(5), 722–728.

Lerman, C., Caporaso, N. E., Audrain, J., Main, D., Bowman, E. D., Lockshin, B., et al. (1999). Evidence suggesting the role of specific genetic factors in cigarette smoking. *Health Psychology, 18*(1), 14–20.

Lesch, K. P., Bengel, D., Heils, A., Sabol, S. Z., Greenberg, B. D., Petri, S., et al. (1996). Association of anxiety-related traits with a polymorphism in the serotonin transporter gene regulatory region. *Science, 274,* 1527–1531.

Leserman, J., Petitto, J. M., Golden, R. N., Gaynes, B. N., Gu, H., Perkins, D. O., et al. (2000). Impact of stressful life events, depression, social support, coping, and cortisol on progression to AIDS. *American Journal of Psychiatry, 157,* 1221–1228.

Lester, D. (1991). Do suicide prevention centres prevent suicide? *Homeostasis in Health and Disease, 33,* 190–194.

Leuchter, A., Cook, I. A., Witte, E. A., Morgan, M., & Abrams, M. (2002). Changes in brain function of depressed subjects during treatment with placebo. *The American Journal of Psychiatry, 159,* 122–129.

Leung, F., Lam, S., & Sze, S. (2001). Cultural expectations of thinness in Chinese women. *Eating Disorders: The Journal of Treatment and Prevention, 9,* 339–350.

Leung, F., Schwartzman, A., & Steiger, H. (1996). Testing a dual-process family model in understanding the development of eating pathology: A structural equation modeling analysis. *International Journal of Eating Disorders, 20,* 367–375.

Leung, G. M., Yeung, R. Y., Chi, I., & Chu L. W. (2003). The economics of Alzheimer disease. *Dementia and Geriatric Cognitive Disorders, 15,* 34–43.

Levenston, G. K., Patrick, C. J., Bradley, M. M., & Lang, P. J. (2000). The psychopath as observer: Emotion and attention in picture processing. *Journal of Abnormal Psychology, 109,* 373–385.

Levin, A., & Hyler, S. (1986). DSM-III personality diagnosis in bulimia. *Comprehensive Psychiatry, 27,* 47.

Levine, M. N., Guyatt, G. H., Gent, M., DePauw, S., Goodyear, M. D., Hryniuk, W. M., et al. (1988). Quality of life in stage II breast cancer: An instrument for clinical trials. *Journal of Clinical Oncology, 6,* 1798–1810.

Levine, M. P., & Smolak, L. (1996). Media as a context for the development of disordered eating. In L. Smolak, M. P. Levine, & R. Striegel-Moore (Eds.), *The developmental psychopathology of eating disorders: Implications for research, prevention, and treatment* (pp. 235–257). Mahwah, NJ: Erlbaum.

Levinson, D. F., Mahtami, M. M., Nancarrow, D. J., Brown, D., Kruglyak, L., Kirby, A., et al. (1998). Genome scan of schizophrenia. *American Journal of Psychiatry, 155*(6), 741–750.

Levitt, A. J., Boyle, M. H., Joffe, R. T., & Baumal, Z. (2000). Estimated prevalence of the seasonal subtype of major depression in a Canadian community sample. *Canadian Journal of Psychiatry, 45,* 650–654.

Levitt, A. J., Joffe, R. T., Moul, D. F., Lam, R. W., Teicher, M. H., Lebegue, B., et al. (1993). Side effects of light therapy in seasonal affective disorder. *American Journal of Psychiatry, 150,* 650–652.

Levy, B. R., Slade, M. D., Kunkel, S. R., & Kasl, S. V. (2002). Longevity increased by positive self-perceptions of aging. *Journal of Personality and Social Psychology, 83,* 261–270.

Lewinsohn, P. M., Allen, N. B., Seeley, J. R., & Gotlib, I. H. (1999). First onset versus recurrence of depression: Differential processes of psychosocial risk. *Journal of Abnormal Psychology, 108*(3), 483–489.

Lewinsohn, P. M., & Gotlib, I. H. (1995). Behavioral therapy and treatment of depression. In E. E. Beckham & W. R. Leber (Eds.), *Handbook of depression* (pp. 352–375). New York: Guilford Press.

Lewinsohn, P. M., Gotlib, I. H., & Seeley, J. R. (1997). Depression-related psychosocial variables: Are they specific to depression in adolescents? *Journal of Abnormal Psychology, 106*(3), 365–375.

Lewinsohn, P. M., Hops, H., Roberts, R. E., Seeley, J. R., & Andrews, J. A. (1993). Adolescent psychopathology: I. Prevalence and incidence of depression and other DSM-III-R disorders in high school students. *Journal of Abnormal Psychology, 102*(1), 133–144.

Lewinsohn, P. M., Rohde, P., & Seeley, J. R. (1993). Psychosocial characteristics of adolescents with a history of suicide attempt. *Journal of the American Academy of Child and Adolescent Psychiatry, 32*(1), 60–68.

Lewinsohn, P. M., Rohde, P., Seeley, J. R., & Fischer, S. A. (1993). Age-cohort changes in the lifetime occurrence of depression and other mental disorders. *Journal of Abnormal Psychology, 102*(1), 110–120.

Lewinsohn, P. M., Rohde, P., Seeley, J. R., Klein, D. N., & Gotlib, I. H. (2000). Natural course of adolescent major depressive disorder on community sample: Predictors of recurrence in young adults. *American Journal of Psychiatry, 157*(10), 1584–1591.

Lewinsohn, P. M., & Rosenbaum, M. (1987). Recall of parental behavior by acute depressives, remitted depressives and nondepressives. *Journal of Personality and Social Psychology, 52*(3), 611–619.

Lewis, D. O., Yeager, C. A., Swica, Y., Pincus, J. H., & Lewis, M. (1997). Objective documentation of child abuse and dissociation in 12 murderers with dissociative identity disorder. *American Journal of Psychiatry, 154,* 1703–1710.

Lewis, G., Croft-Jeffreys, C., & Anthony, D. (1990). Are British psychiatrists racist? *British Journal of Psychiatry, 157,* 410–415.

Lewis, G., David, A., Andreasson, S., & Allsbeck, P. (1992). Schizophrenia and city life. *Lancet, 340,* 137–140.

Lewis, G., Hawton, K., & Jones, P. (1997). Strategies for preventing suicide. *British Journal of Psychiatry, 171,* 351–354.

Lewy, A. J. (1993). Seasonal mood disorders. In D. L. Dunner (Ed.), *Current psychiatric therapy* (pp. 220–225). Philadelphia: W. B. Saunders.

Lewy, A. J., Kern, H. E., Rosenthal, N. E., & Wehr, T. A. (1982). Bright artificial light treatment of a manic-depressive patient with a seasonal mood cycle. *American Journal of Psychiatry, 139,* 1496–1498.

Lewy, A. J., & Sack, R. L. (1987). Light therapy of chronobiological disorders. In A. Halaris (Ed.), *Chronobiology and psychiatric disorders* (pp. 181–206). New York: Elsevier.

Li, H. Z., & Browne, A. J. (2000). Defining mental illness and accessing mental health services: Perspectives of Asian Canadians. *Canadian Journal of Community Mental Health, 19,* 143–159.

Liberman, R. P., DeRisi, W. D., & Mueser, K. T. (1989). *Social skills training for psychiatric patients.* Boston: Allyn & Bacon.

Lidbeck, J. (1997). Group therapy for somatization disorders in general practice: Effectivenss of a short cognitive-behavioral treatment model. *Acta Psychiatrica Scandinavica, 96,* 14–24.

Lieb, R., Wittchen, H. U., Hofler, M., Fuetsch, M., Stein, M. B., & Merikangas, K. R. (2000). Parental psychopathology, parenting styles, and the risk of social phobia in offspring. *Archives of General Psychiatry, 57,* 859–866.

Lieb, R., Zimmermann, P. Friis, R. H., Hofler, M. Tholen, S., & Wittchen, H. U. (2002). The natural course of DSM-IV somatoform disorders and syndromes among adolescents and young adults: A prospective-longitudinal community study. *European Psychiatry, 17,* 321–331.

Lieberman, J. A., Jody, D., Alvir, J. M. J., Ashtari, M., Levy, D. L., Bogerts, B., et al. (1993). Brain morphology, dopamine, and eye-tracking abnormalities in first-episode schizophrenia. *Archives of General Psychiatry, 50,* 357–368.

Liebeskind, J. (1991). Pain can kill. *Pain, 44,* 3–4.

Liebowitz, M. R., Heimberg, R. G., Schneier, F. R., Hope, D. A., Davies, S., Holt, C. S., et al. (1999). Cognitive-behavioral group therapy versus phenelzine in social phobia: Long-term outcome. *Depression and Anxiety, 10,* 89–98.

Liebowitz, M. R., Schneier, F., Campeas, R., Hollander, E., Hatterer, J., Fyer, A., et al. (1992). Phenelzine vs. atenolol in social phobia: A placebo controlled comparison. *Archives of General Psychiatry, 49,* 290–300.

Liggett, J. (1974). *The human face.* New York: Stein and Day.

Lilienfeld, S. O. (1992). The association between antisocial personality and somatization disorders: A review and integration of theoretical models. *Clinical Psychology Review, 12,* 641–662.

Lilienfeld, S. O., & Hess, T. H. (2001). Psychopathic personality traits and somatization: Sex differences and the mediating role of negative emotionality. *Journal of Psychopathology and Behavioral Assessment, 23,* 11–24.

Lilienfeld, S. O., Kirsch, I., Sarbin, T. R., Lynn, S. J., Chaves, J. F., & Ganaway, G. K. (1999). Dissociative identity disorder and the sociocognitive model: Recalling the lessons of the past. *Psychological Bulletin, 125*(5), 507–523.

Lilienfeld, S. O., & Marino, L. (1995). Mental disorder as a Roschian concept: A critique of Wakefield's 'harmful dysfunction' analysis. *Journal of Abnormal Psychology, 104,* 411–420.

Lilienfeld, S. O., & Marino, L. (1999). Essentialism revisited: Evolutionary theory and the concept of mental disorder. *Journal of Abnormal Psychology, 108,* 400–411.

Lilienfeld, S. O., Van Valkenburg, C., Larntz, K., & Akiskal, H. S. (1986). The relationship of histrionic personality to antisocial personality and somatization disorders. *American Journal of Psychiatry, 143,* 718–722.

Lin, K. M. (1986). Psychopathology and social disruption in refugees. In C. L. Williams & J. Westermeyer (Eds.), *Refugee mental health in resettlement countries* (pp. 61–73). Washington, DC: Hemisphere.

Linden, W., Gerin, W., & Davidson, K. (2003). Cardiovascular reactivity: Status quo and a research agenda for the new millennium. *Psychosomatic Medicine, 65,* 5–8.

Lindquist, P., & Allebeck, P. (1990). Schizophrenia and crime: A longitudinal followup of 644 schizophrenics in Stockholm. *British Journal of Psychiatry, 157,* 345–350.

Lindsay, P. S. (1977). Fitness to stand trial in Canada: An overview in light of the recommendations of the law reform commission of Canada. *Criminal Law Quarterly, 19,* 303–348.

Lindsey, K. P., & Paul, G. L. (1989). Involuntary commitments to public mental institutions: Issues involving the overrepresentation of Blacks and assessment of relevant functioning. *Psychological Bulletin, 106,* 171–183.

Linehan, M. M. (1987). Dialectical behavior therapy for borderline personality disorder: Theory and method. *Bulletin of the Menninger Clinic, 51,* 261–276.

Linehan, M. M. (1993). *Cognitive behavioral treatment of borderline personality disorder.* New York: Guilford Press.

Linehan, M. M., Armstrong,, H. E., Suarez, A., Allmon, D., & Heard, H. L. (1991). Cognitive-behavioral treatment of chronically parasuicidal borderline patients. *Archives of General Psychiatry, 48,* 1060–1064.

Linehan, M. M., Heard, H. L., & Armstrong, H. E. (1992). *Naturalistic follow-up of a behavioral treatment for chronically parasuicidal borderline patients.* Unpublished manuscript, University of Washington, Seattle.

Linehan, M. M., & Kehrer, C. A. (1993). Borderline personality disorder. In D. H. Barlow (Ed.), *Clinical handbook of psychological disorders: A step by step treatment manual.* New York: Guilford Press.

Links, P. S., Heslegrave, R, & van Reekum, R. (1998). Prospective follow-up study of borderline personality disorder: Prognosis, prediction outcome, and Axis II comorbidity. *Canadian Journal of Psychiatry, 43,* 265–270.

Links, P. S., Heslegrave, R., & van Reekum, R. (1999). Impulsivity: Core aspect of borderline personality disorder. *Journal of Personality Disorders, 13,* 1–9.

Links, P. S., Steiner, M., Boiago, I., & Irwin, D. (1990). Lithium therapy for borderline patients: Preliminary findings. *Journal of Personality Disorders, 4,* 173–181.

Links, P., Steiner, M., & Huxley, G. (1988). The occurrence of borderline personality disorder in families of borderline patients. *Journal of Personality Disorders, 2,* 14–20.

Links, P. S., & Van Reekum, R. (1993). Childhood sexual abuse, parental impairment and the development of borderline personality disorder. *Canadian Journal of Psychiatry, 38,* 472–474.

Linnet, K. M., Dalsgaard, S., Obel, C., Wisborg, K., Henriksen, T. B., Rodriguez, A., et al. (2003). Maternal lifestyle factors in pregnancy risk of attention deficit hyperactivity disorder and associated behaviors: Review of the current evidence. *American Journal of Psychiatry, 160,* 1028–1040.

Lipchik, G. L., Holroyd, K. A., & Nash, J. M. (2002). Cognitive-behavioral management of recurrent headache disorders: A minimal-therapist-contact approach. In D. C. Turk & R. J. Gatchel (Eds.), *Psychological approaches to pain management: A practitioner's handbook* (2nd ed.). New York: Guilford Press.

Lipowski, Z. J. (1990). *Delirium: Acute confusional states.* New York: Oxford University Press.

Lipton, A. M., & Weiner, M. F. (2003). Differential diagnosis. In M. F. Weiner & A. M. Lipton (Eds.), *The dementias: Diagnosis, treatment and research* (3rd ed.) (pp. 137–180). Washington, DC: American Psychiatric Press.

Lisspers, J., & Öst, L. (1990). Long-term followup of migraine treatment: Do the effects remain up to six years? *Behaviour Research and Therapy, 28,* 313–322.

Livesley, W. J., & Jang, K. L. (2000). Toward an empirically based classification of personality disorder. *Journal of Personality Disorders, 14,* 137–151.

Livesley, W. J., Jang, K. L., & Vernon, P. A. (1998). Phenotypic and genotypic structure of traits delineating personality disorder. *Archives of General Psychiatry, 55,* 941–948.

Livesley, W. J., Schroeder, M. L., Jackson, D. N., & Jang, K. L. (1994). Categorical distinctions in the study of personality disorder: Implications for classification. *Journal of Abnormal Psychology, 103,* 6–17.

Loeb, K. L., Wilson, G. T., Gilbert, J. S., & Labouvie, E. (2000). Guided and unguided self-help for binge eating. *Behaviour Research and Therapy, 38*(3), 259–272.

Loebel, J. P., Dager, S. R., & Kitchell, M. A. (1993). Alzheimer's disease. In D. L. Dunner (Ed.), *Current psychiatric therapy* (pp. 59–65). Philadelphia: W. B. Saunders.

Loehlin, J. C. (1992). *Genes and environment in personality development*. Newbury Park, CA: Sage.

Loewenstein RJ. (1991). An office mental status examination for complex chronic dissociative symptoms and multiple personality disorder. *The Psychiatric Clinics of North America, 14*, 567–604.

Loftus, E. F. (2003). Make-believe memories. *American Psychologist, 58*, 867–873.

Long, J. C., Knowler, W. C., Hanson, R. L., Robin, R. W., Urbanek, M., Moore, E., et al. (1998). Evidence for genetic linkage to alcohol dependence on chromosomes 4 and 11 from an autosome-wide scan in an American Indian population. *American Journal of Medicine and Genetics, 81*, 216–221.

Looman, J., & Marshall, W. L. (2001). Phallometric assessments designed to detect arousal to children: The responses of rapists and child molesters. *Sexual Abuse: Journal of Research and Treatment, 13*, 3–13.

Looper, K. J., & Kirmayer. L. J. (2002). Behavioral medicine approaches to somatoform disorders. *Journal of Consulting and Clinical Psychology, 70*, 810–827.

Looper, K. J., & Paris, J. (2000). What dimensions underlie Cluster B personality disorders? *Comprehensive Psychiatry, 41*, 432–437.

LoPiccolo, J., Heiman, J. R., Hogan, D. R., & Roberts, C. W. (1985). Effectiveness of single therapists versus cotherapy teams in sex therapy. *Journal of Consulting and Clinical Psychology, 53*(3), 287–294.

LoPiccolo, J., & Stock, W. E. (1987). Sexual function, dysfunction and counseling in gynecological practice. In Z. Rosenwaks, F. Benjamin, & M. L. Stone (Eds.), *Gynecology*. New York: Macmillan.

Lovaas, O. I. (1977). *The autistic child: Language development through behavior modification*. New York: Irvington.

Lovaas, O. I. (1987). Behavioral treatment and normal educational and intellectual functioning in young autistic children. *Journal of Consulting and Clinical Psychology, 55*, 3–9.

Lovaas, O. I., Berberich, J. P., Perloff, B. F., & Schaeffer, B. (1966). Acquisition of imitative speech by schizophrenic children. *Science, 151*, 705–707.

Lowman, R. L. (2001). Constructing a literature from case studies: Promise and limitations of the method. *Consulting Psychology Journal: Practice and Research, 53*, 119–123.

Lucas, A. R., Beard, C. M., O'Fallon, W. M., & Kurlan, L. T. (1991). 50-year trends in the incidence of anorexia nervosa in Rochester, Minn.: A population-based study. *American Journal of Psychiatry, 148*, 917–922.

Luckasson, R., Coulter, D. L., Polloway, E. A., Reiss, S., Schalock, R. L., Snell, M. E., et al. (1992). *Mental retardation: Definition, classification, and systems of supports* (9th ed.). Washington, DC: American Association on Mental Retardation.

Ludwig, A. M. (1985). Cognitive processes associated with "spontaneous" recovery from alcoholism. *Journal of Studies on Alcohol, 46*, 53–58.

Ludwig, A. M. (1995). *The price of greatness: Resolving the creativity and madness controversy*. New York: Guilford Publications.

Ludwig, A., Brandsma, J., Wilbur, C., Bendfeldt, F., & Jameson, D. (1972). The objective study of a multiple personality. *Archives of General Psychiatry, 26*, 298–310.

Lundh, L. G., & Öst, L. G. (1996). Recognition bias for critical faces in social phobics. *Behaviour Research and Therapy, 34*, 787–794.

Lundstrom, B., Pauly, I., & Walinder, J. (1984). Outcome of sex reassignment surgery. *Acta Psychiatrica Scandinavica, 70*, 289–294.

Lutgendorf, S. K., Antoni, M. H., Ironson, G., Klimas, N., Kumar, M., Starr, K., et al. (1997). Cognitive-behavioral stress management decreases dysphoric mood and herpes simplex virus-type 2 antibody titers in symptomatic HIV-seropositive gay men. *Journal of Consulting and Clinical Psychology, 65*, 31–43.

Lydiard, R. B., Brawman-Mintzer, O., & Ballenger, J. C. (1996). Recent developments in the psychopharmacology of anxiety disorders. *Journal of Consulting & Clinical Psychology, 64*, 660–668.

Lyketsos, C. G., Steinberg, M., Tschanz, J. T., Norton, M. C., Steffens, D. C., & Breitner, J. C. S. (2000). Mental and behavioral disturbances in dementia: Findings from the Cache County study on memory and aging. *American Journal of Psychiatry, 157*, 708–714.

Lykken, D. T. (1957). A study of anxiety in the sociopathic personality. *Journal of Abnormal and Social Psychology, 55*, 6–10.

Lykken, D. T. (1982). Fearfulness: Its carefree charms and deadly risks. *Psychology Today, 16*, 20–28.

Lynam, D. R. (1996). Early identification of chronic offenders: Who is a fledgling psychopath? *Psychological Bulletin, 120*, 209–234.

Lyon, D. R., Hart, S. D., & Webster, C. D. (2001). Violence and risk assessment. In R. A. Schuller & J. R. P. Ogloff (Eds.), *Introduction to psychology and law: Canadian perspectives* (pp. 314–350). Toronto: University of Toronto Press.

Lyons, M. J., Eisen, S. A., Goldberg, J., True, W., Lin, N., Meyer, J. M., et al. (1998). A registry-based twin study of depression in men. *Archives of General Psychiatry, 55*, 468–472.

Lyubomirsky, S. (2001). Why are some people happier than others? The role of cognitive and motivational processes in well-being. *American Psychologist, 56*, 239–249.

Maas, J. W., Bowden, C. L., Miller, A. L., Javors, M. A., Funderburg, L. G., Berman, N., et al. (1997). Schizophrenia, psychosis, and cerebral spinal fluid homovanillic acid concentrations. *Schizophrenia Bulletin, 23*, 147–154.

Macciocchi, S. N., & Barth, J. T. (1996). The Halstead-Reitan Neuropsychological Test Battery (HRNTB). In C. S. Newmark (Ed.), *Major psychological assessment instruments* (pp. 431–459). Boston: Allyn & Bacon.

MacDonald, A. B., Baker, J. M., Stewart, S. H., & Skinner, M. (2000). Effects of alcohol on the response to hyperventilation of participants high and low in anxiety sensitivity. *Alcoholism: Clinical and Experimental Research, 24*, 1656–1665.

MacDonald, A. B., Stewart, S. H., Hutson, R., Rhyno, E., & Loughlin, H. L. (2001). The roles of alcohol and alcohol expectancy in the dampening of responses to hyperventilation among high anxiety sensitive young adults. *Addictive Behaviors, 26*, 841–867.

Macdonald, P. T., Waldorf, D., Reinarman, C., & Murphy, S. (1988). Heavy cocaine use and sexual behavior. *Journal of Drug Issues, 18*, 437–455.

MacDougall, J. M., Dembroski, T. M., Dimsdale, J. E., & Hackett, T. P. (1985). Components of Type A, hostility, and anger-in: Further relationships to angiographic findings. *Health Psychology, 4*(2), 137–152.

Mace, C. J. (1992). Hysterical conversion II: A critique. *British Journal of Psychiatry, 161*, 378–389.

MacGregor, M. W., Davidson, K. W., Rowan, P., Barksdale, C., & MacLean, D. (2003). The use of defenses and physician health care costs: Are physician health care costs lower in persons with more adaptive defense profiles. *Psychotherapy and Psychosomatics, 72*, 315–323.

Mack, A. H., Franklin, J. E., & Frances, R. J. (2003). Substance use disorders. In R. E. Hales & S. C. Yudofsky (Eds.), *Textbook of clinical psychiatry* (4th ed.) (pp. 309–377). Washington, DC: American Psychiatric Press.

MacKinnon, D. F., Zandi, P. P., Gershon, E. S., Nurnberger, J. I., & DePaulo J. R. (2003). Association of rapid mood switching with panic disorder and familial panic risk in familial bipolar disorder. *American Journal of Psychiatry, 160*, 1696–1698.

MacLeod, C., Mathews, A., & Tata, P. (1986). Attentional bias in emotional disorders. *Journal of Abnormal Psychology, 95*, 15–20.

MacMartin, C., & Yarmey, A. D. (1999). Rhetoric and the recovered memory debate. *Canadian Psychology, 40*, 343–358.

MacMillan, H. L., Fleming, J. E., Streiner, D. L., Lin, E., Boyle, M. H., Jamieson, E., et al. (2001). Childhood abuse and lifetime psychopathology in a community sample. *American Journal of Psychiatry, 158*, 1878–1883.

MacPherson, P. S. R., Stewart, S. H., & McWilliams, L. A. (2001). Parental problem drinking and anxiety disorder symptoms in adult offspring: Examining the mediating role of anxiety sensitivity. *Addictive Behaviors, 26,* 917–934.

Magee, W. J., Eaton, W. W., Wittchen, H. U., McGonagle, K. A., & Kessler, R. C. (1996). Agoraphobia, simple phobia, and social phobia in the National Comorbidity Survey. *Archives of General Psychiatry, 53,* 159–168.

Magne-Ingvar, U., Ojehagen, A., & Traskman-Bendz, L. (1992). The social network of people who attempt suicide. *Acta Psychiatrica Scandinavica, 86,* 153–158.

Magnusson, A., & Axelsson, J. (1993). The prevalence of seasonal affective disorder is low among descendants of Icelandic emigrants in Canada. *Archives of General Psychiatry, 50,* 947–951.

Maher, B. A., & Maher, W. B. (1985a). Psychopathology: I. From ancient times to the eighteenth century. In G. A. Kimble & K. Schlesinger (Eds.), *Topics in the history of psychology* (pp. 251–294). Hillsdale, NJ: Erlbaum.

Maher, B. A., & Maher, W. B. (1985b). Psychopathology: II. From the eighteenth century to modern times. In G. A. Kimble & K. Schlesinger (Eds.), *Topics in the history of psychology* (pp. 295–329). Hillsdale, NJ: Erlbaum.

Maher, J. J. (1997). Exploring alcohol's effects on liver function. *Alcohol Health and Research World, 21,* 5–12.

Mahler, M. (1952). On childhood psychosis and schizophrenia: Autistic and symbiotic infantile psychosis. *Psychoanalytic Study of the Child, 7,* 286–305.

Mahowald, M. W., & Schenck, C. H. (2000). Violent parasomnias: Forensic medical issues. In M. H. Kryger, T. Roth, and W. C. Dement (Eds.), *Principles and practice of sleep medicine* (3rd ed., pp. 786–795). Philadelphia: W. B. Saunders.

Mahr, G., & Leith, W. (1992). Psychogenic stuttering of adult onset. *Journal of Speech and Hearing Research, 35,* 283–286.

Mailloux, D. L., Forth, A. E., & Kroner, D. G. (1997). Psychopathy and substance use in adolescent male offenders. *Psychological Reports, 81,* 529–530.

Maj, M., Pirozzi, R., Magliano, L., & Bartoli, L. (2002) The prognostic significance of "switching" in patients with bipolar disorder: A 10-year prospective follow-up study. *American Journal of Psychiatry, 159,* 1711–1717.

Malatesta, V. J., & Adams, H. E. (1984). The sexual dysfunctions. In H. E. Adams & P. B. Sutker (Eds.), *Comprehensive handbook of psychopathology* (pp. 725–775). New York: Plenum Press.

Malatesta, V. J., & Adams, H. E. (2001). Sexual dysfunctions. In H. E. Adams & P. B. Sutker (Eds.), *Comprehensive handbook of psychopathology* (3rd ed.). New York: Kluwer Academic/Plenum.

Malchy, B., Enns, M. W., Young, T. K., & Cox, J. (1997). Suicide among Manitoba's Aboriginal people, 1988 to 1994. *Canadian Medical Association Journal, 156,*1133–1138.

Maldonado, J. R., Butler, L. D., & Spiegel, D. (1998). Treatments for dissociative disorders. In P. E. Nathan & J. M. Gorman (Eds.), *A guide to treatments that work.* New York: Oxford University Press.

Maletzky, B. M. (1991). *Treating the sexual offender.* Newbury Park, CA: Sage.

Maletzky, B. M. (1998). The paraphilias: Research and treatment. In P. E. Nathan & J. M. Gorman (Eds.), *A guide to treatments that work* (pp. 472–500). New York: Oxford University Press.

Malhotra, S., & Gupta, N. (1999). Childhood disintegrative disorder. *Journal of Autism and Developmental Disorders, 29,* 491–498.

Malla, A. K., Takhar, J. J., Norman, R. M., Manchanda, R., Cortese, L., Haricharan, R., et al. (2002). Negative symptoms in first episode non-affective psychosis. *Acta Psychiatrica Scandinavica, 105,* 431–439.

Malpass, R. S., & Poortinga, Y. H. (1986). Strategies for design and analysis. In W. J. Lonner & J. W. Berry (Eds.), *Field methods in cross-cultural research* (pp. 47–83). Beverly Hills, CA: Sage.

Mandalos, G. E., & Szarek, B. L. (1990). Dose-related paranoid reaction associated with fluoxetine. *Journal of Nervous and Mental Disease, 178*(1), 57–58.

Mandell, A. J., & Knapp, S. (1979). Asymmetry and mood, emergent properties of seratonin regulation: A proposed mechanism of action of lithium. *Archives of General Psychiatry, 36*(8), 909–916.

Mann, J. J., Malone, K. M., Diehl, D. J., Perel, J., Cooper, T. B., & Mintun, M. A. (1996). Demonstration in vivo of reduced serotonin responsivity in the brain of untreated depressed patients. *American Journal of Psychiatry, 153,* 174–182.

Mann, J. J., Waternaux, C., Haas, G. L., & Malone, K. M. (1999). Toward a clinical model of suicidal behavior in psychiatric patients. *American Journal of Psychiatry, 156*(2), 181–189.

Manni, R., Ratti, M. T., & Tartara, A. (1997). Nocturnal eating: Prevalence and features in 120 insomniac referrals. *Sleep, 20,* 734–738.

Mannino, D. M., Klevens, R. M., & Flanders, W. D. (1994). Cigarette smoking: An independent risk factor for impotence? *American Journal of Epidemiology, 140,* 1003–1008.

Manson, S. M., & Good, B. J. (1993, January). *Cultural considerations in the diagnosis of DSM-IV mood disorders.* Cultural proposals and supporting papers for DSM-IV. Submitted to the DSM-IV Task Force by the Steering Committee, NIMH-Sponsored Group on Culture and Diagnosis.

Marcopulos, B. A., & Graves, R. E. (1990). Antidepressant effect on memory in depressed older persons. *Journal of Clinical and Experimental Neuropsychology, 12*(5), 655–663.

Marcus, M. D., Wing, R. R., Ewing, L., Keern, E., Gooding, W., & McDermott, M. (1990). Psychiatric disorders among obese binge eaters. *International Journal of Eating Disorders, 9,* 69–77.

Marcus, M. D., Wing, R. R., & Hopkins, J. (1988). Obese binge eaters: Affect, cognitions, and response to behavioral weight control. *Journal of Consulting and Clinical Psychology, 3,* 433–439.

Margo, A., Hemsley, D. R., & Slade, P. D. (1981). The effects of varying auditory input on schizophrenic hallucinations. *British Journal of Psychiatry, 139,* 122–127.

Mariani, M. A., & Barkley, R. A. (1997). Neuropsychological and academic functioning in preschool boys with attention deficit hyperactivity disorder. *Developmental Neuropsychology, 13,* 111–129.

Marks, I. M. (1985). Behavioural treatment of social phobia. *Psychopharmacology Bulletin, 21,* 615–618.

Marks, I. M. (1988). Blood-injury phobia: A review. *American Journal of Psychiatry, 145,* 1207–1213.

Marlatt, G. A. (1985). Relapse prevention: Theoretical rationale and overview of the model. In G. A. Marlatt & J. R. Gordon (Eds.), *Relapse prevention: Maintenance strategies in the treatment of addictive behaviors* (pp. 3–70). New York: Guilford Press.

Marlatt, G. A. (Ed.). (1998). *Harm reduction: Pragmatic strategies for managing high-risk behaviors.* New York: Guilford Press.

Marlatt, G. A., & Gordon, J. R. (1985). *Relapse prevention: Maintenance strategies in the treatment of addictive behaviors.* New York: Guilford Press.

Marlatt, G. A., Larimer, M. E., Baer, J. S., & Quigley, L. A. (1993). Harm reduction for alcohol problems: Moving beyond the controlled drinking controversy. *Behavior Therapy, 24,* 461–504.

Marmot, M. G., & Syme, S. L. (1976). Acculturation and coronary heart disease in Japanese Americans. *American Journal of Epidemiology, 104,* 225–247.

Marsden, C. D. (1986). Hysteria—A neurologist's view. *Psychological Medicine, 16,* 277–288.

Marshall, W. L. (1997). Pedophilia: Psychopathology and theory. In D. R. Laws & W. O'Donohue (Eds.), *Sexual deviance: Theory, assessment and treatment* (pp. 152–174). New York: Guilford Press.

Marshall, W. L. (1999). Current status of North American assessment and treatment programs for sexual offenders. *Journal of Interpersonal Violence, 14,* 221–239.

Marshall, W. L., Barbaree, H. E., & Christophe, D. (1986). Sexual offenders against female children: Sexual preferences for age of victims and type of behavior. *Canadian Journal of Behavioral Science, 18,* 424–439.

Marshall, W. L., & Moulden, H. (2001). Hostility toward women and victim empathy in rapists. *Sexual Abuse: Journal of Research and Treatment, 13,* 249–255.

Martin, I. (1983). Human classical conditioning. In A. Gale & J. A. Edward (Eds.), *Physiological correlates of human behavior: Vol. 2. Attention and performance.* London: Academic Press.

Martin, P. R., Pekovich, S. R., McCool, B. A., Whetsell, W. O., & Singleton, C. K. (1994). Thiamine utilization in the pathogenesis of alcohol-induced brain damage. *Alcohol and Alcoholism, 2* (Suppl.), 273–279.

Martin, S. L., Ramey, C. T., & Ramey, S. L. (1990). The prevention of intellectual impairment in children of impoverished families: Findings of a randomized trial of educational daycare. *American Journal of Public Health, 80,* 844–847.

Martin-Cook, K., Svetlik, D., & Weiner, M. F. (2003). Supporting family caregivers. In M. F. Weiner & A. M. Lipton (Eds.), *The dementias: Diagnosis, treatment and research* (3rd ed.) (pp. 321–340). Washington, DC: American Psychiatric Press.

Marx, J. (1998). New gene tied to common form of Alzheimer's. *Science, 281,* 507–509.

Maser, J. D. (1985). List of phobias. In A. H. Tuma & J. D. Maser (Eds.), *Anxiety and the anxiety disorders.* Hillsdale, NJ: Erlbaum.

Mash, E. J., & Wolfe, D. A. (2003). Disorders of childhood and adolescence. In G. Stricker & T. A. Widiger (Eds.), *Handbook of psychology: Clinical psychology* (Vol. 8, pp. 27–63). New York: John Wiley & Sons.

Mason, F. L. (1997). Fetishism: Psychopathology and theory. In D. R. Laws & W. O'Donohue (Eds.), *Sexual deviance: Theory, assessment and treatment* (pp. 75–91). New York: Guilford Press.

Massie, H. N., Miranda, G., Snowdon, D. A., Greiner, L. H., Wekstein, D. R., Danner, D., et al. (1996). Linguistic ability in early life and Alzheimer disease in late life. *Journal of the American Medical Association, 275,* 1879.

Masters, W. H., & Johnson, V. E. (1966). *Human sexual response.* Boston: Little, Brown.

Masters, W. H., & Johnson, V. E. (1970). *Human sexual inadequacy.* Boston: Little, Brown.

Mathews, A. (1997). Information processing biases in emotional disorders. In D. M. Clark & C. G. Fairburn (Eds.), *Science and practice of cognitive-behavior therapy* (pp. 47–66). Oxford, UK: Oxford University Press.

Mathews, A., & MacLeod, C. (1994). Cognitive approaches to emotion and emotional disorders. *Annual Review of Psychology, 45,* 25–50.

Mathews, A., Mogg, K., Kentish, J., & Eysenck, M. (1995). Effective psychological treatment on cognitive bias and generalized anxiety disorder. *Behavior Research and Therapy, 33,* 293–303.

Maticka-Tyndale, E. (2001). Sexual health and Canadian youth: How do we measure up? *Canadian Journal of Human Sexuality, 10,* 1–17.

Matsumoto, D. (1994). *People: Psychology from a cultural perspective.* Pacific Grove, CA: Brooks/Cole.

Matsumoto, D. (1996). *Culture and psychology.* Pacific Grove, CA: Brooks/Cole.

Matthews, K. A. (1988). Coronary heart disease and Type A behaviors: Update on and alternative to the Booth-Kewley and Friedman (1987) quantitative review. *Psychological Bulletin, 104*(3), 373–380.

Mattis, S. G., & Ollendick, T. H. (2002). Nonclinical panic attacks in late adolescence prevalence and associated psychopathology. *Journal of Anxiety Disorders, 16,* 351–367.

Mayville, S., Katz, R. C., Gipson, M. T., & Cabral, K. (1999). Assessing the prevalence of body dysmorphic disorder in an ethically diverse group of adolescents. *Journal of Child and Family Studies, 8*(3), 357–362.

Mazure, C. M. (1998). Life stressors as risk factors in depression. *Clinical Psychology: Science and Practice, 5*(3), 291–313.

Mazure, C. M., Bruce, M. L., Maciejewski, P. K., & Jacobs, S. C. (2000). Adverse life events and cognitive-personality characteristics in the prediction of major depression and antidepressant response. *American Journal of Psychiatry, 157*(6), 896–903.

McAdoo, W. G., & DeMyer, M. K. (1978). Research related to family factors in autism. *Journal of Pediatric Psychology, 2,* 162–166.

McCabe, R. E., & Antony, M. M. (2002). Specific and social phobia. In M. M. Antony & D. H. Barlow (Eds.), *Handbook of assessment and treatment planning for psychological disorders* (pp. 113–146). New York: Guilford.

McCabe, R. E., Antony, M. M., Summerfeldt, L. J., Liss, A., & Swinson, R. P. (2003). A preliminary examination of the relationship between anxiety disorders in adults and self-reported history of teasing or bullying experiences. *Cognitive Behaviour Therapy, 32,* 187–193.

McCabe, R. E., McFarlane, T., Polivy, J., & Olmsted, M. P. (2001). Eating disorders, dieting, and the accuracy of self-reported weight. *International Journal of Eating Disorders, 29,* 59–64.

McCaffrey, R. J., & Bellamy-Campbell, R. (1989). Psychometric detection of fabricated symptoms of combat-related post-traumatic stress disorder: A systematic replication. *Journal of Clinical Psychology, 45,* 76–79.

McCaughrin, W. B. (1988). *Longitudinal trends of competitive employment for developmentally disabled adults: A benefit-cost analysis.* Unpublished doctoral dissertation, University of Illinois at Urbana-Champaign.

McClearn, G. E., Johansson, B., Berg, S., Pedersen, N. L., Ahern, F., Petrill, S. A., & Plomin, R. (1997). Substantial genetic influence on cognitive abilities in twins 80 or more years old. *Science, 276,* 1560–1563.

McCrae, R. R., & Costa, P. T. (1997). Personality trait structure as a human universal. *American Psychologist, 52,* 509–516.

McCreery, J. M., & Walker, R. D. (1993). Alcohol problems. In D. L. Dunner (Ed.), *Current psychiatric therapy* (pp. 92–98). Philadelphia: W. B. Saunders.

McCullough, J. P. Jr., Klein, D. N., Keller, M. B., Holzer, C. E., III, Davis, S. M., Kornstein, S. G., et al. (2000). Comparison of DSM-III-R chronic major depression and major depression superimposed on dysthymia (double depression): Validity of the distinction. *Journal of Abnormal Psychology, 109,* 419–427.

McCullough, P. K., & Maltsberger, J. T. (2001). Obsessive-compulsive personality disorder. In G. O. Gabbard (Ed.), *Treatment of psychiatric disorders* (Vol. 2) (3rd ed.) (pp. 2341–2351). Washington, DC: American Psychiatric Publishing.

McDaniel, K. (1990). Thalamic degeneration. In J. L. Cummings (Ed.), *Subcortical dementia* (pp. 132–144). New York: Oxford University Press.

McDonough, J. (2002). *Shakey: Neil Young's biography.* Toronto: Random House.

McDowell, D. M. (1999). MDMA, ketamine, GHB, and the "club drug" scene. In M. Galanter & H. D. Kleber (Eds.), *Textbook of substance abuse treatment* (2nd ed., pp. 295–305). Washington, DC: American Psychiatric Press.

McEachin, J. J., Smith, T., & Lovaas, O. I. (1993). Long-term outcome for children with autism who received early intensive behavioral treatment. *American Journal on Mental Retardation, 97,* 359–372.

McElroy, S. L., & Keck, P. E. (1993). Rapid cycling. In D. L. Dunner (Ed.), *Current psychiatric therapy* (pp. 226–231). Philadelphia: W. B. Saunders.

McEwen, B. S. (1999). Stress and hippocampal plasticity. *Annual Review of Neuroscience, 22,* 105–122.

McGehee, D. S., Heath, M. J. S., Gelber, S., Devay, P., & Role, L. W. (1995). Nicotine enhancement of fast excitatory synaptic transmission in CNS by presynaptic receptors. *Science, 269,* 1692–1696.

McGinnis, J. M., & Foege, W. H. (1993). Actual causes of death in the United States. *Journal of the American Medical Association, 270*(18), 2207–2212.

McGlashan, T. H., & Fenton, W. S. (1991). Classical subtypes for schizophrenia: Literature review for DSM-IV. *Schizophrenia Bulletin, 17,* 609–623.

McGowin, D. F. (1993). *Living in the labyrinth: A personal journey through the maze of Alzheimer's.* New York: Delacorte Press.

McGrath, J. (2000). Universal interventions for the primary prevention of schizophrenia. *Australian and New Zealand Journal of Psychiatry, 34* (Suppl.), S58.

McGrath, P. A., & DeVeber, L. L. (1986). The management of acute pain evoked by medical procedures in children with cancer. *Journal of Pain and Symptom Management, 1,* 145–150.

McGrath, P. J., Finley, G. A., & Turner, C. J. (1992). *Making cancer less painful: A handbook for parents.* Halifax, NS: IWK Children's Hospital.

McGregor, I., Zanna, M. P., Holmes, J. G., & Spencer, S. J. (2001). Compensatory conviction in the face of personal uncertainty: Going to extremes and being oneself. *Journal of Personality and Social Psychology, 80,* 472–488.

McGue, M. (1999). The behavioral genetics of alcoholism. *Current Directions in Psychological Science, 8*(4), 109–115.

McGue, M., & Christensen, K. (1997). Genetic and environmental contributions to depression symptomatology: Evidence from Danish twins 75 years of age and older. *Journal of Abnormal Psychology, 106*(3), 439–448.

McGue, M., & Lykken, D. T. (1992). Genetic influence on risk of divorce. *Psychological Science, 3*(6), 368–373.

McGue, M., Pickens, R. W., & Svikis, D. S. (1992). Sex and age effects on the inheritance of alcohol problems: A twin study. *Journal of Abnormal Psychology, 101,* 3–17.

McGuffin, P., & Katz, R. (1989). The genetics of depression and manic-depressive disorder. *British Journal of Psychiatry, 155,* 294–304.

McGuffin, P., Katz, R., & Bebbington, P. (1988). The Camberwell Collaborative Depression Study: III. Depression and adversity in the relatives of depressed probands. *British Journal of Psychiatry, 152,* 775–782.

McGuffin, P., & Reich, T. (1984). Psychopathology and genetics. In H. E. Adams & P. B. Sutker (Eds.), *Comprehensive handbook of psychopathology.* New York: Plenum Press.

McGuffin, P., Rijsdijk, F., Andrew, M., Sham, P., Katz, R., & Cardno, A. (2003). The heritability of bipolar affective disorder and the genetic relationship to unipolar depression. *Archives of General Psychiatry, 60,* 497–502.

McGuire, P. K., Shah, G. M. S., & Murray, R. M. (1993). Increased blood flow in Broca's area during auditory hallucinations in schizophrenia. *Lancet, 342,* 703–706.

McIntosh, J. L., Santos, J. F., Hubbard, R. W., & Overholser, J. C. (1994). *Elder suicide: Research, theory and treatment.* Washington, DC: American Psychological Association.

McIsaac, H. K., Thordarson, D. S., Shafran, R., Rachman, S., & Poole, G. (1998). Claustrophobia and the magnetic resonance imaging procedure. *Journal of Behavioral Medicine, 21,* 255–268.

McKay, D., Todaro, J., Neziroglu, F., Campisi, T., Moritz, E. K., & Yaryura-Tobias, J. A. (1997). Body dysmorphic disorder: A preliminary evaluation of treatment and maintenance using exposure with response prevention. *Behaviour Research and Therapy, 35,* 67–70.

McKenzie, S. J., Williamson, D. A., & Cubic, B. A. (1993). Stable and reactive body image disturbances in bulimia nervosa. *Behavior Therapy, 24,* 195–207.

McKeon, P., & Murray, R. (1987). Familial aspects of obsessive-compulsive neuroses. *British Journal of Psychiatry, 151,* 528–534.

McKim, W. A. (1991). *Drugs and behavior: An introduction to behavioral pharmacology* (2nd ed.). Englewood Cliffs, NJ: Prentice Hall.

McKinnon, W., Weisse, C. S., Reynolds, C. P., Bowles, C. A., & Baum, A. (1989). Chronic stress, leukocyte subpopulations, and hormonal response to latent viruses. *Health Psychology, 8,* 399–402.

McKnight, D. L., Nelson-Gray, R. O., & Barnhill, J. (1992). Dexamethasone suppression test and response to cognitive therapy and antidepressant medication. *Behavior Therapy, 23*(1), 99–111.

McLaren, A. (1990). *Our own master race: Eugenics in Canada 1885–1945.* Toronto: McClelland & Stewart.

McLean, P., & Taylor, S. (1992). Severity of unipolar depression and choice of treatment. *Behaviour Research and Therapy, 30*(5), 443–451.

McLean, P. D., Whittal, M. L., Thordarson, D. S., Taylor, S., Socting, I., Koch, W. J., et al. (2001). Cognitive versus behavior therapy in the group treatment of obsessive-compulsive disorder. *Journal of Consulting and Clinical Psychology, 69,* 205–214.

McLintock, B. (2002, July 22). Montreux clinic under fire. *The Province,* A14. Retrieved June 24, 2004, from http://www.anorexiasfallenangel.com/news/22072002.htm.

McMain, S., Korman, L. M., & Dimeff, L. (2001). Dialectical behavior therapy and the treatment of emotion dysregulation. *Journal of Clinical Psychology, 57,* 183–196.

McNally, R. J. (1996). Cognitive bias in the anxiety disorders. In D. A. Hope (Ed.), *Perspectives on anxiety, panic and fear* (The 43rd Annual Nebraska Symposium on Motivation) (pp. 211–250). Lincoln: Nebraska University Press.

McNally, R. J. (1999). EMDR and Mesmerism: A comparative historical analysis. *Journal of Anxiety Disorders, 13,* 225–236.

McNaughton, N., & Gray, J. H. (2000). Anxiolytic action on the behavioral inhibition system implies multiple types of arousal contribute to anxiety. *Journal of Affective Disorders, 61*(3), 161–176.

McNeil, T. F. (1987). Perinatal influences in the development of schizophrenia. In H. Helmchen & F. A. Henn (Eds.), *Biological perspectives of schizophrenia* (pp. 125–138). New York: John Wiley.

McNeil, T. F., Cantor-Graae, E., & Weinberger, D. R. (2001). Relationship of obstetric complications and differences in brain structures in monozygotic twin pairs discordant for schizophrenia. *American Journal of Psychiatry, 157*(2), 203–212.

McTeer, M. (2003). *In my own name.* Toronto: Random House of Canada.

McVey, G., & Davis, R. (2002). A program to promote positive body image: A 1-year follow-up evaluation. *Journal of Early Adolescence, 22,* 96–108.

McVey, G. L., Pepler, D., Davis, R., Flett, G. L., & Abdolell, M. (2002). Risk and protective factors associated with disordered eating during early adolescence. *Journal of Early Adolescence, 22,* 75–95.

McWilliams, L. A., & Asmundson, G. J. G. (2001). Is there a negative association between anxiety sensitivity and arousal-increasing substances and activities? *Journal of Anxiety Disorders, 15,* 161–170.

Meana, M., Binik, I., Khalife, S., & Cohen, D. (1998). Affect and marital adjustment in women's rating of dyspareunic pain. *Canadian Journal of Psychiatry, 43,* 381–385.

Meaney, M. J. (2001). Maternal care, gene expression, and the transmission of individual differences in stress reactivity across generations. *Annual Review of Neuroscience, 24,* 1161–1192.

Mednick, S. A., & Schulsinger, F. (1965). A longitudinal study of children with a high risk for schizophrenia: A preliminary report. In S. Vandenberg (Ed.), *Methods and goals in human behavior genetics* (pp. 255–296). New York: Academic Press.

Mednick, S. A., & Schulsinger, F. (1968). Some premorbid characteristics related to breakdown in children with schizophrenic mothers. *Journal of Psychiatric Research, 6,* 267–291.

Mednick, S. A., Watson, J. B., Huttunen, M., Cannon, T. D., Katila, H., Machon, R., et al. (1998). A two-hit working model of the etiology of schizophrenia. In M. F. Lenzenweger & R. H. Dworkin (Eds.) *Origins and development of schizophrenia: Advances in experimental psychopathology* (pp. 27–66). Washington, DC: American Psychological Association.

Meehan, P. J., Lamb, J. A., Saltzman, L. E., & O'Carroll, P. W. (1992). Attempted suicide among young adults: Progress toward a meaningful estimate of prevalence. *American Journal of Psychiatry, 149*(1), 41–44.

Meehl, P. E. (1962). Schizotaxia, schizotypy, schizophrenia. *American Psychologist, 17,* 827–838.

Meehl, P. E. (1989). Schizotaxia revisited. *Archives of General Psychiatry, 46,* 935–944.

Meichenbaum, D. (1977). Dr. Ellis, please stand up. *Counseling Psychologist, 7,* 43–44.

Meichenbaum, D., & Cameron, R. (1973). Training schizophrenics to talk to themselves: A means of developing attentional controls. *Behavior Therapy, 4,* 515–534.

Meichenbaum, D., & Cameron, R. (1974). The clinical potential of modifying what clients say to themselves. *Psychotherapy: Theory, Research & Practice, 11,* 103–117.

Meichenbaum, D. H. (1971). Nature and modification of impulsive children: Training impulsive children to talk to themselves. *Catalog of Selected Documents in Psychology, 1,* 15–16.

Meichenbaum, D. H. (1994). *A clinical handbook/practical therapist manual for assessing and treating adults with posttraumatic stress disorder.* Waterloo, ON: Institute Press.

Meichenbaum, D. H. (1995). Cognitive-behavioral therapy in historical perspective. In B. M. Bongar & L. E. Beutler (Eds.), *Comprehensive textbook of psychotherapy: Theory and practice* (pp. 140–158). London, UK: Oxford University Press.

Meichenbaum, D. H., & Goodman, J. (1971). Training impulsive children to talk to themselves: A means of developing self-control. *Journal of Abnormal Psychology, 77,* 115–126.

Meloy, J. R. (2001). Antisocial personality disorder. In G. O. Gabbard (Ed.), *Treatment of psychiatric disorders* (Vol. 2) (3rd ed.) (pp. 2251–2271). Washington, DC: American Psychiatric Press.

Melton, G. B., Petrila, J., Poythress, N. G., & Slobogin, C. (1987). *Psychological evaluations for the courts.* New York: Guilford.

Melzack, R. (1993). Pain: Past, present, and future. *Canadian Journal of Experimental Psychology, 47,* 615–629.

Melzack, R. (1999). From the gate to the neuromatrix. *Pain, Supplement 6,* S121–S126.

Melzack, R., & Wall, P. D. (1965). Pain mechanisms: A new theory. *Science, 150,* 971–979.

Melzack, R., & Wall, P. D. (1982). *The challenge of pain.* New York: Basic Books.

Merikangas, K. R., & Risch, N. (2003). Will the genomics revolution revolutionize psychiatry? *American Journal of Psychiatry, 160,* 625–635.

Merikangas, K. R., Mehta, R. L., Molnar, B. E., Walters, E. E., Swendsen, J. D., Auilar-Gaziola, S., et al. (1998). Comorbidity of substance use disorders with mood and anxiety disorders: Results of the international consortium in psychiatric epidemiology. *Addictive Behaviors, 23,* 893–908.

Merikangas, K. R., Zhang, H., Avenevoli, S., Acharyya, S., Neuenschwander, M., Angst, J., et al. (2003). Longitudinal trajectories of depression and anxiety in a prospective community study: The Zurich Cohort Study. *Archives of General Psychiatry, 60,* 993–1000.

Merzenich, M. M., Jenkins, W. M., Johnston, P., Schreiner, C., Miller, S. L., & Tallal, P. (1996). Temporal processing deficits of language-learning impaired children ameliorated by training. *Science, 271,* 77–81.

Meston, C. M. (2000). The psychophysiological assessment of female sexual function. *Journal of Sex Education and Therapy, 25,* 6–16.

Meston, C. M., & Gorzalka, B. B. (1996). The effects of immediate, delayed, and residual sympathetic activation on sexual arousal in women. *Behaviour Research and Therapy, 34,* 143–148.

Meston, C. M., & Heiman, J. R. (2000). Sexual abuse and sexual function: An examination of sexually relevant cognitive processes. *Journal of Consulting and Clinical Psychology, 68,* 399–406.

Meston, C. M., Trapnell, P. D., & Gorzalka, B. B. (1996). Ethnic and gender differences in sexuality: Variations in sexual behavior between Asian and non-Asian university students. *Archives of Sexual Behavior, 25,* 33–72.

Meston, C. M., Trapnell, P. D., & Gorzalka, B. B. (1998). Ethnic, gender, and length-of-residency influences on sexual knowledge and attitudes. *Journal of Sex Research, 35,* 176–188.

Meston, C. M., & Worcel, M. (2002). The effects of yohimbine plus L-arginine glutamate on sexual arousal in post-menopausal women with Sexual Arousal Disorder. *Archives of Sexual Behavior, 31,* 323–332.

Meyer, B., & Carver, C. S. (2000). Negative childhood accounts, sensitivity and pessimism: A study of avoidant personality disorder features in college students. *Journal of Personality Disorders, 14,* 233–248.

Meyer, L. H., Peck, C. A., & Brown, L. (1991). *Critical issues in the lives of people with severe disabilities.* Baltimore: Paul H. Brookes.

Meyerowitz, B. E. (1983). Postmastectomy coping strategies and quality of life. *Health Psychology, 2,* 117–132.

Meyers, A. (1991). Biobehavioral interactions in behavioral medicine. *Behavior Therapy, 22,* 129–131.

Meyers, R. J., Villanueva, M., & Smith, J. E. (2005). The community reinforcement approach: History and new directions. *Journal of Cognitive Psychotherapy, 19,* 251–264.

Mezzich, J. E., Good, B. J., Lewis-Fernandez, R., Guarnaccia, P., Lin, K. M., Parron, D., et al. (1993, September). *Cultural formulation guidelines.* Revised cultural proposals for DSM-IV. Submitted to the DSM-IV Task Force by the Steering Committee, NIMH-Sponsored Group on Culture and Diagnosis.

Mezzich, J. E., Kirmayer, L. J., Kleinman, A., Fabrega, H. Jr., Parron, D. L., Good, B. J., et al. (1999). The place of culture in DSM-IV. *Journal of Nervous and Mental Disease, 187,* 457–464.

Mezzich, J. E., Kleinman, A., Fabrega, H., Jr., Good, B., Johnson-Powell, G., Lin, K. M., et al. (1992). *Cultural proposals for DSM-IV.* Submitted to the DSM-IV Task Force by the Steering Committee, NIMH-Sponsored Group on Culture and Diagnosis.

Miaskowski, C. (1999). The role of sex and gender in pain perception and responses to treatment. In R. J. Gatchel & D. C. Turk (Eds.), *Psychosocial factors in pain: Critical perspectives* (pp. 401–411). New York: Guilford Press.

Middleton, W., Burnett, P., Raphael, B., & Martinek, N. (1996). The bereavement response: A cluster analysis. *British Journal of Psychiatry, 169,* 167–171.

Miklowitz, D. J. (2001). Bipolar disorder. In D. H. Barlow (Ed.), *Clinical handbook of psychological disorders* (3rd ed., pp. 523–561). New York: Guilford Publications.

Miklowitz, D. J., George, E. L., Richards, J. A., Simoneau, T. L., & Suddath, R. L. (2003). A randomized study of family-focused psychoeducation and pharmacotherapy in the outpatient management of bipolar disorder. *Archives of General Psychiatry, 60,* 904–912.

Miklowitz, D. J., & Goldstein, M. J. (1997). *Bipolar disorder: A family focused treatment approach.* New York: Guilford Press.

Millar, W. J. (1998). Multiple medication use among seniors. *Health Reports, 9*(4), 11–17.

Miller, I. W., Keitner, G. I., Epstein, N. B., Bishop, D. S., & Ryan, C. E. (1991). *Families of bipolar patients: Dysfunction, course of illness, and pilot treatment study.* Paper presented at the annual meeting of the Association for the Advancement of Behavior Therapy, New York.

Miller, I. W., & Norman, W. H. (1979). Learned helplessness in humans: A review and attribution-theory model. *Psychological Bulletin, 86*(1), 93–118.

Miller, I. W., Norman, W. H., & Keitner, G. I. (1989). Cognitive-behavioral treatment of depressed inpatients: Six- and twelve-month follow-up. *American Journal of Psychiatry, 146,* 1274–1279.

Miller, J. Rodin, C. D. Belar, M. J. Follick, & Singer J. E. (Eds.), *Health psychology: A discipline and a profession.* Chicago: University of Chicago Press.

Miller, N. E. (1969). Learning of visceral and glandular responses. *Science, 163,* 434–445.

Miller, N. S., Gold, M. S., & Pottash, A. C. (1989). A 12-step treatment approach for marijuana (cannabis) dependence. *Journal of Substance Abuse Treatment, 6,* 241–250.

Miller, P. M., Smith, G. T., & Goldman, M. S. (1990). Emergence of alcohol expectancies in childhood: A possible critical period. *Journal of Studies on Alcohol, 51,* 343–349.

Miller, S., & Watson, B. C. (1992). The relationship between communication attitude, anxiety, and depression in stutterers and nonstutterers. *Journal of Speech and Hearing Research, 35,* 789–798.

Miller, T. J., McGlashan, T. H., Rosen, J. L., Somjee, L., Markovich, P. J., Stein, K., et al. (2002). Prospective diagnosis of the initial prodrome for schizophrenia based on the Structured Interview for Prodromal Syndromes: Preliminary evidence of interrater reliability and predictive validity. *American Journal of Psychiatry, 159,* 863–865.

Miller, T. Q., Smith, T. W., Turner, C. W., Guijarro, M. L., & Hallet, A. J. (1996). A meta-analytic review of research on hostility and physical health. *Psychological Bulletin, 119*(2), 322–348.

Miller, W. R. (1985). Motivation for treatment: A review with special emphasis on alcoholism. *Psychological Bulletin, 98,* 84–107.

Miller, W. R., & Hester, R. K. (1986). Inpatient alcoholism treatment: Who benefits? *American Psychologist, 41,* 794–805.

Miller, W. R., & McCrady, B. S. (1993). The importance of research on Alcoholics Anonymous. In B. S. McCrady & W. R. Miller (Eds.), *Research on Alcoholics Anonymous: Opportunities and alternatives* (pp. 3–11). New Brunswick, NJ: Rutgers Center of Alcohol Studies.

Miller, W. R., Meyers, R. J., & Hiller-Sturmhöfel, S. (1999). The community-reinforcement approach. *Alcohol Research and Health, 23*(2), 116–121.

Millon, T. (1981). *Disorders of personality: DSM-III, Axis II.* New York: John Wiley.

Millon, T. (1986). Schizoid and avoidant personality disorders in DSM-III. *American Journal of Psychiatry, 143,* 1321–1322.

Millon, T. (1991). Classification in psychopathology: Rationale, alternatives, and standards. *Journal of Abnormal Psychology, 100*(3), 245–261.

Millon, T., & Martinez, A. (1995). Avoidant personality disorder. In W. J. Livesley (Ed.), *The DSM-IV personality disorders* (pp. 218–233). New York: Guilford Press.

Mills, J. L., Holmes, L. B., Aarons, J. H., Simpson, J. L., Brown, Z. A., Jovanovic-Peterson, L. G., et al. (1993). Moderate caffeine use and the risk of spontaneous abortion and intrauterine growth retardation. *Journal of the American Medical Association, 269,* 593–597.

Mindell, J. A. (1993). Sleep disorders in children. *Health Psychology, 12,* 152–163.

Mindell, J. A. (1999). Empirically supported treatments in pediatric psychology: Bedtime refusal and night wakings in young children. *Journal of Pediatric Psychology, 24,* 465–481.

Mineka, S. (1985b). The frightful complexity of the origins of fears. In F. R. Bruch & J. B. Overmier (Eds.), *Affect, conditioning, and cognition: Essays on the determinants of behavior.* Hillsdale, NJ: Erlbaum.

Mineka, S., Watson, D., & Clark, L. A. (1998). Comorbidity of anxiety and unipolar mood disorders. *Annual Review of Psychology, 49,* 377–412.

Mineka, S., & Zinbarg, R. E. (1995). Animal-ethological models of social phobia. In R. Heimberg, M. Leibowitz, D. Hope, & F. Schneier (Eds.), *Social phobia: Diagnosis, assessment and treatment* (pp. 134–162). New York: Guilford Press.

Mineka, S., & Zinbarg, R. E. (1996). Conditioning and ethological models of anxiety disorders: Stress-in-dynamic-context anxiety models. In D. A. Hope (Ed.), *Perspectives on anxiety, panic and fear* (The 43rd Annual Nebraska Symposium on Motivation) (pp. 135–210). Lincoln: Nebraska University Press.

Mineka, S., & Zinbarg, R. (1998). Experimental approaches to understanding the mood and anxiety disorders. In J. Adair (Ed.), *Advances in psychological research, vol. 2: Social, personal, and cultural aspects* (pp. 429–454). Hove, UK: Psychology Press/Erlbaum.

Mingdao, Z., & Zhenyi, X. (1990). Delivery systems and research for schizophrenia in China. In A. Kales, C. N. Stefanis, & J. A. Talbott (Eds.), *Recent advances in schizophrenia* (pp. 373–395). New York: Springer-Verlag.

Minino, A. M., Arias, E., Kochanek, K. D., Murphy, S. L., & Smith, B. L. (2002). Deaths: Final data for 2000. *National Vital Statistics Reports, 50,* 1–119.

Minuchin, S., Rosman, B. L., & Baker, L. (1978). *Psychosomatic families.* Cambridge, MA: Harvard University Press.

Mirsky, A. F. (1995). Israeli High-Risk Study: Editor's introduction. *Schizophrenia Bulletin, 21,* 179–182.

Mirsky, A. F., Bieliauskas, L. A., French, L. M., Van Kammen, D. P., Joensson, E., & Sedvall, G. (2000). A 39-year followup on the Genain quadruplets. *Schizophrenia Bulletin, 26,* 699–708.

Misri, S., Kostaras, X., Fox, D., & Kostaras, D. (2000). The impact of partner support in the treatment of postpartum depression. *Canadian Journal of Psychiatry, 45,* 554–558.

Mitchell, J. E., & Pyle, R. L. (1988). The diagnosis and clinical characteristics of bulimia. In B. J. Blinder, B. F. Chaitin, & R. S. Goldstein (Eds.), *The eating disorders: Medical and psychological bases of diagnosis and treatment* (pp. 267–273). New York: PMA.

Mitchell, T., Stewart, S. H., Griffin, K., & Loba, P. (2004). "We Will Never Ever Forget...": The Swissair Flight 111 disaster and its impact on volunteers and communities. *Journal of Health Psychology, 9,* 245–262.

Moak, D. H., & Anton, R. F. (1999). Alcohol. In B. S. McCrady & E. E. Epstein (Eds.), *Addictions: A comprehensive guidebook* (pp. 75–94). New York: Oxford University Press.

Moene, F. C., Spinhoven, P., Hoogduin, K. A., & van Dyck, R. (2002). A randomised controlled clinical trial on the additional effect of hypnosis in a comprehensive treatment programme for in-patients with conversion disorder of the motor type. *Psychotherapy and Psychosomatics, 71,* 66–76.

Mogg, K., Bradley, B. P., Millar, N., & White, J. (1995). A follow-up study of cognitive bias in generalized anxiety disorder. *Behaviour Research and Therapy, 33,* 927–935.

Mogg, K., Mathews, A., & Weinman, J. (1989). Selective processing of threat cues in anxiety states: A replication. *Behaviour Research and Therapy, 27,* 317–323.

Mogil, J. S., Sternberg, W. F., Kest, B., Marek, P., & Liebeskind, J. C. (1993). Sex differences in the antagonism of swim stress-induced analgesia: Effects of gonadectomy and estrogen replacement. *Pain, 53,* 17–25.

Mohr, C., Graves, R. E., Gianotti, L. R. R., Pizzagalli, D., & Brugger, P. (2001). Loose but normal: A semantic association study. *Journal of Psycholinguistic Research, 30,* 475–483.

Molina, B. S., & Pelham, W. E. (2003). Childhood predictors of adolescent substance use in a longitudinal study of children with ADHD. *Journal of Abnormal Psychology, 112,* 497–507.

Moller-Madsen, S., & Nystrup, J. (1992). Incidence of anorexia nervosa in Denmark. *Acta Psychiatrica Scandinavica, 86,* 197–200.

Monahan, J. (1992). "A terror to their neighbors": Beliefs about mental disorder and violence in historical and cultural perspective. *Bulletin of the American Academy of Psychiatry and the Law, 20,* 191–195.

Money, J., & Ehrhardt, A. (1972). *Man and woman, boy and girl.* Baltimore: Johns Hopkins University Press.

Monk, T. H. (2000). Shift work. In M. H. Kryger, T. Roth, & W. C. Dement (Eds.), *Principles and practice of sleep medicine* (3rd ed., pp. 600–605). Philadelphia: W. B. Saunders.

Monk, T. H., Buysse, D. J., & Rose, L. R. (1999). Wrist actigraphic measures of sleep in space. *Sleep, 22,* 948–954.

Monk, T. H., & Moline, M. L. (1989). The timing of bedtime and waketime decisions in free-running subjects. *Psychophysiology, 26,* 304–310.

Monroe, S. M., Bromet, E. J., Connell, M. M., & Steiner, S. C. (1986). Social support, life events, and depressive symptoms: A 1 year prospective study. *Journal of Consulting and Clinical Psychology, 54*(4), 424–431.

Monroe, S. M., Imhoff, D. F., Wise, B. D., & Harris, J. E. (1983). Prediction of psychological symptoms under high-risk psychosocial circumstances: Life events, social support, and symptom specificity. *Journal of Abnormal Psychology, 92*(2), 338–350.

Monroe, S. M., Kupfer, D. J., & Frank, E. (1992). Life stress and treatment course of recurrent depression: I. Response during index episode. *Journal of Consulting and Clinical Psychology, 60*(5), 718–724.

Monroe, S. M., & Roberts, J. E. (1990). Conceptualizing and measuring life stress: Problems, principles, procedures, progress. Special issue: II–IV. Advances in measuring life stress. *Stress Medicine, 6*(3), 209–216.

Monroe, S. M., Roberts, J. E., Kupfer, D. J., & Frank, E. (1996). Life stress and treatment course of recurrent depression: II. Postrecovery associations with attrition, symptom course, and recurrence over 3 years. *Journal of Abnormal Psychology, 105*(3), 313–328.

Monroe, S. M., Rohde, P., Seeley, J. R., & Lewinsohn, P. M. (1999). Life events and depression in adolescence: For first onset of major depressive disorder. *Journal of Abnormal Psychology, 108*(4), 606–614.

Montejo-Gonzalez, A. L., Liorca, G., Izquierdo, J. A., Ledesma, A., Bousono, M., Calcedo, A., et al. (1997). SSRI-induced sexual dysfunction: Fluoxetine, paroxetine, sertraline, and fluvoxamine in a prospective, multicenter, and descriptive clinical study of 344 patients. *Journal of Sex and Marital Therapy, 23,* 176–194.

Montiel-Nava, C., Pena, J. A., & Montiel-Barbero, I. (2003). Epidemiological data about attention deficit hyperactivity disorder in a sample of marabino children. *Revista de Neurologia, 37,* 815–819.

Moore, D. S. (2001). *The dependent gene: The fallacy of "nature vs. nurture."* New York: Henry Holt and Company.

Moore, R. Y. (1999). Circadian rhythms: A clock for the ages. *Science, 284,* 2102–2103.

Moras, K., Clark, L. A., Katon, W., Roy-Byrne, P., Watson, D., & Barlow, D. H. (1996). Mixed anxiety-depression. In T. A. Widiger, A. J. Frances, H. A. Pincus, R. Ross, M. B. First, & W. W. Davis (Eds.), *DSM-IV sourcebook* (Vol. 2, pp. 623–643). Washington, DC: American Psychiatric Press.

Morelli, G. A., Rogoff, B., Oppenheim, D., & Goldsmith, D. (1992). Cultural variation in infants' sleeping arrangements: Questions of independence. *Developmental Psychology, 28,* 604–613.

Moretti, M. M., Segal, Z. V., McCann, C. D., Shaw, B. F., Miller, D. T., & Vella, D. (1996). Self-referent versus other-referent information processing in dysphoric, clinically depressed, and remitted depressed subjects. *Personality and Social Psychology Bulletin, 22,* 68–80.

Morey, L. C. (1988). Personality disorders in DSM-III and DSM-III-R: Convergence, coverage, and internal consistency. *American Journal of Psychiatry, 145,* 573–577.

Morey, L. C., & Ochoa, E. S. (1989). An investigation of adherence to diagnostic criteria: Clinical diagnosis of the DSM-III personality disorders. *Journal of Personality Disorders, 3*(3), 180–192.

Morgan, H. W. (1981). *Drugs in America: A social history, 1800–1980.* Syracuse, NY: Syracuse University Press.

Morgenstern, H., & Glazer, W. M. (1993). Identifying risk factors for tardive dyskinesia among long-term outpatients maintained with neuroleptic medications: Results of the Yale tardive dyskinesia study. *Archives of General Psychiatry, 50,* 723–733.

Morin, C. M. (1993). *Insomnia: Psychological assessment and management.* New York: Guilford Press.

Morin, C. M., & Azrin, N. H. (1988). Behavioral and cognitive treatments of geriatric insomnia. *Journal of Consulting and Clinical Psychology, 56,* 748–753.

Morin, C. M., Colecchi, C., Stone, J., Sood, R., & Brink, D. (1999). Behavioral and pharmacological therapies for late-life insomnia: A randomized controlled trial. *Journal of the American Medical Association, 281,* 991–999.

Morin, C. M., & Edinger, J. D. (2003). Sleep disorders: Evaluation and diagnosis. In M. Hersen & S. M. Turner (Eds.). *Adult psychopathology and diagnosis* (4th ed., pp. 583–612). New York: John Wiley.

Morin, C. M., Kowatch, R. A., Barry, T., & Walton, E. (1993). Cognitive-behavior therapy for late-life insomnia. *Journal of Consulting and Clinical Psychology, 61,* 137–146.

Morin, C. M., Rodrigue, S., & Ivers, H. (2003). Role of stress, arousal, and coping skills in primary insomnia. *Psychosomatic Medicine, 65,* 259–267.

Morin, C. M., Savard, J., Ouellet, M. C., & Daley, M. (2003). Insomnia: Nature, epidemiology and treatment. In A. M. Nezu, C. M. Nezu, & P. A. Geller (Eds.), *Handbook of psychology: Health psychology* (Vol 9, pp. 317–337). New York: John Wiley & Sons.

Morin, C. M., Stone, J., Trinkle, D., Mercer, J., & Remsberg, S. (1993). Dysfunctional beliefs and attitudes about sleep among older adults with and without insomnia complaints. *Psychology and Aging, 8,* 463–467.

Morin, C. M., & Wooten, V. (1996). Psychological and pharmacological approaches to treating insomnia: Critical issues in assessing their separate and combined effects. *Clinical Psychology Review, 16,* 521–542.

Morokoff, P. J. (1993). Female sexual arousal disorder. In W. O'Donohue & J. H. Geer (Eds.), *Handbook of sexual dysfunctions: Assessment and treatment* (pp. 157–199). Boston: Allyn & Bacon.

Morris, D. (1985). *Body watching: A field guide to the human species.* New York: Crown.

Morris, J. K., Cook, D. G., & Shaper, A. G. (1994). Loss of employment and mortality. *British Medical Journal, 308,* 1135–1139.

Morris, J. S., Öhman, A., & Dolan, R. J. (1998). Conscious and unconscious emotion learning in the human amygdala. *Nature, 393,* 467–470.

Morris, M., Lack, L., & Dawson, D. (1990). Sleep-onset insomniacs have delayed temperature rhythms. *Sleep, 13,* 1–14.

Morrow, G. R., & Dobkin, P. L. (1988). Anticipatory nausea and vomiting in cancer patients undergoing chemotherapy treatment: Prevalence, etiology, and behavioral interventions. *Clinical Psychology Review, 8,* 517–556.

Morton, A. (1992). *Diana: Her true story.* New York: Pocket Books.

Moscicki, E. (1997). Identification of suicide risk factors using epidemiological studies. *Psychiatric Clinics of North America, 20,* 499–517.

Mosher, D. L., & Sirkin, M. (1984). Measuring a macho personality constellation. *Journal of Research in Personality, 18,* 150–163.

Mosko, S., Richard, C., & McKenna, J. C. (1997). Maternal sleep and arousals during bedsharing with infants. *Sleep, 20,* 142–150.

Moss, A. R., & Bacchetti, P. (1989). Natural history of HIV infection. *AIDS, 3,* 55–61.

Mostofsky, D. I., & Barlow, D. H. (Eds.). (2000). *The management of stress and anxiety in medical disorders.* Needham Heights, MA: Allyn & Bacon.

Moulton, D. (2004, April 27). N. S.'s concern over OxyContin use rises: Government and college step in to stem narcotic abuse. *Medical Post, 40*(17). Retrieved May 17, 2004, from http://www.medicalpost.com/mpcontent/articl.jsp?content=20040425_093635_5176.

Mucha, T. F., & Reinhardt, R. F. (1970). Conversion reactions in student aviators. *American Journal of Psychiatry, 127,* 493–497.

Mueller, T. I., Leon, A. C., Keller, M. B., Solomon, D. A., Endicott, J., Coryell, W., et al. (1999). Recurrence after recovery from major depressive disorder during 15 years of observational follow-up. *American Journal of Psychiatry, 156*(7), 1000–1006.

Mueller, T., Keller, M. B., Leon, A. C., Solomon, D. A., Shea, M. T., Coryell, W., et al. (1996). Recovery after 5 years of unremitting major depressive disorder. *Archives of General Psychiatry, 53,* 794–799.

Mueser, K. T., & Berenbaum, H. (1990). Psychodynamic treatment of schizophrenia: Is there a future? *Psychological Medicine, 20,* 253–262.

Mueser, K. T., Bellack, A. S., Wade, J. H., Sayers, S. L., Tierney, A., & Haas, G. (1993). Expressed emotion, social skill, and response to negative affect in schizophrenia. *Journal of Abnormal Psychology, 102,* 339–351.

Mueser, K. T., Liberman, R. P., & Glynn, S. M. (1990). Psychosocial interventions in schizophrenia. In A. Kales, C. N. Stefanis, & J. A. Talbott (Eds.), *Recent advances in schizophrenia* (pp. 213–235). New York: Springer-Verlag.

Mueser, K. T., Sengupta, A., Schooler, N. R., Bellack, A. S., Xie, H., Glick, I. D., et al. (2001). Family treatment and medication dosage reduction in schizophrenia: Effects on patient social functioning, family attitudes, and burden. *Journal of Consulting and Clinical Psychology, 69* (1), 3–12.

Mukai, J., Uchid, S., Miyazaki, S., Nishihara, K., & Honda, Y. (2003). Spectral analysis of all-night human sleep EEG in narcoleptic patients and normal subjects. *Journal of Sleep Research, 12,* 63–71.

Mumford, D. B., Whitehouse, A. M., & Platts, M. (1991). Sociocultural correlates of eating disorders among Asian schoolgirls in Bradford. *British Journal of Psychiatry, 158,* 222–228.

Mundy, P., Sigman, M., & Kasari, C. (1990). A longitudinal study of joint attention and language development in autistic children. *Journal of Autism and Developmental Disorders, 20,* 115–128.

Munjack, D. J. (1984). The onset of driving phobias. *Journal of Behavior Therapy and Experimental Psychiatry, 15,* 305–308.

Muñoz, R. F. (1993). The prevention of depression: Current research and practice. *Applied and Preventative Psychology, 2,* 21–33.

Munro, A. (1999). *Delusional disorder: Paranoia and related illnesses.* New York: Cambridge University Press.

Murdoch, D., Pihl, R. O., & Ross, D. (1990). Alcohol and crimes of violence: Present issues. *International Journal of the Addictions, 25,* 1065–1081.

Murray, C. J. L. (1996). *Global health statistics.* Cambridge, MA: Harvard University Press.

Mustafa, G. (1990). Delivery systems for the care of schizophrenic patients in Africa—Sub-Sahara. In A. Kales, C. N. Stefanis, & J. A. Talbot (Eds.), *Recent advances in schizophrenia* (pp. 353–371). New York: Springer-Verlag.

Musto, D. F. (1992). America's first cocaine epidemic: What did we learn? In T. R. Kosten & H. D. Kleber (Eds.), *Clinician's guide to cocaine addiction: Theory, research, and treatment* (pp. 3–15). New York: Guilford Press.

Myers, J. K., Weissman, M. M., Tischler, C. E., Holzer, C. E., III, Orvaschel, H., Anthony, J. C., et al. (1984). Six-month prevalence of psychiatric disorders in three communities. *Archives of General Psychiatry, 41,* 959–967.

Nachmias, M., Gunnar, M., Mangelsdorf, S., Parritz, R. H., & Buss, K. (1996). Behavioral inhibition and stress reactivity: The moderating role of attachment security. *Child Development, 67*(2), 508–522.

Nagasaki, Y., Matsubara, Y., Takano, H., Fujii, K., Senoo, M., Akanuma, J., et al. (1999). Reversal of hypopigmentation in phenylketonuria mice by adenovirus-mediated gene transfer. *Pediatric Research, 45,* 465–473.

Nagayama Hall, G. C. (1995). The preliminary development of theory-based community treatment for sexual offenders. *Professional Psychology: Research and Practice, 26*(5), 478–483.

Nagel, D. B. (1991). Psychotherapy of schizophrenia: 1900–1920. In J. G. Howells (Ed.), *The concept of schizophrenia: Historical perspectives* (pp. 191–201). Washington, DC: American Psychiatric Press.

Nagin, D., & Tremblay, R. E. (1999). Trajectories of boys' physical aggression, opposition, and hyperactivity on the path to physically violent and nonviolent juvenile delinquency. *Child Development, 70,* 1181–1196.

Nagin, D. S., & Tremblay, R. E. (2001). Parental and early childhood predictors of persistent physical aggression in boys from kindergarten to high school. *Archives of General Psychiatry, 58,* 389–394.

NAMHC Workgroup on Mental Disorders Prevention Research (1998). *Priorities for Prevention Research at NIMH.* Bethesda: National Institutes of Health (NIH Publication No. 98–4321).

Nasser, M. (1986). Comparative study of the prevalence of abnormal eating attitudes among Arab female students of both London and Cairo universities. *Psychological Medicine, 16,* 621–625.

Nasser, M. (1988). Eating disorders: The cultural dimension. *Social Psychiatry and Psychiatric Epidemiology, 23,* 184–187.

Nathan, P. E. (1993). Alcoholism: Psychopathology, etiology, and treatment. In P. B. Sutker & H. E. Adams (Eds.), *Comprehensive handbook of psychopathology* (pp. 451–476). New York: Plenum Press.

National Institute of Mental Health. (2003). Breaking ground, breaking through: The strategic plan for mood disorders research. *NIH Publication*, No. 03-5121.

National Sleep Foundation (2002). *2002 "Sleep in America Poll."* Washington, DC: Author.

Navia, B. A. (1990). The AIDS dementia complex. In J. L. Cummings (Ed.), *Subcortical dementia* (pp. 181–198). New York: Oxford University Press.

Neighbors, H. W., Jackson, J. S., Campbell, L., & Williams, D. (1989). The influence of racial factors on psychiatric diagnosis: A review and suggestions for research. *Community Mental Health Journal, 25*(4), 301–311.

Neill, M., & Sider, D. (1992, April 27). On the rebound, *People, 97*. Retrieved June 24, 2004, from http://www.eatingdisorderresources.com/peoplemag/042792carlingbassett.htm.

Nelles, W. B. N., & Barlow, D. H. (1988). Do children panic? *Clinical Psychology Review, 8*(4), 359–372.

Nelson, R. O., & Barlow, D. H. (1981). Behavioral assessment: Basic strategies and initial procedures. In D. H. Barlow (Ed.), *Behavioral assessment of adult disorders.* New York: Guilford Press.

Nestadt, G., Romanoski, A. J., Chahal, R., Merchant, A., Folstein, M. F., Gruenberg, E. M., et al. (1990). An epidemiological study of histrionic personality disorder. *Psychological Medicine, 20,* 413–422.

Nestor, P. G. (2002). Mental disorder and violence: Personality dimensions and clinical features. *American Journal of Psychiatry, 159,* 1973–1978.

Newfoundland brother gets 4 years. (1992, February 8). *Spectator.* Retrieved August 23, 2003, from http://members.fortunecity.com/foul2/can.htm.

Newman, J. P., Patterson, C. M., & Kosson, D. S. (1987). Response perseveration in psychopaths. *Journal of Abnormal Psychology, 96,* 145–148.

Newman, J. P., & Wallace, J. F. (1993). Psychopathy and cognition. In K. S. Dobson & P. C. Kendall (Eds.), *Psychopathology and cognition* (pp. 293–349). New York: Academic Press.

Newman, J. P., Widom, C. S., & Nathan, S. (1985). Passive-avoidance in syndromes of disinhibition: Psychopathy and extraversion. *Journal of Personality and Social Psychology, 50,* 624–630.

Newman, S. C., & Bland, R. C. (1994). Life events and the 1-year prevalence of major depressive episode, generalized anxiety disorder, and panic disorder in a community sample. *Comprehensive Psychiatry, 35,* 76–82.

Newmark, C. S., & McCord, D. M. (1996). The Minnesota Multiphasic Personality Inventory-2 (MMPI-2). In C. S. Newmark (Ed.), *Major psychological assessment instruments* (pp. 1–58). Boston: Allyn & Bacon.

Neylan, T. C., Reynolds, C. F., III, & Kupfer, D. J. (2003). Sleep disorders. In R. E. Hales & S. C. Yudofsky (Eds.), *Textbook of clinical psychiatry* (4th ed.) (pp. 975–1000). Washington, DC: American Psychiatric Press.

Nezu, C. M., Nezu, A. M., Friedman, S. H., Houts, P. S., DelliCarpini, L., Bildner, C., et al. (1999). Cancer and psychological distress: Two investigations regarding the role of social problem-solving. *Journal of Psychosocial Oncology, 16*(3–4), 27–40.

Nichols, M. (with S. Doyle Driedger & D. Ballon). (1995, January 30). Schizophrenia: Hidden torment. *MacLean's.* Retrieved December 11, 2006, from http://www.mentalhealth.com/mag1/p51-sc01.html.

Nicholls, T., Jack, L., & Ogloff, J. R. P. (1998, March). *Comorbidity of violence against self and violence against others in a civil psychiatric population.* Poster presented at the Biennial Meeting of the American Psychology Law Society, Redondo Beach, CA.

Nisbett, R. E., & Ross, L. (1980). *Human inference: Strategies and shortcomings in social judgement.* New York: Century.

Nofzinger, E. A., Schwartz, C. F., Reynolds, C. F., Thase, M. E., Jennings, J. R., Frank, E., et al. (1994). Affect intensity and phasic REM sleep in depressed men before and after treatment with cognitive-behavior therapy. *Journal of Consulting and Clinical Psychology, 62,* 83–91.

Nolen-Hoeksema, S. (1987). Sex differences in unipolar depression: Evidence and theory. *Psychological Bulletin, 101*(2), 259–282.

Nolen-Hoeksema, S. (1990). *Sex differences in depression.* Stanford, CA: Stanford University Press.

Nolen-Hoeksema, S. (2000a). Further evidence for the role of psychosocial factors in depression chronicity. *Clinical Psychology: Science and Practice, 7*(2), 224–227.

Nolen-Hoeksema, S. (2000b). The role of rumination in depressive disorders and mixed anxiety/depressive symptoms. *Journal of Abnormal Psychology, 109,* 504–511.

Nolen-Hoeksema, S., Girgus, J. S., & Seligman, M. E. P. (1992). Predictors and consequences of childhood depressive symptoms: A 5-year longitudinal study. *Journal of Abnormal Psychology, 101*(3), 405–422.

Nolen-Hoeksema, S., Larson, J., & Grayson, C. (1999). Explaining the gender differences in depressive symptoms. *Journal of Personality and Social Psychology, 77*(5), 1061–1072.

Nolen-Hoeksema, S., Wolfson, A., Mumme, D., & Guskin, K. (1995). Helplessness in children of depressed and nondepressed mothers. *Developmental Psychology, 31,* 377–387.

Noonan, D. (2003). Exposing the myth of violence. *Schizophrenia Digest.* Retrieved November 10, 2003, from http://www.schizophreniadigest.com/images/archive/phpVQLG8H.pdf.

Norman, R. M. G., & Townsend, L. A. (1999). Cognitive-behavioural therapy for psychosis: A status report. *Canadian Journal of Psychiatry, 44,* 245–252.

Norton, G. R., Dorward, J., & Cox, B. J. (1986). Factors associated with panic attacks in nonclinical subjects. *Behavior Therapy, 17,* 239–252.

Norton, G. R., Harrison, B., Hauch, J., & Rhodes, L. (1985). Characteristics of people with infrequent panic attacks. *Journal of Abnormal Psychology, 94,* 216–221.

Norton, G. R., Norton, P. J., Cox, B. J., & Belik, S. (in press). Panic spectrum disorders and substance use. In S. H. Stewart & P. J. Conrod (Eds.), *Anxiety and substance abuse disorders.* New York: Springer.

Noyes, R., & Kletti, R. (1977). Depersonalization in response to life-threatening danger. *Comprehensive Psychiatry, 18,* 375–384.

Noyes, R., Clarkson, C., Crowe, R. R., Yates, W. R., & McChesney, C. M. (1987). A family study of generalized anxiety disorder. *American Journal of Psychiatry, 144,* 1019–1024.

Noyes, R., Garvey, M. J., Cook, B., & Suelzer, M. (1991). Controlled discontinuation of benzodiazepine treatment for patients with panic disorder. *American Journal of Psychiatry, 148,* 517–523.

Noyes, R., Hoenk, P., Kuperman, S., & Slymen, D. (1977). Depersonalization in accident victims and psychiatric patients. *Journal of Nervous and Mental Disease, 164,* 401–407.

Noyes, R., Stuart, S. P., Langbehn, D. R., Happel, R. L., Longley, S. L., Muller, B. A., et al. (2003). Test of an interpersonal model of hypochondriasis. *Psychomatic Medicine, 65,* 292–300.

Noyes, R., Woodman, C., Garvey, M. J., Cook, B. L., Suelzer, M., Clancy, J., et al. (1992). Generalized anxiety disorder vs. panic disorder: Distinguishing characteristics and patterns of comorbidity. *Journal of Nervous and Mental Disease, 180,* 369–379.

Nugent, S. A. (2000). Perfectionism: Its manifestations and classroom-based interventions. *Journal of Secondary Gifted Education, 11,* 215–221.

Nurnberg, H. G., Raskin, M., Levine, P. E., Pollack, S., Siegel, O., & Prince, R. (1991). The comorbidity of borderline personality and other DSM-III-R Axis II personality disorders. *American Journal of Psychiatry, 148,* 1371–1377.

Nurnberger, J. I., Jr., Berrettini, W., Tamarkin, L., Hamovit, J., Norton, J., & Gershon, E. S. (1988). Supersensitivity to melatonin suppression by light in young people at high risk for affective disorder: A preliminary report. *Neuropsychopharmacology, 1,* 217–223.

Nyhan, W. L. (1978). The Lesch-Nyhan syndrome. *Developmental Medicine and Child Neurology, 20,* 376–387.

Oades, R. D. (1985). The role of noradrenaline in tuning and dopamine in switching between signals in the CNS. *Neuroscience and Biobehavioral Reviews, 9,* 261–282.

O'Brien, C. P. (1996). Recent developments in the pharmacotherapy of substance abuse. *Journal of Consulting and Clinical Psychology, 64,* 677–686.

O'Brien, C. P., & Cornish, J. W. (1999). Opioids: Antagonists and partial agonists. In M. Galanter & H. D. Kleber (Eds.), *Textbook of substance abuse treatment* (2nd ed., pp. 281–294). Washington, DC: American Psychiatric Press.

O'Brien, K. M., & Vincent, N. K. (2003). Psychiatric comorbidity in anorexia and bulimia nervosa: Nature, prevalence and causal relationships. *Clinical Psychology Review, 23,* 57–74.

O'Brien, M. E., Clark, R. A., Besch, C. L., Myers, L., & Kissinger, P. (2003). Patterns and correlates of discontinuation of the initial HAART regimen in an urban outpatient cohort. *Journal of Acquired Immune Deficiency Syndrome, 34*(4), 407–414.

O'Brien, M. M., Trestman, R. L., & Siever, L. J. (1993). Cluster A personality disorders. In D. L. Dunner (Ed.), *Current psychiatric therapy* (pp. 399–404). Philadelphia: W. B. Saunders.

O'Callaghan, E., Sham, P., Takei, N., Glover, G., & Murray, R. M. (1991). Schizophrenia after prenatal exposure to 1957 A2 influenza epidemic. *Lancet, 337,* 1248–1250.

O'Carroll, P. W. (1990). Community strategies for suicide prevention and intervention. In S. J. Blumenthal & D. J. Kupfer (Eds.), *Suicide over the life cycle: Risk factors, assessment and treatment of suicidal patients.* Washington, DC: American Psychiatric Press.

O'Connor, M., Sales, B. D., & Shuman, D. W. (1996). Mental health professional expertise in the courtroom. In B. D. Sales & D. W. Shuman (Eds.), *Law, mental health, and mental disorder* (pp. 40–59). Pacific Grove, CA: Brooks/Cole.

O'Driscoll, G. A., Benkelfat, C., Florencio, P. S., Wolff, A.-L. V. G., Joober, R., Lal, S., et al. (1999). Neural correlates of eye tracking deficits in first-degree relatives of schizophrenic patients: A positron emission tomography study. *Archives of General Psychiatry, 56,* 1127–1134.

O'Driscoll, G. A., Lenzenweger, M. F., & Holzman, P. S. (1998). Antisaccades and smooth pursuit eye tracking and schizotypy. *Archives of General Psychiatry, 55,* 837–843.

Offord, D. R., Boyle, M. H., Campbell, D., Goering, P., Lin, E., Wong, M., et al. (1996). One-year prevalence of psychiatric disorder in Ontarians 15 to 64 years of age. *Canadian Journal of Psychiatry, 41,* 559–563.

Offord, D. R., Boyle, M. H., Szatmari, P., Rae-Grant, N. I., Links, P. S., Cadman, D. T., et al. (1987). Ontario Child Health Study: II. Six-month prevalence of disorder and rates of service utilization. *Archives of General Psychiatry, 44,* 832–836.

Ogata, S. N., Silk, K. R., Goodrich, S., Lohr, N. E., Westen, D., & Hill, E. M. (1990). Childhood sexual and physical abuse in adult patients with borderline personality disorder. *American Journal of Psychiatry, 147,* 1008–1013.

Ogloff, J. R. P., & Whittemore, K. E. (2001). Fitness to stand trial and criminal responsibility in Canada. In R. A. Schuller & J. R. P. Ogloff (Eds.), *Introduction to psychology and law: Canadian perspectives* (pp. 283–313). Toronto, ON: University of Toronto Press.

Ogloff, J. P. R., Wong, S., & Greenwood, A. (1990). Treating criminal psychopaths in a therapeutic community program. *Sciences and the Law, 8,* 81–90.

O'Hagan, S. (1992, February 22). Raving madness. *The Times Saturday Review,* 10–12.

O'Hanlon, J. F., Haak, J. W., Blaauw, G. J., & Riemersma, J. B. J. (1982). Diazepam impairs lateral position control in highway driving. *Science, 27,* 79–81.

O'Hara, A. (2004). *Missing/murdered First Nations (Native) women.* Retrieved July 4, 2004, from http://www.missingnativewomen.ca/index.html.

O'Hara, M. W. (1986). Social support, life events and depression during pregnancy and the puerperium. *Archives of General Psychiatry, 43*(6), 569–575.

O'Hara, M. W., Stuart, S., Gorman, L. L., & Wenzel, A. (2000). Efficacy of interpersonal psychotherapy for postpartum depression. *Archives of General Psychiatry, 57,* 1039–1045.

O'Hara, M. W., Zekoski, E. M., Philipps, L. H., & Wright, E. J. (1990). Controlled prospective study of postpartum mood disorders: Comparison of child bearing and nonbearing women. *Journal of Abnormal Psychology, 99*(1), 3–15.

Ohayon, M. M., & Schatzberg, A. F. (2003). Using chronic pain to predict depressive morbidity in the general population. *Archives of General Psychiatry, 60,* 39–47.

Öhman, A. (1986). Face the beast and fear the face: Animal and social fears as prototypes for evolutionary analyses of emotion. *Psychophysiology, 23,* 123–145.

Öhman, A. (1996). Preferential pre-attentive processing of threat in anxiety: Preparedness and attentional biases. In R. Rapee (Ed.), *Current controversies in the anxiety disorders* (pp. 253–290). New York: Guilford Press.

Öhman, A., & Dimberg, U. (1978). Facial expressions as conditioned stimuli for electrodermal responses: A case of preparedness? *Journal of Personality and Social Psychology, 36*(11), 1251–1258.

Öhman, A., Flykt, A., & Lundqvist, D. (2000). Unconscious emotion: Evolutionary perspective, psychophysiological data, and neuropsychological mechanisms. In R. Lane & L. Nadel (Eds.), *The cognitive neuroscience of emotion* (pp. 296–327). New York: Oxford University Press.

Öhman, A., & Mineka, S. (2001). Fears, phobias, and preparedness: Toward an evolved model of fear and fear learning. *Psychological Review, 108,* 483–522.

Okuji, Y., Matsuura, M., Kawasaki, N., Kometani, S., Shimoyama, T., Sato, M., et al. (2002). Prevalence of insomnia in various psychiatric diagnostic categories. *Psychiatry and Clinical Neurosciences, 56,* 239–240.

Olds, J. (1956). Pleasure centers in the brain. *Scientific American, 195,* 105–116.

Olds, J., & Milner, P. M. (1954). Positive reinforcement produced by electrical stimulation of septal area and other regions of rat brain. *Journal of Comparative and Physiological Psychology, 47,* 419–427.

O'Leary, A. (1990). Stress, emotion, and human immune function. *Psychological Bulletin, 108*(3), 363–382.

Olin, S. S., Raine, A., Cannon, T. D., Parnas, J., Schulsinger, F., & Mednick, S. A. (1997). Childhood behavior precursors of schizotypal personality disorder. *Schizophrenia Bulletin, 23,* 93–103.

Oliver, M. B., & Hyde, J. S. (1993). Gender differences in sexuality: A meta-analysis. *Psychological Bulletin, 114*(1), 29–51.

Ollendick, T. H., & Huntzinger, R. M. (1990). Separation anxiety disorder in childhood. In M. Hersen & C. G. Last (Eds.), *Handbook of child and adult psychopathology: A longitudinal perspective.* Elmsford, NY: Pergamon Press.

Ollendick, T. H., & Ollendick, D. G. (1990). Tics and Tourette syndrome. In A. M. Gross & R. S. Drabman (Eds.), *Handbook of clinical behavioral pediatrics* (pp. 243–252). New York: Plenum Press.

Olley, M. C., & Ogloff, J. R. P. (1995). Patients' rights advocacy: Implications for program design and implementation. *Journal of Mental Health Administration, 22,* 368–376.

O'Malley, M., & Missio, E. (2003, January 13). *Gordon Campbell's predicament.* CBC News Online. Retrieved June 24, 2004, from http://www.cbc.ca/news/features/campbell_gordon.html.

O'Malley, S. S. (1996). Opioid antagonists in the treatment of alcohol dependence. Clinical efficacy and prevention of relapse. *Alcohol and Alcoholism, 31* (Suppl. 1), 77–81.

O'Malley, S. S., Jaffe, A. J., Chang, G., Schottenfeld, R. S., Meyer, R. E., & Rounsaville, B. (1992). Naltrexone and coping skills therapy for alcohol dependence: A controlled study. *Archives of General Psychiatry, 49,* 881–887.

O'Neill, P. (1998). Teaching ethics: The utility of the CPA code. *Canadian Psychology, 39,* 194–201.

Orbach, I. (1997). A taxonomy of factors related to suicidal behavior. *Clinical Psychology: Science and Practice, 4,* 205–224.

Orne, M. T., Dinges, D. F., & Orne, E. C. (1984). On the differential diagnosis of multiple personality in the forensic context. *International Journal of Clinical and Experimental Hypnosis, 32,* 118–169.

O'Rourke, N., & Cappeliez, P. (2002). Perceived control, coping, and expressed burden among spouses of suspected dementia patients: Analysis of the goodness-of-fit hypothesis. *Canadian Journal on Aging, 21,* 385–392.

O'Rourke, N., Tuokko, H., Hayden, S., & Beattie, B. L. (1997). Early identification of dementia: Predictive validity of the clock test. *Archives of Clinical Neuropsychology, 12,* 257–267.

Orsillo, S. M., Roemer, L., & Barlow, D. H. (2003). Integrating acceptance and mindfulness into existing cognitive-behavioral treatment for GAD: A case study. *Cognitive and Behavioral Practice, 10,* 223–230.

Ortiz, A., & Medicna-Mora, M. E. (1988). Research on drugs in Mexico: Epidemiology of drug abuse and issues among Native American populations. In *Community Epidemiology Work Group Proceedings*, December 1987. Contract No. 271–87–8321. Washington, DC: U.S. Government Printing Office.

Oscar-Berman, M., Shagrin, B., Evert, D. L., & Epstein, C. (1997). Impairments of brain and behavior: The neurological effects of alcohol. *Alcohol Health and Research World, 21*, 65–75.

Oslin, D. W., & Cary, M. S. (2003). Alcohol-related dementia: Validation of diagnostic criteria. *American Journal of Geriatric Psychiatry, 11*, 441–447.

Öst, L. G. (1985). Mode of acquisition of phobias. *Acta Universitatis Uppsaliensis* (Abstracts of Uppsala Dissertations from the Faculty of Medicine), *529*, 1–45.

Öst, L. G. (1987). Age at onset in different phobias. *Journal of Abnormal Psychology, 96*, 223–229.

Öst, L. G. (1989). *Blood phobia: A specific phobia subtype in DSM-IV*. Paper requested by the Simple Phobia subcommittee of the DSM-IV Anxiety Disorders Work Group.

Öst, L. G. (1992). Blood and injection phobia: Background and cognitive, physiological, and behavioral variables. *Journal of Abnormal Psychology, 101*(1), 68–74.

Öst, L. G., Ferebee, I., & Furmark, T. (1997). One session group therapy of spiderphobia: Direct vs. indirect treatments. *Behaviour Research and Therapy, 35*, 721–732.

Öst, L. G., & Sterner, U. (1987). Applied tension: A specific behavioural method for treatment of blood phobia. *Behaviour Research and Therapy, 25*, 25–30.

Öst, L. G., Svensson, L., Hellström, K., & Lindwall, R. (2001). One-session treatment of specific phobia in youths: A randomized clinical trial. *Journal of Consulting and Clinical Psychology, 69*, 814–824.

O'Sullivan, K. (1979). Observations on vaginismus in Irish women. *Archives of General Psychiatry, 36*, 824–826.

Ouimette, P. C., Finney, J. W., & Moos, R. H. (1997). Twelve-step and cognitive-behavioral treatment for substance abuse: A comparison of treatment effectiveness. *Journal of Consulting and Clinical Psychology, 65*, 230–240.

Owens, M. J., Mulchahey, J. J., Stout, S. C., & Plotsky, P. M. (1997). Molecular and neurobiological mechanisms in the treatment of psychiatric disorders. In A. Tasman, J. Kay, & J. A. Lieberman (Eds.), *Psychiatry* (Vol. 1), (pp. 210–257). Philadelphia: W. B. Saunders.

Oyama, O., & Andrasik, F. (1992). Behavioral strategies in the prevention of disease. In S. M. Turner, K. S. Calhoun, & H. E. Adams (Eds.), *Handbook of clinical behavior therapy* (2nd ed., pp. 397–413). New York: John Wiley.

Pagani, L., Tremblay, R. E., Vitaro, F., Kerr, M., & McDuff, P. (1998). The impact of family transition on the development of delinquency in adolescent boys: A 9-year longitudinal study. *Journal of Child Psychology, Psychiatry and Allied Disciplines, 39*, 489–499.

Page, A. C. (1994). Blood-injury phobia. *Clinical Psychology Review, 14*, 443–461.

Page, A. C. (1996). Blood-injury-injection fears in medical practice. *Medical Journal of Australia, 164*, 189.

Page, A. C., & Martin, N. G. (1998). Testing a genetic structure of blood-injury-injection fears. *American Journal of Medical Genetics* (Neuropsychiatric Genetics), *81*, 377–384.

Page, G. G., Ben-Eliyahu, S., Yirmiya, R., & Liebeskind, J. C. (1993). Morphine attenuates surgery-induced enhancement of metastatic colonization in rats. *Pain, 54*(1), 21–28.

Pahl, J. J., Swayze, V. W., & Andreasen, N. C. (1990). Diagnostic advances in anatomical and functional brain imaging in schizophrenia. In A. Kales, C. N. Stefanis, & J. A. Talbott (Eds.), *Recent advances in schizophrenia* (pp. 163–189). New York: Springer-Verlag.

Pajer, K. A. (1998). What happens to "bad" girls? A review of the adult outcomes of antisocial adolescent girls. *American Journal of Psychiatry, 155*, 862–870.

Pandina, R., & Hendren, R. (1999). Other drugs of abuse: Inhalants, designer drugs, and steroids. In B. S. McCrady & E. E. Epstein (Eds.), *Addictions: A comprehensive guidebook* (pp. 171–184). New York: Oxford University Press.

Pantaleo, G., Graziosi, C., & Fauci, A. S. (1993). The immunopathogenesis of human immunodeficiency virus infection. *New England Journal of Medicine, 328*, 327–335.

Pantony, K.-L., & Caplan, P. J. (1991). Delusional dominating personality disorder: A modest proposal for identifying some consequences of rigid masculine socialization. *Canadian Psychology, 32*, 120–135.

Papillo, J. F., & Shapiro, D. (1990). The cardiovascular system. In J. T. Cacioppo & L. G. Tassinary (Eds.), *Principles of psychophysiology: Physical, social, and inferential elements*. New York: Cambridge University Press.

Paquette, V., Lévesque, J., Mensour, B., Leroux, J-M, Beudoin, G., Bourgouin, P., et al. (2003). "Change the mind and you change the brain": Effects of cognitive-behavioral therapy on the neural correlates of spider phobia. *Neuroimage, 18*, 401–409.

Parker, G., & Hadzi-Pavlovic, D. (1990). Expressed emotion as a predictor of schizophrenic relapse: An analysis of aggregated data. *Psychological Medicine, 20*, 961–965.

Parkes, J. D., & Block, C. (1989). Genetic factors in sleep disorders. *Journal of Neurology, Neurosurgery, and Psychiatry, 52*, 101–108.

Parkinson, L., & Rachman, S. (1981a). Intrusive thoughts: The effects of an uncontrived stress. *Advances in Behaviour Research and Therapy, 3*, 111–118.

Parkinson, L., & Rachman, S. (1981b). Speed of recovery from an uncontrived stress. *Advances in Behaviour Research and Therapy, 3*, 119–123.

Parkinson Society of Canada, (2002). *Parkinson's disease: Frequently asked questions*. Retrieved November 24, 2003, from http://www.parkinson.ca/pd/faq.html.

Parloff, M. B. (1986). Placebo controls in psychotherapy research: A sine qua non or a placebo for research problems? *Journal of Consulting and Clinical Psychology, 54*, 79–87.

Parry-Jones, B., & Parry-Jones, W. L. (2002). History of bulimia and bulimia nervosa. In K. D. Brownell & C. G. Fairburn (Eds.), *Eating disorders and obesity: A comprehensive handbook* (2nd ed., pp. 145–150). New York: Guilford Press.

Parry-Jones, W. Li., & Parry-Jones, B. (1994). Implications of historical evidence for the classification of eating disorders. *British Journal of Psychiatry, 165*, 287–292.

Parsons, O. A., & Nixon, S. J. (1993). Behavioral disorders associated with central nervous system dysfunction. In P. B. Sutker & H. E. Adams (Eds.), *Comprehensive handbook of psychopathology* (pp. 689–733). New York: Plenum Press.

Pasewark, R. A., & Seidenzahl, D. (1979). Opinions concerning the insanity plea and criminality among mental patients. *Bulletin of the American Academy of Psychiatry and Law, 7*, 199–202.

Pataki, C. S., & Carlson, G. A. (1990). Major depression in childhood. In M. Hersen & C. Last (Eds.), *Handbook of child and adult psychopathology: A longitudinal perspective*. Elmsford, NY: Pergamon Press.

Patel, V., & Andrade, C. (2003). Pharmacological treatment of severe psychiatric disorders in the developing world: Lessons from India. *CNS Drugs, 17*, 1071–1080.

Patience, D. A. (1994). Cognitive-behavioural therapy for schizophrenia. *British Journal of Psychiatry, 165*, 266–267.

Patten, S. B. (2000). Major depression prevalence in Calgary. *Canadian Journal of Psychiatry, 45*, 923–926.

Patten, S. B. (2002). Progress against major depression in Canada. *Canadian Journal of Psychiatry, 47*, 775–780.

Patten, S. B., & Charney, D. A. (1998). Alcohol consumption and major depression in the Canadian population. *Canadian Journal of Psychiatry, 43*, 502–506.

Patterson, G. R. (1982). *Coercive family process*. Eugene, OR: Castalia.

Patterson, G. R. (1986). Performance models for antisocial boys. *American Psychologist, 41*, 432–444.

Patterson, G. R., Chamberlain, P., & Reid, J. B. (1982). A comparative evaluation of a parent-training program. *Behavior Therapy, 13*, 638–650.

Patterson, G. R., Cobb, J. A., & Ray, R. S. (1972). Direct intervention in the classroom: A set of procedures for the aggressive child. In F. Clark, D. Evans, & L. Hamerlynck (Eds.), *Implementing behavioral programs for schools and clinics*. Champaign, IL: Research Press.

Patterson, G. R., DeBaryshe, B. D., & Ramsey, E. (1989). A developmental perspective on antisocial behavior. *American Psychologist, 44*, 329–335.

Patterson, G. R., & Fleischman, M. J. (1979). Maintenance of treatment effects: Some considerations concerning family systems and follow-up data. *Behavior Therapy, 10*, 168–185.

Patton, G. C. (1988). Mortality in eating disorders. *Psychological Medicine, 18*, 947–951.

Patton, G. C., Johnson-Sabine, E., Wood, K., Mann, A. H., & Wakeling, A. (1990). Abnormal eating attitudes in London school girls—A prospective epidemiological study: Outcome at twelve month follow up. *Psychological Medicine, 20,* 383–394.

Paul, G. L., & Lentz, R. J. (1977). *Psychosocial treatment of chronic mental patients: Milieu versus social learning programs.* Cambridge, MA: Harvard University Press.

Paulhus, D. L., & Williams, K. M. (2002). The Dark Triad of personality: Narcissism, Machiavellianism and psychopathy. *Journal of Research in Personality, 36,* 556–563.

Pauli, P., & Alpers, G. W. (2002). Memory bias in patients with hypochondriasis and somatoform pain disorder. *Journal of Psychosomatic Research, 52,* 45–53.

Pavalko, E. K., Elder, G. H., Jr., & Clipp, E. C. (1993). Worklives and longevity: Insights from a life course perspective. *Journal of Health and Social Behavior, 34,* 363–380.

Paxton, S. J., Schutz, H. K., Wertheim, E. H., & Muir, S. L. (1999). Friendship clique and peer influences on body image concerns, dietary restraint, extreme weight-loss behaviors, and binge eating in adolescent girls. *Journal of Abnormal Psychology, 108*(2), 255–266.

Paykel, E. S., Brayne, C., Huppert, F. A., Gill, C., Barkley, C., Gehlhaar, E., et al. (1994). Incidence of dementia in a population older than 75 years in the United Kingdom. *Archives of General Psychiatry, 51,* 325–332.

Pearson, C. (2002, October 31). MDs refuse to prescribe medicinal pot. *Windsor Star.* Retrieved October 26, 2003, from http://www.medicalmarihuana.ca/refusal.html.

Pechnick, R. N., & Ungerleider, J. T. (1997). Hallucinogens. In J. H. Lowinson, P. Ruiz, R. B. Millman, & J. G. Langrod (Eds.), *Substance abuse: A comprehensive textbook* (pp. 230–238). Baltimore, MD: Williams & Wilkins.

Pelham, W. E., Jr. (1999). The NIMH Multimodal Treatment Study for attention-deficit hyperactivity disorder: Just say yes to drugs alone? *Canadian Journal of Psychiatry, 44,* 981–990.

Pelham, W. E., Jr., Waschbusch, D. A., Hoza, B., Pillow, D. R., & Gnagy, E. M. (2001). Effects of methylphenidate and expectancy on performance, self-evaluations, persistence, and attributions on a social task in boys with ADHD. *Experimental and Clinical Psychopharmacology, 9,* 425–437.

Pendery, M. L., Maltzman, I. M., & West, L. J. (1982). Controlled drinking by alcoholics? New findings and a reevaluation of a major affirmative study. *Science, 217,* 169–175.

Pentz, M. A. (1999). Prevention. In M. Galanter & H. D. Kleber (Eds.), *Textbook of substance abuse treatment* (2nd ed., pp. 535–544). Washington, DC: American Psychiatric Press.

"The People's Courtney" (1995). Retrieved from http://www.geocities.com/SunsetStrip/4925/Alanis/Articles/art9.html), November 21, 2006.

Peplau, L. A. (2003). Human sexuality: How do men and women differ? *Current Directions in Psychological Science, 12,* 37–40.

Pepper, C. M., Klein, D. N., Anderson, R. L., Riso, L. P., Ouimette, P. C., & Lizardi, H. (1995). DSM-III-R Axis II comorbidity in dysthymia and major depression. *American Journal of Psychiatry, 152,* 239–247.

Pericak-Vance, M. A., Johnson, C. C., Rimmler, J. B., Saunders, A. M., Robinson, L. C., D'Hondt, E. G., et al. (1996). Alzheimer's disease and apolipoprotein E-4 allele in an Amish population. *Annals of Neurology, 39,* 700–704.

Perkins, K. A., Ciccocioppo, M., Jacobs, L., & Doyle, T. (2003). The subjective and reinforcing effects of visual and olfactory stimuli in alcohol drinking. *Experimental and Clinical Psychopharmacology, 11,* 269–275.

Perlin, M. L. (1996). The voluntary delivery of mental health services in the community. In B. D. Sales & D. W. Shuman (Eds.), *Law, mental health, and mental disorder* (pp. 150–177). Pacific Grove, CA: Brooks/Cole.

Perlin, M. L. (2000). *The hidden prejudice: Mental disability on trial.* Washington, DC: American Psychological Association.

Perry, A., Tarrier, N., Morriss, R., McCarthy, E., & Limb, K. (1999) Randomised controlled trial of efficacy of teaching patients with bipolar disorder to identify early symptoms of relapse and obtain treatment. *British Medical Journal, 318,* 149–153.

Perry, J. C. (1993). Longitudinal studies of personality disorders. *Journal of Personality Disorders, 7,* 63–85.

Perry, J. C. (2001). Dependent personality disorder. In G. O. Gabbard (Ed.), *Treatment of psychiatric disorders* (Vol. 2) (3rd ed.) (pp. 2353–2368). Washington, DC: American Psychiatric Press.

Perry, J. C., Banon, E., & Ianni, F. (1999). Effectiveness of psychotherapy for personality disorders. *American Journal of Psychiatry, 156,* 1312–1321.

Perry, S. (1993). Psychiatric treatment of adults with human immunodeficiency virus infection. In D. L. Dunner (Ed.), *Current psychiatric therapy* (pp. 475–482). Philadelphia: W. B. Saunders.

Person, D. C., & Borkovec, T. D. (1995, August). *Anxiety disorders among the elderly: Patterns and issues.* Paper presented at the 103rd annual meeting of the American Psychological Association. New York, NY.

Peselow, E. D., Fieve, R. R., Difiglia, C., & Sanfilipo, M. P. (1994). Lithium prophylaxis of bipolar illness: The value of combination treatment. *British Journal of Psychiatry, 164,* 208–214.

Peters, C. P. (1991). Concepts of schizophrenia after Kraepelin and Bleuler. In J. G. Howells (Ed.), *The concept of schizophrenia: Historical perspectives* (pp. 93–107). Washington, DC: American Psychiatric Press.

Petersen, A. C., Compas, B. E., Brooks-Gunn, J., Stemmler, M., Ey, S., & Grant, K. E. (1993). Depression in adolescence. *American Psychologist, 48*(2), 155–168.

Peterson, B. S. (1995). Neuroimaging in child and adolescent neuropsychiatric disorders. *Journal of the American Academy of Child and Adolescent Psychiatry, 34,* 1560–1576.

Peterson, C. B., Mitchell, J. E., Engbloom, S., Nugent, S., Mussell, M. P., & Miller, J. P. (1998). Group cognitive-behavioral treatment of binge eating disorders: A comparison of therapist-led versus self-help formats. *International Journal of Eating Disorders, 24,* 125–136.

Peterson, D. R. (1968). *The clinical study of social behavior.* New York: Appleton-Century-Crofts.

Peterson, J. B., Pihl, R. O., Gianoulakis, C., Conrod, P., Finn, P. R., Stewart, S. H., et al. (1996). Ethanol-induced change in cardiac and endogenous opiate function and risk for alcoholism. *Alcoholism: Clinical and Experimental Research, 20,* 1542–1552.

Peterson, J. B., Pihl, R. O., Seguin, J. R., Finn, P. R., & Stewart, S. H. (1993). Heart rate reactivity and alcohol consumation among sons of male alcoholics and sons of non-alcoholics. *Journal of Psychiatry and Neuroscience, 18,* 190–198.

Peterson, L., Farmer, J., & Kashani, J. H. (1990). Parental injury prevention endeavors: A function of health beliefs? *Health Psychology, 9*(2), 177–191.

Peterson, L., & Roberts, M. C. (1992). Complacency, misdirection, and effective prevention of children's injuries. *American Psychologist, 47*(8), 1040–1044.

Peterson, L., & Thiele, C. (1988). Home safety at school. *Child and Family Behavior Therapy, 10*(1), 1–8.

Petit, L., Azad, N., Byszewski, A., Sarazan, F. F. A., & Power, B. (2003). Non-pharmacological management of primary and secondary insomnia among older people: Review of assessment tools and treatments. *Age and Ageing, 32,* 19–25.

Petry, N. M., Martin, B., Cooney, J. L., & Kranzler, H. R. (2000). Give them prizes, and they will come: Contingency management for treatment of alcohol dependence. *Journal of Consulting and Clinical Psychology, 68*(2), 250–257.

Pfohl, B. (1991). Histrionic personality disorder: A review of available data and recommendations for DSM-IV. *Journal of Personality Disorders, 5,* 150–166.

Pfohl, B. (1993). Proposed DSM-IV criteria for personality disorders. In D. L. Dunner (Ed.), *Current psychiatric therapy* (pp. 397–399). Philadelphia: W. B. Saunders.

Pfohl, B. (1995). Histrionic personality disorder. In W. J. Livesley (Ed.), *The DSM-IV personality disorders* (pp. 173–192). New York: Guilford Press.

Pfohl, B., & Blum, N. (1995). Obsessive-compulsive personality disorder. In W. J. Livesley (Ed.), *The DSM-IV personality disorders* (pp. 261–276). New York: Guilford Press.

Pharmacists.ca (2003). *Products discontinued from the market.* Retrieved August 6, 2004, from http://www.pharmacists.ca/content/hcp/tools/drugnews/discontinued.htm.

Phifer, J. F., & Murrell, S. A. (1986). Etiologic factors in the onset of depressive symptoms in older adults. *Journal of Abnormal Psychology, 95,* 282–291.

Philips, H. C., & Grant, L. (1991). Acute back pain: A psychological analysis. *Behaviour Research and Therapy, 29,* 429–434.

Phillip, M. (2003, May 9). When women run away from their lives. *The Globe and Mail.* Retrieved June 17, 2004, from http://www.globeandmail.com/servlet/ ArticleNews/TPPrint/LAC/20030509/ UAMNEN.

Phillips, K. A. (1991). Body dysmorphic disorder: The distress of imagined ugliness. *American Journal of Psychiatry, 148,* 1138–1149.

Phillips, K. A. (2000). Quality of life for patients with body dysmorphic disorder. *Journal of Nervous and Mental Disease, 188*(3), 170–175.

Phillips, K. A., Dwight, M. M., & McElroy, S. L. (1998). Efficacy and safety of fluvoxamine in body dysmorphic disorder. *Journal of Clinical Psychiatry, 59*(4), 165–171.

Phillips, K. A., & Gunderson, J. G. (2000). Personality disorders. In M. H. Kryger, T. Roth, and W. C. Dement (Eds.), *Principles and practice of sleep medicine* (3rd ed., pp. 795–823). Philadelphia: W. B. Saunders.

Phillips, K. A., McElroy, S. L., Keck, P. E., Jr., Pope, H. G., Jr., & Hudson, J. I. (1993). Body dysmorphic disorder: 30 cases of imagined ugliness. *American Journal of Psychiatry, 150,* 302–308.

Phillips, K. A., Yen, S., & Gunderson, J. G. (2003). Personality disorders. In R. E. Hales & S. C. Yudofsky (Eds.), *Textbook of clinical psychiatry* (4th ed.) (pp. 804–832). Washington, DC: American Psychiatric Press.

Phillips, M. R., Li, X., & Zhang, Y. (2002). Suicide rates in China, 1995–99. *Lancet, 359,* 835–840.

Physicians for a Smoke-Free Canada (2002). *Percentage of Canadians who smoke (on either a daily or occasional basis), federal surveys, 1965–2003.* Retrieved October 26, 2003, from http://www.smoke-free.ca/factsheets/ pdf/prevalence.pdf.

Pickens, R. W., Svikis, D. S., McGue, M., Lykken, D. T., Heston, L. L., & Clayton, P. J. (1991). Heterogeneity in the inheritence of alcoholism. *Archives of General Psychiatry, 48,* 19–28.

Pierce, W. D., & Epling, W. F. (1994). Activity anorexia: An interplay between basic and applied behavior analysis. *Behavior Analyst, 17,* 7–23.

Pierce, W. D., & Epling, W. F. (1996). Theoretical developments in activity anorexia. In W. F. Epling & W. D. Pierce (Eds.), *Activity anorexia: Theory research, and treatment* (pp. 23–41). Mahwah, NJ: Erlbaum.

Pierce, J. P., & Gilpin, E. A. (1995). A historical analysis of tobacco marketing and the uptake of smoking by youth in the United States: 1890–1977. *Health Psychology, 14,* 500–508.

Pihl, R. O., Peterson, J. B., & Lau, M. A. (1993). A biosocial model of the alcohol-aggression relationship. *Journal of Studies on Alcohol,* Suppl. No. 11, 128–139.

Pike, K. M., Devlin M. J., & Loeb, C. (2004). Cognitive-behavioral therapy in the treatment of anorexia nervosa, and binge eating disorder. In J. K. Thompson (Ed.) *Handbook of eating disorders and obesity* (pp. 130–162). New York: John Wiley.

Pike, K. M., Loeb, K., & Vitousek, K. (1996). Cognitive-behavioral therapy for anorexia nervosa and bulimia nervosa. In J. K. Thompson (Ed.), *Body image, eating disorders and obesity* (pp. 253–302). Washington, DC: American Psychological Association.

Pike, K. M., & Rodin, J. (1991). Mothers, daughters, and disordered eating. *Journal of Abnormal Psychology, 100*(2), 198–204.

Pike, K. M., Walsh, B. T., Vitousek, K., Wilson, G. T., & Bauer, J. (2003). Cognitive behavior therapy in the posthospitalization treatment of anorexia nervosa. *American Journal of Psychiatry, 160,* 2046–2048.

Pilowsky, I. (1970). Primary and secondary hypochondriasis. *Acta Psychiatrica Scandinavica, 46,* 273–285.

Pinel, J. P. J., Assanand, S., & Lehman, D. R. (2000). Hunger, eating, and ill health. *American Psychologist, 55,* 1105–1116.

Pinel, P. (1962). *A treatise on insanity.* New York: Hafner (Original work published in 1801).

Piran, N. (1997). Prevention of eating disorders: Directions for future research. *Psychopharmacology Bulletin, 33,* 419–423.

Piran, N. (1998). A participatory approach to the prevention of eating disorders in a school. In W. Vandereycken & G. Noordenbos (Eds.), *Prevention of eating disorders* (pp. 173–186). New York: University Press.

Piran, N. (1999). Eating disorders: A trial of prevention in a high risk school setting. *Journal of Primary Prevention, 20,* 75–90.

Piran, N. (2001). V. Reinhabiting the body. *Feminism and Psychology, 11,* 172–176.

Pirke, K. M., Schweiger, U., & Fichter, M. M. (1987). Hypothalamic-pituitary-ovarian axis in bulimia. In J. I. Hudson & H. G. Pope (Eds.), *The psychobiology of bulimia* (pp. 15–28). Washington, DC: American Psychiatric Press.

Pliner, P., & Haddock, G. (1996). Perfectionism in weight-concerned and unconcerned women: An experimental approach. *International Journal of Eating Disorders, 19,* 381–389.

Plomin, R. (1990). The role of inheritance in behavior. *Science, 248,* 183–188.

Plomin, R., DeFries, J. C., McClearn, G. E., & Rutter, M. (1997). *Behavioral genetics: A primer* (3rd ed.). New York: Freeman.

Plomin, R., McClearn, G. E., Smith, D. L., Skuder, P., Vignetti, S., Chorney, M. J., et al. (1995). Allelic association between 100 DNA markers and high versus low IQ. *Intelligence, 21,* 31–48.

Plomin, R., Owen, M. J., & McGuffin, P. (1994). The genetic basis of complex human behaviors. *Science, 264,* 1733–1739.

Polivy, J. (2001). The false hope syndrome: Unrealistic expectations of self-change. *International Journal of Obesity and Related Metabolic Disorders, 25* (Suppl. 1), 80–84.

Polivy, J. M., & Herman, C. P. (1985). Dieting and binging: A causal analysis. *American Psychologist, 40,* 193–201.

Polivy, J. M., & Herman, C. P. (1993). Etiology of binge eating: Psychological mechanisms. In C. G. Fairburn & G. T. Wilson (Eds.), *Binge eating: Nature, assessment, and treatment.* New York: Guilford Press.

Polivy, J., & Herman, C. P. (2002a). Dieting and its relation to eating disorder. In K. D. Brownell & C. G. Fairburn (Eds.), *Eating disorders and obesity: A comprehensive handbook* (2nd ed., pp. 83–86). New York: Guilford Press.

Polivy, J., & Herman, C. P. (2002b). If at first you don't succeed: False hopes of self-change. *American Psychologist, 57,* 677–689.

Polivy, J., Herman, C. P., Mills, J., & Brock, H. (2003). Eating disorders in adolescence. In G. R. Adams & M. D. Berzonsky (Eds.), *Blackwell handbook of adolescence* (pp. 523–549). Malden, MA: Blackwell.

Pollack, C., & Andrews, G. (1989). Defense styles associated with specific anxiety disorders. *American Journal of Psychiatry, 146,* 1500–1502.

Polloway, E. A., Schewel, R., & Patton, J. R. (1992). Learning disabilities in adulthood: Personal perspectives. *Journal of Learning Disabilities, 25,* 520–522.

Polonsky, D. C. (2000). Premature ejaculation. In S. R. Leiblum & R. C. Rosen (Eds.), *Principles and practice of sex therapy* (3rd ed., pp. 305–332). New York: Guilford Press.

Pomeroy, C. (2004). Assessment of medical status and physical factors. In J. K. Thompson (Ed.), *Handbook of eating disorders and obesity* (pp. 81–111). New York: John Wiley.

Pope, H. D., Jr., Oliva, P. S., Hudson, J. I., Bodkin, J. A., & Gruber, A. J. (1999). Attitudes toward DSM-IV dissociative disorders diagnoses among board-certified American psychiatrists. *American Journal of Psychiatry, 156*(2), 321–323.

Pope, H. G., Jr., Gruber, A. J., Mangweth, B., Bureau, B., deCol, C., Jouvent, R., et al. (2000). Body image perception among men in three countries. *American Journal of Psychiatry, 157,* 1297–1301.

Pope, K. S. (1997). Science as careful questioning: Are claims of a false memory syndrome epidemic based on empirical evidence? *American Psychologist, 52,* 997–1006.

Popper, C., & West, S. A. (1999). Disorders usually first diagnosed in infancy, childhood, or adolescence. In R. E. Hales, S. C. Yudofsky, & J. A. Talbott (Eds.), *Textbook of psychiatry* (3rd ed., pp. 825–954). Washington, DC: American Psychiatric Press.

Popper, C. W., Gammon, G. D., West, S. A., & Bailey, C. E. (2003). Disorders usually first diagnosed in infancy, childhood, or adolescence. In R. E. Hales & S. C. Yudofsky (Eds.), *Textbook of clinical psychiatry* (4th ed.) (pp. 833–974). Washington, DC: American Psychiatric Publishing.

Portenoy, R. K., & Payne, R. (1997). Acute and chronic pain. In J. H. Lowinson, P. Ruiz, R. B. Millman, & J. G. Langrod (Eds.), *Substance abuse: A comprehensive textbook* (pp. 563–589). Baltimore, MD: Williams & Wilkins.

Porter, S., Yuille, J. C., & Lehman, D. R. (1999). The nature of real, implanted, and fabricated memories for emotional childhood events: Implications for the recovered memory debate. *Law and Human Behavior, 23*, 517–537.

Post, R. M. (1992). Transduction of psychosocial stress into the neurobiology of recurrent affective disorder. *American Journal of Psychiatry, 149*(8), 999–1010.

Post, R. M., Rubinow, D. R., Uhde, T. W., Roy-Byrne, P. P., Linnoila, M., Rosoff, A., et al. (1989). Dysphoric mania: Clinical and biological correlates. *Archives of General Psychiatry, 46*, 353–358.

Potenza, M. N. (2001). The neurobiology of pathological gambling. *Seminars in Clinical Neuropsychiatry, 6*, 217–226.

Potkin, S. G., Albers, L. J., & Richmond, G. (1993). Schizophrenia: An overview of pharmacological treatment. In D. L. Dunner (Ed.), *Current psychiatric therapy* (pp. 142–154). Philadelphia: W. B. Saunders.

Potter, S. M., Zelazo, P. R., Stack, D. M., & Papageorgiou, A. N. (2000). Adverse effects of fetal cocaine exposure on neonatal auditory information processing. *Pediatrics, 105*(3), E40.

Potter, W. Z., & Manji, H. K. (1993). Are monoamine metabolites in cerebral spinal fluid worth measuring? *Archives of General Psychiatry, 50*, 653–656.

Powell, R. A., & Howell, A. J., (1998). Effectiveness of treatment for dissociative identity disorder. *Psychological Reports, 83*, 483–490.

Poznanski, E. O., Israel, M. C., & Grossman, J. A. (1984). Hypomania in a four year old. *Journal of the American Academy of Child Psychiatry, 23*(1), 105–110.

Prelior, E. F., Yutzy, S. H., Dean, J. T., & Wetzel, R. D. (1993). Briquet's syndrome, dissociation and abuse. *American Journal of Psychiatry, 150*, 1507–1511.

Preskorn, S. H. (1995). Comparison of the tolerability of bupropion, fluoxetine, imipramine, nefazodone, paroxetine, sertraline, and venlafaxine. *Journal of Clinical Psychiatry, 56* (Suppl. 6), 12–21.

Price, R., & Brew, B. (1988). The AIDS dementia complex. *Journal of Infectious Diseases, 158*, 1079–1083.

Pridal, C. G., & LoPiccolo, J. (2000). Multielement treatment of desire disorders: Integration of cognitive, behavioral and systemic therapy. In S. R. Leiblum & R. C. Rosen (Eds.), *Principles and practice of sex therapy* (3rd ed., pp. 57–81). New York: Guilford Press.

Prien, R. F., & Kupfer, D. J. (1986). Continuation drug therapy for major depressive episodes: How long should it be maintained? *American Journal of Psychiatry, 143*(1), 18–23.

Prien, R. F., & Potter, W. Z. (1993). Maintenance treatment for mood disorders. In D. L. Dunner (Ed.), *Current psychiatric therapy* (pp. 255–260). Philadelphia: W. B. Saunders.

Priest, L. (2003, June 25). Children's Aid closes suspected case of Munchausen's syndrome. *The Globe*. Retrieved June 21, 2004, from http://www.msbp.com/DeSousa.htm.

Prince, M. (1906–1907). Hysteria from the point of view of dissociated personality. *Journal of Abnormal Psychology, 1*, 170–187.

Prizant, B. M., & Wetherby, A. M. (1989). Enhancing language and communication in autism: From theory to practice. In G. Dawson (Ed.), *Autism: Nature, diagnosis, and treatment* (pp. 282–309). New York: Guilford Press.

Project MATCH Research Group (1993). Project MATCH: Rationale and methods for a multisite clinical trial matching patients to alcoholism treatment. *Alcoholism: Clinical and Experimental Research, 17*, 1130–1145.

Project MATCH Research Group (1997). Matching alcoholism treatments to client heterogeneity: Project MATCH: Posttreatment drinking outcomes. *Journal of Studies on Alcohol, 58*, 7–29.

Project MATCH Research Group (1998). Matching alcoholism treatments to client heterogeneity: Treatment main effects and matching effects on drinking during treatment. *Journal of Studies on Alcohol, 59*(6), 631–639.

Proulx, A. (2001). *The shipping news*. New York: Simon & Schuster.

Prout, P. I., & Dobson, K. S. (1998). Recovered memories of childhood sexual abuse: Searching for the middle ground in clinical practice. *Canadian Psychology, 39*, 257–265.

Provencher, H. L., & Fincham, F. D. (2000). Attributions of causality, responsibility and blame for positive and negative symptom behaviours in caregivers of persons with schizophrenia. *Psychological Medicine, 30*, 899–910.

Prudic, J., Sackeim, H. A., & Devanand, D. P. (1990). Medication resistance and clinical response to electroconvulsive therapy. *Psychiatry Research, 31*, 287–296.

Pueschel, S. M., & Goldstein, A. (1991). Genetic counseling. In J. L. Matson & J. A. Mulick (Eds.), *Handbook of mental retardation* (2nd ed., pp. 279–291). Elmsford, NY: Pergamon Press.

Puig-Antich, J. (1982). Major depression and conduct disorder in prepuberty. *Journal of the American Academy of Child Psychiatry, 21*, 118–128.

Purdon, C. (1999). Thought suppression and psychopathology. *Behaviour Research and Therapy, 37*, 1029–1054.

Purdon, C., Antony, M., Monteiro, S., & Swinson, R. P. (2001). Social anxiety in college students. *Journal of Anxiety Disorders, 15*, 203–215.

Purdon, C., & Clark, D. A. (2000). White bears and other elusive intrusions: Assessing the relevance of thought suppression for obsessional phenomena. *Behavior Modification, 24*, 425–453.

Purdy, D., & Frank, E. (1993). Should postpartum mood disorders be given a more prominent or distinct place in DSM-IV? *Depression, 1*, 59–70.

Pury, C. L. S., & Mineka, S. (1997). Covariation bias for blood-injury stimuli and aversion outcomes. *Behavior Research and Therapy, 35*, 35–47.

Putnam, F. W. (1989). *Diagnosis and treatment of multiple personality disorder*. New York: Guilford Press.

Putnam, F. W. (1991). Dissociative phenomena. In A. Tasman & S. M. Goldinger (Eds.), *American Psychiatric Press review of psychiatry* (Vol. 10). Washington, DC: American Psychiatric Press.

Putnam, F. W. (1992). Altered states: Peeling away the layers of a multiple personality. *Sciences, 32*(6), 30–36.

Putnam, F. W. (1997). *Dissociation in children and adolescents: A developmental perspective*. New York: Guilford Press.

Putnam, F. W., Guroff, J. J., Silberman, E. K., Barban, L., & Post, R. M. (1986). The clinical phenomenology of multiple personality disorder: Review of 100 recent cases. *Journal of Clinical Psychiatry, 47*, 285–293.

Putnam, F. W., & Loewenstein, R. J. (1993). Treatment of multiple personality disorder: A survey of current practices. *American Journal of Psychiatry, 150*, 1048–1052.

Quality Assurance Project (1990). Treatment outlines for paranoid, schizotypal and schizoid personality disorders. *Australian and New Zealand Journal of Psychiatry, 24*, 339–350.

Quay, H. C. (1965). Psychopathic personality as pathological stimulation seeking. *American Journal of Psychiatry, 122*, 180–183.

Quay, H. C. (1993). The psychobiology of undersocialized aggressive conduct disorder: A theoretical perspective. *Development and Psychopathology, 5*, 165–180.

Quinsey, V. L., Khanna, A., & Malcolm, P. B. (1998). A retrospective evaluation of the regional treatment centre sex offender treatment program. *Journal of Interpersonal Violence, 13*, 621–644.

Quitkin, F. M., Rabkin, J. G., Gerald, J., Davis, J. M., & Klein, D. F. (2000). Validity of clinical trials of antidepressants. *American Journal of Psychiatry, 157*, 327–337.

Rachman, S. (1978). *Fear and courage*. San Francisco: W. H. Freeman.

Rachman, S. (1991). Neo-conditioning and the classical theory of fear acquisition. *Clinical Psychology Review, 11*, 155–173.

Rachman, S. (1998) A cognitive theory of obsessions: Elaborations. *Behaviour Research and Therapy, 35*, 385–401.

Rachman, S. (2002). Fears born and bred: Non-associative fear acquisition? *Behaviour Research and Therapy, 40*, 121–126.

Rachman, S. (2003). *The treatment of obsessions*. New York: Oxford University Press.

Rachman, S., & de Silva, P. (1978). Abnormal and normal obsessions. *Behaviour Research & Therapy, 16*, 233–248.

Rachman, S., & Hodgson, R. (1968). Experimentally induced "sexual fetishism": Replication and development. *Psychological Record, 18*(1), 25–27.

Rachman, S., & Philips, C. (1980). *Psychology and behavioral medicine*. Cambridge, UK: Cambridge University Press.

Rachman, S., & Shafran, R. (1998). Cognitive and behavioral features of obsessive-compulsive disorder. In R. P. Swinson & M. M. Antony (Eds.), *Obsessive-compulsive disorder: Theory, research, and treatment* (pp. 51–78). New York: Guilford Press.

Rachman, S. J. (1977). The conditioning theory of fear-acquisition: A critical examination. *Behaviour Research and Therapy, 15*, 375–387.

Rachman, S. J. (1984). Agoraphobia: A safety-signal perspective. *Behaviour Research and Therapy, 22*, 59–70.

Rachman, S. J. (1988). Panics and their consequences: A review and prospect. In S. J. Rachman & J. D. Maser (Eds.), *Panic: Psychological perspectives* (pp. 259–304). Hillsdale, NJ: Erlbaum.

Radnitz, C. L., Appelbaum, K. A., Blanchard, E. B., Elliott, L., & Andrasik, F. (1988). The effect of self-regulatory treatment on pain behavior in chronic headache. *Behaviour Research and Therapy, 26*, 253–260.

Rado, S. (1962). Theory and therapy: The theory of schizotypal organization and its application to the treatment of decompensated schizotypal behavior. In S. Rado (Ed.), *Psychoanalysis of behavior* (Vol. 2, pp. 127–140). New York: Grune & Stratton.

Radomsky, A. S., & Otto, M. W. (2001). Cognitive behavioral therapy for social anxiety disorder. *Psychiatric Clinics of North America, 24*, 805–815.

Radomsky, A. S., Rachman, S. J., Thordarson, D. S., McIsaac, H. K., & Teachman, B. A. (2001). The Claustrophobia Questionnaire. *Journal of Anxiety Disorders, 15*, 287–297.

Rahkonen, T., Eloniemi-Sulkava, U., Paanila, S., Halonen, P., Sivenius, J., & Sulkava, R. (2001). Systematic intervention for supporting community care of elderly people after a delirium episode. *International Psychogeriatrics, 13*(1), 37–49.

Rahkonen, T., Makela, H., Paanila, S., Halonen, P., Sivenius, J., & Sulkava, R. (2000). Delirium in elderly people without severe predisposing disorders: Etiology and 1-year prognosis after discharge. *International Psychogeriatrics, 12* (4), 473–481.

Raich, R. M., Rosen, J. C., Deus, J., Perez, O., Requiena, A., & Gross, J. (1992). Eating disorder symptoms among adolescents in the United States and Spain: A comparative study. *International Journal of Eating Disorders, 11*, 63–72.

Ramacciotti, C. E., Dell'Osso, L., Paoli, R. A., Ciapparelli, A., Coli, E., Kaplan, A. S., et al. (2002). Characteristics of eating disorder patients without a drive for thinness. *International Journal of Eating Disorders, 32*, 206–212.

Ramey, C. T., & Ramey, S. L. (1992). Effective early intervention. *Mental Retardation, 30*, 337–345.

Ramey, C. T., & Ramey, S. L. (1994). Which children benefit the most from early intervention? *Pediatrics, 94*, 1064–1066.

Ramey, C. T., & Ramey, S. L. (1998). Prevention of intellectual disabilities: Early interventions to improve cognitive development. *Preventive Medicine, 27*(2), 224–232.

Ramsawh, H. J., Morgentaler, A., Covino, N., Barlow, D. H., & Dewolf, W. C. (2005). Quality of life following simultaneous placement of penile prosthesis with radical prostatectomy. *Journal of Urology, 174*, 1395–1398.

Rao, U., Dahl, R. E., Ryan, N. D., Birmaher, B., Williamson, D. E., Rao, R., et al. (2002). Heterogeneity in EEG sleep findings in adolescent depression: Unipolar versus bipolar clinical course. *Journal of Affective Disorders, 70*, 273–280.

Rapee, R. M. & Melville, L. F. (1997). Recall of family factors in social phobia and panic disorder: Comparison of mother and offspring reports. *Depression and Anxiety, 5*, 7–11.

Rapp, S. R., Parisi, S. A., & Wallace, C. E. (1991). Comorbid psychiatric disorders in elderly medical patients: A 1-year prospective study. *Journal of the American Geriatrics Society, 39*(2), 124–131.

Rapport, M. D. (2001). Bridging theory and practice: Conceptual understanding of treatments for children with attention deficit hyperactivity disorder (ADHD), obsessive-compulsive disorder (OCD), autism, and depression. *Journal of Clinical Child Psychology, 30*(1), 3–7.

Rasmussen, S. A., & Eisen, J. L. (1990). Epidemiology of obsessive-compulsive disorder. *Journal of Clinical Psychiatry, 51*, 10–14.

Rasmussen, S. A., & Tsuang, M. T. (1984). The epidemiology of obsessive-compulsive disorder. *Journal of Clinical Psychiatry, 45*, 450–457.

Rasmussen, S. A., & Tsuang, M. T. (1986). Clinical characteristics and family history in DSM-III obsessive-compulsive disorder. *American Journal of Psychiatry, 143*, 317–322.

Rassin, E., & Koster, E. (2003). The correlation between thought-action fusion and religiosity in a normal sample. *Behaviour Research and Therapy, 41*, 361–368.

Ratnasuriya, R. H., Eisler, I., Szmuhter, G. I., & Russell, G. F. (1991). Anorexia nervosa: Outcome and prognostic factors after 20 years. *British Journal of Psychiatry, 158*, 495–502.

Rauch, S. L., Phillips, K. A., Segal, E., Markis, N., Shin, L. M., Whalen, P. J., et al., (2003). A preliminary morphometric magnetic resonance imaging study of regional brain volumes in body dysmorphic disorder. *Psychiatry Research, 122*, 13–19.

Ray, W. A., Fought, R. L., & Decker, M. D. (1992). Psychoactive drugs and the risk of injurious motor vehicle crashes in elderly drivers. *American Journal of Epidemiology, 136*, 873–883.

Ray, W. A., Griffin, M. R., Schaffner, W., Baugh, D. K., & Melton, L. J. (1987). Psychotropic drug use and the risk of hip fracture. *New England Journal of Medicine, 316*, 363–369.

Ray, W. A., Gurwitz, J., Decker, M. D., & Kennedy, D. L. (1992). Medications and the safety of the older driver: Is there a basis for concern? Special issue: Safety and mobility of elderly drivers: II. *Human Factors, 34*(1), 33–47.

Ray, W. A., Thapa, P. B., & Gideon, P. (2000). Benzodiazepines and the risk of falls in nursing home residents. *Journal of the American Geriatrics Society, 48*, 682–685.

Raymond, N. C., Coleman, E., Ohlerking, F., Christenson, G. A., & Miner, M. (1999). Psychiatric comorbidity in pedophilic sex offenders. *American Journal of Psychiatry, 156*, 786–788.

Razali, S. M., Hasanah, C. I., Khan, A., & Subramaniam, M. (2000). Psychosocial interventions for schizophrenia. *Journal of Mental Health, 9*, 283–289.

Razali, S. M., Khan, U. A. & Hasanah, C. I. (1996). Belief in supernatural causes of mental illness among Malay patients: Impact on treatment. *Acta Psychiatrica Scandinavica, 94*, 221–223.

Razran, G. (1961). The observable unconscious and the inferable conscious in current Soviet psychophysiology: Interoceptive conditioning, semantic conditioning, and the orienting reflex. *Psychological Review, 68*, 81–150.

Rector, N. A., & Beck, A. T. (2001). Cognitive behavioral therapy for schizophrenia: An empirical review. *Journal of Nervous and Mental Disease, 189*, 278–287.

Rector, N. A., Segal, Z. V., & Gemar, M. (1998). Schema research in depression: A Canadian perspective. *Canadian Journal of Behavioural Science, 30*, 213–224.

Redd, W. H., & Andrykowski, M. A. (1982). Behavioral intervention in cancer treatment: Controlling aversion reactions to chemotherapy. *Journal of Consulting and Clinical Psychology, 50*, 1018–1029.

Reeve, R. E., & Kauffman, J. M. (1988). Learning disabilities. In V. B. Van Hasselt, P. S. Strain, & M. Hersen (Eds.), *Handbook of developmental and physical disabilities* (pp. 316–335). Elmsford, NY: Pergamon Press.

Regehr, C., & Glancy, G. (1995). Battered woman syndrome defense in Canadian courts. *Canadian Journal of Psychiatry, 40*, 130–135.

*Regina v. Lavallee.* (1988). 65 C.R. 3d 387.

*Regina v. Prichard.* (1836). 7 Car., and P. 304.

*Regina v. Swain.* (1991). 63 C.C.C. (3d) 481 (S.C.C.).

Reich, J. (1987). Sex distribution of DSM-III personality disorders in psychiatric outpatients. *American Journal of Psychiatry, 144*, 485–488.

Reich, J., Yates, W., & Nduaguba, M. (1989). Prevalence of DSM-III personality disorders in the community. *Social Psychiatry and Psychiatric Epidemiology, 24*, 12–16.

Reich, T., Edenberg, H. J., Goate, A., Williams, J. T., Rice, J. P., Van Eerdewegh, P., et al. (1998). Genome-wide search for genes affecting the risk of alcohol dependence. *American Journal of Medicine and Genetics, 81*, 207–215.

Reichle, J., Mirenda, P., Locke, P., Piche, L., & Johnston, S. (1992). Beginning augmentative communication systems. In S. F. Warren & J. Reichle (Eds.), *Causes and effects in communication and language intervention* (pp. 131–156). Baltimore: Paul H. Brookes.

Reid, D. H., Wilson, P. G., & Faw, G. D. (1991). Teaching self-help skills. In J. L. Matson & J. A. Mulick (Eds.), *Handbook of mental retardation* (2nd ed., pp. 436–450). Elmsford, NY: Pergamon Press.

Reid, G. J., Chambers, C. T., McGrath, P. J., & Finley, G. A. (1997). Coping with pain and surgery: Children's and parents' perspectives. *International Journal of Behavioral Medicine, 4*, 339–363.

Reid, W. J., & Crisafulli, A. (1990). Marital discord and child behavior problems: A meta-analysis. *Journal of Abnormal Child Psychology, 18*, 105–117.

Reilly-Harrington, N. A., Alloy, L. B., Fresco, D. M., & Whitehouse, W. G. (1999). Cognitive styles and life events interact to predict bipolar and unipolar symptomatology. *Journal of Abnormal Psychology, 108*(4), 567–578.

Reiss, S., Peterson, R. A., Gursky, D. M., & McNally, R. J. (1986). Anxiety sensitivity, anxiety frequency, and the prediction of fearfulness. *Behaviour Research and Therapy, 24*, 1–8.

Reissing, E. D., Binik, Y. M., & Khalife, S. (1999). Does vaginismus exist? A critical review of the literature. *Journal of Nervous and Mental Disease, 187*, 261–274.

Reitan, R. M., & Davison, I. A. (1974). *Clinical neuropsychology: Current status and applications.* Washington, DC: V. H. Winston.

Rekers, G. A., Kilgus, M., & Rosen, A. C. (1990). Long-term effects of treatment for gender identity disorder of childhood. *Journal of Psychology and Human Sexuality, 3*(2), 121–153.

Renaud, C. A., & Byers, E. S. (2001). Positive and negative sexual cognitions: Subjective experience and relationships to sexual adjustment. *Journal of Sex Research, 38*, 252–262.

Rende, R., & Plomin, R. (1992). Diathesis-stress models of psychopathology: A quantitative genetic perspective. *Applied and Preventive Psychology, 1*, 177–182.

Renneberg, B., Goldstein, A. J., Phillips, D., & Chambless, D. L. (1990). Intensive behavioral group treatment of avoidant personality disorder. *Behavior Therapy, 21*, 363–377.

Report of the Advisory Panel on Alzheimer's Disease. (1995). *Alzheimer's disease and related dementias: Biomedical update.* Department of Health and Human Services.

Repp, A. C., & Singh, N. N. (1990). *Perspectives on the use of nonaversive and aversive interventions for persons with developmental disabilities.* Sycamore, IL: Sycamore Publishing.

Rescorla, R. A. (1988). Pavlovian conditioning: It's not what you think it is. *American Psychologist, 43*(3), 151–160.

Resner, J., & Hartog, J. (1970). Concepts and terminology of mental disorders among Malays. *Journal of Cross-Cultural Psychology, 1*, 369–381.

Resnick, H. S., Kilpatrick, D. G., Dansky, B. S., Saunders, B. E., & Best, C. L. (1993). Prevalence of civilian trauma in posttraumatic stress disorder in a representative national sample of women. *Journal of Consulting and Clinical Psychology, 61*, 984–991.

Rice, D. P., & MacKenzie, E. J. (1989). *Cost of injury in the United States: A report to Congress.* San Francisco: University of California and Injury Prevention Center, Institute for Health and Aging, and the Johns Hopkins University.

Rice, G., Anderson, C., Risch, N., & Ebers, G. (1999). Male homosexuality: Absence of linkage to microsatellite markers at Xq28. *Science, 284*, 665–667.

Rice, M. E. (1997). Violent offender research and implications for the criminal justice system. *American Psychologist, 52*, 414–423.

Rice, M. E., & Harris, G. T. (2002). Men who molest their sexually immature daughters: Is a special explanation required? *Journal of Abnormal Psychology, 111*, 329–339.

Rice, M. E., Harris, G. T., & Quinsey, V. L. (1990). A follow-up of rapists assessed in a maximum security psychiatric facility. *Journal of Interpersonal Violence, 4*, 435–448.

Richards, R., Kinney, D. K., Lunde, I. Benet, M., & Merzel, A. P. C. (1988). Creativity in manic depressives, cyclothymes, their normal relatives, and control subjects. *Journal of Abnormal Psychology, 97*(3), 281–288.

Richardson, S. A., Katz, M., & Koller, H. (1986). Sex differences in number of children administratively classified as mildly mentally retarded: An epidemiological review. *American Journal of Mental Deficiency, 91*, 250–256.

Richters, J. E. (1993). Community violence and children's development: Toward a research agenda for the 1990's. *Psychiatry, 56*, 3–6.

Rickels, K., Downing, R., Schweizer, E., & Hassman, H. (1993). Antidepressants for the treatment of generalized anxiety disorder. *Archives of General Psychiatry, 50*, 884–895.

Rickels, K., Schweizer, E., Case, W. G., & Greenblatt, D. J. (1990). Long-term therapeutic use of benzodiazepines: I. Effects of abrupt discontinuation. *Archives of General Psychiatry, 47*, 899–907.

Rickels, K., Zaninelli, R., McCafferty, J., Bellew, K., Iyengar, M., & Sheehan, D. (2003). Paroxetine treatment of generalized anxiety disorder: A double-blind, placebo-controlled study. *American Journal of Psychiatry, 160*, 749–756.

Riding, A. (1992, November 17). New catechism for Catholics defines sins of modern world. *New York Times*, p. A14.

Rief, W., Hiller, W., & Margraf, J. (1998). Cognitive aspects of hypochondriasis and the somatization syndrome. *Journal of Abnormal Psychology, 107*, 587–595.

Riggs, J. E. (1993). Smoking and Alzheimer's disease: Protective effect or differential survival bias? *Lancet, 342*, 793–794.

Rihmer, Z., & Pestality, P. (1999). Bipolar II disorder and suicidal behavior. *The Psychiatric Clinics of North America, 22*(3), 667–674.

Ritenbaugh, C., Shisstak, C., Teufel, N., Leonard-Green, T. K., & Prince, R. (1994). Eating disorders: A cross-cultural review in regard to DSM-IV. In J. E. Mezzich, A. Kleinman, H. Fabrega, B. Good, G. Johnson-Powell, K. M. Lin, et al. (Eds.), *Cultural proposals and supporting papers for DSM-IV.* Washington, DC: American Psychiatric Press.

Roberts, G. A. (1991). Delusional belief and meaning in life: A preferred reality? *British Journal of Psychiatry, 159*, 20–29.

Roberts, L. J., & Marlatt, G. A. (1999). Harm reduction. In P. J. Ott & R. E. Tarter (Eds.), *Sourcebook on substance abuse: Etiology, epidemiology, assessment, and treatment* (pp. 389–398). Needham Heights, MA: Allyn & Bacon.

Roberts, M. W. (2001). Clinic observations of structured parent-child interaction designed to evaluate externalizing disorders. *Psychological Assessment, 13*, 46–58.

Roberts, R. E., Kaplan, G. A., Shema, S. J., & Strawbridge, W. J. (1997). Does growing old increase the risk for depression? *American Journal of Psychiatry, 154*, 1384–1390.

Roberts, T. B., & Hruby, P. J. (1984). *Religion and psychoactive sacraments: An entheogen chrestomathy.* Retrieved October 26, 2003, from http://www.csp.org/chrestomathy/pass_it_on.html.

Robertson, G. B. (1994). *Mental disability in the law in Canada* (2nd ed.). Scarborough, ON: Carswell.

Robertson, N. (1988). *Getting better: Inside Alcoholics Anonymous.* New York: William Morrow.

Robins, L. N. (1966). *Deviant children grown up: A sociological and psychiatric study of sociopathic personality.* Baltimore: Williams & Wilkins.

Robins, L. N. (1978). Sturdy childhood predictors of adult antisocial behavior: Replications from longitudinal studies. *Psychological Medicine, 8*, 611–622.

Robins, L. N., Helzer, J. E., & Davis, D. H. (1975). Narcotic use in Southeast Asia and afterwards. *Archives of General Psychiatry, 32*, 955–961.

Robins, S., & Novaco, R. W. (2000). Anger control as a health promotion mechanism. In D. I. Mostofsky & D. H. Barlow (Eds.), *The management of stress and anxiety in medical disorders* (pp. 361–377). Needham Heights, MA: Allyn & Bacon.

Robinson, M. J., & Qaqish, R. B. (2002). Practical psychopharmacology in HIV-1 and acquired immunodeficiency syndrome. *Psychiatric Clinics of North America, 25*, 149–175.

Rockwood, K., & Joffres, C. (2002). Improving clinical descriptions to understand the effects of dementia treatment: Consensus recommendations. *International Journal of Geriatric Psychiatry, 17*, 1006–1011.

Rockwood, K., & Lindesay, J. (2002). Delirium and dying. *International Psychogeriatrics, 14*, 235–238.

Rockwood, K., Stolee, P., & Brahim, A. (1991). Outcomes of admission to a psychogeriatric service. *Canadian Journal of Psychiatry, 36*(4), 275–279.

Rockwood, K., Wolfson, C., & McDowell, I. (2001). The Canadian Study of Health and Aging: Organizational lessons from a national, multicenter, epidemiologic study. *International Psychogeriatrics, 13* (Suppl. 1), 233–237.

Rodin, J., & Salovey, P. (1989). Health psychology. *Annual Review of Psychology, 40*, 533–579.

Roehrich, L., & Kinder, B. N. (1991). Alcohol expectancies and male sexuality: Review and implications for sex therapy. *Journal of Sex and Marital Therapy, 17*(1), 45–54.

Roehrs, T., Carskadon, M. A., Dement, W. C., & Roth, T. (2000). Daytime sleepiness and alertness. In M. H. Kryger, T. Roth, W. C. Dement (Eds.), *Principles and practice of sleep medicine* (3rd ed., pp. 43–52). Philadelphia: W. B. Saunders.

Roehrs, T., & Roth, T. (2000). Hypnotics: Efficacy and adverse effects. In M. H. Kryger, T. Roth, W. C. Dement (Eds.), *Principles and practice of sleep medicine* (3rd ed., pp. 414–418). Philadelphia: W. B. Saunders.

Roelofs, K., Keijsers, G. P., Hoogduin, K. A., Naring, G. W., & Moene, F. C. (2002). Childhood abuse in patients with conversion disorder. *American Journal of Psychiatry, 159*, 1908–1913.

Roemer, L., & Orsillo, S. M. (2002). Expanding our conceptualization of and treatment for generalized anxiety disorder: Integrating mindfulness/acceptance-based approaches with existing cognitive-behavioral models. *Clinical Psychology: Science and Practice, 9*, 54–68.

Roemer, L., Orsillo, S. M., & Barlow, D. H. (2002). Generalized anxiety disorder. In D. H. Barlow (Ed.), *Anxiety and its disorders: The nature and treatment of anxiety and panic* (2nd ed.). New York: Guilford Press.

Roesch, R., Ogloff, J. R. P., Hart, S. D., Dempster, R. J., Zapf, P. A., & Whittemore, K. E. (1997). The impact of Canadian criminal code changes on remands and assessments of fitness to stand trial and criminal responsibility in British Columbia. *Canadian Journal of Psychiatry, 42*, 509–514.

Roesch, R., Zapf, P., Webster, C. D., & Eaves, D. (1999). *The Fitness Interview Test.* Burnaby, BC: Simon Fraser University, Mental Health Law & Policy Institute.

Roffman, R. A., & Barnhart, R. (1987). Assessing need for marijuana dependence treatment through an anonymous telephone interview. *International Journal of the Addictions, 22*, 639–651.

Rogers, C. R. (1961). *On becoming a person.* Boston: Houghton Mifflin.

Rogers, S. L., & Friedhoff, L. T. (1996). The efficacy and safety of donepezil in patients with Alzheimer's disease: Results of a US multicentre, randomized, double-blind, placebo-controlled trial. *Dementia, 7*, 293–303.

Roitt, I. (1988). *Essential immunology* (6th ed.). Oxford, UK: Blackwell.

Roland, C. G. (1990). *Clarence Hincks: Mental health crusader.* Toronto: Hannah Institute & Dundurn Press.

Romano, E., Baillargeon, R. H., Wu, H. X., Robaey, P., & Tremblay, R. E. (2002). Prevalence of methylphenidate use and change over a two-year period: A nationwide study of 2- to 11-year-old Canadian children. *Journal of Pediatrics, 141*, 71–75.

Romano, J. M., Jensen, M. P., Turner, J. A., Good, A. B., & Hops, H. (2000). Chronic pain patient-partner interactions: Further support for a behavioral model of chronic pain. *Behavior Therapy, 31*, 415–440.

Romney, D. M., & Candido, C. L. (2001). Anhedonia in depression and schizophrenia: A reexamination. *Journal of Nervous and Mental Disease, 189*, 735–740.

Room, R. (1993). Alcoholics Anonymous as a social movement. In B. S. McCrady & W. R. Miller (Eds.), *Research on Alcoholics Anonymous: Opportunities and alternatives* (pp. 167–187). New Brunswick, NJ: Rutgers Center of Alcohol Studies.

Rorschach, H. (1951). *Psychodiagnostics.* New York: Grune & Stratton (Original work published 1921).

Rosen, J. C., & Leitenberg, H. (1985). Exposure plus response prevention treatment of bulimia. In D. M. Garner & P. E. Garfinkel (Eds.), *Handbook of psychotherapy for anorexia nervosa and bulimia* (pp. 193–209). New York: Guilford Press.

Rosen, J. C., Reiter, J., & Orosan, P. (1995). Cognitive-behavioral body image therapy for body dysmorphic disorder. *Journal of Consulting Clinical Psychology, 63*, 263–269.

Rosen, R. C. (2000). Medical and psychological interventions for erectile dysfunction: Toward a combined treatment approach. In S. R. Leiblum & R. C. Rosen (Eds.), *Principles and practice of sex therapy* (3rd ed., pp. 276–304). New York: Guilford Press.

Rosen, R. C., & Beck, J. G. (1988). *Patterns of sexual arousal: Psychophysiological processes and clinical applications.* New York: Guilford Press.

Rosen, R. C., & Leiblum, S. R. (1995). Treatment of sexual disorders in the 1990's: An integrated approach. *Journal of Consulting and Clinical Psychology, 63*, 877–890.

Rosenbaum, M. (2000). Psychogenic seizures—why women? *Psychosomatics, 41*(2), 147–149.

Rosenberg, H. (1993). Prediction of controlled drinking by alcoholics and problem drinkers. *Psychological Bulletin, 113*, 129–139.

Rosenberg, R. N., Richter, R. W., Risser, R. C., Taubman, K., Prado-Farmer, I., Ebalo, E., et al. (1996). Genetic factors for the development of Alzheimer's disease in the Cherokee Indian. *Archives of Neurology, 53*, 997–1000.

Rosengren, A., Tibblin, G., & Wilhelmsen, L. (1991). Self-perceived psychological stress and incidence of coronary artery disease in middle-aged men. *American Journal of Cardiology, 68*, 1171–1175.

Rosenman, R. H., Brand, R. J., Jenkins, C. D., Friedman, M., Straus, R., & Wurm, M. (1975). Coronary heart disease in the Western Collaborative Group Study: Final follow-up experience of 8 years. *Journal of the American Medical Association, 233*, 872–877.

Rosenthal, D. (Ed.). (1963). *The Genain quadruplets: A case study and theoretical analysis of heredity and environment in schizophrenia.* New York: Basic Books.

Rosenthal, P. A., & Rosenthal, S. (1984). Suicidal behavior by preschool children. *American Journal of Psychiatry, 141*, 520–525.

Rösler, A., & Witztum, M. D. (1998). Treatment of men with paraphilia with a long-acting analogue of gonadotropin-releasing hormone. *New England Journal of Medicine, 338*, 416–422.

Rosowsky, E., & Gurian, B. (1992). Impact of borderline personality disorder in late life on systems of care. *Hospital and Community Psychiatry, 43*, 386–389.

Ross, A. O., & Pelham, W. E. (1981). Child psychopathology. *Annual Review of Psychology, 32*, 243–278.

Ross, C. A. (1991). Epidemiology of multiple personality disorder and dissociation. *Psychiatric Clinics of North America, 14*, 503–517.

Ross, C. A. (1997). *Dissociative identity disorder.* New York: John Wiley.

Ross, C. A., Anderson, G., Fleisher, W. P., & Norton, G. R. (1991). The frequency of multiple personality disorder among psychiatric inpatients. *American Journal of Psychiatry, 148*, 1717–1720.

Ross, C. A., Miller, S. D., Reagor, P., Bjornson, L., Fraser, G. A., & Anderson, G. (1990). Structured interview data on 102 cases of multiple personality disorder from four centers. *American Journal of Psychiatry, 147*, 596–601.

Ross, M. W., Walinder, J., Lundstrom, B., & Thuwe, I. (1981). Cross-cultural approaches to transsexualism: A comparison between Sweden and Australia. *Acta Psychiatrica Scandinavica, 63*, 75–82.

Rost, K., Kashner, T. M., & Smith, G. R. Jr. (1994). Effectiveness of psychiatric intervention with somatization disorder patients: Improved outcomes at reduced costs. *General Hospital Psychiatry, 16*, 381–387.

Rothblum, E. D. (2002). Gay and lesbian body images. In T. F. Cash & T. Pruzinsky (Eds.), *Body image: A handbook of theory, research and clinical practice* (pp. 257–265). New York: Guilford Press.

Rottenberg, J., Gross, J. J., Wilhelm, F. H., Najmi, S., & Gotlib, I. H. (2002). Crying threshold and intensity in major depressive disorder. *Journal of Abnormal Psychology, 111*, 302–312.

Rouff, L. (2000). Schizoid personality traits among the homeless mentally ill: A quantitative and qualitative report. *Journal of Social Distress and the Homeless, 9*, 127–141.

Rounsaville, B. J., Alarcon, R. D., Andrews G., Jackson, J. S., Kendell, R. E., & Kendler, K. (2002). Basic nomenclature issues for DSM-V. In D. J. Kupfer, M. B. First, & D. A. Regier (Eds.) *A research agenda for DSM-V* (pp. 1–29). Washington, DC: American Psychiatric Press.

Rounsaville, B. J., Sholomskas, D., & Prusoff, B. A. (1988). Chronic mood disorders in depressed outpatients: Diagnosis and response to pharmacotherapy. *Journal of Affective Disorders, 2*, 72–88.

Roush, W. (1997). Herbert Benson: Mind-body maverick pushes the envelope. *Science, 276*, 357–359.

Roy, A., Segal, N. L., & Sarchiapone, M. (1995). Attempted suicide among living co-twins of twin suicide victims. *American Journal of Psychiatry, 152*, 1075–1076.

Roy-Byrne, P. P., & Katon, W. (2000). Anxiety management in the medical setting: Rationale, barriers to diagnosis and treatment, and proposed solutions. In D. I. Mostofsky & D. H. Barlow (Eds.),

*The management of stress and anxiety in medical disorders* (pp. 1–14). Needham Heights, MA: Allyn & Bacon.

Rubin, R. T. (1982). Koro (Shook Yang): A culture-bound psychogenic syndrome. In C. T. H. Friedmann & R. A. Fauger (Eds.), *Extraordinary disorders of human behavior* (pp. 155–172). New York: Plenum Press.

Rubinstein, S., & Caballero, B. (2000). Is Miss America an undernourished role model? *Journal of the American Medical Association, 283,* 1569.

Rudd, M. D., Joiner, Y., & Rajab, M. H. (2001). *Treating suicidal behavior.* New York: Guilford Press.

Rudd, M. D., Rajab, M. H., Orman, D. T., Stulman, D. A., Joiner, T., & Dixon, W. (1996). Effectiveness of an outpatient intervention targeting suicidal young adults: Preliminary results. *Journal of Consulting and Clinical Psychology, 64,* 179–190.

Ruiz, I., Offermanns, J., Lanctot, K. L., & Busto, U. (1993). Comparative study on benzodiazepine use in Canada and Chile. *Journal of Clinical Pharmacology, 33,* 124–129.

Rush, A. J., Giles, D. E., Schlesser, M. A., Orsulak, P. J., Weissenburger, J. E., Fulton, C. L., et al. (1997). Dexamethasone response, thyrotropin-releasing hormone stimulation, rapid eye movement latency, and subtypes of depression. *Biological Psychiatry, 41,* 915–928.

Russell, G. F. M. (1979). Bulimia nervosa: An ominous variant of anorexia nervosa. *Psychological Medicine, 9,* 429–448.

Russell, G. F. M., Szmukler, G. I., Dare, C., & Eisler, I. (1987). An evaluation of family therapy in anorexia nervosa and bulimia nervosa. *Archives of General Psychiatry, 44,* 1047–1056.

Rutherford, J., McGuffin, P., Katz, R. J., & Murray, R. M. (1993). Genetic influences on eating attitudes in a normal female twin population. *Psychological Medicine, 23,* 425–436.

Rutherford, M. D., & Rogers, S. J. (2003). Cognitive underpinnings of pretend play in autism. *Journal of Autism and Developmental Disorders, 33,* 289–302.

Rutter, M. (1978). Diagnosis and definition of childhood autism. *Journal of Autism and Childhood Schizophrenia, 8,* 139–161.

Rutter, M. (1997). Nature-nurture integration: The example of antisocial behavior. *American Psychologist, 52,* 390–398.

Rutter, M. (2002). The interplay of nature, nurture, and developmental influences: The challenge ahead for mental health. *Archives of General Psychiatry, 59,* 996–1000.

Rutter, M., & Giller, H. (1984). *Juvenile delinquency: Trends and perspectives.* New York: Guilford Press.

Rutter, M., Macdonald, H., Le Couteur, A., Harrington, R., Bolton, P., & Baily, A. (1990). Genetic factors in child psychiatric disorders: II. Empirical findings. *Journal of Child Psychology and Psychiatry, 31,* 39–83.

Ryan, W. D. (1992). The pharmacologic treatment of child and adolescent depression. *Psychiatric Clinics of North America, 15,* 29–40.

Saab, P. G., Llabre, M. M., Hurwitz, B. E., Frame, C. A., Reineke, I., Fins, A. I., et al. (1992). Myocardial and peripheral vascular responses to behavioral challenges and their stability in Black and White Americans. *Psychophysiology, 29*(4), 384–397.

Sachs, G. A., & Cassel, C. K. (1989). Ethical aspects of dementia. *Neurologic Clinics, 7,* 845–858.

Sachs, G. S., & Rush, A. J. (2003). Response, remission, and recovery in bipolar disorders: What are the realistic treatment goals? *Journal of Clinical Psychiatry, 64,* 18–22.

Sackeim, H. A., & Devanand, D. P. (1991). Dissociative disorders. In M. Hersen & S. M. Turner (Eds.), *Adult psychopathology and diagnosis* (2nd ed., pp. 279–322). New York: John Wiley.

Sackeim, H. A., Nordlie, J. W., & Gur, R. C. (1979). A model of hysterical and hypnotic blindness: Cognition, motivation and awareness. *Journal of Abnormal Psychology, 88,* 474–489.

Sadeh, A., Raviv, A., & Gruber, R. (2000). Sleep patterns and sleep disruptions in school-age children. *Developmental Psychology, 36,* 291–301.

Sakel, M. (1958). *Schizophrenia.* New York: Philosophical Library.

Sakheim, D. K., Barlow, D. H., Abrahamson, D. J., & Beck, J. G. (1987). Distinguishing between organogenic and psychogenic erectile dysfunction. *Behaviour Research and Therapy, 25,* 379–390.

Sakinofsky, I. (1998). The epidemiology of suicide in Canada. In A. A. Leenars, S. Wenckstern, I Sakinofsky, R. J. Dyck, M. J. Kral, & R. C. Bland (Eds.), *Suicide in Canada* (pp. 37–66). Toronto: University of Toronto Press.

Salge, R. A., Beck, J. G., & Logan, A. (1988). A community survey of panic. *Journal of Anxiety Disorder, 2,* 157–167.

Salkovskis, P. M., Atha, C., & Storer, D. (1990). Cognitive-behavioural problem solving in the treatment of patients who repeatedly attempt suicide: A controlled trial. *British Journal of Psychiatry, 157,* 871–876.

Salkovskis, P. M., & Campbell, P. (1994). Thought suppression induces intrusion in naturally occurring negative intrusive thoughts. *Behaviour Research and Therapy, 32*(1), 1–8.

Salkovskis, P. M., & Clark, D. M. (1993). Panic disorders and hypochondriasis. Special issue: Panic, cognitions and sensations. *Advances in Behavioral Research and Therapy, 5,* 23–48.

Salkovskis, P. M., & Warwick, H. M. C. (2001). Making sense of hypochondriasis: A cognitive theory of health anxiety. In G. J. G. Asmundson, S. Taylor, & B. J. Cox (Eds.), *Health anxiety: Clinical and research perspectives on hypochondriasis and related conditions* (pp. 46–64). New York: Wiley.

Salkovskis, P., Shafran, R., Rachman, S., & Freeston, M. H. (1999). Multiple pathways to inflated responsibility beliefs in obsessional problems: Possible origins and implications for therapy and research. *Behaviour Research and Therapy, 37,* 1055–1072.

Salzman, C. (1991). Pharmacologic treatment of the anxious elderly patient. In C. Salzman & B. D. Lebowitz (Eds.), *Anxiety in the elderly: Treatment and research* (pp. 149–173). New York: Springer.

Sampson, R. J., Raudenbush, S. W., & Earls, F. (1997). Neighborhoods and violent crime: A multilevel study of collective efficacy. *Science, 277,* 918–924.

Samson, J. A., Mirin, S. M., Hauser, S. T., Fenton, B. T., & Schildkraut, J. J. (1992). Learned helplessness and urinary MHPG levels in unipolar depression. *American Journal of Psychiatry, 149*(6), 806–809.

Samuels, J., Bienvenu III, O. J., Riddle, M. A., Cullen, B. A. M., Grados, M. A., Liang, K.-Y., et al. (2002). Hoarding in obsessive compulsive disorder: Results from a case-control study. *Behaviour Research and Therapy, 40,* 517–528.

Samuels, S. C., & Davis, K. L. (1997). A risk-benefit assessment of tacrine in the treatment of Alzheimer's disease. *Drug Safety, 16,* 66–77.

Sandberg, O., Franklin, K. A., Bucht, G., & Gustafson, Y. (2001). Sleep apnea, delirium, depressed mood, cognition, and ADL ability after stroke. *Journal of the American Geriatric Society, 49*(4), 391–397.

Sanders, M. R. (1992). Enhancing the impact of behavioural family intervention with children: Emerging perspectives. *Behaviour Change, 9,* 115–119.

Sanders, M. R., Dadds, M. R., Johnston, B. M., & Cash, R. (1992). Childhood depression and conduct disorder: I. Behavioral, affective and cognitive aspects of family problem solving interactions. *Journal of Abnormal Psychology, 101*(3), 495–504.

Sanderson, C., & Clarkin, J. F. (1994). Use of the NEO-PI personality dimensions in differential treatment planning. In P. T. Costa & T. A. Widiger (Eds.), *Personality disorders and the five-factor model of personality* (pp. 219–235). Washington, DC: American Psychological Association.

Sanderson, W. C., & Barlow, D. H. (1990). A description of patients diagnosed with DSM-III-R generalized anxiety disorder. *Journal of Nervous and Mental Disease, 178,* 588–591.

Sano, M., Ernesto, C., Thomas, R. G., Klauber, M. R., Schafer, K., Grundman, M., et al. (1997). A controlled trial of selegiline, alpha-tocopherol, or both as treatment for Alzheimer's disease. *New England Journal of Medicine, 336,* 1216–1222.

Sansbury, L. L., & Wahler, R. G. (1992). Pathways to maladaptive parenting with mothers and their conduct disordered children. *Behavior Modification, 16,* 574–592.

Santarelli, L., Saxe, M., Gross, C., Surget, A., Battaglia, F., Dulawa, S., et al. (2003). Requirement of hippocampal neurogenesis for the behavioral effects of antidepressants. *Science, 301,* 805–809.

Santor, D. A., & Kusumakar, V. (2001). Open trial of interpersonal therapy in adolescents with moderate to severe major depression: Effectiveness of novice IPT therapists. *Journal of the American Academy of Child and Adolescent Psychiatry, 40,* 236–240.

Sapolsky, R. M. (1990, January). Stress in the wild. *Scientific American,* 116–123.

Sapolsky, R. M. (2000a). Glucocorticoids and hippocampal atrophy in neuropsychiatric disorders. *Archives of General Psychiatry, 57*, 925–935.

Sapolsky, R. M. (2000b). *Why zebras don't get ulcers: An updated guide to stress, stress-related diseases, and coping.* New York: Barnes & Noble.

Sapolsky, R. M., & Meaney, M. J. (1986). Maturation of the adrenal stress response: Neuroendocrine control mechanisms and the stress hyporesponsive period. *Brain Research Review, 11*, 65–76.

Sapolsky, R. M., & Ray, J. C. (1989). Styles of dominance and their endocrine correlates among wild, live baboons. *American Journal of Primatology, 18*(1), 1–13.

Sarwer, D. B., & Durlak, J. A. (1997). A field trial of the effectiveness of behavioral treatment for sexual dysfunctions. *Journal of Sex and Marital Therapy, 23*, 87–97.

Sass, K. J., Sass, A., Westerveld, M., Lencz, T., Novelly, R. A., Kim, J. H., et al. (1992). Specificity in the correlation of verbal memory and hippocampal neuron loss: Dissociation of memory, language, and verbal intellectual ability. *Journal of Clinical and Experimental Neuropsychology, 14*(5), 662–672.

Satel, S. (1992). Craving for and fear of cocaine: A phenomenologic update on cocaine craving and paranoia. In T. R. Kosten & H. D. Kleber (Eds.), *Clinician's guide to cocaine addiction: Theory, research, and treatment* (pp. 172–192). New York: Guilford Press.

Saudino, J. J., Pedersen, N. L., Lichenstein, P., McClearn, G. E., & Plomin, R. (1997). Can personality explain genetic influence on life events? *Journal of Personality and Social Psychology, 72*(1), 196–206.

Saudino, K. J., & Plomin, R. (1996). Personality and behavioral genetics: Where have we been and where are we going? *Journal of Research in Personality, 30*, 335–347.

Saudino, K. J., Plomin, R., & DeFries, J. C. (1996). Tester-rated temperament at 14, 20, and 24 months: Environmental change and genetic continuity. *British Journal of Developmental Psychology, 14*, 129–144.

Savard, J., Laroche, L., Simard, S., Ivers, H., & Morin, C. M. (2003). Chronic insomnia and immune functioning. *Psychosomatic Medicine, 65*, 211–221.

Sawa, A., & Snyder, S. H. (2002). Schizophrenia: Diverse approaches to a complex disease. *Science, 296*, 692–695.

Saxena, S., & Prasad, K. (1989). DSM-III subclassifications of dissociative disorders applied to psychiatric outpatients in India. *American Journal of Psychiatry, 146*, 261–262.

Saxena, S., Winograd, A., Dunkin, J. J., Maidment, K., Rosen, R., Vapnik, T., et al. (2001). A retrospective review of clinical characteristics and treatment response in body dysmorphic disorder versus obsession-compulsive disorder. *Journal of Clinical Psychiatry, 62*, 67–72.

Sayer, K., Kirmayer, L. J., & Taillefer, S. (2003). Predictors of somatic symptoms in depressive disorder. *General Hospital Psychiatry, 25*, 108–114.

Schachar, R., Jadad, A. R., Gauld, M., Boyle, M., Booker, L., Snider, A., et al. (2002). Attention-deficit hyperactivity disorder: Critical appraisal of extended treatment studies. *Canadian Journal of Psychiatry, 47*, 337–348.

Schacter, D. L., Chiu, P., & Ochsner, K. N. (1993). Implicit memory: A selective review. *Annual Review of Neuroscience, 16*, 159–182.

Schachter, H. M., Pham, B., King, J., Langford, S., & Moher, D. (2001). How efficacious and safe is short-acting methylphenidate for the treatment of attention-deficit disorder in children and adolescents? A meta-analysis. *Canadian Medical Association Journal, 165*, 1475–1488.

Schafer, J., & Brown, S. A. (1991). Marijuana and cocaine effect expectancies and drug use patterns. *Journal of Consulting and Clinical Psychology, 59*, 558–565.

Schaztberg, A. F. (2000). New indications for antidepressants. *Journal of Clinical Psychiatry, 61* (Suppl. 11), 9–17.

Scheel, K. R. (2000). The empirical basis of dialectical behavior therapy: Summary, critique, and implications. *Clinical Psychology: Science and Practice, 7*, 68–86.

Scheerenberger, R. C. (1983). *A history of mental retardation.* Baltimore: Paul H. Brookes.

Scheidt, P. C., Harel, Y., Trumble, A. C., Jones, D. H., Overpeck, M. D., & Bijur, P. E. (1995). The epidemiology of nonfatal injuries among US children and youth. *American Journal of Public Health, 85*, 932–938.

Scheier, M. F., Matthews, K. A., Owens, J. F., Magovern, G. J., Sr., Lefebvre, R. C., Abbott, R. A., et al. (1989). Dispositional optimism and recovery from coronary artery bypass surgery: The beneficial effects on physical and psychological well-being. *Journal of Personality and Social Psychology, 57*(6), 1024–1040.

Schenk, L., & Bear, D. (1981). Multiple personality and related dissociative phenomena in patients with temporal lobe epilepsy. *American Journal of Psychiatry, 138*, 1311–1316.

Schiavi, R. C. (1990). Chronic alcoholism and male sexual dysfunction. *Journal of Sex and Marital Therapy, 16*, 23–33.

Schiavi, R. C., White, D, Mandeli, J., & Levine, A. C. (1997). Effect of testosterone administration on sexual behavior and mood in men with erectile dysfunction. *Archives of Sexual Behavior, 26*, 231–241.

Schildkraut, J. J. (1965). The catecholamine hypothesis of affective disorders: A review of supporting evidence. *American Journal of Psychiatry, 122*, 509–522.

Schleifer, S. J., Keller, S. E., Bond, R. N., Cohen, J., & Stein, M. (1989). Major depressive disorder and immunity: Role of age, sex, severity, and hospitalization. *Archives of General Psychiatry, 46*, 81–87.

Schlundt, O. G., & Johnson, W. G. (1990). *Eating disorders: Assessment and treatment.* Boston: Allyn & Bacon.

Schmaling, K. B., Fiedelak, J. I., Katon, W. J., Bader, J. O., & Buchwald, D. S. (2003). Prospective study of the prognosis of unexplained chronic fatigue in a clinic-based cohort. *Psychosomatic Medicine, 65*, 1047–1054.

Schmidt, N. B., & Koselka, M. (2000). Gender differences in patients with panic disorder: Evaluating cognitive mediation of phobic avoidance. *Cognitive Therapy and Research, 24*, 533–550.

Schmidt, N. B., Lerew, D. R., & Jackson, R. J. (1997). The role of anxiety sensitivity in the pathogenesis of panic: Prospective evaluation of spontaneous panic attacks during acute stress. *Journal of Abnormal Psychology, 106*, 355–364.

Schmidt, N. B, Lerew, D. R., & Jackson, R. J. (1999). Prospective evaluation of anxiety sensitivity in the pathogenesis of panic: Replication and extension. *Journal of Abnormal Psychology, 108*, 532–537.

Schmitz, J. M., Schneider, N. G., & Jarvik, M. E. (1997). Nicotine. In J. H. Lowinson, P. Ruiz, R. B. Millman, & J. G. Langrod (Eds.), *Substance abuse: A comprehensive textbook* (pp. 276–294). Baltimore: Williams & Wilkins.

Schneiderman, N., Antoni, M. H., Ironson, G., LaPerriere, A., & Fletcher, M. A. (1992). Applied psychological science and HIV-1 spectrum disease. *Applied and Preventive Psychology, 1*, 67–82.

Schneier, F. R., Liebowitz, M. R., Beidel, D. C., Fyer, A. J., George, M. S., Heimberg, R. G., et al. (1996). Social phobia. In T. A. Widiger, A. J. Frances, H. A. Pincus, R. Ross, M. B. First, & W. W. Davis (Eds.), *DSM-IV sourcebook* (Vol. 2, pp. 507–548). Washington, DC: American Psychiatric Press.

Schoenbach, V. J., Kaplan, B. H., Fredman, L., & Kleinbaum, D. G. (1986). Social ties and mortality in Evans County, Georgia. *American Journal of Epidemiology, 123*, 577.

Schoeneman, T. J. (1977). The role of mental illness in the European witchhunts of the sixteenth and seventeenth centuries: An assessment. *Journal of the History of the Behavioral Sciences, 13*, 337–351.

Schover, L. R., & Jensen, S. B. (1988). *Sexuality and chronic illness: A comprehensive approach.* New York: Guilford Press.

Schreiber, F. R. (1973). *Sybil.* Chicago: Regnery.

Schreiner-Engel, P., & Schiavi, R. C. (1986). Lifetime psychopathology in individuals with low sexual desire. *Journal of Nervous and Mental Disease, 174*, 646–651.

Schroeder, M. L., Wormworth, J. A., & Livesley, W. J. (1993). Dimensions of personality disorder and the five-factor model of personality. In P. T. Costa, Jr., & T. A. Widiger (Eds.), *Personality disorders and the five-factor model of personality* (pp. 117–127). Washington, DC: American Psychological Association.

Schuckit, M. A., Smith, T. L., Anthenelli, R., & Irwin, M. (1993). Clinical course of alcoholism in 636 male inpatients. *American Journal of Psychiatry, 150*, 786–792.

Schulberg, H. C., Block, M. R., Madonia, M. J., Scott, C. P., Rodriguez, E., Imber, S. D., et al. (1996). Treating major depression in primary care practice: Eight-month clinical outcomes. *Archives of General Psychiatry, 53*, 913–919.

Schuller, R. A., & Ogloff, J. R. P. (2001). An introduction to psychology and law. In R. A. Schuller & J. R. P. Ogloff (Eds.), *Introduction to psychology and law: Canadian perspectives* (pp. 3–28). Toronto: University of Toronto Press.

Schuller, R. A., & Yarmey, M. (2001). The jury: Deciding guilt and innocence. In R. A. Schuller & J. R. P. Ogloff (Eds.), *Introduction to psychology and law: Canadian perspectives* (pp. 157–187). Toronto: University of Toronto Press.

Schulsinger, F., Kety, S. S., & Rosenthal, D. (1979). A family study of suicide. In M. Schou & E. Stromgren (Eds.), *Origin, prevention, and treatment of affective disorders.* New York: Academic Press.

Schulz, R., Drayer, R. A., & Rollman, B. L. (2002). Depression as a risk factor for non-suicide mortality in the elderly. *Biological Psychiatry, 52,* 205–225

Schwalberg, M. D., Barlow, D. H., Alger, S. A., & Howard, L. J. (1992). Comparison of bulimics, obese binge eaters, social phobics, and individuals with panic disorder or comorbidity across DSM-III-R anxiety. *Journal of Abnormal Psychology, 101,* 675–681.

Schwartlander, B., Garnett, G., Walker, N., & Anderson, R. (2000). AIDS in a new millennium. *Science, 289,* 64–67.

Schwartz, G. E., & Weiss, S. M. (1978). Behavioral medicine revisited: An amended definition. *Journal of Behavioral Medicine, 1,* 249–252.

Schwartz, M. S., & Andrasik, F. (2003). (Eds.). *Biofeedback: A practitioner's guide* (3rd ed.). New York: Guilford Press.

Schwartz, P. J., Brown, C., Wehr, T. A., & Rosenthal, N. E. (1996). Winter seasonal affective disorder: A follow-up study of the first 59 patients of the National Institute of Mental Health seasonal studies program. *American Journal of Psychiatry, 153,* 1028–1036.

Schweizer, E. & Rickels, K. (1996). Pharmacological treatment for generalized anxiety disorder. In M. R. Mavissakalian & R. F. Prien (Eds.), *Long-term treatments of anxiety disorders.* Washington, DC: American Psychiatric Press.

Schweizer, E., Rickels, K., Case, W. G., & Greenblatt, D. J. (1990). Long-term use of benzodiazepines: II. Effects of gradual taper. *Archives of General Psychiatry, 47,* 908–915.

Scott, J. (1995). Psychotherapy for bipolar disorder. *British Journal of Psychiatry, 167,* 581–588.

Scott, J. E., & Dixon, L. B. (1995a). Assertive community treatment and case management for schizophrenia. *Schizophrenia Bulletin, 21,* 657–668.

Scott, J. E., & Dixon, L. B. (1995b). Psychological interventions for schizophrenia. *Schizophrenia Bulletin, 21,* 621–630.

Seeman, P., Lee, T., Chau Wong, M., & Wong, K. (1976). Antipsychotic drug doses and neuroleptic/dopamine receptors. *Nature, 261,* 717–719.

Segal, S. (1978). Attitudes toward the mentally ill: A review. *Social Work, 23,* 211–217.

Segal, Z. V., Hood, J. E., Shaw, B. F., & Higgins, E. (1988). A structural analysis of the self-schema construct in major depression. *Cognitive Therapy and Research, 12*(5), 471–485.

Segal, Z. V., Vincent, P., & Levitt, A. (2002). Efficacy of combined, sequential and crossover psychotherapy and pharmacotherapy in improving outcomes in depression. *Journal of Psychiatry and Neuroscience, 27,* 281–290.

Segal, Z. V., Williams, J. M. G., & Teasdale, J. D. (2002). *Mindfulness-based cognitive therapy for depression: A new approach to preventing relapse.* New York: Guilford Press.

Segraves, R. T., & Althof, S. (1998). Psychotherapy and pharmacotherapy of sexual dysfunctions. In P. E. Nathan & J. M. Gorman (Eds.), *A guide to treatments that work* (pp. 447–471). New York: Oxford University Press.

Seligman, M. E. P. (1971). Phobias and preparedness. *Behavior Therapy, 2,* 307–320.

Seligman, M. E. P. (1975). *Helplessness: On depression, development and death.* San Francisco: W. H. Freeman.

Seligman, M. E. P. (1998). *Learned Optimism.* (2nd ed.). New York: Simon & Schuster.

Seligman, M. E. P. (2002). *Authentic happiness: Using the new positive psychology to realize your potential for lasting fulfillment.* New York: Free Press/Simon & Schuster.

Seligman, M. E. P., & Binik, Y. (1977). The safety signal hypothesis. In H. Davis & H. Horowitz (Eds.), *Operant-Pavlovian interaction.* Hillsdale, NJ: Erlbaum.

Seligman, M. E. P., Schulman, P., DeRubeis, R. J., & Hollon, S. D. (1999). The prevention of depression and anxiety. *Prevention and Treatment, 2,* 8.

Selye, H. (1936). A syndrome produced by diverse noxious agents. *Nature, 138,* 32.

Selye, H. (1950). *The physiology and pathology of exposure to stress.* Montreal: Acta.

Semans, J. H. (1956). Premature ejaculation: A new approach. *Southern Medical Journal, 49,* 353–358.

Sexton, M. M. (1979). Behavioral epidemiology. In O. F. Pomerleau & J. P. Brady (Eds.), *Behavioral medicine: Theory and practice* (pp. 3–21). Baltimore: Williams & Wilkins.

Seyfort, B., Spreen, O., & Lahmer, V. (1980). A critical look at the WISC-R with Native Indian children. *Alberta Journal of Educational Research, 26,* 14–24.

Shabecoff, P. (1987, October 14). Stress and the lure of harmless remedies. *New York Times,* p. 12.

Shaffer, D. R. (1993). *Developmental psychology: Childhood and adolescence* (3rd ed.). Pacific Grove, CA: Brooks/Cole.

Shaffer, D., Garland, A., Gould, M., Fisher, P., & Trautmen, P. (1988). Preventing teenage suicide: A critical review. *Journal of the American Academy of Child and Adolescent Psychiatry, 27,* 675–687.

Shaffer, D., Garland, A., Vieland, V., Underwood, M., & Busner, C. (1991). The impact of curriculum based suicide prevention programs for teenagers. *Journal of the American Academy of Child and Adolescent Psychiatry, 30*(4), 588–596.

Shafran R., Cooper Z., & Fairburn C. G. (2002). Clinical perfectionism: A cognitive-behavioural analysis. *Behaviour Research Therapy,* 40, 773–791.

Shafran, R., Thordarson, D. S., & Rachman, S. (1996). Thought-action fusion in obsessive compulsive disorder. *Journal of Anxiety Disorders, 10,* 379–391.

Shapiro, D. (1965). *Neurotic styles.* New York: Basic Books.

Shapiro, D. A., Rees, A., Barkham, M., Hardy, G., Reynolds, S., & Startup, M. (1995). Effects of treatment duration and severity of depression on the maintenance of gains after cognitive-behavioral and psychodynamic-interpersonal psychotherapy. *Journal of Consulting and Clinical Psychology, 63,* 378–387.

Shapiro, E. S., & Lentz, F. E. (1991). Vocational-technical programs: Follow-up of students with learning disabilities. *Exceptional Children, 58,* 47–59.

Shapiro, F. (1995). *Eye movement desensitization and reprocessing: Basic principles, protocols, and procedures.* New York: Guilford.

Shapiro, F. (1999). Eye movement desensitization and reprocessing (EMDR) and the anxiety disorders: Clinical and research implications of an integrated psychotherapy treatment. *Journal of Anxiety Disorders, 13,* 35–67.

Sharfstein, S. S. (1987). Reimbursement resistance to treatment and support for the long-term mental patient. *New Directions for Mental Health Services, 33,* 75–85.

Sharpe, M. (1992). Fatigue and chronic fatigue syndrome. *Current Opinion in Psychiatry, 5,* 207–212.

Sharpe, M. (1993). *Chronic fatigue syndrome.* Chichester, UK: John Wiley.

Sharpe, M. (1997). Chronic fatigue. In D. M. Clark & C. G. Fairburn (Eds.), *Science and practice of cognitive behavior therapy* (pp. 381–414). Oxford, U. K.: Oxford University Press.

Sharpe, M., Clements, A., Hawton, K., Young, A., Sargent, P., & Cowen, P. (1996). Increased prolactin response to buspirone in chronic fatigue syndrome. *Journal of Affective Disorders, 41,* 71–76.

Shaywitz, S. (2003). *Overcoming dyslexia: A new and complete science-based program for overcoming reading problems at any level.* New York: Knopf.

Shea, M. T., Pilkonis, P. A., Beckham, E., Collins, J. F., Elkin, I., Sotsky, S. M., et al. (1990). Personality disorders and treatment outcome in the NIMH treatment of depression collaborative research program. *American Journal of Psychiatry, 147,* 711–718.

Sheaffer, R. (1986). *The UFO verdict: Examining the evidence.* Buffalo, NY: Prometheus Books.

Shear, M. K., Brown, T. A., Barlow, D. H., Money, R., Sholomskas, D. E., Woods, S. W., et al. (1997). Multicenter collaborative panic disorder severity scale. *American Journal of Psychiatry, 154,* 1571–1575.

Sheikh, J. I. (1992). Anxiety and its disorders in old age. In J. E. Birren, K. Sloan, & G. D. Cohen (Eds.), *Handbook of mental health and aging* (pp. 410–432). New York: Academic Press.

Shepherd, J. E. (2001). Effects of estrogen on cognition, mood, and degenerative brain diseases. *Journal of the American Pharmacological Association (Wash.), 41*(2), 221–228.

Shepherd, M., Watt, D., Falloon, I., & Smeeton, N. (1989). The natural history of schizophrenia: A five-year follow-up study of outcome and prediction in a representative sample of schizophrenics. *Psychological Medicine Monograph, 15* (Suppl.), 1–46.

Sherbourne, C. D., Hays, R. D., & Wells, K. B. (1995). Personal and psychosocial risk factors for physical and mental health outcomes and course of depression among depressed patients. *Journal of Consulting and Clinical Psychology, 63*, 345–355.

Sherman, S. L., DeFries, J. C., Gottesman, I. I., Loehlin, J. C., Meyer, J. M., Pelias, M. Z., et al. (1997). Recent developments in human behavioral genetics: Past accomplishments and future directions. *American Journal of Human Genetics, 60*, 1265–1275.

Sherrington, R., Rogaev, E. I., Liang, Y., Rogaeva, E. A., Levesque, G., Ikeda, M., et al. (1995). Cloning of a gene bearing missense mutations in early-onset familial Alzheimer's disease. *Nature, 375*, 754–60.

Shiffman, S., Hickcox, M., Paty, J. A., Gnys, M., Kassel, J. D., & Richards, T. J. (1996). Progression from a smoking lapse to relapse: Prediction from abstinence violation effects, nicotine dependence, and lapse characteristics. *Journal of Consulting and Clinical Psychology, 64*, 993–1002.

Shneidman, E. S. (1989). Approaches and commonalities of suicide. In R. F. W. Diekstra, R. Mariss, S. Platt, A. Schmidtke, & G. Sonneck (Eds.), *Suicide and its prevention: The role of attitude and imitation. Advances in Suicidology* (Vol. 1). Leiden, Netherlands: E. J. Brill.

Shneidman, E. S., Farberow, N. L., & Litman, R. E. (Eds.). (1970). *The psychology of suicide.* New York: Science House.

Show, M. (1985). Practical problems of lithium maintenance treatment. *Advances in Biochemical Psychopharmacology, 40*, 131–138.

Shulman, K. I., Shedletsky, R., & Silver, I. (1986). The challenge of time: Clock drawing and cognitive function in the elderly. *International Journal of Geriatric Psychiatry, 1*, 135–140.

Sibley, D. C., & Blinder, B. J. (1988). Anorexia nervosa. In B. J. Blinder, B. F. Chaitin, & R. S. Goldstein (Eds.), *The eating disorders: Medical and psychological bases of diagnosis and treatment* (pp. 247–258). New York: PMA.

Siegel, S. (1982). Opioid expectation modifies opoid effects. *Federation Proceedings, 41*, 2339–2343.

Siegel, S., Hinson, R. E., Krank, M. D., & McCully, J. (1982). Heroin "overdose" death: Contribution of drug-associated environmental cues. *Science, 216*, 436–437.

Sierra, M., & Berrios, G. E. (1998). Depersonalization: Neurobiological

perspectives. *Society of Biological Psychiatry, 44*, 898–908.

Siever, L. J. (1992). Schizophrenia spectrum personality disorders. In A. Tasman & M. B. Riba (Eds.), *Review of psychiatry* (Vol. 11, pp. 25–42). Washington, DC: American Psychiatric Press.

Siever, L. J., Bernstein, D. P., & Silverman, J. M. (1991). Schizotypal personality disorder: A review of its current status. *Journal of Personality Disorders, 5*, 178–193.

Siever, L. J., Bernstein, D. P., & Silverman, J. M. (1995). Schizotypal personality disorder. In W. J. Livesley (Ed.), *The DSM-IV personality disorders* (pp. 71–90). New York: Guilford Press.

Siever, L. J., Davis, K. L., & Gorman, L. K. (1991). Pathogenesis of mood disorders. In K. Davis, H. Klar, & J. T. Coyle (Eds.), *Foundations of psychiatry.* Philadelphia: W. B. Saunders.

Siffre, M. (1964). *Beyond time* (H. Briffault, Ed. and Trans.). New York: McGraw-Hill.

Sigvardsson, S., Cloninger, C. R., Bohman, M., & von-Knorring, A. L. (1982). Predisposition to petty criminality in Swedish adoptees. *Archives of General Psychiatry, 39*, 1248–1253.

Silbersweig, D. A., Stern, E., Frith, C., Cahill, C., Holmes, A., Grootoonk, S., et al. (1995). A functional neuroanatomy of hallucinations in schizophrenia. *Nature, 378*, 176–179.

Silva, P. A. (1980). The prevalence, stability and significance of developmental language delay in preschool children. *Developmental Medicine and Child Neurology, 22*, 768–777.

Silveira, J. M., & Seeman, M. V. (1995). Shared psychotic disorder: A critical review of the literature. *Canadian Journal of Psychiatry, 40*, 389–395.

Silverman, K., Evans, S. M., Strain, E. C., & Griffiths, R. R. (1992). Withdrawal syndrome after the double-blind cessation of caffeine consumption. *New England Journal of Medicine, 327*, 1109–1114.

Silverman, W. K., & La Greca, A. M. (2002). Children experiencing disasters: Definitions, reactions and predictors of outcomes. In A. N. La Greca, W. K. Silverman, & M. C. Roberts (Eds.), *Helping children cope with disasters and terrorism* (Vol. 1, pp. 11–33). Washington, DC: American Psychological Association.

Silverman, W. K., La Greca, A. M., & Wasserstein, S. (1995). What do children worry about? Worries and their relation to anxiety. *Child Development, 66*, 671–686.

Silverman, W. K., & Rabian, B. (1993). Simple phobias. *Child and Adolescent Psychiatric Clinics of North America, 2*, 603–622.

Silverstone, T. (1985). Dopamine in manic depressive illness: A pharmacological synthesis. *Journal of Affective Disorders, 8*(3), 225–231.

Simeon, D., Gross, S., Guralnik, O., Stein, M. B., Schmeidler, J., & Hollander E. (1997). Thirty cases of DSM III-R depersonalization disorder. *American Journal of Psychiatry, 154*, 1107–1113.

Simon, E. J. (1997). Opiates: Neurobiology. In J. H. Lowinson, P. Ruiz, R. B. Millman, & J. G. Langrod (Eds.), *Substance abuse: A comprehensive textbook* (pp. 148–158). Baltimore: Williams & Wilkins.

Simon, G. E., Gureje, O., & Fullerton, C. (2001). Course of hypochondriasis in an international primary care study. *General Hospital Psychiatry, 23*, 51–55.

Simon, R. I. (1999). The law and psychiatry. In R. E. Hales, S. C. Yudofsky, & J. A. Talbott (Eds.), *The American Psychiatric Press textbook of psychiatry* (3rd ed., pp. 1493–1534). Washington, DC: American Psychiatric Press.

Simon, R. I. (2003). The law and psychiatry. In R. E. Hales & S. C. Yudofsky (Eds.), *Textbook of clinical psychiatry* (4th ed.) (pp. 1585–1626). Washington, DC: American Psychiatric Press.

Simoneau, T. L., Miklowitz, D. J., Richards, J. A., Saleem, R., & George, E. L. (1999). Bipolar disorder and family communication: Effects of a psychoeducational treatment program. *Journal of Abnormal Psychology, 108*, 588–597.

Simonoff, E., Bolton, P., & Rutter, M. (1996). Mental retardation: Genetic findings, clinical implications and research agenda. *Journal of Child Psychology and Psychiatry, 37*, 259–280.

Simons, A. D., Murphy, G. E., Levine, J. L., & Wetzel, R. D. (1986). Cognitive therapy and pharmacotherapy for depression: Sustained improvement over one year. *Archives of General Psychiatry, 43*(1), 43–48.

Singer, M., & Flannery, D. J. (2000). The relationship between children's threats of violence and violent behaviors. *Archives of Pediatrics and Adolescent Medicine, 154*, 785–790.

Single, E., Robson, L., Rehm, J., & Xie, X. (1996). *The costs of substance abuse in Canada.* Ottawa: Canadian Centre on Substance Abuse.

Siris, S. G. (2000). Depression in schizophrenia: Perspective in the era of "atypical" antipsychotic agents. *American Journal of Psychiatry, 157*, 1379–1389.

Skhiri, D., Annabi, S., Bi, S., & Allani, D. (1982). Enfants d'immigrés: Facteurs de liens ou de rupture? *Annales Medico-Psychologiques, 140*, 597–602.

Skilling, T. A., Harris, G. T., Rice, M. E., & Quinsey, V. L. (2002). Identifying persistently antisocial offenders using the Hare Psychopathy Checklist and DSM antisocial personality disorder criteria. *Psychological Assessment, 14*, 27–38.

Skinner, B. F. (1948). *Walden two.* New York: Macmillan.

Skinner, B. F. (1971). *Beyond freedom and dignity.* New York: Knopf.

Skodol, A. E., Oldham, J. M., & Gallaher, P. E. (1999). Axis II comorbidity of substance use disorders among patients referred for treatment of personality disorders. *American Journal of Psychiatry, 156*, 733–738.

Slade, J. (1999). Nicotine. In B. S. McCrady & E. E. Epstein (Eds.), *Addictions: A comprehensive guidebook* (pp. 162–170). New York: Oxford University Press.

Sleet, D. A., Hammond, R., Jones, R., Thomas, N., & Whitt, B. (2003). Using psychology for injury and violence prevention in the community. In R. H. Rozensky, N. G. Johnson, C. D. Goodheart, & R. Hammond (Eds.), *Psychology builds a healthy world.* Washington, DC: American Psychological Association.

Slutske, W. S., Heath, A. C., Dinwiddie, S. H., Madden, P. A. F., Bucholz, K. K., Dunne, M. P., et al. (1997). Modeling genetic and environmental influences in the etiology of conduct disorder: A study of 2,682 adult twin pairs. *Journal of Abnormal Psychology, 106,* 266–279.

Slutske, W. S., Heath, A. C., Dinwiddie, S. H., Madden, P. A. F., Bucholz, K. K., Dunne, M. P., et al. (1998). Common genetic risk factors for conduct disorder and alcohol dependence. *Journal of Abnormal Psychology, 107,* 363–374.

Small, G. W. (1991). Recognition and treatment of depression in the elderly. The clinician's challenge: Strategies for treatment of depression in the 1990's. *Journal of Clinical Psychiatry, 52,* 11–22.

Smart, R. G. (1985). Alcohol and alcohol problems research: IV. Canada. *British Journal of Addiction, 80,* 255–263.

Smeets, G., de Jong, P. J., & Mayer, B. (2000). If you suffer from a headache, then you have a brain tumour: Domain-specific reasoning "bias" and hypochondriasis. *Behaviour Research and Therapy, 38,* 763–776.

Smith, D. E., Marcus, M. D., & Kaye, W. (1992). Cognitive-behavioral treatment of obese binge eaters. *International Journal of Eating Disorders, 12,* 257–262.

Smith, D. E. & Wesson, D. R. (1999). Benzodiazepines and other sedative-hypnotics. In M. Galanter & H. D. Kleber (Eds.), *Textbook of substance abuse treatment* (2nd ed., pp. 239–250). Washington, DC: American Psychiatric Press.

Smith, J. E., & Krejci, J. (1991). Minorities join the majority: Eating disturbances among Hispanic and Native American youth. *International Journal of Eating Disorders, 10,* 179–186.

Smith, M. D. (1992). Community integration and supported employment. In D. E. Berkell (Ed.), *Autism: Identification, education, and treatment* (pp. 253–271). Hillsdale, NJ: Erlbaum.

Smith, P. G., & Cousens, S. N. (1996). Is the new variant of Creutzfeldt-Jakob disease from mad cows? *Science, 273,* 748.

Smith, P. M., Kraemer, H. C., Miller, N. H., DeBusk, R. F., & Taylor, C. B. (1999). In-hospital smoking cessation programs: Who responds, who doesn't? *Journal of Consulting and Clinical Psychology, 67*(1), 19–27.

Smith, S. E. (1993). Cognitive deficits associated with fragile X syndrome. *Mental Retardation, 31,* 279–283.

Smith, S. S., & Newman, J. P. (1990). Alcohol and drug abuse-dependence disorders in psychopathic and nonpsychopathic criminal offenders. *Journal of Abnormal Psychology, 99,* 430–439.

Smith, T. E., Bellack, A. S., & Liberman, R. P. (1996). Social skills training for schizophrenia: Review and future directions. *Clinical Psychology Review, 16,* 599–617.

Smith, T. W. (1992). Hostility and health: Current status of a psychosomatic hypothesis. *Health Psychology, 11*(3), 139–150.

Smolak, L., & Levine, M. P. (1996). Adolescent transitions and the development of eating problems. In L. Smolak, M. P. Levine & R. Striegel-Moore (Eds.), *The developmental psychopathology of eating disorders: Implications for research, prevention, and treatment* (pp. 207–233). Mahwah, NJ: Erlbaum.

Snyder, E. Y., Taylor, R. M., & Wolfe, J. H. (1995). Neural progenitor cell engraftment corrects lysosomal storage throughout the MPS VII mouse brain. *Nature, 374,* 367–370.

Snyder, S. H. (1976). The dopamine hypothesis of schizophrenia: Focus on the dopamine receptor. *American Journal of Psychiatry, 133,* 197–202.

Snyder, S. H. (1981). Opiate and benzodiazepine receptors. *Psychosomatics, 22*(11), 986–989.

Snyder, S. H., Burt, D. R., & Creese, I. (1976). Dopamine receptor of mammalian brain: Direct demonstration of binding to agonist and antagonist states. *Neuroscience Symposia, 1,* 28–49.

Sobell, M. B., & Sobell, L. C. (1978). *Behavioral treatment of alcohol problems.* New York: Plenum Press.

Sobell, M. B., & Sobell, L. C. (1993). *Problem drinkers: Guided self-change treatment.* New York: Guilford Press.

Social Worker Action Team (2002). *Info: Homelessness.* Retrieved August 11, 2004, from http://www.swatjobs.com/info_homelessness.htm.

Society for Research in Child Development, Committee for Ethical Conduct in Child Development Research (1990, Winter). SRCD ethical standards for research with children. *SRCD Newsletter,* Chicago.

Sokolov, S., & Kutcher, S. (2001). Adolescent depression: Neuroendocrine aspects. In: I. M. Goodyer (Ed.), *Depressed child and adolescent* (2nd ed., pp. 233–266). New York: Cambridge University Press.

Soloff, P. H., George, A., Nathan, R. S., Schulz, P. M., Cornelius, J. R., Herring, J., et al. (1989). Amitriptyline versus haloperidol in borderlines: Final outcomes and predictors of response. *Journal of Clinical Psychopharmacology, 9,* 238–246.

Soloff, P. H., Lynch, K. G., Kelley, T. M., Malone, K. M., & Mann, J. J. (2000). Characteristics of suicide attempts of patients with major depressive episode and borderline personality disorder: A comparative study. *American Journal of Psychiatry, 157*(4), 601–608.

Solomon, A., & Haaga, D. A. F. (2003). Reconsideration of self-complexity as a buffer against depression. *Cognitive Therapy and Research, 27,* 579–591.

Solomon, D. A., Keller, M. B., Leon, A. C., Mueller, T. I., Lavori, P. W., Shea, T., et al. (2000). Multiple recurrences of major depressive disorder. *American Journal of Psychiatry, 157*(2), 229–233.

Solomon, D. A., Keller, M. B., Leon, A. C., Mueller, T. I., Shea, M. T., Warshaw, M., et al. (1997). Recovery from major depression: A 10-year prospective follow-up across multiple episodes. *Archives of General Psychiatry, 54,* 1001–1006.

Solomon, D. A., Leon, A. C., Endicott, J., Coryell, W. H., Mueller, T. I., Posternak M. A., et al. (2003). Unipolar mania over the course of a 20-year follow-up study. *American Journal of Psychiatry, 160,* 2049–2051.

Solomon, R. L. (1980). The opponent-process theory of acquired motivation: The costs of pleasure and the benefits of pain. *American Psychologist, 35,* 691–712.

Solomon, R. L., & Corbit, J. D. (1974). An opponent process theory of motivation: I. Temporal dynamics of affect. *Psychological Review, 81,* 119–145.

Song, X, & Rusak, B. (2000). Acute effects of light on body temperature and activity in Syrian hamsters: Influence of circadian phase. *American Journal of Physiology: Regulatory, Integrative, and Comparative Physiology, 278,* 1369–1380.

Sonuga-Barke, E. J., Daley, D., Thompson, M., Laver-Bradbury, C., & Weeks, A. (2001). Parent-based therapies for preschool attention-deficit/hyperactivity disorder: A randomized, controlled trial with a community sample. *Journal of the American Academy of Child and Adolescent Psychiatry, 40*(4), 402–408.

Southwick, S. M., Krystal, J. H., Johnson, D. R., & Charney, D. S. (1992). Neurobiology of posttraumatic stress disorder. In A. Tasman & M. B. Riba (Eds.), *Review of psychiatry* (Vol. 11, pp. 347–367). Washington, DC: American Psychiatric Press.

Spangler, D. L., Simons, A. D., Monroe, S. M., & Thase, M. E. (1996). Gender differences in cognitive diathesis-stress domain match: Implications for differential pathways to depression. *Journal of Abnormal Psychology, 105,* 653–657.

Spangler, D. L., Simons, A. D., Monroe, S. M., & Thase, M. E. (1997). Comparison of cognitive models of depression: Relationships between cognitive constructs and cognitive diathesis-stress match. *Journal of Abnormal Psychology, 106,* 395–403.

Spanos, N. P. (1996). *Multiple identities and false memories: A sociocognitive prospective.* Washington, DC: American Psychological Association.

Spanos, N. P., Cross, P. A., Dickson, K., & DuBreuil, S. C. (1993). Close encounters: An examination of UFO experiences. *Journal of Abnormal Psychology, 102,* 624–632.

Spanos, N. P., Weeks, J. R., & Bertrand, L. D. (1985). Multiple personality: A social psychological perspective. *Journal of Abnormal Psychology, 92,* 362–376.

Spector, I. P., & Carey, M. P. (1990). Incidence and prevalence of the sexual dysfunctions: A critical review of the empirical literature. *Archives of Sexual Behavior, 19*(4), 389–408.

Spence, J. D., Barnett, P. A., Linden, W., Ramsden, V., & Taenzer, P. (1999). 7. Recommendations on stress management. *Canadian Medical Association Journal, 160,* S46–S50.

Spiegel, D., & Cardeña, E. (1991). Disintegrated experience: The dissociative disorders revisited. *Journal of Abnormal Psychology, 100*(3), 366–378.

Spiegel, D., Bloom, J. R., Kramer, H. C., & Gotheil, E. (1989). Effect of psychosocial treatment on survival of patients with metastatic breast cancer. *Lancet, 14,* 888–891.

Spiegel, D., Morrow, G. R., Classen, C., Riggs, G., Stott, P. B., Mudaliar, N., Pierce, H. I., Flynn, P. J., & Heard, L. (1996). Effects of group therapy on women with primary breast cancer. *The Breast Journal, 2*(1), 104–106.

Spiegel, D. A., Wiegel, M., Baker, S. L., & Greene, K. A. I. (2000). Pharmacological management of anxiety disorders. In D. I. Mostofsky & D. H. Barlow (Eds.), *The management of stress and anxiety in medical disorders* (pp. 36–65). Needham Heights, MA: Allyn & Bacon.

Spielberger, C. D., & Frank, R. G. (1992). Injury control: A promising field for psychologists. *American Psychologist, 47*(8), 1029–1030.

Spielman, A. J., & Glovinsky, P. (1991). The varied nature of insomnia. In P. J. Hauri (Ed.), *Case studies in insomnia* (pp. 1–15). New York: Plenum Press.

Spiker, D., & Ricks, M. (1984). Visual self-recognition in autistic children: Developmental relationships. *Child Development, 55*, 214–225.

Spinelli, M. G., & Endicott, J. (2003). Controlled clinical trial of interpersonal psychotherapy versus parenting education program for depressed pregnant women. *American Journal of Psychiatry, 160*, 555–562.

Spitzer, R. L. (1999). Harmful dysfunction and the DSM definition of mental disorder. *Journal of Abnormal Psychology, 108*, 430–432.

Spitzer, R. L., Devlin, M. J., Walsh, B. T., Hasin, D., Wing, R., Marcus, M. D., et al. (1991). Binge eating disorder: To be or not to be in DSM-IV. *International Journal of Eating Disorders, 10*, 627–629.

Spoont, M. R. (1992). Modulatory role of serotonin in neural information processing: Implications for human psychopathology. *Psychological Bulletin, 112*(2), 330–350.

Spreen, O. (1988). Prognosis of learning disability. *Journal of Consulting and Clinical Psychology, 56*, 836–842.

Sprich, S., Biederman, J., & Crawford, M. H. (2000). Adoptive and biological families of children and adolescents with ADHD. *Journal of the American Academy of Child and Adolescent Psychiatry, 39*, 1432–1437.

Sprock, J. (2000). Gender-typed behavioral examples of histrionic personality disorder. *Journal of Psychopathology and Behavioral Assessment, 22*, 107–122.

Spurrell, E. B., Wilfley, D. E., Tanofsky, M. B., & Brownell, K. D. (1997). Age of onset for binge eating: Are there different pathways to binge eating? *International Journal of Eating Disorders, 21*, 55–65.

Staal, W. G., Pol, H. E. H., Schnack, H. G., Hoogendoorn, M. L. C., Jellema, K., & Kahn, R. S. (2000). Structural brain abnormalities in patients with schizophrenia and their healthy siblings. *American Journal of Psychiatry, 157*, 416–421.

Stam, H., & Steggles, S. (1987). Predicting the onset or progression of cancer from psychological characteristics: Psychometric and theoretical issues. *Journal of Psychosocial Oncology, 5*(2), 35–46.

Stanley, M. A., Beck, J. G., & Glassco, J. D. (1997). Generalized anxiety in older adults: Treatment with cognitive-behavioral and supportive approaches. *Behavior Therapy, 27*, 565–581.

Statistics Canada (1975). Mental health statistics, volume III: Institutional facilities, services and finances, 1975. Ottawa: Minister of Industry, Trade and Commerce.

Statistics Canada (1991). *Health and activity limitation survey (HALS)*. Ottawa, ON: Author.

Statistics Canada (1995). *Mental health statistics, 1992–93*. Ottawa: Minister responsible for Statistics Canada.

Statistics Canada (1996a). *Ethnocultuiral and social characteristics of the Canadian population* (CD-ROM 94F0004xCB, (ethno.1.ivt)). Ottawa, ON: Author.

Statistics Canada. (1996b). *National longitudinal survey of children and youth: User's handbook and microdata guide* (Microdata documentation: 89M0015GPE). Ottawa: Author.

Statistics Canada (2001a). *Census of population*. Ottawa, ON: Author.

Statistics Canada (2001b). *A profile of disability in Canada*. Ottawa, ON: Author.

Statistics Canada (2002a). *Canadian community health survey: Mental health and well-being*. Ottawa, ON: Author.

Statistics Canada (2002b). *Historical statistics of Canada, Section B. Vital statistics and health (B35-50)*. Ottawa, ON: Author.

Statistics Canada. (2003). *Alcohol consumption, by sex, age group and level of education*. Ottawa, ON: Author.

Steadman, H. J., & Ribner, S. A. (1980). Changing perceptions of the mental health needs of inmates in local jails. *American Journal of Psychiatry, 137*, 1115–1116.

Stefan, S. (1996). Issues relating to women and ethnic minorities in mental health treatment and law. In B. D. Sales & D. W. Shuman (Eds.), *Law, mental health, & mental disorder* (pp. 240–278). Pacific Grove, CA: Brooks/Cole.

Steiger, H., Bruce, K. R., & Israel, M. (2003). Eating disorders. In G. Stricker & T. A. Widiger (Eds.), *Handbook psychology: Clinical psychology* (Vol. 8, pp. 173–194). New York: John Wiley.

Steiger, H., Lehoux, P. M., & Gauvin, L. (1999). Impulsivity, dietary control and the urge to binge in bulimic syndromes. *International Journal of Eating Disorders, 26*, 261–274.

Steiger, H., Stotland, S., Trottier, J., & Ghadirian, A. M. (1996). Familial eating concerns and psychopathological traits: Causal implications of transgenerational effects. *International Journal of Eating Disorders, 19*, 147–157.

Stein, M. B., Forde, D. R., Anderson, G., & Walker, J. R. (1997). Obsessive-compulsive disorder in the community: An epidemiologic survey with clinical reappraisal. *American Journal of Psychiatry, 154*, 1120–1126.

Stein, M. B., Goldin, P. R., Sareen, J., Zorrilla, L. T., & Brown, G. G. (2002). Increased amygdala activation to angry and contemptuous faces in generalized social phobia. *Archives of General Psychiatry, 59*, 1027–1034.

Stein, M. B., Jang, K. L., & Livesley, W. J. (2002). Heritability of social anxiety-related concerns and personality characteristics: A twin study. *Journal of Nervous and Mental Disease, 190*, 219–224.

Stein, M. B., Jang, K. L., Taylor, S., Vernon, P. A., & Livesley, W. J. (2002). Genetic and environmental influences on trauma exposure and posttraumatic stress disorder symptoms: A twin study. *American Journal of Psychiatry, 159*, 1675–1681.

Stein, M. B., & Kean, Y. M. (2000). Disability and quality of life in social phobia: Epidemiologic findings. *American Journal of Psychiatry, 157*, 1606–1613.

Stein, M. B., Liebowitz, M. R., Lydiard, R. B., Pitts, C. D., Bushnell, W., & Gergel, I. (1998). Paroxetine treatment of generalized social phobia (social anxiety disorder): A randomized clinical trial. *Journal of the American Medical Association, 280*, 708–713.

Stein, M. B., Torgrud, L. J., & Walker, J. R. (2000). Social phobia symptoms, subtypes, and severity: Findings from a community survey. *Archives of General Psychiatry, 57*, 1046–1052.

Stein, M. B., Walker, J. R., & Forde, D. R. (1996). Public speaking fears in a community sample: Prevalence, impact on functioning and diagnostic classification. *Archives of General Psychiatry, 53*, 169–174.

Stein, M. T., Zucker, K. J., & Dixon, S. D. (2001). Sammy: Gender identity concerns in a 6-year-old boy. *Journal of Development and Behavioral Pediatrics, 22* (Suppl. 2), 43–47.

Stein, R. M., & Ellinwood, E. H. (1993). Stimulant use: Cocaine and amphetamine. In D. L. Dunner (Ed.), *Current psychiatric therapy* (pp. 98–105). Philadelphia: W. B. Saunders.

Steinberg, A. B., & Phares, V. (2001). Family functioning, body image, and eating disturbances. In J. K. Thompson & L. Smolak (Eds.), *Body image, eating disorders, and obesity in youth: Assessment, prevention and treatment* (127–147). Washington, DC: American Psychological Association.

Steinberg, M. (1991). The spectrum of depersonalization: Assessment and treatment. *Annual Review of Psychiatry, 10*, 223–247.

Steiner, M. (2002). Postnatal depression: A few simple questions. *Family Practice, 19*, 469–470.

Steketee, G., & Barlow, D. H. (2002). Obsessive-compulsive disorder. In D. H. Barlow (Ed.), *Anxiety and its disorders: The nature and treatment of anxiety and panic* (2nd ed.). New York: Guilford Press.

Steketee, G., Quay, S., & White, K. (1991). Religion and guilt in OCD patients. *Journal of Anxiety Disorders, 5*, 359–367.

Stephens, R. S., Roffman, R. A., & Simpson, E. E. (1994). Treating adult marijuana dependence: A test of the relapse prevention model. *Journal of Consulting and Clinical Psychology, 62*, 92–99.

Stephenson, J. (2003). Global AIDS epidemic worsens. *Journal of the American Medical Association, 291*, 31–32.

Stern, C. E., Owen, A. M., Look, R. B., Tracey, I., Rosen, B. R., & Petrides, M.

(2000). Activity in ventrolateral and mid-dorsolateral prefrontal cortex during non-spatial visual working memory processing: Evidence from functional magnetic resonance imaging. *Neuroimage, 11*(5), 392–399.

Stern, Y., Gurland, B., Tatemichi, T. K., Tang, M. X., Wilder, D., & Mayeux, R. (1994). Influence of education and occupation on the incidence of Alzheimer's disease. *Journal of the American Medical Association, 271*, 1004–1010.

Sternberg, R. J. (1988). Intellectual development: Psychometric and information-processing approaches. In M. H. Bornstein & M. E. Lamb (Eds.), *Developmental psychology: An advanced textbook* (2nd ed.). Hillsdale, NJ: Erlbaum.

Stevens, J. (1987). *Storming heaven: LSD and the American dream.* New York: Atlantic Monthly Press.

Stewart, S. H. (1996). Alcohol abuse in individuals exposed to trauma: A critical review. *Psychological Bulletin, 120*, 85–112.

Stewart, S. H. (2002). The history, current prevalence and consequences of drinking problems. *Transactions of the Royal Society of Canada*, Seventh Series, Volume II, ISSN: 1710–2839.

Stewart, S. H., & Asmundson, G. J. G. (2006). Anxiety sensitivity and its impact on pain experiences and conditions: A state of the art. *Cognitive Behaviour Therapy, 35*, 185–188.

Stewart, S. H., & Brown, C. G. (in press). Relationship between eating and substance use problems among women: A critical review. In L. Greaves, N. Poole, & J. Greenbaum (Eds.), *Women and substance use: Current Canadian perspectives.* Toronto: Centre for Addiction and Mental Health.

Stewart, S. H., Brown, C., Devoulyte, K., Theakston, J., & Larsen, S. E. (2006). Why do women with alcohol problems binge eat? *Journal of Health Psychology, 11*, 409–425.

Stewart, S. H., Collins, P., Blackburn, J. R., Ellery, M., & Klein, R. M. (2005). Heart rate increase to alcohol administration and video lottery terminal (VLT) play. *Psychology of Addictive Behaviors, 19*, 94–98.

Stewart, S. H., & Conrod, P. J. (Eds.). *Co-morbid anxiety and substance use disorders: Theoretical and treatment issues.* New York: Springer.

Stewart, S. H., & Devine, H. (2000). Relations between personality and drinking motives in young adults. *Personality and Individual Differences, 29*, 495–511.

Stewart, S. H., Finn, P. R., & Pihl, R. O. (1992). The effects of alcohol on the cardiovascular stress response in men at high risk for alcoholism: A dose response study. *Journal of Studies on Alcohol, 53*, 499–506.

Stewart, S. H., Knize, K., & Pihl, R. O. (1992). Anxiety sensitivity and dependency in clinical and non-clinical panickers and controls. *Journal of Anxiety Disorders, 6*, 119–131.

Stewart, S. H., & Kushner, M. G. (2003). Recent research on the comorbidity of alcoholism and pathological gambling.

*Alcoholism: Clinical and Experimental Research, 27*, 285–291.

Stewart, S. H., Rioux, G. F., Connolly, J. F., Dunphy, S. C., & Teehan, M. D. (1996). The effects of oxazepam and lorazepam on implicit and explicit memory: Evidence for possible influences of time course. *Psychopharmacology, 128*, 139–149.

Stewart, S. H., & Samoluk, S. B. (1997). Effects of short-term food deprivation and chronic dietary restraint on the selective processing of appetitive-related cues. *International Journal of Eating Disorders, 21*, 129–135.

Stewart, S. H., Samoluk, S. B., & MacDonald, A. B. (1999). Anxiety sensitivity and substance use and abuse. In S. Taylor (Ed.), *Anxiety sensitivity: Theory, research and treatment of the fear of anxiety* (pp. 287–319). Mahwah, NJ: Lawrence Erlbaum.

Stewart, S. H., Taylor, S., & Baker, J. M. (1997). Gender differences in dimensions of anxiety sensitivity. *Journal of Anxiety Disorders, 11*, 179–200.

Stewart, S. H., & Watt, M. C. (2000). Illness Attitude Scale dimensions and their association with anxiety-related constructs in a non-clinical sample. *Behaviour Research and Therapy, 38*, 83–99.

Stewart, S. H., & Watt, M. C. (2001). Assessment of health anxiety. In G. J. G. Asmundson, S. Taylor, & B. J. Cox (Eds.), *Health anxiety: Clinical and research perspectives on hypochondriasis and related conditions* (pp. 95–131). New York: Wiley.

Stewart, S. H., & Westra, H. A. (2002). Introduction to the special issue on 'Benzodiazepine side-effects: From the bench to the clinic.' *Current Pharmaceutical Design, 8*, 1–3.

Stewart, W. F., Kawas, C., Corrada, M., & Metter, E. J. (1997). Risk of Alzheimer's disease and duration of NSAID use. *Neurology, 48*, 626–632.

Stice, E., Agras, W. S., Telch, C. F., Halmi, K. A. Mitchell, J. E., & Wilson, G. T. (2001). Subtyping binge eating disordered women along dieting and negative affect dimension. *International Journal of Eating Disorders, 30*, 11–27.

Stice, E., Akutagawa, D., Gaggar, A., & Agras, W. S. (2000). Negative affect moderates the relation between dieting and binge eating. *International Journal of Eating Disorders, 27*, 218–229.

Stice, E., Cameron, R. P., Killen, J. D., Hayward, C., & Taylor, C. B. (1999). Naturalistic weight-reduction efforts prospectively predict growth in relative weight and onset of obesity among female adolescents. *Journal of Consulting and Clinical Psychology, 67*, 967–974.

Stice, E., Schupak-Neuberg, E., Shaw, H. E., & Stein, R. I. (1994). Relation of media exposure to eating disorder symptomatology: An examination of mediating mechanisms. *Journal of Abnormal Psychology, 103*, 836–840.

Stip, E., Caron, J., & Lane, C. J. (2001). Schizophrenia: People's perceptions in Quebec. *Canadian Medical Association Journal, 164*, 1299–1300.

St. John, J., Krichev, A., & Bauman, E. (1976). Northwestern Ontario Indian

children and the WISC. *Psychology in the Schools, 13*, 407–411.

Stock, W. (1993). Inhibited female orgasm. In W. O'Donohue & J. H. Geer (Eds.), *Handbook of sexual dysfunctions: Assessment and treatment* (pp. 253–277). Boston: Allyn & Bacon.

Stokes, J., & Lindsay, J. (1996). Major causes of death and hospitalization in Canadian seniors. *Chronic Diseases in Canada, 17*, 63–73.

Stoller, R. J. (1976). Two feminized male American Indians. *Archives of Sexual Behavior, 5*, 529–538.

Stoller, R. J. (1982). Transvestism in women. *Archives of Sexual Behavior, 11*, 99–115.

Stone, G. C. (1987). The scope of health psychology. In G. C. Stone, S. M. Weiss, J. D. Matarazzo, N. E. Miller, J. Rodin, D. D. Belar, (Eds.), *Health psychology: A discipline and a profession.* Chicago: University of Chicago Press.

Stone, J., Zeidler, M., & Sharpe, M. (2003). Misdiagnosis of conversion disorder. *American Journal of Psychiatry, 160*, 391.

Stone, M. (1983). Psychotherapy with schizotypal borderline patients. *Journal of the American Academy of Psychoanalysis, 11*, 87–111.

Stone, M. H. (1986). Borderline personality disorder. In A. M. Cooper, A. J. Frances, & M. H. Sacks (Eds.), *The personality disorders and neuroses* (pp. 203–217). New York: Basic Books.

Stone, M. H. (1989). The course of borderline personality disorder. In A. Tasman, R. E. Hales, & A. J. Frances (Eds.), *Annual review of psychiatry* (Vol. 8, pp. 103–122). Washington, DC: American Psychiatric Press.

Stone, M. H. (1993). Cluster C personality disorders. In D. L. Dunner (Ed.), *Current psychiatric therapy* (pp. 411–417). Philadelphia: W. B. Saunders.

Stone, M. H. (2001). Schizoid and schizotypal personality disorders. In G. O. Gabbard (Ed.), *Treatment of psychiatric disorders* (Vol. 2) (3rd ed.) (pp. 2237–2250). Washington, DC: American Psychiatric Press.

Stone, R. (2000). Stress: The invisible hand in eastern Europe's death rates. *Science, 288*, 1732–1733.

Stoppard, J. M. (1989). An evaluation of the adequacy of cognitive/behavioural theories for understanding depression in women. *Canadian Psychology, 30*, 39–47.

Stoppard, J. M. (1999). Why new perspectives are needed for understanding depression in women. *Canadian Psychology, 40*, 79–90.

Stoppard, J. M. (2000). *Understanding depression: Feminist social constructionist approaches.* Florence, KY: Taylor & Frances/Routledge.

Stoppard, J. M., & McMullen, L. M. (Eds.). (2003). *Situating sadness: Women and depression in social context.* New York: University Press.

Strahl, C., Kleinknecht, R. A., & Dinnel, D. L. (2000). The role of pain anxiety, coping, and pain self-efficacy in rheumatoid arthritis patient functioning. *Behaviour Research and Therapy, 38*, 863–873.

Strain, E. C., Mumford, G. K., Silverman, K., & Griffiths, R. R. (1994). Caffeine dependence syndrome: Evidence from case histories and experimental evaluations. *Journal of the American Medical Association, 272*, 1043–1048.

Strassberg, D. S., Kelly, M. P., Carroll, C., & Kircher, J. C. (1987). The psychophysiological nature of premature ejaculation. *Archives of Sexual Behavior, 16*, 327–336.

Strathdee, S. A., Patrick, D. M., Currie, S. L., Cornelisse, P. G. A., Rekart, M. L., Montaner, J. S. G., (1997). Needle exchange is not enough: Lessons from the Vancouver injecting drug use study. *AIDS, 11*(8), 59–65.

Straus, S. E. (1988). The chronic mononucleosis syndrome. *Journal of Infectious Disease, 157*, 405–412.

Straus, S. E., Tosato, G., Armstrong, G., Lawley, T., Preble, O. T., Henle, W., et al. (1985). Persisting illness and fatigue in adults with evidence of Epstein Barr virus infection. *Annals of Internal Medicine, 102*, 7–16.

Strauss, J., Carpenter, W. T., Jr., & Bartko, J. (1974). The diagnosis and understanding of schizophrenia: III. Speculations on the processes that underlie schizophrenic symptoms and signs. *Schizophrenia Bulletin, 1*, 61–69.

Stravynski, A., Elie, R., & Franche, R. L. (1989). Perception of early parenting by patients diagnosed avoidant personality disorder: A test of the overprotection hypothesis. *Acta Psychiatrica Scandinavica, 80*, 415–420.

Stravynski, A., Lesage, A., Marcouiller, M., & Elie, R. (1989). A test of the therapeutic mechanism in social skills training with avoidant personality disorder. *Journal of Nervous and Mental Disease, 177*, 739–744.

Striegel-Moore, R. H., Cachelin, F. M., Dohm, F. A., Pike, M., Wifley, D. E., & Fairburn, C. G. (2001). Comparison of binge eating disorder and bulimia nervosa in a community sample. *International Journal of Eating Disorders, 29*, 157–165.

Striegal-Moore, R. H., Silberstein, L. R., & Rodin, J. (1986). Toward an understanding of risk factors for bulimia. *American Psychologist, 3*, 246–263.

Striegal-Moore, R. H., Silberstein, L. R., & Rodin, J. (1993). The social self in bulimia nervosa: Public self-consciousness, social anxiety, and perceived fraudulence. *Journal of Abnormal Psychology, 102*(2), 297–303.

Stringer, R., & Stanovich, K. E. (2000). The connection between reaction time and variation in reading ability: Unravelling covariance relationships with cognitive ability and phonological sensitivity. *Scientific Studies of Reading, 4*, 41–53.

Strobel, M. (2002, February 6). Sheena'd be proud. *Toronto Sun*. Retrieved June 24, 2004, from http://www.canoe.ca/Health0202/06_sheena-sun.html.

Strober, M. (2002). Family–genetic perspectives on anorexia nervosa and bulimia nervosa. In K. D. Brownell & C. G. Fairburn (Eds.), *Eating disorders and obesity: A comprehensive handbook* (2nd ed., pp. 212–218). New York: Guilford Press.

Strober, M., Freeman, R., Lampert, C., Diamond, J., & Kaye, W. (2000). Controlled family study of anorexia nervosa and bulimia nervosa: Evidence of shared liability and transmission of partial syndromes. *American Journal of Psychiatry, 157*, 393–401.

Strober, M., & Humphrey, L. L. (1987). Familial contributions to the etiology and course of anorexia nervosa and bulimia. Special Issue: Eating disorders. *Journal of Consulting and Clinical Psychology, 55*(5), 654–659.

Stuart, H. L., & Arboleda-Florez, J. (2000). Homeless shelter users in the postdeinstitutionalization era. *Canadian Journal of Psychiatry, 45*, 55–62.

Stunkard, A. J., Sorenson, T., & Schusinger, F. (1980). Use of the Danish adoption register for the study of obesity and thinness. In S. Kety (Ed.), *The genetics of the neurological and psychiatric disorders* (pp. 115–120). New York: Raven Press.

Stuss, D. T., & Cummings, J. L. (1990). Subcortical vascular dementias. In J. L. Cummings (Ed.), *Subcortical dementia* (pp. 145–163). New York: Oxford University Press.

Stuss, D. T., & Levine, B. (2002). Adult clinical neuropsychology: Lessons from studies of the frontal lobes. *Annual Review of Psychology, 53*(1), 401–433.

Suarez, E. C., Lewis, J. G., & Kuhn, C. (2002). The relation of aggression, hostility, and anger to lipopolysaccharide-stimulated tumor necrosis factor (TNF) by blood monocytes from normal men. *Behavior and Immunity, 16*, 675–684.

Substance Abuse and Mental Health Services Administration, Office of Applied Studies (2003). *Emergency department trends from the Drug Abuse Warning Network, Final estimates 1995–2002.* DAWN Series D-24, DHHS Publication No. (SMA) 03-3780, Rockville, MD.

Sugiyama, T., & Abe, T. (1989). The prevalence of autism in Nagoya, Japan: A total population study. *Journal of Autism and Developmental Disorders, 19*, 87–96.

Sullivan, G. M., Kent, J. M., & Coplan, J. D. (2000). The neurobiology of stress and anxiety. In D. I. Mostofsky & D. H. Barlow (Eds.), *The management of stress and anxiety in medical disorders* (pp. 15–35). Needham Heights, MA: Allyn & Bacon.

Sullivan, K. A. (2001). The clinical features of binge eating disorder and bulimia nervosa: What are the differences? *Canadian Journal of Counselling, 35*, 315–328.

Sullivan, M. J. (2003). Introduction: Emerging trends in secondary prevention of back pain disability. *The Clinical Journal of Pain, 19*, 77–79.

Sullivan, M. J. L., Bishop, S. R., & Pivik, J. (1995). The Pain Catastrophizing Scale: Development and validation. *Psychological Assessment, 7*, 524–532.

Sullivan, M. J. L., & Stanish, W. D. (2003). Psychologically based occupational rehabilitation: The Pain-Disability Prevention Program. *Clinical Journal of Pain, 19*, 97–104.

Sullivan, M. J. L., Thorn, B., Haythornthwaite, J. A., Keefe, F., Martin, M., Bradley, L. A., et al. (2001). Theoretical perspectives on the relation between catastrophizing and pain. *Clinical Journal of Pain, 17*, 52–64.

Sullivan, P. F. (1995). Mortality in anorexia nervosa. *American Journal of Psychiatry, 152*, 1073–1074.

Summerfeldt, L. J., Richter, M. A., Antony, M. M., & Swinson, R. P. (1999). Symptom structure in obsessive-compulsive disorder: A confirmatory factor-analytic study. *Behaviour Research and Therapy, 37*, 297–311.

Suomi, S. J. (1999). Attachment in rhesus monkeys. In J. Cassidy & P. Shaver (Eds.), *Handbook of attachment: Theory, research, and clinical applications* (pp. 181–197). New York: Guilford Press.

Suppes, T., Baldessarini, R. J., Faedda, G. L., & Tohen, M. (1991). Risk of recurrence following discontinuation of lithium treatment in bipolar disorder. *Archives of General Psychiatry, 48*(12), 1082–1088.

Sussman, S. (1998). The first asylums in Canada: A response to neglectful community care and current trends. *Canadian Journal of Psychiatry, 43*, 260–264.

Sutherland, G. R., & Richards, R. I. (1994). Dynamic mutations. *American Scientist, 82*, 157–163.

Sutherland, S. M. (2001). Avoidant personality disorder. In G. O. Gabbard (Ed.), *Treatment of psychiatric disorders* (Vol. 2) (3rd ed.) (pp. 2327–2340). Washington, DC: American Psychiatric Publishing.

Sutker, P. B., Bugg, F., & West, J. A. (1993). Antisocial personality disorder. In P. B. Sutker & H. E. Adams (Eds.), *Comprehensive handbook of psychopathology* (2nd ed., pp. 337–369). New York: Plenum Press.

Sutton, D. A., Moldofsky, H., & Badley, E. M. (2001). Insomnia and health problems in Canadians. *Sleep and Hypnosis, 24*, 665–670.

Swanson, M. C., Bland, R. C., & Newman, S. C. (1994). Antisocial personality disorders. *Acta Psychiatrica Scandinavica, 89* (376, Suppl.), 63–70.

Swartz, M., Blazer, D., George, L., & Landerman, R. (1986a). Somatization disorder in a community population. *American Journal of Psychiatry, 143*, 1403–1408.

Swartz, M., Blazer, D., Woodbury, M., George, L., & Landerman, R. (1986b). Somatization disorder in a U.S. southern community: Use of a new procedure for analysis of medical classification. *Psychological Medicine, 16*, 595–609.

Swedo, S. E., Pleeter, J. D., Richter, D. M., Hoffman, C. L., Allen, A. J., Hamburger, S. D., (1995). Rates of seasonal affective disorder in children and adolescents. *American Journal of Psychiatry, 152*, 1016–1019.

Swift, R. M. (1999). Medications and alcohol craving. *Alcohol Research and Health, 23*(3), 207–213.

Swinson, R. P., Fergus, K. D., Cox, B. J., & Wickwire, K. (1995). Efficacy of telephone-administered behavioral therapy for panic disorder with agoraphobia. *Behaviour Research and Therapy, 33*, 465–469.

Szasz, T. (1961). *The myth of mental illness: Foundations of a theory of personal conduct.* New York: Hoeber-Harper.

Szatmari, P. (2000). The classification of autism, Asperger's syndrome, and pervasive developmental disorder. *Canadian Journal of Psychiatry, 45,* 731–738.

Szatmari, P. (2003). The causes of autism spectrum disorders. *BMJ: British Medical Journal, 326*(7382), 173–174.

Szatmari, P., Offord, D. R., Siegel, L. S., Finlayson, M. A. J., & Tuff, L. (1990). The clinical significance of neurocognitive impairments among children with psychiatric disorders: Diagnosis and situational specificity. *Journal of Child Psychology, Psychiatry and Allied Disciplines, 31,* 287–299.

Szmukler, G. I., Eisler, I., Gillis, C., & Haywood, M. E. (1985). The implications of anorexia nervosa in a ballet school. *Journal of Psychiatric Research, 19,* 177–181.

Takahasi, T. (1989). Social phobia syndrome in Japan. *Comprehensive Psychiatry, 30,* 45–52.

Takei, N., Lewis, S., Jones, P., Harvey, I., & Murray, R. M. (1996). Prenatal exposure to influenza and increased cerebrospinal fluid spaces in schizophrenia. *Schizophrenia Bulletin, 22,* 521–534.

Talbott, J. A. (1990). Current perspectives in the United States on the chronically mentally ill. In A. Kales, C. N. Stefanis, & J. A. Talbott (Eds.), *Recent advances in schizophrenia* (pp. 279–295). New York: Springer-Verlag.

Tan, E. S. (1980). Transcultural aspects of anxiety. In G. D. Burrows & B. Davies (Eds.), *Handbook of studies on anxiety.* Amsterdam: Elsevier/North-Holland.

Tang, M. X., Jacobs, D., Stern, Y., Marder, K., Schofield, P., Gurland, B., et al. (1996). Effects of estrogen during menopause on risk and age at onset of Alzheimer's disease. *Lancet, 348,* 429–432.

Tanzi, R. E., & Parson, A. B. (2000). *Decoding darkness: The search for the genetic causes of Alzheimer's disease.* Cambridge, MA: Perseus Publishing.

*Tarasoff v. Regents of University of California.* ("Tarasoff I"), 529 P.2d 553 (Cal. Sup. Ct. 1974); ("Tarasoff II"), 551 P.2d 334 (Cal. Sup. Ct. 1976).

Tarrier, N., Kinney, C., McCarthy, E., Humphreys, L., Wittkowski, A., & Morris, J. (2000). Two-year follow-up of cognitive behavioural therapy and supportive counseling in the treatment of persistent symptoms in chronic schizophrenia. *Journal of Consulting and Clinical Psychology 68*(5), 912–922.

Tarrier, N., Wittkowski, A., Kinney, C. McCarthy, E., Morris, J., & Humphreys, L., (1999). Durability of the effects of cognitive-behavioural therapy in the treatment of chronic schizophrenia: 12-month follow-up. *British Journal of Psychiatry, 174,* 500–504.

Tattan, T., & Tarrier, N. (2000). The expressed emotion of case managers of the seriously mentally ill: The influence of expressed emotion on clinical outcomes. *Psychological Medicine, 30,* 195–204.

Tauscher, J., Kapur, S., Verhoeff, P. L. G., Hussey, D. F., Daskalakis, Z. J., Tauscher-Wisniewski, S., et al. (2002). Brain serotonin 5-HT-sub(1A) receptor binding in schizophrenia measured by positron emission tomography and [-super(11)C]WAY-100635. *Archives of General Psychiatry, 59,* 514–520.

Taylor, C. B., Sheikh, J., Agras, W. S., Roth, W. T., Margraf, J., Ehlers, A., et al. (1986). Self-report of panic attacks: Agreement with heart rate changes. *American Journal of Psychiatry, 143,* 478–482.

Taylor, G. M., & Ste-Marie, D. M. (2001). Eating disorders symptoms in Canadian female pair and dance figure skaters. *International Journal of Sport Psychology, 32,* 21–28.

Taylor, L., & Ingram, R. E. (1999). Cognitive reactivity and depressotypic information processing in children of depressed mothers. *Journal of Abnormal Psychology, 108,* 202–210.

Taylor, M. A., & Abrams, R. (1981). Early and late-onset bipolar illness. *Archives of General Psychiatry, 38*(1), 58–61.

Taylor, S. (1994). Comment on Otto et al. (1992): Hypochondriacal concerns, anxiety sensitivity, and panic disorder. *Journal of Anxiety Disorders, 8,* 97–99.

Taylor, S. (1995). Panic disorder and hypochondriacal concerns: Reply to Otto and Pollack (1994). *Journal of Anxiety Disorders, 9,* 87–88.

Taylor, S. (1996). Meta-analysis of cognitive behavioral treatment for social phobia. *Journal of Behavior Therapy and Experimental Psychiatry, 27,* 1–9.

Taylor, S. (Ed.) (1999*). Anxiety sensitivity: Theory, research, and treatment of the fear of anxiety*. Mahwah, NJ: Lawrence Erlbaum.

Taylor, S. (2001). Breathing retraining in the treatment of panic disorder: Efficacy, caveats and indications. *Scandinavian Journal of Behaviour Therapy, 30*(2), 49–56.

Taylor, S., Asmundson, G. J. G., & Coons, M. J. (2005). *Current directions in the treatment of hypochondriasis. Journal of Cognitive Psychotherapy, 19,* 285–304.

Taylor, S., & Koch, W. J. (1995). Anxiety disorders due to motor vehicle accidents: Nature and treatment. *Clinical Psychology Review, 15,* 721–738.

Taylor, S., Koch, W. J., & McNally, R. J. (1992). How does anxiety sensitivity vary across the anxiety disorders? *Journal of Anxiety Disorders, 6,* 249–259.

Taylor, S., Thordarson, D. S., Maxfield, L., Fedoroff, I. C., Lovell, K., & Ogrdniczuk, J. (2003). Comparative efficacy, speed, and adverse effects of three PTSD treatments: Exposure therapy, EMDR, and relaxation training. *Journal of Consulting and Clinical Psychology, 71,* 330–338.

Taylor, S. E. (1999). *Health psychology* (4th ed.). Boston: McGraw-Hill.

Taylor, S. E. (2002). *The tending instinct: How nurturing is essential to who we are and how we live.* New York: Henry Holt and Company.

Taylor, S. E., Klein, L. C., Lewis, B. P., Gruenewald, T. L., Gurung, R. A. R., & Updegraff, J. A. (2000). Biobehavioral responses to stress in females: Tend-and-befriend, not fight-or-flight. *Psychological Review, 107,* 411–429.

Taylor, S. E., Repetti, R. L., & Seeman, T. (1997). Health psychology: What is an unhealthy environment and how does it get under the skin? *Annual Review of Psychology, 48,* 411–447.

Teasdale, J. D. (1993). Emotion and two kinds of meaning: Cognitive therapy and applied cognitive science. *Behaviour Research and Therapy, 31*(4), 339–354.

Teasdale, J. D., Segal, Z. V., Williams, J. M., Ridgeway, V. A., Soulsby, J. M., & Lau, M. A. (2000). Prevention of relapse/recurrence in major depression by mindfulness-based cognitive therapy. *Journal of Consulting and Clinical Psychology, 4,* 615–623.

Teicher, M. H., Glod, C., & Cole, J. O. (1990). Emergence of intense suicidal preoccupation during fluoxetine treatment. *American Journal of Psychiatry, 147*(1), 207–210.

Telch, C. F., & Agras, W. S. (1993). The effects of a very low calorie diet on binge eating. *Behavior Therapy, 24,* 177–193.

Telch, C. F., Agras, W. S., & Rossiter, E. M. (1988). Binge eating increases with increasing adiposity. *International Journal of Eating Disorders, 7,* 115–119.

Telch, M. J. (1988). Combined pharmacologic and psychological treatments for panic sufferers. In S. Rachman & J. D. Maser (Eds.), *Panic: Psychological perspectives.* Hillsdale, NJ: Erlbaum.

Telch, M. J., Lucas, J. A., & Nelson, P. (1989). Nonclinical panic in college students: An investigation of prevalence and symptomatology. *Journal of Abnormal Psychology, 98,* 300–306.

Telch, M. J., Tearnan, B. H., & Taylor, C. B. (1983). Antidepressant medication in the treatment of agoraphobia. A critical review. *Behaviour Research and Therapy, 21,* 505–527.

Tellegen, A. (1978). *Manual for the Multidimensional Personality Questionnaire.* Unpublished manuscript, University of Minnesota, Minneapolis.

Tellegen, A. (1985). Structures of mood and personality and their relevance to assessing anxiety, with an emphasis on self-report. In A. H. Tuma & J. D. Maser (Eds.), *Anxiety and the anxiety disorders* (pp. 681–706). Hillsdale, NJ: Erlbaum.

Teplin, L. A. (1985). The criminality of the mentally ill: A dangerous misconception. *American Journal of Psychiatry, 142,* 593–599.

Teri, L., Gibbons, L. E., McCurry, S. M., Logsdon, R. G., Buchner, D. M., Barlow, W. E., et al. (2003). Exercise plus behavioral management in patients with Alzheimer's disease: A randomized controlled trial. *Journal of the American Medical Association, 290,* 2015–2022.

Terman, M., & Terman, J. S. (2000). Light therapy. In M. H. Kryger, T. Roth, & W. C. Dement (Eds.), *Principles and practice of sleep medicine* (3rd ed., pp. 1258–1274). Philadelphia: W. B. Saunders.

Terman, J. S., Terman, M., Lo, E., & Cooper, T. B. (2001). Circadian time of morning light administration and therapeutic response in winter depression. *Archives of General Psychiatry, 58,* 69–75.

Thaker, G. K., & Avila, M. (2003). Schizophrenia, V: Risk markers. *American Journal of Psychiatry, 160,* 1578.

Thase, M. E. (1990). Relapse and recurrence in unipolar major depression: Shortterm and long-term approaches. *Journal of Clinical Psychiatry, 51*(6, Suppl.), 51–57.

Thase, M. E., & Kupfer, D. J. (1996). Recent developments in the pharmacotherapy of mood disorders. *Journal of Consulting and Clinical Psychology, 64,* 646–659.

Theander, S. (1985). Outcome and prognosis in anorexia nervosa and bulimia: Some results of previous investigations, compared with those of the Swedish long-term study. *Journal of Psychiatric Research, 19,* 493–508.

Thompson, J. K., & Kinder, B. (2003). Eating disorders. In M. Hersen & S. Turner (Eds.), *Handbook of adult psychopathology* (4th ed., pp. 555–582). New York: Plenum.

Thompson, J. K., & Stice, E. (2001). Thin-idea internalization: Mounting evidence for a new risk factor for body-image disturbance and eating pathology. *Current Directions in Psychological Science, 11,* 181–183.

Thompson-Brenner, H., Glass, S., & Westen, D. (2003). A multidimensional meta-analysis of psychotherapy for bulimia nervosa. *Clinical Psychology: Science and Practice, 10,* 269–287.

Thoresen, C. E., & Powell, L. H. (1992). Type A behavior pattern: New perspectives on theory, assessment and intervention. Special issue: Behavioral medicine: An update for the 1990s. *Journal of Consulting and Clinical Psychology, 60*(4), 595–604.

Thorpe, G. L., & Burns, L. E. (1983). *The agoraphobic syndrome.* New York: John Wiley.

Thorpy, M., & Glovinsky, P. (1987). Parasomnias. *Psychiatric Clinics of North America, 10,* 623–639.

Tienari, P. (1991). Interaction between genetic vulnerability and family environment: The Finnish adoptive family study of schizophrenia. *Acta Psychiatrica Scandinavica, 84,* 460–465.

Tienari, P., Wynne, L. C., Laksy, K., Moring, J., Nieminen, P., Sorri, A., et al. (2003). Genetic boundaries of the schizophrenia spectrum: Evidence from the Finnish Adoptive Family Study of Schizophrenia. *American Journal of Psychiatry, 160,* 1567–1594.

Tienari, P., Wynne, L. C., Moring, J., Lahti, I., Naarala, M., Sorri, A., et al. (1994). The Finnish adoptive family study of schizophrenia: Implications for family research. *British Journal of Psychiatry, 23* (Suppl. 164), 20–26.

Tierney, M. C., Snow, W. G., Szalai, J. P., Fisher, R. H., & Zorzitto, M. L. (1996). A brief neuropsychological battery for the differential diagnosis of probable Alzheimer's disease. *Clinical Neuropsychologist, 10,* 96–103.

Tiffany, S. T. (1999). Cognitive concepts of craving. *Alcohol Research and Health, 23*(3), 215–224.

Tiffany, S. T., Cox, L. S., & Elash, C. A. (2000). Effects of transdermal nicotine patches on abstinence-induced and cue-elicited craving in cigarette smokers. *Journal of Consulting and Clinical Psychology, 68*(2), 233–240.

Tiggemann, M. (2002). Media influences on body image development. In T. F. Cash & T. Pruzinsky (Eds.), *Body image: A handbook of theory, research and clinical practice* (pp. 91–98). New York: Guilford Press.

Tingelstad, J. B. (1991). The cardiotoxicity of the tricyclics. *Journal of the American Academy of Child and Adolescent Psychiatry, 30,* 845–846.

Tjio, J. H., & Levan, A. (1956). The chromosome number of man. *Hereditas, 42,* 1–6.

Tobin, D. L., Griffing, A., & Griffing, S. (1997). An examination of subtype criteria for bulimia nervosa. *International Journal of Eating Disorders, 22,* 179–186.

Tollefson, G. D. (1993). Major depression. In D. L. Dunner (Ed.), *Current psychiatric therapy.* Philadelphia: W. B. Saunders.

Tomac, A., Lindqvist, E., Lin, L. F. H., Ögren, S. O., Young, D., Hoffer, B. J., et al. (1995). Protection and repair of the nigrostriatal dopaminergic system by GDNF in vivo. *Nature, 373,* 335–339.

Tondo, L., Jamison, K. R., & Baldessarini, R. J. (1997). Effect of lithium maintenance on suicidal behavior in major mood disorders. In D. M. Stoff & J. J. Mann (Eds.), *The neurobiology of suicide: From the bench to the clinic* (Vol. 836, pp. 339–351). New York: Academy of Sciences.

Torgersen, S. (1986). Genetics of somatoform disorder. *Archives of General Psychiatry, 43,* 502–505.

Torgersen, S., Onstad, S., Skre, I., Edvardsen, J., & Kringlen, E. (1993). "True" schizotypal personality disorder: A study of co-twins and relatives of schizophrenic probands. *American Journal of Psychiatry, 150,* 1661–1667.

Torrey, E. F. (1988a). *Nowhere to go: The tragic odyssey of the homeless mentally ill.* New York: Harper & Row.

Torrey, E. F. (1988b). Stalking the schizovirus. *Schizophrenia Bulletin, 14,* 223–229.

Torrey, E. F., Bowler, A. E., Taylor, E. H., & Gottesman, I. I. (1994). *Schizophrenia and manic-depressive disorder: The biological roots of mental illness as revealed by the landmark study of identical twins.* New York: Basic Books.

Torrey, E. F., Rawlings, R., & Waldman, I. (1988). Schizophrenic births and viral diseases in two states. *Schizophrenia Research, 1,* 73–77.

Trebbe, A. (1979, September 15). Ideal is body beautiful and clean cut. *USA Today,* 1–2.

Trimbell, M. R. (1981). *Neuropsychiatry.* Chichester, UK: John Wiley.

Trudel, G., Marchand, A., Ravart, M., Aubin, S., Turgeon, L., & Fortier, P. (2001). The effect of a cognitive-behavioral group treatment program on hypoactive sexual desire in women. *Sexual and Relationship Therapy, 16,* 145–164.

True, W. R., Rice, J., Eisen, S. A., Heath, A. C., Goldberg, J., Lyons, M. J., et al. (1993). A twin study of genetic and environmental contributions to liability for posttraumatic stress symptoms. *Archives of General Psychiatry, 50,* 257–264.

Tsai, L. Y., & Ghaziuddin, M. (1992). Biomedical research in autism. In D. E. Berkell (Ed.), *Autism: Identification, education, and treatment* (pp. 53–74). Hillsdale, NJ: Erlbaum.

Tsuang, M. T., Stone, W. S., & Faraone, S. V. (2002). Understanding predisposition to schizophrenia: Toward intervention and prevention. *Canadian Journal of Psychiatry, 47,* 518–526.

Tuchman, B. (1978). *A distant mirror.* New York: Ballantine Books.

Tucker, G. J., Ferrell, R. B., & Price, T. R. P. (1984). The hospital treatment of schizophrenia. In A. S. Bellack (Ed.), *Schizophrenia: Treatment, management, and rehabilitation* (pp. 175–191). New York: Grune & Stratton.

Tulsky, D. S., Zhu, J., & Prifitera, A. (2000). Assessment of adult intelligence with the WAIS-III. In G. Goldstein & M. Hersen (Eds.), *Handbook of psychological assessment* (pp. 97–129). New York: Pergamon Press.

Tuokko, H., Hadjistavropoulos, T., Rae, S., & O'Rourke, N. (2000). A comparison of alternative approaches to the scoring of clock drawing. *Archives of Clinical Neuropsychology, 15,* 137–148.

Turk, C. L, Heimberg, R. G., & Hope, D. A. (2001). Social phobia and social anxiety. In D. H. Barlow (Ed.), *Clinical handbook of psychological disorders: A step-by-step treatment manual* (3rd ed., pp. 99–136). New York: Guilford Press.

Turk, D. C. (2002). A cognitive-behavioral perspective on treatment of chronic pain patients. In D. C. Turk & R. J. Gatchel (Eds.), *Psychological approaches to pain management: A practitioner's handbook* (2nd ed.). New York: Guilford Press.

Turk, D. C., & Gatchel, R. J. (2002). *Psychological approaches to pain management: A practitioner's handbook* (2nd ed.). New York: Guilford Press.

Turk, D. C., Meichenbaum, D., & Genest, M. (1983). *Pain and behavioral medicine: A cognitive-behavioral perspective.* New York: Guilford Press.

Turk, D. C., & Monarch, E. S. (2002). Biopsychosocial perspective on chronic pain. In D. C. Turk & R. J. Gatchel (Eds.), *Psychological approaches to pain management: A practitioner's handbook* (2nd ed.). New York: Guilford Press.

Turkat, I. D., & Maisto, S. A. (1985). Personality disorders: Applications of the experimental method to the formulation and modification of personality disorders. In D. H. Barlow (Ed.), *Clinical handbook of psychological disorders.* New York: Guilford Press.

Turkel, S. B., & Tavaré, C. J. (2003). Delirium in children and adolescents. *Journal of Neuropsychiatry and Clinical Neuroscience, 15,* 431–435.

Turkheimer, E. (1998). Heritability and biological explanation. *Psychological Review, 105,* 782–791.

Turkheimer, E., & Parry, C. D. H. (1992). Why the gap? Practice and policy in civil commitment hearings. *American Psychologist, 47,* 646–655.

Turkheimer, E., & Waldron, M. C. (2000). Nonshared environment: A theoretical, methodological, and quantitative review. *Psychological Bulletin, 126,* 78–108.

Turkington, C. (1994, January). Wexler wins Lasker award for her work on Huntington's. *APA Monitor,* pp. 20–21.

Turner, S. M., Beidel, D. C., & Jacob, R. G. (1994). Social phobia: A comparison of behavior therapy and atenolol. *Journal of Consulting Psychology, 62,* 350–358.

Turovsky, J., & Barlow, D. H. (1996). Generalized anxiety disorder. In

J. Margraf (Ed.), *Textbook of behavior therapy* (pp. 87–106). Berlin: Springer-Verlag.

Tyler, D. B. (1955). Psychological changes during experimental sleep deprivation. *Diseases of the Nervous System, 16,* 293–299.

Tyler, J. (2003). *New clinical guidelines for blood pressure released.* Retrieved July 8, 2004, from Baylor College of Medicine Web site: http://www.bcmfindings.net /vol1/is6/03june_n2.htm.

Tynes, L. L., White, K., & Steketee, G. S. (1990). Toward a new nosology of obsessive-compulsive disorder. *Comprehensive Psychiatry, 31,* 465–480.

Tyrer, P., & Davidson, K. (2000). Cognitive therapy for personality disorders. In J. G. Gunderson & G. O. Gabbard (Eds.), *Psychotherapy for personality disorders* (pp. 131–149). Washington, DC: American Psychiatric Press.

Uchino, B. N., Cacioppo, J. T., & Kiecolt-Glaser, J. K. (1996). The relationship between social support and physiological processes: A review with emphasis on underlying mechanisms and implications for health. *Psychological Bulletin, 119*(3), 488–531.

Uchino, B. N., Uno, D., & Holt-Lunstad, J. (1999). Social support, physiological processes, and health. *Current Directions in Psychological Science, 8,* 145–148.

Uddo, M., Malow, R., & Sutker, P. B. (1993). Opioid and cocaine abuse and dependence disorders. In P. B. Sutker & H. E. Adams (Eds.), *Comprehensive handbook of psychopathology* (pp. 477–503). New York: Plenum Press.

Uhde, T. (1994). The anxiety disorders: Phenomenology and treatment of core symptoms and associated sleep disturbance. In M. Kryger, T. Roth, & W. Dement (Eds.), *Principles and practice of sleep medicine* (pp. 871–898). Philadelphia: Saunders.

Umbricht, D., & Kane, J. M. (1996). Medical complications of new antipsychotic drugs. *Schizophrenia Bulletin, 22,* 475–483.

Unger, J. B., Yan, L., Shakib, S., Rohrbach, L. A., Chen, X., Qian, G., et al. (2002). Peer influences and access to cigarettes as correlates of adolescent smoking: A cross-cultural comparison of Wuhan, China, and California. *Preventive Medicine, 34*(4), 476–484.

Urbszat, C., Herman, C. P., & Polivy, J. (2002). Eat, drink, and be merry, for tomorrow we diet: Effects of anticipated deprivation on food intake in restrained and unrestrained eaters. *Journal of Abnormal Psychology, 11,* 396–401.

Vaillant, G. E. (1979). Natural history of male psychological health. *New England Journal of Medicine, 301,* 1249–1254.

Vaillant, G. E. (1983). *The natural history of alcoholism.* Cambridge, MA: Harvard University Press.

Vaillant, G. E., Bond, M., & Vaillant, C. D. (1986). An empirically validated hierarchy of defense mechanisms. *Archives of General Psychiatry, 43,* 786–794.

Vaillant, G. E., & Hiller-Sturmhöfel, S. (1997). The natural history of alcoholism. *Alcohol Health and Research, 20,* 152–161.

Vallee, B. (1986). *Life with Billy.* Toronto: McClelland & Stewart.

Vallee, B. L. (1998). Alcohol in the western world. *Scientific American, 278*(6), 80–85.

Vallis, T. M., Howes, J. L., & Standage, K. (2000). Is cognitive therapy suitable for treating individuals with personality dysfunction? *Cognitive Therapy and Research, 24,* 595–606.

Vallis, T. M., Ruggiero, L., Greene, G., Jones, H., Zinman, B., Rossi, S., et al. (2003). Stages of change for healthy eating in diabetes: Relation to demographic, eating-related, health care utilization, and psychosocial factors. *Diabetes Care, 26,* 1468–1474.

Van Acker, R. (1991). Rett syndrome: A review of current knowledge. *Journal of Autism and Developmental Disorders, 21,* 381–406.

Van Dongen, H. P. A., Maislin, G., Mullington, J., & Dinges, D. F. (2003). The cumulative cost of additional wakefulness: Dose-response effects on neuro-behavioral functions and sleep physiology from chronic sleep restriction and total sleep deprivation. *Sleep, 26,* 117–126.

van Kammen, D. P., Docherty, J. P., & Bunney, W. E. (1982). Prediction of early relapse after pimozide discontinuation by response to d-amphetamine during pimozide treatment. *Biological Psychiatry, 17,* 223–242.

Van Laar, M., Volkerts, E., & Verbaten, M. (2001). Subcronic effects of the GABA-agonist lorazepam and the 5- HT2A/2C antagonist ritanserin on driving performance, slow wave sleep and daytime sleepiness in healthy volunteers. *Psychopharmacology (Berlin), 154,* 189–197.

Van Praag, H. M., & Korf, J. (1975). Central monamine deficiency in depressions: Causative of secondary phenomenon? *Pharmakopsychiatr Neuropsychopharmakol, 8,* 322–326.

Vandenberg, S. G., Singer, S. M., & Pauls, D. L. (1986). *The heredity of behavior disorders in adults and children.* New York: Plenum Press.

Vander Plate, C., Aral, S. O., & Magder, L. (1988). The relationship among genital herpes simplex virus, stress, and social support. *Health Psychology, 7,* 159–168.

Vanderwal, J. S., & Thelen, M. H. (2000). Predictors of body image dissatisfaction in elementary-age school girls. *Eating Behaviors, 1,* 105–122.

VanKammen, W. B., Loeber, R., & Stouthamer-Loeber, M. (1991). Substance use and its relationship to conduct problems and delinquency in young boys. *Journal of Youth and Adolescence, 20,* 399–413.

Vasterling, J. J., Brailey, K., Constans, J. I., & Sotker, P. B. (1998). Attention and memory dysfunction in posttraumatic stress disorders. *Neuropsychology, 12*(1), 125–133.

Veale, D. (2000). Outcome of cosmetic surgery and "DIY" surgery inpatients with body dysmorphic disorder. *Psychiatric Bulletin, 24*(6), 218–221.

Veale, D., Boocock, A., Gournay, K., Dryden, W., Shah, F., Willson, R., et al. (1996). Body dysmorphic disorder: A survey of 50 cases. *British Journal of Psychiatry, 169,* 196–201.

Veale, D., & Riley, S. (2001). Mirror, mirror on the wall, who is the ugliest of them all? The psychopathology of mirror gazing in body dysmorphic disorder. *Behaviour Research and Therapy, 39,* 1381–1393.

Venables, P. H. (1996). Schizotypy and maternal exposure to influenza and to cold temperature: The Mauritius study. *Journal of Abnormal Psychology, 105,* 53–60.

Ventura, J., Nuechterlein, K. H., Hardesty, J. P., & Gitlin, M. (1992). Life events and schizophrenic relapse after withdrawal of medication: A prospective study. *British Journal of Psychiatry, 161,* 615–620.

Ventura, J., Nuechterlein, K. H., Lukoff, D., & Hardesty, J. P. (1989). A prospective study of stressful life events and schizophrenia relapse. *Journal of Abnormal Psychology, 98,* 407–411.

Ventura, J., Nuechterlein, K. H., Subotnik, K. L., Hardesty, J. P., & Mintz, J. (2000). Life events can trigger depressive exacerbation in the early course of schizophrenia. *Journal of Abnormal Psychology, 109*(1), 139–144.

Ventura, S. L., Peters, K. D., Martin, J. A., & Mauer, J. D. (1997). Births and deaths: United States, 1996. *Monthly Vital Statistics Report, 46* (Suppl. 2) 1–41.

Verma, K. K., Khaitan, B. K., & Singh, O. P. (1998). The frequency of sexual dysfunction in patients attending a sex therapy clinic in North India. *Archives of Sexual Behavior, 27,* 309–314.

Vernberg, E. M., La Greca, A. M., Silverman, W. K., & Prinstein, M. J. (1996). Prediction of posttraumatic stress symptoms in children after Hurricane Andrew. *Journal of Abnormal Psychology, 105,* 237–248.

Verrier, R. L., Harper, R. M., & Hobson, J. A. (2000). Cardiovascular physiology: Central and autonomic regulation. In M. H. Kryger, T. Roth, & W. C. Dement (Eds.), *Principles and practice of sleep medicine* (3rd ed., pp. 179–191). Philadelphia: W. B. Saunders.

Viens, M., De Koninck, J., Mercier, P., St-Onge, M., & Lorrain, D. (2003). Trait anxiety and sleep-onset insomnia: Evaluation of treatment using anxiety management training. *Journal of Psychosomatic Research, 54,* 31–37.

Vinken, P. J., & Bruyn, G. W. (1972). The phakomatoses. In P. J. Vinken & G. W. Bruyn (Eds.), *Handbook of clinical neurology* (Vol. 14). New York: Elsevier.

Virag, R. (1999). Indications and early results of sildenafil (Viagra) in erectile dysfunction. *Urology, 54,* 1073–1077.

Visser, F. E., Aldenkamp, A. P., van Huffelen, A. C., Kuilman, M., Overweg, J., & van Wijk, J. (1997). Prospective study of the prevalence of Alzheimer-type dementia in institutionalized individuals with Down syndrome. *American Journal on Mental Retardation, 101,* 400–412.

Vitiello, B., & Lederhendler, I. (2000). Research on eating disorders: Current status and future prospects. *Biological Psychiatry, 47,* 777–786.

Vitousek, K., Watson, S., & Wilson, G. T. (1998). Enhancing motivation for change in treatment-resistant eating disorders. *Clinical Psychological Review, 18,* 391–420.

Voglmaier, M. M., Seidman, L. J., Niznikiewicz, M. A., Dickey, C. C., Shenton, M. E., & McCarley, R. W. (2000). Verbal and nonverbal neuropsychological test performance in subjects with schizotypal personality disorder. *American Journal of Psychiatry, 157*, 787–793.

Vohs, K. D., Bardone, A. M., Joiner, T. E., Jr., Abramson, L. Y., & Heatherton, T. F. (1999). Perfectionism, perceived weight status, and self-esteem interact to predict bulimic symptoms: A model of bulimic symptom development. *Journal of Abnormal Psychology, 108*, 695–700.

Volkmar, F. R., & Cohen, D. J. (1991). Nonautistic pervasive developmental disorders. In R. Michels (Ed.), *Psychiatry* (pp. 201–210). Philadelphia: J. B. Lippincott.

Volkmar, F. R., & Klin, A. (2000). Diagnostic issues in Asperger syndrome. In A. Klin, F. R. Volkmar, & S. S. Sparrow (Eds.), *Asperger syndrome* (pp. 25–71). New York: Guilford Press.

Volkmar, F. R., Klin, A., Siegel, B., Szatmari, P., Lord, C., Campbell, M., et al. (1994). Field trial for autistic disorder in DSM-IV. *American Journal of Psychiatry, 151*, 1361–1367.

Volkmar, F. R., Szatmari, P., & Sparrow, S. S. (1993). Sex differences in pervasive developmental disorders. *Journal of Autism and Developmental Disorders, 23*, 579–591.

Volkow, N. D., & Swanson, J. M. (2003). Variables that affect the clinical use and abuse of methylphenidate in the treatment of ADHD. *American Journal of Psychiatry, 160*, 1909–1918.

von Ranson, K. M., Iacono, W. G., & McGue, M. (2002). Disordered eating and substance use in an epidemiological sample: I. Associations within individuals. *International Journal of Eating Disorders, 31*, 389–403.

Vuchinich, S., Bank, L., & Patterson, G. R. (1992). Parenting, peers, and the stability of antisocial behavior in preadolescent boys. *Developmental Psychology, 28*, 510–521.

Wade, T. D., Bulik, C. M., Neale, M., & Kendler, K. S. (2000). Anorexia nervosa and major depression: Shared genetic and environmental risk factors. *American Journal of Psychiatry. 157*, 469–471.

Wadsworth, S. J., DeFries, J. C., Stevenson, J., Gilger, J. W., & Pennington, B. F. (1992). Gender ratios among reading-disabled children and their siblings as a function of parent impairment. *Journal of Child Psychology and Psychiatry, 33*, 1229–1239.

Wagner, A. W., & Linehan, M. M. (1994). Relationship between childhood sexual abuse and topography of parasuicide among women with borderline personality disorder. *Journal of Personality Disorders, 8*, 1–9.

Wagner, B. M. (1997). Family risk factors for child and adolescent suicidal behavior. *Psychological Bulletin, 121*, 246–298.

Wagner, M. (1990, April). *The school programs and school performance of secondary students classified as learning disabled: Findings from the National Longitudinal Transition Study of special education students.* Paper presented at Division G, American Educational Research Association Annual Meeting, Boston.

Wahlbeck, K., Cheine, M., Essali, A., & Adams, C. (1999). Evidence of clozapine's effectiveness in schizophrenia: A systematic review and meta-analysis of randomized trials. *American Journal of Psychiatry, 156*, 990–999.

Wakefield, J. C. (1992). The concept of mental disorder: On the boundary between biological facts and social values. *American Psychologist, 47*, 373–388.

Wakefield, J. C. (1999). Evolutionary versus prototype analyses of the concept of disorder. *Journal of Abnormal Psychology, 108,*(3) 374–399.

Wakefield, J. C. (2003). Dysfunction as a factual component of disorder. *Behavior Research and Therapy, 41*, 969–990.

Wald, J. (2004). Efficacy of virtual reality exposure therapy for driving phobia: A multiple baseline across-subjects design. *Behavior Therapy, 35*, 621–635.

Wald, J., Taylor, S., & Scamvougeras, A. (2004). Cognitive-behavioural and neuropsychiatric treatment of post-traumatic conversion disorder: A case study. *Cognitive Behaviour Therapy, 33*(1), 12–20.

Waliszewski, B., & Smithouser, B. (1997). Plugged in music review—Sarah McLachlan [Review of the album *Surfacing*]. Retrieved June 25, 2004, from http://www.pluggedinonline.com/music/music/a0001196.cfm.

Walker, E. (1991). Research on life-span development in schizophrenia. In E. F. Walker (Ed.), *Schizophrenia: A life-course developmental perspective* (pp. 1–6). New York: Academic Press.

Walker, E. F., Grimes, K. E., Davis, D. M., & Smith, A. J. (1993). Childhood precursors of schizophrenia: Facial expressions of emotion. *American Journal of Psychiatry, 150*, 1654–1660.

Walker, L. (1979). *The battered woman.* New York: Harper & Row.

Wallace, C. S., Kilman, V. L., Withers, G. S., & Greenough, W. T. (1992). Increases in dendritic length in occipital cortex after 4 days of differential housing in weanling rats. *Behavioral and Neural Biology, 58*, 64–68.

Wallace, J., & O'Hara, M. W. (1992). Increases in depressive symptomatology in the rural elderly: Results from a cross-sectional and longitudinal study. *Journal of Abnormal Psychology, 101*(3), 398–404.

Waller, N. G., Putnam, F. W., & Carlson, E. B. (1996). Types of dissociation and dissociative types: A taxometric analysis of dissociative experiences. *Psychological Methods, 1*, 300–321.

Waller, N. G., & Ross, C. A. (1997). The prevalence and biometric structure of pathological dissociation in the general population: Taxometric and behavior genetic findings. *Journal of Abnormal Psychology, 106*, 499–510.

Walsh, B. T. (1991). Fluoxetine treatment of bulimia nervosa. *Journal of Psychosomatic Research, 35*, 471–475.

Walsh, B. T. (1995). Pharmacotherapy of eating disorders. In K. D. Brownell & C. G. Fairburn (Eds.), *Eating disorders and obesity: A comprehensive handbook* (pp. 313–317). New York: Guilford Press.

Walsh, B. T., Agras, W. S., Devlin, M. J., Fairburn, C. G., Wilson, G. T., Kahn, C., et al. (2000). Fluoxetine for bulimia nervosa following poor response to psychotherapy. *American Journal of Psychiatry, 157*, 1332–1334.

Walsh, B. T., Hadigan, C. M., Devlin, M. J., Gladis, M., & Roose, S. P. (1991). Long-term outcome of antidepressant treatment of bulimia nervosa. *Archives of General Psychiatry, 148*, 1206–1212.

Walsh, B. T., Wilson G. T., Loeb, K. L., Devlin, M. J., Pike, K. M., Roose, S. P., et al. (1997). Medication and psychotherapy in the treatment of bulimia nervosa. *American Journal of Psychiatry, 154*, 523–531.

Walsh, J., & Ustun, T. B. (1999). Prevalence and health consequences of insomnia. *Sleep, 22* (Suppl. 3), S427–S436.

Walsh, N. P. (2001, October 14). "I never discuss my mistresses or my tailors." *The Observer*. Retrieved October 25, 2003, from http://observer.guardian.co.uk/life/story/0,6903,573496,00.html.

Walters, E. E., & Kendler, K. S. (1995). Anorexia nervosa and anorexia-like syndromes in a population based female twin sample. *American Journal of Psychiatry, 152*, 64–71.

Wang, J., & Patten, S. B. (2001). Perceived work stress and major depression in the Canadian employed population, 20–49 years old. *Journal of Occupational Health Psychology, 6*, 283–289.

Wang, J., & Patten, S. B. (2002). Prospective study of frequent heavy alcohol use and the risk of major depression in the Canadian general population. *Depression and Anxiety, 15*, 42–45.

Wang, P. S., Bohn, R. L., Glynn, R. J., Mogun, H., & Avorn, J. (2001). Hazardous benzodiazepine regimens in the elderly: Effects of half-life, dosage, and duration on risk of hip fracture. *American Journal of Psychiatry, 158*, 892–898.

Ward, M. M., Swan, G. E., & Chesney, M. A. (1987). Arousal-reduction treatments for mild hypertension: A meta-analysis of recent studies. *Handbook of Hypertension, 9*, 285–302.

Wardman, D., el-Guebaly, N., & Hodgins, D. (2001). Problem and pathological gambling in North American Aboriginal populations: A review of the empirical literature. *Journal of Gambling Studies, 17*, 81–100.

Warneke, L. B. (1991). Benzodiazepines: Abuse and new use. *Canadian Journal of Psychiatry, 36*, 194–205.

Warren, S. F., & Reichle, J. (1992). *Causes and effects in communication and language intervention.* Baltimore: Paul H. Brookes.

Warwick, H. M. C., Clark, D. M., Cobb, A. M., & Salkovskis, P. M. (1996). A controlled trail of cognitive-behavioural treatment of hypochondriasis. *British Journal of Psychiatry, 169*, 189–195.

Warwick, H. M., & Salkovskis, P. M. (1990). Hypochondriasis. *Behavior Research Therapy, 28*, 105–117.

Waschbusch, D. A., & Hill, G. P. (2001). Alternative treatments for children with attention-deficit/hyperactivity disorder: What does the research say? *Behavior Therapist, 24*(8), 161–171

Waschbusch, D. A., & Hill, G. P. (2003). Empirically supported, promising, and unsupported treatments for children with attention-deficit/hyperactivity disorder. In S. O. Lilienfeld & S. J. Lynn (Eds.), *Science and pseudoscience in clinical psychology* (pp. 333–362). New York: Guilford Press.

Waschbusch, D. A., Kipp, H. L., & Pelham, W. E. Jr. (1998). Generalization of behavioral and psychostimulant treatment of attention-deficit/hyperactivity disorder (ADHD): Discussion and examples. *Behaviour Research and Therapy, 36*, 675–694.

Waterhouse, L., Wing, L., & Fein, D. (1989). Re-evaluating the syndrome of autism in light of empirical research. In G. Dawson (Ed.), *Autism: Nature, diagnosis and treatment* (pp. 263–281). New York: Guilford Press.

Waters, B. G. H. (1979). Early symptoms of bipolar affective psychosis: Research and clinical implications. *Canadian Psychiatric Association Journal, 2*, 55–60.

Watson, D., Clark, L. A., & Harkness, A. R. (1994). Structures of personality and their relevance to psychopathology. *Journal of Abnormal Psychology, 103*, 18–31.

Watson, J. B. (1913). Psychology as a behaviorist views it. *Psychology Review, 20*, 158–177.

Watt, M. C., & Stewart, S. H. (2000). Anxiety sensitivity mediates the relationships between childhood learning experiences and elevated hypochondriacal concerns in young adulthood. *Journal of Psychosomatic Research, 49*, 107–118.

Watt, M. C., & Stewart, S. H. (2003). The role of anxiety sensitivity components in mediating the relationship between childhood exposure to parental dyscontrol and adult anxiety symptoms. *Journal of Psychopathology and Behavioral Assessment, 25*, 167–176.

Watt, M. C., Stewart, S. H., & Cox, B. J. (1998). A retrospective study of the learning history origins of anxiety sensitivity. *Behaviour Research & Therapy, 36*, 505–525.

Watt, M. C., Stewart, S. H., Lefaivre, M. J., & Uman, L. (2006). A brief cognitive-behavioural approach to reducing anxiety sensitivity decreases pain-related anxiety. *Cognitive Behaviour Therapy, 35*(4), 248–256.

Webster, C. D., Douglas, K. S., Eaves, D., & Hart, S. D. (1997b). Assessing risk of violence to others. In C. D. Webster & M. A. Jackson (Eds.), *Impulsivity: Theory, assessment, and treatment* (pp. 251–277). New York: Guilford Press.

Webster-Stratton, C., & Hammond, M. (1997). Treating children with early-onset conduct problems: A comparison of child and parent training interventions. *Journal of Consulting and Clinical Psychology, 65*, 93–109.

Weems, C. F., Silverman, W. K., & La Greca, A. M. (2000). What do youths referred for anxiety problems worry about?: Worry and its relation to anxiety and anxiety disorders in children and adolescents. *Journal of Abnormal Child Psychology, 28*, 63–72.

Wegner, D. M. (1989). *White bears and other unwanted thoughts: Suppression, obsession, and the psychology of mental control.* New York: Guilford Press.

Wehr, T. A., Duncan, W. C. Jr., Sher, L., Aeschbach, D., Schwartz, P. J., Turner, E. H., et al. (2001). A circadian signal of change of season in patients with seasonal affective disorder. *Archives of General Psychiatry, 58*, 1108–1114.

Wehr, T. A., Goodwin, F. K., Wirz-Justice, A., Breitmeier, J., & Craig, C. (1982). Forty-eight-hour sleep-wake cycles in manic-depressive illness: Naturalistic observations and sleep-deprivation experiments. *Archives of General Psychiatry, 39*, 559–565.

Wehr, T. A., & Sack, D. A. (1988). The relevance of sleep research to affective illness. In W. P. Koella, F. Obal, H. Schulz, & P. Visser (Eds.), *Sleep '86* (pp. 207–211). New York: Gustav Fischer Verlag.

Wehr, T., Sack, D., Rosenthal, N. E., & Cowdry, R. W. (1988). Rapid cycling affective disorder: Contributing factors and treatment response on 51 patients. *American Journal of Psychiatry, 145*, 179–184.

Weiden, P. J., Dixon, L., Frances, A., Appelbaum, P., Haas, G., & Rapkin, B. (1991). In C. A. Tamminga & S. C. Schulz (Eds.), *Advances in neuropsychiatry and psychopharmacology. 1: Schizophrenia research* (pp. 285–296). New York: Raven Press.

Weinberg, R. A. (1989). Intelligence and IQ: Landmark issues and great debates. *American Psychologist, 44*, 98–104.

Weinberger, D. R. (1995). Schizophrenia as a neurodevelopmental disorder. In S. R. Hirsch & D. R. Weinberger (Eds.), *Schizophrenia* (pp. 293–323). Oxford, UK: Blackwell.

Weiner, D. N. (1996). *Premature ejaculation: An evaluation of sensitivity to erotica.* Unpublished doctoral dissertation, State University of New York, Albany.

Weiner, J. M. (2000). Integration of nature and nurture: A new paradigm for psychiatry. *American Journal of Psychiatry, 157*, 1193–1194.

Weiner, M. F. (2003). Clinical diagnosis of cognitive dysfunction and dementing illness. In M. F. Weiner & A. M. Lipton (Eds.), *The dementias: Diagnosis, treatment and research* (3rd ed.) (pp. 1–48). Washington, DC: American Psychiatric Press.

Weiner, M. F., & Schneider, L. S. (2003). Drugs for behavioral, psychological, and cognitive symptoms. In M. F. Weiner & A. M. Lipton (Eds.), *The dementias: Diagnosis, treatment and research* (3rd ed.) (pp. 219–283). Washington, DC: American Psychiatric Press.

Weisburg, R. B., Brown, T. A., Wincze, J. P., & Barlow, D. H. (2001). Causal attributions and male sexual arousal: The impact of attributions for a bogus erectile difficulty on sexual arousal, cognitions, and affect. *Journal of Abnormal Psychology, 110*, 324–334.

Weiskrantz, L. (1980). Varieties of residual experience. *Quarterly Journal of Experimental Psychology, 32*, 365–386.

Weiskrantz, L. (1992, September/October). Unconscious vision: The strange phenomenon of blindsight. *The Sciences,* 23–28.

Weisman, A. G. (1997). Understanding cross-cultural prognostic variability for schizophrenia. *Cultural Diversity and Mental Health, 3*(1), 23–35.

Weisman, A. G., & Lopez, S. R. (1997). An attributional analysis of emotional reactions to schizophrenia in Mexican and Anglo-Americans. *Journal of Applied Social Psychology, 27*(3), 223–244.

Weisse, C. S. (1992). Depression and immunocompetence: A review of the literature. *Psychological Bulletin, 111*(3), 475–489.

Weissman, M. (1995). *Mastering depression: A patient's guide to interpersonal psychotherapy.* Albany, NY: Graywind.

Weissman, M. M. (1993). The epidemiology of personality disorders: A 1990 update. *Journal of Personality Disorders, Supplement, Spring,* 44–62.

Weissman, M. M., Bland, R. C., Canino, G. J., Faravelli, C., Greenwald, S., Hwu, H. G., et al. (1997). The cross-national epidemiology of panic disorder. *Archives of General Psychiatry, 54*, 305–312.

Weissman, M. M., Bland, R., Canino, G., Greenwald, S., Hwo, H., Lee, C., et al. (1994). The cross national epidemiology of obsessive compulsive disorder. *Journal of Clinical Psychiatry, 55*, 5–10.

Weissman, M. M., Bland, R. C., Canino, G. J., Greenwald, S., Lee, C.-K., Newman, S. C., et al. (1996). The cross-national epidemiology of social phobia: A preliminary report. *International Clinical Psychopharmacology, 11*, 9–14.

Weissman, M. M., Bruce, M. L., Leaf, P. J., Florio, L. P., & Holzer, C. (1991). Affective disorders. In L. N. Robins & D. A. Regier (Eds.), *Psychiatric disorders of America: The epidemiologic catchment area study* (pp. 53–80). New York: Free Press.

Weissman, M. M., & Klerman, G. L. (1977). Sex differences and the epidemiology of depression. *Archives of General Psychiatry, 34*, 98–111.

Weissman, M. M., & Olfson, M. (1995). Depression in women: Implications for health care research. *Science, 269*, 799–801.

Weissman, M. M., Wolk, S., Wickramaratne, P., Goldstein, R. B., Adams, P., Greenwald, S., et al. (1999). Children with prepubertal-onset major depressive disorder and anxiety grown up. *Archives of General Psychiatry, 56*, 794–801.

Weitze, C., & Osburg, S. (1996). Transsexualism in Germany: Empirical data on epidemiology and application of the German transsexuals' act during its first ten years. *Archives of Sexual Behavior, 25*, 409–465.

*Wenden v. Trikha* (1991), 116 A.R. 81 (Q.B.).

Wender, P. H., Kety, S. S., Rosenthal, D., Schlusinger, F., Ortmann, J., & Lunde, I.

(1986). Psychiatric disorders in the biological and adoptive families of adopted individuals with affective disorders. *Archives of General Psychiatry, 43,* 923–929.

Westen, D. (1997). Divergence between clinical and research methods for assessing personality disorders: Implications for research and the evolution of Axis II. *American Journal of Psychiatry, 154,* 895–903.

Westen, D. (2000). The efficacy of dialectical behavior therapy for borderline personality disorder. *Clinical Psychology: Science and Practice, 7,* 92–94.

Westermeyer, J. (1989). *Mental health for refugees and other migrants: Social and preventive approach.* Illinois: C. C. Thomas.

Westra, H. A., & Stewart, S. H. (1998). Cognitive behavioural therapy and pharmacotherapy: Complementary or contradictory approaches to the treatment of anxiety? *Clinical Psychology Review, 18,* 307–340.

Westra, H. A., & Stewart, S. H. (2002). As-needed use of benzodiazepines in managing clinical anxiety: Incidence and implications. *Current Pharmaceutical Design, 8,* 59–74.

Wetherell, J. L., Gatz, M., & Craske, M. G. (2003). Treatment of generalized anxiety disorder in older adults. *Journal of Consulting and Clinical Psychology, 71,* 31–40.

Wetter, D. W., Smith, S. S., Kenford, S. L., Jorenby, D. E., Fiore, M. C., Hurt, R. D., et al. (1994). Smoking outcome expectancies: Factor structure, predictive validity, and discriminant validity. *Journal of Abnormal Psychology, 103,* 801–811.

Wexler, N. S., Lorimer, J., Porter, J., Gomez, F., Moskowitz, C., Shackell, E., et al. (2004). Venezuelan kindreds reveal that genetic and environmental factors modulate Huntington's disease age of onset. *Proceedings of the National Academy of Science, 101,* 3498–3503.

Whiffen, V. E. (1992). Is postpartum depression a distinct diagnosis? *Clinical Psychology Review, 12*(5), 485–508.

Whiffen, V. E., & Gotlib, I. H. (1989a). Infants of postpartum depressed mothers: Temperament and cognitive status. *Journal of Abnormal Psychology, 98,* 274–279.

Whiffen, V. E., & Gotlib, I. H. (1989b). Stress and coping in maritally distressed and nondistressed couples. *Journal of Social and Personal Relationships, 6*(3), 327–344.

Whiffen, V. E., & Gotlib, I. H. (1993). Comparison of postpartum and nonpostpartum depression: Clinical presentation, psychiatric history, and psychosocial functioning. *Journal of Consulting and Clinical Psychology, 61*(3), 485–494.

White, D. P. (2000). Central sleep apnea. In M. H. Kryger, T. Roth, & W. C. Dement (Eds.), *Principles and practice of sleep medicine* (3rd ed., pp. 827–839). Philadelphia: W. B. Saunders.

White, J. L., Moffitt, T. E., & Silva, P. A. (1989). A prospective replication of the protective effects of IQ in subjects at high risk for juvenile delinquency. *Journal of Consulting and Clinical Psychology, 57,* 719–724.

White, K. S., & Barlow, D. H. (2002). Panic disorder with agoraphobia. In D. H. Barlow, (Ed.) *Anxiety and its disorders: The nature and treatment of anxiety and panic.* (2nd ed.). New York: Guilford Press.

Whitehurst, G. J., Fischel, J. E., Lonigan, C. J., Valdez-Menchaca, M. C., DeBaryshe, B. D., & Caulfield, M. B. (1988). Verbal interaction in families of normal and expressive-language-delayed children. *Developmental Psychology, 24,* 690–699.

Whiting, P., Bagnall, A., Sowden, A. J., Cornell, J. E., Mulrow, C. D., & Ramirez, G. (2001). Interventions for the treatment and management of chronic fatigue syndrome. *Journal of the American Medical Association, 286,* 1360–1366.

Whitnam, F. L., Diamond, M., & Martin, J. (1993). Homosexual orientation in twins: A report on 61 pairs and three triplet sets. *Archives of Sexual Behavior, 22*(3), 187–206.

Whitney, C. W., Enright, P. L., Newman, A. B., Bonekat, W., Foley, D., & Quan, S. F. (1998). Correlates of daytime sleepiness in 4578 elderly persons: The cardiovascular health study. *Sleep, 21,* 27–36.

Whittal, M. L., Agras, W. S., & Gould, R. A. (1999). Bulimia nervosa: A meta-analysis of psychosocial and pharmacological treatments. *Behavior Therapy, 30,* 117–135.

Wickramaratne, P. J., Weissman, M. M., Leaf, D. J., & Holford, T. R. (1989). Age, period and cohort effects on the risk of major depression: Results from five United States communities. *Journal of Clinical Epidemiology, 42,* 333–343.

Widiger, T. A. (1991). Personality disorder dimensional models proposed for the DSM-IV. *Journal of Personality Disorders, 5,* 386–398.

Widiger, T. A., & Corbitt, E. M. (1995). Antisocial personality disorder. In W. J. Livesley (Ed.), *The DSM-IV personality disorders* (pp. 103–126). New York: Guilford Press.

Widiger, T. A., & Rogers, J. H. (1989). Prevalence and comorbidity of personality disorders. *Psychiatry Annual, 19,* 132.

Widiger, T. A., & Sankis, L. M. (2000). Adult psychopathology: Issues and controversies. *Annual Review of Psychology, 51,* 377–404.

Widiger, T. A., & Spitzer, R. L. (1991). Sex bias in the diagnosis of personality disorders: Conceptual and methodological issues. *Clinical Psychology Review, 11,* 1–22.

Widiger, T. A., & Trull, T. J. (1993). Borderline and narcissistic personality disorders. In P. B. Sutker & H. E. Adams (Eds.), *Comprehensive handbook of psychopathology* (2nd ed., pp. 371–394). New York: Plenum Press.

Widiger, T. A., & Weissman, M. M. (1991). Epidemiology of borderline personality disorder. *Hospital and Community Psychiatry, 42,* 1015–1021.

Widiger, T. A., Frances, A. J., Pincus, H. A., Ross, R., First, M. B., & Davis, W. W. (Eds.). (1996). *DSM-IV sourcebook* (Vol. 2). Washington, DC: American Psychiatric Press.

Widiger, T. A., Frances, A. J., Pincus, H. A., Ross, R., First, M. B., Davis, W., et al. (Eds.). (1998). *DSM-IV sourcebook* (Vol. 4). Washington, DC: American Psychiatric Press.

Widom, C. S. (1977). A methodology for studying noninstitutionalized psychopaths. *Journal of Consulting and Clinical Psychology, 45,* 674–683.

Widom, C. S. (1984). Sex roles, criminality, and psychopathology. In C. S. Widom (Ed.), *Sex roles and psychopathology* (pp. 183–217). New York: Plenum Press.

Wieczorek, S., Gencik, M., Rujescu, D., Tonn, P., Giegling, I., Epplen, J. T., et al. (2003). TNFA promoter polymorphisms and narcolepsy. *Tissue Antigens, 61,* 437–442.

Wiegel, M. (2004). The self-reported behaviors and characteristics of adult female child sexual abusers. Dissertation Prospectus.

Wiegel, M., Scepkowski, L. A., & Barlow, D. H. (In press). Cognitive-affective processes in sexual arousal and sexual dysfunction. In E. Janssen (Ed.), *The psychophysiology of sex.* Indiana: Indiana University Press.

Wiegel, M., Wincze, J. P., & Barlow, D. H. (2002). Sexual dysfunction. In M. M. Antony & D. H. Barlow (Eds.), *Handbook of assessment and treatment planning for psychological disorders* (pp. 481–522). New York: Guilford Press.

Wilfley, D. E., & Rodin, J. (1995). Cultural influences on eating disorders. In K. D. Brownell & C. G. Fairburn (Eds.), *Eating disorders and obesity: A comprehensive handbook* (pp.78–82.) New York: Guilford Press.

Wilfley, D. E., Schwartz, J. N. B., Spurrell, B., & Fairburn, C. G. (2000). Using the Eating Disorder Examination to identify the specific psychopathology of binge eating disorder. *International Journal of Eating Disorders, 27,* 259–269.

Wilfley, D. E., Welch, R., Stein, R. I. Spurrell, E. B., Cohen, L. R., Saelens, B. E., et al. (2002). A randomized comparison of group cognitive-behavioral and group interpersonal psychotherapy for treatment of overweight individuals with binge-eating disorder. *Archives of General Psychiatry, 59,* 713–721.

Wilgosh, L., Mulcahy, R., & Watters, B. (1986). Assessing intellectual performance of culturally different, Inuit children with the WISC-R. *Canadian Journal of Behavioural Science, 18,* 270–277.

Wilhelm, S., Otto, M. W., Lohr, B., & Deckersbach, T. (1999). Cognitive behavior group therapy for body dysmorphic disorder: A case series. *Behaviour Research and Therapy, 37,* 71–75.

Wilkie, C., Macdonald, S., & Hildahl, K. (1998). Community case study: Suicide cluster in a small Manitoba community. *Canadian Journal of Psychiatry, 43,* 823–828.

Wilkinson-Ryan, T., & Westen, D. (2000). Identity disturbance in borderline personality disorder: An empirical investigation. *American Journal of Psychiatry, 157,* 528–541.

Willi, J., & Grossman, S. (1983). Epidemiology of anorexia nervosa in a defined region of Switzerland. *American Journal of Psychiatry, 140,* 564–567.

Williams, C. J., & Weinberg, M. S. (2003). Zoophilia in men: A study of sexual interest in animals. *Archives of Sexual Behavior, 32,* 523–535.

Williams, L. (1994). Recall of childhood trauma: A prospective study of women's memories of child sexual abuse. *Journal of Consulting and Clinical Psychology, 62,* 1167–1176.

Williams, R. B., Barefoot, J. C., & Schneiderman, N. (2003). Psychosocial risk factors for cardiovascular disease: More than one culprit at work. *Journal of the American Medical Assocation, 290,* 2190–2192.

Williams, R. B., Jr., Haney, T. L., Lee, K. L., Kong, V., & Blumenthal, J. A. (1980). Type A behavior, hostility, and coronary atherosclerosis. *Psychosomatic Medicine, 42,* 529–538.

Williams, R. B., Marchuk, D. A., Gadde, K. M., Barefoot, J. C., Grichnik, K., Helms, M. J., et al. (2001). Central nervous system serotonin function and cardiovascular responses to stress. *Psychosomatic Medicine, 63,* 300–305.

Williams, R. B., & Schneiderman, N. (2002). Resolved: Psychosocial interventions can improve clinical outcomes in organic disease (Pro). *Psychosomatic Medicine, 64,* 552–557.

Williams, R. J., & Schmidt, G. G. (1993). Frequency of seasonal affective disorder among individuals seeking treatment at a northern Canadian mental health center. *Psychiatry Research, 46,* 41–45.

Williams, S., Connolly, J., & Segal, Z. V. (2001). Intimacy in relationships and cognitive vulnerability to depression in adolescent girls. *Cognitive Therapy and Research, 25,* 477–496.

Williams, W. L. (1986). *The spirit and the flesh: Sexual diversity in American Indian culture.* Boston: Beacon Press. (Reprint 1991, with a new preface).

Wills, T. A., Vaccaro, D., McNamara, G., & Hirky, A. E. (1996). Escalated substance use: A longitudinal grouping analysis from early to middle adolescence. *Journal of Abnormal Psychology, 105,* 166–180.

Willwerth, J. (1993, August 30). Tinkering with madness. *Time,* pp. 40–42

Wilson, G. T. (1977). Alcohol and human sexual behavior. *Behaviour Research and Therapy, 15,* 239–252.

Wilson, G. T. (1987). Cognitive studies in alcoholism. *Journal of Consulting and Clinical Psychology, 55,* 325–331.

Wilson, G. T. (1993). Psychological and pharmacological treatments of bulimia nervosa: A research update. *Applied and Preventive Psychology, 2,* 35–42.

Wilson, G. T., & Fairburn, C. G. (2002). Treatments for eating disorders. In P. E. Nathan, & J. M. Gorman (Eds.), *A guide to treatments that work* (2nd ed.) (pp. 559–592). New York: Oxford University Press.

Wilson, G. T., & Pike, K. M. (2001). Eating disorders. In D. H. Barlow (Ed.), *Clinical handbook of psychological disorders* (3rd ed.). New York: Guilford Press.

Wilson, G. T., Loeb, K. L., Walsh, B. T., Labouvie, E., Petkova, E., Liu, S., et al. (1999). Psychological versus pharmacological treatments of bulimia nervosa: Predictors and processes of change. *Journal of Consulting and Clinical Psychology, 67,* 451–459.

Wilson, K. G., Sandler, L. S., Asmundson, G. J., Larsen, D. K., & Ediger, J. M. (1991). Effects of instructional set on self-reports of panic attacks. *Journal of Anxiety Disorders, 5,* 43–63.

Winchel, R. M., Stanley, B., & Stanley, M. (1990). Biochemical aspects of suicide. In S. J. Blumenthal & D. J. Kupfer (Eds.), *Suicide over the life cycle: Risk factors, assessment and treatment of suicidal patterns* (pp. 97–126). Washington, DC: American Psychiatric Press.

Wincze, J. P., & Barlow, D. H. (1997). *Enhancing sexuality: A problem-solving approach client workbook.* San Antonio: Graywind Publications/The Psychological Corporation.

Wincze, J. P., & Carey, M. P. (1991). *Sexual dysfunction: A guide for assessment and treatment.* New York: Guilford Press.

Wincze, J. P., & Carey, M. P. (2001). *Sexual dysfunction: A guide for assessment and treatment* (2nd ed.). New York: Guilford Press.

Windgassen, K. (1992). Treatment with neuroleptics: The patient's perspective. *Acta Psychiatrica Scandinavica, 86,* 405–410.

Winick, B. J. (1997). *The right to refuse mental health treatment.* Washington, DC: American Psychological Press.

Winker, M. A. (1994). Tacrine for Alzheimer's disease: Which patient, what dose? *Journal of the American Medical Association, 271,* 1023–1024.

Winokur, G. (1985). Familial psychopathology in delusional disorder. *Comprehensive Psychiatry, 26,* 241–248.

Winokur, G., Coryell, W., Endicott, J., & Akiskal, H. (1993). Further distinctions between manic-depressive illness (bipolar disorder) and primary depressive disorder (unipolar depression). *American Journal of Psychiatry, 150,* 1176–1181.

Winokur, G., Pfohl, B., & Tsuang, M. (1987). A 40-year follow-up of hebephrenic-catatonic schizophrenia. In N. Miller & G. Cohen (Eds), *Schizophrenia and aging* (pp. 52–60). New York: Guilford Press.

Winter, A. (1998). *Mesmerized powers of mind in Victorian Britain.* University of Chicago Press: Chicago.

Winters, R. W., & Schneiderman, N. (2000). Anxiety and coronary heart disease. In D. I. Mostofsky & D. H. Barlow (Eds.), *The management of stress and anxiety in medical disorders* (pp. 206–219). Needham Heights, MA: Allyn & Bacon.

Wirshing, D. A., Wirshing, W. C., Marder, S. R., Liberman, R. P., & Mintz, J. (1998). Informed consent: Assessment of comprehension. *American Journal of Psychiatry, 155,* 1508–1511.

Wirtz-Justice, A. (1998). Beginning to see the light. *Archives of General Psychiatry, 55,* 861–862.

Wise, M. G., Gray, K. F., & Seltzer, B. (1999). Delirium, dementia, and amnestic disorders. In R. E. Hales, S. C. Judofsky, & J. A. Talbott, (Eds.), *Textbook of psychiatry* (3rd ed.) (pp. 317–362). Washington, DC: American Psychiatric Press.

Wise, M. G., Hilty, D. M., & Cerda, G. M. (2001). Delirium due to a general medical condition, delirium due to multiple etiologies, and delirium not otherwise specified. In G. O. Gabbard (Ed.),

*Treatment of psychiatric disorders* (Vol. 1) (3rd ed.) (pp. 387–412). Washington, DC: American Psychiatric Press.

Wise, R. A. (1988). The neurobiology of craving: Implications for the understanding and treatment of addiction. *Journal of Abnormal Psychology, 97,* 118–132.

Wiseman, C. V., Gray, J. J., Mosimann, J. E., & Ahrens, A. H. (1992). Cultural expectations of thinness in women: An update. *International Journal of Eating Disorders, 11,* 85–89.

Witherington, R. (1988). Suction device therapy in the management of erectile impotence. *Urologic Clinics of North America, 15,* 123–128.

Wittchen, H. U., Knauper, B., & Kessler, R. C. (1994). Lifetime risk of depression. *British Journal of Psychiatry, 165,* 116–122.

Wittchen, H. U., Zhao, S., Kessler, R. C., & Eaton, W. W. (1994). DSM-III-R generalized anxiety disorder in the National Comorbidity Survey. *Archives of General Psychiatry, 51,* 355–364.

Wolf, M. M. (1978). Social validity: The case for subjective measurement or how applied behavior analysis is finding its heart. *Journal of Applied Behavior Analysis, 11,* 203–214.

Wolf, S. S., Jones, D. W., Knable, M. B., Gorey, J. G., Lee, K. S., Hyde, T. M., et al. (1996). Tourette syndrome: Prediction of phenotypic variation in monozygotic twins by caudate nucleus D2 receptor binding. *Science, 273,* 1225–1227.

Wolfe, D. A. (1991). *Preventing physical and emotional abuse of children.* New York: Guilford Press.

Wolff, S. (2000). Schizoid personality in childhood and Asperger syndrome. In A. Klin, F. R. Volkmar, & S. S. Sparrow (Eds.), *Asperger syndrome* (pp. 278–305). New York: Guilford Press.

Wolff, S., Townshed, R., McGuire, R. J., & Weeks, D. J. (1991). "Schizoid" personality in childhood and adult life. II: Adult adjustment and continuity with schizotypal personality disorder. *British Journal of Psychiatry, 159,* 615–620.

Wolf-Maier, K., Cooper, R. S., Banegas, J. R., Giampaoli, S., Hense, H., Joffres, M., et al. (2003). Hypertension prevalence and blood pressure levels in 6 European countries, Canada, and the United States. *Journal of the American Medical Association, 289,* 2362–2369.

Wolfson, C., Wolfson, D. B., Asgharian, M., M'Lan, C. E., Ostbye, T., Rockwood, K., et al. (2001). Clinical Progression of Dementia Study Group: A reevaluation of the duration of survival after the onset of dementia. *New England Journal of Medicine, 344,* 1111–1116.

Wolpe, J. (1958). *Psychotherapy by reciprocal inhibition.* Stanford, CA: Stanford University Press.

Wood, E., Kerr, T., Small, W., Li, K., Marsh, D. C., Montaner, J. S. G., et al. (2004). Changes in public order after the opening of a medically supervised safer-injecting facility for illicit injection drug users. *Canadian Medical Association Journal, 171,* 731–734.

Wood, E., Tyndall, M. W., Qui, Z., Zhang, R., Montaner, J. S. G., & Kerr, T. (2006).

Service uptake and characteristics of injection drug users utilizing North America's first medically supervised safer injecting facility. *American Journal of Public Health, 96,* 770–773.

Wood, J. M., Nezworski, M. T., & Stejskal, W. J. (1996). The comprehensive system for the Rorschach: A critical examination. *Psychological Science, 7,* 3–17.

Woodman, C. L., Noyes, R., Black, D. W., Schlosser, S., & Yagla, S. J. (1999). A 5-year follow-up study of generalized anxiety disorder and panic disorder. *Journal of Nervous and Mental Disease, 187,* 3–9.

Woods, E. R., Lin, Y. G., Middleman, A., Beckford, P., Chase, L., & DuRant, R. H. (1997). The associations of suicide attempts in adolescents. *Pediatrics, 99,* 791–796.

Woodside, D. B., Bulik, C. M., Halmi, K. A., Fichter, M. M., Kaplan, A., Berrettini, et al. (2002). Personality, perfectionism, and attitudes towards eating in parents of individuals with eating disorders. *International Journal of Eating Disorders, 31,* 290–299.

Woodside, D. B., Garfinkel, P. E., Lin, E., Goering, P., & Kaplan, A. S. (2001). Comparisons of men with full or partial eating disorders, men without eating disorders, and women with eating disorders in the community. *American Journal of Psychiatry, 158,* 570–574.

Woodworth, M., & Porter, S. (2002). In cold blood: Characteristics of criminal homicides as a function of psychopathy. *Journal of Abnormal Psychology, 111,* 436–445.

Woody, G. E., & Cacciola, J. (1997). Diagnosis and classification: DSM-IV and ICD-10. In J. H. Lowinson, P. Ruiz, R. B. Millman, & J. G. Langrod (Eds.), *Substance abuse: A comprehensive textbook* (pp. 361–363). Baltimore: Williams & Wilkins.

Wootton, J. M., Frick, P. J., Shelton, K. K., & Silverthorn, P. (1997). Ineffective parenting and childhood conduct problems: The moderating role of callous-unemotional traits. *Journal of Consulting and Clinical Psychology, 65,* 301–308.

Worell, J., & Remer, P. (1992). *Feminist perspectives in therapy: An empowerment model for women.* New York: John Wiley.

World Health Organization. (1992). *The ICD-10 classification of mental and behavioural disorders: Clinical descriptions and diagnostic guidelines.* Geneva, Switzerland: Author.

World Health Organization. (2000). *Women and HIV/AIDS: Fact sheet no. 242.* Available at http://www.who.int/inf-fs/en/fact242.html.

World Health Organization. (2001). *The World Health Report 2001. Mental health: New understanding, new hope.* Geneva, Switzerland: Author.

World Health Organization. (2002). *World report on violence and health.* Geneva: World Health Organization.

*Wyatt v. Stickney.* (1972). 344 F. Supp. 373 (Ala.).

Wyllie, E., Glazer, J. P., Benbadis, S., Kotagal, P., & Wolgamuth, B. (1999). Psychiatric features of children and adolescents with pseudoseizures. *Archives of Pediatrics and Adolescent Medicine, 153,* 244–248.

Yairi, E., & Ambrose, N. (1992). Onset of stuttering in preschool children: Selected

factors. *Journal of Speech and Hearing Research, 35,* 782–788.

Yamamoto, J., Silva, A., Sasao, T., Wang, C., & Nguyen, L. (1993). Alcoholism in Peru. *American Journal of Psychiatry, 150,* 1059–1062.

Yan, L. L., Liu, K., Matthews, K. A., Daviglus, M. L., Ferguson, T. F., & Kiefe, C. I. (2003). Psychosocial risk factors and risk of hypertension: The coronary artery risk development in young adults (CARDIA) study. *Journal of the American Medical Association, 290,* 2138–2148.

Yatham, L., Liddle, P. F., Shiah, I.-S., Lam, R. W., Ngan, E., Scarrow, G., et al. (2002). PET study of [-sup-1-sup-8F]6-fluoro-L-dopa uptake in neuroleptic- and mood-stabilizer-naive first-episode nonpsychotic mania: Effects of treatment with divalproex sodium. *American Journal of Psychiatry, 159,* 768–774.

Ye, X., Mitchell, M., Newman, K., & Batshaw, M. L. (2001). Prospects for prenatal gene therapy in disorders causing mental retardation. *Mental Retardation and Developmental Disabilities Research Review, 7,* 65–72.

Yeaton, W. H., & Bailey, J. S. (1978). Teaching pedestrian safety skills to young children: An analysis and one-year follow-up. *Journal of Applied Behavior Analysis, 11,* 315–329.

Yeh, A. H., Taylor, S., Thordarson, D. S., & Corcoran, K. M. (2003). Efficacy of telephone-administered CBT for obsessive-compulsive spectrum disorders: Case studies. *Cognitive Behaviour Therapy, 32*(2), 75–81.

Yerkes, R. M., & Dodson, J. D. (1908). The relation of strength of stimulus to rapidity of habit-formation. *Journal of Comprehensive Neurology and Psychology, 18,* 459–482.

Yonkers, K. A., Warshaw, M., Massion, A. O., & Keller, M. B. (1996). Phenomenology and course of generalized anxiety disorder. *British Journal of Psychiatry, 168,* 308–313.

Young, A. M., & Herling, S. (1986). Drugs as reinforcers: Studies in laboratory animals. In S. R. Goldberg & I. P. Stolerman (Eds.), *Behavioral analysis of drug dependence* (pp. 9–67). Orlando, FL: Academic Press.

Young, A. R., & Beitchman, J. H. (2001). Learning disorders. In G. O. Gabbard (Ed.), *Treatment of psychiatric disorders* (Vol. 1) (3rd ed.) (pp. 109–124). Washington, DC: American Psychiatric Press.

Young, J. E., Weinberger, A. D., & Beck, A. T. (2001). Cognitive therapy for depression. In D. H. Barlow (Ed.), *Clinical handbook of psychological disorders* (3rd ed., pp. 264–308). New York: Guilford Publications.

Yutzy, S. H., Cloninger, C. R., Guze, S. B., Pribor, E. F., Martin, R. L., Kathol, R. G., et al. (1995). DSM-IV field trial: Testing a new proposal for somatization disorder. *American Journal of Psychiatry, 152,* 97–101.

Zack, M., Toneatto, T., & MacLeod, C. M. (1999). Implicit activation of alcohol concepts by negative affective cues distinguishes between problem drinkers with

high and low psychiatric distress. *Journal of Abnormal Psychology, 108,* 518–531.

Zadra, A., & Donderi, D. C. (2000). Nightmares and bad dreams: Their prevalence and relationship to well-being. *Journal of Abnormal Psychology, 109,* 273–281.

Zajonc, R. B. (1984). On the primacy of affect. *American Psychologist, 39*(2), 117–123.

Zajonc, R. B. (1998). Emotions. In D. Gilbert, S. T. Fiske, & G. Lindzey (Eds.), *Handbook of social psychology* (4th ed., Vol. 1, pp. 591–632). New York: McGraw-Hill.

Zakzanis, K. K., Troyer, A. K., Rich, J. B., & Heinrichs, W. (2000). Component analysis of verbal fluency in patients with schizophrenia. *Neuropsychiatry, Neuropsychology, and Behavioral Neurology, 13,* 239–245.

Zanarini, M. C., & Frankenberg, F. R. (1997). Pathways to the development of borderline personality disorder. *Journal of Personality Disorders, 11,* 93–104.

Zanarini, M. C., Frankenburg, F. R., Dubo, E. E., Sickel, A. E., Trikha, A., Levin, A., et al. (1998). Axis I comorbidity of borderline personality disorder. *American Journal of Psychiatry, 155,* 1733–1739.

Zanarini, M. C., Gunderson, J., Marino, M., Schwartz, E., & Frankenburg, F. (1988). DSM-III disorders in the families of borderline outpatients. *Journal of Personality Disorders, 2,* 292–302.

Zanarini, M. C., Williams, A. A., Lewis, R. E., Reich, R. B., Vera, S. C., Marino, M. F., et al. (1997). Reported pathological childhood experiences associated with the development of borderline personality disorder. *American Journal of Psychiatry, 154,* 1101–1106.

Zapf, P. A., & Roesch, R. (1997). Assessing fitness to stand trial: A comparison of institution-based evaluations and a brief screening interview. *Canadian Journal of Community Mental Health, 16,* 53–66.

Zelazo, P. D., Burack, J. A., Boseovski, J. J., Jacques, S., & Frye, D. (2001). A cognitive complexity and control framework for the study of autism. In J. A. Burack & T. Charman (Eds.), *Development of autism: Perspectives from theory and research* (pp. 195–217). Mahwah, NJ: Lawrence Erlbaum.

Zelazo, P. D., Jacques, S., Burack, J. A., & Frye, D. (2002). The relation between theory of mind and rule use: Evidence from persons with autism-spectrum disorders. *Infant and Child Development, 11,* 171–195.

Zelkowitz, P., & Milet, T. H. (2001). The course of postpartum psychiatric disorders in women and their partners. *Journal of Nervous and Mental Disease, 189,* 575–582.

Zhou, J. N., Hofman, M. A., Gooren, L. J., & Swaab, D. F. (1995). A sex difference in the human brain and its relation to transsexuality. *Nature, 378,* 68–70.

Zigler, E., & Balla, D. (1982). *Mental retardation: The developmental-difference controversy.* Hillsdale, NJ: Erlbaum.

Zigler, E., & Cascione, R. (1984). Mental retardation: An overview. In E. S. Gollin (Ed.), *Malformations of development: Biological and psychological sources and consequences* (pp. 69–90). New York: Academic Press.

Zigler, E., & Hodapp, R. M. (1986). *Understanding mental retardation.* Cambridge, UK: Cambridge University Press.

Zigler, E. F., & Stevenson, M. F. (1993). *Children in a changing world: Development and social issues* (2nd ed.). Pacific Grove, CA: Brooks/Cole.

Zilbergeld, B. (1992). *The new male sexuality.* New York: Bantam Books.

Zilboorg, G., & Henry, G. (1941). *A history of medical psychology.* New York: W. W. Norton.

Zimmerman, M., & Coryell, W. (1989). DSM-III personality disorder diagnoses in a nonpatient sample. *Archives of General Psychiatry, 46,* 682–689.

Zimmerman, M., & Coryell, W. (1990). Diagnosing personality disorders in the community: A comparison of self-report and interview measures. *Archives of General Psychiatry, 47,* 527–531.

Zimmerman, M., & Mattia, J. I. (1998). Body dysmorphic disorder in psychiatric outpatients: Recognition, prevalence, comorbidity, demographic, and clinical correlates. *Comprehensive Psychiatry, 39*(5), 265–270.

Zinbarg, R. E., & Barlow, D. H. (1996). Structure of anxiety and the anxiety disorders: A hierarchical model. *Journal of Abnormal Psychology, 105,* 181–193.

Zipfel, S., Lowe, B., Deter, H. C., & Herzog, W. (2000). Long-term prognosis in anorexia nervosa: Lessons from a 21-year follow-up study. *Lancet, 355,* 721–722.

Zohar, J., Judge, R., & the OCD Paroxetine Study Investigators. (1996). Paroxetine vs. clomipramine in the treatment of obsessive-compulsive disorder. *British Journal of Psychiatry, 169,* 468–474.

Zucker, K. J., & Bradley, S. J. (1995). *Gender identity disorder and psychosexual problems in children and adolescents.* New York: Guilford Press.

Zucker, K. J., Bradley, S. J., & Ipp, M. (1993). Delayed naming of a newborn boy: Relationship to the mother's wish for a girl and subsequent cross-gender identity in the child by the age of two. *Journal of Psychology and Human Sexuality, 6,* 57–68.

Zuroff, D. C., Blatt, S. J., Sanislow, C. A., III, Bondi, C. M., & Pilkonis, P. A. (1999). Vulnerability to depression: Reexamining state dependence and relative stability. *Journal of Abnormal Psychology, 108,* 76–89.

Zvolensky, M. J., Schmidt, N. B., & Stewart, S. H. (2003). Panic disorder and smoking. *Clinical Psychology: Science and Practice, 10,* 29–51.

# Name Index

Aarestad, S. L., 358
Abbeduto, L., 548
Abbey, S., 292, 293
Abbott, D. W., 317
Abdolell, M., 319
Abe, T., 535
Abel, G. G., 332, 364, 383, 385
Abela, J., 242
Abi-Darham, A., 505
Abikoff, H. B., 528
Abrahamson, D. J., 373
Abrams, G. M., 472
Abrams, K., 142
Abrams, M., 55
Abrams, R., 225
Abramson, L. Y., 59, 239, 240, 241, 242, 243, 244, 326
Abuelo, D. N., 545
Acampora, A., 436
Adair, J. G., 69
Adair, R., 339, 340
Adams, C., 505
Adams, H. E., 371, 375
Adams, L. P., 259
Adams, M., 89
Adelson, N., 233
Ader, R., 278
Adlaf, E., 411, 413, 416, 530
Adler, A., 23, 24
Adler, C. M., 181
Adler, P. S., 37, 285
Adrian, C., 237
Afari, N., 294
Agras, W. S., 152, 309, 313, 315, 316, 317, 321, 322, 326, 328, 329, 331, 332, 364, 373
Agrawal, P., 414
Agyei, Y., 358
Ahrens, A. H., 321
Aigner, M., 192
Ainslie, R. C., 104
Akiskal, H. S., 220, 222, 225, 227, 237, 450
Aktar, S., 201
Akutagawa, D., 317

Albano, A. M., 153, 156, 159, 165, 169
Albers, L. J., 511
Albert, M. L., 506
Alberta Family and Social Services, 566
Albertini, R. S., 193
Albin, J. M., 548
Alcoholics Anonymous, 436
Alden, L., 158, 475
Aldous, J., 514
Alexander, F. G., 9, 13, 14, 271, 285
Alford, B. A., 252
Alger, S. A., 313
Allan, J. S., 345
Allani, D., 469
Allebeck, P., 581
Allen, J., 536
Allen, J. M., 228
Allen, K., 67
Allen, L. S., 358
Allen, N. B., 240
Allen-Hauser, W., 189
Aller, G., 592–593
Allerdings, M. D., 290
Allmon, D., 470
Alloul, K., 556
Alloy, L. B., 240, 242, 246
Allsbeck, P., 67
Almeida, D. M., 430
Alper, C. M., 276
Alpers, G. W., 181
Alpert, M., 492
Altay, B., 376
Althof, S., 368, 369, 375, 380, 381, 382
Altmuller, J., 115
Alzheimer, A., 556
Alzheimer's Association, 562
Alzheimer's Society of Canada, 559
Ambrose, M., 568
Ambrose, N., 531
American Academy of Pediatrics, 524
American Psychiatric Association, 4, 76,

127, 183, 248, 249, 250, 251, 259, 263, 331, 341, 403, 404, 424, 425, 435, 446, 448, 448–449, 451, 453, 455, 457, 489, 495, 496, 511, 512, 513, 514, 529, 533, 535, 536, 543, 550, 552, 553, 555, 557, 568
Amering, M., 142
Amir, N., 170
Anagnos, A., 345
Anand, S. S., 287
Anastasi, A., 85, 86
Anch, A. M., 349
Ancoli-Israel, S., 107
Anders, T. F., 338
Andersen, B. L., 358
Andersen, P. M., 190
Anderson, C., 358, 366
Anderson, D. J., 135
Anderson, E., 360–361
Anderson, E. R., 466
Anderson, G., 169, 205
Anderson, R., 279, 281, 282
Andrade, C., 500
Andrasik, F., 273, 295, 296, 298
Andreasen, N. C., 89, 196, 489, 490, 493, 495, 506, 507
Andreasson, S., 67, 507
Andreski, M. A., 420
Andrew, M., 236
Andrews, B., 208
Andrews, G., 21, 531
Andrews, J. A., 230
Andrykowski, M. A., 26
Aneshensel, C. S., 566
Anglin, M. D., 421
Angst, J., 218, 219, 225, 226
Anguilo, M. J., 206
Anisman, H., 43
Annabi, S., 469
Annas, P., 60
Anthenelli, R., 412, 427

Anthony, D., 500
Anthony, W. A., 515
Anton, R. F., 410
Antoni, M. H., 280, 281, 282
Antoniw, E., 89
Antony, M. M., 146, 151, 152, 153, 154, 155, 156, 158, 168, 196–197, 409, 430
Antrobus, J., 335
Apfelbaum, B., 370
Appelbaum, K. S., 298
Appelbaum, P. S., 120, 593
Applegate, B., 525
Applewhite, M., 260
Appolinario, J. C., 331
Aral, S. O., 276
Arbisi, P., 51
Arboleda-Florez, J., 513, 587
Archer, R. P., 86
Arendt, J., 343
Arias, E., 259
Aristotle, 16
Armstrong, H. E., 335, 470, 513
Arnold, L. E., 528
Arnow, B., 217, 326, 331
Arrindell, W. A., 142, 152, 155
Asarnow, J. R., 499
Asberg, M., 261
Aschoff, J., 343
Asmundson, G. J. G., 78, 99, 101, 106, 141, 145, 179, 180, 183, 290
Asnis, L., 468
Assanand, S., 326
Atha, C., 263
Atkinson, J. M., 486
Attia, E., 328
Attie, I., 319, 324
Attwood, A., 539
Aubry, T., 69
Auchterlonie, S., 556
Austin, G. W., 589
Austin, J. B., 392

Avila, M., 503
Avison, W. R., 245
Avorn, J., 137
Awad, A. G., 486
Ayllon, T., 28, 513
Azad, N., 340
Azrin, N. H., 347, 513

Baasher, T. A., 118
Bacchetti, P., 279
Bacchiochi, J. R., 590
Bach, A. K., 366, 368, 373, 378, 380
Bach, M., 192
Bachicha, D. L., 29
Bachrach, L. L., 583
Bader, J. O., 293
Badley, E. M., 335
Baer, D. M., 83
Baer, J. S., 437, 439
Baer, L., 168
Bagby, R. M., 250, 448, 590
Bages, N., 142, 152
Bailey, J. M., 85, 358, 360, 524
Bailey, J. S., 300
Baillargeon, R. H., 528
Bakalar, J. B., 423
Baker, A., 360
Baker, B., 287, 288, 509
Baker, C. D., 378
Baker, J. M., 140, 142, 145
Baker, L., 324
Baker, T. B., 429
Bakker, A., 146
Balabanis, M., 83
Baldessarini, R. J., 249, 250
Baldwin, J. D., 390
Baldwin, J. I., 390
Ball, J. C., 434
Balla, D., 547
Ballenger, J. C., 146, 166
Ban, T. A., 511
Bancroft, J., 358, 363, 366, 372, 373, 383, 384, 390
Bandura, A., 25, 29, 59–60, 131, 276, 290, 292
Bank, L., 466
Banon, E., 446
Baralow, D. H., 165
Barban, L., 203
Barbaree, H., 373, 387, 392

Barchas, J. D., 428
Bardach, J., 196
Bardenhagen, F., 568
Bardone, A. M., 326
Barefoot, J. C., 272, 288
Bargh, J. A., 60
Barinaga, M., 90
Barker, E. T., 430
Barkley, R. A., 524, 525, 526, 527
Barlow, D. H., 5, 56, 58, 60, 92, 109, 127, 128, 129, 130, 131, 132, 133, 134, 135, 136, 137, 138, 139, 140, 141, 142, 143, 144, 145, 146, 147, 148, 150, 151, 152, 153, 154, 155, 156, 158, 159, 162, 163, 164, 165, 167, 169, 170, 181, 234, 240, 241, 242, 244, 245, 246, 273, 275, 276, 296, 297, 298, 313, 332, 364, 366, 368, 373, 374, 376, 377, 382, 384, 385, 390, 392
Barnard, A., 196
Barnes, J., 372, 378, 513
Barnett, P. A., 243, 253, 286
Barnhardt, T. M., 60
Barnhart, R., 423
Barnhill, J., 256
Baron-Cohen, S., 468, 535
Barr, C. E., 507, 527
Barraclough, C., 310
Barrera, M., 429
Barrett, D. H., 465
Barrett, P. M., 138
Barrios, L. C., 260
Barrowclough, C., 515
Barry, T., 347, 411
Barsky, A. J., 179, 180, 181
Bartak, L., 536
Barth, J. Y., 88
Bartko, J., 495
Bartlett, N., 364
Bartlik, B., 368
Bartoli, L., 227
Basoglu, M., 108
Bass, D., 466
Bassett, A. S., 500, 502
Bassett, C., 323–324
Bassiri, A. G., 343

Basson, R., 375–376
Bateson, G., 509
Batshaw, M. L., 549
Baucher, H., 339
Bauchner, H., 339, 340
Bauer, J., 329
Bauer, M. S., 227
Baugh, D. K., 552
Baum, A., 281, 282
Baumal, Z., 228, 277
Bauman, E., 87
Baumeister, R. F., 326
Baumgart, D., 539
Baxter, L. R., 55, 89
Baxter, L. R., Jr., 55
Bazelmans, E., 294
Beach, F., 243, 244
Bear, D., 207
Beard, C. M., 309
Beard, G. M., 292
Beard, J. H., 515
Beardslee, W. R., 254
Beattie, B. L., 558
Bebbington, P. E., 42, 508, 509, 515
Beck, A. T., 62, 134, 138, 145, 230, 234, 242, 243, 252, 254, 259, 261, 364, 372, 373, 453, 455, 456, 474, 476, 477, 515
Becker, D., 469, 472, 473
Becker, E. A., 528
Becker, J. V., 223, 383, 393
Becker, R., 373
Beckham, J., 291
Bedrosian, R. C., 254
Beevers, D. G., 564
Beglin, S. J., 318
Beitchman, J. H., 529, 530, 532
Beitman, B. D., 142
Belitsky, R., 450, 499
Belknap, J. K., 427
Bell, C. C., 143
Bell, I. R., 185
Bellack, A. S., 514
Bellak, L., 85
Bellamy-Campbell, R., 548, 590
Bellavance, F., 552
Bellis, D. J., 434
Belluardo, P., 255
Bem, D. J., 358–359, 466
Bem, D. L., 359
Ben-Abdallah, A., 407
Benbadis, R. R., 189, 190

Benbadis, S., 189, 190
Benca, R. M., 338
Bendfeldt, F., 202
Benedetti, A., 180
Ben-Eliyahu, S., 294
Benet, M., 234
Benishay, D. S., 358
Benkelfat, C., 237
Bennett, A. H., 382
Bennett-Branson, S. M., 282
Benowitz, N. L., 419
Ben-Porath, Y. S., 86
Benson, H., 296
Berberich, J. P., 539
Berenbaum, H., 492, 513
Bergeron, S., 372
Bergin, A. E., 108
Bergson, C., 505
Berkman, L., 67, 223
Berlin, M. D., 387
Berman, A. L., 259
Berman, K. F., 507
Berman, T., 527
Bernardo, P., 385
Bernat, J. A., 385
Bernstein, D. A., 296
Bernstein, D. P., 416, 418, 422, 449, 453, 454, 455, 456, 457
Berrios, G. E., 199, 500
Berry, J., 66
Bertelsen, B., 236, 502
Bertrand, L. D., 204
Berzins, K. M., 486
Besch, C. L., 279
Besier, M., 68, 508, 509
Best, C. L., 162
Bettelheim, B., 536, 538
Bezemer, P. D., 360
Bhagwanjee, A., 134
Bianchi, K., 203–204
Biederman, J., 157, 226, 231, 469, 526, 527, 528
Bierut, L. J., 236, 237, 246
Bigelow, L. B., 508
Biglan, A., 244
Billingsley, R. L., 61, 349
Binet, A., 86–87
Binik, I., 380
Binik, Y. M., 136, 372
Binzer, M., 190
Birch, D. E., 589
Birchwood, M., 515
Bird, D., 89, 332
Bird, S., 136

Birley, J. L. T., 508
Birmingham, C., 313, 328
Biron, M., 115
Bishop, D. S., 256, 290
Blaauw, G. J., 136
Black, D. W., 135, 168,
    251, 288, 489, 490
Black, S. E., 567
Blackburn, I. M., 254, 434
Blagys, M. D., 24
Blanchard, E. B., 84, 106,
    223, 295, 296, 298,
    363, 364, 373, 385
Blanchard, J. J., 512
Blanchard, R., 358, 359
Bland, R. C., 134, 135,
    152, 229, 232,
    244, 459
Blansjaar, B. A., 555
Blashfield, R. K., 96
Blatt, S. J., 242
Blazer, D. G., 107, 134,
    135, 153, 161, 184,
    190, 231, 338, 453
Bleackley, C., 278
Blechman, E. A., 70
Blehar, M. C., 242, 251
Bleijenberg, G., 294
Blendell, K. A., 159
Bleuler, E., 454, 487, 493
Blinder, B. J., 315
Bliss, E. L., 203
Block, C., 341
Bloom, F. E., 50, 51, 53
Bloom, J. R., 282
Bloomquist, M., 528
Bloscovitch, J., 67
Blue, A. V., 118
Blum, N., 477
Blumenthal, J. A., 65
Blumenthal, S. J., 258,
    259, 261, 262
Boag, T., 142
Bock, G. R., 463
Bockoven, J. S., 13–14, 16
Bockting, W. O., 360
Bodkin, J. A., 204
Bodlund, O., 363
Boehnlein, J., 233
Bogaert, A., 359
Bohac, D. L., 568
Bohman, M., 185, 465
Bohn, R. L., 137
Bohus, M., 468, 470
Boiago, I., 469
Boivin, D. B., 343
Boll, T. J., 88
Bolton, B., 312

Bolton, P., 549
Bonanno, G. A., 223
Bond, A., 21, 53
Bond, C. F., 582
Bond, G. R., 277, 515
Bondi, C., 242
Bonnet, M. H., 336
Boocock, A., 193,
    194, 196
Boon, S., 198, 205
Boothroyd, L. J., 233,
    259, 262
Bootzin, R. R., 107, 339,
    342, 347, 420
Borchardt, C., 142
Borkovec, T. D., 134,
    135, 137, 296
Bornath, L. M., 314
Bornstein, M. H., 43
Bornstein, R. F., 476
Borteyru, J. P., 411
Boseovski, J. J., 535
Boskind-Lodahl, M., 317
Bouchard, S., 454, 515
Bouchard, T. J., Jr., 40
Bourassa, M. G., 288
Bourgeois, J. A., 552,
    553, 556, 557, 558,
    560, 562, 563, 565,
    566, 567
Bouton, M. E., 58,
    131, 144
Bowden, S., 568
Bowen, J., 508, 509
Bowen-Bravery, M., 544
Bowers, C. A., 439
Bowlby, J., 476
Bowler, A. E., 499, 524
Bowles, C. A., 277
Bowman, E. P., 372
Bowman, E. S., 205, 207
Bowman, M., 531
Boyd, T. A., 568
Boyer, R., 134
Boyle, R., 228, 231, 300
Bracha, H. S., 508
Bradford, J., 387, 393
Bradley, B. P., 136,
    138, 242
Bradley, M. M., 63, 464
Bradley, S. J., 362, 364
Bradley, W., 527
Brady, J. P., 190, 531
Brady, T. J., 90
Brahim, A., 231
Brailey, K., 164
Brandon, S., 251
Brandon, T. H., 429

Brandsma, J., 202
Brandt, J., 561
Brandt, K. M., 430
Brannon, L., 273, 284,
    285, 288
Braswell, L., 528
Brauchi, J. T., 335
Brauer, L., 23
Brawman-Mintzer, O.,
    137, 166
Brechtl, J. R., 279
Breier, A., 430, 497
Breitbart, W., 279
Breitmeier, J., 238
Brekke, J. S., 515
Bremner, J. D., 164
Brener, N. D., 260, 261
Brennan, P. A., 246
Brenner, D. E., 562
Brenner, I., 201
Brent, D. A., 261, 263
Breslau, N., 235, 420
Breuer, J., 19, 61, 104
Brew, B., 560
Brewin, C. R., 208
Briere, M., 387
Brink, D., 347
Briquet, P., 183
British Columbia
    Schizophrenia
    Society, 486
Broadhead, W. E., 272
Brock, H., 319
Brodeur, D. A., 527
Bromet, E., 162, 243
Bromfield, E., 207
Brondino, M. J., 466
Brondolo, E., 285
Brook, J. S., 333
Brooker, C., 515
Brooks-Gunn, J.,
    319, 324
Brotto, L., 372
Broude, G. J., 358
Broughton, R. J., 348, 349
Browman, C. P., 349
Brown, C., 228
Brown, C. G., 313, 316
Brown, D. C., 566
Brown, G. B., 239
Brown, G. G., 157
Brown, G. K., 259, 274
Brown, G. W., 239, 240,
    245, 508, 509
Brown, J., 115, 116
Brown, S. A., 429
Brown, S. L., 462,
    464, 476

Brown, T. A., 131, 132,
    133, 134, 135, 136,
    141, 146, 151, 153,
    234, 373, 382
Brown, T. M., 549, 553
Browne, A. J., 68
Brownell, K. D., 313,
    317, 321, 323, 392
Brownlee, K., 345
Brownmiller, S., 195
Bruce, M. L., 221, 242,
    243, 245, 317
Bruch, H., 314, 324, 326
Bruch, M. A., 158
Bruck, M., 530, 532
Brugger, P., 457
Brunshaw, J., 23
Bruyn, G. W., 545
Bryant, D. M., 550
Bryant, R. A., 162, 300
Bryson, S. E., 535
Brzustowicz, 500, 502
Bucht, G., 553
Buchwald, D. S.,
    293, 294
Buck, K. J., 427
Buda, M., 259
Budenz, D., 254
Buehler, R. E., 119
Buffery, A. W. H., 185
Buffett-Jerrott, S. E., 61,
    135, 136, 137, 345
Buffum, J., 375
Bufka, L. F., 147
Bugg, F., 449, 460
Buis, T., 590
Bukowski, W. M., 364
Bulik, C. M., 312, 325
Bunney, W. E., 505
Burack, J., 523–524,
    524, 535
Burge, D., 237
Burggraf, K., 321
Burke, J. C., 536
Burke, K. C., 220
Burke, W. J., 568
Burnett, R., 298
Burney, E., 237
Burns, A., 564
Burns, L. E., 142
Burrowes, K., 207, 412
Burt, D. R., 54, 505
Burton, R., 12
Bury, A. S., 590
Busheikin, J., 514
Bushman, B. J., 413
Bushnell, W., 317

Busner, C., 263
Buss, K., 164
Bustillo, J., 515
Busto, U., 415
Butcher, J. N., 86
Butera, E., 240
Butler, G., 136
Butler, L. D., 204, 206, 207, 208, 332
Buysse, D. J., 337, 338, 348
Byers, E. S., 371, 376
Byne, W., 358
Byrne, D., 376, 378
Byszewski, A., 340

Caballero, B., 321
Caballo, V. E., 142, 152
Cabral, K., 194
Cacciola, J., 403
Cacioppo, J. T., 281
Cadoret, R. J., 185, 463
Caine, E. D., 259
Cairney, J., 245
Callaway, E., 91
Callender, J. S., 310
Camargo, C. A., 317
Cameron, E., 120
Cameron, R. P., 62, 314, 322
Campbell, D., 416
Campbell, G., 401
Campbell, L., 232
Campbell, L. A., 132, 234
Campbell, P., 170
Campo, J. V., 191
Canadian Charter of Rights and Freedoms, 591
Canadian Council on Smoking & Health and Physicians for a Smoke-Free Canada, 273, 430
Canadian Down Syndrome Society, 546
Canadian Institutes of Health Research, 592
Canadian Press, 416
Canadian Psychological Association, 589
Canadian Study of Health and Aging Working Group, 555, 556, 558, 562, 564
Candido, C. L., 492

Canestrarir, R., 255
Canino, G., 184, 412
Cannon, T. D., 507, 516
Cannon, W. B., 62, 64, 66
Canter, A., 88
Canterbury Farms, 249
Cantor, J. M., 359
Cantor-Graae, E., 499
Capobianco, D. J., 298
Cappeliez, P., 565
Cappell, H., 428
Capreol, M. J., 475
Caputo, G. C., 142
Cardeña, E. A., 198, 206, 207
Cardno, A., 236
Carey, G., 114
Carey, M. P., 366, 369, 370, 372, 373, 374, 375, 378, 381
Carlat, D. J., 317, 323
Carleton, R. N., 106
Carlson, E. B., 206
Carlson, G. A., 230, 231
Carlsson, A., 504
Carmody, D. L., 361
Carmody, J. T., 361
Caron, C., 451, 489
Carpenter, G., 256
Carpenter, L., 324–325
Carpenter, S., 324–325
Carpenter, W. T., 120, 489, 490, 495
Carr, K., 539
Carrington, P. J., 258
Carroll, B. J., 218, 238
Carroll, C., 371
Carroll, E. M., 162, 164
Carroll, K. M., 439
Carroll, R. A., 362, 363
Carskadon, M. A., 337
Carson, R. C., 98, 505, 507
Carstairs, G. M., 509
Carstensen, L. L., 69, 566
Carter, J., 331
Carter, J. R., 516
Carter, R. M., 134, 135
Cartwright, R., 349
Caruso, J. C., 87
Carver, C. S., 475
Cary, M. S., 561
Cascione, R., 547
Case, W. G., 137, 486
Cash, R., 320
Cashman, L., 170, 254
Casper, R. C., 331

Caspi, A., 41, 42, 44, 51, 57, 236, 448, 466
Cassano, G. B., 220
Cassel, C. K., 566
Cassem, N. H., 299
Cassidy, F., 218
Castellanos, F. X., 526
Castelli, W. P., 287
Castle, D., 499
Castonguay, L. G., 316
Cates, D. S., 288
Cautela, J. R., 391, 437
CBC News Online, 561
CCSA, 411, 412
Ceci, S. J., 208, 318
Center, B., 565
Centers for Disease Control, 259, 273, 300
Cepeda-Benito, A., 434
Cerda, G. M., 553
Cerny, J. A., 146
Cest, C.L., 163
Chakrabarti, S., 535
Chalder, T., 293, 294
Chamberlain, P., 466
Chambless, D. L., 142, 475
Champoux, M., 56
Chan, C. C., 436
Chandarana, P. C., 319
Chandler, M. J., 258
Chang, G., 438
Chapin, H. N., 332
Chapman, T. F., 159
Charcot, J., 18–19
Charlebois, P., 462
Charles, S. T., 69, 425
Charney, D. S., 52, 53, 130, 164, 407
Chartier, M., 180
Chartrand, T. L., 60
Chassin, L., 117, 429, 430
Chaturvedi, S. K., 319
Chau Wong, M., 505
Check, J. R, 188
Cheine, M., 505
Chen, I. G., 319
Chen, N., 512
Cherney, J., 142
Chernick, A. B., 362
Chesney, M. A., 65, 288, 298
Cheung, F., 67
Chevron, E. S., 330
Cheyne, L., 261

Chilcott, L. A., 335
China UN Theme Group, 279
Ching, S., 197
Chiu, P., 61, 319
Chivers, M. L., 360
Choate, M., 152
Chodirker, B. N., 534
Chodoff, P., 189, 450
Chorpita, B. F., 127, 131, 153, 163, 234, 242, 245, 246
Chow, E. W., 500
Christ, M. A. G., 525
Christensen, K., 236, 492
Christenson, G. A., 383
Christenson, R., 453
Christiansen, B. A., 429
Christie, A., 200–201
Christie, C., 500
Christophe, D., 387
Chronic Pain Association of Canada, 289
Chrousos, G. P., 237
Chudley, A. E., 534
Chung, S. Y., 535, 556
Ciaranello, R. D., 50
Cicchetti, D. V., 70
Ciccocioppo, M., 430
Cipani, E., 544
Ciraulo, D. A., 429
Clark, A., 447
Clark, D., 62
Clark, D. A., 170, 252
Clark, D. M., 145, 146, 181, 182, 293
Clark, L. A., 4, 127, 476, 477, 492, 515
Clark, R., 285
Clark, R. A., 279
Clarke, C. E., 567
Clarkin, J. F., 256, 446
Clarkson, S., 135
Classen, C., 282
Claude-Pierre, P., 332
Clayton, P. J., 185, 223
Cleare, A., 293
Cleary, P. D., 180
Cleckley, H. M., 460, 461
Cleghorn, J. M., 491, 506
Clement, U., 357
Clements, C. M., 242
Clementz, B. A., 503
Clipp, E. C., 277
Cloninger, C. R., 96, 184, 185, 465, 472
Closser, M. H., 418

Clum, G. A., 261
Clyburn, L. D., 564
Coates, T. J., 281
Cobain, K., 259
Cobb, A. M., 182
Cobb, J. A., 119
Cobb, S., 67
Cochran, S. D., 515
Cockell, S. J., 326
Cocores, J. A., 375
Coderre, T. J., 295
Cohen, F., 272
Cohen, J., 272, 276, 534, 535
Cohen, J. D., 90
Cohen, L., 401
Cohen, L. J., 196
Cohen, N., 278
Cohen, P., 333
Cohen, S., 67, 276, 277, 279, 372
Cohen, S. E., 287
Col, N., 552
Colakoglu, Z., 376
Cole, J. O., 249
Cole, M., 509
Cole, M. G., 552, 568
Colecchi, C., 347
Coleman, E., 360, 383, 425
Collins, A., 434
Collins, B. E., 300
Collins, J. F., 425
Collins, P., 51
Collins, R. P., 592
Collins, W. A., 43, 44
Comas-Diaz, L., 201
Comeau, M., 439
Compas, B. E., 231
Compton, W. M., 407
Condelli, W. S., 434
Condon, W., 204
Condray, R., 499
Conn, D. K., 551
Connell, M. M., 243
Conners, C. K., 525, 528
Connett, J. E., 287
Connolly, J. F., 137, 240, 532
Conrod, P. J., 115, 142, 407, 410, 429, 438, 439, 440
Constans, J. I., 164
Contandriopoulos, A., 556
Conti, S., 255, 381
Conwell, Y., 259, 261
Cook, B. L., 137

Cook, D. G., 272
Cook, E. H., 537
Cook, E. W., 60
Cook, I. A., 55
Coon, P. M., 209
Coones, W. H., 25
Cooney, J. L., 437
Coons, P. M., 183, 205, 207, 208, 209
Cooper, A. J., 375
Cooper, A. M., 428, 429
Cooper, M. L., 332, 449, 472, 473
Cooper, T. B., 252, 259
Cooper, Z., 312, 315, 317, 318, 326
Cooperstock, R., 414
Coplan, J. D., 56
Corbit, J. D., 429
Corbitt, E. M., 459, 460
Corcoran, C. M., 196, 230
Cordingley, G. E., 298
Coren, S., 335, 342, 343
Corkum, P., 335–336
Cornish, J. W., 434
Corrada, M., 565
Corrado, R., 259
Corrigan, P. W., 514
Corson, S., 140–141
Coryell, W. H., 220, 225, 226, 227, 449, 453
Costa, E., 46
Costa E Silva, J. A., 292, 293
Costa, P. T., Jr., 287, 447, 448
Côté, G., 165, 179, 180, 181, 182, 280
Cottler, L. B., 407
Coughlin, A. M., 582
Courchesne, E., 534, 538
Courchesne, R. Y., 538
Courneya, K. S., 282
Cousens, S. N., 561
Cousins, N., 298
Covey, L. S., 420
Cowdry, R., 227
Cowdry, R. W,, 227
Cowen, P. J., 325
Cox, A., 536
Cox, B. C., 116
Cox, B. J., 127, 140, 142, 145, 147, 159, 179, 180
Cox, C., 259, 261
Cox, L. S., 434
Coyle, J. T., 506

Coyle, N., 559
Crabbe, J. C., 427
Craddock, N., 115
Crafti, N. A., 330
Crago, M., 318, 319
Craig, C., 238
Craig, I.W., 42, 289
Craig, K., 289
Craighead, L. W., 60, 254, 256, 282
Craighead, W. E., 60, 256, 282
Cramer, P., 508
Craske, M. G., 136, 137, 139, 140, 141, 143, 146, 147, 155, 179, 180
Crawford, M., 526, 584
Creese, I., 54, 505
Cremniter, D., 261
Crichton, P., 298
Crisafulli, A., 104
Crisanti, A., 587
Crisp, A. H., 310
Cristi, C., 250
Crockford, D., 407, 435
Croft-Jeffreys, C., 500
Crosby, R. D., 317
Cross, P. A., 342
Cross-National
    Collaborative
    Group, 221
Crow, S. J., 312, 315, 317
Crow, T. J., 495
Crowe, L. C., 375
Crowe, R. R., 135, 251, 463
Crowley, P. H., 546
Cruickshank, J. K., 564
Cubic, B. A., 326
Cullen, B. A. M., 372
Cummings, J. L., 559
Cunniff, C., 508
Cunningham-Rathner,
    J., 383
Curran, P. J., 429
Curry, C., 539
Curtis, G. C., 151
Cuthbert, B., 63
Cutting, J., 493
Cyranowski, J. M., 244, 245, 358, 378
Czeisler, C. A., 345

Daamen, M., 356
Dadds, M. R., 138, 254

Dager, S. R., 566
Dahl, A. A., 435, 457
Dailey, R. C., 408
Dalack, G. W., 420
Daley, D., 107, 528
Dallaire, A., 586
Dallaire, R., 166
Dana, R. H., 85
D'Angelo, E. J., 469
Dannon, P. N., 251
Dansky, B.S., 162, 163
Dare, C., 328
Darkes, J., 429
Darvish, H. S., 223
Darwin, C., 62, 63
David, A., 67
Davidson, J., 161, 163, 226, 246
Davidson, K., 285, 286, 288, 454
Davidson, K. W., 21
Davidson, M., 505, 507
Davidson, R. J., 239
Davies, B., 238, 314, 420
Davis, C., 312, 314, 315, 317, 319, 322, 323, 326, 327, 329, 330, 332, 333
Davis, D. H., 429
Davis, D. M., 493
Davis, J. M., 108, 512
Davis, K. L., 46, 505, 565
Davis, M., 52, 130, 164
Davis, R., 333
Davis, S., 586, 587
Davison, I. A., 88
Dawson, D., 339, 407
Dawson, G., 535, 537
Day, J., 508
Day, R., 560
de Almeidia-Filho,
    N., 431
de Bono, J., 136
de Carvalho-Neto,
    414, 431
de Jong, P. J., 180, 182
de Koninck, J., 346
de la Monte, S. M., 564
de Marco, R. R., 229
de Zwaan, M., 317, 326
Deakin, J. F. W., 130
Deale, A., 294
Dean, C., 226
Dean, J. T., 178
Dean, P., 237
Dean, R. R., 50

DeBacker, G., 287
DeBaryshe, B. D., 465
DeBuono, B. A., 356
DeBusk, R. F., 436
DeCandia, C. G., 582
Deckel, A. W., 299
Decker, M. D., 137, 552
Deckersbach, T., 196
DeCourville, N. H., 207
DeFries, J. C., 39, 530
DeGirolamo, G., 292
Deiter, P. J., 194
Del Boca, F. K., 429
DeLissovoy, V., 537
Delizonna, L. L., 382
Dell, P. F., 205
DeMaso, D. R., 469
DeMayo, R., 245
Dembroski, T. M., 65, 287
Dement, W. C., 337, 345
DeMyer, M., 536
DeMyer, M. K., 536
Dennis, C., 434
Denton, F., 68
Denzin, N. K., 436
Depression Guideline
    Panel, 225, 226,
    248, 251
Deptula, D., 249
Depue, R. A., 51, 54,
    226, 237
DeRisi, W. D., 514
Derry, P. A., 243
Dersh, J., 289, 290
Dershewitz, R. A., 300
Dershowitz, A., 584
DeRubeis, R. J., 254, 255
Desilets, J., 527
DeSilva, P., 169, 378
Deter, H. C., 309
Deutch, A. Y., 164
Devanand, D. P., 199,
    201, 204, 206, 251
Devay, P., 420
DeVeber, L. L., 283
Devine, H., 447
Devins, G. M., 345
Devinsky, O., 207
Devlin, M. J., 328, 329
Devoulyte, K., 313
DeWitt, D., 413
DeWolfe, W., 382
DeYoung, J., 500
Diamond, M., 325,
    358, 359
Diamond, S., 282
DiBartolo, P. M., 136, 156

Dickey, C. C., 457
Dickson, K., 342
Dickstein, S., 222
Diehl, S. R., 501
Diener, E., 59
Difiglia, C., 250
Dihle, P. H., 204
DiLalla, L. F., 463
Dimberg, U., 157
Dimeff, L. A., 439,
    440, 470
Dimsdale, J. E., 65
Dineen, T., 332
Dinges, D. F., 203, 335
Dinnel, D. L., 157, 290
Diorio, J., 43, 130
Ditto, B., 37, 285
Dix, D., 17
Dixie-Bell, D. D., 143
Dixon, J. C., 197
Dixon, K., 286
Dixon, L. B., 513,
    514, 515
Dixon, S. D., 364
Dobkin, P. L., 26
Dobson, K., 5, 96, 208,
    242, 514
Docherty, J. P., 505
Doctor, R. F., 385
Dodge, C. S., 242
Dodick, D. W., 298
Dodson, J. D., 127
Doghramji, K., 345
Doherty, M., 300
Dohrenwend, B. P., 508
Doidge, N., 23
Dolan, R. J., 60
Dolberg, O. T., 251
Doll, H. A., 314, 315,
    317, 318
Dominion Bureau of
    Statistics, 583
Donahoe, C. P., 164
Donderi, D., 348
Dongier, M., 410, 511
Doraiswamy, P. M., 274
Dorian, B., 310, 316
Dorward, J., 145
Douglas, K. S., 462, 579,
    580, 581, 582, 583,
    590, 591, 592
Douglas, V. I., 525,
    527, 530
Downing, R., 137
Doyle, W. J., 67, 276
Draguns, J. G., 67, 117
Draijer, N., 198, 205

Drake, R. E., 515
Dramaix, M., 287
Drayer, R. A., 232
Drevets, W. C., 52,
    53, 130
Drury, V., 515
Dube, K. C., 439
Duberstein, P. R., 259
Dubovsky, S. L., 118
DuBreuil, S. C., 342
Duffy, A. L., 138
Dugas, M., 135, 136, 137
Dulit, R. A., 449, 450,
    460, 468, 472
Duma, C. M., 565
Dumas, J., 466
Duran, R. E. F., 206
Durand, V. M., 82, 84,
    335, 340, 347, 348,
    481, 523, 533, 535,
    538, 539, 548, 549
Durbin, C. E., 5, 236
Durkheim, E., 260
Durlak, J. A., 380
Dusseldorp, E., 286
Dwight, M. M., 196
Dwyer, E., 118
Dyck, R. J., 263
Dykens, E., 543, 547

Eagles, J. M., 309
Earls, F., 465
Earnst, K. S., 489
Earp, J. L., 300
Eaton, W. W., 135, 141,
    152, 217, 219, 222
Eaves, L. J., 135, 236,
    237, 462, 582, 588
Ebers, G., 358
Ebigno, P. O., 118, 181
Eckman, T. A., 514
Eddy, K. T., 315, 328
Edelmann, R. J., 152
Ediger, J. M., 145, 326
Edinger, J. D., 107
Edvarsen, J., 457
Edwards, A. J., 561
Efon, S., 310
Egeland, J. A., 114
Egri, C., 508
Ehrhardt, A., 361
Eich, E., 204
Eiseman, M., 142, 152
Eisen, J., 169
Eisenberg, L., 538

Eisler, I., 309, 323,
    328, 332
Elash, C. A., 434
Elder, G. H., 277, 466
Eldredge, K. L., 316,
    317, 331
El-Guebaly, N., 404,
    407, 435
Elie, R., 475, 552
Ellason, J. W., 205, 209
Ellenbogen, M. A., 237
Ellery, M., 101, 102,
    407, 434
Ellicott, A. G., 240
Ellinwood, E. H.,
    416, 417
Elliot, D. M., 208
Elliott, G., 439, 528
Elliott, R., 298
Ellis, A., 62
Ellis, N. R., 547
Emery, R. E., 104
Emrick, C. D., 436
Emslie, G. J., 336
Endicott, J., 220, 225,
    227, 254
Endler, N., 140, 145, 152,
    233–234, 249, 250,
    251, 298
Engebretson, T. O., 65
Engle-Friedman, M., 107
English, T., 190
Enns, M., 127, 159, 183,
    259, 261
Epling, W. F., 102, 326
Eppright, T. D., 462
Eppstein, D., 295
Epstein, C., 410
Epstein, J., 256
Erdberg, P., 85
Erhardt, D., 525
Erickson, S. A., 508, 509
Erikson, E., 23, 69
Erkinjuntti, T., 556
Ernberg, G., 500
Eron, L., 467
Ertekin, C., 376
Escobar, J. I., 180, 184
Espindle, D., 358
Esposito, C. L., 261
Essali, A., 505
Esterling, B., 280
Estes, L. S., 318
Eth, S., 161
Eubanks, L., 188
Evans, D. A., 555
Evans, D. D., 272

Evans, J. A., 546
Evans, L., 318
Evans, M. D., 255
Evans, S. M., 420
Evenson, B., 527
Everaerd, W., 373
Everett, J., 507
Evert, D. L., 410
Exner, J., 85
Eysenck, H., 27, 138, 447, 463
Eysenck, M., 130
Eysenck, S. B. G., 447, 463
Ezzel, C., 280

Fackelmann, K. A., 423
Faden, R. R., 273
Faedda, G. L., 250
Fagan, P. J., 387, 390, 393
Fahrner, E. M., 375
Fairbank, J. A., 434
Fairburn, C. G., 293, 309, 312, 313, 314, 315, 316, 317, 318, 321, 323, 324, 325, 326, 327, 328, 329, 330, 331, 332
Fallon, A. E., 195, 321, 322
Falloon, I., 499, 515
Fanale, J. E., 552
Faraone, S. V., 115, 231, 500, 525, 526
Farberow, N. L., 260
Farde, L., 455
Farmer, J., 300
Fauci, A. S., 279
Fausto-Sterling, A., 363
Fava, G. A., 249, 255
Faw, G. D., 548
Fawzy, F. I., 298
Feaver, C. H., 68
Federoff, B., 389, 390
Federoff, I. C., 159
Federoff, J. P., 389, 390
Feightner, J., 567
Fein, D., 536
Fein, G., 91
Feinberg, M., 238
Feingold, B. F., 526
Feinleib, M., 287
Feinstein, A., 189
Feist, J., 273, 284, 285, 288
Feldman, E., 207

Feldman, H. A., 369, 375
Feldman, J. J., 321
Feldman, L., 142, 152
Fellenius, J., 155
Fennell, P. A., 293
Fenton, B. T., 246
Fenton, W. S., 495
Fenwick, J. W., 434
Ferber, R., 340
Ferebee, I., 155
Fergus, K. D., 147
Ferguson, K. L., 478
Fernandez, F., 251, 393
Ferreira, C., 478
Ferrell, R. B., 513
Ferster, C. B., 28, 536
Fewell, R. R., 549
Fichter, M. M., 315
Fiedelak, J. I., 293
Field, A., 322
Field, T., 230
Fiester, S. J., 479
Fieve, R., 250
Figueroa, E., 469
Fils-Aime, M. L., 414
Fincham, F. D., 244, 245, 510
Fine, J., 189
Fink, M., 511
Finlayson, M. A. J., 527
Finley, G. A., 282, 283
Finn, P., 428, 429–430
Finney, J. W., 436
Finney, M. L., 65, 115, 116
Fiore, T. A., 528
Fiorino, A. S., 337
Firestone, P., 387, 388
First, M., 4, 23, 94, 96
Fischer, G., 115
Fischer, M., 502
Fischer, S. A., 221
Fish, B., 499, 506
Fishell, A., 389
Fisher, J. D., 88, 300, 301
Fisher, J. E., 566
Fisher, L., 586
Fisher, M., 547
Fisher, P., 261
Fisher, W. A., 300, 301
Fitts, S. N., 194
Fitzgerald, J., 495, 497
Fitzgerald, P. B., 251
Fitzpatrick, A. L., 559
Flanders, W. D., 375
Flannery, D. J., 467
Flater, S. R., 328

Flavin, D., 259
Fleisher, W. P., 205
Fleming, B., 453
Fleming, J. E., 231
Fletcher, M. A., 282
Flett, G. L., 152, 319, 326
Flint, A. J., 135
Flor, H., 291
Florio, L. P., 221
Flykt, A., 60, 64
Foa, E. B., 164, 167, 170, 171
Foege, W. H., 273
Foley, D. J., 107
Folks, D. G., 189
Follette, W. C., 98
Follman, M., 439
Folstein, M. F., 557
Folstein, S. E., 534, 557, 561
Fombonne, E., 535, 536
Ford, C. V., 187
Ford, M. R., 450
Forde, D. R., 156, 169, 189, 338
Fordyce, W. E., 289, 291
Forest, K., 218
Forestell, C. A., 322
Fort, C., 223
Forth, A. E., 449, 450, 460, 462, 463, 464, 465, 466
Fortin, C., 300
Fossati, A., 479
Foster, J. D., 141
Fought, R. L., 552
Fouts, G., 321
Fowles, D. C., 390, 464
Fox, D., 246
Fox, M. J., 561
Fox, P. T., 531
Foy, D. W., 162, 164
France, C., 285, 295
France, C. R., 290
France, J., 285
Frances, A. J., 449, 458, 525
Frances, R., 259, 261
Frances, R. J., 403, 414, 418, 425
Franche, R. L., 475
Francis, D., 43, 61, 130
Francis, G., 109
Frank, E., 227, 234, 240, 244, 250, 256, 300, 366, 367, 593

Frankenburg, F. R., 468, 469
Franklin, B., 18, 170, 180, 250, 403, 406, 414, 418
Franklin, D., 404
Franklin, J., 259
Franklin, J. E., 425, 553
Franko, D. L., 312, 315
Fraser, G. A., 186, 198, 199
Fraser, S., 243
Frasure-Smith, N., 288
Fratiglioni, L., 558, 564
Fredman, L., 67
Fredrikson, M., 60, 285
Freedman, M., 560
Freeman, A., 218, 317, 325, 453, 454, 455, 456, 472, 473, 474, 476, 477
Freeston, M., 170, 182
Freimer, N. B., 500
French-Belgian Collaborative Group, 287
Fresco, D. M., 240
Freud, A., 22
Freud, S., 18, 19–22, 23, 24, 61, 104, 127, 178, 190, 260, 335
Freund, K., 385
Frick, P. J., 466, 525
Friedenreich, C. M., 282
Friedhoff, L. T., 565
Friedl, M., 205
Friedman, B., 589
Friedman, M., 286, 287
Frisch, G. R., 404
Frith, C., 539
Fromm, E., 23
Fromm-Reichmann, F., 509
Frone, M. R., 429
Frost, R. O., 168, 169
Fryer, A. J., 535
Fugl-Meyer, S., 366
Fullerton, C., 180
Furer, P., 180, 182
Furmark, T., 155
Furniss, J. M., 119
Fyer, A., 146, 154, 159

Gabrielli, W. F., 408
Gacano, C. B., 590
Gadde, K. M., 285
Gadsby, J., 414

Gaggar, A., 317
Gagliese, L., 192, 291
Gagnon, C., 462
Gagnon, J., 378
Gagnon, M., 507, 531
Gajdusek, D. C., 564
Galambos, N., 69, 430
Galietta, M., 279
Gallagher, P. E., 460
Gallagher, T. F., 299
Gallagher-Thompson, D., 259
Gallant, D., 410, 435
Gallo, J., 259
Galper, Y., 558
Gammon, G. D., 524
Ganne-Vevonec, M. O., 469
Gara, M., 180
Garb, H. N., 85
Garber, S. W., 528
Garcia, J., 60
Gardner, E. L., 240, 414, 427
Gareau, C., 207
Garfield, A. F., 263
Garfinkel, P. E., 292, 293, 310, 312, 313, 314, 315, 316, 317, 318, 320, 326, 332
Garland, A. F., 259, 261, 263
Garlow, S. J., 237
Garmezy, N., 70
Garner, D. M., 309, 314, 315, 317, 318, 320, 323, 328, 329
Garnett, G., 279
Garre-Olmo, J., 559
Garrison, B., 261
Garvey, M. J., 137, 255
Gatchel, R. J., 289, 290, 291, 292, 295
Gatsonis, C., 222, 259
Gatz, M., 68, 137
Gauthier, J., 290, 292, 545
Gautier, T., 361
Gauvin, L., 322
Gawin, F. H., 429
Gay, M., 479
Gearhart, J. P., 362
Gebhard, P. H., 356
Geen, T., 169
Geist, R., 332
Gelber, S., 420
Gelfand, L. A., 254
Gelinas, L., 585

Geller, B., 249
Geller, J., 313, 332
Gemar, M., 242
Gendall, K., 328
Genest, M., 285
George, E. L., 251, 256, 258
George, L., 134, 135, 153, 161, 184, 190
George, L. K., 565
George, W. H., 375, 429
Gerald, J., 108
Gerin, W., 285
Gernert-Dott, P., 340
Gershon, E. S., 40, 227, 236
Ghadirian, A. M., 324
Ghaemi, S. N., 225, 240, 250
Ghaziuddin, 537
Gianotti, L. R. R., 457
Gianoulakis, C., 410, 422
Gibb, R., 41, 56, 57, 69
Gibb, W. R., 560
Gibson, P., 194
Gideon, P., 415
Giedke, H., 238
Gieser, L., 85
Gigante, R. A., 204
Gilbert, J. S., 331
Gilboa, E., 243
Gilger, J. W., 530
Gilham, J. E., 254, 291
Gillberg, C., 535
Gillies, L., 253
Gillin, J. C., 336, 338, 343, 345
Gillis, C., 323
Gilpin, E. A., 430
Gipson, M. T., 194
Girgus, J. S., 241
Gitlin, M., 508
Gitlin, M. J., 250
Gladis, M., 328
Gladue, B. A., 361
Glancy, G., 584
Glaser, R., 276, 277, 281, 282
Glass, S., 329
Glassco, J. D., 138
Glassman, A. H., 420
Glatt, A. E., 372
Glatt, C. E., 500
Glazer, J. P., 190
Glazer, W. M., 512
Gleason, O. C., 553

Gleaves, D. H., 198, 199, 205, 208, 312
Glick, I. D., 256, 512
Glick, M. P., 549
Glisky, M. L., 206
Glod, C. A., 249
Glover, G., 507
Glovinsky, P., 340, 349
Glynn, R. J., 137
Glynn, S. M., 515
Gnagy, E. M., 528
Goater, N., 500
Goering, P., 5, 317
Goff, D. C., 506
Gold, M. S., 436, 439
Gold, P. W., 237
Goldapple, K., 55
Goldberg, D. P., 184
Goldberg, J., 368, 493
Goldberg, J. F., 499
Goldberg, L., 447, 448
Goldberg, S. C., 458
Goldberger, J., 106, 226
Goldbloom, D., 310
Golden, C. J., 88, 157
Goldfarb, W., 536
Golding, J. M., 169
Goldman, M. S., 404, 429
Goldman, S. J., 469
Goldman-Rakic, P. S., 505
Goldner, E. M., 313, 326, 328, 332, 499
Goldner, V., 544
Goldsmith, D., 340
Goldstein, A., 420, 428, 434, 506, 546
Goldstein, A. J., 475
Goldstein, B., 436
Goldstein, E. B., 45, 46, 88, 375
Goldstein, I., 369, 381
Goldstein, I. B., 285
Goldstein, M. J., 256
Goldston, D., 259
Gonzalez-Lavin, A., 321
Good, A. B., 291
Good, B. J., 66, 232, 292
Good, K. P., 512
Goode, J. A., 463
Goodkin, K., 280
Goodman, S. H., 5, 62, 242, 246
Goodwin, D. W., 185, 408
Goodwin, F. K., 218, 219, 225, 226, 228, 233, 237, 238, 240, 250, 256, 282

Gooren, L., 360, 361
Gordis, E., 427, 428, 435, 440
Gordon, J. R., 438
Gorenstein, E. E., 185
Gorman, J., 148
Gorman, J. M., 279
Gorman, L. K., 46
Gorman, L. L., 254
Gorski, R. A., 358
Gorzalka, B., 373, 378
Gossard, D., 290
Gosselin, N., 136, 507
Gotheil, E., 282
Gotlib, I. H., 208, 217, 227, 230, 231, 232, 239, 240, 242, 243, 245, 246, 253
Gotowiec, A., 68
Gottesman, I. I., 40, 106, 463, 499, 500, 502, 507, 508
Gottlieb, B. H., 565
Gottlieb, G., 44, 56
Gould, M. S., 261, 262
Gould, R. A., 137, 328
Gould, S. J., 18
Grabe, H. J., 191
Grace, M. C., 162
Graeff, F. G., 130
Graf, P., 60, 61
Graham, D. L., 86
Graham-Hole, V., 515
Grandi, S., 255
Grandy, T., 418
Grant, B. F., 407
Grant, D., 23
Grant, I., 68, 232, 272
Grant, L., 289, 290
Gratzer, T. G., 591
Graves, R. E., 249, 457
Gray, J. A., 53, 130, 185, 428, 464
Gray, J. J., 321
Gray, K. F., 558
Grayson, C., 245
Graziosi, C., 279
Graziottin, A., 372
Grazzi, L., 298
Grcevich, S., 527
Greden, J. F., 420
Greeley, J., 428
Green, B. A., 312
Green, D., 278
Green, K. F., 60
Green, R., 361, 362

Greenberg, A. H., 278
Greenberg, D. M., 387
Greenberg, L., 25, 234
Greenberg, M. P., 60
Greenblatt, D. J., 137
Greene, K. A., 145, 162
Greene, R., 358, 514, 527
Greene, R. W., 83
Greenhill, L. L., 528
Greenhouse, W. J., 246
Greenlick, M. R., 287
Greenough, W. T., 56
Greenwood, A., 462
Greer, S., 281
Gregoire, A., 382
Greist, J. H., 170
Grenier, L. H., 371
Grey, J.P., 13, 13–14, 15, 29
Griffin, J., 17, 160, 552
Griffin, K., 161
Griffing, A., 312
Griffith, E. E. H., 190, 201
Griffiths, R. R., 420
Grilo, C. M., 317
Grimes, K. E., 493
Grinspoon, L., 423
Grisham, J. R., 132, 234, 259
Grisso, T., 593
Grissom, R. J., 103
Grob, C. S., 416
Groleau, D., 67, 68
Groom, C., 136
Groopman, L. C., 473
Gross, J., 62, 63, 317
Grossman, J. A., 231
Grossman, L. S., 226
Grossman, S., 309
Gross-Tsur, V., 529
Grosz, H. J., 189
Grove, W. M., 85, 255, 451
Gruber, A. J., 204, 336, 338
Gruder, C. L., 439
Gruen, R., 468
Gruenberg, A. M., 453
Grunhaus, L., 251
Gudanowski, D. M., 162
Guijarro, M. L., 285
Guild, D., 385
Guilhem, A., 10
Guilleminault, C., 341, 342, 343, 345

Gulati, D. K., 546
Gull, W. W., 310
Gündel, H., 223
Gunderson, J. G., 447, 449, 450, 453, 454, 467, 468, 469, 470, 473
Gunnar, M., 164
Gupta, M., 319
Gupta, N., 534
Gur, R. E., 507
Gureje, O., 180, 184, 189
Gurian, B., 450, 468
Gurlanick, O., 199
Guroff, J. J., 203
Gursky, D. M., 145
Gurvits, T. V., 164
Gurwitz, J., 137
Gusella, J., 332, 561
Guskin, K., 131
Gust, S. W., 434
Gustafson, Y., 553
Gustavsson, J. P., 455
Gutierrez, E., 534
Guttmacher, M. S., 585
Guydish, J., 436
Guyton, A., 285
Guze, B. H., 89
Guze, S. B., 185
Gwaltney, J. M., Jr., 67

Haaga, D. A. F., 234
Haak, J. W., 136
Haas, A. P., 423
Haas, G. L., 256, 261
Hachinski, V., 556
Hackett, T. P., 65, 299
Haddock, G., 326
Hadigan, C. M., 328
Hadjistavropoulos, T., 558, 564
Hadzi-Pavlovic, D., 509
Haenen, M. A., 180, 182
Hagnell, O., 559
Haig-Brown, C., 68
Haiman, C., 328
Hakstian, A. R., 460
Halek, C., 310
Hall, A., 309
Hall, D. E., 188
Hall, S. M., 420, 434
Hallet, A. J., 285
Halsey, N. A., 537
Hamer, D. H., 358, 458
Hamilton, D. A., 411
Hammeke, T. A., 88

Hammen, C., 237, 245, 246, 250
Hammerton, J. L., 546
Hammett, E., 163
Hammond, M., 466
Hammond, R., 300
Handman, M, 282
Haney, J. I., 300
Hankin, B. L., 70, 240, 242, 244
Hankins, C., 418
Hanks, D. L., 220
Hanley, I., 566
Hanna, G. L., 169
Hanna, L., 513
Hanrahan, G. E., 511
Hans, S. L., 506
Hans, V. P., 587
Hansen, F., 223
Harada, N., 157
Harbert, T. L., 392
Hardesty, J. P., 508
Harding, K., 222
Hardy-Bayle, M. C., 495
Hare, R. D., 86, 90, 96, 446, 449, 450, 459, 460, 461, 462, 463, 464, 465, 466
Hargrave, C., 582, 583
Hariri, A. R., 40
Harkness, A. R., 447
Harold, G. T., 244
Harousseau, H., 411
Harper, R. M., 336
Harpur, T. J., 460
Harrington, H., 42, 201
Harris, E. C., 310
Harris, G. T., 387, 392, 461, 462
Harris, J. E., 246
Harris, T. O., 239, 240, 245
Harrison, B., 145
Harrison, P. J., 325
Harriss, L., 261
Harrist, A. W., 104
Harrow, M., 226, 499
Hart, A. B., 254
Hart, E. L., 525
Hart, S. D., 460, 462, 463, 581, 582, 589
Harvald, B., 236
Harvey, A. G., 162
Harvey, I., 506
Hasanah, C. I., 118
Haslam, J., 476
Hassan, S. S., 260

Hassman, H., 137
Hathaway, S. R., 85
Hatsukami, D. K., 434
Hatzichristou, C., 142, 152
Hatzichristou, D. G., 369
Hauch, J., 145
Hauri, P. J., 340
Hauser, S. T., 246
Haw, C., 261
Hawkins, R. P., 78
Hawton, K., 261, 263, 367, 369, 371, 372, 381
Hay, P. J., 309, 312, 316, 318
Hayden, T. L., 546, 558
Hayes, M., 283
Hayes, S. C., 5, 109, 111, 392
Haynes, S. G., 287
Haynes, S. N., 83
Hays, R. D., 246, 253
Hayward, C., 314, 322
Hayward, G., 141
Haywood, M. E., 323
Hazell, P., 69
Hazelwood, L., 107
Hazlett-Stevens, H., 296
Health Canada, 249, 300, 301, 448
Heard, H. L., 470
Heath, A. C., 135, 236, 237, 318, 420
Heathcote, D., 69
Heatherington, D., 200–201
Heatherton, T. F., 318, 326
Heaton, R. K., 560
Hechtman, L., 525, 528
Hecker, M. H. L., 288
Hedley, A. J., 301
Heim, C., 56, 130
Heiman, J. R., 370, 377, 378, 379, 380
Heimberg, R. G., 156, 158, 159, 164, 242
Heinman, J. R., 330, 332
Heinrichs, N., 152
Heinrichs, R. W., 486, 507
Helenius, P., 532
Hellekson, K. L., 545
Heller, M. R., 50
Heller, W., 92, 246, 250
Hellman, I., 299
Hellman, R. E., 361

Hellstrom, K., 155
Helmes, E., 86, 556
Helmstetter, E., 539
Helweg-Larsen, M., 300
Helzer, J. E., 412, 429
Hemsley, D. R., 491
Hendin, H., 423
Hendren, R., 425, 426
Henggeler, S. W., 466
Henrich, C., 314
Henry, D, 69
Henry, G., 10, 16
Henschel, A., 323
Hepburn, K. W., 565
Hepworth, C., 240
Herbert, T. B., 272, 276, 277, 278
Herdt, G. H., 361
Herling, S., 428
Herman, C. P., 317, 319, 320, 322, 323, 324, 327, 328, 390
Herman, J. L., 469
Hermelin, B., 539
Hernandez, J., 180
Herrero, M. E., 525
Hersen, M., 392
Herz, M. I., 336
Herzog, D. B., 309, 312, 317, 318, 332, 333
Heslegrave, R., 468
Hess, T. H., 185
Hesselink, J. R., 538
Hester, R. K., 436
Hetherington, E. M., 43, 70, 466
Hettema, J. M., 240, 253
Hewitt, P. L., 326
Higgins, E., 242
Higgins, S. T., 437
Hildahl, K., 259
Hilgard, E. R., 60
Hill, A. E., 534
Hill, D. E., 414, 526
Hill, E. M., 151
Hiller, W., 180
Hiller-Sturmhöfel, S., 413, 438
Hillhouse, J., 181
Hillman, E., 336
Hilsenroth, M., 24
Hilts, P. J., 593
Hilty, D. M., 553
Hinchley, J., 532
Hincks, C., 17–18
Hindmarch, I., 136
Hinshaw, S. P., 525, 528

Hinshelwood, J. A., 531
Hinson, R., 430
Hippocrates, 12
Hirky, A. E., 432
Hirsch, S., 508, 509
Hirschfeld, R. M. A., 157, 476
Hiruma, N., 157
Hitchcock, P. B., 181
Hitler, A., 434
Ho, B. C., 489, 491, 494, 495, 499, 505, 506, 507
Ho, S. Y., 301
Hoaken, P. N., 413
Hobson, J. A., 336
Hodapp, R. M., 543, 545, 547
Hodes, R. L., 60
Hodgins, D., 259, 404
Hodgkinson, K. A., 502
Hodgson, R., 390
Hoehn-Saric, R., 135
Hoek, H. W., 309, 317
Hoenk, P., 197
Hoeper, E. W., 230
Hoffman, R. E., 491
Hoffmann, A., 423
Hofman, M. A., 361
Hofmann, S. G., 150, 151, 156, 158, 159
Hogan, D. R., 379
Hogarty, G. E., 514, 515
Hoge, S. K., 512
Holder, H. D., 440
Holford, T. R., 221
Hollander, E., 196
Holleen, H., 590
Holley, H., 587
Hollifield, M., 142
Hollis, J. F., 287
Hollon, S. D., 254, 255
Holm, J. E., 540
Holman, A., 180
Holmes, L. B., 21
Holroyd, K. A., 292, 295, 296, 298
Holt, C. S., 159
Holt-Lunstad, J., 276
Holzer, C., 221
Holzman, P. S., 503
Hommer, D. W., 430
Homolka, K., 385, 462
Honda, Y., 342
Hood, J. E., 242
Hoogduin, K. A., 190, 191
Hook, E. B., 546

Hooley, J. M., 469, 509
Hope, D. A., 159
Hope, R. A., 329
Hopkins, J., 331
Hops, H., 230, 291
Horan, W., 515
Horen, S. A., 205
Hornblow, A. R., 317
Horney, K., 23
Horowitz, M. J., 223, 472
Horwath, E., 142
Hounsell, S., 61, 323
House, J. S., 67, 232, 245
Houston, B. K., 288
Houston, K., 261
Houts, A. C., 4, 98
Hovdestad, W. E., 207
Howard, L. J., 313
Howard, R., 499
Howell, A. J., 209
Howes, J. L., 446
Howie, P., 531
Hoyt, R., 458
Hoza, B., 528
Hruby, P. J., 424
Hser, Y., 421
Hsu, L. K. G., 310, 312, 313, 314, 315, 319, 324, 331, 332
Hu, N., 358
Hu, S., 358
Hubbard, R. W., 259
Hubert, N. C., 283
Hucker, S. J., 385
Hudson, J. I., 193, 204, 237, 325
Huesmann, R., 467
Huey, S. J., 466
Hufford, M. R., 83, 143
Hughes, D., 134, 135
Hughes, J. R., 434
Hughes, M., 153, 161, 162, 285
Hull, J., 256
Humphrey, L. L., 322, 324, 325
Hunnicut, C. P., 321
Hunsley, H., 69
Hunsley, J., 5, 69, 85, 135
Hunt, W. A., 14
Hunter, D., 309
Hunter, J. A., 390
Huntington's Disease Collaborative Research Group, 561
Huntzinger, R. M., 152
Hurd, H. M., 17

Hurshman, J., 584
Husain, K., 294
Hussian, R. A., 566
Hutchins, G. M., 564
Hutson, R., 108
Huxley, G., 468
Hyde, J. S., 357
Hyler, S., 468
Hyman, S. E., 108
Hyman, S. L., 537
Hymowitz, P., 458
Hynd, G. W., 532
Hypercium Depression Trial Study Group, 249

Iacono, W. G., 237, 313, 509
Ianni, F., 446
Iarocci, G., 524
Iguchi, M. Y., 434
Ihara, H., 500
Ikels, C., 564
Ilardi, S. S., 60, 254
Imber, S. D., 120
Imhoff, D. F., 246
Imperato-McGinley, J., 361
IMS Health Canada, 371, 381
Inayatulla, M., 261
Ingram, R. E., 246
Insel, T. R., 56, 169
Institute Of Medicine, 263
Ipp, M., 362
Iribarren, C., 288
Ironson, G., 65, 272, 280, 281, 282, 288
Irvin, J. E., 439
Irwin, D., 335, 412, 469
Isaacowitz, D., 69
Israel, M., 231, 317
Israeli, A. L., 323
Iversen, L. L., 422
Ivis, F. J., 411, 413, 416, 530
Iwawaki, S., 142, 152
Izard, C. E., 63
Izquierdo, J. A., 375

Jablensky, A., 500
Jack, L., 582
Jackson, D. N., 447
Jackson, M., 196, 232

Jackson, R. J., 145
Jacobi, W., 506
Jacobs, J. L., 407
Jacobs, L., 430
Jacobs, S., 223
Jacobs, S. C., 242
Jacobsberg, L., 458
Jacobson, E., 290, 296
Jacques, D., 535, 565
Jaffe, A. J., 438
Jaffe, J. H., 429
Jaffe, P., 589
Jaffee, S. R., 246, 335
James, S. A., 272
Jameson, D., 202, 226
Jamison, K. R., 218, 219, 225, 228, 233, 237, 238, 240, 250, 256
Jamison, R. N., 291
Jamner, L. D., 285
Jang, K. L., 42, 114, 159, 163, 207, 447, 463
Janicak, P. G., 251
Jarvik, M. E., 419
Jasiukaitis, P., 206
Jason, L. A., 293
Jaspers, K., 489
Jay, S. M., 283
Jaycox, L. H., 254
Jeffrey, 29, 563
Jellinek, M. S., 413
Jenike, M. A., 55, 168, 171
Jenkins, J. H., 232
Jenkins, W. M., 509
Jensen, E. J., 435
Jensen, M. P., 291
Jensen, P. S., 528
Jensen, S. B., 368, 375
Jernigan, T. L., 538
Jerome, A., 298
Jessell, T., 51
Jessell, T. M., 56
Jethanandani, V., 231
Jilek, W. G., 201
Jindal, R. D., 238
Jobes, D. A., 259
Jocelyn, L. J., 534
Joffe, R., 228, 256, 448
Joffres, M., 565
Johannes, C. B., 369
John, O. P., 515
Johns, M. B., 299
Johnson, B., 426
Johnson, B. A., 130, 164, 423, 435
Johnson, B. T., 381
Johnson, J., 565
Johnson, J. G., 333

Johnson, J. M., 539
Johnson, L., 365, 419
Johnson, S. C., 188
Johnson, S. L., 240, 246
Johnson, V., 104, 379, 380
Johnson, W. G., 314, 317, 319
Johnson-Sabine, E., 322
Johnston, B. M., 254
Johnston, C., 5, 525
Johnston, D. W., 286
Johnston, M. I., 309
Johnston, S., 548
Johnston-Cronk, 514
Joiner, T. E., 243, 246, 261, 262, 263, 318, 326
Jonas, J. M., 325
Jones, I., 115
Jones, K. L., 411
Jones, M.C., 27, 164
Jones, P., 263, 506
Jones, R., 329, 330
Jones, R. T., 300
Jones, W., 499
Jonsson, E., 455
Jordan, B. D., 563
Joyce, P., 317
Judd, L. L., 219, 221, 222, 227
Judge, R., 146
Juneau, F., 288
Jung, C., 23, 24
Junginger, J., 384
Juul-Dam, N., 534


Kafka, M. P., 390
Kagan, J., 157
Kahana, E., 558
Kahn, R. S., 505
Kahn, S., 192
Kahn, U. A., 118
Kalat, J. W., 47, 48, 49, 50, 53, 54
Kallmann, F. J., 500
Kaltman, S., 223
Kalus, O., 454, 455, 456
Kamerow, D. B., 338
Kaminen, N., 531
Kandel, D. B., 420
Kandel, E., 51, 56
Kane, J. M., 512
Kanigel, R., 419
Kannel, W. B., 287
Kanner, L., 536, 538
Kaplan, A. S., 313, 317, 332

Kaplan, B. H., 67
Kaplan, G. A., 232
Kaplan, H. S., 365, 367, 368
Kaplan, M., 450
Kaplan, N. M., 285
Kapur, S., 492, 505
Karakowski, L. M., 154, 159, 240
Karlberg, A. M., 259
Karno, M., 169
Karon, B. P., 85
Kasari, C., 535
Kasch, K. L., 217
Kasen, S., 333
Kashani, J. H., 230, 300, 462
Kashner, T. M., 186
Kasl, S., 223
Kasl, S. V., 59
Kass, D. J., 472
Katon, W., 135, 142, 184, 275, 277, 293
Katschnig, H., 142
Katz, J., 192, 295, 299
Katz, M., 544, 553
Katz, R., 42, 231, 235, 236, 313, 323, 325, 326
Katz, R. C., 194
Katzman, D. K., 332
Kauffman, J. M., 532
Kavanagh, D. J., 509
Kawamura, K. Y., 319
Kawas, C., 565
Kaye, W., 312, 316, 325, 326, 328, 331
Kayz, J., 291
Kazarian, S. S., 272, 509
Kazdin, A. E., 83, 261, 300, 466
Keane, T. M., 157, 162, 164
Kearns, R. D., 291
Keck, P. E., Jr., 193, 227, 250
Keefe, F., 290, 291, 295, 298
Keel, P., 309, 310, 312, 313, 315, 316, 318, 326, 333
Keenan, K., 434
Kegeles, L. S., 505
Kehrer, C. A., 263, 470
Keijsers, G. P., 190
Keith, S., 515
Keitner, G. I., 246, 254, 256

Keller, M., 135, 217, 219, 220, 222, 227, 231, 254, 277
Kellner, R., 180, 181, 182
Kelly, K. A., 242, 261
Kelly, M. P., 261, 371, 377
Kelsey, J. E., 50
Kemeny, M. E., 273, 274, 275
Kemp, S., 9, 11, 12
Kendell, R. E., 226
Kendler, G. S., 318
Kendler, K., 40, 42, 44, 130, 135, 154, 236, 237, 240, 253, 312, 317, 318, 325, 326, 327, 453, 501
Kennedy, D. L., 137
Kennedy, Q., 69
Kennedy, S., 96, 272, 280, 281, 310, 313, 317, 326, 328, 330
Kennedy, W., 556
Kenney, R. D., 188
Kent, J. M., 56
Kentish, J., 138
Kern, H. E., 251
Kernberg, O., 22
Kerr, M. M., 105
Kertzner, R. M., 279
Kessler, R. C., 40, 134, 135, 141, 152, 156, 162, 219, 221, 222, 229, 232, 235, 236, 239, 240, 318
Kest, B., 292
Kety, S. S., 261
Keys, A., 323
Khaitan, B. K., 378
Khalifé, S., 372, 380
Khan, A., 118
Khanna, A., 393
Khantzian, E. J., 429
Kiang, M., 492
Kiecolt-Glaser, J. K., 272, 276, 277, 281, 282
Kiesler, D. J., 103
Kihlstrom, J. F., 60, 178, 206, 207
Kilbey, M. M., 420
Kilgus, M., 364
Killen, J. D., 314, 322, 333
Killinger-Johnson, S., 227
Kilman, V. L., 56
Kilpatrick, D. G., 162, 163
Kilzieh, N., 227
Kim, E. D., 369, 382
Kim, J. J., 103

Kim, K. M., 243, 245
Kinder, B., 309
Kinder, B. N., 375
King, A., 87
King, D. W., 162, 164
King, G. R., 416
King, L. A., 162, 164
King, N. J., 153
King, S., 510, 528
King, S. A., 192
Kingdon, D., 515
Kinney, D. K., 234
Kinsey, A., 356
Kinzie, J. D., 233
Kipp, H. L., 528
Kirch, D. G., 507
Kircher, J. C., 371
Kircher, J. R., 377
Kirkley, B. G., 321
Kirmayer, L. J., 67, 68,
   157, 180, 181, 184,
   186, 190, 217, 232,
   233, 259, 262
Kirschenbaum, B., 564
Kissinger, P., 279
Kita, M., 534
Kitchell, M. A., 566
Kittel, F., 287
Kivlahan, D. R., 439
Kjernisted, K. D.,
   127, 183
Kleban, M., 231
Kleber, H. D., 429, 434
Klein, D., 4, 159, 220,
   222, 231, 236, 434
Klein, M., 22
Klein, R., 401
Kleinbaum, D. G., 67, 108
Kleinknecht, E. E., 157
Kleinknecht, R. A.,
   157, 290
Kleinman, A., 66, 118,
   196, 220, 232, 292
Klerman, G. L., 179,
   180, 220, 221, 245,
   251, 330
Kletti, R., 206
Klevens, R. M., 375
Klin, A., 534
Klosko, J. S., 146, 242
Kluft, R. P., 203, 204,
   205, 206, 208, 209
Klumker, A., 196
Klump, K. L., 325
Knapp, C. M., 429
Knapp, S., 237
Knauper, B., 229

Knight, R. A., 385
Ko, G., 505
Koch, G. G., 300
Koch, W. J., 145, 162,
   579, 580, 581, 582,
   583, 591, 592
Kochanek, K. D., 259
Kodituwakku, P., 411
Koegel, L. K., 537
Koegel, R. L., 536
Koh, P. O., 505
Kohut, H., 473
Kolb, B., 41, 56, 57,
   61, 69
Kolko, D., 261
Koller, H., 544
Kong, V., 65
Koocher, G. P., 282
Koopman, C., 206
Kopyov, O. V., 565
Korczyn, A. D., 558, 564
Korenman, S. G., 428
Korf, J., 237
Korfine, L., 469
Korman, L. M., 470
Kornitzer, M., 287
Korol, C., 289
Korten, A., 500
Koselka, M., 142
Kosson, D. S., 464
Kostaras, X., 246
Koster, E., 170
Kotagal, P., 190
Kotsaftis, A., 449, 456
Kovacs, M., 222, 259, 261
Kowatch, R. A., 347
Kozak, J. M., 171
Kraaij, V., 286
Kraemer, H., 282,
   329, 436
Kraepelin, E., 15, 93–94,
   486, 486–487,
   503, 511
Krane, R. J., 369
Krank, M., 430
Krantz, D. S., 299
Kranzler, H. R., 435, 437
Krasnoperova, E., 242
Kraus, N., 532
Krejci, J., 319
Krichev, A., 87
Kring, A. M., 489, 493
Kringlen, E., 457
Kripke, D. F., 336
Krishnamurthy, R., 86
Krishnan, K. R., 274
Krishnan, R. R., 163

Kristensen, H., 531
Kristiansen, C., 207
Krivo, S., 279
Kroner, D. G., 460
Kronholm, P., 552
Krueger, R. F., 448
Krug, E. G., 262
Kruger, S., 328
Krystal, J. H., 164
Kuban, M., 373, 385
Kuch, K., 142
Kuhn, C., 65
Kuiper, N., 243
Kuipers, E. A., 509
Kullgren, G., 190, 363
Kunkel, S. R., 59
Kuno, R., 281
Kuo, W. H., 259, 412
Kuperman, S., 197
Kupfer, D. J., 4, 53, 96,
   98, 99, 238, 240, 250,
   262, 335, 348, 593
Kurita, H., 534
Kurlan, L. T., 309
Kurtzman, H. S., 242
Kushner, M. G., 142,
   404, 407
Kusumakar, V., 221, 222,
   230, 254
Kutcher, S., 89, 237
Kwasnik, D., 525

La Greca, A. M., 161, 164
La Rue, A., 560
Laan, E. T. M., 373
Labouvie, E., 331
Lacey, J. H., 309
Lachar, B. L., 251
Lachar, D., 83
Lack, L., 339
Lacks, P., 346
Ladd, C. O., 56, 130,
   164, 237
Lader, M. H., 130, 190
Lader, M. L., 53
Ladouceur, R., 135, 136,
   137, 138, 149, 151,
   155, 404, 531
Lahey, B. B., 525
Lahmer, V., 87
Laing, R. D., 500
Lakin, K. C., 382
Lalonde, J. K., 204, 258
Lalumiére, M., 358
Lam, R., 228, 251,
   301, 345

Lamb, J. A., 260
Lambert, J. C., 559
Lambert, M., 108, 117,
   118, 256, 325
Lancee, W. J., 23
Lanctot, K. L., 415
Lander, M., 183
Landerman, R., 184, 190
Landis, K. R., 67, 232
Landis, S. E., 300
Lane, C. J., 489
Lane, R. D., 223
Lang, P. J., 60, 63, 430
Lang, R. D., 189
Langewisch, M. W. J., 404
Langford, S., 464, 528
Langstroth, D., 325
LaPerrier, A., 282
Lapierre, Y. D., 249
Larimer, M. E., 437
Larivée, S., 462
Larntz, K., 450
Laroche, L., 335
Larsen, S. E., 145, 313
Larson, E. B., 544
Larson, J., 245
Laruelle, M., 505
Lasch, C., 473
Latham, K. S., 180
Lau, M. A., 245
Laub, J. H., 460
Laumann, E. O., 366,
   367, 369, 370, 371,
   377, 378, 413
Lauriello, J., 515
Laurier, C., 556
Lavalle, C., 233
Laver-Bradbury, C., 528
Laverdure, J., 233
Lavoie, P., 37, 507
Lavori, P., 220, 222
Laws, D. R., 392
Lawson, W. B., 205
Laxenaire, M., 469
Laxova, R., 544
Lazarus, R., 63, 64
Lazerson, A., 50
Le Greca, A. M., 134
Leadbeater, B. J., 69
Leader, J. B., 220
Leaf, P. J., 221
Leary, T., 424
Lebedinskaya, K. S., 535
LeBlanc, M., 462
Leckman, J., 168,
   531, 547
Lecrubier, Y., 146

Lederhendler, I., 310, 316, 318, 325, 328

LeDoux, J. E., 50, 51, 64, 130

Lee, C. K., 412, 431

Lee, C. M., 68, 69

Lee, K., 340

Lee, K. L., 65

Lee, M.A., 424

Lee, P. W. H., 535

Lee, S., 310, 319

Lee, T., 505

Lee, T. M., 228

Leenaars, A. A., 258

Leff, J., 500

Lehman, A. F., 515

Lehman, C. L., 132, 137, 146, 150, 159, 161, 164, 234, 326

Lehman, D., 208

Lehman, H., 14

Lehmann, H. E., 511, 515

Lehoux, P. M., 322

Leiblum, S. R., 372, 378, 380

Leichner, P. P., 205

Leitenberg, H., 326, 332, 373

Leith, W., 531

Lejeune, J., 545

Lemoine, P., 411

Lendon, C., 559

Lenke, R. R., 545

Lentz, R. J., 513

Lentzf, E., 530

Lenze, E. J., 232

Lenzenweger, M. F. A., 503

Leon, A., 51

Leonard-Green, T. K., 319

Lerew, D. R., 145

Lerman, C., 427

Lesage, A., 475

Lesch, K. P., 130

Leserman, J., 67, 280

Leshen, E., 231

Lesperance, F., 288

Lester, D., 258, 263

Leuchter, A., 55

Leung, F., 319, 324

Leung, G. M., 556

Leung, P. K., 233

Levan, A., 545

Levenson, S., 339, 340

Levenston, G. K., 464

Levine, A. C., 381

Levine, B., 89

Levine, J. L., 255

Levine, M. P., 321, 326

Levine, R. J., 120

Levinson, D. F., 468, 503

Levitt, A. J., 228, 251, 255

Levitt, J. T., 147

Levy, B. R., 59

Levy, D. L., 251, 532, 545

Lewine, R. R. J., 506

Lewinsohn, P. M., 220, 221, 222, 230, 231, 236, 239, 240, 243, 245, 261

Lewis, D. O., 206

Lewis, G., 263, 500

Lewis, J. A., 151

Lewis, J. G., 65, 67

Lewis, M., 206

Lewis, S., 506, 507

Lewis-Fernandez, R., 207

Lewy, A. J., 228, 251

Li, H. Z., 68

Li, X., 259

Liberman, R. P., 514, 515, 593

Lichtenstein, P., 42

Lidbeck, J., 186

Lidow, M. S., 505

Lieb, R., 131, 184

Lieberman, A., 565

Lieberman, J. A., 503

Liebeskind, J. C., 289, 292, 294

Liebowitz, M. R., 133, 135, 151, 159, 171, 184, 196

Lieff, S., 551

Lietaer, G., 25

Liggett, J., 195

Lilienfeld, S. O., 4, 185, 204, 208, 450, 471, 472

Limb, K., 257

Lin, E., 317

Lin, K. M., 564

Lind, D. L., 190

Linden, W., 285, 286

Lindesay, J., 552

Lindquist, P., 581

Lindsay, J., 559

Lindsey, K. P., 500

Lindwall, R., 155

Lindy, J. D., 162

Linehan, M., 263, 469, 470

Links, P., 96

Links, P. S., 468, 469, 470

Linnet, K. M., 527

Lipchik, G. L., 292, 298

Lipowski, Z. J., 551

Lipshultz, L. I., 369, 382

Lipton, A. M., 560

Lisanby, S. H., 251

Liss, A., 158

Litman, R., 260

Little, D., 312

Little, L., 436

Littrell, L., 223

Litz, B. T., 382

Liu, D., 43

Livanou, M., 108

Livesley, J., 114, 207, 328

Livesley, W. J., 42, 96, 159, 163, 447, 448, 463

Loba, P., 101, 160, 161, 407

Lobban, M., 309

Locke, P., 548

Lockshin, B., 278

Loeb, K., 329, 331, 332

Loebel, J . P., 566

Loeber, R., 462, 525

Loewenstein, R. J., 199, 204, 209

Loewi, O., 50

Loftus, E. F., 208

Loftus, J., 366

Logan, A., 145

Lohr, B., 196

Loiseau, B., 260

Long, J., 366, 427, 515

Looman, J., 391

Looper, K., 180, 186, 448

Lopez, S. R., 509

LoPiccolo, J., 366, 367, 370, 378, 379, 380, 381

Lord, S., 468

Lorrain, D., 346

Loughlin, H. L., 108

Lovaas, O. I., 539

Lowe, M. R., 309, 312

Lowman, R. L., 104

Lucas, A. R., 309

Lucas, J. A., 145

Luciana, M., 51

Luckasson, R., 540, 542, 543

Ludwig, A. M., 202, 234

Ludwig, D., 412

Luk, S. L., 535

Lukasson, R., 540

Lukoff, D., 508

Lunde, I., 234

Lundh, L. G., 157

Lundqvist, D., 60, 64

Lundstrom, B., 360, 363

Lusty, K., 566

Lutgendorf, S. K., 280

Lydiard, R. B., 166, 170

Lyketsos, C., 555

Lykken, D. T., 40, 105, 464

Lynam, D. R., 462

Lynch, K. G., 261

Lyon, D. R., 589

Lyons, M. J., 236, 237

Lytle, R., 137

Lyubomirsky, S., 59

Maas, J. W., 504

McAdoo, W. G., 536

McAndrews, M. P., 61

Macauley, D., 204

McCabe, R., 146, 155, 156, 158, 196, 197, 314

McCaffrey, R. J., 590

McCarthy, E., 257

McCaughrin, W. B., 549

McChesney, C. M., 135

Macciocchi, S. N., 88

McClearn, G. E., 39, 40, 42

McConaha, C. W., 312

McCool, B. A., 568

McCord, D. M., 86

McCormack, W. M., 356, 372

McCrae, R. R., 447, 448

McCreery, J. M., 435

McCullough, J. P., 223

McCullough, P. K., 478

McDaniel, K., 561

Macdonald, 259, 375

MacDonald, A. B., 66, 108, 140

MacDonald, C., 29

McDonough, J., 401

MacDougall, J. M., 65, 514

McDowell, D. M., 426, 555

McDuff, P., 105

Mace, C. J., 186

McEachin, J. J., 539

McElroy, S. L., 193, 196, 218, 227, 250

McEwen, B., 238

McFarlane, T., 314

McGee, R., 448
McGehee, D. S., 420
McGinnis, J. M., 273
McGlashan, T. H., 495, 499
McGonagle, K. A., 152
McGowan, B. K., 60
McGowin, D. F., 553, 563
McGrath, J., 516
McGrath, P., 282, 283
MacGregor, M. W., 21, 286
McGue, M., 105, 236, 313, 427
McGuffin, P., 42, 130, 235, 236, 246, 323, 503
McGuire, P. K., 491
McGuire, R. J., 456
McHugh, P. R., 557
McHugo, G. J., 515
Maciejewski, P. K., 242
McIntosh, J. L., 259
MacIsaac, A., 3
McIsaac, H., 89, 151
Mack, A. H., 403, 408, 410, 413, 417, 418, 419, 421, 422
McKay, D., 196
Mackay, K., 200
McKenna, J. C., 340
McKenna, P., 500
MacKenzie, E. J., 300, 326
McKeon, P., 478
McKim, W. A., 413, 421
McKinley, J. C., 85
MacKinnon, D. F., 227, 234, 277, 300
MacKinnon, J., 582
McKissick, F. C., 537
McKnight, D. L., 256
McKunlay, J. B., 369
McKusick, L., 281
McLachlan, S., 219, 496–497
McLaren, A., 549
McLaughlin, S., 226
MacLean, C., 21, 318, 439
MacLean, D., 286
McLean, P., 171, 254
McLeod, D. R., 135, 136, 429
McLeod, J. D., 242
McLintock, B., 332
McMain, S., 470

MacMartin, C., 207
MacMillan, F., 469, 515
McMullen, L. M., 245
McNally, R. J., 18, 60, 136, 145
McNamara, G., 432
McNaughton, N., 53, 130
McNeil, T. F., 499, 507
McPherson, L., 131, 449, 450, 466
McTeer, M., 226
McVey, G., 313, 319, 330, 333
McWilliams, L., 131, 141
Maes, S., 286
Magder, L., 276
Magee, W. J., 141, 152, 156, 157
Magliano, L., 227
Magne-Ingvar, U., 260
Magnuson, V. L., 358
Magnusson, A., 228
Maher, B. A., 9, 12, 16
Maher, J. J., 409
Maher, W. B., 9, 12, 16
Mahler, M., 536
Mahowald, M. W., 349
Mahr, G., 531
Mailloux, D. L., 460, 465
Maislin, G., 335
Maisto, S. A., 453
Mak, K. H., 301
Malamud, T. J., 515
Malatesta, V. J., 371, 375
Malchy, B., 259
Malcolm, P. B., 393
Maldonado, J. R., 204, 209
Maletzky, B. M., 391, 392, 393
Malhotra, S., 534
Malkin, I., 439
Malla, A. K., 491, 492, 509
Malone, K. M., 261
Malow, R., 417
Malpass, R. S., 118
Maltsberger, J. T., 478
Maltzman, I. M., 437
Malus, M., 259, 262
Manber, R., 342, 420
Mancill, R. B., 132, 234
Mandalos, G. E., 249
Mandel, H., 168
Mandeli, J., 381
Mandell, A. J., 237
Mandler, G., 60

Mangelsdorf, S., 164
Manji, H. K., 505
Mank, D. M., 548
Mankowski, S., 410
Mann, J. J., 237, 261, 322
Manni, R., 349
Mannino, D. M., 375
Mannuzza, S., 159
Manor, O., 529
Manson, S. M., 232
Mapstone, E., 340, 533
Marcellino, B., 527
March, J. S., 525, 528
Marchand, A., 381
Marchuk, D. A., 285
Marcopulos, B. A., 249
Marcouiller, M., 475
Marcus, J., 506
Marcus, M. D., 329, 331
Marder, S. R., 514, 593
Marek, P., 292
Margo, A., 491
Margraf, J., 180
Mariani, M. A., 524
Marin, D. B., 449
Marino, L., 4, 468
Marks, I., 294
Marks, I. M., 35, 108
Marks, T., 245
Marlatt, A., 437, 438, 439
Marmot, M. G., 287
Marnell, M., 331
Marsden, C. D., 189
Marshall, W. L., 387, 390, 391, 393
Marten, P. A., 134
Martin, B., 437
Martin, C., 356, 358
Martin, I., 131
Martin, J. A., 259
Martin, N. G., 154, 237, 238, 531, 549
Martin, P. R., 568
Martin, R. L., 185
Martin-Cook, K., 567
Martinez, A., 475
Martlatt. G. A., 431
Marx, J., 563
Maser, J. D., 150
Mash, E. J., 523
Masheb, R. M., 317
Maslow, A., 24, 25
Mason, F. L., 383
Massie, H. N., 557
Massion, A. O., 135
Masters, W., 104, 365, 379, 380

Matas, M., 591
Mathews, A., 136, 138, 181, 242
Mathews, R., 390
Maticka-Tyndale, E., 356, 357
Matsuanga, D., 233
Matsumoto, D., 287, 431
Matthews, K. A., 285, 287
Mattia, J. I., 193, 194, 195
Mattis, S. G., 145
Maurer, T. A., 259
Maxwell, K. L., 550
Mayberg, H., 55
Mayer, B., 182
Mayer, J., 321
Mayfield, U., 190
Mayville, S., 194
Maziade, M., 454, 515
Mazure, C. M., 240, 242, 243, 491
Mazurick, J. L., 466
Meadows, E. A., 164
Meana, M., 372
Meaney, M., 43, 130, 274
Medicna-Mora, M. E., 431
Mednick, S. A., 507, 508, 516
Meduna, J. Von, 14
Meehan, P. J., 260
Meehl, P. E., 98, 457, 493
Meichenbaum, D., 25, 62, 165, 285
Meisler, A. W., 373
Melino, G., 278
Meloy, J. R., 466
Melton, G. B., 552, 589, 590
Melville, L. F., 158
Melzack, R., 192, 289, 291, 292, 295
Mendes, W. B., 67
Menuet, J. C., 411
Merali, Z., 43
Mercer, C. H., 339
Merikangas, K. R., 114, 115, 235, 407, 563
Merzel, A. P., 234
Merzenich, M. M., 532
Mesmer, A., 18
Meston, C. M., 357, 358, 373, 377, 378, 380, 381
Metalsky, G. I., 242
Metter, E. J., 565
Metzner, H. M., 67

Meulman, J., 286
Meyer, A., 29–30
Meyer, B., 246
Meyer, J. M., 475
Meyer, L. H., 549
Meyer, R. E., 438
Meyer-Bahlburg,
    H. F. L., 361
Meyerowitz, B. E., 299
Meyers, A., 272
Meyers, R. J., 438
Meyyazhagan, S., 188
Mezzacappa, E., 469
Mezzich, J. E., 97, 201
Miaskowski, C., 292
Michael, R., 28, 378
Michaels, S., 378
Michelson, O., 323
Miklowitz, D. J., 256, 258
Milet, T., 227
Millar, H. R., 309, 552
Millar, N., 138
Miller, G. A., 92
Miller, I., 240, 241, 246
Miller, I. W., 59, 254, 256
Miller, K., 312, 333, 336
Miller, N., 295
Miller, N. S., 375, 436
Miller, P. M., 285, 288,
    429, 436, 438
Miller, P. P., 165
Miller, S., 531
Miller, W. R., 433, 436
Millon, T., 93, 94, 449,
    474, 475
Mills, J. L., 420
Mills, J. R, 319
Milner, P., 427
Milstein, V., 205
Mindell, J. A., 84, 340,
    347, 348
Mineka, S., 58, 60, 127,
    131, 157, 242
Miner, M., 383
Mingdao, Z., 516
Minichiello, W. E., 168
Minino, A. M., 259
Mintz, J., 508, 514, 593
Minuchin, S., 324, 328
Mirenda, P., 548
Mirin, S. M., 246
Mirsky, A. F., 501, 516
Misovich, S. J., 300
Misri, S., 246
Missio, E., 401
Mitchell, J., 160, 163,
    312, 314, 315, 317,
    318, 326, 333

Mitchell, M., 549
Mitchell, T. L., 161
Mitler, M. M., 349
Mittelman, M., 383
Mittlehold, J., 207
Miyake, Y., 534
Miyazaki, S., 342
Moak, D. H., 409, 410
Moene, F. C., 190, 191
Moffitt, T. E., 42, 448, 461
Mogg, K., 136, 138
Mogil, J. S., 292
Mogun, H., 137
Moher, D., 450, 528
Mohr, D. C., 457
Moldofsky, H., 315,
    335, 336
Molina, B. S., 527
Molina, B. S. G., 429
Moline, M. L., 339
Moller-Madsen, S., 309
Monahan, P., 582
Monarch, E. S., 289,
    290, 292
Monck, E. M., 509
Money, J., 120, 361
Monjan, A. A., 107
Monk, T. H., 337, 339
Monroe, M., 414
Monroe, S. M., 239, 240,
    243, 244, 246
Monteiro, S., 155
Montejo-Gonzalez,
    A. L., 375
Montgomery, H., 436
Montiel-Barbero, I., 526
Montiel-Nava, C., 526
Moore, D. S., 43
Moore G. W., 564
Moore, R. G., 254
Moore, R. Y., 238, 246
Moos, R. H., 436
Moras, K., 234
Morelli, G. A., 340
Moretti, M., 243
Morey, L. C., 95, 451
Morgan, M., 55
Morgantaler, A., 382, 436
Morgenstern, H., 512
Morin, C. M., 107, 335,
    338, 339, 340,
    346, 347
Morissette, A., 128
Morokoff, P., 369
Morris, D., 195
Morris, J., 568
Morris, J. K., 272, 277
Morris, J. S., 60

Morris, M., 339
Morrison, M., 254
Morriss, R., 257
Morris-Yates, A., 531
Morrow, G. R., 26
Morton, A., 310
Moscicki, E., 259
Mosher, P., 24
Mosimann, J. E., 321
Mosko, S., 340
Moss, A. R., 279
Mostofsky, D. I., 273
Mottron, L., 524
Moulden, H., 393
Moulton, D., 421
Mount, J. H., 227
Mucha, T. F., 189
Mudar, P., 429
Mueller, T. I., 219,
    222, 227
Mueser, K. T., 509, 513,
    514, 515
Muir, S. L., 322
Mukai, J., 342
Mulchahey, J. J., 41
Mullan, J. T., 566
Mullington, J., 335
Mumford, D. B., 318
Mumford, G. K., 420
Mumme, D., 131
Mundy, P., 535
Munjack, D. J., 153
Muñoz, R. F., 63,
    254, 420
Munro, A., 497
Murdoch, D., 413
Murphy, H. A., 525
Murphy, J., 502
Murphy, S., 375
Murphy, S. L., 255, 259
Murphy-Eberenz,
    K. P., 312
Murray, A., 323, 325
Murray, C. J. L., 259
Murray, R., 478, 491, 499
Murray, R. M., 506, 507
Murry, E., 218
Mussell, M. P., 317
Mustafa, G., 510, 516
Musto, D. F., 417
Myers, J. K., 142,
    149, 152
Myers, L., 279

Nachmias, M., 164
Nagasaki, Y., 550
Nagayama Hall,
    G. C., 393

Nagel, D. B., 511, 513
Nagin, D., 117
Naring, G. W., 190
Nash, J., 292, 298
Nasrallah, A., 251
Nasser, M., 318
Nathan, P. E., 435
Nathan, S., 185
National Institute of
    Mental Health,
    237, 250
National Sleep
    Foundation, 334, 338
Natural Sciences and
    Engineering
    Research Council of
    Canada, 592
Navia, B. A., 560
Nduaguba, M., 449
Neale, M., 318
Neale, M. C., 135, 236,
    325, 358, 449, 456,
    493, 512
Needleman, L. D., 328
Negrini, B. J., 191
Neighbors, H. W., 232
Neill, M., 324
Neitzert, C. S., 326
Nelles, W. B. N., 142
Nelson, C. A., 50
Nelson, C. B., 145, 162
Nelson, R. O., 5
Nelson-Gray, R. O., 5,
    109, 256
Nemeroff, C. B., 56,
    164, 237
Nero, R. C., 528
Nesbitt, N., 515
Nestadt, G., 449, 450
Nestor, P. B., 413
Neufeld, R., 516
Newcorn, J. H., 528
Newman. I. A., 321
Newman, J. P., 134, 135,
    137, 152, 185, 459,
    460, 464, 465
Newman, K., 549
Newman, S., 536
Newmark, C. S., 86
Newton, T. L., 272, 276
Neylan, T. C., 335, 338,
    343, 347, 349
Nezu, A. M., 282
Nezu, C. M., 282
Nezworski, M. T., 85
Nguyen, L., 412
Nicassio, P. M., 339
Nicholls, T., 582

Nichols, L., 513, 515
Nichols, M., 332
Nicholson, R. A., 590
Nikolskaya, O. S., 535
NIMH, 251. *See also*
   National Institute of
   Mental Health
Nisbett, R. E., 104
Nishihara, K., 342
Nitschke, J. B., 92, 246
Nixon, S. J., 562
Noble, J., 295
Nofzinger, E. A., 336
Nolan, S. A., 232
Nolen-Hoeksema, S., 131,
   234, 241, 245, 246
Noonan, D., 489
Nordlie, J. W., 189
Nordstrom, P., 261
Norman, P. A., 317, 318
Norman, R. M., 515
Norman, W. H., 59,
   241, 254
Norton, G. R., 78, 140,
   145, 205
Norton, J., 290, 536
Novaco, R. W., 272
Novosel, S., 556
Noyes, R., 135, 137, 182,
   197, 206
Nuechterlein, K. H., 508
Nugent, S., 478
Nunes, K. L., 387
Nurnberg, H. G., 451
Nurnberger, J. I.,
   238, 531
Nyhan, W. L., 545
Nystrup, J., 309

Oades, R. D., 54
Oakley-Browne,
   M. A., 317
Obermeyer, W. H., 338
O'Brien, C. P., 434
O'Brien, K. M., 313, 316
O'Brien, M. E., 279
O'Brien, M. M., 449,
   453, 458
O'Callaghan, E., 507
O'Carroll, P. W., 260, 262
Ochoa, E. S., 95
Ochsner, K. N., 61
O'Connell, D., 69
O'Connor, K., 198
O'Connor, M., 223, 314,
   317, 318, 329, 589
O'Donnell, S., 593

O'Donohue, W., 392
O'Driscoll, G. A., 503, 507
Oei, T. P. S., 142, 152
O'Fallon, W. M., 309
Offermanns, J., 415
Offord, D. R., 221,
   231, 527
Offord, K. P., 413
Ogata, S. N., 469
Ogborne, A. C., 413
Ogloff, J. P. R., 462, 582,
   585, 586, 587, 588,
   589, 590, 591
Ogston, W., 204
O'Hagan, S., 416
O'Hanlon, J. F., 136
O'Hara, M. W., 200, 226,
   232, 243, 254
Ohayon, M. M., 290
Ohlerking, F., 383
Öhman, A., 60, 63,
   64, 157
Ojehagen, A., 260
Okuji, Y., 338
Oldham, J. M., 23, 460
Olds, J., 427
O'Leary, K. D., 244
O'Leary, T. A., 137,
   278, 290
Olfson, M., 244
Olin, S. S., 457
Oliva, P. S., 204
Oliveau, D., 152
Oliver, M. B., 357, 362
Ollendick, T. H., 83, 145,
   152, 300, 531
Olmsted, M. P., 309, 314,
   323, 330
Olson, C., 104, 462
Oltmanns, T. F., 492
O'Malley, M., 401
O'Malley, S. O., 434, 438
O'Neill, P., 121
O'Neill, R. E., 536
O'Neill, S., 502
Onstad, S., 457
Oppenheim, D., 340
Orbach, I., 261
Oresme, N., 9–10
Orne, E. C., 203
Orne, M. T., 203
Orosan, P., 196
O'Rourke, 558, 565
Orsillo, S. M., 135, 138
Ortiz, A., 431
Osborne, L. N., 244
Osburg, S., 360

Oscar-Berman, M., 410
Osgood, N. J., 259
O'Shaughnessy, M. V., 315
Oslin, D. W., 561
Osmond, H., 424
Öst, L. G., 36, 37, 141,
   151, 153, 154, 155,
   157, 296
Ostbye, T., 556
Ostfeld, A., 223
Ostwald, S. W., 565
O'Sullivan, K., 372, 378
Otis, J. D., 291
Otto, M. W., 137, 159, 196
Ouellet, M. C., 107
Ouimette, P. C., 436
Overholser, J. C., 259
Owen, M. J., 503
Owens, M. J., 41, 51,
   56, 237
Oyama, O., 273

Pacoe, L., 204
Pagani, L., 105
Page, A. C., 35, 154, 294
Paglia, A., 416
Pahl, J. J., 506
Paik, A., 366
Paivio, S. C., 25, 69
Pajer, K. A., 460
Pakianathan, I., 207
Palmer, L. J., 115
Palmour, R. M., 237
Pandina, R., 425, 426
Pantaleo, G., 279
Papageorgiou, A. N., 418
Papillo, J. F., 285
Pappenheim, B., 19
Paquette, V., 55, 155
Parekh, A., 134
Paris, J., 184, 207, 448
Parisi, S. A., 231
Parker, G., 298, 448, 509
Parkinson, L., 169, 170
Parkinson Society of
   Canada, 560
Parloff, M. M., 108
Parritz, R. H., 164
Parrone, P. L., 222
Parry, C. D. H., 583
Parry-Jones, W. L., 317
Parson, A. B., 358, 558
Parsons, O. A., 562
Paruk, Z., 134
Pasewark, R. A., 587
Paslemin, C., 200
Passerieux, C., 495

Pasteur, L., 13
Pataki, C. S., 230
Patel, V., 500
Paterson, J. G., 359
Pathak, D., 180
Patience, D. A., 515
Patrick, C. J., 464
Pattatucci, A. M., 358
Patten, S. B., 229,
   245, 407
Patterson, C., 567
Patterson, C. M., 466
Patterson, G. R., 119,
   464, 465, 466
Patterson, T. L., 68,
   232, 272
Patton, G. C., 310, 322
Patton, J. R., 530
Paty, J., 83
Paul, G. L., 513
Paul, R., 547
Paulauskas, S. L., 222
Paulhus, M. P., 473
Pauli, P., 181
Pauls, D., 500, 531
Pauly, I., 363
Pavalko, E. K., 277
Pavlov, I. P., 25–26, 58
Paykel, E. S., 556
Payne, R., 405
Peacock, E. B., 25
Pearlin, L. I., 566
Pearlson, G. D., 507
Pearson, G., 423
Pechnick, R. N., 424
Peck, C. A., 549
Pedersen, N. L., 42
Pekovich, S. R., 568
Pelayo, R., 341, 342
Pelham, W. E., 525, 526,
   527, 528
Pena, J. A., 526
Pendery, M. L., 437
Pennington, B. F., 530
Pentz, M. A., 439
Penzien, D. B., 295, 296
Pepine, C. J., 381
Peplau, L. A., 357
Pepler, C., 280, 319
Pepper, C. M., 222
Pericak-Vance,
   M. A., 559
Perkins, K. A., 430
Perlin, M. L., 579, 582
Perlis, M. L., 342, 420
Perloff, B. F., 539
Perry, A., 257

Perry, J. C., 446, 449, 469, 477
Perry, S., 560
Person, D. C., 134
Peselow, E. D., 250
Pestality, P., 226
Petch, A., 486
Peters, C. P., 487
Petersen, A. C., 231, 259
Petersen, I., 134
Peterson, B. S., 538
Peterson, C. B., 331
Peterson, D. R., 78
Peterson, E., 235
Peterson, J. B., 410, 413, 422, 428
Peterson, L., 300
Peterson, R. E., 361
Petit, L., 340, 347
Peto, R., 301
Petrila, J., 589
Petry, N. M., 437
Peveler, R. C., 329
Pfister, H., 134
Pfohl, B., 471, 477, 479, 499
Pham, T., 528
Phares, V., 324
Philips, H. C., 272, 289, 290
Phillipp, B., 339, 340
Phillips, K. A., 192, 193, 194, 196, 200, 227, 259, 339, 449, 450, 453, 454, 468, 475, 479, 557
Physicians for a Smoke Free Canada, 419
Piasecki, W. M., 255
Piche, L., 548
Pickens, R. W., 427
Pickrel, S. G., 466
Pidlubny, S. R., 127
Pierce, J. P., 430
Pierce, W. D., 102, 326
Pihl, R. O., 410, 413, 428, 429, 476
Pike, K. M., 312, 324, 326, 329, 332
Pike, M., 312
Pillard, R. C., 358
Pillow, D. R., 429, 528
Pilowsky, I., 182
Pincus, A. L., 137
Pincus, D. B., 152, 206
Pinel, J., 326, 460
Pinel, P. H., 16

Pingel, J. D., 298
Pinsky, D., 287
Pinto, O., 225, 431
Piran, N., 334
Pirke, K. M., 315
Pivik, J., 290
Pizzagalli, D., 457
Platts, M., 318
Pliner, P., 326
Plomin, R., 39, 40, 42, 114, 130, 237, 501, 503, 506
Plotsky, P. M., 41, 130
Polak, D., 251
Poland, R. E., 416
Polatin, P. B., 289
Polivy, J., 96, 309, 317, 320, 322, 323, 324, 327, 328, 390
Pollack, M. H., 21, 137
Polloway, E. A., 530
Polonsky, D. C., 371, 380
Pomara, N., 249
Pomeroy, C., 312
Pomeroy, W. B., 356
Pond, M., 527
Pontius, W., 536
Poole, G., 89
Poortinga, Y. H., 118
Pope, H. G., Jr., 193, 204, 208, 323, 325
Popper, C. W., 524, 525, 526, 527, 529, 531, 532, 544, 547
Portenoy, R. K., 405
Porter, S., 161, 208, 462, 464
Post, R. M., 203, 227, 240, 246
Potkin, S. G., 511
Pottash, A. C., 375, 436
Potter, S. M., 418
Potter, W. Z., 250, 505
Pouget, E. R., 492
Powell, L. H., 286
Powell, R. A., 209
Power, B., 340
Powers, K., 421
Poythress, N. G., 589
Poznanski, E. O., 231
Prasad, K., 201
Preizig, M., 219
Prelior, E. F., 178
Prentky, R. A., 385
Prescott, C. A., 154, 240
Preskorn, S. H., 249
Presson, C. C., 117

Pretzer, J., 453
Price, R., 560
Price, T. R. P., 513
Pridal, C. G., 366, 367, 381
Prien, R. F., 250
Priest, L., 188
Prifitera, A., 87
Primeau, F. J., 552
Prince, M., 197
Prince, R., 319
Prince, V., 385
Prins, J., 294
Prinstein, M. J., 164
Prizant, B. M., 537
Project MATCH Research Group, 438
Propst, R. N., 515
Protection Advocacy System for Persons with Development Disabilities, 591
Prout, P. I., 208
Provencher, H. L., 510
Prudic, J., 251
Prusoff, B. A., 222
Pruzinsky, T., 320
Public Works and Government Services Canada, 120
Pueschel, S. M., 546
Puig-Antich, J., 231
Pule, L., 142
Purdon, C., 155, 170
Purdy, D., 227
Pury, C. L. S., 60
Putnam, F. W., 198, 203, 204, 205, 206, 207, 209
Pyle, R. L., 314, 317

Qaqish, R. B., 560
Quality Assurance Project, 454, 455
Quay, H. C., 170, 463, 464
Quigley, L. A., 437
Quinlan, D. M., 491
Quinney, H. A., 282
Quinsey, V. L., 461, 462
Quitkin, F. M., 108

Rabian, B., 153
Rabin, B. S., 67
Rabkin, J. G., 108
Rachal, J. V., 434

Rachman, S. J., 27, 77, 89, 139, 140, 151, 153, 162, 169, 170, 272, 390
Radnitz, C. L., 298
Rado, S., 457
Radomsky, A. S., 151, 159
Rae, D. S., 221, 558
Raeburn, S. D., 326
Rafanelli, C., 255
Rahkonen. T., 551, 553
Raich, R. M., 319
Rajab, M. H., 263
Ralevski, E., 326
Ramey, C. T., 549
Ramey, S. L., 549
Ramsden, V., 286
Ramsey, E., 465
Ranganath, C., 239
Rao, R., 238
Rao, U., 238
Rapaport, J., 491
Rapee, R. M., 138, 140, 158, 275, 276, 296, 297, 298
Rapp, S. R., 231
Rapport, M. D., 527
Rasmussen, S. A., 169
Rassin, E., 170
Rather, B. C., 404
Ratnasuriya, R. H., 309
Ratti, M. T., 349
Rauch, S. L., 196
Raudenbush, S. W., 465
Raviv, A., 336, 338
Rawlings, R., 507
Ray, R. S., 119
Ray, W. A., 137, 415, 552
Raymond, N. C., 317, 383
Razali, S. M., 118
Razran, G., 131
Rebgetz, M., 254
Rector, N. A., 242, 515
Redd, W. H., 26
Redding, C. A., 194
Reddon, J. R., 86
Reed, D., 274, 287
Reed, D., 274, 287
Reeve, R. E., 532
Regan, W. M., 189
Regehr, C., 584
Regier, D. A., 4, 221, 229
Reich, J., 427, 449
Reich, T., 130
Reichle, J., 548
Reichman, J. T., 142

Reid, D. H., 548
Reid, G. J., 282, 283, 591
Reid, J. B., 466
Reid, J. C., 462
Reid, W. J., 104
Reilly-Harrington, N. A., 240, 242, 243
Reinarman, C., 375
Reinhardt, R. F., 189
Reisner, L. C., 275, 276, 296, 297, 298
Reiss, S., 145
Reissing, E., 372, 380
Reitan, R. M., 88
Reiter, J., 196
Reivich, 254
Rekers, G. A., 364
Remer, P., 86
Remick, R. A., 228, 313
Remington, G., 492, 505
Remsberg, S., 339
Renaud, C. A., 376
Rende, R., 42
Rennenberg, B., 475
Repetti, R. L., 273
Report of the Advisory Panel on Alzheimer's Disease, 558, 563
Repp, A. C., 548
Rescorla, R. A., 58
Resnick, H. S., 162, 163, 458
Reus, V. I., 420
Reynolds, C. A., 89
Reynolds, C. F., 335, 338, 348
Reynolds, C. P., 277
Reynolds, E. J., 364
Reznick, J. S., 157
Rheinstein, B. J. G., 142
Rhodes, R. E., 145, 282, 548
Rhyno, E., 108
Riba, M. B., 455
Ribner, S. A., 581
Rice, D. P., 300
Rice, G., 358, 462
Rice, J., 392
Rice, M. E., 387, 461, 582, 590
Richards, C., 222, 340
Richards, J. A., 256, 258
Richards, R., 234
Richards, R. I., 547
Richardson, S. A., 507, 544

Richie, J. C., 274
Richmond, G., 511
Richter, J., 68, 142, 152, 168, 287
Rickels, K., 136, 137
Ricks, M., 537
Riding, A., 401
Ridler, M. A. C., 544
Rief, W., 180, 182
Riemersma, J. B. J., 136
Rietschlin, J., 245
Riggs, J. E., 562
Rihmer, Z., 226
Rijsdijk, F., 236
Riley, S., 193
Rintelmann, J. W., 336
Riordan, C. E., 429
Rioux, G. F., 137
Risch, N., 114, 115, 358, 563
Risley, T. R., 83
Ritchie, P., 69
Ritenbaugh, C., 319
Robaey, P., 528
Robbins, C., 67
Robbins, J. M., 180, 184
Robbins, L. N., 229
Roberts, C. W., 379
Roberts, G. A., 490
Roberts, J. E., 239, 243
Roberts, L. J., 439
Roberts, M. C., 300
Roberts, M. W., 82
Roberts, R. E., 226, 230, 232, 240
Roberts, T. B., 424
Robertson, J., 69
Robertson, M. J., 581
Robertson, N., 436
Robins, L. N., 462, 465
Robins, S., 272
Robinson, L. C., 560
Robinson, M. J., 233
Robinson, T. E., 41, 56, 69
Robison, B. D., 462
Rockert, W., 323, 330
Rockwood, K., 231, 552, 555, 565
Rodin, J., 287, 319, 321, 324, 326
Rodrigue, S., 335
Rodway, M. R., 478
Roehling, P. V., 429
Roehrich, L., 375
Roehrs, T., 337, 345
Roelofs, K., 190

Roemer, L., 135, 136, 137, 138
Roerig, J. L., 326
Roesch, R., 587, 588
Roffman, R. A., 423, 439
Roffwarg, H. P., 336
Rogers, C., 25
Rogers, J. H., 468
Rogers, R. L., 565
Rogers, S. L., 565
Rogoff, B., 340
Rohde, P., 221, 231, 236, 239, 261
Roitt, I., 278
Roland, C. G., 17, 18
Role, L. W., 420
Rollman, B. L., 232
Romano, J. M., 291, 528
Rommens, J., 113
Romney, D. M., 492
Ronningstam, E., 449, 472, 473
Room, R., 436
Roose, S. P., 328
Rorschach, H., 84, 85
Rose, 337
Rose, J. S., 117
Rosen, B. R., 90
Rosen, J. C., 196, 317, 326
Rosen, R. C., 364, 366, 368, 372, 373, 378, 380, 381, 382
Rosenbaum, J. F., 189, 249
Rosenbaum, M., 243
Rosenberg, H., 437
Rosenberg, S., 548, 559
Rosenbloom, L., 534
Rosenfeld, B., 279
Rosenfeld, J. P., 239
Rosengren, A., 286
Rosenman, R. H., 286, 287
Rosenthal, D., 259, 501
Rosenthal, N. E., 227, 228
Rosenthal, P. A., 251, 261
Rosenthal, S., 251
Rösler, A., 393
Rosman, B. L., 324
Rosowsky, E., 450, 468
Ross, A., 434
Ross, A. O., 526
Ross, C. A., 204, 205, 206, 207, 209
Ross, D., 413

Ross, M. W., 360
Ross, R., 104, 525
Rossiter, E. M., 331
Rossman, E., 515
Rost, K., 186
Roth, S., 373
Roth, T., 337, 345
Rottenberg, J., 217, 234
Rouff, L., 455
Rouleau, J. L., 383
Rounsaville, B. J., 5, 94, 222, 330, 438
Roush, W., 296
Rowane, W. A., 527
Rowe, M. K., 143
Roy, A., 261, 454, 515
Roy-Byrne, P., 135
Rozin, P., 321, 322
Rubin, R. T., 181
Rubinstein, S., 321, 366
Rudd, D. M., 243
Rudd, M. D., 261, 263
Rueger, D. B., 162, 164
Ruiz, I., 415
Rusak, B., 339
Ruscio, A., 137
Rush, A., 238, 250, 336
Rush, B., 16
Russell, G. F., 309, 310
Russell, G. F. M., 317, 328
Russell, M., 428, 429
Rutherford, J., 323, 325, 535
Ruttan, L., 486
Rutter, M., 40, 44, 69, 70, 105, 451, 463, 535, 536, 549
Ryan, C. E., 249, 256
Ryder, A. G., 250, 590

Sabo, A. N., 469
Sachs, G., 250, 566
Sack, D., 227, 228, 238
Sackeim, H. A., 189, 199, 201, 204, 206, 251, 373, 511
Sadeh, A., 336, 338
Sadovnick, A. D., 228
St. John, J., 87
Sakel, M., 14
Sakinofsky, I., 258
Saleem, R., 256
Sales, B. D., 589
Salge, R. A., 145
Salkovskis, P., 170, 181, 182, 263
Salmelin, R., 532

Salovey, P., 287
Saltoun, M., 283
Saltzman, L. E., 260
Salvio, M., 342, 420
Salzman, C., 135
Salzman, D. G., 159
Samoluk, S. B., 66, 323
Sampson, R. J., 465
Samson, J. A., 246
Samuels, J., 168
Samuels, S. C., 565
Sanavio, R., 142, 152
Sandberg, O., 553
Sandeen, E. E., 244
Sanders, B. E., 163
Sanders, M. R., 254, 466
Sanderson, W. C., 134, 135, 446
Sandler, L. C., 145
Sands, J. R., 499
Sanfilipo, M. P., 250
Sanislow, C. A., 242, 505, 507
Sankis, L. M., 4
Sano, M., 155, 565
Sansbury, L. L., 465
Santana, V. S., 431
Santangelo, S. L., 534
Santarelli, L., 238, 248
Santor, D., 221, 222, 230, 254
Santos, J. F., 259
Sapolsky, R. M., 273, 274, 275
Sarazan, F. F. A., 340
Sarchiapone, M., 261
Sareen, J., 157
Sarfati, Y., 495
Sarin, S., 242
Sartorius, N., 190, 500
Sarwer, D. B., 380
Sasao, T., 412
Sass, A., 164
Sass, K. J, 164
Satel, 418
Saudino, J. J., 42, 240
Saunders, B. E., 162
Sauriol, L., 556
Savage, D. D., 411
Savard, J., 107, 335, 337
Sawa, A., 498, 502
Saxena, 196, 201
Sayers, S. L., 217
Scanlan, J., 56
Scepkowski, L. A., 376
Schachter, H. M., 528
Schacter, D. L., 56, 60

Schade, M. L., 514
Schaeffer, B., 539
Schafer, J., 429
Schatzberg, A. F., 290
Scheel, K. R., 470
Scheerenberger, R. C., 540, 545
Scheidt, P. C., 300
Scheier, M. F., 298
Schenck, C. H., 349
Schenk, L., 207
Scherb, H., 115
Scherer, S., 113
Schewel, R., 530
Schiavi, R. C., 367, 375, 381
Schildkraut, J. J., 46, 246
Schleifer, S. J., 277
Schlosser, S., 135
Schlundt, O. G., 314, 317
Schmaling, K. B., 293
Schmeidler, J., 199
Schmidt, A. J. M., 180
Schmidt, C. W., 387, 420
Schmidt, E., 435
Schmidt, L., 493
Schmidt, N. B., 130, 142, 145
Schneider, J. A., 326
Schneider, L. S., 565
Schneiderman, N., 272, 281, 282, 285, 286, 288, 419
Schneidman, E., 260–261
Schneier, F. R., 156
Schoenbach, V. J., 67
Schottenfeld, R. S., 438
Schover, 368, 375
Schreiber, F. R., 205, 251
Schreibman, L., 536
Schreiner-Engel, P., 367
Schroeder, M. L., 328, 447, 448
Schuckit, M. A., 412, 413, 427
Schulberg, H. C., 254
Schuller, R. A., 448, 584, 589
Schulman, I. D., 142
Schulman, P., 254
Schulsinger, F., 261, 322, 516
Schulte, L., 376
Schultz, C., 458
Schultz, L., 235
Schultz, R., 232

Schupak-Neuberg, E., 321
Schutz, H. K., 322
Schwalberg, M. D., 313, 327
Schwartlander, B., 279
Schwartz, D, 320
Schwartz, E., 468
Schwartz, G. E., 272
Schwartz, J., 51
Schwartz, J. E., 220
Schwartz, M. S., 295, 296
Schwartz, P. J., 228
Schwartzman, A., 324
Schwarzler, F., 238
Schweiger, U., 315
Schweizer, E., 136, 137
Scott, C. P., 256
Scott, J. E., 513, 514, 515
Seaman, J. S., 552
Seeley, J. R., 220, 221, 222, 230, 236, 239, 240, 261
Seeman, P., 497, 505
Seeman, T., 273
Sees, K. L., 420
Segal, G. M., 255, 256, 261
Segal, S., 99
Segal, Z. V., 240, 242, 245, 255
Segraves, R. T., 368, 369, 375, 380, 381, 382
Seguin, J. R., 428
Seidenzahl, D., 587
Seim, H. C., 317
Sela, R. A., 282
Selesnick, S. T., 9, 13, 14
Seligman, M. E. P., 58–59, 59, 60, 136, 241, 243, 254
Sellaro, R., 218, 225, 226
Seltzer, B., 558
Seltzer, C. C., 321
Selye, H., 273, 276
Semrud-Clikeman, M., 532
Servis, M. E., 532, 552
Seto, M. C., 385, 392
Severe, J. B., 528
Sexton, M. M., 299
Seyfort, B., 87
Shabecoff, P., 414
Shadick, R., 242
Shaffer, D., 69, 261, 263

Shafran, R., 89, 170, 326, 332
Shagrin, B., 410
Shah, G. M. S., 491
Shalev, R. S., 529
Sham, P., 236, 507
Shaper, A. G., 272
Shapiro, D., 108, 254, 284, 285, 335, 471
Shapiro, E. S., 530
Shapiro, F., 165, 166
Shapiro, P. A., 285
Shapre, M., 293
Sharfstein, S. S., 583
Sharkansky, E. J., 430
Sharpe, M., 187, 293, 294
Shaw, B. F., 242
Shaw, H. E., 321
Shaywitz, S., 47
Shea, T., 446, 476
Sheaffer, R., 342
Shear, K. J., 148
Shear, M. K., 141, 244
Shedletsky, R., 558
Sheikh, J. I., 153, 157
Shelton, K. K., 466
Shelton, R. C., 255
Shema, S. J., 232
Shepherd, J. E., 559, 567
Shepherd, M., 499
Sher, K. J., 142, 169
Sherbourne, C. D., 246, 253
Sherman, S. J., 117
Sherman, S. L., 501, 527
Sherrington, R., 563
Shiah, I.-S., 251
Shields, A. L., 83
Shiffman, S., 83, 439
Shisslak, C. M., 318
Shisstak, C., 319
Sholomskas, D., 222
Shore, D., 108
Show, M., 250
Shulman, K. I., 142, 558, 589
Sibley, D. C., 315
Sica, C., 142, 152
Sickles, M., 458
Siegel, S., 430, 527
Sierra, M., 199
Siever, L. J., 46, 449, 453, 454, 455, 456, 457
Siffre, M., 343
Sigman, M., 535

Sigvardsson, S., 185, 465
Silberman, E. K., 203
Silberstein, L. R., 319, 326
Silbersweig, D. A., 491
Silk, K. R., 469
Silva, A., 412
Silva, P. A., 448, 461, 531
Silver, E., 558
Silveria, J. M., 497
Silverman, J., 456, 457
Silverman, K., 420
Silverman, W. K., 134, 153, 161, 180
Silverstein, M. L., 472, 499
Silverstone, T., 237
Silverthorn, P., 466
Simard, S., 335
Simeon, D., 196, 198, 199
Simon, B., 23
Simon, G. E., 180, 184
Simon, K. M., 453
Simon, R. I., 120, 568, 590, 591
Simon, T., 86–87
Simoneau, T. L., 256, 258
Simonoff, E., 549
Simons, A. D., 244, 254, 255, 422
Simonsick, E. M., 107, 243
Simpson, E. E., 439
Singer, M., 467
Singer, S. M., 531
Singer, W., 256
Singh, N. N., 548
Singh, O. P., 378
Singleton, C. K., 568
Sipprelle, R. C., 162
Siris, S. G., 496
Sirkin, M., 450
Sizemore, C., 204
Skene, D., 343
Skhiri, D., 469
Skillings, J. R., 461
Skinner, B. F., 27–28, 109, 140
Skinner, J. B., 429
Skodol, A. E., 460, 468
Skoner, D. P., 67, 276
Skoog, K., 434
Skre, I., 457
Slade, J., 419, 420
Slade, M. D., 59

Slade, P. D., 491
Sleet, D. A., 300
Slobogin, C., 589
Slutske, W. S., 463
Slymen, D., 197
Small, G. W., 231, 251
Smart, R., 408, 411, 413, 416, 530
Smeeton, N., 499
Smeets, G., 182
Smith, A. J., 493, 514
Smith, B. L., 259
Smith, D. E., 414
Smith, D. W., 411
Smith, G. P., 331
Smith, G. R., 186
Smith, G. T., 429
Smith, I. M., 535
Smith, J. E., 319
Smith, L. E., 473
Smith M. D., 539
Smith, M. L., 61
Smith, P. G., 561
Smith, P. M., 436, 438
Smith, R. H., 436
Smith, S. E., 547
Smith, S. M., 208
Smith, S. S., 460
Smith, T., 539
Smith, T. L., 412
Smith, T. T., 69
Smith, T. W., 285, 288
Smolak, L., 321, 326
Smyer, M. A., 68
Snidman, N., 157
Snow, A. C., 88, 312
Snyder, E. Y., 549
Snyder, S. H., 46, 54, 498, 502, 505
Sobell, E., 515
Sobell, L., 412, 413, 437
Sobell, M., 412, 413, 437
Social Sciences and Humanities Research Council of Canada, 592
Social Worker Action Team, 582
Society for Research in Child Development, 121
Sokolov, S., 237
Soloff, P. H., 261, 469
Solomon, A., 234
Solomon, D., 218, 219, 227
Solomon, R. L., 429

Song, S., 339
Sonnega, A., 162
Sonuga-Barke, E. J., 528
Sood, R., 347
Sorensen, J. L., 322, 436
Sotker, P. B., 164
Southwick, S. M., 164
Spain, D., 142
Spangler, D. L., 243, 244, 245
Spanos, N., 204, 342
Sparrow, S. S., 535
Spector, I. P., 372
Spence, J. D., 286
Spencer, T,, 527
Spiegel, D., 145, 146, 204, 206, 207, 208, 281, 282
Spielberger, C. D., 300
Spielman, A. J., 340
Spiker, D., 537
Spinelli, M. G., 254
Spinhoven, P., 191
Spitzer, R., 4, 316, 451
Spitznagel, E., 407
Spizman, R. F., 528
Spoont, M. R., 51, 54, 261
Spreen, O., 87, 530
Spreng, S., 259
Sprich, S., 526
Sprock, J., 471
Spurrell, E. B., 317
Squire, L. R., 60
Srikameswaran, S., 326, 328
Staal, W. G., 506
Stack, D. M., 418
Stam, H., 282
Standage, K., 446
Stanish, W. D., 291
Stanley, B., 261
Stanley, M., 134, 138, 261
Stanley-Hagan, M., 466
Stanovich, K. E., 532
Statistics Canada, 69, 106, 271, 411, 412, 529, 530, 551, 583
Steadman, H. J., 581
Steart, K., 323, 410
Steenhuis, R., 556
Steer, R. A., 259, 261, 476
Stefan, S., 582
Steggles, S., 282
Steiger, H., 317, 322, 324
Stein, M., 277

Stein, M. B., 42, 78, 156, 157, 159, 163, 169, 180
Stein, M. I., 85
Stein, M. T., 364
Stein, R. I., 321, 328
Stein, R. M., 416, 417
Steinberg, A. B., 324
Steinberg, L., 43
Steinberg, M., 198
Steiner, B. W., 363
Steiner, M., 227, 243, 468, 469
Steinhauer, S. R., 499
Stejskal, W. J., 85
Steketee, G., 167, 168, 169, 170, 195
Ste-Marie, D., 323
Stephens, R. S., 332, 439
Stephenson, J., 279
Stergiopoulos, V., 189
Stern, Y., 558
Sternberg, W. F., 88, 90, 292
Sterner, U., 155
Stevens, A., 23, 180, 287
Stevens, J., 423
Stevenson, J., 530
Stevenson, M. F., 547
Stewart, M. A., 438
Stewart, S. H., 61, 66, 101, 108, 115, 116, 130, 131, 135, 136, 137, 140, 142, 160, 161, 179, 182, 290, 313, 316, 322, 323, 338, 340, 345, 404, 407, 408, 409, 411, 413, 414, 420, 428, 429, 434, 439, 447, 463, 476
Stewart, W. F., 565
Stice, E., 314, 317, 321, 322
Stip, E., 489
Stites, D. P., 281
Stock, W., 369
Stock, W. E., 370
Stokes, J., 559
Stolee, P., 231
Stoller, R. J., 361
Stone, M. H., 272, 277, 339, 343, 347, 449, 450, 456, 458, 468, 469, 476, 478
Stones, M. J., 564

Stoney, C. M., 65, 115, 187
St-Onge, M., 346
Stoppard, J., 245
Storck, M., 163
Storer, D., 263
Stotland, S., 324
Stout, S. C., 41
Stouthamer-Loeber, M., 462
Strachan, S., 314, 323, 465
Strahl, C., 290
Strain, E. C., 420
Strain, J. J., 192
Strassberg, D. S., 371, 377
Strathdee, S. A., 418, 421
Straus, S. E., 293
Strauss, C. C., 525
Strauss, J., 495
Stravynski, A., 475
Strawbridge. W. J., 232
Streiff, O., 469
Streissguth, A. P., 411
Striegel-Moore, R. H., 319, 326
Stringer, R., 532
Stritzke, W. G. K., 430
Strobel, M., 325
Strober, M., 325, 328
Stuart, S., 254, 513
Stuhr, J., 286
Stunkard, A. J., 322
Sturla, E., 361
Stuss, D. T., 89, 559
Suarez, A., 470
Suarez, E. C., 65
Subedar, H., 134
Subotnik, K. L., 508
Subramaniam, M., 118
Substance Abuse and Mental Health Services Administration, 421
Suddath, R. L., 256, 258
Suelzer, M., 137
Sugden, K., 42
Sugiyama, T., 535
Sullivan, G. M., 56, 130, 164
Sullivan, K., 316
Sullivan, M., 290
Sullivan, M. J, 192
Sullivan, M. J. L., 290, 291, 309, 312

Sullivan-Hurst, S., 527
Summerfeldt, L. J., 158, 168, 298
Suomi, S. J., 43, 56
Suppes, T., 250
Sussman, S., 16, 17
Sutherland, G. R., 547
Sutherland, R. J., 411
Sutherland, S. M., 475
Sutker, P. B., 417, 449, 460
Sutton, D. A., 335, 338, 339
Svensson, L., 155
Svetlik, D., 567
Svikis, D. S., 427
Swaab, D. F., 361
Swan, G. E., 298
Swanson, J. M., 527, 528
Swanson, J. W., 298
Swanson, M. C., 459
Swartz, M., 134, 163, 184, 190
Swayze, V. W., 89, 506
Swedo, S. E., 228
Sweeney, J. A., 503
Sweeney, M., 381
Swendsen, J., 250
Swica, Y., 206
Swift, R. M., 430
Swinson, R. P., 96, 108, 140, 142, 145, 147, 148, 155, 158, 168
Sylvester, D., 152
Syme, S. L., 67, 287
Szalai, J. P, 88
Szarek, B. L., 249
Szasz, T., 500
Szatmari, P., 527, 533, 535, 536
Sze, S., 319
Szmukler, G., 309, 323, 328

Tager-Flusberg, H., 535
Taillefer, S., 180, 217
Takahasi, T., 157
Takei, N., 506, 507
Talajic, M., 288
Talbott, J. A., 513
Tam, E. M., 251
Tampilic, M., 500
Tan, E. S., 66
Tanaka-Matsumi, J., 117
Tang, M. X., 565
Tang, T. Z., 254
Tanner, E., 233, 314

Tannock, R., 336
Tanofsky, M. B., 317
Tanzi, R. E., 558
Tarasoff, T., 589
Tarrier, N., 257, 513, 515
Tartara, A., 349
Tasman, A., 455
Tassinari, R., 146
Tata, P., 136
Tataryn, D. J., 60
Tattan, T., 515
Tauscher, J., 52
Tavaré, C. J., 553
Taylor, A., 42, 142, 146, 159, 162, 163, 166, 179, 196, 293
Taylor, C. B., 106, 143, 145, 147, 290, 314, 322, 323, 436
Taylor, E. B., 222
Taylor, E. H., 499
Taylor, G., 323
Taylor, L., 246
Taylor, M. A., 225
Taylor, R. M., 549
Taylor, S., 145, 159, 180, 183, 187, 254, 289, 296
Taylor, S. E., 66, 273, 274, 299
Teachman, B. A., 151
Tearnan, B. H., 146
Teasdale, J. D., 59, 64, 241, 255, 256
Teehan, M. D., 61, 136, 137
Teicher, M. H., 249
Telch, C. F., 145, 146, 322, 326, 331
Tellegen, A., 234, 447, 451
Teplin, L. A., 581
Teri, L., 566
Terman, L., 87, 252, 345
Tessier, G., 556
Teufel, N., 319
Thaker, G. K., 503
Thapa, P. B., 415
Thase, M. E., 222, 243, 244, 250, 255
Theakston, J., 313
Theander, S., 309
Thiele, C., 300
Thisted, R. A., 338
Thomas, N., 300
Thomassen, R., 555
Thompson, B., 143

Thompson, J. K., 309
Thompson, M., 320, 321, 528
Thompson-Brenner, H., 329
Thordarson, D. S., 89, 151, 170, 196
Thoresen, C. E., 286
Thorndike, E. L., 27–28
Thorpe, G. L., 142, 245
Thorpy, M., 349
Thuras, P., 315
Thuwe, I., 360
Tibblin, G., 286
Tienari, P., 43, 259, 502
Tierney, A., 88
Tiffany, S. T., 430, 434
Tiggemann, M., 321
Tingelstad, J. B., 249
Titchener, E., 26, 162
Tjio, J. H., 545
Toews, J., 513
Tohen, M., 250
Tollefson, G. D., 217, 219
Tomac, A., 565
Tondo, L., 250
Toneatto, T., 429
Tonigan, J. S., 436
Torgersen, S., 185, 457
Torgrud, L. J., 156
Tornatore, J., 565
Torres, B., 142, 152
Torrey, E. F., 499, 507, 508, 583
Townsend, E., 261
Townsend, J., 515, 534
Townshed, R., 456
Trapnell, P. D., 357, 378
Traskman-Bendz, L., 260, 261
Trautmen, P., 261
Trebbe, A., 322
Tremblay, R., 105, 117, 119, 462, 528
Trestman, R. L., 449, 453
Trimbell, M. R., 189
Trinkle, D., 339
Trottier, J., 324
Troughton, E., 463
Troyer, A. K., 507
Trudel, G., 381
Trull, T. J., 468
Tsai, L. Y., 537
Tsuang, M., 115, 169, 259, 499, 500

Tsui, L., 113
Tuason, V. B., 255
Tuchman, B., 9, 10
Tucker, G. J., 513
Tuff, L., 527
Tuke, W., 16
Tuma, A. H., 150
Tuokko, H., 558, 564
Turcotte, N., 430
Turk, C. L., 159
Turk, D. C., 285, 289, 290, 291, 292, 295, 298
Turkat, I. D., 453
Turkel, S. B., 553
Turkheimer, E., 43, 44, 583
Turkington, C., 515, 561
Turner, C. W., 283, 285
Turner, J. A., 291
Turner, R., 276
Turovsky, J., 127, 136
Turpin, R., 545
Tyler, D. B., 335
Tynes, L. L., 195
Tyrer, P., 454

Uchid, S., 342
Uchino, B. N., 276, 281, 285
Uddo, M., 417
Uhde, T., 143
Umberson, D., 67, 232
Umbricht, D., 512
Underwood, M., 263
Undie, A. S., 505
Ungerleider, J. T., 424
Uno, D., 276
Urbszat, C., 323
Useda, D., 449, 453
Ustun, T. B., 184, 335

Vaccarino, V., 295
Vaccaro, D., 432
Vaillant, G. E., 21, 275, 277, 412, 413, 460
Vajk, F. C., 256
Vallee, B., 408, 584
Vallieres, A., 454, 515
Vallis, M., 446
Vallis, T. M., 299
Van Acker, R., 534
van Der Ende, J., 142, 152
van Der Kolk, B. A., 469
van Der Velde, J., 373
Van Dongen, H. P. A., 335
van Dyck, R., 191
van Elderen, T., 286
van Kammen, D. P., 505

van Kammen, W. B., 462
van Kesteren, P. J., 360
Van Laar, M., 136
Van Praag, H. M., 237
Van Reekum, R., 468, 469
van Schaick, H. W., 555
Van Valkenburg, C., 450
Vandenberg, S. G., 531
Vander Plate, C., 276
Vanderwal, J. S., 322
Vandrei U., 496
Varley, C. K., 540
Vasey, P. L., 364
Vasterling, J. J., 164
Veale, D., 193, 194, 196
Venables, P. H., 457, 507
Venkataraman, S., 274
Ventura, J., 259, 508
Verbaten, M., 136
Verma, K. K., 378
Vernon, P., 42, 114, 163, 463
Verrier, R. L., 336
Vieland, V., 263
Viens, M., 346
Villanueva, M., 438
Vincent, L., 255, 313, 316
Vinken, P. J., 545
Virag, R., 381
Virts, K. L., 291
Visser, F. E., 546
Visser, L., 180
Vitaro, F., 105
Vitiello, B., 310, 316, 318, 325, 328, 528
Vitousek, K., 329, 332
Voglmaier, M. M., 457
Vohs, K. D., 326
Volkerts, E., 136
Volkmar, F. R., 534, 535
Volkow, F. R., 527
Von Knorring, A. L., 185, 465
Von Ranson, K. M., 313
Vuchinich, S., 466

Wade, T. D., 325
Wadsworth, S. J., 530
Wagner, A. W., 469
Wagner, B. M., 262
Wagner, M., 530
Wahlbeck, K., 505, 512
Wahler, R. G., 465, 466
Waitzkin, H., 180
Wakefield, J. C., 4
Wakeling, A., 322

Wald, J., 111–112, 187, 190, 191
Waldman, I., 507
Waldorf, D., 375
Waldron, M. C., 43
Walinder, J., 360, 363
Walker, E. F., 493, 499
Walker, J., 182
Walker, J. R., 127, 156, 159, 169
Walker, L., 584
Walker, N., 279
Walker, R. D., 435
Wall, P. D., 289, 291, 292
Wallace, C. E., 232
Wallace, C. J., 514
Wallace, C. S., 56
Wallace, J., 227, 231
Wallace, J. F., 465
Wallace, R. B., 107
Waller, N. G., 206, 207, 208
Walsh, B. T., 326, 328, 329, 330, 335, 349, 401
Walsh, M., 436
Walters, A., 420
Walters, E. E., 318, 325, 326
Walton, L. A., 347
Wang, C., 407, 412
Wang, J., 245
Wang, M. C., 439
Wang, P. S., 137
Waraich, P., 499
Ward, M. M., 298
Warneke, L. B., 414, 415
Warren, S. F., 548
Warshaw, M., 135
Warwick, H. M. C., 181, 182
Waschbusch, D. A., 526, 528
Wasserstein, S., 134
Wasylenki, D., 5
Waterhouse, L., 536
Waternaux, C., 261
Waters, B. G. H., 226
Waterworth, D. M., 500
Watson, D., 127, 447
Watson, J. B., 25
Watson, J.B., 26–27, 40, 332
Watson, J. B., 531
Watson, M., 547
Watt, D., 116, 131, 141, 179, 182, 499

Watt, M., 182
Watters, B., 87
Webster, C. D., 462, 582, 588, 589, 590
Webster-Stratton, C., 466
Weeks, A., 528
Weeks, D. J., 456
Weeks, J. R., 204
Weems, C. F., 134
Wegner, D. M., 170
Wehr, T. A., 227, 228, 238, 251
Weiden, P. J., 512
Weihofen, H., 585
Weinberg, M. S., 383
Weinberg, R. A., 88
Weinberg, W. A., 336
Weinberger, A. D., 252
Weinberger, D. R., 499, 507, 508
Weiner, D. N., 371, 376
Weiner, H., 299
Weiner, I. B., 85
Weiner, J. M., 70
Weiner, M. F., 550, 551, 556, 560, 565, 567
Weinman, J., 136
Weise, R. E., 476
Weiskrantz, L., 60, 188
Weisman, A. G., 509
Weiss, M., 181
Weiss, S. M., 272
Weisse, C. S., 277
Weissman, M. M., 142, 157, 169, 221, 225, 229, 231, 232, 244, 253, 330, 449
Weitze, C., 360
Welch, S. L., 314, 315, 316, 318
Wells, J. E., 317
Wells, J. M., 253
Wells, K., 525, 528
Wells, K. B., 246
Weltzin, T. E., 312
Wender, P. H., 261
Wenzel, A., 254
Werdager, D., 436
Wessely, S., 293, 294, 499
Wesson, D. R., 414
West, J. A., 460
West, L. J., 335, 449
West, S. A., 524, 544, 547
Westen, D., 329, 468, 470

Westermeyer, J., 564
Westra, H. A., 137, 340, 345, 414, 437
Wetherby, A. M., 537
Wetherell, J. L., 137
Wetra, H., 414
Wetter, D. W., 429
Wetzel, R. D., 178, 255
Wever, R., 343
Wexler, D. B., 561
Whelan, G., 568
Whetsell, W. O., 568
Whiffen, V. E., 226, 227, 243
Whishaw, I. Q., 56, 61
Whisman, M. A., 137
White, D. P., 343, 381
White, J., 136, 138
White, J. L., 263
White, K., 170, 195
White, K. S., 141, 144
Whitehouse, A. M., 318
Whitehouse, W. G., 240
Whitehurst, G. J., 461, 531
Whiting, P., 294
Whitlatch, C. J., 566
Whitnam, F. L., 358
Whitney, C. W., 338
Whitt, B., 300
Whittal, M. L., 328, 329, 330
Whittemore, K., 585, 587, 588, 589
Wickramaratne, P., 221
Wickwire, K., 147
Widiger, T. A., 4, 96, 447, 449, 450, 451, 459, 460, 468
Widom, C. S., 185, 461
Wiegel, 373
Wiegel, M., 145, 373, 374, 375, 376, 378, 390
Wigal, T., 528
Wik, G., 60
Wilbur, C., 202
Wilens, T., 527
Wilfley, D. E., 317, 318, 319
Wilgosh, L., 87
Wilhelm, S., 196
Wilhelmsen, L., 286
Wilkie, C., 259
Wilkins, J.-A., 37
Wilkinson-Ryan, T., 468
Willi, J., 309

Williams, C. J., 383
Williams, C. L., 86
Williams, J. M. G., 255
Williams, K. M., 473
Williams, L., 168, 208
Williams, R. B., 272, 281, 282, 285, 288, 291
Williams, R. B., Jr., 65
Williams, R. J., 228, 232
Williams, S., 240
Williams, W. L., 361
Williamson, D. A., 326
Williamson, J. W., 300
Wills, T. A., 432
Willwerth, J., 592
Wilner, P., 256
Wilson, B., 530
Wilson, D., 145
Wilson, G. T., 312, 316, 317, 326, 328, 329, 330, 331, 332, 375
Wilson, P. G., 548
Wilson, W., 424, 436
Winchel, R. M., 196, 261
Wincze, J. P., 366, 368, 369, 370, 372, 373, 374, 375, 378, 381, 382, 384, 390
Windgassen, K., 512
Winett, C. A., 246
Wing, L., 130, 509, 536
Wing, R. R., 331
Wing, Y. K., 319
Winick, B. J., 591
Winkelman, M. D., 568
Winker, M. A., 565
Winkler, H., 506
Winokur, G., 225, 251, 497, 499
Winter, A., 18
Winters, R. W., 285, 286, 288
Wirshing, D. A., 514, 593
Wirtz-Justice, A., 228, 238
Wise, B. D., 246
Wise, E. A., 291
Wise, M. G., 553, 558
Wise, R. A., 428
Wise, T. N., 387
Wiseman, C. V., 321
Witherington, R., 382
Withers, G. S., 56
Wittchen, H. U., 134, 135, 141, 152, 229
Witte, E. A., 55

Witztum, M. D., 393
Wjst, M., 115
Wolf, M. M., 83, 103
Wolfe, D., 82
Wolfe, J. H., 523, 531, 549
Wolff, S., 455, 456
Wolf-Maier, K., 284, 285
Wolfson, A., 131, 555, 558
Wolgamuth, B., 190
Wolpe, J., 27, 28, 104
Wonderlich, S. A., 312
Wong, K., 505
Wong, S., 462
Wood, J. M., 85
Wood, K., 322
Wood, S. C., 439
Woodbury, M., 190
Woodman, C. L., 135
Woods, E. R., 261
Woods, S. W., 148
Woodside, D. B., 317, 324, 326
Woodworth, G., 462, 463, 464
Woody, G. E., 403
Wooten, V., 347
Wootton, J. M., 466
Worcel, M., 381
Worell, J., 86
World Health Organization, 68, 258, 300
Wormworth, J. A., 448
Wright, E. J., 227
Wright, K. D., 106
Wu, H. X., 528
Wunder, J., 231, 420
Wyatt, J. K., 342, 420
Wyllie, E., 190
Wyshak, G., 179, 180, 181

Yager, J., 68, 232, 272
Yagla, S. J., 135
Yairi, E., 531
Yamamoto, J., 412
Yan, L. L., 284, 285
Yang, G., 536
Yap, L., 137
Yarmey, A. D., 207, 584
Yates, W. R., 135, 449, 463
Yatham, L., 251
Yeager, C. A., 206
Yeaton, W. H., 300

Yeh, A. H., 196
Yen, S., 449
Yerkes, R. M., 127
Yeung, R. Y., 556
Yeung-Courchesne, R., 538, 549
Yirmiya, R., 294
Yonkers, K. A., 135
Young, A. M., 428
Young, A. R., 529, 530, 532
Young, D., 259
Young, J. E., 244, 252, 254
Young, M. A., 237
Yuille, J., 161, 208, 590
Yurgelun-Todd, D., 325
Yutzy, 184
Yutzy, S. H., 178

Zabinski, M. F., 318
Zack, M., 429
Zadra, A., 348
Zaharia, M. D., 43
Zajonc, R. B., 64
Zakeri, Z., 278
Zakzanis, K., 486, 507
Zald, D., 51
Zanarini, M. C., 468, 469
Zandi, P. P., 227
Zanna, M. P., 21
Zapf, P. A., 588
Zarit, S., 566
Zeaman, D., 547
Zeidler, M., 187
Zekoski, E. M., 226
Zelazo, P., 418, 535
Zelkowitz, P., 227
Zhang, Y., 259
Zhao, S., 135
Zhenyi, X., 516
Zhou, J. N., 361
Zhu, J., 87
Zielezny, M., 255
Zigler, E., 259, 263, 544, 547
Zilbborg, G., 10
Zilbergeld, B., 378
Zimmerli, W. D., 135
Zimmerman, J. C., 193
Zimmerman, M., 189, 194, 195, 449
Zimmermann, P., 453, 514
Zinbarg, R., 58, 157, 234
Zinner, S. H., 356, 372

Zipfel, S., 309
Zipursky, R. B., 505
Zohar, J., 170

Zorilla, L. T., 157
Zorzitto, M. L., 88
Zubin, J., 499

Zucker, K., 358, 362, 364
Zuckerman, B., 339, 340
Zuroff, D., 62, 242

Zvolensky, M. J.,
130, 420
Zweig-Frank, H., 207

# Subject Index

## A

A-beta fibres, 292
A-delta fibres, 292
AA. *See* Alcoholics Anonymous
Abnormal behaviour. *See also* Psychological disorders
historical conceptions of, 8
problems defining, 2–5
Aboriginal peoples
psychological disorders in, 68
suicide rates in, 258–259
Acamprostate, 435
Acedia (sloth), 9–10
Acetylcholine, 50
Acquired immune deficiency syndrome (AIDS), 279–281. *See also* Human immunodeficiency virus
as divine punishment, 11
and immune system, 278, 280
and opiate users, 421
preventing, 300–301
psychological factors in, 272, 280–281
Acquired sexual dysfunctions, 365
Actigraph, 337
"Activity anorexia," 326
Acute onset, 7
Acute pain, 289
Acute PTSD, 161
Acute stress disorder, 161–162, 198
Adderall, 527
Addictive behaviours. *See also* Substance-related disorders
and willpower, 71
ADHD. *See* Attention deficit/hyperactivity disorder (ADHD)

Adolescents
eating disorders, 313, 317–319, 321–324
mood disorders, 230–231, 254
sexual partners, 356–357
sleep disorders, 338
suicide rates in, 259
Adoption studies, 113–114, 502
Adrenal glands, 49
Adrenaline, 49, 50
Adulthood, 69
Advanced sleep phase type, 344
Affect, 63, 80
Affective flattening, 492–493
African Americans
dissociative trances in, 201
eating disorders in, 318
hypertension in, 284
schizophrenia in, 500
Age of onset, 6, 7, 542
Aggression, 185, 413
Agnosia, 555
Agonist substitution, 434
Agonistic effects, 504
Agonists, 51
Agoraphobia, 138. *See also* Panic disorder
causes, 143–144
development of, 139–141
Agreeableness, 447
AIDS. *See* Acquired immune deficiency syndrome (AIDS)
AIDS-related complex (ARC), 279
Akinesia, 512
Alarm response to stress, 273
Alcohol dependence, 413
Alcohol intoxication, 409
Alcohol use/abuse, 411–412

and bulimia nervosa, 313
as coping mechanism, 66
and panic disorder, 140
sexual dysfunction as side effect of, 375
and sleep disorders, 338
and suicide, 261
Alcohol use disorders, 408–413
alcohol effects, 409–411
clinical description, 409
DSM-IV criteria summary, 409
progression of, 412–413
research on, 428
statistics, 411–412
treatment, 433–440
Alcohol withdrawal delirium, 403
Alcoholics Anonymous (AA), 436, 437
Allan Memorial Institute, 592
Allegiance effect, 108
Alogia, 492
Alpha-adrenergic receptors, 53
Alpha waves, 91, 239
Alters, 202
Altruistic suicide, 260
Aluminum, 562
Alzheimer's disease, 556–559, 576. *See also* Dementia
Ambien, 345
Amenorrhea, 315–316
*American Journal of Insanity*, 13
*American Journal of Psychiatry*, 13
American Law Institute (ALI) rule, 585
Amitriptyline, 298
Amnesia, 199–200
Amnestic disorder, 550, 567–568, 575
Amniocentesis, 546

Amotivational syndrome, 423
Amphetamine use disorders, 416–417
Amphetamines, 345, 415, 426, 505
Amygdala, 48
Amyloid plaques, 562–563
Amyloid protein, 563
Anabolic-androgenic steroids, 425–426
Analgesics, 298, 421
Analogue models, 101–102
Anandamide, 423
*Anatomy of Melancholy* (Burton), 12
Anger, and the heart, 65, 272, 285–286, 288
Angina pectoris, 286
Anhedonia, 217, 492
Animal magnetism, 18
Animal phobias, 151
Animal studies
on anxiety disorders, 127
baboons and stress, 274–275
classical conditioning, 57–58
pain in rats, 294–295
on posttraumatic stress disorder, 164
Anna O., 19, 61, 104
Anomia, 557
Anomic suicide, 260
Anorexia nervosa, 309, 313–316
*See also* Eating disorders
associated psychological disorders, 316
binge-eating-purging type, 315, 316
clinical description, 314–315
drug treatments for, 328

DSM-IV-TR criteria
summary, 316
medical consequences,
315–316
psychological
treatments for,
331–332
restricting type, 315
statistics, 318
Antabuse, 435
Antagonist treatments,
434–435
Antagonistic effects, 504
Antagonists, 51
Antianxiety drugs, 375
Antibodies, 278
Antidepressants, 248–250
for eating disorders,
328, 330
for headaches, 298
for panic disorder, 145
sexual dysfunction as
side effect of, 375
for sleep disorders,
345, 348
tricyclic, 52, 145, 159,
248, 375
Antigens, 277
Antihypertensive
medications, 375
Antipsychotic drugs, 54,
505, 511–512, 553
Antisocial personality
disorder (ASPD),
448, 459–467
clinical description,
460–462
and conduct
disorder, 462
and criminality,
461–462
developmental
influences, 465
gender differences
in, 450
genetic influences, 463
integrative approach
to, 465–466
neurobiological
influences,
463–464
prevention, 466–467
psychological and
social dimensions,
464–465
and somatization
disorder, 185
treatment, 466

Anxiety
and defence
mechanisms, 20–21
defined, 127
and depression,
234–235, 237
Anxiety disorders,
126–176. *See also*
Panic disorder;
Phobias
animal research on, 127
and anorexia
nervosa, 316
biological
contributions,
130–131
and bulimia
nervosa, 313
causes of, 129–132
comorbidity, 132
and coronary heart
disease, 288
and eating disorders,
313, 316, 326
fear, 128
generalized anxiety
disorder, 132–138
integrated model,
131–132
obsessive-compulsive
disorder, 166–171
panic, 128–129, 132
psychological
contributions, 131
separation anxiety
disorder, 152
and sleep disorders,
336, 346
social
contributions, 131
vs. stress, depression,
and excitement,
275–276
Anxiety management
training, 346
Anxiety Sensitivity
Index, 145
Anxiolytic effect, 428
Anxiolytics, 413–415
Apathy, 491–492
Aphasia, 557
Appearance, assessment
of, 79
Applied muscle
tension, 37
Arbitrary inference, 242
ARC. *See* AIDS-related
complex

Arousal phase of sexual
response cycle, 365
Arterial insufficiency, 375
Artists, 233–234
Asociality, 493
Asperger's disorder, 533,
534, 574
Assertiveness
training, 298
Assessing psychological
disorders, 76–92
behavioural
assessment, 82–83
clinical assessment, 76
clinical interview, 79–81
key concepts, 78–79
neuroimaging, 89–90
neuropsychological
testing, 88–89
physical examination,
81–82
psychological testing,
84–88
psychophysiological
assessment, 90–92
Assessment gender
bias, 451
Association studies,
114–115, 502
Associative splitting, 487
Astrology, 11
Asylums, 16
development of first
Canadian, 17
and moral therapy, 16
reform, 16–18
Atherosclerosis, 286
Attention
deficit/hyperactivity
disorder (ADHD),
524–528, 573. *See
also* Developmental
disorders
amphetamines for, 416
causes, 526–527
clinical description,
524–525
DSM-IV criteria
summary, 525
and sleep disorders,
335–336
statistics, 525–526
treatment, 527–528
Atypical responses, 3–4
Auditory hallucinations,
205, 491

Augmentative
communication
strategies, 548
Autistic disorder, 82, 455,
523, 533–538, 574.
*See also*
Developmental
disorders
causes, 536–538
clinical description,
533–535
DSM-IV criteria
summary, 536
statistics, 535–536
Autohypnotic model,
206–207
Autoimmune disease, 278
Autonomic nervous
system (ANS), 48–50
Autonomy, 476
Aversion therapy, 437
Aversive treatment, 435
Avoidant personality
disorder, 448, 449,
474–476
Avolition, 491–492
Awakenings,
scheduled, 348
Axons, 44–45

**B**
B cells, 277–278
Baboons and stress,
274–275
Bad dreams, 348
Ballet dancers and
eating disorders,
323, 324, 334
Barbiturates, 413–415
Basal ganglia, 47, 48
Baselines, 111–112
Battered woman
syndrome, 584
Beauty pageant
contestants, 319–322
BED. *See* Binge-eating
disorder
Behaviour
assessment of, 79,
82–83
and emotion, 63–64
studying across
cultures, 117–118
studying over time,
115–117

Behaviour modification, 299–302

*Behaviour of Organisms, The* (Skinner), 27

Behaviour rating scales, 83

Behavioural factors, 35, 57–62

Behavioural family therapy, 515

Behavioural inhibition system (BIS), 130, 464

Behavioural medicine, 272

Behavioural model, 25–29
  beginnings of behaviour therapy, 27
  Pavlov and classical conditioning, 25–26
  Skinner and operant conditioning, 27–28
  Waston and behaviourism, 26–27

Behavioural rehearsal, 475

Behavioural therapy (BT), 27, 329

Behaviourism
  defined, 18
  and Watson, 26–27

Beirut, Lebanon, 232

Bender Visual-Motor Gestalt Test, 88

Benzodiazepines, 14, 53
  dependence on, 414
  for generalized anxiety disorder, 136–137
  for panic disorder, 145, 146
  for sleep disorders, 344–345, 348

Beta-adrenergic receptors, 53

Beta-blockers, 53, 375

*Beyond Freedom and Dignity* (Skinner), 28

Bile, 12

Binge-eating disorder (BED), 316–317, 331. *See also* Eating disorders

Binge-eating-purging type of anorexia nervosa, 315, 316

Binges, 309

Biofeedback, 92, 295–296

Biological factors, 35–57
  anxiety disorders, 130–131
  autism, 537–538
  chronic pain, 291–292
  dementia, 562–563
  dissociative identity disorder, 207
  eating disorders, 325–326
  gender identity disorder, 361–362
  mental retardation, 545–547
  mood disorders, 235–238
  sexual dysfunctions, 374–375
  sexual orientation development, 358, 359
  sleep disorders, 340
  substance-related disorders, 427–428

Biological model, 8

Biological tradition, 12–15
  19th century, 13–14
  consequences of, 15
  Grey, John P., 13–14, 15
  Hippocrates and Galen, 12–13
  syphilis, 13
  treatments, 14–15

Biological treatments. *See also* Drug therapy
  for dementia, 565
  for pervasive developmental disorders, 539–540
  for substance-abuse disorders, 434–435

Bipolar disorders, 218, 223–226, 269. *See also* Mood disorders

Bipolar I disorder, 224

Bipolar II disorder, 224, 225

psychological treatments for, 256–257

and stress, 240

Bisexuality, 362. *See also* Sexual orientation development

Blackouts, 202

Blacks. *See* African Americans

Bleeding, 12

Blind sight, 60

Blindness, 186, 189

Blood, 12

Blood-injury-injection phobia, 2, 35–38, 150–151

Bloodletting, 12

Body dysmorphic disorder (BDD), 192–197, 212
  causes and treatment, 195–196
  clinical description, 193–194
  DSM-IV criteria summary, 194
  and plastic surgery, 196–197
  statistics, 194–195

Body image perception, 320–322, 323, 326, 333–334

Body temperature and sleep disorders, 339

Borderline personality disorder, 448, 467–470
  and bulimia nervosa, 313
  gender differences in, 450
  statistics and development, 449

Bradykinesia, 560

Brain circuits, 50

Brain damage
  and alcohol abuse, 410
  and dementia, 559, 560, 563, 568

Brain function
  images of, 89–90
  interactions of psychosocial factors with, 56–57
  and personality, 54–55

and psychopathy, 464

psychosocial influences on, 55–56

Brain, neuroimaging, 89–90

Brain stem, 46

Brain structure, 46–48
  images of, 89, 491
  interactions of psychosocial factors with, 56–57
  psychosocial influences on, 55–56
  and schizophrenia, 506–507

Brain surgery, 14

Brain tumours, 81

Brain wave activity, and mood disorders, 238–239

Brazil, 431

Breast cancer, 281, 282

Breath analyzer tests, 409

Breathing-related sleep disorders, 336, 341, 342–343, 345

Brief psychotic disorder, 497

Briquet's syndrome, 183

Broca's area, 491

Bromides, 14–15

BT. *See* Behavioural therapy

Bulimia nervosa, 309, 310–313. *See also* Eating disorders
  associated psychological disorders, 313
  case study, 310–312
  clinical description, 312
  drug treatments for, 328
  DSM-IV-TR criteria summary, 313
  and gender, 66
  medical consequences, 312–313
  psychological treatments for, 329–331

purging and non-purging types, 312, 317
statistics, 317–318
Burma, 195

# C

C fibres, 292
Caffeine, 415
Caffeine use disorders, 420
Canada
  AIDS prevention programs in, 300–301
  alcohol use in, 411–412
  availablility of treatment in, 69
  chronic pain in, 288–289
  death, leading causes of, 271
  eating disorders in, 309, 319, 330–331
  sex reassignment surgery in, 363
  sexual dysfunction in, 378
  suicide rates in, 258
*Canadian Code of Ethics for Psychologists* (CPA), 121
Canadian Psychological Association (CPA), 121, 594
Cancer, 281–283
Cannabinoids, 423
*Cannabis sativa*, 422–423
Capgras syndrome, 490
Cardiovascular problems, 283–288
  and anorexia nervosa, 316
  coronary heart disease, 286–288
  hypertension, 284–286
Cardiovascular system, 283
Case study method, 104
Castration anxiety, 22
Castration, chemical, 393

CAT (computerized axial tomography) scans, 89
Cataplexy, 342, 345
Catastrophizing, pain, 290–291
Catatonia, 486
Catatonic immobility, 494
Catatonic type of schizophrenia, 495
Catharsis, 19, 164
Catholic Church, 9, 10, 11
Causality
  multidimensional model of, 35–38
  one-dimensional model of, 35
Causation, vs. correlation, 104–105
CBT. *See* Cognitive-behavioural therapy
Cellular branch of immune system, 277, 278
Central nervous system (CNS), 44–46
Central sleep apnea, 343
Cerebral cortex, 48, 491
Cerebral reserve hypothesis, 558
Cerebral vascular accidents, 283
CFS. *See* Chronic fatigue syndrome
Charles VI, 10, 12, 29
CHD. *See* Coronary heart disease
Chemical castration, 393
Chemical transporter, 41
Child abuse
  and borderline personality disorder, 469
  vs. Munchausen syndrome by proxy, 188
Childhood disintegrative disorder, 533, 534, 574
Childhood disorders, 523
Children
  and anti-depressants, 249

antisocial behaviour in, 461, 465, 466
cancer in, 282–283
with conduct disorder, 462
control studies, 131
depression in, 221, 230–231
gender identity disorder in, 364
and injury prevention, 300
memories of traumatic events by, 161
misdiagnosis of, 7
mood disorders in, 230–231, 254
normal fears and anxieties in, 153
pain coping strategies of, 282–283
panic attacks in, 141–142
pedophilia, 387–388
resilient, 70
separation anxiety disorder in, 152
sexual abuse of, 367, 375–376, 381
sleep disorders, 338, 339–340, 347, 348–349
China, 69, 118
  eating disorders in, 319
  foot binding in, 195
  *koro*, 181
  neurasthenia in, 292
  *Pa-leng*, 153
  schizophrenia in, 516
  smoking in, 301–302
  suicide rates in, 259
Choleric personality, 12
Chromosomes, 39
Chronic course, 6
Chronic fatigue syndrome (CFS), 292–294
Chronic illness and sexual dysfunctions, 375
Chronic negative emotions and coronary heart disease, 287–288
Chronic pain, 288–292
  biological aspects, 291–292

gender
  differences, 292
  psychological aspects, 289–291
  social aspects, 291
Chronic PTSD, 161
Chronic stress, 277
Chronological age, 87
Cialis, 381
Cigarette advertising, 430
Cigarette smoking
  and anxiety disorders, 130–131
  in China, 301–302
  as unhealthy behaviour, 273
Circadian rhythm sleep disorders, 336, 343–344
Circadian rhythms, 238
Civil commitment, 578–583
  criteria for, 579–580
  and dangerousness, 581–582
  and defining mental illness, 581
  and deinstitutionaliza-tion, 582–583
  overview of, 583
Civil commitment laws, 579
Classical categorical approach, 93–94
Classical conditioning, 25–26, 57–58, 278
Classical psychoanalysis, 23–24
Classification
  categorical and dimensional approaches, 93–96
  defined, 93
  reliability, 95
  validity, 95–96
Claustrophobia, 151
Clinical assessment
  behavioural assessment, 82–83
  clinical interview, 79–81
  defined, 76
  key concepts, 78–79
  neuroimaging, 89–90
  neuropsychological testing, 88–89

physical examination, 81–82

psychological testing, 84–88

psychophysiological assessment, 90–92

Clinical description, 6–7

Clinical efficacy, 594

Clinical interview, 79–81

Clinical practice guidelines, 594–596

Clinical psychologists, 5

Clinical significance, 102–103

Clinical utility, 594–595

Clomipramine, 196

Clonidine, 435

Clozapine, 54, 505

Coca leaves, 417

Cocaine, 375, 415

Cocaine use disorders, 417–419

Cognitive-behavioural group therapy (CBGT), for social phobia, 159

Cognitive-behavioural model. *See* Behavioural model

Cognitive-behavioural therapy (CBT), 62
for AIDS, 280
for anorexia nervosa, 332
for binge-eating disorder, 331
for bulimia nervosa, 328–330
for chronic fatigue syndrome, 294
for depression, 336
for headaches, 298
for hypochon-driasis, 183
for mood disorders, 252–253
for panic disorder, 147–148
for schizophrenia, 515

Cognitive coping skills for AIDS, 280

Cognitive disorders, 550–568, 575
amnestic disorder, 550, 567–568
delirium, 550, 551–553
dementia, 550, 553–567

organic causes of, 550–551

Cognitive factors
of emotion, 63–65
in substance-related disorders, 429–430

Cognitive processes
and conditioning, 57–58
and social learning, 59–60

Cognitive relaxation, 346

Cognitive schemas, negative, 252

Cognitive science, 57, 60–61

Cognitive styles, negative, 242–243

Cognitive therapy, 252
for insomnia, 346
for stress reduction, 296–298

Cohort effect, 116

Cohorts, 116

Colds and stress, 276

Collaborative Study on the Genetics of Alcoholism, 427

Colombia, 500

Colour naming, 61

Communication disorders, 530–531, 573

Community reinforcement approach, 438

Comorbidity, 98
of anxiety disorders, 132
personality disorders, 451–452
of substance-related disorders, 407

Comparative treatment research, 108–109

Comprehensive system, 85

Compulsions, 167, 168

Concurrent validity, 78–79

Conditioned response (CR), 26

Conditioned stimulus (CS), 26

Conduct disorder, 462

Confidentiality, 80–81

Confound, 101

Conscience, 20

Conscientiousness, 448

Construct validity, 96

Content validity, 96

Context, 35, 82, 239–240

Contingency management, 437–438

Control
and biofeedback, 296
and chronic pain, 290
and stress, 274–275, 277

Control groups, 101, 107–108

Controlled drinking, 436–437

Conversion disorder, 186–191, 212
causes, 190–191
clinical description, 186–187
closely related disorders, 187–188
DSM-IV criteria summary, 186
statistics, 189–190
treatment, 191
unconscious mental processes, 188–189

Conversion hysteria, 178

Conversion symptoms, 183, 186–187

Coping mechanisms, 66

Coping styles, 21

Coronary heart disease (CHD), 286–288

Correlation, 104–107
epidemiological research, 106–107
negative, 105–106
positive, 105

Correlation coefficient, 105

Correlation research, 115–116

Cortical arousal, 463–464

Cortical immaturity hypothesis, 464

Corticotropin-releasing factor (CRF) system, 130, 274

Cortisol, 50, 237–238, 274

Cosmetic surgery, 196–197

Cotard's syndrome, 490

Counselling psychologists, 5

Countertransference, 23

Course, 6

Covert sensitization, 391–392, 437

Cravings, 430

Creative people, and mood disorders, 233–234

Creutzfeldt-Jakob disease, 559, 561

CRF. *See* Corticotropin-releasing factor

Criminal commitment, 584–590
duty to warn, 589
and expert witnesses, 589–590
fitness to stand trial, 588
insanity defence, 585–588

Criminality, 461–462

Criterion gender bias, 451

Criterion validity, 96

Cross-dressing, 360, 385

Cross-generational effect, 117

Cross-National Collaborative Panic Study, 142

Cross-National Collaborative Study, 232–233

Cross-sectional designs, 115–116

Cultural context, 67–68

Cultural expectations, 3–4

Cultural factors. *See also* Social factors
in body dysmorphic disorder, 195
in conversion disorder, 190–191
in dissociative trance disorder, 201–202
and DSM-IV, 97
in eating disorders, 310, 318–319
fears and phobias, 66
IQ testing, 87–88
in mood disorders, 232–233, 243–246
in panic disorder, 142

in PTSD, 164
in schizophrenia, 500
sexual
    dysfunctions, 378
studying behaviour,
    117–118
in substance-related
    disorders, 431
Cultural-familial
    retardation, 547
*Culture of Narcissism,
    The* (Lasch), 473
Cyclothymic disorder,
    225, 226
Cylert, 527
Cyproterone acetate, 393

**D**
Dalmane, 345
Dangerousness, 581–582
Daytime sequelae, 337
Death
    from eating
        disorders, 310
    leading causes in
        Canada, 271
Deep muscle relaxation,
    296, 298
Defective genes, 39
Defence mechanism,
    20–21
Deinstitutionalization,
    14, 513–514,
    582–583
Delayed sleep phase
    type, 344
Delirium, 550,
    551–553, 575
Delirium tremens (DTs),
    403, 410
Delta waves, 91
Delusional, 193–194
Delusional disorder,
    496–497
Delusions, 489–490, 581
Delusions of
    grandeur, 489
Delusions of
    persecution, 489–490
Dementia, 410, 550,
    553–567, 576
    Alzheimer's disease,
        556–559, 576
    causes, 553, 562–564

clinical description
    and statistics,
    555–556
due to other medical
    conditions,
    559–561, 576
prevention, 567
substance-induced,
    561–562, 576
testing for, 557
treatment, 564–567
vascular, 559, 576
Dementia of the
    Alzheimer's type, 556.
    *See also* Alzheimer's
    disease
Dementia praecox, 486
Dementia
    pugilistica, 563
Demons, 9, 10
Dendrites, 44
Denial, 21, 298–299
Dependence, 185
Dependent personality
    disorder, 448, 449,
    476–477
Dependent variable, 100
Depersonalization,
    197, 198
Depersonalization
    disorder,
    198–199, 213
Depo-Provera, 393
Depressants, 408–415
    alcohol, 408–413
    barbiturates, 413–415
    hypnotics, 413–415
    sedatives, 413–415
Depression
    and anorexia
        nervosa, 316
    and anxiety,
        234–235, 237
    vs. anxiety, stress, and
        excitement,
        275–276
    and bulimia
        nervosa, 313
    clinical description,
        219–220
    and coronary heart
        disease, 288
    and cultural context,
        67–68
    feelings of, 216–217
    genetic factors in,
        235–237

historical conceptions
    of, 9–10
and immune
    system, 277
learned helplessness
    theory of, 241–242
overview of, 216–218
and serotonin, 51
and sleep
    disorders, 336
Depressive cognitive
    triad, 242
Depressive disorders,
    219–223, 269. *See
    also* Mood disorders
    and antidepressants,
        248–250
    causes, 235–247
    in children and
        adolescents,
        230–231
    cultural influences,
        243–246
    double depression, 220
    in the elderly, 231–232
    and grief, 223
    major depressive
        episode, 217
    onset and duration,
        220–223
    postpartum
        depression,
        226–227
    psychological
        dimensions,
        239–243
    relapse prevention,
        255–256
    seasonal affective
        disorder, 228
    social contributions,
        243–246
    and suicide, 258–264
Depressive personality
    disorder, 479
Derealization, 197–198
Descriptive validity,
    78–79
Designer drugs, 416,
    425, 426
Desipramine, 435
Desire phase of sexual
    response cycle, 365
Developing countries,
    psychological
    disorders in, 68–69

Developmental
    disorders, 523–540,
    573–574
    attention
        deficit/hyperactivity
        disorder, 524–528
    learning disorders,
        528–533
    mental retardation,
        540–549
    pervasive, 533–540
    prevention, 549–550
Developmental factors,
    37, 69–70
Developmental
    psychopathology,
    69–70, 523
Developmental stages,
    23, 523
Deviation IQ, 87
Dexamethasone
    suppression test, 238
*Dhat*, 181
Diabetes, 299, 374–375
Diagnosing
    psychological
    disorders, 92–99
    classification issues,
        93–96
    defined, 76
    reliability, 95
    validity, 95–96
*Diagnostic and
    Statistical Manual of
    Mental Disorders*
    (DSM-IV-TR),
    4, 96–99
    alcohol intoxication
        criteria
        summary, 409
    Alzheimer's disease
        criteria
        summary, 557
    amnestic disorder
        criteria
        summary, 568
    amphetamine
        intoxication
        criteria
        summary, 416
    anorexia nervosa
        criteria
        summary, 316
    antisocial personality
        disorder criteria
        summary, 461

attention deficit/hyperactivity disorder criteria summary, 525

autistic disorder criteria summary, 536

avoidant personality disorder criteria summary, 475

bipolar disorder criteria summary, 225

body dysmorphic disorder criteria summary, 194

borderline personality disorder criteria summary, 468

bulimia nervosa criteria summary, 313

caffeine intoxication criteria summary, 420

cannabis intoxication criteria summary, 423

cocaine intoxication criteria summary, 418

conversion disorder criteria summary, 186

criticisms of, 97–98

cyclothymic disorder criteria summary, 226

defence mechanisms in, 21

delirium criteria summary, 552

delusional disorder criteria summary, 496

dependent personality disorder criteria summary, 477

depersonalization disorder criteria summary, 199

diagnosis using, 93

dissociative amnesia criteria summary, 200

dissociative fugue criteria summary, 201

dissociative identity disorder criteria summary, 203

dysthymic disorder criteria summary, 222

evaluation of criteria in, 76

exhibitionism criteria summary, 385

factitious disorder criteria summary, 188

fetishism criteria summary, 384

gender identity disorder criteria summary, 361

generalized anxiety disorder criteria summary, 134

hallucinogen intoxication criteria summary, 425

histrionic personality disorder criteria summary, 471

hyopchondriasis criteria summary, 179

hypoactive sexual desire criteria summary, 367

learning disorders criteria summary, 529

major depressive episode criteria summary, 218

manic episode criteria summary, 218

mental retardation criteria summary, 543

multiaxial system in, 96–97

narcissistic personality disorder criteria summary, 473

nicotine withdrawal criteria summary, 420

obsessive-compulsive disorder criteria summary, 168

obsessive-compulsive personality disorder criteria summary, 478

opioid intoxication criteria summary, 422

orgasmic disorder criteria summary, 370

pain disorder criteria summary, 191–192

panic attack criteria summary, 130

panic disorder criteria summary, 140

paranoid personality disorder criteria summary, 453

pathological gambling criteria summary, 406

pedophilia criteria summary, 388

posttraumatic stress disorder criteria summary, 163

schizoid personality disorder criteria summary, 455

schizophrenia criteria summary, 489

schizotypal personality disorder criteria summary, 457

scizophreniform disorder criteria summary, 496

sedative, hypnotic, or anxiolytic intoxication criteria summary, 414

sexual arousal disorder criteria summary, 369

sexual dysfunction categories, 365–366

sexual masochism criteria summary, 386

sexual pain disorders criteria summary, 373

sexual sadism criteria summary, 386

sleep disorders descriptions, 336

social and cultural considerations in, 97

social phobia criteria summary, 157

somatization disorder criteria summary, 184

specific phobia criteria summary, 150

substance abuse criteria summary, 403

substance dependence criteria summary, 404

substance intoxication criteria summary, 403

trance and possession disorder criteria summary, 202

voyeurism criteria summary, 385

Diagnostic categories, 98

Dialectical behaviour therapy (DBT), 470

Diastolic blood pressure, 284

Diathesis-stress model, 41–42

Dietary restraint, 321, 322–324

Dilators, 380

Dimensional approach, 94

Dimethyltryptamine (DMT), 424

Directionality, 106

Discrimination, 68

Discrimination training, 539

Disease conviction, 180

Disease model of dependence, 430–431

Disintegrated experience, 198

Disorder of written expression, 529

Disorganized speech, 493–494
Disorganized type of schizophrenia, 495
Displacement, 21
Dissociation, 60, 178, 197
Dissociative amnesia, 199–200, 208–209, 213
Dissociative disorders, 178, 197–209, 213
  depersonalization disorder, 198–199
  dissociative amnesia, 199–200, 208–209, 213
  dissociative fugue, 200–203, 208–209, 213
  dissociative identity disorder, 202–209, 213
  dissociative trance disorder, 201–202, 213
Dissociative fugue, 200–203, 208–209, 213
Dissociative identity disorder (DID), 202–209, 213
  causes, 205–207
  characteristics, 203
  clinical description, 202–203
  DSM-IV criteria summary, 203
  faking, 203–204
  real memories and false, 207–208
  statistics, 204–205
  treatment, 208–209
Dissociative trance disorder, 201–202, 213
*Distant Mirror, A* (Tuchman), 9
Distress, 3
Disulfiram (Antabuse), 435
DNA, 38, 39
Dominance and stress, 274–275
Dominant genes, 39
Dopamine, 45, 46, 51, 53–54

and schizoid personality disorder, 455
and schizophrenia, 51, 53–54, 504–506
Dopaminergic system, 428
Dorsal horns of the spinal column, 292
Double bind communication, 509
Double-blind control, 108
Double depression, 220
Down syndrome, 545–546
Dream analysis, 23
Dream anxiety disorder, 336
Dream sleep. *See* Rapid eye movement (REM) sleep
Dreams, bad, 348
Drug holidays, 111
Drug-seeking behaviours, 403–404
Drug therapy, 14. *See also* Biological treatments
  for ADHD, 527–528
  delirium caused by, 552–553
  for eating disorders, 328
  for headaches, 298
  non-compliance with, 512
  for paraphilias, 393
  sexual dysfunction as side effect of, 375
  for sexual dysfunctions, 381–382
  for sleep disorders, 340, 341, 344–345
Drugs, addictiveness of, 406
DSM-IV-TR. *See Diagnostic and Statistical Manual of Mental Disorders*
Durham rule, 585
Duty to warn, 589
Dyslexia, brain structure and, 48
Dysmorphophobia, 193
Dyspareunia, 371–372, 373

Dyssocial behaviour, 463
Dyssomnias, 336–337
Dysthymic disorder, 219–220
  DSM-IV criteria summary, 222
  onset and duration, 222–223

**E**
Eating disorders, 309–334. *See also* Anorexia nervosa; Binge-eating disorder; Bulimia nervosa; Obesity
  biological dimensions, 325–326
  causes of, 320–328
  cross-cultural considerations, 310, 318–319
  developmental considerations, 319
  dietary restraint, 321, 322–324
  and endogenous opioids, 292
  family influences, 324–325
  and gender, 66
  integrative model of, 327–328
  prevention of, 333–334
  psychological dimensions, 326
  psychological treatments for, 328–332
  social dimensions, 320–325
  statistics, 309–310, 317–318
  treatment, 328–332
  types of, 309–319
Echolalia, 523, 535, 537
Ecstasy, 416, 426
Educable mental retardation, 544
Effect size, 103
Effeminate boys, 362, 364
Ego, 20

Dyssocial behaviour, 463
*Ego and the Mechanisms of Defense* (Freud), 22
Ego psychology, 22
Egoistic suicide, 260
Egypt, 12–13, 169, 318
Ejaculation
  premature, 371, 376, 378, 379, 380
  retarded, 370
  retrograde, 370
Elder abuse, 566
Elderly
  anxiety disorders in, 232
  delirium in, 552–553
  erectile dysfunction in, 369
  GAD in, 135
  hypochondriasis in, 180
  mood disorders in, 231–232
  sleep disorders in, 338, 345
  social and interpersonal influences on, 68
  and social networks, 272
  suicide rates in, 259
Electra complex, 22
Electrocardiogram, 337
Electroconvulsive therapy (ECT), 14, 247, 251, 511, 595
Electrodermal activity, 91
Electroencephalogram (EEG), 91, 337
Electrolyte imbalance, 312–313, 316
Electromyograph, 337
Electrooculograph, 337
Emotion
  components of, 63–65
  and coronary heart disease, 287–288
  defined, 63
  expressed, 509
Emotional disorders. *See* Mood disorders
Emotional factors, 37, 62–65
Empathy, 25, 393
Endocrine system, 49, 50, 237–238
Endogenous opioids, 292

Endorphins, 292
Enkephalins, 292
Environmental factors, interaction of genetic factors and, 38–43
Environmental treatments for sleep disorders, 345–346
Epidemiology, 106–107
Epinephrine, 49, 50
Episodic course, 6–7
Equifinality, 70, 432
Erectile dysfunction, 368–369, 374–377, 381–382
Ergotism, 423
Erotomanic delusions, 496–497
Erotophobia, 376–377
Essential hypertension, 284, 285
Estrogen replacement therapy, 565
*Ethical Conduct for Research Involving Humans*, 120
Ethics, research, 120–121, 592–593
Etiology, defined, 7
Eugenics, 549
Event-related potential, 91
Evil, 9
Evil eye, 65–66
Evoked potential, 91
Excitement, 275–276
Exercise, and eating disorders, 312, 314–315, 326
Exhaustion stage of stress, 273
Exhibitionism, 384, 385
Exorcism, 9, 11
*Exorcist, The* (film), 11
Expectancy effect, 429–430
Experimental research, 107–112
  comparative treatment research, 108–109
  control groups, 107–108
  group experimental designs, 107
  single-case experimental designs, 109–112

Experiments, 107
Expert witnesses, 589–590
Explicit memory, 61
Exposure and response prevention, 55
Exposure-based therapy for phobias, 155
  for social phobia, 159
Expressed emotion, 509
Expressive language disorder, 530–531
External validity, 100, 101–102
Extinction, 26
Extrapyramidal symptoms, 512
Extraversion, 447
Eye-movement desensitization and reprocessing (EMDR), 165–166

**F**
Facial agnosia, 555
Factitious disorder by proxy, 188
Factitious disorders, 187–188
"False hope syndrome," 323
False memories, 207–208
False Memory Syndrome Foundation, 208
False negatives, 88–89
False positives, 88–89
Familial aggregation, 113
Family factors
  in antisocial personality disorder, 465
  eating disorders, 324–325
  gender identity disorder, 362
  in mood disorders, 235–236
  and schizophrenia, 509–510
  in substance-related disorders, 427
  and suicide, 261

Family studies, 113, 235–236, 500–501
Family therapy for anorexia nervosa, 332
Fatal familial insomnia, 337
Fatalistic suicide, 260
Fear, 62
  in anxiety disorders, 128
  and chronic pain, 290
  and coronary heart disease, 288
  emotion of, 63
  fright disorders, 65–66
  and panic, 129
  physiology and purpose of, 62–63
Fearlessness hypothesis, 464
Female orgasmic disorder, 370, 380
Female sexual arousal disorder, 368–369, 381
Fenfluramine, 52
Fetal alcohol syndrome (FAS), 411, 544
fetishism, 384
Fetus, affect of cocaine on, 418
Fight/flight system (FFS), 130, 464
Fight or flight response, 62–63, 128
Figure skaters and eating disorders, 323
First Nations people
  dissociative trances in, 201
  mood disorders in, 233
  suicide rates in, 258–259
Fitness to stand trial, 588
Five-factor model, 447–448
Fixation, 21
Flashbacks, 160
Flat affect, 492–493
Flight/fight syndrome, 288
Flight of ideas, 218
Fluoxetine, 183, 249, 328

Flurazepam, 345
Fluvoxamine, 196
Forebrain, 46, 47
Formal observation, 83
Fragile X syndrome, 546–547
Framingham Heart Study, 287
Freckles, 195
Free association, 23
Fright disorders, 65–66
Frigidity, 368. *See also* Sexual dysfunctions
Frigo phobia, 153
Frontal lobe, 48
Frotteurism, 383–384
Functional genomics, 427

**G**
Galen, 12–13
Galvanic skin response, 91
Gambling addiction, 404, 406
Gamma aminobutyric acid (GABA), 45, 46, 52–53
  affect of alcohol on, 409–410
  and anxiety, 130
Gamma hydroxybutyrate (GHB), 426
GAS. *See* General adaptation syndrome
Gate control theory, 292
Gender differences
  in ADHD, 525
  in alcohol consumption, 411–412
  dependence and, 185
  in depression, 230–231, 232
  in mood disorders, 244–245
  and pain, 292
  in panic disorder, 142
  in personality disorders, 450–451
  in specific phobia, 152
  in suicide, 259

Gender identity disorder, 356, 359–364
causes of, 361–362
definition, 360–361
DSM-IV-TR criteria summary, 361
incidence of, 360
treatment, 362–364
Gender roles, 66
Gene therapy, 549–550
General adaptation syndrome (GAS), 273
General paresis, 13
Generalizability, 102
Generalizations, 103
Generalized amnesia, 199
Generalized anxiety disorder (GAD), 132–138
causes, 135–136
clinical description, 133–134
DSM-IV criteria summary, 134
statistics, 134–135
symptoms, 134
treatment, 136–138
Generalized biological vulnerability, 131
Generalized psychological vulnerability, 131, 163
Generalized sexual dysfunctions, 365
Genes, 38–39
nature of, 39–40
new developments in, 40
nongenomic inheritance of behaviour, 43–44
research on, 112–115
Genetic factors
in Alzheimer's disease, 563
in antisocial personality disorder, 463
in autism, 537
interaction of environmental effects and, 38–43
in mental retardation, 545–547

in mood disorders, 235–237
in personality, 54
in PTSD, 163
in schizophrenia, 500–503
in schizotypal personality disorder, 457
in substance-related disorders, 427
Genetic linkage studies, 114–115, 502
Genetic markers, 114
Genetic screening, 549
Genital surgery, 363
Genome, 113
Genotypes, 113
Germ theory of disease, 13
Gila, 118
Ginkgo biloba, 565
Glial cell-derived neurotrophic factor, 565
Globus hystericus, 186
Glutamate system, 410
Gonadal glands, 49
Graduated extinction, 346, 347
Grandiose delusions, 497
Grandiosity, 83
Greeks, 12
Grief, 223
Group experiments, 107–108
Guilt feelings, 83
Gun control, 258
Gynecomastia, 363

**H**
HAART. See Highly active antiretroviral therapy
Halcion, 345
Hallucinations, 80, 342, 490–491, 581
Hallucinogen use disorder, 422
Hallucinogens, 408, 422–425
LSD, 423–425
marijuana, 422–423

Halstead-Reitan Neuropsychological Battery, 88
Hara-kiri, 260
Harm reduction, 439
Head trauma, 559, 560, 563, 568
Headaches, 92, 295–296, 298
Health
factors affecting, 271–278
and social relationships, 67
Health psychology, 272
Heart attack, 286, 375
Heart, effect of anger on, 65, 272
Heart rate, 53
Hebephrenia, 486
Heloperidol, 553
Helper T cells, 278
Heredity. See Genetic factors
Hermaphrodites, 360, 363
Heroin, 375, 421–422, 429, 434
Hierarchy of needs, 24
High blood pressure. See Hypertension
Highly active antiretroviral therapy (HAART), 279
Hillside Strangler, 203–204
Hindbrain, 46, 47
Hippocampus, 48, 274
and PTSD, 164
and stress hormones, 238
Hippocrates, 12–13
Historical context, 1–31
Histrionic personality disorder, 448, 470–472
gender differences in, 450
statistics and development, 449
HIV. See Human immunodeficiency virus
Holiday of Darkness (Endler), 234

Homelessness, 582–583
Homosexuality, 358–359
and eating disorders, 323
vs. gender identity disorder, 360
and sexual dysfunctions, 365
Hopelessness, 242
Hormones, 49, 361
Hostility
and coronary heart disease, 288
and hypertension, 285–286
HPA axis (hypothalamic-pituitary-adrenalcortical axis), and stress, 274
Human genome project, 113
Human immunodeficiency virus (HIV), 11, 278, 279–281, 560. See also Acquired immune deficiency syndrome
prevention interventions, 300–301
Human potential movements, 25
Human Sexual Inadequacy (Masters and Johnson), 379
Humanistic theory, 24–25
Humoral branch of immune system, 277–278
Humoral theory, 12
Humours, 12
Huntington's disease, 559, 560–561
Hyperactivity, 524
Hypericum, 249
Hypersomnia, primary, 336, 340–342, 345
Hypertension, 53, 92, 284–286
Hyperthyroidism, 81
Hypnagogic hallucinations, 342
Hypnosis, 18
Hypnotics, 413–415
Hypnotizability, 206

Hypoactive sexual desire disorder, 366–367, 375–376, 381
Hypochondriasis, 179–183, 212
causes, 181–182
clinical description, 179–180
DSM-IV criteria summary, 179
statistics, 180–181
treatment, 182–183
Hypofrontality, 507
Hypomanic episode, 218
Hypothalamic-pituitary-adrenalcortical axis (HPA axis), 50
Hypothalamus, 48, 50, 325–326
Hypothesis, 100–101
Hypothesis testing, 253
Hypothyroidism, 81
Hypoventilation, 343
Hypoxiphilia, 385
Hysteria, 12–13, 178
Hysterical neurosis, 178

I
ICD-10. See International Classification of Diseases and Health Related Problems (ICD0–10)
Id, 20
Ideas of reference, 456
Illness, chronic, and sexual dysfunctions, 375
Illness phobia, 180
Illusions, 456
Imaginal exposure, 164–165
Imaginary playmates, 206–207
Imagined ugliness. See Body dysmorphic disorder
Imipramine, 145, 248, 348
Immune response and stress, 276–278
Immune system, 276
and AIDS, 278, 280
and depression, 277

and pain, 295
workings of, 277–278
Impacted grief reaction, 223
Impairment, 3
Implicit memory, 60–61
Impotence, 368. See also Sexual dysfunctions
Impulse control disorders, and bulimia nervosa, 313
Impulsivity, 468, 524
Inappropriate affect, 494
Incest, 387
Incidence, 6
Independent living skills programs, 514
Independent variable, 100
India
dhat, 181
dissociative trances in, 201
eating disorders in, 319
OCD in, 169
schizophrenia in, 500
sexual dysfunctions in, 378
Infants, sleep disorders in, 339–340
Informal observation, 83
Information transmission, 153–154
Informed consent, 120, 592–593
Inhalents, 425
Inhibited orgasm, 369–370
Injection drug users, safe injection sites for, 439
Injury prevention, 300
Inpatient treatment facilities, for substance-abuse disorders, 435–436
Insanity defence, 585–588
Insidious onset, 7
Insight, 19
Insomnia, 337
primary, 336, 337–340, 344–347
rebound, 340, 345

Insulin coma therapy, 511
Insulin shock therapy, 14
Integrative approach, 29–30
Intellectual functioning, assessment of, 80
Intelligence quotient (IQ), 40, 86–88
and autism, 535–536
criminality and, 461
and mental retardation, 543–544
Intelligence testing, 84, 86–88
Internal validity, 100, 101–102
International Classification of Diseases and Health Related Problems (ICD-10), 93, 96
Interoceptive avoidance, 141
Interpersonal psychotherapy (IPT), 246, 253–254
Interpersonal relationships, 25, 68
Interpersonal therapy (IPT)
for binge-eating disorder, 331
for bulimia nervosa, 329–330
Interrater reliability, 78
Intersexed individuals, 360, 363
Intoxication, 402–403
Intrapsychic conflicts, 20
Introspection, 26
Inuit people, 142, 259
Inverse agonists, 51
IPT. See Interpersonal therapy
Ischemia, 286

J
Jamaica, 118
Japan, 118
coronary heart disease in, 287

eating disorders in, 319
hara-kiri in, 260
shinkeishitsu, 157, 196
suicide rates in, 259
Jet lag, 340, 343

K
Kayak-angst, 97, 142
Ketamine, 426
Killer T cells, 278, 295
Korea, 431
Koro, 181

L
L-arginine glutamate, 381
L-dopa, 54, 505
La belle indifférence, 187, 190
Labelling, 98–99
Lanugo, 316
Large fibres (A-beta fibres), 292
Latin America, 68
Law of effect, 28
Learned alarms, 132
Learned helplessness, 58–59, 241–242
Learned helplessness theory of depression, 241–242
Learned optimism, 59
Learning
observational learning, 59
prepared, 60
social learning, 59–60
Learning disorders, 528–533, 573. See also Developmental disorders
causes, 531–532
clinical description, 529
DSM-IV criteria summary, 529
statistics, 529–530
treatment, 532
Learning factors, in substance-related disorders, 429–430

Lesch-Nyhan syndrome, 545
Leukocytes, 277
Level, 110
Levitra, 381
Libido, 20
Librium, 14
Life expectancy, and social relationships, 67
Life-span developmentalists, 69–70
Lifelong sexual dysfunctions, 365
Lifestyles, unhealthy, 273, 299–302
Light sensitivity, 238
Light therapy, for sleep disorders, 345–346
Limbic system, 47, 48, 130, 274
Linear causal model, 35
Lithium, 250–251, 256
Localized amnesia, 199–200
Longitudinal course specifiers, 227
Longitudinal designs, 116–117
LSD (d-lysergic acid diethylamide), 423–425
Lunatic, 11
Luria-Nebraska Neuropsychological Battery, 88
Lymphocytes, 277
Lysergic acid amide, 424

**M**
Ma-huang, 416
Magic, 9
Magical ideation (MI), 457
Maintenance treatment, 255–256
Major depressive episode, 217, 219. *See also* Depressive disorders
 criteria for, 95
 DSM-IV criteria summary, 218

onset and duration, 220–222
recurrent, 219
single episode, 219
Malaysia, 117–118
Male erectile disorder, 368–369, 374–377, 381–382
Male orgasmic disorder, 370
Malingering, 187, 189
Mania
 in children and adolescents, 231
 overview of, 217–218
Manic depressive disorder. *See* Bipolar disorder
Manic episodes, 219
 bipolar disorder, 223–226
 DSM-IV criteria summary, 218
 and lithium, 250–251
*Manie sans delire*, 460
Manipulating a variable, 107
Mantra, 296
Marijuana, 375, 422–423
Marital relations, and depression, 243–244
Marker genes, 502–503
Marriage and family therapists, 5
Masturbation, 357, 367, 370, 380, 390
Mathematics disorder, 529
Mature age, 23
MDMA, 416, 426
Meaning, of life events, 239–240
Media and eating disorders, 321
Medical treatments
 for sexual dysfunctions, 381–382
 for sleep disorders, 344–345
Medications. *See* Drug therapy
Meditation, 296
Medroxyprogesterone acetate, 393
Melancholic, 12
Melancholy, 9–10, 12

Melatonin, 344
Memory
 and amnestic disorder, 567–568
 and dissociative disorders, 197–209
 explicit, 61
 false, 207–208
 implicit, 60–61
Memory B cells, 278
Memory loss, 553
Memory T cells, 278
Men
 coronary heart disease in, 287
 eating disorders in, 317, 319, 321, 323
 erectile dysfunction in, 368–369, 374–377, 381–382
 gender identity disorder in, 362
 hypoactive sexual desire in, 367
 inhibited orgasm in, 369, 370
 pain in, 292
 response of to stress, 66
 sexual aversion disorder in, 368
 sexual dysfunction categories, 365, 366
 sexual practices of, 356, 357–358
Menstruation cessation, 315–316
Mental age, 87
Mental health counsellors, 5
Mental health practitioners, 5–6
Mental health services, 577–600
 civil commitment, 578–583
 clinical practice guidelines, 594–596
 criminal commitment, 584–590
 patients' rights, 590–593
Mental hospitals
 and moral therapy, 16
 reform of, 16–18
 size of, 13–14

Mental hygiene movement, 17
Mental illness
 and dangerousness, 581–582
 defining, 581
Mental retardation, 540–550, 574. *See also* Developmental disorders
 causes, 544–547
 clinical description, 542–544
 DSM-IV criteria summary, 543
 statistics, 544
 treatment, 547–549
Mental status exam, 79–81
Mescaline, 424
Mesmerism, 18
Methadone, 434
Methylene-dioxymethamphetamine (MDMA), 416, 426
Methylphenidate, 345
Mexico, 431
Micronesia, 68
Microsleeps, 337
Midbrain, 47, 48
Middle Ages, 9, 10, 11
Migraine headaches, 298
Mind, structure of, 20, 21
Mindfulness-based cognitive therapy, 255–256
Minnesota Multiphasic Personality Inventory (MMPI), 85–86, 590
Miracle cures, 6
Mixed manic episode, 218
Mixed sleep apnea, 343
M'Naghten rule, 585
Modafinil, 345
Modelling, 59
Monoamine oxidase (MAO) inhibitors, 159, 248–249
Montreux clinic, 332
Mood, 63, 80

Mood disorders, 63, 215–266, 268–269
across cultures, 232–233
and anorexia nervosa, 316
biological dimensions, 235–238
bipolar disorders, 223–226
and bulimia nervosa, 313
causes, 235–247
in children and adolescents, 230–231
in creative people, 233–234
cultural influences, 243–246
defined, 216–218
depression, 217
depressive disorders, 219–223
differences in course of, 227–228
in the elderly, 231–232
integrative approach to, 246–247
mania, 217–218
postpartum depression, 226–227
prevalence of, 229–235
prevention, 254
psychological dimensions, 239–243
relapse prevention, 255–256
seasonal affective disorder, 228
social contributions, 243–246
structure of, 218–219
and suicide, 258–264
treatment, 247–257, 269
in women, 244–245
Mood-stabilizing drugs, 250–251
Moon, 11
Moral principles, 20
Moral therapy, 16–18
Moral weakness, 430–431
Morphine, 421

Motivation and anorexia nervosa treatment, 332
Mount Cashel Orphanage, 388
MRI (magnetic resonance imaging), 89, 506
Multidimensional integrative approach, 35–72
behavioural contributions, 57–62
biological contributions, 38–57
conclusions, 70–71
developmental contributions, 69–70
dimensions in, 35–37
emotional contributions, 62–65
one-dimensional vs. multidimensional models, 35–38
social contributions, 65–69
Multidimensional model of causality, 35–38
Multiple baselines, 111–112
Munchausen syndrome by proxy, 188
Murderers, 462
Muscle relaxation, 296, 298, 346
MUSE, 382
Myocardial infarction, 286, 375
Myocardium, 286

N
Naltrexone, 434–435
Narcissistic personality disorder, 448, 449, 472–473
Narcolepsy, 336, 342, 345, 416
Natural environment phobias, 151
Natural opioids, 292

Nature vs. nurture debate, 39
Nefazodone, 249
Negative affect symptoms, 234
Negative cognitive schemas, 252
Negative correlation, 105–106
Negative emotions and coronary heart disease, 287–288
Negative reinforcement, 428–429
Negative symptoms, 491–493
Negativistic personality disorder, 479
Nervous breakdowns, 162
Nervous system, 45
Neurasthenia, 292, 293
Neurobiological influences
antisocial personality disorder, 463–464
autism, 537–538
schizophrenia, 503–508
substance-related disorders, 427–428
suicide, 261
Neurobiological procedures, 84
Neurochemical abnormalities, 505
Neurofibrillary tangles, 562
Neurohormones, 250, 274
Neuroimaging, 89–90
Neuroleptics, 14, 15, 505, 511–512
Neurology, 54
Neurons, 44–46, 56, 428
Neuropsychological testing, 84, 88–89
Neuroses, 22
Neurosis, 24, 178
Neuroticism, 448
Neurotransmitters, 45–46, 50–54
effect of alcohol on, 409–410
effect of cocaine on, 418

and antidepressants, 248–250
dopamine, 51, 53–54, 455, 504–506
drug interactions on, 50–51
and eating disorders, 325–326
GABA, 52–53, 130, 409–410
and mood disorders, 237
norepinephrine, 53
and psychosocial factors, 56
research on, 51
serotonin, 45, 46, 51–52, 55, 238, 248–250, 325–326
New Zealand, eating disorders in, 317
Nicotine, 415
Nicotine dependence. See also Cigarette smoking
and bulimia nervosa, 313
Nicotine use disorders, 419–420
Nicotinic acetylcholine-receptors, 420
Nigeria, 118, 201, 500
Nightmare disorder, 336, 347–348
Nocturnal eating syndrome, 349
Nocturnal panic, 142–143
Nocturnal penile tumescence (NPT), 373
Nomenclature, 93
Non-compliance, 512
Non-demand pleasuring, 379
Non-genital pleasuring, 379
Non-purging type of bulimia nervosa, 312
Non-rapid eye movement (NREM) sleep, 347, 348
Nongenomic inheritance of behaviour, 43–44
Noradrenaline. See Norepinephrine

Norepinephrine, 45, 53, 248–250
Nosology, 93
Not criminally responsible on account of mental disorder (NCRMD), 585–588
Not guilty by reason of insanity (NGRI), 585–588
NPT. *See* Nocturnal penile tumescence
NREM sleep. *See* Non-rapid eye movement (NREM) sleep

**O**

Obesity. *See also* Eating disorders
   and sleep disorders, 345
Object relations, 22–23
Observational assessment, 82–83
Observational learning, 59
Obsessions, 167, 168
Obsessive-compulsive disorder (OCD), 80, 166–171
   and anorexia nervosa, 316
   and body dysmorphic disorder, 195–196
   and brain function, 54–55
   causes, 169–170
   clinical description, 167–168
   and delusions, 193
   DSM-IV criteria summary, 168
   statistics, 169
   treatment, 170–171
Obsessive-compulsive personality disorder, 448, 449, 477–478
Obstructive sleep apnea (OSA), 343
Occipital lobe, 48
OCD. *See* Obsessive-compulsive disorder
Oedipus conflict, 22

*Oedipus Rex*, 22
Older adults. *See* Elderly
Olfactory bulb, 47
Oncology, 281
Ondansetron, 435
One-dimensional model of causality, 35
Onset, 7
Ontario, sex reassignment surgery in, 363
Openness to experience, 448
Operant conditioning, 27–28, 58
Operant control of pain, 291
Operational definition, 83
Opioid-releasing neurons, 428
Opioid use disorders, 421–422
Opioids, 292, 408, 421–422
Opium, 14, 421–422
Opponent-process theory, 429
Optic nerve, 47
Optimism, and physical disorders, 298–299
Oral stage, 21–22
Orbital surface, 55
Organic mental disorders, 550–551
Orgasm disorders, 369–371
Orgasm phase of sexual response cycle, 365
Orgasmic reconditioning, 392
OSA. *See* Obstructive sleep apnea
Overgeneralization, 242
Oxycodone, 421

**P**

*Pa-leng*, 153
Pain
   acute, 289
   chronic, 288–292
   and immune system, 295
   operant control of, 291

phantom limb, 291
   in rats, 294–295
Pain behaviours, 289
Pain catastrophizing, 290–291
Pain disorder, 191–192
Panic
   in anxiety disorders, 128–129, 132
   nocturnal, 142–143
Panic attacks, 128–129
   causes, 144
   and cocaine withdrawal, 81–82
   DSM-IV criteria summary, 130
Panic control treatment (PCT), 146–147
Panic disorder, 138–148
   and alcohol abuse, 140
   causes, 143–145
   clinical description, 139–141
   cultural influences, 142
   DSM-IV criteria summary, 140
   and hypochindriasis, 180
   nocturnal panic, 142–143
   and sexual aversion disorder, 367–368
   statistics, 141–143
   treatment, 145–148
Panic disorder with agoraphobia (PDA), 138
Panic disorder without agoraphobia (PD), 139
Papaverine, 381–382
Paradoxical intention therapy, 346
Paranoia, 486
Paranoid personality disorder, 448, 449, 452–454
Paranoid type of schizophrenia, 494–495
Paraphilias, 356, 383–394
   assessing, 391
   causes of, 389–391
   exhibitionism, 384, 385
   fetishism, 384

incest, 387
   pedophilia, 387–388
   sadistic rape, 386
   sexual sadism and sexual masochism, 385–386
   transvestic fetishism, 360, 385
   treatment, 391–394
   voyeurism, 384–385
   in women, 389
Parasomnias, 336–337, 347–349
Parasympathetic nervous system (PNS), 48–50
*Parens patriae*, 579
Parietal lobe, 48
Parkinson's disease, 54, 559, 560
Partialism, 384
Pathological gambling, 404, 406
Pathological grief reaction, 223
Patient uniformity myth, 103
Patient's rights, 590–593
Pedophilia, 387–388
Penile prostheses or implants, 382
Penile strain gauge, 373
Penis envy, 22
Perfectionism and eating disorders, 326
Performance anxiety, 156
Performance scales, 87
Peripheral nervous system, 45, 48–50
Person-centred therapy, 25
Personal distress, 3
Personality
   and brain function, 54–55
   dimensions of, 447–448
   and hierarchy of needs, 24
Personality disorders, 445–484
   antisocial, 459–467
   aspects of, 446–447
   avoidant, 474–475, 476
   borderline, 467–470

categorical and
dimensional
models, 447–448
cluster A, 452–458
cluster B, 458–474
cluster C, 474–479
comorbidity, 451–452
defined, 446
dependent, 476–477
gender differences in,
450–451
histrionic, 470–472
narcissistic, 472–473
obsessive-compulsive,
477–478
paranoid, 452–454
proposed, 479
schizoid, 454–456
schizotypal, 456–458
statistics and
development,
448–450
Personality inventories,
85–86
Pervasive development
disorder-not
otherwise specified,
533, 534
Pervasive development
disorders,
533–540, 574
autistic disorder,
533–538
treatment, 538–540
PET (positron emission
tomography), 89–90
Pets, 67
Phallic stage, 22
Phantom limb pain, 291
Phase advances, 345
Phase delays, 345
Ph.D. degree, 5
Phelgm, 12
Phencyclidine
(PCP), 426
Phenotypes, 113, 457
Phenylketonuria, 545
Phlegmatic
personality, 12
Phobias
animal, 151
blood-injury-injection,
2, 35–38, 150–151
causes, 153–155
and culture, 65–66
defined, 2
and gender, 66

illness, 180
natural
environment, 151
situational, 151
social phobia, 155–159
specific phobia,
149–155
treatment, 155
Phobic avoidance, 139
Phototherapy, 251–252
Physical abuse
and dissociative
identity disorder,
205–206
and suicide, 262
Physical disorders, 271.
*See also* Eating
disorders; Sleep
disorders
AIDS, 279–281
cancer, 281–283
cardiovascular
problems, 283–288
chronic fatigue
syndrome,
292–294
chronic pain, 288–292
coronary heart
disease, 286–288
hypertension, 284–286
psychological
treatment,
294–302
psychosocial effects
on, 279–294
Physical drives, 20
Physical examination,
81–82
Physiology
of emotion, 63–64
of stress, 274
Pick's disease, 559, 561
Pituitary gland, 49,
50, 274
Placebo control
groups, 108
Placebo effect, 107–108
Plastic surgery, 196–197
Plateau phase of sexual
response cycle, 365
Plato, 15
*Playboy* centrefolds,
320–321
Pleasure centre, 427–428
Pleasure principle, 20
PNI. *See* Psychoneuro-
immunology

Poets, 233
Political dissidents, 4
Polygenic factors, 39
Polysomnographic (PSG)
evaluation, 337
Polysubstance abuse, 401
Positive correlation, 105
Positive psychology, 59
Positive
reinforcement, 428
Positive symptoms,
489–491
Positron emission
tomography (PET),
89–90
Possession
across cultures,
201–202
treatments, 11
Postpartum depression,
226–227, 246
Posttraumatic stress
disorder (PTSD),
160–166
and borderline
personality
disorder, 469
causes, 162–164
clinical description,
160–162
delayed onset, 161
DSM-IV criteria
summary, 163
statistics, 162
treatment, 164–166
Poverty, 68
Predictive validity, 79, 96
Predisposing
conditions, 340
Preintervention
research, 115
Premarital sex, 358
Premature ejaculation,
371, 376, 378,
379, 380
Prenatal gene therapy,
549–550
Prepared learning, 60
Presenting a problem, 6
Prevalence, 6
Prevention research, 115
Primary gain, 190
Primary hypersomnia,
336, 340–342, 345
Primary insomnia, 336,
337–340
causes of, 339–340

clinical
description, 338
integrative model
of, 340
medical treatments
for, 344–345
psychological
treatments for,
346–347
statistics, 338
Primary process, 20
Privileged
communication,
80–81
Proband, 113
Prognosis, 7, 93
Program of research,
119–120
Progressive muscle
relaxation, 296, 346
Project MATCH, 438
Projection, 21
Projective tests, 84–85
Propranolol, 375
Prostaglandin, 381
Prototypes, 4
Prototypical approach,
94–95
Prozac, 52, 249, 328, 375
PSG evaluation. *See*
Polysomnographic
(PSG) evaluation
Psilocybin, 424
Psyche, 8
Psychiatric nurses, 5
Psychiatric social
workers, 5
Psychiatrists, 5
Psycho-oncology, 281
Psychoactive
substances, 402
Psychoanalysis, 18
Psychoanalysts, 23
Psychoanalytic
model, 19
Psychoanalytic
psychotherapy,
23–24
Psychoanalytic theory,
18–24
Anna O., 19
and case studies, 104
defence mechanisms,
20–21
Freud and Breuer,
18–24

later developments in, 22–23
psychoanalytic psychotherapy, 23–24
psychosexual stages of development, 21–22
structure of the mind, 20, 21
Psychodynamic psychotherapy, 24
Psychoeducation
for anorexia nervosa, 332
for bulimia nervosa, 330
Psychological autopsy, 260–261
Psychological dependence, 404
Psychological dimensions
AIDS, 272, 280–281
anxiety disorders, 131
chronic pain, 289–291
dementia, 563–564
eating disorders, 326
and health, 271–278
mood disorder, 239–243
psychopathy, 464–465
schizophrenia, 508–510
sexual dysfunctions, 375–376
sleep disorders, 340
substance-related disorders, 428–429
Psychological disorders
assessing, 76–92
defined, 2–5
diagnosing, 92–99
global incidence of, 68–69
historical conceptions of, 8
vs. mental illness, 581
and suicide, 261
Psychological dysfunction, 3
Psychological model, 8
Psychological testing, 84–88
intelligence testing, 86–88

personality inventories, 85–86
projective tests, 84–85
Psychological tradition, 15–29
asylum reform and declines of moral therapy, 16–18
behavioural model, 25–29
humanistic theory, 24–25
moral therapy, 16
psychoanalytic theory, 18–24
Psychological treatment of physical disorders, 294–302
behaviour modification, 299–302
biofeedback, 295–296
denial as means of coping, 298–299
drugs and stress-reduction programs, 298
relaxation and meditation, 296
stress- and pain-reduction program, 296–298
Psychological treatments
for anorexia nervosa, 331–332
for binge-eating disorder, 331
for bipolar disorder, 256–257
for bulimia nervosa, 329–331
for cancer, 281–282
for eating disorders, 328–332
for generalized anxiety disorder, 137–138
for mood disorders, 252–254
for OCD, 170–171
for panic disorder, 146–148
for paraphilias, 391–393
for posttraumatic stress disorder, 164–166

for sleep disorders, 346–347
Psychologists, 5
Psychology profession, regulation of, 5
Psychoneuro-immunology (PNI), 278
Psychopathology, 2–8
behavioural contributions to, 57–62
biological contributions to, 38–57
and brain function, 54–55
causation, treatment, and outcomes, 7–8
clinical description, 6–7
defined, 5
developmental contributions to, 69–70
emotional contributions to, 62–65
historical conceptions of, 8–29
integrative approach to, 29–30
multidimensional integrative approach to, 36–38
scientist-practitioner, 5–6
social contributions, 65–69
Psychopathy, 460. *See also* Antisocial personality disorder
and the brain, 464
and criminality, 461–462
and narcissism, 473
Psychophysiological assessment, 90–92
Psychophysiological disorders, 271
Psychosexual stages of development, 21–22
Psychosocial approaches, 16

Psychosocial effects on physical disorders, 279–294
Psychosocial factors
brain structure and function, 55–56
interactions of, with brain structure and function, 56–57
Psychosocial treatments
for dementia, 565–567
for gender identity disorder, 364
for schizophrenia, 513–515
for sexual dysfunctions, 379–381
for substance-abuse disorders, 435–439
Psychosomatic medicine, 271
Psychosurgery, 171, 511
*Psychotherapy by Reciprocal Inhibition* (Wolpe), 104
Psychotic, 488
Psychotic behaviour, 489
Psy.D. (Doctor of Psychology) degree, 5
Puberty. *See also* Adolescents
and panic attacks, 141–142
Purging techniques, 312
Purging type of bulimia nervosa, 312, 317

**Q**
Quantitative genetics, 39–40
Quantitative trait loci, 503

**R**
Randomization, 101
Rape, sadistic, 386
Rapid-cycling specifier, 227
Rational-emotive therapy, 62

Rationalization, 21
Rats and pain, 294–295
Raynaud's disease, 283
Reaction formation, 21
Reactivity, 83
Reading disorder, 529
Reality principle, 20
Rebound headaches, 298
Rebound insomnia, 340, 345
Receptors, 44
Reciprocal gene-environment model, 42–43, 240
Redux, 52
*Regina v. Swain*, 585–586
Reinforcement, 28
Relapse prevention, 392, 438–439
Relaxation response, 296
Relaxation techniques, 296, 298, 346
Reliability, 78, 84, 95, 98
REM (rapid eye movement) sleep, 143, 335, 336, 342, 345, 347
Repeated measurements, 109–110
Replication, 120
Repression, 21
Research, 99–121
  adoption studies, 113–114, 502
  association studies, 114–115
  behaviour across cultures, 117–118
  behaviour over time, 115–117
  case study method, 104
  comparative treatment, 108–109
  components of research study, 100–102
  by correlation, 104–107
  epidemiological, 106–107
  ethics, 120–121, 592–593
  experimental, 107–112
  family studies, 113
  genetics, 112–115

methods, 104–112
  patient uniformity myth, 103
  prevention, 115
  program of, 119–120
  replication, 120
  single-case experimental designs, 109–112
  statistical vs. clinical significance, 102–103
  twin studies, 114
Research design, 100
Research participants, informed consent by, 120, 592
Reserpine, 14, 29, 53–54
Residual type of schizophrenia, 495
Resistance stage of stress, 273
Resolution phase of sexual response cycle, 365
Restricting type of anorexia nervosa, 315
Retarded ejaculation, 370
Reticular activating system, 48
Retrograde ejaculation, 370
Retrospective information, 116
Retrospective studies, 475
Rett's disorder, 533, 534, 574
Reuptake, 51
Revised Psychopathy Checklist (PCL-R), 86
Reward system (REW), 464
Rheumatoid arthritis, 278
Rhythm Test, 88
Right to refuse treatment, 591–592
Right to treatment, 591
Ritalin, 341, 345
Ritualistic behaviours, 535
Rituals, 168
Role-playing, 455, 514

Roman Catholic Church, 9, 10, 11
Rorschach inkblot test, 84–85
"Runners' high," 292

**S**
Sadistic personality disorder, 479
Sadistic rape, 386
Safe injection sites (SISs), 439
Salem witch trials, 9
Sanguine, 12
Saudi Arabia, 118, 169
Scheduled awakenings, 348
Schedules of reinforcement, 28
Schizoaffective disorder, 496
Schizoid personality disorder, 448, 449, 454–456
Schizophrenia, 485–521
  and brain function, 551
  and brain structure, 506–507
  cultural factors, 500
  defined, 486
  development of, 499–500
  disorganized symptoms, 489, 493–494
  and dopamine, 51, 53–54, 504–506
  DSM-IV criteria summary, 489
  early figures in diagnosing, 486–487
  early treatments for, 14
  genetic influences, 500–503
  negative symptoms, 489, 491–493
  neurobiological influences, 503–508
  positive symptoms, 489–491
  prevention, 516

psychological and social influences, 508–510
  and sleep disorders, 336
  and social networks, 67
  statistics, 498–499
  subtypes, 494–495
  symptoms, 487–494, 521
  treatment, 510–516
  and viral infections, 507–508
Schizophreniform disorder, 496
Schizophrenogenic mothers, 509
Schizotypal personality disorder, 448, 449, 456–458, 497
Scientific method, 29–30
Scientist-practitioners, 5–6, 596
Script theory of sexual functioning, 378
SE. *See* Sleep efficiency
Seasonal affective disorder (SAD), 228, 251–252
Secondary gain, 190
Secondary process, 20
Sedatives, 413–415
Seizure disorders, diagnosis of, 91
Selective amnesia, 199–200
Selective mutism, 530–531
Selective serotonin reuptake inhibitors (SSRIs), 52, 249. *See also* Antidepressants
  for eating disorders, 330
  for panic disorder, 145–146
  sexual dysfunction as side effect of, 375
Self-actualization, 23, 24
Self-defeating personality disorder, 479
Self-efficacy, 276
Self-help procedures for binge-eating disorder, 331

Self-injurious
behaviour, 82
Self-instructional
training, 62
Self-medication, 428–429
Self-monitoring, 83
Self-observation, 83
Semistructured clinical
interviews, 81
Sensate focus, 379
Sensorium, 80
Separation anxiety
disorder, 152
Sequential design, 117
Serial killers, 478
Serotonin, 45, 46,
51–52, 55
and alcohol, 409
and antidepressants,
248–250
and depression, 51
and eating disorders,
325–326
and mood
disorders, 238
Severe mental
retardation, 544
Sex chromosomes, 39
Sex ratio, 6
Sex reassignment
surgery, 360, 363
Sexual abuse, 367,
375–376, 381
and borderline
personality
disorder, 469
and dissociative
identity disorder,
205–206
and false memories,
207–208
and suicide, 262
Sexual arousal, 376, 377
Sexual arousal disorders,
368–369, 381
Sexual aversion
disorder, 367–368
Sexual desire disorders,
366–368
Sexual dysfunctions,
356, 365–382
acquired, 365
assessing, 373
causes of, 374–378
DSM-IV-TR categories
of, 365–366
generalized, 365
incidence of, 366

lifelong, 365
orgasm disorders,
369–371
psychophysiological
assessment of, 91
sexual arousal
disorders,
368–369, 381
sexual desire
disorders, 366–368
sexual pain disorders,
371–373
and sexual
satisfaction, 366
as side effect of
medication,
145–146, 248, 249
situational, 365
treatment, 378–382
Sexual fantasies, 22,
357–358
Sexual masochism,
385–386
Sexual orientation
development,
358–359
Sexual pain disorders,
371–373
Sexual response
cycle, 365
Sexual sadism, 385–386
Sexual satisfaction, 366
Sexual self-schemas, 358
Sexuality, 356–359
cultural differences, 358
gender differences,
357–358
myths of, 356, 378
number of sexual
partners, 356–357
sexual orientation
development,
358–359
Shaping, 28, 539
Shared psychotic
disorder (folie á
deux), 497
Shift work type sleep
disorders, 343
*Shinkeishitsu*, 157
Shock treatments, 11, 14
Shyness, 155, 156, 455
Sildenafil, 381
Silver nitrate, 435
Sin, 11
Single-case experimental
designs, 109–112
Situational phobias, 151

Situational sexual
dysfunctions, 365
Situationally bound
panic attacks, 129
Situationally
predisposed panic
attacks, 129
Sleep
and mood
disorders, 238
and nocturnal panic,
142–143
Sleep apnea, 341,
343, 345
Sleep attacks, 343
Sleep disorders, 334–349
breathing-related, 336,
341, 342–343, 345
circadian rhythm, 336,
343–344
DSM-IV-TR
descriptions, 336
dyssomnias, 336–337
narcolepsy, 336,
342, 345
overview of, 335–337
parasomnias, 336–337,
347–349
prevention of, 347
primary hypersomnia,
336, 340–342, 345
primary insomnia,
336, 337–340,
344–347
treatment, 344–349
Sleep efficiency (SE), 337
Sleep hygiene, 346, 347
Sleep paralysis, 342
Sleep restriction, 346–347
Sleep stages, 335
Sleep stress, 340
Sleep terror disorder,
336, 348
Sleepwalking disorder,
336, 348–349
Small fibres (A-delta and
C fibres), 292
Smooth-pursuit eye
movement, 503
Snake pits, 11
Snap gauge, 373
Social factors, 37. *See
also* Cultural factors
antisocial personality
disorder, 464–465
anxiety disorders, 131
chronic pain, 291

conversion disorder,
190–191
culture, 65–66
dementia, 563–564
eating disorders,
320–325
and the elderly, 68
gender, 66
and health, 271–278
mood disorders,
243–246
psychopathology, 65–69
PTSD, 164
schizophrenia, 508–510
sexual dysfunctions,
376–378
substance-related
disorders, 430–431
Social learning,
59–60, 513
Social learning model.
*See* Behavioural
model
Social learning theory, 59
Social norms, 3–4
Social phobia, 129,
155–159
and bulimia
nervosa, 313
causes, 157–159
clinical
description, 156
DSM-IV criteria
summary, 157
statistics, 156–157
treatment, 159
Social relationships,
272, 291
and health, 67
and mood disorders,
245–246
Social validity, 103
Society for Research
in Child
Development, 121
Sociocognitive
model, 204
Sociopathic personality
disturbances, 406
Sociotropy, 476
Somatic concern, 83
Somatic nervous
system, 48
Somatic symptoms, 217
Somatization disorder,
183–186, 212
causes, 184–185

clinical description, 183–184

DSM-IV criteria summary, 184

statistics, 184

treatment, 186

Somatoform disorders, 12–13, 178–197, 212

body dysmorphic disorder, 192–197, 212

conversion disorder, 186–191, 212

hypochondriasis, 179–183, 212

pain disorder, 191–192

somatization disorder, 183–186, 212

Somnambulism, 336, 348–349

Sorcery, 9, 10

Soul, 8

Specific phobia, 129, 149–155

animal phobias, 151

blood-injury-injection phobia, 2, 35–38, 150–151

causes, 153–155

clinical description, 149–152

DSM-IV criteria summary, 150

natural environment phobias, 151

separation anxiety disorder, 152

situational phobias, 151

statistics, 152–153

treatment, 155

Specific psychological vulnerability, 170

SPECT (single photon emission computed tomography), 90, 91, 491

Spinal cord, 44

Squeeze technique for premature ejaculation, 380

SSRIs. See Selective serotonin reuptake inhibitors

St. John's wort, 249

Standardization, 79

Stanford-Binet, 87

Stars, 11

Statistical significance, 102–103

Statistics, 6

Sterilization, of mentally retarded, 549

Steroids, 425–426

Stimulant medications, 527–528

Stimulants, 408, 415–420

amphetamine use disorders, 416–417

caffeine use disorders, 420

cocaine use disorders, 417–419

nicotine use disorders, 419–420

Stimulus control, 346

Stimulus generalization, 26

Strength of Grip Test, 88

Stress, 9–10, 273–278

alarm response to, 273

and antisocial personality disorder, 465

and anxiety, 131

vs. anxiety, depression, and excitement, 275–276

body's reaction to, 49–50

chronic, 277

and chronic fatigue syndrome, 293–294

contributions to stress response, 274–275

and conversion symptoms, 187

and coronary heart disease, 288

and hypertension, 285–286

and immune response, 276–278

and mood disorders, 239–242, 246

nature of, 273

and panic, 132, 144

physiology of, 274

and sleep disorders, 339, 340

and suicide, 261–262

Stress- and pain-reduction program, 296–298

Stress hormones, 237–238, 274

Stress-reduction programs, 280–281, 286, 298

Stress-reduction treatments, 91

Strokes, 283, 559

Stroop colour-naming paradigm, 61, 181

Stuttering, 530–531

Subcortical dementia, 560

Sublimation, 21

Subordinates and stress, 274–275

Substance abuse, 403

and anorexia nervosa, 316

and bulimia nervosa, 313

and dementia, 561–562

sexual dysfunction as side effect of, 375

and suicide, 261

Substance dependence, 403–406

Substance-induced dementia, 576

Substance intoxication, 402–403

Substance-related disorders, 400–444

biological dimensions, 427–428

causes, 427–433

cognitive and learning factors in, 429–430

comorbidity, 407

cultural influences, 431

depressants, 408–415

diagnostic issues, 406–408

hallucinogens, 422–425

integrative approach to, 431–432

levels of involvement, 402–406

opioids, 421–422

other drugs of abuse, 425–426

polysubstance abuse, 401

prevention, 439–440

psychological dimensions, 428–429

relapse prevention, 438–439

social contributions, 430–431

stimulants, 415–420

treatment, 433–440

Substance use, 402

Suffering and pain, 289

Suggestibility, 206–207

Suicidal attempts, 259

Suicidal ideation, 259–260, 263

Suicide, 258–264. See also Mood disorders and anti-depressants, 249

causes, 260

contagiousness of, 262

risk factors, 260–262

statistics, 258–260

treatment, 262–264

Sundowner syndrome, 556

Superego, 20

Supernatural model, 8

Supernatural tradition, 9–11

demons and witches, 9

moon and stars, 11

possession treatments, 11

stress and melancholy, 9–10

Supported employment, 548–549

Suppressant, alcohol as, 375

Suppressor T cells, 278

Suprachiasmatic nucleus, 343

Susto, 65–66, 142

Sweden, suicide rates in, 259

Switch, 203

Switzerland, eating disorders in, 309

Sybil, 205

Sympathetic nervous system (SNS), 48–50, 285

Symptom substitution, 23

Syncope, 35–36

Synaptic cleft, 45

Syphilis, 13

Systematic desensitization, 27, 475
Systemic perspective, 35
Systolic blood pressure, 284

**T**
T cells, 277, 278
Tactile Performance Test, 88
*Taijin kyofusho*, 157, 196
Taiwan
    mood disorders in, 232
    panic disorder in, 142
Tardive dyskinesia, 512
Target behaviours, 82
Task analysis, 548
Taxonomy, 93
Teenagers. *See* Adolescents
Television and eating disorders, 321
Temperance Movement, 408–409
Temporal lobe, 48
Tend and befriend, 66
Tennis players and eating disorders, 323–324
Tension headaches, 295–296, 298
Test-retest reliability, 78
Testability, 101
Tetrahydrocannabinols, 423
Thailand, dissociative trances in, 201
Thalamus, 48
Thanatos, 20
Thematic Apperception Test (TAT), 85
Therapeutic alliance, 24
Theta waves, 464
Theurapetic relationship, 25
Thought-action fusion, 170
Thought processes, assessment of, 79–80
*Three Faces of Eve, The*, 204
Thresholds, 118
Thyroid gland, 49

Thyroid problems, 81
Tic disorder, 530–531
Time-limited course, 7
Time management, 298
Token economy, 513
Tolerance, 403
Trainable mental retardation, 544
Traits, familial aggregation of, 113
Trance states, 201–202
Tranquillizers, 14
Transcendental meditation, 296
Transcranial magnetic stimulation (TMS), 251
Transference, 23
Transinstitutionalization, 583
Transsexualism, 360. *See also* Gender identity disorder
Transvestic fetishism, 360, 385
Traumatic events. *See also* Posttraumatic stress disorder (PTSD)
    and dissociative identity disorder, 205–206
    memories of, 161, 207–208
Treatment. *See also specific types*
    right to, 591
    right to refuse, 591–592
Treatment approaches, 7–8
Trend, 110
Triazolam, 345
Tricyclic antidepressants, 52, 248, 375. *See also* Antidepressants
    for panic disorder, 145
    for social phobia, 159
Twin studies, 114, 236
    antisocial personality disorder, 463
    eating disorders, 317–318, 325
    genetic factors in behaviour, 40

schizophrenia, 501–502, 506–507
sexual orientation development, 358, 359
suicide, 261
Type A behaviour pattern, 286–288
Type B behaviour pattern, 286–287
Tyramine, 248

**U**
UFO experiences, 342
Unconditional positive regard, 25
Unconditioned response (UCR), 26
Unconditioned stimulus (UCS), 26
Unconscious, 19, 60–61
Unconscious mental processes, in conversion disorder, 188–189
Unconscious vision, 60
Underarousal hypothesis, 463–464
Undifferentiated type of schizophrenia, 495
Unemployment and risk of death, 272
Unexpected panic attacks, 129
Unipolar mood disorder, 218
United States
    alcohol use in, 411–412
    suicide rates in, 258, 259
Unstructured interviews, 81

**V**
Vacuum device therapy, 382
Vaginal lubrication, 368
Vaginal photoplethysmograph, 373
Vaginismus, 372, 373, 380

Validity, 78–79, 84, 95–96, 98
    in research studies, 100–102
Valium, 14
Variability, 110
Variables
    correlation between, 104–107
    manipulating, 107
Vascular dementia, 559, 576
Vascular disease, 375
Vascular surgery, 382
Vasovagal syncope, 35–36
Vegetative symptoms, 217
Venlafaxine, 249
Venous leakage, 375
Ventricles, 506
Verbal scales, 87
Viagra, 381
Vibrators, 380
Violent behaviour
    and alcohol abuse, 413
    and schizophrenia, 489
Viral infections, and schizophrenia, 507–508
Vomiting, induction of, 12
Voodoo, 65–66
Voyeurism, 384–385
Vulnerability, 41, 358

**W**
*Walden Two* (Skinner), 28
Wandering uterus, 13
Waxy flexibility, 494
Wechsler Intelligence Scale for Children (WISC), 87–88
Weight gain strategies for anorexia nervosa, 331–332
Wernicke-Korsakoff syndrom, 568, 575
Wernicke's area, 491
Wernicke's disease, 410
Western Collaborative Group Study, 287
Wisconsin Card Sorting Task, 507
Witches, 9, 10
Withdrawal, 403

Withdrawal delirium, 410
Withdrawal designs, 111
Women
   coronary heart disease
      in, 287
   eating disorders in,
      310, 316–322
   hypoactive sexual
      desire in, 367,
      375–376, 381
   inhibited orgasm in,
      369–370, 380

   mood disorders in,
      244–245
   pain in, 292
   paraphilia in, 389
   response of to stress, 66
   sexual arousal disorder
      in, 368–369, 381
   sexual dysfunction
      categories, 365, 366
   sexual pain disorders
      in, 372, 373
   sexual practices of,
      356, 357–358
   sleep disorders in, 338

World Health
   Organization
   (WHO), 68, 93
Worry, 133
Wrestlers and eating
   disorders, 317
*Wyatt v. Stickney*, 591

**X**
X chromosomes, 39

**Y**
Y chromosomes, 39
Yerkes-Dodson curve, 464
Yohimbine, 381

**Z**
Zolpidem, 345